Vietnam

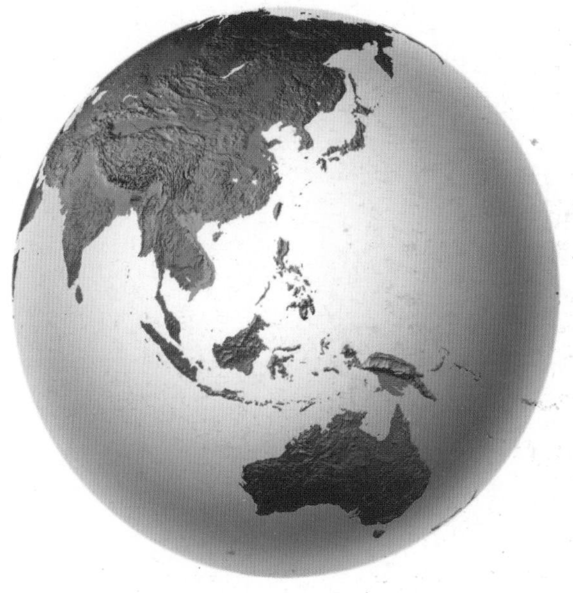

Nick Ray,
Yu-Mei Balasingamchow, Iain Stewart

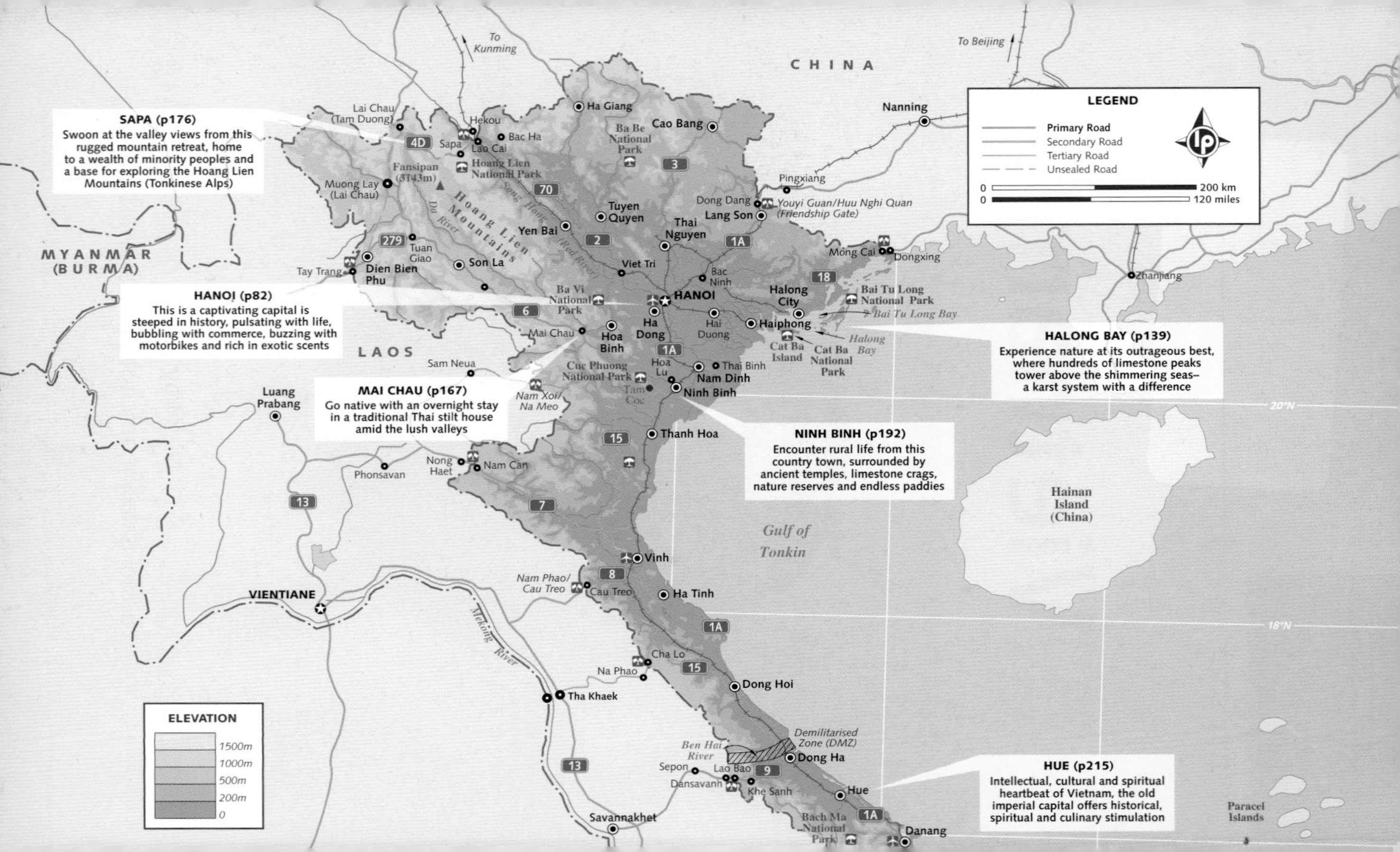
SAPA (p176)
Swoon at the valley views from this rugged mountain retreat, home to a wealth of minority peoples and a base for exploring the Hoang Lien Mountains (Tonkinese Alps)
HANOI (p82)
This is a captivating capital is steeped in history, pulsating with life, bubbling with commerce, buzzing with motorbikes and rich in exotic scents
MAI CHAU (p167)
Go native with an overnight stay in a traditional Thai stilt house amid the lush valleys
NINH BINH (p192)
Encounter rural life from this country town, surrounded by ancient temples, limestone crags, nature reserves and endless paddies
HALONG BAY (p139)
Experience nature at its outrageous best, where hundreds of limestone peaks tower above the shimmering seas– a karst system with a difference
HUE (p215)
Intellectual, cultural and spiritual heartbeat of Vietnam, the old imperial capital offers historical, spiritual and culinary stimulation
LEGEND
Primary Road
Secondary Road
Tertiary Road
Unsealed Road
0 200 km
0 120 miles
ELEVATION
1500m
1000m
500m
200m
0
CHINA
LAOS
MYANMAR (BURMA)
To Kunming
To Beijing
Nanning
Pingxiang
Zhanjiang
Dongxing
Hainan Island (China)
Gulf of Tonkin
Paracel Islands
20°N
18°N
HANOI
Lai Chau (Tam Duong)
Hekou
Sapa
Lao Cai
Bac Ha
Hoang Lien National Park
Fansipan (3143m)
Muong Lay (Lai Chau)
Hoang Lien Mountains
Song Hong (Red River)
Da River
Tuan Giao
Dien Bien Phu
Tay Trang
Son La
Ha Giang
Ba Be National Park
Cao Bang
Tuyen Quyen
Yen Bai
Thai Nguyen
Lang Son
Dong Dang
Youyi Guan/Huu Nghi Quan (Friendship Gate)
Viet Tri
Bac Ninh
Mong Cai
Halong City
Bai Tu Long National Park
Bai Tu Long Bay
Halong Bay
Haiphong
Cat Ba Island
Cat Ba National Park
Ba Vi National Park
Ha Dong
Hai Duong
Mai Chau
Hoa Binh
Cuc Phuong National Park
Hoa Lu
Tam Coc
Thai Binh
Nam Dinh
Ninh Binh
Thanh Hoa
Sam Neua
Nam Xoi/Na Meo
Luang Prabang
Phonsavan
Nong Haet
Nam Can
Vinh
Nam Phao/Cau Treo
Cau Treo
Ha Tinh
VIENTIANE
Mekong River
Cha Lo
Na Phao
Tha Khaek
Dong Hoi
Demilitarised Zone (DMZ)
Ben Hai River
Dong Ha
Sepon
Lao Bao
Dansavanh
Khe Sanh
Hue
Bach Ma National Park
Savannakhet
Danang
4D
279
70
3
2
1A
18
6
15
7
8
13
9

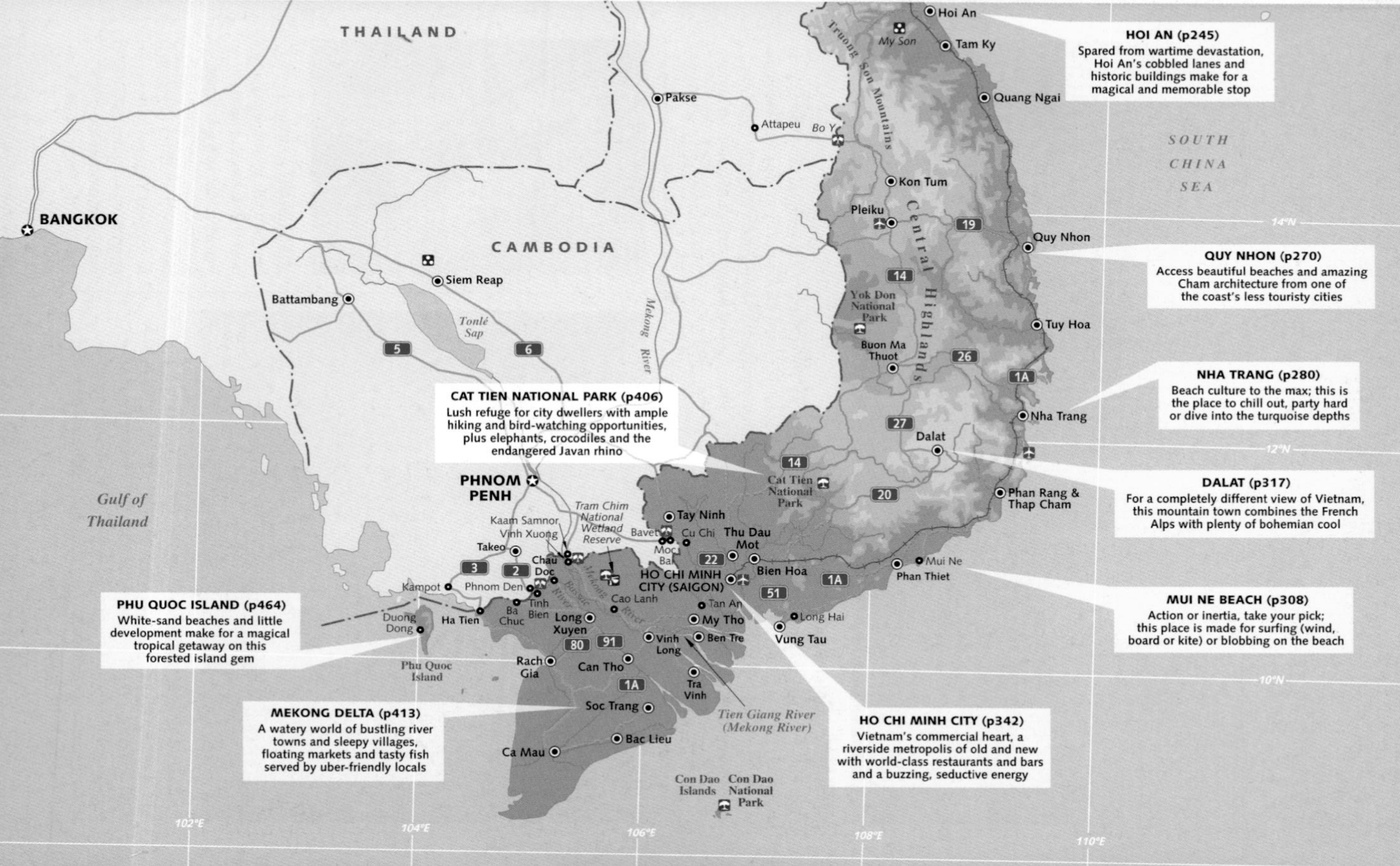
HOI AN (p245)
Spared from wartime devastation, Hoi An's cobbled lanes and historic buildings make for a magical and memorable stop
QUY NHON (p270)
Access beautiful beaches and amazing Cham architecture from one of the coast's less touristy cities
NHA TRANG (p280)
Beach culture to the max; this is the place to chill out, party hard or dive into the turquoise depths
DALAT (p317)
For a completely different view of Vietnam, this mountain town combines the French Alps with plenty of bohemian cool
MUI NE BEACH (p308)
Action or inertia, take your pick; this place is made for surfing (wind, board or kite) or blobbing on the beach
HO CHI MINH CITY (p342)
Vietnam's commercial heart, a riverside metropolis of old and new with world-class restaurants and bars and a buzzing, seductive energy
CAT TIEN NATIONAL PARK (p406)
Lush refuge for city dwellers with ample hiking and bird-watching opportunities, plus elephants, crocodiles and the endangered Javan rhino
PHU QUOC ISLAND (p464)
White-sand beaches and little development make for a magical tropical getaway on this forested island gem
MEKONG DELTA (p413)
A watery world of bustling river towns and sleepy villages, floating markets and tasty fish served by uber-friendly locals
THAILAND
CAMBODIA
SOUTH CHINA SEA
Gulf of Thailand
BANGKOK
PHNOM PENH
HO CHI MINH CITY (SAIGON)
Hoi An
Tam Ky
Quang Ngai
My Son
Truong Son Mountains
Central Highlands
Pakse
Attapeu
Bo Y
Kon Tum
Pleiku
Quy Nhon
Tuy Hoa
Yok Don National Park
Buon Ma Thuot
Nha Trang
Dalat
Cat Tien National Park
Phan Rang & Thap Cham
Siem Reap
Battambang
Tonlé Sap
Mekong River
Tay Ninh
Cu Chi
Thu Dau Mot
Bavet
Moc Bai
Bien Hoa
Phan Thiet
Mui Ne
Long Hai
Vung Tau
Tan An
My Tho
Ben Tre
Vinh Long
Tra Vinh
Tram Chim National Wetland Reserve
Kaam Samnor
Vinh Xuong
Takeo
Chau Doc
Phnom Den
Kampot
Ha Tien
Ba Chuc
Tinh Bien
Long Xuyen
Cao Lanh
Bassac River
Mekong River
Duong Dong
Phu Quoc Island
Rach Gia
Can Tho
Soc Trang
Bac Lieu
Ca Mau
Tien Giang River (Mekong River)
Con Dao Islands
Con Dao National Park
1A
5
6
3
2
14
19
20
22
26
27
51
80
91
14°N
12°N
10°N
102°E
104°E
106°E
108°E
110°E

On the Road

NICK RAY Coordinating Author
Most folk don't realise that the Ho Chi Minh Highway (Hwy 1A) connects Hanoi and Ho Chi Minh City via the Truong Son Mountains and is breathtakingly beautiful. I crossed the border from Laos into Vietnam at Bo Y and headed north. The scenery is sublime with jagged peaks, raging rivers and little oases of green where rice is grown. The scenery around Phong Nha is Halong Bay on land, and continues almost all the way to the suburbs of Hanoi.

YU-MEI BALASINGAMCHOW My first day on the job and my motorbike driver gleefully deposited me at the foot of a small hill outside Ninh Binh. 'Up, up – nice to see!' he exhorted. Five hundred steep stone steps later, I had an incredible view of rice fields and limestone landscapes. Well worth the climb, but I wish someone had warned me to bring some water.

IAIN STEWART Punting a bamboo raft on the Quay Son river that forms the border between Vietnam and China, with the Ban Gioc waterfall in the background. Ho Chi Minh re-entered Vietnam in this remote region (after decades in exile) and plotted the overthrow of the French from a cave close by.

For full author biographies see p535

Vietnam Highlights

From the steaming mangrove swamps of the Mekong Delta to the frenetic pace of the chameleonlike cities, from the indolent rhythm of the tropical islands to the delectable cuisine and defiant history, Vietnam is a study in contrasts. Embrace them.

Here, travellers, authors and Lonely Planet staff share their top experiences in Vietnam. Do you agree with their choices, or have we missed your favourites? Go to www.lonelyplanet.com/vietnam and tell us your highlights.

NOBORU KOMINE

1 HALONG BAY

If you can get out of bed after being lulled to sleep by the swaying boat, your morning on Halong Bay (p139) will truly be one for the books. The mountains meet the sea in this archipelago, huge peaks rising all around you as you sail by. Every view is picture worthy, especially in the morning light. If you like rice for breakfast, you're really in luck.

Lucy Anne Kagan, Traveller, USA

MICHELLE BENNETT

2 CHAM RUINS, MY SON

Described as the holy land of what was the Champa kingdom, this UNESCO-listed site (p262) once served as a magnet for religious pilgrims, an intellectual centre and the final resting place of kings. The ruins at My Son have survived the demise of the civilisation that built them, together with centuries of pillaging, neglect and successive wars. The fragments that remain here still evoke some of the grandeur that was.

Debra Herrmann, Lonely Planet Staff

STU SMUCKER

3 TREKKING THROUGH SAPA

As you trek through Sapa (p176), the landscape becomes even more spectacular, giving way to high mountains, steep valleys and rice paddies. Visiting minority villages and staying overnight in a homestay makes you feel privileged and humbled to be a guest in the locals' homes, and despite their meagre surroundings, their warmth and hospitality is truly delightful.

Marina Kosmatos, Traveller, USA

HILL TRIBES

Tote a questionably heavy bag of marbles into the mountains. Watch the hill-tribe children's faces light up as you play. At five, they work full time, slinging a younger sibling on their back while selling handicrafts to tourists.

Heather Narynski, Traveller, Canada

4

JULIET COOMBE

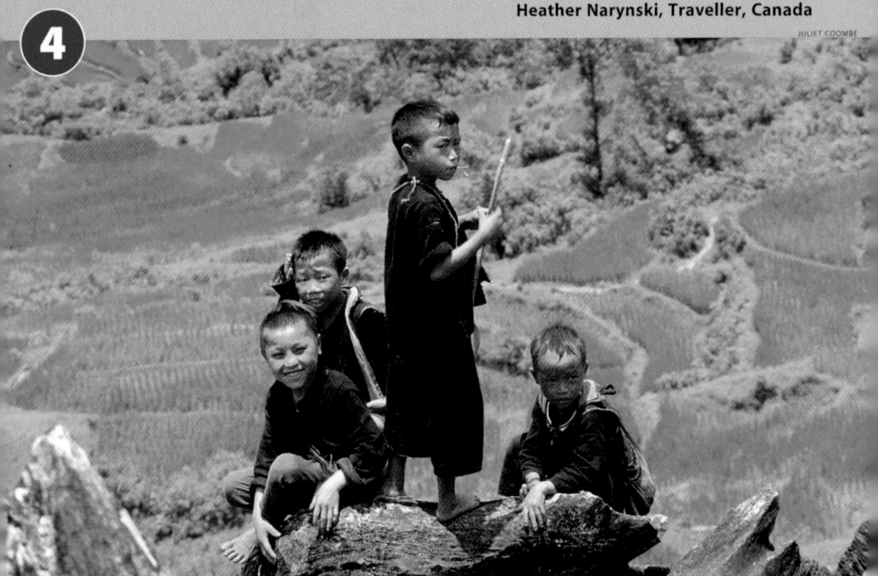

NHA TRANG

If you like to include a bit of beach bumming on your travels then Nha Trang (p280) is the place to be. There's lots to do: you can go on boat trips, snorkelling and scuba-diving. If you're like me however, then sipping cocktails on the beach, feasting on sumptuous seafood and partying the night away is enough activity for one day.

Paul "Cuz" Williams, Traveller, Australia

5

JOHN BANAGAN

JOHN BANA

6 VINH LONG, MEKONG DELTA

We had a fantastic day in the Mekong Delta, cruising down the narrow canals of the Co Chien River in a wooden canoe, sucking on freshly cut sugar cane and visiting the beautiful little islands of Vinh Long (p423).

Ben Dillon, Traveller, Australia

MICAH WI

7 SAND DUNES OF MUI NE

If you're after a break from the ever-present fish sauce smell of Mui Ne, then charter yourself a motorbike tour and head for the red-and-white sand dunes (p309). You'll especially appreciate the sight if it's overcast, as the colour of the dunes can change dramatically from one second to the next. And if you feel like a spot of surfing – sand dune–style – then there's an abundance of local kids on hand to lend you a plastic board. For a small fee, of course.

Naomi Jennings, Lonely Planet Staff

HOI AN

Tile-roofed wooden houses, streets lit with hanging red lanterns, and Chinese temples give small, riverside Hoi An (p245) great charm. It has few cars but a busy river life, and is good for tailor-made clothes and original art.

onesmallbag, Traveller

8

CHRISTOPHER GROENHOUT

BEN THANH MARKET, HO CHI MINH CITY

This market (p384) offers mind-blowing shopping, from sequins to squid, tea sets to tiaras and everything in between. Bargain hard (start at 30%) but stay friendly. Scrumptious, safe, authentic food. And then there's Binh Tay Market in Cholon (p385) – unmissable.

ronan82, Traveller

9

RICHARD CUMMINS

JOHN BANAGAN

10 DALAT

Dalat (p317) is a beautiful city set in the mountains, known for its flowers and strawberries. The weather is cooler than throughout the rest of the country and provides a nice break from the heat on the coast. You can travel to Dalat very easily from the surrounding cities. Go to relax, enjoy the food and see the city's agriculture and beauty.

Elizabeth Trexler, Traveller, USA

11 PERFUME PAGODA, HANOI

Venture out of Hanoi's Old Quarter past the luminous green rice paddies – you will feel like you are drifting back in time while you watch water buffalo graze and locals go about life as if from a bygone era.

mike81, Traveller

JON ARMSTRO

JULIET COO

12 CRAZY HOUSE

The charming town of Dalat (p317) houses perhaps the country's strangest attraction – Hang Nga Crazy House (p318), a surreal labyrinth of walkways and bizarre themed rooms. You can stay the night, but you may have to share the room with a kangaroo with red glowing eyes.

Chris Girdler, Lonely Planet Staff

HO CHI MINH HIGHWAY

Ride the Ho Chi Minh Highway on two wheels and get off Vietnam's well-worn tourist trail. Rent a motorcycle and hire an Easy Rider guide (p325) in either Hoi An or Dalat for the 800km, four-day trip through the mountains and villages of the striking central highlands.

Cheryn Flanagan, Traveller, USA

13

GUENTER FISCHER/IMAGEBROKER / ALAMY

PHU QUOC ISLAND

You can't go past Phu Quoc Island (p464)…especially the snorkelling off the southern tip and the pearl market on the eastern side.

Bruce Taylor, Lonely Planet Staff

14

JOHN BORTHWICK

RADIUS IMAGES / ALA

15 MUI NE FAIRY SPRING

Slosh through the muddy, ankle-deep water in Mui Ne's Fairy Spring (p309), which is also used as a 'road' for ox-carts! The cool, clear waterfalls at the end of the hike make for a refreshing end.

Catherine Bodry, Lonely Planet Author, USA

ANDERS BLOMQV

16 TEMPLE OF LITERATURE, HANOI

Around Hanoi you can find a variety of temples containing a great mix of religions. Buddhism, Taoism and Confucianism are all blended together, with a harmonious – if confusing! – result. Make sure you check out the Temple of Literature (p96) and the Ngoc Son Temple (p96) on the island in the centre of Hoan Kiem Lake.

moontorch, Traveller

Contents

Regional Map Contents

Destination Vietnam

If there is one country in Southeast Asia that everyone has heard about long before they discover the region, it's Vietnam. Of course, such infamy wasn't always for the right reasons, but this is the new Vietnam and it's one of the most intoxicating places on earth. It's a kaleidoscope of vivid colours and subtle shades, of exotic sights and curious sounds, of compelling history and contrasting cultures.

Nature has blessed Vietnam with a bountiful harvest. From the soaring mountains of the far north to the carpet of emerald-green rice paddies in the south, Vietnam is little short of stunning. The curvaceous coastline is defined by endless beaches, lovely lagoons and hidden coves. Inland, peasant women in conical hats still tend to their fields, children ride buffalo along country paths, and minority people scratch out a living from impossible gradients.

If Vietnam has a soundtrack, it's the buzz of a million motorbikes, the cries of street hawkers plying their wares and the tinkle of pagodas drawing the faithful to prayer. Here, the modern and medieval collide. The big cities are strikingly sophisticated, with gourmet restaurants and designer boutiques, but turn a random corner and find yourself travelling back in time. Embrace the street life with a bowl of *pho* at a pint-sized plastic table.

For culinary crusaders, Vietnam is a treasure trove of more than 500 different dishes. It's a wonderful world of pungent herbs and secret spices. Dip delicate spring rolls in *nuoc mam,* a fish sauce that, for the Vietnamese, is as compulsory as ketchup. Or play 'down-in-one' with *ruou* (pronounced 'xeo'), the whisky of the mountains.

'Nam' to a generation, the sorrow of war weighs heavily on the consciousness of all who can remember it, and the Vietnamese side of the story is told at poignant sites across the country. Although fiercely protective of their independence and sovereignty, the Vietnamese are graciously welcoming of foreigners who come as guests not would-be conquerors. Of course, the country's history did not begin and end with the American War and the country is littered with vestiges of empires past and battles fought, all of which are elements in piecing together the story of Vietnam today.

Politically, Vietnam remains a perplexing place. Apparently, it's a communist country, but capitalism is no longer a four-letter word. The cities are awash with money, but not everyone is getting a share. Transparency International rated Vietnam 121st out of 179 countries surveyed for its corruption index, on a par with Nigeria. Some observers argue this is why Vietnam needs to embrace democracy, to hold the politicians accountable for their actions; others argue that a firm hand drives the country forward economically, creating a stable environment for investors. Either way, there is no doubt the latest Asian dragon has awoken from its slumber.

Tourism has had a huge impact on Vietnam in the past two decades, helping plug the Vietnamese back into the world. It has spread into areas that other businesses cannot reach, and empowered a new generation of young Viets to a better life. The Vietnamese people are dynamic in commerce and dedicated to their families. They love to share a joke, a story, and getting to know some Vietnamese beyond the tourism industry can be the highlight of a visit. The Vietnamese have a vitality as tangible as the traffic on the street.

Vietnam is in top gear. Try and catch it before it reinvents itself as another Malaysia or Thailand. For now, it remains one of the most enriching, enlivening and enticing countries on earth.

FAST FACTS

Population: 86 million

Life expectancy: 68 for men, 74 for women

Infant mortality: 24 per 1000 births

GDP: US$70.2 billion

Adult literacy rate: 94%

Annual rice production: 34.4 million tonnes

Tonnage of bombs dropped on Vietnam during the American War: 15 million

Number of motorbikes: 16 million and counting

Litres of *nuoc mam* (fish sauce) produced per year: 200 million plus

Members of Communist Party: 2 million

Getting Started

Vietnam is the flavour of the month these days and it's not just down to the delectable cuisine. The country offers an intoxicating blend: vibrant yet traditional cities, unashamedly idyllic coastline, incredible scenery, pulsating history and culture, and a kaleidoscope of people. Vietnam has it all, but it's also raw in places, so pack some flexibility, humour and patience. Come expecting the unexpected, be ready for an adventure as much as a holiday, and Vietnam will deliver.

WHEN TO GO

When it comes to weather, it's a tough call, as Vietnam's climate is so diverse. Think frosts and occasional snow in the mountains of the north, and temperatures soaring to 40°C in the south during the dry season.

Vietnam's weather is dictated by two monsoons, meaning double trouble on the rain front. The winter monsoon comes from the northeast between October and March, bringing damp and chilly winters to all areas north of Nha Trang, and dry and warm temperatures to the south. From April or May to October, the summer monsoon brings hot, humid weather to the whole country except for those areas sheltered by mountains. For the best balance, we'd vote for the months of April, May or October. For those sticking to the south, November to February is dry and a touch cooler. From July to November, violent and unpredictable typhoons hit central and northern Vietnam, which can dampen the spirits of even the most enthusiastic traveller.

See Climate Charts (p480) for more information.

It gets pretty crowded from November to March and in July and August during high season. Domestic tourists are a major force now and they tend to travel in numbers during July and August as well. Prices peak over the Christmas and New Year period, and if you don't fancy sharing the sites with the masses, try to avoid this busy time. May, June and September are usually the quietest months.

Some travellers like to time a visit with Tet (Vietnamese New Year; see p54), the biggest festival in the calendar, which falls in late January or early February. It's a nice idea in principle, but not in practice, as the whole country is on the move and prices rise dramatically. Transport is crammed in the run-up and aftermath, the Reunification Express shuts down during festivities, and most shops and businesses are closed for the best part of a week.

DON'T LEAVE HOME WITHOUT...

Bring as little as possible, as Vietnam has pretty much anything you can find back home but at lower prices. All the soaps and smellies are cheap and plentiful, and clothing, shoes and backpacks are all manufactured in Vietnam and available at a snip. Tampons are available in all major towns and cities, but not in very remote areas.

A Swiss army knife or equivalent comes in handy, but you don't need 27 separate functions, just one blade and an opener. A torch (flashlight) and compass are also useful.

Other handy things to bring are business cards, as Vietnamese deal them out like a deck of cards; ear plugs to block the ever-present soundtrack that is Vietnam; a universal plug adaptor; a rain cover for the backpack; a sweater for the highlands and air-con bus trips; and mosquito repellent to keep the bugs at bay.

Finally, the secret of successful packing: plastic bags, as not only do they keep things separate and clean, but also dry. That means a lot at the end of a long, wet day.

COSTS & MONEY

The cost of travel in Vietnam varies from bargain basement to sky high, depending on taste and comfort. Ascetics could just about get by on US$15 a day, while a conventional budget traveller can live it up from US$25 to US$35. Midrange travellers can have a ball from US$50 to US$150 a day, staying comfortably, eating well and travelling flexibly. At the top end, spending US$250 or more a day, anything is possible. Vietnam is not quite as cheap as it used to be thanks to rampant inflation, but it is still a great deal compared with many parts of the world.

The official currency is the Vietnam dong (d), but the US dollar is pretty widely accepted. In tourist centres, most hotels will accept either, while other businesses may prefer dong. As you venture off the trail, make sure you are packing plenty of local currency. Rooms start from as little as US$5 in busy tourist centres. Spending US$10 to US$30 will boost the comforts quickly, and rooms will generally include air-con, satellite TV, fridge and hot water. Make the step up to US$50 and three-star frills are available. At US$100 and above, it's five-star territory in many destinations, although Hanoi and Ho Chi Minh City (HCMC) tend to be more expensive than the provinces. Don't be afraid to negotiate for a discount if it is low season or if numbers are down.

HOW MUCH?

Restaurant meal US$3-10

Hotel room with air-con US$10-30

Internet access US$0.20-0.50 per hour

Short *cyclo* ride US$0.50

Two-kilometre taxi ride US$1-2

Dining out is where Vietnam comes into its own. Surfing the street stalls and markets, meals can be found for US$1 or less. Local restaurants are more comfortable and you can eat well for between US$2 and US$5. Then there are the Vietnamese gourmet restaurants, where you can still only spend around US$15 with drinks; with the right wines you could easily spend US$50.

Domestic flights are quite good value for longer journeys, particularly with lowcost carrier Jetstar Pacific on the scene. A one-way ticket from Hanoi to HCMC is around US$100, although Jetstar can be cheaper. Trains are great value and overnight sleepers are a good way to cover long distances like Hanoi to Hue or HCMC to Nha Trang.

Bus travel is a bargain by Western standards, as long as you manage to pay the local price. Public buses between major destinations have fixed fares, but for bus travel in remote areas, overcharging is the rule. For maximum flexibility, many travellers prefer to rent a car or 4WD and go exploring with a guide. Costs run from about US$30 around town to US$100 or more a day up-country (including the driver's food and lodging). A guide costs from US$15 to US$50, depending on the destination.

Foreigners are sometimes overcharged, particularly when buying souvenirs and occasionally in restaurants. Transport prices are sometimes bumped up to several times the Vietnamese price. However, don't assume that everyone is trying to rip you off. Despite widespread poverty, many Vietnamese will only ask the local price for many goods and services.

TRAVELLING RESPONSIBLY

Since our inception in 1973, Lonely Planet has encouraged readers to tread lightly, travel responsibly and experience the magic of independent travel. International travel is growing at a jaw-dropping rate, and we still firmly believe in the benefits it can bring – but, as always, we encourage you to consider the impact your visit will have on both the global environment and the local economies, cultures and ecosystems.

Staying longer, travelling further and spreading the wealth is obvious advice, but even for those on a short stay, it is possible to engage with locals in markets and spend money in restaurants and outlets that assist disadvantaged Vietnamese in places like Hanoi, HCMC and Hoi An.

TOP 10

Thailand

VIETNAM

TOP EATS, TOP DRINKS

Vietnam's cuisine is full of sensual flavours, subtle aromas and super-fresh ingredients. *Bia hoi* (beer) is the new tea, but in the mountains it is all about *ruou* (rice wine; pronounced 'xeo').

1. *Bia hoi* – The world's cheapest draught beer keeps on flowing
2. *Ca phe* – Caffeine cravers unite: Vietnam's coffee has a real kick
3. *Cao lau* – Hoi An's answer to fried noodles, made with water from a well
4. *Nem* – Spring rolls are the country's most famous export, fried or fresh
5. *Nuoc mam* – Fermented fish sauce, the pungent secret of Vietnamese cuisine
6. *Pho bo* – Rice-noodle soup with beef, the meal that built a nation
7. *Rau muong* – Just the thing on a glorious morning, with a dash of garlic and chilli
8. *Thit cho* – Dog lover has a whole different meaning in this part of the world
9. *333 – Ba ba ba,* learn to count with the leading local beer in the south
10. *Ruou* – The local firewater, particularly potent is the 'five times a night' variety

MUST-SEE MOVIES

Film-makers have found a rich vein of material in the tales of Vietnamese history. There are a whole host of films dealing with the American experience in Vietnam, and some that deal with both Americans and Vietnamese coming to terms with life after so much death.

1. *Apocalypse Now* (1979) Director: Francis Ford Coppola
2. *Cyclo* (1995) Director: Anh Hung Tran
3. *The Deer Hunter* (1978) Director: Michael Cimino
4. *The Lover* (1992) Director: Jean-Jacques Annaud
5. *Platoon* (1986) Director: Oliver Stone
6. *The Quiet American* (2002) Director: Phillip Noyce
7. *The Rebel* (2007) Director: Charlie Nguyen
8. *Rescue Dawn* (2007) Director: Werner Herzog
9. *The Scent of Green Papaya* (1992) Director: Anh Hung Tran
10. *We Were Soldiers* (2002) Director: Randall Wallace

VIETNAM EXPERIENCES

Travel is not just about visiting, it's about experiencing. Try to get beneath the skin of the country: this can take many shapes or forms. It might be a culinary adventure or a walk on the wild side. It could be a cultural encounter or perhaps spiritual enlightenment.

1. Cross the road in a busy city like a local, one step at a time
2. Delve into the bustling markets, the life-blood of every community
3. Get the measure of a tailor, the only time you want to be stitched up in Vietnam
4. Haggle with a *cyclo* driver about the price before enjoying the ride
5. Meet the minorities, a multicoloured mosaic of mountain people
6. Play *tram phan tram* (100%) or bottoms up with the locals in a backstreet bar
7. See the sunrise over the South China Sea from a beautiful beach
8. Take some time out in a temple, the spiritual sanctuary of the Vietnamese
9. Turn down the volume and meander down the Mekong by sampan
10. Wander through the emerald-green paddy fields to discover rural Vietnam

For more on sustainable tourism and some tips on responsible travel while still having the trip of a lifetime, try the following websites:

Responsible Travel (www.responsible-travel.org) A no-nonsense website with common sense advice on how to travel with a conscience.

Stay Another Day (www.stay-another-day.org) A great website dedicated to tempting tourists into staying longer in Vietnam. It's packed with ideas on day trips, project visits and alternative things to see and do.

TRAVEL LITERATURE

Vietnam: A Traveller's Literary Companion (1996), edited by Qui Doc Nguyen, is a good way to learn more about the culture of the country. It has an engaging collection of stories by various Vietnamese writers, ranging from folklore and the tragedy of war to love and family ties, all set against evocative backdrops from Hanoi to Dalat.

Vietnam: Journeys of Body, Mind and Spirit (2003), edited by Van Huy Nguyen, is a beautifully shot photographic journey that travels to the heart of Vietnam. It's put together by locals and residents of Vietnam and offers an intimate portrait of the country.

'No one is spared, not the locals, not the travellers, not even hallowed guidebook authors.'

Fragrant Palm Leaves (1998) is a remarkable, poetic collection of journal entries by Zen monk and peace crusader Nhat Hanh Thich, written in Vietnam and the USA during the 1960s. As the American War in Vietnam rages on, he tries to make sense of it all, and there are some vivid scenes from South Vietnam.

Written by writers who know and love their countries, *To Asia with Love: A Connoisseur's Guide to Cambodia, Laos, Thailand and Vietnam* (2004), an anthology edited by Kim Fay, is a delightful introduction to Vietnam and the Mekong region for those looking for some inspiration and adventure. A new *To Vietnam with Love* (2008) has just come out brimming with stories.

The Indochina Chronicles (2005) by Phil Karber is a lively travelogue taking in adventures and misadventures in Cambodia, Laos and Vietnam.

Sparring with Charlie: Motorbiking down the Ho Chi Minh Trail (1996), by Christopher Hunt, is a light-hearted travelogue about modern Vietnam that takes you off the tourist trail and into some less-travelled parts of the country.

Derailed in Uncle Ho's Victory Garden (1995) by Tim Page is the story of the author's quest to erect a war memorial in the Demilitarised Zone (DMZ) to honour the fallen war correspondents on all sides.

A Dragon Apparent (1952) is Norman Lewis' fascinating account of his journeys through Vietnam, Laos and Cambodia in 1950, and is an eloquent insight into the last days of colonial rule.

Karin Muller's *Hitchhiking Vietnam* (1998) is a travelogue detailing one woman's tumultuous seven-month journey through Vietnam.

Part memoir and part travel narrative, *Catfish and Mandala* (1999) is Vietnamese-American Andrew X Pham's fascinating account of his escape from the war-torn Vietnam of 1977 and his subsequent return two decades later, equipped with a bicycle and a need to work out his mixed-up cultural identity.

The ultimate spoof guidebook, *Phaic Tan: Sunstroke on a Shoestring* (2004) makes fun of us all. No one is spared, not the locals, not the travellers, not even hallowed guidebook authors. An absolute must for anyone travelling through Vietnam and the region beyond.

INTERNET RESOURCES

Jewels of the Mekong Delta (www.travelmedia.com/mekong) Features travel information and news about countries along the Mekong River.

Living in Vietnam (www.livinginvietnam.com) One of the most popular expat websites on Vietnam and a good source of information on settling down here, including job adverts.
Lonely Planet (www.lonelyplanet.com) Provides summaries on travelling to Vietnam, the Thorn Tree forum travel news and loads of links to other useful travel resources.
Things Asian (www.thingsasian.com) Bubbling with information on the culture of Vietnam, this site has everything, including architecture, literature and fashion.
Vietnam Adventures Online (www.vietnamadventures.com) Another fine site full of practical travel information that features monthly adventures and special travel deals.
Vietnam Online (www.vietnamonline.com) Loaded with useful travel lore and handy coverage of employment and business opportunities in Vietnam.

Itineraries
CLASSIC ROUTES

THE GREAT OCEAN ROAD Three to Four Weeks / Hanoi to HCMC

Acclimatise in the capital, **Hanoi** (p82); see the sights, wine and dine, and prepare for the long ride south. Head to nearby **Ninh Binh** (p192), gateway to the striking scenery of **Tam Coc** (p193) and **Hoa Lu** (p195), and the funky gibbons of **Cuc Phuong National Park** (p196).

Experience **Hue** (p215), imperial capital of old, then head up and over (or under) the mighty Hai Van Pass to **Danang** (p235), gateway to charming **Hoi An** (p245), the perfect place for some time out – sightseeing, shopping and sunning yourself on the beach.

Head to the golden sands of **Quy Nhon** (p275) for some relaxation. Enter **Nha Trang** (p280), the biggest and brashest beach resort in Vietnam, and try a hedonistic boat trip to nearby islands. If it's all too much, carry on south to **Mui Ne Beach** (p308), a tropical idyll with smart resorts, blissed-out budget options, towering dunes and crazy kitesurfing.

Finish up in **Ho Chi Minh City** (HCMC; p342), where you can indulge in sophisticated shopping, delectable dining and the liveliest night scene in the country.

Many tour companies offer this trip in a two-week timeframe, but this barely allows enough time to unpack your bags in each place. Train, bus or opt for a car and driver for this 1710km epic.

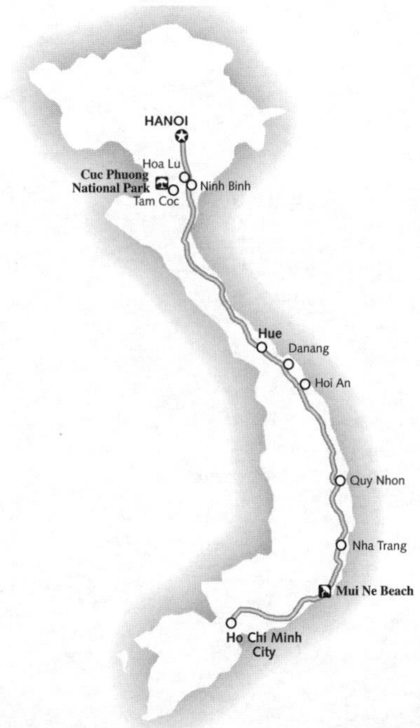

THE WORKS

One Month or More / HCMC to Sapa

Run this one in reverse, and start out in the cauldron of commerce that is **Ho Chi Minh City** (p342). Hit the markets, browse a couple of museums and go underground into the alternate world that is the **Cu Chi Tunnels** (p390). Carry on to **Tay Ninh** (p393), headquarters of the Cao Dai sect, and its fairy-tale temple for a morning service.

Dip into the Mekong Delta for a day or two. Stay at **Can Tho** (p434), the social and commercial heart of the region, and take to the water to cruise through the watery world of the floating markets.

Head up into the central highlands to the romantic hill station of **Dalat** (p317). Back down on the coast, take in the stops from the Great Ocean Road itinerary (see opposite), including the beach resort of **Nha Trang** (p280), the cultured charmer that is **Hoi An** (p245) and the old imperial capital of **Hue** (p215). North of Hue is the former Demilitarised Zone (DMZ) that divided North and South Vietnam. All around this area are famous sites from the American War, including **Khe Sanh Combat Base** (p212) and the **Vinh Moc Tunnels** (p209). All aboard the night train to **Hanoi** (p82), gateway to the north, or cruise up the coast checking out the up-and-coming beach destination of **Dong Hoi** (p203), with a side trip to the **Phong Nha Cave** (p202), a World Heritage Site, and a run up the stunning Ho Chi Minh Highway to the capital.

To the east of the capital lies **Halong Bay** (p139), with more than 2000 limestone outcrops dotting the scenic bay. Cruise through the bay to the rugged, foreboding **Cat Ba Island** (p146) before looping back to the capital through **Haiphong** (p135), for the feel of old Hanoi.

Take a night train to **Sapa** (p176), unofficial capital of the northwest hill-tribe region and a beautiful base for hiking and biking.

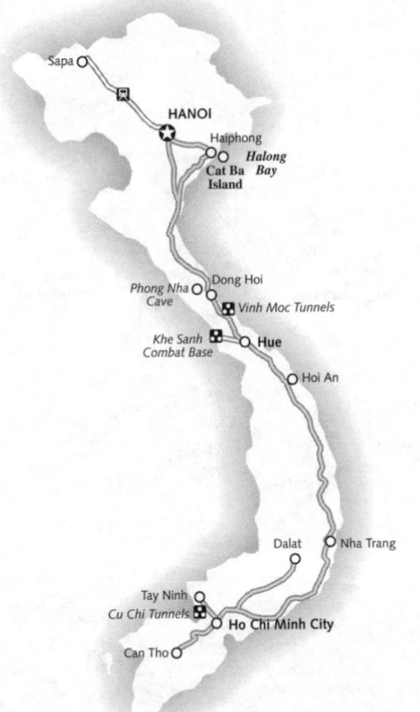

Trains and buses stop at most destinations, but to cover this huge distance of more than 3000km, a Hue–Hanoi flight could save time. Travel by boat around the Halong Bay area – the only way to get a good look at the crazy karsts.

ROADS LESS TRAVELLED

MINORITY REPORT

One to Three Weeks / Hanoi to Cao Bang

Northern Vietnam is a world unto itself, a land of brooding mountains, a mosaic of ethnic minorities, a region of overwhelming beauty. Hit the road by 4WD or motorbike more for an adventure than a holiday.

Leaving Hanoi, head west to the villages of **Mai Chau** (p167), which are home to the White Thai people and a perfect introduction to the life of the minorities. Northwest of here, where the road begins to climb into the Hoang Lien Mountains (Tonkinese Alps), a logical stop is **Son La** (p169).

Dien Bien Phu (p171) is a name that resonates with history; it was here that the French colonial story ended with their overwhelming defeat at the hands of the Viet Minh in one of the most celebrated military victories in Vietnamese history.

Climb over the mighty **Tram Ton Pass** (p179) to **Sapa** (p176). This is the premier destination in the northwest, thanks to the infinite views (on a clear day!), an amazing array of minority peoples and some of the region's most colourful markets. Head by train to **Lao Cai** (p183), or continue further east to **Bac Ha** (p184), home to the Flower H'mong. Adventurers can continue on to **Ha Giang** (p187), a realm of mythical landscapes and uncharted territory. From here head to the lovely lakes of **Ba Be National Park** (p162) before journeying northeast to **Cao Bang** (p158), a province peppered with karsts, caves and beautiful waterfalls.

The snaking roads on this journey are some of the most treacherous in Vietnam, and landslides and floods are common. The motorbiking here is pure heaven for seasoned two-wheelers, but for the majority a 4WD is the sanest way to tackle this 1000km trip through the mountains.

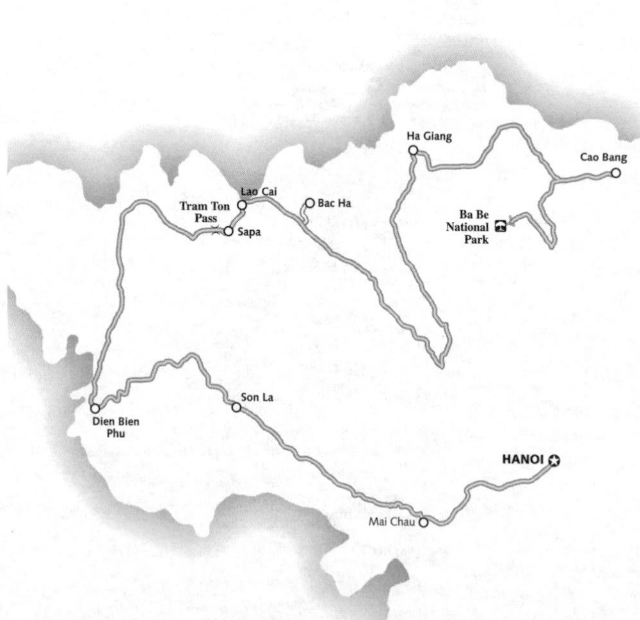

MEKONG MEANDERS

Two Weeks / Ben Tre to Phu Quoc Island

With their own wheels, travellers can tear up the three-day tourist trail through the Mekong byways and delve deeper into the delta to be rewarded with its rhythms, fragrances and colours.

Beginning in **Ben Tre** (p420), take a boat trip to the islands around Vinh Long and overnight in a bungalow set in a small longan orchard. Take the road down to **Tra Vinh** (p426), one of the most charming towns in the Mekong Delta, with graceful tree-lined boulevards and a sizeable Cambodian community and their wonderful *wats* (temples). From Tra Vinh, a trek to **Can Tho** (p434) takes you to the home of the famous Ho Chi Minh 'Tin Man' statue and the delta's most cosmopolitan and commercial city.

Drift by boat through the local floating markets before moving on to charming **Chau Doc** (p449), a border-crossing town for those pushing westward into Cambodia via river or road. Check out the views of the pancake delta from the heights of **Sam Mountain** (p453).

Leave behind the roads more travelled once again, heading southwest to **Ba Chuc** (p455) and its bone pagoda, and then through **Ha Tien** (p456), another border town with a beach to boot. Even more bucolic a beach can be found at **Hon Chong** (p460), where the sunset meets the sea and the rocky coastal geography contrasts sharply with the sandy beaches east of Ho Chi Minh City.

Fast boat connections are available from both Ha Tien and Hon Chong to the serene **Phu Quoc Island** (p464). Phu Quoc affords rest and relaxation, *nuoc mam* (fish sauce) and forest reserves – a spectacular end to the Mekong Delta experience.

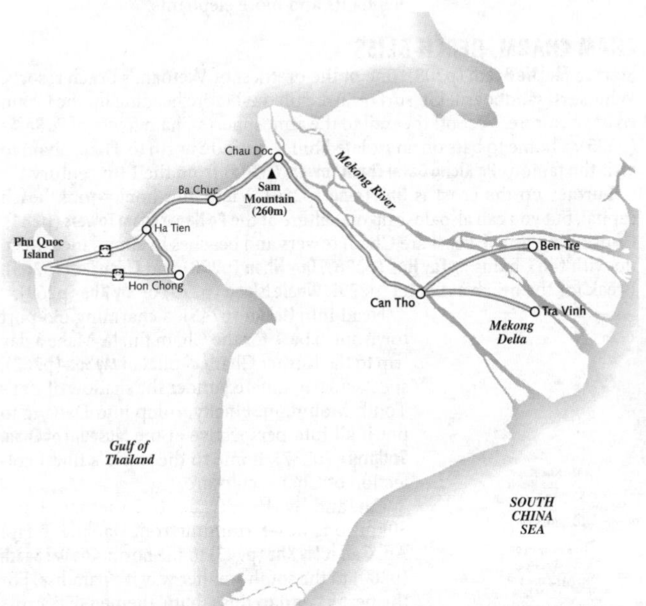

Down to Chau Doc, public transport is a breeze; after that, it's sparse and requires flexibility. Flights from Phu Quoc Island to HCMC run daily; if flying back to HCMC, book return flights well before hitting the delta to guarantee a quick getaway and avoid the 500km return trip.

TAILORED TRIPS

NATURAL HIGHS

For adrenalin junkies or nature lovers, Vietnam has plenty to offer. Start out with a visit to **Halong Bay** (p139) for some sea kayaking among the karsts. Experienced climbers with their own gear might leave the water far below, as these limestone outcrops offer some excellent ascents, plus there is organised climbing around **Cat Ba Island** (p146).

Further northeast in **Bai Tu Long Bay** (p153), take to the water by local boat to see the 'new' Halong Bay without the tourists. Boating, kayaking, even surfing are possibilities here and there are some beautiful beaches on Quan Lan's east coast.

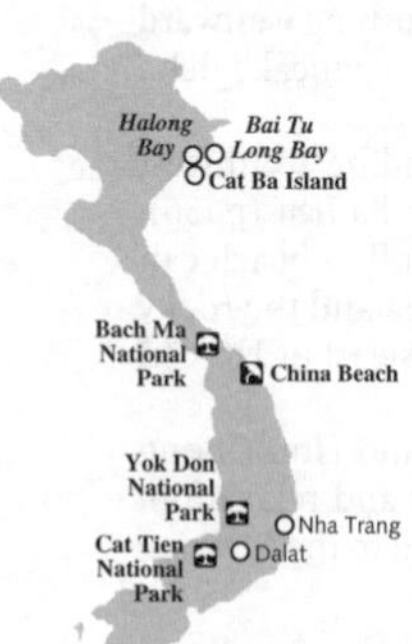

Heading south to central Vietnam, **Bach Ma National Park** (p232) is well geared up for walkers and has a series of lush trails to secluded waterfalls. Down on the coast below Bach Ma is **China Beach** (p243), a base for serious surfers.

Or go under the waves at **Nha Trang** (p280), dive capital of Vietnam, before heading up towards the hills of the central highlands. Wind up, or down, in **Dalat** (p317), a base for abseiling, cycling or rock climbing. Don't forget two of Vietnam's best-known national parks: the birding hot spot of **Cat Tien** (p406), with a population of rare Javan rhinos, and **Yok Don** (p332), home to elephants, elephants and more elephants.

CHAM CHARM, BEACH BLISS

Start in **Mui Ne Beach** (p308), one of the prettiest of Vietnam's beach resorts. Windsurf, sandboard, kitesurf or just chill out before heading up the Cham coast of culture. Veer off the trail to the atmospheric Cham tower of **Po Ro Me** (p305), a home to bats on an isolated hill. Continue north to Thap Cham to visit the famous **Po Klong Garai Cham Towers** (p304) from the 13th century.

Further up the coast is **Nha Trang** (p280), Vietnam's honky-tonk beach capital, but you can also dose up on culture at the **Po Nagar Cham Towers** (p284). Continuing up the coast are Cham towers and beaches in abundance. Keep up with the Chams at **Tuy Hoa** (p278), **Quy Nhon** (p270) and **Chien Dan** (p265). Break for the beach at **Doc Let** (p279), **Whale Island** (p279) or **My Khe** (p269).

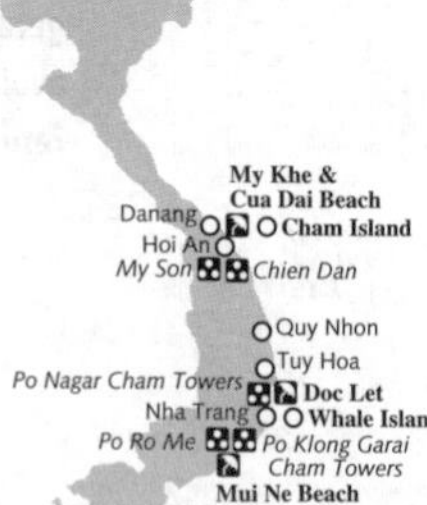

Head into **Hoi An** (p245), a charming old port town and a base for the Cham finale. Make a day trip to the former Cham capital of **My Son** (p262), spectacularly situated under the shadow of Cat's Tooth Mountain. Finally, romp into Danang to put it all into perspective at the **Museum of Cham Sculpture** (p237), home to the world's finest collection of Cham sculpture.

Oh, and by the way, central Vietnam has a 30km-long beach running from Danang to Hoi An. Call it **My Khe** (p243) to the north, **Cua Dai Beach** (p260) to the south – either way it's paradise. For the perfect end to this Cham-themed trip, cross to **Cham Island** (p261) and chill out on the quiet beaches.

History

Vietnam has a history as rich and evocative as anywhere on earth. Sure, the American War in Vietnam captured the attention of the West, but centuries before that Vietnam was scrapping with the Chinese, the Khmers, the Chams and the Mongols. Vietnamese civilisation is as sophisticated as that of its mighty northern neighbour China, from where it drew many of its influences under a 1000-year occupation. Later came the French and the humbling period of colonialism from which Vietnam was not to emerge until the second half of the 20th century. The Americans were simply the last in a long line of visitors who had come and gone through the centuries and, as far as Ho Chi Minh was concerned, no matter what was required or how long it took, they too would be vanquished. A number of commentators and historians have since observed that had the military planners in Washington paid just a little more attention to the history of this proud nation, then Vietnam might have avoided the trauma and tragedy of a bloody war.

Visitors to Vietnam can't help but notice that the same names occur again and again on the streets of every city and town. These are Vietnam's national heroes who, over the last 2000 years, have led the country in its repeated expulsions of foreign invaders and whose exploits have inspired subsequent generations of patriots.

The people of the Bronze Age Dong Son period were major traders in the region and bronze drums from northern Vietnam have been found as far afield as the island of Alor, in eastern Indonesia.

Archaeologists conducting excavations at Oc-Eo discovered a Roman medallion dating from AD 152, bearing the likeness of Antoninus Pius.

THE EARLY DAYS

Recent archaeological finds suggest that the earliest human habitation of northern Vietnam began about 500,000 years ago. Neolithic cultures were roaming around the same area just 10,000 years ago and engaged in primitive agriculture as early as 7000 BC. The sophisticated Bronze Age Dong Son culture, which is famous for its bronze *moko* drums, emerged sometime around the 3rd century BC. The Dong Son period also saw huge advances in rice cultivation and the emergence of the Red River Delta as a major agricultural centre.

From the 1st to 6th centuries AD, southern Vietnam was part of the Indianised Cambodian kingdom of Funan – famous for its refined art and architecture. Known as Nokor Phnom to the Khmers, this kingdom was centred on the walled city of Angkor Borei, near modern-day Takeo, but was likely a series of feudal states rather than a unified empire. The people of Funan constructed an elaborate system of canals both for transportation and the irrigation of rice. The principal port city of Funan was Oc-Eo in the Mekong Delta and archaeological excavations here suggest there was contact between Funan and China, Indonesia, Persia and even the Mediterranean. It remains a sensitive area of study in Vietnam, as some groups in Cambodia

In AD 679 the Chinese changed the name of Vietnam to Annam, which means the 'Pacified South'. Ever since this era, the collective memory of Chinese control has played an important role in shaping Vietnamese identity and attitudes towards the northern neighbour.

TIMELINE

2789 BC

The Van Lang kingdom is founded, considered the first independent Vietnamese state (Lac Viet), under the stewardship of the Hung Vuong kings. Van Lang is referred to in both Chin and Tang dynasty sources in China.

2000 BC

The Bronze Age Dong Son culture emerges in the Red River Delta around Hanoi, renowned for its rice cultivation and the production of bronzeware, including drums and gongs.

250 BC

Van Lang is conquered by a Chinese warlord and a new kingdom known as Au Lac is established at Co Loa, close to the modern-day capital of Hanoi.

IN THE BEGINNING...

Every country has a creation myth and Vietnam is no exception. The Vietnamese are supposed to be descended from a union of Dragon Lord Lac Long Quan and the fairy Au Co. Their relationship was fruitful, producing 100 sons, 50 migrating with their mother to the mountains and the other half travelling with their father to the sea. These sons founded the first Vietnamese dynasty, the Hung, who ruled over the kingdom of Van Lang, whose people were the first to be known as the Lac Viet.

still claim the Mekong Delta as their own and refer to it as Kampuchea Krom (lower Cambodia), despite the fact that the area has been settled by a majority Vietnamese population since the 17th century.

The Hindu kingdom of Champa emerged around present-day Danang in the late 2nd century AD (see p264 for more information). Like Funan, it adopted Sanskrit as a sacred language and borrowed heavily from Indian art and culture. By the 8th century Champa had expanded southward to include what is now Nha Trang and Phan Rang. The Cham were a feisty bunch who conducted raids along the entire coast of Indochina, and thus found themselves in a perpetual state of war; with the Vietnamese to the north and the Khmers to the south. Ultimately this cost them their kingdom, as they found themselves squeezed between these two great powers. Check out some exquisite sculptures in the Museum of Cham Sculpture in Danang (p237).

Meanwhile, back in the Mekong Delta, the Chenla empire of Cambodia was controlling affairs. Geographically, the Chenla empire was a continuation of the Funan kingdom, but as its control of neighbouring territory grew, the empire developed into Upper and Lower Chenla, spread along the Mekong River. Historians still debate the areas of control between Chenla and Champa and there is evidence to suggest that these empires were fluid, with both powers occupying the sacred site of Wat Phu in southern Laos at different times.

Archaeologists used to assume that bronze casting originated in China and spread southwards, but evidence from northern Thailand and Vietnam suggests it originated in Southeast Asia and spread north.

1000 YEARS OF CHINESE OCCUPATION

The Chinese conquered the Red River Delta in the 2nd century BC. Over the following centuries, large numbers of Chinese settlers, officials and scholars moved south seeking to impress a centralised state system on the Vietnamese.

In the most famous act of resistance, in AD 40, the Trung Sisters (Hai Ba Trung) rallied the people, raised an army and led a revolt against the Chinese. In AD 43 the Chinese counter-attacked and, rather than suffer the ignominy of surrender, the Trung Sisters threw themselves into the Hat Giang River. There were numerous small-scale rebellions against Chinese rule – which was

111 BC

The Han emperors of China annex the Red River Delta region of Vietnam, heralding 1000 years of Chinese rule. Confucianism prevails as the governing philosophy.

AD 40

The Trung Sisters (Hai Ba Trung) lead a rebellion against the Chinese occupiers, raising an army that sends the Chinese governor fleeing. They proclaim themselves queens of an independent Vietnam.

263

The powerful Mekong Delta kingdom of Funan, one of the pre–Angkorian Khmer kingdoms, pays tribute to the Chinese emperor. The emperor orders the establishment of an institute of Funanese music.

characterised by tyranny, forced labour and insatiable demands for tribute – from the 3rd to 6th centuries, but all were defeated.

However, the early Vietnamese learned much from the Chinese, including the advancement of dykes and irrigation works. These innovations helped reinforce the role of rice as the 'staff of life', and paddy agriculture remains the foundation of the Vietnamese way of life to this day. As food became more plentiful the population expanded, forcing the Vietnamese to seek new lands. The ominous Truong Son Mountains prevented westward expansion, as the climate was harsh and terrain unsuited to mass rice cultivation, so instead the Vietnamese moved south along the coast.

For a closer look at China's 1000-year occupation of Vietnam, which was instrumental in shaping the country's outlook and attitude today, try *The Birth of Vietnam* by Keith Weller Taylor.

During this era, Vietnam was a key port of call on the sea route between China and India. The Chinese introduced Confucianism, Taoism and Mahayana Buddhism to Vietnam, while the Indians brought Theravada Buddhism and Hinduism (to Champa). Monks carried with them the scientific and medical knowledge of these two great civilisations and Vietnam was soon producing its own doctors, botanists and scholars.

LIBERATION FROM CHINA

In the early 10th century the Tang dynasty in China collapsed. The Vietnamese seized the moment and launched a revolt against Chinese rule in Vietnam. In AD 938 popular patriot Ngo Quyen vanquished the Chinese armies at a famous battle on the Bach Dang River, ending 1000 years of Chinese rule. He lured the Chinese fleet up the river in a feigned retreat, only to counter-attack and impale the Chinese ships on a wall of sharpened stakes hidden beneath the waters. However, this was not to be the last time the Vietnamese would tussle with their mighty northern neighbour.

Ngo Quyen died a premature death provoking a struggle for power among rival claimants to the throne, the first of many periods of civil strife that have punctuated Vietnam's independent history. It was only the prospect of Chinese dominance that eventually unified the country under the leadership of one emperor.

From the 11th to 13th centuries, Vietnamese independence was consolidated under the emperors of the Ly dynasty, founded by Ly Thai To. This was a period of progress and prosperity that saw the introduction of an elaborate dyke system for flood control and cultivation, and the establishment of the country's first university. During the Ly dynasty, many neighbours launched attacks on Vietnam, among them the Chinese, the Khmer and the Cham, but all were repelled. Meanwhile, the Vietnamese continued their expansion southwards and slowly but surely began to consolidate control of the Cham kingdom.

In the 11th century, Emperor Ly Thai To changed the name of the country to Dai Viet, which translates as 'Great Viet'.

Mongol warrior Kublai Khan completed his conquest of China in the mid-13th century. For his next trick, he planned to attack Champa and demanded the right to cross Vietnamese territory. The Vietnamese refused,

446

Relations between the kingdom of Champa and the Chinese deteriorate. China invades Champa, sacks the capital of Simhapura and plunders a 50-tonne golden Buddha statue.

938

The Chinese are kicked out of Vietnam after a thousand years of occupation, as Ngo Quyen leads his people to victory in the battle of the Bach Dang River, luring the Chinese ships onto sharpened stakes.

1010

Thanh Long (City of the Soaring Dragon), known today as Hanoi, is founded by Emperor Ly Thai To and becomes the new capital of Vietnam.

DYNASTIES OF VIETNAM

Dynasty	Year
Ngo dynasty	939–965
Dinh dynasty	968–980
Early Le dynasty	980–1009
Ly dynasty	1010–1225
Tran dynasty	1225–1400
Ho dynasty	1400–1407
Post-Tran dynasty	1407–1413
Chinese rule	1414–1427
Later Le dynasty	1428–1524
Mac dynasty	1527–1592
Trinh Lords of the North	1539–1787
Nguyen Lords of the South	1558–1778
Tay Son dynasty	1788–1802
Nguyen dynasty	1802–1945

but the Mongol hordes – all 500,000 of them – pushed ahead. They met their match in the revered general Tran Hung Dao; he defeated them in the battle of Bach Dang River, one of the most celebrated scalps among many the Vietnamese have taken. See the boxed text on p141 for more on this battle.

CHINA BITES BACK

The Chinese took control of Vietnam again in the early 15th century, taking the national archives and some of the country's intellectuals to China – a loss that was to have a lasting impact on Vietnamese civilisation. Heavy taxation and slave labour were also typical of the era. The poet Nguyen Trai (1380–1442) wrote of this period:

> Were the water of the Eastern Sea to be exhausted, the stain of their ignominy could not be washed away; all the bamboo of the Southern Mountains would not suffice to provide the paper for recording all their crimes.

LE LOI ENTERS THE SCENE

In 1418 wealthy philanthropist Le Loi sparked the Lam Son Uprising by refusing to serve as an official for the Chinese Ming dynasty. By 1428, local rebellions had erupted in several regions and Le Loi travelled the countryside to rally the people against the Chinese. Following Le Loi's victory over the Chinese, poet Nguyen Trai, Le Loi's companion in arms, wrote his infamous Great Proclamation (Binh Ngo Dai Cao). Still guaranteed to fan the flames of

1076

Founded by King Ly Thanh Tong, Vietnam's first university, the Temple of Literature in Hanoi, opens its doors to scholars and is the nation's centre of learning for nearly 800 years.

1288

The Mongols attempt to invade Dai Viet for a third time, but General Tran Hung Dao employs the same strategy as Ngo Quyen at the first battle of Bach Dang, and spears the Mongol fleet on sharpened stakes.

1371

In a last hurrah, King Binasuos of Champa leads an attack on the Vietnamese, sacking Hanoi. However, following his death in 1390, the kingdom is steadily eclipsed.

Vietnamese nationalism almost six centuries later, it articulated the country's fierce spirit of independence:

> Our people long ago established Vietnam as an independent nation with its own civilisation. We have our own mountains and our own rivers, our own customs and traditions, and these are different from those of the foreign country to the north…We have sometimes been weak and sometimes powerful, but at no time have we suffered from a lack of heroes.

One of the most prominent early missionaries was French Jesuit Alexandre de Rhodes (1591–1660), widely lauded for his work in devising *quoc ngu,* the Latin-based phonetic alphabet in which Vietnamese is written to this day.

Le Loi and his successors launched a campaign to take over Cham lands to the south, which culminated in the occupation of its capital Vijaya, near present-day Quy Nhon, by Le Thanh Thong in 1471. This was the end of Champa as a military power and the Cham people began to migrate southwards as Vietnamese settlers moved in to their territory. Parts of eastern Laos kowtowed to the Vietnamese, including Luang Prabang, which came under their control for a time.

THE COMING OF THE EUROPEANS

The first Portuguese sailors came ashore at Danang in 1516 and were soon followed by a party of Dominican missionaries. During the following decades the Portuguese began to trade with Vietnam, setting up a commercial colony alongside those of the Japanese and Chinese at Faifo (present-day Hoi An, p245). With the exception of the Philippines, which was ruled by the Spanish for 400 years, the Catholic Church eventually had a greater impact on Vietnam than on any country in Asia.

Ho Chi Minh City (Saigon) began life as humble Prey Nokor in the 16th century, a backwater of a Khmer village in what was then the eastern edge of Cambodia.

LORDING IT OVER THE PEOPLE

In a dress rehearsal for the tumultuous events of the 20th century, Vietnam found itself divided in half throughout much of the 17th and 18th centuries. The powerful Trinh Lords were later Le kings who ruled the North. To the South were the Nguyen Lords, who feigned tribute to the kings of the North but carried on like an independent kingdom. The powerful Trinh failed in their persistent efforts to subdue the Nguyen, in part because their Dutch weaponry was matched by the Portuguese armaments supplied to the Nguyen. By this time, several European nations were interested in Vietnam's potential and were jockeying for influence. For their part, the Nguyen expanded southwards again, absorbing the Cambodian territories of the Mekong Delta.

TAY SON REBELLION

In 1765 a rebellion erupted in the town of Tay Son near Qui Nhon, ostensibly against the punitive taxes of the Nguyen family. The Tay Son Rebels, as they were known, were led by the brothers Nguyen, who espoused the sort of Robin

1428

Le Loi triumphs over the Chinese occupiers, declaring himself Emperor Le Thai To, the first in the long line of the Le dynasty. He is revered as one of the nation's greatest heroes.

1442

National poet Nguyen Trai is executed when Emperor Le Thai Tong dies unexpectedly during a visit. The punishment is known as *tru di tam toc*.

1471

The Vietnamese inflict a humbling defeat on the kingdom of Champa, killing more than 60,000 Cham soldiers and capturing 36,000, including the king and most of the royal family.

Hood–like philosophy of take from the rich and redistribute to the poor. It was clearly popular and in less than a decade they controlled the whole of central Vietnam. In 1783 they captured Saigon and the South from the Nguyen Lords, killing the reigning prince and his family. Nguyen Lu became king of the South, while Nguyen Nhac was crowned king of central Vietnam.

Continuing their conquests, the Tay Son Rebels overthrew the Trinh Lords in the North, while the Chinese moved in to take advantage of the power vacuum. In response, the third brother, Nguyen Hue, proclaimed himself Emperor Quang Trung. In 1789 Nguyen Hue's armed forces overwhelmingly defeated the Chinese army at Dong Da in another of the greatest hits of Vietnamese history.

In the South, Nguyen Anh, a rare survivor from the original Nguyen Lords – yes, know your Nguyens if you hope to understand Vietnamese history! – gradually overcame the rebels. In 1802 Nguyen Anh proclaimed himself Emperor Gia Long, thus beginning the Nguyen dynasty. When he captured Hanoi, his work was complete and, for the first time in two centuries, Vietnam was united, with Hue as its new capital city.

Buddhism flourished during the 17th and 18th centuries and many pagodas were erected across the country. However, it was not pure Buddhism, but a peculiarly Vietnamese blend mixed with ancestor worship, animism and Taoism.

THE TRADITIONALISTS PREVAIL

Emperor Gia Long returned to Confucian values in an effort to consolidate his precarious position. This was a calculated move to win over conservative elements of the elite who appreciated the familiar sense of order, which had all but vanished in the dizzying atmosphere of reform stirred up by the Tay Son Rebels.

Gia Long's son, Emperor Minh Mang, worked to strengthen the state. He was profoundly hostile to Catholicism, which he saw as a threat to Confucian traditions, and extended this antipathy to all Western influences.

The early Nguyen emperors continued the expansionist policies of the preceding dynasties, pushing into Cambodia and westward into the mountains along a wide front. Huge areas of Lao territory were seized and clashes with Thailand broke out in an attempt to pick apart the skeleton of the fractured Khmer empire.

The return to traditional values may have earned support among the elite at home, but the isolationism and hostility to the West ultimately cost the Nguyen emperors as they failed to modernise the country fast enough to compete with the well-armed Europeans.

THE FRENCH TAKEOVER

France's military activity in Vietnam began in 1847, when the French Navy attacked Danang harbour in response to Emperor Thieu Tri's imprisonment of Catholic missionaries. Saigon was seized in early 1859 and, in 1862, Emperor Tu Duc signed a treaty that gave the French the three eastern provinces of Cochinchina (the southern part of Vietnam during the French-colonial

1516

Portuguese traders land at Danang, sparking the start of European interest in Vietnam. They set up a trading post in Faifo (present-day Hoi An) and introduce Catholicism to small numbers of Vietnamese.

1651

The first *quoc ngu* (romanised Vietnamese) dictionary, the Dictionarium Annamiticum Lusitanum et Latinum, is produced, following many years of work by Father Alexandre de Rhodes.

1765

The Tay Son Rebellion erupts near Quy Nhon, led by the brothers Nguyen, and they take control of the whole country over the next 25 years.

era). However, over the next four decades the French colonial venture in Indochina was carried out haphazardly, seemingly without any preconceived plan. It faltered repeatedly and, at times, only the reckless adventures of a few mavericks kept it going.

In 1872 Jean Dupuis, a merchant seeking to supply salt and weapons to a Yunnanese general via the Red River, seized the Hanoi Citadel. Captain Francis Garnier, ostensibly dispatched to rein in Dupuis, instead took over where Dupuis left off and began a conquest of the North.

A few weeks after the death of Tu Duc in 1883, the French attacked Hue and the Treaty of Protectorate was imposed on the imperial court. There then began a tragi-comic struggle for royal succession that was notable for its palace coups, the death of emperors in suspicious circumstances and heavy-handed French diplomacy.

The Indochinese Union proclaimed by the French in 1887 may have ended the existence of an independent Vietnamese state, but active resistance continued in various parts of the country for the duration of French rule. The expansionist era came to a close and the Vietnamese were forced to return territory seized from Cambodia and Laos.

The French colonial authorities carried out ambitious public works, such as the construction of the Saigon–Hanoi railway, which were funded by heavy government taxes; these taxes were to have a devastating impact on the rural economy. Such operations became notorious for the abysmal wages paid by the French and the subhuman treatment of Vietnamese workers.

INDEPENDENCE ASPIRATIONS

Throughout the colonial period, the desire of many Vietnamese for independence simmered under the surface. Nationalist aspirations often erupted into open defiance of the French. This ranged from the publishing of patriotic periodicals to a dramatic attempt to poison the French garrison in Hanoi.

'modernisation was the key to an independent Vietnam'

The imperial court in Hue, although allegedly quite corrupt, was a centre of nationalist sentiment and the French orchestrated a game of musical thrones, as one emperor after another turned against their patronage. This culminated in the accession of Emperor Bao Dai in 1925, who was just 12 years old at the time and studying in France.

Leading patriots soon realised that modernisation was the key to an independent Vietnam. Phan Boi Chau launched the Dong Du (Go East) movement which planned to send Vietnamese intellectuals to Japan for study with a view to fomenting a successful uprising in the future. Phan Tru Chinh favoured the education of the masses, the modernisation of the economy and working with the French towards independence. It was at this time that the Roman script of *quoc ngu* came to prominence, as educators

1802

Emperor Gia Long takes the throne and the Nguyen dynasty is born, ruling over Vietnam until 1945. The country is reunited for the first time in more than 200 years.

1825

Emperor Minh Mang issues several proclamations outlawing missionary work in Vietnam. Missionaries are imprisoned and persecuted, giving the French the pretext they need for more forceful intervention.

1862

Following French attacks on both Danang and Saigon, Emperor Tu Duc signs a treaty ceding control of the Mekong Delta provinces to France, renaming them Cochinchina (Cochinchine).

realised this would be a far easier tool with which to educate the masses than the elaborate Chinese-style script of *nom*.

However, the most successful of the anticolonialists were the communists, who were able to tune into the frustrations and aspirations of the population – especially the peasants – and effectively channel their demands for fairer land distribution.

'Ho appeared pragmatic, patriotic and populist and understood the need for national unity'

The story of Vietnamese communism, which in many ways is also the political biography of Ho Chi Minh (see opposite), is convoluted. The first Marxist grouping in Indochina was the Vietnam Revolutionary Youth League, founded by Ho Chi Minh in Canton, China, in 1925. This was succeeded in February 1930 by the Vietnamese Communist Party. In 1941 Ho formed the League for the Independence of Vietnam, much better known as the Viet Minh, which resisted the Vichy French government, as well as Japanese forces, and carried out extensive political activities during WWII. Despite its nationalist platform, the Viet Minh was, from its inception, dominated by Ho's communists. However, as well as a communist, Ho appeared pragmatic, patriotic and populist and understood the need for national unity.

WWII BREAKS OUT

When France fell to Nazi Germany in 1940, the Indochinese government of Vichy France collaborators acquiesced to the presence of Japanese troops in Vietnam. The Japanese left the French administration in charge of the day-to-day running of the country and, for a time, Vietnam was spared the ravages of Japanese occupation, with things continuing much as normal. However, as WWII drew to a close, Japanese rice requisitions, combined with floods and breaches in the dykes, caused a horrific famine in which two million of North Vietnam's 10 million people starved to death. The only force opposed to both the French and Japanese presence in Vietnam was the Viet Minh, and Ho Chi Minh received assistance from the US government during this period. As events unfolded in mainland Europe, the French and Japanese fell out and the Viet Minh saw its opportunity to strike.

A FALSE DAWN

By the spring of 1945 the Viet Minh controlled large swathes of the country, particularly in the North. In mid-August, Ho Chi Minh formed the National Liberation Committee and called for a general uprising, later known as the August Revolution, to take advantage of the power vacuum. In central Vietnam, Bao Dai abdicated in favour of the new government, and in the South the Viet Minh soon held power in a shaky coalition with noncommunist groups. On 2 September 1945, Ho Chi Minh declared independence at a rally in Hanoi's Ba Dinh Square. Throughout this period, Ho wrote no fewer than eight letters to US president Harry Truman and the US State

1883

The French impose the Treaty of Protectorate on the Vietnamese, marking the start of 70 years of colonial control, although active resistance continues throughout this period.

1887

The French proclaim the Indochinese Union, which brings together the countries of Vietnam, Cambodia and Laos under French rule, binding their fates in the tumultuous events of the 20th century.

1897

Paul Doumer becomes governor general of Indochina, inaugurating an infrastructure program of roads and railways across Vietnam. In 1931 he becomes president of France, but is assassinated a year later.

UNCLE OF THE PEOPLE

Ho Chi Minh (Bringer of Light) is the best known of some 50 aliases assumed by Nguyen Tat Thanh (1890–1969) over the course of his long career. He was founder of the Vietnamese Communist Party and president of the Democratic Republic of Vietnam from 1946 until his death. The son of a fiercely nationalistic scholar-official of humble means, he was educated in the Quoc Hoc Secondary School in Hue. In 1911 he signed up as a cook's apprentice on a French ship, sailing the seas to North America, Africa and Europe. He stopped off in Europe where, while odd-jobbing as a gardener, snow sweeper, waiter, photo retoucher and stoker, his political consciousness began to develop.

Ho Chi Minh moved to Paris, where he adopted the name Nguyen Ai Quoc (Nguyen the Patriot). During this period he mastered a number of languages (including English, French, German and Mandarin) and began to promote the issue of Indochinese independence. During the 1919 Versailles Peace Conference, he tried to present an independence plan for Vietnam to US president Woodrow Wilson.

Ho Chi Minh was a founding member of the French Communist Party, which was established in 1920. In 1923 he was summoned to Moscow for training by Communist International and from there to Guangzhou (Canton), China, where he founded the Revolutionary Youth League of Vietnam.

During the early 1930s the English rulers of Hong Kong obliged the French government by imprisoning Ho for his revolutionary activities. After his release he travelled to the USSR and China. In 1941 Ho Chi Minh returned to Vietnam for the first time in 30 years. That same year, at the age of 51, he helped found the Viet Minh, the goal of which was the independence of Vietnam from French colonial rule and Japanese occupation. In 1942 he was arrested and held for a year by the Nationalist Chinese. As Japan prepared to surrender in August 1945, Ho Chi Minh led the August Revolution, and his forces then established control throughout much of Vietnam.

The return of the French shortly thereafter forced Ho Chi Minh and the Viet Minh to flee Hanoi and take up armed resistance. Ho spent eight years conducting a guerrilla war until the Viet Minh's victory against the French at Dien Bien Phu in 1954. He led North Vietnam until his death in September 1969 – he never lived to see the North's victory over the South. Ho is affectionately referred to as 'Uncle Ho' (Bac Ho) by his admirers.

The party has worked hard to preserve the image of Bac Ho who, like his erstwhile nemesis South Vietnamese president Ngo Dinh Diem, never married. His image dominates contemporary Vietnam more than three decades after his death. No town is complete without a statue of Ho, and no city is complete without a museum in his name. This cult of personality is in stark contrast to the simplicity with which Ho lived his life. For the fullest picture of Ho's legendary life, check out *Ho Chi Minh*, the excellent biography by William J Duiker.

Department asking for US aid, but received no replies, as events in Europe and Japan were occupying the department's attention.

A footnote on the agenda of the Potsdam Conference of 1945 was the disarming of Japanese occupation forces in Vietnam. It was decided that the

1911

Nguyen Tat Thanh, later known as Ho Chi Minh, leaves Vietnam aboard a steamship to travel the world, eventually settling in Europe where his political consciousness evolves.

1925

Ho Chi Minh moves towards organised political agitation, establishing the Revolutionary Youth League of Vietnam in Canton in southern China, an early incarnation of the Vietnamese Communist Party.

1927

Drawing on the ideals of popular nationalist leader Phan Boi Chau, the Vietnamese Nationalist Party is founded. Modelled on the Chinese Kuomintang, the party pledges to overthrow the French.

Chinese Kuomintang would accept the Japanese surrender north of the 16th Parallel and that the British would do the same to the south.

When the British arrived in Saigon in September, anarchy ruled. The Japanese were defeated, the French were vulnerable, the Viet Minh was looking to assert itself, and private militias were fuelling trouble. In order to stabilise the situation, defeated Japanese troops helped the British restore order as part of a so-called Gremlin force. Then 1400 armed French paratroopers were released from imprisonment by the Japanese and, looking for vengeance after Ho Chi Minh's declaration of independence, immediately took to the streets, breaking into the homes and shops of the Vietnamese and attacking civilians. The Viet Minh responded by calling a general strike and by launching a guerrilla campaign against the French. On 24 September French general Jacques Philippe Leclerc arrived in Saigon, declaring 'We have come to reclaim our inheritance'.

Between 1944 and 1945, the Viet Minh received funding and arms from the US Office of Strategic Services (OSS; today the CIA). When Ho Chi Minh declared independence in 1945, he had OSS agents at his side and borrowed liberally from the American Declaration of Independence.

In the north, Chinese Kuomintang troops were fleeing the Chinese communists and making their way southward towards Hanoi. Ho tried to placate them, but as the months of Chinese occupation dragged on, he decided to accept a temporary return of the French. For the Vietnamese, the French colonisers were a safer bet than the Chinese; they had only occupied Vietnam for 60-odd years, the Chinese for more than 1000 years. The French were to stay for five years in return for recognising Vietnam as a free state within the French Union.

WAR WITH THE FRENCH

The French had managed to regain control of Vietnam, at least in name. However, following the French shelling of Haiphong in November 1946, which killed hundreds of civilians, the détente with the Viet Minh began to unravel. Only a few weeks later fighting broke out in Hanoi, marking the start of the Franco-Viet Minh War. Ho Chi Minh and his forces fled to the mountains, where they would remain for the next eight years.

In May 1954 the Viet Minh dug a tunnel network under the French defences on Hill A1 and rigged it with explosives. Comrade Sapper Nguyen Van Bach volunteered himself as a human fuse in case the detonator failed. Luckily for him it didn't and he is today honoured as a national hero.

In the face of determined Vietnamese nationalism, the French proved unable to reassert their control. Despite massive US aid in an effort to halt the communist domino effect throughout Asia, and the existence of significant indigenous anticommunist elements, for the French it was ultimately an unwinnable war. As Ho said to the French at the outset: 'You can kill 10 of my men for every one I kill of yours, but even at those odds you will lose and I will win.'

After eight years of fighting, the Viet Minh controlled much of Vietnam and neighbouring Laos. On 7 May 1954, after a 57-day siege, more than 10,000 starving French troops surrendered to the Viet Minh at Dien Bien Phu (p171). This defeat brought an end to the French colonial adventure in Indochina. The following day, the Geneva Conference opened to negotiate an end to the conflict, but the French had no cards left to bring to the table.

1940

The Japanese occupation of Vietnam begins, as the pro–Vichy France colonial government offers the use of military facilities in return for the continued control over administration.

1941

Ho Chi Minh forms the Viet Minh (short for the League for the Independence of Vietnam), a liberation movement seeking independence from France and fighting the Japanese occupation of WWII.

Mid-1940s

The combination of Japanese rice requisitions and widespread flooding leads to a disastrous famine in which 20% of North Vietnam's population dies.

Resolutions included an exchange of prisoners; the 'temporary' division of Vietnam into two zones at the Ben Hai River (near the 17th Parallel) until nationwide elections could be held; the free passage of people across the 17th Parallel for a period of 300 days; and the holding of nationwide elections on 20 July 1956. In the course of the Franco-Viet Minh War, more than 35,000 French fighters had been killed and 48,000 wounded; there are no exact numbers for Vietnamese casualties, but they were certainly higher.

A SEPARATE SOUTH VIETNAM

After the Geneva Accords were signed and sealed, the South was ruled by a government led by Ngo Dinh Diem, a fiercely anticommunist Catholic. His power base was significantly strengthened by 900,000 refugees, many of them Catholics, who had fled the communist North during the 300-day free-passage period.

Nationwide elections were never held, as the Americans rightly feared that Ho Chi Minh would win with a massive majority. During the first few years of his rule, Diem consolidated power fairly effectively, defeating the Binh Xuyen crime syndicate and the private armies of the Hoa Hao and Cao Dai religious sects. During Diem's 1957 official visit to the USA, President Eisenhower called him the 'miracle man' of Asia. As time went on Diem became increasingly tyrannical in dealing with dissent, closing Buddhist monasteries, imprisoning monks and banning opposition parties. Running the government became a family affair. His younger brother, Ngo Dinh Ngu, became his chief political adviser during his rule, while his sister-in-law Madame Nhu effectively became First Lady, as Diem himself never married.

In the early 1960s the South was rocked by anti-Diem unrest led by university students and Buddhist clergy, which included several highly publicised self-immolations by monks that shocked the world (see p229). The US began to see Diem as a liability and threw its support behind a military coup. A group of young generals led the operation in November 1963. Diem was to go into exile, but the generals executed both Diem and his brother. Diem was succeeded by a string of military rulers who continued his policies.

The 2002 remake of *The Quiet American*, starring Michael Caine, is a must-see. Beautifully shot, it is a classic introduction to Vietnam in the 1950s, as the French disengaged and the Americans moved in to take their place.

The USA closed its consulate in Hanoi on 12 December 1955 and would not officially reopen an embassy in the Vietnamese capital for more than 40 years.

A NEW NORTH VIETNAM

The Geneva Accords allowed the leadership of the Democratic Republic of Vietnam to return to Hanoi and assert control of all territory north of the 17th Parallel. The new government immediately set out to eliminate those elements of the population that threatened its power. Tens of thousands of landlords, some with only tiny holdings, were denounced to security committees by their neighbours and arrested. Hasty trials resulted in between 10,000 and 15,000 executions and the imprisonment of thousands more. In 1956, the party, faced with widespread rural unrest, recognised that things had got out of control and began a Campaign for the Rectification of Errors.

1945

Ho Chi Minh proclaims Vietnamese independence on 2 September in Ba Dinh Square in central Hanoi, but the French aim to reassert their authority and impose colonial rule once more.

1946

Strained relations between the Viet Minh forces and the French colonialists erupt into open fighting in Hanoi and Haiphong, marking the start of the eight-year Franco-Viet Minh War.

1949

Mao Tse Tung and the Chinese communists take power in Beijing, offering an alternative road to revolution to that of Moscow and the Soviet Union. Vietnam, Cambodia and Laos later find themselves caught up in the politics of the Sino-Soviet split.

In Hanoi and the North, Ho Chi Minh created a very effective police state. The regime was characterised by ruthless police power; denunciations by a huge network of secret informers; and the blacklisting of dissidents, their children and their children's children.

THE NORTH–SOUTH WAR

The communists' campaign to liberate the South began in 1959. The Ho Chi Minh Trail, which had been in existence for several years, reopened for business. In April 1960 universal military conscription was implemented in the North. Eight months later, Hanoi announced the formation of the National Liberation Front (NLF), which came to be known as the Viet Cong or the VC.

As the NLF launched its campaign, the Diem government quickly lost control of the countryside. To stem the tide, the Strategic Hamlets Program was implemented in 1962, based on British tactics in Malaya. This involved forcibly moving peasants into fortified 'strategic hamlets' in order to deny the VC the oxygen of the people and their potential bases of support. This program was abandoned with the death of Diem, but years later the VC admitted that it had caused them significant problems.

And for the South it was no longer just a battle with the VC. In 1964 Hanoi began sending regular North Vietnamese Army (NVA) units down the Ho Chi Minh Trail. By early 1965 the Saigon government was on its last legs. Desertions from the Army of the Republic of Vietnam (ARVN) had reached 2000 per month. The South was losing a district capital each week, yet in 10 years only one senior South Vietnamese army officer had been wounded. The army was getting ready to evacuate Hue and Danang, and the central highlands seemed about to fall.

Viet Cong and VC are both abbreviations for Viet Nam Cong San, which means Vietnamese communist. American soldiers nicknamed the VC 'Charlie', as in 'Victor Charlie'.

ENTER THE CAVALRY

The Americans saw France's war in Indochina as an important element in the worldwide struggle against communist expansion. Vietnam was the next domino and could not topple. In 1950, the US Military Assistance Advisory Group (MAAG) rolled into Vietnam, ostensibly to train local troops in the use of advanced weaponry. American soldiers would remain on Vietnamese soil for the next 25 years, initially as advisers, and then as active combatants. As early as 1954, US military aid to the French topped US$2 billion.

A decisive turning point in US strategy came with the August 1964 Gulf of Tonkin Incident. Two US destroyers, the *Maddox* and the *Turner Joy*, claimed to have come under unprovoked attack while sailing off the North Vietnamese coast. Subsequent research suggests that there was a certain degree of provocation; the first attack took place while the *Maddox* was in North Vietnamese waters assisting a secret South Vietnamese commando raid and, according to an official National Security Agency report in 2005, the second one never happened.

US presidential candidate John McCain spent five and a half years in the notorious 'Hanoi Hilton', the Hoa Lo Prison in the Vietnamese capital.

However, on US president Lyndon Johnson's orders, 64 sorties unleashed bombs on the North – the first of thousands of such missions that would hit every single road and rail bridge in the country, as well as 4000 of North Vietnam's 5788 villages. Two US aircraft were lost in the raids and Lieutenant

1954

French forces surrender en masse to Viet Minh fighters as the siege of Dien Bien Phu comes to a dramatic close on 7 May, marking the end of colonial rule in Indochina.

1955

Vietnam is 'temporarily' divided at the 17th Parallel into communist North Vietnam and 'free' South Vietnam and Catholics and communists are given 300 days to relocate to the South and North, respectively.

1959

The Ho Chi Minh Trail reopens for business in readiness for a protracted guerrilla war in the South. Originally established to fight the French throughout Indochina, the trail is used to supply Vietnamese communist forces in the South.

TRACKING THE AMERICAN WAR

The American War in Vietnam was *the story* for a generation. Follow in the footsteps of soldiers, journalists and politicians on all sides with a visit to the sites where the story unfolded.

- **China Beach** (p243) The strip of sand near Danang where US soldiers dropped in for some rest and relaxation.
- **Cu Chi Tunnels** (p390) The Vietnamese dug an incredible and elaborate tunnel network to evade American forces, just 30km from Saigon and right under the noses of a US base.
- **Demilitarised Zone** (DMZ; p208) The no-man's land at the 17th Parallel, dividing North and South Vietnam after 1954, soon became one of the most heavily militarised zones in the world.
- **Dien Bien Phu** (p171) The ultimate historic battle site, where the French colonial story came to a close in May 1954.
- **Ho Chi Minh Trail** (p334) The supply route for the South; the North Vietnamese moved soldiers and munitions down this incredible trail through the Truong Son Mountains in an almost unparalleled logistical feat.
- **Hue Citadel** (p217) The ancient citadel was razed to the ground during street-to-street fighting in early 1968 when the Americans retook the city from the communists after a three-week occupation.
- **Khe Sanh** (p213) This was the biggest smokescreen of the war, as the North Vietnamese massed forces around this US base in 1968 to draw attention away from the coming Tet Offensive.
- **Long Tan Memorial** (p400) The Australian contingent who fought in Vietnam, mostly based near Vung Tau in the south, is remembered here with the Long Tan Memorial Cross.
- **My Lai** (p270) The village of My Lai is infamous as the site of one of the worst atrocities in the war, when American GIs massacred hundreds of villagers in March 1968.
- **Vinh Moc Tunnels** (p209) The real deal: these tunnels haven't been surgically enlarged for tourists and they mark yet another feat of infrastructural ingenuity.

Everett Alvarez became the first American prisoner of war (POW) of the conflict – he remained in captivity for eight years.

A few days later, the US Congress overwhelmingly passed the Tonkin Gulf Resolution, which gave the president the power to 'take all necessary measures' to 'repel any armed attack against the forces of the United States and to prevent further aggression'. Until its repeal in 1970, the resolution gave the president the power to take any action in Vietnam without congressional control.

As the military situation of the Saigon government reached a new nadir, the first US combat troops splashed ashore at Danang in March 1965. By

1960

The National Liberation Front (better known as the Viet Cong) launch a guerrilla war against the Diem government in the South, sparking the 'American War'.

1962

Based on the British experience fighting communist forces in Malaya, the Diem government, with the support of the Americans, initiates the Strategic Hamlets Program, which cuts off the Viet Cong from its network of village support systems.

1963

South Vietnam's president Ngo Dinh Diem is overthrown and killed in a coup backed by the USA, which brings a new group of young military commanders into power.

Hitch a ride with Michael Herr and his seminal work *Dispatches*. A correspondent for *Rolling Stone* magazine, Herr tells it how it was, as some of the darkest events of the American War unfolded around him, including the siege of Khe Sanh.

December 1965 there were 184,300 US military personnel in Vietnam and 636 Americans had died. By December 1967 the figures had risen to 485,600 US soldiers in country and 16,021 dead. There were 1.3 million soldiers fighting for the Saigon government, including the South Vietnamese and other allies.

By 1966 the buzz words in Washington were 'pacification', 'search and destroy' and 'free-fire zones'. Pacification involved developing a pro-government civilian infrastructure in each village, and providing the soldiers to guard it. To protect the villages from VC raids, mobile search-and-destroy units of soldiers moved around the country hunting VC guerrillas. In some cases, villagers were evacuated so the Americans could use heavy weaponry such as napalm and tanks in areas that were declared free-fire zones.

These strategies were only partially successful: US forces could control the countryside by day, while the VC usually controlled it by night. Even without heavy weapons, VC guerrillas continued to inflict heavy casualties in ambushes and through extensive use of mines and booby traps. Although free-fire zones were supposed to prevent civilian casualties, plenty of villagers were nevertheless shelled, bombed, strafed or napalmed. These attacks turned out to be a fairly efficient recruiting tool for the VC.

Neil Sheehan's account of the life of Colonel John Paul Vann, *Bright Shining Lie,* won the Pulitzer Prize and is the portrayal of one man's disenchantment with the war, mirroring America's realisation it could not be won.

THE TURNING POINT

In January 1968 North Vietnamese troops launched a major attack on the US base at Khe Sanh (p213) in the Demilitarised Zone (DMZ). This battle, the single largest of the war, was in part a massive diversion from the Tet Offensive.

The Tet Offensive marked a decisive turning point in the war. On the evening of 31 January, as the country celebrated the Lunar New Year, the VC broke an unofficial holiday ceasefire with a series of coordinated strikes in more than 100 cities and towns, including Saigon. As the TV cameras rolled, a VC commando team took over the courtyard of the US embassy in central Saigon. However, the communists miscalculated the mood of the population, as the popular uprising they had hoped to provoke never materialised. In cities such as Hue, the VC were not welcomed as liberators and this contributed to a communist backlash against the civilian population.

Oliver Stone has never been one to shy away from political point-scoring and in the first of his famous trilogy about Vietnam, *Platoon,* he earns a maximum ten. A brutal and cynical look at the conflict through the eyes of rookie Charlie Sheen, with great performances from Tom Berenger and Willem Dafoe.

US forces had long been eager to engage the VC in open battle and the Tet Offensive delivered. Although utterly surprised – a major failure of US military intelligence – the South Vietnamese and Americans immediately counter-attacked with massive firepower, bombing and shelling heavily populated cities as they had the open jungle. The counter-attack devastated the VC, but also traumatised the civilian population. In Ben Tre, a US officer bitterly remarked that they 'had to destroy the town in order to save it'.

The Tet Offensive killed about 1000 US soldiers and 2000 ARVN troops, but VC losses were more than 10 times higher, at around 32,000 deaths. In

1964

Although the US is not officially at war, it launches Operation Pierce Arrow and bombs North Vietnam for the first time in retaliation for the Gulf of Tonkin incident.

1965

The first US Marines wade ashore at Danang, greeted by garland-bedecked girls on the beach, marking the start of the US ground war in Vietnam.

1967

By the end of the year, there are 1.3 million soldiers fighting for the South – nearly half a million of these are from the US.

addition, some 500 American and 10,000 North Vietnamese troops had died at the battle of Khe Sanh the preceding week.

The VC may have lost the battle, but this was the critical turning point on the road to winning the war. The military had long been boasting that victory was just a matter of time. Watching the killing and chaos in Saigon beamed into their living rooms, many Americans stopped swallowing the official line. While US generals were proclaiming a great victory, public tolerance of the war and its casualties reached breaking point. For the Vietnamese communists, the Tet Offensive ultimately proved a success, as the cost of fighting the war became unbearable for the Americans.

Simultaneously, stories began leaking out of Vietnam about atrocities and massacres carried out against unarmed Vietnamese civilians, including the infamous My Lai Massacre (see p270). This helped turn the tide and a coalition of the concerned emerged that threatened the establishment. Antiwar demonstrations rocked American university campuses and spilled onto the streets.

The Tet Offensive was a long-term success, but in the short-term it fundamentally weakened the VC's military capacity and ensured that North Vietnamese soldiers would play a decisive role in the future of the war.

NIXON & HIS DOCTRINE

Richard Nixon was elected president in part because of a promise that he had a 'secret plan' to end the war. The Nixon Doctrine, as it was called, was unveiled in July 1969 and it called on Asian nations to be more 'self-reliant' in matters of defence. Nixon's strategy called for 'Vietnamisation', which meant making the South Vietnamese fight the war without the support of US troops.

Even with the election of the man referred to as 'Tricky Dicky', the first half of 1969 saw the conflict escalate further. In April the number of US soldiers in Vietnam reached an all-time high of 543,400. While the fighting raged, Nixon's chief negotiator, Henry Kissinger, pursued peace talks in Paris with his North Vietnamese counterpart Le Duc Tho.

In 1969 the Americans began secretly bombing Cambodia in an attempt to flush out Vietnamese communist sanctuaries across the border. Given the choice between facing US troops and pushing deeper into Cambodia, the VC fled west. In 1970, US ground forces were sent into Cambodia to extricate ARVN units, whose combat ability was yet to match the enemy's. The North Vietnamese moved deeper into Cambodian territory and together with their Khmer Rouge allies controlled half of the country by the summer of 1970, including the world-famous temples of Angkor.

This new escalation provoked violent antiwar protests in the US and elsewhere. A peace demonstration at Kent State University in Ohio resulted in four protesters being shot dead by National Guard troops. The rise of organisations such as Vietnam Veterans Against the War demonstrated that it wasn't just those fearing military conscription who wanted the USA out of Vietnam. It was clear that the war was tearing America apart.

The definitive American War movie has to be *Apocalypse Now*. Marlon Brando plays renegade Colonel Kurtz who has gone AWOL, and native, in the wilds of northeast Cambodia. Martin Sheen is sent to bring him back and the psychotic world into which he is drawn is one of the most savage indictments of war ever portrayed.

1968

The Viet Cong launches the Tet Offensive, an attack on towns and cities throughout the South that catches the Americans, who were diverted by the siege of Khe Sanh, unaware.

1968

In one of the worst atrocities of the war, between 347 and 504 Vietnamese civilians are killed in what is to become known as the My Lai Massacre.

1969

President Nixon authorises the secret bombing of Cambodia in an attempt to flush out Vietnamese communist forces there. Operation Menu, as it was known, commences on 18 March 1969.

For a human perspective on the North Vietnamese experience during the war, read *The Sorrow of War* by Bao Ninh, a poignant tale of love and loss that shows the soldiers from the North had the same fears and desires as most American GIs.

In the spring of 1972 the North Vietnamese launched an offensive across the 17th Parallel; the USA responded with increased bombing of the North and by laying mines in North Vietnam's harbours. The 'Christmas bombing' of Haiphong and Hanoi at the end of 1972 was calculated to wrest concessions from North Vietnam at the negotiating table. Eventually, the Paris Peace Accords were signed by the USA, North Vietnam, South Vietnam and the VC on 27 January 1973, which provided for a ceasefire, the total withdrawal of US combat forces and the release of 590 American POWs. The agreement failed to mention the 200,000 North Vietnamese troops still in South Vietnam.

In total, 3.14 million Americans (including 7200 women) served in the US armed forces in Vietnam during the war. Officially, 58,183 Americans were killed in action or are listed as missing in action (MIA). The direct cost of the war was officially put at US$165 billion, though its real cost to the economy was likely to have been considerably more.

Pentagon figures indicate that by 1972, 3689 fixed-wing aircraft and 4857 helicopters had been lost and 15 million tonnes of ammunition had been expended.

By the end of 1973, 223,748 South Vietnamese soldiers had been killed in action; North Vietnamese and VC fatalities have been estimated at one million. Approximately four million civilians (or 10% of the Vietnamese population) were injured or killed during the war. At least 300,000 Vietnamese and 2200 Americans are still listed as MIA. US teams continue to search Vietnam, Laos and Cambodia for the remains of their fallen comrades. In more recent years, the Vietnamese have been searching for their own MIAs in Cambodia and Laos. Individual family members often use mediums to try and locate the remains of their loved ones.

OTHER FOREIGN INVOLVEMENT

Australia, New Zealand, South Korea, the Philippines and Thailand also sent military personnel to South Vietnam as part of what the Americans called the 'Free World Military Forces', whose purpose was to help internationalise the American war effort in order to give it more legitimacy.

The American War in Vietnam claimed the lives of countless journalists. For a look at the finest photographic work from the battlefront, *Requiem* is an anthology of work from fallen correspondents on all sides of the conflict and a fitting tribute to their trade.

Australia's participation in the conflict constituted the most significant commitment of its military forces since WWII. Of the 46,852 Australian military personnel who served in the war, casualties totalled 496, with 2398 soldiers wounded.

Most of New Zealand's contingent, which numbered 548 at its highest point in 1968, operated as an integral part of the Australian Task Force, which was stationed near Baria, just north of Vung Tau.

THE FALL OF THE SOUTH

Most US military personnel departed Vietnam in 1973, leaving behind a small contingent of technicians, advisors and CIA agents. The bombing of North Vietnam ceased and the US POWs were released. Still the war rumbled on, only now the South Vietnamese were fighting alone.

1970

The North Vietnamese move deeper into Cambodia, proving Operation Menu to be counterproductive. By the summer the Vietnamese occupy the temples of Angkor.

1973

All sides put pen to paper to sign the Paris Peace Accords on 27 January 1973, stipulating an end to hostilities, but the conflict rumbles on with the US taking a back seat.

1975

Nguyen Van Thieu, South Vietamese president, flees the country after seven years in power.

CHILDREN OF THE DUST

One tragic legacy of the American War was the plight of thousands of Amerasians. Marriages, relationships and commercial encounters between Americans and Vietnamese were common during the war. But when the Americans headed home, many abandoned their 'wives' and mistresses, leaving them to raise children who were half-American or half-Vietnamese in a society not particularly tolerant of such racial intermingling.

After reunification, the Amerasians – living reminders of the American presence – were often mistreated by Vietnamese and even abandoned, forcing them to live on the streets. They were also denied educational and vocational opportunities, and were sadly referred to as 'children of the dust'.

At the end of the 1980s, the Orderly Departure Program (ODP) was designed to allow Amerasians and political refugees who otherwise might have tried to flee the country by land or sea to resettle in the West (mostly in the USA).

Unfortunately, many Amerasian children were adopted by Vietnamese eager to emigrate, but were then dumped after the family's arrival in the USA. For more on this forgotten chapter from the American War, pick up *Surviving Twice: Amerasian Children of the Vietnam War* (2005) by Trin Yarborough.

In January 1975 the North Vietnamese launched a massive ground attack across the 17th Parallel using tanks and heavy artillery. The invasion provoked panic in the South Vietnamese army, which had always depended on US support. In March, the NVA occupied a strategic section of the central highlands at Buon Ma Thuot. South Vietnam's president, Nguyen Van Thieu, decided on a strategy of tactical withdrawal to more defensible positions. This was to prove a spectacular military blunder.

Whole brigades of ARVN soldiers disintegrated and fled southward, joining hundreds of thousands of civilians clogging Hwy 1. City after city – Hue, Danang, Quy Nhon, Nha Trang – were simply abandoned with hardly a shot fired. The ARVN troops were fleeing so quickly that the North Vietnamese army could barely keep up.

Nguyen Van Thieu, in power since 1967, resigned on 21 April 1975 and fled the country, allegedly carting off millions of dollars in ill-gotten wealth. The North Vietnamese pushed on to Saigon and on the morning of 30 April 1975 their tanks smashed through the gates of Saigon's Independence Palace (now called Reunification Palace). General Duong Van Minh, president for just 42 hours, formally surrendered, marking the end of the war.

Just a few hours before the surrender, the last Americans were evacuated by helicopter from the US embassy roof to ships stationed just offshore. Iconic images of US Marines booting Vietnamese people off their helicopters were beamed around the world. And so more than a quarter of a century

The concept of 'embedded' journalists was a direct result of bad press coverage during the war in Vietnam. Journalists were allowed to travel anywhere and everywhere during the conflict and told both sides of the story. Some American military commanders maintain it was the press that lost the US the war.

1975

On 30 April 1975 Saigon falls to the North Vietnamese and is renamed Ho Chi Minh City, as the last Americans scramble to leave the city before the communists take over.

1977

Talks between the US and Vietnam on the normalisation of relations stall, as Washington cosies up to China. The US$3.5 billion war reparations package agreed to by the US in 1973 is never repaid.

1978

Vietnam invades Cambodia on Christmas Day, sweeping through the shattered country and overthrowing the Khmer Rouge government on 7 January 1979.

of American military involvement came to a close. Throughout the entire conflict, the USA never actually declared war on North Vietnam.

The Americans weren't the only ones who left. As the South collapsed, 135,000 Vietnamese also fled the country; over the next five years, at least half a million of their compatriots would do the same. Those who left by sea would become known to the world as 'boat people'. These refugees risked everything to undertake perilous journeys on the South China Sea, but eventually some of these hardy souls found a new life in places as diverse as Australia and France.

The majority of Vietnamese 'boat people' who fled the country in the late 1970s were not in fact Vietnamese, but ethnic Chinese whose wealth and business acumen, to say nothing of their ethnicity, made them an obvious target for the revolution.

REUNIFICATION OF VIETNAM

On the first day of their victory, the communists changed Saigon's name to Ho Chi Minh City (HCMC). This was just the first of many changes.

The sudden success of the 1975 North Vietnamese offensive surprised the North almost as much as it did the South. Consequently, Hanoi had no detailed plans to deal with the reintegration of the North and South, which had totally different social and economic systems.

The party faced the legacy of a cruel and protracted war that had literally fractured the country. There was bitterness on both sides, and a daunting series of challenges. Damage from the fighting was extensive, including anything from unmarked minefields to war-focused, dysfunctional economies; from a chemically poisoned countryside to a population who were physically or mentally scarred. Peace may have arrived, but the struggle was far from over.

Until the formal reunification of Vietnam in July 1976, the South was ruled by the Provisional Revolutionary Government. The Communist Party did not trust the Southern urban intelligentsia, so large numbers of Northern cadres were sent southward to manage the transition. This fuelled resentment among Southerners who had worked against the Thieu government and then, after its overthrow, found themselves frozen out.

The Paris Peace Accords of 1973 included a provision for US reparations to Vietnam totalling US$3.5 billion and this became the main stumbling block to normalising relations in 1978. No money has ever been paid to Vietnam.

The party opted for a rapid transition to socialism in the South, but it proved disastrous for the economy. Reunification was accompanied by widespread political repression. Despite repeated assurances to the contrary, hundreds of thousands of people who had ties to the previous regime had their property confiscated and were rounded up and imprisoned without trial in forced-labour camps, euphemistically known as re-education camps. Tens of thousands of businesspeople, intellectuals, artists, journalists, writers, union leaders and religious leaders – some of whom had opposed both the Southern government and the war – were held in terrible conditions.

Contrary to its economic policy, Vietnam sought a rapprochement with the USA and by 1978 Washington was close to establishing relations with Hanoi. But the China card was ultimately played: Vietnam was sacrificed for the prize of US relations with Beijing and Hanoi moved into the orbit of the Soviet Union, on whom it was to rely for the next decade.

1979

China invades northern Vietnam in February in a retaliatory attack against the Vietnamese for attacking their Khmer Rouge allies, but the Vietnamese emerge relatively unscathed. Thousands of ethnic Chinese in Vietnam flee the country.

1984

In response to Khmer Rouge attacks from safe havens on the Thai border, Vietnamese forces begin to lay the longest land-mine belt in the world, known as K-5, which stretches the full length of the Cambodia–Thailand border.

1986

Doi moi (economic reform), Vietnam's answer to perestroika and the first step towards re-engaging with the West, is launched with a rash of economic reforms.

Relations with China to the north and its Khmer Rouge allies to the west were rapidly deteriorating. War-weary Vietnam felt encircled by enemies. An anticapitalist campaign was launched in March 1978, seizing private property and businesses. Most of the victims were ethnic Chinese – hundreds of thousands soon became refugees or 'boat people', and relations with China soured further.

Meanwhile, repeated attacks on Vietnamese border villages by the Khmer Rouge forced Vietnam to respond. Vietnamese forces entered Cambodia on Christmas Day 1978. They succeeded in driving the Khmer Rouge from power on 7 January 1979 and set up a pro-Hanoi regime in Phnom Penh. China viewed the attack on the Khmer Rouge as a serious provocation. In February 1979 Chinese forces invaded Vietnam and fought a brief, 17-day war before withdrawing (see the boxed text Neighbouring Tensions, p156).

Liberation of Cambodia from the Khmer Rouge soon turned to occupation and a long civil war, which exacted a heavy toll on Vietnam. The command economy was strangling the commercial instincts of Vietnamese rice farmers. Today one of the world's leading rice exporters, back in the early 1980s Vietnam was a rice *importer*. War and revolution had brought the country to its knees and a radical change in direction was required.

During the occupation of Cambodia in the 1980s, the Vietnamese laid the world's longest minefield belt, K-5, as a defence against Khmer Rouge guerrilla attacks from Thailand. It stretched from the Mekong River to the Gulf of Thailand and remains one of the most heavily mined areas in the world.

OPENING THE DOOR

In 1985 President Mikhael Gorbachev came to power in the Soviet Union. *Glasnost* (openness) and *perestroika* (restructuring) were in, radical revolutionaries were out. Vietnam followed suit in 1986 by choosing reform-minded Nguyen Van Linh to lead the Vietnamese Communist Party. *Doi moi* (economic reform) was experimented with in Cambodia and introduced to Vietnam. As the USSR scaled back its commitments to the communist world, the far-flung outposts were the first to feel the pinch. The Vietnamese decided to unilaterally withdraw from Cambodia in September 1989, as they could no longer afford the occupation. The party in Vietnam was on its own and needed to reform to survive.

However, dramatic changes in Eastern Europe in 1989 and the collapse of the Soviet Union in 1991 were not viewed with favour in Hanoi. The party denounced the participation of noncommunists in Eastern bloc governments, calling the democratic revolutions 'a counter-attack from imperialist circles' against socialism. Politically, things were moving at a glacial pace, but economically the Vietnamese decided to embrace the market. Capitalism has since taken root and it is unlikely that Ho Chi Minh would recognise the dynamic Vietnam of today.

Author and documentary film-maker John Pilger was ripping into the establishment long before Michael Moore rode into town. Get to grips with his hard-hitting views on the American War at www.johnpilger.com.

VIETNAM TODAY

Relations with Vietnam's old nemesis, the USA, have improved in recent times. In early 1994 the USA lifted its economic embargo, which had been

1989

Vietnamese forces pull out of Cambodia in September as the Soviet Union scales back its commitment to its communist partners, and Vietnam is at peace for the first time in decades.

1994

The US trade embargo on Vietnam, in place in the North since 1964 and extended to the reunified nation since 1975, is revoked.

1995

Vietnam joins the Association of South-East Asian Nations (ASEAN), an organisation originally founded as a bulwark against the expansion of communism in the region.

THE NORTH–SOUTH DIVIDE

Vietnam knows more about north–south divides than most, as the country spent 21 years partitioned along the 17th Parallel, à la Korea.

War and politics are not the only explanation for two Vietnams. Climatically, the two regions are very different and this has an impact on productivity, the Mekong Delta yielding three rice harvests a year and the Red River just two. There are two dialects with very different pronunciation. There is different food. And, some say, a different persona.

The war amplified the differences. The North experienced communist austerity and US bombing. The South experienced the roller-coaster ride that was the American presence in Nam. As the war came to a close and Southerners began to flee, thousands settled abroad, known as the Viet Kieu. Many have returned, confident thanks to an overseas education and savvy in the ways of the world. Their initiative and investment has helped to drive the economy forward.

This meant that it was the south of the reunified country that benefited most from the economic reforms of *doi moi*, with self-confident Saigon the dynamo driving the rest of it forward. Until the recent global economic crisis, the economy had been growing rapidly for a decade and a half, but this has been more heavily skewed to the south. Much of this is down to the attitude of government officials and the fact that many northern cadres were far more suspicious of reform than their southern cousins.

The government is aware of these divisions and tries to ensure a fair balance of the offices of state. It wasn't always so and many southern communists found themselves frozen out after reunification, but these days the party ensures that if the prime minister is from the south, the head of the Communist Party is from the north.

When it comes to the older generation, the south has never forgiven the north for bulldozing their war cemeteries, imposing communism and blackballing whole families. The north has never forgiven the south for siding with the Americans against their own people. Luckily for Vietnam, the new generation seems to have less interest in their harrowing history and more interest in making money. Today there is only one Vietnam and its mantra is business.

in place in the North since the 1960s. Full diplomatic relations with the USA have been restored and in 2000 Bill Clinton became the first US president to visit northern Vietnam. George W Bush followed suit in 2006, as Vietnam was welcomed into the World Trade Organization (WTO) in January 2007. In 2008, Vietnam became a nonpermanent member of the UN Security Council for the first time in its history, further bolstering its international standing.

While the international rehabilitation of Vietnam continues apace, political rehabilitation at home has been considerably slower. The central highlands continues to be an Achilles heel for the Hanoi government. As more and more highland areas are settled by ethnic Vietnamese, the ethnic minorities have protested against this Vietnamisation of their traditional land and culture. The Vietnamese government has cracked down hard, sending hundreds of

2000

Bill Clinton visits Vietnam at the end of his presidency and becomes the first American president to set foot in Hanoi, cementing a new chapter in Vietnamese–US relations.

2003

Crime figure Nam Can goes on trial for corruption, embezzlement, kidnap, murder and more. The case implicates dozens of police and politicians, rocking the reputation of the government. He is eventually sentenced to death.

2004

Bird flu (avian influenza) sweeps through Vietnam, leaving several dozen people dead and severely denting the tourism trade.

political refugees fleeing to Cambodia where they have often been sent back by an unsympathetic government in Phnom Penh. Today there is a tense stalemate in the region and there are still some sensitive areas for foreigners, especially those carrying professional camera equipment.

Corruption remains a real problem in Vietnam. Although the authorities have embarked on several campaigns to stamp it out, there was a severe setback in the summer of 2008 when two journalists were jailed for exposing a major scandal in which public officials were using state money to bet on major football matches in Europe. This has cast a shadow over the media establishment in Vietnam and will undoubtedly lead to even more caution among editors and journalists alike when it comes to exposing government malpractice.

Back on the international front, relations have also improved with the historic enemy China. Vietnam is still overshadowed by its northern neighbour and some observers suggest that China still views Vietnam as a renegade province. But Vietnam's economic boom has caught Beijing's attention and it sees northern Vietnam as the fastest route from Yunnan and Sichuan to the South China Sea. Cooperation towards the future seems more important than the conflict of the past.

Vietnam is an active member of ASEAN, an organisation originally established as a bulwark against communism, and this is all adding up to a rosy economic picture. Vietnam's economy has been moving full steam ahead and tourists just can't get enough of the place. The future is bright, but ultimate success depends on how well the Vietnamese can follow the Chinese road to development: economic liberalisation without political liberalisation. With only two million paid-up members of the Communist Party and 85 million Vietnamese, it is a road they must tread carefully.

2006

Vietnam's rehabilitation is virtually complete as it plays host to the glitzy APEC summit, welcoming US president number two in the shape of George W Bush, and prepares to join the WTO.

2008

Rampant inflation grips the country, as commodity prices soar; the local stock-market bubble bursts and house prices spiral downwards leaving many saddled with high debts.

2010

Hanoi celebrates its 1000th birthday. The government plans events and celebrations throughout the year and hopes to secure Unesco World Heritage status for the city.

The Culture

THE NATIONAL PSYCHE

The Vietnamese have been shaped by their history, which is littered with the scars of battles against enemies old and new. The Chinese have been the traditional threat and the proximity of this northern giant has cast a long shadow over Vietnam and its people. They respect but fear China, and in the context of 2000 years of history, the French and the Americans are but a niggling annoyance that were duly dispatched. The Vietnamese are battle-hardened, proud and nationalistic, as they have earned their stripes in successive skirmishes with the world's mightiest powers.

But that's the older generation, who remember every inch of the territory for which they fought, and every bomb and bullet that rained upon them during the long, hard years. For the new generation, Vietnam is a different place: a place to succeed, a place to ignore the staid structures set in stone by the communists, and a place to go out and have some fun. While Uncle Ho (Chi Minh) is respected and revered down the generations for his dedication to the national cause, the young are more interested in David Beckham's current haircut than the Party's latest pronouncements.

It's not only young and old who are living a life apart, but also the urban and rural populations, and the rich and poor. Communism is dead; long live the one-party capitalist dictatorship, where survival of the fittest is the name of the game. Some have survived the transition better than others, and this has created strains in the shape of rural revolts and political backlash. One of the great ironies of the Vietnamese revolution is that it strove to impose a communist system on a society with a competitive instinct to do business and to do it at any hour of the day or night. To the Vietnamese, business, work, commerce – call it what you like – is life.

Shadows and Wind (1999) by journalist Robert Templer is a snappily written exploration of contemporary Vietnam, from Ho Chi Minh personality cults to Vietnam's rock-and-roll youth.

The north–south divide lingers on. The war may be history, but prejudice is alive and well. Ask a southerner what they think of northerners and they'll say they have a 'hard face', that they take themselves too seriously and don't know how to have fun. Ask a northerner what they think of southerners and they will say they are too superficial, obsessed by business and, well, bling. Caricatures they may be, but they shed light on the very real differences between north and south that go beyond the language. Climate plays its part too; just think of the differences between northern and southern Europe and you have a snapshot of how one people can become two. Not forgetting that the north has lived with communism for more than half a century, while the south had more than two decades of freewheelin' free-for-all with the Americans. For more on this, see the North–South Divide on p46.

Finally, don't forget 'face' – or, more importantly, the art of not making the locals lose face. Face is all in Asia, and in Vietnam it is above all. Having 'big face' is synonymous with prestige, and prestige is particularly important in Vietnam. All families, even poor ones, are expected to have big wedding parties and throw their money around like it's water in order to gain face. This is often ruinously expensive but far less important than 'losing face'. And it is for this reason that foreigners should never lose their tempers with the Vietnamese; this will bring unacceptable 'loss of face' to the individual involved and end any chance of a sensible solution to the dispute.

LIFESTYLE

Traditionally, Vietnamese life has revolved around family, fields and faith, with the rhythm of rural existence continuing for centuries at the same pace.

For the majority of the population who still live in the countryside, these constants have remained unchanged, with several generations sharing the same roof, the same rice and the same religion. But in recent decades these rhythms have been jarred by war and ideology, as the peasants were dragged from all they held dear to defend their motherland, and were later herded into cooperatives as the Party tried to take over as the moral and social beacon in the lives of the people.

For an in-depth insight into the culture of Vietnam, including fashion, film and music, check out www.thingsasian.com.

The Communist Party failed to move the masses in the post–American War period. Communism only converted a few, just as the French and Americans had only corrupted a few before it, and, for the majority, it was to the familiar they looked to define their lives. Today this is beginning to change and it's not due to Uncle Ho or the man known as Tricky Dicky (Nixon), but to a combination of a population shift from the countryside to the cities and a demographic shift from old to young.

Like China and Thailand before it, Vietnam is experiencing its very own '60s swing, as the younger generation stand up for a different lifestyle to that of their parents. This is creating plenty of feisty friction in the cities, as sons and daughters dress as they like, date who they want and hit the town until all hours. But few live on their own and they still come home to Mum and Dad at the end of the day, where arguments might arise, particularly when it comes to marriage and settling down.

Extended family is important to the Vietnamese and that includes second or third cousins, the sort of family that many Westerners may not even realise they have. The extended family comes together during times of trouble and times of joy, celebrating festivals and successes, mourning deaths or disappointments. This is a source of strength for many of the older generation, while for the younger generation it's likely to be friends, girlfriends or gangs who play the role of anchor.

Failing businesses often call in a geomancer (feng-shui expert). Sometimes the solution is to move a door or a window. If this doesn't do the trick, it might be necessary to move an ancestor's grave.

With so many family members traditionally under one roof, the Vietnamese generally don't share Western concepts of privacy and personal space. Don't be surprised if people walk into your hotel room without knocking: you may be sitting starkers when the maid unlocks the door and walks in unannounced.

One tradition that remains central to Vietnamese life is geomancy, or feng shui as most of us know it today. Known as *phong thuy* to the locals, this is the art (or science) of living in tune with the environment. The orientation of houses, tombs, *dinh* (communal meeting halls) and pagodas is determined by geomancers. The location of an ancestor's grave is an especially serious matter: if the grave is in the wrong spot or facing the wrong way, there's no telling what trouble the spirits might cause. The same goes for the location of the family altar, which can be found in nearly every Vietnamese home. Westerners planning to go into business with a Vietnamese partner will need to budget for a geomancer to ensure the venture is successful.

GOVERNMENT & ECONOMY

Vietnam is a paradox. It's a communist government with a capitalist economy. Telling it how it is, communism, socialism – call it what you will – is dead. This is a one-party capitalist bureaucracy that doesn't need to sweat about bothersome elections and democratic rights. Officially, communism is still king, but there can be few party hacks who really believe Vietnam is a Marxist utopia. Market-oriented socialism is the new mantra, although socially responsible capitalism might be nearer the mark.

Vietnam now produces and uses more cement each year than its former colonial ruler France.

It's full steam ahead, with Vietnam consistently one of the world's fastest growing economies for more than a decade now, but there are signs the global downturn is slowing things down considerably. Ho Chi Minh may be a hero, but it is Deng Xiaoping's school of economics that has prevailed,

MALTHUS VS MARX

Thomas Robert Malthus (1766–1834) was a political economist and the first to publish the theory that population growth would lead to mass poverty. The 'Malthusian Theory' had many critics at the time, including the Pope. Another detractor was Karl Marx (1818–83), who believed that more people meant more production, and he accused Malthus of being an apologist for the capitalists.

Not surprisingly, when the Vietnamese government adopted Marxism as its economic model, birth control was viewed as a capitalist plot to make developing countries weak. In this regard, the Vietnamese were encouraged by their Soviet mentors, who ruled a country where family planning was prohibited and 'hero mothers' were rewarded for having more than 10 children. But with the collapse of the Soviet Union in 1991, the Vietnamese had to take a critical look at their family-planning policies and moved from Marx to Malthus, limiting urban families to no more than two children, which continues today.

not the austere collectivism once espoused by Ho. And it's working well. Vietnam has become the new darling among international investors, providing garments galore for Western fashion houses and playing host to hi-tech investors such as Intel. Let the good times roll: Vietnam's economy is in top gear. It's not only the big ticket industries that are doing well; Vietnam is going head to head with Thailand for the crown of the world's largest rice exporter, proving that the rural economy is also roaring along. However, Vietnam is preparing for some tough times as the global downturn spreads. Vietnam's stock market was the worst performing index in Asia in 2008, falling almost 70%. At the same time, the property bubble burst and investments started to dry. Like the rest of the world, the Vietnamese are looking ahead for signs of recovery.

Vietnam joined the World Trade Organization at the start of 2007. This will eventually have a big impact on the economy, but even more interesting is to see how the government deals with the issues of piracy and intellectual property rights. Vietnam, like China, has long been a nation where copycatting is a national pastime. Not just software, music, books (including guidebooks...) and the usual suspects, but even hotels, restaurants and travel agents.

Vietnamese who have emigrated are called Viet Kieu. They have traditionally been maligned by locals as cowardly, arrogant and privileged. In the '90s, returning Viet Kieu were often followed by police but now official policy is to welcome them, and their money, back to the motherland.

POPULATION

Vietnam's population hovers at around 85.5 million, ranking it the 13th most populous country in the world, and with its population growth rate it could soon hit the top 10. Vietnam is a young country, with an incredible 65% of the population under the age of 30, and, after years of revolutionary initiatives encouraging large families, a two-child policy is now enforced in urban areas (see above).

Traditionally a rural agrarian society, the race is on for the move to the cities. Like Thailand and Malaysia before it, Vietnam is experiencing a tremendous shift in the balance of population, as increasing numbers of young people desert the fields in search of those mythical streets paved with gold in Hanoi or Ho Chi Minh City (HCMC). The population of HCMC and its suburbs is already more than seven million, Hanoi has around four million, and both Danang and Haiphong are millionaires. As economic migrants continue to seek their fortune, these numbers look set to soar.

THE PEOPLE OF VIETNAM

Vietnamese culture and civilisation have been profoundly influenced by the Chinese, and to many observers of Vietnamese history, China has long treated Vietnam as a sort of renegade province rather than an independent entity.

However, the Vietnamese existed as a people in the Red River Delta region long before the first waves of Chinese arrived more than 2000 years ago.

History has of course influenced the mix of Vietnamese minorities. The steady expansion southwards in search of cultivable lands absorbed first the Kingdom of Champa and later the eastern extent of the Khmer empire, and both the Chams and the Khmers are sizeable minorities today. There are perhaps one million Khmers inhabiting the Mekong Delta, or what they refer to as Kampuchea Krom (lower Cambodia; see p431), and almost as many Chams living along the coastal regions between Phan Rang and Danang.

Traffic was not only one way. Many of the 50 or more ethno-linguistic minority groups that inhabit the far northwest only migrated to these areas from Yunnan (China) and Tibet in the last few centuries. They moved into the mountains that the lowland Vietnamese considered uncultivable and help make up the most colourful part of the ethnic mosaic that is Vietnam today. For more on Vietnam's minority hill-tribe groups, see p285.

While the invasions and occupations of old may be over, the largest minority group in Vietnam has always been the ethnic-Chinese community, which makes up much of the commercial class in the cities. While the government has traditionally viewed them with suspicion, and drove many of them out of the country as 'boat people' in the late 1970s, many are now comfortably resettled and play a major part in driving economic development.

In the past, the term *lien xo!* (Soviet Union) was often shouted at Westerners, all of whom were assumed to be the legendary and very unpopular Russians residing in Vietnam. These days, depending on your dress, a more common name is *tay balo!* (literally, 'Westerner backpack'), a contemporary term for scruffy-looking backpackers.

RELIGION

Four great religions and philosophies have shaped the spiritual life of the Vietnamese: Buddhism, Confucianism, Taoism and, later, Christianity. Over the centuries, Confucianism, Taoism and Buddhism have fused with popular Chinese beliefs and ancient Vietnamese animism to create the Tam Giao (Triple Religion). When discussing religion, most Vietnamese people are likely to say that they are Buddhist, but when it comes to family or civic duties they are likely to follow the moral and social code of Confucianism, and turn to Taoist concepts to understand the nature of the cosmos.

Although the majority of the population has only a vague notion of Buddhist doctrines, they invite monks to participate in life-cycle ceremonies, such as funerals. Buddhist pagodas are seen by many Vietnamese as a physical and spiritual refuge from an uncertain world.

Buddhism

Buddhism, like other great religions, has been through a somewhat messy divorce, and arrived in Vietnam in two forms: Mahayana Buddhism (the Northern school) proceeded north into Nepal, Tibet, China, Korea, Mongolia and Japan, while Theravada Buddhism (the Southern school) took the more southerly route through India, Sri Lanka, Myanmar and Cambodia.

To learn more about Buddhism in Vietnam, check out the website www.quangduc.com. The official website of the Quang Duc Monastery in Melbourne, Australia, it is a gateway to all things Buddhist.

The Theravada school of Buddhism is an earlier and, according to its followers, less corrupted form of Buddhism than the Mahayana schools found around East Asia and the Himalayan regions. As Theravada followers tried to preserve and limit the Buddhist doctrines to only those canons codified in the early Buddhist era, the Mahayana school gave Theravada Buddhism the pejorative name 'Hinayana' (meaning 'Lesser Vehicle'). Its followers considered themselves 'Greater Vehicle' primarily because they built upon the earlier teachings.

The predominant school of Buddhism, and indeed religion, in Vietnam is Mahayana Buddhism (Dai Thua, or Bac Tong, meaning 'From the North'). The largest Mahayana sect in the country is Zen (Dhyana, or Thien), also known as the school of meditation. Dao Trang (the Pure Land school), another important sect, is practised mainly in the south.

WHEN IN NAM… DO AS THE VIETS

Take your time to learn a little about the local culture in Vietnam. Not only will this ensure you don't inadvertently cause offence or, worse, spark an international incident, but it will also endear you to your hosts. Here are a few top tips to help you go native.

Dress Code

Respect local dress standards: shorts to the knees, women's tops covering the shoulder, particularly at religious sites. Always remove your shoes before entering a temple. Nude sunbathing is considered *totally* inappropriate, even on beaches.

Meet & Greet

The traditional Vietnamese form of greeting is to press your hands together in front of your body and bow slightly. These days, the Western custom of shaking hands has almost completely taken over.

It's on the Cards

Exchanging business cards is an important part of even the smallest transaction or business contact. Get some printed before you arrive in Vietnam and hand them out like confetti.

Deadly Chopsticks

Leaving a pair of chopsticks sitting vertically in a rice bowl looks very much like the incense sticks that are burned for the dead. This is a powerful sign and is not appreciated anywhere in Asia.

Mean Feet

Like the Chinese and Japanese, Vietnamese strictly maintain clean floors and it's usual to remove shoes when entering somebody's home. It's rude to point the bottom of your feet towards other people. Never, ever point your feet towards anything sacred, such as a Buddha image.

Hats Off to Them

As a form of respect to elderly or other esteemed people, such as monks, take off your hat and bow your head politely when addressing them. In Asia, the head is the symbolic highest point – never pat or touch an adult on the head.

Theravada Buddhism (Tieu Thua, or Nam Tong) is found mainly in the Mekong Delta region, and is mostly practised by ethnic Khmers.

Vietnamese Buddhist monks *(bonze)* minister to the spiritual needs of the peasantry, but it is largely up to the monks whether they follow the lore of Taoism or the philosophy of Buddhism.

Taoism

Taoism (Lao Giao, or Dao Giao) originated in China and is based on the philosophy of Laotse (The Old One), who lived in the 6th century BC. Little is known about Laotse and there is some debate as to whether or not he actually existed. He is believed to have been the custodian of the imperial archives for the Chinese government, and Confucius is supposed to have consulted him.

Understanding Taoism is not easy. The philosophy emphasises contemplation and simplicity. Its ideal is returning to the Tao (The Way, or the essence of which all things are made), and it emphasises *am* and *duong*, the Vietnamese equivalents of yin and yang. Much of Taoist ritualism has been absorbed into Chinese and Vietnamese Buddhism, including, most commonly, the use of dragons and demons to decorate temple rooftops.

Confucianism

More a philosophy than an organised religion, Confucianism (Nho Giao, or Khong Giao) has been an important force in shaping Vietnam's social system and the lives and beliefs of its people.

Confucius (Khong Tu) was born in China around 550 BC. He saw people as social beings formed by society yet also capable of shaping their society. He believed that the individual exists in and for society and drew up a code of ethics to guide the individual in social interaction. This code laid down a person's obligations to family, society and the state, which remain the pillars of Vietnamese society today.

Cao Daism

Cao Daism is a Vietnamese sect that seeks to create the ideal religion by fusing the secular and religious philosophies of both East and West. It was founded in the early 1920s based on messages revealed in seances to Ngo Minh Chieu, the group's founder. At present there are about two million followers of Cao Daism in Vietnam. The sect's colourful headquarters is in Tay Ninh (p393), 96km northwest of HCMC.

Mahayana Buddhists believe in Boddhisatvas (Quan Am in Vietnam) or Buddhas that attain nirvana but postpone their enlightenment to stay on earth to save their fellow beings.

Hoa Hao Buddhism

The Hoa Hao Buddhist sect (Phat Giao Hoa Hao) was founded in the Mekong Delta in 1939 by Huynh Phu So. After he was miraculously cured of an illness, So began preaching a reformed Buddhism based on the common people and embodied in personal faith rather than elaborate rituals. His Buddhist philosophies involve simplicity in worship and no intermediaries between humans and the Supreme Being. Hoa Hao Buddhists are thought to number approximately 1.5 million.

Christianity

Catholicism was introduced in the 16th century by missionaries. Today, Vietnam has the second-highest concentration of Catholics (8% to 10% of the population) in Asia after the Philippines. Under the communist government, Catholics faced severe restrictions on their religious activities. In Vietnam, as in the USSR, churches were viewed as a capitalist institution and a rival centre of power that could subvert the government. Since 1990, the government has taken a more liberal line and Catholicism is making a comeback.

Protestantism was introduced to Vietnam in 1911 and most of the 200,000 followers today are Montagnards living in the central highlands. Protestants were doubly unfortunate in that they were persecuted first by the pro-Catholic government of Diem and later by the communists.

Islam

Muslims, mostly ethnic Chams, make up about 0.5% of the population. The Chams consider themselves Muslims, but in practice they follow a localised

PAGODA OR TEMPLE?

Travelling around Vietnam, there are a lot of pagodas and temples, but how does the average person know which is which? The Vietnamese regard a *chua* (pagoda) as a place of worship where they make offerings or pray. A Vietnamese *den* (temple) is not really a place of worship, but rather a structure built to honour a great historical figure (Confucius, Tran Hung Dao, and even Ho Chi Minh).

The Cao Dai temple seems to somehow fall between the cracks. Given the mixture of ideas that is part and parcel of Cao Daism, it's arguably a blend of temple, pagoda, church and mosque.

adaptation of Islamic theology and law. Though Muslims usually pray five times a day, the Chams pray only on Fridays and celebrate Ramadan for only three days. In addition, their Islam-based religious rituals co-exist with animism and the worship of Hindu deities. Circumcision is symbolically performed on boys at age 15, when a religious leader makes the gestures of circumcision with a wooden knife.

Hinduism

Champa was profoundly influenced by Hinduism, and many of the Cham towers, built as Hindu sanctuaries, contain *lingas* that are still worshipped by ethnic Vietnamese and ethnic Chinese alike. After the fall of Champa in

TET: THE BIG ONE

Tet is Christmas, New Year and birthdays all rolled into one. Tet Nguyen Dan (Festival of the First Day) ushers in the Lunar New Year and is the most significant date in the Vietnamese calendar. It's a time when families reunite in the hope of good fortune for the coming year, and ancestral spirits are welcomed back into the family home. And the whole of Vietnam celebrates a birthday; everyone becomes one year older.

The festival falls some time between 19 January and 20 February, the same dates as Chinese New Year. The first three days after New Year's Day are the official holidays but many people take the whole week off, particularly in the south.

Tet rites begin seven days before New Year's Day. This is when the Tao Quan – the three Spirits of the Hearth, found in the kitchen of every home – ascend to the heavens to report on the past year's events to the Jade Emperor. Altars, laden with offerings, are assembled in preparation for the gods' departure, all in the hope of receiving a favourable report and ensuring good luck for the family in the coming year.

As Tet approaches other rituals include visiting cemeteries and inviting the spirits of dead relatives home for the celebrations. Absent family members return home so that the whole family can celebrate Tet under the same roof. All loose ends are tied up so that the new year can be started with a clean slate; debts are paid and cleaning becomes the national sport.

A New Year's tree *(cay neu)* is constructed to ward off evil spirits. Kumquat trees are popular throughout the country, while branches of pink peach blossoms *(dao)* grace houses in the north, and yellow apricot blossoms *(mai)* can be found in homes further south. For a spectacular sight, go to ĐL Nguyen Hue in Ho Chi Minh City, much of which is taken over by the annual Tet flower market. In Hanoi, the area around Pho Hang Dau and Pho Hang Ma is transformed into a massive peach-blossom and kumquat-tree market.

On New Year's Eve the Tao Quan return to earth. At the stroke of midnight all problems from the previous year are left behind and mayhem ensues. The goal is to make as much noise as possible. Drums and percussion are popular, as were firecrackers until they were banned in 1995.

The events of New Year's Day are crucial as it's believed they affect the course of life in the year ahead. People take extra care not to be rude or show anger. Other activities that are believed to attract bad spirits include sewing, sweeping, swearing and breaking things.

It's crucial that the first visitor of the year to each household is suitable. They're usually male – best of all is a wealthy married man with several children. Foreigners are sometimes welcomed as the first to enter the house, although not always, so it's unwise to visit any Vietnamese house on the first day of Tet unless explicitly invited.

Apart from New Year's Eve itself, Tet is not a particularly boisterous celebration. It's like Christmas Day, a quiet family affair. It's not the ideal time to visit the country, as transport can be a nightmare for a week or more, plus a lot of places close down for a few days. However, it can be interesting to witness the contrasting frenzied activity before the New Year and the calm (and quiet streets!) that follows. Wherever you're staying, you're sure to be invited to join in the celebrations.

If you are visiting Vietnam during Tet, be sure you learn this phrase: *chuc mung nam moi* – Happy New Year!

ANCESTOR WORSHIP

Vietnamese ancestor worship dates from before the arrival of Confucianism or Buddhism. Ancestor worship is based on the belief that the soul lives on after death and becomes the protector of its descendants. Because of the influence the spirits of one's ancestors exert on the living, it is considered not only shameful for the spirits to be upset or restless, but downright dangerous.

Traditionally, the Vietnamese worship and honour the spirits of their ancestors regularly, especially on the anniversary of a particular ancestor's death. To request help for success in business or on behalf of a sick child, sacrifices and prayers are given to the ancestral spirits. Important worship elements are the family altar and a plot of land, the income of which is set aside for the support of the ancestors.

the 15th century, most Chams who remained in Vietnam became Muslims (Arab traders brought Islam to Indonesia and Malaysia; these merchants then brought it to Champa) but continued to practise various Hindu rituals and customs. Hundreds of thousands more migrated southwest to Cambodia, where they make up an important minority today.

WOMEN IN VIETNAM

As in many parts of Asia, Vietnamese women take a lot of pain for little gain, with plenty of hard work to do but little authority at the decision-making level. Vietnamese women were highly successful as guerrillas in the American War and brought plenty of grief to US soldiers. After the war, their contributions were given much fanfare, but most of the government posts were given to men. In the countryside, you'll see women doing backbreaking jobs, such as crushing rocks at construction sites and carrying heavy baskets.

The country's two-children-per-family policy is once again being strictly enforced, at least in urban areas, and is boosting the independence of Vietnamese women, with more delaying marriage to get an education. Around 50% of university students are female, but they're not always given the same opportunity as males to shine after graduation.

Cao Daism is a cocktail of the world's faiths and philosophies. Its prophets include Buddha, Confucius, Jesus Christ, Moses and Mohammed, and some wacky choices, such as Joan of Arc, William Shakespeare and Victor Hugo.

A substantial number of women end up in prostitution of some sort or another, working in massage parlours, karaoke clubs or dubious bars. The trafficking of poor, rural women into the sex industry in Cambodia has been a huge problem and in many cases this has involved family members sacrificing one of their daughters in order for the rest to survive.

The Vietnamese consider pale skin to be beautiful. On sunny days, trendy Vietnamese women can often be seen strolling under the shade of an umbrella in order to keep from tanning. Women who work in the fields will go to great lengths to preserve their pale skin by wrapping their faces in towels and wearing long-sleeved shirts, elbow-length silk gloves and conical hats. To tell a Vietnamese woman that she has white skin is a great compliment; telling her that she has a 'lovely suntan' is a grave insult.

MEDIA

To the untrained eye, Vietnam looks like it has a flourishing free press, with plenty of newspapers and glossy magazines. However, in reality it is not possible to get a publishing licence unless you are affiliated with the Communist Party. As many in the media say, there is no censorship in Vietnam, only self-censorship. Newspapers and magazines that cross the line are periodically closed down, sometimes for good. TV is even more tightly controlled, although the advent of satellite TV and the internet have made it much easier to get unbiased information from overseas. Vietnam uses the same filtering technology as China to block access to (politically) undesirable websites.

LUNAR CALENDAR

The Vietnamese lunar calendar closely resembles that of the Chinese. Year one of the Vietnamese lunar calendar corresponds to 2637 BC and each lunar month has 29 or 30 days, resulting in years with 355 days.

Approximately every third year is a leap year; an extra month is added between the third and fourth months to keep the lunar year in time with the solar year. If this was not done, the seasons would shift around the lunar year, playing havoc with all elements of life linked to the agricultural seasons. To check the Gregorian (solar) date corresponding to a lunar date, pick up any Vietnamese or Chinese calendar.

The Vietnamese have 12 zodiacal animals, each of which represents one year in a 12-year cycle. If you want to know your sign in the Vietnamese zodiac, look up your year of birth in the following chart. Don't forget that the Vietnamese New Year falls in late January or mid-February. If your birthday is in the first half of January it will be included in the zodiac year before the calendar year of your birth.

Buffalo *(suu):* stubborn, conservative, patient							
1925	1937	1949	1961	1973	1985	1997	2009
Tiger *(dan):* creative, brave, overbearing							
1926	1938	1950	1962	1974	1986	1998	2010
Cat *(mao):* timid, affectionate, amicable							
1927	1939	1951	1963	1975	1987	1999	2011
Dragon *(thin):* egotistical, strong, intelligent							
1928	1940	1952	1964	1976	1988	2000	2012
Snake *(ty):* luxury seeking, secretive, friendly							
1929	1941	1953	1965	1977	1989	2001	2013
Horse *(ngo):* emotional, clever, quick thinker							
1930	1942	1954	1966	1978	1990	2002	2014
Goat *(mui):* charming, good with money, indecisive							
1931	1943	1955	1967	1979	1991	2003	2015
Monkey *(than):* confident, humorous, fickle							
1932	1944	1956	1968	1980	1992	2004	2016
Rooster *(dau):* diligent, imaginative, needs attention							
1933	1945	1957	1969	1981	1993	2005	2017
Dog *(tuat):* humble, responsible, patient							
1934	1946	1958	1970	1982	1994	2006	2018
Pig *(hoi):* materialistic, loyal, honest							
1935	1947	1959	1971	1983	1995	2007	2019
Rat *(tý):* generous, social, insecure, idle							
1936	1948	1960	1972	1984	1996	2008	2020

ARTS
Music
TRADITIONAL

Heavily influenced by the Chinese to the north and Indian-influenced Khmer and Cham musical traditions to the south, this blend has produced an original style and instrumentation for Vietnamese music. Written music and the five note (pentatonic) scale may be of Chinese origin, but Vietnamese choral music is unique, as the melody and the tones move as one; the melody cannot rise during a verse that has a falling tone.

Vietnamese folk music is usually sung without any instrumental accompaniment and was adapted by the Communist Party for many a patriotic marching song.

Classical, or 'learned music', is rather formal and frigid. It was performed at the imperial court for the entertainment of the mandarin elite. There are two main types of classical chamber music: *hat a dao* from the north and *ca Hue* from central Vietnam.

Traditional music is played on a wide array of indigenous instruments, dating back to ancient *do son* drums, which are sought-after works of art. The best known traditional instrument in use is the *dan bau,* a single-stringed zither that generates an astounding array of tones. Also common at performances of traditional music is the *dan tranh,* a 16-string zither with a haunting melody, and the *to rung,* a large bamboo xylophone.

Each of Vietnam's ethno-linguistic minorities has its own musical traditions that often include distinctive costumes and instruments, such as reed flutes, lithophones (similar to xylophones), bamboo whistles, gongs and stringed instruments made from gourds.

The easiest way to catch a performance of Vietnamese music is to dine at one of the many local restaurants offering traditional performances. Hanoi and HCMC are good hunting grounds or the cultural hub of Hue is another option. Some museums also offer short performances.

For a look at the impact of *doi moi* (economic reform) on some Vietnamese women, Vu Xuan Hung's film *Misfortune's End* (1996) tells the tale of a silk weaver deserted by her husband for an upwardly mobile businesswoman.

CONTEMPORARY & POP

Like the rest of Southeast Asia, Vietnam has a thriving domestic pop scene. The most celebrated artist is Khanh Ly, who left Vietnam in 1975 for the USA. She is massive both in Vietnam and abroad. Her music is widely available in Vietnam, but the government frowns on her recently composed lyrics that recall the trials of her life as a refugee.

Vietnam's number-one domestic heart-throb is Hue-born Quang Linh, whose early popularity in Saigon shot him up the local pop charts. He is adored by Vietnamese of all ages for his love songs.

Other celebrated local pop singers include sex symbol Phuong Thanh, Vietnam's answer to Madonna or Britney Spears (only with more clothes), and Vietnamese girls are seriously into heart-throb Lam Truong, a Robbie Williams–style performer who woos his crowds.

Of the legion of legendary Vietnamese contemporary-music composers, the leader of the pack was Trinh Cong Son, who died in HCMC in 2001. A former literature student from Hue, he wrote more than 500 songs, making him perhaps the most prolific Vietnamese composer in history.

Tieng Hat Que Huong, which was founded in 1981, has a mission to preserve, develop and promote Vietnamese traditional music, building a bridge between artists, old and new. Visit it at www.tienghatquehuong.com and look up details of forthcoming performances in HCMC.

Dance

Traditionally reserved for ceremonies and festivals, Vietnamese folk dance is again mainstream thanks to tourism. The Conical Hat Dance is one of the most visually stunning dances. A group of women wearing *ao dai* (the national dress of Vietnam) shake their stuff and spin around, whirling their classic conical hats like Fred Astaire with his cane.

Vietnam's ethnic minorities have their own dancing traditions, which are distinctly different from the Vietnamese majority. A great deal of anthropological research has been carried out in recent years in order to preserve and revive important indigenous traditions.

Some upmarket restaurants host dance performances at the weekend. Minority dances are organised in some of the more popular tourist stops in northwest Vietnam such as Mai Chau (p167).

Theatre & Puppetry

Vietnamese theatre fuses music, singing, recitation, dance and mime into an artistic whole. These days, the various forms of Vietnamese theatre are performed by dozens of state-funded troupes and companies around the country.

Classical theatre is known as *hat tuong* in the north and *hat boi* in the south and is based on Chinese opera. Classical theatre is very formal, employing fixed gestures and scenery similar to the Chinese classics. The accompanying orchestra, which is dominated by the drum, usually has six musicians. Often, the audience also has a drum so it can pass judgment on the onstage action. It has a limited cast of characters, each of whom is easily identifiable through their make-up and costume. Red face paint represents courage, loyalty and faithfulness, while traitors and cruel people have white faces. A male character expresses emotions (pensiveness, worry, anger) by fingering his beard in different ways.

To learn more about the unique art of water puppetry or 'Punch and Judy in a pool', visit www.thanglongwaterpuppet.org

Popular theatre *(hat cheo)* expresses social protest through satire, although there has been less protest and more satire since 1975. The singing and verse are in everyday language and include many proverbs and sayings, accompanied by folk melodies.

Modern theatre *(cai luong)* originated in the south in the early 20th century and shows strong Western influences. Spoken drama *(kich noi* or *kich)*, with its Western roots, appeared in the 1920s and is popular among students and intellectuals.

Conventional puppetry *(roi can)* and the uniquely Vietnamese art form of water puppetry *(roi nuoc)*, draw their plots from the same legendary and historical sources as other forms of traditional theatre. It is believed that water puppetry developed when determined puppeteers in the Red River Delta managed to continue performances despite annual flooding (see the boxed text, p116).

Dancing Girl, directed by Le Hoang, caused a major splash with its release in 2003. It tells the story of two HIV-positive prostitutes, and Hoa (played by My Duyen), is seen mainlining heroin.

Cinema

One of Vietnam's earliest cinematographic efforts was a newsreel of Ho Chi Minh's 1945 Proclamation of Independence. Later, parts of the battle of Dien Bien Phu (p173) were restaged for the benefit of movie cameras.

Prior to reunification, the South Vietnamese movie industry produced a string of sensational, low-budget flicks. Conversely, North Vietnamese film-making efforts were dedicated to 'the mobilisation of the masses for economic reconstruction, the building of socialism and the struggle for national reunification'. Yawn.

In recent years, Vietnamese cinema has evolved from the realm of propaganda to a world that more closely reflects the lives of modern Vietnamese people and the challenges they face. Contemporary films span a wide range of themes, from warfare to modern romance.

In Nguyen Khac's *The Retired General* (1988), the central character copes with adjusting from his life as a soldier during the American War to life as a civilian family man, symbolising Vietnam's difficult transition to the postwar era.

Returning to Ngo Thuy (1977), directed by Le Manh Thich and Do Khanh Toan, pays homage to the women of Ngo Thuy village. In 1971, these women were the subject of a propaganda film to encourage people to sign up for the war effort.

Dang Nhat Minh is perhaps Vietnam's most prolific film-maker. In *The Return* (1993), Minh hones in on the complexities of modern relationships, while *The Girl on the River* (1987) tells the stirring tale of a female journalist who joins an ex-prostitute in search of her former lover, a Viet Cong soldier whose life she had saved and heart she'd been promised.

Young overseas-Vietnamese film directors are steadily carving a niche for themselves in the international film industry and snapping up awards at film festivals worldwide.

Tran Anh Hung's touching *The Scent of Green Papaya* (1992), filmed in France, celebrates the coming of age of a young girl who works as a servant for an affluent Saigon family during the 1950s. *Cyclo* (1995), his visually stunning masterpiece, cuts to the core of HCMC's gritty underworld and its violent existence.

Vietnamese-American Tony Bui made a splash in 1999 with his exquisite feature debut *Three Seasons* (1999). Set in HCMC, this beautifully made film weaves together the lives of four unlikely characters with that of a US war veteran, played by Harvey Keitel, who comes to Vietnam in search of his long-lost daughter.

See p19 for more must-see movies.

The Sacred Willow (2000), by Duong Van Mai Elliot, spans four tumultuous generations of an upper-class Vietnamese family. This enlightening historical memoir traces French colonisation, WWII and the wars with the French and Americans.

Literature

There are three veins of Vietnamese literature. Traditional oral literature *(truyen khau)* began long before recorded history and includes legends, folk songs and proverbs. Sino-Vietnamese literature was written in Chinese characters *(chu nho)*. Dominated by Confucian and Buddhist texts, it was governed by strict rules of metre and verse. Modern Vietnamese literature *(quoc am)* includes anything recorded in *nom* characters. The earliest text written in *nom* was the late-13th-century *Van Te Ca Sau* (Ode to an Alligator).

One of Vietnam's literary masterpieces, *Kim Van Kieu* (The Tale of Kieu) was written during the first half of the 19th century by Nguyen Du (1765–1820), a poet, scholar, mandarin and diplomat.

Architecture

The Vietnamese have not been prolific builders like their Khmer neighbours, or the Chams, whose graceful brick towers adorn many parts of the southern half of Vietnam. For more on the Chams, check out the boxed text on p264 or follow in their footsteps (p26).

Traditionally, most Vietnamese constructions were made of wood and other materials that decayed in the tropical climate. This, coupled with the fact that almost all stone structures erected by the Vietnamese were destroyed in countless feudal wars and invasions, means that very little premodern Vietnamese architecture remains.

Paradise of the Blind, by Duong Thu Huong, was the first Vietnamese novel to be published in the USA. It is set in a northern village and a Hanoi slum, and recalls the lives of three women and the hardships they faced over some 40 years.

Plenty of pagodas and temples that were founded hundreds of years ago are still functioning, but they have usually been rebuilt many times with little concern for the original. As a result, many modern elements have been casually introduced into pagoda architecture – those garish neon haloes for statues of Buddha are a shining example.

Thanks to the custom of ancestor worship, many graves from previous centuries survive today. These include temples erected in memory of high-ranking mandarins, royal-family members and emperors.

Memorials for Vietnamese who died in the wars against the Chinese, French and Americans usually contain cement obelisks inscribed with the words *to quoc ghi cong* ('the country will remember their exploits').

Painting & Sculpture

Painting on frame-mounted silk dates from the 13th century and was at one time the preserve of scholar-calligraphers, who painted grand scenes

INSIDE LACQUER

Lacquer *(son mai)* is made from resin extracted from the rhus tree. It is creamy white in raw form, but is darkened with pigments in an iron container for 40 hours. After the object has been treated with glue, the requisite 10 coats of lacquer are applied. Each coat must be dried for a week and then thoroughly sanded with pumice and cuttlebone before the next layer can be applied. A specially refined lacquer is used for the 11th and final coat, which is sanded with a fine coal powder and lime wash before the object is decorated. Designs include engraving in low relief, or inlaying mother-of-pearl, egg shell or precious metals.

The art of making lacquerware was brought to Vietnam from China in the mid-15th century. During the 1930s, the Fine Arts School in Hanoi had several Japanese teachers who introduced new styles and production methods.

from nature. Before the advent of photography, realistic portraits for use in ancestor worship were produced. Some of these – usually of former head monks – can still be seen in certain Buddhist pagodas.

Vietnamese Painting – From Tradition to Modernity, by Corinne de Ménonville, is a lush look at Vietnamese contemporary painting. For the contributions of women to the art scene, check out *Vietnamese Women Artists* (2004).

During the past century, Vietnamese painting has been influenced by Western trends. Much recent work has had political rather than aesthetic or artistic motives. These propagandist pieces are easy to spot at the Fine Arts Museum (p98) in Hanoi.

The recent economic liberalisation has convinced many young artists to abandon the revolutionary themes and concentrate on producing commercial paintings. Some have gone back to the traditional-style silk or lacquer paintings, while others experiment with contemporary subjects.

The Chams produced spectacular carved sandstone figures for their Hindu and Buddhist sanctuaries. Cham sculpture was profoundly influenced by Indian art but over the centuries it managed to also incorporate Indonesian and Vietnamese elements. The largest single collection of Cham sculpture in the world is found at the Museum of Cham Sculpture (p237) in Danang. For the lowdown on Cham architecture, see p304.

If you're crazy about your china, or pots about your pottery, try to find a copy of *Viet Nam Ceramics*, an illustrated insight into Vietnamese pottery over the centuries.

Ceramics

The production of ceramics *(gom)* has a long history in Vietnam. In ancient times, ceramic objects were made by coating a wicker mould with clay and baking it. Later, ceramic production became very refined, and each dynastic period is known for its particular techniques and motifs.

It's possible to view ancient ceramics in museums throughout Vietnam. Excavations of archaeological sites are still revealing ancient examples, as are the ongoing discoveries of shipwreck treasures.

Bat Trang (p122), located near Hanoi, is famous for its contemporary ceramic industry.

SPORT

For more on the story of salvaging ceramics from ancient wrecks, check out *Dragon Sea: A True Tale of Treasure Archaeology and Greed off the Coast of Vietnam*. It is part love story with the country and its troubled history, and part adventure.

Football (soccer) is Vietnam's number-one spectator sport and the country is mad for it. During the World Cup, the European Champions League or other major clashes, half the country stays up all night to watch live games in different time zones around the world. Postgame fun includes hazardous high-speed motorbike cruising in the streets of Hanoi and HCMC, horns blaring, and flags waving. Sadly the national team has not kept pace with this obsession and although one of the stronger teams in Southeast Asia, they remain minnows on the international stage. Think World Cup 2030 or beyond.

Tennis has considerable snob appeal these days and trendy Vietnamese like to both watch and play. Similarly, golf has taken off as a way to earn brownie points with international investors or local movers and shakers. Golf courses have been developed all over the country, although membership fees ensure it remains a game for the elite.

The Vietnamese are a nation of badminton players and every street is a potential court. Other favourite sports include volleyball and table tennis.

Food & Drink

If you're the sort of traveller who believes that eating locally is one of the best ways to immerse yourself in a culture, prepare to be amazed by Vietnam. From traditional street stalls to contemporary big-city temples of upscale dining, the country serves up an endless banquet of exquisite eating.

Diverse landscapes – fertile highlands, water-logged rice paddies, forest-cloaked mountains and sandy coasts – lend the country its cuisine variety, while a long history of contact with outsiders brings complexity. Over the centuries locals have absorbed and adapted Chinese, Indian, French and even Japanese techniques and specialities to their own kitchens and palates, and, more recently, expatriates and those Vietnamese chefs who have spent time cooking overseas have breathed new life into white-tablecloth dining scenes in Hanoi and Ho Chi Minh City (HCMC). In Vietnam, to 'eat local' can mean anything from supping on rice-flour vermicelli flavoured with fish sauce, to feasting on beef stew accompanied by a crispy baguette.

The country's vast range of excellent edibles invites experimentation. Though Vietnam's well-known classics – *pho*, spring rolls, and shrimp paste grilled on sugar cane – are all well and tasty, it pays to venture into the unknown. Every bustling wet market, every bicycle-riding vendor and every open-air eatery is a potential trove of delights that rarely make it beyond the country's borders. Keep your eyes open, follow your nose, and you'll depart with mouth-watering memories that will have you saying '*Hen gap lai*' (see you again).

Andrea Nguyen's *Into the Vietnamese Kitchen* demystifies the country's cuisine with easy-to-follow recipes that will have you whipping up everything from *pho* to charcuterie in no time.

FLAVOURS

Vietnamese palates vary from north to south, but no matter where they are, local cooks work to balance hot, sour, salty and sweet flavours in each dish. Sugar's centrality to the cuisine is best illustrated by the ever popular *kho*: sweet-savoury dishes of fish or meat simmered in a clay pot with fish sauce and one of the Vietnamese cuisine's most oft-used seasonings – bitter caramel sauce, made from cane sugar. Vietnamese cooks also use sugar to sweeten dipping sauces, sticky rice-based and other desserts and, of course, coffee.

Sugar's sweetness is countered with fruity tartness, derived from the lime wedges mounded in bowls on restaurant tables (to squeeze into noodle soups and dipping sauces) and from *kalamansi* (a small green-skinned, orange-fleshed citrus fruit that tastes like a cross between a lime and a mandarin orange), the juice of which is combined with salt and black pepper as a dip for seafood, meats and omelettes. The tart pulp of the tamarind pod is mixed with water and strained, then added as a souring agent to a fish and vegetable soup called *canh chua* and a delectable dish of whole prawns coated with sticky sweet-and-sour sauce. Northern cooks who seek sourness are more likely to turn to vinegar. A clear yellowish vinegar made from wine lees, mixed with chopped ginger, is often served alongside snail specialities such as *bun oc* (rice noodle and snail soup).

Vietnamese cooks generally use fewer extremely hot chillies than Thai cooks, while central Vietnamese use more of them than their fellow nationals. Local chillies vary from a long, red, fleshy, mild variety that appears in many southern dishes and are served chopped to accompany noodles, to a smallish pale chartreuse specimen that is chopped and served with a saucer of fish sauce in restaurants specialising in Hue cuisine. Beware – the latter really pack a punch. Dried ground chillies and spicy chilli sauces are tabletop condiments in many a central Vietnamese eatery.

Vietnam is a huge peppercorn exporter (though it is said that much of the black pepper labelled 'Vietnamese' originates in southern Cambodia), and ground black and white peppercorns season everything from *chao* (rice porridge) to beef stew. Wonderfully fragrant, pungent Vietnamese black peppercorns put what's sold in supermarkets back home to shame; if your country's customs will allow it in, a half-kilogram bag, purchased at a Vietnamese wet market for a very reasonable 50,000d, makes a fine edible souvenir.

Vietnamese food's saltiness comes from, well, salt – the coastal area around Nha Trang is the site of numerous salt flats – but most prevalently from the fermented seafood sauces that grace the shelves of every Vietnamese pantry. The most common is *nuoc mam* or fish sauce, which is so elemental to the cuisine that, sprinkled over a bowl of rice, it's considered a meal. *Nuoc mam* is made from small fish (most often anchovies) that are layered with salt in large earthenware, concrete or wooden containers, weighted to keep the fish submerged in their own liquid, and left in a hot place for up to a year. As they ferment the fish release a fragrant (some might say stinky) liquid that is drawn off through a spigot near the container's bottom. The first extraction, called *nuoc mam cot*, is dark brown and richly flavoured, and is essentially an 'extra virgin' fish sauce reserved for table use. The second extraction, obtained by adding salted water to the already fermented fish and leaving them for a few more months, is used for cooking. Phu Quoc Island (p464) is famous for its *nuoc mam*, though some cooks prefer the milder version that's made around coastal Phan Thiet (p314).

'fish sauce... is so elemental to the cuisine that, sprinkled over a bowl of rice, it's considered a meal'

When it comes to fermented fish products, *nuoc mam* is only the tip of the iceberg. At some point most travellers come face-to-face with *mam tom*, a reeking violet paste of salted, fermented shrimp. At the table, it's added to noodle soups, smeared onto rice-paper rolls, and even serves as a dip for sour fruits like green mango. It's also used extensively in cooking, lending a pungent salty backbone to specialities like the southern fish and vegetable noodle soup-stew *bun mam*. *Mam tom* has close cousins in the cuisines of every Southeast Asian nation, as well as many versions in Vietnam, including ones made from crabs, shrimp of all sizes (*mam tep*, a southern speciality, is made from especially small shrimp) and various varieties of fish. Try to work past the ingredient's odour to sample a range of dishes made with it: the flavour it lends to food is much more subtle than its stench might imply!

Fish flavours also come from dried seafood. Vietnamese cooks are quite choosy about their dried shrimp; market stalls display up to fifteen grades. You'll also find all varieties and sizes of dried fish, both whole and in fillets, and dried squid. The latter is often barbecued and sold from a roving stall.

Beyond *nuoc mam* and *mam*, Vietnamese cooks use quite a few sauces, such as soy, oyster and fermented bean – culinary souvenirs of China's almost 1000-year rule over the country's north. Warm spices like star anise, cinnamon and cloves are essential to a good *pho*. Curries were introduced to Vietnam by Indian traders, probably through the once-important port of Hoi An; now they're cooked up using packets of locally made curry powder and small jars of curry paste packed in oil. Vietnamese curries, such as *ka ri ga* (chicken cooked with curry, coconut milk and lemongrass) and *lau de* (curried goat hotpot), tend to be more aromatic than fiery, and slightly sweet.

Vietnamese food is often described as 'fresh' and 'light' owing to the plates heaped with gorgeous fresh herbs that seem to accompany every meal. Coriander, mint and anise-flavoured Thai basil will be familiar to anyone who's travelled elsewhere in the region. Look also for green-and-garnet *perilla* or *shiso* leaves; small and pointy, pleasantly peppery astringent *rau ram* leaves; and *rau om* (rice-paddy herb), which has delicate leaves that hint of lemon and cumin. *Rau om* invariably shows up atop bowls of *canh chua*.

Shallots, thinly sliced and slowly fried in lots of oil until caramelised, add a bit of sweetness when sprinkled atop salad and noodle dishes.

STAPLES

Rice

Rice, or *com*, is the very bedrock of Vietnamese cuisine. In the Hue of imperial times rice with salt was served to distinguished guests by royal mandarins; these days locals eat at least one rice-based meal every day and offer a bowl of rice to their departed ancestors. If a Vietnamese says '*An com*' (literally 'let's eat rice') it's an invitation to lunch or dinner, and you can also get your fill of the stuff, accompanied by a variety of stir-fried meat, fish and vegetable dishes, at specialised eateries called *quan com binh danh*. Cooked to a soupy state with chicken, fish, eel or duck, rice becomes *chao* (rice porridge); fried in a hot wok with egg, vegetables and other ingredients, it's *com rang*; and 'broken' into short, uneven grains, steamed, topped with barbecued pork, an egg, and sliced cucumber, and accompanied by sweetened *nuoc mam* with chillies, it's *com tam*. Sticky or glutinous rice (white, red and black) is mixed with pulses or rehydrated dried corn, peanuts and sesame seeds for a filling breakfast treat called *xoi* (*ngo* in central Vietnam), mixed with sugar and coconut milk and moulded into sweet treats, or layered with pork and steamed in bamboo or banana leaves for a filling Tet speciality called *banh chung*. Soaked and ground into flour, rice becomes the base for everything from noodles and sweets to crackers and the dry round, translucent 'papers' that Vietnamese moisten before using to wrap salad rolls and other specialities.

'Rice, or *com*, is the very bedrock of Vietnamese cuisine'

Noodles

Noodles are an anytime-of-the-day Vietnamese meal or snack. *Pho* is made with *banh pho* (flat rice noodles). Though this unofficial national dish gets all the culinary press, the truth is that truly fine versions, featuring a rich, carefully made broth are hard to come by. If you're a noodle lover do yourself a favour and look also for dishes featuring *bun* (round rice noodles) such as *bun thit nuong*, a zesty, cool noodle 'salad' topped with smoky grilled pork, and *bun bo Hue*, a spicy, beefy speciality from central Vietnam. Keep an eye open also for *banh hoi*, very thin rice-flour noodles that are formed into delicate nests and eaten rolled with grilled meat in leafy greens. Chinese-style egg noodles known as *mi* are thrown into soups (think Chinese wonton noodles) or fried and topped with a savoury stir-fried mixture of seafood, meats and vegetables in a thickish gravy for a dish called *mi xao*. *Mien*, made from mung-bean starch and also known as bean-thread noodles, are stir-fried with *mien cua* (crab meat) and eaten with steamed fish.

Rice-Paper Rolls

Vietnamese will wrap almost anything in crackly rice paper. Steamed fish and grilled meats are often rolled at the table with herbs, lettuce and slices of super-sour star fruit and green banana, and dipped in fish sauce mixed with sugar and chillies. Fat *goi cuon*, a southern speciality popularly known as 'salad' or 'summer' rolls, contain shrimp, pork, round rice noodles and herbs and are meant to be dipped in bean paste or hoisin sauce. *Bo pia*, thin rice-paper cigars filled with slices of Chinese sausage, dried shrimp, cooked jicama, lettuce and chilli paste, are usually knocked up to order by street vendors with mobile carts. And then there's *nem ran ha noi*, northern-style crispy deep-fried spring rolls.

Bread

A legacy of the French, *banh mi* refers to both the crackly crusted rice and wheat-flour baguettes sold everywhere (eaten plain or dipped in beef stew and soups) to the sandwiches stuffed with meats, vegies and daikon, and carrot pickles that are made with them. If you haven't tried a stuffed *banh mi* you haven't eaten in Vietnam. Enough said.

Fish, Meat & Fowl

Thanks to Vietnam's long coastline and plentiful river deltas, seafood is a major source of protein. From the ocean comes fish such as tuna, pomfret, red snapper and sea bass, as well as prawns, crabs and clams. Flooded rice paddies yield miniscule crabs and golf ball–sized snails, and favourite freshwater eats include the well-loved *ca loc* (snakehead fish), catfish and, along the central coast, tiny clams called *hen*. Chicken and pork are widely eaten. In the mornings the tantalising aroma of barbecuing *nuoc mam*–marinated pork, intended to fill breakfast baguette sandwiches and top broken rice, scents the air of many a city street. Beef is less frequently seen but does show up in bowls of *pho*, in *kho bo* (beef stew with tomato), in *thit bo bit tet* (Vietnamese pan-seared beefsteak), and wrapped in *la lot* (wild pepper leaves) and grilled. Other sources of protein include goat (eaten in hotpot with a curried broth), frogs, insect larvae and – yes, in the Mekong Delta – rat.

Vegetables and Fruits

If you come across a knobby fruit that looks like an orange durian don't eat it. *Gac* is used only for its juice, which colours sticky rice lucky red for Tet and weddings.

Vegetables range from the mundane – tomatoes, potatoes, eggplants (delicious grilled and topped with ground pork and *nuoc mam*), cucumbers, asparagus – to the exotic. Banana blossoms and lotus-flower stems are made into *goi* (salads), a thick, spongy plant stem called *bac ha* is added to soups, and *thien ly*, a wild plant with tender leaves and fragrant blossoms, is eaten stir-fried with garlic. Bunches of sunshine-yellow squash blossoms are a common sight in southern markets; locals like them simply stir-fried with garlic. All sorts of delicious wild mushrooms sprout on forest floors during the rainy season, and if you're off the beaten track then you might also be treated to tender fern tips which, like the more common *rau muong* (water spinach), get the stir-fry treatment. Especially loved are leafy greens such as lettuce, watercress, and mustard, which Vietnamese use to wrap *banh xeo* (crispy pork and shrimp pancakes) into bite-sized parcels suitable for dipping in *nuoc mam*.

If you're a fruit lover you've come to the right place. Depending on when you're travelling you'll be able to gorge on mangoes, crispy and sour green or soft and tartly floral pink guavas, juicy lychees and longans, and exotic mangosteen, passionfruit and jackfruit. Keep an eye out for *sinh to* stalls stocked with a variety of fruits (including avocado, which Vietnamese treat as a fruit rather than a vegetable) and a blender, where you can treat yourself to a refreshing blended-to-order iced fruit smoothie. It doesn't get much fresher than that.

Sweets

Do ngot (Vietnamese sweets) and *do trang mieng* (desserts) are popular everywhere, and are especially prevalent during festivals, when *banh* (traditional cakes) come in a wide variety of shapes and flavours. Rice flour is the base for many desserts, sweetened with sugar and coconut milk and enriched with lotus seeds, sesame seeds and peanuts. Yellow mung beans turn up in many desserts, while the French influence is evident in crème caramel. Cold sweets like *kem* (ice cream), *thach*, lovely layered agar-agar jellies in flavours like pandan and coffee-and-coconut, and locally made sweetened yoghurt sold in small glass pots, hit the spot on steamy days.

Che are sweet 'soups' that combine ingredients like lotus seeds or tapioca pearls and coconut milk; they're also a scrumptious shaved-ice treat, for

CELEBRATIONS

Food is an important part of Vietnamese holidays, and Tet in particular. You'll know Tet is just around the corner when *banh chung*, square and circular sticky rice cakes filled with pork and mung beans and wrapped in bamboo leaves, start appearing everywhere. They're not the Vietnamese version of the Christmas fruit cake, but delicious (if awfully filling) specialities that are looked forward to and eaten sliced plain, fried, or sandwiched between rice crackers. Other foods eaten at Tet include labour-intensive dishes such as the Hanoi fish-and-meat noodle dish *bun thang*, pickled and preserved vegetables (especially those with auspiciously rosy hues), sausages, and long-cooked dishes like *kho bo* or beef stew. As in China, moon cakes are eaten for Tet Trung Thu, the autumn moon festival. Should you be lucky enough to score an invitation to a home-cooked festive meal it might not be a bad idea to fast beforehand; Vietnamese are generous hosts and as a special guest you'll be expected to carry your weight at the table.

which a mound of ice crystals with your choice of toddy palm seeds, bits of agar-agar jelly, white or red beans, corn, and other bits is doused with coconut milk, condensed milk, sugar syrup or all three. The combination of beans, corn, and sweet liquid might sound strange, but in addition to being delicious, *che* is surprisingly refreshing.

REGIONAL SPECIALITIES

Travel the length of Vietnam and you'll notice subtle and not-so-subtle differences in its regional cuisines. Generally speaking, northern dishes tend to be mild, somewhat rustic, and more Chinese-influenced than those in the south; central Vietnamese produce dainty edibles and like their food salty and spicy; and southern cuisine plays up the region's lush abundance and tends to be on the sweet side.

North

It is northern Vietnamese food that most clearly bears the imprint of the centuries of Chinese occupation. There, soy is used as frequently as fish sauce, vinegar is more likely to add sourness than lime juice and tamarind, chillies give way to black pepper, and long-cooking is used as a means of coaxing maximum flavour from unpretentious ingredients. A good *pho bo dac biet* ('special' beef *pho*) perfectly embodies the northern approach to cooking, hinging as it does on the broth, which is made from little more than beef bones boiled for hours in water alongside onions, ginger, fish sauce, star anise, cinnamon and cloves. Pretty simple really, but connoisseurs insist that a perfectly made *pho bo* sits firmly at the top of the Vietnamese noodle pyramid.

That said, there are other noodle specialities worth seeking out in Hanoi and surrounds, such as *bun cha*, barbecued sliced pork or pork patties served with thin rice vermicelli, a heap of fresh herbs and green vegetables, and a bowl of sweetened *nuoc mam* with floating slices of pickled daikon and carrot. Stuffed noodle sheets called *banh cuon* recall Hong Kong–style noodle rolls and are made from rice-flour batter that's poured onto a piece of muslin cloth stretched over a steamer; once firm the pancake is scattered with chopped pork, mushrooms and dried shrimp, then rolled up, sprinkled with crispy shallots, and served alongside a tangle of bean sprouts, slivered cucumber and chopped Thai basil, with a saucer of *nuoc mam* for dipping.

Long ago ingenious northerners figured out how to make the most of two freshwater crustaceans that grow in flooded rice paddies: tiny crabs, and golf ball–sized snails called *oc*. The former go into *bun rieu cua*, thin rice noodles in a crimson-hued broth made from tomatoes and pulverised crab shells; on top floats a heavenly layer of crab fat that, after being extricated from the crabs' carcasses, is sautéed with shallots. *Bun rieu cua* is accompanied by the usual assortment of herbs but gets extra punch from crunchy slivered banana-tree stem; some cooks also add *oc* (in which case the dish is called *bun rieu cua oc*). You'll also find the snails in their own delicious tomato and noodle soup (*bun oc*), or chopped with lemongrass and herbs, stuffed into their own shells, and steamed, for *oc nhoi hap la xa* (a sort of Vietnamese escargot). A length of lemongrass leaf protrudes from each snail shell – give it a tug to pull out the meat. Northerners often eat pickled small round white eggplants with snail dishes, especially in the summer, when vinegar's cooling properties are a most welcome counter to the region's thick humidity.

Other northern water-creature specialities include *sup rieu ca*, a comforting fish soup with tomato and dill; *cha ca*, grilled and fried turmeric-marinated catfish scattered with lots of dill and eaten wrapped in rice paper; and *banh tom*, deep-fried sweet potato and shrimp fritters.

KOTO: A Culinary Journey Through Vietnam, written by a former chef at the Hanoi non-profit restaurant (p109) and her partner, is a loving ode to Vietnam's regional cuisines.

Centre

Everything seems smaller in the centre; baguettes and herbs are miniature versions of their southern selves, while Hue's own imperial cuisine is comprised of a procession of dainty dishes. Emperor Tu Duc was a demanding diner, but his legacy is some of the best food in Vietnam. Imperial-style banquets, which can be booked at a few high-end hotels, might include up to fifteen dishes. But one edible legacy of the royal court is easily found on the street: *banh*, delicate steamed cakes made from glutinous rice flour. One type of *banh* is a small, thick patty encasing a single whole prawn; another is flat, dotted with bits of mushroom, and steamed in a banana-leaf packet; still another comprises a minipancake served plain or dusted with chopped dried shrimp. All are eaten with a sprinkle of *nuoc mam* (in Hoi An they add a spoonful of chilli sauce).

Another Hue speciality is the pinky nail–sized freshwater clam called *hen*. These are eaten in broth with noodles or sautéed with peppery Vietnamese coriander and ladled over rice (to make *com hen*) or noodles or scooped up with rice crackers (*banh da*). Hue cooks treat young jackfruit as a vegetable, boiling the flesh (which tastes like a cross between artichoke and asparagus), shredding it, dressing it with fish sauce, scattering the lot with sesame seeds, and serving the dish (called *nom mit non)* with rice crackers. The centre also has its own way with pork, which is chopped, mixed with rice and fiery chillies, allowed to ferment, and wrapped in banana leaves for *nem Hue*. And the imperial city has its own version of the spring roll: soft, fresh *nem cuon Hue*, filled with sweet potato, pork, crunchy pickled prawns, water spinach and herbs.

The central Vietnamese proclivity for spicy food is illustrated by *bun bo Hue*, a fantastically fiery rice-noodle soup with beef and pork. Like most Vietnamese noodle soups it's accompanied by a riot of herbs and leafy greens that diners can stir into the broth at will. *My quang*, named for its home province of Quang Nam, is a dish of rice noodles tinted yellow with annatto seeds or pale pink (if made from red rice flour) topped with pork, shrimp, slivered banana blossoms, herbs and chopped peanuts, and doused with just enough broth to moisten. It's eaten with rice crackers (which diners crumble over to add crunch) and sweet-hot chilli jam. *Cao lau*, a noodle dish specific to the ancient port town of Hoi An, features thick, rough-textured noodles that are said to have origins in the soba noodles Japanese traders brought with them on trade missions. Like *my quang*, *cao lau* is moistened with just a smidge of richly flavoured broth; it is topped with slices of stewed pork, blanched bean sprouts, fresh greens and herbs, and crispy square 'croutons' made from the same dough as the noodles. Truly authentic *cao lau* features noodles made with water from a particular well in Hoi An's old town, though few believe that every bowl served in the town today carries that pedigree.

Another dish worth keeping your eye out for in central Vietnam is *banh khoai*. These dessert plate-sized thin crepes are made with rice-flour batter and cooked with copious amounts of oil in special long-handled pans. They feature a spare filling of shrimp, pork and bean sprouts, are rolled with fresh herbs and lettuce in a square of rice paper, and then dunked in a yellow bean-based dipping sauce.

South

In southern Vietnam the food reflects the region's natural abundance and year-round growing season. Here, dishes are bigger, more colourful and, some say, more visually attractive. When it migrated south, *banh khoai* morphed into a typically southern oversized version of its central self: a larger-than-plate-sized shocking-yellow crepe stuffed to bursting with filling called *banh xeo* (so named for the 'sssssst' sound the crepe's batter makes when it hits a hot pan).

No matter the season, vendors at southern markets display heaps of lush, big-leafed herbs, fruits in every colour of the rainbow, and the freshest fish possible. *Canh chua* is the Mekong Delta in a bowl: plentiful fish (usually snakehead or catfish), fruit (tomato and pineapple) and vegetables (bean sprouts, okra and *bac ha* or taro stem) in a broth that's tart from tamarind and salty from *nuoc mam*. Topped with vivid green herbs and golden fried garlic, it's as lovely to look at as it is to taste. Tamarind is a typically southern ingredient; it also sauces shelled or unshelled prawns in *tom rang me*, a messy but rewarding sweet-tart dish. But lest you think southerners only prefer their food on the tart side, know that *kho ca to*, catfish simmered in a clay pot with sweet caramel sauce and fish sauce, is a solid favourite.

Though its author no longer resides in Saigon, www.noodlepie.typepad.com is still the best go-to for info on the city's street foods. www.stickyrice.typepad.com has Hanoi similarly covered.

In the south coconut milk, an ingredient rarely used elsewhere in Vietnam, is the base for sweet, mild, Indianesque curries of chicken, pork and goat. The southern love of fresh herbs, fruit and vegetables comes to the fore in the region's numerous *goi* (salads), which feature ingredients like shredded green papaya, grapefruitlike pomelo, lotus stems and banana flower. *Banh trang phoi suong*, a do-it-yourself rice-paper affair with thinly sliced pork and pickled shallots, features a veritable hedgerow of unusual fresh greens, some spicy, some sour, some bitter, and some just saladish; many are picked wild. Southerners lay claim to a number of noodle specialities as well, such as the cool salad noodle *bun thit nuong*; *hu tieu nam vang*, a mild, soupy pork-and-shrimp import from neighbouring Cambodia; and *bun mam*, a strong fish-flavoured rice-noodle broth made with *mam* that, like *canh chua*, also includes tomatoes, pineapple and *bac ha*. (An identically named but significantly more challenging dish of cool rice noodles, bean sprouts, and herbs dressed with straight *mam* is found in central Vietnam.)

DRINKS

You're unlikely to go thirsty in Vietnam where, thanks to a healthy drinking culture there exists all manner of beverages to slake your parched throat. Sooner or later every traveller succumbs to *bia hoi* ('fresh' or draught beer) – local brands are served straight from the keg by the glass for a pittance in restaurants, eateries and specialist shops on seemingly every street corner. If you're looking to pay a little more for a beer of better quality, Saigon Beer isn't horrible, and La Rue, brewed on the central coast and more often available bottled than draught, is quite good. While imported liquor can be expensive, Vietnam brews a number of its own spirits, including drinkable, dirt-cheap vodka called Ha Noi. Distilled sticky-rice wine called *ruou* (which means,

DINING WITH CHILDREN

Family is at the centre of life in Vietnam, and you can consider almost every restaurant family friendly. Vietnamese love children, and restaurant staff will welcome yours with open arms. Fussy young palates should do well with mild rice and noodle-based dishes. Don't expect to find children's menus in any restaurants except those in the fanciest resorts, but food in Vietnam is so affordable that there is little room to quibble.

literally, 'alcohol') is often flavoured with herbs, spices, fruits and even animals. Travel to the northern highlands and you may be offered *ruou can*, sherrylike rice wine drunk through long bamboo straws from a communal vessel. And you'll undoubtedly encounter *ruou ran* (snake wine), an elixir that's thought to cure everything from night blindness to impotence. (Cobras and many other snakes in Vietnam are officially listed as endangered, a fact that producers rarely heed.)

In Vietnam the preparation, serving and drinking of tea (*tra* in the south and *che* in the north) has a social importance seldom appreciated by Western visitors. Serving tea in the home or office is more than a gesture of hospitality, it is a ritual. Northerners favour hot green tea, while in the south the same is often served over big chunks of ice. Chrysanthemum and jasmine infusions are also popular; particularly delicious is a fragrant noncaffeinated tea made from lotus seeds.

Vietnam is also a major coffee producer; when the country flooded the world market with robusta beans (arabica's cheaper, less aromatic cousin) nearly 10 years ago the bottom dropped out of the wholesale coffee market. Whiling away a morning or an afternoon over endless glasses of iced coffee, with or without milk (*ca phe sua da* or *ca phe da*) is somewhat of a ritual for Vietnam's male population, and cafes (the term can refer to a proper shop with tables and chairs as well as to a one-vendor stall that serves customers seated on tiny plastic stools) are as ubiquitous as *bia hoi* joints. Vietnamese coffee is thick and strong, which is why coffee jockeys measure it out with small cups that resemble shot glasses, and mixed with sweetened condensed milk it becomes almost chocolatey. Other liquid options in Vietnam include *mia da*, a freshly squeezed sugar-cane juice that is especially refreshing served over ice with a squeeze of *kalamansi*; *sinh to* (fresh fruit smoothies blended to order); and soy milk.

WHERE TO EAT & DRINK

Whatever your likes and dislikes, one eatery or another in Vietnam is almost certain to cater to them, be it the humble peddler with his yoke, a roadside stall, a simple *pho* shop or a fancy-pants restaurant. If you're new to the cuisine and not squeamish about street food, wet-market food courts, with vendors serving everything from coffee and fruit juices to noodles and steamed rice with side dishes, are the perfect place to graze.

Don't neglect French and Chinese restaurants. Though not as common as they used to be (except in HCMC's Cholon, or Chinese district), they serve up an important part of Vietnam's culinary and cultural legacy. And in recent years a flood of expatriates to Ho Chi Minh City and Hanoi have precipitated an explosion of truly international eateries serving Turkish and Thai, Malaysian and Moroccan, Indian and Italian.

There are often no set dining hours, but as a general rule of thumb cafes are open most of the day and into the night. Street stalls are open from very early in the morning until late at night. Restaurants usually open for lunch between 11am and 3pm, and dinner between 5pm or 6pm and 10pm or 11pm.

VEGETARIANS & VEGANS

The good news is that there is now more choice than ever before when it comes to vegetarian dining. The bad news is that you have not landed in Veg Heaven, for the Vietnamese are voracious omnivores. While they dearly love their vegies, they also adore much of what crawls on the ground, swims in the sea or flies in the air. In keeping with Buddhist precepts many vendors and eateries go vegie on the 1st and 15th of each lunar month; this is a great time to scour the markets and sample dishes that would otherwise be off-limits. Otherwise, be wary. Any dish of vegetables may well have been cooked with fish sauce or shrimp paste. If you're vegan, you're facing a bigger challenge. 'Mock meat' restaurants are something to seek out for those who want to remain true to their vegetarian principles but secretly miss their bacon butties. Found throughout Vietnam, they put tofu and gluten to use to create meatlike entities that even hardened carnivores enjoy.

HABITS & CUSTOMS

Enter the Vietnamese kitchen and you will be convinced that good food comes from simplicity. Essentials consist of a strong flame, basic cutting utensils, a mortar and pestle, and a well-blackened pot or two. The kitchen is so sacred that it is inhabited by its own deity, *Ong Tao* or the Kitchen God. The spiritual guardian of the hearth must have its due and the most important object in the kitchen is its altar.

Gain insight into aspects of Vietnamese culinary culture such as festival food traditions and the role of tea with *The Cuisine of Vietnam: Nourishing a Culture.*

Vietnamese generally eat three meals a day and snack in between. Breakfast is simple and may be noodles or *chao*. Baguettes are available at any time of day or night, and go well with coffee or tea. Lunch starts early, around 11am. In earlier years workers went home to eat with their families, but most now eat at nearby street cafes. Dinner is a time for family bonding. The dishes are arranged around a central rice bowl and diners each have a small eating bowl. When ordering from a restaurant menu don't worry about the succession of courses. All dishes are placed in the centre of the table as soon as they are ready and diners serve themselves. If it's a special occasion the host may drop a morsel or two into your rice bowl.

TABLE ETIQUETTE

Sit at the table with your bowl on a small plate, chopsticks and a soup spoon at the ready. Each place will include a small bowl at the top right-hand side for the *nuoc mam* or other dipping sauces. When serving yourself from the central bowls, use the communal serving spoon so as not to dip your chopsticks into it. Pick up the bowl with the left hand, bring it close to your mouth and use the chopsticks to manoeuvre the food. If you're eating noodles, lower your head till it hangs over the bowl and slurp away. It is polite for the host to offer more food than the guests can eat, and it is polite for the guests not to eat everything.

STREET SMARTS

Vietnamese entrepreneur Hoai Tan Duong is the brains behind the wildly successful restaurant Quan An Ngon, which has branches in both HCMC (p373) and Hanoi (p107), and which features vendors serving up classic street foods in an upscale, nostalgic setting. Though his ventures (Hoai also owns a travel company) have earned him a mint, he still enjoys hunting for the country's best street eats. Taking the plunge into street food can be daunting, but Hoai has a couple of tips for identifying promising vendors. First, look for lots of parked motorbikes rather than pedicabs; a profusion of the latter might indicate cheap rather than delicious grub. Secondly, make sure the vendor is serving from a huge pot, which indicates that their dish is so delish they sell heaps of it every day.

Also, remember not to leave chopsticks in a V-shape in your bowl – this is a symbol of death.

COOKING COURSES

The best way to tackle Vietnamese cuisine head-on is to sign up for a cooking course during your stay. For those who fall in love with the food, there is no better experience than re-creating the real recipes back home. It's also a great way to introduce your Vietnam experience to friends; they may not want to hear the stories or see the photos, but offer them a mouth-watering meal and they'll come running. Cooking courses have really taken off in the last few years as more and more travellers combine the twin passions of eating and exploring, and range from budget classes in the local specialities of Hoi An to gastronomic gallops through the country's classic cuisine at five-star hotels in Hanoi and HCMC. If you are set on serious studies, try a short course in Hoi An and negotiate for something longer once you've had a taste of the experience.

EAT YOUR WORDS

Speaking some of the local lingo always helps and never more than when it's time for a meal. Locals will appreciate your efforts, even if your pronunciation is off the mark, and might just introduce you to some regional specialities you would otherwise never have discovered.

Useful Phrases

restaurant
nhà hàng — nyaà haàng

Do you have a menu in English?
Bạn có thực đơn bằng tiếng Anh không? — baạn káw tụhrk đern bùhng díng aang kawm

I'm a vegetarian.
Tôi ăn chay. — doy uhn jay

I'd like ...
Xin cho tôi ... — sin jo doy ...

What's the speciality here?
Ở đây có món gì đặc biệt? — ẻr đay kó món zeè dụhk bee·ụht

Not too spicy please.
Xin đừng cho cay quá. — sin đùrng jo ğay gwaá

No sugar.
Không đường. — kawm dur-èrng

No salt.
Không muối. — kawm moo-eé

Can I get this without the meat?
Cho tôi món này không thịt được không? — jo doi món này kawm tịt đuhr-ẹrk kawm

I'm allergic to ....
Tôi bị dị ứng với ... — doy beẹ zeẹ úhrng ver-eé ...

I don't eat ...
Tôi không được ăn ... — doy kawm đuhr-ẹrk uhn ...

beef
thịt bò — tịt bò

chicken
thịt gà — tịt gaà

fish
cá kaá
fish sauce
nước mắm nuhr-érk múhm
pork
thịt heo tịt hay-o
peanuts
lạc/đậu phộng lạc (N/S) lak/dọh fọm

Can you please bring me ...?
Xin mang cho tôi...? sin maang jo doy ...
a spoon
cái thìa ğaí tee-ùh
a knife
con dao ğon zow
a fork
cái dĩa/cái nĩa (N/S) ğaí deẽ-uh/ğaí neẽ-uh
chopsticks
đôi đũa đoy-ee đoõ-uh
a glass
cái cốc/cái ly (N/S) ğaí káwp/ğaí lee

Can I have a (beer) please?
Xin cho tôi (chai bia)? sin jo doy (jai bee-uh)
No ice.
Không đá. Kawm đaá.
Thank you, that was delicious.
Cám ơn, ngon lắm. ğaám ern, ngon lúhm
The bill, please.
Xin tính tiền. sin díng dee-ùhn

Menu Decoder

TYPICAL DISHES

bánh bao (baáng bow) – sweet, doughy Chinese pastry filled with meat and vegetables and dunked in soy sauce
bánh chưng (baáng juhrng) – square cakes made from sticky rice and filled with beans, onion and pork, boiled in leaves for 10 hours
bánh cuốn (baáng ğoo-úhn) – steamed rice-paper rolls with minced pork, dried shrimp and pressed pork
bò bảy món (bò bảy món) – seven beef dishes
bún bò huế (bún bò hwé) – spicy beef noodle soup
bún chả (bún jaả) – rice vermicelli with pork and vegetables
bún thịt nướng (bún tịt nuhr-érng) – rice vermicelli with char-grilled pork
canh khổ qua (ğaáng kảw gwaa) – a bitter soup
chả (jaả) – pressed pork, a cold meat/cold cut
chả cá (jaả ğaá) – filleted fish slices grilled over charcoal
chả cá lã vọng (jaả ğaá laã vọm) – grilled fish cooked with noodles, dill, turmeric and spring onions in a charcoal brazier
chả quế (jaả gwé) – pressed pork prepared with cinnamon
chạo tôm (jọw dawm) – grilled sugar cane rolled in spiced shrimp paste
ếch tẩm bột rán (ék dủhm bạwt zaán) – frog meat soaked in a thin batter and fried in oil
gỏi ngó sen (gỏy ngó san) – lotus-stem salad
khoai tây rán/chiên (N/S) (kwai day zaán/jee-uhn) – french fries
lẩu (lỏh) – Vietnamese hotpot, with fish *(lẩu cá)*, goat *(lẩu dê)* or vegetables only *(lẩu rau)*

ốc nhồi (áwp nyòy) – snail meat, pork, chopped green onion, fish sauce and pepper rolled up in ginger leaves and cooked in snail shells
rau muống xào (zoh moo-úhng sòw) – stir-fried water spinach

NOODLES
bún bò (bún bò) – braised beef with rice vermicelli
hủ tiếu bò kho (hoỏ dee-oó bò ko) – beef stew with flat rice noodles
mì gà (meè gaà) – chicken soup with thin egg noodles
miến cua (mee-úhn ğoo-uh) – cellophane-noodle soup with crab
phở gà/bò (fẻr gaà/bò) – rice-noodle soup with chicken/beef

VEGETARIAN
đậu phụ/tàu hũ (N/S) *kho* (đọw fụ/tòw hoõ ko) – braised tofu
đậu phụ/tàu hũ (N/S) *xào xả ớt* (đọw fụ/tòw hoõ sòw saả ért) – tofu fried with lemon grass and chilli
gỏi cuốn chay (gỏy ğoo-úhn jay) – vegetarian rice-paper rolls
nấm rơm kho (núhm zerm ko) – braised straw mushrooms
rau cải xào thập cẩm (zoh ğaỉ sòw tụhp ğẩhm) – stir-fried mixed vegetables
súp rau (súp zoh) – vegetable soup

DESSERTS
bánh đậu xanh (baáng đọh saang) – mung-bean cake
bánh ít nhân đậu (baáng ít nyuhn đọh) – pastry made of sticky rice, beans and sugar that's steamed in a banana leaf folded into a triangular pyramid
chè (jà) – served in a tall ice cream–sundae glass containing beans, fruit, coconut and sugar
kem dừa (ğam zuhr-ùh) – mix of ice cream, candied fruit and the jellylike flesh of young coconut
mứt (mút) – candied fruit or vegetables, made with carrot, coconut, kumquat, gourd, ginger root, lotus seeds or tomato
sữa chua (sũhr-uh joo-uh) –sweetened yogurt

Food Glossary

RICE

cơm rang thập cẩm (N)	ğerm zaang tụhp ğủhm	mixed fried rice
cơm chiên (S)	ğerm jee-uhn	
cháo	jów	rice porridge
cơm	ğerm	rice
cơm trắng	ğerm chaáng	steamed rice

MEAT & SEAFOOD

thịt bò	tịt bò	beef
thịt gà	tịt gaà	chicken
cua	ğoo-uh	crab
lươn	luhr-ern	eel
cá	ğaá	fish
ếch	ék	frog
thịt dê	tịt ze	goat
thịt lòng	tịt lòm	offal
thịt lợn/heo (N/S)	tịt lẹrn/hay-o	pork
tôm	dawm	shrimp/prawns
ốc	áwp	snail
mực	mụhrk	squid

FRUIT

táo/bơm (N/S)	dów/berm	apple
chuối	joo-eé	banana

dừa	zuhr-ùh	coconut
nho	nyo	grapes
chanh	chaang	lemon
vải	vaỉ	lychee
quýt	gweét	mandarin
xoài	swaì	mango
cam	ğaam	orange
đu đủ	đoo đỏo	papaya
dứa	zuhr-úh	pineapple
dâu	zoh	strawberry
dưa hấu	zuhr-uh hóh	watermelon

VEGETABLES

bắp cải	búhp ğaỉ	cabbage
cà rốt	ğaà záwt	carrot
ngô/bắp (N/S)	ngow/búp	corn
dưa leo	zuhr-uh lay-o	cucumber
cà tím	ğaà dím	eggplant
đậu xanh	đọh saang	green beans
ớt xanh	ért saang	green pepper
rau diếp	zoh zee-úhp	lettuce
nấm	núhm	mushrooms
đậu bi	đọh bee	peas
khoai tây	kwai day	potato
bí ngô	beé ngaw	pumpkin
khoai lang	kwai laang	sweet potato
cà chua	ğaà joo-uh	tomato

DRINKS

bia	bi-a	beer
cà phê	ğaà fe	coffee
sinh tố	sing dáw	fruit shake
cà phê đen nóng	ğaà fe đen nóm	hot black coffee
trà nóng	chaà nóm	hot black tea
trà sữa nóng	chaà sũhr-uh nóm	hot milk black tea
nâu nóng (N)	noh nóm	hot milk coffee
cà phê sữa nóng (S)	ğaà fe sũhr-uh nóm	
sữa nóng	sũhr-uh nóm	hot milk
đá	đaá	ice
cà phê đá	ğaà fe đaá	iced black coffee
cacao đá	ğa-ğow đaá	iced chocolate
chanh đá	jaang đaá	iced lemon juice
nâu đá (N)	noh đaá	iced milk coffee
	cà phê sữa đá (S)	ğaà fe sũhr-uh đaá
sữa đá	sũhr-uh đaá	iced milk
sữa	sũhr-uh	milk
nước khoáng (N)	nuhr-érk kwaáng	mineral water
	nước suối (S)	nuhr-érk soo-eé
cam vắt	ğaam vúht	orange juice
soda chanh	so-daa jaang	soda water and lemon
sữa đậu nành	sũhr-uh đọh naàng	soy milk
chè/trà (N/S)	jà/chaà	tea

Environment

THE LAND

Vietnam is a long, stretched-out country spanning 1600km along the eastern edge of the Indochinese peninsula. The country's land area is 326,797 sq km, making it a bit bigger than Italy and slightly smaller than Japan; 3451km of its borders are convoluted coastlines fronting the Gulf of Tonkin in the north and the South China Sea in the south, plus it shares 3818km of land borders with China, Laos, and Cambodia.

Geologically, Southeast Asia is formed from fragments of ancient Gondwanaland that splintered off and started migrating north about 350 million years ago. As these fragments ran into the Asian continent the collisions crumpled ancient sea floors (indicated by the presence of limestone) into mountain ranges or, in other areas, formed suture lines where rivers now flow. The Truong Son Range was uplifted about 250 million years ago, and the Red River of northern Vietnam follows the contact line where one massive fragment (the Indochina Block) collided with South China. The Indochina Block is thought to underlie much of Southeast Asia (though buried under sediments and later formations), but an exposed portion of this block can still be seen on the 60,000-sq-km Kontum Massif in central Vietnam.

'The country is S-shaped, broad in the north and south and very narrow in the centre'

The most significant of these northward-drifting fragments was India, which collided with Asia about 50 million years. This collision had such incredible force that it uplifted the Himalaya (the highest mountains in the world) and twisted the neighbouring Indochinese peninsula into its characteristic S-shaped curve. The Himalayan uplift had a profound impact on Southeast Asia which included altering weather patterns so they are now strongly seasonal with powerful monsoons, and creating steep slopes that send immense amounts of sediment down the Red and Mekong Rivers to form vast, productive deltas at their mouths on the Vietnam coast.

Vietnam is also a land shaped by its history. Dominated by the Chinese for a thousand years the Vietnamese pushed southwards, putting a bit of distance between them and their northern neighbours and seeking new lands for cultivation. Hemmed in by the Truong Son Mountains to the west, they had little choice but to continue down the coast, eating up the Kingdom of Champa and taking a bite-sized chunk out of Cambodia.

The result is the map of Vietnam today. As the Vietnamese are quick to point out, it resembles a *don ganh,* or the ubiquitous bamboo pole with a basket of rice slung from each end. The baskets represent the main rice-growing regions of the Red River Delta in the north and the Mekong Delta in the south. The country is S-shaped, broad in the north and south and very narrow in the centre, where at one point it is only 50km wide.

The coastline is one of the big draws for tourists and it doesn't disappoint, with sweeping beaches, towering cliffs, undulating dunes and countless uninhabited islands along its length. The largest of these islands is Phu Quoc (p464), off the coast of Cambodia in the Gulf of Thailand. Other major islands include Cat Ba (p146) and Van Don (p153) in the Halong Bay area, and a splattering of dots off Nha Trang (p280).

Both the Red River and the Mekong River Deltas are pancake flat and prone to flooding. Silt carried by the Red River and its tributaries, confined to their paths by 3000km of dykes, has raised the level of the river beds above the surrounding plains so that breaches in the dykes result in disastrous flooding. The Mekong Delta has no such protection and when *cuu long* 'the nine dragons' (the nickname for the nine channels of the Mekong where it splits in the delta) burst their banks it creates havoc for communities and crops. The Mekong Delta continues to expand at a rate of about 100m per year, through global warming; the consequent rise in sea levels around the world could one day submerge it.

Three-quarters of the country consists of rolling hills (mostly in the south) and mighty mountains (mostly in the north), the highest of which is 3143m-high Fansipan (p178) in the far northwest. The Truong Son Mountains, which form the central highlands, run almost the full length of Vietnam along its borders with Laos and Cambodia. The coastal ranges near Nha Trang and those at Hai Van Pass (Danang) are composed of granite, and the giant boulders littering the hillsides are a surreal sight. The western part of the central highlands, near Buon Ma Thuot and Pleiku, is well known for its incredibly fertile, red volcanic soil.

The most striking geological features in Vietnam are karst formations of limestone in which erosion has produced fissures, sinkholes, caves and underground rivers. Northern Vietnam is a showcase for these outcrops, with stunning examples at Halong Bay (p139) and Bai Tu Long Bay, (p153) and around Ninh Binh (p192) and the Perfume Pagoda (p121). At Halong and Bai Tu Long Bays, an enormous limestone plateau has dramatically eroded so that old mountain tops stick out of the sea like bony vertical fingers pointing towards the sky.

The forces that erode limestone into such fantastic formations are the region's torrential monsoon rains. First there are winter monsoons from mid-November to late March that bring cooler weather and rain from the north. Then, after a transition period in April and May, the winds shift to the southwest and bring heavy summer monsoons out of the Indian Ocean until September (with some rains continuing through October). However, northern Vietnam (north of Ngang Pass) sees strong seasonal changes in rainfall and temperature, while southern Vietnam has more uniform year-round conditions.

WILDLIFE

Despite some disastrous bouts of deforestation, Vietnam's flora and fauna continue to be as exotic, abundant and varied as any tropical country. Intensive surveys by the World Wildlife Fund along the Mekong River (including both Vietnam and its neighbouring areas), have found a total of 1068 new species from 1997 to 2007, placing this area on Conservation International's list of the top five biodiversity hot spots in the world. Numerous areas inside Vietnam remain unsurveyed or poorly known and many more species are likely to be found.

The scientific and conservation value of these recent discoveries has not been lost on authorities, and the Vietnamese government has been expanding the size of its national parks and nature reserves, and banning logging within these areas.

Many interesting environmental articles are published in the online edition of *Thanh Nien*, where you can keep up with current issues and stories (www.thanhniennews.com).

Animals

On paper, Vietnam has plenty to offer those who are wild about wildlife, but in reality many animals live in remote forested areas and encountering them is extremely unlikely. Most of the wildlife in readily accessible areas is disappearing rapidly thanks to a growing resource-hungry human population and the destruction of habitats. Hunting, poaching and pollution are taking their toll too.

With a wide range of habitats – from equatorial lowlands to high, temperate plateaus and even alpine peaks – the wildlife of Vietnam is enormously diverse. One recent tally listed 275 species of mammals, more than 800 birds, 180 reptiles, 80 amphibians, hundreds of fish and tens of thousands of invertebrates, but new species are being discovered at such a rapid rate that this list is constantly being revised upward.

More than any location in the world, Vietnam is revealing new creatures that elude scientific classification. Since Vietnam reopened for business around 1990, biologists have discovered several previously unknown species of large mammal in Vietnam, including finding three new hoofed animals within a span of four years. Most significant among these was a large antelopelike wild ox named the saola; scientists have yet to see one in the wild, despite intensive efforts, but they have a couple skins, skulls, and photographs taken with remote cameras to confirm the saola's existence.

Twitchers with a serious interest in the birdlife of Vietnam should carry a copy of *Birds of Southeast Asia* (2005) by Craig Robson, which includes a thorough coverage of Vietnam.

Rare and little-known birds previously thought to be extinct have been spotted and no doubt there are more in the extensive forests along the Lao border. Edwards' pheasant, previously believed to be extinct, was found on a scientific expedition, and other excursions have yielded the white-winged wood duck and white-shouldered ibis.

Even casual visitors will spot a few bird species: swallows and swifts flying over fields and along watercourses; flocks of finches at roadsides and in paddies; and bulbuls and mynahs in gardens and patches of forest. Vietnam is on the east-Asian flyway and is an important stopover for migratory waders en route from Siberian breeding grounds to their Australian winter quarters.

ENDANGERED SPECIES

Tragically, Vietnam's wildlife has been in stunning decline as forest habitats are destroyed and waterways polluted. Most significantly, widespread illegal and subsistence hunting has decimated local animal populations, in some cases wiping out entire species. Continued deforestation and poaching means that many endangered species are on a one-way ticket to extinction. Captive-breeding programs may be the only hope for some, but rarely is there money and resources available for such expensive efforts.

Officially, the government has recognised 54 species of mammal and 60 species of bird as endangered. Of large animals, the tapir and Sumatran rhinoceros are already extinct in Vietnam, but no one knows how many lesser-known animals are gone forever. Larger animals at the forefront of the country's conservation efforts include elephant, tiger, leopard, black bear, honey bear, snub-nosed monkey, flying squirrel, crocodile and turtle. In the early 1990s a small population of Javan rhinos, the world's rarest rhinoceros, was discovered in Cat Tien National Park (p406), northeast of Ho Chi Minh City. There are probably only 10 to 20 left in the entire country, but their two main blocks of habitat are separated by heavily used agricultural areas and it's not clear if there are even enough males or females left to build a self-sustaining population.

If you see endangered animals for sale, or listed on a restaurant menu, call the toll-free hotline run by Education for Nature Vietnam: 1800 1522.

Cat Tien is also the site of a remarkable wildlife recovery story involving the Siamese crocodile, which was extinct in the wild due to excessive hunting and cross-breeding with introduced Cuban crocodiles. It took a lot of detective work, but scientists tested the DNA of individual crocodiles in captivity until they found a handful of pure Siamese crocodiles that were then reintroduced to an isolated lake in the park where they are now thriving.

Another positive sign is that some wildlife populations are re-establishing themselves in reforested areas. Birds, fish and crustaceans have reappeared in replanted mangrove forests. Areas in which large animals were thought to have been wiped out by war are now hot spots of biodiversity and abundance. The extensive forests of the central highlands and far north remain a home to some of nature's most noble creatures, such as tigers, elephants, clouded leopards and sun bears. Their chances of survival rest in the balance, as Vietnam's population continues to expand, eating up more and more of the remaining wilderness areas.

Plants

Years ago Vietnam was almost completely blanketed in forest, from vast mangrove swamps fringing the coast to dense rainforest in mountainous regions. Over the centuries, these habitats have been progressively pushed back: first by the clearing of land for cultivation, and later by a booming population and the ravages of war.

Vietnam: A Natural History, a collaboration between American and Vietnamese biodiversity experts, is by far the best book for those who want to learn more about the country's extraordinary flora and fauna.

Although the scars of war are still visible and much of the damage is irreversible, reforestation programs have been implemented and today the landscape is showing signs of recovery in many protected areas. Natural forests at higher elevations, such as those in the northwest, feature wild rhododendrons, dwarf bamboos and numerous types of orchids; the central coast is drier and features stands of pines; while the river deltas support mangrove forests, which are valuable nurseries for fish and crustaceans as well as feeding sites for many bird species.

The diverse habitats of Vietnam are estimated to contain more than 12,000 plant species; only around 7000 of which have been identified and 2300 of which are known to be valuable to humanity. Recently the islands and caves of Halong Bay yielded seven previously unknown plants – the largest and most conspicuous of the new flora has been christened the Halong Fan Palm. Other surveys along the Mekong River have confirmed that Southeast Asia has the highest levels of plant diversity found anywhere in the world.

The Vietnamese make good use of a wide variety of wild and domestic plants for medicines and remedies. Villagers forage in the forests for barks, roots, herbs and flowers, which go into making cures for all sorts of ailments.

NATIONAL PARKS: THE TOP TEN

Park (size in hectares)	Features	Activities	Best time to visit	Page
Ba Be (9022)	lakes, rainforest, waterfalls, towering peaks, caves, bears, langurs	hiking, boating, bird-watching	Apr-Nov	p162
Bai Tu Long (15,600)	karst peaks, caves, hidden beaches	boating, kayaking, swimming, surfing, hiking	Apr-Nov	p153
Bach Ma (37,500)	waterfalls, tigers, primates	hiking, bird-watching	Feb-Sep	p232
Cat Ba (15,331)	jungle, caves, langurs, boars, deer, waterfowl	hiking, swimming, bird-watching	Apr-Aug	p152
Cat Tien (71,457)	primates, elephants, birdlife, rhinos, tigers	jungle exploration, hiking	Nov-Jun	p406
Con Dao (19,991)	dugongs, turtles, beaches	bird-watching, snorkelling	Nov-Jun	p409
Cuc Phuong (22,406)	jungle, grottoes, primates, birding centre, caves	endangered-primate viewing, hiking	Nov-Feb	p196
Hoang Lien (28,500)	mountains, birdlife, minority communities	hiking, cycling, bird-watching, mountain climbing	Sep-Nov, Apr-May	p178
Phong Nha–Ke Bang (125,362)	caves, karsts, birds	boat trips, caving, birding	Apr-Sep	p202
Yok Don (112,102)	stilt houses, minority communities	elephant rides, hiking	Nov-Feb	p332

NATIONAL PARKS

Thanks to a decision in 2000 to begin re-gazetting its parks, Vietnam has been aggressively expanding the size and number of national parks in the country and there are now 30, from Hoang Lien in the far north to Mui Ca Mau on the very southern tip of Vietnam. There is also an ever-growing number of nature reserves (58 reserves as of 2008); a reserve is often a stepping stone towards an area being declared a national park. Levels of infrastructure and enforcement vary widely from park to park, but unlike other countries there are no 'paper parks' in Vietnam because everything is very official here and every park has at least a ranger station and some rangers.

Ho Chi Minh, taking time off from the war in 1963 to dedicate Cuc Phuong National Park, said: 'Forest is gold. If we know how to conserve it well, it will be very precious. Destruction of the forest will lead to serious effects on both life and productivity.'

The staffing and management of national parks is a continuing source of conflict because Vietnam has yet to figure out an effective way to bring dense rural populations in and around park boundaries into the process of protecting and caring for their local natural resources. Rangers are often vastly outnumbered by local villagers who rely on the forests for food and income. Some parks now use high-tech mapping software to track poaching and logging activity to help rangers use their limited time and resources more effectively.

Most of Vietnam's national parks are seldom visited by travellers, who tend to get stuck on the 'must-see' tourist trail, without the time or wanderlust to explore new destinations. Access can be problematic with some parks hidden in remote areas, but others are easy to reach. For those who make the effort to seek them out, national parks reveal a whole different face to Vietnam. They also have the added appeal of being among the few places in Vietnam where tourists are unlikely to be hassled to buy anything. However, if you are wanting a bit of peace and quiet to soak up the serenity and splendour it is better to visit the more popular parks during the week, as hordes of Vietnamese descend during the weekend. Prepare to be shocked if you encounter lots of noisy people and trash in a national park.

The most interesting and accessible parks are Cat Ba (p152), Bai Tu Long (p153), Ba Be (p162), Hoang Lien (p178) and Cuc Phuong (p196) in the north; Bach Ma (p232) in the centre; and Cat Tien (p406) and Yok Don (p332) in the south. All of the parks levy some sort of admission charge, but it is usually very reasonable at around 10,000d or less than US$1. Many parks have accommodations available, most often a mix of rooms and bungalows, and camping is sometimes possible if you have your own gear.

Flora and Fauna International produce an excellent Nature Tourism Map of Vietnam, which includes detailed coverage of all the national parks in Vietnam (www.fauna-flora.org/maps.php). All proceeds from sales of the map go towards supporting primate conservation in Vietnam.

Cat Ba National Park is on a beautiful island, and during the summer months it attracts a steady stream of foreign travellers willing to make the boat journey. In 2000, Vietnam also created Bai Tu Long National Park, a protected reserve situated to the northeast of Halong Bay, which includes more than 15,000 hectares of tropical evergreen forest, plenty of hidden beaches and a spot of surf.

Ba Be National Park features spectacular waterfalls and is accessible by hired 4WD or motorbike from Hanoi. Hoang Lien National Park was recently created to protect the landscape and peoples around Sapa. Cuc Phuong National Park is less visited, but easily reached from Hanoi and offers great hiking, plus an amazing array of rescued primates that are being rehabilitated. Bach Ma National Park, near Hue, receives far fewer visitors than its attractions deserve, but is demonstrating good potential for responsible ecotourism.

Cat Tien National Park, in the southern part of the central highlands, is relatively easy to reach from Ho Chi Minh City or Dalat, and very popular with bird-watchers. Also in the central highlands is Yok Don National Park, which is home to many elephants and local minority tribes.

One other park in the south that is a must for any serious birder is Tram Chim National Park (p433), east of Chau Doc in Tham Chap province. This is home to the magnificent rare Sarus Crane and one of only two nesting sites in the world. The other is at Ang Trapeng Thmor in northwest Cambodia.

ENVIRONMENTAL ISSUES

Vietnam's environment is not yet teetering on the brink, but there are some worrying signs. Vietnam is a poor, densely populated, agricultural country, so humans are competing with native plants and animals for the same limited resources. The population is also expected to nearly double from 85 million in 2008 to over 150 million in 2050, putting tremendous strain on already over-stressed systems.

Deforestation is one serious problem facing the country today. Originally, almost all of Vietnam was covered with dense forests. Since the arrival of human beings many millennia ago, Vietnam has been progressively denuded of forest cover. While 44% of the original forest cover was extant in 1943, by 1983 only 24% was left and in 1995 it was down to 20%. In a positive turnaround, recent reforestation projects by the Forest Ministry, including the banning of unprocessed timber exports in 1992, have produced a rise in the amount of forest cover. However this has been bad news for the neighbours, because it simply means Vietnam buys its timber from Laos and Cambodia where environmental enforcement is lax. It is also important to read between the lines when hearing about Vietnam's reforestation programs and improved 'forest cover'. Nearly all planting programs involve planting non-native trees in homogenous plantations of trees in straight rows. This looks great on paper but has almost no ecological merit.

Another major problem is the prolific hunting of animals within the forest. This includes both illegal poaching and the 'legitimate' hunting of animals by people simply looking to put food on the table. One serious issue is the widespread use of snares that capture and kill animals indiscriminately, whether they're common or critically endangered. So many animals are killed and trapped for the wildlife and 'bush meat' trades that vast areas of intact forest are increasingly devoid of wildlife. And attempts to curtail

DOING YOUR BIT

- Vietnam has a low level of environmental awareness and responsibility, and many people remain unaware of the implications of littering. Try and raise awareness of these issues by example, and dispose of your litter as responsibly as possible.
- Vietnam's fauna populations are under considerable threat from domestic consumption of 'bush meat' and the illegal international trade in animal products. Though it may be 'exotic' to drink snake wine, or eat wild meat such as muntjac, bat, deer, sea horse, shark fin and so on – or to buy products made from endangered plants and animals – doing so will indicate your support or acceptance of such practices and add to the demand for them.
- When visiting coral reefs and snorkelling or diving, or simply boating, be careful not to touch live coral or anchor boats on it, as this hinders the coral's growth. If it's possible to anchor in a sandy area, try to convince the operator to do so and indicate your willingness to swim to the coral. Don't buy coral souvenirs.
- When visiting limestone caves, be aware that touching the formations hinders growth and turns the limestone black. Don't break off the stalactites or stalagmites as they take lifetimes to regrow. Don't carve graffiti onto limestone formations, cave walls or other rock.
- Do not remove or buy 'souvenirs' that have been taken from historical sites and natural areas.

these trades on the local level are thwarted by bribery, corruption and the simple fact that everyone is somebody's friend, neighbour or relative so it's hard to enforce the law.

Ecotourism is increasingly on the rise, and it would seem that that would be a bright spot because the government has set aside tens of thousands of square kilometres of forest land with plans to create even more national parks, nature reserves and ecotourism areas. However, there are development interests that are not particularly amenable to boosting the size of Vietnam's national parks and nature reserves. As in the West, even the best-laid plans can sometimes go awry. Massive infrastructure projects such as new highways are threatening protected areas, as it is cheaper for the government to use park land than compensate villagers for farm land. A case in point is the Ho Chi Minh road, Hwy 14, which cuts through Cuc Phuong National Park.

The Vietnam Association for Conservation of Nature and Environment acts as a bit of a clearing house for stories and projects related to Vietnam's environment; www.vacne.org.vn/Index_e.htm.

The government also has an active program for leasing plots of forest to individuals, communities and corporations so they can develop reforestation and ecotourism projects that benefit the country. It was discovered in 2008, however, that 30,000 hectares of leases in one area alone had instead been logged for profit, and it turned out that loopholes in the lease contracts made it almost impossible to hold anyone responsible.

That said, ecotourism is still held up as a growth industry as more and more international visitors demand environmentally friendly activities. As well as trekking in national parks and mountain areas, cycling is increasingly popular and kayaking has taken off in Halong Bay. However, the fact is that ecotourism remains a much used and abused phrase and many of the so-called 'ecotourism' products in Vietnam are more about marketing than the environment. On a similar note, a survey of 418 businesses in 2008 found that 80% did not follow through on their promise to protect the environment.

Vietnam has a rapidly growing industrial base that spells environmental trouble ahead. Until recently, it could be said that there was little pollution because there was relatively little industry, but doctors in Ho Chi Minh City (HCMC) are already noticing a sharp increase in respiratory ailments because the air contains from 1.5 to three times more pollutants than permitted. Doctors now advise that people who spend time on the street in HCMC wear respirators or masks, and these kinds of problems are likely to spread to other cities, especially with the dramatic increase in the number of noisy, smoke-spewing motorbikes in recent years.

The Vietnam Green Building Council posts articles about current environmental and global-warming issues on its website, www.vsccan.org/vgbc.

Groundwater in Hanoi and HCMC has also become polluted. At the same time so much water is being pumped out of the aquifers that the land itself is actually dropping. Groundwater wells in coastal areas are now increasingly salty and polluted as well.

Vietnam is also ranked as one of the most vulnerable countries in the world in the face of global warming, because rising tides, flooding and hurricanes will likely inundate low-lying areas. A 2008 conference determined that a

LENDING A HAND

Vietnam has a growing number of very effective local NGOs, plus many international organisations are active in the country, creating a tremendous number of fascinating opportunities to volunteer on environmental projects in the country. Try starting with the Volunteer for Community Development and Environment Education Organization (VFCD), which has active projects in education, conservation, and community development; www.vfcd.org. PanNature is a Vietnamese NGO promoting nature-friendly solutions to environmental problems and sustainable development issues. It occasionally offers volunteer opportunities; www.nature.org.vn. And you can find many volunteer projects through www.idealist.org.

sea-level rise of only 1m would flood over 6% of the country and displace more than 10 million people. Similar flooding will increasingly happen as the run-off from severe monsoons flood the vast deltas of the Red River and Mekong River.

Much has been written about the human and economic devastation wrought by the USA during the American War, but there was also ecocide – the war saw the most intensive attempt to destroy a country's natural environment the world has ever seen. American forces sprayed 72 million litres of herbicides (named Agents Orange, White and Blue after the colour of their canisters) over 16% of South Vietnam to destroy the Viet Cong's natural cover.

Another environmentally disastrous method of defoliation employed during the war involved the use of enormous bulldozers called 'Rome ploughs' to rip up the jungle floor. Large tracts of forest, agricultural land, villages and even cemeteries were bulldozed, removing both the vegetation and topsoil. Flammable melaleuca forests were ignited with napalm. In mountain areas, landslides were deliberately created by bombing and spraying acid on limestone hillsides. Elephants, useful for transport, were attacked from the air with bombs and napalm. By the war's end, extensive areas had been taken over by tough weeds (known locally as 'American grass'). The government estimates that 20,000 sq km of forest and farmland were lost as a direct result of the American War.

Some 13 million tonnes of bombs – equivalent to 450 times the energy of the atomic bomb used on Hiroshima – were dropped on the Indochina region. This equates to 265kg for every man, woman and child in Vietnam, Cambodia and Laos.

Scientists have yet to conclusively prove a link between the residues of chemicals used by the USA and spontaneous abortions, stillbirths, birth defects and other human health problems. However, the circumstantial evidence is certainly compelling. In 2002, on the heels of a landmark Agent Orange conference in Hanoi, the USA and Vietnam initiated a joint investigation into the health effects of this damaging herbicide. Delegates from Vietnam's National Environmental Agency and the US National Institute of Environmental Health Sciences cosigned a directive for scientists to explore possible links between Agent Orange and various physical illnesses such as cancers in adults and leukaemia in children.

Hanoi

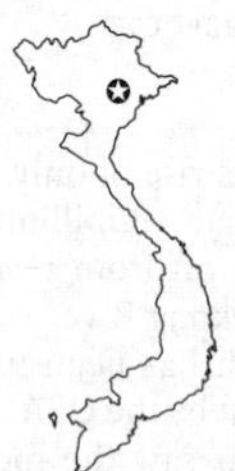

The grand old dame of the orient, Hanoi is perhaps the most graceful, atmospheric and exotic capital city in Asia. Its appeal is instant, with sweeping boulevards, tree-fringed lakes, ancient pagodas and a relatively compact historic centre that's best explored on foot.

Hanoi is very much a city on the move. The pace of life is relentless and the energy and enterprise remarkable – indeed, it seems that all of Hanoi's defiant, ambitious citizens are determined to make up for all that lost time. A constant tide of motorbikes swarms through the quixotic web of streets of the Old Quarter, a cauldron of commerce for almost 1000 years and still the best place to check the pulse of this resurgent city. Life is carried out on the street, as hawkers in conical hats ply their wares while locals sip drip-coffee and *bia hoi* (beer). Witness synchronised t'ai chi on the shores of Hoan Kiem Lake at dawn while goateed grandfathers tug at their wisps over the next chess move.

It is a city of sharp contrasts. In Lenin Park the Communist Party youth go through military drills and keep the red flag flying high. A street or two away, Hanoi's bright young things dine in cosmopolitan restaurants before heading on to a cutting-edge bar where the soundtrack is Ibiza-style house music or Berlin electro.

Huge challenges now confront Hanoi, as rapacious developers target prime plots and traffic increasingly threatens to choke the character out of the city. But for now it retains a unique blend of Parisian grace and Asian pace, for in Hanoi the medieval and modern coexist and enthral.

HIGHLIGHTS

- Experience Asia at its raw, pulsating best in the labyrinthine streets of the **Old Quarter** (p91)
- Step into history, and a spiritual retreat from the busy streets beyond, at the **Temple of Literature** (p96)
- Check out the best of Hanoi's unique bar scene at the '**bia hoi junction**' (p113)
- Pay your respects to 'Uncle Ho' himself at **Ho Chi Minh's Mausoleum** (p94)
- Piece together the country's ethnic mosaic at the wonderful **Vietnam Museum of Ethnology** (p97)

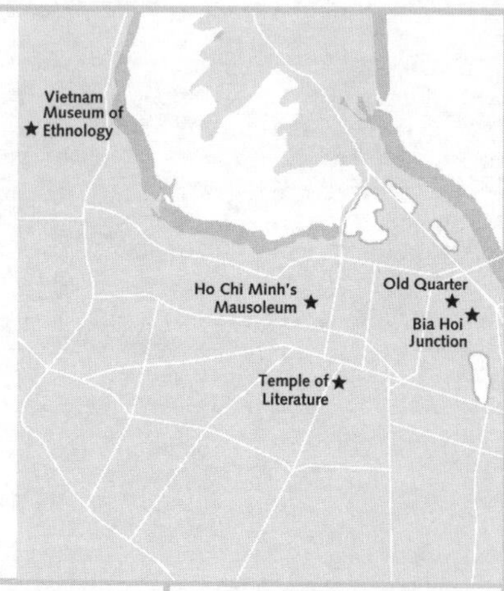

- TELEPHONE CODE: 04
- POPULATION: 3.7 MILLION
- BEST TIMES TO VISIT: MAR–MAY & SEP–NOV

HISTORY

The site where Hanoi stands today has been inhabited since the neolithic period. Emperor Ly Thai To moved his capital here in AD 1010, naming it Thang Long (City of the Soaring Dragon). Spectacular celebrations in honour of the 1000th birthday of the city are planned for 2010.

The decision by Emperor Gia Long, founder of the Nguyen dynasty in 1802, to rule from Hue relegated Hanoi to the status of a regional capital for a century. The city was named Hanoi (The City in a Bend of the River) by Emperor Tu Duc in 1831. From 1902 to 1953, Hanoi served as the capital of French Indochina.

Hanoi was proclaimed the capital of Vietnam after the August Revolution of 1945, but it was not until the Geneva Accords of 1954 that the Viet Minh, driven from the city by the French in 1946, were able to return.

During the American War, US bombing destroyed parts of Hanoi and killed hundreds of civilians. One of the prime targets was the 1682m-long Long Bien Bridge. US aircraft repeatedly bombed the strategic bridge, yet after each attack the Vietnamese managed to improvise replacement spans and return it to road and rail services. It is said that the US military ended the attacks when US POWs were put to work repairing the structure.

As recently as the early 1990s motorised transport was rare; most people got around on bicycles and the only modern structures were designed by Soviet architects. Times have changed, and today Hanoi's unique character is under attack on many fronts as conservationists fight to save historic structures, and the city struggles to cope with a booming population, soaring pollution levels and an inefficient public transport system – work is slated to begin on the first line of a metro in 2009.

ORIENTATION

Hanoi sprawls along the banks of Song Hong (Red River), which is spanned by two bridges – the Long Bien Bridge (now used only by nonmotorised vehicles and pedestrians) and, 600m to the south, the newer Chuong Duong Bridge.

The elegant heart of Hanoi is centred on the Hoan Kiem Lake. Just north of this lake is the Old Quarter (known to the French as the Cité Indigène), which is characterised by narrow streets with names that change every one or two blocks and alleys that are too narrow for cars. Most visitors prefer to base themselves in this part of town thanks to the incredible energy of the area.

Along the western periphery of the Old Quarter is the ancient Hanoi Citadel, which was originally constructed by Emperor Gia Long. Today the citadel is a military base, home to high-ranking officers and their families, and closed to the public. Most of the ancient buildings were destroyed by French troops in 1894, and US bombers took care of the rest. There are persistent rumours that this area will soon be opened up to development, but for now it's a still a military compound.

Further west is Ho Chi Minh's Mausoleum. Many foreign embassies, museums and temples are found in this neighbourhood.

South of Hoan Kiem Lake is the French Quarter, an upmarket area home to the Opera House, grand hotels, imposing colonial mansions and swish restaurants.

Ho Tay (West Lake), Hanoi's largest lake, lies 2km northwest of the Old Quarter. The residential suburbs around the lake are popular with expats and there's an exciting drinking and dining scene on the Xuan Dieu strip here.

Maps

Hanoi city maps come in every size and scale. Some are freebies subsidised by advertising and others precise works of cartography.

Leading maps include detailed ones at a scale of 1:10,000 or 1:17,500. Covit produces a couple of hand-drawn 3-D maps of Hanoi, including a detailed Old Town map, which make nice souvenirs. These maps are available at leading bookshops in Hanoi.

There is also an excellent bus map available: *Xe Buyt Ha Noi* (5000d).

INFORMATION

Bookshops

Hanoi has some good bookstores and many of the budget hotels in the Old Quarter have small book exchanges. The shelves in the office of tour operator Ethnic Travel are also well worth checking.

Bookworm (Map pp88-9; ☎ 3747 8778; bookworm@fpt.vn; 4B P Yen The; ⏲ 10am-7pm Tue-Sun) Stocks over 5000 new and used English-language books. There's plenty of fiction, and independent travel advice is offered. It's a 10-minute walk east of the Temple of Literature.

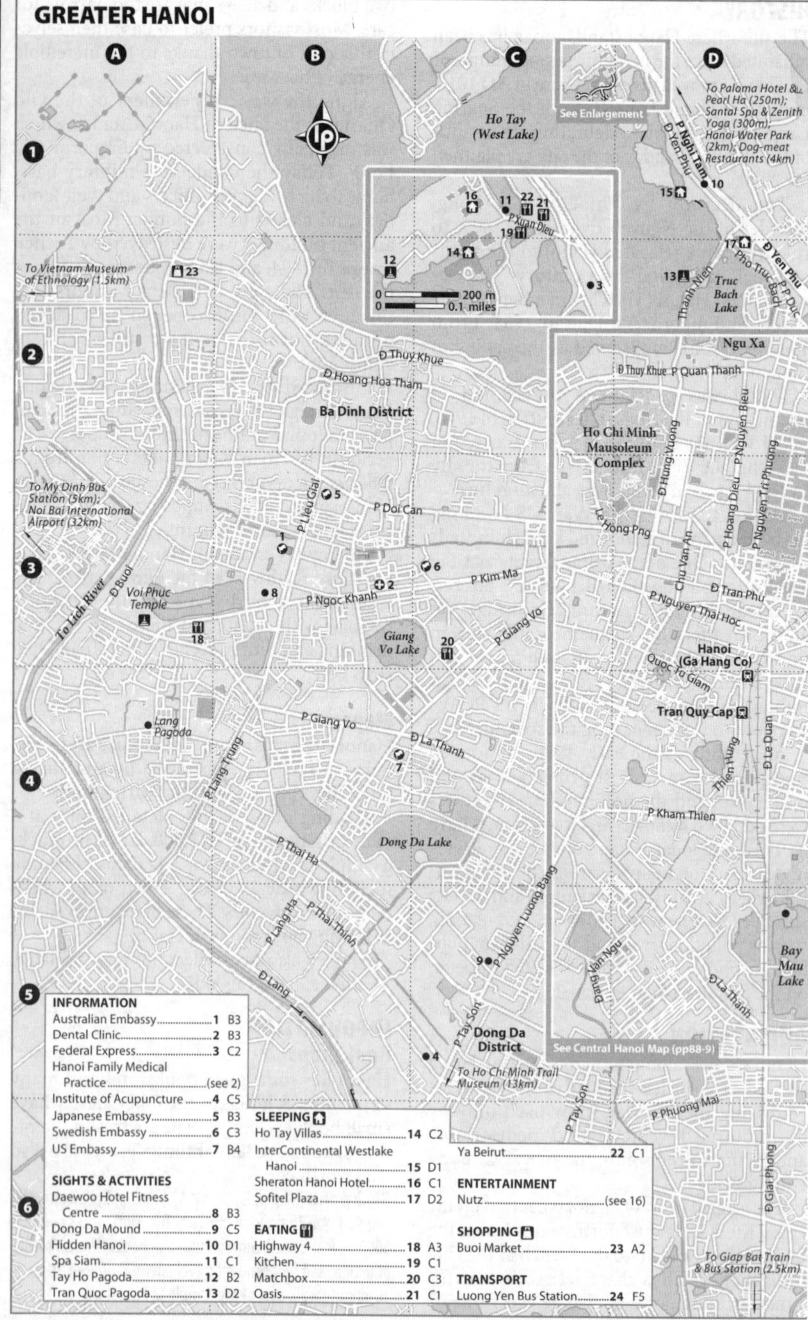
GREATER HANOI
Ho Tay
(West Lake)
See Enlargement
To Paloma Hotel & Pearl Ha (250m); Santal Spa & Zenith Yoga (300m); Hanoi Water Park (2km); Dog-meat Restaurants (4km)
P Nghi Tam
Đ Yen Phu
P Xuan Dieu
0 200 m
0 0.1 miles
Truc Bach Lake
Thanh Nien
Pho Truc Bach
P P Duc
Ngu Xa
To Vietnam Museum of Ethnology (1.5km)
Đ Thuy Khue
Đ Hoang Hoa Tham
Ba Dinh District
P Quan Thanh
Ho Chi Minh Mausoleum Complex
Đ Hung Vuong
P Nguyen Bieu
P Nguyen Tri Phuong
P Hoang Dieu
Le Hong Png
Chu Van An
Đ Tran Phu
P Nguyen Thai Hoc
To My Dinh Bus Station (5km); Noi Bai International Airport (32km)
P Lieu Giai
P Doi Can
P Kim Ma
P Ngoc Khanh
To Lich River
Đ Buoi
Voi Phuc Temple
Giang Vo Lake
P Giang Vo
Hanoi (Ga Hang Co)
Quoc Tu Giam
Tran Quy Cap
Lang Pagoda
P Lang Trung
Đ La Thanh
Thien Hung
Đ Le Duan
P Kham Thien
Dong Da Lake
P Thai Ha
P Lang Ha
P Thai Thinh
P Nguyen Luong Bang
Dang Van Ngu
Bay Mau Lake
Đ Lang
P Tay Son
Dong Da District
See Central Hanoi Map (pp88-9)
To Ho Chi Minh Trail Museum (13km)
P Phuong Mai
Đ Giai Phong
To Giap Bat Train & Bus Station (2.5km)
INFORMATION
Australian Embassy 1 B3
Dental Clinic 2 B3
Federal Express 3 C2
Hanoi Family Medical Practice (see 2)
Institute of Acupuncture 4 C5
Japanese Embassy 5 B3
Swedish Embassy 6 C3
US Embassy 7 B4
SIGHTS & ACTIVITIES
Daewoo Hotel Fitness Centre 8 B3
Dong Da Mound 9 C5
Hidden Hanoi 10 D1
Spa Siam 11 C1
Tay Ho Pagoda 12 B2
Tran Quoc Pagoda 13 D2
SLEEPING
Ho Tay Villas 14 C2
InterContinental Westlake Hanoi 15 D1
Sheraton Hanoi Hotel 16 C1
Sofitel Plaza 17 D2
EATING
Highway 4 18 A3
Kitchen 19 C1
Matchbox 20 C3
Oasis 21 C1
Ya Beirut 22 C1
ENTERTAINMENT
Nutz (see 16)
SHOPPING
Buoi Market 23 A2
TRANSPORT
Luong Yen Bus Station 24 F5

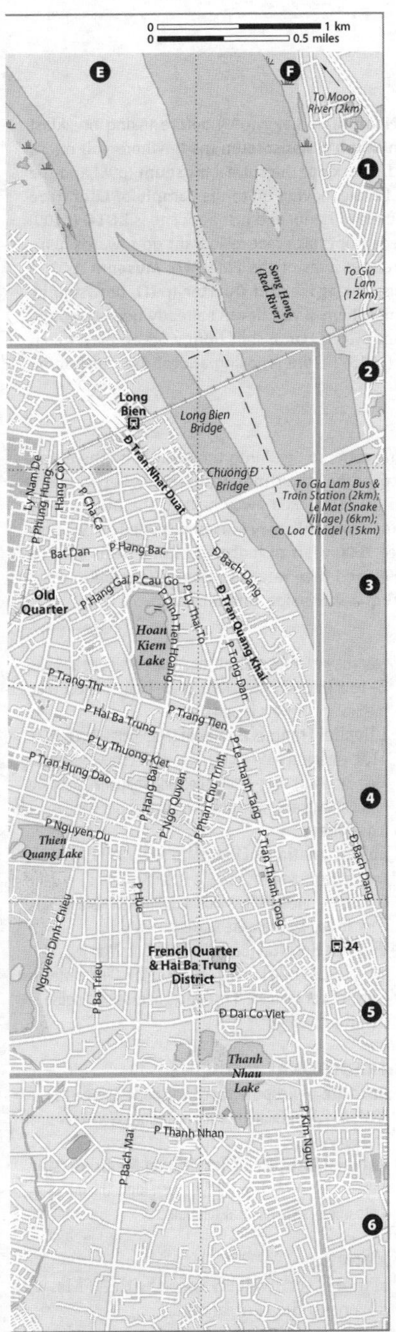

Love Planet (Map p92; ☎ 3828 4864; www.loveplanet travel.com; 25 P Hang Bac) Book exchange and lots of second-hand titles, though the categorisation is nonexistent.

Thang Long Bookshop (Map p92; ☎ 3825 7043; 53-55 P Trang Tien) One of the biggest bookshops in town with English and French titles, plus some international newspapers and magazines.

Cultural Centres

Homesick? Head to the following places, which all have periodicals and newspapers to browse.

American Club (Map p92; ☎ 3824 1850; hanoiric@ hotmail.com; 19-21 P Hai Ba Trung) Also has a huge DVD library.

British Council (Map pp88-9; ☎ 3728 1922; www .britishcouncil.org/vietnam; 20 Thuy Khue, Tay Ho). Hosts cultural events, exhibitions, workshops and fashion shows.

Centre Culturel Français de Hanoi (Map p92; ☎ 3936 2164; 24 P Trang Tien) In the L'Espace building near the Opera House.

Emergency

The emergency services should be able to transfer you to an English-speaker.

Ambulance (☎ 115)

Fire (☎ 114)

Police (☎ 113)

Internet Access

Most budget and midrange hotels offer free internet access as standard: the fancier places in the room, the cheaper places in the lobby.

Internet cafes are ubiquitous in central Hanoi, particularly around P Hang Bac and P Hang Be in the Old Quarter. Many places do not display prices, so make sure you check before you notch up a couple of hours online. Rates start as low as 3000d per hour.

Wi-fi is becoming quite common in many of the city's tourist-geared hotels, cafes and bars, though the connection speeds can be pretty pedestrian.

Internet Resources

There are several good websites to help get the most out of Hanoi.

Hanoi Grapevine (www.hanoigrapevine.com) A culture vulture's paradise, this site is the place for information about concerts, art exhibitions and cinema and has a very useful events calendar.

Infoshare (www.infosharehanoi.com) Geared towards expats but has plenty of useful content for visitors, including a hilarious, all-too-true article about Hanoi traffic.

ay

Begin with an early morning walk around misty **Hoan Kiem Lake** (p99) before taking breakfast in an Old Quarter cafe. Then head over to **Ho Chi Minh's Mausoleum** (p94), where you might be lucky enough to catch a changing of the guard. Check out the surreal **museum** (p95) and the balancing act that is the **One Pillar Pagoda** (p95) before moving on to the **Temple of Literature** (p96). This is a great escape from the hustle and bustle of Hanoi and just opposite is **KOTO** (p109) on Van Mieu, an essential lunch stop as all proceeds from this great restaurant go towards helping street children. After lunch take in the cultural treasures of the **Fine Arts Museum** (p98) a five-minute walk away. It's now time for a serious look at the **Old Quarter** (p91), browsing its buildings, shops or bars to soak up the unique atmosphere. If you haven't already been tempted, stop for a *bia hoi* (draught beer) around sunset and watch Hanoi shift from work to play. Catch a performance of the wonderful **water puppets** (p115) before enjoying a local meal and some beers on nearby P Bao Khanh.

Two Days

Hanoi has some terrific sights away from the central zone, so head into the suburbs to the excellent **Vietnam Museum of Ethnology** (p97) to discover the ethnic mosaic that makes up Vietnam today. Have a local lunch in **Nha Hang Lan Chin** (p113), tucked away next to the **Museum of Vietnamese Revolution** (p98) and hop across the road to the **History Museum** (p97). The building is stunning and the contents a fine introduction to 2000 years of highs and lows. Head back to the Old Quarter for a look at **Memorial House** (p98) and then return to **Hoan Kiem Lake** (p99), for a lingering look at this magical oriental city from a shore-side cafe table.

New Hanoian (www.newhanoian.com) A terrific website, this is the premier online resource for visitors and expats and is well worth checking out for its up-to-date restaurant, bar and accommodation reviews. The forums buzz with life and the site also hosts a monthly get-together in a Hanoi restaurant with complimentary scoff for members.
Sticky Rice (http://stickyrice.typepad.com) Foodie website, with the lowdown on everything from gourmet Vietnamese to Hanoi street kitchens, plus some bar reviews.

Libraries

National Library and Archives (Map p92; ☎ 3825 3357; 31 P Trang Thi) This grand old building has some English and French material available, but it's mostly Vietnamese.

Medical Services

Dental Clinic (Map pp84-5; ☎ 3823 0281; thedental@netnam.vn; Van Phuc Diplomatic Compound, 298 P Kim Ma) Tooth issues? Deal with them at this clinic, part of the Hanoi Family Medical Practice, which offers 24-hour cover.
French Embassy Clinic (Map pp88-9; ☎ 3825 2719; 49 P Ba Trieu) A 24-hour clinic for French nationals.
Hanoi Family Medical Practice (Map pp84-5; ☎ 3843 0748; www.vietnammedicalpractice.com; Van Phuc Diplomatic Compound, 298 P Kim Ma) Includes a team of well-respected international physicians and has 24-hour emergency cover. Prices are high, so check your medical insurance is in order.
L'Hopital Français de Hanoi (Map pp88-9; ☎ 3577 1100, emergency 3574 1111; www.hfh.com.vn; 1 Phuong Mai; 24hr) Long-established, international-standard hospital with A&E, intensive care, dental clinic and consulting services.
SOS International Clinic (Map p92; ☎ 3934 0666; www.internationalsos.com; 31 P Hai Ba Trung; 24hr) Centrally located and has a dental clinic. English, French, German and Japanese are spoken.
Viet Duc Hospital (Benh Vien Viet Duc; Map p92; ☎ 3825 3531; 40 P Trang Thi; 24hr) Old Quarter unit for emergency surgery; the doctors here speak English, French and German.

TRADITIONAL MEDICINE

Institute of Acupuncture (Map pp84-5; ☎ 3853 3881; 49 P Thai Thinh) Holistic medicine? Well, very small holes anyway.
National Institute of Traditional Medicine (Map pp88-9; ☎ 3826 3616; 29 P Nguyen Binh Khiem) Vietnamese-style medical solutions.

Money

Hanoi is very well endowed with ATMs, with dozens in the central area.

ANZ Bank (Map p92; ☎ 3825 8190; 14 P Le Thai To; 🕑 8.30am-4pm Mon-Fri) On the western edge of Hoan Kiem Lake, offering cash advances in dong and dollars, plus an ATM.

Industrial & Commercial Bank (Map p92; ☎ 3825 4276; 37 P Hang Bo) In a convenient location in the Old Quarter, this bank's commission rates are 0.5% for dong and 1.25% for US dollars for cashing travellers cheques; credit-card cash advances cost 3%.

Vietcombank (Map p92; ☎ 3826 8045; 198 P Tran Quang Khai) This towering HQ is located a few blocks east of Hoan Kiem Lake. It has an ATM and offers most currency services.

Post

Domestic post office (Buu Dien Trung Vong; Map p92; ☎ 3825 7036; 75 P Dinh Tien Hoang; 🕑 7am-9pm) For internal postal services in Vietnam, and sells philatelic items.

International postal office (☎ 3825 2030; Map p92; cnr P Dinh Tien Hoang & P Dinh Le; 🕑 7am-8pm) With its own entrance to the right of the domestic office. The place to dispatch all those hefty souvenirs.

Courier companies:

DHL (Map pp88-9; ☎ 3733 2086; 49 P Nguyen Thai Hoc)

Federal Express (Map pp84-5; ☎ 3824 9054; 63 Đ Yen Phu)

Telephone

Guesthouses and internet cafes are convenient for local calls within Hanoi. For international telephone services, call centres and internet cafes offer the cheapest rates; there are plenty of places in the Old Quarter with inexpensive tariffs and two on P Ta Hien.

International Call Service (Map p92; ☎ 3828 3549; 3 P Ta Hien; 🕑 7am-10pm). Tiny hole-in-the-wall operation with a couple of booths, clear lines and bargain rates: 1000d to 1500d per minute to most countries.

Tourist Information

The flash **Tourist Information Center** (☎ 3926 3366; www.vntourists.com; P Dinh Tien Hoang) has free information and plenty of glossy handouts but it's privately run and it also sells tours. You'll find that the government-run tourist office at the airport isn't exactly a font of knowledge either.

For the best tourism information in Hanoi, try the travel agencies listed here or consult the websites recommended on p85.

Travel Agencies

Hanoi has hundreds of travel agencies, most of a pretty dubious quality, while a few are downright dodgy. Many of the sketchy agencies operate from the lobbies of budget hotels in the Old Quarter, where pushy staff will attempt you get you to sign up for a tour before you've even had the chance to slide the backpack off your shoulders. Most of the torrent of complaints we receive about travel agents in Hanoi relate to budget hotel–based agents. Few deliver what they promise (especially when a two-day trip to Halong Bay costs as little as US$40).

Beware that some cheap hotels have been known to kick out travellers who book tours elsewhere. To avoid possible problems you could say that you're travelling independently (and, as transport connections to Cat Ba Island on the west side of Halong Bay, or up to Sapa, are pretty straightforward, consider doing just that).

Look out too for clones of the popular agencies, it's common for a rival business to set up shop close to a well-respected agency and attempt to cream off a slice of their business. Check the address and website carefully; often these impostors are staffed by ill-informed workers adopting a very hard sell.

There are some superb agencies out there, with professional, knowledgeable staff who speak fluent English and coordinate well-organised trips – inevitably these agencies tend to charge more for their services. We suggest that you take time to seek out tour operators who stick to small groups, use their own vehicles and guides and offer trips away from the main tourist trail. Here are some well-regarded companies:

ET Pumpkin (Map p92; ☎ 3926 0739; www.et-pumpkin.com; 89 P Ma May) Operates tours throughout the north including a 10-day trip for US$595per person, and operates its own private carriage on the night train to Sapa.

Ethnic Travel (Map p92; ☎ 3926 1951; www.ethnictravel.com.vn; 35 P Hang Giay) Specialises in off-the-beaten-track trips across the north in small groups (maximum six people). Some trips are low-impact using public transport and homestays, others are activity based (including hiking, cycling and cooking). Offers Bai Tu Long Bay tours.

Explorer Tours (Map p92; ☎ 3923 0713; www.explorer.com.vn; 85 P Hang Bo) Well-priced sailing trips to Halong Bay on junk boats and tailored trips around the north.

Free Wheelin' Tours (Map p92; ☎ 3747 0545; www.freewheelin-tours.com; 28 Dao Duy Tu) Adventurous motorbike (p507) and 4WD tours around the north, including an eight-day trip to the northeast on Minsk bikes, plus trips to Bai Tu Long Bay and the Pu Luong national park. Based in Café Ket Noi (p110).

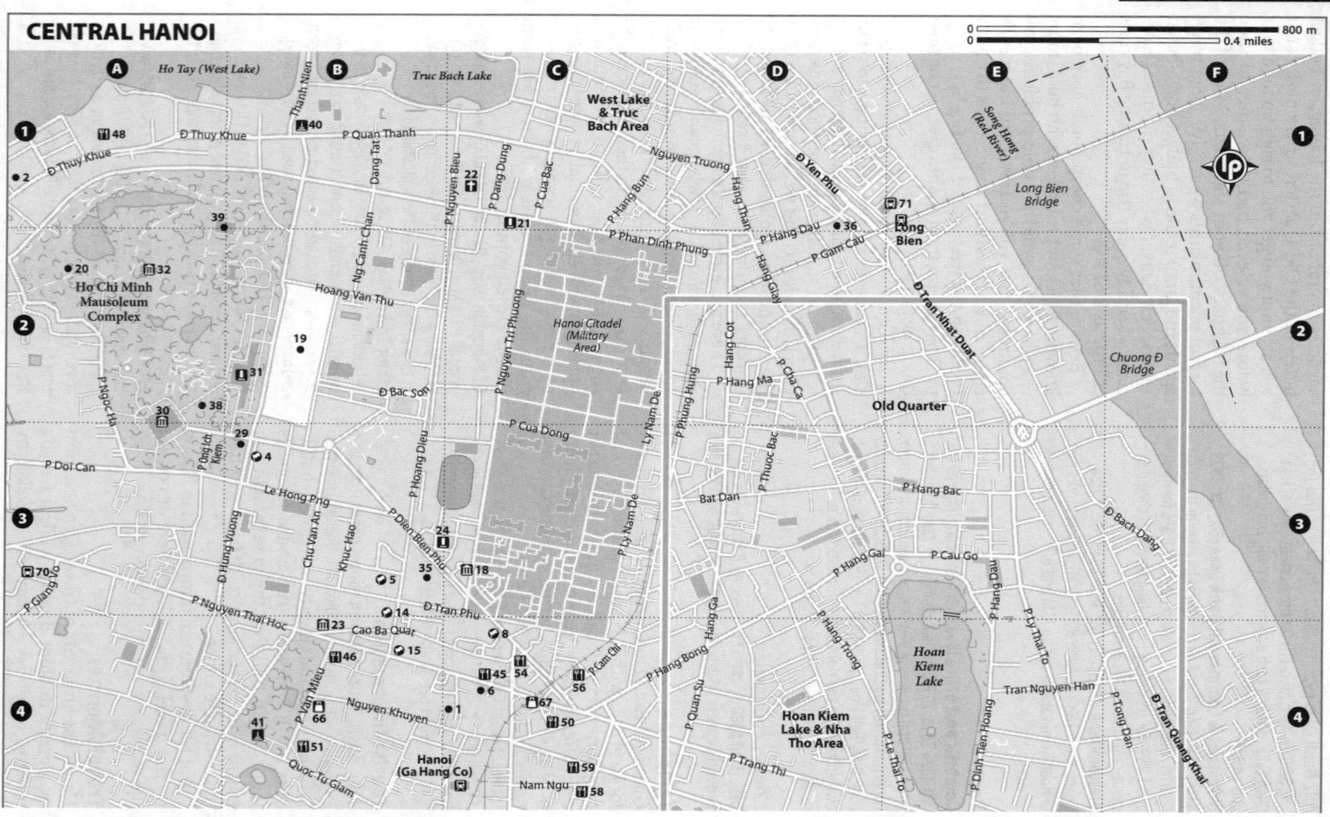
CENTRAL HANOI
0.4 miles
800 m
Ho Tay (West Lake)
Truc Bach Lake
West Lake & Truc Bach Area
Ho Chi Minh Mausoleum Complex
Hanoi Citadel (Military Area)
Old Quarter
Hoan Kiem Lake
Hoan Kiem Lake & Nha Tho Area
Song Hong (Red River)
Long Bien Bridge
Chuong Đ Bridge
Long Bien
Hanoi (Ga Hang Co)
Đ Thuy Khue
P Quan Thanh
Thanh Nien
P Ngoc Ha
P Doi Can
P Giang Vo
Đ Hung Vuong
Le Hong Png
Chu Van An
Khuc Hao
Cao Ba Quat
P Nguyen Thai Hoc
Đ Tran Phu
P Dien Bien Phu
P Hoang Dieu
Đ Bac Son
Hoang Van Thu
Ng Canh Chan
Dang Tat
P Nguyen Bieu
P Dang Dung
P Cua Bac
P Nguyen Tri Phuong
P Cua Dong
P Phan Dinh Phung
P Hang Bun
Nguyen Truong
Hang Than
Hang Giay
P Hang Dau
P Gam Cau
Đ Yen Phu
Đ Tran Nhat Duat
Đ Tran Quang Khai
Đ Bach Dang
P Tong Dan
P Ly Thai To
Tran Nguyen Han
P Dinh Tien Hoang
P Hang Dau
P Cau Go
P Hang Bac
P Hang Gai
P Le Thai To
P Hang Trong
P Cha Ca
P Thuoc Bac
P Hang Ma
Hang Cot
Bat Dan
P Phung Hung
Hang Ga
P Hang Bong
P Quan Su
P Trang Thi
Ly Nam De
P Ly Nam De
P Cam Chi
Nam Ngu
Nguyen Khuyen
P Van Mieu
Quoc Tu Giam
P Ong Ich Kiem

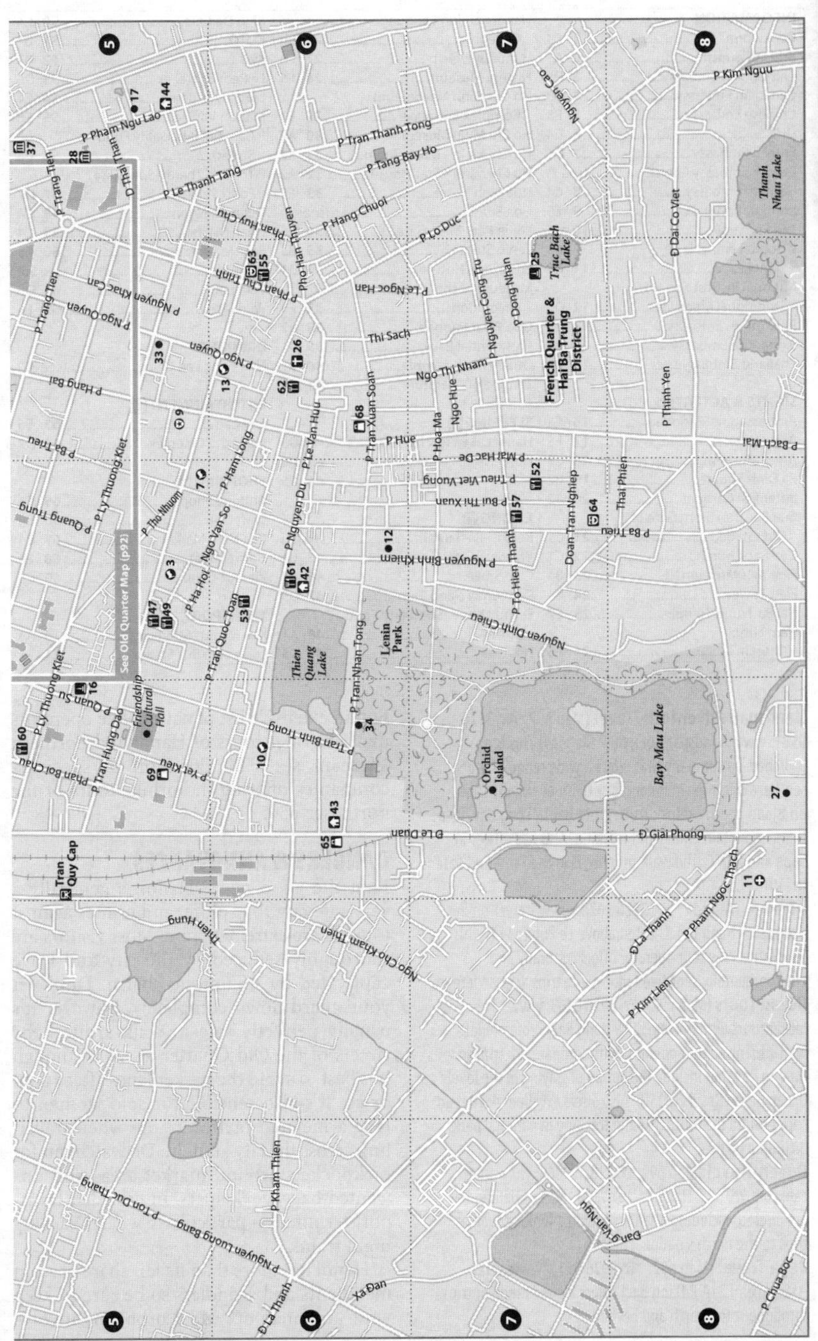

HANOI
French Quarter & Hai Ba Trung District
See Old Quarter Map (p92)
Thien Quang Lake
Lenin Park
Bay Mau Lake
Orchid Island
Truc Bach Lake
Thanh Nhau Lake
Friendship Cultural Hall
Tran Quy Cap
P Pham Ngu Lao
D Thai Than
P Trang Tien
P Le Thanh Tang
P Tran Thanh Tong
P Tang Bay Ho
Phan Huy Chu
P Hang Chuoi
P Lo Duc
Nguyen Cao
P Kim Nguu
D Dai Co Viet
P Phan Chu Trinh
Pho Han Thuyen
P Le Ngoc Han
P Nguyen Cong Tru
P Dong Nhan
P Nguyen Khac Can
P Ngo Quyen
Thi Sach
Ngo Thi Nham
P Hang Bai
P Le Van Huu
P Tran Xuan Soan
P Hoa Ma
Ngo Hue
P Thinh Yen
P Ba Trieu
P Ly Thuong Kiet
P Ham Long
P Hue
P Bach Mai
P Mai Hac De
P Trieu Viet Vuong
P Bui Thi Xuan
Doan Tran Nghiep
Thai Phien
P Quang Trung
P Tho Nhuom
P Ngo Van So
P Nguyen Du
P Nguyen Binh Khiem
P To Hien Thanh
P Ha Hoi
P Tran Quoc Toan
Nguyen Dinh Chieu
P Tran Nhan Tong
P Quan Su
P Tran Hung Dao
Phan Boi Chau
P Yet Kieu
P Tran Binh Trong
D Le Duan
D Giai Phong
Thien Hung
Ngo Cho Kham Thien
D La Thanh
P Pham Ngoc Thach
P Kim Lien
P Kham Thien
P Ton Duc Thang
P Nguyen Luong Bang
Xa Dan
Dang Van Ngu
P Chua Boc
5
6
7
8
3
7
9
10
11
12
13
16
17
25
26
27
28
33
34
37
42
43
44
47
49
52
53
55
57
60
61
62
63
64
65
68
69

INFORMATION

Bookworm 1 C4
British Council 2 A1
Cambodian Embassy 3 D5
Canadian Embassy 4 B3
Chinese Embassy 5 B3
DHL 6 C4
French Embassy 7 D5
French Embassy Clinic .... (see 7)
German Embassy 8 C4
Immigration Police 9 E5
Lao Embassy 10 C6
L'Hopital Francais de Hanoi 11 C8
National Institute of Traditional Medicine 12 D6
Philippines Embassy 13 E6
Singapore Embassy 14 B3
Thailand Embassy 15 B4

SIGHTS & ACTIVITIES

Ambassadors' Pagoda 16 C5
Army Hotel 17 F5
Army Museum 18 C3
Ba Dinh Square 19 B2
Botanical Gardens 20 A2
Cua Bac (Northern Gate of Old Citadel) 21 C1
Cua Bac Church 22 C1
Fine Arts Museum 23 B4
Flag Tower 24 B3
Hai Ba Trung Temple 25 E7
Ham Long Church 26 E6
Hanoi Foreign Language College .... (see 28)
Hanoi University 27 C8
History Museum 28 F5
Ho Chi Minh Mausoleum Complex Entrance 29 B3
Ho Chi Minh Museum 30 A2
Ho Chi Minh's Mausoleum 31 B2
Ho Chi Minh's Stilt House 32 A2
Hoa Binh Hotel 33 E5
Hoa Sua .... (see 49)
Lenin Park Main Gate 34 C6
Lenin Statue 35 B3
Long Bien Hotel II 36 D1
Museum of the Vietnamese Revolution 37 F5
One Pillar Pagoda 38 A2
Presidential Palace 39 A1
Quan Thanh Temple 40 B1
Temple of Literature 41 B4

SLEEPING

Hanoi Lake View Hotel 42 D6
Hotel Nikko Hanoi 43 C6
M.O.D. Palace 44 F5

EATING

Benkay Restaurant .... (see 43)
Brothers Café 45 C4
Café Smile 46 B4
Com Chay Nang Tam 47 D5
Đ Thuy Khue (Speciality Food Street) 48 A1
Hoa Sua 49 D5
Kinh Do Café 50 C4
KOTO 51 B4
Ky Y 52 D7
Le Petit Bruxelles 53 D6
Luna d'Autumno 54 C4
Maison Vanille 55 E6
P Cam Chi (Speciality Food Street) 56 C4
P To Hien Thanh (Speciality Food Street) 57 D7
Quan An Ngon 58 C4
Quan Malay 59 C4
San Ho Restaurant 60 C5
Van Anh .... (see 56)
Wild Lotus 61 D6
Wild Rice 62 E6

DRINKING

Nha Hang Lan Chin .... (see 37)

ENTERTAINMENT

Cay Cau 63 E6
Megastar Cineplex 64 D7

SHOPPING

Antique Shops 65 C6
Craft Link 66 B4
Cua Nam Market 67 C4
Hom Market 68 E6
Viet Art Centre 69 C5

TRANSPORT

Kim Ma Bus Station 70 A3
Long Bien Bus Station 71 E1

Handspan Adventure Travel (Map p92; ☎ 3926 0581; www.handspan.com; 80 P Ma May) This is a switched-on company that offers a wide range of tours: sea-kayaking trips in Halong Bay (with overnight stays on island beach camps), cruises into Bai Tu Long Bay, jeep tours, mountain biking and trekking. Also has offices in Sapa and HCMC. The walk-in office is in the Tamarind Café (p110).

I Travel (Map p92; ☎ 3926 3678; www.itravel-online.com; 25 P Hang Be). Located above Le Pub (p114), this innovative new tour operator offers culturally and environmentally sensitive tailor-made trips across Vietnam.

Ocean Tours (Map p92; ☎ 3926 0463; www.oceantoursvietnam.com; 22 P Hang Bac) Professional, well-organised tour operator with some superb trips to Halong Bay that include the option of staying in the lovely Ocean Beach Resort (p150). Also offers excellent 4WD road trips around the northeast and trekking in national parks including Ba Be.

Queen Travel (Map p92; ☎ 3826 0860; www.queencafe.com.vn; 65 P Hang Bac) Several tours to Halong Bay are offered, including a sailing trip on a junk, as well as trips to the north's national parks.

Vega Travel (Map p92; ☎ 3926 0910; www.vega-travel.com; 24A P Hang Bac) Offers a good range of trips throughout the north and beyond.

For an extensive list of nationwide operators that also offer tours of Hanoi and northern Vietnam, see p500. For more on specialist companies offering motorbike tours of the north, see p507.

DANGERS & ANNOYANCES

First the good news: Hanoi is generally a very safe city to explore, and crimes against tourists are extremely rare. Most visitors are thoroughly seduced by the city and leave captivated by its unique charm. Don't let your guard down completely, however it's usually perfectly safe to walk around the streets of the Old Quarter at night, though it is best to avoid the darker lanes after 10pm or so. It's also sensible for solo women to take a metered taxi or *xe om* when travelling across the city at night. Do watch out for pickpockets around market areas and unwanted baggage 'helpers' in crowded transport terminals – particularly when boarding night trains.

Hanoi has more than its fair share of scam merchants and swindlers so be sure to keep your antennae up. Most problems involve

MAKE THAT COMPLAINT COUNT...

We get a lot of letters complaining about hotels, guesthouses, travel companies and more. It's great to give us feedback about all these things, as it helps to work out which businesses care about their customers and which don't. As well as telling us, make sure you tell the **Vietnam National Administration of Tourism** (Map p92; ☎ 3824 7652; www.hanoitourism.gov.vn; 3 Le Lai); its Hanoi office is reasonably helpful and needs to know about the problems before it can do anything about them. Make a complaint here, and in time it might well pressure the cowboys into cleaning up their act.

budget hotels and tours (p87). Very occasionally things can get quite nasty and we've received reports of verbal aggression and threats of physical violence towards tourists who've decided against a hotel room or a tour. Stay calm and back away slowly or things could quickly flare up.

Traffic and pollution are other irritants. The city's traffic is so dense and unrelenting that simply crossing the street can be a real headache, and weaving a path through a tide of motorbikes (two million and counting) can be a hairy experience (see p506 for advice!). Keep your wits about you as you explore the Old Quarter, as motorbikes come at you from all directions and pavements are obstructed by cooking stalls and yet more parked motorbikes. Pollution levels are punishing, and air quality is poor, with levels of some contaminants higher than in Bangkok.

Scams

Whilst there's no need to be paranoid, Hanoi is riddled with scams, many of them inextricably linked. The taxi and minibus mafia at the airport shuttle unwitting tourists to the wrong hotel. Invariably, the hotel has copied the name of another popular property and will then attempt to appropriate as much of your money as possible. For more on the airport–hotel scam and how to avoid it, see the boxed texts on p104 and p120. Taxi swindles are also becoming increasingly common; see p120 for a warning. Some shoeshine boys and cyclo drivers attempt to add a zero or two to an agreed price for their services; stick to your guns and give them the amount you originally agreed.

Watch out for friendly, smooth-talking strangers approaching you around the Hoan Kiem Lake. There are many variations, but sometimes these con-artists pose as students and suggest a drink or a meal. Gay men are also targeted in this way. Your new friend may then suggest a visit to a karaoke bar, snake-meat restaurant or some other venue and before you know it you're presented with a bill for hundreds of dollars. Be careful and follow your instincts, as these crooks can seem quite charming.

SIGHTS

Old Quarter

This is the Asia we dreamed of from afar. Steeped in history, pulsating with life, bubbling with commerce, buzzing with motorbikes and rich in exotic scents, the Old Quarter is Hanoi's historic heart. The streets are narrow and congested, and crossing the road is an art form, but remember to look up as well as down, as there is some elegant old architecture in and among the chaos. Hawkers pound the streets with sizzling and smoking baskets that hide cheap meals for the locals. *Pho* stalls and *bia hoi* dens hug every corner, resonant with the sound of gossip and laughter. Modern yet medieval, there is no better way to spend time in Hanoi than walking the streets, soaking up the sights, sounds and smells.

Home to 1000 years of history, the commercial quarter of the city evolved alongside the Red River and the smaller To Lich River, which once flowed through the city centre in an intricate network of canals and waterways that teemed with boats. Waters could rise as high as 8m during the monsoon. Dykes were constructed to protect the city and these can still be seen along Tran Quang Khai.

In the 13th century Hanoi's 36 guilds established themselves here, each taking a different street – hence the original name '36 Streets'. Today, there are more than 50 streets in today's Old Quarter. *Hang* means 'merchandise' and is usually followed by the name of the product that was traditionally sold in that street. Thus, P Hang Gai translates as 'Silk Street' (see the boxed text on p95 for the rest); these days the street name may not indicate what businesses are there, otherwise there would be lots of P Hang Du Lich (Tourism Streets).

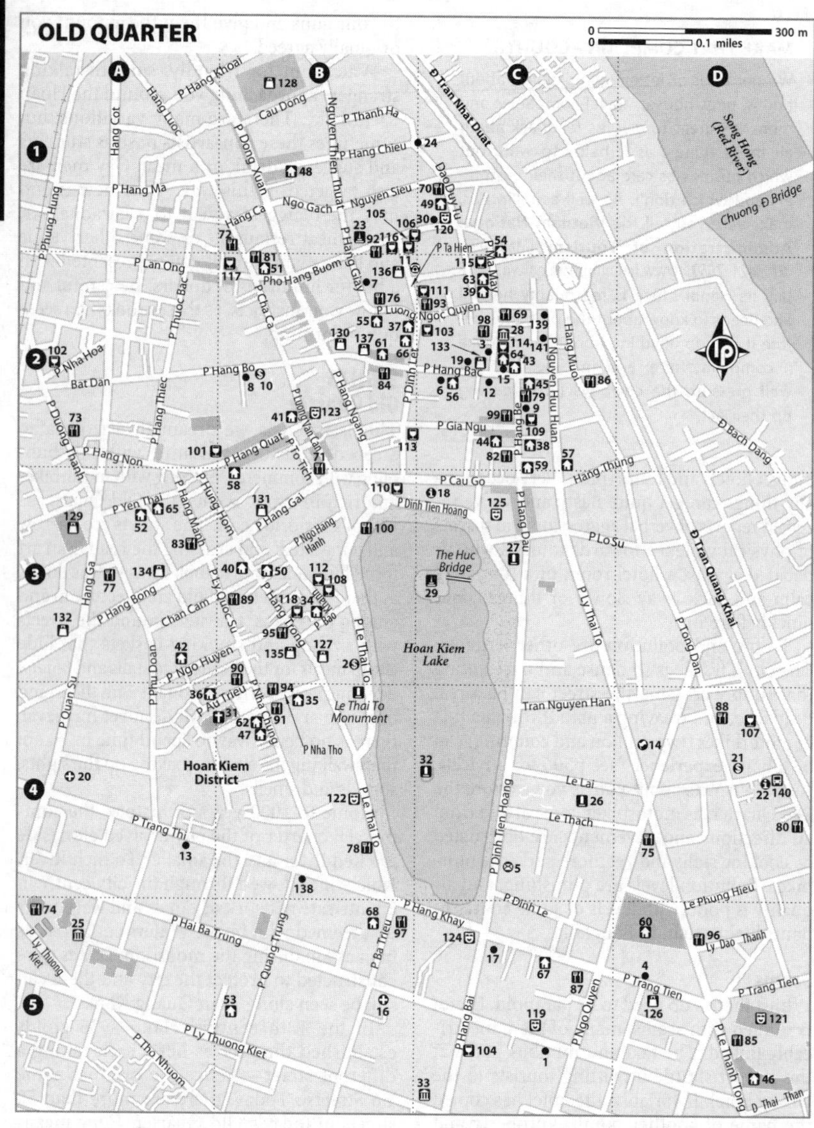

Exploring the maze of back streets is fascinating: some streets open up while others narrow into a warren of alleys. The area is known for its tunnel (or tube) houses – so called because of their narrow frontages and long rooms. These tunnel houses were developed to avoid taxes based on the width of their street frontage. By feudal law, houses were also limited to two storeys and, out of respect for the king, could not be taller than the Royal Palace. These days there are taller buildings, but no real high-rise buildings.

Opportunities to dispense with your dong are endless. As you wander around you'll find clothes, cosmetics, fake sunglasses, luxury food, T-shirts, musical instruments, plumbing

INFORMATION

- American Club 1 C5
- ANZ Bank 2 B3
- British Embassy (see 16)
- Buffalo Tours 3 C2
- Centre Culturel Français de Hanoi 4 D5
- Domestic Post Office 5 C4
- ET Pumpkin 6 C2
- Ethnic Travel 7 B2
- Explorer Tours 8 B2
- Free Wheelin' Tours (see 70)
- Handspan (see 98)
- Handspan Adventure Travel (see 98)
- I Travel 9 C2
- Industrial & Commercial Bank 10 B2
- International Call Service 11 B2
- International Post Office (see 5)
- Love Planet 12 C2
- National Library & Archives 13 A4
- New Zealand Embassy 14 D4
- Ocean Tours 15 C2
- Queen Travel (see 56)
- SOS International Clinic 16 B5
- Thang Long Bookshop 17 C5
- Tourist Information Center 18 C3
- UK Embassy (see 16)
- Vega Travel 19 C2
- Viet Duc Hospital 20 A4
- Vietcombank 21 D4
- Vietnam National Administration of Tourism 22 D4

SIGHTS & ACTIVITIES

- Bach Ma Temple 23 B1
- Cua O Quan Chuong (Old East Gate) 24 C1
- Dong Xuan Market (see 128)
- Hoa Lo Prison Museum 25 A5
- Ly Thai Tho Statue 26 C4
- Martyrs' Monument 27 C3
- Memorial House 28 C2
- Ngoc Son Temple 29 C3
- SF Salon & Spa 30 C1
- St Joseph Cathedral 31 B4
- Thap Rua (Tortoise Tower) 32 C4
- Women's Museum 33 C5

SLEEPING

- Artist Hotel (see 119)
- Bamboo Hotel 34 B3
- Church Hotel 35 B4
- Cinnamon Hotel 36 A4
- Classic 1 Hotel 37 B2
- Classic Street Hotel 38 C2
- Dong A Hotel 39 C2
- Especen Hotel (see 141)
- Golden Lotus Hotel 40 B3
- Green Mango 41 B2
- Hanoi Backpackers Hostel 42 A3
- Hanoi Elegance Hotel 43 C2
- Hanoi Spirit House 44 C2
- Hanoi Stars Hotel 45 C2
- Heart Hotel (see 105)
- Hilton Hanoi Opera 46 D5
- Hotel Thien Trang 47 B4
- Khanh Sinh Hotel 48 B1
- Kim Tuc Hotel 49 C1
- Maison D'Hanoi Hanova Hotel 50 B3
- Majestic Salute Hotel 51 B2
- Manh Dung Guesthouse 52 A3
- Melia Hotel 53 B5
- Old Street Hotel 54 C1
- Prince 1 Hotel 55 B2
- Queen Hotel 56 C2
- Queen of Heart Hotel 57 C2
- Real Darling Café 58 B3
- Rising Dragon Hotel 59 C2
- Sofitel Metropole Hotel 60 D5
- Sports Hotel 61 B2
- Spring Hotel 62 B4
- Sunshine Hotel 63 C2
- Sunshine Hotel 3 64 C2
- Thu Giang Guesthouse 65 A3
- Thuy Nga Guesthouse 66 B2
- Trang Tien Hotel 67 C5
- Zephyr Hotel 68 B5

EATING

- 69 Bar-Restaurant 69 C2
- Café Ket Noi 70 C1
- Café Pho Co 71 B2
- Cha Ca La Vong 72 B1
- Cha Ca Thang Long 73 A2
- Cine Café (see 119)
- Citimart 74 A5
- Club 51 Ly Thai To 75 D4
- Culi Café 76 B2
- Cyclo 77 A3
- Fanny Ice Cream 78 B4
- Five 79 C2
- Fivimart 80 D4
- GoldenLand Restaurant 81 B2
- Green Mango (see 41)
- Green Tangerine 82 C2
- Hanoi Garden 83 A3
- Havana Club 84 B2
- Highlands Opera 85 D5
- Highway 4 86 C2
- Kem Dac Diet Trang Tien 87 C5
- Khazaana 88 D4
- La 89 B3
- La Place 90 B3
- La Salsa 91 B4
- Ladybird Restaurant 92 B1
- Le Beaulieu (see 60)
- Little Hanoi 1 93 C2
- Mediterraneo (see 91)
- Moca Café 94 B4
- Old Hanoi (see 19)
- Pho 24 (see 21)
- Puku 95 B3
- Restaurant 96 D5
- Restaurant Bobby Chinn 97 B5
- Tamarind Café 98 C2
- Tandoor 99 C2
- Thuy Ta Café 100 B3

DRINKING

- Angelina (see 60)
- Bia Hoi 68 Hang Quat 101 A2
- Bia Hoi Ha Noi 102 A2
- Bia Hoi Junction 103 C2
- Bia Hoi Viet Ha 104 C5
- Cheeky Quarter 105 B1
- Dragonfly 106 B1
- Funky Monkey (see 61)
- Gambrinus 107 D4
- GC Pub 108 B3
- Green Mango (see 41)
- Le Pub 109 C2
- Legends Beer 110 B3
- Mao Red Lounge 111 C2
- Polite Pub 112 B3
- Quan Bia Minh 113 B2
- Red Beer 114 C2
- Roots (see 70)
- Studio 115 C2
- Tet 116 B1
- Thanh Binh 117 B2
- The Warehouse 118 B3

ENTERTAINMENT

- Centre Culturel Francais de Hanoi (see 4)
- Cinematheque 119 C5
- Club Opera (see 96)
- Egypt Club 120 C1
- Hanoi Opera House 121 D5
- I-Box 122 B4
- Jazz Club By Quyen Van Minh 123 B2
- Loop 124 C5
- Municipal Water Puppet Theatre 125 C3
- Terrace Bar (see 96)

SHOPPING

- Chi Vang 126 D5
- Dome 127 B3
- Dong Xuan Market 128 B1
- Hadong Silk (see 131)
- Hang Da Market 129 A3
- Hanoi Gallery 130 B2
- Khai Silk 131 B3
- Mai Gallery 132 A3
- Old Propaganda Posters (see 130)
- Pan Flute 133 C2
- Pearl Ha 134 A3
- Shoe Market (see 27)
- Suffusive 135 B3
- Things of Substance (see 35)
- Three Trees (see 35)
- Viet Hien 136 B2
- Vietnamese House 137 B2

TRANSPORT

- Airport Minibus 138 B4
- Cuong's Motorbike Adventure 139 C2
- Hong Ha Tourism 140 D4
- Offroad Vietnam 141 C2
- Vietnam Airlines (see 138)

supplies, herbal medicines, jewellery, religious offerings, spices, woven mats and much, much more (see p116 for details).

Some of the specialised streets include P Hang Quat, with its red candlesticks, funeral boxes, flags and temple items; and the more glamorous P Hang Gai, with its silk, embroidery, lacquerware, paintings and water puppets – silk sleeping-bag liners and elegant *ao dai* (the national dress of Vietnam) are popular here. Finally, no trip to the Old Quarter would be complete without a visit to the **Dong Xuan Market** (Map p92; cnr P Hang Khoai & P Dong Xuan), rebuilt after a fire in 1994.

A stroll through the historic Old Quarter can last anywhere from an hour to the better part of a day, depending on your pace. However long, or whatever detours you might take, the walking tour on p101 will provide you with a heady dose of Vietnamese culture, lots of shopping opportunities and some insight into the city's long history.

Ho Chi Minh Mausoleum Complex

This is the holiest of the holies for many Vietnamese. To the west of the Old Quarter, the **Ho Chi Minh Mausoleum Complex** (Map pp88-9; entrance cnr P Ngoc Ha & P Doi Can) is an important place of pilgrimage. A traffic-free area of parks, monuments, memorials and pagodas, it's usually crowded with groups of all ages, from all over the nation, who have come to pay their respects.

HO CHI MINH'S MAUSOLEUM

In the tradition of Lenin and Stalin before him – and Mao afterwards – **Ho Chi Minh's Mausoleum** (Map pp88-9; admission free; 8-11am Tue-Thu, Sat & Sun Dec-Sep, last entry usually 10.15am) is a monumental marble edifice. Contrary to his desire for a simple cremation, the mausoleum was constructed from materials gathered from all over Vietnam between 1973 and 1975. The roof and peristyle are said to evoke either a traditional communal house or a lotus flower, though to many tourists it looks like a concrete cubicle with columns. Set deep in the bowels of the building in a glass sarcophagus is the frail, pale body of Ho Chi Minh. The mausoleum is closed for about two months each year while Ho Chi Minh's embalmed corpse goes to Russia for maintenance.

The queue, which moves quite quickly, usually snakes for several hundred metres to the mausoleum entrance itself. Inside, adopt a slow but steady walking pace as you file past Ho's body. Guards, regaled in snowy white military uniforms, are posted at intervals of five paces, giving an eerily authoritarian aspect to the slightly macabre spectacle of the body with its wispy white hair.

The following rules are strictly applied to all visitors to the mausoleum:

- People wearing shorts, tank tops and so on will not be admitted.
- Nothing (including day packs, cameras and mobiles) can be taken inside.
- Maintain a respectful demeanour at all times: no talking or sniggering.
- Photography is absolutely prohibited inside the mausoleum.
- It is forbidden to put your hands in your pockets.
- Hats must be taken off inside the mausoleum building.

Most of the visitors are Vietnamese and it's interesting to watch their reactions. Most show deep respect for Ho Chi Minh, who is honoured for his role as the liberator of the Vietnamese people from colonialism, as much as for his communist ideology. This view is reinforced by Vietnam's educational system, which emphasises Ho's deeds and accomplishments.

If you're lucky, you'll catch the changing of the guard outside Ho's mausoleum – the pomp and ceremony displayed here rivals the British equivalent at Buckingham Palace.

Photography is permitted outside the building but not inside and visitors must leave their bags and mobile phones at a counter just inside the entrance.

HO CHI MINH'S STILT HOUSE & THE PRESIDENTIAL PALACE

Behind Ho Chi Minh's Mausoleum is a humble **stilt house** (Nha San Bac Ho; Map pp88-9; admission 5000d; 8-11am & 2-4pm), where Ho lived on and off from 1958 to 1969. The house is an interpretation of a traditional rural dwelling, and has been preserved just as Ho left it. It's set in a well-tended garden next to a carp-filled pond. Just how much time he actually spent here is questionable – the house would have been a tempting target for US bombers had it been suspected that Ho was hanging out here.

In stark contrast to the understated stilt house is the imposing **Presidential Palace** (Map pp88-9), a beautifully restored colonial building constructed in 1906 as the Palace of the

OLD QUARTER STREET NAMES

Street name	Description	Street name	Description
Bat Dan	wooden bowls	Hang Giay	paper or shoes
Bat Su	china bowls	Hang Hanh	onions
Cha Ca	roasted fish	Hang Hom	cases
Chan Cam	string instruments	Hang Huong	incense
Cho Gao	rice market	Hang Khay	trays
Gia Ngu	fishermen	Hang Khoai	sweet potatoes
Hai Tuong	sandals	Hang Luoc	combs
Hang Bac	silversmiths	Hang Ma	votive papers
Hang Be	rafts	Hang Mam	pickled fish
Hang Bo	baskets	Hang Manh	bamboo screens
Hang Bong	cotton	Hang Muoi	salt
Hang Buom	sails	Hang Ngang	transversal street
Hang But	brushes	Hang Non	hats
Hang Ca	fish	Hang Phen	alum
Hang Can	scales	Hang Quat	fans
Hang Chai	bottles	Hang Ruoi	clam worms
Hang Chi	threads	Hang Than	charcoal
Hang Chieu	mats	Hang Thiec	tin
Hang Chinh	jars	Hang Thung	barrels
Hang Cot	bamboo lattices	Hang Tre	bamboo
Hang Da	leather	Hang Trong	drums
Hang Dao	(silk) dyers	Hang Vai	cloth
Hang Dau	beans or oils	Lo Ren	blacksmiths
Hang Dieu	pipes	Lo Su	coffins
Hang Dong	copper	Ma May	rattan
Hang Duong	sugar	Ngo Gach	bricks
Hang Ga	chicken	Thuoc Bac	herbal medicines
Hang Gai	silk		

Governor General of Indochina. It is now used for official receptions and isn't open to the public. There is a combined entrance gate to the stilt house and Presidential Palace grounds on P Ong Ich Kiem, inside the mausoleum complex; when the main mausoleum entrance is closed, enter from Đ Hung Vuong near the palace building.

HO CHI MINH MUSEUM

Adjacent to Ho's Mausoleum, the huge concrete Soviet-style **Ho Chi Minh Museum** (Bao Tang Ho Chi Minh; Map pp88-9; (☎ 3846 3757; admission 10,000d; ⏲ 8-11.30am & 2-4.30pm Tue-Thu, Sat & Sun) is a triumphalist monument dedicated to the life of the founder of modern Vietnam, and the onward march of revolutionary socialism. Mementos of Ho's life are showcased, and there are some fascinating photos and dusty old official documents relating the overthrow of the French and rise of communism.

You'll also find some striking, conceptual art displays that are supposed to signify themes including 'peace', 'progress' and 'freedom'. The symbolism is tricky to interpret unless you take an English-speaking guide, though the 1958 Ford Edsel bursting through the wall – a US commercial failure to symbolise its military failure – is a knockout.

Photography is forbidden and, upon entry, you must leave bags and cameras at reception.

ONE PILLAR PAGODA

A Hanoi landmark, the **One Pillar Pagoda** (Chua Mot Cot; Map pp88-9; P Ong Ich Kiem) was built by the Emperor Ly Thai Tong, who ruled from 1028 to 1054. According to the annals, the heirless emperor dreamed that he had met Quan The Am Bo Tat, the Goddess of Mercy, who, while seated on a lotus flower, handed him a male child. Ly Thai Tong then married a young peasant girl and had a son and heir by her. As a way of expressing his gratitude for this event, he constructed this pagoda in 1049.

The delicate One Pillar Pagoda, built of wood on a single stone pillar, is designed to resemble a lotus blossom, the symbol of purity, rising out of a sea of sorrow. One of the last acts of the French before quitting Hanoi in 1954 was to destroy the original One Pillar Pagoda; the structure was rebuilt by the new government. The pagoda is between the mausoleum and the museum.

Temples & Pagodas

TEMPLE OF LITERATURE

About 2km west of Hoan Kiem Lake, the **Temple of Literature** (Van Mieu; Map pp88-9; ☎ 3845 2917; P Quoc Tu Giam; admission 5000d, English-speaking guide 75,000d; 🕑 8am-5pm) is a rare example of well-preserved traditional Vietnamese architecture. The temple complex, consisting of five courtyards, is extensive and well kept, and makes a welcome retreat from the frenetic streets of Hanoi.

Founded in 1070 by Emperor Ly Thanh Tong, the temple is dedicated to Confucius (Khong Tu) and honours Vietnam's finest scholars and men of literary accomplishment. Vietnam's first university was established here in 1076, though originally entrance was only granted to those of noble birth. After 1442, a more egalitarian approach was adopted and gifted students from all over the nation headed to Hanoi to study the principles of Confucianism, literature and poetry here.

In 1484 Emperor Le Thanh Tong ordered that stelae be erected to record the names, places of birth and achievements of exceptional scholars: 82 stelae remain standing. Though the inscriptions have faded with time, the monuments commemorate graduates including historian Ngo Sy Lien, famous mathematicians and poets.

The imposing tiered gateway (on P Quoc Giam) which forms the main entrance is preceded by a curious plaque, whose inscription requests that visitors dismount their horses before entering. Make sure you do.

Paths then lead through formal gardens to the Khué Van pavilion, constructed in 1802, beyond which is a large square pond known as the Well of Heavenly Clarity. The 82 stelae, considered to be the most precious artefacts in the temple, are arrayed to either side of here; each one sits on a stone tortoise.

The secular intrudes on the spiritual these days, and the plazalike Thai Hoc courtyard at the rear is a slightly tawdry commercial affair with all manner of trinkets and souvenirs for sale (and even an ATM). The northern side of this courtyard is marked by a low-slung pagoda housing an extraordinary statue of a majestic-looking Confucius, depicted with a goatee and bearing scarlet robes, flanked by four of his disciples.

NGOC SON TEMPLE

Perhaps the most visited temple in Hanoi, **Ngoc Son Temple** (Jade Mountain Temple; Map p92; admission 3000d; 🕑 8am-5pm) sits pretty on a delightful little island in the northern part of Hoan Kiem Lake. An elegant scarlet bridge, known as Huc (Rising Sun) Bridge, constructed in classical Vietnamese style and lined with flags, connects the island to the lakeshore. Surrounded by water and shaded by trees, this small temple is dedicated to General Tran Hung Dao, who defeated the Mongols in the 13th century, La To, the patron saint of physicians, and the scholar Van Xuong. Inside you'll find some fine ceramics, a gong or two, some ancient bells and a glass case containing a stuffed lake turtle, which is said to have weighed a hefty 250kg.

The nearby **Martyrs' Monument** was erected as a memorial to those who died fighting for Vietnam's independence.

AMBASSADORS' PAGODA

The official centre of Buddhism in Hanoi, the **Ambassadors' Pagoda** (Chua Quan Su; Map pp88-9; ☎ 3825 2427; 73 P Quan Su) attracts quite a crowd on holidays. During the 17th century there was a guesthouse here for the ambassadors of Buddhist countries. Today there are about a dozen monks and nuns based at the Ambassadors' Pagoda. Next to the pagoda is a shop selling Buddhist ritual objects.

The Ambassadors' Pagoda is located between P Ly Thuong Kiet and P Tran Hung Dao.

BACH MA TEMPLE

In the heart of the Old Quarter, the small **Bach Ma Temple** (Map p92; cnr P Hang Buom & P Hang Giay) is said to be the oldest temple in the city, though much of the current structure dates from the 18th century and a shrine to Confucius was added in 1839. It was originally built by King Ly Thai To in the 11th century to honour a white horse that guided him to this site, where he chose to construct his city walls. Pass through the wonderful old wooden doors of the pagoda to see a statue of the legendary white horse, as well as a beautiful red-lacquered funeral palanquin.

HAI BA TRUNG TEMPLE

Two kilometres south of Hoan Kiem Lake, this **temple** (Map pp88-9; P Tho Lao) was founded in 1142. A statue shows the two Trung sisters (who lived in the 1st century AD) kneeling with their arms raised in the air, as if they are addressing a crowd. Some say the statue shows the sisters, who had been proclaimed the queens of the Vietnamese, about to dive into a river. They are said to have drowned themselves rather than surrender following their defeat at the hands of the Chinese.

QUAN THANH TEMPLE

Shaded by huge trees, **Quan Thanh Temple** (Map pp88-9; P Quan Thanh) was established during the Ly dynasty (1010–1225) and was dedicated to Tran Vo (God of the North), whose symbols of power were the tortoise and the snake. A bronze statue and bell date from 1677. The temple is on the shores of Truc Bach Lake, near the intersection of Đ Thanh Nien and P Quan Thanh.

TAY HO PAGODA

Jutting into West Lake, beautiful **Tay Ho Pagoda** (Map pp84-5; P Tay Ho) is perhaps the most popular place of worship in Hanoi. Throngs of people come here on the first and 15th day of each lunar month in the hope of receiving good fortune from the Mother Goddess, to whom the temple is dedicated. The entrance includes a colourful lane of stalls selling temple offerings and food, while a line of good fresh -seafood restaurants fronts the lake. It's a great place to watch the world go by.

TRAN QUOC PAGODA

One of the oldest in Vietnam, **Tran Quoc Pagoda** (Map pp84-5) is on the eastern shore of West Lake, just off Đ Thanh Nien, which divides this lake from Truc Bach Lake. A stela here, dating from 1639, tells the history of this site. The pagoda was rebuilt in the 15th century and again in 1842. There are a number of monks' funerary monuments in the garden.

Museums

It's worth noting that in addition to the usual two-hour lunch break, most museums are closed on Mondays.

VIETNAM MUSEUM OF ETHNOLOGY

The outstanding **Vietnam Museum of Ethnology** (Bao Tang Dan Toc Hoc Viet Nam; off Map pp84-5; ☎ 3756 2193; www.vme.org.vn; Đ Nguyen Van Huyen; admission 25,000d, guide 50,000d, camera fee 50,000d; 🕑 8.30am-5.30pm Tue-Sun) is one of the country's premier museums. Occupying a fine modern structure, the terrific collection features well-presented tribal art, artefacts and everyday objects gathered from across the nation. Displays are well labelled in Vietnamese, French and English. For anyone with an interest in Vietnam's minorities, it's an essential visit – though it is located way out in the suburbs.

Alongside some outstanding textiles are displays portraying the making of conical hats, and a Tay shamanic ceremony, while videos show the real-life contexts. In the grounds are examples of traditional village houses – a Tay stilt house, impressive Bahnar communal structure and a Yao home – these are popular places for formal wedding photos, quite a surreal sight. Don't miss the soaring, thatched-roofed Giarai tomb, complete with risqué wooden statues. Special exhibitions are regularly held on subjects as diverse as Vietnamese Catholic ritual to life in the early 1980s under the coupon system.

A craft shop – affiliated with Craft Link, which is a fair-trade organisation – sells books, beautiful postcards, and arts and crafts from ethnic communities. The museum is wheelchair friendly.

Getting There & Away

The museum is in the Cau Giay district, about 7km from the city centre and around 60,000d each way in a taxi. Local bus 14 (3000d), departs from P Dinh Tien Hoang on the east side of Hoan Kiem Lake and passes within a couple of blocks of the museum – get off at the Nghia Tan bus stop and head to Đ Nguyen Van Huyen.

HISTORY MUSEUM

A must for the architecture more than the collection, the **History Museum** (Bao Tang Lich Su; Map pp88-9; 1 P Trang Tien; admission 20,000d; 🕑 8-11.30am & 1.30-4.30pm Tue-Sun) was formerly home to the École Française d'Extrême Orient in Vietnam. It is an elegant, ochre-coloured structure built between 1925 and 1932. French architect Ernest Hebrard was among the first in Vietnam to incorporate a blend of Chinese and French design elements in his creations, and this particular building remains one of Hanoi's most stunning architectural showpieces.

Collections here cover the ups more than the downs of Vietnamese history. Highlights include some excellent bronzes from the Dong Son culture (3rd century BC to 3rd century AD) and some striking Hindu statuary from the Khmer and Champa kingdoms. More recent history is a little one-sided and includes the struggle against the French and the story of the Communist Party.

MUSEUM OF THE VIETNAMESE REVOLUTION

A must for all budding revolutionaries, the history of the Vietnamese Revolution is enthusiastically presented in this **museum** (Bao Tang Cach Mang; Map pp88-9; 216 Đ Tran Quang Khai; admission 15,000d; 8-11.45am & 1.30-4.15pm Tue-Sun). It's diagonally across the road from the History Museum.

MEMORIAL HOUSE

One of the Old Quarter's best restored properties, this traditional merchants' **house** (Map p92; 87 P Ma May; admission 5000d; 8am-5pm) is sparsely but beautifully decorated, with rooms set around two courtyards and plenty filled with fine furniture. Note the high steps between rooms, a traditional design incorporated to stop the flow of bad energy around the property. There are plenty of crafts and trinkets for sale here including silver jewellery, basketware and Vietnamese tea sets and there's usually a calligrapher or another craftsperson at work too.

FINE ARTS MUSEUM

Hanoi's excellent **Fine Arts Museum** (Bao Tang My Thuat; Map pp88-9; www.vnfineartsmuseum.org.vn; 66 P Nguyen Thai Hoc; admission 20,000d; 9.15am-5pm Tue-Sun) is housed in two buildings that were once the French Ministry of Information.

There's some outstanding art here, with a collection of superb textiles, furniture and ceramics in the first building, which also showcases some terrific temporary exhibitions. But over in the magnificent main building things get even more impressive as room after room reveals artistic treasures from Vietnam including ancient Chapa stone carvings and some astonishing effigies of Guan Yin (the thousand-eyed, thousand-armed) goddess of compassion. Look out too for the remarkable lacquered-wood statues of robed Buddhist monks, complete with drooping earlobes and fabulously expressive faces, from the Tay Son dynasty. There's also a large collection of contemporary art.

The museum is also a good starting point for anyone interested in acquiring some local art. There's are a couple of galleries with contemporary art, folk-naive paintings, as well as some intriguing books devoted to Vietnamese culture. Reproductions of antiques are also on sale here, but be sure to ask for a certificate to clear these goods through customs when you leave Vietnam.

The Fine Arts Museum is on the corner of P Cao Ba Quat, across the street from the northern wall of the Temple of Literature.

WOMEN'S MUSEUM

Hanoi's **Women's Museum** (Bao Tang Phu Nu; Map p92; 36 P Ly Thuong Kiet; admission 20,000d; 9am-4.30pm) is the subject of an ongoing modernisation program that is introducing better displays and updated facilities. It's a work in progress, so you might encounter some ongoing renovations. There are some powerful tributes to women soldiers and great exhibits from the international women's movement protesting against the American War. And there's much more in terms of cultural and political information. On the 4th floor, you'll find different costumes worn by the women of the ethnic minority groups, and examples of tribal basketware and fabric motifs. Many of the exhibits have multilingual explanations, and regular exhibitions are held on topics as diverse as human trafficking and traditional medicine.

ARMY MUSEUM

Easy to spot thanks to a large collection of weaponry out front, the **Army Museum** (Bao Tang Quan Doi; Map pp88-9; 3823 4264; P Dien Bien Phu; admission 20,000d; 8-11.30am & 1-4.30pm Tue-Sun) displays Soviet and Chinese equipment alongside French- and US-made weapons captured during years of warfare. The centrepiece is a Soviet-built MiG-21 jet fighter, triumphant amid the wreckage of French aircraft downed at Dien Bien Phu, and a US F-111. The exhibits include English translations and some excellent war photography.

Next to the Army Museum is the hexagonal **Flag Tower**, one of the symbols of Hanoi. Museum guards may offer to show you this tower, but will then ask for US$10 to pay for the privilege. Opposite the museum is small park with a commanding **statue of Lenin**.

HOA LO PRISON MUSEUM

This thought-provoking site is all that remains of the former **Hoa Lo Prison** (Map p92; ☎ 3824 6358; 1 P Hoa Lo, cnr P Hai Ba Trung; admission 5000d; 🕑 8-11.30am & 1.30-4.30pm Tue-Sun), ironically nicknamed the 'Hanoi Hilton' by US POWs during the American War. Those incarcerated at Hoa Lo included Pete Peterson, who later became the first US Ambassador to a unified Vietnam in 1995, and Senator John McCain (the Republican nominee for the US presidency in 2008).

The vast prison complex was built by the French in 1896. Originally intended to house around 450 inmates, records indicate that by the 1930s there were close to 2000 prisoners. Hoa Lo was never a very successful prison, and hundreds escaped its walls over the years, many squeezing out through sewer grates.

Much of the prison was razed to make room for the Hanoi Towers skyscraper, though the section at the front of the site has been preserved and restored as a museum – look for the sign over the gate reading 'Maison Centrale'. There are some English and French labels corresponding with the displays, and it is possible to find an English-speaking guide on-site.

The bulk of the exhibits here relate to the prison's use up to the mid-1950s, focusing on the Vietnamese struggle for independence from France. Notable gruesome exhibits in the dark chambers include an ominous French guillotine that was used to behead Vietnamese revolutionaries during the colonial period, and the fetters with which prisoners were chained to the bunks. There are also mug shots on display of Americans and Vietnamese who served time at Hoa Lo. Missing in Action (MIA) teams continue to search for remains of missing US air personnel all over Vietnam.

Lakes & Parks

HOAN KIEM LAKE

The epicentre of old Hanoi, **Hoan Kiem Lake** (Map p92) is an enchanting body of water. Legend has it that, in the mid-15th century, Heaven sent Emperor Le Thai To (formerly Le Loi) a magical sword, which he used to drive the Chinese out of Vietnam. One day after the war he happened upon a giant golden tortoise swimming on the surface of the water; the creature grabbed the sword and disappeared into the depths of the lake. Since that time, the lake has been known as Ho Hoan Kiem (Lake of the Restored Sword) because the tortoise restored the sword to its divine owners.

Ngoc Son Temple (p96) sits on an island near the northern end of Hoan Kiem Lake. The ramshackle **Thap Rua** (Tortoise Tower), on an islet near the southern end of the lake, is topped with a red star and is often used as an emblem of Hanoi. Early risers should make for the lake, as every morning around 6am local residents can be seen doing their traditional t'ai chi on the shore. It's a graceful sight, plus there are joggers and games of badminton.

HO TAY (WEST LAKE)

The city's largest lake, **Ho Tay** (Map pp84-5) is some 13km in circumference and ringed by upmarket suburbs. On the south side of the lake, along Đ Thuy Khue, there's a string of popular seafood restaurants (p112) that are de rigueur for a local night out. To the east, the Xuan Dieu strip is lined with fancy restaurants, cafes, boutiques and spas and some of Hanoi's best hotels including the InterContinental and Sheraton (p107). You'll also find two temples on its shores; the Tay Ho (p97) and Tran Quoc pagodas (p97).

Two legends explain the origins of Ho Tay, which is also known as the Lake of Mist and the Big Lake. According to one legend, Ho Tay was created when the Dragon King drowned an evil nine-tailed fox in his lair, which was in a forest on this site. Another legend relates that in the 11th century a Vietnamese Buddhist monk, Khong Lo, rendered a great service to the emperor of China, who rewarded him with a vast quantity of bronze which he cast into a huge bell. The sound of the bell could be heard all the way to China, where the Golden Buffalo Calf, mistaking the ringing for its mother's call, ran southward, trampling on the site of Ho Tay and turning it into a lake.

The geological explanation is that the lake was created when Song Hong (Red River) overflowed its banks. The flood problem has been partially controlled by building dykes – the highway along the eastern side of Ho Tay is built upon one.

LENIN PARK

The nearest green lung to the Old Quarter, **Lenin Park** (Map pp88-9; admission 2000d; 🕑 4am-9pm) is about 2km south of Hoan Kiem Lake. It's a great place to escape urban Hanoi (and incorporates Bau Mau Lake, where there are pedal boats) and has a couple of cafes. You'll find fitness bars for pull-ups and dips, and its shady paths are popular with joggers.

THE TORTOISES OF HOAN KIEM LAKE: FACT OR FICTION?

Unbelievably, there *are* tortoises in the mysterious and murky waters of Hoan Kiem Lake.

Surfacing on rare occasions, and bringing luck to anyone fortunate enough to see one, the Sword Lake tortoise (*Rafetus leloii*) is not just your common garden-variety tortoise: it is a huge beast. A specimen that died in 1968 weighed in at 250kg and was 2.1m long! Its preserved remains are on show in the Ngoc Son Temple complex (p96), together with a photo taken of a tortoise that appeared in the lake in 2000. No one is sure how many there still are, or how they have survived in this urban setting.

Rumours abound. Are these really the lake-dwelling descendants of the golden tortoise of Le Thai To? Or are they safeguarded in enclosures elsewhere and transported to the lake from time to time, where their occasional appearance is simply an orchestrated ploy to keep the legend of the lake alive?

Those ripples on the lake surface will never seem so innocent again.

TRUC BACH LAKE

This **lake** (Ho Truc Bach; Map pp84-5) is separated from Ho Tay by Đ Thanh Nien, which is lined with flame trees. During the 18th century the Trinh lords built a palace on the lakeside; it was later transformed into a reformatory for wayward royal concubines, who were condemned to spend their days weaving pure white silk.

St Joseph Cathedral

The striking neo-Gothic **St Joseph Cathedral** (Map p92; P Nha Tho; main gate 5-7am & 5-7pm) was inaugurated in 1886, and boasts a soaring facade that faces a little plaza. Its most noteworthy features are its twin belltowers, elaborate altar and fine stained-glass windows.

The main gate to St Joseph Cathedral is open when Mass is held. Guests are welcome at other times of the day, but must enter the cathedral via the compound of the Diocese of Hanoi, the entrance to which is a block away at 40 P Nha Chung. Walking through the main gate, go straight and then turn right. When you reach the side door to the cathedral, ring the small bell high up to the right-hand side of the door and someone should let you in.

Try to drop by on Sunday for the evening Mass (usually at 6pm), when the congregation spills out on the streets, hymns are beamed across this pretty corner of the Old Quarter and the devout sit on motorbikes listening intently to the sermon.

ACTIVITIES

Fitness Clubs

The **Daewoo Hotel Fitness Centre** (Map pp84-5; ☎ 3835 1000; 360 Đ Kim Ma) has a day-use fee of US$20 for all facilities including the pool.

Golf

King's Island (☎ 3772 3160; www.kingsislandgolf.com), 45km west of Hanoi, close to the base of Ba Vi Mountain, is north Vietnam's first 36-hole golf course. The course offers a lakeside or mountain-view course, and visitors can play here for US$80 during the week. Clubs and shoes are available for rent.

There is a popular new course at Tam Dao Hill Station; see p123 for more details.

Hash House Harriers

For the uninitiated, these are drinkers with a running problem. The 'hash' meets at the American Club (p85) on Saturday afternoons; check the website www.hanoih3.com for the latest information. It costs around US$6 and includes a lot of drinks.

Massage & Spa

Hanoi has an expanding choice of spas and massage centres, and because rates at many places are a fraction of those in the West, or richer Asian countries, it's a great place for a little indulgence. There are also plenty of dubious massage parlours where naughty 'extra services' are on offer.

Just north of the Old Quarter, **Long Bien Hotel II** (Map pp88-9; ☎ 3927 1330; 78 Đ Yen Phu; admission incl 1hr massage 130,000d) is a great place to mingle with the locals and have a good scrub, with steam rooms, showers and large baths.

For a serious treat, the smartest spa in town is **Santal Spa** (off Map pp84-5; ☎ 3718 4686; www.santalgroup.com; 112 P Xuan Dieu; 9am-10pm) which has gorgeous facilities, and treatments including a range of massages (from US$50) and herbal baths (US$30), facials and body wraps. Just down the road, **Spa Siam** (Map pp84-

5; ☎ 3719 0385; www.spasiam.com.vn; 30 P Xuan Dieu; ⌚ 9am-9.30pm) is a more economical, simple place, offering massages (from US$12) and facials (US$16). Or in the Old Quarter, head to **SF Salon & Spa** (Map p92; ☎ 3926 2032; 16 P Hang Buom; ⌚ 8.30am-11pm) for Swedish or Thai massages (US$12) and plenty of reasonably priced spa treatments.

Swimming

In central Hanoi, the **Army Hotel** (Khach San Quan Doi; Map pp88-9; ☎ 3825 2896; 33C P Pham Ngu Lao) charges US$3 for day use of its pool, which is big enough for laps and open all year. You can get cold drinks here but it gets very busy in the afternoon with children.

Hanoi Water Park (off Map pp84-5; ☎ 3753 2757; ⌚ 9am-9pm Wed-Mon Apr-Nov) is a family-geared water park around 5km north of the city centre with pools, slides and a lazy river. Entry costs 50,000d for those over 110cm tall, and 30,000d for shorter people, translating roughly to adults and children. Again, it gets extremely busy here on hot summer afternoons.

Yoga

Getting good feedback, **Zenith Yoga** (off Map pp84-5; ☎ 090-4641 171; www.zenithyoga.com; 111 P Xuan Dieu; per class US$10) has daily Asthanga, Iyengar and Hatha yoga sessions in a smart studio. Consult the website for a full schedule of classes.

For up-to-date yoga information, check the noticeboard at Kitchen (p112).

WALKING TOUR

If the Old Quarter is the heart of Hanoi, there is no better way to check its beat than pounding the narrow streets on foot. Start by paying your respects at the **Ngoc Son Temple** (**1**; p96) at the northern end of Hoan Kiem Lake. Cross back over the arched red **Huc Bridge (2)**, and stop for a quick look at the **Martyrs' Monument** (**3**; p96). Follow the lake around on P Dinh Tien Hoang and pick up some tickets for an evening performance at the **Water Puppet Theatre** (**4**; p115) on So Lau. Head north on P Hang Dau and you'll soon be swimming in **shoe shops (5)** selling every shape, size and style. Cross over P Cau Go to P Hang Be, and browse the (very local) **market (6)** with its dried fish and bundles of fresh herbs, which occupies the eastern end of P Gia Ngu.

Back on P Hang Be, continue north to P Hang Bac. At the T-junction there are always artisans hand-carving intricate **gravestones (7)**, most bearing an image of the deceased. Next head up P Ma May to the **Memorial House** (**8**; p98) at No 87, a beautifully restored old Chinese merchant's home.

Return to P Hang Bac and head west past a strip of snazzy **jewellery shops (9)**. Don't miss the small entry to **house 102 (10)**, which includes a fully functioning temple where most people would have a lounge room. This street is plagued by heavy traffic, but if you retrace your steps for a few metres and head north up narrow **P Ta Hien (11)** things are much more peaceful, as the lane passes through a close-knit community and then a strip of low-key bars. Turn left once you reach P Hang Buom and you'll soon reach the impressive **Bach Ma Temple** (**12**; p96), staffed by white-bearded guardians, who spend their days sipping tea.

Legend has it that Ly Thai To used the pagoda to pray for assistance in building the city walls because they persistently collapsed, no matter how many times he rebuilt them. His prayers were finally answered when a white horse appeared out of the temple and guided him to the site where he could safely build his walls. Evidence of his success is still visible at **Cua O Quan Chuong (13)**, the quarter's well-preserved Old East Gate at the eastern end of P Hang Chieu, near the intersection with P Tran Nhat Duat.

Continue north along the narrow P Thanh Ha, which has a **traditional street market (14)**, with squirming fish, chunky frogs and heaped produce. Follow this round to the left and emerge near **Dong Xuan Market** (**15**; p117), one of the most important in the city.

Backtrack south on Nguyen Thien Thuat and turn right on to P Hang Chieu, past a handful of **shops (16)** selling straw mats and rope. This becomes one of Hanoi's most interesting streets, **P Hang Ma (17)** – the name translates as Counterfeit Street – where imitation 'ghost money' is sold for burning in Buddhist ceremonies – there are even US$5000 bills! Loop around and follow your ears to the sounds of **blacksmiths (18)** pounding metal on metal near the corner of P Lo Ren and P Thuoc Bac. Moving south on P Thuoc Bac, at the junction with P Lan Ong, the Thanh Binh store is well-stocked with **rice wine** (**19**; p114), many bottles infused with all the trimmings, including scorpions and snakes. Continue along Lan Ong and you'll pass a row of **herb merchants (20)**, their wares filling the street with pungent aromas.

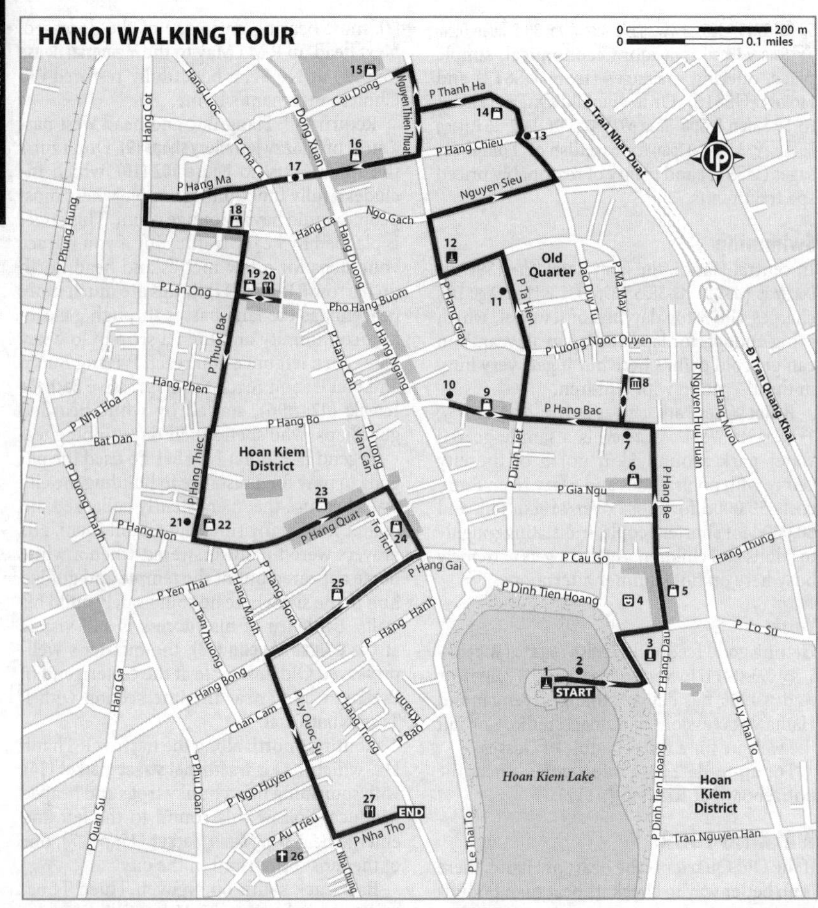

Double back to P Thuoc Bac and head south past the **tin-box makers (21)**, opposite the **mirror shops (22)** on P Hang Thiec, then turn left towards the interesting shops selling **Buddhist altars and statues (23)** along P Hang Quat.

From here, head south on P Luong Van Can past all the **toy shops (24)**, which could save the day if you are following this walk with flagging children. Then wander west along P Hang Gai, window shopping as you pass the elegant designer **silk shops (25)**. Head south on P Ly Quoc Su to the imposing Gothic-style **St Joseph Cathedral** (26; p100). And after all that exercise, you deserve a break from the streets, so dive into one of the stylish **restaurants and cafes (27)** on P Nha Tho, a few steps from the church.

WALK FACTS

Distance 3.5km
Duration Minimum two hours; more with sights and stops
Start Ngoc Son Temple, Hoan Kiem Lake
Finish P Nha Tho

COURSES

Cooking

Hanoi is an excellent place to get to a grip on Vietnamese cooking, and to distinguish your *thit gaa* from your *thit bo*.

Hidden Hanoi (Map pp84-5; ☎ 091-225-4045; www.hiddenhanoi.com.vn; 137 P Nghi Tam; per class US$40) offers cooking classes from its kitchen near Ho Tay.

Highway 4 (p108) also has half-day cooking classes. Prices range from US$26 to US$51 depending on numbers and include a trip to a street market, two hours of cooking supervision and a slap-up feed.

Hoa Sua (p109) offers classes for a cause to raise funds for its training program for disadvantaged youth. Costs vary from US$32 to US$47, and market trips can be arranged for an extra fee.

Language

Hanoi Foreign Language College (Map pp88-9; ☎ 3826 2468; 1 P Pham Ngu Lao), housed in the History Museum compound, is a branch of Hanoi National University where foreigners can study Vietnamese for about US$7 per lesson.

Hidden Hanoi (see opposite) also offers a study program (US$140 for 12 classes) that includes two field trips.

HANOI FOR CHILDREN

Hanoi is a fun city for children thanks to the all-action Old Quarter (p91) and the city's many parks and lakes. Wandering the Old Quarter can be tiring for young ones, and you'll have to maintain a watchful eye for motorbikes, but there are enough diversions to keep them entertained, and plenty of ice-cream shops and fruit markets for those little treats along the way.

Boating is a fun family activity and there is the choice of bigger boats on Ho Tay (p99) or pedal-powered boats in Lenin Park (p99). Hanoi Water Park (p101) is a great place to take children to cool off, but it is only open half the year. Come the evening, there is only one place for any self-respecting child to be, and that is at a water-puppet show (p115), a Punch and Judy pantomime on the water.

TOURS

Anyone arriving in Hanoi on an organised trip will have a city tour included. Most people prefer to explore the city at their own pace but there are some interesting tours offered by Hidden Hanoi (see opposite). These include walking tours of the Old Quarter (US$20) and French Quarter (US$15) and a Temple Tour (US$15); a minimum of two people is required.

FESTIVALS & EVENTS

Tet (Tet Nguyen Dan/Vietnamese Lunar New Year; late January or early February) During the week preceding Tet, there is a flower market on P Hang Luoc. There's also a colourful, two-week flower exhibition and competition, beginning on the first day of the new year, that takes place in Lenin Park near Bay Mau Lake. For much, much more on Tet, see the boxed text on p54.

Quang Trung Festival (February/March) Wrestling competitions, lion dances and human chess take place on the 15th day of the first lunar month at Dong Da Mound, site of the uprising against the Chinese led by Emperor Quang Trung (Nguyen Hué) in 1788.

Vietnam's National Day (2 September) Celebrated with a rally and fireworks at Ba Dinh Sq, in front of Ho Chi Minh's Mausoleum. There are also boat races on Hoan Kiem Lake.

SLEEPING

Virtually all Hanoi's cheap accommodation is in or around the Old Quarter. Be warned, we receive numerous complaints about budget-hotel owners pressuring guests to book tours with them. Some travellers have even been turfed out into the street for not complying, while others have found mysterious taxes added to their bills. In addition, Old Quarter traffic is oppressive, particularly on the streets Hang Be, Hang Bac and Ma May.

Hanoi has experienced a property boom in recent years and the cost of rooms here has risen sharply, so expect to pay at least US$12 to US$15 for a decent budget room. Pay a little more and you get better value: there's a wide selection of hotels with rates in the US$20 to US$40 bracket and most have rooms loaded with gadgets and facilities including air-con, satellite TV, wi-fi, a computer and minibar.

Several small boutique hotels boasting contemporary design features are now up and running in Hanoi, with tariffs averaging around US$50 to US$80 a night. Above and beyond US$100, you're looking at the large luxury hotels, all of which boast pools, fitness centres and restaurants; these places often have good internet promotions.

Most of the budget and midrange hotels include free internet access. Most of the top-end hotels levy a charge. Always check whether tax and service is included.

Old Quarter

BUDGET

Dong A Hotel (Map p92; ☎ 3926 2353; www.dongahotels.com; 50 P Ma May; dm/r US$3/15; ❄ 💻) A good-value place in a central location, the nine rooms here are quite roomy and all have bathtubs and TV. The no-frills dorm in the basement

DO THE HUSTLE

Hanoi is not only the political capital of Vietnam, it is also the capital of hotel hustles. Copycat hotels and fly-by-night hotels abound. These sharks rent a building, appropriate the name of another hotel, and then work with touts to bring unwitting tourists to their 'chosen' accommodation. Visitors who question the alternative location are told the hotel has moved and it is not until they check the next day that they realise they have been had. These hotels overcharge on anything they can, often giving a price for the room on check-in and a price per person on check out. The best way to avoid this is to prebook a room by phone or via email. This way, you know the hotel is still open, still in the same location and not full. Airport taxis and minibuses often work in partnership with these copycat hotels, as they give the biggest commissions.

There have even been reports of desperate Westerners working in tandem with these hotels, steering backpackers their way. For more on scams and how to avoid them, see p91 and the boxed text on p120.

has 14 beds, separated by fabric screens, with slim-line mattresses, fans and lockers.

Hanoi Backpackers Hostel (Map p92; ☎ 3828 5372; www.hanoibackpackershostel.com; 48 P Ngo Huyen; dm US$7.50, r US$30-36; ⊠ 🖳) An efficient, perennially popular hostel that now occupies two buildings on a quiet lane. It's impressively organised, with custom-built bunk beds and lockers, and the dorms all have en-suite bathrooms. You'll also find a rooftop terrace for barbecues and a bar downstairs.

Thu Giang Guesthouse (Map p92; ☎ 3828 5734; 5A P Tam Thuong; r US$7-15; ⊠ 🖳) Hidden at the end of a narrow alley, this modest place in a quiet neighbourhood is owned and run by a hospitable family who go out of their way to help travellers. There's a second branch for overspills at 35A P Hang Dieu.

Manh Dung Guesthouse (Map p92; ☎ 3826 7201; tranmanhdungvn@yahoo.com; 2 P Tam Thuong; r US$12-18; ⊠ 🖳) Opposite the Thu Giang, this is a step up in quality, and has a lift, though most rooms are on the small side.

Thuy Nga Guesthouse (Map p92; ☎ 3826 6053; 24C P Ta Hien; s/d US$12/14; ⊠ 🖳) The garish 'design' which combines plastic flowers and mismatched furniture is pretty bizarre, but this homely little place is run by an accommodating family and the six rooms, though small, do have plenty of natural light, a TV and fridge.

our pick **Especen Hotel** (Map p92; ☎ 3824 4401; www.especen.vn; 28 P Tho Xuong & 41 P Ngo Huyen; s/d US$14/17; ⊠ 🖳) Trying harder than most bog-standard budget places, this hotel has a great location near St Joseph Cathedral. The big, airy and light rooms – most with balcony and all with wi-fi – are in good shape, while the location is almost tranquil (by Old Quarter standards anyway). The two branches are a few doors apart, and have near-identical facilities.

Hotel Thien Trang (Map p92; ☎ 3826 9823; thientranghotel24@hotmail.com; 24 P Nha Chung; r US$15-20; ⊠ 🖳) This place enjoys a terrific, quiet location in the stylish Nha Tho area, and it's run by a friendly old soul. This hotel's spacious rooms retain a degree of period character alongside somewhat less pleasing modern additions.

Sports Hotel (Map p92; ☎ 3926 0154; www.hanoistays.com; 96 P Hang Bac; r US$15-28; ⊠ 🖳) Located on busy Hang Bac, this place has a long narrow lobby with several computer terminals and smart, well-presented (and equipped) rooms. The cheaper rooms on the upper floors are excellent value and there's wi-fi.

Bamboo Hotel (Map p92; ☎ 3926 2378; www.tnktravel.com; 32 P Hang Be; r US$15-35; ⊠ 🖳) This new place has been tastefully designed, and the very spacious rooms have an understated elegance with whitewashed walls, bamboo furniture and terracotta-tile floors. You'll find a neat little cafe downstairs, where a complimentary breakfast is served.

Spring Hotel (Map p92; ☎ 3826 8500; spring.hotel@fpt.vn; 8A P Nha Chung; r US$16-30; ⊠ 🖳) This hotel, in a classy historic building with high ceilings and gorgeous old floor tiles, is run by a friendly family. However note that many of the miniscule en-suite bathrooms are more suited to waiflike supermodels than sumo wrestlers.

Prince 1 Hotel (Map p92; ☎ 3828 0155; www.hanoiprincehotel.com; 51 P Luong Ngoc Quyen; r US$18-28; ⊠ 🖳) The original Prince hotel has a grand-looking lobby, helpful staff and large rooms with imposing Chinese carved furniture and all the trimmings (including TV and minibar).

Artist Hotel (Map p92; ☎ 3825 3044; vietcultour@hn.vnn.vn; 22A P Hai Ba Trung; r US$20-30; ❄) Twelve en-suite rooms that are pretty basic but in fair shape. However the real appeal is the setting around a leafy courtyard, well off the street, with a bar-restaurant and the Cinematheque (p114) downstairs.

Also worth a peek:

Real Darling Café (Map p92; ☎ 3826 9386; darling_café@hotmail.com; 33 P Hang Quat; r US$5-12; ❄ 💻) Almost as old as the Old Quarter, it's still one of the cheapest in town.

Hanoi Spirit House (Map p92; ☎ 3826 7356; 50 Hang Be; r US$10-20; ❄ 💻) Looks a little weary, but all the cheap rooms have TV, fridge and reliable air-con.

MIDRANGE

Rising Dragon Hotel (Map p92; ☎ 3926 3494; www.risingdragonhotel.com; 61 P Hang Be; r US$20-35; ❄ 💻) The attentive, helpful staff and spacious rooms make this place, though those at the rear only have a tiny (or no) window and there's no lift. Breakfast is served in the huge lobby area, which has computers for guests and even a few toys for children.

our pick **Queen of Heart Hotel** (Map p92; ☎ 3926 2911; www.queenofhearthotel.com; 65 Nguyen Huu Huan; r US$20-39; ⊠ ❄ 💻) This excellent place's location on a traffic-heavy street isn't very enticing but noise isn't much of an issue as the glazing is good. Step inside and you'll find an extremely well-run, modern hotel, with very attractive, Swiss-clean rooms that have comfort and a degree of minimalist style. Breakfast is included and the management is very helpful.

Hanoi Elegance Hotel (Map p92; ☎ 3825 3740; www.hanoielegancehotel.com; 8 P Hang Bac; r US$24-55; ❄ 💻) With large rooms, each kitted out with a computer, wooden floors, modern furniture and cable TV, this is a solid choice. Two other branches are close by.

Sunshine Hotel 3 (Map p92; ☎ 3926 3763; www.hanoisunshinehotel.com; 73 P Ma May; r US$24-38, ste US$66; ❄ 💻) This is the best of the three Sunshine hotels, with bright, well-appointed accommodation. All rooms have a computer and fridge; those at the front are very generously proportioned but suffer a degree of street noise.

Khanh Sinh Hotel (Map p92; ☎ 3929 0397; khanhsinhinnhotel@gmail.com; 95 P Hang Chieu; r US$25-35; ❄) An impressive little hotel that opened in late 2008 with well-trained reception staff and 16 very comfortable, attractive and clean rooms. There's wi-fi, a lift, restaurant and the roof terrace is a great spot for an evening beer with a view.

Classic Street Hotel (Map p92; ☎ 3825 2421; www.classicstreet-phocohotel.com; 41 P Hang Be; r US$30-38; ❄) This place, on ever-busy Hang Be, is a little more homely than most hotels, with cosy rooms that all have large beds and satellite TV, and plenty of paintings and ceramics brightening up the communal spaces and corridors.

Hanoi Stars Hotel (Map p92; ☎ 3825 0273; www.hanoistarshotel.com; 25 P Hang Mam; r US$33-55; ❄ 💻) The attention to detail here is excellent, with well-trained, English-speaking staff and attractive, spacious rooms benefiting from good quality beds and linen, fridge and laminate flooring. A complimentary breakfast is served in the lobby, and there's a lift. Periodic promotions offer substantial discounts; check the hotel website.

Golden Lotus Hotel (Map p92; ☎ 3928 8583; www.goldenlotushotel.com.vn; 32 P Hang Trong; r US$50-65; ❄ 💻) An elegant, polished lobby sets the tone at this atmospheric little hotel, which blends Eastern flavours and Western chic. All rooms have wooden floors, silk trim, art aplenty and broadband internet connections, though most at the rear do not enjoy any natural light. Breakfast is included.

Green Mango (Map p92; ☎ 3928 9916; greenmangohanoi@gmail.com; 18 P Hang Quat; r US$55-100; ❄ 💻). The seven rooms here are right above the eponymous bar-lounge-restaurant (see p110), and with great food, killer cocktails and company on tap you could live in this place for weeks and be quite content. Savour the silk sheets and period features (including lovely French Mediterranean–style doors) though the hip feel is slightly let down by some cheap-looking furniture and the bathrooms lack a 'wow' factor.

Church Hotel (Map p92; ☎ 3928 8118; www.churchhotel.com.vn; 9 P Nha Tho; r US$57-90; ❄ 💻) Classy minihotel with real boutique appeal. Some rooms are smallish, but all have stylish furnishings and there's an elegant dining room for your complimentary breakfast. Locationwise this is as good as it gets, as Nha Tho is the epicentre of Old Quarter chic.

Queen Hotel (Map p92; ☎ 3826 0860; www.queencafe.com.vn; 65 P Hang Bac; r US$65-79; ❄ 💻) The quirky but stylish entrance, complete with classic Vespas, is a give-away – this place is no identikit Hanoi hotel. Everything is done a little better here, from the lovely parquet floors to the modish furniture, but the upwardly mobile tariffs are now looking ambitious. Traffic noise is also an issue on the street-facing lower levels.

our pick Cinnamon Hotel (Map p92; ☎ 3938 0430; www.cinnamonhotel.net; 26 P Au Trieu; r US$70-80;) Very hip new hotel overlooking St Joseph Cathedral in the smartest enclave of the Old Quarter. The design is outstanding, combining the historic features of the building – wrought-ironwork and window shutters – with Japanese-influenced interiors and modern gadgetry. Of the six rooms, all with balcony and tropical names, 'Lime' has a commanding perspective of the cathedral. There's wi-fi and a small bar-restaurant. Book well ahead.

Or try these places:

Classic 1 Hotel (Map p92; ☎ 3826 6224; www.hanoiclassichotel.com; 22A P Ta Hien; r US$25-50;) The decor is a bit garish but it's comfortable enough. Some rooms boast nice old French-style window shutters.

Heart Hotel (Map p92; ☎ 3928 6682; www.heart-hotel.com; 11B P Hang Hanh; r US$32-45;) Popular little hotel with 10 neat rooms, some with lake views. Has a lift.

Kim Tuc Hotel (Map p92; ☎ 3929 0366; 32 Dao Duy Tu; r US$45-60;) Smart mini-hotel with attentive staff, a bar and restaurant.

TOP END

Maison D'Hanoi Hanova Hotel (Map p92; ☎ 3938 0999; www.hanovahotel.com; 35-37 P Hang Trong; r from US$136;) Adopting the attention to detail of the boutique-hotel concept but adapting it to a large Old Quarter structure, this impressive new place has 55 rooms, all with a distinctive Oriental design. Benefits from a very central location about a three-minute walk from Hoan Kiem Lake, and breakfast is included.

Hilton Hanoi Opera (Map p92; ☎ 3933 0500; www.hanoi.hilton.com; 1 P Le Thanh Tong; r from US$216;) Built in 1998, this impressive neoclassical edifice blends in well with its surrounds, which include the magnificent Opera House. Rooms are spacious and plush, but the decor is a little dated and there's no wi-fi. Business facilities are impressive, but on the leisure side things are pretty average and the pool is small.

our pick Sofitel Metropole Hotel (Map p92; ☎ 3826 6919; www.sofitel.com; 15 P Ngo Quyen; r from US$245;) A historic hotel and a supremely refined place to stay. Boasts an immaculately restored colonial facade, mahogany-panelled reception rooms and two well-regarded restaurants. Rooms in the old wing offer unmatched colonial style, while the modern Opera Wing has sumptuous levels of comfort, but doesn't have the character.

Zephyr Hotel (Map p92; ☎ 3934 1256; www.zephyrhotel.com.vn; 4 P Ba Trieu; s/d from US$104/112;) The contemporary rooms here boast sharp lines and subtle trim. Has a small gym and a great location.

Melia Hotel (Map p92; ☎ 3934 3343; www.meliahanoi.com; 44B P Ly Thuong Kiet; r from US$155;) An ugly duckling on the outside, but has all the four-star comfort anyone could need.

Central Hanoi

M.O.D Palace (Nha Khach Bo Quoc Phong; Map pp88-9; ☎ 3826 5540; gmd@fpt.vn; 33A P Pham Ngu Lao; r US$50-60;) Owned and operated by the military, and though it's certainly not a palace it's far from a boot camp. Rooms are large and in decent shape, with wi-fi and two double beds, and the linen is good quality. There's an impressive pool.

Hotel Nikko Hanoi (Map pp88-9; ☎ 3822 3535; www.hotelnikkohanoi.com.vn; 84 P Tran Nhan Tong; s/d from US$180;) Sixteen-storey luxury hotel with a renowned Japanese restaurant, and the Sky Lounge bar here has panoramic city views. Comfortable rooms, with fairly standard-issue international hotel chain–style decor, though the bathrooms have fab all-singing, all-dancing Japanese toilets.

Or consider:

Hanoi Lake View Hotel (Map pp88-9; ☎ 3944 7583; www.hanoilakeviewhotel.com.vn; 57A P Quang Trung; r US$45-63;) New mini-hotel with modern rooms and facilities opposite Thien Quang Lake. Slightly overpriced though, so be sure to ask for a discount.

Greater Hanoi

our pick Paloma Hotel (off Map pp84-5; ☎ 3718 4861; www.hanoipalomahotel.com; 70 P Xuan Dieu; r US$28-60;) Opening in late 2008, this fashionable, modern hotel has a prime position on happening Xuan Dieu facing the West Lake. There are four price categories (though all adopt a minimalist style with modish furniture and flat-screen TV). The windowless 'superior' rooms are an absolute steal, but book a lake-view room and you'll get floor-to-ceiling windows and a great balcony – 501 or 505 are the ones to try and secure. Breakfast is included.

Moon River (off Map pp84-5; ☎ 3871 1658; wildrice@fpt.vn; Bac Cau, Gia Lam; r US$90-120;) A real hideaway, this retreat is situated on the banks of the Red River. Rooms here are decorated with antiques and Japanese art and the owners speak good English. It's way out in the Gia Lam suburb, 3km north of the Chuong Duong Bridge.

InterContinental Westlake Hanoi (Map pp84-5; ☎ 4270 8888; www.intercontinental.com/hanoi; 1A Nghi Tam, Tay Ho; r from US$235;) Unquestionably the most luxurious address in the north of the city, this hotel is setting new standards in the luxury sector, with a contemporary Asian-design theme running throughout. The whole complex juts into the lake, with many of the stunning rooms (all with balconies) set on stilts right above the water. The Italian and Asian restaurants, both featuring open kitchens, are some of the city's best and the pool and fitness facilities are top notch.

Other options:

Ho Tay Villas (Map pp84-5; ☎ 3804 7772; hotayvillas@fmail.vnn.vn; Đ Dang Thai Mai; r US$75-140;) Once the Communist Party guesthouse and even hosted Ho himself. However, today you might consider its ageing facilities have been surpassed by the capitalist competition.

Sofitel Plaza (Map pp84-5; ☎ 3823 8888; www.sofitel.com; 1 Đ Thanh Nien; r from US$175;) Sofitel's not-so-historic other half, it boasts the region's first indoor-outdoor swimming pool with a retractable roof.

Sheraton Hanoi Hotel (Map pp84-5; ☎ 3719 9000; www.sheraton.com/hanoi; 11 P Xuan Dieu; r from US$185;) Rooms enjoy sweeping views over West Lake and the hotel is a short walk from the trendy Xuan Dieu strip.

EATING

Hanoi is an international city, and whatever your budget (or your tastes) it's available here. If you've just flown in you're likely to want to get stuck into the local cuisine, which is wonderfully tasty, fragrantly spiced and inexpensive. But if you've been up in the hills subsisting on noodles and rice, the capital's cosmopolitan dining – surf-fresh sushi bars, Parisian-style cafes and authentic Italian and Lebanese food – will come as a welcome relief, with menu prices set at a fraction of what you'd pay in other countries.

Vietnamese

For authentic, flavoursome Vietnamese food, Hanoi is your oyster. Some of the finest grub is dispensed right on the street in the Old Quarter: squat down one of the tiny stools with the locals and chow down – a bowl of steaming *pho* costs a dollar or so. Most of Vietnam's greatest hits are available if you shop around, and almost every corner and alley in the Old Quarter has a street kitchen. Some lanes in the Old Quarter have stalls dedicated to a specific local dish; see p112.

However long you're in town, and no matter what budget you're on, you should treat yourself to a meal or two in one of the city's terrific gourmet Vietnamese restaurants (see p108). Vietnamese food is complex, its flavours created from subtle spice combinations and the generous use of fresh herbs and you'll find some really stylish places to enjoy a memorable meal.

You'll also find plenty of fine international restaurants, staffed by talented chefs who are cooking exciting modern Western and fusion cuisine. Again, menu prices are very reasonable; Hanoi really is a foodie's paradise.

Note that all the innumerable *bia hoi* joints (see the boxed text, p113) around the city also have minimenus.

Little Hanoi 1 (Map p92; ☎ 3926 0168; 9 P Ta Hien; meals from 20,000d; breakfast, lunch & dinner) Venerable travellers' hang-out that's popular for its do-it-yourself fish spring rolls, a delicious dish.

Pho 24 (Map p92; ☎ 3747 4840; www.pho24.com.vn; 1 P Hang Khay; meals 25,000d; breakfast, lunch & dinner) Upmarket noodle chain offering street-style noodles without the street-side location (and exhaust fumes). It's all very well done indeed: the *pho* is great and the restaurants are modern and inviting. Choose by the cut.

our pick **Quan An Ngon** (Map pp88-9; ☎ 3942 8162; 15 P Phan Boi Chau; dishes 35,000-70,000d; 11.30am-10.30pm) Fancy that street-food experience, but afraid to take the plunge? Head to this incredibly busy, popular place that's rammed with locals and a smattering of expats. Minikitchens turn out terrific food, including specialities from all over the nation like squid with lemongrass and chilli or *chao tom* (grilled sugar cane rolled in spiced shrimp paste). Be prepared to wait for a table.

our pick **69 Bar-Restaurant** (Map p92; ☎ 3926 0452; 69 P Ma May; www.69mamay.com; mains 35,000-90,000d; breakfast, lunch & dinner) A highly atmospheric and enjoyable restaurant, 69 occupies a historic house and features heavy old wooden beams and subtle lighting. The creative menu is predominantly Vietnamese (try grilled fish mousse served on lemongrass sticks, or the green papaya and beef salad) and there's a commendably decent vegetarian selection. Reserve one of the two balcony tables for a romantic setting.

ourpick Highway 4 (Map p92; ☎ 3926 0639; www.highway4.com; 5 P Hang Tre; meals 50,000-120,000d; ⏰ lunch & dinner) Providing a memorable dining experience, this is the original location (inside a tottering old house) of an expanding family of restaurants that specialise in Vietnamese cuisine from the northern mountains. There's an astounding array of dishes: from bite-sized snacks through to meaty dishes like *lin luec mam tep* (pork fillet with shrimp sauce) and true exotica like *cha de men* (meat patties with crickets…crunch!). Wash it all down with a bottle or two of delicious Son Tinh rice wine, which comes in flavours including mulberry and apricot. There is another **branch** (Map pp84-5; ☎ 3976 2647; 5 P Mai Hac De; ⏰ lunch & dinner) away from the city centre, which has an atmospheric, sociable vibe, and decor that combines bamboo furnishings and low-level seating, as well as another two branches on Hang Tre.

Hanoi Garden (Map p92; ☎ 3824 3402; 36 P Hang Manh; meals 80,000d-220,000d; ⏰ lunch & dinner) Popular with locals, this restaurant serves Southern Vietnamese and spicy Chinese dishes in a relaxed setting with an open-air courtyard.

One of Hanoi's most famous food specialities is *cha ca* (filleted fish slices grilled over charcoal); your very own fresh fish barbecue. Two good authentic places are the casual, busy **Cha Ca Thang Long** (Map p92; ☎ 3824 5115; 21 P Duong Thanh; cha ca 80,000d; ⏰ lunch & dinner) and the more formal **Cha Ca La Vong** (Map p92; ☎ 3825 3929; 14 P Cha Ca; cha ca 80,000d; ⏰ lunch & dinner) which has been family run for five generations and draws more tour groups. It's DIY at both places: you grill your own succulent fish with a little shrimp paste and plenty of herbs.

Other places to seek out:

Old Hanoi (Map p92; ☎ 3824 5251; 106 P Ma May; meals 30,000-85,000d; ⏰ lunch & dinner) A sophisticated little eatery with tasty Vietnamese specialities.

Golden Land Restaurant (Map p92; ☎ 3828 1056; 15 P Cha Ca; meals 40,000-80,000d; ⏰ breakfast, lunch & dinner) A fairly upmarket place that serves everything from *cha ca* to noodles.

Gourmet Vietnamese

Wild Rice (Map pp88-9; ☎ 3943 8896; 6 P Ngo Thi Nham; mains 60,000-210,000d; ⏰ lunch & dinner) Deceptively simple from the outside, the elegant interior – with leather sofas, exposed stone walls, slate floors and plush seating – is a fine setting for the contemporary Vietnamese cuisine. Seafood is particularly strong here; the fresh fish spring rolls are divine. Try the prawns with peanut and tamarind sauce, or tuna steamed in a banana leaf.

Club 51 Ly Thai To (Map p92; ☎ 3936 3069; 51 P Ly Thai To; meals 70,000-280,000d; ⏰ lunch & dinner) Set in an elegant old residence, this restaurant's impressive dining room is a great location for a gourmet meal – try the memorable green mango and dried anchovy salad.

Club Opera (Map p92; ☎ 3824 6950; 59 P Ly Thai To; mains US$7-17; ⏰ lunch & dinner) Delectable Vietnamese dining in refined, intimate surrounds that resemble a private club. Seafood dishes include fried soft-shell crab with lemon sauce, or try the roast duck.

ourpick Wild Lotus (Map pp88-9; ☎ 3943 9342; www.wildlotus.com.vn; 55A P Nguyen Du; mains 80,000-150,000d, set menus US$18-30; ⏰ lunch & dinner) Seriously upmarket restaurant in a converted colonial mansion with a stately dining room full of imposing artwork. The menu includes three spice journeys: set menus that guide you through the highlights of the Vietnamese table.

And there's more:

Brothers Café (Map pp88-9; ☎ 3733 3866; www.brothercafe.com; 26 P Nguyen Thai Hoc; lunch/dinner buffet US$11/14; ⏰ lunch & dinner) The location is wonderful (in the courtyard of a beautifully restored Buddhist temple) even if the buffet food is less memorable.

Other Asian

Quan Malay (Map pp88-9; ☎ 3941 1443; 65 P Hai Ba Trung; dishes from 25,000d; ⏰ lunch & dinner) Moderately priced Malay restaurant that's a great place to sate your appetite for satay, a nasi campur or Chinese Malay dishes. The set meal (55,000d) is a great deal.

Ky Y (Map pp88-9; ☎ 3978 1386; 166 P Trieu Viet Vuong; meals 30,000-100,000d; ⏰ lunch & dinner) Very popular, moderately priced Japanese restaurant over three floors. Authentic sushi and sashimi, miso soup and teppanyaki dishes, and a convivial atmosphere.

Van Anh (Map pp88-9; ☎ 3928 5163; 5A P Tong Duy Tan; meals 30,000-100,000d; ⏰ lunch & dinner) This was the first non-Vietnamese restaurant to dare to take on the mass of Vietnamese restaurants in speciality food street P Cam Chi (p112). The taste of Thailand.

Tandoor (Map p92; ☎ 3824 5359; 24 P Hang Be; mains 45,000-95,000d, set menu 90,000d; ⏰ lunch & dinner) With a handy Old Quarter location, this is an ideal place to spice up your life with a tandoori chicken, good-value thali or the Goan-style fish curry. There's plenty of choice for vegetarians and the food is halal.

Khazaana (Map pp88-9; ☎ 3934 5657; 1C P Tong Dan, meals 100,000-270,000d; lunch & dinner) Very pukka, upmarket Indian restaurant with delicious cooking from the north and south of the subcontinent. There's plenty of vegetarian choice and the filling thalis offer great value. Mr Gopi, the ever-helpful manager will offer suggestions from the menu, and a delivery service is offered.

Benkay Restaurant (Map pp88-9; ☎ 3822 3535; Hotel Nikko, 84 Tran Nhan Tong; set lunches around US$10, dinner from US$25; lunch & dinner) For authentic Japanese dining, Hotel Nikko's restaurant is hard to beat, and the lunch specials are a steal.

International

Ladybird Restaurant (Map p92; ☎ 3926 1863; 57 P Hang Buom; meals 25,000-45,000d; breakfast, lunch & dinner) Inexpensive place that serves hearty Vietnamese food like stir-fried rice noodles and filling Western grub including pasta and burgers.

Café Smile (Map pp88-9; ☎ 3843 8850; 5 P Van Mieu; meals 50,000-120,000d breakfast, lunch & dinner;) Part of the Hoa Sua family (see right), this relaxed cafe-restaurant is renowned for its cakes and pastries, but also serves delicious Vietnamese (try the *pho*) and Western dishes.

La Salsa (Map p92; ☎ 3828 9052; 25 P Nha Tho; meals 50,000-180,000d; 10.30am-midnight) Informal place on two floors that's good for tapas or something more substantial off the menu, which has both Spanish (try the paella) and French dishes (such as cassoulet).

our pick **KOTO** (Map p92; ☎ 3747 0338; www.koto.com.au; 59 P Van Mieu; meals 55,000-79,000d; closed dinner Mon;) Stunning four-storey modernist cafe-bar-restaurant overlooking the Temple of Literature, where the interior design has been taken very seriously, from the stylish seating to the fresh flowers by the till. Daily specials are chalked up on a blackboard and the shortish menu has everything from yummy pita wraps to Red River fish 'n' chips. The bar also has a mighty fine cocktail list. KOTO is an extraordinarily successful not-for-profit project that provides career training and guidance to disadvantaged kids (see the boxed text on p111). All the staff here are graduates of the training program and the service is a testament to its success: polished and professional, yet warm and receptive.

our pick **Matchbox** (Map pp84-5; ☎ 3726 3904; 12 Nui Truc; meals 60,000-180,000d; breakfast, lunch & dinner) Outstanding new Kiwi-owned rest[...] hip, urban decor and a very mo[...] based on simple cooking of prime in[...] (try the Aussie steak with mash). Not cheap, but great value given the quality and dining experience; visit on Tuesday and pasta is just 50,000d. Doubles as a cafe, and the breakfasts are equally impressive.

Cyclo (Map p92; ☎ 3828 6844; 38 P Duong Thanh; mains from 70,000d; lunch & dinner) No one ever forgets this place…no, it's not down to the tasty Vietnamese and French food, but the *cyclos* that have been creatively transformed into tables. The set lunch is a good deal at 90,000d.

Havana Club (Map p92; ☎ 3926 4146; 135 P Hang Bac; meals from 70,000d; breakfast, lunch & dinner) Feast on delicious Mexican food (try the mixed burritos), a steak or choice Vietnamese cuisine including wonderful green-mango salad with grilled pork. Also hosts the odd salsa night too, when the margaritas really start flowing.

Hoa Sua (Map pp88-9; ☎ 3824 0448; www.hoasuaschool.com; 28A P Ha Hoi; set meals from 80,000d; lunch & dinner;) A shady retreat by day, a dignified diner by night, this restaurant offers a menu of Western dishes (including a strong French influence) alongside some terrific Vietnamese cooking. The set menus are a good deal. Hoa Sua is an excellent project that trains disadvantaged kids for culinary careers and also offers cooking classes (p102).

Ya Beirut (Map pp84-5; ☎ 3718 4844; 28 P Xuan Dieu; meals from 90,000d; dinner) For authentic Middle Eastern cuisine, including kofta kebabs and plenty of vegetarian choices, try this casual Lebanese-owned place. It's down a short alley, just off Xuan Dieu.

our pick **Five** (Map p92; ☎ 3926 3761; 5 P Hang Be; mains 90,000-140,000d; breakfast, lunch & dinner;) Occupying a tastefully restored old building this intimate restaurant is setting new gastro standards in the Old Quarter. It delivers a contemporary take on fine dining, with a short well-chosen menu of Western food including ravioli, lamb and very fine desserts (try the fig cheesecake). A selection of wines are available by the glass and the service is refined, pleasant and professional. There's a little deli counter for takeaways, and it's also great for breakfast: the eggs Benedict is absolutely legendary.

La (Map p92; ☎ 3928 8933; 49 P Ly Quoc Su; mains 140,000-280,000d; lunch & dinner) An intimate, modest-looking and yet atmospheric bistro with a creative menu that includes seared tuna with sesame-seed crust and some good Vietnamese options. Commendably, La offers a diverse selection of wines by the glass.

our pick Green Mango (Map p92; ☎ 3928_9917; 18 P Hang Quat; meals 130,000-340,000d; ⏰ breakfast, lunch & dinner; 💻) Probably Hanoi's hippest hang-out, this highly successful restaurant-cum-lounge has a real vibe as well as great cooking. The stunning dining rooms, complete with rich silk drapes, evoke the feel of an opium den while the huge rear courtyard comes into its own on summer nights. Menu-wise there's everything from pasta to mod-Asian fusion creations like red snapper with curried veg and fettuccini.

Le Petit Bruxelles (Map pp88-9; ☎ 3942 5958; 58B P Tran Quoc Toan; www.le-petit-bruxelles.com; set lunch 65,000d, meals 140,000-300,000d; ⏰ lunch & dinner) Brussels-style brassiere occupying a fine old colonial mansion and its shady courtyard. The set-lunch deal is superb value, but venture à la carte and you'll find mussels, frites and plenty of classic European fare. This is a favoured meeting place for French expats.

Green Tangerine (Map p92; ☎ 3825 1286; 48 P Hang Be; mains US$12-20; ⏰ lunch & dinner; ⊠) Experience the mood and flavour of 1950s Indochine at this elegant restaurant, located in a beautifully restored colonial house, which has a cobbled courtyard and a formal dining room. Dine on inventive French, Vietnamese and fusion dishes; the set lunch (US$9) is a great value.

Restaurant (Press Club; Map p92; ☎ 3934 0888; www.hanoi-pressclub.com; 59A P Ly Thai To; meals from US$18; 💻) Smart, impressive (and expensive) restaurant opposite the Metropole that's popular with Western businesspeople and embassy staff on generous expense accounts. The set lunch buffet (US$9.50) in the deli offers good value, and features imported salmon and cured meats plus a smattering of seafood.

Le Beaulieu Restaurant (Map p92; ☎ 3826 6919 ext 8028; Sofitel Metropole Hotel, 15 P Ngo Quyen; mains from US$22; ⏰ breakfast, lunch & dinner) Hotel restaurants don't come much more elegant (or pricey) than this in Asia. Le Beaulieu is the home of fine French food, with gastronomic cooking, regular regional specialities, an epic cheese board and a professional wine list.

Italian

Luna d'Autunno (Map pp88-9; ☎ 3823 7338; 11B P Dien Bien Phu; pizza from 70,000d, fresh pasta from 90,000d; ⏰ lunch & dinner) Well-established Italian restaurant that has good antipasto, fresh pasta (try the walnut and eggplant ravioli) but is really famous for its pizza, which is baked in a wood-fired oven. Service can be spotty, and at times seriously distracted.

Mediterraneo (Map p92; ☎ 3826 6288; 23 P Nha Tho; mains US$5-7; ⏰ lunch & dinner) Popular, authentic little Italian restaurant that serves up great home-made pasta: try the gorgonzola ravioli or gnocchi, which both go down perfectly with a crisp salad.

Seafood

San Ho Restaurant (Map pp88-9; ☎ 3934 9184; 58 P Ly Thuong Kiet; meals around 200,000d; ⏰ lunch & dinner) Set in an attractive French-era villa, San Ho is considered one of the best seafood restaurants in Hanoi. Crustaceans and molluscs come in every shape and size, bathed in delicious sauces. Most prices are by the kilogram.

Vegetarian

Com Chay Nang Tam (Map pp88-9; ☎ 3826 6140; 79A P Tran Hung Dao; meals from 40,000d; ⏰ lunch & dinner) Dishes of vegetables that look like meat, reflecting an ancient Buddhist tradition designed to make carnivore guests feel at home.

Tamarind Café (Map p92; ☎ 3926 0580; 80 P Ma May; meals US$3-7; ⏰ 6am-midnight; 💻) A relaxed cafe-restaurant with lounge-around cushioned seating, plenty of space and wi-fi. Offers an eclectic menu but is best for tabouli, eggplant claypot and salads. Drinks include heavenly lassis, zesty juices and wine by the glass. Our only quibble is that it's a tad on the expensive side and all prices are in dollars.

Cafes

Maison Vanille (Map pp88-9; ☎ 3933 2355; 49 P Phan Chu Trinh; snacks 12,000-50,000d; ⏰ 7am-9pm) Renowned for its fine pastries, and the folks here also bake their own bread so it's a good place for a lunchtime baguette.

Café Ket Noi (Map p92; ☎ 3926 2743; 28 P Dao Duy Tu; snacks & meals from 25,000d; ⏰ 8.30am-midnight; 💻) An intimate little cafe that's part of the Hoa Sua training school (p109). This branch employs staff from ethnic minority groups. Head here for a bite to eat, coffee or beer or drop by to check out one of the cultural exhibitions and events held on the upper floor.

Café Pho Co (Map p92; ☎ 3928 8153; 11 P Hang Gai; shakes/snacks 18,000/25,000d; ⏰ breakfast, lunch & dinner) One of Hanoi's best-kept secrets, this place has plum views over Hoan Kiem Lake. Enter through the Feeling Gallery, which sells paint-

LOCAL VOICE: KOTO FOUNDER, JIMMY PHAM

Born in Ho Chi Minh City in 1972, Jimmy is of mixed Korean and Vietnamese descent. He escaped South Vietnam after the American retreat, and lived in a compound in Singapore for 2½ years before emigrating to Saudi Arabia and then Australia. His mum worked all hours as a machinist and in a butcher's shop.

'We were Catholics and I was a good altar boy at church but I went through a stage of rebellion, leaving home in my teenage years, but returned to finish my education. I started working for a travel business because I wanted to work in the tourism industry, and my company had an Indochina division.'

'This company's main destination was Vietnam, and I returned here in 1996 to check out hotels in Saigon. I went for a walk and met some street kids selling coconuts. I noticed their ulcers and blisters and asked them if they showered. They told me they washed next to a open sewer. They told me it wasn't safe to sleep on the streets so they slept up a tree, in baskets balanced on branches. I was shocked. I bought them clothes and *pho* and extended my stay from two to 20 weeks, trying to help these kids.'

'I became a Vietnam-based tour guide with Intrepid so I could visit HCMC. I wanted to make a difference. I travelled through Vietnam and met street kids in every town. All of the kids were desperately poor, but after three years of buying them meals and putting them through English classes, some kids in Hanoi said to me, "We trust you now. But what you are doing is not helping us. We need jobs".'

'So in 1999 I opened a sandwich shop called KOTO ('Know One Teach One') near Hanoi train station. It was tough but none of my kids jumped ship, all stuck by me. I then borrowed money from family and friends and moved to a larger place, and employed about 20 kids. After two months Bill Clinton came.'

'We then started the process of becoming an NGO, applying for funding and dealing with the police and tax guy for the first time. Now we have a 24-month training program that empowers not just street children but many disadvantaged kids. The training is very intense, taking in hygiene, health and safety training and every aspect of the restaurant and service industry. About half the kids in each intake make it through to graduation day. Our program has been so successful that the InterContinental took our entire year of graduates in 2008; the whole year. We have other graduates at the Sheraton, and now working in Macao, Australia and Dubai.'

'We use appraisals, training and development to nurture careers. We employ a 50/50 ratio of boys and girls at KOTO. We've women role models – Vietnamese women are amazing, they are so tough. They're in rice fields, bricklayers, road workers and they have the strength to be income earners and manage – KOTO's manager is a woman.'

'Home is Vietnam for now, but though I speak fluent Vietnamese I still feel Australian, it's the education I guess. But one day soon I may go to Saigon and – who knows – start a KOTO scheme there.'

KOTO (p109) is located near the Temple of Literature in Hanoi.

ings, and continue up the stairs up to the top floor for the mother-of-all vistas.

Kinh Do Café (Map pp88-9; ☎ 3825 0216; 252 P Hang Bong; light meals from 40,000d; 🕑 7am-10pm) Fans of Catherine Deneuve will want to make a pilgrimage here, as this was the setting for her morning cuppa during the making of the film *Indochine*. It serves healthy yoghurt, plus tasty French pastries and feisty coffee.

Moca Café (Map p92; ☎ 3825 6334; 14-16 P Nha Tho; snack & meals from 45,000d; 🕑 7.30am-11pm) A large, stylish cafe-restaurant on chic Nha Tho, Moca really looks the part and is a good bet for a coffee or a civilised beer (brewed on the premises). The menu has both Western (from sandwiches to steaks) and Vietnamese food, though both can be a little bland.

Highlands Opera (Map p92; ☎ 3933 4947; www.highlandscoffee.com.vn; P 1A Trang_Tien; sandwiches from 49,000d; 🕑 breakfast & lunch) The classy Highlands chain's most elegant cafe; this branch is situated right next to the fabulously grand presence of the Opera House. Pasta and sandwiches are served but Highlands is best for just a cappuccino and a slab of cake. It's an open-air affair, so not the best place on a chilly January morning.

our pick La Place (Map p92; ☎ 3928 5859; 4 P Au Trieu; meals from 60,000d; 🕑 7.30am-10.30pm). Stylish, popular little cafe adjacent to St Joseph Cathedral with walls covered in propaganda art and an East-West menu: try the coconut chicken curry from the former and a salad or pasta from the latter. Plenty of wine by the glass is on offer and the coffee has a kick.

our pick Kitchen (Map pp84-5; ☎ 3719 2679; http://so-9.com; 9 P Xuan Dieu; snacks & meals 60,000-130,000d; 🕑 7am-9pm; 💻) Truly a metropolitan animal, this hip basement cafe ticks all the right boxes with a mellow buzz and a creative, healthy menu of delicious sandwiches and salads sourced from 'virtually' organic ingredients. Also great for breakfast, a juice (try the ginger and watermelon tonic), or just a quick espresso. Prices are expat wallet-friendly rather than backpacker money belt-geared though.

Or try these:

Cine Café (Map p92; ☎ 3433 9362; 22A P Hai Ba Trung; drinks US$1-3; 🕑 7am-10.30pm) The Cinematheque's (p114) cafe-bar offers a quiet retreat from the fury of Hanoi's streets; enjoy a fresh juice, espresso or a snack in the courtyard.

Puku (Map p92; ☎ 3928 5244; upstairs 60 P Hang Trong; snacks 45,000-70,000d; 🕑 7am-10pm; 💻) Bohemian-style place, with a relaxed vibe and a simple food menu. Hosts regular art exhibitions and has wi-fi.

Culi Café (Map p92; ☎ 3926 2241; 40 P Luong Ngoc Quyen; meals around 50,000d; 🕑 7.30am-11pm; 💻) Casual cafe above a laundry with Aussie-style tucker. The balcony seats offer a good vantage of Old Quarter life and there's free wi-fi.

Thuy Ta Café (Map p92; ☎ 3828 8148; 1 P Le Thai To; coffee US$2-3.50; 🕑 6am-11pm) A sublime lakeside setting for a morning coffee, though the food menu is well overpriced.

Ice Cream

Kem Dac Diet Trang Tien (Map p92; 35 P Trang Tien; ice creams from 5000d) It's barely possible to walk down the road to get to this parlour on hot summer nights, such is its popularity. In truth the ice cream is not that memorable (and some flavours are artificial), but it's certainly well priced.

Fanny Ice Cream (Map p92; ☎ 3828 5656; 48 P Le Thai To; ice creams from 10,000d) The place for French-style ice cream and sorbets in Hanoi. During the right season try the *com*, a delightful local flavour extracted from young sticky rice; other innovative options include ginger and green tea.

Speciality Food Streets

If you would like to combine eating with exploration, most of the following food streets are in central Hanoi. Most places don't have anything as fancy as a seat – just squat down with the locals on one of the kiddie-sized plastic stools and get stuck in.

PHO CAM CHI

The narrow lane **Pho Cam Chi** (Map pp88-9) is crammed with street stalls turning out cheap, tasty food for a buck or two a feed. Cam Chi translates as 'Forbidden to Point' and dates from centuries ago. It is said that the street was named as a reminder for the local residents to keep their curious fingers in their pockets when the king and his entourage went through the neighbourhood. Cam Chi is about 500m northeast of Hanoi train station.

DUONG THUY KHUE

On the southern bank of Ho Tay, **Đuong Thuy Khue** (Map pp88-9) features dozens of outdoor seafood restaurants with a lakeside setting. The level of competition is evident by the daredevil touts who literally throw themselves in front of oncoming traffic to steer people to their tables. You can eat well here for about 100,000d a head.

PHO NGHI TAM

About 10km north of central Hanoi, P Nghi Tam has a 1km-long stretch of about 60 **dog-meat restaurants** (off Map pp84-5; meals from 80,000d). The street runs along the embankment between West Lake and Song Hong (Red River) and the restaurants are on the right as you leave town: look for the words *thit cho*. Even if you have no interest in eating dog meat, it's interesting to cruise this stretch of road on the last evening of the lunar month. Hanoians believe that eating dog meat in the first half of the month brings bad luck, so the restaurants are deserted. Business picks up in the second half of the month and the last day is particularly auspicious with the restaurants packed. Now we know why dogs howl at the moon!

Self-Catering

Fivimart (Map p92; 210 Đ Tran Quang Khai) One of the best-stocked supermarkets in the centre of town.

Citimart (Map p92; Hanoi Towers, 49 Hai Ba Trung) Supermarket that's full of deli-style treats.

Oasis (Map pp84-5; 24 P Xuan Dieu) Italian-owned deli with excellent bread, cheese and salami as well as home-made pasta and sauces.

DRINKING

Bars

Hanoi has a lively drinking scene, with an eclectic selection of places: grungy dive bars, a Western-style pub or two, sleek lounge bars and hundreds of *bia hoi* joints (see the boxed text, below, for more).

However, as the no-fun police supervise a strict curfew, and regularly show up to enforce the closure of places that flout this law, there's little or no action after midnight. Lock-ins do occur here and there, but are increasingly rare, though some bars in luxury hotels can open until 2am. The best place for a pub crawl is P Ta Hien, which has a strip of atmospheric little bars popular with travellers.

Cheeky Quarter (Map p92; ☎ 093-6143 3999; 1 P Ta Hien) Quirky, sociable little bar owned by a Vietnamese–English couple, that comes complete with patterned wallpaper and intriguing framed portraits (that look vaguely like they're depicting some eccentric titled family). Table footy (foosball) is taken very seriously here and the tunes are contemporary: drum 'n' bass or house music. It's at the top end of the Ta Hien strip.

Funky Monkey (Map p92; ☎ 3928 6113; 31 P Hang Thung) This place is very popular with fashion-conscious locals and keeps shifting location (probably in a bid to dodge the no-fun police). On weekend nights things can take off here with Hanoi's party people grooving to pumping house music.

Gambrinus (Map p92; ☎ 3935 1114; 198 P Tran Quang Khai) For a Prague-style brew head to this vast, impressive *brauhaus*, which has shiny vats of freshly brewed Czech beer. Very popular with the Vietnamese.

Green Mango (Map p92; ☎ 3928 9917; 18 P Hang Quat) This acclaimed hotel-restaurant also

BIA AHOY!

'Tram phan tram!' Remember these words, as all over Vietnam, glasses of *bia hoi* are raised and emptied, and cries of '100%' or 'bottoms up' echo around the table.

Bia hoi (beer) is Vietnam's very own draught beer or microbrew. This refreshing, light-bodied pilsener was first introduced to Vietnam by the Czechs. Decades later *bia hoi* is still brewed and delivered daily to drinking establishments throughout Ho Chi Minh City (HCMC), Hanoi and all points between. Brewed without preservatives, it is meant to be enjoyed immediately. And enjoyed it is! Many tourists and expats have never heard of this nectar, but that's their loss, especially given it costs as little as 3000d a glass.

If you think you're ready to try *bia hoi*, be prepared – drinking with the pros is not for the meek. A Western face is a bit unusual at any *bia hoi* establishment and inevitably attracts curious attention from fellow patrons. Raising your glass in toast more often than not results in an invitation to join a group.

Hanoi is the *bia hoi* capital of Vietnam and there are microbars on almost every street corner. Hitting the Old Quarter for a *bia hoi* crawl is a brilliant way to get beneath the skin of the capital. Put US$10 in your pocket and you will be able to afford dozens of beers, so you'll soon make lots of friends. One of the best places to sample this bargain beer is *'bia hoi* junction' (Map p92) in the heart of the Old Quarter where P Ta Hien meets P Luong Ngoc Quyen. Here are three bustling *bia hoi* places occupying different corners, all packed with backpackers and locals every night as they knock back the ale. Don't forget that most *bia hoi* places also serve delicious and inexpensive food.

An alternative *bia hoi* junction that is more local in flavour is where P Nha Hoa meets P Duong Thanh on the western edge of the Old Quarter. **Bia Hoi Ha Noi** (Map p92; 2 P Duong Thanh) does the best spare ribs in town for a little something to go with the beer.

For the best quality *bia hoi*, try **Bia Hoi Viet Ha** (Map p92; P Hang Bai), which is well loved by Hanoi insiders, as it has the biggest chillers in town. It recently relocated to a much bigger premises on Hang Bai, but it's still hard to get a table.

Other good spots to sample the brew include **Bia Hoi 68 Hang Quat** (Map p92; P Hang Quat) and **Nha Hang Lan Chin** (Map pp88-9; 2 P Trang Tien), one of the most popular local lunch spots in town.

has arguably the city's best lounge bar, with stylish seating, a tempting cocktail list and plenty of beautiful people enjoying the relaxed vibe.

ourpick **Le Pub** (Map p92; ☎ 3926 2104; 25 P Hang Be) Sociable and enjoyable, Le Pub is a great place to hook up with others, as there's always a good mix of travellers and foreign residents here. There's a cosy, tavernlike interior (with big screens for sports fans), street-facing terrace and a rear courtyard. Bar snacks are served and the service is prompt.

Legends Beer (Map p92; ☎ 3557 1277; 109 P Nguyen Tuan) Yes, it's extremely touristy, but as every beer comes with fine balcony views of Hoan Kiem Lake it's still worth dropping by for a cold one. Home brews include excellent *weiss* (white) beer.

Mao Red Lounge (Map p92; 5 P Ta Hien) Probably the most popular place on Ta Hien, the place is rammed with a sociable crowd on weekend nights. It's a classic dive bar with dim lighting and air thick with tobacco smoke.

Polite Pub (Map p92; ☎ 3825 0959; 5 P Bao Khanh) Don't forget your manners at this long-running place, unless of course your favourite English Premier League team is 3-0 down at half-time. Classic publike atmosphere and decor.

Roots (Map p92; 2 P Luong Ngoc Quyen; 🕑 8pm-late) Primarily a reggae bar, this is the place for some serious bassline pressure (though other musical genres are tolerated, and played) and can be a riot on the right night with plenty of dance-floor skanking. Lock-ins have been known. Hosts a salsa/latin night on Wednesdays.

Studio (Map p92; ☎ 3926 3882; 32 P Ma May) Quite possibly the most beautiful space in Hanoi, this sleek and sexy new lounge bar-cum-restaurant has a Le Corbusier–influenced modernist design with subtle lighting and soaring white walls that form a blank canvas for the statement art. The cocktails are wonderful, the music is chilled and contemporary, there's a fine food menu and prices are relatively moderate.

Tet (Map p92; ☎ 3928 2618; 2A P Ta Hien) Formally Le Marquis, this intimate little bar has dim lighting and a great little mezzanine table for an intimate drink. It's popular with French speakers.

Or try these:

Angelina (Map p92; ☎ 3826 6919; Sofitel Metropole Hotel, 15 P Ngo Quyen; 🕑 noon-2am) Flash hotel bar with glitzy decor and a late licence. DJs spin funky house and chill-out tunes here on weekend nights.

Dragonfly (Map p92; 15 P Hang Buom) Bar-club with a handy Old Quarter location, though draws a (very) young crowd, and the music is pretty mainstream.

GC Pub (Map p92; ☎ 3825 0499; 7 P Bao Khanh) Looks pretty run down from the street but it gets very lively on weekend nights. Popular with gay Hanoians and has pool tables.

Quan Bia Minh (Map p92; ☎ 3934 5233; 7A P Dinh Liet) An old backpacker fave, this no-frills bar has an upper terrace and cheap beer.

Wine and Liquor Shops

Thanh Binh (Map p92; ☎ 3844 6669; 62 P Lan Ong) After something pretty gruesome to impress your mates at home? Forget Mescal, this rice-wine store has bottles marinated with all kind of exotica including geckos, snakes and scorpions.

Warehouse (Map p92; ☎ 3928 7666; 59 P Hang Trong) Excellent wine store with a superb selection from France, Italy, Spain, Australia, New Zealand and South America.

ENTERTAINMENT

Cinemas

Centre Culturel Français de Hanoi (Map p92; ☎ 3936 2164; 24 P Trang Tien) Set in the sublime L'Espace building near the Opera House, it offers a regular program of French flicks.

Cinematheque (Map p92; ☎ 3936 2648; 22A Hai Ba Trung) A mecca for art-house film lovers, this is a Hanoi institution. There's a great little cafe-bar (p112) here too.

Megastar Cineplex (Map pp88-9; ☎ 3974 3333; www.megastarmedia.net/en; 6th fl, Vincom Tower, 191 Ba Trieu) Multiplex cinema with quality screen and audio, comfortable seats starting at US$2, and sweet and salty popcorn.

Nightclubs

Hanoi is not far short of a clubbing wasteland. In recent years nearly all the city's club venues have been forced to close, leaving Hanoi's dwindling band of DJs left in search of a dance floor. The midnight curfew has been strictly enforced in recent years, but should this change (and there are often rumours that things will be relaxed) then the action will undoubtedly pick up. There are plenty of clubbers in search of a good time, but for the moment dancing is pretty much confined to bar-clubs in and around the Old Quarter, p113, or discos in the luxury hotels.

GAY & LESBIAN HANOI

There are very few gay venues in Hanoi, but plenty of places that are gay-friendly. However official attitudes are still fairly conservative and Hanoi is home to these official attitudes. Police raids in the name of 'social reform' aren't unknown and that tends to ensure gays and lesbians keep a low profile.

The **GC Pub** (opposite) is one of the key gay bars in Hanoi, while another place that is gay-friendly is the **Funky Monkey** (p113).

There's a bustling cruising area along P Bao Khanh, plus nearby Hoan Kiem Lake, although gay males should watch out for an extortion scam linked to the latter (see p91).

The website www.utopia-asia.com has up-to-date information about gay Hanoi and a popular forum.

Egypt Club (Map p92; ☎ 3926 4185; 8 P Hang Buom; 🕑 9am-midnight) There's a vaguely Egyptian theme running through this bar-club, including shisha pipes to puff on. You can get a coffee here during the day, but this is primarily a club venue; DJs spin electronic music and club anthems in the rear section, which has a decent-sized dance floor.

Loop (Map p92; ☎ 6270 0595; 6 P Hang Bai; 🕑 8pm-late) Opening in late 2008, this hip new place created quite a stir by flying in hip electro DJs (including Jonty Scrufff) in its opening weeks. The sound system is terrific and it attracts a good mix of Westerners and locals. Postmidnight dance-floor action has been known.

Nutz (Map pp84-5; ☎ 3719 9000; Sheraton Hotel, 11 P Xuan Dieu; 🕑 5pm-2am) This upmarket hotel disco has a late licence, cool lighting and a decent sound system but atmosphere-wise it's more of an '80s disco than a cutting-edge club. Wednesday is salsa night, with beginners' classes at 8pm.

Live Music

CLASSICAL

Check the website www.ticketvn.com for forthcoming performances.

Hanoi Opera House (Nha Hat Lon; Map p92; ☎ 3993 0113; P Trang Tien) This magnificent 900-seat venue, dating back to 1911 and built in wonderfully elaborate French-colonial style, has been restored to its former glory. On 16 August 1945 the Viet Minh–run Citizens' Committee announced that it had taken over the city from a balcony on this building. Performances of classical music and opera are periodically held here in the evenings – a wonderful experience. The theatre's Vietnamese name appropriately translates to 'House Sing Big'.

JAZZ & MODERN

I-Box (Map p92; ☎ 3828 8820; 32 P Le Thai Tho) Stylish cafe-bar that resembles a private members' club with luxurious drapes and elegant seating. There's live music most nights, including jazz and cover bands. Highly popular with wealthy Vietnamese; drinks are expensive.

Jazz Club By Quyen Van Minh (Cau Lac Bo; Map p92; ☎ 3825 7655; 31-33 P Luong Van Can; 🕑 performances 9-11.30pm) This atmospheric venue is the place in Hanoi to catch some live jazz. There's a full bar, food menu, and high-quality gigs featuring father–son team Minh and Dac, plus other local and international jazz acts. Nonsmokers will suffer though, as the ventilation is poor.

Terrace Bar (Press Club; Map p92; ☎ 3934 0888; 59A P Ly Thai To) Not as popular as it was, but it's worth dropping by this upmarket place for happy hour (from 6pm), particularly on Fridays. Live bands play disco hits.

TRADITIONAL

Live music is performed daily at the Temple of Literature (p96). Upmarket Vietnamese restaurants in central Hanoi are also good places to catch traditional Vietnamese music. **Cay Cau** (Map pp88-9; ☎ 3824 5346; De Syloia Hotel, 17A P Tran Hung Dao) in De Syloia Hotel and **Club Opera** (Map p92; ☎ 3824 6950; 59 P Ly Thai To) are two spots to hit.

Water Puppets

This fascinating art form (see the boxed text, p116) originated in northern Vietnam, and Hanoi is the best place to catch a show.

Performances are held at the **Municipal Water Puppet Theatre** (Roi Nuoc Thang Long; Map p92; ☎ 3824 9494; www.thanglongwaterpuppet.org; 57B P Dinh Tien Hoang; admission 25,000-50,000d, camera fee 15,000d, video fee 50,000d; 🕑 performances 4pm, 5.15pm, 6.30pm, 8pm & 9.15pm). These shows are a real treat for

PUNCH & JUDY IN A POOL

The ancient art of water puppetry *(roi nuoc)* was virtually unknown outside of northern Vietnam until the 1960s. It originated with rice farmers who worked the flooded fields of the Red River Delta. Some say they saw the potential of the water as a dynamic stage, others say they adapted conventional puppetry during a massive flood. Whatever the real story, it is at least 1000 years old.

The farmers carved the puppets from water-resistant fig-tree timber *(sung)* in forms modelled on the villagers themselves, animals from their daily lives and more fanciful mythical creatures such as the dragon, phoenix and unicorn. Performances were usually staged in ponds, lakes or flooded paddy fields.

Contemporary performances use a square tank of waist-deep water for the 'stage'; the water is murky to conceal the mechanisms that operate the puppets. The wooden puppets can be up to 50cm long and weigh as much as 15kg, and are painted with a glossy vegetable-based paint. Each lasts only about three to four months if used continually, so puppet production provides several villages outside Hanoi with a full-time livelihood.

Eleven puppeteers, each one trained for a minimum of three years, are involved in each performance. The puppeteers stand in the water behind a bamboo screen and have traditionally suffered from a host of water-borne diseases – these days they wear waders to avoid this nasty occupational hazard.

Some puppets are simply attached to a long pole, while others are set on a floating base, in turn attached to a pole. Most have articulated limbs and heads, some also have rudders to help guide them. In the darkened auditorium it looks as if they are literally walking on water.

The considerable skills required to operate the puppets were traditionally kept secret and passed only from father to son; never to daughters through fear that they would marry outside the village and take the secrets with them.

The music, which is provided by a band, is as important as the action on stage. The band includes wooden flutes *(sao)*, gongs *(cong)*, cylindrical drums *(trong com)*, bamboo xylophones and the fascinating single-stringed zither *(dan bau)*.

The performance consists of a number of vignettes depicting pastoral scenes and legends. One memorable scene tells of the battle between a fisherman and his prey, which is so electric it appears as if a live fish is being used. There are also fire-breathing dragons (complete with fireworks) and a flute-playing boy riding a buffalo.

The performance is a lot of fun. The water puppets are both amusing and graceful, and the water greatly enhances the drama by allowing the puppets to appear and disappear as if by magic. Spectators in the front-row seats can expect a bit of a splash.

children. Multilingual programs allow the audience to read up on each vignette as it's performed. Book well ahead, especially during high season.

SHOPPING

See p112 for supermarket listings and p114 for details of wine and liquor shops.

Boutiques

P Nha Tho is one of the best areas for browsing for good-quality furnishing stores and clothes boutiques. Most places will ship your purchases abroad.

Chi Vang (Map p92; ☎ 3824 0933; 17 P Trang Tien) Renowned for its exquisite lace creations, including clothing and homewares.

Dome (Map p92; ☎ 3928 7677; www.dome.com.vn; 71 P Hang Trong) An elegant emporium with stylish furniture, gorgeous curtains and cushions made from Vietnamese fabrics. Also has very high-quality basketry, lacquerware and gifts.

Khai Silk (Map p92; ☎ 3825 4237; khaisilk@fpt.vn; 96 P Hang Gai) Upmarket, nationwide store offering stylish, fashionable silk clothing, as well as more classical creations.

Hadong Silk (Map p92; ☎ 3928 5056; 102 P Hang Gai) One of the biggest silk shops on (appropriately enough) 'silk street', with a terrific choice of designs.

Pearl Ha (Map pp84-5; ☎ 091 232 0332; www.pearlha.com; 65 P Xuan Dieu) Renowned designer Ha Linh Thu produces cool clothing, designer jewellery and quirky accessories. The main showroom is on Xuan Dieu, and you'll find outlets in major hotels including the Hilton.

Things of Substance (Map p92; ☎ 3828 6965; 5 P Nha Tho) Tailored fashions and some rack items at moderate prices. The staff are professional and speak decent English.

Three Trees (Map p92; ☎ 3928 8725; 15 P Nha Tho) Stunning, very unusual designer jewellery, including many delicate necklaces, which make very special gifts. There's another branch inside the Sheraton Hotel.

Galleries

The highest concentration of upmarket galleries is on P Trang Tien, between Hoan Kiem Lake and the Opera House – just stroll down the strip. It's also worth dropping by the Fine Arts Museum (p98) which has a couple of interesting galleries featuring talented artists.

Most art galleries have some English-speaking staff, and are open daily until 8pm or 9pm. Prices range from a few dollars to a few thousand and polite bargaining is the norm.

Mai Gallery (Map p92; ☎ 3828 5854; www.maigallery-vietnam.com; 183 P Hang Bong) Run by resident artist Mai, this is a good place to learn more about Vietnamese art before making a purchase.

Suffusive (Map p92; ☎ 3828 8359; www.suffusiveart.com; 2B P Bao Khanh) Gallery dedicated to showcasing innovative paintings from talented young Vietnamese artists. Features regularly changing exhibitions.

Viet Art Centre (Map pp88-9; ☎ 3942 9085; www.vietartcentre.vn; 42 P Yet Kieu) Fine place to browse contemporary Vietnamese art including paintings, photography and sculpture. You can contemplate any prospective purchases in the attractive little cafe here too.

For communist-propaganda art posters there are several good places on Hang Bac in the Old Quarter, including **Hanoi Gallery** (Map p92; 110 P Hang Bac) and **Old Propaganda Poster** (Map p92; ☎ 3926 2493; 122 P Hang Bac).

Handicrafts & Antiques

Some of the best Vietnamese handicrafts include textiles, lacquerware, mother-of-pearl–inlaid furniture, ceramics and sandalwood statuettes. To browse for these, as well as watercolours, oil paintings, prints and assorted antiques, head to the stores along P Hang Gai, P To Tich, P Hang Khai and P Cau Go.

Craft Link (Map pp88-9; ☎ 3843 7710; .com.vn; 43 P Van Mieu) A not-for-profit tion near the Temple of Literature quality tribal handicrafts and weavings at fair-trade prices.

Viet Hien (Map p92; ☎ 3826 9769; 8B P Ta Hien) An enormous warehouse of antiques, paintings, furniture and handicrafts, including rattan creations that are a hell of a lot cheaper than at home.

Vietnamese House (Map p92; ☎ 3826 2455; 92 P Hang Bac) Small, attractive shop dealing in a mix of old and new treasures.

Markets

Buoi Market (Map pp84-5) Located out in the far northwest. Notable for live animals (chickens, ducks, pigs and so on), it also features ornamental plants.

Cua Nam Market (Map pp88-9) A few blocks north of the Hanoi train station. The market is itself of no great interest (except maybe for the flowers), but Đ Le Duan between the market and the train station is a treasure-trove of household goods, such as electronics.

Dong Xuan Market (Map p92) A large nontouristy market located in the Old Quarter of Hanoi, 900m north of Hoan Kiem Lake. There are hundreds of stalls here, and it's a fascinating place to explore if you want to catch a flavour of Hanoian street life.

Hang Da Market (Map p92) A relatively small market, but has a decent selection of imported foods, wine, beer and flowers. The 2nd floor is good for fabric and ready-made clothing. It's located off P Hang Ga, 300m west of Hoan Kiem Lake.

Hom Market (Map pp88-9) On the northeast corner of P Hué and P Tran Xuan Soan, is a good general-purpose market and excellent for local fabric, if you plan to have clothes made.

There's also a **night market** (7pm-midnight) running north to south through the heart of the Old Quarter, starting on P Hang Giay and heading down to P Hang Dao. Content-wise it's something of a spillover for the area's shops, but at least the streets are closed to traffic. Watch out for pickpockets.

Souvenirs & Other Shops

The streets Hang Bong and Hang Gai, just northwest of Hoan Kiem Lake, have shops and market stalls selling souvenirs with a Vietnam theme including T-shirts, Viet Cong (VC) headgear and so on.

P Hang Gai and its continuation, P Hang Bong, are good places to look for embroidered tablecloths, T-shirts and wall hangings. P Hang Gai is also a fine place to have clothes custom-made. Take a look along P Hang Dao, just north of Hoan Kiem Lake, for souvenir Russian-made watches.

For tribal ethnic-minority garb and handicrafts head to P To Tich or P Hang Bac where there are a dozen or so places, including **Pan Flute** (Map p92; ☎ 0913-5387 4338; 42 P Hang Bac) which has an excellent selection including some old textiles.

Several shops along P Hang Bong and P Trang Tien stock CDs and DVDs, many of very dubious quality. For dirt-cheap eyeglasses, made in a mere 10 minutes using imported lenses from France or Japan, again P Trang Tien is the place.

GETTING THERE & AWAY

Air

Hanoi has fewer direct international flights than Ho Chi Minh City, but with a change of aircraft in Singapore, Hong Kong or Bangkok you can get almost anywhere. For further information about international flights, see p493.

Vietnam Airlines (Map p92; ☎ 3943 9660; www.vietnamair.com.vn; 25 P Trang Thi; ⏲ 7am-6.30pm Mon-Fri, 8-11.45am & 2-5pm Sat, Sun & holidays) links Hanoi to destinations throughout Vietnam. Popular routes include Hanoi to Dalat, Danang, Dien Bien Phu, HCMC, Hue and Nha Trang, all served daily.

Jetstar Airways (☎ 3955 0550) operates low-cost flights to Danang, HCMC, Hue and Nha Trang.

Bus & Minibus

Hanoi has four main long-distance bus stations. They are fairly well organised, with ticket offices, fixed prices and schedules. Consider buying tickets the day before you plan to travel on the longer-distance routes to ensure a seat.

Gia Lam bus station (off Map pp84-5; ☎ 3827 1569; Đ Ngoc Lam) has buses to the northeast of Hanoi, with services every 15 minutes to Halong Bay (66,000d, 3½ hours), Haiphong (50,000d, two hours) and Lang Son (60,000d to 80,000d, three hours). There are also nine daily buses to Lao Cai (155,000d, nine hours), the last at 1pm. It's located around 3km northeast of the centre on the other bank of the Song Hong (Red River).

Loung Yen bus station (Map pp84-5; ☎ 3942 0477; Tran Quang Khai & Nguyen Khoai), 3km southeast of the Old Quarter, serves the same places plus Cao Bang (110,000d, eight hours), Mong Cai (110,000d to 150,000d, eight hours) and Ha Giang (110,000d, eight hours).

Transport to Cat Ba Island is best organised from this terminal. Two companies run eight daily bus connections to Cat Ba Town; Hoang Long Buses (4½ hours, 5.15am, 7.15am, 11.15am and 1.15pm, 170,000d) is usually the more efficient. Your ticket includes a large bus to Haiphong, a minibus transfer to the ferry pier at Dinh Vu, a 40-minute boat ride to Cai Vieng harbour on Cat Ba Island, and the final bus journey to Cat Ba Town. It sounds complicated, but the transfers work quite efficiently and there's little or no time hanging around. Be sure to buy your ticket from the bus driver.

Giap Bat bus station (off Map pp84-5; ☎ 3864 1467; Đ Giai Phong) serves points south of Hanoi, including Ninh Binh (50,000d, two hours) and Hue (185,000d, 12 hours). It is 7km south of the Hanoi train station.

My Dinh bus station (off Map pp84-5; ☎ 3768 5549, Đ Pham Hung) is an option in the west of town, which serves a range of destinations, including Halong City, Lang Son, Cao Bang, Ha Giang and Dien Bien Phu.

Some buses also leave from **Kim Ma bus station** (Map pp88-9; P Nguyen Thai Hoc), 2km east of the Old Quarter, including routes for the northwestern part of Vietnam: Hoa Binh (45,000d, two hours) and Dien Bien Phu (from 235,000d, 14 hours).

Two daily services (at 7.30am and 9.30am) to Nanning, China (300,000d, eight hours) leave from the private terminal of **Hong Ha Tourism** (Map p92; ☎ 3824 7339; Hong Ha Hotel, 204 Tran Quang Khai). Tickets should be purchased in advance, though little English is spoken. You may be asked to show your Chinese visa. The bus runs to the border at Dong Dang where you have to pass through Chinese immigration (look smart!) and then change to a Chinese bus which continues to the Lang Dong bus station in Nanning. Reports from Nanning-bound travellers indicate that this bus route is less hassle and quicker than travelling by train.

Tourist-style minibuses can be booked through most hotels and travel agents. Popular destinations include Halong Bay and Sapa. Prices are usually about 30 to 40%

higher than the regular public bus, but include a hotel pick-up.

Many open-ticket tours through Vietnam start or finish in Hanoi – for more details see p503.

Car & Motorbike

Car hire is best arranged via a travel agency (p87) or hotel. Rates (virtually) always include a driver, a necessity as many roads and turnings are not signposted. Generally, the roads in both the northeast and northwest are in reasonable shape, but are certainly not highways in the Western sense, with narrow lanes, potholes and plenty of blind corners. Progress is always slow – reckon on an average of just 35km to 40km per hour. During the rainy season expect serious delays as landslides are cleared and bridges repaired.

You'll need a 4WD. Toyota Landcruisers are the most popular option; daily rates start at about US$90 a day (including driver and petrol). Make sure the driver's expenses are covered in the rate you're quoted.

If you plan to tour the north by bike, you'll find several good tour operators in Hanoi which offer well-maintained bikes, and who can help you with itinerary planning (and guides). Check out p507 for more details.

For a reliable Honda trail (starting from US$20 daily) and road bikes (US$15) or a moped (US$5 to US$8), as well as great advice, head to **Offroad Vietnam** (Map p92; ☎ 3926 3433; www.offroadvietnam.com; 36 P Nguyen Huu Huan). **Cuong's Motorbike Adventure** (Map p92; ☎ 3926 1534; cuongminsk@yahoo.com; 1 P Luong Ngoc Quyen) is also highly recommended for Minsks (US$7), Hondas and 650cc Urals. Both places rent out bikes that come with a full range of spare parts and tools.

Train

The main **Hanoi train station** (Ga Hang Co; Map pp88-9; ☎ 3825 3949; 120 Đ Le Duan; ⏰ ticket office 7.30am-12.30pm & 1.30-7.30pm) is at the western end of P Tran Hung Dao; trains from here go to southern destinations. Foreigners can buy tickets for southbound trains at counter 2, where the staff speak English. We recommend buying your tickets at least one day before departure to ensure a seat or sleeper.

To the right of the main entrance of the train station is a separate ticket office for northbound trains to Lao Cai (for Sapa) and China. Tickets to China must be bought from counter 13. Note that all northbound trains leave from a separate station (just behind) called **Tran Quy Cap station** (B Station; P Tran Qui Cap; ☎ 3825 2628).

To make things even more complicated, some northbound (Lao Cai and Lang Son included) and eastbound (Haiphong) trains depart from **Gia Lam train station** (Map pp84-5) on the eastern side of the Song Hong (Red River), and **Long Bien** (Map pp88-9; ☎ 3826 8280) on the western (city) side of the river. Be sure to ask just where you need to go to catch your train. Tickets can be bought at the main station until about two hours before departure. Of course any travel agency (and many tour operators) can book train tickets for you for a commission, taking the hassle out the equation.

Trains from Hanoi to Beijing (2,317,000d) depart the capital on Tuesdays and Fridays at 6.30pm, a 43-hour journey; once you're in China the train is a comfortable, air-conditioned service with four-bed sleeper compartments and a restaurant. There's also a daily train between Hanoi and Nanning (US$38 in soft sleeper), leaving at 7.30pm and arriving in Nanning at 8am; which could be a great connection but for the two-hour border and immigration formalities and change of train that you have to do between midnight and 2am. You cannot board these international trains in Lang Son or Dong Dang. Check all schedules in Hanoi, as they may change.

Consult **Vietnam Rail** (Duong Sat Viet Nam; www.vr.com.vn) for current timetables. For more information on trains see p507.

GETTING AROUND

To/From the Airport

Hanoi's Noi Bai International Airport (off Map pp84–5) is about 35km north of the city. The trip here takes 45 minutes to an hour, along a fast modern highway.

There are numerous scams involving taxi drivers and dodgy hotels, see the boxed text (p120) for the full rundown.

Vietnam Airlines minibuses between Hanoi and Noi Bai airport run about every half-hour and charge US$2 a seat. They arrive and depart from the Vietnam Airlines office (Map p92) on P Trang Thi. It's best – though not essential – to book the day before.

The cheapest way to get between Noi Bai airport and central Hanoi is to use public buses 7 or 17, which run to/from Kim Ma bus station and Long Bien bus station (Map pp88–9) respectively. Services depart every 15 minutes from around 5am to 9pm and tickets are just 5000d. It can take more than an hour, however. Arrange an onward metered taxi from the bus station to your chosen hotel.

Airport Taxi (☎ 3873 3333) charges US$12 for a taxi ride door-to-door to or from Noi Bai airport. They do *not* require that you pay the toll for the bridge you cross en route. Some other taxi drivers require that you pay the toll, so ask first.

From the terminal, look out for the official taxi drivers who wear bright yellow jackets. The price to anywhere in central Hanoi is a fixed 250,000d. Don't use freelance taxi drivers touting for business – the chances of a rip-off are too high.

There's always a collection of taxi drivers just outside the Vietnam Airlines office or at the northern end of Hoan Kiem Lake.

Bicycle

Given the traffic, Hanoi is very challenging to get around by bicycle. However many guesthouses and cafes will rent you a bike for about US$1 to US$2 per day.

Bus

Hanoi has an extensive and complex public bus system, though few tourists take advantage of the rock-bottom fares (3000d). If you're up for a challenge pick up a copy of the *Xe Buyt Hanoi* (Hanoi bus map; 5000d) from recommended bookstores on P Trang Tien. It is all in Vietnamese but easy enough to follow with routes and numbers clearly marked.

Car & Motorbike

Until you've had a few weeks (preferably a lifetime) in Hanoi, avoid attempting to get around the city by motorbike. Signposts are tricky to spot or missing, the roads change name every few hundred metres, the traffic is relentless, the air is toxic, road manners are nonexistent and street lighting is hopelessly inadequate. Then there are the hassles of dealing with parking and possible theft, and bribe-happy police. That said, most guesthouses and hotels can arrange mopeds for around US$5 a day!

Cyclo

Sadly, the *cyclos* of Hanoi are on the way out. You're only likely to see them in the Old Quarter, and they're mainly booked by tour operators to give video camera–toting punters a trundle around town. Some *cyclo* drivers still hang around the Old Quarter looking for business, and if you've only a short distance to cover it's still a great way to experience the city (despite the fumes). Settle on a price first and watch out for overcharging – a common ploy when carrying two passengers is to agree on a price, and then *double* it upon arrival, gesturing 'no, no, no…that was per person'.

Aim to pay around 15,000d for a shortish journey; night rides are more. Few *cyclo* drivers speak English so take a map with you.

Motorbike Taxi

You won't have any trouble finding a *xe om* (motorbike taxi) in Hanoi. Just stroll along any major street and you'll get an offer from a driver almost every 10 seconds.

Expect to pay around 10,000d for a short ride, or 20,000d for a journey of over 3km.

Taxi

Several reliable companies offer metered taxis. All charge fairly similar rates. Flag fall is around 10,000d to 15,000d, which takes you 1km or 2km; every kilometre thereafter

MIND THE MAFIA

It happens all over the world and Hanoi is no exception. Many of the drivers who hang out at Noi Bai airport are working in cahoots with hotels in Hanoi to fill their rooms. They know every trick in the book and usually carry the cards of all the popular budget hotels. 'It's full today' is popular, as is 'they have a new place, much nicer, number two'. Usually it's a bunch of lies. The best defence is to insist you already have a reservation. Even if the place does turn out to be full, you can plot your own course from there. When it comes to the Vietnam Airlines minibus, the best bet is to bail out at the Vietnam Airlines office, usually the first stop in the centre. Otherwise you will be dragged around endless commission-paying hotels in the Old Quarter. Another option to avoid the nonsense is to book a room in advance and arrange an airport pick-up. Someone will be waiting with a name board and you can wave to the taxi touts as you exit the airport.

costs 10,000d or so. Bear in mind that there are dodgy operators with high-speed meters. There are also a few upmarket taxis cruising the streets with upmarket tariffs to match. Try and use the more reliable companies:

Airport Taxi (☎ 3873 3333)
Hanoi Taxi (☎ 3853 5353)
Mai Linh Taxi (☎ 3822 2666)
Van Xuan (☎ 3822 2888)

AROUND HANOI

The rich alluvial soils of the Red River Delta nurture a rich rice crop and many of the communities surrounding Hanoi are still engaged in agriculture. The contrast between the modern face of Hanoi and the medieval lifestyle of the villages is stark. Many of the small tour operators in Hanoi offer cycling tours to villages near Hanoi, which are a great way to discover a different world. **Onbike Tour** (☎ 3732 4788) specialises in cycling tours (from US$23) around Hanoi, on some trips they guarantee you won't see another tourist. These tours also avoid having to struggle through Hanoi's ferocious traffic, as a minibus takes the strain through the suburbs.

HO CHI MINH TRAIL MUSEUM

The **Ho Chi Minh Trail Museum** (Bao Tang Duong Ho Chi Minh; ☎ 034-382 0889; Hwy 6; admission 10,000d; 🕒 7-11.30am & 1.30-4pm Tue-Sun) is dedicated to the famous supply route from the communist north to the occupied south of Vietnam. The displays, including a barrage of American ammunition and weaponry as well as some powerful photography, document all too clearly the extreme effort and organisation needed to keep the show on the road – and the death and destruction involved. Quite simply, defeat was simply not an option for the VC, whatever the odds. There's a model of the trail, which shows the nightmarish terrain through which it passed. It's located about 13km southwest of Hanoi and can be combined with a visit to Van Phuc handicraft village (p122), or visited on the way to the Perfume Pagoda.

PERFUME PAGODA

North Vietnam's very own Marble Mountains (p242), the **Perfume Pagoda** (Chua Huong; admission incl return boat trip 40,000d) is a striking complex of pagodas and Buddhist shrines built into the karst cliffs of Huong Tich Mountain (Mountain of the Fragrant Traces). Among the better-known sites here are Thien Chu (Pagoda Leading to Heaven); Giai Oan Chu (Purgatorial Pagoda), where the faithful believe deities purify souls, cure sufferings and grant offspring to childless families; and Huong Tich Chu (Pagoda of the Perfumed Vestige). This is a domestic drawcard and it is an interesting experience just to see the Vietnamese tourists at play.

The entertaining boat trip along the scenic waterways between limestone cliffs takes about two hours return; allow a couple more hours to climb to the top and return. The path to the summit is steep in places and if it's raining the ground can get *very* slippery. However, the good news is that there is now a cable car to the summit, costing 30,000d one way. A smart combination is to use the cable car to go up and then walk down.

Great numbers of Buddhist pilgrims come here during a festival that begins in the middle of the second lunar month and lasts until the last week of the third lunar month (usually corresponding to March and April). It's *very* busy during this period, especially on the even dates of the lunar month; you'll have a much easier time if you establish the lunar date and plan to go on an odd date. Weekends tend to draw crowds year-round, when pilgrims and other visitors spend their time boating, hiking and exploring the caves. Litter and hawkers are part and parcel of the visit, and some hawkers are persistent enough to hassle visitors all the way to the top; you have been warned!

Getting There & Away

The Perfume Pagoda is about 60km southwest of Hanoi by road. Getting there requires a journey first by road, then by river, then on foot or by cable car.

First, travel from Hanoi by car for two hours to the township of My Duc. Vehicles usually drop you about a 15-minute walk from the boat ramp, or you can hop on a *xe om*. Then take a small boat, usually rowed by women, for one hour to the foot of the mountain.

The main pagoda area is a steep 3km hike from the boat dock. Allow yourself at least two hours to make the return trip, longer if it's been raining and is slippery.

Most tour operators and some travellers' cafes in Hanoi offer inexpensive tours to the pagoda, for as little as US$10 (inclusive of guide and lunch). Small-group around US$25. This is one of those places where it is easier to take a tour as it's a pain by public transport.

HANDICRAFT VILLAGES

Numerous villages surrounding Hanoi specialise in cottage industries. Visiting these settlements can make a rewarding day trip, though having a good guide helps make the journey really worthwhile.

Bat Trang is known as the 'ceramic village'. Here artisans mass-produce ceramic vases and other pieces in their kilns. It's hot, sweaty work, but the results are superb and very reasonably priced compared with the boutiques in town. There are masses of ceramic shops but poke around down the lanes and behind the shops to find the kilns. Bat Trang is 13km southeast of Hanoi. Public bus 47 runs here from Long Bien bus station (Map pp88–9).

Van Phuc specialises in silk. Silk cloth is produced here on looms and lots of visitors like to buy or order tailor-made clothes. Many of the fine silk items you see on sale in Hanoi's P Hang Gai are made in Van Phuc. There's a small daily fruit-and-vegetable market here in the mornings, and a pretty village pagoda with a lily pond. Van Phuc is 8km southwest of Hanoi; take city bus 1 from Long Bien bus station.

Dong Ky was known as the 'firecracker village' until 1995, when the Vietnamese government banned firecrackers. With that industry now extinguished, the village survives by producing beautiful traditional furniture inlaid with mother-of-pearl. You can have handcrafted beds, chairs and tables and wardrobes custom-made here and exported directly to your door. Dong Ky is 15km northeast of Hanoi.

Le Mat, 7km northeast of central Hanoi, is a snake village (in every sense). Locals have been employed as snake catchers throughout Vietnam for generations, and consequently there's a great deal of local expertise about snake venom, tonics and potions. Today they breed snakes here for upmarket restaurants in Hanoi, and traditional medicine. The village has several places where you can try fresh snake cuisine and snake elixir, and for around US$15 you can try a set course consisting of grass-snake meat prepared in around 10 different ways (cobra is far more expensive). On the 23rd day of the third lunar month is the colourful **Le Mat Festival**, featuring 'snake dances' and other activities.

Other handicraft villages in the region produce conical hats, delicate wooden bird cages and herbs.

THAY & TAY PHUONG PAGODAS

Stunning limestone outcrops loom up from the emerald-green paddy fields and clinging to the cliffs are these two pagodas, about 20 minutes apart from each other by road.

Thay Pagoda (Master's Pagoda; admission 5000d), also known as Thien Phuc (Heavenly Blessing), is dedicated to Thich Ca Buddha (Sakyamuni, the historical Buddha). To the left of the main altar is a statue of the 12th-century monk Tu Dao Hanh, the master in whose honour the pagoda is named. To the right is a statue of King Ly Nhan Tong, who is believed to have been a reincarnation of Tu Dao Hanh.

In front of the pagoda is a small stage built on stilts in the middle of a pond; water-puppet shows are staged here during festivals. Follow the path around the outside of the main pagoda building, and take a steep 10-minute climb up to a beautiful smaller pagoda perched high on the rock. Thay Pagoda is a big and confusing complex for non-Buddhists – consider hiring a guide to get the most from a visit.

The pagoda's **annual festival** is held from the fifth to the seventh days of the third lunar month. Pilgrims and other visitors enjoy watching water-puppet shows, hiking and exploring caves in the area.

Tay Phuong Pagoda (Pagoda of the West; admission 5000d), also known as Sung Phuc Pagoda, consists of three single-level structures built in descending order on a hillock said to resemble a buffalo. The figures representing 'the conditions of man' are carved from jackfruit wood, many dating from the 18th century, and are the pagoda's most celebrated feature. The earliest construction here dates from the 8th century. Take the steep steps up to the main pagoda building, then find a path at the back that loops down past the other two pagodas and wander through the hillside village surrounding the complex.

Getting There & Away

The pagodas are about 30km west of Hanoi in Ha Tay province. Hanoi travel agents and tour operators offer day trips that take in both pagodas, from US$40 per person. Alternatively, hire a car and driver for about US$80, and plot a rewarding day trip that combines the pagodas and Ba Vi National Park.

BA VI NATIONAL PARK

☎ 034

Formerly a French hill station, the triple-peaked Ba Vi Mountain (Nui Ba Vi) has been attracting visitors for decades and remains a popular weekend escape for Hanoians. The limestone mountain is now part of the **Ba Vi National Park** (☎ 388 1205; per person/motorbike 10,000d/5000d) which has several rare and endangered plants in its protected forest, mammals including two species of rare 'flying' squirrel and bountiful bird life.

There's an orchid garden and a bird garden, and **hiking** opportunities through the forested slopes. A **temple** dedicated to Ho Chi Minh sits at the mountain's summit (1276m) – it's a hard but beautiful 30-minute climb up 1229 steps through the trees. Fog often shrouds the peak, but despite the damp and mist it's eerily atmospheric – visit between April and December for the best chance of clear views down to the Red River valley and Hanoi in the distance.

Sleeping & Eating

Ba Vi Guesthouse (☎ 388 1197; r weekdays 130,000-190,000d, weekends 180,000-240,000d) spreads over several blocks in the heart of the park and has a big swimming pool and a moderately priced restaurant (meals 50,000d). Go for one of the less-noisy guesthouses away from the pool and restaurant area if you're here on a weekend. You'll definitely need your passport to check in.

Getting There & Away

Ba Vi National Park is about 65km west of Hanoi, and the only practical option for visiting is by hired vehicle from Hanoi. Travelling by motorbike, it is possible to visit Ba Vi before taking a beautiful riverside road down to Hoa Binh and onwards into the northwest.

There has been some confusion between attractions near Ba Vi town, which is well away from the park boundaries, and Ba Vi National Park. Make sure your driver knows you want the national park.

CO LOA CITADEL

Dating from the 3rd century BC, **Co Loa Citadel** (Co Loa Thanh; admission per person/car 3000/5000d; 8am-5pm) was the first fortified citadel in Vietnamese history and became the national capital during the reign of Ngo Quyen (AD 939–44). Only vestiges of the ancient ramparts, which enclosed an area of about 5 sq km, remain.

In the centre of the citadel are temples dedicated to the rule of King An Duong Vuong (257–208 BC), who founded the legendary Thuc dynasty, and his daughter My Nuong (Mi Chau). Legend tells that My Nuong showed her father's magic crossbow trigger (which made him invincible in battle) to her husband, the son of a Chinese general. He stole it and gave it to his father. With this not-so-secret weapon, the Chinese defeated An Duong Vuong, beginning 1000 years of Chinese occupation.

Co Loa Citadel is 16km north of central Hanoi in Dong Anh district, and can be visited as a short detour while on the way to or from Tam Dao Hill Station (below). Public bus 46 runs here from My Dinh bus station (off Map pp84–5) in Hanoi.

TAM DAO HILL STATION

☎ 0211 / elevation 930m

Nestling below soaring forest-clad peaks, Tam Dao is a former French hill station in a spectacular setting northwest of Hanoi. Today it's a popular summer resort, a favoured weekend escape for Hanoians, who come here to revel in the temperate climate and make merry in the extensive numbers of restaurants and bars. Founded in 1907 by the French, most of its stock of colonial villas was destroyed during the Franco-Viet Minh War, only to be replaced with by brutalist-style concrete architecture. Tam Dao is a useful base for hiking, but the town itself is an unattractive sprawl of hotel blocks.

Tam Dao National Park was designated in 1996 and covers much of the area around the town. Tam Dao means 'Three Islands', and the three summits of Tam Dao Mountain, all about 1400m in height, are sometimes visible to the northeast of the hill station, floating like islands in the mist. There are at least 64 mammal species (including langurs) and 239 bird species in the park, but you'll need a good local guide and be prepared to do some hiking to find them. Illegal hunting remains a big problem.

Remember that it is cool up in Tam Dao and this part of Vietnam has a distinct winter.

Don't be caught unprepared. Hikes vary from half an hour return to the **waterfall**, to day-treks taking in bamboo forest and primary tropical forest. A guide is essential for the longer hikes and can be hired from 50,000d; ask about these at the Mela Hotel (opposite). The best time to visit is between late April and mid-October, when the mist sometimes lifts and the weather can be fine. As with other popular sites in Vietnam, weekends can be packed, weekdays are far less busy.

The **Tam Dao Golf and Resort** (☎ 04-3736 6457; http://tamdaogolf.com) is set against the beautiful backdrop of the 'Three Islands'. A round of golf here costs from US$36 during the week.

Sleeping & Eating

There's a host of hotels and guesthouses in Tam Dao. The town is easy to navigate, so look around and negotiate.

Huong Lien Hotel (☎ 382 4282; r 160,000d) Offering decent value for the price, most of the rooms here have balconies to make the most of those misty mountain views. There's a little restaurant too.

Hang Khong Hotel (☎ 382 4208; r US$20-28;) A good new midrange place where the rooms have plenty of sparkle and space as well as comfortable beds, balconies and en-suite shower rooms.

Mela Hotel (☎ 382 4321; r US$57-95;) A modern, attractive, European-managed hotel with 20 spacious comfortable rooms (some include fireplaces) and most with balconies and wonderful valley views. The in-house Bamboo restaurant (meals US$4 to US$12) has an eclectic menu which features everything from French cuisine to the ubiquitous Vietnamese spring rolls.

There are plenty of other hotel restaurants and good *com pho* places. Try to avoid eating the local wildlife.

Getting There & Away

Tam Dao is 85km northwest of Hanoi in Vinh Phuc province. Buses run from Kim Ma bus station in Hanoi to Vinh Yen (25,000d, one hour). From there you can hire a motorbike (about 70,000d one way) to travel the 24km single-lane road that leads to the national park.

On a motorbike from Hanoi, the journey time is a little over two hours, and the last part of the ride into the park is beautiful.

VIETNAM BY THE LETTER

It was simply inevitable that Vietnam would have more to offer than your average tourist destination. Stretching from the misty mountains on the Chinese border to the azure waters of the Gulf of Thailand, Vietnam is a place of adventures to set your pulse racing, a land of beaches to slow it back down again, and a culinary destination to tease the palette, thanks to a flair for flavours. To experience the very best the country has to offer, follow our ABC guide.

Adventures

Dense jungles, brooding mountains, endless waterways, towering cliffs, hairpin bends: the potential for adrenalin-fuelled adventure is limitless in Vietnam. Whether you prefer to scale the heights of jagged peaks or plumb the depths of coral reefs, Vietnam will deliver something special. Heck, just being here is one long adventure, but these experiences will take it to a whole new level.

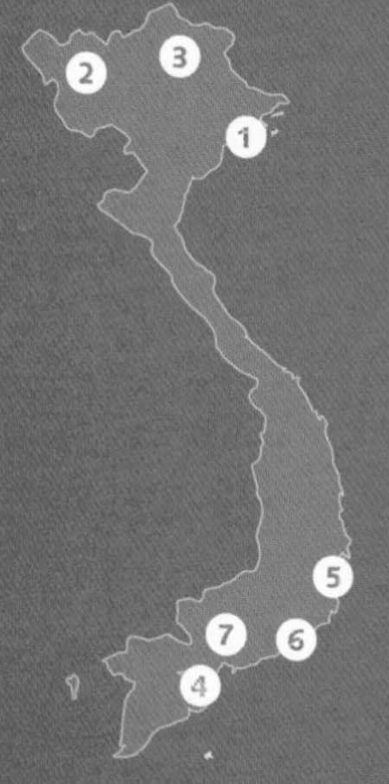

❶ Kayak Halong Bay

Use paddle power to explore this incredible forest of karsts (p139), which jut out of the South China Sea like stone sentinels. Kayaks go where other boats cannot, such as into hidden caves and secret lagoons, and will reveal to you the very best of the bay.

❷ Conquer Mount Fansipan

OK, so it's not Mt Everest, but at 3143m, it is the highest peak in the country (p178). Meet some of the minority peoples on the trek before tackling the elements to arrive on the roof of Vietnam.

❸ Motorbike through the Deep North

Saddle up for the ride of a lifetime into the mountains of Vietnam's deep north (p165). The roads are absolute roller coasters, the scenery is simply stunning and the ethnic mosaic of the population is incredibly hospitable.

❹ Cycle the Mekong Delta

Forget about those newfangled engines and pedal through the back roads of the Mekong Delta (p413) – a patchwork of emerald greens. Stick to the roads less travelled or jump on the odd boat or two for the full Mekong experience.

❺ Dive Beneath

See Vietnam from a different angle by scuba diving off its curvaceous coast. Tank up, buddy down and explore the reefs off Nha Trang (p280). Other options are Phu Quoc Island (p464) or, the final frontier, Con Dao (p407).

❻ Kitesurf Above

If all that underwater stuff sounds too deep, then float above it all with something more carefree like kitesurfing. Mui Ne (p308) is the unashamed kitesurfing capital, but the sport is (literally) taking off, up and down the coast.

❼ Explore the National Parks

Vietnam's jungle is massive – well at least in some of the protected areas. Track shy wildlife, hike to hidden waterfalls or mountain-bike down paths less travelled in one of the country's remote national parks, such as magnificent Cat Tien (p406).

Beaches

Vietnam might have been late to Southeast Asia's beach party, but it was worth the wait. The country boasts more than 3400km of coastline, with infinite stretches of powdery sand, hidden coves, lovely lagoons, impossible boulder formations and tropical islands ringed with yet *more* beaches. Help! Too many choices!

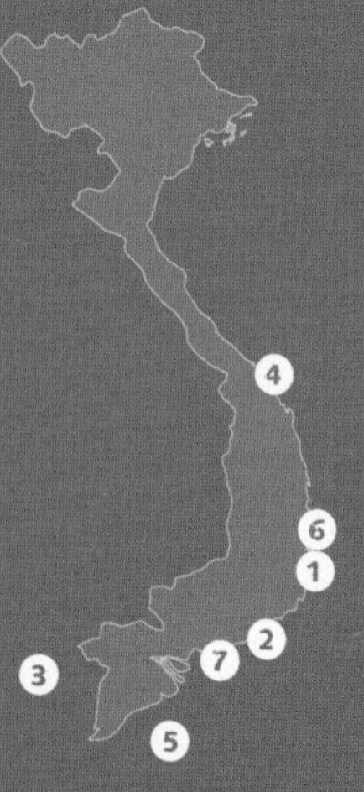

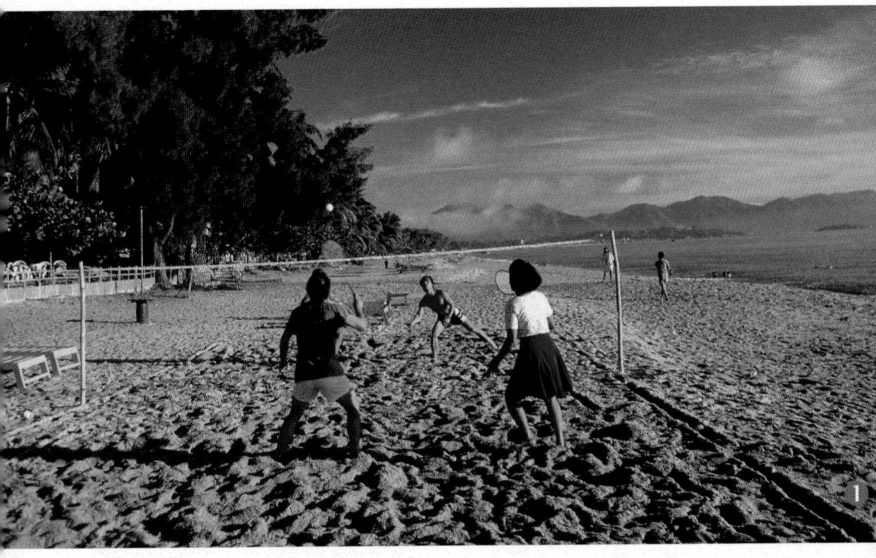

1 Nha Trang

The heavyweight champion of Vietnam, Nha Trang (p280) has been knocking out visitors for years. True, the town is brazen and brash, but the beach is bold and beautiful and a gateway to a cluster of quieter islands.

2 Mui Ne

Set on a seductive swathe of sand, Mui Ne (p308) is an absolute charmer with swaying palms and towering dunes. Get pummelled on the beach by a masseur or pummelled by the waves with some water sports – this place blends action and inertia to perfection.

3 Phu Quoc

Simply the most beautiful island in Vietnam, Phu Quoc (p464) is liberally sprinkled with picture-perfect white-sand beaches and cloaked in dense, impenetrable jungle. Long Beach is sophisticated, Ong Lan Beach romantic, and Bai Sao simply irresistible.

4 China Beach

OK, so we are using artistic licence with the name, but whether you call it My Khe to the north or Cua Dai to the south, it's all just one long, luscious stretch of sand. Try surfing off the shores of Danang (p235) or just pamper yourself at the resorts near Hoi An (p260).

5 Con Dao

The Con Dao Islands (p407) have been protected from over-exposure by their isolated location off the coast. Enjoy it while it lasts, with their smattering of resorts and an overdose of idyllic beaches, as this is sure to be the next big thing in Vietnamese beaches.

6 Doc Let

While the rest of the world is sunning itself in Nha Trang, slip up the coast to this little teaser (p279), home to some atmospheric resorts and some squeaky white sand; a place to get away from it all.

7 Ho Coc

Vung Tau to Phan Thiet is almost one long beach, but much of it remains mercifully inaccessible to the masses. Sample its potential with a retreat to Ho Coc (p405), a glorious sandbar about midway along this stretch.

Cuisine

Travel for just a week in Vietnam and you'll realise how few of its gastronomic specialities see the light of day beyond its borders. Every region lays claim to unique edible delights – well-known classics such as northern *pho*, Hue imperial banquet fare, and southern salad rolls are just the tip of the culinary iceberg.

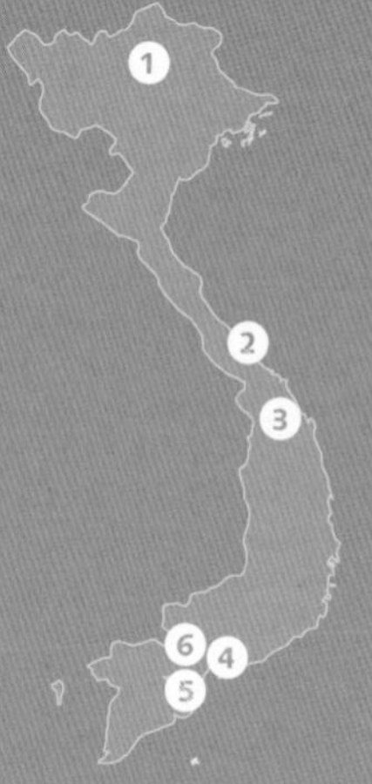

❶ Bun Rieu Cua
Thank the northern knack for turning humble ingredients into something sublime for this crustacean-flavoured soup. It's made from paddy crabs, packed with tomato chunks, green onions and *bun* (rice vermicelli), and capped with a floater of sautéed crab fat. Some cooks add bean curd and *oc* (large snails, in which case the dish is called *bun rieu cua oc*). Green leaves and herbs, along with sliced banana tree stem, are mainstay accompaniments.

❷ Banh
One of the tastiest relics of Emperor Tu Duc's reign is *banh*, steamed rice cakes eaten with a drizzle of fish sauce. Whether eaten plain, dotted with chopped mushrooms, or stuffed with chopped dried shrimp, these dainty Hue bites make the perfect light breakfast or between-meal snack. Heat-loving central Vietnamese often add a dollop of chilli sauce.

❸ My Quang
Thick and chewy turmeric-yellow noodles are topped with shrimp, pork, bean sprouts, herbs and chopped peanuts, and are moistened with just a bit of rich broth. Named for its native province of Quang Nam, the dish comes with rice crackers for crumbling and is finished in characteristically central-Vietnamese style, with a dab of sweet-hot chilli jam.

❹ Banh Trang Phoi Suong
A veritable hedgerow of unusual greens and herbs, many of which are gathered wild from riverbanks and rice paddies, features in this Trang Bang District do-it-yourself roll-up of thinly sliced pork and cucumber, accompanied by pickled garlic, daikon and carrots. Everything's bundled into rustic rice papers, which have, as the name of the dish suggests, been 'exposed in the dew at night', and dipped in *nuoc cham*.

❺ Canh Chua
This beautiful, tangy tamarind-flavoured soup embodies the Mekong Delta's abundance: from its waterways come fish; from its fruit plantations, pineapple; and from its fertile soil, tomato and spongy *bac ha* or taro stem. The region's rice paddies contribute the cuminlike herb *rau rom*. Accompanied by rice it's an unpretentious yet appetising meal in a bowl.

❻ Banh Khot
These small sweet-and-savoury prawn pancakes are made from ground rice and coconut milk batter that's cooked in special half-spherical moulds, resulting in a crispy crust enclosing a soft centre. A speciality of Ba Ria-Vung Tau province, they're eaten rolled with herbs in a lettuce leaf.

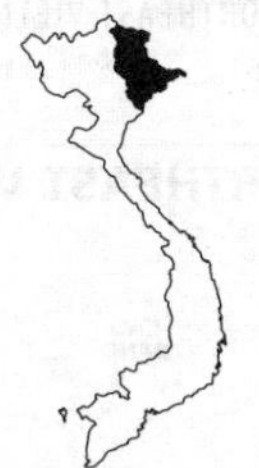

Northeast Vietnam

Northeast Vietnam's top ticket is Halong Bay, and a boat trip through the sublime World Heritage site is undoubtedly an enchanting experience. But the region also has some of Vietnam's most impressive and rugged highland scenery, defined by craggy limestone peaks and extensive tropical forests, as well as a smattering of interesting historic sights, caves and waterfalls.

Bizarre but beautiful, Halong Bay is geology gone wild, with thousands of limestone pinnacles protruding from the waters. Fringing the southern part of the bay is Cat Ba, a verdant island that's fast emerging as an important travellers' base for its hiking, biking, sailing and world-class rock climbing. East of Halong Bay is the less-visited Bai Tu Long Bay, where nature's spectacular show continues all the way to the Chinese border.

Looming above the coast, the brooding mountains of the northeast are another world entirely. The karst connection continues into Cao Bang province, and the surreal scenery is some of the most stunning in all Vietnam. With northwest Vietnam well and truly on the map, this is the region to head for if you really want to explore remote backroads. In a week you can take in the lakes of Ba Be National Park and the waterfalls and scenery around Cao Bang and loop back down via Lang Son to Halong City.

This area is also a popular route for travelling overland between China and Vietnam and there are two important border crossings at Mong Cai and Dong Dang.

HIGHLIGHTS

- Discover the supernatural beauty of **Halong Bay** (p139) on a cruise through its emerald waters and limestone islands
- Delve into the great outdoors on **Cat Ba Island** (p146), which has superb hiking, biking and a fascinating national park
- Get right off the tourist trail in undeveloped **Lan Ha Bay** (p152), an emerging area of gorgeous islands and beaches with superb rock climbing, sailing and kayaking
- Board a boat to glide through lakes and rivers, and spend the night with a local Tay family in **Ba Be National Park** (p162)
- Check out the crazy karst scenery of **Cao Bang** (p158) and the province's waterfalls, caves, lakes and historic sights

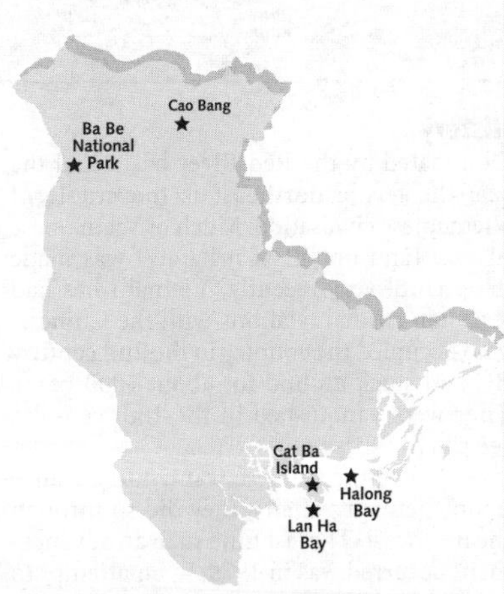

- ELEVATION: 0–1980M
- BEST TIME TO VISIT: MAR–MAY & SEP–NOV

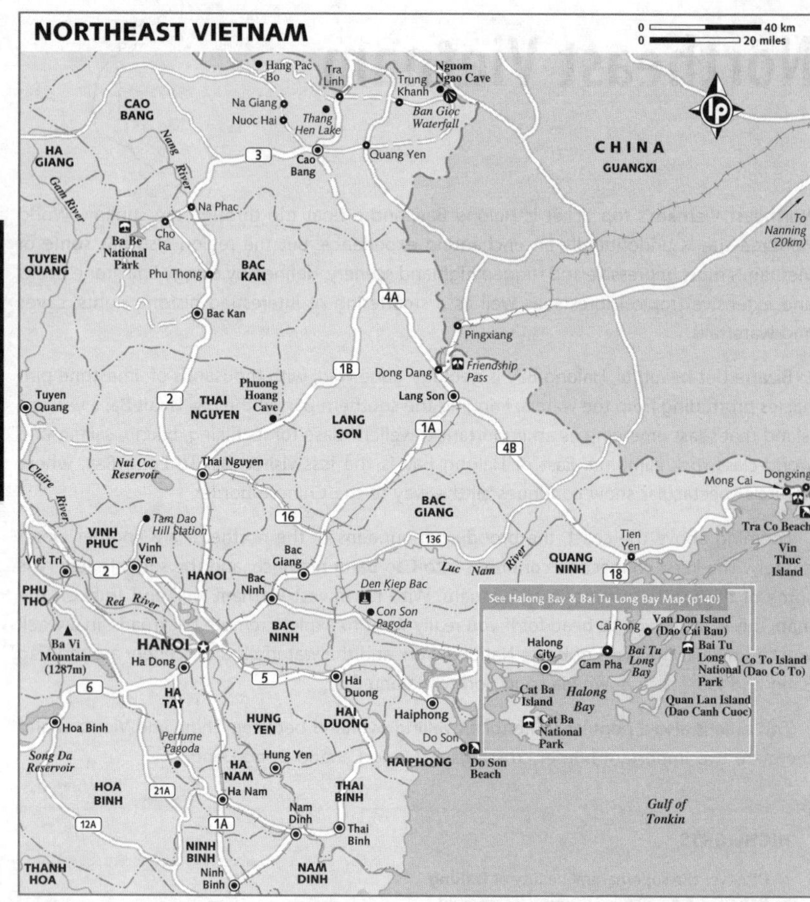

History

Dominated by the Red River basin and the sea, the fertile northeast is the cradle of Vietnamese civilisation. Much of Vietnamese history (and not all of it happy) was made here. Until very recently, Vietnam has had less than cordial relations with the Chinese, who occupied the country in the 2nd century BC and stuck around for about 1000 years. They were vanquished in the 10th century; see p141.

Any time the Chinese wanted to advance upon Vietnam's affairs, they did so through the northeast. The last time such an advancement occurred was in 1979, in an attempt to punish the Vietnamese for their occupation of Cambodia (p156). Thousands of ethnic Chinese also fled through this region in the 1970s and 1980s in search of a better life.

Today things have settled down considerably. Border trade is surging ahead and Chinese tourists now flock to the region in their thousands during the summer months.

National Parks

The beautiful national parks of the northeast all involve a certain amount of water-based activity. Cat Ba National Park, near Halong Bay, is a rugged island jutting out of the sea, liberally cloaked in lush jungle. This park also includes the 300 or so limestone islands of Lan Ha Bay, and dozens of deserted beaches.

Further northeast, Halong Bay becomes Bai Tu Long National Park, a stunning scene of karsts that is every bit the equal of its illustrious neighbour. Bai Tu's isolation gives visitors the chance to savour its beauty without the tourists and explore the hidden beaches.

Ba Be National Park has some gorgeous emerald lakes, hemmed in by soaring mountains and lush forest on all sides. Almost alpine, this is a great area for hiking, biking and boat trips to caves and waterfalls. Consider a homestay in a minority village in the park.

Getting There & Away

Hanoi is the gateway to the northeast. Road connections from the capital to Haiphong, Halong City and Lang Son are fast, but as the terrain gets more mountainous, things slow down considerably. Buses are fast and frequent in the lowlands, but slow and creaking in the highlands. There are also rail links to Haiphong and Lang Son, but the trains move at a snail's pace.

CON SON & DEN KIEP BAC

More appealing to domestic travellers than foreigners, Con Son and Den Kiep Bac are nonetheless potential diversions en route to Haiphong or Halong City.

Con Son was home to Nguyen Trai (1380–1442), the famed Vietnamese poet, writer and general. Nguyen Trai assisted Emperor Le Loi in his successful battle against the Chinese Ming dynasty in the 15th century. **Con Son pagoda complex** (admission per person/vehicle 3000/5000d) has a temple honouring Nguyen Trai atop a nearby mountain. It's a 600-step climb to reach it – a serious workout. Alternatively, take the loop walk past a spring, heading up through pine forests, and return down the steps.

Several kilometres away, **Den Kiep Bac** (Kiep Bac Temple; admission per person/vehicle 3000/5000d) is dedicated to Tran Hung Dao (1228–1300). An outstanding general, his armies defeated 500,000 Mongol invaders in the late 1280s and he is a revered Vietnamese folk hero.

This beautiful temple was founded in 1300 and built on the site where Tran Hung Dao is said to have died. It also honours his family. Quyen Thanh, one of the general's daughters, married Tran Nhat Ton, who was credited with founding the Truc Lam sect of Vietnamese Buddhism.

Within the temple complex there's a small exhibition on Tran Hung Dao's exploits, but you'll need a Vietnamese speaker to translate the details. The **Tran Hung Dao Festival** is held at Den Kiep Bac every year from the 18th to the 20th day of the eighth lunar month, usually in October.

Den Kiep Bac and Con Son are in Hai Duong province, about 80km east of Hanoi. With wheels, it's easy to visit on the way to Haiphong or Halong Bay. There are several hotels and guesthouses nearby.

HAIPHONG

☎ 031 / pop 1,884,600

With graceful tree-lined boulevards, an impressive array of colonial-era buildings and an unhurried air, Haiphong is a very approachable city. It's an important seaport and industrial centre but few visitors stop here long, probably because sights are thin on the ground. If you do pass through, you'll find far fewer hassles than in Vietnam's other main tourism centres, with barely a tout to be found.

Cafe culture is very strong here, so be sure to take in one of the myriad excellent places in the city centre, many with street tables for people-watching, and wi-fi.

The city is a transport hub, and very well connected to Cat Ba Island and Hanoi by bus, boat and train.

History

The French took possession of Haiphong in 1874 when it was just a small market town. The city developed rapidly, becoming a major port. Heavy industry was a natural choice thanks to its proximity to coal supplies.

The city was the site of one of the most immediate causes of the Franco-Viet Minh War; the French bombardment of 1946, which killed thousands. Between 1965 and 1972 it also came under air and naval attack from the US, which mined the city's harbour in an attempt to cut the flow of Soviet military supplies. In the late 1970s and the 1980s Haiphong experienced a mass exodus, including many ethnic Chinese refugees, who took much of the city's fishing fleet with them.

Today the city is on the up again, and has attracted massive inward investment from multinational corporations drawn here by its port facilities and transport linkS.

Information

INTERNET ACCESS

There are centrally located internet cafes on P Dien Bien Phu, charging around 3000d per hour. Several of the cafes on P Minh Khai have free wi-fi.

MEDICAL SERVICES

If you need medical treatment it's best to head to Hanoi.

Vietnam-Czech Friendship Hospital (Benh Vien Viet-Tiep; ☎ 370 0514; ; P Nha Thuong) The best of the hospitals, but rely on it for emergencies only.

MONEY

There are plenty of ATMs in the city centre.

Vietcombank (11 P Hoang Dieu) Can deal with cash and travellers cheques and has an ATM.

POST

Main post office (3 P Nguyen Tri Phuong) A grand old yellow dame on the corner of P Hoang Van Thu.

Sights & Activities

Have half a day on your hands in Haiphong? There are a few low-key sights to keep you busy, but the museums have the most obscure opening times in the country.

The **Haiphong Museum** (66 P Dien Bien Phu; admission free; 8-10.30am Tue & Thu, 7.30-9.30pm Wed & Sun), in a splendid colonial building, concentrates on the city's history; some of the displays have English translations. Nearby, the **Navy Museum** (Bao Tang Hai Quan; P Dien Bien Phu; 8-11am Tue, Thu & Sat) is possibly popular with visiting sailors and veterans.

Check out the neoclassical **Opera House** (Nha Hat Lon; P Quang Trung) which dates from 1904, its facade embellished with white columns. If you can get inside its interior is even more ornate.

Du Hang Pagoda (Chua Du Hang; 121 P Chua Hang) was founded three centuries ago. Though it has been rebuilt several times, it remains a fine example of traditional Vietnamese architecture and sculpture. P Chua Hang itself is narrow and bustling with Haiphong street life, and is fun to wander along.

Sleeping

Accommodation in central Haiphong is pretty limited, with lots of ageing government places typified by dusty corridors and gloomy rooms.

Kim Thanh Hotel (☎ 374 5264; 67 P Dien Bien Phu; r US$17-21;) Nothing fancy, but probably the best bet for a reasonably priced hotel in Haiphong. The rooms are old-fashioned but kept clean, and have TV and minibar. Breakfast is included.

our pick **Monaco Hotel** (☎ 374 6468; monacohotel@vnn.vn; 103 P Dien Bien Phu; r US$25, ste US$35-50;) An excellent deal, this bright, modern and very central hotel has a real polish about it, including the smart lobby where the helpful reception staff speak some English. The very spacious, spotless rooms with two double beds and attractive bathrooms are well presented and chintz-free, while the suites can easily accommodate four.

Harbour View Hotel (☎ 382 7827; www.harbourviewvietnam.com; 4 P Tran Phu; s/d US$118/132;) This stately hotel does have plenty of class, though not quite as much as the tariffs suggest, so be sure to ask for a discount. Designed in classic colonial style, the 122 rooms are comfortable and have excellent facilities, plus there's a gym, spa and restaurant. Breakfast is included.

Other options:

Hotel du Commerce (☎ 384 2706; 62 P Dien Bien Phu; r US$12-22;) Occupies a fine historic building, and though the rooms are now very dated and unloved, it does have a good central location.

Duyen Hai Hotel (☎ 384 2134; 6 Đ Nguyen Tri Phuong; r 240,000-340,000d;) Offers fair value and is worth a try if other places are full.

Huu Nghi Hotel (☎ 382 3244; www.huunghihotel.vn; 60A P Dien Bien Phu; r US$70-80;) It's overpriced and it looks like a Soviet-style concrete block but the rooms are in decent shape. Insist on a discount.

Eating

Haiphong is noted for its sumptuous fresh seafood. P Quang Trung has a strip of places with point-and-cook tanks as well as *bia hoi* (beer) joints. For stylish cafes and restaurants take a wander along P Minh Khai.

Com Vietnam (☎ 384 1698; 4A P Hoang Van Thu; mains 20,000-60,000d; lunch & dinner) Diminutive, unpretentious restaurant with a small patio, this place hits the spot for its affordable local seafood and Vietnamese specialities.

Van Tue (☎ 374 6338; 1 P Hoang Dieu; mains 25,000-160,000d; lunch & dinner) Capacious place that's renowned for its seafood, including an amazing selection of crab dishes. Wash it all down with home-brewed Czech beer.

our pick **BKK** (☎ 382 1018; 22 P Minh Khai; mains 34,000-90,000d; lunch & dinner) The card proclaims 'trendy Thai restaurant' and it's damn right. A lot of thought has gone into the dining experience here, and whether you eat inside the lovely, carefully restored old townhouse or outside on the little front patio, it's the perfect

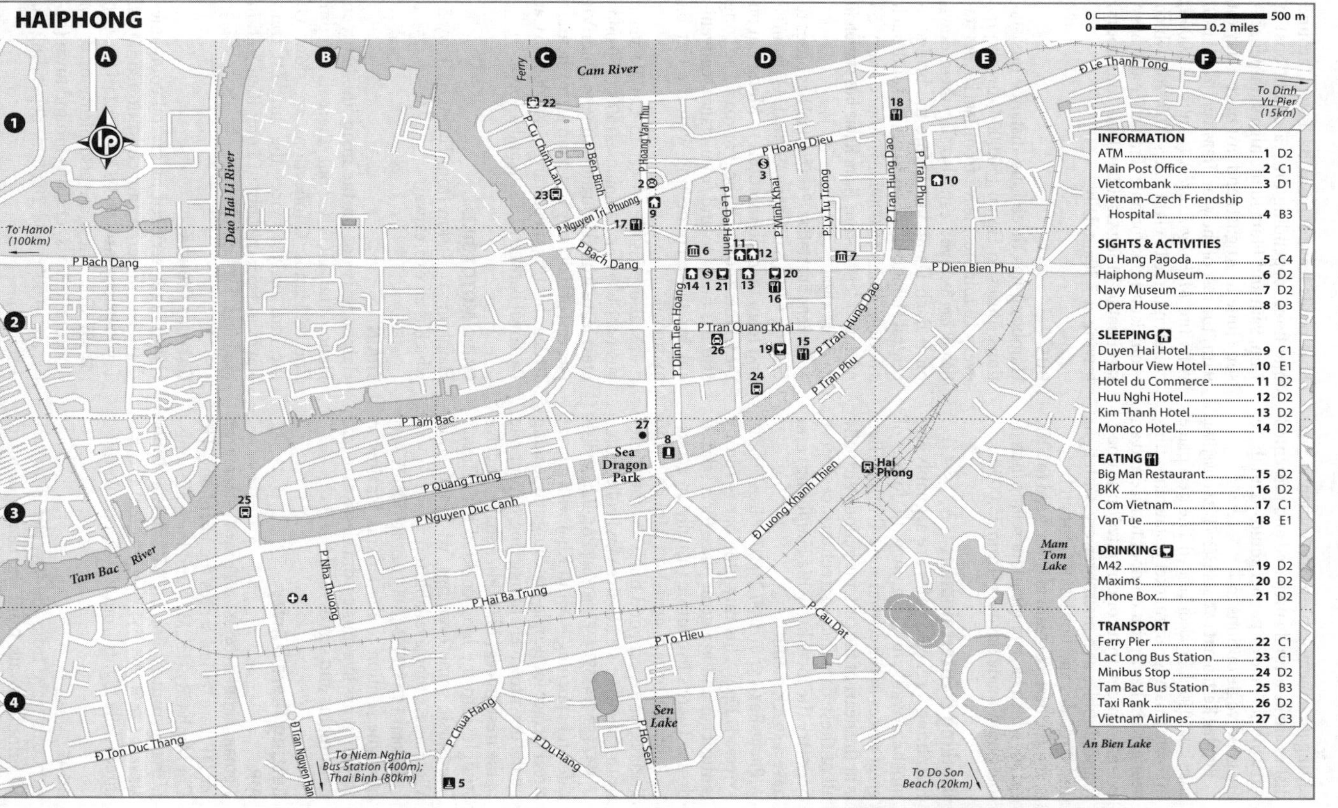
HAIPHONG
0 500 m
0 0.2 miles
INFORMATION
ATM....1 D2
Main Post Office....2 C1
Vietcombank....3 D1
Vietnam-Czech Friendship Hospital....4 B3
SIGHTS & ACTIVITIES
Du Hang Pagoda....5 C4
Haiphong Museum....6 D2
Navy Museum....7 D2
Opera House....8 D3
SLEEPING
Duyen Hai Hotel....9 C1
Harbour View Hotel....10 E1
Hotel du Commerce....11 D2
Huu Nghi Hotel....12 D2
Kim Thanh Hotel....13 D2
Monaco Hotel....14 D2
EATING
Big Man Restaurant....15 D2
BKK....16 D2
Com Vietnam....17 C1
Van Tue....18 E1
DRINKING
M42....19 D2
Maxims....20 D2
Phone Box....21 D2
TRANSPORT
Ferry Pier....22 C1
Lac Long Bus Station....23 C1
Minibus Stop....24 D2
Tam Bac Bus Station....25 B3
Taxi Rank....26 D2
Vietnam Airlines....27 C3
To Dinh Vu Pier (15km)
To Hanoi (100km)
To Do Son Beach (20km)
To Niem Nghia Bus Station (400m); Thai Binh (80km)
Cam River
Dao Hai Li River
Tam Bac River
Mam Tom Lake
An Bien Lake
Sen Lake
Sea Dragon Park
Hai Phong
Ferry
Đ Le Thanh Tong
P Tran Phu
P Tran Hung Dao
P Dien Bien Phu
P Ly Tu Trong
P Minh Khai
P Hoang Dieu
P Le Dai Hanh
P Tran Quang Khai
P Dinh Tien Hoang
P Hoang Van Thu
P Nguyen Tri Phuong
Đ Ben Binh
P Cu Chinh Lan
P Bach Dang
P Tam Bac
P Quang Trung
P Nguyen Duc Canh
P Hai Ba Trung
P Nha Thuong
Đ Tran Nguyen Han
Đ Ton Duc Thang
P Chua Hang
P Du Hang
P Ho Sen
P To Hieu
P Cau Dat
Đ Luong Khanh Thien

setting for a memorable meal. Authentic Thai dishes are beautifully prepared and presented – try the *lab moo* or pepper squid – and there are good vegie options too.

Big Man Restaurant (☎ 384 2383; 7 P Tran Hung Dao; mains from 50,000d; 🕑 lunch & dinner) The new place in town, this huge upmarket restaurant-cum-beer garden has a great outdoor terrace and an extensive menu that concentrates on seafood. It also doubles as a microbrewery, with light and dark ales and bottles of German beer.

For the best ice cream in town, head to BKK (p136) which has a miniparlour selling incredible home-made flavours (from 25,000d).

Drinking & Entertainment

Haiphong's relaxed cafes are arguably the most enjoyable in Vietnam, with dozens of great places in the central zone: P Minh Hieu is at the heart of the caffeine action. Virtually all of these cafes have street terraces, serve beer (try the local brew Bia Haiphong) and have a snack menu.

Phone Box (☎ 0123 487 2873; 79 P Dien Bien Phu; 🕑 noon-11.30pm) This tiny little bar is run by a musician and is a great place for a relaxed drink. There's live music (usually an acoustic guitarist or jazz artist) on Mondays and Fridays, or expect good tunes at other times from the owner's extensive vinyl collection.

M42 (☎ 374 5659; 42 P Minh Khai) Popular, stylish cafe on happening P Minh Khai with a great street terrace for people-watching and soaking up the downtown Haiphong vibe. Savour one of the fresh juices (25,000d), a shake, or delve straight into the long cocktail list. There's live music some evenings, wi-fi and good Vietnamese food available too.

Maxims (☎ 382 2934; 51B P Dien Bien Phu) A sort of vague relation to the famous Maxims in Saigon, it has live music from classical to jazz most nights and serves food.

Getting There & Away

AIR

Vietnam Airlines (☎ 381 0890; www.vietnamair.com.vn; 30 P Hoang Van Thu) serves the Haiphong–Ho Chi Minh City (HCMC) and the Haiphong–Danang routes. For HCMC, **Jetstar Pacific Airways** (☎ 04-3955 0550; www.jetstar.com) also has direct daily flights from US$66 one-way.

BOAT

All boats leave from the **ferry pier** (Đ Ben Binh), 10 minutes' walk from the centre of town. Hydrofoils leave for Cat Ba Town (around one hour, depending on sea conditions) at 7am, 9am and 11am in the high summer season (June to August) and just once a day (at 9am) the rest of the year. **Transtour** (☎ 384 1009) runs the *Mekong Express* (adults 135,000d, children three to eight years 70,000d), which is quick and comfortable. Transtour also has a fast boat to Mong Cai (280,000d, four hours) leaving at 7.30am daily.

BUS

Haiphong has three long-distance bus stations. Buses to Hanoi (50,000d, two hours, every 10 minutes) leave from **Tam Bac bus station** (P Tam Bac); you can also flag them down on P Bach Dang, just before the bridge in central Haiphong. Buses to points south such as Ninh Binh (65,000d, 3½ hours, every 30 minutes) leave from **Niem Nghia bus station** (Đ Tran Nguyen Han).

Lac Long bus station (P Cu Chinh Lan) has buses to Halong City (Bai Chay; 35,000d, 1½ hours), and from there connections to Mong Cai on the Chinese border by boat or road. Lac Long also has buses to and from Hanoi, convenient for those connecting with the Cat Ba hydrofoil.

It's also possible to get to Cat Ba via a bus-boat-bus route. Minibuses (5000d, 30 minutes) leave from P Quang Trung to Dinh Vu pier east of Haiphong City from where there are 10 daily boat/bus departures (100,000d) to Cat Ba Town between 7.15am and 5.15pm.

CAR & MOTORBIKE

Haiphong is 103km from Hanoi on Hwy 5, which is an expressway.

TRAIN

Haiphong is not on the main line between Hanoi and HCMC, but there is a spur line to Hanoi. Connections are slow. Of the four daily services the quickest train leaves at 8.55am daily to Long Bien station (33,000d, 2½ hours).

Getting Around

Haiphong is serviced by several companies that use metered, air-conditioned taxis. Try **Haiphong Taxi** (☎ 383 8383) or **Taxi Mai Linh** (☎ 383 3833). There are also plenty of *xe om* (motorbike taxis) cruising around town (between 10,000d and 20,000d, depending on distance).

AROUND HAIPHONG

Do Son Beach

Do Son Beach, 21km southeast of central Haiphong, is a honky-tonk seaside resort that is popular with Vietnamese for karaoke and massage. The 4km-long promontory ends with a string of islets, and the peninsula's nine hills are known as Cuu Long Son (Nine Dragons). There are plenty of colourful fishing boats on the water and a long promenade, but the beaches are disappointingly small and disappear completely at high tide.

The final part of the peninsula, lined with pine trees and small hotels, is the most attractive stretch of beach. This is also where you'll find Vietnam's first casino, the **Doson Resort Hotel** (☎ 031-386 4888; www.dosonresorthotel.com.vn), which is open to foreigners but not Vietnamese.

Do Son town is famous for its ritual **buffalo fights**, the finals of which are held annually on the 10th day of the eighth lunar month, usually late September or October, and which commemorates the date when the leader of an 18th-century peasant rebellion was killed here.

HALONG BAY

☎ 033

Majestic and mysterious, inspiring and imperious: words alone cannot do justice to the natural wonder that is Halong Bay. Imagine 2000 or more incredible islands rising from the emerald waters of the Gulf of Tonkin and you have a vision of breathtaking beauty.

The area was designated a World Heritage site in 1994. Many visitors can't help but compare the magical, mystical landscape of limestone islets to Guilin in China and Krabi in southern Thailand, but in reality Halong Bay is more spectacular. These tiny islands are dotted with grottoes created by wind and waves, and have sparsely forested slopes ringing with birdsong.

Beyond the breathtaking vistas on a boat cruise through the bay, visitors to Halong come to explore the caves – some of which are illuminated for the benefit of tourists – and to hike in Cat Ba National Park. There are few real beaches in Halong Bay, but Lan Ha Bay (p152) has dozens of idyllic sandy coves, dozens of which lie within a short hop of Cat Ba Town.

Sprawling Halong City is the main gateway to Halong Bay but not the ideal introduction to this incredible site. Most visitors sensibly opt for tours that include sleeping on a boat in the bay, while some travellers are now dodging Halong City completely and heading straight for Cat Ba Town, from where trips to less-visited (but arguably more alluring) Lan Ha Bay are easily set up. For more on tours around Halong Bay, see the boxed text on p142.

As the number-one tourist attraction in the northeast, Halong Bay draws a steady stream of visitors year-round. From February to April the weather in this region is often cool and drizzly. The ensuing fog can make visibility low, but this adds an ethereal air to the place and the temperature rarely falls below 10°C. During the summer months tropical storms are frequent, and tourist boats may have to alter their itineraries, depending on the weather.

Halong Bay is the stuff of myths and naturally the Vietnamese have concocted one. *Halong* translates as 'where the dragon descends into the sea'. Legend has it that the islands of Halong Bay were created by a great dragon that lived in the mountains. As it charged towards the coast, its flailing tail gouged out valleys and crevasses. When it finally plunged into the sea, the area filled with water, leaving only the pinnacles visible.

Information

All visitors must purchase a 30,000d entry ticket to the national park; this is usually included for those on a tour.

The official **Halong Bay Tourist Information Centre** (☎ 384 7481; www.halong.org.vn; 7am-4pm) is at Bai Chay dock in Halong City. Here you'll find English-speaking staff, free internet and excellent maps (20,000d) of the Halong Bay area.

For a virtual 360-degree tour of Halong Bay in full panorama, go to www.world-heritage-tour.org/asia/vn/halongbay/island.html.

Sights & Activities

CAVES

Halong Bay's limestone islands are peppered with caves of all shapes and sizes, many illuminated with technicolour lighting effects. Sadly, litter and trinket-touting vendors are very much part of the experience.

Hang Dau Go (Cave of Wooden Stakes) is a huge cave consisting of three chambers, which you reach via 90 steps. Among the stalactites

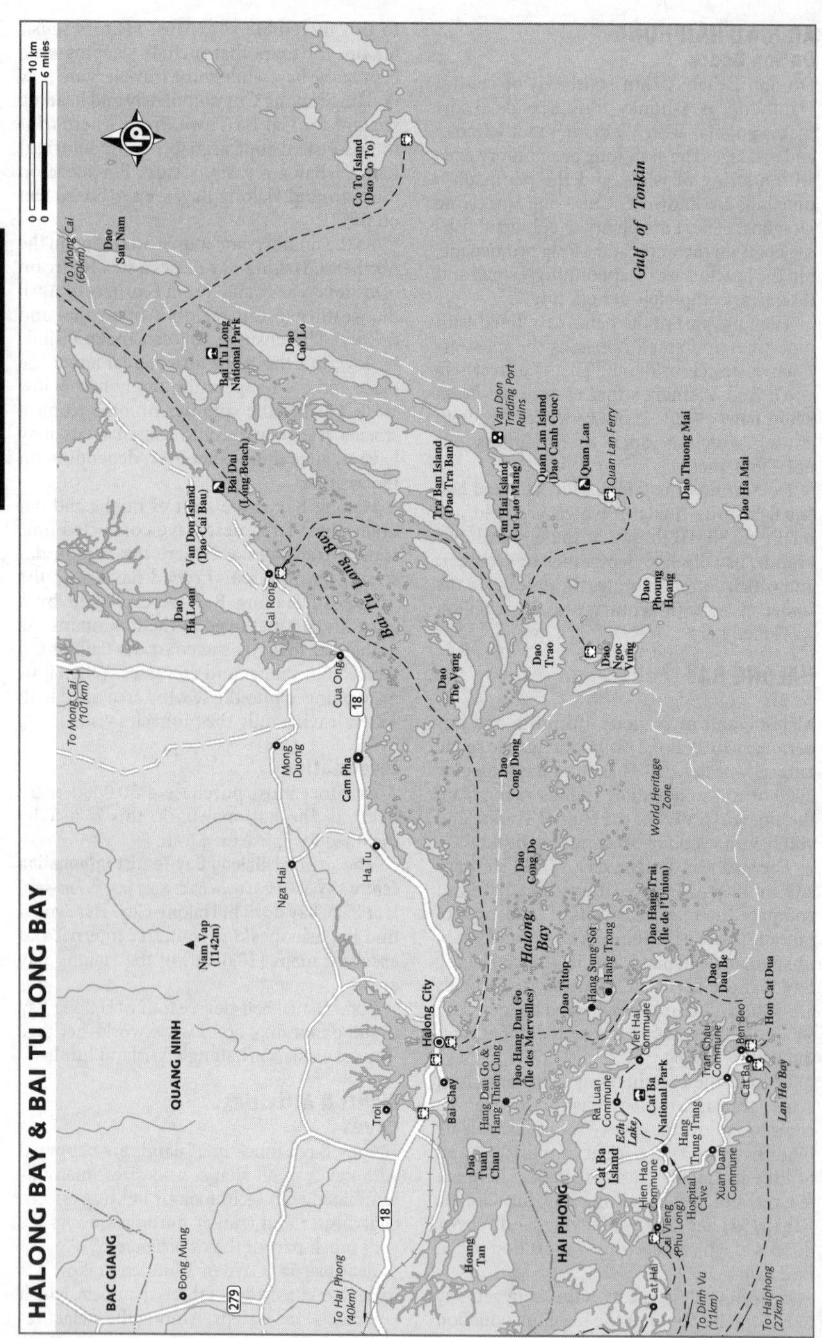
HALONG BAY & BAI TU LONG BAY
0 10 km
0 6 miles
BAC GIANG
QUANG NINH
HAI PHONG
Dong Mung
279
18
To Hai Phong (40km)
To Mong Cai (101km)
To Mong Cai (60km)
Nam Vap (1142m)
Troi
Bai Chay
Halong City
Nga Hai
Ha Tu
Cam Pha
Mong Duong
Cua Ong
Cai Rong
Dao Ha Loan
Van Don Island (Dao Cai Bau)
Bai Dai (Long Beach)
Bai Tu Long National Park
Dao Sau Nam
Dao Cao Lo
Co To Island (Dao Co To)
Gulf of Tonkin
Bai Tu Long Bay
Tra Ban Island (Dao Tra Ban)
Van Hai Island (Cu Lao Mang)
Van Don Trading Port Ruins
Quan Lan Island (Dao Canh Cuoc)
Quan Lan
Quan Lan Ferry
Dao Thuong Mai
Dao Ha Mai
Dao Phoung Hoang
Dao Ngoc Vung
Dao Trao
Dao The Vang
Dao Cong Dong
World Heritage Zone
Dao Cong Do
Dao Hang Trai (Île de l'Union)
Halong Bay
Hang Sung Sot
Hang Trong
Dao Titop
Dao Dau Be
Hon Cat Dua
Dao Hang Dau Go (Île des Merveilles)
Hang Dau Go & Hang Thien Cung
Dao Tuan Chau
Hoang Tan
Viet Hai Commune
Ra Luan Commune
Cat Ba National Park
Ech Lake
Cat Ba Island
Hang Trung Trang
Hien Hao Commune
Hospital Cave
Xuan Dam Commune
Tran Chau Commune
Ben Beo
Cat Ba
Lan Ha Bay
Cai Vieng (Phu Long)
Cat Hai
To Dinh Vu (11km)
To Haiphong (27km)

of the first hall, scores of gnomes appear to be holding a meeting. The walls of the second chamber sparkle if bright light is shone on them. The cave derives its Vietnamese name from the third chamber. This chamber is said to have been used during the 13th century to store the sharp bamboo stakes that Vietnamese folk hero and war general Tran Hung Dao planted in the bed of the Bach Dang River to impale Mongolian general Kublai Khan's invasion fleet. It's the closest cave site to the mainland. Part of the same system, the nearby **Hang Thien Cung** has 'cauliflower' limestone growths as well as stalactites and stalagmites.

Hang Sung Sot (Surprise Cave) is a popular cave to visit. It too has three vast and beautiful chambers; in the second there's an astonishing pink-lit rock phallus, called the 'Cock Rock' by some guides which is (not surprisingly) regarded as a fertility symbol. You have to hike up steps to reach it, and can take a loop walk through the cool interior and via a wooden bridge back to the bay.

Hang Trong (Drum Grotto) is so named because when the wind blows through its many stalactites and stalagmites, the effect resembles the sound of distant drumbeats.

Exactly which of the caves you visit is usually decided on the day you travel. It depends on several factors, including the weather and the number of other boats in the vicinity.

ISLANDS

Dao Tuan Chau (Tuan Chau Island), just 7km west of Halong City, was Ho Chi Minh's summer residence. Today it's connected to the mainland by a bridge, and home to the swanky 300-room **Tuan Chau Resort** (☎ 384 2115; r US$79-123;), which has a golf course and luxurious private villas, some facing an artificial white-sand beach. Be warned: some visitors may not appreciate the animal circus and dolphin shows.

Dao Titop (Titop Island) is a small island in the middle of the bay with a somewhat scruffy little beach. Ignore the beach's dubious charms and make for the summit of the island, which offers one of the best panoramic views of Halong Bay. It's cheaper than a chopper.

There are also several **floating villages** in the bay, which consist of a collection of ramshackle houses, some connected by wooden walkways. Each home has a ferocious dog (which never gets ashore). These villagers farm fish for a living, which are caught offshore and then fattened up in netted enclosures. Some tour operators include a visit to these villages as part of their Halong Bay itineraries.

Cat Ba Island (p146) is the best known and most developed of Halong Bay's islands. Cat Ba Town is very close to the gorgeous Lan Ha Bay region, in the southwest of Halong Bay, which has hundreds of limestone islets and sandy beaches and is less visited by tourists.

KAYAKING

A leisurely paddle among the karsts is an activity that has taken off in recent years and many tour operators include the option in their Halong Bay tours. This usually consists of about an hour (or less) exploring part of

PLAYING FOR HIGH STAKES

A military general and one of Vietnam's greatest heroes, Tran Hung Dao (1228–1300) defeated the Mongol warriors of the Chinese army no fewer than three times as they attempted to invade Vietnam.

His most famous victory was at the Bach Dang River in northeast Vietnam in 1288, which secured the country's sovereignty. He borrowed the military strategy of Ngo Quyen, who had regained Vietnam's independence in 939, following 1000 years of Chinese rule. After dark, sharpened bamboo poles – of a length designed to remain hidden underwater at high tide – were set vertically in the river, near the bank where it was shallow. At high tide, Tran Hung Dao sent small boats out – passing easily between the posts – to goad the Chinese warships to approach. As the tide receded, the impaled Chinese boats were left high and dry, and flaming arrows destroyed the fleet. In Halong Bay you can visit Hang Dau Go (Cave of Wooden Stakes; p139), where Tran Hung Dao's forces are said to have prepared and stored the bamboo poles.

Now you know why he is commemorated in all of those Tran Hung Dao streets in every Vietnamese town, and why every street parallel to a river is called Bach Dang, in memory of the victory.

NORTHEAST VIETNAM

the bay and kayaking through a hollow karst or to a floating village. A word of warning: be very careful when exploring the caves – we have received a report from two travellers who were sucked deep into a tunnel by a strong current and had to inch their way back in complete darkness. Remember that many tour operators use inexperienced guides and have inadequate safety standards.

If you're really keen on kayaking in Halong Bay, contact specialist operator **Handspan Adventure Travel** (☎ 04-3926 0581; www.handspan.com; 80 P Ma May, Hanoi), which runs professionally organised trips, has qualified guides and operates two beach camps; trips start from US$159.

Getting There & Away

AIR

Northern Airport Flight Service Company (☎ 04-3827 4409; 173 P Truong Chinh, Hanoi) offers a helicopter charter service from Gia Lam airport in Hanoi to Halong Bay on Saturdays from 8am. Free transfers are available from the Sofitel Metropole Hotel (p106). The cost for the charter service is US$230 per person, but it only runs with a minimum of six guests. The same helicopters can be privately chartered for US$3895 round trip.

BUS & BOAT

For the full picture on Halong Bay tours, see the boxed text below. Taking a tour is certainly convenient, and many are very cheap. But it's perfectly possible and increasingly popular for travellers to steer their own course to the region (although you will still need to take a tour to explore the islands). There are two possible routes to Halong Bay from Hanoi for independent travellers. The regular run is by bus from Hanoi to Halong City, and then heading to the Bai Chay harbour. Here you can either jump aboard a tour boat, or a Cat Ba tourist boat which takes in the main sites in Halong Bay before dropping you off in Cat Ba Town.

CRUISING THE KARSTS: TOURS TO HALONG BAY

There are many ways to experience the ethereal beauty of Halong Bay. Unless you have a private yacht (or you're an Olympian kayaker), you'll have to take a tour or set up a trip of some kind.

For a serious splurge, cruising the karsts aboard a luxury Chinese-style junk is hard to beat. There's also a very luxurious paddle ship, based on a French craft from the early 20th century. Halong from the deck of a junk over a gin and tonic as the sun sinks into the horizon is certainly a mighty fine sight. But be aware that nearly all of these luxury trips operate on a fixed itinerary, taking in the well-known caves and islands, and simply do not have the time to stray far from Halong City. Many 'two-day' tours actually involve less than 24 hours on a boat (and cost hundreds of dollars per person).

At the other end of the scale, budget tours sold out of Hanoi start from a rock-bottom US$20 per person for a dodgy day trip and rise to around US$140 for two nights on the bay with kayaking. We get heaps of complaints about poor service, bad food and rats running around boats, but these tend to be on the ultrabudget tours. Spend a little more and enjoy the experience a lot more. Most tours include transport, meals and, sometimes, island hikes. Drinks are extra (and generally quite pricey). Do bear in mind that most of these budget trips also follow a strict itinerary, with planned stops at illuminated caves and so on, and operate out of Halong City (where hundreds of tour boats are based).

For those that have a little more time and want to experience Halong Bay without the crowds, consider heading for Cat Ba Island. Here you'll find a couple of new adventure tour operators (p148) which concentrate on Lan Ha Bay, which is less frequented and still has an untouched, virgin feel, and some sublime sandy beaches. At the moment this is a backpacker-geared (and priced) experience on small sailing boats, with beach camping and bonfires, plus the option of some kayaking and fishing.

A word of warning about the weather. Boat tours are sometimes cancelled because of storms, and you'll probably be offered a (very partial) refund. You may want to ascertain in advance what that will be.

For a list of reliable Hanoi-based tour operators operating in Halong Bay see p87 or the Transport chapter (p506).

BOAT OPERATORS

This is just a selection of the most interesting companies.

Cruise Halong (☎ 04-3984 2807; www.cruisehalong.com; d from US$437) This company has two beautiful, very classy junks (and another under construction) with trademark ginger sails. Three-day cruises can be booked; there's 24-hour room service and great cuisine.

Emeraude Classic Cruise (☎ 04-3934 0888; www.emeraude-cruises.com; s/d US$339/413) A 56m replica paddle steamer with 38 air-conditioned cabins, all with elegant wooden furniture and smart hot-water showers. Lavish buffet-style meals are served. It is pricey, however, for a cruise that's less than 24 hours.

Indochina Sails (☎ 04-3984 2362; www.indochinasails.com; cabins from US$351) Cruise Halong on a traditional junk kitted out to a three-star standard. Indochina operates two 42m junks and one smaller craft; all have attractive wooden cabins and great viewing decks.

Tropical Sails (☎ 04-3923 2559; www.tropical-sails.com; s/d from US$127/196) This small outfit operates junks with large sails, allowing the boats to get up a head of steam on a windy day. The longer trips reach the Bai Tu Long Bay area.

The disadvantage of doing it this way is that you'll have to deal with Halong City and its chaotic harbour.

If you'd prefer to tailor your own trip, head to Loung Yen bus station in Hanoi and book a combined bus-boat-bus ticket to Cat Ba (p118). Once you're in Cat Ba Town you can set up a boat trip into Lan Ha Bay which has some of the most dramatic and least spoilt islands in the Halong Bay region, many with white-sand beaches ideal for camping out. However, trips from Cat Ba don't normally involve an overnight on a boat.

Getting Around

Virtually all boat tours leave from Bai Chay tourist dock in Halong City. Prices are officially regulated and depend upon the route, length of trip and class of boat. Some staff speak English and can usually hook you up with other people. This dock is something of a circus, with hundreds of people milling about as dozens of boats unload one set of passengers and welcome another. The swirling diesel fumes are hardly the best introduction to the delights of Halong Bay.

Official tour prices are quite reasonable at 50,000d to 60,000d per person per hour, on top of which you'll have to factor in the hire price of the boat (this cost is divided between the total number of people on board). A four-hour cruise on a one-star boat costs around 280,000d, or it's around 440,000d for a six-hour cruise on a two-star boat. You can rent out a whole two-star boat for the day for 4,000,000d. Tourist boats (five hours) to Cat Ba Island cost 140,000d per person; one leaves at noon daily.

HALONG CITY

☎ 033 / pop 193,700

Halong City is the main gateway to Halong Bay. Until 2008, this port was very much a city of two halves, with ferries the only means of transport between its east and west banks, but there's now a sweeping new suspension bridge across the divide. Though the city enjoys a stunning position on the cusp of Halong Bay, developers have not been kind to it, and have dumped a succession of high-rise hotels along the shoreline. However, the majority of food, accommodation and other life-support systems for Halong Bay are found here.

Most travellers no longer stay in town, preferring to spend a night out in Halong Bay itself, and increased competition for a dwindling clientele has meant that budget hotel rates are some of the cheapest in Vietnam. Indeed many locals are now studying Chinese in preference to English, and looking to the east and the domestic market to fill the void.

Orientation

Halong City occupies two peninsulas that jut into the northern part of Halong Bay. By far the most important district for travellers is the western half, Bai Chay, which has the vast majority of hotels and restaurants, and the tourist boat dock.

Hon Gai district, on the eastern side of the bay, is much grittier. Its port concerns itself with coal exports rather than tourism, which means it's a bit grubby, but at least there is some local flavour.

Note that many long-distance buses will be marked 'Bai Chay' or 'Hon Gai' rather than 'Halong City'.

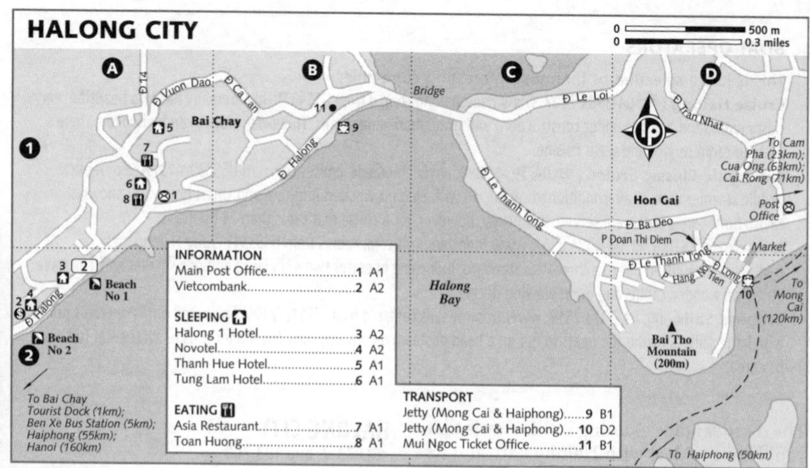

Information

Main post office (Đ Halong) Conveniently placed at the bottom of Vuon Dao.

Vietcombank (Đ Halong) Cashes travellers cheques and has an ATM.

Beaches

Local 'beaches' were basically mud and rock until the authorities corrected things with tonnes of imported white sand. However they're not great for swimming as the water is pretty murky.

HALONG BAY'S VERY OWN LOCH NESS MONSTER

The dragon that gave birth to Halong Bay may be legend (see p139), but sailors have often reported sightings of a mysterious marine creature of gargantuan proportions known as the *tarasque*. The more paranoid elements of the military suspect it's an imperialist spy submarine, while eccentric travellers believe they have discovered Vietnam's version of the Loch Ness monster. Meanwhile, the monster – or whatever it is – continues to haunt Halong Bay, unfettered by the marine police, Vietnam Tourism and the immigration authorities. Enterprising Vietnamese boat owners have made a cottage industry out of the creature, offering cash-laden tourists the chance to rent a junk and pursue the *tarasque* before it gets bored and swims away.

Sleeping

Most people stay on a boat in the bay rather than in a hotel in Halong City. But if you do spend a night here you'll find hundreds of hotels in Bai Chay, and prices are very reasonable outside the peak season (June to August) or during the Tet festival.

Virtually all budget accommodation is on the 'hotel alley' of Đ Vuon Dao, which is home to around 50 near-identical mini-hotels, with comfortable doubles available at US$10 or less a night. Midrange and top-end hotels are scattered along bay-facing Đ Halong, many commanding great views.

Tung Lam Hotel (☎ 364 0743; 29 Đ Vuon Dao; r US$8-12; ❄) This mini-hotel is making a little more effort than most on this strip. The rooms – all with two beds, TV, minibar and attractive en-suite bathrooms – have been recently renovated, and those at the front are really spacious and have a balcony.

Thanh Hue Hotel (☎ 384 7612; Đ Vuon Dao; r US$12-15; ❄ 💻) Continue up, up, up the hill from the Tung Lam and you come to this great-value hotel – look for the powder-blue paint job. Most rooms have cracking views of the bay from their balconies.

Halong 1 Hotel (☎ 384 6320; Đ Halong; r US$35, ste US$55; ❄ 💻) Set back from the harbour road, this grand old hotel has a peaceful setting and plenty of colonial character. However it is a government-run place so don't expect snappy service, and the furnishings are looking a tad tired. Catherine Deneuve stayed here during the filming of *Indochine*. Breakfast is included.

CLIMBING THE KARSTS

The word is out. If you've ever considered it, or been tempted to climb, Halong Bay is a superb place to go for it – the karst cliffs here offer exceptional climbing amid stunning scenery. Most climbers in Cat Ba are complete novices, but as the instruction is excellent, many leave Cat Ba completely bitten by the bug.

You don't need great upper-body strength to climb, as you actually use your legs far more. The karst limestone of Halong Bay is not too sharp and quite friendly on the hands, and as many of the routes are sheltered by natural overhangs that prevent the climbable portion of the rock from getting wet, climbing is almost always possible, rain or shine.

Beginners' climbing trips, organised by Slo Pony Adventures (p149), are located on walls inland on Cat Ba Island or out on beautiful Lan Ha Bay. You'll be kitted up with a harness and climbing shoes, given instruction and taught the fundamentals of the climbing and belaying technique, then given a demonstration. Then it's over to you (with your climbing instructor talking you through each move, and anchoring you, of course!). Most people are able to complete a couple of climbs at Hai Pai and Moody's Beach, which are ideal for beginners.

The vertical cliffs of Halong and Lan Ha bays are also perfect for deep-water soloing, which is basically climbing alone, without ropes or a harness, and using the ocean as a water bed in case you fall. This is obviously only for the experienced, and it's essential to know the depth of water and tidal patterns. It's customary to finish a solo climb with a controlled freefall (or 'tombstone') into the sea and a swim back to the shore, or your boat.

our pick **Novotel** (☎ 384 8108; www.novotelhalongbay.com; Đ Halong; r from US$103; ⊠ ⊞ ⊟ ⊡) The interior designers have done an amazing job here, creating a sleek, hip hotel by fusing Asian and Japanese influences with contemporary detailing. The rooms are simply stunning, with teak floors, marble bathrooms and sliding screens to divide living areas. Facilities include an oval infinity pool, an espresso bar and a great restaurant. Rates are hefty, but the website often has promotions that drop room prices as low as US$75.

There's also a luxury hotel on the nearby island of Dao Tuan Chau (p141) but it's very much geared towards the local market.

Eating

For cheap, filling food there are some modest places at the bottom of Đ Vuon Dao with English menus and low prices. Seafood lovers should gravitate to the harbourfront Đ Halong, where there's a cluster of good places – many have fish tanks out front.

Toan Huong (☎ 384 4651; 1 Đ Vuon Dao; meals from 25,000d) A simple place with friendly staff, a street terrace and an extensive menu (in English) that has a bit of everything: Western breakfasts, salads, fresh seafood and imported wine.

Asia Restaurant (☎ 384 6927; 24 Đ Vuon Dao; mains 35,000-60,000d) A clean, attractive place that's geared to travellers' tastes, with good Vietnamese food and a smattering of Western favourites. The owner speaks excellent German and pretty good English.

Getting There & Away

BOAT

For all the details on boat trips throughout Halong Bay, see p142.

With a marked improvement in roads around the region, boat transport is not nearly as popular as it once was. The hydrofoil to Mong Cai remains a good option for anyone overlanding to China. Slow boats occasionally still sail to Haiphong; these leave from Hon Gai harbour, but very irregularly now.

From Bai Chay, **Mui Ngoc** (☎ 384 7888; Đ Halong) operates hydrofoils to Mong Cai (US$20, three hours) leaving at 8am and 11am. The trip is definitely preferable to the long road journey. Book ahead, as demand often outstrips supply.

The best way to get to Cat Ba Island is to hop onto the regular tourist boats from Bai Chay boat dock. It costs 160,000d one-way, including a leisurely cruise through the most beautiful parts of the bay. An extra 30,000d allows entry to the most important caves and grottoes. The whole trip takes about five or six hours; there's one daily departure at noon (and more in high season, June to early September).

As always, be prepared for changes to these schedules.

WATCH THOSE VALUABLES!

Take real care with your valuables when cruising the waters of Halong Bay. Do not leave them unattended as they might grow legs and walk. Always try and ensure there is someone you know and trust watching your gear on a day cruise. When it comes to overnight cruises, most boats have lockable cabins.

BUS

All buses leave from the new **Ben Xe bus station** which is 6km south of central Bai Chay, just off Hwy 18. Buses leave from here to all stations in Hanoi (65,000d, 3½ hours) every 15 minutes. Other destinations include Haiphong (35,000d, 1½ hours) every 20 minutes; Mong Chai (65,000d, 4½ hours) every 15 minutes; Cai Rong (35,000d, 1½ hours) for Van Don Island (Dao Cai Bau) every 30 minutes; and Lang Son (80,000d, six hours) daily at 12.30pm.

CAR & MOTORBIKE

Halong City is 160km from Hanoi and 55km from Haiphong. The one-way trip from Hanoi to Halong City takes about three hours by private vehicle.

Getting Around

Bai Chay is fairly spread out, so metered taxis are a good option for moving around. **Mai Linh** (☎ 382 2226) is a reliable option. Taxis also wait by the bus station and post office.

CAT BA ISLAND

☎ 031 / pop 13,500

Rugged, craggy and jungle-clad Cat Ba, the largest island in Halong Bay, is fast emerging as Vietnam's adventure sport and ecotourism mecca. There's a terrific roll-call of activities here – sailing trips, bird-watching, biking, hiking and rock climbing – and some fine tour operators organising them.

Except for a few fertile pockets, Cat Ba's terrain is too rocky for serious agriculture; most residents earn their living from the sea, while others cater to the tourist trade. In recent years the main settlement of Cat Ba Town has experienced a hotel boom, and a chain of ugly concrete hotels now frames a once-lovely bay. But as the rest of the island is untouched, and the idyllic islands of Lan Ha Bay lie just offshore, it's easy to forget the over-development of Cat Ba Town after a day or two.

Almost half of Cat Ba Island (which has a total area of 354 sq km) and 90 sq km of the adjacent waters were declared a national park in 1986 to protect the island's diverse ecosystems. These include subtropical evergreen forests on the hills, freshwater swamp forests at the base of the hills, coastal mangrove forests, small freshwater lakes and coral reefs. Most of the coastline consists of rocky cliffs, but there are some sandy beaches hidden away in small coves and some tiny fishing villages dotted around the shore.

There are numerous lakes, waterfalls and grottoes in the spectacular limestone hills, the highest of which rises 331m above sea level. The largest permanent body of water on the island is **Ech Lake**, which covers an area of 3 hectares. Almost all of the surface streams are seasonal; most of the island's rainwater flows into caves and follows underground streams to the sea, which creates a shortage of fresh water during the dry season.

Lan Ha Bay (p152), encompassing the southern seas off Cat Ba, is dotted with hundreds of jungle-topped limestone islands and offers numerous deserted beaches to explore. You could spend a year here discovering a different islet every day, swimming and snorkelling the bay's turquoise waters.

The best weather on Cat Ba Island is from late September to November, when air and water temperatures are mild and skies mostly clear. December to February is cooler, but still pleasant. From February to April is another good time to visit though you can expect some rain, while the summer months, from June through August, are hot and humid, with occasional thunderstorms. This is also peak season and the island is packed with Vietnamese tourists from Hanoi and beyond.

Cat Ba Town

First impressions of Cat Ba Town are not great; the ageing mirrored windows of its skinny high-rise hotels look like a low-rent Manhattan. But appearances are deceptive in this case, for this town is all front, and only extends for a street or two behind the promenade.

Most of the year Cat Ba Town is actually a pretty laid-back place and it certainly makes a handy base for some serious adventures of the hiking, biking and climbing kind around the island, or sailing and kayaking around Lan Ha Bay. But on summer weekends Cat Ba turns into a roaring resort, filling up with vacationing Vietnamese. Hotel prices double or treble and there's an excess of karaoke joints and hubbub. So many people flood into town that cars are banned from the promenade, which is taken over by a sea of strolling holidaymakers. Weekdays are saner, but still busy between June and August.

Ho Chi Minh paid a visit to Cat Ba Island on April 1 1951 and there is a large annual festival on the island to commemorate the event.

INFORMATION

Internet Access

Cat Ba has several internet places on the waterfront but, at 15,000d an hour or more, prices are quite high, and the connections sluggish.

Money

Agribank has an ATM on the harbour, and a **branch** (☎ 388 8227) 1km north of town, for changing dollars. **Vu Binh Jewellers** (☎ 388 8641) cashes travellers cheques at 3% commission and does credit-card cash advances at 5%.

Post

The **main post office** (Đ 1-4) is a one-stop shop for postal needs and telephone calls.

Tourist Information

The best impartial advice is at **Slo Pony Adventures** (p149), where the helpful crew can bring you up to speed on everything from transport connections to the best *pho bo* (beef noodle soup) joint. *Cat Ba Biosphere Reserve* maps are available.

Don't expect much help from the official **Tourism Information & Development Centre** (☎ 368 8215; www.catba.com.vn; Đ 1-4) where staff are more interested in peddling tours than information.

SIGHTS

A **monument** to Ho Chi Minh stands up on Mountain No 1, the hillock opposite the pier in Cat Ba Town. The **market** at the northern end of the harbourfront is a fascinating, authentically local affair with twitching crabs, jumbo shrimps and pyramids of fresh fruit.

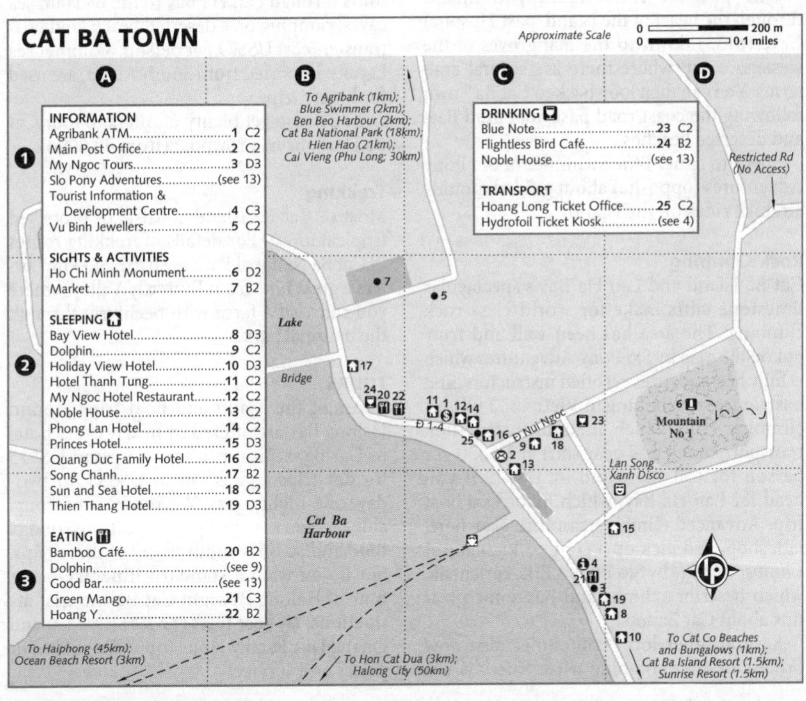

MONKEY BUSINESS

Monkey Island in Cat Ba National Park is included in many itineraries. However the troop of monkeys here is pretty aggressive and many travellers have been bitten. The bite itself can be painful and shocking, but worse are the rabies shots that follow. You might like to save the monkey business for somewhere more interesting like Cuc Phuong National Park (p196).

ACTIVITIES

Above all else, Cat Ba really is a superb base for all manner of adventure sports – on the island itself and in, on and over the water.

Mountain Biking

Rented bicycles are a great way to explore the island and many of the hotels can arrange Chinese mountain bikes (around 80,000d per day), while Blue Swimmer rents Trek bikes for US$12 per day. There are also some tandems available for double the pedal power.

One possible route takes you inland through the heart of the island, past Hospital Cave (p153) down to the mangroves of the western coast, where there are several crab farms. You can then loop back to Cat Ba Town following the coast road past tidal mud flats and deserted beaches.

Speak to either Blue Swimmer or Slo Pony Adventures (opposite) about guided mountain bike rides on the island.

Rock Climbing

Cat Ba Island and Lan Ha Bay's spectacular limestone cliffs make for world-class rock climbing. The area has been well and truly put on the map by Slo Pony Adventures which is fully licensed, uses certified instructors, and has pioneered climbing in Vietnam. Full-day climbing trips which include instruction, transport, lunch and gear start at US$50 per person for Cat Ba Island or US$75 if you head for Lan Ha Bay, which involves a boat trip. Advanced climbers can hire gear here, talk shop, and pick up a copy of *Vietnam: A Climber's Guide* by Slo Pony's Erik Ferjentsik, which describes climbs and has some great tips about Cat Ba too.

Several other local companies also now profess to offer climbing trips. Safety is not something you want to gamble with. See the boxed text Climbing the Karsts (p145) for the full rundown.

Sailing & Kayaking

You certainly shouldn't miss the spectacular islands and beaches of Lan Ha Bay (p152) while you're here. Blue Swimmer offers wonderful **sailing excursions** at reasonable rates to the myriad islands around Cat Ba. Overnight sailing trips through Lan Ha Bay to Nam Cat beach, including a night sleeping in a bamboo hut, cost US$39 per person. Full-day trips on a Chinese junk to Long Chau lighthouse (built by the French in the 1920s and still bearing bomb scars from the American War) are US$49. Private boat charters with a skipper start at US$60 for a half-day trip.

Plenty of hotels in Cat Ba can rent you a **kayak** for the day, with rates starting at around US$8 per day. Blue Swimmer has good quality kayaks (US$12), which you can use to explore the Cat Ba coast. Overnight kayak-and-camp packages (US$20) take in a paddle over to Nam Cat with accommodation and dinner on the beach. Guided overnight kayak tours through Lan Ha Bay to the Ba Ham sea caves, camping on a deserted beach, and boat transfers cost US$79 per person. Skimmer sea kayaks, imported from South Africa, are used for longer trips.

You'll also get plenty of offers to tour Cat Ba Harbour in a rowboat (from 40,000d).

Trekking

Most of Cat Ba Island consists of protected tropical forest. For details of trekking routes in Cat Ba National Park see p152. Slo Pony offers a great hike from Butterfly Valley (where you can visit a farm with beehives) through the national park.

TOURS

Tours of the island and boat trips around Halong Bay are offered by nearly every hotel in Cat Ba; typical prices are around US$15 for day trips and as low as US$35 for two-day, one-night tours. We receive unfavourable feedback – cramped conditions, dodgy food and so on – about many of these trips, but if you want a standard itinerary-based tour of Halong Bay and Cat Ba's tourist attractions, **My Ngoc Tours** (☎ 388 8199; Đ 1-4) and Quang Duc Family Hotel (opposite) offer fair prices and service.

If you're looking for a different experience, the following adventure tour operators understand travellers' needs and will steer you away from the tourist trail to really special areas of Cat Ba, Lan Ha Bay and beyond.

Blue Swimmer (☎ 368 8237; www.blueswimmersailing.com; Ben Beo harbour) A very well-organised, environmentally conscious new outfit set up by Vinh, one of the founders of Handspan, a respected tour operator. Superb sailing and kayak trips, trekking and biking excursions are offered.

Slo Pony Adventures (☎ 368 8450; www.slopony.com; Noble House, Đ 1-4) A highly professional company run by two uberpassionate climbers and explorers: Onslow Carrington and Erik Ferjentsik. Climbing instruction is their real expertise but they also offer excellent well-structured sailing, biking and hiking trips.

SLEEPING

Cat Ba has dozens of hotels, in all price categories. Many are tall, thin ugly concrete numbers painted all shades of a faded rainbow, but some better options are starting to emerge. Most hotels are situated on (or just off) the waterfront in Cat Ba Town and have at least one staff member who speaks English. For more of a back-to-nature scene there are a couple of beachfront options close to Cat Ba Town, including one on a private island.

Room rates fluctuate greatly. In the high-season summer months (June to August) you can expect to pay a minimum of US$15 per room; rates sink to below US$10 for a decent room outside this time. The rates given here are for low season. Peak season rates are impossible to determine as hotel owners tend to pick a number out of their head depending on demand.

Budget

Song Chanh (☎ 388 8402; Đ 1-4 178; r US$7-10; ❄) A well-maintained place with spacious, airy rooms that all come with good-quality beds and bathrooms attached. All those at the front boast stunning harbour views.

Phong Lan Hotel (☎ 388 8605; Đ 1-4; r US$7-10; ❄) It is worth requesting a room at the front of this hotel, right in the middle of the seafront strip, which has balconies overlooking the harbour. The English-speaking owner is helpful and there's a travel agency here too.

Dolphin (☎ 388 8804; Đ Nui Ngoc; r US$8-10; ❄) It's quite plain, but this place has five simple, functional tiled rooms (all with two beds and a TV) and the en-suite bathrooms have hot water and tubs. Owner Trung speaks fluent English and understands travellers' needs; there's a restaurant on the ground floor too. Also known as the Luong Son Quan.

Bay View Hotel (☎ 368 8241; Đ 1-4; r US$8-15; ❄) An excellent new English/Vietnamese-owned mini-hotel with a prime harbourfront spot and very competitive rates. All the modern rooms are spruce indeed: pick one at the front for a huge bay-view window. There's a little cafe downstairs.

our pick Noble House (☎ 388 8363; thenoblehousevn@yahoo.com; Đ 1-4; r US$8-17; ❄) A cut above the competition, this excellent place is well geared to travellers' needs. Check in here and you've got the town's best bar, a good cafe and Slo Pony Adventures right on site. Rooms are really stylish and excellent value, with simple yet elegant furniture, TV, fridge and shower room. Prices double between June and August though. Book ahead.

Quang Duc Family Hotel (☎ 388 8231; Đ 1-4; r from US$10; ❄) Deservedly popular for years, this cheap and friendly family hotel has just seven rooms, and satellite TV and hot water come as standard.

Sun and Sea Hotel (☎ 388 8315; www.sunseahotel.com.vn; Đ Nui Ngoc; r US$12-15; ❄) A good choice, this harbourfront hotel has 31 well-presented rooms with satellite TV and minibar, some with bay views. A breakfast is thrown in for good measure and kayaks are available for hire.

Tien Thang Hotel (☎ 388 8568; tienthanghotel@yahoo.com; Đ 1-4; r US$12-15; ❄) Offering more comfort and space than most in this price range, these rooms have satellite TV and big bathrooms and some come with sea-view balconies.

Other options:

My Ngoc Hotel Restaurant (☎ 388 8363; Đ 1-4; r US$8; ❄) Long-running place with sparse but well-scrubbed, good-value rooms, plus a restaurant and kayaks for hire.

Hotel Thanh Tung (☎ 388 8364; Đ 1-4; r US$8-11; ❄) Right on the seafront strip, this clean place boasts that it has 'bed rooms forward sea', which is sea-view rooms to the uninitiated.

Travelling through Vietnam can mean sleeping in a lot of noisy towns and cities, but in Cat Ba you have the chance to stay right on a sandy beach at Cat Co 2, where there are nine little thatched wooden **bungalows** (☎ 031-350 8408; 250,000d). Though the bungalows are tiny and represent nothing much more than a mattress, a fan and a roof over your head, they are well spaced around an attractive, leafy beachside plot. There's a shower block and cafe for meals (around 50,000d).

Alternatively, the small village of Hien Hao offers homestays in local houses. This is quite an authentic experience and what's more the villagers are very friendly. For details contact **Mr Tuan** (☎ 388 8737). Hien Hao is just over 20km from Cat Ba Town or 12km from the ferry landing at Cai Vieng (also known as Phu Long).

Midrange & Top End

Princes Hotel (☎ 388 8899; www.princeshotel-catba.com; Đ Nui Ngoc; r US$25-35;) Despite the incredibly uninviting lobby, this is actually supposed to be one of the smarter addresses in town. The frilly net curtains and furniture won't win any style awards, but the rooms are at least well equipped and spick and span. It also has a rooftop bar and basement nightclub.

Holiday View Hotel (☎ 388 7200; www.holidayviewhotel-catba.com; Đ 1-4; r US$45-70;) It's destroyed the Cat Ba skyline, but if you can live with that, this 13-storey landmark does offer unrivalled views of the bay. Rooms here are certainly stylish, with wooden floors, cream bed linen, modern bathrooms and balconies. Breakfast is included and there's a large restaurant.

our pick **Ocean Beach Resort** (☎ 321 2668; www.oceanbeachresort.com.vn; r per person from US$35) Located on a private island about 4km from Cat Ba Town, this special place makes a wonderful quiet base for a few days, with its own slim sandy beach, restaurant and kayaks. All seven Thai-style bungalows are simply constructed from wood and bamboo, but have top-quality beds, fans and front porches for sea gazing. At dinner time, tables are often placed right on the beach and guests eat together. Most people visit here as part of a tour run by Hanoi's Ocean Tours (p90) but independent travellers are always welcome. Cat Ba Town is a 20-minute boat ride away, with free connections for guests. The owner plans to open a low-key chill-out bar here in the future.

Cat Ba Island Resort (☎ 368 8686; www.catbaislandresort-spa.com; Cat Co 1; r US$105-185;) Large water-park resort with a huge pool and plenty of tubes and slides to keep the family splash-happy. The main hotel structure is an attractive, vaguely neocolonial affair. All rooms look over the hotel grounds to the bay, and have tropical-style decor, with wooden flooring and rattan furniture. It's a better bet in the low season, as the water park draws huge crowds during the summer months (June to August).

Sunrise Resort (☎ 388 7360; www.catbasunriseresort.com; Cat Co 3; r from US$110;) This beachfront resort has been quite thoughtfully and tastefully planned, with low-rise tiled-roofed blocks sitting below green cliffs. Rooms are spacious and smart, all with sea-view balconies, and the facilities include a swimming pool and spa and kiddies' playground. Breakfast is included.

EATING

Most of the best places are dotted along the seafront strip, though you shouldn't neglect the floating restaurants offshore (see opposite). For a cheap feed, head to the food stalls in front of the market where there's plenty of cheap grub.

our pick **Bamboo Café** (☎ 388 7552; Đ 1-4; dishes 30,000-75,000d) The best for a casual bite on the seafront, this enjoyable little place has a small harbour-facing terrace and an intimate bamboo-walled interior. Tuan, the genial owner, is a fluent English speaker and serves up very generous portions of Vietnamese and international food, and there's wine available by the glass.

Hoang Y (☎ 090 403 7902; Đ 1-4; dishes 30,000-90,000d) The extensive menu at this well-run restaurant, run by the highly talkative chef-patron Mr Long, includes a few Western treats (including shakes and pancakes) and some vegie choices, but it's the fresh seafood that really stands out.

Dolphin (☎ 388 8804; Đ Nui Ngoc; mains 35,000-50,000d) Popular with travellers for its pasta, pizza and breakfasts but also serves up tasty Vietnamese food. Don't worry, definitely no dolphin!

our pick **Green Mango** (☎ 388 7151; Đ 1-4; mains 80,000-220,000d) For inventive, creative cuisine this is the restaurant of choice in Cat Ba Town. There's an incredibly tempting menu that includes lamb shank, smoked duck and blackened barramundi (160,000d) as well as more inexpensive pasta dishes. It is also a great venue for a cocktail or three, either in the lounge bar–style interior or outside on the terrace.

Otherwise you could try:

Good Bar (☎ 388 8363; Đ 1-4; meals 45,000d-80,000d). The most popular backpacker hang-out in town, with a

FLOATING RESTAURANTS

There are numerous 'floating' seafood restaurants just offshore on Cat Ba Harbour. It's best to work out the price in advance, as well as the cost of a boat to get you out there and back, as we've heard reports of overcharging. Locals advise heading around the bay to the couple of floating restaurants in Ben Beo Harbour which are less touristy. A boat ride there and back, including waiting time, should cost around 60,000d. Ask your hotel to recommend a boat.

One of these restaurants is **Xuan Hong** (☎ 388 8485), a fish-farm-cum-restaurant at Ben Beo Pier, where you can get up close and personal with your dinner first. Select a live victim or two from the pen and they'll be grilled, fried or steamed for your table in no time. Prices simply go by weight and type of seafood; you can eat your fill of a selection of fish for around 100,000d per person.

(mainly) Western menu; try the lumberjack burger. Also sells wine and has a full cocktail list.

DRINKING

Bar culture is casual and relaxed in Cat Ba Town. There are a couple of publike places, or you can head to the drink stalls at the eastern end of the harbour, crack open a cold one, and watch the world go by.

our pick **Noble House** (☎ 388 8363; Đ 1-4) Party HQ for travellers, this superb upper-floor bar has a real vibe, and the drinking, flirting and story-telling goes on until late most nights. It comes fully equipped with pool tables, plenty of space and terrific harbour views.

Flightless Bird Café (☎ 388 8517; Đ 1-4; 🕒 from 6.30pm) Small pub with a dart board, chilled beer, Californian wine and posters of the Kiwi motherland plastered over the walls. There's also a small book exchange.

Blue Note (Đ Nui Ngoc) Although not quite as popular as it once was, this singalong-style bar has a karaoke list including alt-rock anthems, alongside plenty of the usual cheesy hits.

GETTING THERE & AWAY

Cat Ba Island is 45km east of Haiphong and 50km south of Halong City. Be aware that there are several piers. Most handy is the jetty directly in front of Cat Ba Town from where the hydrofoils to Haiphong depart. A second popular one is at Ben Beo, about 2km from Cat Ba Town where most of the tourist boats berth. There's a third pier at Cai Vieng (also known as Phu Long), 30km northwest of Cat Ba Town which is the one used by bus-boat-bus connections from Hanoi and Haiphong. At Cai Vieng, motorbike drivers wait to whisk passengers from the ferries to town (or the 15km to Cat Ba National Park) for about 70,000d. Some public buses also meet the boats.

If you're heading for Hanoi it's often easiest to buy a combined bus-boat-bus ticket (160,000d, 4½ hours). There are between seven and ten daily departures, operated by two companies based on the seafront: **Hoang Long** (☎ 031-268 8008), which offers a slightly more reliable service, and **Hoang Yen** (☎ 098 294 1285). Travelling this way involves a bus to Cai Vieng harbour, a 40-minute boat trip to the mainland, a minibus to the bus company terminal and a large bus to Hanoi. Though it sounds a hassle, the system is well set up and reliable and you won't have to spend long waiting for a connection. You can also travel this way to Haiphong (120,000d, 2½ hours).

Hydrofoils (which take over an hour, though they are advertised as taking 45 minutes) also link Cat Ba directly to Haiphong. Several companies run the route, with three departures a day in the high summer season and just one a day the rest of the year. Summer season services depart between 10am and 5pm. **Transtour** (☎ 388 8314) runs the *Mekong Express* (120,000d, 2.45pm departure), which is the safest and most comfortable option. Tickets are available from the hydrofoil ticket kiosk on the harbour.

For details about boat connections from Halong City to Cat Ba see p145. Heading the other way is less organised; check schedules at Slo Pony Adventures (p149).

GETTING AROUND

Bicycle and motorbike rentals are available from most of the hotels (both around US$5 to US$7 per day). If you're heading out to the beaches or national park, pay the parking fee for security. If you're looking for a decent mountain bike or a guided bike tour, contact one of the tour operators on p149.

Beaches

A 15-minute walk southeast from Cat Ba Town, the three beautiful **Cat Co cove beaches** boast white sand and good swimming. Cat Co 2, backed by limestone cliffs, is the beach to head for; here you'll find a lovely sheltered sandy bay, a snack bar and some simple thatched beach huts (see p149). However, as developers have been eyeing up this beach for some time, check first to see if it remains a haven of tranquillity.

Cat Co 1 and 3 were once equally as attractive, but both have now been developed as resorts. On weekends in summer they get packed with Vietnamese tourists and litter becomes a real blight. The wooden cliffside walkway that once connected Cat Co 1 and 2 is broken.

Other beaches include Cai Vieng, Hong Xoai Be and Hong Xoai Lon.

Lan Ha Bay

The 300 or so karst islands of Lan Ha Bay are directly south and east of Cat Ba Town. Geologically they are very much an extension of Halong Bay, but geographically these islands lie in a different province of Vietnam. They share the same emerald sea, and the limestone pinnacles and scenery are every bit as beautiful as Halong Bay, but these islands have the additional attraction of numerous white sand beaches. Lan Ha Bay is a long way from Halong City, so virtually no tourist boats based there venture to this side of the bay. In short, Lan Ha Bay has a more isolated, off-the-beaten-track appeal (and far fewer visitors).

Around 200 species of fish, 500 species of mollusc, 400 species of arthropod and numerous hard and soft coral live in Lan Ha Bay. Larger marine animals in the area include seals and three species of dolphin.

Sailing and kayak trips here are best organised in Cat Ba Town. With hundreds of **beaches** to choose from it's easy to find your own private patch of sand for the day. Camping is permitted on gorgeous **Hai Pie beach** (also known as Tiger beach) which is used as a base camp by the Cat Ba adventure tour operators and also hosts occasional full-moon parties. Lan Ha Bay also offers superb rock climbing and is the main destination for trips run by Slo Pony Adventures (p149).

Cat Ba National Park

This accessible **national park** (☎ 321 6350; admission up to 2hr 15,000d, 4-7hr 35,000d, with guide 50,000-150,000d; ⏰ dawn-dusk) is home to 32 types of mammals – langurs and macaques, wild boar, deer, civets, several species of squirrel including the giant black squirrel – and more than 70 species of birds, including hawks, hornbills and cuckoos. The golden-headed langur is officially the world's most endangered primate with around 65 remaining, most in this park. Cat Ba lies on a major migration route for waterfowl, which feed and roost on the beaches in the mangrove forests. Over a thousand species of plants have been recorded here, including 118 trees and 160 plants with medicinal value. The park is also home to the Cay Kim Gao tree. In ancient days, kings and nobles would eat only with chopsticks made from this timber, as anything poisonous it touches is reputed to turn the light-coloured wood to black.

A guide is not mandatory, but is definitely recommended; otherwise, all you are likely to see is a canopy of trees. The multi-chambered **Hang Trung Trang** (Trung Trang Cave) is easily accessible, but you will need to contact a ranger to make sure it is open. Bring a torch (flashlight) as it is gloomy inside.

There's a challenging 18km hike through the park and up to one of the mountain summits. Arrange a guide for this six-hour hike, and organise a bus or boat transport to the trailhead and a boat to get back to town. All of this can be easily organised with rangers at the national park headquarters or at Slo Pony Adventures (p149) in Cat Ba if you're travelling independently.

Many hikes end at Viet Hai, a remote minority village just outside the park boundary, from where boats shuttle back to Cat Ba Town (about 300,000d per boat). Don't get stranded here or you'll get stuck. Take proper hiking shoes, a raincoat and a generous supply of water for this hike. Independent hikers can buy basic snacks at the kiosks in Viet Hai, which is where many hiking groups stop for lunch. This is *not* an easy walk, and is much harder and more slippery after rain. There are shorter hiking options that are less hard-core.

To reach the national park headquarters at Trung Trang, take a public minibus from the market place in Cat Ba Town (12,000d, 20 minutes). Another option is to hire a motorbike for around 40,000d one-way.

Hospital Cave

Hospital Cave (☎ 368 8215; admission 15,000d; 🕐 7am-4.30pm) oozes historical significance, as it served both as a secret, bomb-proof hospital during the American War and as a safe house for VC leaders. Built between 1963 and 1965 (with assistance from China), this incredibly well-constructed three-storey feat of engineering was in constant use until 1975. A guide (most know a few words of English) will show you around the 17 rooms, point out the old operating theatre and take you to the huge natural cavern which was used as a cinema (and even had its own small swimming pool). The cave is about 10km north of Cat Ba Town on the road to the national park entrance.

BAI TU LONG BAY

☎ 033

There's more to northeastern Vietnam than Halong Bay. The sinking limestone plateau, which gave birth to the bay's spectacular islands, continues for some 100km to the Chinese border. The area immediately northeast of Halong Bay is part of **Bai Tu Long National Park** (☎ 379 3365).

Bai Tu Long Bay is every bit as beautiful as its famous neighbour. Indeed, in some ways it's more beautiful, since it has scarcely seen any tourist development. This is both good news and bad news. The bay is unpolluted and undeveloped, but there's little tourism infrastructure. It's pretty hard travelling around and staying here and it's difficult to get information.

Charter boats can be arranged to Bai Tu Long Bay from Halong Bay; rates start at 200,000d per hour and the trip there takes about five hours. A cheaper alternative is to travel overland to Cai Rong and visit the outlying islands by boat from here. Foreigners are almost always charged double the going rate on the ferries around Bai Tu Long Bay.

Van Don Island (Dao Cai Bau)

Van Don is the largest (around 30 sq km), most populated and most developed island in the archipelago. However, there remains only very limited tourism development here to date. **Cai Rong** (pronounced Cai Zong) is the main town on the island. **Bai Dai** (Long Beach) runs along much of the southern side of the island and is hard-packed sand with some mangroves. Just offshore there are stunning limestone **rock formations**.

The only hotels are at Cai Rong Pier (Cai Rong Pha), about 8km north of the bridge to the mainland. Cai Rong is an unattractive, bustling port full of karaoke bars and motor bikes but it does have a couple of decent hotels: **Hung Toan Hotel** (☎ 387 4220; r 140,000d; ❄) is good value while **Viet Linh Hotel** (☎ 379 3898; r 210,000d; ❄) is fancier. Down on Bai Dai the **Bai Tu Long Ecotourism Resort** (☎ 379 3156; www.atiresorts.com; bungalows 275,000-500,000d; ❄) is a far more attractive place to stay, with fine beachside bungalows or more traditional rooms in stilt houses.

Frequent buses run between Hon Gai (Halong City) and Cai Rong bus station (32,000d, 1½ hours) along a road lined with coal mines. There's also a hydrofoil operated by **Mui Ngoc** (☎ 379 3335), which leaves Halong City (US$12, one hour) at 8am and returns to Halong City at 4pm. These boat schedules are dependent on the weather.

Hanoi tour operators (p87) including Ethnic Travel run trips here. **ATI** (www.atiresorts.com) operates ecolodges on Van Don and Quan Lan Islands, and offers a combination of tours around the bay.

Other Islands

Cai Rong Pier is on the edge of Cai Rong town. Boat charters (from 150,000d per hour) can be organised here to the outlying islands.

QUAN LAN ISLAND (DAO CANH CUOC)

The main attraction here is a beautiful, 1km-long **white-sand beach** shaped like a crescent moon. The water is clear blue and the waves are suitable for surfing. There are several other blissful beaches on the eastern seaboard, though sea temperatures are a bit chilly between January and April.

The northeastern part of the island has some battered **ruins** of the old Van Don Trading Port. There are several cheap accommodation options on the island: **Minh Vu Guesthouse** (☎ 387 7479) and **Vinh Ly Guesthouse** (☎ 387 7354) both have solar-powered hot water and rooms around the 140,000d mark. The beachfront **Quan Lan Ecotourism Resort** (☎ 387 7417; www.atiresorts.com; bungalows 190,000-400,000d) has a choice of comfortable bungalows or a large stilt house for larger groups.

Daily ferries connect Quan Lan and Cai Rong (40,000d, two hours), departing Cai Rong at 2pm and Quan Lan at 7am, so a trip to the island requires an overnight stay.

TRA BAN & NGOC VUNG ISLANDS

One of the largest islands in the Bai Tu Long region, Dao Tra Ban offers some of the most dramatic karst scenery in the bay. The southern part of the island is blanketed in thick jungle and provides a habitat for many colourful butterflies. There are boats to and from Van Don Island's Cai Rong Pier at 7am and 2pm (35,000d, 90 minutes).

Dao Ngoc Vung borders Halong Bay and has some dramatic limestone cliffs and a great beach on its southern shore, where you'll find some basic **beach huts** (150,000d). Daily boats link Cai Rong (departing 1pm) and Dao Ngoc Vung (departing 6am), costing 75,000d for foreigners and taking three hours.

CO TO ISLAND

In the northeast, Dao Co To is the furthest inhabited island from the mainland. Its highest peak reaches a respectable 170m. There are numerous other hills, and a large lighthouse atop one of them. The coastline is mostly cliffs and large rocks, but there's at least one fine sandy **beach**. Fishing boats usually anchor just off here, and you can walk to some of the boats during low tide. There is a small and very basic guesthouse on the island.

Ferries bound for Dao Co To depart Cai Rong Pier on Mondays, Wednesdays and Fridays at unspecified times; check the schedule in Cai Rong. They return from Dao Co To on Tuesdays, Thursdays and Fridays. The one-way fare is 50,000d and the journey takes about five hours, depending on the winds.

MONG CAI & THE CHINESE BORDER

☎ 033 / pop 76,700

A bustling border city, Mong Cai is an upwardly mobile place which thrives on booming trade with China. Huge industrial zones are being created on its outskirts, and plots are being snapped up by Chinese and foreign corporations. Vast new buildings and shopping malls are under construction in the city centre. For the Vietnamese, the big draw here is the chance to purchase low-priced (and low-quality) Chinese-made consumer goods. For the Chinese, the attraction is mostly gambling (two huge casinos are nearly complete).

Chinese speakers will find plenty of opportunity to practice in Mong Cai. Other than the prospect of crossing the border, Mong Cai is of no real interest to tourists.

Information

Vietcombank (P Van Don) changes travellers cheques and has an ATM. Internet access is available in a cluster of places just off P Hung Vuong near the post office for around 3000d per hour.

Sleeping & Eating

The nearby beach retreat of Tra Co (opposite) is a good alternative to staying in town, but there are masses of hotels in Mong Cai.

Two huge casino resorts, the Loi Lai and the Hoang Van, were nearing completion when we passed by, and should be open by the time you read this.

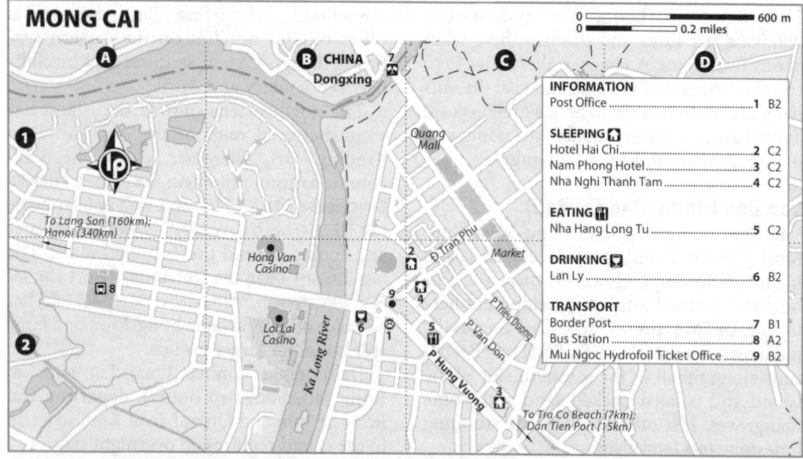

Nha Nghi Thanh Tam (☎ 388 1373; 71 Đ Trieu Duong; r 150,000d; ❄) A family-run place with simple, clean, comfortable rooms which have hot-water bathrooms that (for those who have just arrived and can't sort their dong from their yuan) cost just US$9. There are plenty of other comparable options on this street.

Hotel Hai Chi (☎ 388 7939; 52 P Tran Phu; r 180,000d; ❄) A clean, well-kept place where the attractive rooms have wooden furniture and wood-panelling. Most are triples.

Nam Phong Hotel (☎ 388 7775; P Hung Vuong; r 225,000-250,000d; ❄ 💻) An upmarket place with spacious, well-equipped rooms that have satellite TV and wi-fi. On the ground floor there's a flashy lobby, bar and restaurant serving good Chinese and Vietnamese dishes. As there's no lift, rooms on the 5th floor are discounted.

Ngha Hang Long Tu (☎ 377 0489; P Hung Vuong; mains 25,000-60,000d) A long-running restaurant, this place is best for its table-top barbecues, steamboats or seafood.

Lan Ly (☎ 388 4336; 2 P Ho Xuan Houng; coffee from 10,000d) In need of a caffeine fix before you deal with the border? Rev up here at this friendly coffee bar which has a street terrace with a view of Mong Cai's traffic action.

There are also plenty of food stalls on P Hung Vuong, inc½luding several good spots near the Nam Phong Hotel.

Getting There & Away

BOAT

Mui Ngoc (☎ 322 2988; P Hung Vuong) runs daily air-conditioned hydrofoils from Mong Cai to Halong City (320,000d, three hours) at 2pm and 5pm (returning at 8am and 11pm from Halong City). **Transtour** (☎ 388 1214; 43 P Tran Phu) also operates a daily hydrofoil (four hours) between Mong Cai and Haiphong at 2.30pm.

From Mong Cai, shuttle vans leave the hydrofoil ticket offices for the pier at Dan Tien Port, about 15km away. Arriving in Mong Cai, the hydrofoils often berth in the middle of the open sea; don't worry, you haven't broken down! Low tides require a transfer by small boat.

BUS

Mong Cai is located 340km from Hanoi. The bus terminal is on Hwy 18, about 3km from the border. Buses run to and from all bus stations in Hanoi (110,000d to150,000d, eight hours) roughly every 20 minutes until 1pm, then less frequently until 10.30pm. Buses head to Halong City (65,000d, 4½ hours) every 10 minutes.

From Mong Cai to Lang Son (100,000d, seven hours) there is just one bus a day at 1pm.

> **BORDER CROSSING: MONG CAI–DONGXING**
>
> Mong Cai is located on the Chinese border in the extreme northeastern corner of Vietnam. One of three official international overland border crossings with China, it's open from 7am to 7.30pm daily. It's about 3km between the border and Mong Cai bus station; aim to pay around 15,000d on a *xe om* (motorbike taxi).

AROUND MONG CAI

Tra Co Beach

☎ 033

Located in the extreme northeast of Vietnam, right by the Chinese border, Tra Co is a fine, gently shelving beach of pale sand some 17km in length. This is one of the longest stretches of sandy beachfront real estate in Vietnam and, inevitably, it's succumbing to tourist development.

It's still a small-scale resort, but there's a high season between May and August, with many Vietnamese, Chinese and even a few Malaysian tourists. Out of season it's well worth the detour (from Mong Cai, not Hanoi). It's peaceful, clean and beautiful, and the shore is lined with coastal pine trees. And the beach restaurants could not have fresher seafood.

There are plenty of hotels and guesthouses; those described here have direct beach frontage. Low-season rates are given; expect inflation in high season.

Tra Co Beach Hotel (☎ 388 1264; r 140,000-200,000d; ❄) This rambling old government hotel has a prime location on the beach. The rooms are looking a little weary these days but are still serviceable enough for a night or two.

Hotel Gio Bien (☎ 388 5802; r from 150,000d; ❄) Owned and managed by the very hospitable Van Bong family, this small hotel has a welcoming atmosphere. The rooms are a little cluttered, with a few frilly touches, but have a certain charm. If you're here in the quiet season you should be able to get a room at the front with a (shared) sea-view balcony.

NEIGHBOURING TENSIONS

Mong Cai is a free-trade zone with plenty of frenetic activity in the city's booming markets and malls. It wasn't always so. From 1978 to 1990 the border was virtually sealed. How two former friends became such bitter enemies and were reconciled is a spicy story.

China was on good terms with North Vietnam from 1954 (when the French left) until the late 1970s. But relations began to sour shortly after reunification, as the Vietnamese government became more and more friendly with China's rival, the USSR.

In March 1978 the Vietnamese government launched a campaign in the south against 'commercial opportunists', seizing private property to complete the country's 'socialist transformation'. The campaign hit the ethnic Chinese particularly hard.

The anti-capitalist and anti-Chinese campaign caused up to 500,000 of Vietnam's 1.8 million ethnic Chinese citizens to flee the country. Those in the north fled overland to China, while those in the south left by sea. The creation of Chinese refugees in the south proved to be lucrative for the government – to leave, refugees typically had to pay up to US$5000 each in 'exit fees'. Chinese entrepreneurs in Ho Chi Minh City (HCMC) had that kind of money, but refugees in the north were mostly dirt poor. In response, China cut all aid to Vietnam, cancelled dozens of development projects and withdrew 800 technicians. Vietnam's invasion of Cambodia in late 1978 was the final straw: Beijing – alarmed because the Khmer Rouge was its close ally, and worried by the huge build-up of Soviet military forces on the China–USSR border – became convinced that Vietnam had fallen into the Russian camp, which, it believed, was trying to encircle China with hostile forces. Ironically enough, this was exactly what Vietnam suspected about the Chinese–Khmer Rouge alliance.

In February 1979 China invaded northern Vietnam at several points along the border, but soon learned that Vietnam's troops, battle-hardened by many years of fighting the USA, were

Opposite Tra Co Beach Hotel, there are three seafood **restaurants** (meals US$5-8). **Thanh Hai** (☎ 378 0124) is the most popular, with tanks and bowls full of live crab, squid, grouper, tiger prawns and huge clams. Pick your victim(s) and you're charged per kilo; the prices are on the board.

GETTING THERE & AWAY

Tra Co is 8km from Mong Cai and connected by a regular bus service. Taxis charge around 80,000d one-way, or it's about 30,000d in a *xe om*.

LANG SON

☎ 025 / pop 79,200 / elev 270m

Lang Son is a booming border city, connected by a fast highway to Hanoi and very close to Chinese border. Surrounded by a nest of karst peaks, Lang Son is in an area populated largely by Tho, Nung, Man and Dzao tribal people, though their influence is not that evident in the city itself.

The city was partially destroyed in February 1979 by Chinese forces (see the boxed text, above); the ruins of the town and the devastated frontier village of Dong Dang were frequently shown to foreign journalists as evidence of Chinese aggression. Although the border is still heavily fortified, both towns have been rebuilt and Sino–Vietnamese trade is in full swing again.

This is not a town to linger in, but if you find yourself with a few hours to spare there's enough to explore, and the night market is fascinating. Most travellers come to Lang Son when crossing between Vietnam and China: the border is actually just outside Dong Dang, 18km to the north.

Information

There are very few internet places in central Lang Son, but guests (and nonguests) can get online for 5000d per hour at the Van Xuan Hotel (opposite), which has several terminals in its lobby.

Vietin Bank (51 Đ Le Loi) has an ATM and can aid all your currency needs; the **main post office** (Đ Le Loi) is next door.

Sights & Activities

There are two large and beautiful **caves** (admission 5000d; 🕑 6am-6pm) in the suburbs of Lang Son. Both are illuminated, which makes for easy exploration, and have Buddhist altars inside. **Tam Thanh Cave** is vast and seductive.

no pushovers. Although China's forces were withdrawn after 17 days, and the operation was officially declared a great success, most observers concurred that China's army of 200,000 troops had been badly mauled by the Vietnamese. The Chinese fought without a military hierarchy, failed to use air power to support ground forces, and used runners instead of radios for communication. China suffered around 20,000 casualties in 29 days of fighting – despite many of Vietnam's strongest troops being in Cambodia at the time. There are no accurate figures for Vietnamese casualties but it's estimated that around 15,000 militia and civilians were killed or wounded.

Officially, this conflict is considered ancient history. Commerce across the China–Vietnam border is roaring ahead and both countries profess to be on good terms. In practice, trade may be booming but political tensions continue. Disputes over the Spratly Islands and oil-drilling rights in the South China Sea continue and the border area remains militarily sensitive.

If you visit China and discuss this border war, you will almost certainly be told that China acted in self-defence because the Vietnamese were launching raids across the border and murdering innocent Chinese villagers. Virtually all Western observers, from the US government's Central Intelligence Agency to historians, disagree. The war, according to Gerald Segal, author of *Defending China*, was a complete failure: 'China failed to force a Vietnamese withdrawal from [Cambodia], failed to end border clashes, failed to cast doubt on the strength of the Soviet power, failed to dispel the image of China as a paper tiger, and failed to draw the United States into an anti-Soviet coalition.'

For the inside story on how the communist comrades fell out, read *Brother Enemy* (1988) by Nayan Chanda, an excellent account of Cold War power plays and the making and breaking of alliances.

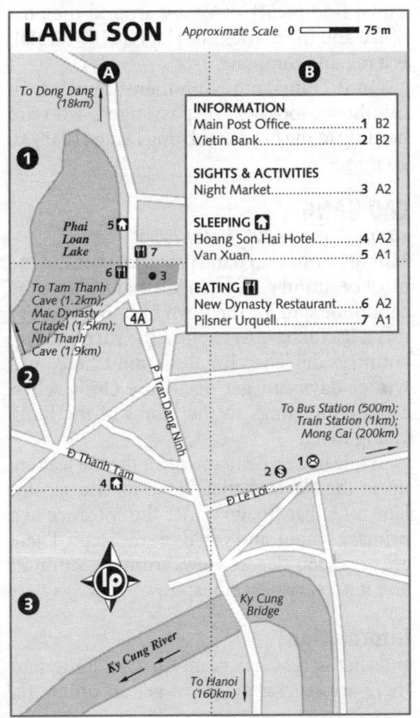

There's an internal pool and a viewing point or natural 'window' offering a sweeping view of the surrounding rice fields. Just a few hundred metres up a stone staircase are the ruins of the **Mac Dynasty Citadel**. It's a lovely, deserted spot, with stunning views across the countryside.

The Ngoc Tuyen River flows through **Nhi Thanh Cave**, 700m beyond Tam Thanh. The cave entrance has a series of carved poems written by the cave's discoverer, a soldier called Ngo Thi San, in the 18th century. There's also a carved stone plaque commemorating an early French resident of Lang Son, complete with his silhouette in European clothing.

Lang Son's huge **night market** (5pm-11pm) is a credit cruncher's delight, with hundreds of stalls selling cheapo electrical goods and fake clothes by 'Adides' and 'Versache'.

Sleeping & Eating

Van Xuan Hotel (371 0440; 147 P Tran Dang Ninh; r from 190,000d) A big glass-fronted structure that offers the best value in town. All the rooms are really well kept (and swept), light and airy, but the family rooms (320,000d) are particularly enormous and extremely comfortable; if you can, book room 606 which has

BORDER CROSSING: YOUYI GUAN–HUU NGHI QUAN

The Friendship Pass at Dong Dang–Pingxiang is the most popular border crossing in the far north. The border post itself is at Huu Nghi Quan (Friendship Gate), 3km north of Dong Dang town; a *xe om* (motorbike taxi) ride here will cost 20,000d per person. The border is open from 7am to 5.30pm daily, and there's a 500m walk between the Vietnamese and Chinese frontiers.

Entering Vietnam this way, there's an Agribank ATM at the border (and another in Dong Dang). Ignore touts offering bus tickets at the border and head straight to the Dong Dang minibus terminal which has services (80,000d, 3¼ hours) leaving every 30 minutes until 6pm. Otherwise head straight to Lang Son bus station and get a connection there; local minibuses are very regular and cost 10,000d for the 18km journey. A *xe om* is about 40,000d.

On the Chinese side, it's a 20-minute drive from the border to Pingxiang by bus or shared taxi. Pingxiang is connected by train and bus to Nanning, the capital of China's Guangxi province.

Three trains also link Hanoi and Lang Son daily, but these are very slow, taking over five hours – the bus is a much better option. Trains from Hanoi to Nanning and Beijing pass through this border, but it's not possible to jump aboard these services in Lang Son or Dong Dang. For the full picture about these cross-border trains see p119.

a balcony overlooking Phai Loan lake and the surrounding karst hills.

Hoang Son Hai Hotel (☎ 371 0479; 57 Đ Thanh Tam; r US$20-25; ❄) This slender mini-skyscraper is not quite as grand as its imposing marble lobby would suggest, but it does offer well-maintained, spacious rooms all with bathtubs, fridges and TV. Triples and quadruples are available.

Pilsner Urquell (☎ 371 3683; 208 P Tran Dang Ninh; dishes from 22,000d) A modern take on a traditional beer hall, this place has huge glass windows that look down over the lake. The menu has plenty of tempting plates from Central Europe including Czech sausages and German-style stewed pork, plus Vietnamese dishes. It doubles as a microbrewery with gorgeous dark or gold beer on tap.

New Dynasty Restaurant (☎ 389 8000; Phai Loan Lake; steamboat 100,000d) The most famous place in town, this slightly tacky bar-restaurant complex sits on a little peninsula that juts into the lake and has tables facing the water. Everyone is here for the steamboats, but there's also a draught-beer emporium.

There are plenty of other hotels and guesthouses in town, of much the same standard. Few have restaurants, but there are some *com pho* places in town and a couple of cheap restaurants near the bus station.

Getting There & Away

All buses leave from the large open terminal on Đ Le Loi. Buses for Hanoi (60,000d to 80,000d, three hours) leave every ten minutes until 6pm. Four daily buses (at 6am, 8am, 10am and 2pm) depart for Cao Bang (70,000d, five hours) along a rough road. There's also one daily service to Mong Cai (100,000d, seven hours) at 5am.

There are only very slow trains between Lang Son and Hanoi (42,000d, 5½ hours).

Getting Around

You'll find plenty of *xe om* around the post office and the market. **Taxi Tam Gia** (☎ 381 8181) is a reliable company.

On P Tran Dang Ninh there are plenty of minibuses looking for passengers who are heading to the border at Dong Dang (10,000d, 20 minutes).

CAO BANG

☎ 026 / pop 48,200 / elev 290m

Mountainous Cao Bang province is one of the most beautiful regions in Vietnam. The same cannot be said for the town of Cao Bang, but it is a useful base to explore the surrounding countryside. The climate is mild here, and winter days can get decidedly chilly when a thick fog clings to the banks of the Bang Giang River.

While in Cao Bang town, hit the hill leading up to the **War Memorial**. Head up the second lane off Đ Pac Bo, go under the entrance to a primary school, and you'll see the steps. There are great 360-degree views from the summit, and it's a very peaceful spot.

Information

Internet access has come to Cao Bang and there are several places to get an online fix on P Vuon Cam, just north of the Thanh Loan Hotel.

Cao Bang has several ATMs, including an **Agribank machine** in the grounds of the Bang Giang Hotel. The **Bank for Foreign Investment and Development** will change US dollars, but be prepared for a wait.

Sleeping & Eating

Nguyet Nga Hotel (☎ 385 6445; r from 150,000d) If you're on a real economy drive, this guest house fits the bill. The furniture is ancient, and the rooms are a bit gloomy, but they do all have a TV and fridge.

ourpick Hoanh Anh Hotel (☎ 385 8969; 131 Đ Kim Dong; r 200,000-220,000d) An exceptional new place, this smart mini-hotel has a positively sparkling lobby and very friendly staff who speak a little English. All the rooms are really attractive, with modern furnishings, quality mattresses, wi-fi, stylish shower rooms and chintz-free minimalist decor. See if you can book the room ending in 'one' on each floor (for example 201, 301 to 701) – these have balconies, so you'll also get a breathtaking view over the Bang Giang River.

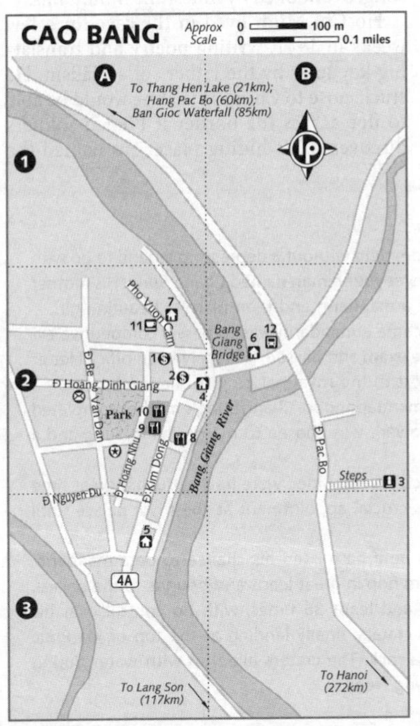

Thanh Loan Hotel (☎ 385 7026; 159 P Vuon Cam; thanh_loan_hotel@hn.vnn.vn; r 280,000d) Situated on a pleasant, quiet street with a cafe or two on its doorstep, this is a really efficient, spotless place where the spacious rooms all have high ceilings, dark wood furniture wi-fi and most have bathrooms with tubs. There's even a little bar area that's perfect for a nightcap. Rates include breakfast.

Bang Giang Hotel (☎ 385 3431; Đ Kim Dong; s/d 300,000/400,000d) Vast government-owned, Soviet-style concrete colossus, complete with shops and restaurants, which is starting to show her age. Rooms are large and in fair shape, and some have wonderful river views from their balconies. Service is spotty however.

Men Quyen Restaurant (☎ 385 6433; meals 25,000-50,000d) Tucked away behind the market, this modest little place has a buffet style set-up – just point to the dishes you want. Be sure to try the delicious *cha la lot* (cabbage rolls).

Huong Sen Hotel & Restaurant (☎ 385 4654; 100 Đ Kim Dong; meals 30,000-50,000d) This nine-storey hotel (rooms from 210,000d) has clean, perfectly adequate rooms (with wi-fi) but its ground-floor restaurant is the best in the town centre, with really fresh food, including river fish and some vegie choices at moderate prices. There's also a cafe on the top floor with great views.

Cao Bang also has some good cafes. **Coffee Pho** (☎ 395 0240; 140 P Vuon Cam) is a stylish little place with pavement tables that serves good Vietnamese coffee, cappuccino, juices and beer plus a snack or two.

INFORMATION
ATM.....1 A2
Bank for Foreign Investment and Development.....2 A2

SIGHTS & ACTIVITIES
War Memorial.....3 B2

SLEEPING
Bang Giang Hotel.....4 A2
Hoanh Anh Hotel.....5 A3
Nguyet Nga Hotel.....6 B2
Thanh Loan Hotel.....7 A2

EATING
Huong Sen Hotel & Restaurant.....8 A2
Men Quyen Restaurant.....9 A2
Trung Tau Market.....10 A2

DRINKING
Coffee Pho.....11 A2

TRANSPORT
Bus Station.....12 B2

NORTHEAST VIETNAM

You'll find cheap food stalls near the **Trung Tau market** (meals from 15,000d), and if you really want to taste the local delicacy, there's a line of late-night tripe stalls opposite the Hoanh Anh Hotel.

Getting There & Away

Cao Bang is 272km north of Hanoi, along Hwy 3. This is a sealed road, but due to the mountainous terrain, it's a full day's drive. From the **bus station** (Đ Pac Bo) there are 12 daily buses to and from Hanoi (105,000d to 117,000d, nine hours), and very regular buses to Thai Nguyen. Four daily buses go to and from Lang Son (70,000d, 4½ hours). If you're heading for the Ba Be Lakes you'll have to hop on a local bus to Na Phuc and then another to Cho Ra, where you'll need to hire a *xe om* for the final stretch into the national park.

AROUND CAO BANG

Thang Hen Lake

This large lake can be visited year-round; however, what you get to see varies according to the seasons. During the rainy season, from about May to September, the 36 lakes in the area are separated by convoluted rock formations. In the dry season, most of the lakes – except Thang Hen itself – are dry. However during this time of year the lake level drops low enough to reveal a large **cave**, which can be explored by bamboo raft – if you can locate anyone at all in the vicinity to ask. There are opportunities for good day walks throughout this area, but you'll need a local guide; try the hotels in Cao Bang for assistance.

There are no restaurants or hotels at Thang Hen, nor is there any public transport. To get here from Cao Bang, drive 20km to the top of Ma Phuc Pass. From there carry on for 1km to the fork in the highway – take the left branch and continue another 4km. A return trip to/from Cao Bang on a *xe om* should cost around 80,000d.

Hang Pac Bo (Water-Wheel Cave)

After 30 years of exile, Ho Chi Minh re-entered Vietnam in January 1941 and took shelter in a small cave in one of the most remote regions of Vietnam, 3km from the Chinese border. The cave itself, Hang Pac Bo (Water-Wheel Cave), and the surrounding area are sacred ground for Vietnamese revolutionaries, for this is the base from where Ho launched the revolution that he had long been planning.

Even if you have little interest in the history of Vietnamese communism, the cave is located in a beautiful location, surrounded by evergreen forests filled with butterflies and birdsong, overlooked by limestone mountains.

Ho Chi Minh lived in the cave for a few weeks in 1941, writing poetry and translating key texts by the fathers of socialism. He stuck close to China so that he would be able to flee across the border if French soldiers discovered his hiding place. Ho named the

THE LEGEND OF THE LAKES

The charming setting of Thang Hen wouldn't be complete without a depressing legend to go with it. It seems that there was a very handsome and clever young man named Chang Sung. His mother adored him and deemed that he should become a mandarin and then marry a beautiful girl.

Under Confucian tradition, the only way to become a mandarin was to pass a competitive examination. Chang Sung, being a clever boy, sat the exam and passed. He received an official letter bearing the good news and ordering him to report to the royal palace just one week later.

With her son virtually guaranteed admission to mandarinhood, Chang Sung's mother completed her plan. A beautiful girl, Biooc Luong (Yellow Flower), was chosen to marry Chang Sung and a big wedding was hastily arranged.

Chang Sung couldn't have been happier. In fact, he and Biooc were having such a great time on their honeymoon that he forgot all about his crucial appointment at the royal palace until the night before the deadline.

Knowing how disappointed his mother would be if he missed his chance to be a mandarin, Chang Sung summoned magical forces to help him hop in great leaps and bounds to the palace. Unfortunately, he messed up the aerodynamics and leapt 36 times, with no control over his direction or velocity, and wound up creating 36 craters, finally landing at the top of Ma Phuc Pass, where he died of exhaustion and became a rock. The craters filled up with water during the rainy season and became the 36 lakes of Thang Hen.

stream in front of his cave Lenin Creek and the jungle-clad mountain that overlooks this stream Karl Marx Peak.

There's a modest Uncle Ho **museum** (admission 15,000d; 7.30-11.30am & 1.30-5pm Wed-Sun) at the entrance to the Pac Bo area. About 2km beyond this is a parking area. The cave is a 10-minute walk away along a shady stone path that follows the riverbank. You can step inside the mouth of the small cave, but not enter inside. The path then loops past various other points of interest, including a **rock table** that Ho is said to have used as a kind of jungle office for his translations and writing.

About a 15-minute walk in the opposite direction, in a patch of forest is a **jungle hut**, another of Ho's hideouts. On the way to the hut is a rock outcrop used as a 'dead-letter box', where he would leave and pick up messages.

Hang Pac Bo is 58km northwest of Cao Bang. Allow three hours to make the return trip by road, plus an hour to look around. To do this as a return half-day trip by *xe om*, expect to pay around US$20. No permits are currently needed, despite the proximity to the Chinese border.

Ban Gioc Waterfall & Nguom Ngao Cave

Ban Gioc Waterfall (admission 15,000d; 7.30am-5pm) is one of Vietnam's best-known waterfalls, and its image adorns the lobby of many a cheap guesthouse. The falls are actually an impressive sight in a highly scenic location, and are fed by the Quay Son River that marks the border with China.

The waterfall is the largest, although not the highest, in the country. The vertical drop is around 30m, but it has an impressive 300m span; one side of the falls is in China, the other is in Vietnam. Water volume varies considerably between the dry and rainy seasons: the falls are most impressive from May to September.

Boatmen will punt you on bamboo **rafts** (per trip 100,000d) close enough to the waterfall so you can feel the spray on your hair (bring some shampoo!) and skin. Rafts on the Vietnamese side have green canopies, those on the Chinese side blue (and life rings). You're allowed to swim in the large natural pool on the Vietnamese side, but not in the river or close to the main waterfall.

It's a very picturesque 10-minute stroll through paddy fields to reach the base of the falls from the parking area. If you're here at harvest time in September or October the farmers will try to encourage you to try out their pedal-powered threshing machines.

A police permit (200,000d for up to 10 people) is required to visit this region, which has to be organised in advance; any hotel in Cao Bang will sort it out for you.

About 4km from the waterfall, **Nguom Ngao Cave** (admission incl guide 20,000d; 7.30am-4.30pm) is one of the most spectacular cave systems in Vietnam, extending for several kilometres underground. Villagers sheltered here during the 1979 war with China. Visitors are permitted in one section of the cave, where a 1km-long concrete path and excellent lighting have been installed. A guide (very few words of English are spoken) accompanies you on an hour-long tour of the cave network, which was created by an underground river, past huge stalagmite and stalactite outcrops that resemble a waterfall and chandelier, and through a vast 100m chamber. The 10-minute walk from the parking lot to the cave is also very beautiful, threading through the limestone hills that characterise Cao Bang province, past fields of soya beans.

A second, even bigger branch of the cave system, is said to extend almost all the way to the waterfall, though there's currently no visitor access to this section.

GETTING THERE & AWAY

The journey to the falls and cave is absolutely stunning, the road weaving through soaring karst peaks and following a beautiful river valley for much of the trip. It's an 87km journey along a decent paved road, and takes about 2½ hours.

Twelve daily buses (38,000d, two hours) connect Cao Bang with Trung Khanh, 27km short of the falls. Negotiate for a *xe om* in Trung Khanh to take you onward, which should come to around 80,000d including a two-hour wait for the . Alternatively, hotels and guesthouses in Cao Bang can arrange a motorbike (self-drive) or vehicle (with driver).

There are snack and drink stalls by both the cave and waterfall.

Montagnard Markets

In the province of Cao Bang, Kinh (ethnic Vietnamese) are a distinct minority. The largest ethnic groups are the Tay (46%), Nung (32%), H'mong (8%), Dzao (7%)

and Lolo (1%). Intermarriage and mass education are gradually eroding tribal and cultural distinctions.

Check out Tim Doling's *Mountains and Ethnic Minorities: North East Vietnam* for detailed accounts of tribal people in the region It's available from the Vietnam Museum of Ethnology (p97) and bookshops in Hanoi.

Most of Cao Bang's Montagnards remain blissfully unaware about the ways of the outside world. Cheating in the marketplace, for example, is virtually unknown and even tourists are charged the same price as locals without bargaining. Whether or not this innocence can withstand the onslaught of even limited tourism remains to be seen.

The following big Montagnard markets in Cao Bang province are held every five days, according to lunar calendar dates.

Nuoc Hai 1st, 6th, 11th, 16th, 21st and 26th day of each lunar month.

Na Giang 1st, 6th, 11th, 16th, 21st and 26th day of each lunar month. Attracting Tay, Nung and H'mong, this is one of the best and busiest markets in the provinces.

Tra Linh 4th, 9th, 14th, 19th, 24th and 29th day of each lunar month.

Trung Khanh 5th, 10th, 15th, 20th, 25th and 30th day of each lunar month.

BA BE NATIONAL PARK

☎ 0281 / elev 145m

Often referred to as the Ba Be Lakes, **Ba Be National Park** (☎ 389 4014; www.babenationalpark.org; admission per person/car 3000/20,000d) was established in 1992 as Vietnam's eighth national park. The scenery here is breathtaking, with towering limestone mountains peaking at 1554m, plunging valleys, dense evergreen forest, waterfalls, caves and, of course, the lakes themselves.

There are 13 tribal villages in the Ba Be region, with most belonging to the Tay minority, who live in stilt homes, plus smaller numbers of Dao and Mong. A village homestay program is now well established, allowing travellers to experience life in a tribal village.

The park is a rainforest area with over 550 named plant species, and the government subsidises the villagers not to cut down the trees. The hundreds of wildlife species here include 65 (mostly rarely seen) mammals, 353 butterflies, 106 species of fish, four kinds of turtle, the highly endangered Vietnamese salamander and even the Burmese python. Ba Be birdlife is equally prolific, with 233 species recorded, including the spectacular crested serpent eagle and oriental honey buzzard. Hunting is forbidden, but villagers are permitted to fish.

Ba Be (Three Bays) is in fact three linked lakes, which have a total length of 8km and a width of about 400m. Over a hundred species of freshwater fish inhabit the lake. Two of the lakes are separated by a 100m-wide strip of water called Be Kam, sandwiched between high walls of chalk rock.

Park staff can organise several **tours**. Costs depend on the number of people, starting at about US$22 per day for solo travellers, and less if there's a group of you. The most popular excursion is a **boat trip** (boat hire 300,000-550,000d) along the Nang River and around the lake – keep an eye out for kingfishers and raptors. The boats can accommodate up to 12 people and the tour usually takes in the tunnel-like **Hang Puong** (Puong Cave), which is about 40m high and 300m long, and completely passes through a mountain. As many as 7000 bats (belonging to 18 species) are said to live in this cave. Further stops can be made at the pretty Tay village of Cam Ha (where every timber house has a satellite dish) and to the startling circular, jungle-rimmed lagoon of Ao Tien before finishing at **An Ma Pagoda**, situated on a little island in the middle of the lake.

The **Thac Dau Dang** (Dau Dang or Ta Ken Waterfall), consisting of a series of spectacular cascades between sheer walls of rock, is another possible destination. Just 200m below the rapids is a small Tay village called Hua Tang.

Other options include dugout-canoe tours or combination cycling, boating and walking possibilities. Longer treks can also be arranged.

The park entrance fee is payable at a checkpoint on the road into the park, about 15km before the park headquarters, just beyond the town of Cho Ra.

Sleeping & Eating

The only hotel rooms inside the park are in a **government-owned complex** (☎ 389 4026) next to the park headquarters. The best rooms here are in attractive semidetached **bungalows** (300,000d), each with two double beds, while the **chalets** (200,000d) are small and fairly basic. A few **rooms** (from 200,000d) are available too. The complex has two **restaurants** (meals from 50,000d), though you should place your order an hour

THE LEGEND OF WIDOW'S ISLAND

A tiny islet in the middle of the Ba Be Lakes is the source of a local legend. The Tay people believe that what is a lake today was once farmland, and in the middle was a village called Nam Mau.

One day, the Nam Mau residents found a buffalo wandering in the nearby forest. They caught it, butchered it and shared the meat. However, they didn't share any with a certain lonely old widow.

Unfortunately for the villagers, this wasn't just any old buffalo. It belonged to the river ghost. When the buffalo failed to return home, the ghost went to the village disguised as a beggar. He asked the villagers for something to eat, but they refused to share their buffalo buffet and ran the poor beggar off. Only the widow was kind to him and gave him some food and a place to stay for the night.

That night the beggar told the widow to take some rice husks and sprinkle them on the ground around her house. Later in the evening, it started to rain, and then a flood came. The villagers all drowned, and the flood washed away their homes and farms, thus creating the Ba Be Lakes. Only the widow's house remained: it's now Po Gia Mai (Widow's Island).

or so before you want to eat. For a less formal setting, you'll find a line of cookshacks by the chalets, which sell cheap meals and snacks and are run by local villagers.

It's also possible to stay in Pac Ngoi village, where a successful **homestay** (per person 60,000d) program has been established so visitors can stay in a stilt house. The park office usually organises this, but you can just rock up and check in too. The very well-kept **Hoa Son guesthouse** (☎ 389 4065) is one of the best, with a huge balcony and lake views, but there at least a dozen other options, all of which have hot-water bathrooms. Meals (20,000d to 60,000d) are available, and can include fresh fish from the lake.

Take enough cash for your visit – there are no money-exchange facilities, although there are banks in Bac Kan, the provincial capital.

Getting There & Away

Ba Be National Park is 240km from Hanoi, 61km from Bac Kan and 18km from Cho Ra.

Most people visit Ba Be as part of tour, or by chartered vehicle from Hanoi (a 4WD is not necessary). The one-way journey from Hanoi takes about six hours.

Reaching the park by public transport is possible, but not easy. Take a bus from Hanoi to Phu Thong (90,000d, five hours) via Thai Nguyen and/or Bac Kan, and from there take another bus to Cho Ra (25,000d, one hour). In Cho Ra arrange a motorbike (about 50,000d) to cover the last 18km.

If you're heading northeast, it's best to get a local bus from Cho Ra to Na Phac and get a connection there to Cao Bang.

THAI NGUYEN

☎ 0280 / pop 236,000

It's definitely not northeast Vietnam's most interesting town, but the industrial city of Thai Nguyen is home to an informative and enjoyable **Museum of Ethnology** (Bao Tang Van Hoa Cac Dan Toc; ☎ 385 5781; admission 20,000d; 🕑 8am-5.30pm Tue-Sun). It's worth dropping by here on the way either to or from Ba Be National Park, as this large museum has a wide array of colourful exhibits dedicated to Vietnam's 50-odd hill tribes and their textile traditions, crafts and customs. There are English translations and some excellent photography.

Thai Nguyen is 76km north of Hanoi, and the road here is in good shape. Buses and minibuses to Thai Nguyen (35,000d, two hours) depart from Hanoi's Gia Lam station very regularly between 5am and 5pm.

AROUND THAI NGUYEN

Phuong Hoang Cave

Phuong Hoang Cave is one of the largest and most accessible caverns in northeastern Vietnam. There are four main chambers of the cave, two of which are illuminated by the sun when the angle is correct. Most of the stalactites and stalagmites are still in place, although unfortunately quite a few have been broken off by souvenir hunters. Like many caves throughout Vietnam, this one served as a hospital and ammunition depot during the American War. Note that if you want to see anything, it's important to bring a good torch.

The cave is located 40km northeast of Thai Nguyen, just off Highway 1B.

Nui Coc Reservoir

A scenic spot popular with locals, **Nui Coc Reservoir** (admission 10,000d; hotel rooms 90,000-300,000d) is 25km west of Thai Nguyen. It's a pretty stretch of water and a major draw-card for Hanoi residents looking to get away from it all. On summer weekends it can get particularly crowded. A one-hour, circular motorboat tour of the lake is *the* thing to do and costs about 250,000d. You can use the water park's swimming pool for 20,000d, and also rent rowboats. It could be worth a visit if you're travelling to Ba Be National Park, with your own wheels, and fancy a dip.

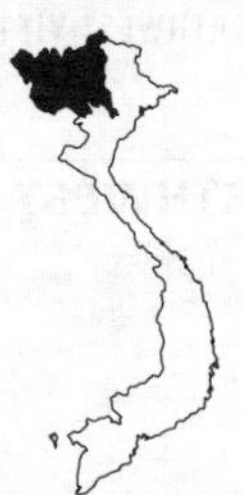

Northwest Vietnam

A heady landscape of towering evergreen peaks, fertile river valleys and scattered hill-tribe villages, northwest Vietnam is the most dramatic and mountainous region in the country. It's a sparsely populated area (most of the towns are little more than overgrown villages) so it's a great place to get off the beaten path and escape the urban sprawl and heavy traffic that characterises much of the travellers' trail in Vietnam.

The northwest is a heartland of hill-tribe culture, and the displays of textiles and traditional costume are mesmerising. The weaving skills of the women are astounding, and you'll witness a riot of colour in the markets: the scarlet headdresses of the Dzao women, the indigo fabrics of the sociable and chatty Black H'mong, and the incredibly intricate brocaded aprons of the Flower H'mong.

Sapa, an old French hill station, makes a great base for a few days, with some superb hiking and stunning vistas of Fansipan, Vietnam's highest peak. Northeast is Bac Ha, home to an astonishing Sunday market, and the province of Ha Giang, where you'll find the valley of Dong Van. The fabled northwest loop road snakes an incredibly scenic path across to Dien Bien Phu and down to Mai Chau through lush lowland valleys and over chilly high mountain passes.

Public bus services are improving, and though they are slow it's perfectly feasible to get around this way. However most travellers opt to explore the region by motorbike or 4WD. The main roads are virtually all paved, but still gruelling, and are regularly wiped out by landslides during the wet season.

HIGHLIGHTS

- Walk misty mountain trails through sublime scenery and hill-tribe villages around **Sapa** (p176)
- Marvel at the fecund landscape and stay in a traditional stilt house in the **Mai Chau** (p168) region
- Make for the minority markets – a blaze of colour when the Flower H'mong are in town – around **Bac Ha** (p185)
- Strap on your trekking boots for an ascent of Vietnam's highest peak, **Fansipan** (p178)
- Explore the bunkers, museums and war memorials of **Dien Bien Phu** (p171), the end of the road for the French in Vietnam

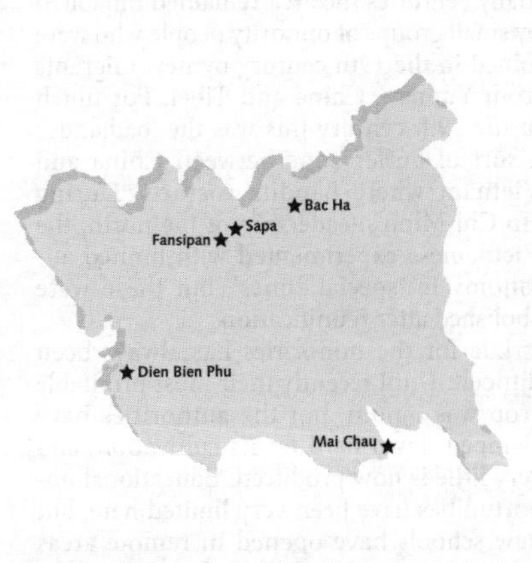

- ELEVATION: 100–3143M
- BEST TIME TO VISIT: MAR–MAY & SEP–NOV

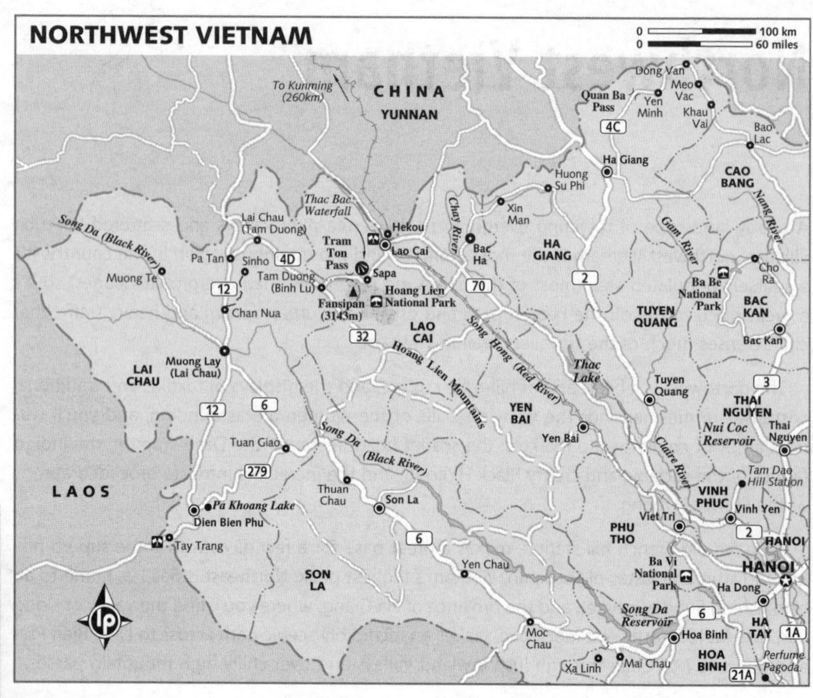

History

The history of the northwest is a separate saga to that of lowland Vietnam. The Vietnamese traditionally steered clear of the mountains, as the unforgiving terrain was not seen as suitable for large-scale rice production. For many centuries the area remained inhabited by small groups of minority people who were joined in the 19th century by new migrants from Yunnan, China and Tibet. For much of the 19th century this was the 'badlands'; a sort of buffer zone between China and Vietnam where bandits roamed. During Ho Chi Minh's leadership of the north, the Vietnamese experimented with limited autonomy in 'special zones', but these were abolished after reunification.

Life for the minorities has always been difficult. Until recently their most profitable crop was opium, but the authorities have clamped down hard on its cultivation, and very little is now produced. Educational opportunities have been very limited here, but new schools have opened in remote areas across the north in the last decade and the vast majority of children are now receiving an education. Economic prospects remain limited however, and many highlanders move to Hanoi or other cities in search of work.

Getting There & Away

Remote and mountainous, the northwest is the one region of Vietnam where it pays to consider the 'ins and outs' carefully. The main airport is at Dien Bien Phu, which has daily connections to Hanoi. The most popular way to reach the region is aboard the train from Hanoi to Lao Cai, the gateway to Sapa. It's either that or the mountain roads, which can be somewhat unforgiving on a public bus. Even better is the option of a private 4WD if you have the funds or can muster a group together. But perhaps the best way to experience this wonderful region is from the seat of a motorbike.

The most rewarding journey in these parts is the 'northwest loop'. Head for Mai Chau, then Son La and Dien Bien Phu, then north to Lai Chau, Sapa and back to Hanoi. Or do it in reverse. The loop is best with a 4WD or motorbike, for though the highways are much improved, they are still rough in parts. Allow at least a week for this journey, and considerably more time if braving the local buses. And three cheers for the hardy cyclists who pump up and down these roads.

HOA BINH

☎ 0218 / pop 112,000 / elev 22m

Hoa Binh means 'peace' and the easy-going nature of this town is quite a relief after the ferocious traffic that plagues the suburbs of Hanoi. The surrounding region is home to many hill-tribe people, including the H'mong and Thai, who add colour to the town's market. Hoa Binh is a handy pit stop on the road to Mai Chau, but most visitors don't stay overnight.

Information

There are several banks with ATMs along Hwy 6.

Hoa Binh Tourism Company (☎ 385 4374; www.hoabinhtourism.com; Hoa Binh Hotels I & II) Has offices at both hotels; regional tours are offered.

Main post office Internet access is available here (per hr 3000d), plus international phone services.

Sights

In Hoa Binh there is a small **museum** (admission free; 8-10.30am & 2-4.30pm Mon-Fri) that has war memorabilia, including a rusty old French amphibious vehicle.

Cross the new bridge towards Phu Tho and to the right you will see the **dam wall** of a vast and impressive hydroelectric station built by the Russians; over the river is an impressive memorial to the 161 workers who died during its construction.

Sleeping & Eating

Thap Vang Hotel (☎ 385 2864; 213 Đ Cu Chinh Lan; r 150,000d;) Set just off the main street in town, this smart mini-hotel has neat rooms with fridge and satellite TV. Heading west of the centre along Hwy 6, **Hoa Binh Hotels I & II** (☎ 385 2051 & 385 2537; s/d US$25/31;) have comfortable accommodation in mock stilt houses.

You'll find *com pho* places lining Hwy 6 and both the Hoa Binh hotels have restaurants.

Getting There & Away

Hoa Binh is 74km southwest of Hanoi and accessible by public bus (35,000d, two hours). Those with transport can visit Ba Vi National Park (p123) and follow a riverbank road to Hoa Binh.

SONG DA RESERVOIR (HO SONG DA)

Stretching west from Hoa Binh is Song Da Reservoir (Ho Song Da), one of Vietnam's largest. The flooding of the Da River has displaced a large number of farmers for about 200km upstream, and is part of a major hydroelectric scheme generating power for northern Vietnam. In 1994 a 500kV power line was extended to the south, temporarily freeing Ho Chi Minh City (HCMC) from seasonal power shortages.

Easiest access to the reservoir is by taking a spur road that cuts off from Hwy 6 at Dong Bang Junction (60km west of Hoa Binh and just outside Mai Chau). From the junction it's about a 5km drive to Bai San Pier. There's no obvious jetty here – hang around and someone will come out from a house and ask where you want to go. You'll need a Vietnamese speaker to help make arrangements.

One of the trips you can take is to the **Ba Khan Islands**, which are the tops of submerged mountains. The return trip to the islands takes three hours and costs about 350,000d per boat (each boat can seat 10).

Another possible boat trip is to **Than Nhan village**, home to members of the Dzao tribe. The two-hour return trip costs about 260,000d. The boat leaves you at a pier from where it's a steep 4km uphill walk to the village.

MAI CHAU

☎ 0218 / pop 12,000 / elev 300m

In the heart of an idyllic valley, a world away from the hustle and bustle of Hanoi, the Mai Chau region is a very tranquil place to spend a few days. The small town of Mai Chai is unappealing, but close by are Thai villages that enjoy a delightfully rustic setting surrounded by paddy fields. The lush countryside could not be more peaceful – there's little or no traffic to contend with and the rural soundtrack is defined by gurgling irrigation streams and birdsong. Even the dogs seem mellow.

The villagers are mostly White Thai, distantly related to tribes in Thailand, Laos and China. Most no longer wear traditional dress, but the Thai women are masterful weavers who ensure that there is plenty of traditional-style clothing (and souvenirs) to buy in the village centre. You'll see women weaving on looms under or inside their houses. Locals do not employ strong-arm sales tactics here: polite bargaining is the norm.

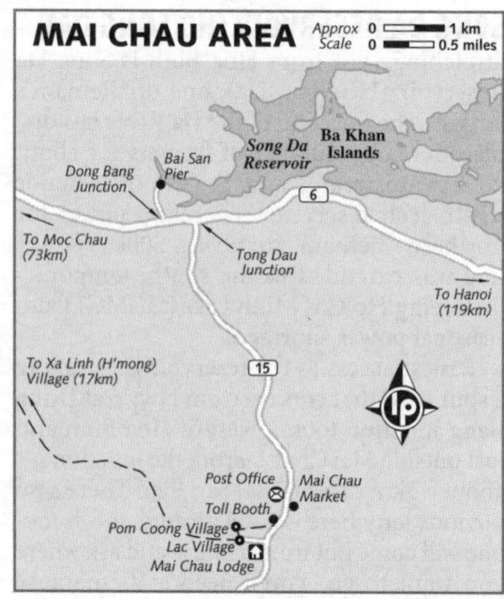

Mai Chau is a very successful grassroots tourism project, though some might find the experience a little too sanitised, and the villages are on the tour-group agenda. If you're looking for hard-core exploration, this is not the place; but as useful base for some hiking and relaxation Mai Chau could fit the bill nicely.

Sights & Activities

This is one of the closest places to Hanoi where you can stay in a tribal village and sleep in a stilt house. There's some fine **walking** past rice fields and **trekking** to minority villages. A typical trek further afield covers 7km to 8km; a local guide can be hired for about US$5.

There is a popular 18km trek from **Lac village** (Ban Lac) in Mai Chau to **Xa Linh village**, near a mountain pass (elevation 1000m) on Hwy 6. Lac village is home to the White Thai people, while the inhabitants of Xa Linh are H'mong. The trek is quite strenuous to undertake in a day, so most people spend the night in a village along the way. Arrange a local guide and a car to meet you at the mountain pass for the journey back to Mai Chau. Be warned that there is a 600m climb in altitude and the trail can be slippery in the rain.

Longer treks of three to seven days are possible. Ask around in Mai Chau. Many travel agencies in Hanoi run inexpensive trips to Mai Chau (see p87).

Sleeping & Eating

Virtually everyone stays in **Thai stilt houses** (80,000-150,000d per person) in the villages of Lac or Pom Coong, which are a five-minute stroll apart. See the boxed text (opposite) for more information.

Mai Chau Lodge (☎ 386 8959; www.maichaulodge.com; r US$165-185;) This seriously upmarket new hotel has broken the Mai Chau mould, setting itself up as a place where you can 'live the culture but stay in comfort'. The latter promise is certainly fulfilled, as the stylish rooms show fine attention to detail: the wooden floors, hip lighting and contemporary theme are offset nicely by the use of local textiles. Most rooms have balconies with rice-paddy views. The thatched-roofed **restaurant** (meals US$10-14) overlooks a small lake and the pool.

Most people eat where they stay. Establish the price of meals first as some places charge up to 150,000d for dinner. The women here have learned to cook everything from fried eggs to French fries, but as the local food is delicious it's best to stick with that.

Getting There & Away

Mai Chau is 135km from Hanoi and just 5km south of Tong Dau junction on Hwy 6. There's no direct public transport to Mai Chau from Hanoi, but it's easy enough to catch a Son La–bound bus as far as Tong Dau (45,000d, 3½ hours) and a *xe om* (motorbike taxi) from there to Mai Chau for around 20,000d.

You may have to pay a 5000d entry fee to Mai Chau, but the toll booth is usually not attended.

MOC CHAU

☎ 022 / pop 67,400 / elevation 797m

This highland town produces some of the best tea in Vietnam and is a good place to stock up. The surrounding area is also home to several ethnic minorities, including Green H'mong, Dzao, Thai and Muong.

Moc Chau boasts a pioneering dairy industry that started in the late 1970s with Australian (and later UN) assistance. The dairy provides Hanoi with such delectable luxuries as fresh milk, sweetened condensed milk and little tooth-rotting bars called *banh sua*. Not surprisingly, Moc Chau is a good place to sample some fresh milk and yoghurt. Indulge yourself at one of the dairy shops that line Hwy 6 as it passes through Moc Chau.

Should you get stuck in Moc Chau, the family-run **Duc Dung Guesthouse** (☎ 386 6181;

r 140,000d;) is a reliable option. It's about 300m from the post office on Hwy 6.

Moc Chau is 200km from Hanoi (75,000d, 5½ hours); all buses on the Son La–Hanoi run pass through the town.

YEN CHAU

022 / pop 31,200

Predominantly agricultural, this district is known for its abundant fruits. Bananas aside, all fruits grown here are seasonal – mangoes, plums and peaches are harvested from April to June, longans in July and August, and custard apples in August and September.

The mangoes are considered to be some of the tastiest in Vietnam, although travellers may find them disappointing at first, as they are small and green rather than big, yellow and juicy like those of the tropical south. However, many Vietnamese prefer the somewhat tart taste and aroma of the green ones, especially dipped in *nuoc mam* (fish sauce) and sugar.

Yen Chau is 260km from Hanoi (90,000d), and approximately seven hours by road. A bus from Yen Chau to Son La costs 25,000d.

SON LA

022 / pop 66,500

Son La has prospered on the back of its location as a natural transit point between Hanoi and Dien Bien Phu. It may not be one of Vietnam's must-see destinations, but the surrounding scenery is impressive and there are enough diversions to occupy half a day.

The surrounding region is one of Vietnam's most ethnically diverse and home to more than 30 different minorities including Black Thai, Meo, Muong and White Thai. Vietnamese influence in the area was minimal until the 20th century; from 1959 to 1980 the region was part of the Tay Bac Autonomous Region.

Information

In central Son La, **Agribank** (8 Đ Chu Van Thinh) has an ATM and changes dollars and travellers cheques. The **main post office** is west of here.

Sights & Activities

The **Old French Prison & Museum** (Nha Tu Cu Cua Phap; admission 10,000d; 7.30-11am & 1.30-5pm) in Son La was once the site of a French penal colony where anticolonial revolutionaries were incarcerated. It was destroyed by the infamous 'off-loading' of unused ammunition by US warplanes that were returning to their bases after bombing raids, but it has been partially restored. Rebuilt turrets and watchtowers stand guard over the remains of cells, inner walls and a famous lone surviving peach tree. The tree, which blooms with traditional Tet flowers, was planted in the compound by To Hieu, a former inmate from the 1940s. To Hieu has subsequently been immortalised, with various landmarks now named after him.

A narrow road leads uphill to the prison, off the main highway. Nearby is a **People's Committee office** with a small **museum** on the top floor, where there are some local hill-tribe displays and a good view of the prison ruins; no English translations are available however.

Perched above the town, a **lookout tower** offers a sweeping overview of Son La and the surrounding area. It's a 20-minute hike away; follow the stone steps leading up to the left of the Trade Union Hotel.

NORTHWEST VIETNAM

SLEEPING ON STILTS

If you are anticipating an exotic Indiana Jones encounter – sharing a bowl of eyeball soup, taking part in an ancient fertility ritual or entering a shamanic trance with the local medicine man – think again. Spending a night in one of Mai Chau's minority villages is a very civilised experience: electricity flows, there are Western-style toilets and hot showers, and roll-up mattresses and mosquito nets are provided. While this is eminently more comfortable, it may not live up to your rustic hill-tribe trekking expectations.

Despite – or perhaps because of – the modern amenities, it's still a memorable experience and many people end up staying longer than planned. The surrounding area is lush and extremely beautiful, the Thai villages are attractive and kept very tidy, and locals are exceedingly friendly. Even with a TV on and the hum of the refrigerator, it *is* a peaceful place and you're still sleeping in a thatched-roof stilt house on split-bamboo floors.

Reservations are not necessary. Just show up, but try and arrive before dark, just to get your bearings as much as anything else.

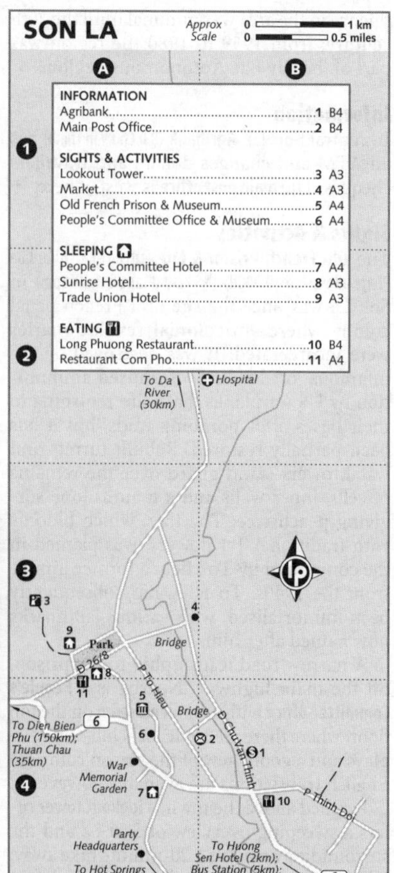

You can find a small selection of colourful woven shoulder bags, scarves, silver buttons and necklaces, clothing and other Montagnard crafts at Son La's **market**.

The township of Thuan Chau is about 35km northwest of Son La. Try and pass through early in the morning when the small daily local **market** is full of incredibly colourful hill-tribe women.

Sleeping & Eating

Son La is an ideal place to break the journey between Hanoi and Dien Bien Phu. There are a few budget options in town, but if you pay US$25 you'll get a pretty plush room.

Sunrise Hotel (☎ 385 8798; 53 Đ 26/8; r US$12-16; ❄) Rooms here are a little dated in terms of furnishings, but are in decent shape and come with satellite TV and gleaming tiled floors.

Huong Sen Hotel (☎ 385 1980; 228 Đ Truong Chinh; r 150,000-200,000d; ❄) A smart mini-hotel, located between the bus station and centre of town, that is popular with businessmen and offers excellent value. Rooms are comfortable and quite spacious, and also include a smart bathroom. There's a lift too.

Trade Union Hotel (Khach San Cong Doan; ☎ 385 2804; r US$18-25; ❄) This large, rambling government-run place isn't ageing particularly well but there are some benefits to staying here. Staff are welcoming (even bordering on overhelpful at times) and can arrange transport and tours. All the rooms are large, and have desks, wardrobes, two beds and bathrooms with tubs. Rates include a hearty breakfast in the reliable restaurant (meals around 50,000d).

People's Committee Hotel (Khach UBND Tinh; ☎ 385 2080; r US$20-30; ❄ 💻) Just off Hwy 6, this huge, imposing state-owned place is a kind of 21st-century take on the Trade Union Hotel. All the carpeted rooms are excellent value and in tip-top condition, with good quality furniture and plenty of space; some even have sofas.

Restaurant Com Pho (☎ 385 4444; 8 Đ 26/8; dishes 18,000-30,000d) A very humble but friendly place where no English is spoken. Point to whatever takes your fancy.

Long Phuong Restaurant (☎ 385 2339; P Thinh Doi; mains 20,000-60,000d) Located at one of the busier junctions in town, this restaurant is the place to sample some local minority dishes. Consider the sour *mang dang* (bamboo shoots) soup, and wash it down with sticky rice dipped in sesame-seed salt.

Getting There & Away

Son La lies 340km from Hanoi and 140km from Dien Bien Phu.

Son La's large bus station is 5km southwest of town. Buses run about every 30 minutes between 5am to 1pm to Hanoi (125,000d, 8½ hours), regularly between 5.30am and 1.30pm to Dien Bien Phu (88,000d, 5½ hours), and to Ninh Binh at 5.30am (135,000d, nine hours).

TUAN GIAO

☎ 0230 / pop 28,000 / elev 600m

This remote mountain town is at the junction of Hwy 279 to Dien Bien Phu (three hours, 80km) and Hwy 6 to Muong Lay (three hours, 98km). Few people spend the night here unless they are running behind schedule and can't make it to Dien Bien Phu, but it's a perfectly reasonable place to bed down for the night. There's an Agribank (with ATM) 200m east of the main T-junction in town.

Tuan Giao Hotel (☎ 386 2613; r 160,000-200,000d) is a plain but clean place with hot showers ,though the beds are pretty hard (even compared with sleeping on the floor in Mai Chau). It's opposite the Agribank.

About 500m west of the junction, heading towards Dien Bien Phu, **Hoang Quat Restaurant** (☎ 386 2482; dishes 15,000-45,000d) is a very popular lunchtime stop for small groups touring the northwest, with business cards from all over the world providing the wallpaper. The Vietnamese food here is plentiful, tasty and includes great grilled chicken with ginger and 'mountainous' rice.

Tuan Giao's bus station is just east of the junction. There are (roughly hourly) buses to Dien Bien Phu (42,000d, 2½ hours) from 6.30am until 3.30pm and also to Son La (55,000d, three hours). Hanoi buses (198,000d, 11½ hours) run between 5am and 2pm.

The government is busy improving roads in this remote region, but it's very much a work in progress, with stretches of smooth paved road giving way to mud-bound rutted trails, and plenty of hairpin bends. Reckon on an average speed of just 30km/h on a motorbike, and a little more in a 4WD.

PA KHOANG LAKE

A beautiful body of water, Pa Khoang Lake is 17km east of Dien Bien Phu on the road from Son La, and 4km off the highway. About a 15km drive around the lake's edge, or an hour's boat ride plus a 3km forest walk, is the recently restored **bunker of General Giap** (admission 5000d; ⌚ 7.30-11.30am & 1.30-4pm), the Vietnamese commander of the Dien Bien Phu campaign. The network of bunkers, tunnels, sentry boxes and huts here could be better set up for visitors, but make an interesting diversion for those attracted by Vietnam's legendary military tactician. There is also a remote **Thai village** that can be visited across the lake. Hire a motor boat (200,000d return) to the bunker or villages, and stay for a spot of lunch.

DIEN BIEN PHU

☎ 0230 / pop 72,700 / elev 491m

Dien Bien Phu is famous as the site of a battle that was truly decisive. The French colonial forces were roundly defeated at the hands of the Viet Minh on 7 May 1954 and the days of their Indochina empire became numbered.

Located in one of the most remote parts of Vietnam, Dien Bien Phu (or DBP for short) sits in the flat, heart-shaped Muong Thanh Valley, surrounded by heavily forested, distant hills. The scenery on the journey to or from Dien Bien Phu is stunning, the approach roads scything through thick forests and steep terrain, but the city itself lies in a broad, dry plain.

Dien Bien Phu is expanding and developing quickly. Previously just a very minor settlement, it only achieved town status in 1992, became a city in 2003, and was upgraded to a provincial capital the following year. Huge new boulevards and civic buildings have been constructed and the airport now has daily flight connections with Hanoi. With the nearby Tay Trang–Sop Hun border post now officially open to foreigners (see p174), more and more travellers are passing through the city.

Border crossing aside, history is the main attraction here and there are numerous bunkers and museums to visit.

Thai, H'mong and Si La people live in the mountains around DBP, but the city and valley are mainly inhabited by ethnic Vietnamese.

Orientation & Information

Dien Bien Phu is a sprawling city. The Ron River splits the town in half, but most of the accommodation and attractions are on the east bank. To the west is the airport, bus station and some dusty suburbs.

There are a couple of internet cafes on Đ Hoang Van Thai.

Agribank (☎ 382 5786; Đ 7-5) Has an ATM and changes cash dollars. There's a second ATM on Đ Hoang Van Thai.

Main post office (Đ 7-5) Post and phone services and internet access.

Sights & Activities

The site of the 1954 battle is now marked by several monuments, including the **Dien Bien Phu Museum** (☎ 382 4971; Đ 7-5; admission 5000d; ⌚ 7-11am & 1.30-5pm), which contains a startlingly eclectic collection of exhibits. Alongside the usual weaponry and guns there's a bathtub that belonged to Colonel de Castries, a bicycle capable of carrying 330kg of ordnance, and plenty of photographs and documents, some with English translations.

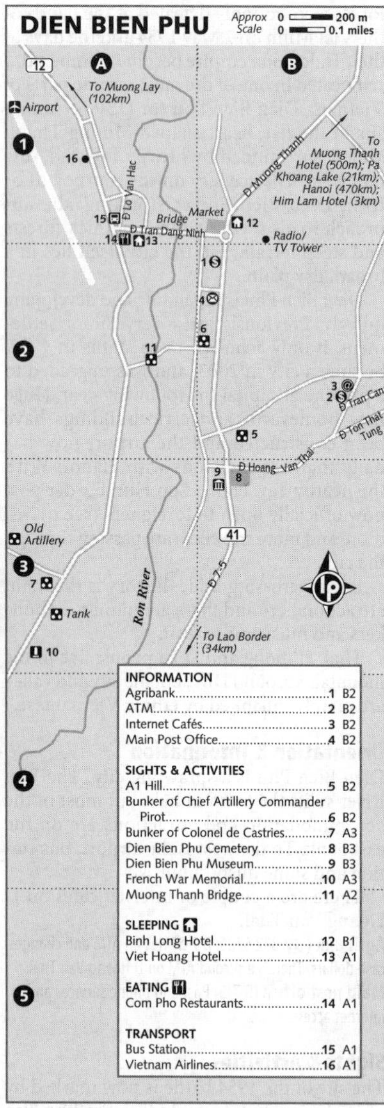

Across the river the **bunker headquarters** (admission 3000d; 7-11am & 1.30-5pm) of the French commander, Colonel Christian de Castries, has been re-created, and there are old French tanks and artillery pieces close by. There are more tanks and a monument to Viet Minh casualties on the site of the former French position, known to the French as Eliane and to the Vietnamese as **A1 Hill** (admission 5000d; 7-11am & 1.30-5pm), where bitter fighting took place. The elaborate trenches at the heart of the French defences have also been re-created.

The old **Muong Thanh Bridge** is preserved and closed to four-wheeled traffic. Near the southern end of the bridge – though not much more than a crater in the ground overgrown with weeds – is the **bunker** where Chief Artillery Commander Pirot committed suicide.

A formal **memorial** to the 3000 French troops buried under the rice paddies was erected in 1984 on the 30th anniversary of the battle. On the other bank of the Ron River, the poignantly designed and immaculately maintained **Dien Bien Phu Cemetery** commemorates the Vietnamese dead, each gravestone bearing the gold star of the Vietnamese flag and a clutch of incense sticks. Looking across the endless headstones begs the question: are there any victors in war?

Sleeping

Viet Hoang Hotel (373 5046; 67 Đ Tran Dang Ninh; s/d 100,000/120,000d;) Right opposite the bus station, this friendly new guesthouse is the ideal base if you're doing the early-morning border run. Rooms are smallish but neat and come with a splash of colour (well, the frilly net curtains are pink). Owner Mr Duc and his family are hospitable and serve up free tea for guests.

Binh Long Hotel (382 4345; 429 Đ Muong Thanh; tw US$14;) Another small, friendly family-run place, but on a busy junction in the thick of things. The twin rooms aren't exactly huge, but they're neat and tidy, and a breakfast is included.

Muong Thanh Hotel (381 0043; Đ Muong Thanh; r US$20-25;) Ignore the scary-looking 'fantasy' carved furniture in the lobby; this place is pretty efficient and the accommodation is decent value. Rooms are scattered around several blocks, and all are very clean with good mattresses and water coolers, but try to book either 224 or 225, which have the best views (and share a balcony). There's also a roadside cafe, a huge barnlike restaurant, a murky pool and a dodgy-looking massage parlour.

Him Lam Hotel (381 1999; www.himlamhotel.com.vn; Hwy 279; r US$20-30;) This resort-style place is one of Vietnam's best government-run places, with very attractive, spacious bungalows and rooms in modern blocks, extensive grounds with tennis courts, pools, a bar, a restaurant and a massage block. But as there's also a little 'zoo' section with bears and monkeys kept in small cages you may choose to take your custom elsewhere.

Eating & Drinking

Dining options are quite limited in DBP, though the Muong Thanh Hotel (opposite) also has a good restaurant.

Lien Tuoi Restaurant (☎ 382 4919; Đ Hoang Van Thai; mains 20,000-65,000d) A long-running place famous for its filling Vietnamese and Chinese food, Lien Tuoi has a menu in English and French with some imaginative translations.

For a cheap pit stop, check out the inexpensive *pho* stalls and simple restaurants opposite the bus station; some serve delicious fresh sugar-cane juice.

The beer halls on Đ Hoang Van Thai are the best place to sink a local brew or two.

Getting There & Away

The overland trip to Dien Bien Phu can be more intriguing than the actual battlefield sites for which the town is so celebrated. Of course, you miss out on this if you fly. For information about getting to or from Laos see the boxed text on p174.

AIR

Vietnam Airlines (☎ 382 4948; www.vietnamairlines.com; Hwy 12; ⏰ 7.30-11.30am & 1.30-4.30pm) operates daily flights between Dien Bien Phu and Hanoi. The office is just before the airport, about 1.5km from the town centre, along the road to Muong Lay.

BUS

The bus station is on Hwy 12, at the corner of Đ Tran Dang Ninh. There are 11 daily buses to Hanoi (235,000d to 285,000d, 14 hours) between 4.30am and 11.30am via Son La (88,000d, 5½ hours).

Seven daily buses run to Lai Chau (107,000d, six hours) via Muong Lay (52,000d, three hours) between 5am and 2pm.

CAR & MOTORBIKE

The 480km drive from Hanoi to Dien Bien Phu on Hwys 6 and 279 takes at least 12

THE SIEGE OF DIEN BIEN PHU

In early 1954 General Henri Navarre, commander of the French forces in Indochina, sent 12 battalions to occupy the Muong Thanh Valley in an attempt to prevent the Viet Minh from crossing into Laos and threatening the former Lao capital of Luang Prabang. The French units, of which about 30% were ethnic Vietnamese, were soon surrounded by a Viet Minh force under General Vo Nguyen Giap, which consisted of 33 infantry battalions, six artillery regiments and a regiment of engineers. The Viet Minh force, which outnumbered the French by five to one, was equipped with 105mm artillery pieces and anti-aircraft guns, carried by porters through jungles and across rivers in an unbelievable feat of logistics. The guns were placed in carefully camouflaged positions dug deep into the hills that overlooked the French positions.

When the guns eventually opened up, French Chief Artillery Commander Pirot committed suicide. He had assumed there was no way the Viet Minh could get heavy artillery to the area. Now it was a reality, Dien Bien Phu would only end in defeat. A failed Viet Minh human-wave assault against the French was followed by weeks of intense artillery bombardments. Six battalions of French paratroopers were parachuted into Dien Bien Phu as the situation worsened, but bad weather and the Viet Minh artillery, impervious to French air and artillery attacks, prevented sufficient French reinforcements and supplies from arriving. An elaborate system of trenches and tunnels allowed Viet Minh soldiers to reach French positions without coming under fire. The trenches and bunkers were overrun by the Viet Minh after the French decided against the use of US conventional bombers – and the Pentagon's proposal to use tactical atomic bombs. All 13,000 men in the French garrison were either killed or taken prisoner; Viet Minh casualties were estimated at 25,000.

Just one day before the Geneva Conference on Indochina was set to begin half a world away, Viet Minh forces overran the beleaguered French garrison at Dien Bien Phu after a 57-day siege. This shattered French morale and forced the French government to abandon its attempts to re-establish colonial control of Vietnam. For the full story of this incredible siege, pick up a copy of *Hell in a Small Place: The Siege of Dien Bien Phu* by legendary French reporter Bernard S Fall.

BORDER CROSSING: TAY TRANG–SOP HUN

The Lao border at Tay Trang is 34km from Dien Bien Phu (DBP). After years of rumours it's now well and truly open (daily between 7am and 5pm). You need to get a visa arranged in advance to enter Vietnam here, but if you're crossing into Laos most nationalities are able to get a visa on arrival (one-month stamp) at the border. There are no banks on either side of the frontier, so have some cash dollars to pay for your Laos visa if you need one.

Buses from DBP currently leave at 5.30am only on Sundays, Mondays, Wednesdays and Fridays. This bus takes you through the border crossing and drops you off in Muang Khua, Laos. The journey typically takes between seven and eight hours, but could be longer depending on the state of the roads and border formalities. In the other direction, buses leave Muang Khua for DBP at 7am on Sundays, Tuesdays, Wednesdays and Fridays.

It is possible to hire a *xe om* (motorbike taxi) from DBP to the border for around 120,000d, but you'll probably have to walk 5km to the nearest Lao village for transport to Muang May. Muang May has basic guesthouses (both 45,000 kip) and a daily 9am bus to Muang Khua. You'll need some cash dollars or kip to do the trip this way.

hours (if you're lucky). The road is generally in pretty good shape (but has heavy traffic) until Son La, but things slow down considerably after that town.

MUONG LAY

☎ 0231 / pop 8800 / elev 531m

Formerly known as Lai Chau, this small town is nestled in a pretty valley carved from spectacular mountains by the Da River, and makes a good lunch or overnight stop for people travelling between Dien Bien Phu and Sapa.

Beneath Muong Lay's beauty lies a difficult existence for locals. Far from busy trade routes, normal commerce is limited and the town has historically only been successful in harvesting cash crops such opium and timber. Needless to say, opium cultivation does not find favour with the central government.

In recent years the forest cover has been reduced and periodic floods have swept through the valley, killing hundreds in 1990 and 1996: the ruins of the former cultural hall can be seen in the middle of town.

One day soon Muong Lay will flood again, for a huge dam is under construction, just above the current Song Da Reservoir, which will fill the valley with water. Locals do not expected this to happen until 2012 at the very earliest.

Sleeping & Eating

our pick **Lan Anh Hotel** (☎ 385 2682; www.lananhhotel.com; r US$15-30;) These guys run a tight ship, which is pretty fortunate given the town will be under water in the next few years. It's efficiently managed by a hard-working team that offers tourist information, good food (meals from 35,000d) and a steady stream of cold beer. The accommodation is looking a little frayed around the edges these days, but there's still plenty of character with cowboy-style log cabins, stilt houses and slightly pokey wooden rooms scattered around the large leafy compound. Tours and boat trips can be arranged, or follow one of the maps available to get to local sights and villages.

There are plenty of market and food stalls on either bank of the bridge.

Getting There & Away

Muong Lay is connected by regular buses to Dien Bien Phu (54,000d, three hours) and Lai Chau (68,000d, 3 hours 45 minutes). There are also services to Tuan Giao (three hours), which is 96km away.

For Sapa, take the first available bus to Lai Chau and an onward connection from there. This road is one of the most beautiful in the north, tracing a broad river valley dotted by the thatched-roofed homes of minority people, with rickety suspension bridges connecting the two banks.

If you've got your own wheels you'll find that signposts are virtually nonexistent (and often bear the old town names). It's not easy to get lost, but be sure to check your progress carefully by asking locals and using a map.

MUONG TE

☎ 0231 / pop 15,200 / elev 900m

Muong Te is one of Vietnam's most remote outposts, 98km northwest of Muong Lay along the scenic Song Da River. The majority of the population is ethnic Thai, although they have assimilated enough to be nearly indistinguishable from the Vietnamese. Other minority groups found in the area include the Lahu (Khau Xung), Si La and Ha Nhi.

Apart from a small Sunday **market** and some nearby **villages**, there is not much to see or do in Muong Te. The only accommodation available in town is the shabby People's Committee Guesthouse, which also has a small restaurant. Three daily minibuses (62,000d, 3½ hours) connect Muong Lay with Muong Te along a very rough highland road.

SINHO

☎ 0231 / pop 8500 / elev 1054m

Sinho is a scenic mountain village that is home to a large number of ethnic minorities. It should attract more tourists, but the police have a poor reputation here and there is a 'You ain't from around here' look on the faces of many locals. There is a colourful Sunday **market**, although the dingy People's Committee Guesthouse has the only beds in town and they have to be pressured into accepting foreigners.

Sinho is a 38km climb on a road that is steadily being paved, but still very slow going – even though it is one of the most spectacular runs in the region. The turn-off is about 1km north of Chan Nua, on the road from Muong Lay, and it takes about 1½ hours each way. Irregular minibuses (28,000d) run between Muong Lay and Sinho; there's usually a morning departure at 11am.

LAI CHAU

☎ 0231 / pop 37,000

After passing through one of remotest regions in the country, the spanking new eight-lane high street and monumental half-built government buildings of Lai Chau appear like some Vietnamese El Dorado. The reality is more prosaic.

Formerly known as Tam Duong, this remote town was renamed Lai Chau when a decision was made to create a reservoir that would flood 'old' Lai Chau (now humble Muong Lay). Confused? So are locals.

Grand designs have been set in motion, and one day soon there may be a car or two on the absurdly grandiose streets. For the moment though this is still something of a one-horse town, despite its upgrade to provincial capital status.

Fortunately the scenery remains as beguiling as ever, for Lai Chau is set in a verdant valley of conical peaks that resemble diminutive volcanoes. Most visitors stop here because it makes a handy lunch break between Muong Lay and Sapa.

Lai Chau is split between the old town, with its **market**, full of hill-tribe people from nearby villages, and the concrete new town emerging 3km to the southeast. There's an Agribank and two ATMs on the main street in the old town.

The drive from Lai Chau to Sapa along Hwy 4D, threading through the Fansipan Mountain Range near the Chinese border, is a beautiful stretch of road.

Sleeping & Eating

Tay Bac Hotel (☎ 387 5879; r 135,000-175,000d; ❄) The best cheapie, this place has a bit of character, as the rooms are in an attractive Thai-style wooden house. There's a 'safe big car park'.

Muong Thanh Hotel (☎ 379 0888; r US$20; ❄ 🏊) This huge seven-storey government hotel is the smartest in town with 120 spacious, comfortable and well-equipped rooms that represent very good value. The facilities are great, with a tennis court, gardens and a vast

ALL CHANGE IN THE NORTH

There have been a lot of confusing name changes in the northwest over the past couple of years. A large chunk of old Lai Chau province, including the provincial capital, is due to go under water in a few years. The government struck first and created the new province of Dien Bien Phu and relocated the province of Lai Chau to the northeast. The old town of Lai Chau is now Muong Lay; the old town of Tam Duong is now Lai Chau, the provincial capital of the new province; and the old town of Binh Lu is now Tam Duong. Confused? So were we. Not all signposts and road markers reflect the new status quo so progress carefully. More than a few travellers have been jumping off the bus in the new town of Lai Chau, hunting for the popular Lan Anh Hotel. No, that's in Muong Lay – the old Lai Chau. Aarrgghh!

restaurant meals from 50,000d that sits on stilts above a minilake. Staff are friendly and some English is spoken on reception. It's situated between the two halves of town, just off the highway, and even has its own ATM.

Tuan Anh Restaurant (meals 20,000-40,000d) Offers the best food in town for those on a lunch run. There are also plenty of *com pho* spots nearby.

SAPA

☎ 020 / pop 36,200 / elev 1650m

Established as a hill station by the French in 1922, the charming highland town of Sapa is the one place in the northwest where tourism is booming. The magnificent scenery is on a very grand scale, and the town is orientated to make the most of the spectacular views that open up on clear days. Perched on a steep slope, Sapa overlooks a plunging valley of cascading rice terraces, with mountains towering above the town on all sides.

Tantalising glimpses of the epic scenery are more common than full-frontal vistas, for the town is often wrapped in a thick mist that rolls back and forth along the peaks. But even if it's damp and cloudy, Sapa has a lot going for it – this is an important market town for hill-tribe people, who fill the cobbled lanes with colour.

History has not always been kind to Sapa. From WWII, successive wars against the French, USA and China took their toll and the old colonial hotels were allowed to fall into disrepair.

With the advent of tourism, Sapa has experienced a renaissance. Countless new hotels and boutiques have popped up and the dining scene is now almost as cosmopolitan as that of Hanoi. The downside is a building boom that has seen one hotel after another raise the roof in a continual quest for better views. Height restrictions are rarely enforced and the Sapa skyline is changing for the worse.

Inherent in all of this prosperity is a sharp cultural change for the hill-tribe people, the future prosperity of whom has become closely tied with the tourism influx.

The H'mong people, once the poorest of the local tribes, are very canny traders, and you'll encounter them all over town urging you to buy handicrafts and trinkets. Most

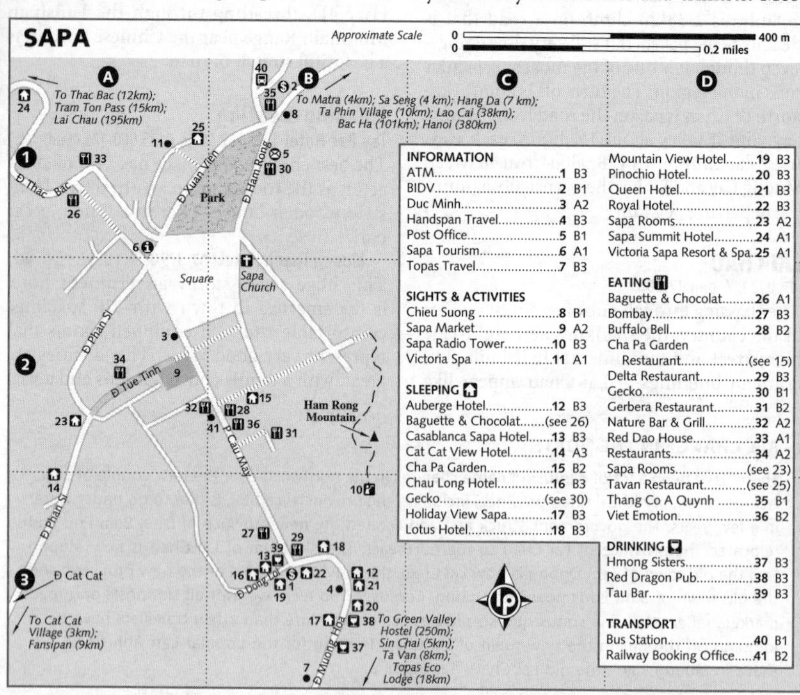

have had little formal education and are illiterate, yet all the youngsters have a good command of English, French and a handful of other languages (as well as a mobile phone and an email address). Plenty of H'mong have used their language skills to good effect and work as trekking guides or in hotels and restaurants in Sapa. Other minorities like the Red Dzao are visible all over town, their billowing red headdresses a surreal sight amid the accelerating development.

If you visit Sapa off-season, don't forget your winter woollies. Not only is it cold (0°C), but winter brings fog and drizzle. The chilly climate does have its advantages, however. The area boasts temperate-zone fruit trees bearing peaches and plums, and gardens for raising medicinal herbs.

The dry season in Sapa lasts from around January to June. January and February are the coldest (and foggiest) months. From March to May the weather is often excellent, and the summer is warm despite the rains between June and August. The window from September to mid-December is a rewarding time to be in Sapa, though there is a bit of lingering rain at the start and the temperature dips by December.

If possible, try to visit during the week, when Sapa is less crowded and more intimate. Crowds flock to Sapa for the Saturday market, but a smaller market is held every day. There is plenty to see on weekdays, and there are lots of interesting villages within walking distance of the centre.

Orientation

Sapa is hilly and quite spread out. Many guesthouses catering to Vietnamese tourists are in the north side of town around the bus station. Western-geared places are in the lower, southern half of town. There's a large square and church between the two.

The main street in Sapa with all the restaurants and cafes is called P Cau May, which becomes Đ Muong Hoa a little south of the junction with Đ Dong Loi.

MAPS

The *Sapa Tourist Map* is an excellent 1:75,000 scale map of the walking trails and attractions around Sapa. The *Sapa Trekking Map* is a nice little hand-drawn map showing trekking routes and the town, produced by Covit. Both cost around 30,000d.

Information

INTERNET ACCESS

Internet access is available in dozens of cybercafes, hotels and travel offices around town, usually priced at about 5000d per hour. Otherwise head to the tourist office, where it's free.

MONEY

There are two ATMs in Sapa and many of the hotels and businesses will change US dollars and euros.

BIDV (☎ 387 2569; Đ Ngu Chi Son; ⏲ 7-11.30 & 1.30-4.30pm) Has an ATM and will exchange travellers cheques and cash.

POST

Main post office (Đ Ham Rong) International phone calls can also be made here.

TOURIST INFORMATION

Sapa Tourism (☎ 387 3239; www.sapa-tourism.com; 103 Đ Xuan Vien; ⏲ 7.30-11.30am & 1.30-5pm) This is a rarity: a well-run and informative tourism office with helpful English-speaking staff who don't try and peddle (well, maybe occasionally) tours. Transport, trekking and weather information is offered, and there's even a pleasant little cafe and free internet. A stilt house at the rear of the office hosts folk dances, and a permanent handicraft market is under construction here too.

TRAVEL AGENCIES

There are several reliable travel companies in Sapa for trekking, mountain biking and other adventure activities.

Duc Minh (☎ 387 1881; www.sapatourist.com.vn; 3 P Cau May) This is a reliable local tour operator and agency. Check it out for trekking up Fansipan and to hill-tribe villages; it can also arrange transport.

Handspan Travel (☎ /fax 387 2110; www.handspan.com; 8 P Cau May) Offers trekking and mountain-biking tours to villages and markets. Exact prices depend upon numbers, but a two-day trek with a night in a hill-tribe village costs around US$100.

Topas Travel (☎ 387 1331; www.topastravel.vn; 24 Đ Muong Hoa) A Sapa-based operator that has high-quality trekking, biking and village encounters. Many options include a stay in their fab Eco Lodge (p180). Topas also employs many guides from minority groups.

Sights & Activities

The easiest trek in town is to follow the steps up to the **Sapa radio tower** (admission 15,000d) for killer views of the valley.

Hill-tribe people from surrounding villages don their best clothes and go to the **Sapa market** most days. Saturday is the busiest day, and the town is choking with tourists as the evening 'love market' is a big magnet for organised tour groups from Hanoi. If you'd rather enjoy Sapa at a more sedate pace, avoid the Saturday market.

The love market is speed dating minority-style. Tribal teenagers trek into town to find a mate. It's all very coy, but unlike many of the more remote love markets in the region, it has become very commercial in recent years. These days there are more camera-toting tourists than love-sick Montagnards, as well as a smattering of opportunist prostitutes on the scene.

TREKKING TO LOCAL VILLAGES

It's quite possible to hike around Sapa without the assistance of a guide, but you're likely to get much more out of the experience if you do take an informed local along. For overnight stays in villages and longer treks into the mountains, it's definitely best to hook up with someone who knows the terrain and culture and speaks the language. We recommend using minority guides, as this offers them a means of making a living.

There are endless options for trekking. Speak to freelance guides and travel agencies, pick up a decent map and plot your course. The villages and the surrounding landscape are now part of Hoang Lien National Park.

The nearest village within walking distance is **Cat Cat** (admission 5000d), 3km south of Sapa. Like everywhere in this area, it's a steep and very beautiful hike down; if you're too exhausted or unfit to hike back up, there are plenty of *xe om* ready and willing to cart you back to your hotel.

Another popular hike is to **Ta Phin village** (admission 5000d), home to Red Dzao and about 10km from Sapa. Most people take a *xe om* to a starting point about 8km from Sapa, and then make a 14km loop through the area, passing through Black H'mong and Red Dzao villages.

For spectacular valley views (if the mist and cloud gods relent that is) there's a beautiful hike along a high ridge east of Sapa through the Black H'mong settlements of **Sa Seng** and **Hang Da** down to the Ta Van River, where you can get transport back to Sapa.

There are also community-based tours to the nearby H'mong village of **Sin Chai** with an overnight in the village to learn about textiles or music and dance. Other popular communities to visit include the Giay village of **Ta Van** and the H'mong village of **Matra**.

Most hotels offer guided day and half-day treks; depending on the number of people and what, if any, vehicles are needed, expect to pay somewhere between US$12 and US$35. Good places to ask about guided treks include the Cha Pa Garden (p180), where tailor-made trips can be set up in advance, Auberge Hotel (p180), Cat Cat View Hotel (p180) and Mountain View Hotel (opposite). There are also several tour-booking offices on the main street.

FANSIPAN

Surrounding Sapa are the Hoang Lien Mountains, nicknamed the Tonkinese Alps by the French. These mountains include Fansipan, which at 3143m is Vietnam's highest peak. The summit towers above Sapa, although it is often obscured by clouds and occasionally dusted with snow. The peak is accessible all year to those in good shape and properly equipped, but don't underestimate the challenge. It is very wet, and can be perilously slippery and generally cold, so you must be prepared. Do not attempt an ascent if the weather is terrible in Sapa, as limited visibility on Fansipan could be treacherous.

The summit of Fansipan is 19km from Sapa and can be reached only on foot. The terrain is rough and adverse weather is frequent. Despite the short distance, the round trip usually takes three days; some very fit and experienced hikers do it in two days, but this is rare. After the first morning you won't see any villages: just the forest, striking mountain vistas and perhaps some local wildlife such as monkeys, mountain goats and birds.

No ropes or technical climbing skills are needed, just endurance. There are no mountain huts or other facilities along the way (yet), so you need to be self-sufficient. This means taking a sleeping bag, waterproof tent, food, stove, raincoat or poncho, compass and other miscellaneous survival gear. Hiring a reputable guide is vital, and porters are also recommended.

For recommendations on trekking guides, see above and p177. If you organise the climb through a local operator, you'll find yourself paying an all-inclusive rate of around US$100 per person for a couple, US$90 per person for a group of four and US$75 per person for the sensible maximum group size of six.

Weather-wise the best time for making the ascent is from mid-October to mid-December, and again in March, when wildflowers are in bloom.

TRAM TON PASS

The incredible road between Sapa and Lai Chau crosses the Tram Ton Pass on the northern side of Fansipan, 15km from Sapa. At 1900m this is the highest mountain pass in Vietnam and acts as a dividing line between two weather fronts. Even if you are not planning to tour the northwest, it's worth coming up here to experience the incredible views from the top of this pass (clouds, mist and rain permitting that is!). Descending by mountain bike is a seriously spectacular ride.

On the Sapa side of the mountain the weather is often cold, foggy and generally miserable. Drop down a few hundred metres below the pass on the Lai Chau side and it will often be sunny and warm. Ferocious winds come ripping over the pass, which is not surprising given the temperature differences – Sapa is the coldest place in Vietnam while Lai Chau can be one of the warmest in summer.

Alongside the road, about 3km towards Sapa, is **Thac Bac** (Silver Waterfall). With a height of 100m, it's a big one, and the **loop track** (admission 3000d) is steep and scenic.

MASSAGE & SPA

Hiking those mountain trails can be tough on your joints. These places will help soothe away any highland tensions.

Chieu Suong (☎ 387 1919; 16 P Thach Son; massages from 120,000d) It looks pretty uninspiring from the street, but this humble place offers bona fide foot and body massages at very fair rates.

Victoria Spa (☎ 387 1522; www.victoriahotels-asia.com; Victoria Sapa Resort & Spa; massages from US$40, treatments from US$30) State-of-the-art spa complex, with gorgeous massage and treatment rooms. Swedish, Thai and aromatherapy massages, and some wonderfully revitalising body wraps and scrubs.

Sleeping

Sapa has almost a hundred hotels, from bare-bones cheapies to a luxury hilltop resort. There's even a metropolitan-style boutique hotel now (and some less convincing wannabes). Most hotels listed here offer rooms with a view – but be aware that Sapa's ongoing building boom can wipe out a view overnight; always check before you rent the room. Sadly, the local government does little or nothing to enforce height restrictions. Very few hotels have air-conditioning as it's never hot enough to warrant it.

The sheer amount of places keeps prices competitive. However, prices can fluctuate wildly according to tourist numbers and often double on busy weekends. Look around and negotiate. Needless to say, it's wise to avoid the weekend rush. There are *plenty* of other hotels not listed here that are also good value, especially in the northern part of town, but they lack the scenic setting of those om the cusp of the valley.

Beware of hotels using old-style charcoal burners for heat, as the fumes can cause severe breathing problems if the room's not well ventilated. Most hotels have switched over to electric heaters or open fireplaces for the winter.

BUDGET

If you haven't made a booking try the cluster of ever-popular budget places on Đ Muong Hoa first (though new buildings here have largely obscured their views and this strip does suffer a little traffic noise). It's well worth noting that some of the midrange places also have excellent budget rooms.

our pick **Pinochio Hotel** (☎ 387 1876; quysapa1978@yahoo.com; 15 Đ Muong Hoa; r US$6-9; 💻) The young, lively and very friendly staff that run this excellent guesthouse really make this place. The rooms, all with simple but attractive decor, creep higher and higher up the hillside – those at the top enjoying a terrific valley aspect from their balconies. And to top it all there's a rooftop restaurant.

Queen Hotel (☎ 387 1301; Đ Muong Hoa; r US$5-12) This long-running place has been hosting backpackers for years and remains a solid choice. Size matters when it comes to price, but all rooms have hot water and TV. Cheap tours are offered too.

Mountain View Hotel (☎ 387 1334; 54A Đ Cau May; r US$10-25; 💻) A few paces away from the real cheapie strip, but a step up in quality, this large, well-run place has a prime location with 180-degree views of the valley. The cheapest rooms are simply huge for the price, with two beds, TV, phone and reading lights. Pay US$25 for doubly dramatic vistas and a balcony.

Other good options:

Green Valley Hostel (☎ 387 1449; 45 Đ Muong Hoa; r US$6-10) The HI choice in town. Could be a little better maintained, but still offers cheap rooms and unobstructed views.

Lotus Hotel (☎ 387 1308; 5 Đ Muong Hoa; r US$6-12; 💻) Offers decent value, fairly spacious if plain rooms, all with a fireplace and many with a balcony.

MIDRANGE

Sapa Summit Hotel (☎ 387 2967; 10 Đ Thac Bac; r US$10-35; 💻) Excellent value, this chaletlike hotel has a selection of attractive, light and airy rooms, all with two beds and great views across terracotta-tiled rooftops towards Fansipan. Superior rooms get a balcony and bathtub. There's a bar-restaurant and gardens with a kids' play area. It's located up a steep hill, a ten-minute walk from the dining and drinking action.

Cat Cat View Hotel (☎ 387 1946; www.catcathotel.com; 1 Đ Phan Si; r US$10-60; 💻) Owned by an English-Vietnamese couple, this efficient place has now expanded to 40 rooms over nine floors, many with great views. There's something for every budget, with homely, comfortable pine-trimmed accommodation, and even a seriously spacious two-bed apartment (US$150). The cheaper rooms are the best value: bargain hunters should check out the wing across the road for excellent budget rooms in the US$10 to US$15 range. There's a cafe, restaurant and lift.

Gecko (☎ 387 1504; www.geckosapa.com; Đ Ham Rong; s/d US$15/25) Another place with real character; five rustic-style rooms each have a wood stove, a little balcony, a wardrobe, reading lights and a TV. It's located above a good cafe-restaurant and a hearty breakfast is included.

our pick **Casablanca Sapa Hotel** (☎ 387 2667; casablancasapahotel@gmail.com; Đ Dong Loi; r US$15-30) For boutique on the cheap, this atmospheric little hotel is just the ticket and has a great central location. A lot of thought has gone into this place, and all 12 rooms have modish furniture, wooden floors, cream bed linen, fireplaces, TV and electric heaters. For a bargain, book a room at the rear, while the upper floors have balconies with that valley view. Mr Kien, the attentive owner, speaks fluent English and could not be more helpful.

Baguette & Chocolat (☎ 387 1766; www.hoasuaschool.com; Đ Thac Bac; r US$18) Operated by Hoa Sua (a group helping disadvantaged youth), this place has plenty of charm and some style, though as there are just four rooms it's essential to book ahead. The guesthouse is above an excellent French cafe, and rates include a great breakfast.

Sapa Rooms (☎ 387 2131; www.saparooms.com; Đ Phan Si; r US$27-44; 💻) Billing itself as a boutique hotel, this zany new place has been decorated in a highly quirky style – check out the lobby cafe. The rooms are more prosaic, but show some nice touches, including fresh flowers (though the cheapo floor tiles spoil the effect). Prices are a tad ambitious but do include a good breakfast, and the Australian owner is helpful and friendly.

our pick **Cha Pa Garden** (☎ 387 2907; www.chapagarden.com; 23B P Cau May; r US$60-80; ✖ 💻) Bucking the local trend for views at all cost, this exquisite new boutique hotel concentrates on class, elegance and atmosphere instead. Cha Pa occupies a sensitively restored colonial villa in the heart of Sapa, and is owned and run by a hospitable young Norwegian-H'mong couple who really look after their guests well. There are just four rooms (though more are planned), all presented in contemporary style, with uncluttered lines and hip bathrooms. The restaurant is one of the best in town, the gardens are spacious and a spa should open in late 2009. Considered travel advice is offered too, and bespoke tours can be set up.

Other places worth checking out:

Royal Hotel (☎ 387 1313; royalhotelsapa@hotmail.com; 54B P Cau May; r US$12-30; 💻) It's a little impersonal, but the location is handy and views are impressive.

Auberge Hotel (☎ 387 1243; auberge@fpt.vn; 7 Đ Muong Hoa; r US$18-34; 💻) A venerable place that still has character, but the rooms would benefit from a makeover (and some efficient heating). You can organise good tours here.

Holiday View Sapa (☎ 387 2989; 16 P Cau May; r US$45-65; 💻) Formerly the Royal View Sapa, this castle-esque hotel has had a name change but is still looking a little weary. It does have great views (if the sun's out).

TOP END

Chau Long Hotel (☎ 387 1245; www.chaulonghotel.com; 24 Đ Dong Loi; r US$125-185; 💻 🏊) Four-star hotel in a quiet location just off the main street. There are plenty of spacious, comfortable rooms and though they lack a 'wow' factor, the very fine balcony views certainly help compensate. The pool is tiny and often murky. The old wing has rooms for about a third of the price.

Topas Eco Lodge (☎ 387 2404; www.topas-eco-lodge.com; s/d US$131/143) Perched on a slope overlooking a plunging valley, this high-quality ecolodge has 25 lovely stone-and-thatch bungalows, each with front balconies to make the most of the magnificent views. The attention to detail is thoughtful with simple, stylish furniture and sleek bathrooms. The whole project has been designed to be as sustainable and environmentally friendly as possible, with sunlight providing the power and minority people the hotel staff and guides (for local treks and mountain biking). Tariffs are quite steep but do include three hearty meals in the stilt house restaurant and free transfers from Sapa. It's near Tan Kim village, about 18km from Sapa, and located at a much milder (and warmer) altitude.

Victoria Sapa Resort & Spa (☎ 387 1522; www.victoriahotels-asia.com; r from US$175;) This large hotel on the crest of a hill resembles an alpine lodge, and the log fire in the lobby sets a welcoming tone. It's a well-maintained establishment, right down to the clipped scrubs and manicured lawns, and though the rooms are not large they do have hand-carved furniture, balconies and all the trimmings you'd expect for the price. The restaurant is well regarded, there are two bars and the facilities are top-notch: there's a heated 15m indoor swimming pool, a fitness centre, a tennis court and a terrific, very tasteful spa (p179). Get here in style from Hanoi on one of the resort's luxury *Victoria Express* train carriages; return tickets start at US$165 without meals.

Eating

For Western food in comfortable surrounds, head to the main drag P Cau May which has a dozen or so choices.

our pick **Baguette & Chocolat** (Đ Thac Bac; cakes from 10,000d, snacks & meals 40,000-120,000d; breakfast, lunch & dinner) If you're craving a genuine European-style cafe, head to this elegant converted villa for a fine breakfast (sets cost 60,000d to 78,000d), tartine, baguette or a slab of gateau. There are also good salads, pasta and Asian and Vietnamese dishes, and the 'picnic kits' are a smart option for trekkers.

Viet Emotion (☎ 387 2559; 27 P Cau May; www.vietemotion.com; meals 40,000-120,000d; breakfast, lunch & dinner) Perhaps the pick of the places on busy P Cau May, this stylish, intimate little place has a bistro feel about it, with bottles of wine hanging from the ceiling, plus a fireplace. Try the trekking omelette, home-made soup, or something from the tapas menu like *gambas al ajillo* (garlic prawns). If the weather really sets in there are books and magazines to browse and games including chess.

Bombay (36 P Cau May; mains US$2-5; breakfast, lunch & dinner) Indian food in Sapa? Certainly – all your favourite curries, dhal, naan and vegie dishes are present and correct here, though the restaurant lacks a little in terms of atmosphere.

Buffalo Bell (☎ 387 3455; 25 P Cau May; meals from 40,000d; breakfast, lunch & dinner) Another good option on the main drag, this place has a slim street terrace, take-away cakes, and a menu that includes delicious, filling baguettes and Italian food – try the penne arrabiata.

Sapa Rooms (☎ 387 2131; www.saparooms.com; Đ Phan Si; snacks 30,000d, meals around 70,000d; breakfast, lunch & dinner;) A flamboyantly decorated cafe, complete with hanging statement art, that looks like it should be in New York or London rather than the highlands of northern Vietnam. Great for a snack (think corn fritters or a BLT baguette), meal (try the 'caramelised' pork fillet or fish 'n' chips), or just a pot of tea and a piece of cake.

Gecko (☎ 377 1504; Đ Ham Rong; mains US$5-9, sets US$6.50-10; lunch & dinner) This large enjoyable French-owned place resembles an auberge, with a rustic feel and a menu of flavoursome country cooking: try the boeuf bourguignon or the 'gecko' soup (with potato, bacon and cheese). There's a bar area and a little park-facing front terrace.

Delta Restaurant (☎ 387 1799; P Cau May; mains US$5; lunch & dinner) Another stylish and atmospheric place, Delta Restaurant is renowned for its pizzas, which are the most authentic in town, though the pasta is pretty decent too. Wash it all down with a drop of Aussie red.

Cha Pa Garden Restaurant (☎ 387 2907; www.chapagarden.com; 23B P Cau May; mains US$7-12; dinner) No room at the inn? Eat there instead. Sapa's boutique hotel has a terrific restaurant, with a select menu of well-chosen European dishes, including Scandinavian meatballs and marinated rainbow trout with roast potatoes. The dining room has a real intimacy and warmth (which is aided by a log fire), and there are plenty of wines – from France, Spain and the USA – to indulge in.

Tavan Restaurant (☎ 387 1522; Victoria Sapa Hotel; mains US$4-28; lunch & dinner) This hotel restaurant has a good rep, and is the place for a ser ious splurge. The Parisian chef has been here for years, and while there are Asian dishes on the menu it's best to stick to European classics like the rack of lamb (US$20), raclette (US$28) or pasta (from US$4).

Also worth a try:

Gerbera Restaurant (☎ 387 1064; P Cau May; mains from 20,000d; ⌚ breakfast, lunch & dinner) An old travellers' fave that's best for its filling, inexpensive Vietnamese food. Choose from the looooong menu.

Nature Bar & Grill (P Cau May; meals 35,000-50,000d; ⌚ breakfast, lunch & dinner) Has a large wood-panelled interior and a central fireplace. The menu is a typical Sapa mix of Vietnamese and Western dishes.

Red Dao House (☎ 387 2927; 4B Đ Thac Bac; meals from 65,000d; ⌚ breakfast, lunch & dinner; 💻) Smart new restaurant in a mock hill-tribe house with a nice front terrace. There are set breakfasts, and plenty of Vietnamese seafood and chicken dishes. Staff wear Dzao-style costume here.

There's a cluster of humble, more authentically Vietnamese restaurants below the market on Đ Tue Tinh where the setting usually combines plastic stools and fluorescent lighting with cheap prices.

Vietnamese-style hot pot (meat stew cooked with local vegetables, cabbage and mushroom) is a very popular local dish; the area just south of the bus station has several good places to try it. For a very local experience, **Thang Co A Quynh** (☎ 387 1555; 15 Thach Son; hot pot for 4-6 people 250,000d) is about as hard-core as it gets, as it only serves horse (yes, and including plenty of boiled blood and offal) and rice wine, and you sit on the floor.

If that sounds a step too far, the night-market stalls just south of the church can't be beaten for *bun cha* (barbecued pork).

Drinking & Entertainment

A bar crawl in Sapa will take in a maximum of three or four venues – this is not a party town.

Red Dragon Pub (☎ 387 2085; 23 Đ Muong Hoa) Looking like something transplanted from the Pembrokeshire coast, this genteel place resembles a Welsh tearoom, with plenty of knick-knacks on show. It's good for a quiet drink, and serves filling pub grub including shepherd's pie.

Tau Bar (☎ 387 1322; 42 P Cau May) With an exterior tagged with graffiti and an interior of unforgiving concrete this bunker-cum-bar is as urban as it gets in Sapa. There's a bass-heavy sound system, a DIY jukebox that's strong on hip hop, and always a crowd around the pool tables.

Hmong Sisters (Đ Muong Hoa) This bar with pool tables could be half-decent if the staff were half-polite or, as was the case when we were there, the owner stopped asking people to move tables to accommodate his friends.

Shopping

Sapa is the top shopping destination in the northwest. Most of the items are clothing, accessories and jewellery produced by the multitude of minority peoples in the area. More recently some Vietnamese designers have also been getting in on the act, producing clothes and household furnishings inspired by tribal motifs and patterns. The stores on P Cau May and along Đ Phan Si have the best stuff.

Lots of the minority women and young girls have gone into the souvenir business; the older women in particular are known for their strong-armed selling tactics. One frequent Sapa sight is a frenzy of elderly H'mong women clamouring around a hapless traveller to hawk their goods, which range from colourful ethnic garb to little pouches of opium stashed away in matchboxes. When negotiating prices, you do need to hold your ground, but avoid aggressive bargaining.

A word of warning on the clothes: as beautiful and cheap as they are, the dyes used are not set. Much of the stuff sold has the potential to turn anything it touches (including your skin) a muddy blue-green colour – check out the hands and arms of the H'mong for an idea. Wash the fabric separately in cold salt water as it helps to stop the dye from running. Wrap anything you buy in plastic bags before stuffing it in your luggage.

Getting There & Away

The gateway to Sapa is Lao Cai, 38km away on the Chinese border via a smooth, well-maintained highway. Sapa's bus station is in the north of town, but you can also check schedules at the tourist office.

Minibuses make the trip to and from Lao Cai about every half-hour between 5am and 5pm (26,000d, 1½ hours). Services to Lao Cai wait in front of the church, and also run from the bus station.

Public buses run from Sapa to Dien Bien Phu at 7.30am and 9am (145,000d, nine hours). Slower local buses also head west to towns including Lai Chau (42,000d, 2½ hours) and Muong Lau (88,000d, 5½ hours).

Hotels and travel agents offer direct minibus services to Bac Ha (from US$12 return) for the Sunday market. Departure from Sapa is at 6am and from Bac Ha at around 1pm. It's cheaper to go to Bac Ha by public minibus, changing buses in Lao Cai.

Driving a motorbike from Hanoi to Sapa is feasible, but it's a very long trip, at 380km. Wise bikers put their motorbikes on a train to Lao Cai and save themselves the hassle and danger of dealing with Vietnam's busy highways. The 38km between Lao Cai and Sapa is straight uphill – and unless you've been training for the Olympics, it's hell on a bicycle.

There's no train line to Sapa, but very regular services from Hanoi to Lao Cai (p184). You can book tickets at the **Railway Booking Office** (☎ 387 1480; ⏲ 7.30-11am & 1.30-4pm) on P Cau May, which charges a small commission.

Getting Around

The best way to get around Sapa is to walk, and almost everywhere it's steep! Bicycles can be hired, but you might spend half the time pushing it up vertiginous hills. For excursions further afield motorbikes are available from about US$5 a day. If you've never ridden a motorbike before this is probably not the place to learn. The weather can be wet and treacherous at any time of the year, and roads are steep and regularly damaged by floods and heavy rain. Accident rates are high. Consider hiring a bike with a local driver (about US$12 a day).

Cars, 4WDs and minibuses are also available for hire through hotels, guesthouses and travel agents. Rates vary widely depending on the destination and the distance.

LAO CAI

☎ 020 / pop 46,700 / elev 232m

Lao Cai, the end of the line so to speak, is right on the Vietnam–China border. The town was razed in the Chinese invasion of 1979, so most of the buildings are new. The border crossing here slammed shut during the 1979 war and only reopened in 1993.

Today Lao Cai is a major destination for travellers journeying between Hanoi or Sapa and Kunming in China, but Lao Cai is no place to linger, with Sapa just an hour or so away.

The border town on the Chinese side is called Hekou – you would have to be an enthusiast of Chinese border towns to want to hang out there.

Information

Be especially wary of black marketeers, especially on the Chinese side – they frequently short-change tourists. If you do black-market dealings, it's best to change only small amounts.

There are two ATMs by the train station. **BIDV Bank** (Đ Thuy Hoa) on the west bank of the river exchanges cash and travellers cheques, and also has an ATM.

Sleeping & Eating

Terminus Hotel & Restaurant (☎ 383 5470; 242 P Nguyen Hue; r from 150,000d; ✇) Right across the

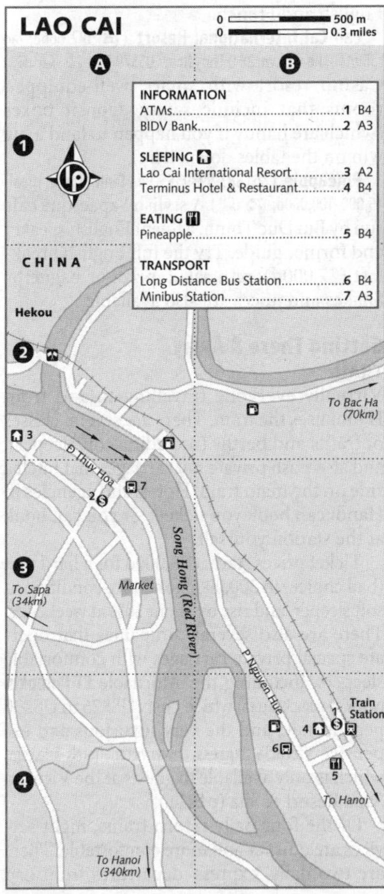

BORDER CROSSING: LAO CAI–HEKOU

The Lao Cai–Hekou crossing is a direct route between northern Vietnam and Yunnan in China. The border is open daily between 7am and 7pm. China is separated from Vietnam by a road bridge and a separate rail bridge over the Red River. Pedestrians pay a toll of 3000d to cross.

The border is about 3km from Lao Cai train station, a journey that is easily done on a *xe om* (motorbike taxi; 20,000d). Note that travellers have reported Chinese officials confiscating Lonely Planet *China* guides at this border, so you may want to try masking the cover.

Trains no longer run from Hekou to Kunming, but there are several 'sleeper' buses (87 RMB) which have sleeping berths that are a bit of a squeeze for anyone over 1.8m but reasonably comfortable. One bus leaves at 7pm and arrives in Kunming around 7am, but there are also earlier departures.

square from the train station this is a good spot for an early breakfast or a filling meal. The rooms are very clean and tidy, and have a few frilly decorative touches. Staff speak English and French.

Lao Cai International Resort (☎ 382 6668; laocaihotel@hn.vnn.vn; 88 Đ Thuy Hoa; r US$79-95;) Casino resort with smart, well-equipped rooms that include safety deposit boxes (which are handy if you happen to land a big win on the tables downstairs).

Pineapple (☎ 383 5939; 55 Pha Dinh Phung; meals 45,000-100,000d;) A stylish Sapaesque cafe run by Bui Duc Thinh, a fluent English speaker and former guide. Try the full English breakfast (77,000d), or a salad, pizza or baguette. Shakes and juices are also available.

NORTHWEST VIETNAM

Getting There & Away

TRAIN

Virtually everyone travelling to and from Hanoi uses the train. There are several classes of trains and berths (including soft sleeper), and also posh private rail carriages that hitch a ride on the main train. Hotels and agencies in Hanoi can book you tickets, or you can book at the station yourself.

Ticket prices start at 98,000d for a hard seat (bad choice) to 300,000d for an air-conditioned soft sleeper, and rise by about 10% at weekends. There are also several companies that operate special private carriages with comfortable sleepers, including the affordable **ET Pumpkin** (www.et-pumpkin.com) which costs US$25 to US$30 per journey, and the very luxurious and expensive **Victoria Express** (www.victoriahotels-asia.com) which is only available to guests at the Victoria Sapa Resort & Spa (p181).

Of the four daily return trains, night services are quicker and more comfortable. There are two daily 'express' departures from Lao Cai to Hanoi at 8.15pm and 9pm. The journey takes about eight hours. From Hanoi the best trains leave at 9.15pm and 9.55pm. Check with **Vietnam Rail** (Duong Sat Viet Nam; www.vr.com.vn) for current timetables, or www.seat61.com for additional information.

BUS & TAXI

Lao Cai is about 340km from Hanoi. Nine daily buses make the journey to Hanoi (155,000d, nine hours), leaving early in the morning from the **long distance bus station** (P Nguyen Hue), but most travellers sensibly prefer taking the train.

Minibuses for Sapa (28,000d, 1½ hours) wait by the station for trains that arrive from Hanoi, and also run regularly from the minibus terminal next to the Red River bridge. Minibuses to Bac Ha (50,000d, 2½ hours) also leave from here; there are five daily services, at 6am, 7am, 10am, noon and 3pm.

A taxi to Sapa costs about US$28; it's around US$40 to Bac Ha.

BAC HA

☎ 020 / pop 7400 / elev 800m

An unhurried, friendly and remote town, Bac Ha makes a wonderfully relaxed base for a few days exploring the northern highlands and hill-tribe villages. The atmosphere is very different from Sapa, and you can walk the streets freely without being accosted by hawkers. If you want to experience life in a small untouristy mountain town, this is an excellent destination.

Bac Ha has a certain charm, though its stock of traditional old adobe houses is dwindling and being replaced by concrete structures. Wood smoke fills the morning air and chickens and pigs poke around the back lanes. For six days a week Bac Ha slumbers, but its lanes fill up to choking point each Sunday when visitors and Flower H'mong flood in for the weekly market. Bac Ha's Sunday market is one of the finest in Vietnam, a riot of colour and commerce that simply should not be missed.

Bac Ha is a good base to explore the surrounding highlands: it has an improving choice of inexpensive hotels and the climate here is noticeably warmer than in Sapa. There are 10 Montagnard groups that live around Bac Ha: the colourful Flower H'mong are the most visible, but other groups include Dzao, Giay (Nhang), Han (Hoa), Xa Fang, Lachi, Nung, Phula, Thai and Thulao.

One of Bac Ha's main industries is the manufacture of alcoholic home brews (rice wine, cassava wine and corn liquor). The *ruou* corn hooch produced by the Flower H'mong is so potent it can ignite; there's an entire area devoted to it at the Sunday market. Swill some down before deciding whether to buy a buffalo or cow.

Information

There's no ATM in Bac Ha but the **Agribank** will change cash dollars. Or head to the Sao Mai Hotel (p187) which will change US bucks, Chinese currency, euros, sterling and Aussie dollars, plus travellers cheques; they also plan to offer credit-card advances here.

You'll find a tiny internet place next to the Hoang Vu Hotel (p186). There's no official tourist information in Bac Ha, but there's excellent advice available at the Hoang Yen Restaurant (p187) or Hoang Vu Hotel; speak to **Mr Nghe** (☎ 091-200 5952; hoangvutours@hotmail.com) who owns both these places or consult the website www.bachatourism.com.

Sights & Activities

There are few real sights in town, but you should certainly check out the outlandish **Vua Meo** ('Cat King' House; free admission; 8am-5.30pm), a palace constructed in a kind of bizarre 'oriental baroque' architectural style on the northern edge of town. Dating from 1921, it was built by the French to keep the Flower H'mong chief Hoang A Tuong happy and looks like a cross between an exotic church and a French chateau. A museum may open here some time in the future.

HILL-TRIBE MARKETS

There are several terrific markets in and around Bac Ha.

Bac Ha Market

This outstanding Sunday market is Bac Ha's big draw. There are a few handicrafts for sale, but this is very much a local affair, and it's all about experiencing a highland market rather than shopping for souvenirs. Bac Ha market is a magnet for the local hill-tribe people, above all the exotically attired Flower H'mong, and it makes a technicolour dream for photographers.

Flower H'mong women wear several layers of dazzling clothing. These include an elaborate collar-cum-shawl that's pinned at the neck and an apron-style garment; both

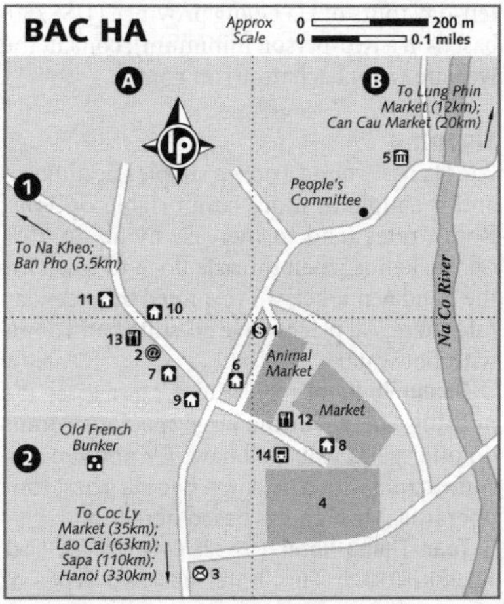

INFORMATION
Agribank....1 B2
Internet....2 A2
Post Office....3 A2

SIGHTS & ACTIVITIES
Bac Ha Market....4 B2
Vua Meo....5 B1

SLEEPING
Congfu Hotel....6 A2
Hoang Vu Hotel....7 A2
Minh Quan Hotel....8 B2
Quynh Trang Hotel....9 A2
Sao Mai Hotel....10 A1
Toan Thang Hotel....11 A1

EATING
Duc Tuan Restaurant....12 B2
Hoang Yen Restaurant....13 A2

TRANSPORT
Bus Station....14 B2

are made of tightly woven strips of multicoloured fabric, often with a frilly edge. Highly ornate cuffs and ankle fabrics are also part of their costume as is a checked headscarf (often electric pink or lime green).

The market itself is compartmentalised. The huge animal section, held on a muddy open field, is fascinating, as prospective vendors prise open the mouths of water buffalo and horses for an impromptu dental examination; prod pigs; and size up dogs on strings. Bordering this are food stalls with giant vats of bubbling broths, tables displaying glistening entrails and drink tents dedicated to merrymaking where you can join the locals for shots of corn hooch. On the east side are handicraft stalls selling local fabrics and silver jewellery.

If you can, stay overnight in Bac Ha and get here early before hundreds of day-trippers from Sapa start arriving. Bac Ha market starts at sunrise and winds down by about 2pm.

Can Cau Market

This fascinating open-air morning market, 20km north of Bac Ha and just 9km from the Chinese border, only attracts a trickle of outsiders. It's a mecca for the local tribal people, including Flower H'mong and Blue H'mong (look out for the striking zigzag costume of the latter).

It spills down a hillside with cookshacks on one level and livestock at the bottom of the valley, including plenty of dogs. Locals will implore you to drink the local *ruou* (corn moonshine) with them. The market is only open on Saturday. Some trips from Bac Ha include the option of an afternoon trek (for those still standing after *ruou* shots) to the nearby village of Fu La.

Other Markets

Lung Phin market is between Can Cau market and Bac Ha, about 12km from the town. It's less busy than other markets, and is open on Sunday. It is a good place to move onto once the tour buses arrive in Bac Ha from Sapa, and has a really local feel.

The impressive Tuesday **Coc Ly** market attracts Dzao, Flower H'mong, Tay and Nung people from the surrounding hills. It's about 35km southwest of Bac Ha along reasonably good roads. Tour operators in Bac Ha can arrange day trips here, after which you can do a boat trip down the Chay River before heading back to Bac Ha.

TREKKING & TOURS TO LOCAL VILLAGES

There's great hiking and some remarkable hill-tribe villages in the Bac Ha region. The Flower H'mong village of **Ban Pho** is one of the nearest to town, from where you can walk to the Nung settlement of **Na Kheo** then head back to Bac Ha. Other nearby villages include **Trieu Cai**, an 8km return walk, and **Na Ang**, a 6km return walk.

To see a bit more of the region, it's best to set up a trip with a local guide. Until very recently most of the minority people in these hills had no formal education but the government has opened several schools in the last few years. Most hill-tribe children now receive an education (in the Vietnamese language). Boarding schools are favoured because the communities are so spread out, so children spend the week away from their families and sleep in dormitories. Tour guides in Bac Ha can arrange visits to rural schools as part of a motorbike or trekking day trip.

There's also a **waterfall** near Thai Giang Pho village, about 12km east of Bac Ha, which has a pool big enough for swimming.

Mr Nghe (p185), who owns the Hoang Yen Restaurant (opposite) and operates tours from the Hoang Vu Hotel (below), is a one-man dynamo intent on developing tourism in Bac Ha. He'll set you up with a local guide, organise motorbikes and can help out with transport. You're sure to encounter him at one of the above places, wearing his usual attire of a suit. There are all sorts of possibilities: from half-day trips (around 100,000d per person) to ten-day tours of Ha Giang province (US$750, based on a two-person minimum); consult the website www.bachatourism.com.

Sleeping

Bac Ha has around a dozen simple guesthouses and a couple of more comfortable options. Room rates tend to increase by about 20% on weekends when tourists flock to town for the Sunday market; we've quoted the weekday rates here. All places have en-suite bathrooms with hot water.

Hoang Vu Hotel (☎ 388 0264; r from US$6) It's nothing fancy, but the large spacious rooms do offer good value; all have TV and fan and some come with a balcony. Bac Ha's best tour operator, Mr Nghe, is based here too.

Toan Thang Hotel (☎ 388 0444; old/new block 125,000/280,000d) This hotel has two types of rooms; those in the old wooden block are OK for the tariff asked, with two beds, TV and fan, though a little dark. The newer rooms are overpriced. Staff are friendly, and some English is spoken.

Quynh Trang Hotel (☎ 388 0450; r from 150,000d) A well-run place, owned by a dynamic lady who speaks almost no English but does have spotless rooms with wood-panelled walls, solid furniture, fans and TV.

our pick **Congfu Hotel** (☎ 388 0254; congfuhotel@gmail.com; r from 260,000d;) This new place has got most things correct, with 21 very attractive rooms, almost minimalist in design, that show a notable absence of chintz. The bed linen is good quality (though beds are a little hard); showers are modern; there's wi-fi, parking, internet in the lobby and helpful staff; and the restaurant (meals from 30,000d) is very decent. Book rooms 205, 208, 305 or 308 and you'll get a floor-to-ceiling window overlooking Bac Ha market.

Sao Mai Hotel (☎ 388 0288; saomaibh@vnn.vn; r US$20-35;) Once the only proper hotel in town, this place has had little or no competition for years. The 54 rooms are all looking a bit weary, typified by unattractive brown tiled floors and pink bath suites. However a new five-storey block is under construction here (it should open in late 2009), which should offer better quality accommodation in the US$35 to US$40 range. The large restaurant is pretty gloomy too.

Also worth trying:

Ngan Nga Gia Huy (☎ 388 0231; r 100,000-160,000d;) A friendly place with basic rooms (some with balconies) above a popular restaurant.

Minh Quan Hotel (☎ 388 0222; r from 150,000d;) Rooms here have good views of the market and mountains.

Eating

Of all the hotel restaurants in Bac Ha, the Congfu has great views of the animal market area through huge plate-glass windows, while the Ngan Nga Gia Huy is cheap, cheerful and slightly chaotic. But the best place in town is undoubtedly **Hoang Yen Restaurant** (mains 15,000-40,000d) opposite the Sao Mai Hotel, which has a great front terrace and a well-priced menu with good breakfast choices, fresh and dried noodle dishes, tasty pumpkin soup, cheap beer and Dalat wine. Otherwise head to **Duc Tuan Restaurant** (mains 30,000-50,000d) near the market for reliable Vietnamese food and big portions.

Getting There & Away

For transport information from Lao Cai see p184. Buses leave Bac Ha for Lao Cai (50,000d) at 6am, 7am, noon, 2pm and 3pm, and the journey takes about 2½ hours.

A motorbike/taxi to Lao Cai costs US$15/40, or to Sapa US$25/60. Tours to Bac Ha from Sapa cost from US$12 per person; on the way back you can bail out in Lao Cai and catch the night train back to Hanoi. These tour buses will take you one-way to Sapa for about US$10.

Bac Ha is about 330km (10 hours) from Hanoi. Tour operators in Hanoi offer four-day bus trips to Sapa, with a visit to Bac Ha included.

HA GIANG PROVINCE

Ha Giang is the final frontier in northern Vietnam, a lunar landscape of limestone pinnacles and granite outcrops. The far north of the province has some of the most spectacular scenery in the country and the trip between Dong Van and Meo Vac is a mind-blower for motorbikers, but not much fun on buses. It should be one of the most popular destinations in this region, but is one of those rare provinces that still requires a travel permit and the bureaucratic baloney keeps most at bay.

Ha Giang

☎ **0219 / pop 49,000 / elev 102m**

Ha Giang is somewhere to recharge the batteries on the long road north. This town, bisected by the broad river Lo, is a provincial capital with clean streets and an understated provincial ambience. The scenery is a good taste of things to come, with limestone outcrops soaring skywards over the suburbs. Those heading further north to explore the districts of Yen Minh, Dong Van, Meo Van and Bac Me need to arrange a permit (around US$20 per person, with discounts for groups) here.

ORIENTATION & INFORMATION

The main drag is P Nguyen Trai, which runs north–south paralleling the west bank of the Lo for 3km or so. You'll find the bus station, hotels, banks and restaurants on this road.

Travel permits are best organised through your hotel or the **Ha Giang Tourist Company** (☎ 386 7054; P Tran Hung Dao). The tourist company can also provide guides (US$30 per day), though it's no longer essential to have one.

The stone-faced police can organise permits, but routinely overcharge tourists.

Agribank has a branch on P Nguyen Trai with an ATM. There's a second ATM on the same street, and also a couple of places for internet access.

SLEEPING & EATING

There are plenty of good budget places in Ha Giang.

Duc Giang Hotel (☎ 387 5648; 14 P Nguyen Trai; s/d/tr 140,000/150,000/200,000d;) Right opposite the bus station, it's ideally placed for an early-morning getaway. A family-run place with clean, light and airy tiled rooms; triples are also available.

Huy Hoan Hotel (☎ 386 1288; P Nguyen Trai; r 150,000-250,000d) About 2km north of the bus station, this tall slim place is smartest hotel in town. Offers large, clean well-kept rooms with dark oriental furniture and (very) firm beds. There's also a lift and plenty of parking.

Khanh Huyen Hotel (☎ 386 7009; 115 P Tran Hung Dao; r 160,000d;) Just off the main street, this is another slimline hotel, with good spacious and inexpensive rooms with bathrooms, though some lack windows.

You'll find several cheap restaurants scattered along P Nguyen Trai, but for something exotic **Bien Nho Thanh Thu Restaurant** (☎ 328 2558; 17 P Duong Huu Nghi; meals from 70,000d) has crocodile, seafood, goose and traditional food from the ethnic minorities of Ha Giang. The only cafe in town, **A...Lo** (P Nguyen Trai) is a friendly but smoky place that has wi-fi.

GETTING THERE & AWAY

Ha Giang is 290km north of Hanoi. Ten daily buses (115,000d, seven hours) make the run down to Hanoi from the main bus station on P Nguyen Trai. Three daily minibuses trundle over to Meo Vac (75,000d, five hours), leaving from a separate minibus terminal on the east bank of town.

The road to Bac Ha is rough and only for the strongest 4WD or very experienced bikers; no buses run there from Ha Giang. The route is very beautiful and passes through the lively towns of Xin Man and Huong Su Phi.

Around Ha Giang

It's all about the trip north to the districts of Dong Van and Meo Vac, nestled against the border with China. It's also now possible to complete a kind of 'extreme north' loop, continuing on from Bao Lac down towards Hwy 3 and Cao Bang. However make sure you have your Ha Giang permit in order as travellers entering this region without permission are heavily fined by the officious police in Meo Vac and sent straight back to Ha Giang.

Leaving Ha Giang, the road climbs over the **Quan Ba Pass** (Heaven's Gate). Poetic licence is a national pastime in Vietnam, but this time the romantics have it right. The road winds over a saddle and opens up on to an awesome vista. It's dizzying to think of the forces of nature that carved out these incredible limestone towers.

Dropping into **Yen Minh** through pine forests, it is worth stopping for a drink before the final leg into the surreal scenery near China. **Dong Van** is just a small, dusty outpost, but don't be disappointed as it is the gateway to the best road trip in Vietnam: the 22km that snakes its way along the mountainside to **Meo Vac**. The road has been cut into the side of a cliff face and far below are the distant waters of the Nho Que River and towering above, the rock face of this mighty gorge. Take your time and soak it up, as this journey is one to savour.

Meo Vac is a district capital hemmed in by mountains and, like many towns in the northwest, it is steadily being settled by Vietnamese from elsewhere. There are several small faceless guesthouses in town, charging around 80,000d for a basic room with shared bathroom. Best is the **Viet Hung Guesthouse** (r 80,000d) with comfy beds and a TV, located on the road to Khau Vai district. You need to show your travel permit when checking in at any guesthouse. There are a couple of *com pho* places around town, plus the market has some food stalls.

SOUTH TO CAO BANG

Foreigners are now permitted to travel from Meo Vac to Bao Lac (around five hours) in Cao Bang province. Of course you must have your Ha Giang permit to do this spectacular trip. Most of the road is now paved, though it's best on trail bikes.

Heading south from Meo Vac you'll pass through the town of Khau Vai after about 20km, which is famous for its annual **love market** where the tribal minorities swap wives and husbands. Though it's undoubtedly a fascinating tradition, around fifty busloads of Vietnamese tourists now gatecrash the

TAKING THE HIGH ROAD

With spectacular scenery, little traffic and improved roads, more and more travellers are choosing to take a motorbike around the northwest loop from Hanoi up to Lao Cai, over to Dien Bien Phu and back to the capital.

Hanoi, where you'll find several specialist motorbike-tour operators, is the place to start making arrangements. Consider joining a tour (p507) or hiring a guide, who will know the roads and can help with mechanical and linguistic difficulties. Be sure to get acquainted with your bike first and check current road conditions and routes.

Most motorbikes in Vietnam are small capacity (under 250cc). For years the sturdy Minsk, built in Belarus, was the bike of choice for travellers and it still has many devoted aficionados. For the full story, consult www.minskclubvietnam.com, which even has a free PDF breakdown manual to download. Minsks are quirky bikes, not known for their reliability (though they will deal with rutted, rough roads well). They were common in northern Vietnam for years, and many mechanics know how to fix them. But today numbers have dwindled as mopeds and Chinese road bikes have proliferated.

Honda road bikes (such as the Honda GL160) and trail bikes are other good choices. These bikes have a good reputation for reliability and have decent shock absorbers. Some folk bike it around Vietnam on mopeds (like the 100cc Honda Wave), which tend to be reliable and their automatic gears make things easier for inexperienced riders. However you'll find bumps tough on your butt.

Rental agencies will help with checklists but some essentials include a good helmet, local mobile phone for emergencies, rain gear, a spare parts and repair kit (including spark plugs, spanners, inner tube and tyre levers), air pump and decent maps. Knee and elbow pads and gloves are also a good idea.

Highways can be hell in Vietnam, so it's wise to let the train take the strain on the long route north to Lao Cai. Load your bike into a goods carriage (180,000d) while you sleep in a berth. You'll have to (almost) drain it of petrol. Then in Lao Cai, pick it up, fill up, fire it up and off you go.

Take it slowly, particularly in the rain: smooth paved roads can turn into muddy tracks in no time. Do not ride during or immediately after heavy rain storms as this is the time a landslide might occur (many mountain roads are quite new and the cliff embankments can be unstable). Expect to average about 35km per hour. Only use safe hotel parking. Fill up from petrol stations where the gas is less likely to have been watered down.

And if you're running short on time or energy remember that many bus companies will let you put your bike on the roof of a bus (around 500,000d from Son La to Hanoi), but get permission first from your bike rental company.

Recommended motorbike specialists in Hanoi include Cuong's Motorbike Adventure (p119) and Off Road Vietnam (p119).

dating scene, and this unique event has become something of a circus. It takes place on the 27th day of the 3rd lunar month in the Vietnamese calendar, usually from late April to mid-May.

After Khau Vai, there's a new bridge, which should open in 2009 or 2010, being built over the Nho Que River. Until it does you have to cross the river on a bamboo raft; a local will pole you over for a small fee. From Bao Lac to Cao Bang is another seven hours on bumpy roads via Nguyen Binh.

It's not currently possible to do this trip in reverse from Cao Bang province, as you have to have a permit issued in Ha Giang town to enter this border region. Check the latest situation on the forums of www.gt-rider.com.

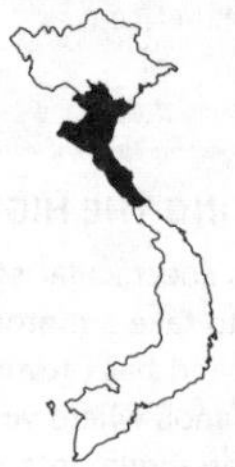

North-Central Vietnam

Looking for the 'real' Vietnam? Try the north-central region on for size. It's overlooked by most travellers scurrying between Hanoi and Hue, which may be why it's still so charming and unassuming. The countryside is extraordinarily beautiful yet largely free of tourist traps, the towns are filled with regular folk who won't try to sell you a conical hat, and there's still a blissful dearth of people who speak English.

The jewel in the crown is Ninh Binh, blessed with a karst-studded landscape set off by lush green rice paddies. People come for a day, then stay for several when they realise that beyond the pleasant-enough Tam Coc is even more beautiful backcountry, the kind that's best explored on two wheels. There are also a number of churches here, the *grande dame* being the cathedral at Phat Diem (immortalised in Graham Greene's *The Quiet American*).

Further south, the land turns dour, the after-effects of wartime bombing exacerbated by unimaginative postwar architecture. Few foreigners show up here unless they're heading to Laos. While the only thing of beauty is the majestic Phong Nha Cave, if you're tired of the tourist trail you could easily take a break and disappear into Dong Hoi for a couple of days. Take your time – no one's going to hassle you about it either way.

HIGHLIGHTS

- Gawk at the limestone monoliths of **Tam Coc** (p193) as you're lulled in a rowboat down the Ngo Dong River
- Confound your imagination with the East-meets-West architecture at **Phat Diem Cathedral** (p198)
- Go underground and explore the nooks and crannies of **Phong Nha Cave** (p202)
- Head out for a nature ramble at **Cuc Phuong National Park** (p196)
- Lap up the royal view at **Hoa Lu's ancient temples** (p195)

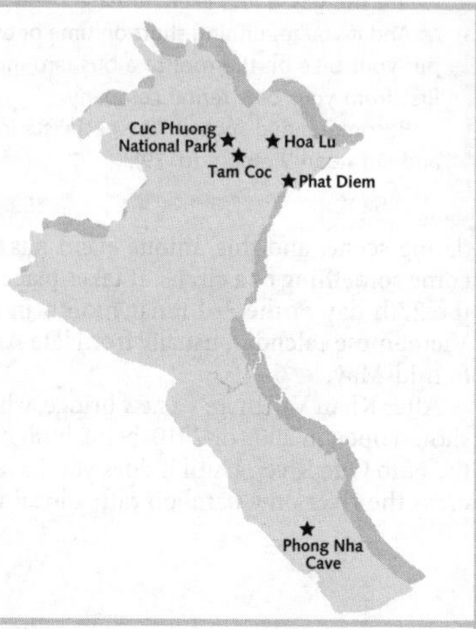

- ELEVATION: 1–2711M
- BEST TIME TO VISIT: APR–OCT

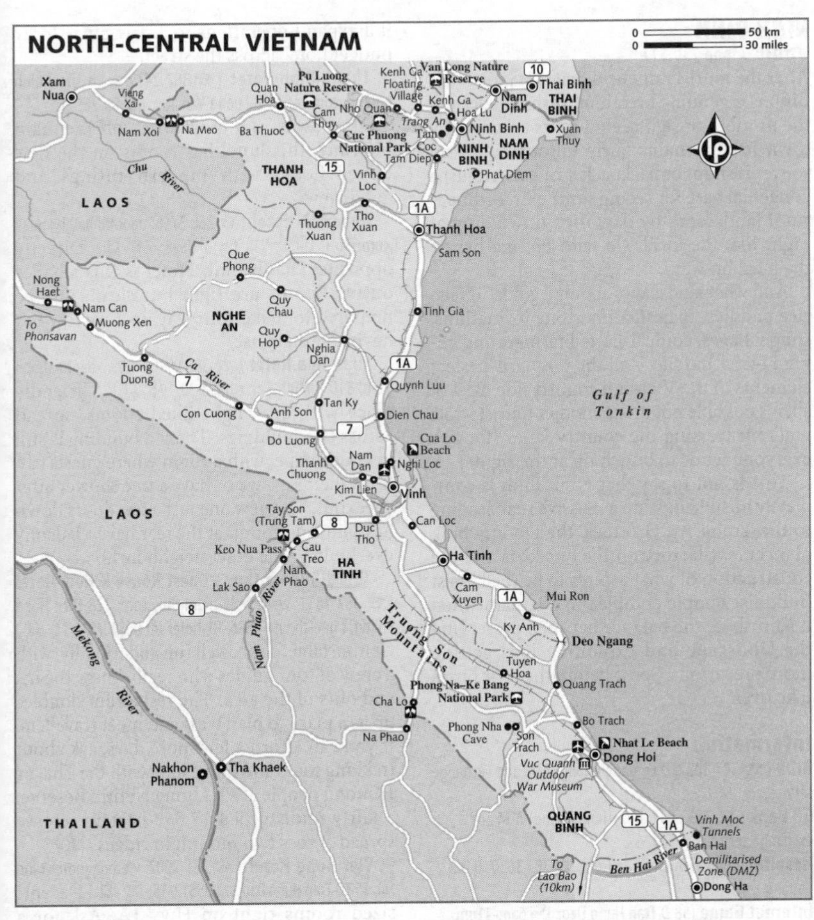

History

Quiet though it is today, this region has seen its fair share of historical moments. After Vietnam shook off almost a millennium of Chinese rule in the 10th century, one of the earliest emperors established the capital at Hoa Lu, setting his citadel amid the protection of towering limestone cliffs. In the 13th and 14th centuries, the Tran dynasty based in Thang Long (present-day Hanoi) introduced a peculiar administrative arrangement: the heirs to the throne partially succeeded their fathers as king, while the latter shared power in an unofficial capital in Tuc Mac, about 5km from Nam Dinh. This prevented succession disputes and made the Tran dynasty one of the most politically stable and prosperous in Vietnamese history.

During the American War, the region suffered tremendous damage from US bombing, reducing most towns to rubble and debris. Vinh and Dong Hoi were key military targets: the former was a port supplying the Ho Chi Minh Trail, the latter was the North Vietnamese Army's main staging area.

Getting There & Away

The major north–south rail route cuts a swathe directly through the region, as does Hwy 1A. There are airports at Vinh and Dong Hoi, with flights to Ho Chi Minh City (HCMC) and Hanoi.

NINH BINH

☎ 030 / pop 130,517

After the tourist minefield that is Hanoi, Ninh Binh is a genuine breath of fresh air. Despite the number of sightseeing spots around, the town itself remains fairly untouristed – no souvenir shops or backpacker cafes here, just a congenial base for seeing some extraordinary rural landscapes by day, then unwinding at night like the locals do with *bia hoi* beside the local brewery.

And what landscapes abound: golden-green rice paddies, majestic limestone formations, snug villages, conical-hatted farmers and benign water buffalo – all the postcard-perfect elements of the Vietnam countryside. Best of all, it's possible not to see another tourist while you're traversing the country lanes (though everyone tends to bunch up at the sights).

This is not to say that Ninh Binh is completely unsullied. With a massive road leading to the Trang An Grottoes, the gloomy bulk of a cement factory on the outskirts and the construction of what aspires to be the largest Buddhist temple complex in Vietnam when it's finished, the balance between preserving the landscape and exploiting it is getting more precarious. See it before the tour buses take over.

Information

BIDV (☎ 387 1082; Đ Le Hong Phong) ATM and exchange service.

GP Bank (☎ 389 6637; Đ Le Hong Phong) ATM and exchange service.

Hospital (Benh Vien Da Khoa Tinh; ☎ 387 1030; Đ Hai Thuong Lan)

Internet Game (58 Đ Tran Hung Dao; 6am-11pm; per hr 10,000d)

Main post office (Đ Tran Hung Dao)

Vietin Bank & ATM (☎ 388 2057; Đ Tran Hung Dao)

Vietin Bank ATM (Đ Tran Hung Dao)

Sleeping

Ninh Binh hoteliers have a well-deserved reputation for friendly service and some of the best-value accommodation in Vietnam. Most can make tour arrangements, and hotel staff and guides often speak good English.

Queen Mini Hotel (☎ 387 1874; luongvn2001@yahoo.com; 21 Đ Hoang Hoa Tham; dm US$2, r US$5-7;) Located right by the train station, this small hotel has simple rooms and runs popular tour services – it has a big book of travellers' comments to prove it. By the end of 2009, it'll expand operations to a new nine-storey budget hotel across the street.

Thanh Binh Hotel (☎ 387 2439; www.thanhbinhhotelnb.com.vn; 31 Đ Luong Van Tuy; r US$5-25;) Tucked away in a quiet street off the main highway, this hotel has rooms on the new upper floors with modern fittings and good views.

Ngoc Anh Hotel (☎ 388 3768; ngocanhhotel@gmail.com; 30 Đ Luong Van Tuy; r US$8;) Directly opposite Thanh Binh Hotel is this smaller outfit. Rooms are tight but clean; just be prepared to make your way up a narrow but navigable staircase.

Xuan Hoa Hotel (☎ 388 0970; www.xuanhoahotel.com; 31D P Minh Kai; r US$8-30;) A friendly place with airy, light-filled rooms, spread across two buildings. The old building is still in good shape, with a room where guests can leave their luggage or have a free shower after checkout. The new one just a few doors down has a lift, and rooms at the rear have a balcony overlooking the quiet neighbourhood.

our pick **Thanhthuy's Guest House & New Hotel** (☎ 387 1811; www.hotelthanhthuy.com; 128 Đ Le Hong Phong; r guesthouse US$6-10, hotel s/d US$10/12;) Comfortable, clean, well run and friendly, with a crew of tour guides who really know the ins and outs of the area. The restaurant doubles up as a place to plan trips and meet travellers. If you can afford a few more days, ask about trekking tours and homestays with the Thai or H'mong people at Pu Luong Nature Reserve, a fairly undisturbed 17,662-hectare reserve spread across two mountain ridges.

Viet Hung Hotel (☎ 387 2002; viethunghotel@vnn.vn; 150 Đ Tran Hung Dao; s/d US$12/15;) Decent-sized rooms right on Hwy 1A. Ask for a room at the back to avoid the noise. Prices include breakfast.

Thuy Anh Hotel (☎ 387 1602; www.thuyanhhotel.com; 55A Đ Truong Han Sieu; s/d old wing US$20/25, new wing US$30/35;) This is as swanky as it gets in Ninh Binh. Rooms are comfortable and welcoming, while the top-floor bar offers a breezy spot to watch the Ninh Binh rooftops. The owner will open a second upmarket Ninh Binh Legend Hotel near the Trang An Grottoes in late 2009.

Eating & Drinking

Although Ninh Binh is popular with backpackers, the town doesn't have much in the way of restaurants. The local speciality is *de* (goat meat), usually served with fresh herbs

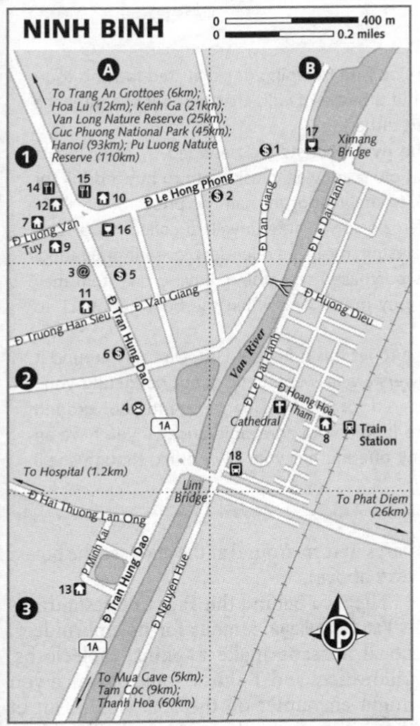

INFORMATION

BIDV	1	B1
GP Bank	2	B1
Internet Game	3	A2
Main Post Office	4	A2
Vietin Bank	5	A2
Vietin Bank ATM	6	A2

SLEEPING

Ngoc Anh Hotel	7	A1
Queen Mini Hotel	8	B2
Thanh Binh Hotel	9	A1
Thanhthuy's Guesthouse & New Hotel	10	A1
Thuy Anh Hotel	11	A2
Viet Hung Hotel	12	A1
Xuan Hoa Hotel	13	A3

EATING

Casual Eateries	(see 15)	
Huong Mai Restaurant	14	A1
Pho Ngan Eateries	15	A1

DRINKING

Bia hoi	16	A1
Bia hoi	17	B1

TRANSPORT

Bus Station	18	B2

and rice paper to wrap it in. A good place to try this is the blue-walled **Huong Mai Restaurant** (☎ 387 1351; 12 Đ Tran Hung Dao; dishes 10,000-80,000d; ⏰ lunch & dinner). There is an English menu, though the staff don't speak English. Try the fried goat with chilli and citronella, and don't let the oversized goat's head mounted over the counter intimidate you.

There are **casual eateries** (near Xuan Hoa Hotel) and delicious **pho ngan eateries** (duck noodle soup; Đ Tran Hung Dao) around the corner from Thanhthuy's. Otherwise, most travellers eat at their hotel (dishes from 20,000d to 60,000d). Mrs Xuan's cooking at Xuan Hoa Hotel is legendary.

For *bia hoi*, try the sidewalk setups directly opposite Thanhthuy's or the equally casual riverside places near Ximang Bridge beside the local brewery.

Getting There & Away

BUS

Ninh Binh's **bus station** (Đ Le Dai Hanh) is located near the Lim Bridge, just below the overpass to Phat Diem. Public buses leave almost every 15 minutes for the Giap Bat bus station in Hanoi (45,000d, 2½ hours, 93km). Ninh Binh is also a stop for open-tour buses between Hanoi (US$5, two hours) and Hue (US$11, 10 hours), which can deposit and pick up passengers at some hotels.

CAR & MOTORBIKE

The nearest major towns are Hanoi (93km) and Vinh (230km).

TRAIN

The **train station** (Ga Ninh Binh; ☎ 367 3619; 1 Đ Hoang Hoa Tham) is a scheduled stop for Reunification Express trains, with destinations including Hanoi (40,000d, two to 2½ hours, four daily), Vinh (80,000d, six hours, three daily) and Hue (235,000d, 12½ to 13½ hours, four daily).

Getting Around

Most hotels rent out bicycles (per day US$1 to US$2) and motorbikes (per day US$5 to US$6). A motorbike driver's rates will depend on distance and time, but for a full day is likely to be around US$10.

AROUND NINH BINH

Tam Coc

This is what most travellers come to Ninh Binh to see: limestone karsts sweeping up from serene rice paddies, best appreciated on a languorous rowboat ride down the river, to the soundtrack of water lapping against the oars.

SURVIVING THE TAM COC TANGO

It's not surprising to see boats returning from Tam Coc with frowning or exhausted-looking tourists. It's not any physical test that's bested them, but a battle of wills that requires the patience of a saint (a little devilish good humour won't hurt either).

Here's the setup: as boats reach the end of the river, tourists are beseiged by other boats selling snacks and drinks. If repeatedly declined, an old scam was to ask them to buy a drink for their rower, which the rower would later sell back to the vendor for half the price.

When the boats turn to head upstream, the female rower now unveils a collection of embroidered pictures, tablecloths and T-shirts. The sales pitch can be relentless, even intimidating. Some rowers have refused to budge until visitors purchased something. Buying one item may not halt the hard sell; rowers simply parrot, 'You buy more!' And when the boat gets back to shore, they *still* expect a tip.

Despite the potential aggro, it would be a shame to let this ruin your visit. One way around it is to go late in the day, when most sellers and rowers are less energetic about badgering you.

Alternatively, forewarned is forearmed: be prepared for the little dance, stand your ground politely and don't buy anything unless you want to (and get an agreeable price). If you have an elderly rower, you can appease your conscience by offering her your own drink, though she'll probably refuse.

It's de rigueur to describe the area around Tam Coc as the inland version of Halong Bay, but that's not exactly a fair comparison. Halong Bay (p139) sweeps across 3000 islands; at **Tam Coc** (admission 30,000d, boat 60,000d) the encounter is much more intimate. Along a mere 2km of the Ngo Dong River, undisturbed by engine noise, the limestone outcrops loom closer, larger – this is the kind of landscape that would have suited the Romantic poets just fine.

Except that isn't most visitors' experience of Tam Coc. The scenery is spectacular but given its immense popularity, the river's often filled with a crooked procession of boats inching by, with all the accompanying babble and noise. To really enjoy the view, come in the early morning or late afternoon.

Each boat carries two visitors, as well as the main rower and a secondary rower. The route takes boats through the three caves for which Tam Coc is named: Hang Ca (127m long), Hang Giua (70m long) and Hang Cuoi (45m long). Eagle-eyed travellers may spot a small temple perched on an apparently inaccessible hilltop (see opposite).

Tickets are sold at the small booking office by the car park. The journey takes about two hours. It's not necessary to have a torch (flashlight), but remember to bring sunscreen and a hat or umbrella, as the boats aren't shaded. Rowers are adept at using their feet to propel the oars, which makes for a tourist-pleasing Kodak moment. Less pleasing is the hard sell that kicks in as the boat prepares to turn around at the end (see the boxed text, above).

The area behind the Tam Coc restaurants is **Van Lan village**, famous for its embroidery. Local artisans make napkins, tablecloths, pillowcases and T-shirts, some of which you might encounter on the boat ride. A lot of these items are sold on Hanoi's Pho Hang Gai (p117), but it's cheaper to buy them here, direct from the artisans.

BICH DONG PAGODA

This charming cluster of **cave temples** (Jade Grotto; admission free) is a couple of kilometres north of Tam Coc. The Lower Pagoda is located at the foot of the outcrop, from which it's a climb of about 100 steps to the Middle Pagoda, then a shorter but still steep ascent to the Upper Pagoda.

Inside each cave temple, looming statues and the smoke of burning incense create an otherworldly atmosphere. Outside the reverse couldn't be more true: there are some incredible views of the countryside.

SLEEPING & EATING

It's possible to stay in Van Lan village and get an early start on the river the next day.

Lang Khanh Guest House (☎ 361 8073; langkhanhtc@yahoo.com.vn; r US$5-10; ✖) About 100m from the jetty on the road from Ninh Binh, this family-run guesthouse has small but clean rooms, and a simple restaurant (dishes 40,000d to 60,000d; open breakfast, lunch and dinner).

Anh Dzung Hotel (☎ 361 8020; anhdzung_tamcoc@yahoo.com; r US$20-30;) A few steps down the road is this more upmarket option, with comfortable rooms and a huge restaurant (dishes 40,000d to 80,000d; open breakfast, lunch and dinner).

GETTING THERE & AWAY

Tam Coc is 9km southwest of Ninh Binh. Follow Hwy 1A south and turn west at the Tam Coc turn-off, marked by giant totem pole–like pillars. Ninh Binh hotels run day tours, or make your own way by bicycle or motorbike. Hotel staff can advise you on some beautiful back roads.

Budget cafes in Hanoi book day trips to Tam Coc and Hoa Lu. The standard version goes for about US$20, but expect to pay US$30 and up for a smaller group, comfortable vehicle and professional guide.

Mua Cave

Tucked away at the end of a road running between rice paddies, **Mua Cave** (Cave of Dance; admission 20,000d) is not terribly impressive, but the main attraction is the panoramic view from the peak above. A stone staircase beside the cave entrance zigzags up the side of the karst (beware the goat droppings) and it's almost 500 steps to the top where there's a simple altar to Quan Am (Goddess of Mercy). Look west and you'll see the Ngo Dong River winding through Tam Coc.

The climb is paved but pretty steep in sections, so bring some water and allow an hour for the trip (including time at the top for picture-taking). Mua Cave is 5km from Ninh Binh and a popular stop on motorbike tours heading to Tam Coc.

Hoa Lu

Hoa Lu was the capital of Vietnam during the Dinh (968–80 AD) and early Le (980–1009 AD) dynasties. The Dinh chose the site to put some distance between them and China, as well as to take advantage of the protection of the region's rocky outcrops, as spectacular as Tam Coc's. Most of the ancient citadel has been destroyed, but it used to cover about 3 sq km.

Yen Ngua Mountain provides a scenic backdrop for Hoa Lu's two surviving **temples** (admission 10,000d), both intimate spaces dominated by beautiful dark-red lacquered pillars. The first, Dinh Tien Hoang, was restored in the 17th century and is dedicated to the Dinh dynasty. At the front of the main temple building is the stone pedestal of a royal throne; inside are bronze bells and a statue of Emperor Dinh Tien Hoang with his three sons.

The second temple is dedicated to Le Dai Hanh, an early Le monarch. Inside the main hall is the usual assortment of drums, gongs, incense burners, candle holders and weapons, with a statue of the king in the middle, his queen on the right and their son on the left. In the left-hand section of this complex a museum features part of the excavations of the 10th-century citadel wall.

Given how much of it is in ruins, perhaps the best way to appreciate Hoa Lu is to hike up to the tomb of Emperor Dinh Tien Hoang, 80m up the flight of steps at the hill opposite the ticket office. It takes about 20 minutes to go up, and for the best view of Hoa Lu, stop and look back just before you reach the tomb.

GETTING THERE & AWAY

Hoa Lu is 12km northwest of Ninh Binh; turn left 6km north of town on Hwy 1A. There is no public transport available. Ask your hotel about the blissful back roads linking Hoa Lu to Tam Coc.

Kenh Ga

The village of Kenh Ga (Chicken Canal) gets its name, apparently, from the number of wild chickens that used to live here, but it's the riverine way of life that's the main draw. While it's on a smaller scale than in the Mekong Delta, the Delta doesn't have the stunning limestone formations that so dramatically punctuate the landscape here.

The local people seem to spend most of their lives on or in the water: watching over their floating fish-breeding pens, harvesting river grass for fish feed or selling vegies boat-to-boat. Even the children commute to school by boat. The river is used for everything from bathing, to washing plucked chickens, to defecating in.

While this used to be largely a floating village, as fortunes have improved there are more houses on the riverbanks, leading off in from the yellow cathedral at the village centre. You'll still see some tiny wooden shelters on boats – the poorest of the poor.

From the pier you can hire a **motorboat** (☎ 386 8560; 50,000d) for a 1½-hour ride along the river around the village. Ask the boatman to stop and let you walk around. You'll be the subject of curious stares, but no one speaks English and no one will try to sell you anything (not even a cold drink).

GETTING THERE & AWAY

Kenh Ga is 21km from Ninh Binh off the road to Cuc Phuong National Park. Follow Hwy 1A north for 11km, then it's a 10km drive west to the boat pier.

Van Long Nature Reserve

Set amid yet more glorious limestone pinnacles, this tranquil **reserve** (admission 15,000d, boat 40,000d) comprises a reedy wetland that's popular with bird-watchers. Among the bird species that have been spotted here are the rare black-faced spoonbill, cotton pygmy goose and white-browed crake. Van Long is also one of the last wild refuges of the endangered Delacour's langur, partly because the wetlands keep predators and poachers at bay. Langurs are not easy to spot; try your luck early in the morning or in the evening.

As the nature reserve doesn't get as busy as Tam Coc, a boat ride (maximum two people per boat) is considerably more relaxing. The shallow waters are about 2m deep and rowers rely on a combination of rowing and punting with a bamboo pole.

Van Long is 2km east of Tran Me, a small town 23km from Ninh Binh along the road to Cuc Phuong. It can be easily combined with a visit to Kenh Ga and, at a stretch, both can be visited en route to Cuc Phuong National Park.

Trang An Grottoes

At the time of research, the government was constructing a new tourism complex at **Trang An**, touting it as a bigger, better version of Tam Coc. It will offer boat rides along the Sao Khe River through 15 limestone caves, many of them longer and deeper than those at Tam Coc. The journey should take 2½ to three hours and is supposed to be free of the infamous boat vendors (see the boxed text, p194).

Trang An is likely to be marketed as an ecotourism destination, but its development has entailed relocating farmers and fishermen from the area, expanding dirt tracks into carriageways for tour buses, and drilling tunnels through some of the very limestone terrain that travellers come here to admire. If this is the shape of things to come, it doesn't augur well for the natural beauty of the province.

The Trang An Grottoes are about 7km northwest of Ninh Binh. Follow the wide highway heading out of town.

CUC PHUONG NATIONAL PARK

☎ 030 / elevation 150-656m

Established in 1962, this **national park** (☎ 384 8006; www.cucphuongtourism.com; adult/child 20,000/10,000d) is one of Vietnam's most important protected areas. Though wildlife has suffered a precipitous decline in Vietnam in recent decades, the park's 222 sq km of primary tropical forest remains home to an amazing variety of animal and plant life: 307 species of bird, 133 species of mammal, 122 species of reptile, 2000 plant species and counting.

The national park covers an area that spans two limestone mountain ranges across three provinces. Its highest peak is Dinh May Bac (Silver Cloud Peak) at 656m. No less an eminence than Ho Chi Minh took time off from the war in 1963 to declare this Vietnam's first national park, saying: 'Forest is gold. If we know how to conserve it well, it will be very precious. Destruction of the forest will lead to serious effects on both life and productivity.'

Despite his exhortations, poaching and habitat destruction continue to plague the park. Improved roads have led to more illegal logging, and many native species – the Asiatic black bear, Siamese crocodile, wild dog and tiger – have vanished as a result of human activity.

To learn more about the park's conservation efforts, visit the excellent **Endangered Primate Rescue Center** and **Turtle Conservation Center** (see the boxed text, opposite). The former is located about 500m before the **national park visitor centre** (☎ 384 8006; near park entrance), the latter a little farther down from it. You'll have to get a guide (10,000d) from the visitor centre, but entry to both centres is free so consider purchasing some souvenirs or making a donation.

The park is also home to the minority Muong people, whom the government relocated from the park's central valley to its western edge in the late 1980s. This was ostensibly to encourage a shift from their slash-and-burn practices to sedentary farming, but the government's star project, the Ho Chi Minh Highway, subsequently cut across some of the former Muong parklands.

SAVING MONKEYS AND TURTLES

Cuc Phuong's **conservation centres** (admission free, with guide 10,000d) provide a glimpse of their work and the fascinating animals they're trying to help. The **Endangered Primate Rescue Center** (☎ 384 8002; www.primatecenter.org; 🕑 9-11am & 1-4pm) is home to over 140 creatures from 15 species of gibbon, langur and loris. The gibbon is a long-armed, fruit-eating ape, the langur is a long-tailed, tree-dwelling monkey, and the loris is a smaller nocturnal primate with large eyes.

All the centre's animals were either bred here or rescued from cages or illegal traders, who transport them mostly to China to become medicinal ingredients. These rare animals can fetch anywhere between US$200 and US$1000 for their 'medicinal worth', such as for gallstone relief or as an aphrodisiac.

The centre has bred 100 offspring in all, including the world's first Cat Ba langur and grey-shanked Douc langur bred in captivity. As a preliminary step to reintroduce these primates into their natural habitat, about 20 gibbons, Hatinh langurs and Douc langurs have been released into a semi-wild area adjacent to the centre, as well as into another site at Phong Nha–Ke Bang National Park.

The **Turtle Conservation Center** (☎ 384 8090; www.asianturtlenetwork.org/project%20profiles/vietnam/cuc_phuong.htm; 🕑 9-11.15am & 2-4.45pm) houses over 1000 turtles from 20 of Vietnam's 25 native species. This includes animals that were confiscated from smugglers; again it's China generating the demand, for culinary and medicinal value.

In 2007 the Center successfully bred 127 turtles from 11 different species including six native endangered species. Its new interpretation centre has insightful displays (including incubation and hatchling viewing areas).

The best time of year to visit the park is in the dry months from November to February. From April to June it becomes increasingly hot, wet and muddy, and from July to October the rains arrive, bringing lots of leeches. Visitors in April and May may see some of the millions of butterflies that breed here. Avoid the place on weekends – it fills up with Vietnamese visitors and all the accompanying ruckus.

The visitor centre near the entrance is low key and informative, while the **park centre** (Bong) is the main hub of activity.

Hiking

Excellent hiking opportunities abound in the park. Short walks include a large **botanic garden** near the park headquarters with deer, civets, gibbons and langurs. Another short trail leads to a steep 220-step stairway to the **Cave of Prehistoric Man**. Human graves and tools were found here dating back 7500 years, making it one of the oldest sites of human habitation in Vietnam. Sadly the artefacts were handed to the local museum, leaving the unlit cave with three old tomb mounds and many bats.

Popular day trails include a 6km-return walk to the massive, 1000-year-old **'old tree'** (*Tetrameles nudiflora*) and a longer four-hour hike to **Silver Cloud Peak**. There's also a strenuous five-hour hike to **Kanh**, a Muong village. You can overnight here with local families (p198) and raft on the Buoi River (50,000d).

Park staff can provide you with basic maps, but a guide is recommended for day trips and mandatory for longer treks. For a group of up to five people, a guide for the Silver Cloud Peak hike costs US$20 per day and one for the hike to the Kanh Village costs US$25 per day.

Sleeping & Eating

There are three accommodation areas in the park. The park centre at Bong, 18km from the park entrance, is the best place to be for an early morning walk or bird-watching. There are some forlorn rooms with no hot water in a **pseudo stilt house** (per person US$6), a building with large **four-bed rooms** (r US$16) and a few **bungalows** (r US$25).

At the visitor centre beside the park entrance the setup is similar: tight, dark rooms in a faux **stilt house** (per person US$5), **guesthouse rooms** (r US$20) and one stand-alone **bungalow for two** (US$25). The nicest accommodations are the **bungalows** (r US$20) around the artificial Mac Lake, 2km inside the park.

Camping (per person US$2, with a tent US$4) is available at the visitor centre or Mac Lake. There are **restaurants** (meals 20,000-40,000d) at the park centre and visitor centre; meals can be ordered for those camping or staying at Mac Lake.

Homestays with Muong families are available at **Kanh village** (per person US$5). The dwellings are predictably basic.

The park can get very busy here at weekends and during school holidays. Reservations can be made through the national park visitor centre (p196).

Getting There & Away

Cuc Phuong National Park is 45km from Ninh Binh. The turn-off from Hwy 1A is north of Ninh Binh and follows the road that goes to Kenh Ga and Van Long Nature Reserve.

From Ninh Binh, there is a regular bus to Cuc Phuong (15,000d). From Hanoi, a bus from Giap Bat bus station runs directly to Cuc Phuong (70,000d) at 9am, returning from Cuc Phuong at 3pm. Alternatively, take a bus to Nho Quan (40,000d, 2½ to 3½ hours, six daily) and grab a motorbike (50,000d) to the park entrance.

PHAT DIEM

The Tay Ninh (p393) of the north, Phat Diem is the home of a celebrated **cathedral** (admission free), which is remarkable for its vast dimensions and inimitable Sino-Vietnamese architecture, with a dash of European dressing for good measure.

During the French era this was an important centre of Catholicism and Phat Diem's bishop ruled the area with his private army, Middle Ages–style, until French troops took over in 1951. The cathedral (1891) featured prominently in Graham Greene's novel *The Quiet American*, and it was from the bell tower that the author watched battles between the North Vietnamese Army and the French.

The cathedral complex is fronted by an ornamental lake with a statue of an open-armed Christ rising from a small island. At busy times you may have to negotiate with aggressive sellers and beggars to earn your entrance, but inside it's peaceful in a sepulchre-like way. The cathedral itself is dominated by cool wood, with a vaulted ceiling supported by massive columns almost 1m in diameter and 10m tall. Above the altar (made from a single block of granite), Vietnamese-looking cherubs with golden wings swarm, while Chinese-style clouds drift across the blue ceiling. Beneath them are icons of the martyrs slaughtered by Emperor Tu Duc during the anti-Catholic purges of the 1850s.

Opposite the cathedral's main doors is the free-standing bell tower, with stone columns carved to look like bamboo. At its base lie two enormous stone slabs. Their sole purpose was to provide a perch for mandarins to sit and observe – no doubt with great amusement – the rituals of the Catholic mass. Atop the tower is a gloriously enormous bell.

Between the tower and the cathedral is the tomb of the Vietnamese founder, Father Six. Behind the main building is a large pile of limestone boulders – Father Six piled them up to test whether the boggy ground would support his plans. The rock heap has been used to form a Lourdes grotto, with a somewhat spooky bust of Father Six beside it.

Hordes of Vietnamese tourists come to this place, few of them Catholic but many curious about churches and Christianity. Daily mass is celebrated at 5am and 5pm, when the massive bell is rung and the faithful stream into the cathedral, all dressed up.

Not far from this cathedral is a **covered bridge** dating from the late 19th century. **Dong Huong Pagoda** is the largest pagoda in the area, catering to the Buddhist community. Many of its congregation are from the minority Muong people. To find it, turn right at the canal as you're approaching town from the north and follow the small road alongside the water for 3km.

A Gothic counterpoint to Phat Diem is the **cathedral** at Ton Dao, along route 10 about 5km from Phat Diem. It looks beatifically out over rice fields and, at the rear of the churchyard, a statue of the Virgin Mary keeps unexpected company with porcelain images of Quan Am.

Getting There & Away

Phat Diem, sometimes known by its former name Kim Son, is 121km south of Hanoi and 26km southeast of Ninh Binh. There are direct buses from Ninh Binh to Phat Diem (16,000d, one hour), or you can go by bicycle or motorbike (140,000d for a motorbike and driver, including waiting time).

VINH

☎ **038 / pop 283,000**

Practically obliterated during the American War, Vinh was hastily rebuilt with East German aid, hence the frightful blockish

NORTH-CENTRAL VIETNAM

BORDER CROSSING BLUES 1

Crossing the border between north-central Vietnam and Laos is at best uneventful, at worst an exercise in exasperation that might make a good travel story someday. If you've got the time, head south to Lao Bao (p216).

Those seeking some kind of backwoods adventure can try crossing at **Nam Xoi–Na Meo** (7am-5pm) in Thanh Hoa province. It's the most remote crossing, 175km northwest of Thanh Hoa (Vietnam) and 70km east of Xam Nua (Laos), and visas for either country are not available. It takes at least a day, but be prepared to overnight in either border town (preferably Na Meo).

From Xam Nua, catch a *songthaew* (pick-up truck, 25,000 kip, four hours) to Nam Xoi. Once in Vietnam, there ought to be motorbikes for hire but we've heard that bus operators have cornered the market, demanding up to US$30 for the journey to Thanh Hoa every Tuesday, Thursday and Saturday (it should cost about US$8). An alternative is the direct bus from Xam Nua to Thanh Hoa every Saturday, leaving at 7.40am (100,000 kip, five hours), though again travellers get overcharged and the bus doesn't always run when it's scheduled.

In the opposite direction, there is a bus from Thanh Hoa to Xam Nua, scheduled to leave every Friday at 8am (160,000d). Onward transport into Laos is extremely irregular; expect to hitch a ride on a truck to Xam Nua or Vieng Xai for US$5 to US$10.

architecture that dominates the downtown drag. Unlike other Vietnamese towns, it has wide boulevards with equally wide pavements that are surprisingly devoid of street stalls – easy to walk down but there's nothing to see.

Despite attempts to prettify the place with trees and parks, this is an industrial city through and through. There are precious few reasons to stop here unless you are a Ho Chi Minh devotee (he was born in a nearby village) or passing through the Laos border.

History

Vinh came to prominence as the 'Phoenix Capital City' of the Tay Son Rebellion and under French rule in the late 19th century, it began its transformation into an industrial city. A May Day demonstration in 1930 was suppressed by the police, who killed seven people. Nonetheless revolutionary fervour spread, with Vinh's communist cells, trade unions and farmers' organisations earning it the appellation 'Red-Glorious City'.

In the early 1950s, the city was reduced to rubble by a three-punch whammy: French aerial bombing, the Viet Minh's scorched-earth policy and finally a huge fire. During the American War, the port of Vinh became a key supply point for the Ho Chi Minh Trail (see the boxed text, p334). Vinh was thus the target of the first American bombing of North Vietnam and was relentlessly pounded for eight years – eventually leaving only two buildings intact.

Orientation

As Hwy 1A enters Vinh from the south, it crosses over the mouth of the Lam River (Ca River), also known as the Cua Hoi Estuary.

Information

BIDV ATM (Đ Quang Trung)

Main post office (☎ 356 1408; Đ Nguyen Thi Minh Khai) For phone calls and postal services. Also has an internet centre attached (per 15min 500d).

Saigon Commercial Bank (☎ 358 8502; 25 Đ Quang Trang) ATM and exchange services.

Vietcombank ATM (33 Đ Le Mao)

Vinh City Hospital (Benh Vien Da Khoa Thanh Pho Vinh; ☎ 383 5279; 178 Đ Tran Phu)

Sights & Activities

There's not a lot left to see of Vinh's **citadel** (1831) apart from the sludgy green moat and three gates: **Left Gate** (Cua Ta; Đ Dao Tan), **Right Gate** (Cua Huu; Đ Dao Tan) and **Front Gate** (Cua Tien; Khoi 5 Đ Dang Thai Than). The walk between the Left and Right Gates provides a pleasant interlude and passes the little-visited **Xo Viet Nghe Tinh Museum** (admission free; Đ Dao Tan; 7-11am & 1-5pm), which memorialises local heroes of the nationalist movement against the French in 1930–31. Outside, in true socialist-art style, is a large stone **monument** to those who perished at the hands of the French.

Sleeping

Hai Cafe Guesthouse (☎ 358 5121; 77 Đ Le Loi; r 110,000d;) This cheapie has rooms in a quiet lane just behind the bus station. Enquire at the Hai

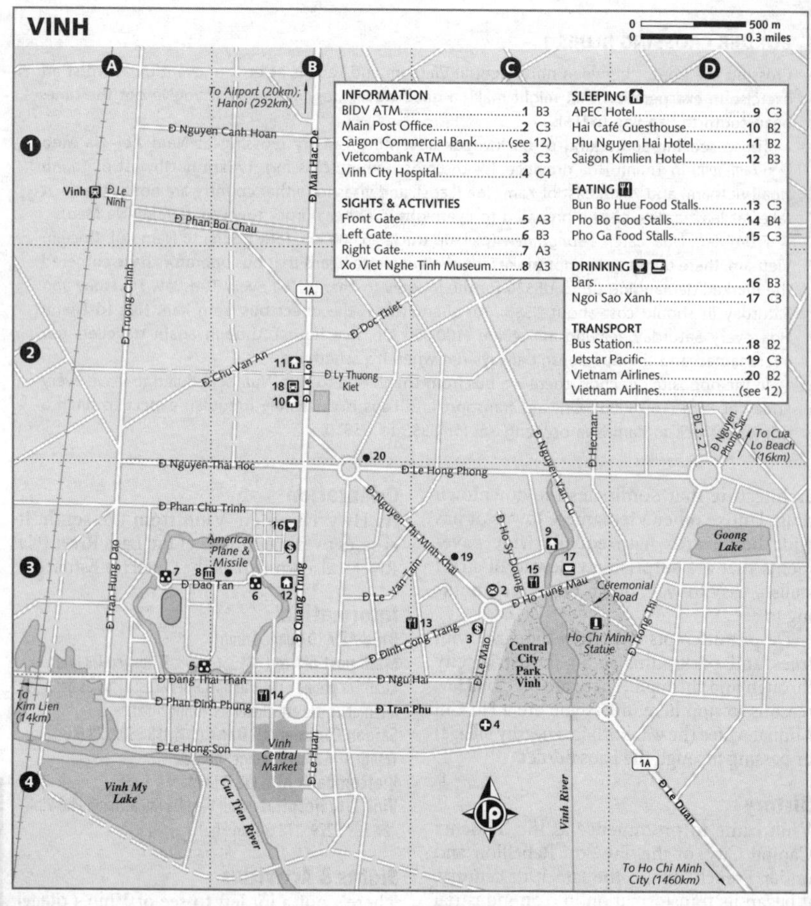

Café office at the bus station (on your left after you enter the parking lot).

APEC Hotel (☎ 358 9466; apec_hotel_na@yahoo.com; Ngo 1 Đ Ho Tung Mau; r 160,000-190,000d;) This spanking new hotel with bright spiffy rooms is an unexpected find. It's tucked away in an alley behind Đ Ho Tung Mau (follow the signs from the main road).

Phu Nguyen Hai Hotel (☎ 384 8429; ctpnh@hn.vnn.vn; 81 Đ Le Loi; s/d US$15/20;) Pretty much the only reason to stay here is to be right next to the bus station. High ceilings make the rooms appear less dingy, but the traffic noise is phenomenal.

Saigon Kimlien Hotel (☎ 383 8899; www.saigonkimlien.com.vn; 25 Đ Quang Trung; s US$22-32, d US$32-38;) Probably the nicest hotel in the central area, a short walk from the bus station. All rooms face Hwy 1A and eyeball the East German–style housing across the street. Fortunately it also has a serviceable restaurant.

Eating & Drinking

Dining selections are pretty paltry in Vinh, though there's always Saigon Kimlien Hotel. Street-food options include the Central Market; **pho bo food stalls** (beef noodle soup; Đ Phan Dinh Phung); **bun bo Hue food stalls** (Hue-style spicy beef noodle soup; off Đ Dinh Cong Trang); and **pho ga food stalls** (chicken noodle soup; Đ Ho Sy Doung).

There are some **bars** (Đ Quang Trung) strung along the street. To people-watch (inasmuch as one can in Vinh) try **Ngoi Sao Xanh** (☎ 356 7878; 17 Đ Ho Tung Mau) which overlooks the park.

Getting There & Away

AIR

Vietnam Airlines (☎ 359 5777; 2 Đ Le Hong Phong) and **Jetstar Pacific** (☎ 355 0550; 46 Đ Nguyen Thi Min Khai) each have a daily flight to HCMC. There is another Vietnam Airlines booking office in the foyer of the Saigon Kimlien Hotel (see opposite). The airport is about 20km north of the city.

BUS

The chaotic **bus station** (☎ 383 3997; Đ Le Loi) is easy to locate right in the centre of town. Regular buses head to Hanoi (90,000d, six hours) and Hue (100,000d, 6½ hours); buses on the latter route stop at Dong Hoi (four hours) and Dong Ha (5½ hours) on the way. Open-tour buses pass through town between Hanoi and Hue, and while it's easy to ask to jump off here, it's harder to arrange a pick-up.

Buses also head to Tay Son (formerly called Trung Tam and this is usually what's written on the bus) on Hwy 8, near the Lao border (see the boxed text, p202), and there are services through to Phonsavan on Hwy 7 (see the boxed text, below).

CAR & MOTORBIKE

From Vinh it's 96km to the Lao border, 197km to Dong Hoi and 292km to Hanoi.

TRAIN

The **Vinh train station** (Ga Vinh; ☎ 385 3158; Đ Le Ninh) is on the northwestern edge of town. The Reunification Express heads to destinations including Hanoi (145,000d, 5½ to eight hours, eight daily), Ninh Binh (90,000d, 3½ to 4½ hours, five daily), Dong Hoi (98,000d, 3½ to 6½ hours, eight daily) and Hue (177,000d, 6½ to 10½ hours, eight daily).

AROUND VINH

Cua Lo Beach

It's pleasant enough, with white sand, clean water and a shady grove of pine trees – but the concrete, karaoke, massage parlours and litter won't suit many travellers. Nevertheless, if you have time to kill, come for a cooling dip and a seafood lunch at one of the beach restaurants.

There are heaps of huge government hotels facing the beach and behind them, uninspired **guesthouses** (r 200,000-250,000d). Most hotels offer 'massage' and karaoke; some attract prostitutes. In summer, rooms can go for triple (or more) the usual price and reservations are advisable.

Cua Lo is 16km northeast of Vinh and can be reached easily by motorbike (90,000d including waiting time) or taxi (120,000d).

Kim Lien

Ho Chi Minh's birthplace in Hoang Tru, and the village of Kim Lien where he spent some of his formative years, are 14km northwest of Vinh. For all that these are popular pilgrimage spots for the party faithful, there's little to see other than recreated **houses** of bamboo and palm leaves, dressed (barely) with a few pieces of furniture.

Ho Chi Minh was born in Hoang Tru in 1890 and raised there till 1895, when the family moved to Hue. They returned in 1901, but

BORDER CROSSING BLUES 2

The often mist-shrouded **Nong Haet–Nam Can** (🕑 7am-5pm) is 119km east of Phonsavan and 250km northwest of Vinh. Thirty-day Lao visas are available on arrival; Vietnamese visas are not.

Buses between Vinh and Phonsavan cross here, leaving Phonsavan at 6am on Tuesday, Thursday, Friday and Saturday (110,000 kip, 13 hours, 403km) and returning from Vinh on Wednesday, Friday, Saturday and Sunday (235,000d). Some buses from Phonsavan claim to continue to Hanoi or Danang, but unceremoniously discharge all their passengers in Vinh.

For a go-it-yourself journey, take a morning bus from Phonsavan to Nong Haet (30,000 kip, four hours, 119km), then hire a *songthaew* (30,000 kip but travellers have been charged double or triple) for the 13km run to the border. On the Vietnam side, you'll haggle over a motorbike ride to the nearest town, Muong Xen. The route is breathtaking but only 25km downhill and should cost around US$5; drivers may ask for up to US$15. From Muong Xen there's a bus to Vinh (90,000d, eight hours, 250km).

For Laos-bound travellers, the bus leaves Vinh in the morning for Muong Xen. Get a motorbike to take you uphill to the border. Transport on the Laos side to Nong Haet is erratic, but once you get there, you can pick up a bus to Phonsavan.

BORDER CROSSING BLUES 3

The **Nam Phao–Cau Treo border crossing** (7am-6pm) is 96km west of Vinh and about 30km east of Lak Sao in Laos. Thirty-day Lao visas are available, but Vietnamese visas must be arranged in advance.

While the most travelled and shortest distance of the crossings in north-central Vietnam, it's also an area familiar to drug smugglers and other dodgy dealers. A lot of travellers have reported bad experiences on local buses, including chronic overcharging and threatening to eject travellers in the middle of nowhere unless they cough up an extra US$20. Lao Bao (see p216) is a much better option.

Local buses from Vinh to Tay Son (formerly Trung Tam) leave regularly throughout the day (70,000d, three hours, 70km). From Tay Son, it's another 25km through some richly forested country to the border. It should cost about 50,000d by motorbike or taxi, but drivers will demand several times that. On the Laos side, a jumbo or *songthaew* between the border and Lak Sao runs to about 35,000 kip (bargain hard).

Upon entering Vietnam, expect to get mobbed by hard-nosed drivers to Vinh, quoting up to US$30 for a bus ride. A metered taxi costs US$35 to US$40 while a motorbike fare is about 200,000d. Try to hook up with as many people as possible at the border to improve your bargaining position. Some buses from Lak Sao claim to run to Danang or Hanoi, but in fact terminate in Vinh.

One way to avoid the circus altogether is to book a direct bus to Vientiane (360,000d, departs 8am daily) or Phonsavan (300,000d, departs 7am daily) through **Hai Cafe** (090-927 5992) at the Vinh bus station. It's located immediately to the left of the station gate and Mr Hai speaks excellent English.

it was to the house in Kim Lien, about 2km from Hoang Tru. Not far from this house is a shrine-like **museum**, enclosed by pale green walls. If you want to hit the real motherlode of Ho Chi Minh memorabilia, drop by the store outside the museum.

No English-language information is available at either **site** (admission free; 7-11.30am & 2-5pm Mon-Fri, 7.30am-noon & 1.30-5pm Sat & Sun). You can get to either village by motorbike (60,000d including waiting time) or taxi (100,000d) in Vinh.

PHONG NHA CAVE

052

The largest and most stunning cave in Vietnam is **Phong Nha Cave** (367 5110; admission 30,000d, boat 200,000d; 7am-4pm). It was reliably mapped for the first time only in 1990, by an expedition led by the British Cave Research Association. Further exploration has revealed that Phong Nha Cave alone is nearly 55km long, though only the first kilometre is open to visitors. The name means Cave of Teeth, but the 'teeth' (stalagmites) by the entrance are long gone. The cave is an incredible otherworldly landscape to explore – except for the garish lights that illuminate certain formations.

Tien Son Cave (367 5110; admission 20,000d; 7am-4pm) is a dry cave in the mountainside above Phong Nha Cave. Boats on the way to Phong Nha Cave stop at a landing five minutes' walk from the foot of the steep 330-step climb to Tien Son. Inside, the remains of Cham altars and inscriptions date back to the 9th and 10th centuries, while the entrance bears evidence of American aerial attacks. The cave was used as a hospital and ammunition depot during the American War. The Americans also heavily strafed and bombed the area because it was a key entrance point to the Ho Chi Minh Trail (see the boxed text, p334).

For tickets, go to the Phong Nha Reception Department in **Son Trach village**. Boats leave from the jetty here (maximum 10 people per boat). In November and December the river is prone to flooding and Phong Nha Cave may be closed. Both caves are dimly lit so bring a torch (flashlight). On weekends they're extremely popular with Vietnamese visitors, whose presence is magnified by the spectacular echoes and unventilated cigarette smoke.

Phong Nha Cave is the linchpin of the **Phong Nha–Ke Bang National Park**. The park was designated a Unesco World Heritage site in 2003 and contains the oldest major karst area in Asia, formed approximately 400 million years ago.

In 2008 the national park opened the **Nuoc Mooc Eco-Trail** (admission free), a 1km route that winds through scenic forest. The trail is 15km from Son Trach and can also be reached by boat (two hours).

Sleeping & Eating

There is better accommodation in Dong Hoi, but staying in Son Trach may help you to beat the crowds. **Saigon Phong Nha** (☎ 367 7016; sgphongnhahotel@yahoo.com.vn; r US$20-25; ✈ 🖳) has decent rooms and a restaurant right beside the Reception Department. Make sure you bring cash as there are no banks here.

Getting There & Away

Son Trach village is 50km northwest of Dong Hoi; from Dong Hoi head 20km north on Hwy 1A to Bo Trach, then turn west for another 30km. The turn-off to Son Trach is marked by a giant sign (just like the Hollywood sign) on the side of a mountain.

Some hotels in Dong Hoi offer tours (800,000d with a guide and lunch) or you can try A2Z Tours in Dong Hoi (195,000d with a guide). A cheaper option is by motorbike (150,000d, including waiting time).

The cave entrance is 5km by river from Son Trach. Allow two to three hours if you're visiting both caves.

DONG HOI

☎ 052 / pop 104,000

Pleasantly untouristed, Dong Hoi is a simple seaside resort town with a fair selection of hotels but no souvenir shops and no hassling. While the town itself isn't incredibly attractive, the modest beaches to the north and south, and the Nhat Le River (complete with fishing boats bobbing on the tide) make up for it. It's the most likeable spot to break up the journey between Hanoi and Hue.

Like its southern neighbour Dong Ha, Dong Hoi suddenly found itself a border town in 1954 with the partition of Vietnam at the 17th Parallel. As the main staging area for the North Vietnamese Army, it suffered more than most during the American War. It has since recovered as a congenial provincial capital and makes a good base for visiting Phong Nha Cave (see opposite).

Information

Main post office (☎ 382 2560; 1 Đ Tran Hung Dao)

Agribank (☎ 382 5656; 2 Đ Me Suot) Has an ATM and exchange services. There is a **Vietcombank ATM** (Đ Tran Hung Dao) opposite the post office.

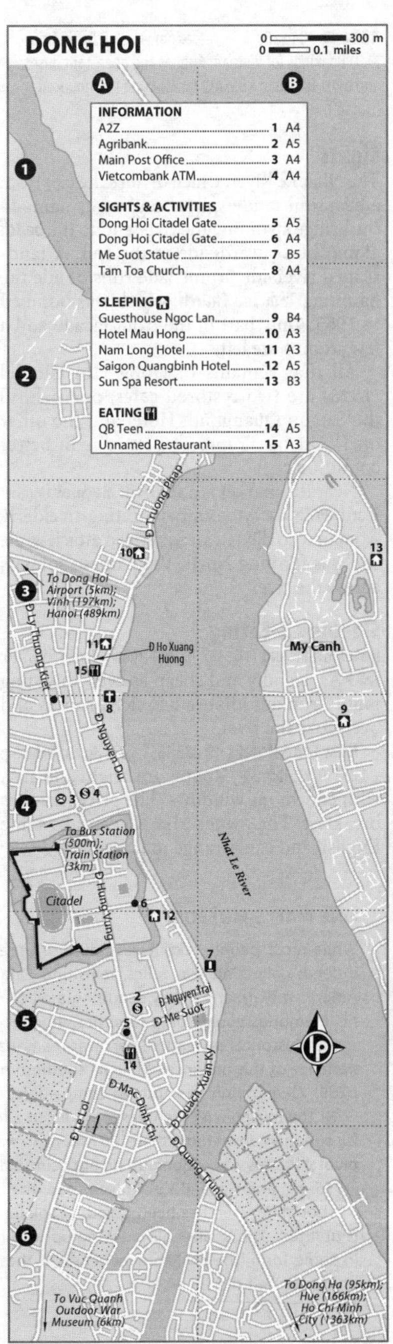

A2Z (☎ 384 5868; info@atoz.com.vn; 29 Đ Ly Thuong Kiet) Bookings for Vietnam Airlines and open-tour buses, and tours to Phong Nha. Ask for Mr Dung (pronounced 'zuhng').

Sights

The Nhat Le River, which divides the city from a beautiful sandy spit, also gives its name to the bridge spanning the river and to the **beach** along the seaward side of the spit. A landscaped riverside promenade runs beside the haunting **Tam Toa Church**, which was bombed in 1965. Only part of the front facade and a few stumps are left.

All that remains of Dong Hoi Citadel (1825) are two restored **gates**, one behind the Saigon Quangbinh Hotel and the other on Đ Quang Trung. The latter is in better condition.

Near the market is a **statue of Me Suot** (Mother Suot; Đ Quach Xuan Ky), commemorating an elderly woman who died in an American attack while she was ferrying North Vietnamese soldiers across the river.

Sleeping & Eating

Hotel Mau Hong (☎ 382 1804; Đ Truong Phap; r US$7-10;) As friendly and cheap as ever, this snug family-run guesthouse has clean rooms and overlooks the river.

Nam Long Hotel (☎ 382 1851; 22 Đ Ho Xuan Huong; s/d US$10/12;) Rooms are bright and airy, with enormous windows. The price includes breakfast. The owner Mrs Nga speaks some English and can arrange tour services.

Guesthouse Ngoc Lan (☎ 384 3732; My Canh; r 200,000d;) The only budget accommodation within walking distance of Nhat Le Beach.

Saigon Quangbinh Hotel (☎ 382 2276; www.sgquangbinhtourist.com.vn; 20 Đ Quach Xuan Ky; r US$50-80, ste US$120;) This is the poshest riverside accommodation and the only one with a pool. Rooms are comfortable and modern.

Sun Spa Resort (☎ 384 2999; www.sunsparesortvietnam.com; My Canh; r US$100-140, ste US$280;) This sprawling compound on Nhat Le Beach is tricked out with a resort-style pool, tennis courts, landscaped garden and good rooms. For a small fee, visitors can use the hotel's facilities.

QB Teen (☎ 382 4694; qb_fastfood@yahoo.com; 3 Đ Le Loi; meals 20,000-70,000; lunch & dinner) is the only place with Western fare, and true to its name the staff look like they're just out of their teens.

A casual **unnamed restaurant** (Đ Ho Xuang Huong; meals 40,000-60,000d) directly opposite Nam Long Hotel serves Vietnamese food.

Getting There & Away

AIR

Located 6km north of town, Dong Hoi Airport started operations in May 2008. At the time of research only Vietnam Airlines was offering flights to Hanoi. Book through a local travel agency.

BUS

From the **bus station** (☎ 382 2150; Đ Tran Hung Dao) you can catch services south to Danang

ONE MAN'S MUSEUM

While most people take it easy during retirement, Mr Lien Xuan Nguyen has been very busy indeed: collecting war relics, revisiting Quang Binh province (where he worked during the American War), and finally acquiring a piece of land outside Dong Hoi where his collection and his memories could come together, in what he calls the Vuc Quanh Outdoor War Museum.

Part historical recreation, part war memorial, this is Mr Lien's attempt to enshrine the war experience of this province. While its southern neighbour Quang Tri has the Vinh Moc Tunnels (see p209), Quang Binh has nothing comparable, even though it too was close to the front line.

At the museum Mr Lien has reproduced a letter from Ho Chi Minh, commending the province for shooting down more than 100 American warplanes. Quang Binh was also the birthplace of two pivotal figures who wound up on opposing sides: Ngo Dinh Diem, the president of South Vietnam (1955–63) and General Vo Nguyen Giap, the brilliant military commander of North Vietnam.

Though Mr Lien has been called a kook for funding this project himself, the unassuming man is unfazed. Age is, after all, catching up with his generation. If they don't put down their stories in some form, the civilian experience of the war will fade back into the forest, just as the Ho Chi Minh Trail did.

(120,000d, five hours, five daily), Hue (70,000d, four hours, two daily) via Dong Ha (50,000d, two hours), and north to Vinh (120,000d, four hours, six daily). It's easy to leave an open-tour bus in Dong Hoi, but for a pick-up go through a travel agency.

It's possible to get a bus south to the busy Lao border at Lao Bao (80,000d, four hours, 180km) and directly to the Lao city of Muang Khammouan (200,000d, 11 hours). The latter leaves Dong Hoi on Monday, Wednesday and Friday, returning the next day. It crosses at the little-used **Cha Lo–Na Phao border crossing** (7am-5pm) situated between Don Bai Dinh (Vietnam) and Na Phao (Laos). Vietnam and Lao visas are not available at this border.

CAR & MOTORBIKE

Dong Hoi is on Hwy 1A, 166km north of Hue, 95km north of Dong Ha and 197km south of Vinh.

TRAIN

The **train station** (Ga Dong Hoi; ☎ 382 0558; Đ Thuan Ly) is 3km from Hwy 1A. Follow Đ Tran Hung Dao until it crosses a bridge. Take the next right (signposted), then another right and the station is directly ahead.

The Reunification Express runs to Hanoi (243,000d, nine to 12½ hours, seven daily), Vinh (98,000d, 3½ to 6½ hours, seven daily), Dong Ha (47,000d, two to three hours, seven daily) and Hue (80,000d, 2½ to six hours, nine daily), among other destinations.

AROUND DONG HOI

Vuc Quanh Outdoor War Museum

Think of it as a raw version of the Cu Chi Tunnels (see p390) – minus the tunnels. This **'outdoor museum'** (Khu Du Lich Sinh Thai – Van Hoa Vuc Quanh; admission 20,000d; ☎ 224 0042; vucquanh@yahoo.com; Nghia Ninh; by appointment only) is one man's private effort (see the boxed text, opposite) to remember the civilian war experience in Quang Binh province. His approach: build a replica village for his personal collection of war relics and memorabilia.

On a 3-hectare site said to be part of the Ho Chi Minh Trail (see the boxed text, p334), the village consists of thatched huts scattered haphazardly along a maze of dirt paths and trenches. Each hut reproduces some aspect of village life: farmhouse, schoolroom, hospital or crêche. While many items are replicas, more poignant items include an authentic baby basket and plaques listing the names of school or hospital staff from the province who perished during the war.

There's also the requisite display of military relics, such as the American bomb casings artfully arranged around an artificial bomb crater. An unusual item is the American intrusion detector – 20,000 of these were dropped along the 'McNamara Line' in an attempt to stymie the Trail.

The museum's got a hokey charm, but it feels makeshift and unfinished – this is very much a personal project that's moving at its own pace. Don't expect anything slick.

GETTING THERE & AWAY

The museum is 7km from Dong Hoi. To get there, follow Đ Le Loi to the end, turn left (towards Quang Tri) and continue for just over 1km. At the signs for *chao sang bun be*, turn right and proceed for another kilometre. Alternatively, enquire at A2Z about tours (see opposite).

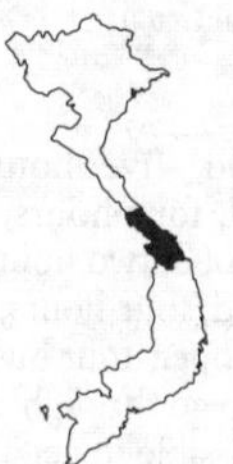

Central Vietnam

History, culture, food and fresh air – central Vietnam's got them all (oh, and tourists too). This is a region that packs in the country's third-largest city, its former imperial capital and its bloodiest modern battle sites, but also a seaport that time forgot, an ancient religious capital and nature reserves so dense scientists are still discovering new creatures in them.

Most travellers dash through the 'greatest hits' in a week: the Citadel and imperial tombs of Hue, the Old Town of Hoi An and the ruins of My Son. They're all Unesco World Heritage sites, so they're heavy on history, culture and tourist numbers. But you could easily amble along for two weeks without running out of things to do. For a change of pace, run for the beach or the hills. Near Danang are My Khe Beach and Ba Na Hill Station, while Bach Ma National Park is near Hue.

And then there's the food. Hue specialises in royal cuisine; Hoi An has its homegrown *cao lau* (flat noodles with croutons, vegies and pork slices) and 'white rose' (shrimp encased in rice paper and steamed), not to mention an astonishing range of effortlessly superb restaurants. Even Danang is starting to show a little mettle.

For some, this part of Vietnam will always be associated with the American War, even though many sites in the Demilitarised Zone (DMZ) are long overgrown and the memories resonate more strongly than the places. For others, central Vietnam is the place to see a little of everything the country has to offer, and perhaps even revel in the touristy buzz of it all.

HIGHLIGHTS

- Travel back in time in the old houses and quaint streets of **Hoi An** (p245) – and sit down to a fabulous meal while you're at it
- Tread in the footsteps of emperors from the Forbidden Purple City to the imperial tombs of **Hue** (p215)
- Wonder while you wander amid the enigmatic Cham ruins at **My Son** (p262)
- Slip underground at the **Vinh Moc Tunnels** (p209) in the Demilitarised Zone
- Skitter up the **Marble Mountains** (p242) for some great views and cave-temples

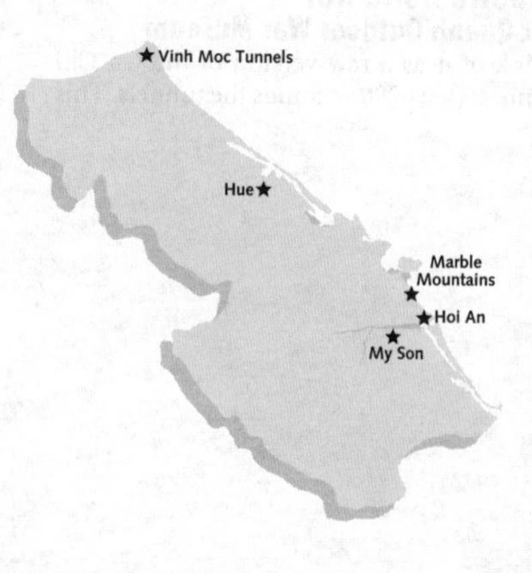

- ELEVATION: 1–1865M
- BEST TIME TO VISIT: FEB–SEP

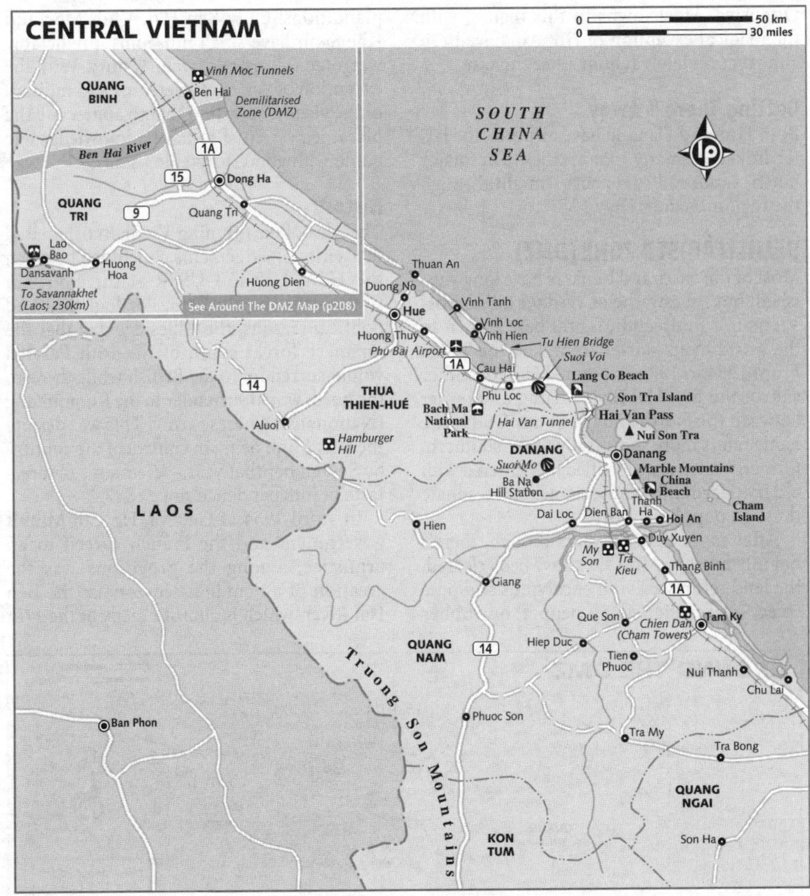

History

This region's seen them all: kings and kingmakers, warriors and occupiers, Vietnamese forces and many non-Vietnamese contenders. The ancient kingdom of Champa (see the boxed text, p264) began here in the 2nd century and flourished for more than a thousand years. It left its mark in the many towers dotting the landscape; the most renowned are at My Son.

As the Vietnamese pushed southwards, they subdued Champa in the 15th century, most likely because they had acquired firearms and the Chams hadn't. The following century the first Europeans showed up: Portuguese traders at Danang. They were followed by more foreign traders as Hoi An rose to prominence as an international port in the 17th century.

In 1802 Vietnam's last royal dynasty, the Nguyens, set up court at Hue, which became the centre of political intrigue, intellectual excellence and spiritual guidance. Later emperors were subdued by expanding French ambitions in Vietnam, and by the time of independence the locus of national power had shifted back to Hanoi.

In 1954 Vietnam was fatefully partitioned into North and South, creating a DMZ that saw some of the heaviest fighting in the American War. Thousands of lives were lost in bloody battles for strategic hills and valleys whose names are still murmured halfway around the world – Khe Sanh and Hamburger Hill among them. Even the former imperial capital of Hue was not spared during the Tet

Offensive. Most towns in this region, with the magical exception of Hoi An, have been almost completely rebuilt since the war.

Getting There & Away

Both Hue and Danang have airports, the latter linked to many major cities. The major north–south rail route cuts straight through the region, as does Hwy 1A.

DEMILITARISED ZONE (DMZ)

Most of the bases and bunkers have long vanished, but this swathe of verdant hills across Vietnam's midsection is still best known to the world by its war-era moniker, the DMZ. From 1954 to 1975 it spanned 5km on either side of the Ben Hai River, acting as a buffer between the North and the South. Today the name refers more specifically to the southern, formerly American-fortified half, littered with old battlegrounds whose names still resonate through popular culture.

After more than 30 years though, there's not much to see. Most sites have been cleared, the land reforested with eucalyptus and pine trees, or reassigned as pepper or rubber plantations. Only Ben Hai, Vinh Moc and Khe Sanh have small museums, predictably weighted towards the victor's story. With the exception of American veterans and military buffs, visitors may find that to appreciate the place, it's essential to have a knowledgeable guide with good storytelling skills.

History

The idea of partitioning Vietnam originated in a series of agreements concluded between the USA, UK and USSR at the Potsdam Conference in July 1945. For logistical and political reasons, the Allies decided that the Japanese forces south of the 16th Parallel would surrender to the British while those to the north would surrender to the Kuomintang (Nationalist) Chinese army. This was despite the Viet Minh being in control of the country by September that year – Vietnam's first real taste of independence since 1887.

In April 1954 at Geneva, Ho Chi Minh's government and the French agreed to an armistice; among the provisions was the creation of a demilitarised zone at the Ben Hai River, which is almost exactly at the 17th

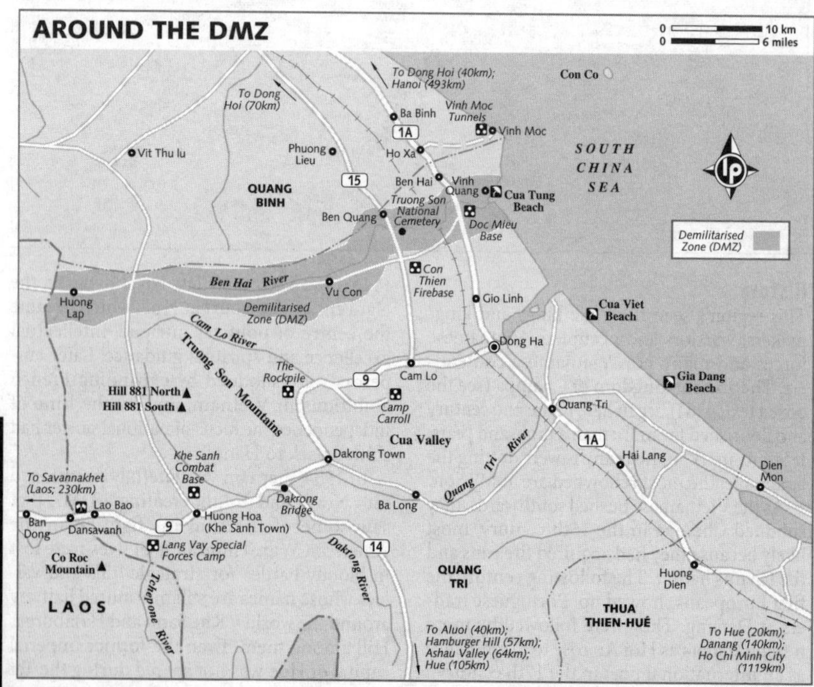

WATCH YOUR STEP

The war may be over, but death and injury still happen more often in the Demilitarised Zone (DMZ) than you'd think. At many of the places listed in this section there is still a chance of encountering live mortar rounds, artillery projectiles and mines. Watch where you step and don't leave the marked paths. Never touch any left-over ordnance – if the locals haven't carted it off for scrap it means that even they are afraid to disturb it.

It's not just the DMZ that's affected. It's estimated that as much as 20% of Vietnam remains uncleared, with more than 3.5 million mines and 350,000 to 800,000 tonnes of unexploded ordnance (UXO). This represents a staggering 46 tonnes of UXO per square kilometre. Between 1975 and 2000 it resulted in the deaths of 39,206 people and 66,380 injuries nationwide. Every year on average 1110 people die and 1882 are injured – a disproportionate number of them children or ethnic minorities.

The People's Army is responsible for most ongoing mine clearance. They're joined by foreign NGOs such as the Mines Advisory Group (www.maginternational.org) and Clear Path International (www.clearpathinternational.org), whose efforts are well worth supporting.

Parallel. The agreement stated explicitly that the division of Vietnam was temporary and that the demarcation line did not constitute a political boundary. But when the South cancelled nationwide general elections planned for July 1956 (it anticipated the Viet Minh would win), the North and South became separate states, eyeing each other warily across the river.

During the American War, the DMZ ironically became one of the most militarised zones in the world, what in 1967 *Time* magazine called 'a running sore'. The area just south of the DMZ was the scene of some of the bloodiest battles in America's first TV war, turning Quang Tri, The Rockpile, Khe Sanh, Lang Vay and Hamburger Hill into household names.

Since 1975, over 5000 people have been injured or killed in and around the DMZ by mines and ordnance left over from the war (see the boxed text, above), and the province has the highest such casualty rate in Vietnam. Although left-over metal is less visible and not worth much these days, the poor still risk their lives to forage for it.

Orientation

The area known as the DMZ extends from the coast westward to the Lao border. Hwy 1A runs across the Ben Hai River, while Hwy 9 runs almost parallel to the old DMZ about 10km south of it. The road southeast from Dakrong Bridge on Hwy 9 goes to Aluoi and the Ashau Valley (site of the infamous Hamburger Hill).

Information

DMZ sites range from well-signposted destinations with museums, parking lots and toilets to unmarked patches of grass reached by dirt path (or no path). Bus tours sweep through the former in one day or less, while locating the latter requires the expertise of a guide. Visiting all the DMZ sites takes about two days.

Almost any hotel or cafe in Hue (p215) or Dong Ha (p213) can handle tour bookings. Only a few agencies run the tours, so no matter where you sign up you'll probably wind up as part of a group. Expect to pay US$12 to US$16 for a day-long outing that leaves Hue at 6.30am. Tour guides (even the young ones) have a well-rehearsed litany of war stories. Some veterans of the Army of the Republic of Vietnam (ARVN) also work as guides.

A more meaningful experience, particularly for American veterans, is to see the DMZ independently. A car and English-speaking guide from Hue may set you back around US$100. Motorbike tours are also available, but check that the bike seat is well-padded before committing yourself. Tours cost US$15 to US$20 a day from Dong Ha and US$25 from Hue.

A common complaint about any DMZ tour is that more time is spent driving than sightseeing. These tours cover considerable distances: Hue is 77km from Dong Ha for starters, and Khe Sanh, the westernmost stop for most bus tours, is 65km from Dong Ha.

Military Sites off Highway 1A

VINH MOC TUNNELS

An impressive rabbit's warren of tunnels, **Vinh Moc** (admission 20,000d; 7am-4.30pm) is a coastal North Vietnamese village that literally went underground in response to unremitting American bombing. More than 90 families

GONE UNDERGROUND

In 1966 the USA began a massive aerial and artillery bombardment of North Vietnam. Just north of the Demilitarised Zone (DMZ), the villagers of Vinh Moc found themselves living in one of the most heavily bombed and shelled strips of land on the planet. Small family shelters could not withstand this onslaught and villagers either fled or began tunnelling by hand and with simple tools into the red-clay earth.

The Viet Cong (VC) found it useful to have a base here and encouraged the villagers to stay. After 18 months of work, an enormous complex was established underground, creating new homes on three levels from 12m to 23m below ground. Whole families lived here, their longest sojourn lasting 10 days and 10 nights. Over the years 17 babies were born underground. Later, the civilians and VC were joined by North Vietnamese soldiers, whose mission was to keep communications and supply lines to nearby Con Co Island open.

Other villages north of the DMZ also built tunnel systems, but none were as elaborate as Vinh Moc. The poorly constructed tunnels of Vinh Quang village (at the mouth of the Ben Hai River) collapsed after repeated bombing, killing everyone inside.

US warships stationed off the coast consistently bombarded the Vinh Moc tunnels (craters are still visible) and occasionally the tunnel mouths that faced the sea were struck by naval gunfire. The only ordnance that posed a real threat was the 'drilling bomb'. It scored a direct hit once but failed to explode, and no one was injured; the inhabitants adapted the bomb hole for use as an air shaft.

disappeared into three levels of tunnels running 2km in all, and continued to live and work while bombs rained down around them (see the boxed text, above).

Most of the tunnels are open to visitors, and are kept in their original form unlike those at Cu Chi (p390). The Vinh Moc tunnels are also larger and taller, so walking through them is more comfortable, albeit still claustrophobic (try not to dwell on the fact that you might be 23m below the surface). Close your eyes, let the sounds of the sea wash over you – and imagine living here for five years.

The tunnels are accessible from 12 entrances and up to 100 visitors can enter at a time. There are lights inside, a luxury the villagers certainly didn't have, but you may want to bring a torch (flashlight). The **museum** has photos and relics of tunnel life, including a full map of the tunnel network. The museum caretaker, who cannot speak, lived in the tunnels during the war.

The turn-off to Vinh Moc from Hwy 1A is 6.5km north of the Ben Hai River in the village of Ho Xa. Follow this road east for 13km.

CUA TUNG BEACH

This long, secluded stretch of sand where Vietnam's last emperor, Bao Dai, used to holiday is just north of the mouth of the Ben Hai River; there are beaches on the southern side as well. Bomb craters are still visible on the road that runs above the beach.

Cua Tung Beach is about 7km south of Vinh Moc via the road that runs along the coast. Turn east off Hwy 1A at a point 1.2km north of the Ben Hai River.

DOC MIEU BASE

Part of the McNamara Line, an elaborate electronic system intended to prevent infiltration along the Ho Chi Minh Trail (see the boxed text, p334) and across the DMZ, Doc Mieu Base was once protected by barbed-wire fences, mines and trenches. Little remains today. If you climb up to the rusting tank standing vigil beside a monument, there's a good view of the Ben Hai flag tower and the sea.

Doc Mieu Base is next to Hwy 1A on a low slope 16km north of Dong Ha or 8km south of the Ben Hai River.

BEN HAI FLAG TOWER & MUSEUM

Once the iconic border crossing between North and South Vietnam, Ben Hai has been spruced up on both sides of the river. Two bridges span the river: a modern one bearing Hwy 1A and the reconstructed pedestrian-only Hien Luong Bridge, which replaced the wartime bridge destroyed by American bombing in 1967. At the southern end of the bridge, a new reunification monument stands tall and proud, its stylised palm leaves oddly resembling missiles. At the northern end of the bridge is a yellow archway – a perhaps unexpected colour choice given that it was the southern half of the bridge that was painted yellow during the war (the northern half was painted red, of course).

The northern bank of the river is dominated by a reconstructed **flag tower** and the **Museum of the 17th Parallel and Dreams of Reunification** (admission 20,000d, 7am-5pm). Most tour buses stop at the flag tower for an obligatory, if unexciting, photo op. The museum, despite its name, is just as bland.

Ben Hai is 22km north of Dong Ha on Hwy 1A.

TRUONG SON NATIONAL CEMETERY

More effective than the nationalist propaganda that papers Vietnam's museums, this sprawling cemetery is a sobering memorial to the legions of North Vietnamese soldiers who died in the Truong Son mountain range along the Ho Chi Minh Trail. More than 10,000 graves dot these hillsides, each marked by a simple white tombstone headed by the inscription *liet si* (martyr).

The gravestones of 13 war heroes, including two women, are singled out in a separate area. All other soldiers are buried in five zones according to the part of Vietnam that they came from, with each zone further subdivided into provinces. During the war they would have been buried near where they were killed, but after reunification their remains were transferred here or to one of the four other national cemeteries. However, many graves are empty, simply bearing names – a fraction of Vietnam's 300,000 soldiers missing in action.

The cemetery site was used as a base by the May 1959 Army Corps from 1972 to 1975. The corps had the mission of constructing and maintaining the Ho Chi Minh Trail. A sculpture garden and three-sided stele pay tribute to their memory.

The road to Truong Son National Cemetery intersects Hwy 1A 13km north of Dong Ha and 9km south of the Ben Hai River; the cemetery is 17km from the highway. A rocky path, passable by motorbike, links Cam Lo (on Hwy 9) with the cemetery (18km). This track passes rubber plantations and the homes of Bru (Van Kieu) people.

CON THIEN FIREBASE

Only one bunker remains of the US Marine Corps base that used to cover the three small hills here. Established as part of the McNamara Line to stop infiltration across the DMZ, on a good day the base had a clear view all the way to the Ben Hai River.

In September 1967 Con Thien was besieged by North Vietnamese forces; the US responded with 4000 bombing sorties that dropped more than 40,000 tonnes of bombs on the North Vietnamese forces around the base. The North Vietnamese withdrew after three weeks, but their real mission was accomplished: to divert US attention from South Vietnam's cities in preparation for the Tet Offensive. The unintended consequence was that the area around the base was rendered utterly desolate, with enough unexploded ordnance to maim or kill people for decades to come.

The land was cleared of mines in 2003 and rubber plantations are springing up, but it's still best to follow the beaten path and keep your eyes open.

Con Thien Firebase is 15km west of Hwy 1A and 8km south of Truong Son National Cemetery along the road that links the highway with the cemetery. Follow the dirt path, accessible only by motorbike or on foot, for about 1.5km through the plantations.

Military Sites on Highway 9

The legendary Ho Chi Minh Trail (see p334) was the main artery of supplies for the North's war effort and the bane of American military commanders who were never able to cut it off. In an effort to sever it near the border, the Americans established a series of bases along Hwy 9, including (from east to west) Cua Viet, Gio Linh, Dong Ha, Cam Lo, Camp Carroll, The Rockpile, Ca Lu (now called Dakrong Town), Khe Sanh and Lang Vay. Despite all the firepower and technology they threw at it, they never succeeded and the Trail was in use till the end of the war.

CAMP CARROLL

Camp Carroll was named after a Marine Corps captain who was killed while trying to seize a nearby ridge. Its gargantuan 175m cannons were used to shell targets as far away as Khe Sanh.

These days there isn't much to see except a Vietnamese memorial marker to Tan Lam Hill 241 (the Vietnamese name for the site) and parts of the camp's cement foundation. Eagle-eyed visitors might spot bits of old sandbags among the pepper, rubber and eucalyptus plants around.

The turn-off to Camp Carroll is 10km west of Cam Lo and 23km northeast of Dakrong Bridge. The base is 3km from Hwy 9.

THE ROCKPILE

Visible from Hwy 9, this 230m-high pile of rocks once had a US Marine Corps lookout on top and a base for American long-range artillery nearby. There isn't much left and you'll probably need a guide to point it out to you.

The Rockpile is 29km west of Dong Ha on Hwy 9. A 2km-long road from the highway leads to the base of the mountain only.

DAKRONG BRIDGE

Crossing the Dakrong River 13km east of the Khe Sanh bus station, this bridge was rebuilt in 2001 and bears a marker hailing its importance as a conduit for the Ho Chi Minh Trail. The road to Aluoi was once part of the Trail and heads southeast from the bridge.

HUONG HOA (KHE SANH)

☎ 53 / elev 600m

The town has been officially renamed Huong Hoa, but the Western world remembers it as Khe Sanh. Set amid beautiful hills, valleys and fields, it's known for its coffee plantations, and many inhabitants are of the Bru tribe. You'll notice their different clothing, with women wearing saronglike skirts, and woven baskets taking the place of plastic bags.

About the only reason for staying here is if you're planning to hit the road to Laos the next morning. **May Hong** (☎ 388 0189; Km 64 Khe Sanh; r US$10; ❄) has serviceable rooms.

The bus station is on Hwy 9, about 600m towards the Lao frontier from the triangular intersection where the road to Khe Sanh Combat Base branches off. Buses to Dong Ha (30,000d, 1½ hours) and Lao Bao (20,000d, one hour) depart regularly. Change at Dong Ha for other destinations.

KHE SANH COMBAT BASE

The site of the most famous siege – and one of the most controversial battles – of the American War, Khe Sanh Combat Base was never overrun, but it was completely stripped and dismantled before the Americans left. Today the site is occupied by a small **museum** (admission 20,000d; 🕒 7am-5pm), a few reconstructed bunkers, a few captured or downed American aircraft and a red dirt swathe where the airstrip used to be.

In early 1968, Khe Sanh saw the bloodiest battle of the war (see the boxed text, opposite). About 500 Americans (the official figure of 205 was arrived at by statistical sleight of hand), 10,000 North Vietnamese troops and uncounted civilian bystanders died amid the din of machine guns and the fiery explosions of 1000kg bombs, white phosphorus shells, napalm, mortars and artillery rounds of all sorts. Despite the fierce fighting and loss of life, Khe Sanh was probably never the North's real target, but merely a diversionary gambit in preparation for the Tet Offensive.

The place continues to evoke a strong reaction in many war veterans, as a review of comments left in the visitors' book will show. Besides the usual photographs and war relics in the museum, there are also displays depicting local minority people using their traditional weapons and tactics against the Americans. In reality, minority groups often aided the Americans against the North Vietnamese (and suffered for it after the war).

Getting There & Away

From Huong Hoa bus station, head 600m towards Dong Ha then turn northwest at the triangular intersection. The base is 2.5km further on, 500m off the eastern side.

LANG VAY SPECIAL FORCES CAMP

A solemn North Vietnamese Army tank mounted on a grey memorial commemorates the 1968 battle in which the North first rolled out tanks against the enemy. Americans remember it as the battle where they were severely outnumbered. After one night of hand-to-hand combat, 10 out of 24 US Army Special Forces soldiers and 316 out of 400 South Vietnamese, Bru and Montagnards (a French term referring to ethnic minorities) were killed.

There's nothing left except the Vietnamese memorial. The base is on a ridge southwest of Hwy 9, between Khe Sanh bus station (9km) and Lao Bao (7km).

ALUOI

The most far-flung of the DMZ sites, Aluoi is the town closest to **landing zones Cunningham**, **Erskine** and **Razor**, **Hill 1175** (west of the valley), **Hill 521** (in Laos) and the most well known of all, Apbia Mountain in the Ashau Valley, better known as **Hamburger Hill**. US Army Special

THE FIGHT FOR NOWHERE

Despite opposition from Marine Corps brass, the small US Army Special Forces (Green Beret) base at Khe Sanh was turned into a Marines' stronghold in late 1966. In April 1967 a series of 'hill fights' began between US forces and the well-dug-in North Vietnamese infantry, who held the hills 8km to the northwest. In only a few weeks, 155 Marines and thousands of North Vietnamese were killed.

In late 1967 American intelligence detected the movement into the hills around Khe Sanh of tens of thousands of North Vietnamese regulars, armed with mortars, rockets and artillery. General Westmoreland became convinced that the North Vietnamese were planning another Dien Bien Phu (see the boxed text, p173). This analogy was foolhardy, given American firepower and the proximity of Khe Sanh to supply lines and other US bases. President Johnson himself became obsessed by the spectre of 'Din Bin Foo', as he famously referred to it. He had a sand-table model of the Khe Sanh plateau constructed in the White House situation room and took the unprecedented step of requiring a written guarantee from the Joint Chiefs of Staff that Khe Sanh could be held.

Determined to avoid another Dien Bien Phu at all costs, Westmoreland assembled a force of 5000 planes and helicopters and increased the number of troops at Khe Sanh to 6000. He even ordered his staff to study the feasibility of using tactical nuclear weapons.

The 75-day siege of Khe Sanh began on 21 January 1968 with a small-scale assault on the base's perimeter. As the Marines and South Vietnamese Rangers braced for a full-scale ground attack, Khe Sanh became the focus of global media attention. It was the cover story for both *Newsweek* and *Life* magazines, and made the front pages of countless newspapers around the world. During the next two months the base was subjected to continuous ground attacks and artillery fire, and US aircraft dropped 100,000 tonnes of explosives in its vicinity. But the expected attempt to overrun the base never came. On 7 April 1968, after heavy fighting, US troops reopened Hwy 9 and linked up with the Marines, ending the siege.

It now seems clear that the siege was an enormous diversion to draw US attention away from the South Vietnamese population centres in preparation for the Tet Offensive, which began a week after the siege started. However, at the time, Westmoreland considered the entire Tet Offensive to be a 'diversionary effort' to distract attention from Khe Sanh.

After Westmoreland's tour of duty in Vietnam ended in July 1968, US forces in the area were redeployed. Holding Khe Sanh, for which so many men had died, was deemed unnecessary. After everything at Khe Sanh was buried, trucked out or blown up (leaving nothing recognisable that could be used in a North Vietnamese propaganda film), US forces upped and left under a curtain of secrecy. The American command had finally realised what a Marine officer had expressed long before: 'When you're at Khe Sanh, you're not really anywhere. You could lose it and you really haven't lost a damn thing.'

Forces bases in Aluoi and Ashau were overrun and abandoned in 1966. The area then became an important centre for supplies coming down the Trail.

In May 1969 US forces on a search-and-destroy operation near the Lao border fought in one of the fiercest battles of the war. In less than a week of fighting, 241 American soldiers died at Hamburger Hill – a fact that was very well publicised in the US media. A month later, after the US forces withdrew to continue operations elsewhere, the hill was reoccupied by the North Vietnamese.

Hamburger Hill is about 8km from Aluoi and there are still bunkers, trenches and craters visible. You'll need a guide, both to find the sites and to arrange a permit. Although the vegetation looks healthy, the land and people living around Aluoi still suffer from the effects of Agent Orange.

DONG HA

☎ 053 / pop 82,046

With a rougher edge than you'd expect for a provincial capital, Dong Ha feels more like the border town it used to be when Vietnam was divided into North and South. Most people seem to be passing through the dismal town on their way elsewhere, and travellers don't usually see more than its dusty main drag, where they're likely to be badgered (sometimes quite forcefully) about hotel or tour arrangements.

From 1968 to 1969 Dong Ha was a US Marine Corps command and logistics centre. During the Tet Offensive, North Vietnamese troops crossed the DMZ and attacked the town. They were repelled, but captured Dong Ha in the Easter Offensive of 1972. No traces of the wartime town remain.

Situated at the intersection of Hwys 1A and 9, Dong Ha makes a useful base for exploring the DMZ if you want to save time on the commute from Hue. The only other reason to come here is to catch a bus to the Lao Bao border crossing (see the boxed text, p216).

Orientation

Hwy 1A is called Đ Le Duan as it passes through Dong Ha. Hwy 9, with signs reading 'Lao Bao', intersects Hwy 1A next to the bus station.

Information

Post office (☎ 385 6192; 183 Đ Le Duan) Has basic postal services.

Vietcombank ATM (189 Đ Le Duan) In front of Sepon Travel.

Vietin Bank ATM (66 Đ Le Duan) At Mekong Hotel.

Tours

There are now a number of tour agencies running DMZ tours, as enterprising and experienced tour guides from state-run agencies have struck out on their own.

Annam Tour (☎ 090-514 0600; vudmz@yahoo.com; 207 Đ Nguyen Du) Head honcho Mr Vu speaks excellent English, loves military history and has been a DMZ tour guide for more than 10 years.

DMZTours (☎ 356 4056; www dmztours.net; 260 Đ Le Duan) A group of energetic tour guides formerly from Quang Tri Tourism, offering DMZ tours as well as adventure trips, village homestays and itineraries for American veterans.

Quang Tri Tourism (☎ 385 2927; dmzqtri@dng.vnn.vn; 66 Đ Le Duan) This state office at the Mekong Hotel arranges DMZ tours and car rentals.

Sepon Travel (☎ 385 5289; www.sepon.com.vn; 189 Đ Le Duan) Handles bookings for DMZ tours, buses to Savannakhet (Laos) and Vietnam Airlines.

Sleeping

DMZ Café (☎ 385 7026; dmzcafedh@yahoo.com; 88 Đ Le Duan; r US$5-8) It's a cheapie – no attached bathrooms, no satellite TV – but a goodie too. Owner Mr Tinh is an ARVN veteran and will regale you with stories if you let him. He also organises good motorbike tours (US$15 to US$20) led by fellow veterans.

Thuy Dien Guesthouse (☎ 385 7187; 9 Đ Le Van Huu; r 120,000d) A smart new mini-hotel opposite the bus station, with clean rooms that are a good bang for your buck.

Melody Hotel (☎ 355 4664; www.melodyhotel.net; 62 Đ Le Duan; r 150,000-200,000d) Probably the nicest hotel on the main strip, with pleasant, newish rooms. The hotel also handles motorbike rentals and can arrange DMZ tours.

Mekong Hotel (☎ 385 2292; 66 Đ Le Duan; r 200,000-250,000d) This large hotel was in the middle of a much-needed facelift at the time of research. Even the best refurbishment can't totally block out the traffic noise from Hwy 1A though, so get a room at the rear. Don't be deceived by the restaurant's apparent popularity – it's a breakfast and lunch stop for DMZ bus tours.

Eating

There isn't much that's remarkable in Dong Ha for foodies. There are some *com pho* (rice-noodle soup) places along Đ Le Duan and Đ Le Van Huu that will tide you over. For vegetarian fare, try **Quan Chay Vegetarian House** (☎ 385 4634; 34 Đ Nguyen Trai; meals 20,000d), a small, tidy place on Dong Ha's nicest street.

Getting There & Away

BUS

Dong Ha bus station (Ben Xe Khach Dong Ha; ☎ 385 1488; 68 Đ Le Duan) is near the intersection of Hwys 1A and 9. Vehicles to Dong Hoi (50,000d, two hours), Hue (40,000d, 1½ hours), Danang (60,000d, 3½ hours), Khe Sanh (30,000d, 1½ hours) and Lao Bao (35,000d, two hours) depart regularly.

It is sometimes necessary to change buses in Khe Sanh for Lao Bao. Buses are also advertised to Savannakhet in Laos, but the station won't book a ticket for foreigners. For that, you'll need to cross the road to Sepon Travel (left).

CAR & MOTORBIKE

Road distances from Dong Ho: Dong Hoi (95km), Hue (77km), Danang (190km), Khe Sanh (65km), Lao Bao (85km) and Vinh Moc (41km).

Motorbike tours to the DMZ start from US$15. A one-way car trip to the Lao Bao border will set you back US$40. Motorbikes can be hired from DMZ Café or Melody Hotel for about US$10 per day.

TRAIN

Reunification Express trains stop in Dong Ha's **train station** (Ga Dong Ha; ☎ 385 0631; 2 Đ Le Thanh Ton). Destinations include Hanoi (290,000d, 12½ to 16 hours, five daily), Dong Hoi (47,000d, 1½ to three hours, seven daily) and Hue (30,000d, 1½ to 2½ hours, seven daily).

To get to the Dong Ha train station from the bus station, head 1km southeast on Hwy 1A to a big guesthouse called Nha Khach 261. Turn right here and the back of the train station is about 150m over the tracks.

LAO BAO

☎ 053 / pop 30,000

Lao Bao, on the Sepon River (Song Xe Pon) that marks the VietnamLaos border, is an important crossing for trade and tourism between the two countries. Towering above the town on the Lao side is Co Roc Mountain, once a North Vietnamese artillery stronghold.

There is a huge border market on the Vietnamese side, where goods smuggled from Thailand are readily available. Merchants accept either Vietnamese dong or Lao kip. Try not to change currency here unless you have to: the rate can be about 50% lower than at banks.

There's no reason to linger in Lao Bao, but if you miss the border opening hours (see the boxed text, p216), **Sepon Hotel** (☎ 377 7129; www.seponhotel.com.vn; 82 Lao Bao; r US$20-27; ❄ 💻) is a newish business hotel with spacious rooms. Slightly further away from the bus station is the ageing **Bao Son Hotel** (☎ 387 7848; r US$15-17; ❄). There are *com pho* places in the centre of town.

Lao Bao town is 18km west of Khe Sanh, 85km from Dong Ha, 152km from Hue, 45km east of Sepon (Laos) and 255km east of Savannakhet (Laos).

QUANG TRI

☎ 053 / pop 22,760

Quang Tri was once an important citadel city, but little of its old glory remains. In the Easter Offensive of 1972, four divisions of North Vietnamese regulars, backed by tanks, artillery and rockets, poured across the DMZ into this province. They laid siege to Quang Tri town, shelling it heavily before capturing it along with the rest of the province.

The South struck back: over the next four months the city was almost completely levelled by South Vietnamese artillery and carpet bombing by US fighter-bombers and B-52s. The ARVN suffered 5000 casualties in rubble-to-rubble fighting to retake the city.

Today all that might interest a visitor are the remnants of the moat, ramparts and gates of the **citadel**, which the North and South fought bitterly over in 1972. It's off Đ Tran Hung Dao, 1.6km north of Hwy 1A.

Outside Quang Tri, along Hwy 1A towards Hue, is the skeleton of **Long Hung Church**. It bears countless bullet holes and mortar damage from the 1972 bombardment, and is a common stop on DMZ tours.

The **bus station** (Đ Tran Hung Dao) is about 1km from Hwy 1A, but buses can just as easily be flagged down on the side of the road.

HUE

☎ 054 / pop 335,747

Palaces and pagodas, tombs and temples, culture and cuisine, history and heartbreak – there's no shortage of poetic pairings to describe Hue (pronounced 'hway'). Ordained by Unesco as a World Heritage site in 1993, this capital of the Nguyen emperors is where tourists come to see something of old, pre-communist Vietnam, even though none of the buildings are older than 150 years and many of them have borne the brunt of war and wilful neglect (the latter due to communist disapproval of imperial emblems).

Hue owes its charm partly to its location on the Perfume River – picturesque on a clear day, sleekly mysterious even in less flattering weather. There's always restoration work going on to recover some of its lost imperial splendour, but the city is very much a jumble of new and old: modern homes sit cheek by jowl with crumbling century-old Citadel walls, and colourless new hotels tower over stately colonial-era properties.

The new has also meant the influx of mass tourism into the heart of Hue, bringing tour buses that charge down its narrow streets and touts who dog your every step. However, unlike sister site Hoi An, Hue has managed to absorb tourists while retaining its reputation as a conservative, quiet town. You'll be hard-pressed to find a party place that's open into the wee hours of the night, and local tourism authorities have lamented the fact that locals go to bed at 10pm. On the flip side, just

BORDER CROSSING: LAO BAO–DANSAVANH

The **Lao Bao border** (⌚ 7am-6pm) is the most popular and least problematic crossing between Laos and Vietnam. You can get a 30-day Lao visa on arrival, but Vietnamese visas need to be arranged in advance; drop in at the Vietnamese consulate in Savannakhet.

Dong Ha is the junction town for Lao Bao. Sepon Travel in Dong Ha (p214) has buses to Savannakhet (180,000d, 7½ hours). They leave Dong Ha at 8am every odd-numbered date and return from Savannakhet's Savanbanhao Hotel (90,000 kip) the next day. These buses also start from Hue (US$20, add 1½ hours) and can be booked from hotels or travel agencies (see opposite).

To cross the border on your own, take a bus from Dong Ha to Lao Bao (two hours, 85km, 50,000d). From the bus station the local price for a *xe om* (motorbike taxi) to the border is 5000d (foreigners pay about 10,000d), or walk it in about 20 minutes. Between the Vietnam and Laos border posts is a short walk of a few hundred metres.

Once in Laos there is only one public bus a day direct to Savannakhet (five hours, 250km, 60,000 kip), which leaves when full. *Songthaew* (pick-up trucks) head regularly to Sepon, from where you can get a bus or another *songthaew* to Savannakhet.

Coming the other way, the bus from Savannakhet to Dansavanh runs regularly during the day and there is an overnight bus that leaves at 10pm for Hue; be warned that the latter arrives at Dansavanh around 3am and is known to make passengers disembark and wait by the road till morning. No public buses from Laos go directly to Hue, despite what drivers may tell you.

If you're taking a tourist bus, confirm (preferably in writing) that the same bus continues through the border. Travellers have reported being bundled off nice buses on the Vietnamese side and onto overcrowded local buses in Laos. If the bus is likely to arrive at the border after it's closed, check if your ticket includes accommodation for the night, or be prepared to sleep on an overcrowded bus.

venture a couple of streets from the tourist enclave and you'll find the good people of Hue going about their (nontourist) business as usual.

Having fallen into obscurity before, Hue seems determined not to let it happen again. The city hosts a biennial arts festival, the Festival of Hue (www.huefestival.com), in even-numbered years, featuring local and international artists and performers. Events take place at historical sites and arts centres all over the city. There's also talk of turning Hue into Vietnam's first 'festival city' (whatever that is).

History

Before Hue, the citadel city of Phu Xuan, 5km northeast, was the capital of the southern part of Vietnam under the Nguyen lords in 1744. The Tay Son Rebels occupied the city from 1786 until 1802, when it fell to Nguyen Anh. He crowned himself Emperor Gia Long, thus founding the Nguyen dynasty, which ruled the country – at least in name – until 1945.

Gia Long ordered the building of the Citadel, which has become synonymous with Hue. In 1885, when the advisers of 13-year-old Emperor Ham Nghi objected to French activities in Tonkin, French forces encircled the city. Unwisely, the outnumbered Vietnamese forces launched an attack; the French responded mercilessly. According to a contemporary French account, the French took three days to burn the imperial library and remove from the palace every single object of value – from gold and silver ornaments to mosquito nets and toothpicks. The French replaced Ham Nghi with the more pliable Dong Khanh, thus ending any pretence of genuine independence for Vietnam.

The emperors continued to reside in Hue but were very much sidelined from events of national import. It was only in 1968 that attention shifted to Hue again, this time as the site of a vicious battle in the Tet Offensive; it was the only city in South Vietnam to be held by the communists for more than a few days. While the American command was concentrating its energies on Khe Sanh, North Vietnamese and Viet Cong (VC) troops skirted the American stronghold and seized most of Hue within 24 hours.

Immediately, political cadres began to remove Hue's 'uncooperative' elements. Thousands of people were rounded up in extensive house-to-house searches, according to name-lists meticulously prepared months before. During the 3½ weeks that the National Liberation Front flag flew over the Citadel, more than 2500 people were summarily shot, clubbed to death or buried alive. The North called them 'lackeys who owed blood debts' – ARVN soldiers, wealthy merchants, government workers, monks, priests and intellectuals.

When the South Vietnamese army was unable to dislodge the occupying North Vietnamese and VC forces, General Westmoreland ordered US troops to recapture the city. Over the next few weeks, whole neighbourhoods were levelled by VC rockets and US bombs. Most of the area inside the Citadel was battered by the South Vietnamese air force, US artillery (who used napalm on the imperial palace) and brutal house-to-house fighting. According to remarks attributed to an American soldier involved in the assault, they had to 'destroy the city in order to save it'. Approximately 10,000 people died in Hue, including thousands of VC troops, 400 South Vietnamese soldiers and 150 US Marines – but most of those killed were civilians.

In March 1975, the North Vietnamese forces returned, fresh from their success in the central highlands, and captured Hue after three days.

Journalist Gavin Young's 1997 memoir *A Wavering Grace* is a moving account of his 30-year relationship with a family from Hue and with the city itself, during and beyond the American War. It makes a good literary companion for a stay in the city.

Orientation

The city of Hue lies along either side of the Perfume River (Song Huong). The north side of the river is largely dominated by the Citadel and has a quieter, local feel, while the south side, once a French enclave, has most of the hotels and restaurants. Aside from the Citadel, the other imperial landmarks and sightseeing spots are scattered across the countryside.

Most hotels are clustered off Đ Hung Vuong immediately southeast of the Hotel Saigon Morin, or in the narrow streets between Đ Pham Ngu Lao and Đ Chu Van An. The island on which the Phu Cat and Phu Hiep subdistricts are located can be reached by crossing the Dong Ba Canal near Dong Ba Market.

Information

BOOKSHOPS

Phu Xuan Bookstore (☎ 352 2000; 131 Đ Tran Hung Dao; 🕒 8am-noon & 1-10pm) has a selection of English-language books. The rooftop cafe has free wi-fi.

INTERNET ACCESS

There are lots of internet cafes on the tourist strips of Đ Hung Vuong and Đ Le Loi.

MEDICAL SERVICES

Hue Central Hospital (Benh Vien Trung Uong Hue; ☎ 382 2325; 16 Đ Le Loi)

MONEY

Vietcombank (30 Đ Le Loi; 🕒 7am-10pm, closed Sun) Located at the Hotel Saigon Morin.

Vietin Bank (☎ 383 0212; 12 Đ Hung Vuong; 🕒 7.30am-6pm Tue-Sat, 8-11.30am Sun) Has an ATM and exchange services.

Vietin Bank ATM Outside the Imperial Hotel.

POST

Post office Đ Le Loi (☎ 383 2072; 44 Đ Le Loi); Đ Tran Hung Dao (☎ 353 1927; Đ 91 Tran Hung Dao); main post office (☎ 382 3468; 8 Đ Hoang Hoa Tham); train station (☎ 382 3109; 1 Đ Bui Thi Xuan). They offer postal, internet and telephone services.

TRAVEL AGENCIES

Café on Thu Wheels (☎ 383 2241; minhthuhue@yahoo.com; 3/34 Đ Nguyen Tri Phuong) Cycling and motorbiking tours around Hue, overseen by the gregarious and inimitable Mrs Thu.

Mandarin Café (☎ 382 1281; mandarin@dng.vnn.vn; 24 Đ Tran Cao Van) Watched over by the eagle eyes of photographer Mr Cu (who speaks English and French), this place is great for information, transport and tours.

Sinh Café (☎ 382 3309; www.sinhcafevn.com; 7 Đ Nguyen Tri Phuong) Books open-tour buses and buses to Laos.

Stop and Go Café (☎ 382 7051; stopandgocafetours@yahoo.com; 25 Đ Tran Cao Van) Top-notch, personalised motorbike and car tours. It also offers highly rated DMZ tours guided by Vietnamese veterans.

Sights & Activities

CITADEL

Most of Hue's sights and a sizable chunk of its population reside within the 2m-thick, 10km-long walls of its **Citadel** (Kinh Thanh) on the north bank of the river. Begun in 1804 on a site chosen by Emperor Gia Long's geomancers, three sides of the Citadel are straight; the

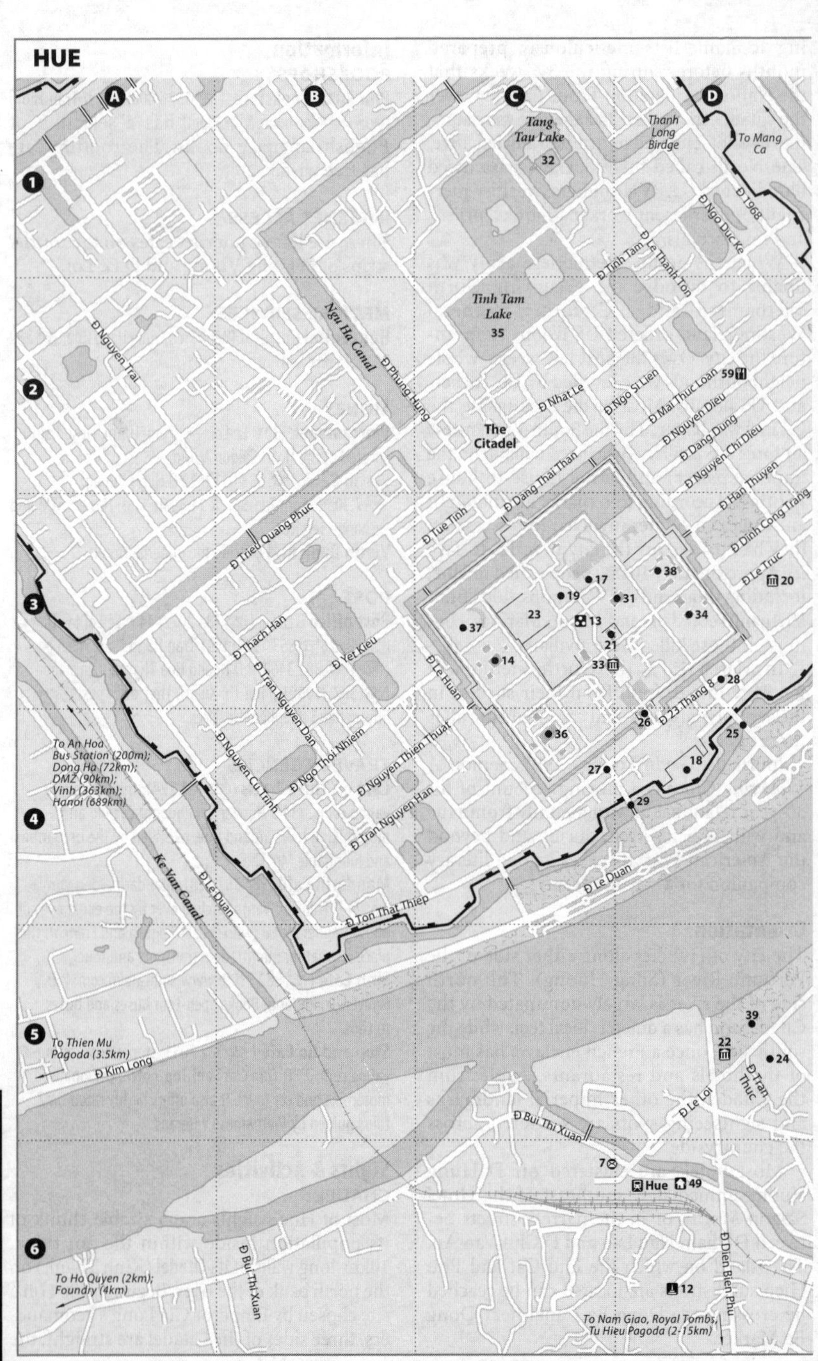

HUE
Tang Tau Lake
Thanh Long Birdge
To Mang Ca
Tinh Tam Lake
Ngu Ha Canal
The Citadel
Ke Van Canal
To An Hoa Bus Station (200m); Dong Ha (72km); DMZ (90km); Vinh (363km); Hanoi (689km)
To Thien Mu Pagoda (3.5km)
To Ho Quyen (2km); Foundry (4km)
To Nam Giao, Royal Tombs, Tu Hieu Pagoda (2-15km)
Hue
Đ Nguyen Trai
Đ Phung Hung
Đ Tinh Tam
Đ Le Thanh Ton
Đ Ngo Duc Ke
Đ 1968
Đ Nhat Le
Đ Ngo Si Lien
Đ Mai Thuc Loan
Đ Nguyen Dieu
Đ Dang Dung
Đ Nguyen Chi Dieu
Đ Han Thuyen
Đ Dinh Cong Trang
Đ Le Truc
Đ Dang Thai Than
Đ Tue Tinh
Đ Trieu Quang Phuc
Đ Thach Han
Đ Yet Kieu
Đ Le Huan
Đ Tran Nguyen Dan
Đ Nguyen Cu Trinh
Đ Ngo Thoi Nhiem
Đ Nguyen Thien Thuat
Đ Tran Nguyen Han
Đ 23 Thang 8
Đ Le Duan
Đ Ton That Thiep
Đ Kim Long
Đ Bui Thi Xuan
Đ Le Loi
Đ Tran Thuc
Đ Dien Bien Phu

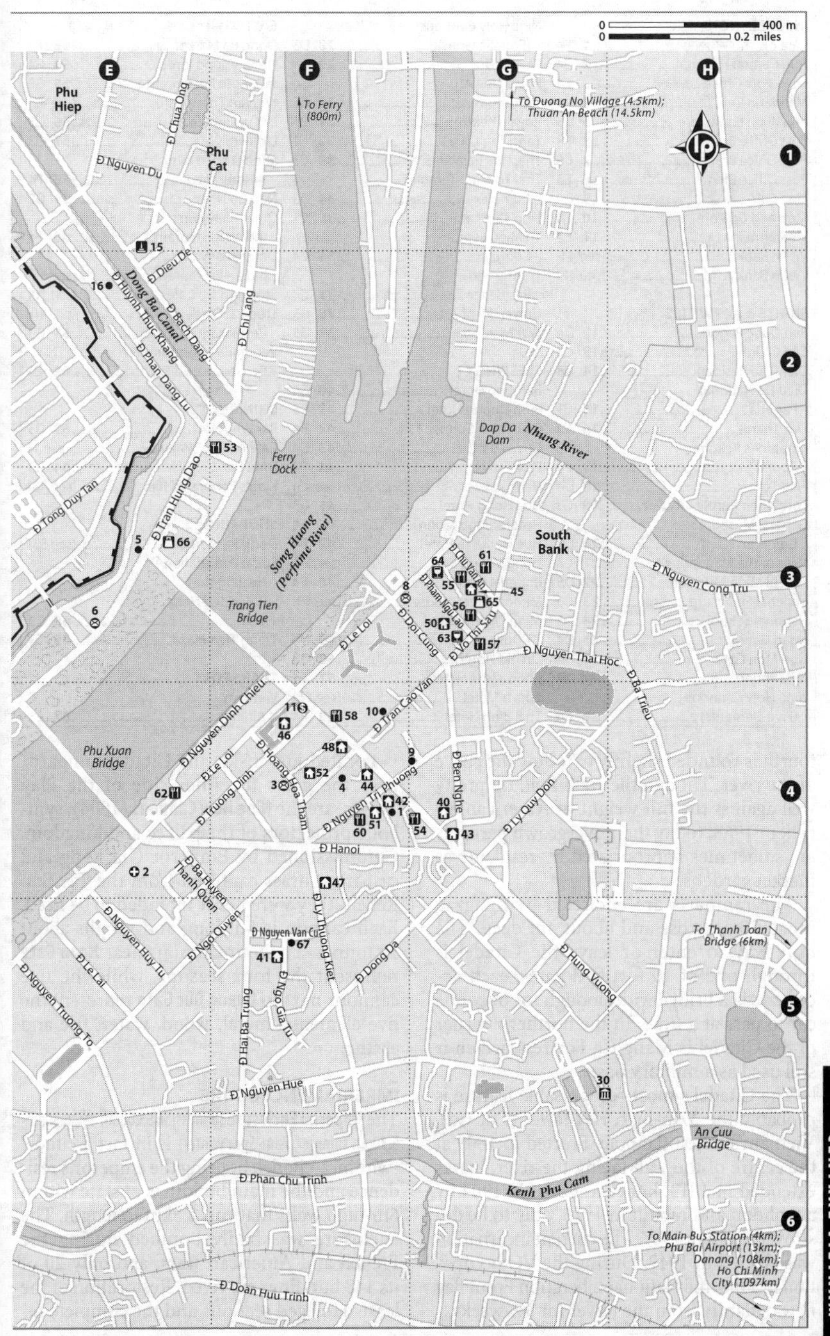

CENTRAL VIETNAM

INFORMATION
- Café on Thu Wheels 1 F4
- Hue Central Hospital 2 E4
- Main Post Office 3 F4
- Mandarin Café 4 F4
- Phu Xuan Bookstore 5 E3
- Post Office Branch 8 F3
- Post Office Branch 7 C6
- Post Office Branch 6 E3
- Sinh Café 9 G4
- Stop and Go Café 10 F4
- Vietcombank 11 F4
- Vietin Bank (see 44)
- Vietin Bank ATM (see 48)

SIGHTS & ACTIVITIES
- Bao Quoc Pagoda 12 D6
- Can Chanh Palace 13 C3
- Dien Tho Residence 14 C3
- Dieu De National Pagoda 15 E1
- Duc Thanh 16 E2
- Emperor's Reading Room 17 C3
- Flag Tower 18 D4
- Forbidden Purple City 19 C3
- General Museum Complex 20 D3
- Halls of the Mandarins 21 C3
- Ho Chi Minh Museum 22 D5
- Imperial Enclosure 23 C3
- National School 24 D5
- Ngan Gate 25 D4
- Ngo Mon Gate 26 D4
- Ngu Phung (see 26)
- Nine Holy Cannons (Five Elements) 27 C4
- Nine Holy Cannons (Four Seasons) 28 D3
- Quang Duc Gate 29 D4
- Royal Fine Arts Museum 30 G5
- Royal Theatre 31 D3
- Tang Tau Lake 32 C1
- Thai Hoa Palace 33 C3
- Thai To Mieu Temple Complex 34 D3
- Tinh Tam Lake 35 C1
- To Mieu Temple Complex 36 C4
- Truong San Residence 37 C3
- University of Arts 38 D3
- War Memorial 39 D5

SLEEPING
- Bamboo Hotel 40 G4
- Binh Duong Hotel 2 41 F5
- Binh Minh Sunrise 1 42 F4
- Chau Loan 43 G4
- Duy Tan Hotel 44 F4
- Halo (see 45)
- Hoa Hong Hotel 45 G3
- Hotel Saigon Morin 46 F4
- Hue Heritage Hotel 47 F4
- Hung Vuong Inn (see 54)
- Imperial Hotel 48 F4
- Mimosa Guesthouse (see 45)
- Minh Quang Guest House 49 D6
- Orchid Hotel 50 G3
- Phong Nha Hotel 51 F4
- Sports Hotel (see 56)
- Thai Binh Hotel 2 52 F4

EATING
- Dong Ba Market 53 F2
- Hung Vuong Inn 54 G4
- Japanese Restaurant 55 G3
- Khuyen Trang Café (see 42)
- La Carambole 56 G3
- Little Italy 57 G3
- Minh & Coco Mini Restaurant 58 F4
- Ngo Co Nhan 59 D2
- Omar Khayyam's Indian Restaurant 60 F4
- Omar Khayyam's Indian Restaurant (see 63)
- Stop and Go Café (see 10)
- Tropical Garden Restaurant 61 G3
- Vegetarian Restaurant Bo De 62 E4

DRINKING
- Bar Why Not? 63 G3
- Café on Thu Wheels (see 1)
- DMZ Bar 64 G3
- King's Panorama Bar (see 48)

SHOPPING
- Dong Ba Market (see 53)
- Spiral Foundation Healing the Wounded Heart Center 65 G3
- Trang Tien Plaza 66 E3

TRANSPORT
- Vietnam Airlines 67 F5

fourth is rounded slightly to follow the curve of the river. Though the walls held up pretty well against the full weight of American attack in 1968, today their overgrown parapets are sometimes appropriated by residents as market gardens.

The ramparts are encircled by a zigzag moat, 30m across and about 4m deep. The only way to enter or leave the Citadel is through one of 10 fortified gates, each accessed via a bridge wide enough for only one car to pass at a time. In the northern corner of the Citadel is Mang Ca Fortress, which is still used as a military base.

The Citadel's most recognisable feature is probably the 37m-high **Flag Tower** (Cot Co), Vietnam's tallest flagpole. Erected in 1809 at the centre of the wall facing the river, it was extended in 1813, knocked down in 1904 by a typhoon and rebuilt in 1915, only to be destroyed again in 1947. The current incarnation was erected in 1949. During the VC occupation in 1968, the National Liberation Front flag flew defiantly from the tower for 3½ weeks.

Located just inside the Citadel ramparts, near the gates to either side of the Flag Tower, are the **Nine Holy Cannons** (1804), symbolic protectors of the palace and kingdom. Commissioned by Emperor Gia Long and cast from brass captured from the Tay Son Rebels, they were never intended to be fired. Each cannon is 5m long and weighs about 10 tonnes. The four cannons near **Ngan Gate** represent the four seasons, while the five cannons next to **Quang Duc Gate** represent the five elements: metal, wood, water, fire and earth.

IMPERIAL ENCLOSURE

The **Imperial Enclosure** (admission 55,000d; 6.30am-5.30pm summer, 7am-5pm winter) is in fact a citadel-within-a-citadel, housing the emperor's residence and the main buildings of state within 6m-high walls that run 2.5km in length. The enclosure was badly bombed during the French and American wars, and only 20 of its 148 buildings survived. Restoration of the least-damaged sections and the complete rebuilding of others is ongoing, but a large part of it languishes in ruin.

The Enclosure is divided into several walled sections, with the Forbidden Purple City at its centre. The formal state palaces are between this and the main gate. Around the perimeter is a collection of temples and residences, the better preserved of which are along the southwestern wall. Situated along the opposite wall, nearest to the main gate, are the ruins of the **Thai To Mieu temple complex** (now a plant nursery) and behind it the **University of Arts**, housed in the former Royal Treasury. To the rear of this are some untended gardens, a park and lake.

This is a fascinating site, worth exploring for the better part of a day. It's enjoyable as a leisurely stroll and some of the less-visited areas can be quite atmospheric to linger in.

Ngo Mon Gate

The principal entrance to the Imperial Enclosure is **Ngo Mon Gate** (Noontime Gate; 1833), which faces the Flag Tower. The central passageway, with its yellow doors, was reserved for the use of the emperor, as was the bridge across the lotus pond.

On top of the gate is **Ngu Phung** (Belvedere of the Five Phoenixes), where the emperor appeared on important occasions, most notably for the promulgation of the lunar calendar. On 30 August 1945 the Nguyen dynasty ended here when Emperor Bao Dai abdicated to a delegation sent by Ho Chi Minh's Provisional Revolutionary Government.

Thai Hoa Palace

This **palace** (Palace of Supreme Harmony; 1803) is a spacious hall with an ornate timber roof supported by 80 carved and lacquered columns. It was used for the emperor's official receptions and other important court ceremonies, such as anniversaries and coronations. On state occasions the emperor sat on his elevated throne. Nine stelae divide the

CRAFTSMANSHIP FIT FOR A KING

Building the imperial monuments of Hue took the work of thousands of craftsmen and labourers, not only to erect the structures but also to fill them with the requisite appurtenances and objets d'art. Though the days of imperial patronage are long over, descendants of some craftsmen still make a living from these skills today.

At **Duc Thanh** (☎ 352 7707; 82 Đ Phan Dang Luu) in the Citadel, proprietor Mr Kinh Van Le is passing down the tradition of silk embroidery art. His father was a third-generation embroidery artisan who worked for Emperors Khai Dinh and Bao Dai, and Mr Kinh learned the way all apprentices do: from observing his father and relatives. When he was eight he embarked on his first solo project (still framed and displayed in his shop), but by the time he was an adult the days of the Nguyen dynasty were numbered.

Mr Kinh kept up his skills and later established a cooperative for embroidery artisans. He had to stop practising when his eyesight worsened with age, but now he runs classes that teach advanced embroidery techniques, such as how to make images appear more fanciful and lively, or to create an illusion of changing colours if one looks at the artwork from different angles. He also gives free classes to some disabled children. He'll tell you with pride that all the embroidery art in his shop is painstakingly hand-stitched, which is why he gets orders all the way from Japan.

Also toiling away at the family métier is 71-year-old Mr De Van Nguyen, who runs a small **foundry** (☎ 383 2151; 324/7 Đ Bui Thi Xuan) by the Perfume River southwest of the city. This is where he casts bells, statues and cauldrons, some for temples in Hue and neighbouring provinces.

Mr De's family has been in Hue since the early 19th century and their work for the royal family included some of the Citadel's cannons. His own particular skill is in the making of *kham tam khi* – a type of bronzework that uses a blend of bronze, silver and gold. He has 10 workers in his foundry, including his son; even then it takes them two months to complete a larger-than-life Buddha statue.

Mr Kinh and Mr De are happy to train new blood, but the hard part is finding young people who are interested. It takes years to hone one's skill, not to mention a lot of sweat and intense concentration – yet the earning power, even of a master artisan, can't compare with that of a modern job. These crafts aren't quite dying out yet, but former imperial prestige will only go so far.

two-level courtyard into separate areas for officials in each of the nine ranks of the mandarinate; administrative mandarins stood to one side, military mandarins to the other.

Halls of the Mandarins

Located immediately behind Thai Hoa Palace on either side of a courtyard, these **halls** were used by mandarins as offices and to prepare for court ceremonies. They were restored in 1977. In the courtyard you will find two gargantuan 17th-century bronze *vac dong* (cauldrons).

The hall to the left has been set up for cheesy tourist photos; you can pose in imperial costume (20,000d to 100,000d) on the throne or with an entourage of 'imperial maids and mandarins'. The opposite hall showcases a collection of gowns, photographs and porcelain from the Nguyen era, including a ferocious gilt decorative piece featuring two elephant tusks.

Behind the courtyard are the ruins of the **Can Chanh Palace**, a large hall for receptions. It was being rebuilt at the time of research.

Forbidden Purple City

Behind the palaces, in the very centre of the Imperial Enclosure, the **Forbidden Purple City** (Tu Cam Thanh) was a citadel-within-a-citadel-within-a-citadel. Almost entirely destroyed in the wars, it was once a walled compound solely for the personal use of the emperor. The only servants allowed were eunuchs who would pose no threat to the royal concubines. During the reign of the last emperor, Bao Dai, it even held a tennis court, a modern version of which now sits on the site (restored for 'tourist purposes').

Most of the area is now overgrown. Take care as you wander around the ruins as there are some gaping holes.

To the right the **Royal Theatre** (Duyen Thi Duong; ☎ 351 4989; www.nhanhac.com.vn; tickets 50,000d; 🕐 9am, 10am, 2.30pm & 3.30pm), begun in 1826, has been rebuilt on its former foundations. During the imperial period it hosted classical opera *(tuong)*, dance and music *(nha nhac)* performances for the emperor and his guests; today these traditional art forms are performed by the Theatre of Hue Traditional and Royal Arts.

Behind this, the two-storey **Emperor's Reading Room** (Thai Binh Lau) was the only part of the Forbidden Purple City to escape damage during the French reoccupation of Hue in 1947. The structure is not open to visitors, but it's worth popping by to see the intricate roof mosaics.

To Mieu Temple Complex

Taking up the south corner of the Imperial Enclosure, this walled complex dedicated to the Nguyen emperors has been beautifully restored.

The first structure after you enter is the three-tiered **Hien Lam Pavilion**, which at 13m stands at the height limit for Citadel buildings. On the other side of it stand **Nine Dynastic Urns** *(dinh)*, cast between 1835 and 1836, each dedicated to one Nguyen sovereign. About 2m in height and weighing 1900kg to 2600kg each, the urns symbolise the power and stability of the Nguyen throne. The central urn, also the largest and most ornate, is dedicated to dynasty founder Gia Long. Also in the courtyard are two dragons, trapped in what look like red phone boxes.

On the other side of the courtyard is the solemn **To Mieu Temple**, which houses shrines to each of the emperors, topped by their photos. Under the French only the seven who met with colonial approval were honoured; Ham Nghi, Thanh Thai and Duy Tan were added in 1959.

The temple is flanked to its right by a small robing house and to its left by a shrine to a soil god. Behind each of these, a gate leads into the small walled enclosure which houses the **Hung To Mieu Temple.** The temple sits between a Divine Kitchen and Divine Storehouse and is a restored 1951 reconstruction of the original, built in 1804 to honour Gia Long's parents. Both temples were used by the court on death anniversaries, but women (including the Empress) were strictly forbidden.

Dien Tho Residence

Behind the two temples is this stunning, partially ruined residence (1804). This comprised the apartments and audience hall of the Queen Mothers of the Nguyen dynasty. The audience hall houses an exhibition of photos and a display of royal garments.

Just outside is their Highnesses' enchanting pleasure pavilion, a carved wooden building set above a lily pond. Sitting pretty to the left of the audience hall is Tinh Minh Building, Bao Dai's private residence.

Truong San Residence

In 1844 Emperor Thieu Tri described this as one of the top 20 beautiful spots in Hue, but it was utterly devastated by war. At the time of research it was still being rebuilt. If the sumptuous entrance gate is anything to go by (check out the prancing dragons and phoenixes), the completed complex will be quite worthy of that accolade again.

TINH TAM LAKE

In the middle of Tinh Tam Lake, which is 500m north of the Imperial Enclosure, are two islands connected by bridges. The emperors used to come here to relax; now it's a fishermen's haunt.

TANG TAU LAKE

An island on Tang Tau Lake, which is northeast of Tinh Tam Lake, was once the site of a royal library. It is now occupied by the small Ngoc Huong Pagoda.

MUSEUMS

Royal Fine Arts Museum

This **museum** (150 Đ Nguyen Hue; admission free; 6.30am-5.30pm summer, 7am-5pm winter) moved to An Dinh Palace in 2008 when its former home Long An Palace was closed for renovation. The museum's most precious artefacts were lost during the American War, but the ceramics, paintings, furniture and royal clothing that remain are well worth a visit.

The museum's new home is the Baroque-influenced An Dinh Palace (1918), commissioned by Emperor Khai Dinh and full of elaborate murals, floral motifs and trompe lœil details. The structure was built with both Western-style steel-reinforced concrete and traditional Vietnamese wood, bricks and tiles. Emperor Bao Dai lived here with his family after abdicating in 1945. It was recently restored by a German-led team.

General Museum Complex

Formerly a school for princes and the sons of high-ranking mandarins, this exquisite albeit somewhat rundown building now forms part of the **General Museum Complex** (☎ 352 2397; Đ 23 Thang 8; admission free; 7.30-11am & 1.30-5pm, closed Mon), a hodgepodge of small, dissimilar museums. There's a pagoda devoted to archaeology, a small Natural History Museum and a building about anticolonial resistance in Thua Thien Hue province. Out front are war relics from the 1975 battle when Hue fell to the North.

Ho Chi Minh Museum

Every town's got one, and while Hue's **museum** (☎ 382 2152; 7 Đ Le Loi; admission 10,000d; 7.30-11am & 1.30-4.30pm, closed Mon) is a modern version more cheerful than most, the collection is as humdrum as usual. English captions are available.

PAGODAS

Bao Quoc Pagoda

Last renovated in 1957, this **pagoda** (Pagoda Which Serves the Country; ☎ 382 0488; Ham Long Hill; admission free) was founded in 1670. It was given its present name in 1824 by Emperor Minh Mang, who celebrated his 40th birthday here in 1830.

Follow the wide staircase up the hill to the triple-gated entrance to the pagoda. To the right is a school for training monks, which has been functioning since 1940. To the left is a cemetery for monks.

To get here, head south from Đ Le Loi on Đ Dien Bien Phu and take the first right after crossing the railway tracks.

Dieu De National Pagoda

Overlooking Dong Ba Canal, this **pagoda** (Quoc Tu Dieu De; 102 Đ Bach Dang) was built under Emperor Thieu Tri's rule (1841–47) and is one of the city's three 'national pagodas' that were once under the direct patronage of the emperor. It is famous for its four low towers, one to either side of the gate and two flanking the sanctuary.

During the regime of Ngo Dinh Diem (1955–63) and through the mid-1960s, Dieu De was a stronghold of Buddhist and student opposition to the South Vietnamese government and the war. In 1966 the pagoda was stormed by police, who confiscated radio equipment and arrested many monks, laypeople and students.

The pavilions on either side of the main sanctuary entrance contain the 18 La Ha, whose rank is just below that of Bodhisattva, and the eight Kim Cang, protectors of Buddha. In the back row of the main dais is Thich Ca Buddha, flanked by two assistants.

NATIONAL SCHOOL

One of the most famous secondary schools in Vietnam, the **National School** (Truong Quoc Hoc; 10 Đ Le Loi; 11.30am-1pm & from 5pm) was founded in 1896 and run by Ngo Dinh Kha, the father of South Vietnamese president Ngo Dinh Diem. Many of its pupils later rose to prominence: General Vo Nguyen Giap, strategist of the Viet Minh victory at Dien Bien Phu and North Vietnam's long-serving deputy premier, defence minister and commander-in-chief; Pham Van Dong, North Vietnam's prime minister for more than a quarter of a century; and Do Muoi, former Communist Party secretary-general and prime minister. Ho Chi Minh attended the school briefly in 1908.

The school admits students aged 16 to 18. It looks pleasant enough, with cheerful red buildings set along leafy avenues, but entrance examinations are notoriously difficult.

The National School can only be visited during the lunch break and after classes finish. Directly opposite its front entrance is a commanding but weather-beaten **war memorial** to Vietnamese and French soldiers who died in France during WWI.

BOAT TRIPS

Many sights around Hue, including Thien Mu Pagoda (p228) and several of the Royal Tombs (p229), can be reached by a journey along the Perfume River. Rates for chartering a boat are around US$8 for an hour's sightseeing on the river; a half-day charter to one or more sites will cost about US$15.

Ask directly at any of the four main riverboat moorings on the south side of the river; it's cheaper than going through an agency and you can negotiate your own route. However, be clear on your requirements, preferably in writing. Don't get scammed into paying more for lunch or motorbike fees (to get from the river to the tombs).

Most hotels and travellers' cafes are keen to push shared tours, hitting the tombs of Tu Duc, Minh Mang, Khai Dinh and Thien Mu Pagoda. Prices may be as implausible as US$3 per person (including a meagre lunch but not entry fees). The tour usually runs from 8am to 4pm. Given the time constraints, you'll need to ride a motorbike to get from the moorings to the first tomb. The second tomb is less than a 1km walk, but guides will try to get you on a bike for that too. The third tomb is 1.5km inland, a considerable hike, especially since it's usually one of the later stops on the cruise. Once the various fees have been factored in, many travellers wish they had cycled or arranged a motorbike instead.

Sleeping

BUDGET

There are two clusters of accommodation on the south side of the river. One is in the triangle formed by Đ Hung Vuong, Đ Nguyen Tri Phuong and Đ Hanoi. The other is a few blocks north in the little alleyways between Đ Le Loi and Đ Vo Thi Sau. This makes it easy to shop around, though both areas are in the heart of tourist town, where demanding *cyclo* drivers lurk on every street corner.

Mimosa Guesthouse (☎ 382 8068; 10/66 Đ Le Loi; r US$7-8; ❄) This cheapie has spartan rooms and is run by an affable former French teacher who also speaks good English.

Phong Nha Hotel (☎ 382 7729; phongnha_hotel@yahoo.com; 10/10 Đ Nguyen Tri Phuong; r US$8-15; ❄ 💻) Strategically located next to Café on Thu Wheels, this newish mini-hotel has rooms that are good value for money.

Halo (☎ 382 9371; huehalo@yahoo.com; 10A/66 Đ Le Loi; r US$8-15; ❄ 💻) Gleaming, immaculate rooms right in the heart of backpacker alley. Rooms at the front enjoy the use of a large balcony.

Binh Duong Hotel 2 (☎ 384 6466; binhduong2@dng.vnn.vn; 8 Đ Ngo Gia Tu; r US$8-15; ❄ 💻) A short walk away from the main tourist circuit in a quiet residential neighbourhood, this friendly outfit has everything from cheapies to spacious rooms with modern bathrooms.

Minh Quang Guest House (☎ 382 4152; 16 Đ Phan Chu Trinh; r US$12; ❄) Spotless accommodation near the railway station, way off the tourist track. Little English is spoken, but rooms are well equipped with modern appliances and bathroom fixtures.

Hung Vuong Inn (☎ 382 1068; truongdung2000@yahoo.com; 20 Đ Hung Vuong; r US$12-15; ❄ 💻) There's a lively restaurant downstairs and nine good-sized rooms upstairs; from up here you'll be guaranteed all the peace and quiet you want.

our pick **Binh Minh Sunrise 1 Hotel** (☎ 382 5526; www.binhminhhue.com; 36 (12) Đ Nguyen Tri Phuong; s US$12, d US$15-20; ❄ 💻) This hotel has all the ingredients for a pleasant stay: a central location, effortlessly pleasant staff and clean, fair-sized rooms. To sweeten the deal, there's complimentary in-room coffee and tea. Staff are helpful but not pushy about tours.

Bamboo Hotel (☎ 832 8888; huuthuan@dng.vnn.vn; 61 Đ Hung Vuong; r US$15; ❄ 💻) The name of the hotel also inspired its decor, with bamboo lamps, wooden floors and green accents in all the rooms. There's an enormous family room for US$35 that sleeps six.

Sports Hotel (☎ 382 8096; www.huestays.com; 15 Đ Pham Ngu Lao; r US$15-25;) Tasteful contemporary decor and cheerful staff set this a class apart from other mini-hotels. The price includes breakfast and every room has a bar fridge.

MIDRANGE

Thai Binh Hotel 2 (☎ 382 7561; www.thaibinhhotel-hue.com; 2 Đ Luong The Vinh; r US$20-30;) One street away from the tourist thoroughfare, this smart hotel is near to the action, yet blessed with lots of peace and quiet. The view from the higher floors is excellent (and a bargain, considering the price).

Duy Tan Hotel (☎ 382 5001; www.duytanhotel.com.vn; 12 Đ Hung Vuong; r US$25-60;) This centrally located hotel is popular with tour groups. Rooms in the old building are cheaper but there's no lift; those in the new building are better appointed.

Hoa Hong Hotel (☎ 382 4377; hoahonghotel@gmail.com; 1 Đ Pham Ngu Lao; s US$25-50, d US$30-60;) There's a lot of heavy Vietnamese wooden furniture in the lobby and the decor looks somewhat dated, but the rooms are well appointed, with large bathrooms. Prices include breakfast.

Orchid Hotel (☎ 383 1177; www.orchidhotel.com.vn; 30A Đ Chu Van An; r US$35-39;) This sparkling new hotel has been receiving rave reviews for impeccable service and sterling accommodation that outstrips its three-star competitors. Beyond the usual mod cons, every room has a DVD player and stereo, and pricier rooms have a desktop computer for in-room internet access.

Hue Heritage Hotel (☎ 383 8888; www.hueheritagehotel.com; 9 Đ Ly Thuong Kiet; r US$50-70, ste US$120;) Dressed up in mock-classical style, this hotel has stately rooms with high ceilings and a rooftop swimming pool. The massage showers aren't bad either.

TOP END

Hotel Saigon Morin (☎ 382 3526; www.morinhotel.com.vn; 30 Đ Le Loi; s US$100-140, d US$120-160, ste US$250-500;) Built in 1901, this was the first hotel in central Vietnam and the centre of French colonial life for most of the pre-WWII period. Even after a 1997 makeover into a four-star hotel, it retains much of its colonial charm, with spacious long rooms that are well appointed but not overdone.

Imperial Hotel (☎ 388 2222; www.imperial-hotel.com.vn; 8 Đ Hung Vuong; r US$159-179, ste US$239;) This 16-storey tower wouldn't look out of place in a more cosmopolitan city; here in Hue, it seems to have arrived ahead of its time. It's posh as all get out, with everything you'd expect of a five-star debutante: gleaming chandeliers, rooms with sweeping views, chic restaurants and the aptly named rooftop King's Panorama Bar.

Eating

We have the famed fussy eater Emperor Tu Duc to thank for the culinary variety of Hue (see p66). While the elaborate decoration of imperial cuisine may seem profligate, even a little silly, the *degustation*-style banquets can be sublime, well worthy of a splurge.

A local speciality worth trying is the royal rice cakes, the most common of which is *banh khoai*. You'll find these along with other variations *(banh beo, banh loc, banh it* and *banh nam)* in street stalls and restaurants at **Dong Ba Market** (Đ Tran Hung Dao; dishes 5000-10,000d) and around town. Other street-food options include the noodle stalls set up around the Citadel at night and the *com pho* places along Đ Tran Cao Van.

Vegetarian food has a long tradition in Hue. Stalls in Dong Ba Market serve lots of options on the first and 15th days of the lunar month. You'll find several vegie options on most menus in town, some using soya-bean mock meat.

VIETNAMESE

Vegetarian Restaurant Bo De (☎ 382 5959; 11 Đ Le Loi; dishes 10,000-50,000d; lunch & dinner) Fill up on inexpensive Vietnamese vegetarian fare (and we don't mean mock meat). Situated on a quiet riverside stretch, this is a pleasant nook to escape the town hubbub for a while. Menus are in English and French, and patio seating is available.

Chau Loan (☎ 382 2777; 78 Đ Ben Nghe; meals 15,000-50,000d; breakfast, lunch & dinner) Eat with the locals at this hole-in-the-wall joint serving Chinese-style food. Just don't look too closely at the walls and floor – they probably haven't been scrubbed in years. An English menu is available.

Khuyen Trang Café (☎ 384 9793; 40 Đ Nguyen Tri Phuong; meals 15,000-50,000d; breakfast, lunch & dinner) A friendly no-frills place offering simple Vietnamese and backpacker fare, it's a good spot to unwind over a beer at the end of the day.

Tropical Garden Restaurant (☎ 384 7143; tropicalgarden@vnn.vn; 27 Đ Chu Van An; dishes 25,000-140,000d;

THE JASS MAN

Warning: visiting Vietnam can change your life.

When Mr Michio Koyama visited Ho Chi Minh City (HCMC) in 1992, he encountered street children whose daily concerns were a far cry from the children he had been teaching in Tokyo. Here in Vietnam were youngsters living in extreme poverty and turning to crime to fill their bellies. Many were orphaned or had been abandoned by families who couldn't (or didn't want to) afford their upkeep anymore.

The next year, determined to do something for them, he left his life in Tokyo. First he got a job teaching Japanese at the university in Hue, earning money to set up a house. This he built in 1994, and he has not looked back since. The Streetchildren's Home can take in about 60 children aged six to 19. In almost 15 years it has seen more than 400 children pass through its doors, receiving not only safe refuge, but education and vocational guidance. Twenty children have gone on to university or technical schools.

Mr Koyama has also set up a Japanese restaurant (below) and a vocational centre which provides training in motorcycle repair or sewing and embroidery; both employ former street children. At Hue Municipal Hospital, he set up a centre where children with disabilities can receive free or subsidised medical care and rehabilitiation.

All these efforts reflect Mr Koyama's extraordinary ability to work with communists and capitalists alike, under the aegis of his NGO, The Japanese Association of Supporting Streetchildren Home (JASS). This extraordinary man has the support of the local People's Committee and was the first Japanese person to be granted citizenship of Hue. He was also awarded a Friendship medal by the Vietnamese government.

Funding for JASS has largely come from Japanese sources, including government grants and donations from about 1400 individuals and companies. Eating at the restaurant is an inexpensive way to support this cause, but if you feel like doing more, information is available on the JASS website (www001.upp.so-net.ne.jp/jass/).

dinner) It's a little naff but still good fun, serving central Vietnamese cuisine along with traditional Hue music (7pm to 9pm nightly). It's popular with tour groups, so service can be a bit spotty if you're on your own.

Ngo Co Nhan (☎ 351 3399; 47 Đ Nguyen Dieu; dishes 30,000-100,000d; lunch & dinner) Tucked away in a residential area of the Citadel, this restaurant looks like a giant bamboo hut raised up on stilts. It serves grilled seafood and beer to a mainly Vietnamese clientele. An English menu is available.

INTERNATIONAL

Minh & Coco Mini Restaurant (☎ 382 1822; 1 Đ Hung Vuong; mains 10,000-35,000d; breakfast, lunch & dinner) Run by two lively sisters, this neighbourhood dive has inexpensive food and attracts the locals for beer at night. It also books tours; the DMZ tour gets rave reviews for its tour leader who's an ARVN veteran.

Omar Khayyam's Indian Restaurant (☎ 381 0310; 22 Đ Pham Ngu Lao; dishes 10,000-89,000d; lunch & dinner) There are now two places to get Indian fare in town: the new space at Đ Pham Ngu Lao or the original but renovated location at 34 Đ Nguyen Tri Phuong. The former is warmly decorated in more traditional style, while the latter has a sparkling new rooftop terrace and also serves Italian and Vietnamese dishes.

Hung Vuong Inn (☎ 382 1068; 20 Đ Hung Vuong; pastries 15,000d, meals 30,000-60,000d; breakfast, lunch & dinner) The kind of casual yet clean eatery where everyone knows your name – or tries to, anyway, despite a constant stream of travellers passing through. There's a decent wine list and French-style pastries and bread.

Stop and Go Café (☎ 382 7051; 25 Đ Tran Cao Van; meals 20,000-60,000d; breakfast, lunch & dinner) Run by the very mellow Mr Do, this indoor-outdoor cafe has good Vietnamese and backpacker fare, including home-made tacos.

Japanese Restaurant (☎ 382 5146; 12 Đ Chu Van An; dishes US$1.50-9.00; dinner) Decent sushi and other Japanese delights in a restaurant that employs street children and supports a home for them (see the boxed text, above).

Little Italy (☎ 382 6928; www.littleitalyhue.com; 2A Đ Vo Thi Sau; dishes 20,000-100,000d; breakfast, lunch & dinner) Despite the bamboo decor and *ao dai*–wearing waitresses, this casual trattoria is as Italian as it gets in Hue. The menu is pretty extensive, with a wide range of reasonable pasta and pizzas.

La Carambole (☎ 381 0491; www.lacarambole.com; 19 Đ Pham Ngu Lao; mains 28,000-140,000d; ⏰ breakfast, lunch & dinner) Dressed up with colourful lanterns and signature red tablecloths, this bistro-style place run by a Frenchman and his Vietnamese wife serves both cuisines, including imperial-style Hue specialities.

Drinking

Café on Thu Wheels (☎ 383 2241; minhthuhue@yahoo.com; 10/2 Đ Nguyen Tri Phuong) It's small but packs a powerful punch, with the energetic owner keeping the chatter going every night. A great place for meeting people, swapping on-the-road tales and, of course, sampling Hue beer.

DMZ Bar (☎ 382 3414; www.dmz-bar.com; 60 Đ Le Loi) As popular as ever, this joint's always abuzz with rocking music, free pool and lively conversation. It serves food till midnight, including the entire menu from Little Italy.

Bar Why Not? (☎ 382 4793; www.whynotbarhue.com; 21 Đ Vo Thi Sau) At the other end of Đ Pham Ngu Lao is this less-raucous hang-out, also with a pool table. There's a sensational list of cocktails.

King's Panorama Bar (☎ 388 2222; 8 Đ Hung Vuong) If you want a fancy nightcap, head to this oh-so-swanky rooftop bar at the Imperial Hotel and soak up the incredible views along with your preferred poison.

Shopping

Hue produces the finest conical hats in Vietnam. The city's speciality is 'poem hats', which, when held up to the light, reveal shadowy scenes of daily life. It's also home to one of the largest and most beautiful selections of rice-paper and silk paintings in Vietnam, but the prices quoted are usually inflated to about four times the 'real' price.

Dong Ba Market (Đ Tran Hung Dao; ⏰ 6.30am-8pm) Just north of Trang Tien Bridge, this is Hue's largest market, selling anything and everything.

Trang Tien Plaza (6 Đ Tran Hung Dao; ⏰ 8am-10pm) A small, modern shopping centre between Trang Tien Bridge and Dong Ba Market. There's a Coopmart supermarket with all the comforts of wide aisles and price tags.

Spiral Foundation Healing the Wounded Heart Center (☎ 383 3694; 23 D Vo Thi Sau) This social enterprise sells a wide array of handicrafts made by 40 disabled artisans. Many of the items are eco-friendly or made with recycled materials, and make good souvenirs. Sales proceeds go towards paying fair salaries and medical insurance for the disabled employees, and funding heart surgery for children in need through the Hue College of Medicine and Pharmacy.

Getting There & Away

AIR

The main office of **Vietnam Airlines** (☎ 382 4709; 23 Đ Nguyen Van Cu; ⏰ closed Sun) handles reservations. Three flights a day connect Hue to both Hanoi and HCMC.

BUS

The main bus station is 4km to the southeast of the city on the continuation of Đ Hung Vuong (it becomes Đ An Duong Vuong and Đ An Thuy Vuong). The first main stop south is Danang (40,000d, three hours, every 15 minutes). **An Hoa bus station** (Hwy 1A), northwest of the Citadel, serves northern destinations, including Dong Ha (30,000d, 1½ hours, every halfhour).

Hue is a regular stop on open-tour bus routes. Most will drop passengers off around the Đ Hung Vuong tourist ghetto and pick them up from hotels. Expect a complete circus when you hop off, as you're likely to be followed by several persistent hotel touts.

Mandarin, Sinh and Stop and Go Cafés (p217) can arrange bookings for buses to Savannakhet, Laos (see the boxed text, p216).

CAR & MOTORBIKE

Some of the principal destinations from Hue include Hanoi (689km), Dong Ha (77km), Lao Bao (152km), Danang (108km) and HCMC (1097km).

TRAIN

The **Hue train station** (☎ 382 2175; 2 Đ Phan Chu Trinh) is at the southwestern end of Đ Le Loi. Destinations include Ninh Binh (268,000d, 10½ to 14½ hours, five daily), Vinh (177,000d, 6½ to 10 hours, seven daily), Dong Hoi (80,000d, 2½ to 5½ hours, nine daily), Dong Ha (30,000d, 1½ to 2½ hours, seven daily) and Danang (50,000d, 2½ to six hours, nine daily).

Getting Around

TO/FROM THE AIRPORT

Hue is served by Phu Bai Airport, once an important US air base, 14km south of the city centre. Taxi fares are typically around US$10, although you may save a few bucks with a share-taxi – enquire at your hotel. **Vietnam Airlines** (☎ 382 4709; 23 Đ Nguyen Van Cu; closed Sun) runs its own airport shuttle, which can collect you from your hotel (tickets 45,000d).

BICYCLE, MOTORBIKE & CAR HIRE

Pedal power is a fun way to tour Hue and the nearby Royal Tombs. Many hotels rent out bicycles for US$1 to US$2 per day. Self-drive motorbikes are available from US$3 to US$10, depending on the model and condition of the bike. A car with driver is available from US$30 per day.

CYCLO & XE OM

While Hue is an easy city to walk around, a typical street scene is a foreigner walking down the street with two *cyclos* and a motorbike in hot pursuit – the drivers yelling, 'hello cyclo' and 'hello motorbike' and the foreigner yelling, 'no, thank you, no!' Both types of drivers will quote outrageous prices, but a fair rate is 10,000d per kilometre.

TAXI

There are several metered taxi companies: **Gili** (☎ 382 8282), **Mai Linh** (☎ 389 8989), **Dong Ba** (☎ 384 8484) or **Thanh Do** (☎ 385 8585).

AROUND HUE

Thien Mu Pagoda

Built on a hillock overlooking the Perfume River, 4km southwest of the Citadel, this **pagoda** (Linh Mu; admission free) is an icon of Vietnam and as potent a symbol of Hue as the Citadel. The 21m-high octagonal tower, Thap Phuoc Duyen, was constructed under the reign of Emperor Thieu Tri in 1844. Each of its seven storeys is dedicated to a *manushi-buddha* (a Buddha that appeared in human form).

Thien Mu Pagoda was originally founded in 1601 by Nguyen Hoang, governor of Thuan Hoa province, after he heard that a Fairy Woman (Thien Mu) had told the people that a lord would build a pagoda for the country's prosperity. Over the centuries its buildings have been destroyed and rebuilt several times. Since the 1960s it has been a flashpoint of political demonstrations (see the boxed text, opposite).

To the right of the tower is a pavilion containing a stele dating from 1715. It is set on the back of a massive marble turtle, a symbol of longevity. To the left of the tower is another six-sided pavilion, this one sheltering an enormous bell (1710), which weighs 2052kg and is said to be audible 10km away.

The temple itself is a humble building in the inner courtyard, past the triple-gated entrance where three statues of Buddhist guardians stand at the alert. In the temple's main sanctuary behind the bronze laughing Buddha are three statues: A Di Da, the Buddha of the Past; Thich Ca, the historical Buddha (Sakyamuni); and Di Lac Buddha, the Buddha of the Future.

The best time to visit is early in the morning, before the tour groups show up. For a nice bicycle ride, head southwest (parallel to the Perfume River) on riverside Đ Tran Hung

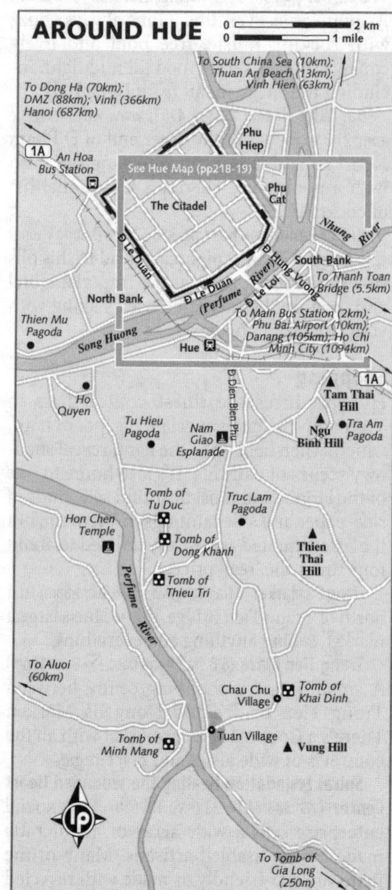

A FIERY PROTEST

Behind the main sanctuary of the Thien Mu Pagoda is the Austin motorcar that transported the monk Thich Quang Duc to the site of his 1963 self-immolation. He publicly burned himself to death in Saigon to protest the policies of South Vietnamese President Ngo Dinh Diem. A famous photograph of this act was printed on the front pages of newspapers around the world, and his death inspired a number of other self-immolations.

The response of the president's notorious sister-in-law, Tran Le Xuan (Madame Nhu), was to happily proclaim the self-immolations a 'barbecue party', saying 'Let them burn and we shall clap our hands'. Her statements greatly aggravated the already substantial public disgust with Diem's regime. In November both President Diem and his brother Ngo Dinh Nhu (Madame Nhu's husband) were assassinated by Diem's military. Madame Nhu was overseas at the time.

Another self-immolation sparked fresh protest in 1993. A man arrived at the pagoda and, after leaving offerings, set himself alight chanting the word 'Buddha'. Although his motivation remains a mystery, this set off a chain of events whereby the pagoda's leading monks were arrested, linked with the independent United Buddhist Church of Vietnam, the banned alternative to the state-sanctioned Vietnam Buddhist Church. This led to an official complaint to the UN by the International Federation of Human Rights accusing the Vietnamese government of violating its own constitution, which protects freedom of religion.

Dao, which turns into Đ Le Duan after Phu Xuan Bridge. Cross the railway tracks and keep going on Đ Kim Long. Thien Mu Pagoda can also be reached by boat.

Tu Hieu Pagoda

Nestled in a pine forest, this popular **pagoda** (admission free) was built in 1843 and later coopted by eunuchs from the Citadel, so that the monks would worship and honour them after their death. The small cemetery to the left of the pagoda was exclusively for the burial of eunuchs, and is filled with neat mossy tombs.

Today the temple is better known for its association with Zen master Thich Nhat Hanh, who entered its monastery in the early 1940s. When he left Vietnam on a peace mission to the West in 1966, he was barred from returning by both the North and the South. It was only in 2005 that he was permitted to return to the country.

Tour groups usually stop by at 10am and 4pm to hear the monks chant. At other times it's quite tranquil amidst the whistle of pine trees, particularly by the small lake to the right of the pagoda.

Tu Hieu Pagoda is about 5km from the centre of Hue, on the way to the tomb of Tu Duc.

Royal Tombs

The **tombs** (🕒 6.30am-5.30pm summer, 7am-5pm winter) of the rulers of the Nguyen dynasty (1802–1945) are extravagant mausoleums, spread out along the banks of the Perfume River between 2km and 16km south of Hue. Almost all were planned by the emperors during their lifetimes, and some were even used as residences while they were still alive.

Although each tomb is unique, most of the mausoleums consist of five essential elements. The first is a stele pavilion in which the accomplishments, exploits and virtues of the deceased emperor are engraved on a marble tablet. Next is a temple for the worship of the emperor and empress. Third, an enclosed sepulchre where the emperor's remains are buried. Fourth, an honour courtyard with stone elephants, horses, and civil and military mandarins. And finally, a lotus pond surrounded by frangipani and pine trees.

Unfortunately, many valuable objects went missing from the tombs during Vietnam's wars, so they seem rather scantily decorated today.

While many of the tombs can be reached by boat, you'll have more time to enjoy them by renting your own bicycle or motorbike. Alternatively hire a *xe om* or car and driver for the day (see opposite).

TOMB OF TU DUC

The majestic and serene **tomb** (admission 55,000d) is set amid frangipani and pine trees. Emperor Tu Duc designed the exquisitely harmonious tomb, which was constructed between 1864 and 1867, for use both before and after his death. The enormous expense of the tomb and the forced labour used in its construction spawned a coup plot that was discovered and suppressed in 1866.

It is said that Tu Duc, who had the longest reign of any Nguyen monarch (1848–83), lived a life of ultimate imperial luxury. Though he had 104 wives and countless concubines, he had no offspring. One theory has it that he became sterile after contracting smallpox.

The tomb is entered from the southeast. A path leads to a boat landing on the shore of **Luu Khiem Lake**. The island to the right, Tinh Khiem, is where Tu Duc used to hunt small game. Across the water to the left is Xung Khiem Pavilion, where he would sit with his concubines, composing or reciting poetry.

Across the courtyard from the landing are steps leading to **Hoa Khiem Temple**, where Tu Duc and his wife, Empress Hoang Le Thien Anh, are worshipped. Before his death, Tu Duc used this as an office. Today it houses a jumble of dusty, unlabelled royal artefacts. The larger throne was for the empress; Tu Duc was only 153cm tall.

Minh Khiem Chamber, to the right behind Hoa Khiem Temple, was originally meant to be a theatre. It's inherited some of the touristy aspects of the Citadel: cheesy dress-up photo ops from 30,000d and cultural performances by the same troupe that performs in the Forbidden Purple City. Directly behind Hoa Khiem Temple is the quieter Luong Khiem Temple, where Tu Duc's mother, Tu Du, is worshipped.

Following the shore of the lake, the path continues to the **Honour Courtyard**. After walking between the honour guard of elephants, horses and diminutive mandarins (they were made even shorter than the emperor), you reach the Stele Pavilion, which shelters a 20-tonne stone tablet. Tu Duc drafted the inscriptions himself. He freely admitted that he had made mistakes and chose to name his tomb Khiem ('modest').

The **tomb**, enclosed by a wall, is on the other side of a half-moon-shaped lake. It's a drab grey monument, and the emperor was never interred here. The site where his remains were buried (along with great treasure) is not known. To keep it a secret from grave robbers, all of the 200 servants who buried the king were beheaded.

Across the lake are the **tombs** of Tu Duc's adopted son, Emperor Kien Phuc, who ruled for only seven months before dying at the age of 15, and Empress Hoang Le Thien Anh.

Tu Duc's tomb is about 5km south of Hue on Van Nien Hill in Duong Xuan Thuong village.

TOMB OF MINH MANG

Perhaps the most majestic of all of the royal tombs is this **tomb of Minh Mang** (admission 55,000d), who ruled from 1820 to 1840. Renowned for its architecture, which harmoniously blends into the natural surroundings, the tomb was planned during Minh Mang's lifetime and built between 1841 and 1843 by his successor Thieu Tri.

The **Honour Courtyard** is reached via three gates on the eastern side of the wall. Three granite staircases lead from the courtyard to the square Stele Pavilion (Dinh Vuong).

Sung An Temple, which is dedicated to Minh Mang and his empress, is reached via three terraces and the rebuilt Hien Duc Gate. On the other side of the temple, three stone bridges span Trung Minh Ho (Lake of Impeccable Clarity). The central bridge, constructed of marble, was for the emperor's use only. Minh Lau Pavilion (Pavilion of Light) stands on the top of three superimposed terraces that represent the 'three powers': the heavens, the earth and water. To the left is the Fresh Air Pavilion, to the right the Angling Pavilion.

From a stone bridge across crescent-shaped Tan Nguyet Lake (Lake of the New Moon), a monumental staircase with dragon banisters leads to the **sepulchre**, which is surrounded by a circular wall symbolising the sun. Behind the bronze door in the middle of the enclosure is the emperor's burial place: a mound of earth covered with mature pine trees and dense shrubbery. The gate to the tomb is opened only once a year on the anniversary of the emperor's death.

The tomb of Minh Mang, which is on Cam Ke Hill in An Bang village, is over the bridge on the west bank of the Perfume River, about 12km from Hue.

TOMB OF KHAI DINH

A striking departure from the architectural styles of the other royal tombs, this hillside **monument** (admission 55,000d) is a synthesis of Vietnamese and European elements. Most of the tomb's grandiose exterior is covered in blackened concrete, creating an unexpectedly gothic air, while the interiors resemble an explosion of colourful mosaic.

Khai Dinh was the penultimate emperor of Vietnam, from 1916 to 1925, and widely seen by young nationalists as a puppet of the French. The construction of his flamboyant tomb took 11 years (1920–31) – two years longer than his reign.

Be prepared to climb stairs if you visit this tomb. The first flight of 36 wide steps leads to a courtyard flanked by two pavilions. The **Honour Courtyard** is 26 steps further up the hillside. Note the stone faces of the mandarin honour guards, sculpted with a mixture of Vietnamese and European features.

Up three more flights of stairs is the stupendous main building, **Thien Dinh**. The walls and ceiling are decorated with murals of the Four Seasons, Eight Precious Objects and Eight Fairies. Under a graceless, gold-speckled concrete canopy is a gilt bronze statue of Khai Dinh. His remains are interred 18m below the statue and he is worshipped in the last hall. Be warned that the fluorescent lighting makes everything look even more over the top.

The tomb of Khai Dinh is 10km from Hue in Chau Chu village.

TOMB OF GIA LONG

Emperor Gia Long founded the Nguyen dynasty in 1802 and ruled until 1819. According to royal annals, the emperor himself chose the site after scouting the area on the back of an elephant. Both the emperor and his queen are buried here. The rarely visited **tomb** (admission free) is presently in a state of ruin. It is around 14km south of Hue and 3km from the west bank of the Perfume River.

TOMB OF DONG KHANH

The smallest of the royal tombs, **Dong Khanh's mausoleum** was built in 1889. He was the nephew and adopted son of Tu Duc, and was placed on the throne by the French in 1885 after they exiled his predecessor, Ham Nghi. Predictably, Dong Khanh was docile till his death three years later.

This tomb was closed for restoration at the time of research. It is just over 5km from the city, 500m behind the tomb of Tu Duc.

TOMB OF THIEU TRI

The only royal tomb not enclosed by a wall, the **tomb of Thieu Tri** (1848) has a similar floor plan to his father Minh Mang's tomb but is substantially smaller. It was closed for restoration at the time of research.

The tomb is about 7km from Hue. There's a pretty 2km cross-country track that leads here from the tomb of Dong Khanh.

NAM GIAO ESPLANADE

Barely visible from the road amid a thick pine forest, this three-tiered **esplanade** (admission free) was once the most important religious site in Vietnam. In an annual (later triennial) ritual, the Nguyen emperors made animal sacrifices and elaborate offerings to the All-Highest Emperor of the August Heaven (Thuong De), to ensure the stability and prosperity of their rule. The topmost esplanade, which represents heaven, is round, while the middle terrace, representing earth, is square, as is the lowest terrace representing humanity.

The ceremony involved a lavish procession from the Citadel and a three-day fast by the emperor at the nearby **Fasting Palace** before the ritual. The last ceremony was held in 1945, presided over by Bao Dai.

Since 2006 the ceremony has been re-enacted in full regalia (minus the fasting and animal sacrifices) as part of the Festival of Hue. The Fasting Palace, located at the furthest end of the park from the entrance, has an informative display of photographs and English captions.

Nam Giao Esplanade is at the southern end of Đ Dien Bien Phu, about 2km from the railway tracks.

HO QUYEN

Wildly overgrown but still evocative, **Ho Quyen** (Tiger Arena; admission free) was built in 1830 for the royal pastime of watching elephants and tigers face off in combat. The tigers were usually declawed and had their teeth removed, so that the elephants – a symbol of the emperor's power – triumphed every time. The last fight was held here in 1904.

At only 44m across, the arena is hardly *Gladiator*-sized. The interior is closed off, but you can climb up to the grassy ramparts and look down on where the animals once rumbled. The south-facing section was reserved for the royal family, while diametrically opposite are the tiger cages. The elephants were brought in through the doorway that's almost 4m high.

Ho Quyen is about 3km outside Hue in Truong Da village. Follow Đ Bui Thi Xuan west from the train station, then look out for the blue sign near the market that indicates the turn-off on the left. Follow this lane for about 200m to a fork in the road and go right.

Thanh Toan Bridge

This is a classic covered Japanese **footbridge** (admission free), architecturally similar to its cousin in Hoi An but receiving far fewer visitors due to its out-of-the-way location. With picturesque countryside nearby and not a souvenir shop in sight, it makes for a lovely diversion from Hue's ostentatious tombs and temples.

The bridge is in sleepy Thuy Thanh village, 7km east of Hue. Finding it is a bit tricky; getting lost is part of the fun. Head north for a few hundred metres on Đ Ba Trieu until you see a sign to the Citadel Hotel. Turn right and follow the bumpy dirt road for another 6km past villages, rice paddies and several pagodas.

Thuan An to Vinh Hien

Thuan An Beach, 15km northeast of Hue, is on the splendid Tam Giang–Cau Hai Lagoon near the mouth of the Perfume River, at the tip of a long, thin island. It's quite undeveloped except for a few kiosks, but between September and April the water's often too rough to swim in.

Beyond the beach a 50km road stretches the length of the island from Thuan An to Vinh Hien. This makes a great day trip by motorbike or car from Hue. It also offers an alternative route to or from Hue for travellers making their way along the coast road.

Coming from Thuan An, the road winds past villages alternating with shrimp lagoons and vegetable gardens. Most extraordinary are the colourful and opulent **graves and family temples** lining the ocean side of the road. The area is known as the 'city of tombs' or 'city of ghosts' – families, often with funding from their overseas Vietnamese relatives, vie to outdo their neighbours' ancestral monuments.

From Vinh Hien, the new Tu Hien Bridge connects the island to the mainland, where the road hugs the southeastern shore of the lagoon all the way to Hwy 1A.

BACH MA NATIONAL PARK

☎ 054 / elevation 1450m

A French-era hill station, this **national park** (Vuon Quoc Gia Bach Ma; ☎ 387 1330; www.bachma.vnn.vn; adult/child/child under 6 20,000d/10,000d/free) reaches a peak of 1450m at Bach Ma mountain, only 18km from the coast. The cool climate attracted the French, who started building villas here in 1930; by 1937 the number of holiday homes had reached 139 and it became known as the 'Dalat of central Vietnam'. Not surprisingly the Viet Minh tried hard to spoil the holiday – the area saw some heavy fighting in the early 1950s.

Bach Ma has some stunning views across the coastline near the Hai Van Pass, which the Americans used to their advantage: during the war, US troops turned the area into a fortified bunker. The VC did their best, but couldn't dislodge the Americans. Between the eerie remains of forgotten French villas and memories of the American War, spooky stories abound among locals, who maintain that the park is a realm of ghosts.

In 1991, land stretching from the coast to the Annamite mountain range at the Lao border was set aside as a nature preserve and designated Bach Ma National Park. Efforts are now underway to regenerate patches of forest that were destroyed during the American War. More than 1400 species of plants have been discovered here, representing a fifth of the flora of Vietnam. Forty-three species of mammal have been definitively recorded within the boundaries of the park, with a further 76 species potentially present.

A recent victory in the wildlife stakes came with the discovery in 1992 of evidence of the sao la, a previously unknown antelopelike creature. Two other animals were discovered here in the late 1990s: the deerlike Truong Son muntjac and the giant muntjac. Additional reserves in the provinces neighbouring Bach Ma National Park have been created to help protect the natural habitat and there is hope that wild elephants will return from the Lao side of the border.

As most of the park's resident mammals are nocturnal, sightings demand a great deal of effort and patience. Bird-watching is fantastic but you need to be up at dawn for the best sightings. Of the 800-odd bird species known to inhabit Vietnam, the park is home to 358, including the fabulous crested argus pheasant and the tenacious Edwards' pheasant. As far as back as 1925 conservationists had proposed protecting the latter species; it went unseen for 50 years and was thought to be extinct, until it was rediscovered in the park in the late 1990s.

The **visitor centre** at the park entrance has a small exhibition on the park's flora and fauna. You can book village and bird-watching tours, English- or French-speaking guides (200,000d per day), and eight-seater minibuses (one way/return 350,000/500,000d) to take you to the summit. Motorbikes and cycles are strictly prohibited.

If you're keen on hiking, pick up the detailed booklet on hiking trails (10,000d) from the visitor centre. Rangers still issue warnings about possible unexploded ordnance in the area, so it's best to stick to the trails. Each trail is several kilometres long, and a popular option is the steep 500m ascent to the summit of Bach Ma mountain. A recent influx of Buddhist visitors making pilgrimages to the peak has led to the construction of a new pagoda, Bach Van Tu, near the top.

Bach Ma is the wettest place in Vietnam, with the heaviest of the rain falling in October and November (and bringing out the leeches). It's not out of the question to visit then, but check road conditions first. The best time to visit Bach Ma is from February to September, particularly between March and June.

Sleeping & Eating

National Park Guesthouse (☎ 387 1330; camp sites per person 10,000d, entrance r 150,000d, summit r 150,000-300,000d) The park authority has a small camping ground, two guesthouses near the entrance and four guesthouses near the summit. One of the summit guesthouses has a 12-person dorm with a shared bathroom. The more expensive twin-bed rooms are a better bet for views and facilities. Give at least four hours' notice for meal requirements, as fresh food is brought up to the park on demand.

Near the summit are two guesthouses, **Cam Tu** (☎ 387 1802) and **Phong Lan** (☎ 387 1801); rates were not available at the time of research. A nicer option is the **Morin-Bach Ma Hotel** (☎ 387 1199; www.huonggiangtourist.com/huonggiangtourist/hotel/Bachma_Hotel.htm; s/d US$35/40). Built in a French style, it has acceptable rooms and a restaurant (order meals in advance).

Getting There & Away

Bach Ma is 28km west of Lang Co and 40km southeast of Hue. The turn-off is signposted in the town of Cau Hai on Hwy 1A. The entrance is 3km in. You can also enter from the town of Phu Loc – look for the red gateway leading to the park.

From the visitor centre, it's another steep and meandering 16km on the sealed road to the summit. Private transport is available from the visitor centre. Walking down from the summit takes about three to four hours; carry plenty of water and wear a hat, as there is little canopy protection on the lower part of the road.

There are buses to the park from Danang (35,000d, two hours) and Hue (20,000d, one hour). Local buses stop at Cau Hai, where *xe om* drivers can ferry you to the entrance. Cau Hai has a **train station** (☎ 387 1362; Loc Dien village), but the two daily services in either direction are slow and pass through at antisocial times.

Getting Around

Your visit will be much easier if you hire a vehicle for your time in the park, especially if you plan to hit the trails – they're spread out along the 16km access road.

SUOI VOI (ELEPHANT SPRINGS)

About 15km north of Lang Co Beach, **Suoi Voi** (admission 10,000d, motorbike/car 3000/10,000d) is a secluded recreation area that's a good pitstop for those with their own wheels. The crystal-clear waters and lush forest all around are great for destressing after being on the road.

The main springs are a short walk from the parking area. The natural pool is ringed by huge boulders, one vaguely in the shape of an elephant's head and cosmetically enhanced to look more like it. Further exploration will lead to less-populated swimming holes.

Foreign visitors here are scarce and on weekdays you may have the whole place to yourself. Weekends and holidays are jam-packed with locals, both families and young couples exploring the birds and bees.

The turn-off to the springs from Hwy 1A is well signposted near the road markers reading 'Danang 52km' (if coming from the north) or 'Phu Bai 44km' (from the south). You will see the 19th-century Thua Luu Church just ahead of you. Keep the church on your left and follow the dirt road for 5km to the entry gate. Buy a ticket here and keep it in case you have to show it again. From here it's a bumpy 1.5km to the parking area.

There are some food stalls at the springs, but they're only open when the park is busy. It's better to bring a picnic anyway.

LANG CO BEACH

☎ 054

Lang Co is an attractive, islandlike stretch of palm-shaded white sand, with a crystal-clear, turquoise lagoon on one side and 10km of beachfront on the other. Many open-tour buses make a lunch stop here and if the weather's nice, it's a fine place to hop off for a night or two.

The beach is best enjoyed between April and July. From late August till November rains are frequent, and from December to March it can get chilly.

There are spectacular views of Lang Co from the Hai Van Pass and from the trains linking Danang and Hue. Most of the accommodation is north of the town along the highway.

Sleeping & Eating

Chi Na Guesthouse (☎ 387 4597; s/d 100,000/120,000d; ❄) Rooms are basic and the family speaks a little English. Cheaper fan-cooled rooms are available.

Thanh Tam Seaside Resort (☎ 387 4456; www.thanhtamresort-langcobeach.com.vn; r US$23-55; ❄) This resort has a range of accommodation: old and new, rooms and bungalows. Choose carefully, as the newer building has more contemporary furniture and a warmer feel, while older rooms look quite tired, even dismal. The terrace restaurant is a popular stop for buses journeying between Hue and Danang, but the food was overpriced and mediocre when we visited.

Lang Co Beach Resort (☎ 387 3555; www.langcobeachresort.com.vn; r US$40, villa US$75-95; ❄ 💻 🏊) There's a faintly Balinese feel to the main lobby, and the lavishly landscaped gardens certainly add a stylish note. The beach-facing villas have large balconies and excellent views.

Getting There & Away

Lang Co is just on the other side of the Hai Van Tunnel from Danang, which has reduced the distance to 20km. Tourist buses pass through daily. However, those on two wheels will still need to take the 35km scenic route over the Hai Van Pass.

Lang Co's **train station** (☎ 387 4423) is located 3km from the beach, in the direction of the lagoon. Getting a *xe om* to get you to the beach shouldn't be difficult. The train journey from here to Danang (15,000d, 1½ to two hours, four daily) is one of the most spectacular in Vietnam. Services also connect to Hue (28,000d, 1½ to two hours, three daily).

HAI VAN PASS & TUNNEL

The **Hai Van (Sea Cloud) Pass** crosses over a spur of the Truong Son mountain range that juts into the sea. About 30km north of Danang, the road climbs to an elevation of 496m, passing south of the Ai Van Son peak (1172m). It's an incredibly mountainous stretch of highway with spectacular views. The railway track, with its many tunnels, goes around the peninsula, following the beautiful and deserted shoreline.

In the 15th century this pass formed the boundary between Vietnam and the kingdom of Champa. Until the American War it was heavily forested. At the summit is a bullet-scarred French fort, later used as a bunker by the South Vietnamese and US armies.

If you cross in winter, the pass serves as something of a visible dividing line between the climates of the north and south, protecting Danang from the fierce 'Chinese winds' that sweep in from the northeast. From about November to March the exposed Lang Co side of the pass can be wet and chilly, while just to the south it's warm and dry. When the winter weather is lousy in Hue, it's usually good in Danang.

The top of the pass is the only place you can pull over for a while. The view is well worth it, but you'll have to fight off a rather large crowd of very insistent vendors. Don't change money here – you'll get short-changed.

In 2005 the 6280m-long **Hai Van Tunnel** opened, bypassing the pass and shaving an hour off the journey between Danang and Hue. Motorbikes and bicycles are not permitted in the tunnel, nor are vehicles carrying live animals or flammable materials, but most cars and buses now take this route. Sure, it saves time, but on a nice day it really is a shame to miss the views from the pass.

Despite the odd hair-raising encounter, the pass road is safer than it used to be. If you can take your eyes off the road, keep them peeled for the small altars on the roadside – sobering reminders of those who have died in accidents on this winding route.

BA NA HILL STATION

☎ 0511 / elev 1485m

Another hill-resort inherited from the French, lush **Ba Na** (admission 10,000d, per motorbike/car 5000/10,000d) has refreshingly cool weather and gorgeous countryside views – well worth the steep climb up a winding road. When it's 36°C on the coast, it's likely to be between 15°C and 26°C on the mountain. Rain often falls in the section between 700m and 1200m above sea level, but around the hill station itself, the sky is usually clear (except during the impossible rainy months of October and November).

Mountain tracks lead to some waterfalls and viewing points. Near the top, the **Linh Ung Pagoda** (1999) is a supremely peaceful spot, with a 24m-high white seated Buddha visible for miles around.

Established in 1919, the resort area once held 200-odd villas, but only a few tattered ruins remain. Until WWII the French were carried up the last 20km of rough mountain road by sedan chair. Today's tourists arrive by more mundane means, although a new cable-car system was being built at the time of research.

The provincial government aspires to make Ba Na the Dalat of the province, but progress is slow and the proliferation of karaoke and litter leaves much to be desired. Nonetheless, if you avoid weekends and the high-season rush, this can be an idyllic place to pass a few days.

There are no ATMs up here, but there is a small **post office** (☎ 379 1500) near Le Nim.

Sleeping

Ba Na By Night Resort (☎ 379 1056; bananight@dng.vnn.vn; r 200,000-500,000d) Don't let the name fool you – this place is a hubbub of activity all day long. There are rooms in *rong* houses (thatched-roof stilt houses) and villas; opt for one away from the main hotel if you want some peace and quiet. One of the old villas beside the restaurant contains a colonial-era wine cellar built into the side of the mountain. A path from the hotel leads down to Linh Ung Pagoda.

Le Nim (☎ 379 1504) Undergoing a massive overhaul at the time of research, this resort is similarly priced to Ba Na By Night, while overlooking a different vista. Hopefully the new hotel rooms will continue to take full advantage of its views and dial down the noisy activities.

Getting There & Away

Ba Na is 42km west of Danang along a beautiful winding road that was being improved at the time of research. From the Reception Centre it's a steep climb uphill, and many motorbikes won't attempt it. Shuttle buses (return 40,000d) head up the mountain when full. Otherwise you can hire a local with a high-powered motorcycle to take you (80,000d).

DANANG

☎ 0511 / pop 788,500

The third-largest city in Vietnam, Danang manages to be the least touristed as well – and that's a good thing. People here are too busy making a living, whether they're selling *mi quang* (soup noodles served with pork slices, half a hard-boiled egg, shrimp, peanuts and vegies) on the street or investing in joint-stock companies, to bother about tourists, and the city itself has little by way of conventional sightseeing spots. Yet with the constant flow of business travellers and a burgeoning expat community, there's a healthy hotel, dining and nightlife scene – good for whiling away a few days off the tourist trail.

By no stretch of the imagination is this a beautiful city, but Danang is gradually coming into its own as a thoroughly modern one. Downtown Danang has unveiled several sparkling skyscrapers. Out to the west, the local government is developing Da Phuoc International New Town (trendily abbreviated to D-City), while all the beaches south of My Khe have been colonised by five-star hotel developments. As Danang's trying its darnedest to go glitzy as a playground for the rich, it remains to be seen if it'll be hamstrung by its lingering war-era reputation for sleaze (gentlemen, beware of attempts in bars to importune you).

Most travellers who linger in Danang come to lie on the beach or explore Monkey Mountain or the Marble Mountains (Monkey is to the north and there's only one mountain, Marble is to the south and there are five of them). If you're staying downtown, the riverfront promenade can be a charming, less dramatic version of the Bund in Shanghai, particularly in the evening when it attracts canoodling couples, families out for an evening constitutional and teenagers just hanging out (and sometimes breakdancing). Despite the city's size, not that many people speak English. You're not likely to be hassled about buying anything; even the *xe om* drivers are tame compared with their brethren in Hue or Hoi An.

History

Known during French colonial rule as Tourane, Danang succeeded Hoi An as the most important port in central Vietnam during the 19th century, and it remains the principal one for central Vietnam.

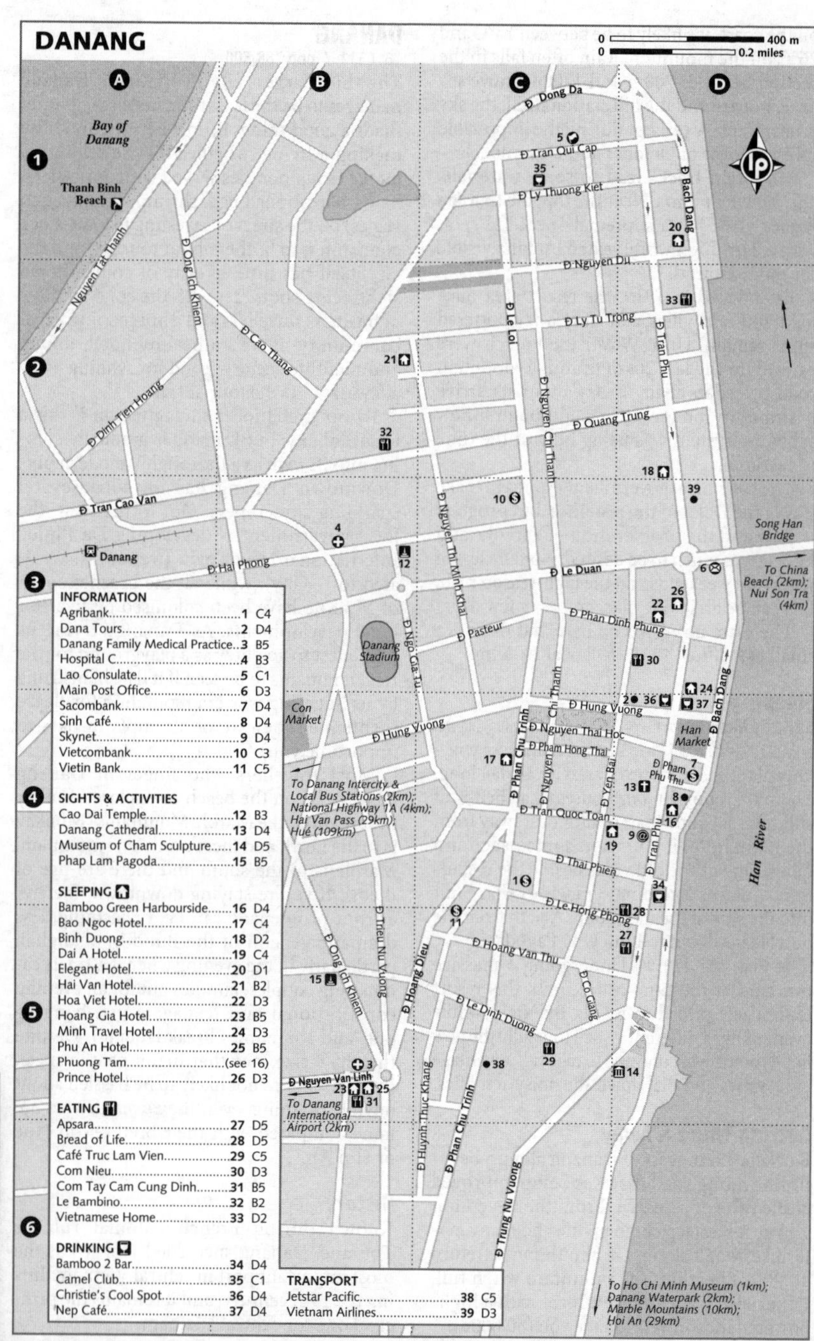
DANANG
0 400 m
0 0.2 miles
A
B
C
D
1
2
3
4
5
6
Bay of Danang
Thanh Binh Beach
Nguyen Tat Thanh
Đ Ong Ich Khiem
Đ Cao Thang
Đ Dinh Tien Hoang
Đ Tran Cao Van
Danang
Đ Hai Phong
Đ Dong Da
Đ Tran Qui Cap
Đ Ly Thuong Kiet
Đ Bach Dang
Đ Nguyen Du
Đ Le Loi
Đ Ly Tu Trong
Đ Tran Phu
Đ Nguyen Chi Thanh
Đ Quang Trung
Đ Nguyen Thi Minh Khai
Đ Le Duan
Song Han Bridge
To China Beach (2km); Nui Son Tra (4km)
Đ Ngo Gia Tu
Danang Stadium
Đ Pasteur
Đ Phan Dinh Phung
Con Market
Đ Hung Vuong
Đ Phan Chu Trinh
Đ Nguyen Thai Hoc
Đ Pham Hong Thai
Han Market
Đ Pham Phu Thu
Đ Yen Bai
Đ Tran Quoc Toan
Đ Thai Phien
Đ Le Hong Phong
Đ Hoang Van Thu
Đ Co Giang
Đ Le Dinh Duong
Đ Hoang Dieu
Đ Trieu Nu Vuong
Đ Huynh Thuc Khang
Đ Trung Nu Vuong
Đ Nguyen Van Linh
Han River
To Danang Intercity & Local Bus Stations (2km); National Highway 1A (4km); Hai Van Pass (29km); Hué (109km)
To Danang International Airport (2km)
To Ho Chi Minh Museum (1km); Danang Waterpark (2km); Marble Mountains (10km); Hoi An (29km)
INFORMATION
Agribank 1 C4
Dana Tours 2 D4
Danang Family Medical Practice 3 B5
Hospital C 4 B3
Lao Consulate 5 C1
Main Post Office 6 D3
Sacombank 7 D4
Sinh Café 8 D4
Skynet 9 D4
Vietcombank 10 C3
Vietin Bank 11 C5
SIGHTS & ACTIVITIES
Cao Dai Temple 12 B3
Danang Cathedral 13 D4
Museum of Cham Sculpture 14 D5
Phap Lam Pagoda 15 B5
SLEEPING
Bamboo Green Harbourside 16 D4
Bao Ngoc Hotel 17 C4
Binh Duong 18 D2
Dai A Hotel 19 C4
Elegant Hotel 20 D1
Hai Van Hotel 21 B2
Hoa Viet Hotel 22 D3
Hoang Gia Hotel 23 B5
Minh Travel Hotel 24 D3
Phu An Hotel 25 B5
Phuong Tam (see 16)
Prince Hotel 26 D3
EATING
Apsara 27 D5
Bread of Life 28 D5
Café Truc Lam Vien 29 C5
Com Nieu 30 D3
Com Tay Cam Cung Dinh 31 B5
Le Bambino 32 B2
Vietnamese Home 33 D2
DRINKING
Bamboo 2 Bar 34 D4
Camel Club 35 C1
Christie's Cool Spot 36 D4
Nep Café 37 D4
TRANSPORT
Jetstar Pacific 38 C5
Vietnam Airlines 39 D3

As American involvement in Vietnam escalated, Danang became the recipient of the first American combat troops in South Vietnam – 3500 Marines in March 1965. Memorably they stormed Nam O Beach in full battle gear, only to be greeted by a bevy of *ao dai*–wearing Vietnamese girls bearing cheerful flower garlands. A decade later, the scene could not have been more different: utter chaos ensued as news broke of Hue and Quang Ngai falling to the North. Desperate civilians tried to flee the city, as some soldiers of the South Vietnamese army engaged in looting, pillage and rape. On 29 March 1975, two truckloads of communist guerrillas, more than half of them women, drove into what had been the most heavily defended city in South Vietnam and, without firing a shot, declared Danang liberated.

Orientation

Danang is on the western bank of the Han River. The city is part of a long, thin peninsula, at the northern tip of which is Nui Son Tra (called Monkey Mountain by US soldiers). China Beach and the Marble Mountains lie south of the city, and the Hai Van Pass overlooks Danang from the northwest.

MAPS

The Danang Tourist Map is a pocket-sized fold-out that is available for 20,000d in bookshops and hotels.

Information

INTERNET ACCESS

There are internet cafes scattered all over Danang. For 24-hour access, try **Skynet** (Map p236; ☎ 356 2604; 172 Đ Tran Phu; per hr 7000d).

MEDICAL SERVICES

Danang Family Medical Practice (Map p236; ☎ 358 2700; www.vietnammedicalpractice.com; 50-52 Đ Nguyen Van Linh) Set up like a minihospital with in-patient facilities, this excellent practice has sister clinics in Hanoi and HCMC. This branch is run by an Australian doctor and the friendly staff speak excellent English.

Hospital C (Map p236; Benh Vien C; ☎ 382 1483; 122 Đ Hai Phong) The most advanced of the four hospitals in town.

MONEY

Agribank (Map p236; ☎ 382 2323; 202 Đ Nguyen Chi Thanh) ATM and exchange service.

Sacombank (Map p236; ☎ 358 2612; 130-132 Đ Bach Dang) ATM and exchange service.

Vietcombank (Map p236; ☎ 381 7441; 140 Đ Le Loi) The only bank that changes travellers cheques.

Vietin Bank (Map p236; ☎ 356 5949; 85 Đ Hoang Dieu) ATM and exchange service.

POST

Main post office (Map p236; ☎ 383 7407; 64 Đ Bach Dang) Near the Song Han Bridge.

TRAVEL AGENCIES

Dana Tours (Map p236; ☎ 382 5653; 76 Đ Hung Vuong; closed Sun) Offers car rentals, boat trips, visa extensions and day trips.

Sinh Café (Map p236; ☎ 384 3258; www.sinhcafevn.com; 154 Đ Bach Dang) Books open-tour buses and makes other travel arrangements.

Trong's Real Easy Riders (☎ 090-359 7971; trongn59@yahoo.com) A group of about 30 Easy Riders (see the boxed text, p325) who operate out of Danang. Trong can arrange day trips (from US$20) or longer tours to Hoi An and the central highlands. He's a friendly chap who speaks good English and doesn't drive like a maniac.

Sights & Activities

MUSEUM OF CHAM SCULPTURE

This one's for the history buffs: a **museum** (Bao Tang Dieu Khac Cham Da Nang; Map p236; 1 Đ Trung Nu Vuong; admission 30,000d; 7am-5pm) with the largest collection of Cham artefacts, housed in buildings that marry French-colonial architecture with Cham elements. Founded in 1915 by the École Française d'Extrême Orient, it has more than 300 pieces on display including altars, *lingas*, garudas, apsaras, Ganeshas and images of Shiva, Brahma and Vishnu – all dating from the 5th to 15th centuries.

The artefacts come from Dong Duong (Indrapura), Khuong My, My Son (p262), Tra Kieu (p265) and other sites, mostly in Quang Nam and Da Nang provinces. The museum's rooms are named after the localities in which the objects displayed were found, which makes for a somewhat disjointed viewing experience, and the English captions are too dense to help. Unless you happen to be an expert in Cham history, this is one place where it's worth hiring a well-informed guide. Alternatively, pick up one of the English-language guidebooks at the museum shop.

An airy rear annexe was added in 2002 and the upper level focuses on the Cham culture today, with a handful of contemporary artefacts and photos of the Kate Festival (the Cham New Year) being celebrated at the Po Klong Garai Towers (p304).

The museum is not very large and is a mandatory stop for tour groups passing through Danang, so it might be a good idea to come at lunchtime to avoid the crowds.

HO CHI MINH MUSEUM

Despite its huge grounds, this **museum** (Map p241; ☎ 361 5982; 3 Đ Nguyen Van Troi; admission free; ⏰ 7-11am & 1.30-4.30pm) is typically unenlightening for a site venerating Ho Chi Minh. At the front is a display of the usual US, Soviet and Chinese weaponry. Hidden behind the Party buildings are a replica of Ho Chi Minh's house in Hanoi and a museum about him.

The museum is 250m west of Đ Nui Thanh. The complex is not often visited by tourists, so you may be escorted by one of the staff.

DANANG WATERPARK

The enormous **water park** (Map p241; adult/child 30,000/20,000d; ⏰ 8.30am-6.30pm Mon-Sat, 7am-9pm Sun) is showing its age but still can be a whirligig of fun on a hot summer day. There are plenty of slides, pools and the like to keep everyone (not just the kids) happy. It's near the riverbank, 2km beyond the Ho Chi Minh Museum.

CAO DAI TEMPLE

After Tay Ninh (p393), this **temple** (Map p236; 63 Đ Hai Phong) is the largest such structure in Vietnam, serving about 50,000 followers in Quang Nam and Da Nang provinces, including 20,000 in Danang itself. As with all Cao Dai temples, prayers are held four times a day: 5.30am, 11.30am, 5.30pm and 11.30pm.

The left-hand gate to the complex is for women; the right-hand gate for men. The doors to the sanctuary are similarly segregated, although priests of either gender use the central door. Behind the main altar sits an enormous globe with the Cao Dai 'divine eye' symbol on it.

A sign reading *van giao nhat ly* (all religions have the same reason) hangs from the ceiling in front of the altar. Behind the gilded letters is a picture of the founders of five of the world's great religions. From left to right are Mohammed, Laotse (wearing Eastern Orthodox–style robes), Jesus, a Southeast Asian–looking Buddha and Confucius (looking as Chinese as could be).

DANANG CATHEDRAL

Known to locals as Con Ga Church (Rooster Church) because of the weathercock on top of the steeple, the candy-pink **Danang Cathedral** (Map p236; Đ Tran Phu) was built for the city's French residents in 1923. Today it serves a Catholic community of 4000 – it's standing room only if you arrive late.

Mass is usually held from Monday to Saturday at 5am and 5.30pm, and on Sunday at 5am, 6.15am, 7.30am, 3.30pm and 5pm.

PHAP LAM PAGODA

Recently rebuilt, this **pagoda** (Map p236; ☎ 382 3870; 574 Đ Ong Ich Khiem; ⏰ 5-11.30am & 1-9.30pm) has three giant Buddha statues in the courtyard, and an equally imposing large gold one in the temple. It's set back from the road noise and at night, a cluster of street-food stalls mushrooms outside the temple gates.

Sleeping

Hotels in Danang cater primarily to business travellers, so budget deals aren't as easy to find as in Hoi An and Hue. For information on accommodation just across the river at My Khe Beach, see p244.

BUDGET

Hai Van Hotel (Map p236; ☎ 382 3750; kshaivan.dng@vnn.vn; 2 Đ Nguyen Thi Minh Khai; s/d US$12/19; ❄) Stepping inside this old-fashioned, airy building is like stepping back into the 1970s. It's in need of a paint job, but rooms are spacious, bathrooms adequate and the location pleasantly away from downtown.

Minh Travel Hotel (Map p236; ☎ 381 2661; minhtraveldn@gmail.com; 105 Đ Tran Phu; r US$15; ❄ 💻) This mini-hotel has the cheapest rooms in the city centre, and they look it too. Expect spartan rooms and shabby paintwork. Fan-cooled rooms are available for US$10.

Binh Duong (Map p236; ☎ 382 1930; ngtbinhduong@yahoo.com; 32-34 Đ Tran Phu; r US$15-30; ❄ 💻) Spread over three adjoining buildings, this family-run hotel is on a fairly deserted street near the Song Han Bridge. Rooms are spacious, just don't mind the somewhat tacky decor.

Hoang Gia Hotel (Map p236; ☎ 369 0250; 47 Đ Nguyen Van Linh; r 220,000-280,000d; ❄ 💻) There's a country feel to the decor at this family-run hotel. Rooms at the front of the building are enormous, but suffer from street noise.

Phu An Hotel (Map p236; ☎ 382 5708; phuanhoteldng@gmail.com; 29 Đ Nguyen Van Linh; s 220,000d, d 250,000-270,000d; ❄ 💻) A few buildings down from Hoang Gia Hotel, this is a slightly better set-up with big rooms, modern bathrooms and helpful staff. Rooms at the front still get the traffic noise, though.

Bao Ngoc Hotel (Map p236; ☎ 381 7711; baongoc hotel@dng.vnn.vn; 48 Đ Phan Chu Trinh; r US$17-20;) It's got uniformed staff, carpeted floors and very comfortable rooms. Rooms at the back are particularly large.

MIDRANGE

Dai A Hotel (Map p236; ☎ 382 7532; www.daiahotel.com .vn; 51 Đ Yen Bai; s US$16, d US$20-35;) You can't miss the Catholic overtones in the lobby, with the papal-crown light fixture and Jesus painting looking down beatifically. Cheaper rooms are plain, almost monastic; pricier ones are plush and more contemporary in style.

our pick **Prince Hotel** (Map p236; ☎ 381 7929; tranthai2003@dng.vnn.vn; 60 Đ Tran Phu; s/d US$17/22;) A great location, very nice rooms and helpful staff make this boutique outfit the best value for money in downtown Danang. The only downside is that some rooms are a little tight.

Hoa Viet Hotel (Map p236; ☎ 384 0111; 8 Đ Phan Dinh Phung; r US$20;) This hotel near the river is clean and well maintained, which is probably why it looks newer than it is. Bathrooms have rather space age–looking shower stalls.

Phuong Tam (Map p236; ☎ 382 4288; 174 Đ Bach Dang, s US$20, d US$25-32;) At the time of research the hotel was undergoing refurbishment. Completed rooms had been spruced up with modern bathroom fittings and new furniture.

Bamboo Green Harbourside (Map p236; ☎ 382 2722; www.bamboogreenhotel.com; 177 Đ Tran Phu; r US$25-35, ste US$45;) This centrally located hotel has nice rooms with (what else?) faux bamboo furniture, though bathrooms and the public hallways are somewhat worn-looking. Many rooms have good views of the river.

Elegant Hotel (Map p236; ☎ 389 2893; elegant@ dng.vnn.vn; 22A Đ Bach Dang; s/d US$28/36, ste US$70;) With a stark white quasimodernist building, this boutique hotel on the riverfront more than lives up to its name. It has good rooms with views to match, and it welcomes backpackers.

Eating

Danang has a very lively street-food scene, and it's hard to find a street in town that doesn't have a resident *bun, com* or *mi quang* stall. There are also a number of *com chay* (vegetarian food) eateries. The restaurant scene is flourishing, with a number of good (primarily Vietnamese) restaurants popping up across town.

VIETNAMESE

Com Tay Cam Cung Dinh (Map p236; ☎ 389 7638; K254/2 Đ Hoang Dieu; dishes 15,000-75,000d; lunch & dinner) A pleasant little restaurant tucked away off an alley, serving local specialities *com nieu* (rice cooked in a claypot) and *hoanh thanh* – a wontonlike combination of minced pork and shrimp served fried or steamed.

Com Nieu (Map p236; ☎ 386 7026; 25 Đ Yen Bai; dishes 14,000-120,000d; lunch & dinner) Very popular with locals, this contemporary restaurant has hearty meals and affable staff. Besides its namesake dish, there's a full spread of Vietnamese fare. Try the savoury grilled beef wrapped in seaweed, or ask about the day's fresh seafood.

Vietnamese Home (Map p236; ☎ 388 9575; 34 Đ Bach Dang; dishes 20,000-90,000d; lunch & dinner) Located just off the northern tip of the riverfront promenade (the entrance is on Đ Ly Tu Trong), this restaurant is popular with locals and has an extensive seafood menu. The live seafood tanks are merrily decorated with blinking fairy lights.

Café Truc Lam Vien (Map p236; ☎ 358 2428; www.truc lamvien.com.vn; 37 Đ Le Dinh Duong; meals 35,000-80,000d; lunch & dinner) Dine alfresco in a pretty garden courtyard or in one of the sleek wooden pavilions. Service is efficient and the menu, including local favourites such as *mi quang*, is available in English. The restaurant is a short walk from the Museum of Cham Sculpture.

Au Lac (Map p241; ☎ 361 1074; 4-6 Đ 2/9; dishes 30,000-100,000d; lunch & dinner) Stylish and colourful, this restaurant specialises in Vietnamese seafood, with some Western and Japanese dishes.

Apsara (Map p236; ☎ 356 1409; 222 Đ Tran Phu; dishes 30,000-400,000d; lunch & dinner) Posh indeed, Apsara pulls out all the stops with Cham-influenced decor, a good wine list and live music (though the playlist sometimes veers towards American pop tunes rather than traditional music). The cuisine is primarily Vietnamese, with an emphasis on seafood. Yeah, it's overpriced, but it's just about the only fancy dining venue of its kind in Danang.

INTERNATIONAL

Bread of Life (Map p236; ☎ 356 5185; breadoflife@ pobox.com; 12 Đ Le Hong Phong; meals 40,000-100,000d; breakfast, lunch & dinner, closed Sun) If the heavenly smells from the bakery don't win you over, the

American menu of pancakes, pizza and other comfort foods (biscuits and gravy, anyone?) surely will. The restaurant is almost entirely run by deaf staff and proceeds go towards training activities for the deaf in Danang (see the boxed text, p260).

Phi Lu Chinese Restaurant (Map p241; ☎ 361 1888; 1-3 Đ 2/9; dishes 40,000-400,000d; ⏲ lunch & dinner) A ballroomlike space decked out in full Chinese style, this popular restaurant has very good food. Warning: splurging on multiple seafood dishes may bust your bank account.

Le Bambino (Map p236; ☎ 389 6386; www.lebambino.com; 122/11 Đ Quang Trung; meals 100,000-300,000d; ⏲ lunch & dinner) Hidden away in a small residential lane, this delightful French oasis is run by a couple (French husband, Vietnamese wife) who turned their home into a restaurant and boutique hotel. The menu (available in Japanese) features hearty French fare, pizza and pasta. Upstairs, three enormous and extremely well-appointed rooms go for US$30 per night.

Drinking

Bamboo 2 Bar (Map p236; ☎ 090-554 4769; 230 Đ Bach Dang) This is the kind of comfortable hole-in-the-wall joint where the walls are covered in customers' drunken scribbles. There's a busy pool table in the back and a Western food menu.

Christie's Cool Spot (Map p236; ☎ 382 4040; ccdng@dng.vnn.vn; 112 Đ Tran Phu) The bar downstairs is where US war veterans hold forth about ongoing American politics vis-à-vis the American War in Vietnam. These days they're joined by Western expats in search of an ice-cold beer or the comfort food available in the restaurant upstairs.

Nep Café (Map p236; ☎ 091-344 1234; 115 Đ Tran Phu) An old trombone, a Che poster and a bicycle poking out of an exposed brick wall are just some of the oddments decorating this indie hang-out right across from Christie's. Live bands play upstairs three times a week.

Camel Club (Map p236; ☎ 388 7462; 16 Đ Ly Thuong Kiet; admission 20,000d) This is pretty much Danang's party central, if you like loud music, expensive drinks and dancing that's quite colourful by Vietnamese standards.

Getting There & Away

AIR

During the American War, Danang had one of the busiest airports in the world. Now it settles for being the third busiest in Vietnam.

Jetstar Pacific (Map p236; ☎ 358 3538; 307 Đ Phan Chu Trinh) has daily flights from Danang to HCMC and Hanoi. **Vietnam Airlines** (Map p236; ☎ 382 1130; 35 Đ Tran Phu) connects Danang with Hanoi, HCMC, Dien Bien Phu, Pleiku, Buon Ma Thuot, Nha Trang, Phu Quoc and Quy Nhon.

BUS

The large **intercity bus station** (Map p241; ☎ 382 1265; 33 Đ Dien Bien Phu) is 3km west of the city centre. A metered taxi to the riverside will cost 50,000d.

Buses leave for all major centres, including Dong Hoi (55,000d to 100,000d, five hours, four daily), Hue (25,000d, three hours, every 30 minutes), Quy Nhon (50,000d to 100,000d, six hours, four daily) and Kon Tum (130,000d, five hours, four daily).

There are three weekly services to Savannakhet (118,000d, 14 hours), crossing the border at Lao Bao. Buses to the Lao Bao border alone are 90,000d (six hours); you may have to change buses at Dong Ha.

Regular buses to Hoi An (10,000d, one hour) are a bright sunflower yellow but have no air-conditioning. They depart from a **local bus station** directly opposite the ticket office in the intercity bus station. Foreigners tend to be overcharged, so check the price before boarding and stand your ground.

With a booking, Sinh Café (p237) open-tour buses will pick-up from its office twice daily en route to Hue (60,000d to 70,000d, 2½ hours) or Hoi An (50,000d to 60,000d, one hour).

CAR & MOTORBIKE

A car to Hoi An (30km) costs around US$15 from your hotel or a local travel agency (see p237). A cheaper option is a *xe om* for around 100,000d. For a slightly higher fee you can ask the driver to stop and wait while you visit the Marble Mountains and China Beach.

You can also reach My Son by motorbike (US$20) or car (US$65), with the option of being dropped off in Hoi An on the way back.

Distances to major destinations from Danang include Hanoi (764km), Hue (108km) and HCMC (972km).

TRAIN

Danang's **train station** (Map p236; ☎ 382 3810; 202 Đ Hai Phong) is served by Reunification Express trains, with stops including Hue (50,000d, 2½ to 4½ hours, nine daily), Lang Co (15,000d, 1½ to 2½ hours, three daily), Quang Ngai (64,000d, 2½ to four hours, nine daily), Tuy Hoa (190,000d, 7½ to 10 hours, seven daily) and Nha Trang (252,000d, 8½ to 12½ hours, nine daily).

The train ride to Hue is one of the best in the country – it's worth taking as an excursion in itself.

Getting Around

TO/FROM THE AIRPORT

Danang's airport is 2km west of the city centre, close enough to reach by *xe om* in 10 minutes (40,000d). A metered taxi costs about 50,000d.

CYCLO & XE OM

Danang has plenty of motorbike taxis and *cyclo* drivers; as usual, be prepared to bargain. Trips around town shouldn't cost more than 10,000d to 15,000d. Be careful of *xe om* drivers at night offering to take you to bars/girls – you may find yourself heavied into parting with hundreds of dollars.

TAXI

If you need a metered taxi, try **Taxi Xanh** (☎ 368 6868) or **Mai Linh** (☎ 356 5656).

AROUND DANANG

☎ 0511

Nam O Beach

Nam O Beach (Map p241), 15km northwest of the city, was where the first US combat troops landed in South Vietnam in 1965. Today it's reverted to more humble form. The beach is

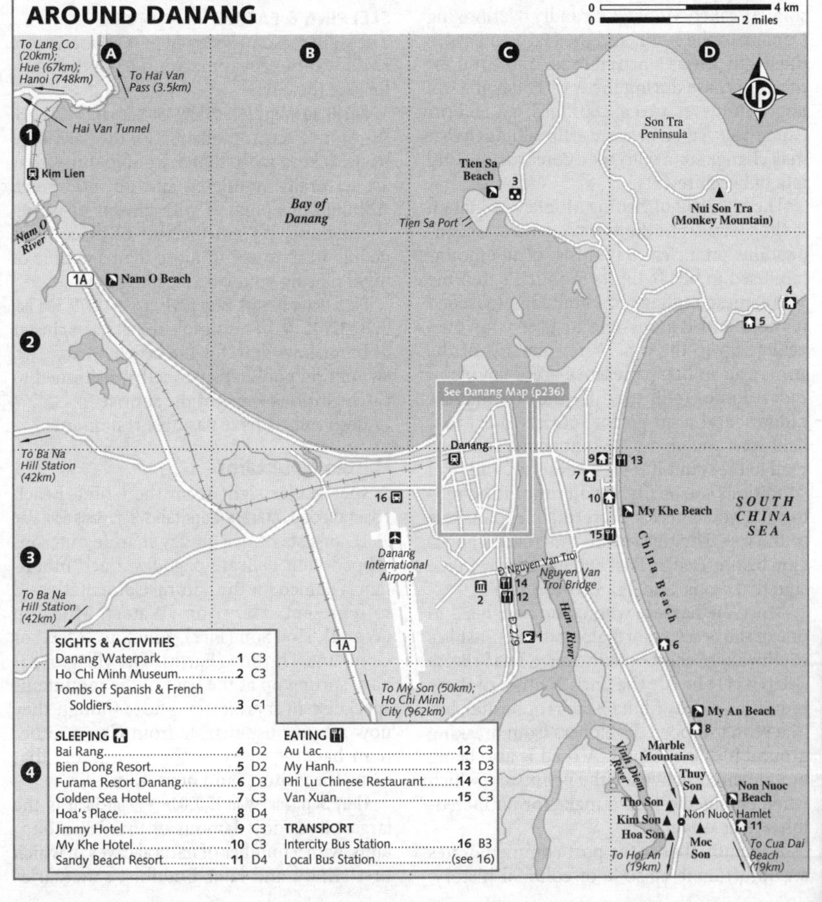

not as attractive as its counterparts to the east and is hardly developed.

Nam O village used to support itself by producing firecrackers until the government imposed a ban on them in 1995. Now the villagers make *nuoc mam* (fish sauce) and *goi ca*. The latter is a kind of Vietnamese sushi: fresh, raw fish fillets marinated in a special sauce and coated in a spicy powder. It's served with fresh vegetables on rice-paper rolls. You'll find it for sale on the beach in the summer or look for it in the village.

Nui Son Tra (Monkey Mountain)

elev 850m

Jutting out into the sea like a giant pair of Mickey Mouse ears, the Son Tra peninsula is crowned by the mountain that the American soldiers called Monkey. Grandly overlooking Danang to the south and the Hai Van Pass to the north, it was a prized radar and communications base during the war. Today it's still largely undeveloped except for Tien Sa Port (Cang Tien Sa) on its eastern tip, although that may change soon with road construction and talk of beach resorts.

The highlight of visiting Monkey Mountain is the views from the **summit**, which are stupendous on a clear day. Most of the mountain used to be off-limits to tourists, but the Vietnamese military has gradually loosened its hold and it's possible to take your own vehicle up to the top. What remains of the American military presence are a couple of radar domes (still used by the Vietnamese military and a no-go for tourists) next to a helicopter pad, now a lookout point. The steep road to the summit is pretty deserted and road conditions can be iffy. If you're going on motorbike, you'll need a powerful one to make it to the top. The turn-off to this road is about 3km before Tien Sa Port and marked by a blue sign that reads 'Son Tra Eco-tourism'.

Most Vietnamese who come here head to one of the beach resorts along the peninsula's southwestern coast or to sheltered **Tien Sa Beach** (Map p241) beside the port. Neither of these is quite as nice as China Beach (opposite), but that hasn't stopped developers from breaking ground for new resorts. A road is also being built to circumnavigate the peninsula, which when completed would make for an incredibly scenic drive.

A memorial near the port commemorates an unfortunate episode of colonial history. Spanish-led Filipino and French troops attacked Danang in August 1858, ostensibly to end Emperor Tu Duc's mistreatment of Catholics. The city quickly fell, but the invaders were hit by cholera, dysentery, scurvy, typhus and mysterious fevers. By the summer of 1859, the number of invaders who had died of illness was 20 times the number who had been killed in combat.

Many of the **tombs of Spanish and French soldiers** (Map p241; admission free) are below a chapel near Tien Sa Port. To get here, cross Song Han Bridge and turn left onto Đ Ngo Quyen, continuing north to the port. The overgrown ossuary, a small white building, stands on the right on a low hill, about 500m before the port's gate.

SLEEPING & EATING

The only reason to stay here is if you really, *really* want to cut yourself off from the comforts of the city.

Bai Rang (Map p241; ☎ 397 1904; Son Tra; r 200,000d; ❄) Simple accommodation for the hard-core backpacker, with thatch-roofed huts that are naturally ventilated and no mod-cons. Although it's popular with groups of young Vietnamese, it's not the sort of place most people want to spend more than a couple of nights. Bring your own sleeping mat.

Bien Dong Resort (Map p241; ☎ 399 0179; Son Tra; US$32-35; ❄ 🏊) This simple resort has a cluster of bungalows and, for the beach-weary, two swimming pools. It's perfectly positioned to catch glorious views of the sunrise.

Both resorts have passable restaurants.

Marble Mountains

A spectacular sight from the China Beach coastal road, **Marble Mountains** (Ngu Hanh Son; Map p241) consists of five craggy marble outcrops topped with delicate pagodas. Each mountain is named for the natural element it's said to represent: Thuy Son (Water), Moc Son (Wood), Hoa Son (Fire), Kim Son (Metal or Gold) and Tho Son (Earth). The villages that have sprung up at the base of the mountains specialise in marble sculpture, though they now astutely use marble from China rather than hacking away at the mountains that bring the visitors (and buyers) in.

Thuy Son (admission 15,000d; ⏰ 7am-5pm) is the largest and most famous of the five mountains, with a number of natural caves in which first Hindu and later Buddhist sanctuaries have been built over the centuries. Of the two paths heading up the mountain, the one closer to the beach (at the end of the village) makes for a better circuit.

At the top of the staircase is a gate, **Ong Chon**, which is pockmarked with bullet holes. This leads to **Linh Ong Pagoda**. Behind it, a path heads left through two short tunnels to several caverns known as Tang Chon Dong, containing several Buddhas and blocks of carved stone of Cham origin. Near one of the altars is a flight of steps leading up to another cave, partially open to the sky, with two seated Buddhas in it.

Immediately to the left as you enter Ong Chon Gate is the main path to the rest of Thuy Son, beginning with **Xa Loi Pagoda**, a beautiful stone tower that overlooks the coast. Stairs off the main pathway lead to **Vong Hai Da**, a viewing point that would yield a brilliant panorama of China Beach if it weren't so untended. The stone-paved path continues to the right and into a canyon. On the left is **Van Thong Cave**, opposite which is a cement Buddha and a narrow passage that leads up to a natural chimney open to the sky.

Exit the canyon through a battle-scarred masonry gate. There's a rocky path to the right leading to **Linh Nham**, a tall chimney-shaped cave with a small altar inside. Nearby, another path leads to **Hoa Nghiem**, a shallow cave with a Buddha. If you go down the passageway to the left of the Buddha, you come to cathedral-like **Huyen Khong Cave**, lit by an opening to the sky. The entrance to this spectacular chamber is guarded by two administrative mandarins (to the left of the doorway) and two military mandarins (to the right).

Scattered about the cave are Buddhist and Confucian shrines; note the inscriptions carved into the stone walls. On the right a door leads to two stalactites, dripping water that comes from heaven, according to local legend. Actually, only one stalactite drips; the other one supposedly ran dry when Emperor Tu Duc touched it. During the American War this chamber was used as a VC field hospital. Inside is a plaque dedicated to the Women's Artillery Group, which destroyed 19 US aircraft from a base below the mountains in 1972.

Back on the main path, just to the left of the masonry gate is **Tam Thai Tu Pagoda**, restored by Emperor Minh Mang in 1826. A path heading obliquely to the right goes to the monks' residence, but before you reach it, take the stairs to the left of the path to **Vong Giang Dai**, which offers a fantastic 180-degree landward view of the other Marble Mountains and their surroundings.

A torch (flashlight) is handy but not essential for exploring the caves. The gradient of the walk is quite comfortable, but whichever end you start at, the ascent up the mountain begins with a fairly strenuous climb.

Local buses between Danang and Hoi An (tickets 10,000d) can drop you at Marble Mountains, 19km north of Hoi An.

China Beach

Thanks to the eponymous TV series, China Beach will forever be associated with pretty young military nurses complaining about their love lives to the accompaniment of the Rolling Stones' *Paint It Black*. During the war the Americans used the name to refer to the beautiful 30km swoop of fine white sand that starts at Monkey Mountain and ends near Hoi An, with the Marble Mountains near its centre. The part they were most familiar with was the area close to Danang where soldiers stationed all over the country would be sent for some R&R. For some, a picnic on the beach was their last meal before returning to combat.

The Vietnamese call sections of the beach by different names, including My Khe, My An, Non Nuoc and Cua Dai. The northernmost stretch, My Khe, is now basically a suburb of Danang, while to the south Cua Dai is widely considered Hoi An's beach. The area in between has been carved up among the likes of the Raffles, Hyatt and other five-star brands, with swanky beach resorts under construction and leaving only a pitiful stretch of beach open to the public. Of course, how they'll fill all those ritzy rooms is another matter.

The best time for swimming at China Beach is from May to July, when the sea is at its calmest. At other times the water can get rough. Be warned that lifeguards patrol only parts of the beach.

In December 1992 China Beach was the site of the first international surfing competition in Vietnam. The surf can be very good from around mid-September to December, particularly in the morning when wind conditions are right. The dangerous winter weather goes hand-in-hand with large breakers, which are ideal for surfing – if you know what you're doing. Boards can be rented at Hoa's Place (right).

MY KHE BEACH

Just across the Song Han Bridge (10,000d by *xe om*), My Khe is fast becoming Danang's easternmost suburb. In the early morning and evening the beach fills up with city folk doing t'ai chi. Tourists emerge during peak suntanning hours, while locals start showing up in the evening. After dark the deckchairs are taken over by young couples seeking a little privacy. Despite its popularity, the beach is still blessedly free of roaming vendors and the only thing you might be coaxed to purchase is time on a lounger (15,000d).

The water has a dangerous undertow, especially in winter. However, it's protected by the bulk of Nui Son Tra and is safer than the rest of China Beach.

This was the part of China Beach well known to American servicemen, and unfortunately a sleazy undertone lingers in parts.

Sleeping

There's no beachfront accommodation here and the older establishments all look rather shabby. Try one of the side streets slightly further in for new outfits that offer better value.

My Khe Hotel (Map p241; ☎ 383 6125; mkbeach@vnn.vn; 241 Đ Nguyen Van Thoai; s US$18-35, d US$22-40, ste US$80;) The architecture and decor are old hat, but the rooms in this low-rise hotel are spacious and many have a decent beach view.

Jimmy Hotel (Map p241; ☎ 394 5888; jimmyhotel danang.com.vn; Lot F 18, An Cu No. 3; s US$20-30, d US$25-40;) Clean white decor and shiny new rooms make this friendly mini-hotel one of the nicest places in the area. While it's a little further from the beach, rooms on the upper floors have incredible views.

Golden Sea Hotel (Map p241; ☎ 393 6666; www.goldenseahotelvn.com; B26-29 Đ Pham Van Dong; s US$28-35, d US$30-40, ste US$60;) Located halfway between the river and the beach, this smart hotel has well-appointed rooms. Pricier ones come with views of the sea or Monkey Mountain.

Eating & Drinking

My Khe Beach is where the locals go to sup on seafood while the sea breeze whips through their hair. There's a row of beachside restaurants along Đ Du Lich Son Tra, some with more pimped-out neon signs or snazzier decor than others.

For a typical Vietnamese experience, try the restaurant at the southern end, **My Hanh** (Map p241; ☎ 383 1494; 18 Đ Du Lich Son Tra; meals 150,000-200,000d; lunch & dinner). It's not shy about having the seafood swim around in open tanks right by the entrance, so you can walk right up and pick what you'd like.

A little further down the road, **Van Xuan** (Map p241; ☎ 394 1235; 233A Đ Nguyen Van Thoai; dishes 18,000-100,000d; lunch & dinner) has opted for a pleasant garden setting. Besides the usual array of seafood (and crocodile), it also serves its own Czech-style microbrew, Five Mountains Beer.

MY AN & NON NUOC BEACHES

Much of the central section of China Beach has been blocked off for new resort developments, but there are a few existing hotels that are good for avoiding the weekend rush at My Khe Beach.

Sleeping & Eating

Hoa's Place (Map p241; ☎ 396 9216; 215/14 Đ Huyen Tran Cong Chua, My An Beach; hoasplace@hotmail.com; r U$9) This budget joint has become a beach icon in its own right. The rooms are backpacker-basic, just a stone's throw from the beach, but the food and convivial atmosphere, presided over by the irrepressible Hoa himself, keep people coming back. This is where things get so laid-back and comfortable, a one-night stay can easily turn into a week long (or longer) sojourn.

Sandy Beach Resort (Map p241; ☎ 383 6216; www.sandybeachdanang.com; 255 Đ Huyen Tran Cong Chua, Non Nuoc Beach; r US$140-180, bungalows US$190-210, villas US$230-250;) The only resort at the southern end of Non Nuoc Beach, this smart four-star operation is replete with swimming pools, dining and drinking options. There's a complimentary shuttle bus to Danang and Hoi An.

Furama Resort Danang (Map p241; ☎ 384 7333; www.furamavietnam.com; 68 Đ Ho Xuan Huong, My An Beach; s US$200-280, d US$220-300, ste US$600-700;) This luxury establishment has been pampering Vietnam's beach-bound for years; cynics might consider it a harbinger of things to come. The five-star set-up includes a diving facility, a golf driving range and two swimming pools (one with a waterfall). Day use of the facilities is US$10 for nonguests.

HOI AN

☎0510 / pop 122,000

Once a sleepy village whose trading fortunes had declined, Hoi An was resurrected with great aplomb as a tourist town in the mid-1990s and received Unesco World Heritage status in 1999. Its pride and joy is the distinctive architecture of the Old Town, remarkably intact despite its age. Wandering through the narrow, blessedly car-free streets, you can almost imagine you've been transported back several centuries – until a souvenir seller hails you, anyway.

More so than with other towns, the tourist economy is both a boon and a bane to little Hoi An. Without it, the alluring houses of the Old Town would have crumbled into the river years ago. With it, the face of the Old Town has been preserved but its people and purpose have changed beyond recognition. Residents and rice fields have been gradually replaced by tourist businesses, and the An Hoi Peninsula across the river has been co-opted for the newest nightlife hot spots.

The upside to Hoi An's development is that it has the best boutique hotels and restaurants in central Vietnam. The downside is that it's so often choked with visitors that it feels more like a movie set than an authentic town. But don't despair. A short bicycle or boat ride away are graceful country landscapes and quiet little villages where foreigners are still a novelty.

To see Hoi An at its prettiest, come during the full moon for 'Hoi An Legendary Night'. Motorbikes are banned from the Old Town, which is transformed into a magical land of silk lanterns, traditional food, song and dance, and street games. It's a little naff, yet very captivating.

Hoi An's riverside location makes it particularly vulnerable to flooding during the rainy season (October and November). It's common for the waterfront to be hit by sporadic floods of about 1m and a typhoon can bring floodwaters of 2m or more. In late 2006 and 2007 the town experienced some of the worst flooding in recent history.

History

The earliest evidence of human habitation here dates back 2200 years: excavated ceramic fragments are thought to belong to the late–Iron Age Sa Huynh civilisation, which is related to the Dong Son culture of northern Vietnam. From the 2nd to the 10th centuries, this was a busy seaport of the Champa kingdom (see the boxed text, p264), and archaeologists have found the foundations of numerous Cham towers around Hoi An.

In 1307 the Cham king presented Quang Nam province as a gift when he married a Vietnamese princess. When his successor refused to recognise the deal, fighting broke out and for the next century chaos reigned. By the 15th century peace was restored, allowing commerce to resume. During the next four centuries Hoi An – also known as Faifoo to Western traders – held sway as one of Southeast Asia's major international ports. Chinese, Japanese, Dutch, Portuguese, Spanish, Indian, Filipino, Indonesian, Thai, French, British and American ships came to call, and the town's warehouses teemed with the treasures of the Orient: high-grade silk (for which the area is famous), fabrics, paper, porcelain, tea, sugar, molasses, areca nuts, pepper, Chinese medicines, elephant tusks, beeswax, mother-of-pearl, lacquer, sulphur and lead.

Chinese and Japanese traders in particular left their mark on Hoi An. Both groups came in the spring, driven south by monsoon winds. They would stay in Hoi An until the summer, when southerly winds would blow them home. During their four-month sojourn in Hoi An, they rented waterfront houses for use as warehouses and living quarters. Some began leaving full-time agents in Hoi An to take care of their off-season business affairs.

The Japanese ceased coming to Hoi An after 1637 when the Japanese government forbade contact with the outside world, but the Chinese lingered, making Hoi An the site of the first Chinese settlement in southern Vietnam. The town's Chinese *hoi quan* (congregational assembly halls) still play a special role among southern Vietnam's ethnic Chinese, some of whom come from all over the region to participate in congregation-wide celebrations.

This was also the first place in Vietnam to be exposed to Christianity. Among the 17th-century missionary visitors was Alexandre de Rhodes, who devised the Latin-based *quoc ngu* script for the Vietnamese language.

Although Hoi An was almost completely destroyed during the Tay Son Rebellion, it was rebuilt and continued to be an important port until the late 19th century, when the Thu Bon River (Cai River), which links Hoi An with the sea, silted up and became too shallow for navigation. Danang (Tourane) took over as the region's main port.

CENTRAL VIETNAM

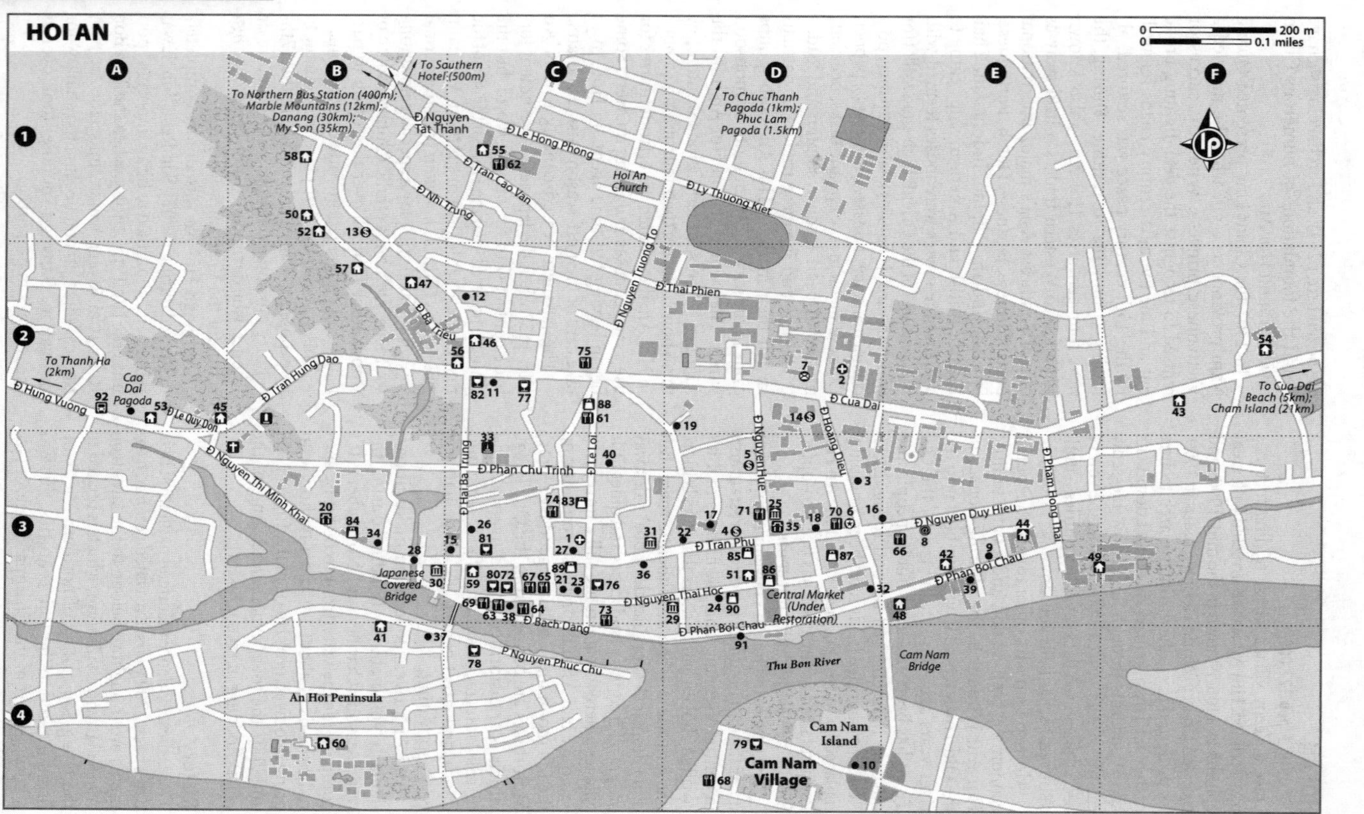

INFORMATION
- Dr Ho Huu Phuoc Practice ... 1 C3
- Hoi An Hospital ... 2 D2
- Hoi An Old Town Booth ... 3 D3
- Hoi An Old Town Booth ... 5 D3
- Hoi An Old Town Booth ... 4 D3
- Hoi An Police Station ... 6 D3
- Main Post Office ... 7 D2
- Min's Computer ... 8 E3
- Nga ... 9 E3
- Randy's Book Xchange ... 10 D4
- Sacombank ... 11 C2
- Sinh Café ... 12 C2
- Vietcombank ... 13 B1
- Vietin Bank ... 14 D2

SIGHTS & ACTIVITIES
- Assembly Hall of the Cantonese Chinese Congregation ... 15 C3
- Assembly Hall of the Chaozhou Chinese Congregation ... 16 D3
- Assembly Hall of the Fujian Chinese Congregation ... 17 D3
- Assembly Hall of the Hainan Chinese Congregation ... 18 D3
- Ba Le Well ... 19 D2
- Cam Pho Temple ... 20 B3
- Cham Island Diving Center ... 21 C3
- Chinese All-Community Assembly Hall ... 22 D3
- Diep Dong Nguyen House ... 23 C3
- Handicraft Workshop ... 24 D3
- Hoi An Museum of History & Culture ... 25 D3
- Hoi An Old Town Booth ... 26 C3
- Hoi An Old Town Booth ... 27 C3
- Japanese Covered Bridge ... 28 B3
- Morning Glory Cooking School ... (see 72)
- Museum of Folklore in Hoi An ... 29 D3
- Museum of Sa Huynh Culture & Museum of the Revolution ... 30 B3
- Museum of Trading Ceramics ... 31 C3
- New Market ... 32 D3
- Phac Hat Pagoda ... 33 C3
- Phung Hung Old House ... 34 B3
- Quan Cong Temple ... 35 D3
- Quan Thang House ... 36 C3
- Rainbow Divers ... 37 B4
- Tan Ky House ... 38 C3
- Tran Duong House ... 39 E3
- Tran Family Chapel ... 40 C3

SLEEPING
- An Hoi Hotel ... 41 B4
- An Huy Hotel ... 42 E3
- Green Field Hotel ... 43 F2
- Ha An Hotel ... 44 E3
- Hoang Trinh Hotel ... 45 A2
- Hoi Pho Hotel ... 46 C2
- Hop Yen Hotel ... 47 B2
- Huy Hoang 1 Hotel ... 48 E3
- Life Heritage Resort Hoi An ... 49 E3
- Long Life Hotel ... 50 B1
- Minh A Ancient Lodging House ... 51 D3
- Nhat Huy Hoang Hotel ... 52 B1
- Nhi Nhi Hotel ... 53 A2
- Phu Thinh II Hotel ... 54 F2
- Phuoc An Hotel ... 55 C1
- Thanh Van Hotel ... 56 C2
- Thien Nga Hotel ... 57 B2
- Thien Thanh Hotel ... 58 B1
- Vinh Hung 1 Hotel ... 59 C3
- Vinh Hung Resort ... 60 B4

EATING
- Bobo Café ... 61 C2
- Café 43 ... 62 C1
- Cargo Club ... 63 C3
- Casa Verde ... 64 C3
- Good Morning Vietnam ... 65 C3
- Green Moss ... 66 E3
- Hai Scout Café ... 67 C3
- Lighthouse Café & Restaurant ... 68 D4
- Mango Rooms ... 69 C3
- Mermaid Restaurant ... 70 D3
- Miss Ly Cafeteria 22 ... 71 D3
- Morning Glory Street Food Restaurant ... 72 C3
- Phone Café ... 73 C3
- Quan Chay Co Dam ... 74 C3
- Shree Ganesh Indian Restaurant ... 75 C2

DRINKING
- Before & Now ... 76 C3
- Re-Treat Café ... 77 C2
- River Lounge ... 78 C4
- Sleepy Gecko ... 79 D4
- Tam Tam Cafe ... 80 C3
- Treat's Café ... 81 C3
- Treat's Same Same But Not Different Café ... 82 C2

SHOPPING
- A Dong Silk ... 83 C3
- Art Galleries ... 84 B3
- B'lan ... 85 D3
- Hoi An Cloth Market ... 86 D3
- Lotus Jewellery ... (see 67)
- Phuoc An ... 87 C2
- Reaching Out ... (see 63)
- Tuoi Ngoc ... 88 C3
- Yaly ... 89 D3

TRANSPORT
- Boat Landing ... 90 D4
- Main Bus Station ... 91 A2

Under French rule Hoi An served as an administrative centre. It was almost completely undamaged after the American War, thanks to the cooperation of both sides.

Orientation

The Thu Bon River forms the southern edge of the Old Town, with bridges across to the An Hoi Peninsula and Cam Nam Island. The newer part of town stretches to the north.

Information

BOOKSHOPS

For a genuine bookshop, head to Cam Nam Island and take the first right to **Randy's Book Xchange** (☎ 093-608 9483; randysbookxchange.com; To 5 Khoi Xuyen Trung). Set up like a personal library, it has more than 5000 used books for sale or exchange.

EMERGENCY

Hoi An Police Station (☎ 386 1204; 84 Đ Hoang Dieu)

INTERNET ACCESS

Min's Computer (☎ 391 4323; 125 Đ Nguyen Duy Hieu; per hr 6000d)

MEDICAL SERVICES

Dr Ho Huu Phuoc Practice (☎ 386 1419; 74 Đ Le Loi; 11am-12.30pm & 5-9.30pm) A local doctor who speaks English.

Hoi An Hospital (☎ 386 1364; 4 Đ Tran Hung Dao) If it's anything serious, make for Danang.

MONEY

Sacombank (☎ 391 1031; 91 Đ Tran Hung Dao), **Vietcombank** (☎ 391 6374; 642 Đ Hai Ba Trung) and **Vietin Bank** (☎ 386 1340; 4 Đ Hoang Dieu) all change cash and travellers cheques, and have ATMs.

POST

Main post office (☎ 386 1480; 6 Đ Tran Hung Dao)

TOURIST INFORMATION

There are four **Hoi An Old Town Booths** (☎ 386 2715; 7am-5pm) that sell Old Town tickets: 30 Đ Tran Phu, 10 Đ Nguyen Hue, 5 Đ Hoang Dieu and 78 Đ Le Loi.

TRAVEL AGENCIES

Competition is pretty fierce, so it's worth checking out a few options and negotiating.

Nga (☎ 386 3485; lenga22us@yahoo.com; 22 Đ Phan Boi Chau) Handles plane, train and open-tour bus bookings, tours to My Son and Cham Island, boat trips and car rentals.

Sinh Café (☎ 386 3948; www.sinhcafevn.com; 587 Đ Hai Ba Trung) Books reputable open-tour buses.

Dangers & Annoyances

Hoi An is one of the safer towns in Vietnam, but there are occasional stories of late-night bag-snatching or assaults on women. If you are a lone female, try to make sure you walk home with somebody.

A worrying trend here, as in other parts of Vietnam, is the use of children to sell trinkets, postcards and newspapers. Don't be fooled into thinking that the kids get to keep the money. One can only hope that if tourists stop buying from the children, their controllers won't exploit them this way.

Sights

By Unesco fiat more than 800 historical buildings in Hoi An have been preserved, so much of the **Old Town** (www.hoianworldheritage.org; tickets 75,000d) looks as it did several centuries ago, barring the ugly power lines and impatient motorbikes. There are restrictions on building alterations, building height and vehicle movement (no cars).

Only 15 buildings are open to visitors and most require an Old Town ticket for admission; the fee goes towards funding conservation work. Buying a ticket at any of the Old Town Booths is easy enough; planning your visit around the byzantine admission options is another matter. Each ticket allows you to visit five different types of heritage attractions, including a traditional music show at the Handicraft Workshop and one each of the following: museums, assembly halls, old houses and an 'other' category (either the Japanese Bridge or Quan Cong Temple). To enter more places, you'll have to buy another ticket. To see everything on offer will take four tickets in all (and at least two days).

For most visitors, one ticket is usually enough. What are the most interesting stops? Among the museums, the Museum of Trading Ceramics is in a well-restored building, with a small exhibition of the architectural qualities of Hoi An's old houses that's handy for swotting up. The most intriguing assembly hall is the Fujian one. Of the old houses, Tan Ky House and the Tran Family Chapel have the most informative tours; to see a traditional trading house, pick the Tan Ky House. For the 'other' category, choose Quan Cong temple; the Japanese Bridge ticket just gets you into a small shrine that is second-best to the bridge itself, which you can enjoy for free.

Most buildings are scrupulous about collecting ticket stubs, and one hopes that the fees go into restoration and preservation. At lunchtime many houses and halls are closed, though the museums stay open.

Not all of Hoi An's old buildings require a ticket, and there's certainly nothing to stop anybody from admiring the houses from the street. Tran Duong House charges an independent admission fee, which is an alternative for those baulking at the Old Town 'package'.

Despite the number of tourists who flood into Hoi An, it is still a conservative town. Visitors should dress modestly, especially since some of the old houses are still private homes.

JAPANESE COVERED BRIDGE

This **bridge** (Cau Nhat Ban; admission free) has become a modern-day icon of Hoi An, although most visitors are surprised by how small it is. The first bridge on this site was constructed in the 1590s by the Japanese community of Hoi An, in order to link them with the Chinese quarters across the stream.

The bridge is very solidly constructed because the original builders were concerned about the threat of earthquakes. Over the centuries the ornamentation has remained relatively faithful to the original understated Japanese design. The French flattened out the roadway for their motor vehicles, but the original arched shape was restored in 1986.

The entrances to the bridge are guarded by weathered statues: a pair of monkeys on one side, a pair of dogs on the other. According to one story, many of Japan's emperors were born in the years of the dog and monkey. Another tale says that construction of the bridge started in the year of the monkey and was finished in the year of the dog. The stelae, listing all Vietnamese and Chinese contributors to a subsequent restoration of the bridge, are written in *chu nho* (Chinese characters) – the *nom* script had not yet become popular.

Built into the northern side of the bridge is a small **temple** (Chua Cau; admission by Hoi An Old Town ticket). According to legend, there once lived an enormous monster called Cu which had its head in India, its tail in Japan and its body in Vietnam. Whenever the monster moved, terrible disasters befell Vietnam. This bridge was built on the monster's weakest point and killed it, but the people of Hoi An took pity and built this temple to pray for its soul. The writing over the temple door is the name given to the bridge in 1719: Lai Vien Kieu (Bridge for Passers-by from Afar). However it never quite caught on.

ASSEMBLY HALLS

The Chinese who settled in Hoi An, like their counterparts in other parts of Asia, identified themselves according to their province of origin. Each community built its own assembly hall, known as *hoi quan* in Vietnamese, for social gatherings, meetings and celebrations.

Assembly Hall of the Fujian Chinese Congregation

What began as a traditional **assembly hall** (Phuc Kien Hoi Quan; opposite 35 Đ Tran Phu; admission by Hoi An Old Town ticket; 🕑 7am-5.30pm) was later transformed into a temple for the worship of Thien Hau, a deity from Fujian province. The grand triple gate to the complex was built in 1975.

The mural on the right-hand wall – if you can see it behind the prayer coils – depicts Thien Hau, her way lit by lantern light as she crosses a stormy sea to rescue a foundering ship. On the wall opposite is a mural of the heads of the six Fujian families who fled from China to Hoi An in the 17th century, following the overthrow of the Ming dynasty.

The penultimate chamber contains a statue of Thien Hau. To either side of the entrance stand red-skinned Thuan Phong Nhi and green-skinned Thien Ly Nhan, deities who alert Thien Hau when sailors are in distress. The replica of a Chinese boat along the right-hand wall is 1:20 scale.

The central altar in the last chamber contains seated figures of the heads of the six Fujian families. The smaller figures below them represent their successors as clan leaders. Behind the altar on the right are three fairies and smaller figures representing the 12 *ba mu* (midwives), each of whom teaches newborns a different skill necessary for the first year of life: smiling, sucking and so forth. Childless couples often come here to pray for offspring.

Assembly Hall of the Cantonese Chinese Congregation

Founded in 1786, this **assembly hall** (Quang Trieu Hoi Quan; 176 Đ Tran Phu; admission by Hoi An Old Town ticket; 🕑 8am-5pm) has a tall, airy entrance hall that opens onto a splendidly over-the-top mosaic statue of a dragon and a carp. The main altar is dedicated to Quan Cong (see p251). The very pleasant garden behind has an even more incredible dragon statue.

Assembly Hall of the Chaozhou Chinese Congregation

Built in 1752, the highlight in this **congregational hall** (Trieu Chau Hoi Quan; opposite 157 Đ Nguyen Duy Hieu; admission by Hoi An Old Town ticket; 🕑 8am-5pm) is the gleaming woodcarvings on the beams, walls and altar – absolutely stunning in their intricacy. You could stand here for hours to unravel the stories, but if you're just popping by quickly, look for the carvings on the doors in front of the altar of two Chinese women wearing their hair in an unexpectedly Japanese style.

Chinese All-Community Assembly Hall

Founded in 1773, this **assembly hall** (Chua Ba; 64 Tran Phu; admission free; 🕑 8am-5pm) was used by Fujian, Cantonese, Hainan, Chaozhou and Hakka congregations in Hoi An. To the right of the entrance are portraits of Chinese resistance heroes in Vietnam who died during WWII. The well-restored red temple is dedicated to Thien Hau and sits between pavilions adorned with French-style balustrades.

Assembly Hall of the Hainan Chinese Congregation

Built in 1851, this **assembly hall** (Hai Nam Hoi Quan; 10 Đ Tran Phu; admission free; 🕑 8am-5pm) is a memorial to 108 merchants from Hainan Island who were mistaken for pirates and killed in Quang Nam province in 1851. The elaborate dais

HOI AN HOUSES: A CLOSER LOOK

The historical buildings of Hoi An not only survived the 20th century's wars, they also retain features of traditional architecture rarely seen today. As they have been for centuries, some shopfronts are shuttered at night with horizontal planks inserted into grooves that cut into the columns that support the roof. Some roofs are made up of thousands of brick-coloured *am* and *duong* (yin and yang) roof tiles – so called because of the way the alternating rows of concave and convex tiles fit snugly together. During the rainy season the lichens and moss that live on the tiles spring to life, turning entire rooftops bright green.

A number of Hoi An's houses have round pieces of wood with an *am-duong* symbol in the middle surrounded by a spiral design over the doorway. These *mat cua* (door eyes) are supposed to protect the residents from harm.

It's not just individual buildings that have survived – it's whole streetscapes. This is particularly true around Đ Tran Phu and waterside promenade Đ Bach Dang. In the former French quarter to the east of Cam Nam Bridge there's a whole block of colonnaded houses, painted in the mustard yellow typical of French-colonial buildings.

Hoi An's historic structures are being gradually, sincerely restored and even the snaking power lines are slowly but surely vanishing underground. Old houses must be licensed for (tasteful) restoration work, which keeps most modernisation attempts within reason. One only hopes that not all buildings will become tailor and souvenir shops when they're done.

contains plaques to their memory. In front of the central altar is a fine gilded woodcarving of Chinese court life.

OLD HOUSES

All houses except Diep Dong Nguyen and Quan Thang now offer short guided tours, usually conducted by a young woman from the family. Efficient but sometimes coming across as perfunctory, she whisks you into a heavy wooden chair and recites a carefully scripted introduction to the house. Visitors can still wander around after the tour. One downside to putting these old houses on show is that what were once living spaces now seem dead and museumlike, the family having sequestered itself away from visitors' eyes.

Tan Ky House

Built two centuries ago as the home of a well-to-do ethnic-Vietnamese merchant, **Tan Ky House** (☎ 386 1474; 101 Đ Nguyen Thai Hoc; admission by Hoi An Old Town ticket; ⏲ 8am-noon & 2-4.30pm) has been lovingly preserved and today looks almost exactly as it did in the early 19th century. Don't be spooked by the portrait of a stern-looking matriarch over the entry hall; this gem of a house is worth lingering in.

Look out for signs of Japanese and Chinese influences on the architecture. Japanese elements include the ceiling (in the sitting area), which is supported by three progressively shorter beams, one on top of the other. There are similar beams in the salon. Under the crab-shell ceiling are carvings of crossed sabres wrapped in silk ribbon. The sabres symbolise force, the silk represents flexibility.

The interior is brightened by a beautiful detail: Chinese poems written in inlaid mother-of-pearl hang from some of the columns that hold up the roof. The Chinese characters on these 150-year-old panels are formed entirely of birds gracefully portrayed in various positions of flight.

The courtyard has several functions: to let in light, provide ventilation, bring a glimpse of nature into the home, and collect rainwater and provide drainage. The carved wooden balcony supports around the courtyard are decorated with grape leaves, which are a European import and further evidence of the unique blending of cultures in Hoi An.

The back of the house faces the river and was rented out to foreign merchants. Marks on one wall record recent flood heights, including the 1964 record when the water covered almost the entire ground level, and a 2m-high mark for the 2007 flood. There are two pulleys attached to a beam in the loft – in the past they were used for moving goods into storage, today for raising furniture for safekeeping from the floods.

The exterior of the roof is made of tiles; inside, the ceiling consists of wood. This design keeps the house cool in summer and warm in winter.

Tran Family Chapel

This **chapel** (21 Đ Le Loi; admission by Hoi An Old Town ticket) was built for worshipping the family ancestors in 1802. It was built by Tran Tu, one of the clan who ascended to the rank of mandarin and served as an ambassador to China. His picture is to the right of the chapel.

The architecture of the building reflects the influence of Chinese and Japanese styles. The central door is reserved for the dead – it's opened at Tet and on 11 November, the death anniversary of the main ancestor. Traditionally, women entered from the left and men from the right, although these distinctions are no longer observed.

The wooden boxes on the altar contain the Tran ancestors' stone tablets, with chiselled Chinese characters setting out the dates of birth and death, along with some small personal effects. On the anniversary of each family member's death, their box is opened, incense is burned and food is offered.

The small garden behind is where the placentas of newborn family members were buried. The practice was meant to prevent fighting between the children, but it hasn't been observed in more than 20 years, now that all babies are born in hospital.

Phung Hung Old House

Just a few steps down from the Japanese Covered Bridge, this **old house** (4 Đ Nguyen Thi Minh Khai; admission by Hoi An Old Town ticket; 8am-7pm) has a wide, welcoming entrance hall decorated with exquisite lanterns, wall hangings and embroidery. There's also an impressive suspended altar.

Tran Duong House

There's a whole block of colonnaded French-colonial buildings on Đ Phan Boi Chau between Nos 22 and 73, among them the 19th-century **Tran Duong House** (25 Đ Phan Boi Chau; admission 20,000d; 9am-6pm). It's mainly a showcase of antique French and Chinese furniture, including a sideboard buffet and a sitting room set with elaborate mother-of-pearl inlay. By contrast, the large plain wooden table in the front room is the family bed.

Diep Dong Nguyen House

Built for a wealthy Chinese merchant in the late 19th century, this **old house** (58 Đ Nguyen Thai Hoc; admission free; 8am-noon & 2-4.30pm) looks like an apothecary from another era. The front room was once a dispensary for *thuoc bac* (Chinese medicine); the medicines were stored in the glass-enclosed cases lining the walls.

Quan Thang House

This **house** (77 Tran Phu; admission by Hoi An Old Town ticket; 7am-5pm) is three centuries old and was built by an ancestor who was a Chinese captain. As usual, the architecture includes Japanese and Chinese elements. There are some especially fine carvings of peacocks and flowers on the teak walls of the rooms around the courtyard, on the roof beams and under the crab-shell roof (in the salon beside the courtyard).

MUSEUMS

All four museums are small and none too engaging.

Museum of Trading Ceramics (80 Đ Tran Phu; admission by Hoi An Old Town ticket; 7am-5.30pm) occupies a simply restored house made of dark wood. The artefacts are from all over Asia, with oddments from as far afield as Egypt. While this reveals that Hoi An had some rather impressive trading links, frankly it would take an expert eye to appreciate the display. However the small exhibition on the restoration of Hoi An's old houses provides a useful crash course in Old Town architecture.

Museum of Folklore in Hoi An (33 Đ Nguyen Thai Hoc/62 Đ Bach Dang; admission by Hoi An Old Town ticket; 7am-5.30pm) occupies a 150-year-old Chinese trading house. The exhibits give some idea of local customs and culture, though it's awfully dusty and decontextualised for a folk history museum. The view of the river from upstairs is very picturesque.

Housed in the Quan Am Pagoda, the **Hoi An Museum of History & Culture** (7 Đ Nguyen Hue; admission by Hoi An Old Town ticket; 7am-5.30pm) provides a sampling of pre-Cham, Cham and port-era artefacts, much of it ceramics.

Museum of Sa Huynh Culture & Museum of the Revolution (149 Đ Tran Phu; admission by Hoi An Old Town ticket; 7am-5.30pm) make odd bedfellows in the same building. The former (downstairs) has assorted fragments and burial jars dating from the early Dong Son civilisation of Sa Huynh. The latter (upstairs) focuses on local contributions to the last two wars.

TEMPLES & PAGODAS

Quan Cong Temple

Founded in 1653, this small **temple** (Chua Ong; 24 Đ Tran Phu; admission by Hoi An Old Town ticket) is dedicated to Quan Cong – a highly esteemed Chinese general who is worshipped as a symbol of loyalty, sincerity, integrity and justice. His partially gilt statue, made of papier-mâché on a wooden frame, is on the central altar at the back of the sanctuary. When someone makes an offering to Quan Cong, the caretaker solemnly strikes a bronze bowl that makes a bell-like sound.

On the left of Quan Cong is a statue of General Chau Xuong, one of his guardians, striking a tough-guy pose. On the right is the rather plump administrative mandarin Quan Binh. The life-sized white horse recalls a mount ridden by Quan Cong.

Check out the carp-shaped rain spouts on the roof surrounding the courtyard. The carp is a symbol of patience in Chinese mythology and is popular in Hoi An.

Shoes should be removed when mounting the platform in front of the statue of Quan Cong.

Chuc Thanh Pagoda

Founded in 1454 by a Buddhist monk from China, this **pagoda** (Khu Vuc 7, Tan An; ⌚ 8am-6pm) is the oldest pagoda in Hoi An. Among the antique ritual objects still in use are several bells, a stone gong that is two centuries old and a carp-shaped wooden gong said to be even older.

To get to Chuc Thanh Pagoda, go north all the way to the end of Đ Nguyen Truong To and turn left. Follow the sandy path for 500m.

Phuoc Lam Pagoda

This **pagoda** (Thon 2A, Cam Ha; ⌚ 8am-5pm) was founded in the mid-17th century. The head monk at the end of that century was An Thiem, a Vietnamese prodigy who became a monk at the age of eight. When he was 18, the king drafted An Thiem's brothers into his army to put down a rebellion. An Thiem volunteered to take the places of the other men in his family and eventually rose to the rank of general. After the war he returned to monkhood, but felt guilty about the many people he had slain. To atone for his sins, he volunteered to clean the Hoi An market for 20 years, then joined this pagoda as its head monk.

To reach the pagoda, continue past Chuc Thanh Pagoda for 400m. The path passes an obelisk that was erected over the tomb of 13 ethnic Chinese who were decapitated by the Japanese during WWII for resistance activities.

Other Temples & Pagodas

Phac Hat Pagoda (673 Đ Hai Ba Trung) has a colourful facade of ceramics and murals. It was being expanded at the time of research, with a large annexe being built at the rear.

The less ornate and newish **Cam Pho Temple** (52 Đ Nguyen Thi Minh Khai; ⌚ 8am-5pm) has a sparkling ceramic dragon roofline. At the time of research the interiors were undergoing restoration.

HANDICRAFT WORKSHOP

Housed in the 200-year-old Chinese trading house, the **Handicraft Workshop** (☎ 391 0216; 9 Đ Nguyen Thai Hoc; admission by Hoi An Old Town ticket) has artisans making silk lanterns and practising traditional embroidery in the back. In the front is your typical tourist-oriented cultural show (10.15am and 3.15pm) with traditional singers, dancers and musicians. It makes a sufficiently diverting break from sightseeing.

BA LE WELL

This square well's claim to fame is that it's the source of water for making authentic *cao lau*, a Hoi An speciality (see p256). The well is said to date from Cham times and elderly people make their daily pilgrimage to fill pails here. To find it, turn down the alley opposite 35 Đ Phan Chu Trinh and take the second laneway to the right.

Hoi An Walking Tour

It's possible to breeze past Hoi An's main sights in half a day. If you want to pop inside some of the buildings, call at an Old Town Booth (p248) first to purchase a ticket.

Start at the **Tran Family Chapel** (**1**; p251). Head south on Đ Le Loi and turn left at the next junction onto Đ Tran Phu. On your right you'll find **Quan Thang House** (**2**; p251) and a little further on the left, the **Museum of Trading Ceramics** (**3**; p251). Continuing along Đ Tran Phu, there is a cluster of interesting buildings on the left-hand side of the road, including the **Chinese All-Community Assembly Hall** (**4**; p249) and the **Assembly Hall of the Fujian Chinese Congregation** (**5**; p249). Keep heading east and at the next junction take a short detour north on Đ Nguyen Hue to the **Hoi An Museum of History & Culture** (**6**; p251). Back on Đ Tran Phu you'll see the **Quan Cong Temple** (**7**; p251).

HOI AN WALKING TOUR

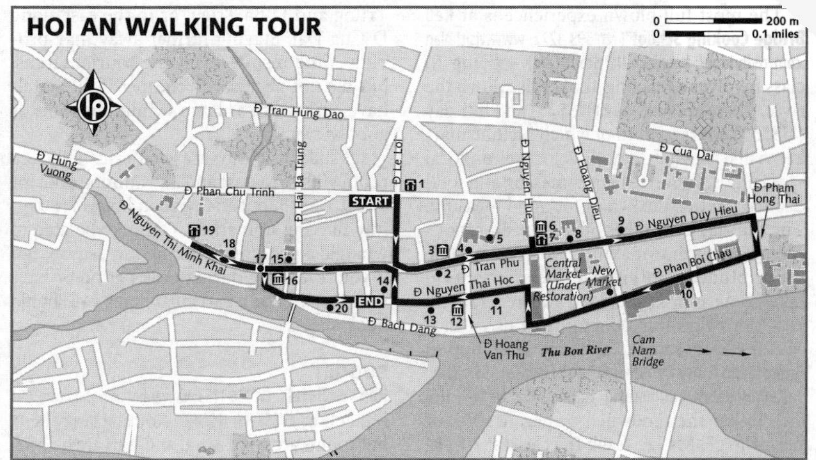

WALK FACTS

Distance: 2.5km
Duration: one to five hours (depending on how many sights you visit)
Start: Tran Family Chapel
Finish: Tan Ky House

Still walking east on Đ Tran Phu, the **Assembly Hall of the Hainan Chinese Congregation** (**8**; p249) is on the left. Cross the next junction and the road becomes Đ Nguyen Duy Hieu. On the left is the **Assembly Hall of the Chaozhou Chinese Congregation** (**9**; p249).

Take the second right on to Đ Pham Hong Thai and turn right again onto Đ Phan Boi Chau. Among the colonnaded French buildings here (Nos 22 to 73) is **Tran Duong House** (**10**; p251). Mosey along Đ Phan Boi Chau, turning right just past the old market, then left into Đ Nguyen Thai Hoc. On the left is the **Handicraft Workshop** (**11**; opposite) – if you time it correctly you might be able to catch a cultural performance. Further down Đ Nguyen Thai Hoc, at the corner with Đ Hoang Van Thu, is the **Museum of Folklore in Hoi An** (**12**; p251). Slightly further along on Đ Nguyen Thai Hoc is the intriguingly named **Hoi An Department of Managing & Gathering Swallows' Nests** (**13**; 53 Nguyen Thai Hoc). The nests are gathered from the Cham Island archipelago (see p261) twice a year; if you're lucky you'll be able to watch workers sorting their precious harvest here (see the boxed text, p303).

Proceed a few steps past the junction of Đ Le Loi and Đ Nguyen Thai Hoc to see the **Diep Dong Nguyen House** (**14**; p251). Return to Đ Le Loi, head north to Đ Tran Phu and turn left. Keep heading west and you'll pass the **Assembly Hall of the Cantonese Chinese Congregation** (**15**; p249). A little further along on the left is the **Museum of Sa Huynh Culture and Museum of the Revolution** (**16**; p251). Beyond is the famed **Japanese Covered Bridge** (**17**; p248), which connects Đ Tran Phu with Đ Nguyen Thi Minh Khai. Continue westward and keep an eye out for the **Phung Hung Old House** (**18**; p251) on the right. Also check out **Cam Pho Temple** (**19**; opposite).

From here retrace your steps across the Japanese bridge, turn right and follow the road onto Đ Nguyen Thai Hoc, where you'll see the **Tan Ky House** (**20**; p250). Now you can settle down for a long, cool drink at one of the nearby bars or cafes.

Activities

For swimming and eco-tours at Cua Dai Beach to the east, see p260.

COOKING COURSES

With so many local specialities (see p256) to its credit, Hoi An is a good place not only to fill up on the food but to learn to make it too. Almost every restaurant offers cooking classes, from no-fuss introductory lessons to more in-depth affairs for the dedicated chef or gourmand. Best of all, at the end of it you get to eat what you cook.

...l-blown experience is at **Red ...chool** (☎ 393 3222; www.visithoian ...okings Hai Scout Café) – going to class ... relaxing 4km cruise down the river. There are half-day (US$23) and full-day (US$39) courses, both of which include market visits. The half-day class focuses on local specialities, with rice paper–making and food decoration tips thrown in for good measure. The full-day class takes on a more ambitious menu, including making *pho* (rice-noodle soup). Students are given recipe print-outs to take home and, as an added sweetener, there is a 20m swimming pool for their use.

A less elaborate but still very swish option is **Morning Glory Cooking School** (☎ 224 1555; www.hoianhospitality.com/morning_c.htm; 106 Đ Nguyen Thai Hoc). Either the renowned owner, Ms Vy, or her protégé, Ms Lu, teach the classes (US$12 to US$55), which range from simple demonstrations of preparing everyday Vietnamese fare to intensive six-hour sessions for hard-core chefs.

More informal classes can be found at Green Moss (choose off the menu and pay a US$2 supplement; see p256), Phone Café (US$11; see p256) and the Lighthouse Café & Restaurant (US$21 with a market tour and boat to the restaurant; see p256).

DIVING

You can book dives at Cu Lao Cham Marine Park (p261) with **Cham Island Diving Center** (☎ 391 0782; www.chamislanddiving.com; 88 Đ Nguyen Thai Hoc; snorkelling US$40, dives US$65-75) and **Rainbow Divers** (☎ 091-422 4102; www.divevietnam.com; 41 Đ Nguyen Phuc Chu; snorkelling US$30, dives US$55-90). Cham Island Diving Center has also opened Dive Bar and Restaurant at the same address as its office.

Sleeping

There's no better indicator of Hoi An's transformation into a tourist town than the sheer explosion of hotels in the last five to seven years. It's hard to believe that tourists once had to commute from Danang, when today you're simply spoilt for choice of accommodation. Hoi An's savvy hoteliers are also constantly trying to keep up with each other: everyone's putting in swimming pools and massage showers these days.

Although there are a couple of hotels in the Old Town, most accommodation is spread out to the northwest around Đ Hai Ba Trung and Đ Ba Trieu, or to the east along Đ Cua Dai. Staying further away may provide some respite from the tourist circus, but it's not necessarily cheaper if the hotels have perks such as large swimming pools or good views.

It's still possible to get a good air-conditioned room with breakfast and a swimming pool for about US$15, but many good hotels are rapidly moving upmarket. You may be able to wrangle a good price during low season, but if you're visiting during peak period or have your heart set on a particular hotel, you should book ahead.

BUDGET

Hop Yen Hotel (☎ 386 3153; hopyenhotel@yahoo.com; 694 Đ Hai Ba Trung; r US$8-15;) Nothing fancy here, but rooms are good-sized and staff are helpful. Dorm beds are available for US$5.

Minh A Ancient Lodging House (☎ 386 1368; 2 Đ Nguyen Thai Hoc; r US$15) Offering about the most authentic experience of living in an Old Town traditional home, this guesthouse occupies a 180-year-old building right by the old central market. As you'd expect, the digs are pretty basic and there's no air-conditioning, but with plenty of antique furniture it's got character and colour in spades.

Hoi Pho Hotel (☎ 391 6382; hoiphohotel@yahoo.com; 627 Đ Hai Ba Trung; r US$15;) This family-owned mini-hotel is known for good service. Rooms are large and have lots of windows.

Huy Hoang I Hotel (☎ 386 1453; kshuyhoang@dng.vnn.vn; 73 Đ Phan Boi Chau; r US$15-18;) One of the oldest hotels in Hoi An, and it looks it too. The building is desperately in need of a new coat of paint, but its strength is its location – right beside the market and Cam Nam Bridge.

Thanh Van Hotel (☎ 391 6916; www.thanhvanhotel.com; 78 Đ Tran Hung Dao; r US$15-20;) One of the best-value places in town, this hotel has comfortable rooms in a good location near the livelier section of the Old Town. Prices include breakfast, served beside the pool, and the staff are forthcoming with information and suggestions.

Hoang Trinh Hotel (☎ 391 6579; www.hoianhoangtrinhhotel.com; 45 Đ Le Quy Don; r US$15-20;) A short stroll from the Old Town is this clean, modern hotel with high ceilings, pleasing decor and good service.

Nhat Huy Hoang Hotel (☎ 386 1665; nhathuyhoang.coltd@vnn.vn; 58 Đ Ba Trieu; r US$15-30;) This new hotel is earning a reputation for clean rooms at good prices. The only caveat is that rooms on the ground floors are windowless, although one is large enough to sleep six.

An Hoi Hotel (☎ 391 1888; www.anhoihotel.com.vn; 69 Đ Nguyen Phuc Chu; r US$15-35;) This was the first hotel to open on the An Hoi Peninsula waterfront facing the Old Town. It's peaceful yet a stone's throw from town. Rooms are good-sized and clean, and the breakfast area overlooks the river.

MIDRANGE

Green Field Hotel (Dong Xanh Hotel; ☎ 386 3484; www.greenfieldhotel.com; 423 Đ Cua Dai; dm US$5, r US$20-45;) This hotel east of town has comfortable rooms and runs an hour of free-flowing cocktails every evening by the pool. Ask about the US$5-a-bed dorm.

Phuoc An Hotel (☎ 391 6757; www.hoianhotels.com.vn; 31/1 Đ Tran Cao Van; r US$18-40;) Good rooms and a winning service record make this place a long-time favourite. The best rooms have an in-room computer, and the rooftop terrace is a nice place to unwind in the evening. Room prices include breakfast and free bicycle rental.

Thien Nga Hotel (☎ 391 6330; thienngahotel@gmail.com; 52 Đ Ba Trieu; s/d US$20/30;) Every room has a balcony at this superb little hotel, with those at the back looking out over pleasant vegetable farms. Extra touches such as being able to have breakfast served in your room make all the difference.

Nhi Nhi Hotel (☎ 391 6718; www.nhinhihotel.com.vn; 60 Đ Hung Vuong; s/d US$20/30;) This is the hotel for those who want to get out of the tourist thicket but still be within a short walk of the Old Town. It's got smart rooms, many of which overlook the swimming pool, and we keep hearing good things about the friendly staff.

Long Life Hotel (Thanh Xuan Hotel; ☎ 391 6696; www.longlifehotels.com; 30 Đ Ba Trieu; r US$20-40;) What looks like a narrow building from the street opens up in the rear to a lovely garden and pool overlooking the rice paddies – and that's just the breakfast area. Rooms are impeccable and cosy (but not small), and have massage bathtubs.

An Huy Hotel (☎ 386 2116; www.anhuyhotel.com; 30 Đ Phan Boi Chau; r US$28-45;) With just 14 rooms, this boutique hotel offers privacy and comfort, while evoking old-world charm with woody decor and pretty tiles. The staff are known for going above and beyond the call of duty.

Phu Thinh II Hotel (☎ 392 3923; www.phuthinhhotels.com; 488 Đ Cua Dai; s/d US$32/40;) A Happy Buddha statue presides over the staircase leading up to the rooms, which are clean and airy with large windows. Rooms at the rear look out onto tranquil rice fields, as do the cleverly situated pool and restaurant.

Thien Thanh Hotel (Blue Sky Hotel; ☎ 391 6545; www.hoianthienthanhhotel.com; 16 Đ Ba Trieu; r US$35-60;) With a covered swimming pool and rear rooms that overlook the rice paddies, this hotel is one of the most tempting along the mini-hotel strip. The decor is fresh and modern, and the best rooms come with a DVD player and complimentary in-room coffee or tea.

Ha An Hotel (☎ 386 3126; www.haanhotel.com; 6-8 Đ Phan Boi Chau; r US$45-70;) Resortlike without the resort prices, this French Quarter hotel is centred on a lovely garden courtyard. The rooms look quite swish, with plenty of light and all the modern trimmings.

Southern Hotel (Phuong Nam Hotel; ☎ 392 3401; www.hoianphuongnamhotel.com; 224 Đ Ly Thai To; r US$49-79;) Stylishly decorated rooms with polished wooden floors make up for the fact that this hotel is some way from the town with nothing much within walking distance. There's a free hourly shuttle to town and there are some very new resort-style rooms overlooking the pool.

TOP END

Vinh Hung Resort (☎ 391 0393; www.vinhhungresort.com; 111 Ngo Quyen, An Hoi Peninsula; r US$70-100, ste US$125;) On a lovely riverfront site, this resort is blissfully isolated from the town. Rooms are enormous and there's a boat service to town (which is also within 10 minutes' walk).

Vinh Hung 1 Hotel (☎ 386 1621; www.vinhhunghotels.com.vn; 143 Đ Tran Phu; r US$90-100;) Soak up that Old Town atmosphere in this 125-year-old Chinese trading house. All the rooms are dressed up with antique furniture and the very best ones were used as dressing rooms by Michael Caine while filming *The Quiet American*.

Life Heritage Resort Hoi An (☎ 391 4555; www.life-resorts.com; 1 Đ Pham Hong Thai; r US$120, ste US$154-279;) It's the only resort within walking distance of the town centre, and one with a truly tranquil air. Recently upgraded, the rooms now have new furniture and fixtures, all very contemporary and stylish.

Eating

Hoi An's main contribution to Vietnamese cuisine is *cao lau,* doughy flat noodles combined with croutons, bean sprouts and greens and topped off with pork slices. It is mixed with crumbled, crispy rice paper immediately before eating. Other local specialities are fried *hoanh thanh* (won ton), *banh xeo* (crispy savoury pancakes rolled with herbs in fresh rice paper) and the delicate 'white rose' (shrimp encased in rice paper and steamed). Most restaurants serve these items, but quality varies widely.

The beauty of Hoi An is that you can snag a spectacular (and spectacularly) cheap meal at the central market and in casual eateries – or you can splash out on excellent fine dining or fusion cuisine. Outside of Hanoi and HCMC, this is the most exciting restaurant scene in Vietnam, helmed by some incredibly talented Vietnamese and foreign chefs. Hoi An specialities will always be a staple, but don't miss the opportunity to get a taste of the new Vietnam. Restaurant prices tend to be higher than in other towns, but good meals are still very affordable for most travellers.

VIETNAMESE

Mermaid Restaurant (☎ 386 1527; www.hoianhospitality.com/mermaid.htm; 2 Đ Tran Phu; dishes 18,000-68,000d; ⏰ lunch & dinner) One of the original Hoi An eateries (since 1991), this place is still going strong with its menu of Hoi An specialities and family recipes. Try the fried spring rolls and the excellent 'white rose'.

Quan Chay Co Dam (☎ 386 3733; 71/20 Đ Phan Chu Trinh; meals 20,000d-30,000d; ⏰ breakfast, lunch & dinner) A hole-in-the-wall place in the middle of the Old Town, yet well-hidden from the main street. It's worth hunting down for the hearty and flavourful vegetarian meals. If the menu stumps you, just choose from what's on the counter.

Café 43 (☎ 386 2587; 43 Đ Tran Cao Van; dishes 20,000-50,000d; ⏰ lunch & dinner) Tucked away in a residential lane, this casual eatery continues to get rave reviews for good food at good prices. The fact that it's run by a very friendly family doesn't hurt.

Phone Café (☎ 324 1988; thanhphone72@yahoo.com; 80B Đ Bach Dang; dishes 20,000d-60,000d; ⏰ lunch & dinner) Don't be fooled by the dingy appearance – this modest operation has excellent food that tastes just like Mum's cooking (assuming your mother cooks Vietnamese). The *cao lau*'s not bad and the claypot specialities are quite delectable.

Green Moss (☎ 386 3728; 341 Đ Nguyen Duy Hieu; dishes 20,000-80,000d; ⏰ lunch & dinner) French-colonial architecture meets a modern Asian aesthetic in this cosy cafe with an air of casual chic. The menu includes Vietnamese and Thai food, with a number of vegetarian options.

Other options that won't break the bank:

Bobo Café (☎ 386 1939; thuyph.ha@dng.vnn.v; 18 Đ Le Loi; dishes 15,000-50,000d; ⏰ breakfast, lunch & dinner) A no-frills family operation that has courtyard seating.

Miss Ly Cafeteria 22 (☎ 386 1603; 22 Đ Nguyen Hue; dishes 20,000-50,000d; ⏰ breakfast, lunch & dinner) A local institution for local specialities.

GOURMET VIETNAMESE

Lighthouse Café & Restaurant (☎ 393 6235; www.lighthousecafehoian.com; To 5 Khoi Xuyen Trung, Cam Nam Island; dishes 20,000-100,000d; ⏰ lunch & dinner, closed Tue) Run by a Dutch man and his Vietnamese wife, this cosy restaurant on Cam Nam Island has good Vietnamese food and great views – plus there's a mean Dutch apple cake for dessert. Walk over Cam Nam Bridge to get here, or catch the free boat (marked 'Hai Dang') from the waterfront in front of Đ Bach Dang. The restaurant is small, so reservations are required after 7pm; the balcony tables are good for couples.

Morning Glory Street Food Restaurant (☎ 224 1555; www.hoianhospitality.com; 106 Đ Nguyen Thai Hoc; dishes 40,000-100,000d; ⏰ breakfast, lunch & dinner) Another stylish, fine dining establishment from the restaurateur who gave Hoi An the Cargo Club and Mermaid. Though this restaurant purports to specialise in street food, its real strength is in modern Vietnamese cuisine. Try the exquisite prawn curry or the roast duck.

our pick **Mango Rooms** (☎ 391 0839; www.mangorooms.com; 111 Đ Nguyen Thai Hoc; meals 100,000-300,000d; ⏰ breakfast, lunch & dinner) Don't look for *cao lau* here. This restaurant specialises in putting a modern spin on Vietnamese cuisine, and chef and owner Duc Tran has concocted fresh, unexpected flavours in every dish. Even Mick Jagger's come to sample the menu. Both the formal dining room and the chilled-out riverside space are decorated with playful splashes of primary colours. Adjoining them is the kitchen, where the staff do all their chopping and cooking in full view of the customers.

INTERNATIONAL

Shree Ganesh Indian Restaurant (☎ 386 4538; rajtikh@yahoo.com; 24 Đ Tran Hung Dao; dishes 20,000-85,000d; ⌚ lunch & dinner) Formerly known as Omar Khayyam's, this is the place for authentic Indian food. Fill up on your masala dishes and curries, with lots of vegetarian choices too.

Hai Scout Café (☎ 386 3210; www.visithoian.com/haicafe.html; 98 Đ Nguyen Thai Hoc; dishes 30,000-110,000d; ⌚ breakfast, lunch & dinner) Making the most of its airy Old Town building, this cafe stretches into a large garden courtyard that breaks into a bar by night. On the menu are good sandwiches, Western breakfasts, Vietnamese dishes and some European mains. There's a display on World Wildlife Fund (WWF) projects in central Vietnam out back, and some minority tribal crafts for sale.

Cargo Club (☎ 391 0489; 107 Đ Nguyen Thai Hoc; dishes 35,000-105,000d; ⌚ breakfast, lunch & dinner) If you're craving a hearty Western meal, come here for a full spread of international cuisine. The freshly baked patisserie and boulangerie selections are 'to die for', in the words of a Hoi An expat. It's a great place for people-watching at any time of the day, and from the upstairs balcony there are lovely views of the river. After dark the place morphs into a groovy bar.

Good Morning Vietnam (☎ 391 0227; 102 Đ Nguyen Thai Hoc; mains 50,000-125,000d; ⌚ lunch & dinner) Yes, it's a chain, but a good one. With Italian owners and chefs running the show, this place serves everything you'd expect of a good trattoria: tip-top pizzas and pastas, and good coffee and wine to round off the meal.

Casa Verde (☎ 391 1594; 99 Đ Bach Dang; mains 85,000-190,000d; ⌚ lunch & dinner) It's not just another cosy Mediterranean restaurant transplanted to the Hoi An riverside – the chef-owner created memorable meals when he was at the Victoria Hoi An Resort and the results here are *bellissimo*. Take your pick of European and Vietnamese classics, given that extra dash of flair. The chef grows his own herbs and makes all the ice cream. It's pricey by Hoi An standards, but still a bargain for the quality of food you get.

Drinking

For a little place, Hoi An has quite the selection of bars, many with helpfully hedonistic happy hours and extensive food menus. Most stay open into the early hours, which is quite unusual, and it's entirely possible to party till dawn if you want to. Just don't wake up the hotel when you bumble in.

Beware of *xe om* drivers offering to take you to out-of-the-way venues at night. We've heard reports of extortionate prices being demanded for the return trip, occasionally accompanied by physical threats.

Before & Now (☎ 391 0599; www.beforennow.com; 51 Đ Le Loi) An energetic bar that's good for its pop-rock-funk playlist, Milan-trained chef and buzzing crowd. If you run out of conversation topics, contemplate the ramifications of Bono-as-Superman, as depicted on one of local artist Tran Trung Linh's pop-art portraits on the walls (the eclectic mix includes Lenin, Mao, Che, Marilyn and Gandhi).

Tam Tam Cafe (☎ 386 2212; 110 Đ Nguyen Thai Hoc) Set in a lovingly restored tea warehouse, this cool hang-out indulges in comfortable tropical decor and plenty of lounge space upstairs. The outdoor seating is good for people-watching, while the scene is livelier around the pool table and the balcony.

Sleepy Gecko (☎ 090-842 6349; sleepygecko@gmail.com; To 5 Khoi Xuyen Trung, Cam Nam Island) To escape the tourist circus, there's no better place than this beach bar–style place on Cam Nam Island, where you can admire the view of Hoi An over an ice-cold beer. The owner, Steve, is there night or day to provide good tunes and good jibes – ask about his very good 'byke tours'.

River Lounge (☎ 391 1700; www.lounge-collection.com; 35 Đ Nguyen Phuc Chu) Very cool, very white, very European – this oh-so-chic chill-out spot is more expensive than most, but the views and ambience aren't like anything else you'll find in Hoi An. Make the most of it by sprawling out on a daybed upstairs.

Treat's Café (☎ 386 1125; 158 Đ Tran Phu) *The* backpacker bar of old Hoi An, this place is regularly full to bursting, particularly during its generous 4pm to 9pm happy hour.

Treat's Café has spawned two virtually identical joints on the same formula:

Re-Treat Café (☎ 391 0527; 69 Đ Tran Hung Dao)

Treat's Same Same But Not Different Café (☎ 386 2278; 93 Đ Tran Hung Dao)

Shopping

Hoi An has a long history of flogging goods to international visitors, and today's residents haven't lost their commercial edge. It's

GETTING CLOTHES THAT MEASURE UP

Let's face it: the tailor scene in Hoi An is out of control. The estimated number of tailors working here ranges anywhere from 300 to 500. Hotels and tour guides all have their preferred partners – 'We give you good price' they promise before shuttling you off to their aunt/cousin/in-law /neighbour (from whom they'll probably earn a nice commission). If you're a Caucasian male, you're likely to be propositioned on the street for new clothes (the girls don't really want to be your girlfriend, they just want you to place an order).

In such a demanding environment, what's an aspiring fashionista, or someone who just wants 'something nice', to do? The first rule of thumb is that while you should always bargain and be comfortable with the price, you also get what you pay for. A tailor who quotes you a price that is drastically lower than a competitor's is probably cutting corners (pun intended) without telling you. Better tailors and better fabrics cost more, as do tighter deadlines. If a shop promises to deliver you a new wardrobe within 24 hours, think about it: either they're working an army of sweatshop apprentices to the bone, or you're probably going to get some dodgy items (or both).

Hoi An's tailors are renowned as master copiers – show them a picture ripped out of a magazine, and they'll whip out an identical outfit in a day or two. If you don't know what you want, the helpful shopgirls will heave out tomes of catalogues for you to leaf through. They don't just do *ao dai* or summer dresses; winter coats, wedding dresses and full two- or three-piece suits are perfectly within their repertoire.

Eavesdrop on other customers while you're deciding and spy on the shop's latest products being fitted before you commit yourself. It also helps if you know your fabrics and preferences, right down to details like thread colour, linings and buttons. When buying silk, make sure you're paying for the real thing. The only real test is with a cigarette or match (synthetic fibres melt, silk burns), so if you're concerned about authenticity ask for a small sample of the material and

common for travellers not planning to buy anything to leave Hoi An laden down with extra bags – which, by the way, you can buy here too.

The biggest lure is the clothes (see the boxed text, above). Hoi An has long been known for fabric production, and the voracity of tourist demand has swiftly shoehorned enough tailor shops for a small province into the tiny Old Town. Pop into the **Hoi An Cloth Market** (Đ Tran Phu) for a selection of local fabrics.

Coming in a close second in popularity are shoes, also copied from Western designs. The cobblers here can imitate anything from sneakers (trainers) to the highest heels or the coolest Cubans. Prices are very low, but as with tailored clothes the quality can vary greatly.

Reaching Out (☎ 386 2460; www.reachingoutvietnam.com; 103 Đ Nguyen Thai Hoc; 🕓 7.30am-9.30pm) is a very worthwhile fair-trade gift shop started by a Vietnamese couple, one of whom is disabled (see the boxed text, p260). The shop employs disabled artisans, and proceeds are ploughed back into the business to train and employ the disabled all over Vietnam.

Chinese lanterns are popular souvenirs, all handily foldable. To watch them being made, try **Tuoi Ngoc** (☎ 386 1920; 103 Đ Tran Phu), which has been making lanterns for three generations, or the Handicraft Workshop (p252).

Woodcarvings are another local speciality. Cross to Cam Nam Village to watch the carvers at work, or hop on a ferry to Cam Kim Island (p260), where many woodcarving workshops are clustered near the jetty. For other types of art, the art galleries near the Japanese Covered Bridge along Đ Nguyen Thi Minh Khai, Đ Tran Phu and Đ Nguyen Thai Hoc are great to browse through. Don't expect to stumble across any genuine antiques – all of them were probably scooped up long ago.

If you're interested in jewellery beyond the bits and bobs sold in souvenir shops, try **Lotus Jewellery** (☎ 391 1664; 100 Đ Nguyen Thai Hoc), which has very affordable and attractive pieces from all over Asia.

Getting There & Away

AIR

The closest airport is 45 minutes away in Danang (see p240).

BUS

The **main bus station** (☎ 386 1284; 96 Đ Hung Vuong) is 1km west of the centre of town. Buses run go outside to test it. Similarly, don't accept on face value that a fabric is 100% cotton or wool without giving it a good feel for the quality. Prices (in US$) currently hover around $10 to $15 for a men's shirt, and about $20 for skirts and trousers. If a suit costs less than $100, make sure the fabric and workmanship is up to scratch; well-made ones with proper lining generally cost more than $100.

Although many travellers try to squeeze in a clothing order within a 48-hour sojourn, that doesn't leave much time for fittings and alterations, which are more important than most people anticipate. Remember to check the seams of the finished garment: a single set of stitching along the inside edges will soon cause fraying and, eventually, gaping holes. Well-tailored garments have a second set of stitches (known in the trade as blanket stitching) which binds the edge, oversewing the fabric so fraying is impossible.

If you have a big order in mind, it might make sense to try out a few different shops on small items first. While some tourists bring an extra bag (or three) for their new outfits, most shops can pack and ship orders to your home country. Although there are occasional reports of packages going astray or the wrong order arriving, the local post office's hit rate is better than most.

In such a crowded field, it's tough to sort the wheat from the chaff, particularly since all the shops outsource their orders to a growing legion of anonymous workers. It may be worth your while to scour the Old Town for a small operation that isn't tainted by overpopularity. If you're pressed for time, places that we regularly hear good things about are (in alphabetical order): **A Dong Silk** (☎ 386 3170; www.adongsilk.com; 40 Đ Le Loi), **B'lan** (☎ 386 1866; www.hoianblan.com; 23 Đ Tran Phu); **Phuoc An** (☎ 386 2615; www.phuocanriver.com; 6 Đ Le Loi), **Thu Thuy** (☎ 386 1699; www.thuthuysilk.com; 60 Đ Le Loi) and **Yaly** (☎ 391 0474; www.yalycouture.com; 47 Đ Nguyen Thai Hoc), which tends to be significantly more expensive.

to Danang (10,000d, one hour), Quang Ngai and other points. More frequent services to Danang leave from the **northern bus station** (Đ Le Hong Phong).

It's easy to pick up an open-tour bus to or from Hue (US$4, four hours) or Nha Trang (seated/sleeping US$8/15, 11 to 12 hours).

CAR & MOTORBIKE

To get to Danang (30km) you can either head north out of town and join up with Hwy 1A, or head east to Cua Dai Beach and follow the China Beach coastal road. The going rate for a motorbike taxi between Danang and Hoi An is 100,000d. A taxi costs approximately US$15.

A journey to Hue starts from US$50 (depending on how many stops you plan to make along the way), while a half-day trip around the surrounding area, including My Son, is US$20 to US$30. Agree on your itinerary in advance and get a copy in writing.

Getting Around

The Old Town is compact and highly walkable. To go further afield, rent a bicycle (20,000d per day). The An Hoi Peninsula is small enough to zip around quickly, and the route east to Cua Dai Beach passes some lovely rice paddies.

A motorbike without/with a driver will cost around US$6/10 per day. A taxi to the beach costs a couple of dollars.

BOAT

A boat trip on the Thu Bon River can be a fascinating experience. A simple rowboat (which comes complete with rower) should cost about 50,000d per hour, and one hour is probably long enough. Some My Son tours cover part of the journey by boat – a lovely but lengthy voyage.

Motorboats for small groups can be hired to visit handicraft and fishing villages in the area; expect to pay 100,000d to 150,000d per hour. Look for the boats near the dock close to the market.

TAXI

For a metered cab, try **Hoi An Taxi** (☎ 391 9919) or **Mai Linh** (☎ 392 5925).

AROUND HOI AN

Thanh Ha

This small village of about 70 families has long been known for its pottery industry, but

ENABLING THE DISABLED

For the nine million or so Vietnamese who are disabled, chances are they won't have the opportunity to go to school or pick up skills that will let them earn a living as independent adults. Most schools aren't equipped to receive students with disabilities and employers don't see the disabled as having employable skills. Most disabled people are cooped up at home with few or no friends, entirely dependent on their families or the government for support.

It's a dismal prospect, but one that individual Vietnamese and expatriates are working hard to change through businesses that train, employ and empower the disabled – and this is where your tourist dollar can make a difference. In Hoi An, Mr Binh Nguyen Le has been running the fair-trade shop Reaching Out (p258) since 2001. Wheelchair-bound due to botched medical treatment when he was 16, he understands all too well the frustrations faced by disabled young people. At Reaching Out, he hires disabled workers who first receive training in new craftsmanship skills, then start work in a comfortable workshop located behind the shop (and open to visitors).

Besides giving the disabled an employable skill, Mr Binh runs his business on fair-trade policies: workers work eight-hour days, are paid salaries about 35% above the norm, and receive Đhealth and social insurance. True to its name, Reaching Out also contracts disabled workers all over Vietnam, paying them a better rate than they would get from other middlemen. Profits go into expanding the business to train and employ more disabled workers.

In Danang the bakery-restaurant Bread of Life (p239) is run by Americans Kathleen and Bob Huff to finance sign-language and vocational training for the hearing-impaired. The operating principles are similar: give the deaf an employable skill – in this case, baking and cooking everything from pizzas to Southern-style biscuits to sloppy Joes – so that they can be financially independent. The Huffs take no salary, so all profits from the business go to support sign-language training for deaf children (which is not taught in school).

Another organisation helping disabled children is the **Kianh Foundation** (www.kianh.org.uk), a UK charity that helps children at the state-run Hoi An Orphanage. Its work ranges from providing special education, physiotherapy and speech therapy programs (the children previously had no schooling, educational stimulation or access to therapies), to employing and training Vietnamese staff.

By visiting some of these charities, such as Reaching Out or Bread of Life, you can see the cheerful, confident vibe they have. In the words of Nam, a disabled artisan at Reaching Out, 'Working here is so much better than feeding buffalo'.

demand has been declining and most villagers have gradually switched from making bricks and tiles to making pots and thingumabobs for the tourist trade (see the boxed text, opposite). The artisans employed in this hot, sweaty and painstaking work don't mind if you come for a gander and a chat, though they're happier if you buy something.

Thanh Ha is 3km west of Hoi An and can be easily reached on bicycle, or on the way back from My Son.

Cam Kim Island

The master woodcarvers, who in previous centuries produced the fine carvings that graced the homes of Hoi An's merchants and the town's public buildings, came from Kim Bong village on Cam Kim Island. Most of the woodcarvings on sale in Hoi An are produced here.

Boats to the island leave from the boat landing at Đ Bach Dang in Hoi An (10,000d to 15,000d, 30 minutes). The village and island are also fun to explore on bicycle, with few tourists and certainly no tailors or souvenir shops.

Cua Dai Beach

This pristine, palm-fringed beach is the closest to the township of Hoi An and part of the coastline that runs all the way up to Danang's My Khe Beach. At this end it's relatively undisturbed, except for a few five-star resorts and the inevitable clump of seafood restaurants; the latter also have deckchairs for hire. While the beach can get busy on weekends, on weekdays it's a restful spot to soak up some sun. Note that safe swimming is only possible between the months of April and October.

Cua Dai Beach is 5km east of Hoi An on Đ Cua Dai. Even if you're not a beach bum, getting there makes for a pleasant bike ride.

TOURS

There are some pricey but unusual tours available near Cua Dai Beach. **Hoi An Eco Tour** (☎ 0510-392 8900; www.hoianecotour.com.vn; Phuoc Hai Village; tours US$34-44) runs tours along the river, where tourists can see traditional village life and try their hand at fishing or paddling a basket boat. A more adrenalin-packed option are the jet-ski tours offered by **Jet Ski Vietnam** (☎ 0510-392 7632; www.jetskivietnam.com; 47 Đ Cua Dai; tours from 700,000d), which cover the delta around Hoi An and as far as Cham Island or My Son.

SLEEPING

Sea and Sand Hotel (Cat Bien Hotel; ☎ 0510-392 7999; www.seaandsandhotel.com; 15 Đ Cua Dai; r US$35-45;) Despite the institutional feeling created by the pale green and white walls, this is the cheapest accommodation near the beach (just 50m away). Rooms are spacious and have a balcony. There's also a shuttle service to Hoi An that runs three times a day.

Victoria Hoi An Resort (☎ 0510-392 7040; www.victoriahotels.asia; r US$160-225, ste US$280-300;) Decked out in fresh Mediterranean colours, this four-star beachfront resort has lovely rooms decorated in Vietnamese, French or Japanese styles. It has all the usual resort trimmings – swimming pools, tennis court, fitness centre and spa – and service is tip-top.

Cham Island

A little isolation can be a good thing. Cham Island (Cu Lao Cham) is only 21km from Hoi An, but because it was until recently closed to visitors (the military won't explain why) and is readily accessible for only about seven months of the year, it remains blessedly undeveloped – and beautiful. There's nothing here except fisherpeople, forest, a couple of villages, a few unobtrusive military types and plenty of unspoiled beach.

And diving – diving is the reason most people visit Cham Island. It's part of the Cu Lao Cham Marine Park, which comprises eight islands and is home to about 135 species of coral, 202 species of fish, five species of lobster and 84 species of mollusc. Diving trips can be arranged through Rainbow Divers or Cham Island Diving Center (p254). Rainbow Divers focuses on dive-only trips where the boats remain offshore, but can organise island visits for large groups. Cham Island Diving Center trips include beach time (hammocks provided) and optional activities such as hiking, village visits or overnight stays. Because of weather and water conditions, diving is only possible from March to September.

There are three guesthouses (rooms US$10 to US$15) on Cham Island, two at the main village of Bay Lang and a state-run operation at Bay Chong beach. There are no restaurants but the guesthouse owners can cook for you. If the villagers take a shine to you, you might get invited to toss back some rice wine with them.

POTTERING ON

Just about every souvenir shop in Hoi An sells little clay figurines and whistles. These are handmade in Thanh Ha village, on the banks of the Thu Bon River. In this dense rabbit warren of homes, sheds, kilns and alleyways, it's easy to get turned and turned about, even lost.

In imperial times this crumbling village was so renowned for pottery that its craftsmen made items for the royal court at Hue. Today the villagers get by churning out knick-knacks for Hoi An's booming tourist trade. They also make bricks and tiles, but it's hard to compete with mechanised factories that make better-quality products.

Ms Nam Ti Hoang, 39, tells it like it is: 'We collect clay from the fields around the village and shape them into figurines and small jars and pots. We can make about 80 to 100 small items every day. Big pots without much decoration are easier – we can make about 200 a day.'

She learned to make pottery because it was the family tradition, but she doesn't want her children to continue it. 'Sometimes they help us to decorate the figurines or whistles. But our work is very hard. The salary is no good.'

A few families in Thanh Ha have switched to fishing, but for most pottery is all they know. They're also too poor to move, even though the village floods every year. As Ms Nam says, 'We don't know when the next order will come from Hoi An. We'll just keep making these things first.'

All boats to Cham Island dock at Bay Lang village. There is a public boat that leaves from the boat landing at Đ Bach Dang in Hoi An (15,000d, two to three hours, 7am daily); foreigners can expect to be charged more. Bring a copy of your passport and visa, as the boat captain needs to prepare a permit. Tour agencies charge US$20 to US$25 for a half-day island tour, which includes a speedboat ride. Cham Island Diving Center charges US$40 for a full-day trip excluding diving (see p254), as well as sailing trips on a trimaran around Cham Island and up the coast.

MY SON

The effusive have described this as Vietnam's Angkor Wat, but that's hardly fair: **My Son** (☎ 373 1309; admission 60,000d; 🕑 6.30am-4pm) contains fewer ruins (and they are very much ruined) within a small area of about 200 sq metres. Still, it's the most extensive of Vietnam's Cham remains, and enchanting in its own way – if appreciated on its own merits.

The ruins are set in a lush jungle valley 55km from Hoi An, surrounded by the burble of streams and overlooked by Cat's Tooth Mountain (Hon Quap). Only about 20 structures survive where at least 68 once stood. The smallness of the site and sparseness of the ruins make a visit here feel at once intimate and enthralling (if you avoid the crowds).

My Son was once the most important intellectual and religious centre of the kingdom of Champa (see the boxed text, p264) and may also have served as a burial place for Cham monarchs. It was rediscovered by the French in the late 19th century. Although they set about restoring and preserving parts of the complex, American bombing later devastated the place. Today it is a Unesco World Heritage site and restoration work is ongoing.

History

My Son (pronounced 'me sun') became a religious centre under King Bhadravarman in the late 4th century and was constantly occupied until the 13th century – the longest period of development of any monument in Southeast Asia. Most of the temples were dedicated to Cham kings associated with divinities, particularly Shiva, who was regarded as the founder and protector of Champa's dynasties.

Because some of the ornamentation work at My Son was never finished, archaeologists know that the Chams first built their structures and only then carved decorations into the brickwork. However, they have yet to figure out for certain how they stuck the baked bricks together. According to one theory, they used a paste prepared with a botanical oil that is indigenous to central Vietnam.

During one period in their history, the summits of some of the towers were completely covered with a layer of gold. After the area fell into decline, much of its glory was stripped over the centuries by the Chinese, Khmer and Vietnamese. When the French found the site and studied it, they moved some of the artefacts to the Museum of Cham Sculpture (p237) in Danang – fortuitously so, because the VC used My Son as a base during the American War and American bombing destroyed some of the most important monuments that were still standing.

Information

It gets very busy, so go early or late to soak up the atmosphere. By departing from Hoi An at 5am or 6am, you will arrive to wake up the gods (and the guards) for sunrise and could be leaving just as the tour groups hit the area.

The Site

The large **Exhibition Buildings** contain Sanskrit-inscribed stones as well as historical information on topics including the hairstyles of Cham women. Take time to review the large map – it'll come in handy later, as the site is not well signposted. The complex includes toilets and a souvenir shop.

Archaeologists have divided My Son's monuments into 10 main groups, uninspiringly named A, A', B, C, D, E, F, G, H and K. Each structure within that group is given a number.

GROUP C

The 8th-century **C1** was used to worship Shiva, portrayed in human form (rather than in the form of a *linga*, as in B1). Inside is an altar where a statue of Shiva, now in the Museum of Cham Sculpture in Danang, used to stand. Note the motifs, characteristic of the 8th century, carved into the brickwork of the exterior walls. With the massive bomb crater in front of this group, it's amazing that anything's still standing.

GROUP B

The main *kalan* (sanctuary), **B1**, was dedicated to Bhadresvara, which is a contraction of the name of King Bhadravarman, who built the first temple at My Son, combined with '-esvara', which means Shiva. The first building on this site was erected in the 4th century, destroyed in the 6th century and rebuilt in the 7th century. Only the 11th-century base, made of large sandstone blocks, remains. The niches in the wall were used to hold lamps (Cham sanctuaries had no windows). The *linga* inside was discovered during excavations in 1985, 1m below its current position.

B5, built in the 10th century, was used for storing sacred books and objects used in ceremonies performed in B1. The boat-shaped roof (the 'bow' and 'stern' have fallen off) demonstrates the influence of Malayo-Polynesian architecture. Unlike the sanctuaries, this building has windows and the Cham masonry inside is original. Over the window on the outside wall facing B4 is a brick bas-relief of two elephants under a tree with two birds in it.

The ornamentation on the exterior walls of **B4** is an excellent example of a Cham decorative style, typical of the 9th century and said to resemble worms. The style is unlike anything found in other Southeast Asian cultures.

B3 has an Indian-influenced pyramidal roof typical of Cham towers. Inside **B6** is a bath-shaped basin for keeping sacred water that was poured over the *linga* in B1; this is the only known example of a Cham basin. **B2** is a gate.

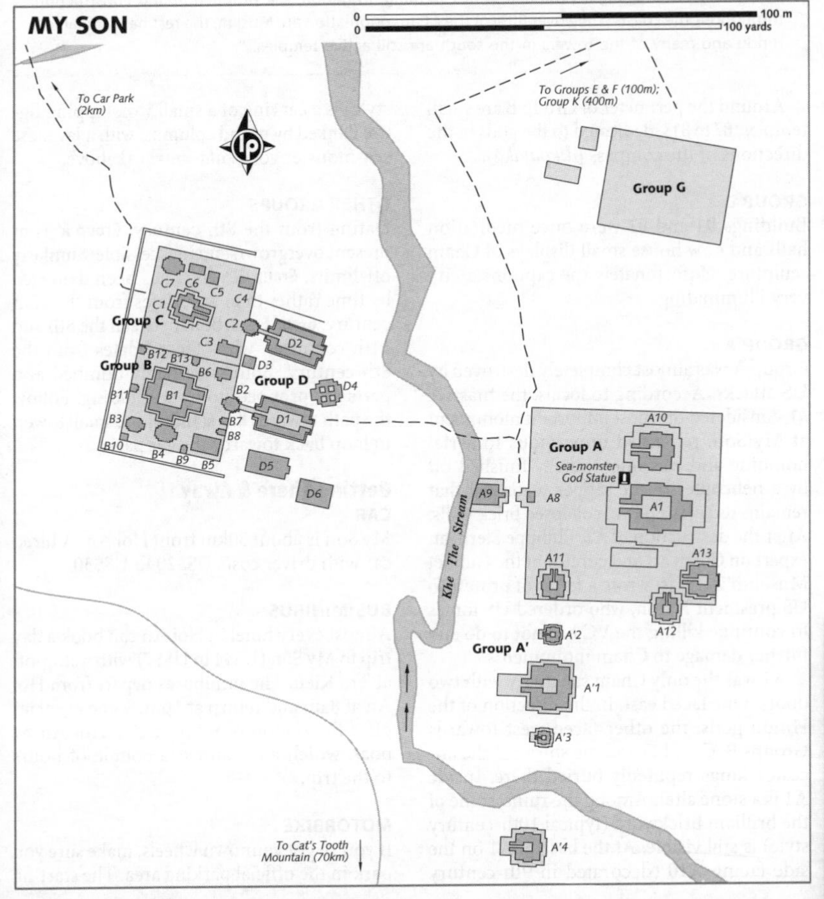

THE KINGDOM OF CHAMPA

The kingdom of Champa flourished between the 2nd and the 15th centuries. It first appeared around present-day Danang and later spread south to what is now Nha Trang and Phan Rang. Champa became Indianised through commercial ties: adopting Hinduism, using Sanskrit as a sacred language and borrowing from Indian art.

The Chams, who lacked enough land for agriculture, were semipiratical and conducted attacks on passing ships. As a result they were in a constant state of war with the Vietnamese to the north and the Khmers to the southwest. The Chams successfully threw off Khmer rule in the 12th century, but were entirely absorbed by Vietnam in the 17th century.

The Chams are best known for the many brick sanctuaries (Cham towers) they constructed throughout the south. The greatest collection of Cham art is in the Museum of Cham Sculpture (p237) in Danang. The major Cham site is at My Son (p262), and other Cham ruins can be found in Quy Nhon (p271) and its surrounds (p276), Tuy Hoa (p278), Nha Trang (p284), Thap Cham (p304) and Mui Ne (p309).

The Cham remain a substantial ethnic minority in Vietnam, particularly around Phan Rang, numbering around 100,000 people. Elements of Cham civilisation can still be seen in techniques for pottery, fishing, sugar production, rice farming, irrigation, silk production and construction throughout the coast. While over 80% of the Cham population are Muslim, the rest have remained Hindu and many of the towers in the south are still active temples.

Around the perimeter of Group B are small temples, **B7** to **B13**, dedicated to the gods of the directions of the compass *(dikpalaka)*.

GROUP D

Buildings **D1** and **D2** were once meditation halls and now house small displays of Cham sculpture. Unfortunately the captions aren't very illuminating.

GROUP A

Group A was almost completely destroyed by US attacks. According to locals, the massive **A1**, considered the most important monument at My Son, remained impervious to aerial bombing and was intentionally finished off by a helicopter-borne sapper team. All that remains today is a pile of collapsed brick walls. After the destruction of A1, Philippe Stern, an expert on Cham art and curator of the Guimet Museum in Paris, wrote a letter of protest to US president Nixon, who ordered US forces to continue killing the VC but not to do any further damage to Cham monuments.

A1 was the only Cham sanctuary with two doors. One faced east, in the direction of the Hindu gods; the other faced west towards Groups B, C and D and the spirits of the ancestor kings reputedly buried there. Inside A1 is a stone altar. Among the ruins, some of the brilliant brickwork (typical 10th-century style) is still visible. At the base of A1 on the side facing A10 (decorated in 9th-century style) is a carving of a small worshipping figure flanked by round columns, with a Javanese sea-monster god *(kala-makara)* above.

OTHER GROUPS

Dating from the 8th century, **Group A'** is at present overgrown and inaccessible. Similarly off-limits, **Group G**, which has been damaged by time rather than war, dates from the 12th century. **Group E** was built between the 8th and 11th centuries, while **Group F** dates from the 8th century. Both were badly bombed and parts are propped up by scaffolding. Follow the path towards **K**, a stand-alone small tower, to loop back towards the car park.

Getting There & Away

CAR

My Son is about 50km from Hoi An. A hired car with driver costs US$20 to US$30.

BUS/MINIBUS

Almost every hotel in Hoi An can book a day trip to My Son (US$4 to US$7) with a stop-off at Tra Kieu. The minibuses depart from Hoi An at 8am and return at 1pm. Some agencies offer the option of returning to Hoi An by boat, which adds an extra couple of hours to the trip.

MOTORBIKE

If you've got your own wheels, make sure you park in the official parking area. The starting price of a *xe om* from Hoi An is 120,000d (including waiting time).

TRA KIEU (SIMHAPURA)

Formerly called Simhapura (Lion Citadel), Tra Kieu was the first capital city of Champa and remained so from the 4th century to the 8th century. Today nothing remains of the ancient city except the rectangular ramparts. A large number of artefacts, including some of the finest carvings in the Museum of Cham Sculpture (p237) in Danang, were found here.

Mountain Church

Standing atop Buu Chau Hill, this modern **church** (Nha Tho Nui) was built in 1970 to replace an earlier church destroyed by an American bomb. A Cham tower once stood on this spot. If the church is open, go in to see a wonderful view of the city's outlines and the surrounding countryside.

A quirky stop is the small **shop** at the bottom of the hill which sells Catholic items. The owner has a picture of what Cham-era Tra Kieu might have looked like and some Cham artefacts stacked haphazardly in a corner.

The Mountain Church is 6.5km from Hwy 1A and 19.5km from My Son. In Tra Kieu, it is 200m from the morning **market** (Cho Tra Kieu) and 550m from Tra Kieu Church.

Tra Kieu Church

This 19th-century **church** (Dia So Tra Kieu) is home to a **museum** (Van Hoa Cham) of Cham artefacts, collected by local people and then amassed by a priest from this church. The artefacts are kept in a locked, dusty room on the 2nd floor of the building to the right of the church.

According to local belief this church was the site of a miracle in 1885, witnessed by 80 people. When the Catholic villagers were under attack by anti-French forces, a vision of a lady in white, believed to be Mary, appeared on top of the church. At the end of a 21-day siege during which 500 shells were fired on the village, the church and those who had sheltered in it remained unharmed. While the miracle is not officially recognised by the Catholic church, this is a popular site for Vietnamese pilgrims. The original Mountain Church was built to commemorate this event – although it didn't enjoy such divine protection during the American War.

Tra Kieu Church is 7km from Hwy 1A and 19km from My Son. It is down a street opposite the town's **Clinic of Western Medicine** (Quay Thuoc Tay Y). Follow the signs from the Mountain Church.

Getting There & Away

Many day trips to My Son from Hoi An include a stop-off at Tra Kieu.

CHIEN DAN

The elegant Cham towers at **Chien Dan** (Chien Dan Cham; Hwy 1A; admission 10,000d; 8-11.30am & 1-5.30pm Mon-Fri) are located just outside the town of Tam Ky on a wide open field; the only other building nearby is a small museum. Dating from the 11th or 12th century, each *kalan* faces east. Many of the decorative friezes remain on the outside walls.

The middle tower was dedicated to Shiva; at the front left-hand edge of its base there are carvings of dancing girls and a fight scene. Look for the grinning faces high up between this and the left tower (honouring Brahma) and the two elephants at the rear. The right-hand tower is dedicated to Vishnu.

Although the towers escaped the bombing that ravaged My Son, scars from the American War are evident. The eerie feel of the interior of the middle tower is heightened by the numerous bullet holes in the wall.

The site is to the right of the road on your approach to Tam Ky, 47km south of Hoi An. It can easily be combined with a trip to My Son. Few visitors come here and you'll be pretty much be left to your own devices to poke around for as long as you please.

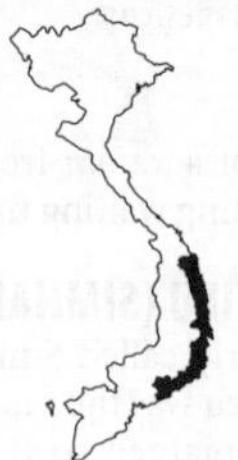

South-Central Coast

Vietnam has an incredibly curvaceous coastline and it is in this region that it is at its most alluring. The country is staking its claim as one of the new coastal meccas in Asia and many of the voluptuous beaches along this stretch are yet to be discovered and developed. Not for long.

Nha Trang and Mui Ne attract the headlines here. Nha Trang is bold and brash, Vietnam's biggest resort with some wonderful offshore islands. Mui Ne is more beguiling, unfurling along one of the most extensive beaches in Vietnam. If your idea of paradise is reclining in front of turquoise waters, weighing up the merits of a massage or a mojito, then you have come to the right place. On hand to complement the sedentary delights are activities to set the pulse racing, including scuba diving, snorkelling, surfing, windsurfing and kitesurfing. Action or inaction, these places bubble with opportunities.

Most visitors never make it beyond these two tourist centres, leaving vast tracts of unexplored coastline with towering cliffs and concealed bays. If adventure and exploration are not your thing, then beat the crowds in style, as there is now a series of ultra-exclusive resorts emerging along the coast.

Those with an eye towards cultural edification will find a wealth of Cham towers and what remains of the Cham population in this region. While not as archaeologically important as the My Son site further north, they're much more accessible and, in many ways, more impressive to the untrained eye.

HIGHLIGHTS

- Surf on sand or water or take off in a new direction with some kitesurfing at the adrenalin capital of the south, **Mui Ne** (p310)
- Crawl your way around the bars of **Nha Trang** (p300) after another tough day lying around on the beach or exploring offshore islands by boat
- Bag a secluded bay to yourself or explore the little-visited vestiges of the Cham kingdom around **Quy Nhon** (p270)
- Forget beach bum, have some beach fun by exploring the blissful **beaches north of Nha Trang** (p278)
- Come face to face with the horrors of war at the poignant **Son My Memorial** (p268)

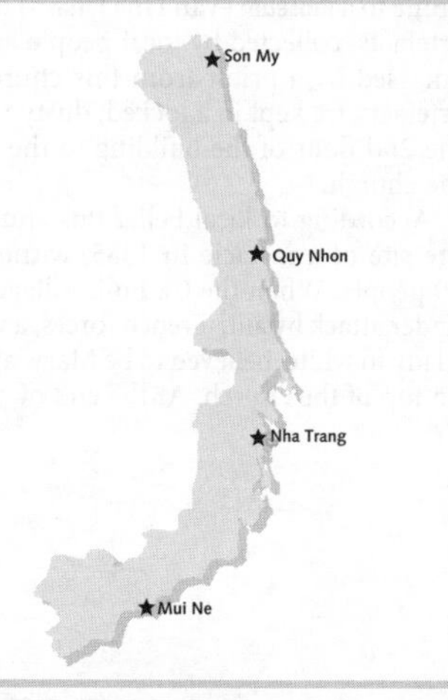

- ELEVATION: 1–1793M
- BEST TIME TO VISIT: FEB–OCT

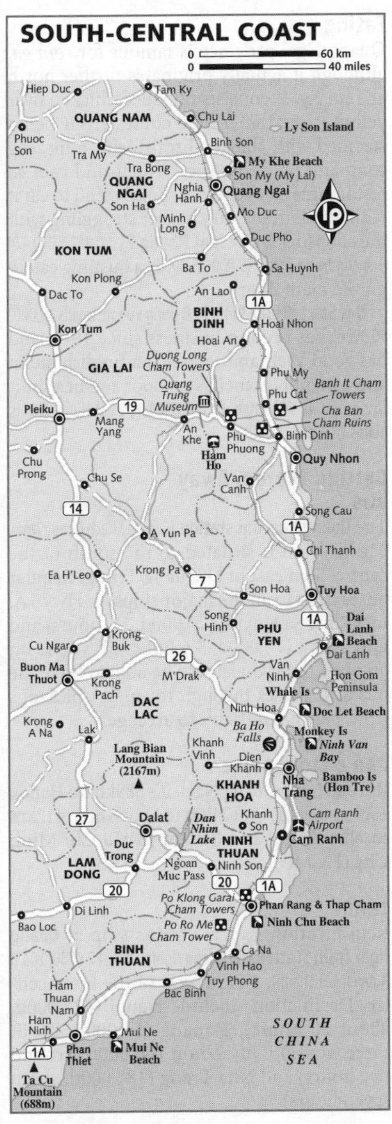

Getting There & Away

Quy Nhon, Tuy Hoa and Cam Ranh, near Nha Trang, have airports, while Danang is a useful air hub to start or finish a trip through this region. The north–south rail route cuts through the region, as does Hwy 1A. Hwy 19, just north of Quy Nhon, links the coast to Pleiku, while Hwy 26 joins Ninh Hoa (north of Nha Trang) to Buon Ma Thuot, and Hwy 20 connects Phan Rang and Dalat. There is also a very handy, and beautiful, direct link between Dalat and Nha Trang, cutting the journey time to just three hours or so.

QUANG NGAI

☎ 055 / pop 134,000

The eponymous capital of Quang Ngai (aka Quang Nhia or Quangai) province only earned city status in 2005, so the impression of a large country town is justified. The city itself offers no obvious attractions, so most visitors only drop by for a spot of grazing at lunchtime. The few travellers that venture here come to pay their respects to the victims of the most famous atrocity of the American War (see p270). Perhaps it's the sombre mood induced by the memorial that has caused tourists to overlook one of Vietnam's less celebrated beaches, a couple of kilometres away.

Even before WWII, Quang Ngai was an important centre of resistance against the French. During the Franco-Viet Minh War, the area was a Viet Minh stronghold. In 1962 the South Vietnamese government introduced its ill-fated Strategic Hamlets Program. Villagers were forcibly removed from their homes and resettled in fortified hamlets, infuriating and alienating the local population and increasing popular support for the Viet Cong. Some of the bitterest fighting of the war took place here.

Orientation

Built on the southern bank of the Tra Khuc River, the city is 15km from the coast. Hwy 1A doubles as the main street Đ Quang Trung as it passes through town. The train station is 1.5km west of the town centre on Đ Hung Vuong.

Information

Deluxe Taxis (☎ 383 8383)

Main post office (☎ 382 2935; 80 Đ Phan Dinh Phung) Internet access available.

Vietcombank (45 Đ Hung Vuong) Branch in the Hung Vuong Hotel with an ATM outside.

Sleeping

Hung Vuong Hotel (☎ 381 8828; 33 Đ Hung Vuong; r 160,000-230,000d; ❄) One of the cheaper spots in town; there is no English spoken here, but the friendly family offers good-value rooms at a fair price. The higher-priced rooms are almost quads.

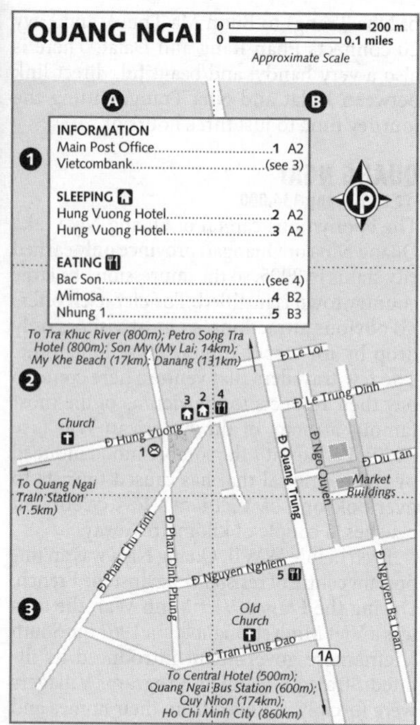

Hung Vuong Hotel (☎ 371 0477; www.hungvuong-hotel.com.vn; 45 Đ Hung Vuong; s/d/tr/ste US$28/35/40/48;) Déjà vu? Yes, it's pretty confusing – there are two hotels on the same street with the same name. This is the more glamorous of the two, although we are talking Quang Ngai glamour here. It has 64 spacious rooms with a reasonable spread of creature comforts.

Petro Song Tra Hotel (☎ 382 2665; www.petrosetco.com.vn; 2 Đ Quang Trung; s US$30-35, d US$35-40, ste US$60-70;) This landmark on the northern edge of town is smarter than it might first appear. Rooms are well decorated and include internet (wired and wireless), plus there's an inviting pool and gym, adding up to good value.

Central Hotel (☎ 382 9999; www.centralhotel.com.vn; 784 Đ Quang Trung; r US$35-150;) At the smartest hotel in town prices have actually dropped as it matures with age, making for a good deal. Standard rooms have shower only, but the VIP rooms have huge bathtubs. Extra touches include free wi-fi, a tennis court and a pool that is verging on Olympic.

If you really feel the urge to stick around for a night, consider staying on the beach at nearby My Khe (opposite).

Eating

Quang Ngai province is famous for *com ga*, although it actually originates further north at Tam Ky. It consists of boiled chicken over yellow rice (the colour comes from being steamed with chicken broth) with mint, egg soup and pickled vegies. You'll find *com ga* restaurants all over town. Locals tend to eat it with a spoon, so don't bother struggling with the chopsticks. Try it at **Nhung 1** (☎ 382 1797; 474 Đ Quang Trung; meals 15,000-25,000d), a bustling eatery on the main drag.

Bac Son (☎ 382 3440; 23 Đ Hung Vuong; mains 20,000-40,000d) has been in business since 1943, and has good Vietnamese food, an English menu and a friendly owner. Next door and in a similar vein is **Mimosa** (☎ 382 2438; 21 Đ Hung Vuong; mains 20,000-40,000d).

Getting There & Away

BUS

The **Quang Ngai bus station** (Ben Xe Khach Quang Ngai; Đ Le Thanh Ton) is situated to the south of the centre, 50m east of Đ Quang Trung. Regular buses head to all the major stops on Hwy 1A, including Sa Huynh (25,000d, 1½ hours) and Quy Nhon (70,000d, 3½ hours). If you're on an open tour you should be able to leave the bus as it passes through town, but pick-ups from here are difficult to arrange.

CAR & MOTORBIKE

By road from Quang Ngai, it's 889km to Hanoi, 100km to Hoi An, 174km to Quy Nhon, 412km to Nha Trang and 860km to Ho Chi Minh City (HCMC).

TRAIN

Reunification Express trains stop at **Quang Ngai Train Station** (Ga Quang Nghia; ☎ 382 0280; 204 Đ Nguyen Chi Thanh), 1.5km west of the town centre. Destinations include Hanoi (428,000d, about 20 hours), Danang (56,000d, about three hours), Quy Nhon (66,000d, around five hours) and Nha Trang (180,000d, about seven hours).

AROUND QUANG NGAI

Son My (My Lai)

It's hard to believe that this tranquil rural spot was the setting for one of the most horrific crimes of the American War. On the morning of 16 March 1968, US troops swept through four hamlets in the Son My subdistrict, killing 504 villagers, many of them elderly and children. The largest mass killing took place in Xom Lang (Thuan Yen) subhamlet, where the **Son My Memorial** (admission 10,000d; 8-11.30am & 1-4.30pm Mon-Fri) now stands. However, it was one of the other hamlets that lent the name the world remembers – the My Lai Massacre.

The memorial is centred on a dramatic stone sculpture of an elderly woman holding up her fist in defiance, a dead child in her arms, surrounded by the injured and dying at her feet. The scene has been recreated to reflect the aftermath of that fateful day. Burnt-out shells of homes stand in their original locations, each marked with a plaque listing the names and ages of the family that once resided there. The concrete connecting the ruins is coloured to represent a dirt path, and indented with the heavy bootprints of American soldiers and the bare footprints of fleeing villagers. However, the overall effect is rather kitsch, making it feel more like a theme park than a memorial for some visitors.

The massacre was painstakingly documented by a US military photographer and these graphic images are now the showcase of a small **museum** on the site. While a distressing experience, the display ends on a hopeful note – chronicling the efforts of the local people to rebuild their lives afterwards. A prominent section honours the GIs who tried to stop the carnage, shielding a group of villagers from certain death, and those responsible for blowing the whistle.

The road to Son My passes through particularly beautiful countryside: rice paddies, cassava patches and vegetable gardens shaded by casuarinas and eucalyptus trees. However, if you look closely you can still make out the odd bomb crater, and the bare tops of hills are testimony to the continuing environmental devastation caused by Agent Orange.

The best way to get to Son My is by motorbike or regular taxi. The return bike trip, including waiting time, will cost about 60,000d. From Quang Ngai head north on Đ Quang Trung (Hwy 1A) and cross the long bridge over the Tra Khuc River. Take the first right (eastward, parallel to the river) where a triangular concrete stela indicates the way and follow the road for 12km. The memorial is just past a small hospital.

My Khe Beach

A world away from the sombre atmosphere of the Son My Memorial, but only a couple of kilometres down the road, My Khe (not to be confused with the other My Khe Beach near Danang) is a superb beach, with fine white sand and clear water. It stretches for kilometres along a long, thin, casuarina-lined spit of sand, separated from the mainland by Song Kinh Giang, a body of water just inland from the beach. The downside is that it has been blighted by litter in the past couple of years. It is to be hoped that the sellers here realise this is a big turn-off before it is too late. Still, if you want a pretty beach largely to yourself, this is one place to come, as most travellers are hotfooting it between Hoi An and Nha Trang.

Find the beach after crossing a bridge 2km further along the road heading past the Son My memorial.

The local commune is hidden away behind a large yellow wall and includes a row of restaurants strung out along the beach. Among them is **My Khe Restaurant** (384 3316; Tinh Khe commune; r 120,000d), offering basic stilt houses to rent, each with its own bathroom, fan and TV. Fresh seafood meals are in the region of 40,000d to 80,000d.

A smart little place, **My Khe Resort** (368 6111; ks_mytra@dng.vnn.vn; Tinh Khe; r US$25-35;) is a good deal, probably down to the fact it gets very few customers. Rooms have satellite TV and free internet access, as well as bathtubs. Breakfast is included at the beachfront restaurant across the road.

There are plenty of other beachfront restaurants to the north of My Khe Resort, although they can be a bit hard-sell. The seafood is fresh and delicious, but agree prices in advance.

SA HUYNH

055

This is a popular stop for lunch on the long road north or south. Approaching the bay, there is a beautiful semicircular beach, but sadly it doesn't look quite so exotic at close quarters due to a surfeit of litter. The little town is also known for its salt marshes and salt-evaporation ponds, as well as a pungent *nuoc mam* (fish sauce) industry. Archaeologists have unearthed remains from the Dong Son civilisation dating from the 1st century AD in the vicinity of Sa Huynh.

Vinh Hotel (386 0385; Hwy 1A; r 120,000d;), a popular restaurant, moonlights in the hotel business, offering eight simple air-con rooms. It's about 1km to the south of the town with

MY LAI MASSACRE

At about 7.30am on 16 March 1968 – after the area had been bombarded with artillery, and the landing zone raked with rocket and machine-gun fire from helicopter gunships – the US Army's Charlie Company landed by helicopter in the west of Son My, regarded as a Viet Cong stronghold. They encountered no resistance during the 'combat-assault', nor did they come under fire at any time during the operation; but as soon as their sweep eastward began, so did the atrocities.

As the soldiers of the 1st Platoon moved through Xom Lang, they shot and bayoneted fleeing villagers, threw hand grenades into houses and bomb shelters, slaughtered livestock and burned dwellings. Somewhere between 75 and 150 unarmed villagers were rounded up and herded to a ditch, where they were executed by machine-gun fire.

In the next few hours, as command helicopters circled overhead and American navy boats patrolled offshore, the 2nd Platoon, the 3rd Platoon and the company headquarters group also became involved in the attacks. At least half a dozen groups of civilians, including women and children, were assembled and executed. Villagers fleeing towards Quang Ngai were shot. As these massacres were taking place, at least four girls and women were raped or gang-raped by groups of soldiers.

According to the memorial here, a total of 504 Vietnamese were killed during the massacre; US army sources determined the total number of dead at 347.

Troops who participated were ordered to keep their mouths shut, but several disobeyed orders and went public with the story after returning to the USA, including helicopter pilot Hugh Thompson Jr who managed to rescue several women and children that fateful day. When it broke in the newspapers it had a devastating effect on the military's morale and fuelled further public protests against the war. It did little to persuade the world that the US Army was fighting on behalf of the Vietnamese people. Unlike WWII veterans, who returned home to parades and glory, soldiers coming home from Vietnam often found themselves ostracised and branded as 'baby killers'.

A cover-up of the atrocities was undertaken at all levels of the US army command, eventually leading to several investigations. Lieutenant William Calley, leader of the 1st Platoon, was court-martialled and found guilty of the murders of 22 unarmed civilians. He was sentenced to life imprisonment in 1971 and spent three years under house arrest at Fort Benning, Georgia, while appealing his conviction. Calley was paroled in 1974 after the US Supreme Court refused to hear his case. Calley's case still causes controversy – many claim that he was made a scapegoat because of his low rank, and that officers much higher up ordered the massacres. What is certain is that he didn't act alone.

For the full story of this event and its aftermath, pick up a copy of *Four Hours in My Lai* by Michael Bilton and Kevin Sim, a stunning piece of journalism.

a little bridge linking it to a quiet section of beach. The seafood restaurant draws a steady crowd thanks to fresh seafood and authentic flavours. Meals cost 30,000d to 80,000d.

Sa Huynh is on Hwy 1A, about 60km south of Quang Ngai (1½ hours by bus) and 114km north of Quy Nhon (two hours by bus). There is no bus station, but it should be easy enough to pick up a passing bus on the highway in either direction. Make sure to agree on a price before you get on. A ticket bought from the bus station at Quang Ngai to Sa Huynh only costs 25,000d. With this as a guide it should only cost about 50,000d to Quy Nhon, although we've heard of people being charged a lot more.

QUY NHON

☎ 056 / pop 260,000

Flanked by beautiful beaches, the surrounding countryside dotted with ancient Cham temples and other overlooked sights, Quy Nhon (Qui Nhon; pronounced 'hwee ngon') has never attracted the numbers it deserves. But this is an attraction in itself, as it is not on the standard tourist trail and the trickle of foreigners will find friendly locals and far fewer hassles than in the more honkytonk beach towns to the south. There are precious few touts, hawkers, beggars, pimps or dealers and it's quite possible to walk down the street without the usual soundtrack of 'Hello. Where you go?'

The capital of Binh Dinh province and one of Vietnam's more active second-string seaports, this is a great spot to sample some fresh seafood. It's perfectly located to break the long journey from Hoi An to Nha Trang, with plenty to keep you occupied for a few days, if lazing around on the beaches isn't enough.

During the American War there was considerable South Vietnamese, US, VC and South Korean military activity in the area. The mayor of Quy Nhon, hoping to cash in on the presence of US troops, turned his official residence into a large massage parlour.

There's a historical connection between Quy Nhon and New Zealand dating back to the early 1960s, when funds and staff from New Zealand were provided to the provincial hospital and later to aid refugees. The strong links continue today, with New Zealand's Volunteer Service Abroad (VSA) involved in projects in health, fisheries management, agriculture and rural development, and the New Zealand Vietnam Health Trust providing training and specialists for the local hospital. At any one time around half of the small expat community in Quy Nhon are Kiwis.

Orientation

Quy Nhon is on the coast, 10km east of Hwy 1A's Phu Tai junction. The main part of town is on an east–west orientated peninsula, shaped like an anteater's nose. The tip of the nose (the port area) is closed to the public. The municipal beach is on the peninsula's south coast, curving around to face east.

Information

Barbara's: The Kiwi Connection (☎ 389 2921; nzbarb@yahoo.com; 19 Đ Xuan Dieu) Free tourist information, bike and motorbike hire, local maps and connections with English-speaking drivers.

Binh Dinh Tourist (☎ 389 2524; fax 891 162; 10 Đ Nguyen Hue) For local tours.

Main post office (☎ 381 2700; 197 Đ Phan Boi Chau; 🕑 6.30am-10pm) Plus cheap internet.

Vietcombank (☎ 382 2266; 148 Đ Le Loi) On the corner of Đ Tran Hung Dao; has a 24-hour ATM. Further ATMs can be found outside the Seagull Hotel (489 Đ An Duong Vuong) and the main post office.

Sights

MUNICIPAL BEACH

The long sweep of Quy Nhon's beachfront extends from the port in the northeast to the hills in the south. It's a beautiful stretch of sand and has been given a major facelift in recent years, making it almost as nice as Nha Trang, but with a fraction of the visitors.

At the top end, the nicest section is near the Kiwi Connection, where a grove of coconut trees lines the road. At dawn and in the evenings this area is packed with locals practising t'ai chi. In the distance you can see a giant **statue of Tran Hung Dao** giving the Chinese the finger on the far headland (see Playing for High Stakes, p141). It is possible to climb the statue if the door is open and peak out through the eyes. Heading south, a striking socialist-realist **war memorial** dominates a small square.

From here, buildings encroach on the waterfront for a kilometre before opening out to a parklike promenade, punctuated by large hotels, stretching to the south end of the bay. Here the beach gets more beautiful and secluded, away from the bustle of town. At night the bright lights of the squid boats give the illusion of a floating town far out to sea.

BINH DINH MUSEUM

This small **museum** (☎ 3822 452; 28 Đ Nguyen Hue; admission free; 🕑 7-11am & 2-5pm Apr-Sep, 7.30-11am & 1.30-4.30pm Oct-Mar) features exhibits on regional history. The entry hall focuses on local communism, including an interesting silk print (by Zuy Nhat, 1959) showing a fat French colonist sitting aloft mandarins, in turn supported by bureaucrats, and cruel bosses, with the struggling masses supporting the whole bunch. The room to the left has a small Natural History section and some Cham statues, while the rear room has the bulk of the excellent Cham collection. The room to the right of the entrance is devoted to the American War, with local relics such as the 'Spittoon of Heroic Vietnamese Mother Huynh Thi Bon'.

THAP DOI CHAM TOWERS

This remarkable pair of **Cham towers** (admission 2000d; 🕑 8-11am & 1-6pm) sits within the city confines in a little park. Steep steps lead up to the former temples, which are open to the sky. Atypically for Cham architecture, they have curved pyramidal roofs rather than the usual terracing. The larger tower (20m tall) retains some of its ornate brickwork and remnants of the granite statuary that once graced its summit. The dismembered torsos of garuda (half human, half bird) can be seen at the corners of the roofs.

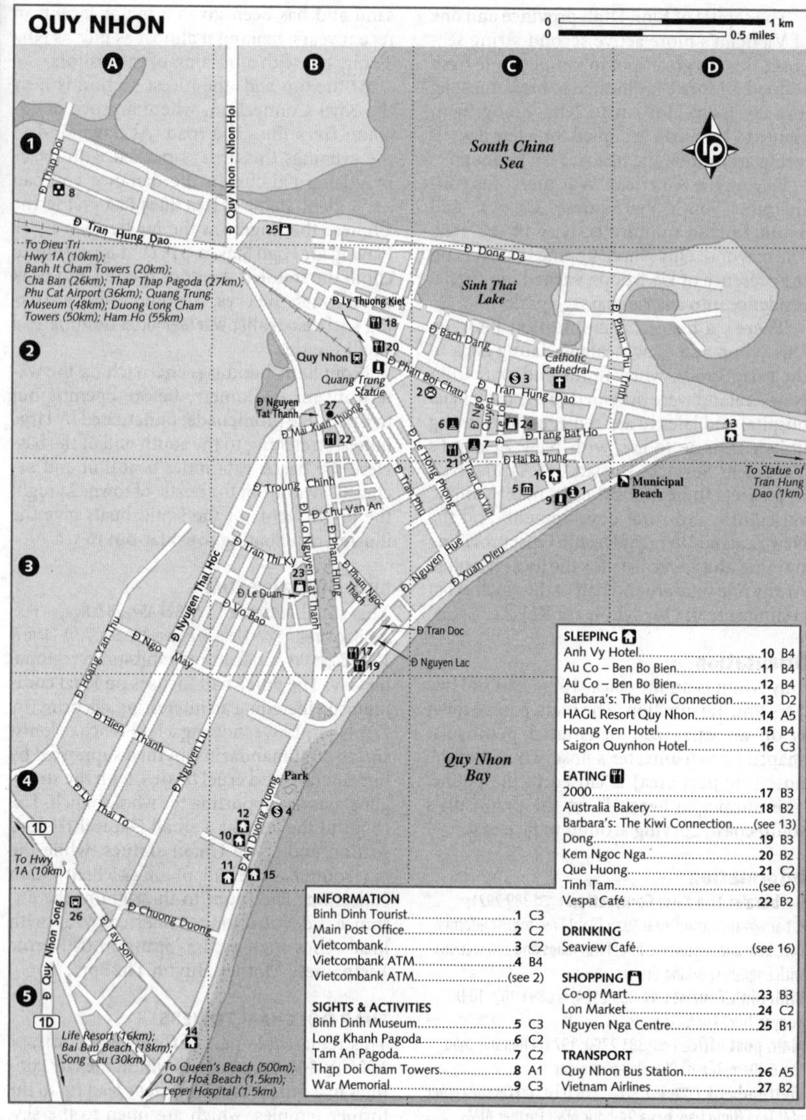

Take Đ Tran Hung Dao west away from the centre and turn right into the lane after number 900 (Đ Thap Doi). The towers are down the first lane on the right.

LONG KHANH PAGODA

It's hard to miss the 17m-high Buddha (built in 1972) heralding Quy Nhon's main pagoda, set back from the road next to 143 Đ Tran Cao Van. The pagoda was founded in 1715 by a Chinese merchant, and the monks who reside here preside over the religious affairs of the city's relatively active Buddhist community.

The pagoda was repaired in 1957 after being damaged during the Franco-Viet Minh War. Mosaic dragons with manes of broken glass lead up to the main building, flanked by towers sheltering a giant drum (on the left) and an enormous bell (right). Inside, in front of the large copper Thich Ca Buddha (with its multicoloured neon halo) is a drawing of multi-armed and multi-eyed Chuan De (the Goddess of Mercy); the numerous arms and eyes symbolise her ability to touch and see all.

TAM AN PAGODA

Quy Nhon's second most active pagoda, **Tam An** (58B Đ Ngo Quyen) is a charming little place that attracts mostly female worshipers, although it's open to all.

Sleeping

Quy Nhon offers great value for midrangers, so it is one destination where you might consider spending a little extra for a lot more comfort.

BUDGET

Barbara's: The Kiwi Connection (☎ 389 2921; nzbarb@yahoo.com; 18 Đ Xuan Dieu; dm 50,000d, r 200,000-300,000d;) There are no-frills dorm beds here for those counting the dong, with shared shower and toilet. The rooms are actually located in a neighbouring mini-hotel called the Lan Anh and aren't great value compared with what is on offer elsewhere.

Anh Vy Hotel (☎ 384 7763; 8 Đ An Duong Vuong; r 120,000-200,000d;) In the south of town near the swish hotel strip, this family-run enterprise has clean rooms with satellite TV and hot-water showers. Some of the upper rooms also include a sea view for anyone willing to tackle the stairs.

Au Co – Ben Bo Bien (☎ 374 7699; hotel_auco@yahoo.com; 8 & 24 Đ An Duong Vuong; r 160,000-300,000d;) Under the same ownership, these two hotels share the same name, one of them confusingly sharing the same street address as the Anh Vy Hotel. The older wing (at number 8) is the slightly more atmospheric of the two – the Vietnamese take on a San Francisco townhouse. Narrow stairs with carved wooden dragons on the balustrades lead to clean rooms with tiny bathrooms but great sea views and balconies. Number 24 is even more kitsch, with fake trees predominating in the lobby.

MIDRANGE & TOP END

HAGL Resort Quy Nhon (☎ 374 7100; www.hagl.com.vn; 1 Đ Han Mac Tu; s US$22-48, d US$25-54, ste US$110;) This is a pretty swanky resort by Quy Nhon standards and the rates are half what they were when it opened, making it an official bargain. It's a huge place with 133 rooms, all equipped with plush furnishings and all the gadgets. Other facilities include an immense pool, a fitness centre, tennis courts and the inevitable massage. There is a nice stretch of sand here, too.

Hoang Yen Hotel (☎ 374 6900; www.hoangyenhotel.com.vn; 5 Đ An Duong Vuong; s US$26-32, d US$28-35;) The smart rooms at this 10-storey pad overlooking the beach in the south of town are a good deal. The trim includes satellite TV and minibar, as well as some heavy Sino-Vietnamese furnishings. Bag a sea view, as the rates aren't much higher.

Saigon Quynhon Hotel (☎ 382 0100; www.saigonquynhonhotel.com.vn; 24 Đ Nguyen Hue; s US$25-50, d US$35-60, ste from US$75;) This place offers a cracking deal for comfort, as the smart, modern rooms include deep-pile carpets and bathrobes. Other facilities include in-room safety boxes, free wi-fi, a small swimming pool and a rooftop bar with serious sea views.

Life Resort (☎ 384 0132; www.life-resorts.com; Ghenh Rang, Bai Dai Beach; r US$132-152, ste US$172;) This gorgeous resort, set on a private beach about 18km south of town, is the most luxurious place in Binh Dinh. A subtle Cham influence pervades the architecture and interior design. The spacious rooms are striking, with stunning open-plan bathrooms. You can indulge in a spa treatment, enjoy t'ai chi on the beach, go snorkelling or take a boat to the resort's little offshore island. The wonderful staff offer friendly service and speak excellent English. The restaurant's food and wine selection is impressive.

Eating & Drinking

Australia Bakery (☎ 382 1071; 543 Đ Tran Hung Dao; meals 5000-20,000d) This new cafe-bakery doubles as a fast-food joint, complete with burgers and fries if you have overdosed on rice.

Tinh Tam (141 Đ Tran Cao Van; mains 10,000-20,000d) Located next to Long Khanh Pagoda, this hole-in-the-wall serves hearty vegetarian meals in basic surrounds.

Vespa Café (☎ 629 2252; 94 Đ Pham Hung; mains 25,000-75,000d) This cool cafe wouldn't look out of place in downtown Saigon. The theme is, unsurprisingly, Vespas and scooters, with creative coffees on the menu and well-presented Vietnamese food. Offering an arty vibe, it's very popular with locals.

Barbara's: The Kiwi Connection (☎ 389 2921; nzbarb@yahoo.com; 19 Đ Xuan Dieu; mains 25,000-75,000d) A popular place for comfort food from home, this place draws a mix of backpackers and expats each night. There are healthy smoothies and international breakfasts, including Kiwi favourites such as French toast with bacon, bananas and maple syrup.

Que Huong (☎ 381 2123; 125 Đ Tang Bat Ho; dishes 30,000-60,000d) Follow the local crowd to this place (set over two floors), which serves everything from seafood to snake. The staff are pretty friendly to foreigners who pass through.

2000 (☎ 381 2787; 1 Đ Tran Doc; dishes 50,000-150,000d; lunch & dinner) At least you won't have to worry about how fresh the seafood is here, as there are tubs and tanks full of live crabs, shrimp and fish downstairs. There is also an upstairs dining area with a balcony if the dinner crowd downstairs is looking rowdy. The seafood hotpots are the stuff of legend.

Dong (☎ 382 4877; 26 Đ Nguyen Lac; dishes 50,000-100,000d; lunch & dinner) In the same backstreet area as 2000, Dong is also popular with the local crowd seeking the bounty of the sea. Check out if fresh scallops are available for an affordable indulgence.

Seaview Café (☎ 382 0100; 24 Đ Nguyen Hue) Set on the 8th floor of the Saigon Quynhon Hotel (p273), this rooftop bar has commanding views over Nha Trang and is worth the diversion for a sundowner. There's also free wi-fi.

Quy Nhon has lots of delicious street food all around the town centre. If you've got a sweet tooth, check out the tasty bakery items and ice cream at **Kem Ngoc Nga** (☎ 382 1562; 326 Đ Phan Boi Chau).

Shopping

Lon Market (Cho Lon, Đ Tang Bat Ho) The famous Lon Market burnt to the ground in December 2006 and plans are afoot to redevelop a new shopping-centre-style market in the coming years. Currently the sellers have set up stalls in the blocks around the old site.

Co-op Mart (☎ 382 1321; 7 Đ Le Duan) This huge shopping complex is officially a supermarket but, like a traditional market, sells a little bit of everything. It's a great place to stock up on treats for a day trip to nearby Cham towers or a long bus ride.

Nguyen Nga Centre (☎ 381 8272; www.nguyennga.org; 91 Đ Dong Da) This shop sells lovely homemade weavings, handicrafts and clothing, with the money going towards running a centre for disabled students. Splashing US$50 here will provide you with a huge swag bag of interesting gifts to take home.

Getting There & Away

AIR

Vietnam Airlines flights link Quy Nhon with HCMC (880,000d) daily. There are daily flights to Danang (880,000d), continuing on to Hanoi (2,060,000d) four times a week.

Vietnam Airlines (☎ 382 5313; 1 Đ Nguyen Tat Thanh) offers a minibus transfer (30,000d) for airline passengers between the office and Phu Cat airport, 36km north of the city.

BUS

Quy Nhon bus station (Ben Xe Khach Quy Nhon; ☎ 384 6246; Đ Tay Son) is on the south side of town. The next major stop north is Quang Ngai (70,000d, 3½ hours), with frequent buses heading on to Danang (80,000d, six hours) and the odd one to Hue (125,000d, nine hours). Heading south there are regular services to Tuy Hoa (60,000d, two hours) and on to Nha Trang (75,000d, five hours), with four heading all the way to HCMC (190,000d, 15 hours).

Quy Nhon is a great access point for the central highlands. There are frequent buses to Pleiku (70,000d, four hours), of which five head on to Kon Tum (85,000d, five hours) and at least one to Buon Ma Thuot (105,000d, seven hours) and Dalat (130,000d, 10 hours).

It is now possible to get a bus all the way to Pakse (250,000d, 20 hours, four per week) in Laos, crossing the border at Bo Y. Lao visas are available here.

CAR & MOTORBIKE

By road from Quy Nhon, it's 677km to HCMC, 238km to Nha Trang, 186km to Pleiku, 198km to Kon Tum, 174km to Quang Ngai and 303km to Danang.

TRAIN

The nearest the Reunification Express trains get to Quy Nhon is Dieu Tri, 10km west of the city. **Quy Nhon train station** (Ga Quy Nhon; ☎ 382 2036; Đ Le Hong Phong) is at the end of a 10km spur off the main north–south track. Only very slow local trains stop here and they are not worth bothering with. It's better to get to/from Dieu Tri by taxi or *xe om* (motorbike taxi) for around 50,000d.

AN AMERICAN WAR VETERAN RETURNS *As told to Josh Krist*

Rod lives in Northern California with his wife, Jean. The couple have travelled all over the world but in 2007 Rod decided to revisit the country where he fought as a young man.

When did you first go to Vietnam? I first knew I was off to 'Nam' as a 20-year-old kid back in '66. I last left the war in 1971.

What was your experience during the war? As an army infantryman, officer and aviator I got to see a lot of the warring country, including the central highlands, the central coast, and too much of the DMZ. I was lucky enough to spend some time with nonmilitary Vietnamese and tribal people – in their space and on their terms. I also spent thousands of hours flying 'slow and low' over what even then was a beautiful piece of the world. I tried to keep my memories of the people and the country separate from the stain of the war.

You've visited countries all over Asia, why not Vietnam until now? I think I was avoiding it. Vietnam made me a different person, for sure. There's the pain of physical wounds, mental pain of losing friends – and memories of pants-peeing fear and gleefully inflicting death. The thought of returning to the sites of these memories brought up new fears. Would I face hatred or guilt, open old wounds, or even sink back into the depression I felt when I left Vietnam and was greeted by an indifferent country?

What was your experience this time? I sought out and found former enemies – they often work for the government. They are now older too. We traded stories, drinks and handshakes with lots of people who seem positive, prospering, and devoid of any ill-will. They were happy to meet me and we were happy to be there; good vibes.

Would you recommend Vietnam to other veterans? Well, it sure is a great tourist destination and it satisfied all the needs of my personal history lessons – and therapy sessions. People there look forward to a future that is far better than their past – a past that for them, and now me, is old history. Yeah, go for it.

Josh Krist is a Lonely Planet author who has contributed to a number of titles including Southeast Asia on a Shoestring.

Tickets for trains departing from Dieu Tri can be purchased at Quy Nhon train station, though if you arrive in Dieu Tri by train, your best bet is to purchase an onward ticket before leaving the station. Ticket prices to destinations include: Danang (142,000d, about six hours), Quang Ngai (66,000d, about three hours), Nha Trang (106,000d, about four hours) and HCMC (303,000d, about 12 hours).

There is also a luxury night-train service, **Golden Trains** (☎ 056-350 1599; www.goldentrains.com.vn). Numbered SN, tickets start from 435,000d for a soft seat and 550,000d for a soft sleeper from Quy Nhon to HCMC (around 12 hours).

AROUND QUY NHON

Beaches

The clarity of the water at the beaches improves considerably once you round the Ganh Rang hill to the south of the town. Several beaches are easily accessible by bicycle.

QUEEN'S BEACH

Popular with locals, this stony little beach at the foot of Ganh Rang was once a favourite holiday spot of Queen Nam Phuong. There's a cafe and great views back over Quy Nhon. To get here, take Đ An Duong Vuong to the far south end of Quy Nhon's beachfront and continue as the road starts to climb. After it crosses a small bridge, turn to the left and head through the gates where you will need to pay the entrance fee (5000d). Follow the path up the hill, keeping to the left where it forks. Queen's Beach is signposted to the left.

QUY HOA BEACH & LEPER HOSPITAL

Leprosy may not conjure up images of fun in the sun, but this really is a lovely spot. As leper hospitals go, this one is highly unusual. Rather than being a depressing place, it's a sort of model village near the seafront, where treated patients live together with their families in small, well-kept houses. Depending on their abilities, the patients work in the rice fields, in fishing, and in repair-oriented businesses or small craft shops – one supported by Handicap International produces prosthetic limbs.

The **hospital grounds** (☎ 364 6343; admission 3000d; ⌚ 8-11.30am & 1.30-4pm) are so well maintained that it looks a bit like a resort, complete with a guitar-shaped pavilion and numerous busts of distinguished and historically important doctors, both Vietnamese and foreign. Fronting the village is **Quy Hoa Beach**, one of the nicer stretches of sand around Quy Nhon and a popular weekend hang-out for the city's expat community. Just up from the beach, there's a dirt path to the hillside **tomb of Han Mac Tu**, a mystical poet who died in 1940.

If travelling by foot or bicycle, continue along the road past Queen's Beach until it descends to the hospital's entrance gates, about 1.5km south of Quy Nhon. It's also accessible from the road to Song Cau by taking a left turn once the water comes back into view after crossing the hills south of town.

BAI BAU BEACH

While the Life Resort charges nonguests US$10 to lounge on their beach (whether they've dined at the restaurant or not), those in the know will head 2km south for an even better beach at a fraction of the price. **Bai Bau** (admission 5000d, deck chair 5000d) is a beautiful white-sand crescent no more than 150m wide, sheltered by rocky headlands, with mountains for a backdrop. It can get busy on the weekend and during Vietnamese holidays, but midweek you'll likely have the place to yourself.

Bai Bau is well signed, just off the road to Song Cau, about 20km south of Quy Nhon.

Cham Sites

The former Cham capital of Cha Ban (also known as Vijay and Quy Nhon) was located 26km north of Quy Nhon and 5km from Binh Dinh. While of archaeological importance, there's not a lot to see for the casual visitor. However, there are several interesting Cham structures dotted around the area.

BANH IT CHAM TOWERS

The most interesting and accessible of the area's Cham sites, this group of four towers sitting atop a hill 20km to the north of Quy Nhon is clearly visible from Hwy 1A. The architecture of each tower is distinctly different, although all were built around the end of the 11th century and the beginning of the 12th. The smaller, barrel-roofed tower has the most intricate carvings, although there's still a wonderfully toothy face looking down on it from the wall of the largest tower. A large Buddhist pagoda sits on the side of the hill under the lowest of the towers. There are great views of the surrounding countryside from the top of the hill.

The **towers** (Phuoc Hiep, Tuy Phuoc district; admission free; 7-11am & 1.30-4.30pm) are easily reached by taking Đ Tran Hung Dao out of town for about 30 minutes, when you'll see the towers in the distance to the right of the road. After the traffic lights joining the main highway, cross the bridge and turn right. Take the left turn heading up the hill to reach the entrance.

DUONG LONG CHAM TOWERS

These **towers** (Binh Hoa, Tay Son district; admission free; 7-11am & 1.30-4.30pm) are harder to find, sitting in the countryside about 50km northwest of Quy Nhon. Dating from the late 12th century, the largest of the three brick towers (24m high) is embellished with granite ornamentation representing *naga* (a mythical serpent being with divine powers) and elephants (Duong Long means 'Towers of Ivory'). Over the doors are bas-reliefs of women, dancers, monsters and various animals. The corners of the structure are formed by enormous dragon heads.

It is best to visit the towers with a driver or a tour, as the site is reached by a succession of pretty country lanes through rice paddies and over rickety bridges.

OTHER TOWERS

Several single towers sprout out of farmland around the area. These are not as well restored as the big sites, and they generally have no gates or admission charges. You'll need an experienced guide and a couple of days to spare if you want to track them all down.

Thu Thien (Binh Nghi, Tay Son district) is not far off Hwy 19, 35km northwest from Quy Nhon, and can easily be combined with a visit to Duong Long and the Quang Trung Museum (below). **Phu Loc** (Nhon Thanh, An Nhon district) translates as 'Gold Tower' and has beautiful views, while **Canh Tien** (Nhon Hau, An Nhon district), built in the 16th century, is named after upturned leaf shapes at the top which are said to resemble fairy wings. **Binh Lam** (Phuoc Hoa, Tuy Phuoc district) sits high on a hill, 22km from Quy Nhon.

Quang Trung Museum

Nguyen Hue, the second-oldest of the three brothers who led the Tay Son Rebellion,

THE LOST CITY OF CHAMPA

Cha Ban, which served as the capital of Champa from the year 1000 (after the loss of Indrapura/Dong Duong) until 1471, was attacked and plundered repeatedly by the Vietnamese, Khmers and Chinese.

In 1044 the Vietnamese prince Phat Ma occupied the city and carried off a great deal of booty along with the Cham king's wives, harem, female dancers, musicians and singers. Cha Ban was under the control of Jayavarman VII and the Khmer empire from 1190 to 1220. In 1377 the Vietnamese were defeated and their king was killed in an attempt to capture Cha Ban. The Vietnamese emperor Le Thanh Ton breached the eastern gate of the city in 1471 and captured the Cham king and 50 members of the royal family. During this, the last great battle fought by the Cham, 60,000 Cham were killed and 30,000 more were taken prisoner by the Vietnamese.

During the Tay Son Rebellion, Cha Ban served as the capital of central Vietnam, and was ruled by the eldest of the three Tay Son brothers. It was attacked in 1793 by the forces of Nguyen Anh (later Emperor Gia Long), but the assault failed. In 1799 they laid siege to the city again, under the command of General Vu Tinh, capturing it at last.

The Tay Son soon reoccupied the port of Thi Nai (modern-day Quy Nhon) and then laid siege to Cha Ban themselves. The siege continued for over a year, and by June 1801, Vu Tinh's provisions were gone. Food was in short supply; all the horses and elephants had long since been eaten. Refusing to consider the ignominy of surrender, Vu Tinh had an octagonal wooden tower constructed. He filled it with gunpowder and, arrayed in his ceremonial robes, went inside and blew himself up. Upon hearing the news of the death of his dedicated general, Nguyen Anh wept.

crowned himself Emperor Quang Trung in 1788. In 1789, Quang Trung led the campaign that overwhelmingly defeated a Chinese invasion of 200,000 troops near Hanoi. This epic battle is still celebrated as one of the greatest triumphs in Vietnamese history.

During his reign, Quang Trung was something of a social reformer. He encouraged land reform, revised the system of taxation, improved the army and emphasised education, opening many schools and encouraging the development of Vietnamese poetry and literature. He died in 1792 at the age of 40. Communist literature portrays him as the leader of a peasant revolution whose progressive policies were crushed by the reactionary Nguyen dynasty, which came to power in 1802 and was overthrown by Ho Chi Minh in 1945.

The **Quang Trung Museum** (Phu Phong; admission 10,000d; ⌚ 8-11.30am & 1-4.30pm Mon-Fri) is built on the site of the brothers' house and encloses the original well and a more-than-200-year-old tamarind tree said to have been planted by the brothers. Displays include various statues, costumes, documents and artefacts from the 18th century, most of them labelled in English. Especially notable are the elephant-skin battle drums and gongs from the Bahnar tribe. The museum is also known for its demonstrations of *vo binh dinh,* a traditional martial art that is performed with a bamboo stick.

The museum is about 50km from Quy Nhon. Take Hwy 19 west for 40km towards Pleiku. The museum is about 5km north of the highway (the turn-off is signposted) in Phu Phong, Tay Son district.

Ham Ho

A beautiful nature reserve 55km from Quy Nhon, **Ham Ho** (☎ 388 0860; Tay Phu; admission 5,000d; ⌚ 7-11.30am & 1-4.30pm) can easily be combined with a trip to the Quang Trung Museum. Taking up a jungle-lined 3km stretch of clean, fish-filled river, the park is best enjoyed by boat (60,000d). The further up river you travel, the better the swimming spots are.

The road to Ham Ho is signposted to the south of Hwy 19 at Tay Son.

Thap Thap Pagoda

This peaceful pagoda in the heart of the countryside was built in the 17th century partly from material stripped from neighbouring Cham towers. It's a lovely piece of Buddhist architecture with a deep verandah surrounded by attractive gardens. Take time to wander through the serene cemetery behind.

To find it, take Hwy 1A for 27km northwest of Quy Nhon. Just past Dong Da village turn left before a small bridge labelled Cau Van Thuan 2 onto a tiny country lane leading to Nhon Hau village.

SONG CAU

☎ 057

The village of Song Cau is an obscure place that you could easily drive past without ever noticing, but nearby is an immense beautiful bay. It makes a good rest stop for tourists doing the Nha Trang–Hoi An run. Song Cau is along a notorious stretch of Hwy 1A dubbed the 'Happy 16 Kilometres' by long-distance truck drivers, named for the 'taxi girls' who ply their trade by the roadside along this stretch.

Song Cau is 170km north of Nha Trang and 30km south of Quy Nhon. Highway buses can drop off and pick up here (with luck). If travelling with your own wheels, take the newly completed coastal road between Song Cau and Quy Nhon; the scenery is stunning, and there are several good beaches en route.

TUY HOA

☎ 057 / pop 165,000

The capital of Phu Yen province, Tuy Hoa (pronounced 'twee hwa') is a friendly little place with a wide, empty beach with coarse golden sand. It's a possible overnight stop to break up a longer journey, especially for cyclists brave enough to tackle Hwy 1A, but most give it a miss.

The few sights the town has are all on hilltops visible from the main highway. There's a huge **seated Buddha** that greets you if you're approaching from the north. To the south of town the **Nhan Cham Tower** is an impressive sight, particularly when it's illuminated at night. The climb to the tower takes you through a small **botanic garden** and is rewarded with great views. On the same hill is a massive white **war memorial**, designed with sails a little like the Sydney Opera House.

Orientation & Information

Hwy 1A forms the western edge of town with the Da Rang River to the south. The main street, Đ Tran Hung Dao, runs several kilometres from the highway to the beach in the east.

Incombank ATM (239 Đ Tran Hung Dao) Opposite the market.

Main post office (cnr Đ Tran Hung Dao & Nguyen Thai) Plus internet access.

Sleeping & Eating

Cong Doan Hotel (☎ 382 3187; 53 Đ Doc Lap; r 160,000d; ❄) With a prime location opposite the beachfront, this hotel is the best choice in town. It can feel eerily deserted at times, but the rooms are smart enough for the rates, with TV and hot-water showers. Bag a sea view, as the hotel is rarely full.

There are plenty more nondescript minihotels and a glut of humble restaurants and street vendors along the main highway and Đ Tran Hung Dao, but it's not the nicest part of town due to the constant rumble of traffic. The best dining is to be had on the beach, where a stretch of seafood shacks and *bia hoi* (draught beer) joints serve fresh seafood. Many charge by the kilogram, so be sure to agree on prices to avoid an expensive surprise.

Getting There & Away

Tuy Hoa has no bus station, but buses tend to stop for fares at the petrol station on Hwy 1A, not far from the Cham tower. There are regular buses to Quy Nhon (60,000d, two hours, 110km) and Nha Trang (70,000d, 3½ hours, 123km).

A stop on the Reunification Express, **Tuy Hoa Train Station** (Ga Tuy Hoa; ☎ 382 3672; 149 Le Trung Kien) is on the road parallel to the highway, north of the main street. Destinations include Danang (160,000d, eight hours) and Nha Trang (48,000d, 2½ hours).

The **Vietnam Airlines** (☎ 382 6508; 353 Đ Tran Hung Dao) office is in the centre of town and the airport is 8km to the south. There are several flights weekly between Tuy Hoa and HCMC (800,000d).

BEACHES NORTH OF NHA TRANG

☎ 058

The coastal drive between Tuy Hoa and Nha Trang on Hwy 1A provides tantalising glimpses of a number of beautiful remote spots, while others are hidden away in the jungle along promontories or on secluded islands. Inspiring accommodation options are limited, but as a day trip there's plenty to discover if you've got your own wheels. Leave behind the guidebook for a day and go exploring. Money-changing facilities and ATMs are thin on the ground here, so plan ahead in Nha Trang or Quy Nhon.

Dai Lanh Beach

Crescent-shaped Dai Lanh Beach has a split personality: a scruffy fishing village occupying the northern end, but yielding to an attractive beach shaded by casuarina trees. About 1km south is a vast sand-dune causeway worth exploring; it connects the mainland to Hon Gom, a mountainous peninsula almost 30km in length. Boats for Whale Island leave from Hom Gom's main village, **Dam Mon**, set on a sheltered bay.

It's possible to stay overnight under the trees right on Dai Lanh Beach if comfort isn't a concern. **Thuy Ta Restaurant** (☎ 384 2117; tents 20,000d, r 80,000-150,000d) has tents, as well as some very rustic straw-roof beach bungalows, with brick floors, fans and shared toilets. Fresh seafood features prominently on the menu with mains from 30,000d to 60,000d. Keep a close eye on your gear, as there have been some reports of theft.

Dai Lanh is situated 40km south of Tuy Hoa and 83km north of Nha Trang on Hwy 1A. Any highway buses can drop you here and there's a local train station.

Whale Island

Whale Island is a tiny speck on the map and home to the romantic and secluded **Whale Island Resort** (☎ 384 0501; www.whaleislandresort.com; s/d from US$69/79), just a 15-minute boat ride from Dam Mon (above). Resort rates have dropped in recent years and include three hearty meals a day. However, prices no longer include transfers, which are separately priced on the website – a bus-boat combination from Nha Trang costs US$35 per person. The bungalows are atmospheric, but quite basic for the price, as you are really paying for the idyllic location.

Rainbow Divers has a permanent base on the island, and the Nha Trang office (see p295) can make resort bookings and help with transfers. Scuba-diving season ends in mid-October, starting up again in mid-February. Dynamite fishing used to be a real problem in this area, but environmental protection efforts, such as the transplanting of sea coral on to concrete pillars, have brought about a marked increase in the number of marine species – from 40 to around 200.

Doc Let Beach

This lovely stretch of beachfront is tourist-brochure material, with chalk-white sand and shallow waters. Doc Let (pronounced yop lek) is easily accessible from Nha Trang and worth considering as a day trip (beach entrance fee 10,000d) or overnight stop. Although there's a small town nearby, the resorts on the beach are fairly isolated. If you're staying here, be prepared to do nothing but lounge around.

SLEEPING

Jungle Beach (☎ 366 2384; r 350,000d) Just as you were thinking that Vietnam was too conservative to deliver the hippy-trippy vibe of Thailand or Goa, along comes Jungle Beach. It's hard to find, but some say harder to leave, despite the very basic accommodation, which involves camping in the garden or opting for a beachfront lean-to with only rattan blinds for privacy. All meals are included in the price, adding to the atmosphere of a commune where it is all about relaxing. Given the obscure location, it makes sense to come with a *xe om* or taxi driver. No, not to stay with you, just to show you the way.

Paradise Resort (☎ 367 0480; www.vngold.com/doclet/paradise; bungalows s US$20-25, d US$30-35, apt US$60; ⊠ 🖳) This chilled-out retreat is popular with travellers seeking to escape the 24-hour party people of Nha Trang. Set in the quiet village of Dom Hai where the beach is less developed, this French-run place offers accommodation in basic beach-view huts or more upmarket (and air-conditioned) apartments. Prices include three meals a day and free water, tea, coffee and fruits. Follow the blue signs past the turn-off for Doc Let Resort for 2km, turning right at a petrol station and then right again halfway through the village.

White Sand Doclet Resort & Spa (☎ 367 0670; www.whitesandresort.com.vn; r US$75-80, bungalows US$90-130; ⊠ 🖳 ⊠) This is a pretty swanky place, offering tastefully decorated rooms complete with everything from bathrobes to a safety box. All bungalows front the beach, but the fancier ones include a massive TV and DVD player. Rooms are in the low-slung hotel overlooking the pool.

Ki-em Art House (☎ 367 0952; www.ki-em.com; bungalows US$140-180; ⊠ 🖳 ⊠) Set in the grounds of a stunning Vietnamese-German artist's retreat, this is boutique with a capital B. The elegant bungalows are lovingly decorated with works of art and feature lumber four-poster beds, all set amid a gorgeous garden that faces a lovely tropical beach. Other features include an antique museum and art gallery, with works of art produced by the owner. It is not far from Paradise near Dom Hai village.

Wild Beach Resort (☎ 367 0952; www.wildbeachresort.com; r US$149-199, ste from US$349; ⊠ 🖳 ⊠) A newer luxury resort on Doc Let, although website specials suggest it needs more punters.

GETTING THERE & AWAY

Head 35km north of Nha Trang on Hwy 1A, turning right (east) about 4km past Ninh Hoa where there is a big sign for the Hyundai Port. Turn right and continue for 10km past photogenic salt fields, looking out for the signs to the resorts (except Jungle Beach). Make a left turn to take you through Doc Let village and then a right to the beach. There is no public transport, but tour operators in Nha Trang offer day trips often coupled with Monkey Island. Most of the hotels and resorts also offer some sort of transfer service for a fee.

Ninh Van Bay

Welcome to an alternate reality populated by European royalty, film stars and the otherwise rich and secretive. Sadly for the average Joe, this place doesn't really exist. Occupying a secluded beach at the end of a dense jungle-covered peninsula, there are no roads to the unique home of **Evason Hideaway & Six Senses Spa at Ana Mandara** (☎ 372 8222; www.sixsenses.com; villas US$734-2401;). The resort is so sophisticated, it even has its own time zone – setting the clocks an hour ahead in an effort to encourage guests to enjoy the sunrise. The traditionally inspired architecture and the winding paths between buildings give the illusion of a jungle village – albeit one where every dwelling is an elegant two-storey villa, each with its own swimming pool and round-the-clock butler service. As you would expect for the price, the detail is superb and the setting is simply magical.

NHA TRANG

☎ 058 / pop 315,200

Welcome to the beach capital of Vietnam. It may not be a charmer like Mui Ne or a historic jewel like Hoi An, but there is a certain something about Nha Trang that just keeps them coming back for more. For most it is the beautiful beach, the best municipal stretch of sand in the country, while the offshore islands add to the appeal, offering decadent boat trips on the water and some of Vietnam's best diving under it.

The setting is stunning, with towering mountains looming up behind the city and the sweeping beach stretching into the distance, the turquoise waters dotted with little islands. The beachfront has been given a huge makeover in recent years, with parks and sculpture gardens spread along the shorefront, although by night it still reverts to a bit of a circus with motorbike drivers doubling as pimps and dealers, and kamikaze hookers hoping to relieve drunken tourists of their remaining dong.

Nha Trang is a study in contrasts, as the main city is still a bustling Vietnamese entity, buzzing along oblivious to the tourist crowds lining the shore. Hugging the coast for a few blocks is a fully-fledged international resort, complete with high-rise hotels, souvenir shops, stylish restaurants and sophisticated bars. This part of town, complete with a newly built Sheraton and Novotel, could be anywhere in the world, but the steady soundtrack of *xe om* drivers will soon bring you back to the Vietnamese reality.

It is not only the blissful beaches and glorious coastline that define Nha Trang. It also offers some of the best dining beyond Hanoi and Saigon, with a bounty from the sea and an array of international flavours. As the restaurants wind down, the nightlife cranks up, as Nha Trang is a party town at heart, like any self-respecting resort should be. Forget the curfews of the capital; people play late in this town.

If cocktails and shooters aren't your flavour, there are some more sedate activities on offer beyond the waters. Try an old-school spa treatment with a visit to a mud bath or explore centuries-old Cham towers still standing in the centre of town. Or throw culture to the wind and experience Vinpearl Land, Nha Trang's attempt at Disneyworld. Nha Trang has something for everyone.

This part of the country has its very own microclimate and the rains tend to come from October until December, a time best avoided if you are into lazing on the beach or diving in crystal-clear waters.

Orientation

The main coastal boulevard, Đ Tran Phu, runs alongside the beautiful beach and is flanked by major hotels and restaurants, as well as the odd restaurant and resort on the beachside. To the south it eventually hits the port area of Nha Trang, the embarkation point for boat trips to the offshore islands or a cable car to Vinpearl Land. To the north it eventually hits the Hon Chong promontory, a popular local beach.

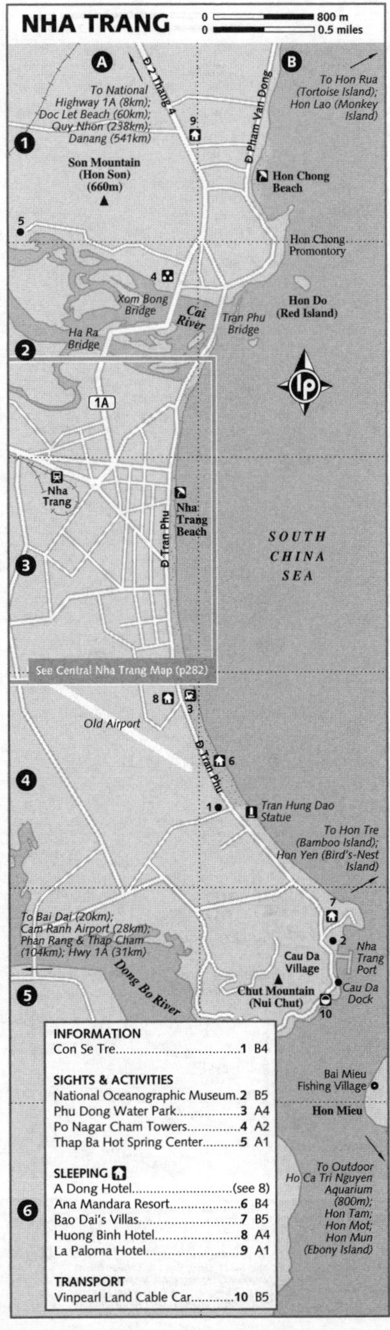

Most of the popular restaurants and bars, plus many of the best-value budget and mid-range hotels, are located on a square block of streets that include Đ Trang Quang Khai and Đ Biet Thu, both intersected by Đ Nguyen Thien Thuat. The airport is now located at Cam Ranh, about 30km south of town, while the railway station is in the centre on Đ Thai Nguyen.

Information

INTERNET ACCESS

Nha Trang has dozens of designated internet cafes all over town, and you can also get online in most hotels and travellers cafes. Loads of places now offer wi-fi: search for a network on Đ Trang Quang Khai or Đ Biet Thu and you'll be overwhelmed with options.

MEDICAL SERVICES

Pasteur Institute (Map p282; ☎ 382 2355; 10 Đ Tran Phu) Offers medical consultations and vaccinations. See p293.

MONEY

There are ATMs all over Nha Trang. **Vietcombank** (Map p282; ☎ 382 2720; 17 Đ Quang Trung; ⏲ Mon-Fri) changes travellers cheques and offers cash advances. There is a handy **Vietcombank ATM** (Map p282; 4 Đ Le Loi) outside the main post office and another **Vietcombank ATM** (Map p282; 60 Đ Tran Phu) outside the Que Huong Hotel. Yet another is located on the junction of Đ Hung Vuong and Đ Nguyen Thi Minh Khai.

POST

Main post office (Map p282; ☎ 382 3866; 4 Đ Le Loi; ⏲ 6.30am-10pm)

Post office branches Đ Le Thanh Ton (Map p282; ☎ 365 2070; 50 Đ Le Thanh Ton; ⏲ 7am-11pm); Đ Tran Quang Khai (Map p282; ☎ 352 2099; 1/29 Đ Tran Quang Khai)

TRAVEL AGENCIES

Highland Tours (Map p282; ☎ 352 4477; www.highlandtourstravel.com; 17B Đ Hung Vuong) Fun boat trips off the coast, plus an extensive program of affordable tours in the central highlands.

Khanh Hoa Tours (Map p282; ☎ 352 6753; khtourism@dng.vnn.vn; 1 Đ Tran Hung Dao) Government-run provincial tourism company with various tour programs, including boat trips.

Mama Linh's Boat Tours (Map p282; ☎ 352 2844; mamalinhvn@yahoo.com; 23C Đ Biet Thu) Known for its boat tours, Mama Linh's can also arrange trips around the province and into the highlands.

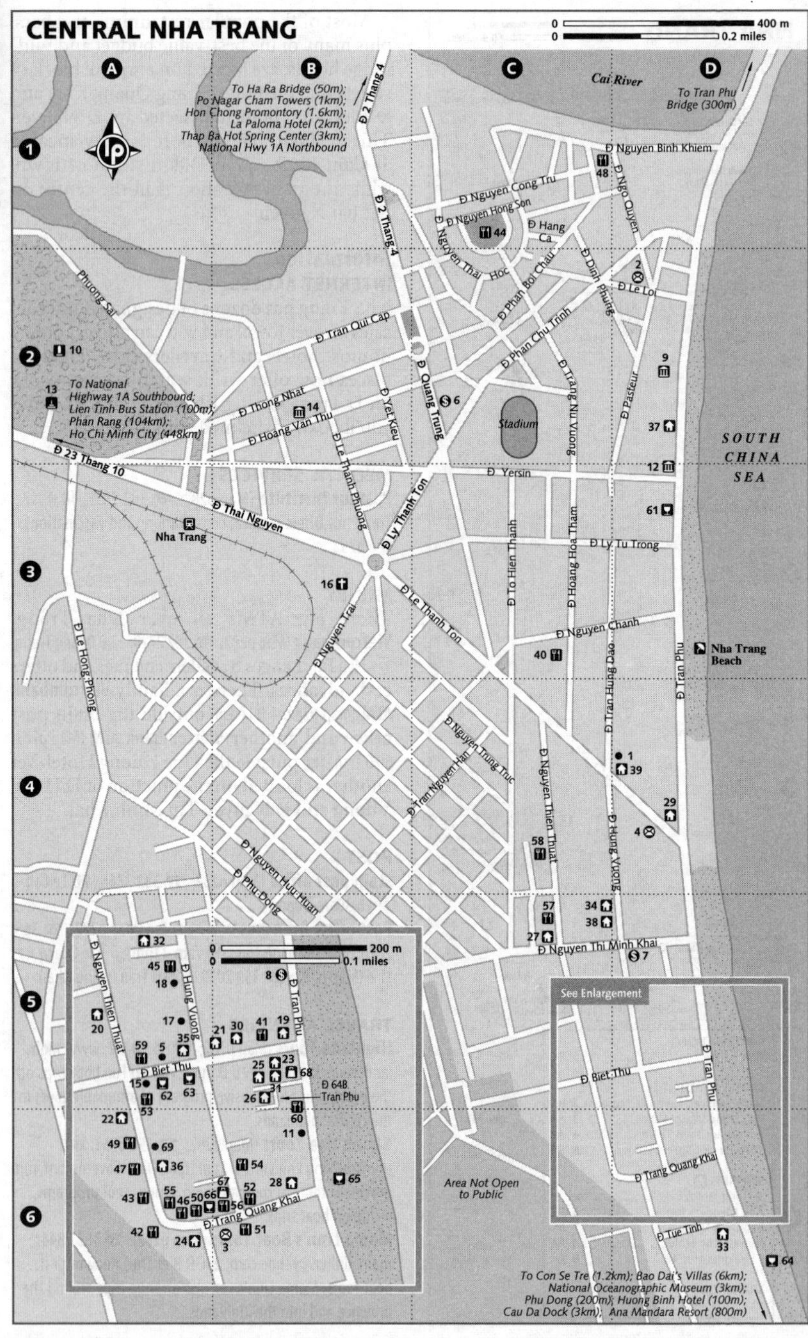
CENTRAL NHA TRANG
0 400 m
0 0.2 miles
To Ha Ra Bridge (50m); Po Nagar Cham Towers (1km); Hon Chong Promontory (1.6km); La Paloma Hotel (2km); Thap Ba Hot Spring Center (3km); National Hwy 1A Northbound
Cai River
To Tran Phu Bridge (300m)
Đ Nguyen Binh Khiem
Đ Nguyen Cong Tru
Đ Nguyen Hong Son
Đ Hang Ca
Đ Ngo Quyen
Đ Nguyen Thai Hoc
Đ Phan Boi Chau
Đ Dinh Phung
Đ Le Loi
Đ 2 Thang 4
Phuong Sai
Đ Tran Qui Cap
Đ Phan Chu Trinh
Đ Quang Trung
Đ Trang Nu Vuong
Đ Pasteur
To National Highway 1A Southbound; Lien Tinh Bus Station (100m); Phan Rang (104km); Ho Chi Minh City (448km)
Đ Thong Nhat
Đ Hoang Van Thu
Đ Yet Kieu
Stadium
SOUTH CHINA SEA
Đ 23 Thang 10
Đ Le Thanh Phuong
Đ Yersin
Đ Thai Nguyen
Đ Ly Thanh Ton
Nha Trang
Đ Ly Tu Trong
Đ To Hien Thanh
Đ Hoang Hoa Tham
Đ Le Thanh Ton
Đ Nguyen Trai
Đ Le Hong Phong
Đ Nguyen Chanh
Nha Trang Beach
Đ Tran Hung Dao
Đ Tran Phu
Đ Nguyen Trung Truc
Đ Tran Nguyen Han
Đ Nguyen Thien Thuat
Đ Hung Vuong
Đ Nguyen Huu Huan
Đ Phu Dong
Đ Nguyen Thi Minh Khai
0 200 m
0 0.1 miles
Đ Biet Thu
Đ 64B Tran Phu
Đ Trang Quang Khai
See Enlargement
Area Not Open to Public
Đ Tue Tinh
To Con Se Tre (1.2km); Bao Dai's Villas (6km); National Oceanographic Museum (3km); Phu Dong (200m); Huong Binh Hotel (100m); Cau Da Dock (3km); Ana Mandara Resort (800m)

INFORMATION

Highland Tours (see 22)
Khanh Hoa Tours 1 D4
Main Post Office 2 D2
Pasteur Institute (see 9)
Post Office 3 B6
Post Office 4 D4
Sinh Café 5 A5
Vietcombank 6 C2
Vietcombank ATM 7 D5
Vietcombank ATM 8 B5
Vietcombank ATM (see 2)

SIGHTS & ACTIVITIES

Alexandre Yersin Museum 9 D2
Buddha 10 A2
Deep Blue Diving 11 B6
Khanh Hoa Museum 12 D3
Long Son Pagoda 13 A2
Long Thanh Gallery 14 B2
Mama Linh's Boat Tours 15 A5
Nha Trang Cathedral 16 B3
Rainbow Divers 17 A5
Sailing Club Divers (see 65)
Su Spa (see 69)
Vietnam Explorer 18 A5
Waves Watersports (see 64)

SLEEPING

62 Tran Phu Hotel 19 B5
AP Hotel 20 A5
Asia Paradise Hotel 21 B5
Backpacker's House 22 A6
Blue Star Hotel 23 B5
Ha Van Hotel 24 A6
Hotel An Hoa 25 B5
Hotel Nhi Hang 26 B5
La Suisse Hotel (see 24)
My Long Hotel 27 C5
Nha Trang Beach Lodge 28 B6
Nha Trang Lodge Hotel 29 D4
Perfume Grass Inn 30 B5
Pho Bien 31 B5
Phong Lan Hotel 32 A5
Phu Quy 2 Hotel 33 D6
Phu Quy Hotel 34 C5
Rainbow Hotel 35 A5
Sao Mai Hotel 36 A6
Sunrise Beach Resort 37 D2
T78 Guesthouse 38 C5
Vien Dong Hotel 39 D4

EATING

Au Lac 40 C3
Bo De (see 40)
Café des Amis 41 B5
Cyclo Café 42 A6
Da Fernando 43 A6
Dam Market 44 C1
El Coyote 45 A5
Gia 46 A6
La Mancha 47 A6
La Taverna (see 55)
Lac Canh Restaurant 48 C1
Lanterns 49 A6
Le Petit Bistro 50 A6
Louisiane Brewhouse (see 64)
Mai Anh 51 B6
Mecca 52 B6
Omar's Tandoori Cafe 53 A5
Pho Cali 54 B6
Same Same But Different Café 55 A6
Something Fishy 56 B6
T2 Sushi Bar 57 C5
Thanh Thanh Cafe 58 C4
Truc Linh 2 59 A5
Veranda 60 B5

DRINKING

City View Café 61 D3
Crazy Kim Bar 62 A5
Crazy Kim Spa & Gym (see 23)
Guava 63 A5
Louisiane Brewhouse 64 D6
Red Apple Club (see 22)
Sailing Club 65 B6
Sailing Club (see 65)
Shamrock Bar (see 22)
Why Not Bar? 66 A6

SHOPPING

A Mart (see 63)
My Village 67 B6
XQ 68 B5

TRANSPORT

Vietnam Airlines 69 A6

Sinh Café (Map p282; ☎ 352 4329; sinhcafent@dng.vnn.vn; 10 Đ Biet Thu) Offers cheap local tours as well as open-tour buses.

Dangers & Annoyances

In Nha Trang there are many ways for you and your money to part company. We've heard reports of thefts on the beach (pickpockets, and jewellery disappearing during an embrace), during massages (a third person sneaks into the room and removes money from clothes) and from hotel rooms (none of those included in this book, but you should still be cautious). Don't carry too much on you, and consider leaving surplus cash at the hotel reception. That way the hotel is responsible if it goes missing, although even this may not protect you from unscrupulous operators. Drive-by bag snatching is on the rise, which can be highly dangerous if you fall victim while on the back of *xe om*. There are also some stories of gangs of youths using tasers around the beachfront at night to stun people before robbing them.

Some female tourists have reported being photographed by young Vietnamese males when emerging from the water or just lying on the beach. These guys are quite blatant about it and are rather persistent.

At tourist sites unobservant foreigners may be overcharged – check the price on pre-printed tickets, check your change and don't get stung for bicycle or motorbike parking.

Sights

NHA TRANG BEACH

The clear turquoise waters of Nha Trang's 6km beach are best enjoyed during the dry season – from June to early October. During heavy rains, run-off from the rivers at each end of the beach flows into the bay, gradually turning it a murky brown. Most of the year, however, the water is as it appears in the tourist brochures. Even in the wettest months, rain usually falls only at night or in the morning. The best beach weather is generally before 1pm; the afternoon sea breezes can make things unpleasant until the wind dies back down after dark.

Beach chairs are available for rent where you can sit and enjoy the drinks, light food or massages that the beach vendors offer. About the only time you'll need to move is to use the toilet or when the tide comes up. The two most popular lounging spots are the Sailing Club and Louisiane Brewhouse.

PO NAGAR CHAM TOWERS

The Cham towers of **Po Nagar** (Thap Ba; Lady of the City; Map p281; admission 10,500d; 6am-6pm) were built between the 7th and 12th centuries, although the site was first used for worship as early as the 2nd century AD. To this day Cham, ethnic Chinese and Vietnamese Buddhists come to Po Nagar to pray and make offerings, according to their respective traditions. This site has a continuing religious significance, so be sure to remove your shoes before entering.

The towers serve as the Holy See, honouring Yang Ino Po Nagar, the goddess of the Dua (Liu) clan, which ruled over the southern part of the Cham kingdom covering Kauthara and Pan Duranga (present-day Khanh Hoa and Thuan Hai provinces). The original wooden structure was razed to the ground by attacking Javanese in AD 774 but was replaced by a stone-and-brick temple (the first of its kind) in 784. There are inscribed stone slabs scattered throughout the complex, most of which relate to history or religion and provide insight into the spiritual life and social structure of the Cham.

Originally the complex covered an area of 500 sq metres and there were seven or eight towers; four towers remain. All of the temples face east, as did the original entrance to the complex, which is to the right as you ascend the hillock. In centuries past, a person coming to pray passed through the pillared meditation hall, 10 pillars of which can still be seen, before proceeding up the steep staircase to the towers.

The 28m-high **North Tower** (Thap Chinh), with its terraced pyramidal roof, vaulted interior masonry and vestibule, is a superb example of Cham architecture. One of the tallest Cham towers, it was built in 817 after the original temples here were sacked and burned. The raiders also carried off a *linga* (stylised phallus venerated by Hindus) made of precious metal. In 918, King Indravarman III placed a gold *mukha-linga* (carved phallus with a human face painted on it) in the North Tower, but it too was taken, this time by the Khmers. This pattern of statues being destroyed or stolen and then replaced continued until 965, when King Jaya Indravarman IV replaced the gold *mukha-linga* with the stone figure, Uma (*shakti*, or female consort of Shiva), which remains to this day.

Above the entrance to the North Tower, two musicians, one of whose feet is on the head of the bull Nandin, flank a dancing four-armed Shiva. The sandstone doorposts are covered with inscriptions, as are parts of the walls of the vestibule. A gong and a drum stand under the pyramid-shaped ceiling of the antechamber. In the 28m-high pyramidal main chamber, there is a black-stone statue of the goddess Uma with 10 arms, two of which are hidden under her vest; she is seated and leaning back against some sort of monstrous animal.

The **Central Tower** (Thap Nam) was built partly of recycled bricks in the 12th century on the site of a structure dating from the 7th century. It is less finely constructed than the other towers and has little ornamentation; the pyramidal roof lacks terracing or pilasters, although the interior altars were once covered with silver. There is a *linga* inside the main chamber.

The **South Tower** (Mieu Dong Nam), at one time dedicated to Sandhaka (Shiva), still shelters a *linga*, while the richly ornamented **Northwest Tower** (Thap Tay Bac) was originally dedicated to Ganesh. To the rear of the complex is a less impressive **museum** with a few examples of Cham stonework; the explanatory signs are in Vietnamese only.

The towers of Po Nagar stand on a granite knoll 2km north of central Nha Trang on the banks of the Cai River. To get here from central Nha Trang, take Đ Quang Trung (which becomes Đ 2 Thang 4) north across the Ha Ra and Xom Bong Bridges. Po Nagar can also be reached via the new Tran Phu Bridge along the beachfront road.

LONG SON PAGODA

This striking **pagoda** (Map p282; 7.30-11.30am & 1.30-8pm) was founded in the late 19th century and has been rebuilt several times over the years. The entrance and roofs are decorated with mosaic dragons constructed of glass and bits of ceramic tile. The main sanctuary is a hall adorned with modern interpretations of traditional motifs. Note the ferocious nose hairs on the colourful dragons wrapped around the pillars on either side of the main altar.

At the top of the hill, behind the pagoda, is a huge white **Buddha** (Kim Than Phat To) seated on a lotus blossom and visible from all over the city. Around the statue's base are fire-ringed relief busts of Thich Quang Duc and six other

(Continued on page 293)

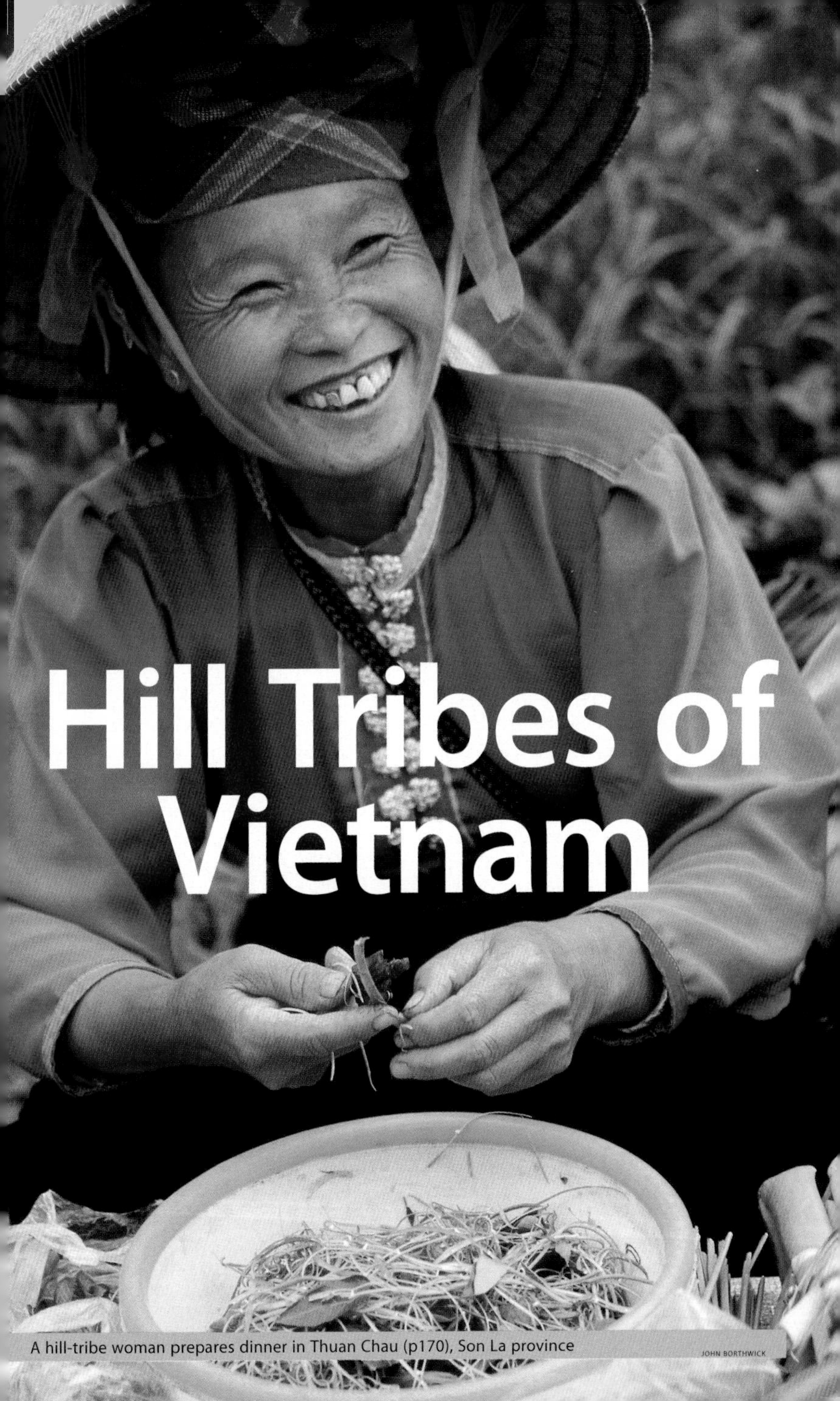

Hill Tribes of Vietnam

A hill-tribe woman prepares dinner in Thuan Chau (p170), Son La province

JOHN BORTHWICK

Commonly known as 'hill tribes', a mosaic of ethnic minorities inhabits the mountainous regions of Vietnam. Encountering these hardy people in their mystical mountain homeland is undoubtedly one of the highlights of a visit to Vietnam. Many of the minorities wear incredible costumes, with some so elaborate that it's easy to believe minority girls learn to embroider before they can walk.

The French called these ethnic minorities Montagnards ('highlanders' or 'mountain people') and this term is still used today. Ethnic Vietnamese traditionally referred to them as *moi*, a somewhat derogatory term meaning savages, which reflects all too common attitudes among many lowland Vietnamese. The current government prefers the term 'national minorities', of which there are more than 15 separate groups.

The most colourful of these minorities live in the far north of Vietnam, carving an existence out of the lush mountain landscapes along the Chinese and Lao borders. Many of the minorities in the central highlands can be difficult to distinguish, at least by dress, from other Vietnamese.

While some of these minorities number as many as a million people, it is feared that other groups have dwindled to as few as 100. Some hill-tribe groups have lived in Vietnam for thousands of years, while others migrated south from China in the past few hundred years. In some ways they are 'fourth world' people in that they belong neither to the first-world powers nor to the developing nations. Rather, they have crossed national borders, often fleeing oppression by other cultures, without regard for recent statehood. The areas inhabited by each group are often delineated by altitude, with more recent arrivals settling higher up. First come, first served even applies to the remote mountains.

Each hill tribe has its own language, customs, mode of dress and spiritual beliefs. Language and culture constitute the borders of their world. Some groups are caught between medieval and modern worlds, while others have assimilated into modern life.

Most groups share a rural, agricultural lifestyle with similar village architecture and traditional rituals. The majority are seminomadic, and cultivate their crops using slash-and-burn methods. The government has been trying to encourage the hill tribes to adopt standard agriculture at lower altitudes, including wet-rice agriculture or tea and coffee, with incentives such as subsidised irrigation, better education and health care. However the hill tribes' long history of independence and a general distrust of the ethnic-Vietnamese majority keep many away from the lowlands.

As in other parts of Asia, the traditional culture of the ethnic minorities is gradually giving way to outside influences. Many no

KHAU VAI LOVE MARKET: SPEED DATING FOR THE MINORITIES

Scenery aside, one of the major drawcards in Ha Giang (p187) is the annual love market of Khau Vai. Forget the weekly jamboree in Sapa, this love market takes place but once a year and draws H'mong, Dzao and Tay from all over the region.

The love market is speed dating minority style. The good folk of Khau Vai have been husband- and wife-swapping for almost 100 years. Youngsters come to find a mate, and old flames fan the dying embers of a lost passion.

It takes place on the 27th day of the 3rd lunar month. For those of us who don't know our dogs from our dragons, it's usually sometime from late April to mid-May, essentially three months after Tet (Vietnamese New Year). Khau Vai is about 20km southeast of Meo Vac.

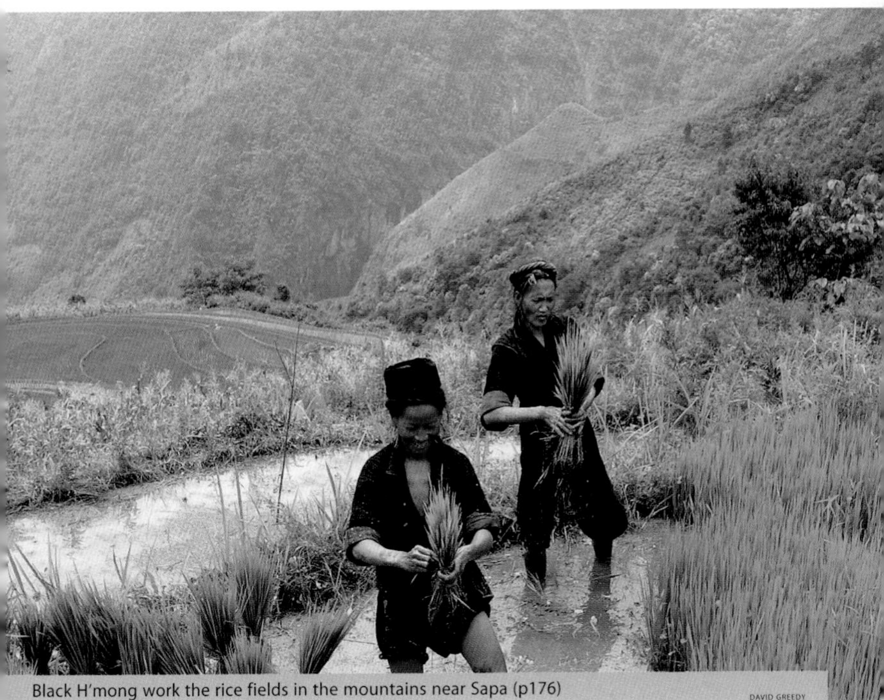

Black H'mong work the rice fields in the mountains near Sapa (p176) DAVID GREEDY

longer dress in traditional clothing and those who do are often found only in the remote villages of the far north. Often it is the women of the community who keep the costume alive, weaving the traditional clothes and passing the knowledge on to their daughters.

A more recent outside influence is tourism. With growing numbers of people travelling to see the different ethnic minorities, increased exposure to business-savvy lowlanders and ever greater commercialism, it is a situation that could get worse before it gets better. It has resulted in some children, particularly in Sapa, expecting hand outs of money or sweets. Worse, domestic tourism has created a market for karaoke, massage and sex, and in some areas unscrupulous ethnic Vietnamese are luring minority women into this trade.

Vietnam's hill-tribe minorities have some autonomy and, though the official national language is Vietnamese, children can still learn their local languages, (see p530 for useful phrases), although this has been a sensitive issue in parts of the central highlands.

While there may be no official discrimination system, cultural prejudice against hill-tribe people helps ensure they remain at the bottom of the educational and economic ladder. Despite improvements in rural schooling and regional healthcare, many minority people marry young, have large families and die early. Put simply, life is a struggle for most of the minority people.

Here we profile some of the better known minority groups in Vietnam, including those that many visitors will encounter on a journey into the mountains.

THE ETHNIC MOSAIC

Bahnar

The Bahnar (population 135,000) are believed to have migrated long ago to the central highlands (p206) from the coast. They are animists and worship trees such as the banyan and ficus. The Bahnar keep their own traditional calendar, which calls for 10 months of cultivation, with the remaining two months set aside for social and personal duties, such as marriage, weaving, ceremonies and festivals. Traditionally when babies reached one month of age, a ceremony was held in which their lobes were pierced to make them a member of the village. Those who died without such holes were believed to be taken to a land of monkeys by a black-eared goddess called Dudyai. The Bahnar are skilled woodcarvers and wear similar dress to the Jarai (opposite).

Dzao

The Dzao (or Zao/Dao) are one of the largest (population 470,000) and most colourful of Vietnam's ethnic groups and live in the northwestern provinces (p165) near China and Laos. The Dzao practise ancestor worship of spirits or *ban ho* (no relation to Uncle Ho) and hold elaborate rituals with sacrifices of pigs and chickens. The Dzao's close proximity to China explains the common use of traditional medicine and the similarity of the *nom dao* script to Chinese characters.

The Dzao are famous for their elaborate dress. Women's clothing typically features intricate weaving and silver-coloured beads and coins. Their long flowing hair, shaved above the forehead, is tied up into a large red or embroidered turban.

Ede

The polytheistic Ede live communally in beamless boat-shaped longhouses on stilts. About one-third of these homes, which often accommodate large extended families, are reserved for communal use, with the rest partitioned into smaller sections to give some privacy to married couples. Speaking of which, like the Jarai, the Ede girls must propose to the men and after marriage the couple resides with the wife's family and bears the mother's name. Inheritance is also the preserve of women, particularly the youngest daughter of the family. Ede women generally wear colourfully embroidered vests with copper and silver jewellery. There are 25,000 living in Kon Tum and Dac Lac.

THE LEGACY OF WAR

During the American War, many of the Montagnards in the central highlands were enrolled in the Civil Irregular Defense Program (CIDG), part of the US Army Special Forces. US special forces considered the Montagnards the hardiest and most loyal forces on the South Vietnamese side.

Following the end of the war in 1975, some of these experienced fighters continued to resist the new communist government based in Hanoi. The United Front for the Liberation of Oppressed Races (FULRO) continued to conduct small-scale attacks on government forces right through the 1980s.

Even today many of the minorities of the central highlands face discrimination by the Vietnamese authorities. There have been several high-profile arrests in the past decade and many Montagnards have fled across the border to Cambodia. The war may be long over, but to some observers and supporters of the Montagnards, it is questionable as to whether the communist government has forgiven them for their role in the conflict.

H'mong

Since migrating from China in the 19th century, the H'mong have grown to become one of the largest ethnic groups in Vietnam. Numbering around half a million, they are spread across the far north, but most visitors will run into them in Sapa (p176) or Bac Ha (p184). The H'mong are animists, and worship spirits.

The H'mong live at high altitudes, cultivate dry rice and medicinal plants (including opium), and raise animals. There are several groups within the H'mong, including Black, White, Red, Green and Flower, each of which has its own subtle dress code. One of the most recognisable are the Black H'mong, who wear indigo-dyed linen clothing, with women typically wearing skirts, aprons, retro leggings and cylindrical hats. The Flower H'mong women wear extrovert outfits, with bright rainbow banding and '70s-style sequins from head to toe. Many H'mong women wear large silver necklaces, earrings and clusters of silver bracelets.

The H'mong are also found in neighbouring Laos and Thailand, and many have fled to Western countries as refugees. Their cultivation of opium has made them the target of much government suspicion over the years.

Flower H'mong girls at Can Cau market (p186)
MASON FLORENCE

Jarai

With a population of 200,000, the Jarai are the most populous minority in the central highlands. Many live around Pleiku (p335), as well as in northeast Cambodia and southern Laos. Villages are often named after a nearby river, stream or tribal chief, and a *nha-rong* (communal house) is usually found in the centre. Jarai women typically propose marriage to men through a matchmaker, who delivers the prospective groom a copper bracelet. Animistic beliefs and rituals still abound, and the Jarai pay respect to their ancestors and nature through a host or *yang* (genie).

The Jarai construct elaborate cemeteries for their dead, which include carved effigies of the deceased. These totems can be found in the forests around villages, but sadly many are being snapped up by culturally insensitive collectors.

Perhaps more than any of Vietnam's other hill tribes, the Jarai are renowned for their indigenous musical instruments, from bamboo tubes, which act as wind flutes and percussion, to bronze gongs.

Muong

Mainly concentrated in Hoa Binh province (p167), the male-dominated Muong live in small stilt-house hamlets. Though their origins lie close to the ethnic Vietnamese, the Muong (population 900,000) have a culture similar to the Thai (opposite).

They are known for producing folk literature, poems and songs, many of which have been translated into Vietnamese. Musical instruments such as the gong, drums, pan pipes, flutes and two-stringed violin are popular.

HIGHLAND POLITICS

Traditionally, highland areas were allowed to remain independent as long as their leaders recognised Vietnamese sovereignty and paid tribute and taxes. This was in part due to difficulties in settling and cultivating highland areas and in part a desire to avoid conflict with the minority peoples. Two autonomous regions were established in the northwest in 1959 and only abolished in 1980. Since this time, a huge number of lowland settlers have moved into highland regions, raising tensions in some areas, however this has been offset by greater political opportunities for minority people. Nong Duc Manh, an ethnic Tay, was elected leader of the Communist Party in April 2001.

Nung

The Nung (population 700,000) inhabit the far northeastern provinces near the Chinese border. Concentrated into small villages, Nung homes are typically divided into two areas: one serves as living quarters and the other is for work and worship.

From ardent ancestral worship to traditional festivities, the Nung are spiritually and socially similar to the Tay people (below). Nung brides traditionally command high dowries from their prospective grooms.

Most Nung villages still have medicine men who are called upon to help get rid of evil spirits and cure the ill. The Nung are also known for their handicrafts, such as basketry.

Sedang

Native to the central highlands, the Sedang (population 95,000) have been adversely affected by centuries of war and outside invasion and may have been raided by both the Cham and the Khmer. They do not carry family names, and there is said to be complete equality between the sexes. The children of one's siblings are also given the same treatment as one's own, creating a strong familial tradition. The Sedang practise unique customs, such as grave abandonment, sharing of property with the deceased and giving birth at the forest's edge.

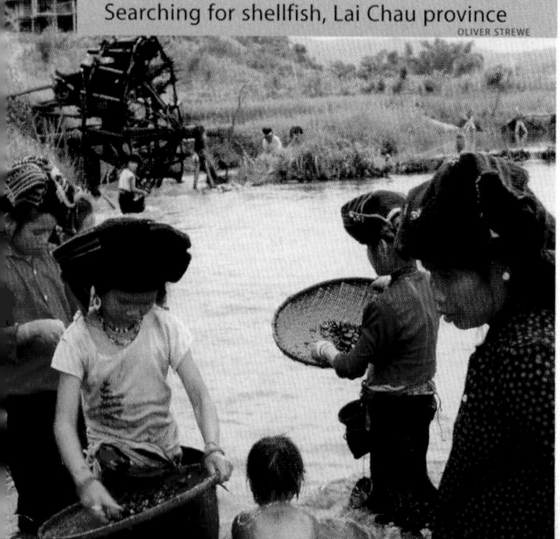
Searching for shellfish, Lai Chau province
OLIVER STREWE

Tay

The Tay (population 1.2 million) are the largest group among the hill tribes, and live at low elevations and in valleys between Hanoi and the Chinese border. They adhere closely to Vietnamese beliefs in Buddhism, Confucianism and Taoism, but also worship genies and local spirits. Since they developed their own script in the 16th century, Tay literature and arts have become famous throughout Vietnam.

Thai

Like the Tay, the Thai (population 1 million) originated in southern China before settling along the fertile riverbeds of the northwest from Hoa Binh (p167) to Muong Lay (p174). Villages typically consist of 40 or 50 thatched houses built on bamboo stilts. The Thai minority are usually categorised by colour, including the Red, Black and White Thai. Black Thai women wear vibrantly coloured blouses and headgear, while the White Thai tend to dress in contemporary clothing. Theories vary on the many colour groupings. Some suggest it corresponds to colours on the women's skirts, while others believe it comes from the nearby Red and Black Rivers.

The Thai, using a script developed in the 5th century, have produced literature ranging from poetry and love songs to folk tales. Travellers staying overnight in Mai Chau (p167) can usually catch a performance of the Thai's renowned music and dance.

You'll be the most popular kid in town among the White Thai children of Hoa Binh province

MARK DAFFEY

WHERE TO VISIT THE HILL TRIBES

The ethnic minorities of Vietnam are spread throughout the highland areas in the north and centre of the country. The old French hill station of Sapa (p176) is the gateway to the northwest and the most popular place in the country to encounter the Montagnards. It is most famous for Black H'mong and Red Dzao villages, and also within striking distance of the colourful Flower H'mong markets around Bac Ha (p184).

Homestays with minority families are a rewarding experience and Mai Chau (p167) is famous for the warm welcome of the White Thai people. Other centres in the northwest also offer opportunities for ethnic minority encounters, including Ha Giang (p187) and Lai Chau (p175).

Further east, the province of Cao Bang (p158) is a less travelled region with several minorities, including the H'mong, the Nung and the Tay. Lang Son (p156) also provides a home to these minority groups, but sees fewer tourists still.

Down in the central highlands, Buon Ma Thuot (p328), Dalat (p317), Kon Tum (p338) and Pleiku (p335) are useful bases to meet the Bahnar, Jarai and Sedang. However, most families here have forsaken their traditional costume, so meet-the-minorities tourism has less pulling power than in the north.

top five MEET THE MINORITIES

Sapa (p176)
Dzao and H'mong people inhabit the dramatic valleys around this hill station

Bac Ha (p184)
Famous for its market, which draws Flower H'mong from far and wide

Mai Chau (p167)
Beautiful valley home of the White Thai and a popular place for a homestay

Cao Bang (p158)
Rugged mountain country in the northeast with a diverse range of minority groups

Kon Tum (p338)
One of the easier places in the Central Highlands to meet the minority people

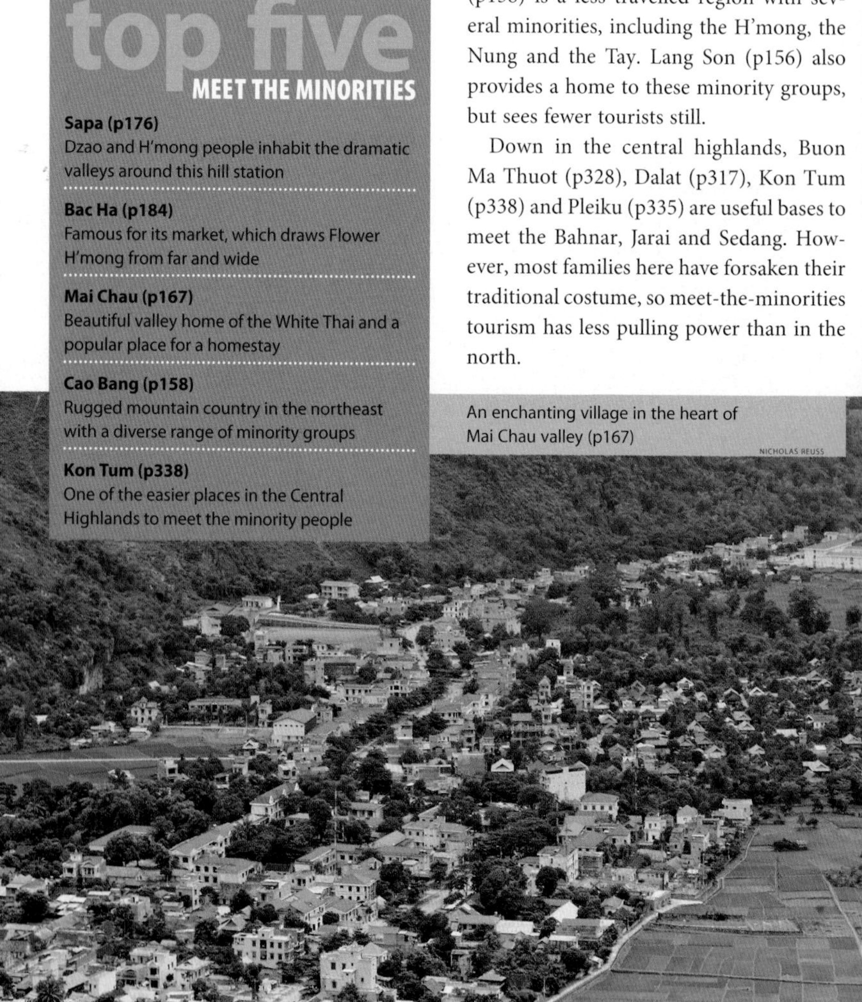

An enchanting village in the heart of Mai Chau valley (p167)

NICHOLAS REUSS

(Continued from page 284)

Buddhist monks who died in self-immolations in 1963 (see p229). The platform around the 14m-high figure has great views of Nha Trang and nearby rural areas. As you approach the pagoda from the street, the 152 stone steps up the hill to the Buddha begin to the right of the structure. You should take some time to explore off to the left, where there's an entrance to another hall of the pagoda.

Genuinely desperate-seeming beggars congregate within the complex, as do a number of scam-artists. There's a persistent scam here, where visitors are approached by children (and occasionally older people) with preprinted name badges claiming to work for the monks. After showing you around the pagoda, whether invited to or not, they will then demand money 'for the monks' or, if that fails, insist that you buy postcards for 100,000d. The best course of action is to firmly let them know you don't require their services when they first appear. If they persist, tell them that you know they don't work for the monks and you're not about to give them any money – this should ensure a quick disappearance. If you want to give money towards the monks and upkeep of the complex, leave it in the donation boxes as you would in any other pagoda.

The pagoda is located about 400m west of the train station, just off Đ 23 Thang 10.

NHA TRANG CATHEDRAL

Built between 1928 and 1933 in French Gothic style, complete with stained-glass windows, **Nha Trang Cathedral** (Map p282; cnr Đ Nguyen Trai & Đ Thai Nguyen) stands on a small hill overlooking the train station. It's a surprisingly elegant building given that it was constructed of simple cement blocks. Some particularly colourful Vietnamese touches include the red neon outlining the crucifix, the pink back-lighting on the tabernacle and the blue neon arch and white neon halo over the statue of St Mary. In 1988 a Catholic cemetery not far from the church was disinterred to make room for a new railway building. The remains were brought to the cathedral and reburied in the cavities behind the wall of plaques that line the ramp up the hill.

LONG THANH GALLERY

Located in the bustling heart of the city, **Long Thanh Gallery** (Map p282; ☎ 382 4875; www.elephantguide.com/photographer/longthanh.htm; 126 Đ Hoang Van Thu; 🕒 8.30-11.30am & 1-6pm Mon-Sat) showcases the work of Vietnam's most prominent photographer. Long Thanh developed his first photo in 1964 and continues to shoot extraordinary black-and-white images of everyday Vietnamese moments.

The powerful images capture the heart and soul of Vietnam. Among his most compelling works, *Under the Rain* is a perfectly timed shot of two young girls caught in a sudden downpour, with a mysterious beam of sunlight streaming down on them. *Afternoon Countryside* is another rare scene – a boy dashing across the backs of a herd of water buffalo submerged in a lake outside Nha Trang.

From the images captured to their processing, there's an honesty to Long Thanh's work. The tactile process of mixing his own chemicals and developing the photos in a makeshift darkroom in his simple kitchen is an integral part of it. 'Colour' and 'digital' are dirty words in his book – let alone 'Photoshop'. His work has been honoured at photographic competitions around the world, showing internationally in nearly 60 group exhibitions, as well as in solo exhibitions in Germany, Japan, Australia and the USA.

NATIONAL OCEANOGRAPHIC MUSEUM

Housed in a grand French-colonial building in the port district of Cau Da at the far south end of Nha Trang is the **National Oceanographic Museum** (Map p281; ☎ 359 0037; haiduong@dng.vnn.vn; 1 Cau Da; adult/child 15,000/7000d; 🕒 6am-6pm). It's attached to the Oceanographic Institute founded in 1923, and signs direct you around the tanks of colourful live marine life and the 60,000 jars of pickled specimens that make up the collection. There are also stuffed birds and sea mammals and displays of local boats and fishing artefacts. Most of the signs have English translations, so a guide is unnecessary.

ALEXANDRE YERSIN MUSEUM

Dr Alexandre Yersin (1863–1943) founded Nha Trang's **Pasteur Institute** in 1895. He was probably the Frenchman most loved by the Vietnamese. Born in Switzerland, he came to Vietnam in 1889 after working under Louis Pasteur in Paris. He learned to speak Vietnamese fluently, and spent the next few years travelling throughout the central highlands and recording his observations. During this period he came upon the site of what is now Dalat and recommended to the government that a hill station be established there.

Yersin also introduced rubber and quinine-producing trees to Vietnam. In 1894, while in Hong Kong, he discovered the rat-borne microbe that causes bubonic plague. At his request, Dr Yersin was buried near Nha Trang.

Today, the Pasteur Institute in Nha Trang coordinates vaccination and hygiene programs for the country's southern coastal region. The institute produces vaccines and carries out medical research and testing to European standards. Physicians at the clinic here offer medical advice to around 70 patients a day. Vietnam's two other Pasteur Institutes are in HCMC and Dalat.

Yersin's library and office are now an interesting **museum** (Map p282; ☎ 382 2355; 10 Đ Tran Phu; admission 26,000d; ⌚ 8-11am & 2-4.30pm Mon-Fri, 8-11am Sat). Items on display include laboratory equipment (such as astronomical instruments), books from Yersin's library, a fascinating 3-D photo viewer and some of the thousand or so letters written to his mother. The model boat was given to him by local fishermen with whom he spent a great deal of his time. Tours of the museum are guided in French, English and Vietnamese, and a short film on Yersin's life is also shown.

KHANH HOA MUSEUM

This sleepy local **museum** (Map p282; ☎ 382 2227; 16 Đ Tran Phu; admission free; ⌚ 8-11am & 2-5pm Mon, Wed, Fri & Sun) features displays of Cham statues and artefacts of the ethnic minorities in the province. The Uncle Ho room features several of Ho Chi Minh's personal effects, such as clothing and the microphone with which he made his famous independence speech in Hanoi on 2 September 1945.

HON CHONG PROMONTORY

The narrow granite promontory of Hon Chong (Map p281) offers views of the mountainous coastline north of Nha Trang and the nearby islands. The beach here has a more local flavour than Nha Trang Beach, but the accompanying refuse makes it a less attractive option for swimming or sunbathing.

There's a gargantuan handprint on the massive boulder balanced at the tip of the promontory. According to legend, a drunken giant male fairy made it when he fell while spying on a female fairy bathing nude at Bai Tien (Fairy Beach), the point of land closest to Hon Rua. They fell in love but the gods intervened, sending the male fairy away. The lovesick female fairy waited patiently for him to return, but after a very long time she lay down in sorrow and turned into **Nui Co Tien** (Fairy Mountain). Looking to the northeast from Hon Chong Promontory, the peak on the right is supposed to be her face, gazing up towards the sky; the middle peak is her breasts; and the summit on the left (the highest) forms her crossed legs.

About 300m south of Hon Chong (towards Nha Trang) and a few dozen metres from the beach is tiny **Hon Do** (Red Island), which has a Buddhist temple on top. To the northeast is **Hon Rua** (Tortoise Island), which really does resemble a tortoise. The two islands of **Hon Yen** (Bird's-Nest Island) are off in the distance to the east.

Activities

BOAT TOURS

The 71 offshore islands around Nha Trang are renowned for the remarkably clear water surrounding them. A trip to these islands is one of Nha Trang's main draws, so try to schedule at least one day for a boat excursion. Virtually every hotel and travel company in town books island-hopping boat tours. Or you can pay more for a less-crowded and more-luxurious boat that takes you to more islands. Indeed, you'll have to do this if you want to get in much snorkelling.

Shallow water prevents boats from reaching shore at some of the fishing villages. In this case, you must sometimes walk several hundred metres across floats. The floats were designed for Vietnamese people, and weightier Westerners might get wet – balance carefully and take care with your camera. Nevertheless, it's all good fun and a visit to these villages is highly recommended.

Mama Linh's Boat Tours (Map p282; ☎ 352 2844; mamalinhvn@yahoo.com; 23C Đ Biet Thu) are the hottest ticket for island-hopping, guzzling fruit wine at the impromptu 'floating bar', and deck-side dancing. Daily trips last from 8.45am until 4.30pm, and typically include stops on Hon Mun, Hon Mot, Hon Tam and Hon Mieu – see p302. Tickets (US$8) are sold at the office, but you can easily book at your hotel for a dollar or two more. There are plenty of other similar options, including the aforementioned Highland Tours (p281) who usually pull a party crowd from the Red Apple Club (p300).

It's definitely the backpacker answer to Club 18–30 and might not be the best environment for families with children (or for recovering alcoholics). If the cultural fanfare of the party-boat experience does not sound up your alley, there are other more orthodox boat tours around.

Con Se Tre (Map p281; ☎ 381 1163; www.consetre.com.vn; 100/16 Đ Tran Phu; 8am-6pm) offers tours to Hon Tre, which include a visit to Vinpearl Land (p296), a look around the village and lunch (from US$17 per person), and snorkelling trips to Hon Mun (from $US15 per person). It also charters speed boats (from US$50) and wooden boats (from US$40), including snorkels and a guide.

If you're brave and a good haggler (use the rates listed earlier as a benchmark) you can charter a boat directly from Cau Da dock at the south end of Nha Trang. Get there early, as all the boats are gone by 10am. An alternative is joining up with one of the local dive boats, most of which will take nondivers along for a discounted rate.

The cheapest way to get out on the water is to take the regular local ferry to Vinpearl Land on Hon Tre (adult/child 45,000/20,000d each way), leaving from Phu Quy harbour just past Cau Da dock. There is also the massive Vinpearl Land cable car which is strung out across the bay and takes 10 minutes. Most people use this in conjunction with their entry ticket to Vinpearl Land (p296).

DIVING

Nha Trang is Vietnam's premier scuba-diving locale. Visibility averages 15m but can be as much as 30m, depending on the season (late October to early January is the worst time of year).

There are around 25 dive sites in the area, both shallow and deep. There are no wrecks to visit, but some sites have good drop-offs and there are a few small underwater caves to explore. The waters support a good variety of soft and hard corals, and a reasonable number of small reef fish.

A full-day outing including boat transport, two dives and lunch typically costs between US$45 and US$75. Most dive operators also offer a range of dive courses, including a 'discover diving' program for uncertified first-time divers to experience the underwater world with the supervision of a qualified dive master.

There are a dozen or so dive operators touting for business on the streets of Nha Trang. The places listed below are all long-running operators with environmentally responsible diving practices.

Deep Blue Diving (Map p282; ☎ 352 7034; www.vietnam-diving.com; 66 Đ Tran Phu) Popular seafront company for recreational dives.

Rainbow Divers (Map p282; ☎ 352 4351; www.divevietnam.com; 90A Đ Hung Vuong) The longest-running dive company in Vietnam, operating out of five centres nationwide. Here at HQ, there is also a popular restaurant and bar.

Sailing Club Divers (Map p282; ☎ 352 2788; www.sailingclubvietnam.com; 72-74 Đ Tran Phu) Formerly Octopus Diving, this is the underwater arm of the famous Sailing Club.

Vietnam Explorer (Map p282; ☎ 352 4490; www.divingvietnam.com; 24 Đ Hung Vuong) Another PADI dive centre with a good reputation in Vietnam.

MORE WATERY FUN

Right on the beachfront, **Phu Dong Water Park** (Map p281; Đ Tran Phu; admission 25,000d, lockers 5000d; 9am-5pm Sat & Sun) has hydroslides, shallow pools and fountains if salt water is not your thing.

If salt water is your thing, check out **Waves Watersports** (Map p282; ☎ 090-544 7393; www.waveswatersports.com; Louisiane Brewhouse, 29 Đ Tran Phu). Offering windsurfing, sea kayaking, wakeboarding, water-skiing and sailing lessons, Waves uses state-of-the-art equipment and has access to some great surfing spots in Cam Ranh Bay.

Or perhaps hot muddy water is your thing? **Thap Ba Hot Spring Center** (Map p281; ☎ 383 4939; www.thapbahotspring.com.vn; 25 Ngoc Son; 8am-8pm) is one of the most fun experiences on offer here. For 180,000d you can sit in a wooden bathtub full of hot thermal mud, or for 60,000d per person you can slop around with a group of friends in a larger pool. The centre also has private mineral baths (50,000d) and a large outdoor heated swimming pool complete with thermal waterfalls (free with a mud or mineral bath, 30,000d otherwise). To get here, follow the signpost on the second road to the left past the Po Nagar Cham Towers and follow the winding road for 2.5km.

SPAS

There is a burgeoning spa industry in Nha Trang. Some of the best places include the following:

CONSIDERATIONS FOR RESPONSIBLE DIVING

The popularity of diving is placing immense pressure on many sites. Please consider the following tips when diving and help preserve the ecology and beauty of Vietnam's reefs.

- Do not anchor on the reef, and take care not to ground boats on coral. Encourage dive operators and regulatory bodies to establish permanent moorings at popular dive sites.
- Avoid touching living marine organisms with your body or dragging equipment across the reef. Polyps can be damaged by even the gentlest contact. Never stand on corals, even if they look solid and robust. If you must hold on to the reef, touch only exposed rock or dead coral.
- Be conscious of your fins. Even without contact, the surge from heavy fin strokes near the reef can damage delicate organisms. When treading water in shallow reef areas, take care not to kick up clouds of sand. Settling sand can easily smother the delicate organisms of the reef.
- Practise and maintain proper buoyancy control. Major damage can be done by divers descending too fast and colliding with the reef. Make sure you are correctly weighted and that your weight belt is positioned so that you stay horizontal. If you have not dived for a while, have a practice dive in a pool before taking to the reef. Be aware that buoyancy can change over the period of an extended trip: initially you may breathe harder and need more weight; a few days later you may breathe more easily and need less weight.
- Resist the temptation to collect or buy coral or shells. Aside from the ecological damage, taking home marine souvenirs depletes the beauty of a site and spoils the enjoyment of others. The same goes for marine archaeological sites (mainly shipwrecks). Respect their integrity; some sites are protected from looting by law.
- Ensure that you take home all your rubbish and any litter you may find as well. Plastics in particular are a serious threat to marine life. Turtles can mistake plastic for jellyfish and eat it.
- Resist the temptation to feed fish. You may disturb their normal eating habits, encourage aggressive behaviour or feed them food that is detrimental to their health.
- Minimise your disturbance of marine animals.

Crazy Kim Spa & Gym (Map p282; ☎ 352 7837; 1D Đ Biet Thu) Helping to fund the 'Hands off the Kids!' campaign run by Kimmy Le (see p300), this is indulgence for a good cause.

Su Spa (Map p282; ☎ 352 3242; www.suspa.vn; 93 Đ Nguyen Thien Thuat) A designer spa with a range of scrubs, rubs and tubs.

VINPEARL LAND

Nha Trang's answer to Disneyland (well, sort of) the island resort of **Vinpearl Land** (☎ 359 0111; www.vinpearlland.com; Hon Tre; adult/child 250,000/175,000d; 🕑 9am-10pm) has fun-fair rides, a water park, arcade games and plenty of other attractions to keep the kiddies amused. There is also an Underwater World aquarium here, but that costs another 60,000/45,000d per adult/child. It's certainly not a world-class adventure park, but it will keep children amused for a full day, and includes the world's longest over-the-sea cable car (oooh!) and the biggest wave pool in Southeast Asia (ahhh!). The leading attraction is undoubtedly the water park, with more than 20 serious slides for adrenalin-seekers.

Most visitors arrive by cable car or fast boat, both included in the ticket price. Both depart from the coast just south of Cau Da dock area.

Sleeping

There is no shortage of hotels in Nha Trang, with 250 or more places to choose from and counting. They range from dives to the divine and there are new places sprouting up all the time, including a number of chain hotels under construction at the time of writing, like Sheraton and Crowne Plaza. It makes sense to stay near the beach, given this is the big attraction. There are many midrange and top-end options lining Đ Tran Phu, the waterfront boulevard. However, there are also several budget options just a stroll away from the beachfront action. Most budget places don't include breakfast, but there are no 'plus plus' (++ or $$) charges for tax and service like at many of the midrange and top-end pads.

For more beachfront options to the north of Nha Trang, see p278.

BUDGET

There is a cluster of mini-hotels in an alleyway at 64 Đ Tran Phu, within striking distance of the beach. All offer similar air-conditioned rooms for around US$10 or so, cheaper if you go with the flow of a fan.

Backpacker's House (Map p282; ☎ 352 3884; www.backpackershouse.net; 54G Đ Nguyen Thien Thuat; dm US$6, r US$17-24; ❄ 💻) This new flashpacker pad opened in summer 2008 and is popular with the party set, as it is only a stumble from the nearby Red Apple Club (p300). The dorms are mixed and have four to six beds. The rooms are a smarter choice, but don't check in here if you need a long sleep, as it can be noisy.

Sao Mai Hotel (Map p282; ☎ 352 6412; saomai2ht@yahoo.com; 99 Đ Nguyen Thien Thuat; r 90,000-180,000d; ❄) This budget crash pad has been around for years, but still offers no-nonsense value for money for those on a budget. The rooms are simple yet clean, plus there is a nice rooftop terrace to escape the bustle below.

Hotel An Hoa (Map p282; ☎ 352 4029; anhoahotel@yahoo.com; 64B/6 Đ Tran Phu; r US$8-12; ❄) A reliable option in the heart of the budget alley, this friendly hostelry has small rooms with no windows or air-con, or bigger and better rooms with larger bathrooms and a smarter trim.

Blue Star Hotel (Map p282; ☎ 352 5447; quangc@dng.vnn.vn; 1B Đ Biet Thu; r US$8-15; ❄ 💻) When it comes to location, this is one of the better budget places, as it's a stone's throw from the beach (don't try it, you might hit someone) and on the doorstep of lots of leading restaurants and bars. The rooms aren't bad value and some have sea views, including corner rooms with big balconies.

Phong Lan Hotel (Map p282; ☎ 352 2647; orchidhotel2000@yahoo.com; 24/44 Đ Hung Vuong; r US$8-15; ❄) Located in a small alley off Hung Vuong, the Orchid Hotel, as it translates, is a friendly, family-run place. The clean rooms include TV and fridge. The owners speak both English and French.

56 Hung Vuong Hotel (Map p282; ☎ 352 4584; 56hungvuonghotel@dng.vnn.vn; 56 Đ Hung Vuong; r US$8-15; ❄) Next door to the Phu Quy, this is a friendly pad with expansive, not expensive, rooms; many have a balcony and a sea view (if you are prepared for stairs).

Phu Quy Hotel (Map p282; ☎ 352 1609; phuquyhotel@dng.vnn.vn; 54 Đ Hung Vuong; r US$8-20; ❄ 💻) At the pad that kickstarted the Phu Quy (pronounced foo hwee) empire, there is a great rooftop terrace which has long lured in backpackers looking to chill out. Rooms are fine for the money and just US$10 will get a balcony and a strained sea view.

our pick **Pho Bien** (Map p282; ☎ 352 4858; phobienhotelint@yahoo.com; 64B/1 Đ Tran Phu; r US$8-20; ❄) The Pho Bien is one of the smarter places hiding away down budget alley. It has a big reception area with free internet and lots of tour information. Rooms are clean and comfortable and include satellite TV, fridge and hot water. There is also a handy lift these days, helpful after a big night out.

There are also some good local hotels on the southern strip of Tran Phu that are aiming for the Vietnamese market. Try **Huong Bing Hotel** (Map p281; ☎ 352 7188; huongbinhhotel@yahoo.com; 98A Đ Tran Phu; r 160,000-320,000d; ❄), overlooking the seafront. It has 35 sparkling rooms, all with satellite TV, IDD phones and modern bathrooms. Bag a balcony to enjoy the view. Or opt for pot luck and try one of the other dozen or more places here.

Other possible budget options:

Hotel Nhi Hang (Map p282; ☎ 352 5837; www.vngold.com/nt/nhihang; 64B/7 Đ Tran Phu; r US$8-15; ❄) Another little teaser down budget alley, which has a similar set-up to Hotel An Hoa (left).

62 Tran Phu Hotel (Map p282; ☎ 352 5095; 62 Đ Tran Phu; r US$8-20; ❄) Really rundown are the first words that spring to mind, but for the party set who don't care about the room, it has a great seafront location.

A Dong Hotel (Map p281; ☎ 352 7768; www.adonghotel.com; 100/10B Đ Tran Phu; r US$10-15; ❄ 💻) Recommended by readers, a reliable place on the Vietnamese hotel strip on southern Tran Phu.

My Long Hotel (Map p282; ☎ 352 1451; lexuannga_nt@yahoo.com; 26A Đ Nguyen Thien Thuat; s/d/tr US$11/12/16; ❄) This is same-same and not that different from many of the other mini-hotels, but the staff here are enthusiastic and friendly.

MIDRANGE

Perfume Grass Inn (Map p282; ☎ 352 4286; www.perfume-grass.com; 4A Đ Biet Thu; r US$10-30; ❄ 💻) Deservedly popular, this welcoming inn has rooms with a touch of character, particularly the more expensive options with wood panelling. Cheaper fan rooms still have a sea view and include satellite TV and hot shower. Add to the mix free internet, breakfast and a cosy little bar downstairs and it's a deal.

Ha Van Hotel (Map p282; ☎ 352 5454; havanhotel@vnn.vn; 3/2 Đ Tran Quang Khai; r US$18-22; ❄ 💻) Under international management, this place is striving to stand out from the pack. The rooms have all the standard comforts, plus a bit more verve on the decorative front.

La Suisse Hotel (Map p282; ☎ 352 4353; www.lasuissehotel.com; 3/4 Đ Tran Quang Khai; r US$15-30;) Switzerland is famous for its hoteliers and there is a touch of *la Suisse* about the efficient service here. Rooms have smart furnishings and some have jacuzzi-style tubs and elegant balconies. It's next door to Ha Van.

Rainbow Hotel (Map p282; ☎ 352 5480; rainbowhotel@dng.vnn.vn; 10A Đ Biet Thu; r US$15-30;) It may not be affiliated with the nearby HQ of Rainbow Divers, but it's still a popular place thanks to 50 rooms at tempting prices. Solar-heated water earns brownie points, as does the top-floor restaurant with views over town.

La Paloma Hotel (Map p281; ☎ 383 1216; datle@dng.vnn.vn; 1 Đ Hon Chong; r US$15-40;) If you don't fancy the circus of downtown Nha Trang, then this family pad offers an escape. It is tucked away in the backstreets near Hon Chong Beach, a local neighbourhood with fewer tourists. Rooms are spacious and comfortable, plus there is a large garden with alfresco dining.

AP Hotel (Map p282; ☎ 352 7544; 34 Đ Nguyen Thien Thuat; r US$20-32;) The official one-star rating seems a bit stingy given the facilities at this mini-hotel, where rooms have satellite TV, minibar and bathtub. The cheaper rooms have no windows, which isn't ideal, but the fancy-pants rooms just about offer a sea view. Plus free internet.

Nha Trang Beach Hotel (Map p282; ☎ 352 4469; www.nhatrangbeachhotel.com.vn; 4 Đ Tran Quang Khai; r 250,000-400,000d;) A pretty slick-looking place for the rates, this friendly hotel offers a good deal. The decoration is simple, but it is very clean and the location is hard to beat.

Vien Dong Hotel (Map p282; ☎ 382 1606; www.nhatrangtourist.com.vn/viendong/viendong_e.htm; 1 Đ Tran Hung Dao; s 270,000-450,000d, d 300,000-500,000d;) Popular with midrange tour groups, this old government hotel has been around for as long as the sands of Nha Trang. Old-wing rooms are ageing now, but the newer rooms are a fair deal given the impressive swimming pool. A brand new wing was underway at the time of writing.

Bao Dai's Villas (Map p281; ☎ 359 0148; www.vngold.com/nt/baodai/; Cau Da village; r US$25-80;) Originally reserved for royalty, Emperor Bao Dai's villas are now open to the masses, provided they have the money to spend. Built in the 1920s, this was a beachside retreat for the last emperor, but it is not particularly opulent these days. Aside from the historical-pull factor and its lush grounds, the rooms themselves are pretty average for the price. However, there is a certain colonial decay about the place with high ceilings and creaking shutters. There is a small beach and a couple of restaurants here.

Phu Quy 2 Hotel (Map p282; ☎ 352 5050; www.phuquyhotel.com.vn; 1 Đ Tue Tinh; r US$30-54, ste US$91;) The upmarket sibling in the Phu Quy family, this towering hotel has a rooftop pool with views to the beach. The rooms are squeaky clean and well appointed, although it is worth investing a few more bucks for a spacious sea-view one. Breakfast and internet access included.

Other options in the mix:

Nha Trang Lodge Hotel (Map p282; ☎ 352 1500; www.nhatranglodge.com; 42 Đ Tran Phu; r US$65-140;) Almost top end, this place offers online deals and discount rates luring it into midrange territory. High-rise and low on atmosphere, it's a business-style place but the views are splendid.

T78 Guesthouse (Map p282; ☎ 352 3445; fax 352 6395; 44 Đ Tran Phu; r 90,000-1,200,000d;) This beautiful old French-colonial building is begging to be a boutique hotel, but it remains a rundown state entity for now, with a certain raffish charm.

TOP END

Asia Paradise Hotel (Map p282; ☎ 352 4686; www.asiaparadisehotel.com; 6 Đ Biet Thu; r US$63-110, ste US$132;) A cut above the midrange competition in this midrange neighbourhood, the Asia Paradise is a modern business-style hotel with smart rooms. The decor is stylish, including attractive bathrooms. There's even a rooftop pool and a gym.

Sunrise Beach Resort (Map p282; ☎ 382 0999; www.sunrisenhatrang.com.vn; 12-14 Đ Tran Phu; s US$170-190, d US$185-205, ste US$220-535;) One of the smartest hotels in Nha Trang, for the time being at least, the design owes much to the wedding-cake school of hotels so loved in Asia. The opulent lobby sets the scene for the impressive rooms, which include the usual array of five-star extras. There are several good restaurants here, including a Japanese one, plus the temptations of a spa or Irish bar, depending on your persuasion.

Ana Mandara Resort (Map p281; ☎ 352 2522; www.evasonresorts.com; Đ Tran Phu; villa US$235-435, ste US$450-520;) Nha Trang's most desirable address, the Ana Mandara is a charming cluster of beach villas on an exclusive strip of sand.

There is more than a hint of Bali about the place with classic furnishings and four-poster beds. Facilities include two swimming pools and an indulgent (and suitably expensive) Six Senses Spa. Personal touches every week include guest appearances by local cooks for a slice of street food and a cocktail evening on the beach.

Eating

Nha Trang is a great destination for dining, with a diverse mix of international flavours. Vietnamese, Japanese, French, Italian, Indian – anything and everything is available. Đ Tran Quang Khai and Đ Biet Thu are popular hunting grounds, but more authentic Vietnamese is found further afield. Seafood-lovers are in for a treat with fresh fish, crab, shrimp and an assortment of exotic molluscs.

VIETNAMESE

Pho Cali (Map p282; ☎ 352 5885; 7G Đ Hung Vuong; dishes 20,000-40,000d; ⌚ breakfast, lunch & dinner) Part of a nationwide chain of soup stores, this place has an ultramodern open-plan kitchen. The speciality is, unsurprisingly, *pho*, but there is a selection of Vietnamese greatest hits on offer as well.

Café des Amis (Map p282; ☎ 352 1009; 2D Đ Biet Thu; dishes 20,000-70,000d; ⌚ breakfast, lunch & dinner) Long a backpacker favourite thanks to cheap eats and plentiful beer, this place has a menu that includes a strong selection of Vietnamese dishes, inexpensive seafood and a pick and mix of international dishes. Look out for local artworks adorning the walls.

Lac Canh Restaurant (Map p282; ☎ 382 1391; 44 Đ Nguyen Binh Khiem; dishes 20,000-100,000d; ⌚ lunch & dinner) Locals flock here in numbers to fire up the tabletop barbecues and grill their own meats, squid, prawns, lobsters and more. There are plenty of accompaniments on the menu making this a popular stop in Nha Trang.

Truc Linh 2 (Map p282; ☎ 352 1089; 21 Đ Biet Thu; dishes 25,000-150,000d; ⌚ lunch & dinner) The Truc Linh empire includes three eateries in the heart of backpackersville. Number 2 has a pretty garden setting and serves authentic dishes at affordable prices.

Cyclo Café (Map p282; ☎ 352 4208; 5A Đ Tran Quang Khai; mains 30,000-90,000d; ⌚ breakfast, lunch & dinner) The Cyclo is a lively little place for an inviting blend of Vietnamese and continental dishes. The food is good value, the service is sharp; the only drawback is the roadshow of sellers that troop through each night, but it can be fun if you can live with the banter.

Mecca (Map p282; ☎ 352 4455; 16 Đ Tran Quang Khai; dishes 30,000-150,000d; ⌚ breakfast, lunch & dinner) Make a pilgrimage to this trendy spot. It started life as a coffee shop, but has morphed into a full restaurant complete with fresh seafood, local specialities and some international offerings. The lush garden is quite an oasis, by day or night.

our pick **Lanterns** (Map p282; ☎ 352 1674; 72 Đ Nguyen Thien Thuat; dishes 40,000-140,000d; ⌚ lunch & dinner) The flavours are predominantly Vietnamese, such as braised pork in claypot or fried tofu with lemongrass, but there are some international offerings for anyone who is riced out. The restaurant supports a local orphanage and invites the children and their carers in to dine each month.

Gia (Map p282; ☎ 352 5220; 30 Đ Tran Quang Khai; dishes 50,000-130,000d; ⌚ lunch & dinner) This stylish venue is an alluring option for sophisticated Vietnamese food. It attracts a mixed crowd of tourists and locals and has a serious selection of seafood.

For a more traditional local experience, try **Dam Market** (Map p282; Đ Trang Nu Vuong; ⌚ breakfast & lunch), which has a colourful collection of stalls, including *com chay* (vegetarian) options, in the 'food court'.

VIETNAMESE VEGETARIAN

There are a couple of specialist vegetarian places of the I-can't-believe-it's-not-meat variety: **Au Lac** (Map p282; ☎ 381 3946; 28C Đ Hoang Hoa Tham; meals from 15,000d; ⌚ breakfast, lunch & dinner) and **Bo De** (Map p282; ☎ 381 0116; 28A Đ Hoang Hoa Tham; meals from 10,000d; ⌚ breakfast, lunch & dinner), are conveniently located side by side near the corner of Đ Nguyen Chanh.

OTHER ASIAN

T2 Sushi Bar (Map p282; ☎ 352 3307; 24C Đ Nguyen Thien Thuat; sushi items 20,000-50,000d; ⌚ lunch & dinner) This tiny little restaurant is highly regarded by local residents for its fresh sushi and sashimi. The menu is often improvised depending on what sort of fish and seafood is available.

Omar's Tandoori Cafe (Map p282; ☎ 352 2459; 89B Đ Nguyen Thien Thuat; dishes 40,000-120,000d; ⌚ breakfast, lunch & dinner) For an authentic sampling of the subcontinent, look no further than Omar's. There is a wide selection of curries available, plus a lot of tandoori specialities. It's the venue of choice with curry-craving expats in town.

FRENCH

Mai Anh (Map p282; ☎ 381 5920; 1/21 Đ Tran Quang Khai; mains 40,000-150,000d; lunch & dinner) A small restaurant with a big personality, Mai Anh promotes 'French grand cuisine'. The nine-course set menu counts as really grand and is 'to be shared with darling from a single plate'. Tender steaks are a reliable choice.

Le Petit Bistro (Map p282; ☎ 352 7201; 26D Đ Tran Quang Khai; mains 50,000-200,000d; lunch & dinner;) Arguably the most popular of the French restaurants with the French crowd (always a good sign), this is the place for the *fromage* you have been pining for or some select cold cuts. The wine list is professional for those that like to quaff.

INTERNATIONAL

Same Same But Different Café (Map p282; ☎ 352 4079; 111 Đ Nguyen Thien Thuat; mains 20,000-80,000d; breakfast, lunch & dinner) With a name like this, it could only be a backpacker cafe and it's one of the better ones in town. All the Vietnamese staples are here, plus some Western favourites, including a healthy smattering of vegie dishes.

La Taverna (Map p282; ☎ 352 2259; www.lataverna vietnam.com; 115 Đ Nguyen Thien Thuat; mains 32,000-96,000d; breakfast, lunch & dinner;) Arguably offering the best-value Italian food in Nha Trang, La Taverna is run by a Swiss-Italian and imports all its ingredients. If authentic pastas and pizzas don't do it for you, there is Vietnamese and even Swiss available.

Veranda (Map p282; ☎ 352 7492; 66 Đ Tran Phu; mains 40,000-100,000d; lunch & dinner) This stylish little restaurant offers a small menu of food with flair, blending Vietnamese ingredients with an international outlook to create some original flavours. The prices are very reasonable given the delicate presentation, and fresh seafood is available for those who like to point and eat.

El Coyote (Map p282; ☎ 352 6320; 76 Đ Hung Vuong; mains 40,000-125,000d; breakfast, lunch & dinner) Spice up your life with some authentic Tex-Mex flavours at the Coyote. The fajitas, burritos and tacos are all designed to sate the appetite. The owner is even more fusion than the food: a mixture of French, Vietnamese, Lao and Cheyenne Indian.

Louisiane Brewhouse (Map p282; ☎ 352 1948; 29 Đ Tran Phu; www.louisianebrewhouse.com.vn; mains 50,000-150,000d; 7am-1am;) It's not only the beer that draws a crowd here, as there is an eclectic menu offering international classics, some fiery Thai dishes and Vietnamese favourites. The beachside pool is a beautiful place to while away some time digesting the meal, and there are some great cakes and pastries for inveterate snackers.

Sailing Club (Map p282; ☎ 382 6528; 72-74 Đ Tran Phu; mains 50,000-250,000d; breakfast, lunch & dinner;) This Nha Trang institution offers not one, but three dining options, including Vietnamese, Italian and Indian, not forgetting a smattering of international dishes. The beachfront terrace is the nicest of the dining areas with people-watching by day and brisk breezes by night. It is possible to order from any of the menus, so don't feel duty bound to sit in the streetside garden if you are hankering for Italian or Indian.

And the beat goes on:

Thanh Thanh Cafe (Map p282; ☎ 382 4413; 10 Đ Nguyen Thien Thuat; meals 25,000-95,000d; breakfast, lunch & dinner) A popular backpacker cafe, with Vietnamese dishes and wholesome pizzas.

La Mancha (Map p282; ☎ 352 7978; 78 Đ Nguyen Thien Thuat; mains 30,000-160,000d; lunch & dinner) This Spanish restaurant-bar is an unexpected surprise in Nha Trang, with tapas bites and larger plates like paella.

Something Fishy (Map p282; ☎ 352 5039; 12A Đ Biet Thu; mains 40,000-80,000d; lunch & dinner) This cosy little cafe-restaurant serves a great range of inexpensive fish and seafood, including a hearty fish and chips.

Da Fernando (Map p282; ☎ 352 8034; 96 Đ Nguyen Thien Thuat; mains 40,000-140,000d; lunch & dinner) Reliable Italian restaurant with freshly made pastas and wines from the homeland.

Drinking & Entertainment

Sailing Club (Map p282; 72-74 Đ Tran Phu;) There was a time when nightlife in Nha Trang was the Sailing Club and debauched partygoers would stumble from the boat trip into the bar, and sometimes back onto the boat again. As Nha Trang has gentrified, so too has the Sailing Club. It's still a great place for a drink and a big night out, but perhaps not as hedonistic as it once was.

Red Apple Club (Map p282; ☎ 352 5599; 54H Đ Nguyen Thien Thuat;) *The* place where backpackers wind down after a boat trip or wind up before the next one. Cheap beer, flowing shots, regular promotions and indie anthems ensure this place is crammed every night. Watch out for the beer funnel, as things can get very messy. Plus pool and free internet.

Crazy Kim Bar (Map p282; ☎ 352 3072; www.crazykim bar.com; 19 Đ Biet Thu;) Run by local personality Kimmy Le, this busy bar is home base for her

WARNING

There have been a number of reports of laced cocktail buckets doing the rounds in popular night spots. This might mean staff using home-made moonshine instead of legal spirits or could mean the addition of some drugs of some sort by other punters. While buckets are fun and communal, take care in Nha Trang and try and keep an eye on what goes into the bucket. You don't want your night to end in paranoia or robbery.

commendable 'Hands off the Kids!' campaign, which works to prevent paedophilia. She's now set up a permanent classroom for vulnerable street kids on the premises. Part of the proceeds from the food, booze and T-shirt sales go towards the cause. Sign up at the bar if you're interested in volunteering to teach English. Crazy Kim's has regular themed party nights, great music, devilish cocktail buckets and free wi-fi. Crazy (happy) hours run pretty much nonstop from noon to midnight.

Guava (Map p282; ☎ 352 4140; www.clubnhatrang.com; 17 Đ Biet Thu; 💻) A hip lounge bar, Guava is the place to come if you are seeking some style while you drink. Choose from sunken sofas inside or a leafy garden patio outside. Regular drink promotions include two-for-one surprises most days, such as Bloody Marys to accompany the Sunday 'hangover breakfast'.

Louisiane Brewhouse (Map p282; ☎ 352 1948; 29 Đ Tran Phu; 💻 📶) Homebrew, Nha Trang–style. All self-respecting beer drinkers will want to stop by here to sample the wares of this elegant microbrewery. Beyond the shiny copper vats lie an inviting swimming pool and a private strip of sand.

Why Not Bar? (Map p282; ☎ 352 2652; 24 Đ Tran Quang Khai) Another lively spot for hedonists, this place offers bargain promotions until 1am. Why not? As well as dangerous drink deals, there's pool and table football. Open late; entry is 30,000d after 1am.

Or down a drink at these places:

City View Café (Map p282; ☎ 382 0090; 18 Đ Tran Phu) Perched atop the Yasaka Saigon Nhatrang hotel, this garden bar has great views over the seafront promenade, making it a good stop for a sundowner.

Shamrock Bar (Map p282; ☎ 352 1117; 34F Đ Nguyen Thien Thu) This hole-in-the-wall Irish bar has cheap booze and hearty pub fare, plus they arrange fishing and rafting trips, although not at night while under the influence.

Shopping

Nha Trang has emerged as a popular place to look for local arts and crafts. A number of shops can be found in the blocks surrounding the corner of Đ Tran Quang Khai and Đ Hung Vuong.

XQ (Map p282; ☎ 352 6579; www.xqhandembroidery.com; 64 Đ Tran Phu; 🕗 8am-8pm) At this place designed to look like a traditional rural village, you are invited to enjoy a complimentary glass of green tea as you wander around. You can watch the artisans at work in the embroidery workshop and gallery.

My Village (Map p282; ☎ 352 4825; 4L Đ Hung Vuong) Located at the epicentre of touristville, this little shop offers lacquerwork, furniture and handicrafts.

Also worth checking out are the hand-painted T-shirts done by a friendly local painter named Kim Quang, who works from his wheelchair at the Sailing Club (opposite) from 2pm to 9pm.

A Mart (Map p282; ☎ 352 3035; 17A Đ Biet Thu) is a centrally located minimart that offers a good selection of imported items.

Getting There & Away

AIR

Vietnam Airlines (Map p282; ☎ 352 6768; 91 Đ Nguyen Thien Thuat) connects Nha Trang with HCMC (from US$45) three times a day, and Hanoi (from US$42) and Danang (from US$35) daily.

BUS

Lien Tinh bus station (Ben Xe Lien Tinh; ☎ 382 2192; Đ 23 Thang 10) is Nha Trang's main intercity bus terminal, 500m west of the train station. Regular daily buses head north to Quy Nhon (from 75,000d, five hours), with a few continuing to Danang (140,000d, 12 hours). Regular buses head south to Phan Rang (30,000d, two hours), with a dozen continuing on to HCMC (130,000d, 11 hours) and a similar number heading into the highlands to Dalat (88,000d, five hours).

Nha Trang is a major stopping point on all of the tourist open-bus tours. These are the best option for accessing Mui Ne, which is not served by local buses. These buses usually depart some time between 7am and 8am reaching Mui Ne at lunchtime, before continuing on to HCMC. There are also regular open buses to Dalat (six hours) and Hoi An (11 hours).

CAR & MOTORBIKE

By road from Nha Trang it's 235km to Quy Nhon, 523km to Danang, 104km to Phan Rang, 250km to Mui Ne, 448km to HCMC, 205km to Dalat and 205km to Buon Ma Thuot.

TRAIN

The **Nha Trang train station** (Map p282; ☎ 382 2113; Đ Thai Nguyen; ⏰ ticket office 7-11.30am, 1.30-5pm & 6-10pm) is down the hill west of the cathedral. Destinations include Danang (220,000d, about 10 hours), Phan Rang (35,000d, about two hours) and HCMC (175,000d, about nine hours).

There is also a luxury train service, **Golden Trains** (☎ 347 1318; www.goldentrains.com.vn), which is numbered SN. Tickets from HCMC to Nha Trang start from 395,000d for a soft seat and 465,000d for a soft sleeper.

Getting Around

TO/FROM THE AIRPORT

Nha Trang is now served by Cam Ranh Airport, about 28km south of the city. A beautiful coastal road links Nha Trang with Cam Ranh. A shuttle bus runs the route (40,000d), leaving from the site of the old airport (near 86 Đ Tran Phu) two hours before scheduled departure times, taking about 30 minutes or so. Departing town, a taxi might be a more convenient option to avoid waiting around at the airport, but is considerably more expensive. Using **Nha Trang Taxi** (☎ 382 4000), the official maroon-coloured cabs, it costs 260,000d from the airport to a downtown destination. Conversely, it is only 180,000d from town out to the airport. Other taxi companies charge by the meter, meaning at least 300,000d.

BICYCLE

It's easy to get around all of the sights, including Thap Ba, by bicycle. Most major hotels have rentals from 30,000d per day. Watch out for the one-way system around the train station, and the chaotic roundabouts.

TAXI, CYCLO & XE OM

Nha Trang has an excessive number of all three. The *xe om* drivers are the most consistently annoying, although like taxis all over the world they seem to disappear when you actually want one. A motorcycle ride anywhere in the centre shouldn't cost more than 15,000d. Be careful at night, when some less reputable drivers moonlight as pimps and drug dealers.

AROUND NHA TRANG

Islands

Island tours are a big part of the Nha Trang experience. For details on boat tours and charters see p294.

HON TRE (BAMBOO ISLAND)

The beauty of Nha Trang's largest and closest offshore island is now marred by a huge Hollywood-style sign advertising Vinpearl Land (p296). You can access this island by cable car or boat.

HON MIEU

All the tourist literature touts Hon Mieu (also called Tri Nguyen Island) as the site of an outdoor aquarium (Ho Ca Tri Nguyen). In fact, the aquarium is an important fish-breeding farm, where over 40 species of fish, crustacean and other marine creatures are raised in three separate areas. There is also a cafe built on stilts over the water. Ask around for canoe rentals.

The main village on Hon Mieu is Tri Nguyen. Bai Soai is a gravel beach on the far side of Hon Mieu from Cau Da, and there are a number of rustic **bungalows** (US$10) on the island.

Most people will take some sort of boat tour booked through a hotel, cafe or Khanh Hoa Tours (p281). Impoverished and less-hurried travellers might catch one of the regular ferries that go to Tri Nguyen village from Cau Da dock.

HON MUN (EBONY ISLAND)

Hon Mun is situated just southeast of Bamboo Island and is well known for its snorkelling.

HON MOT

Sandwiched neatly between Ebony Island and Hon Tam is tiny Hon Mot; it's another great place for snorkelling.

HON YEN (BIRD'S-NEST ISLAND)

Also known as Salangane Island, this is the two lump-shaped islands visible from Nha Trang Beach. These and other islands off Khanh Hoa province are the source of Vietnam's finest *salangane* (swiftlet) nests (see the boxed text, right). There is a small, secluded beach here. The 17km trip out to the islands takes three to four hours by small boat from Nha Trang.

HON LAO (MONKEY ISLAND)

The island is named after its large contingent of resident monkeys and has become a big hit with tourists (mostly Vietnamese). Most of the monkeys have grown quite accustomed to receiving food handouts, providing ample photo opportunities. However, these are wild animals and should be treated as such, particularly if travelling with children. Bear in mind that monkey bites are a possible source of rabies.

Aside from being unwilling to participate in a cuddle, the monkeys are materialistic. They'll grab the sunglasses off your face or snatch a pen from your shirt pocket and run off. So far, we haven't heard of monkeys slitting open travellers' handbags with a razor blade, but keep a close eye (and hand) on your possessions.

A word of warning: though the island itself can make for a fun visit, there's also a bear-and-monkey show that you may want to avoid. Travellers have reported seeing the animals beaten by their trainers during performances.

If you're not part of a tour, head 15km north of Nha Trang on Hwy 1A to **Long Phu Tourist** (☎ 383 9436; Vinh Luong), easily spotted by the huge colourful dragons forming the entrance, not far from a pagoda. Boats will ferry you to the island for 65,000d (15 minutes). Other destinations reached from here include Hoa Lan Springs on Hon Heo (50,000d, 45 minutes) and Hon Thi (30,000d, 20 minutes).

Thanh Citadel

This citadel dates from the 17th-century Trinh dynasty. It was rebuilt by Prince Nguyen Anh (later Emperor Gia Long) in 1793 during his successful offensive against the Tay Son Rebels. Only a few sections of the walls and gates remain. Thanh Citadel is 11km west of Nha Trang near Dien Khanh town.

Ba Ho Falls

The three waterfalls and pools at Ba Ho Falls (Suoi Ba Ho) are in a forested area about 20km north of Nha Trang and about 2km west of Phu Huu village. Turn off Hwy 1A just north of Quyen Restaurant.

Suoi Tien (Fairy Spring)

This enchanting little spring seems to pop out of nowhere. Like a small oasis, the Fairy Spring is decorated with its own natural garden of tropical vegetation and smooth boulders. It has been earmarked as the next big ecotourism site, which paradoxically probably means massive overdevelopment, but it is still peaceful if you hike upstream.

You'll need to rent a motorbike or car to reach the spring. From Nha Trang, drive south on Hwy 1A for 27km to Suoi Cat, turning right (west) at the blue and white 'Ho chua nuoc Suoi Dau' sign. After 5km you'll see a sign directing you to the spring.

Cam Ranh Harbour

The gorgeous natural harbour of **Cam Ranh Bay** starts 25km south of Nha Trang and 56km north of Phan Rang. With the opening of the stunning airport road, beautiful **Bai Dai** (Long Beach), forming the northern head of the harbour, has become much more accessible. Largely unspoilt, the government has been encouraging development and as if to confirm its international arrival, a Miss Universe contest was held at the Diamond Bay Resort in August 2008. What would Ho Chi Minh make of it all?

Driving the beach road, reminders of the American War come in the form of abandoned tanks peering out of the sand. The military still controls access to much of this area but is starting to work with tourist operators. Nha Trang's Waves Watersports (see p295) has negotiated access to some of the best surf breaks in Vietnam.

BIRD-SPIT SOUP

The nests of the *salangane* (swiftlet) are used in bird's-nest soup as well as in traditional medicine, and are considered an aphrodisiac. It is said that the extraordinary virility of Emperor Minh Mang, who ruled Vietnam from 1820 to 1840, was derived from the consumption of swiftlet nests.

The nests, which are built out of silk-like salivary secretions, are 5cm to 8cm in diameter. They are usually harvested twice a year. Red nests are the most highly prized. Annual production in Khanh Hoa and Phu Yen provinces is about 1000kg. At present, swiftlet spit fetches US$2000 per kilogram in the international marketplace.

GOODBYE SAILOR

Cam Ranh Harbour has long been considered one of Asia's prime deep-water anchorages. The Russian fleet of Admiral Rodjestvenski used it in 1905 at the end of the Russo-Japanese War, as did the Japanese during WWII. At this time the surrounding area was still considered an excellent place for tiger hunting. In the mid-1960s the Americans constructed a vast base here, including an extensive port, ship-repair facilities and an airstrip.

After reunification the Russians and their fleet came back, enjoying far better facilities than they had left seven decades before. For a while this became the largest Soviet naval installation outside the USSR. With the collapse of the Soviet Union in 1991 and the end of the Cold War, economic problems forced the Russians to cut back vastly on their overseas military facilities. Although the initial contract on Cam Ranh Bay was due to expire in 2004, the Russians vacated their position by the end of 2002, the last hurrah for the Russian navy in Asia.

To get here you can take the airport shuttle bus (see p302), although you'll need to time your visit around flight times. A one-way journey in a taxi will cost almost 200,000d, but you'll be able to negotiate something considerably cheaper, including waiting time, with a *xe om* (aim for 75,000d).

PHAN RANG & THAP CHAM

☎ 068 / pop 161,000

This really is a tale of two cities: Phan Rang hugging the shoulders of Hwy 1A and Thap Cham straddling Hwy 20 as it starts its long climb to Dalat. Anyone travelling Vietnam from north to south will notice a big change in the vegetation when approaching the joint capitals of Ninh Thuan province. The familiar lush green rice paddies are replaced with sandy soil supporting only scrubby plants. Local flora includes poinciana trees and prickly-pear cacti with vicious thorns. The area is famous for its production of table grapes, and many of the houses on the outskirts of town are decorated with vines on trellises.

The area's best-known sight (and a common stop on the Dalat–Nha Trang route) is the group of Cham towers known as Po Klong Garai (right), from which Thap Cham (Cham Tower) derives its name. There are many more towers dotted about the countryside in this area and the province is home to tens of thousands of Cham people. The Cham, like other ethnic minorities in Vietnam, have suffered from discrimination and are usually poorer than their ethnic-Vietnamese neighbours. There are also several thousand Chinese in the area, many of whom come to worship at the 135-year old **Quang Cong Pagoda** (Đ Thong Nhat), a colourful Chinese temple in the town centre.

With two major highways (1A and 20) intersecting in the town, this is a good pit stop for a coastal trip or the journey to Dalat. Nearby Ninh Chu Beach (p307) is another, quieter alternative to the celebrity beaches on this coast.

Orientation

Hwy 1A is Phan Rang's main commercial street, and becomes Đ Thong Nhat in town. The main part of town is bordered to the south by the Cai River. Thap Cham, 7km from Phan Rang, is strung out along Hwy 20, which heads northwest from Phan Rang towards Dalat.

Information

Agriculture Bank (☎ 382 2714; 540-544 Đ Thong Nhat) Exchanges currency.

Main post office (☎ 382 4943; 217A Đ Thong Nhat) Also offers internet access.

Sights

PO KLONG GARAI CHAM TOWERS

The four brick towers of **Po Klong Garai** (Thap Cham; admission 5000d; ⏰ 7.30am-6pm) were constructed at the end of the 13th and beginning of the 14th century. Built as Hindu temples, they stand on a brick platform at the top of **Cho'k Hala**, a crumbly granite hill covered with some of the most ornery cacti this side of the Rio Grande.

A large modern building in a vaguely Cham style sitting at the base of the hill is dedicated to Cham culture, with separate **galleries** of photographs, paintings and traditional pottery. It's a good reminder that while the Cham kingdom is long gone, the Cham people are alive and kicking (see p264).

Over the entrance to the largest tower (the **kalan**, or sanctuary) is a beautiful carving of a dancing Shiva with six arms. Note the inscriptions in the ancient Cham language on the doorposts. These tell of past restoration efforts and offerings of sacrifices and slaves. If you want to look inside, you'll need to remove your shoes as this is still an active place of worship. Inside the vestibule is a statue of the bull Nandin, symbol of the agricultural productivity of the countryside. To ensure a good crop, farmers would place an offering of fresh greens, herbs and areca nuts in front of Nandin's muzzle. Under the main tower is a *mukha-linga* sitting under a wooden pyramid.

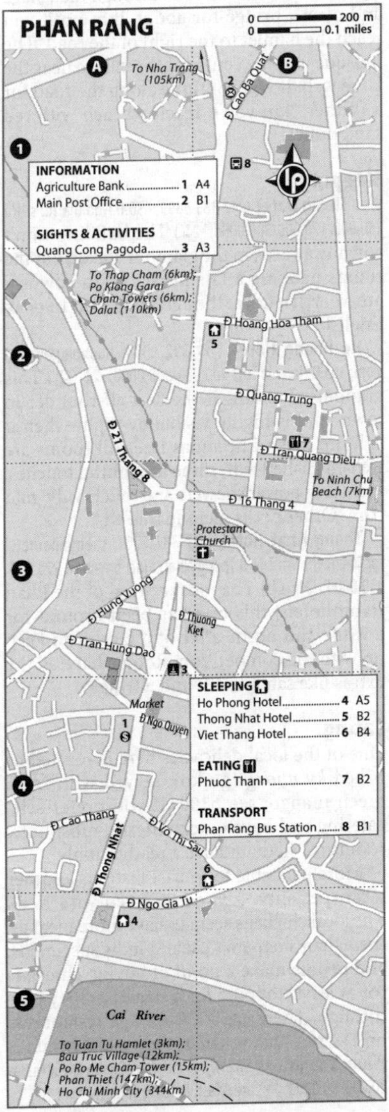

Inside the **smaller tower** opposite the entrance to the sanctuary, you can get a good look at some of the Cham's sophisticated building technology; the wooden columns that support the lightweight roof are visible. The structure attached to it was originally the **main entrance** to the complex.

On the hill directly south of Cho'k Hala is a concrete water tank built by the Americans in 1965. It is encircled by French pillboxes built during the Franco-Viet Minh War to protect the nearby rail yards. To the north of Cho'k Hala, you can see the concrete retaining walls of Thanh Son Airbase, used since 1975 by the Vietnamese Air Force.

Po Klong Garai is just north of Hwy 20, at a point 6km west of Phan Rang towards Dalat. The towers are on the opposite side of the tracks to Thap Cham train station. If you're travelling between Dalat and the coast, you will pass the site. Most of the open-tour buses running the route make a requisite pit stop here.

PO RO ME CHAM TOWER

Po Ro Me (Thap Po Ro Me; admission free) is one of the most atmospheric of Vietnam's Cham towers thanks in part to its isolated setting on top of a craggy hill with sweeping views over the cactus-strewn landscape. The temple honours the last ruler of an independent Champa, King Po Ro Me (r 1629–51), who died as a prisoner of the Vietnamese. His image and those of his family are found on the external decorations. Note the flame motif repeated around the arches, a symbol of purity, cleansing visitors of any residual bad karma.

The temple is still in active use, with ceremonies taking place twice a year. The rest of the time it's locked up, but the caretakers, who are based at the foot of the hill, will open the sanctuary for you. Consider leaving a small donation with them and don't forget to remove your shoes.

The occupants of the temple aren't used to having their rest disturbed, and it can be a little creepy when the bats start chattering and swooping overhead in the confined dark space. Through the gloom you'll be able to

PHAN RANG

0 200 m / 0 0.1 miles

INFORMATION
Agriculture Bank 1 A4
Main Post Office 2 B1

SIGHTS & ACTIVITIES
Quang Cong Pagoda 3 A3

SLEEPING
Ho Phong Hotel 4 A5
Thong Nhat Hotel 5 B2
Viet Thang Hotel 6 B4

EATING
Phuoc Thanh 7 B2

TRANSPORT
Phan Rang Bus Station 8 B1

To Nha Trang (105km)
To Thap Cham (6km); Po Klong Garai Cham Towers (6km); Dalat (110km)
To Ninh Chu Beach (7km)
To Tuan Tu Hamlet (3km); Bau Truc Village (12km); Po Ro Me Cham Tower (15km); Phan Thiet (147km); Ho Chi Minh City (344km)
Đ Cao Ba Quat
Đ Hoang Hoa Tham
Đ Quang Trung
Đ Tran Quang Dieu
Đ 21 Thang 8
Đ 16 Thang 4
Protestant Church
Đ Hung Vuong
Đ Thuong Kiet
Đ Tran Hung Dao
Market
Đ Ngo Quyen
Đ Cao Thang
Đ Vo Thi Sau
Đ Thong Nhat
Đ Ngo Gia Tu
Cai River

make out a blood-red and black centrepiece – a bas-relief representing the deified king in the form of Shiva. Behind the main deity and to the left is one of his queens, Thanh Chanh. Look out for the inscriptions on the doorposts and a stone statue of the bull Nandin.

Cham temple architecture has changed considerably if the small concrete hut dated 1962 at the back of the tower is anything to go by. Inside is a statue of the king's first wife – a Muslim woman called Thanh Cat – with an inscription painted on her chest. A statue of the third wife has been removed to a museum, along with other relics from the site. A *linga* remains at the front right of the tower. The rubble at the front left is all that's left of a preparation room bombed during the American War – revealing how close Po Ro Me came to destruction.

The best way to reach the site is with your own motorbike or a *xe om*. The trip is worthwhile, as long as getting lost is a part of your agenda. Take Hwy 1A south from Phan Rang for 9km. Turn right at the turn-off to Ho Tan Giang, a narrow sealed road just after the petrol station, and continue for a further 6km. Turn left in the middle of a dusty village at a paddock that doubles as a football field and follow the road as it meanders to the right until the tower comes into sight. A sign points the way cross-country for the last 500m. You might like to park and walk the remainder.

BAU TRUC VILLAGE

This Cham village is known for its pottery and you'll see several family shops in front of the mud and bamboo houses. On the way to Po Ro Me turn right off Hwy 1A near the war memorial, into the commune with the banner 'Lang Nghe Gom Bau Truc'. Inside the village take the first left for some of the better pottery stores.

TUAN TU HAMLET

While Cham history was all about Hinduism, significant parts of the remaining population are Islamic. There is a minaret-less mosque in the Cham hamlet of Tuan Tu (population 1000). This community is governed by elected religious leaders (Thay Mun), who can easily be identified by their traditional costume, which includes a white robe and an elaborate white turban with red tassels. In keeping with Islamic precepts governing modesty, the women here often wear head coverings and long dresses.

To get to Tuan Tu Hamlet, head south from Phan Rang along Hwy 1A. Go 250m south of the large bridge to a small bridge. Cross it and turn left (to the southeast) onto Đ Tran Nhat Duat. The road bends right at a Buddhist pagoda. Turn right at the T-junction after a school and follow the road through the village and over a bridge for about 2km until you reach the hamlet to the right of the road. The mosque is at the centre of the village near the large well. If you continue along the road for a further 2km you'll reach a beach with red sand dunes.

Sleeping

Viet Thang Hotel (☎ 383 5899; 430 Đ Ngo Gia Tu; s/d/q 150,000/170,000/300,000d; ❄) The building won't win any awards in the glamour stakes, but the rooms here are a fair price and the owners are very friendly, though they don't speak English.

Ho Phong Hotel (☎ 392 0333; hophong@yahoo.com; 363 Đ Ngo Gia Tu; r 200,000-300,000d; ❄ 💻) This grandiose building is the best all-rounder in town, and is highly visible by night when it is lit up like a Christmas tree. All rooms are well-furnished with some thoughtful touches, including power showers and toilets with gold trim. Other perks include free wi-fi.

Thong Nhat Hotel (☎ 382 7201; thongnhathotel-pr@hcm.vnn.vn; 343 Đ Thong Nhat; r incl breakfast 220,000-330,000d; ❄ 💻) The most central of the Phan Rang hotels, this one has been around for a while and needs a bit of a facelift to keep up with the competition. Rooms have all the extras like satellite TV and a fridge.

Eating

One of the local delicacies here is roasted or baked *ky nhong* (gecko), served with fresh green mango; see p309. If you prefer self-catering and have quick reflexes, most hotel rooms in Vietnam have a ready supply.

More palatable to tourist tastes is another local speciality, *com ga* (chicken with rice). The local chickens seem to have more meat on them than Vietnam's usual spindly specimens, and people make a point of buying chickens (or at least stopping for a snack) as they pass through. There are a few *com ga* restaurants on Đ Tran Quang Dieu, the best of which is **Phuoc Thanh** (☎ 382 4712; 3 Đ Tran Quang Dieu; mains 20,000-30,000d; 🕑 breakfast, lunch & dinner).

CHAMPY NEW YEAR

The Cham New Year *(kate)* is celebrated at Po Klong Garai in the seventh month of the Cham calendar (around October). The festival commemorates ancestors, Cham national heroes and deities such as the farmers' goddess Po Ino Nagar.

On the eve of the festival, a procession guarded by the mountain people of Tay Nguyen carries King Po Klong Garai's clothing, to the accompaniment of traditional music. The procession lasts until midnight. The following morning the garments are carried to the tower, once again accompanied by music, along with banners, flags, singing and dancing. Notables, dignitaries and village elders follow behind. This colourful ceremony continues into the afternoon.

The celebrations then carry on for the rest of the month, as the Cham attend parties and visit friends and relatives. They also use this time to pray for good fortune.

Phan Rang is the table-grape capital of Vietnam. Stalls in the market sell fresh grapes, grape juice and dried grapes (too juicy to be called raisins). Also worth sampling is the green *thanh long* (dragon fruit). Its mild, kiwifruit-like taste is especially refreshing when chilled. It's available in the market or in grocery shops along Đ Thong Nhat.

Getting There & Away

BUS

Phan Rang bus station (Ben Xe Phan Rang; opposite 64 Đ Thong Nhat) is on the northern outskirts of town. Regular buses head north to Nha Trang (from 30,000d, 2½ hours), northwest to Dalat (from 40,000d, four hours), and south to Ca Na (from 12,000d, one hour) and beyond.

CAR & MOTORBIKE

Phan Rang is 344km from HCMC, 147km from Phan Thiet, 104km from Nha Trang and 108km from Dalat.

TRAIN

The **Thap Cham train station** (Ga Thap Cham; ☎ 388 8029; 7 Đ Phan Dinh Phung) is about 6km west of Hwy 1A, within sight of Po Klong Garai Cham towers. Destinations include Nha Trang (39,000d, around two hours) and HCMC (130,000d, around eight hours).

NINH CHU BEACH

☎ 068

Southeast of Phan Rang, Ninh Chu Beach is increasingly popular with local tourists. Apart from the blight of litter in places, the 10km-long beach is quite nice. It makes a quieter alternative to Phan Rang as a base for visiting the Cham ruins.

A bizarre local attraction is the **Hoan Cau Resort** (☎ 3890 077; waterpark adult/child 10,000/5000d), where Disneyland meets Vietnamese folklore. Hilarious plaster statues adorn the grounds and rooms are shaped like tree stumps. A brief visit is more enjoyable than actually staying here.

Sleeping & Eating

Den Gion Resort (☎ 3874 223; www.dengion-resort.com; r 400,000-800,000d; ⌘ 💻) This resort has been lovingly upgraded in recent years and is an atmospheric place to stay. There are a range of bungalows set in a lush garden by the beach, all offering the same trim which includes smart showers and rustic ceiling fans. Breakfast is included, taken at the open-air restaurant (mains 50,000d to 125,000d). Free internet is a bonus, or there is a tennis court for a spot of exercise.

Saigon Ninhchu Hotel (☎ 3876 006; www.saigonninhchuhotel.com.vn; r US$65-105, ste US$150-200; ⌘ 💻 🏊) While prices have ostensibly risen here, online discounts mean it is still a nice place to stay. All rooms come with some sort of sea view and are well appointed with those extra touches like bathrobes and a safety box. The pool is a free-form lagoon and a tempting alternative to the beach. There is also a fitness centre, a couple of restaurants and a business centre.

Getting There & Away

Turn left (southeast) into Đ Ngo Gia Tu, the street immediately before the Cai River bridge in Phan Rang, and continue on, following the signs for 7km. Unless you're driving yourself, it's easiest to take a *xe om* (around 30,000d).

CA NA

☎ 068

During the 16th century, princes of the Cham royal family would fish and hunt tigers, elephants and rhinoceros here. Today Ca Na (pronounced 'kah nah' – not like the site of the biblical booze-up) is better known for its white-sand beaches, which are dotted with huge granite boulders. The best of the beach and accommodation is available right on Hwy 1A, a kilometre north of the fishing village. It's a beautiful spot, but it's tough to ignore the constant honking and rumble of trucks. The payoff, however, is an almost complete lack of hassle from the friendly locals.

The terrain is studded with magnificent prickly-pear cacti. Bright yellow **Lac Son**, a small pagoda on the hillside, makes for an interesting but steep climb. Further afield, **Tra Cang Temple** is about midway between Ca Na and Phan Rang. Unfortunately, you have to sidetrack over an abysmal dirt road in order to reach it. Many ethnic Chinese from Cholon visit the temple.

If you stay here, be aware that there are no banks or ATMs and absolutely no one accepts credit cards or travellers cheques.

Sleeping & Eating

Ca Na Hotel (☎/fax 376 1320; r 160,000-240,000d; ❄) This place feels as old as the boulders that dot the beach. It's a concrete place on the edge of the highway with slightly dilapidated rooms. The beach bungalows are definitely worth the extra dong. Most people only stop for lunch (dishes 25,000d to 75,000d) on the HCMC–Nha Trang run.

Hon Co Ca Na Motel (☎ 376 0999; www.ninhthuantourist.com.vn; r 250,000-300,000d; ❄ 💻) Quite a swanky place for little Ca Na, this resort has eight bungalows and a further 12 rooms in the 'motel' building. The set-up is impressive, but there is a slightly forlorn feel about the place due to a lack of regular guests. The beach is very inviting, plus there's a huge seafood restaurant (dishes 40,000d to 100,000d) and the dangerous diversions of karaoke and massage.

Getting There & Away

Ca Na is 114km north of Phan Thiet and 32km south of Phan Rang. Many long-haul buses cruising Hwy 1A can drop you here, including the open-tour buses on the Nha Trang–Mui Ne leg. Most open-tour buses can also pick up here if you phone ahead. Local buses from Phan Rang (12,000d, one hour) head into Ca Na fishing village – ask to be let out on the highway and catch a *xe om* for the last kilometre.

VINH HAO

☎ 062

Known for its mineral water, which is bottled and sold all over Vietnam, Vinh Hao is an obscure town just off Hwy 1A between Phan Rang and Phan Thiet.

It's also the home of **Vietnam Scuba** (☎ 3853 919; www.vietnamscuba.com), an attractive and well-appointed Korean-run dive centre on a private beach about 3.5km south of Ca Na, easy to spot from the highway. This is very much a by-Koreans for-Koreans resort, but serious scuba divers – and *kimchi* (pickled cabbage) lovers – will appreciate the set-up and some of the best diving in Vietnam. Marine life includes big fish, manta rays, barracuda and sharks.

Daily dive packages (from US$150) include accommodation in nice beachfront villas, boat trips and guides, and three meals a day. A BC (buoyancy compensator) and regulator can be rented for an extra US$50 a day. All dive sites are offshore, anywhere from 30 to 90 minutes from the resort's private jetty.

MUI NE BEACH

☎ 062

Once upon a time, Mui Ne was an isolated stretch of sand. but it was too beautiful to be ignored. Times have changed and it is now a string of resorts, expanding in number every year. However, the beach retains much of its charm and the resorts are, for the most part, mercifully low-rise, set amid pretty gardens by the sea. The original fishing village is still here, but tourists outnumber locals these days. Mui Ne is definitely moving upmarket, as more exclusive resorts open their doors, complemented by swish restaurants and swanky shops, but there is still a surfer vibe to the town.

Mui Ne is the adrenalin capital of southern Vietnam. There's no scuba diving or snorkelling to speak of, but when Nha Trang and Hoi An get the rains, Mui Ne gets the waves. Surf's up from August to December. For windsurfers, the gales blow as well, especially from late October to late April, when swells stir thanks to the Philippine typhoons. Kitesurfing has really taken off and the infinite horizon is often obscured by a pair of dangling legs flapping in the breeze. If this all sounds too much like hard work you can simply lounge around on the beach, watching others take the strain.

Mui Ne sees only about half the rainfall of nearby Phan Thiet. The sand dunes help protect its unique microclimate, and even during the wet season (from June to September) rains tend to be fairly light and sporadic.

One major problem the area faces is the steady creep of coastal erosion. Many resorts have almost completely lost their beaches and rely on sandbagging to keep the little they have left. On the plus side, it's almost impossible to get lost in Mui Ne, as everything is spread out along a 10km stretch of highway. Most accommodation lines the beach side, while restaurants and shops flank the other.

Orientation

The road follows the curve of the beach, running roughly east to west. Until the explosion of resorts it went by the name of Route 706 with addresses designated by their distance in kilometres from Hwy 1A in Phan Thiet (to the west). Half the properties now follow a new numbering system, with Route 706 given proper street numbers and renamed Đ Nguyen Dinh Chieu on the west half of the beach and Đ Huynh Thuc Khang on the east half. Adding to the confusion, some refer to themselves by the old kilometre marking combined with the new street name.

Information

A great resource for information on Mui Ne is www.muinebeach.net. Internet access is available at most hotels and resorts, as well as at many restaurants and travel cafes. There are several ATMs along the main Mui Ne strip.

Fami Tour Office (☎ 374 1030; 121 Đ Nguyen Dinh Chieu) Local tours, internet access and cheap international internet calls.

Main post office (☎ 384 9799; 348 Đ Huynh Thuc Khang) In Mui Ne village.

Post office branch (☎ 384 7480; 44 Đ Nguyen Dinh Chieu) A more convenient location at Swiss Village.

Sinh Café (☎ 3847 542; 144 Đ Nguyen Dinh Chieu) Operates out of Mui Ne Resort, booking open-tour buses and offering credit-card cash advances.

Tam Nam (☎ 374 2457; 49 Đ Nguyen Dinh Chieu) Friendly and cheap laundry service operating out of a small grocery store.

Sights

Mui Ne is famous for its enormous **red and white sand dunes**. These have been a favourite subject for many a Vietnamese photographer, including some who sit like camels on the blazing hot sand for hours, waiting for the winds to sculpt the dunes into that perfect Kodak moment. If you visit, be sure to try the sand-sledding.

You'll need a jeep to explore these properly, but be careful to agree on an itinerary for the tour, preferably in writing. We've heard complaints, particularly about 'sunset tours' that cut short with the sun high in the sky and the drivers getting aggressive when challenged.

Also of interest is the **Fairy Spring** (Suoi Tien), which is really a stream that flows through a patch of dunes with interesting sand and rock formations. It's a beautiful trek wading up the stream from the sea to its source, though it might be wise to hire a local guide. You can do the trek barefoot, but if you're heading out into the big sand dunes, you'll need leather soles on your feet; sandals are even questionable during the midday sun.

Heading west, **Po Shanu Cham Towers** (Km5; admission 2000d; 🕒 7.30-11.30am & 1.30-4.30pm) occupies a hill near Phan Thiet, with sweeping views of the town and a cemetery filled with candylike tombstones. Dating from the 9th century, this complex consists of the ruins of three towers, none of which are in very good shape. There's a small pagoda on the site, as well as a gallery and shop.

LIZARD FISHING

When most people think of fishing in the mountains they conjure up images of hooking river trout or lake bass. But in the arid foothills of the south-central coast (notably around places like Ca Na, Phan Rang, Phan Thiet and Mui Ne) there is a whole other kind of angling, and a walk in these hills can yield one of the strangest sights in Vietnam – lizard fishing.

These lizards, called *than lan nui,* are members of the gecko family and good for eating – some say they taste like chicken. The traditional way of catching the lizards is by setting a hook on a long bamboo fishing pole and dangling bait from the top of a boulder until the spunky little reptiles strike.

Lizards are served grilled, roasted or fried, and are often made up into a paté (complete with their finely chopped bones) and used as a dip for rice-paper crackers. Yum.

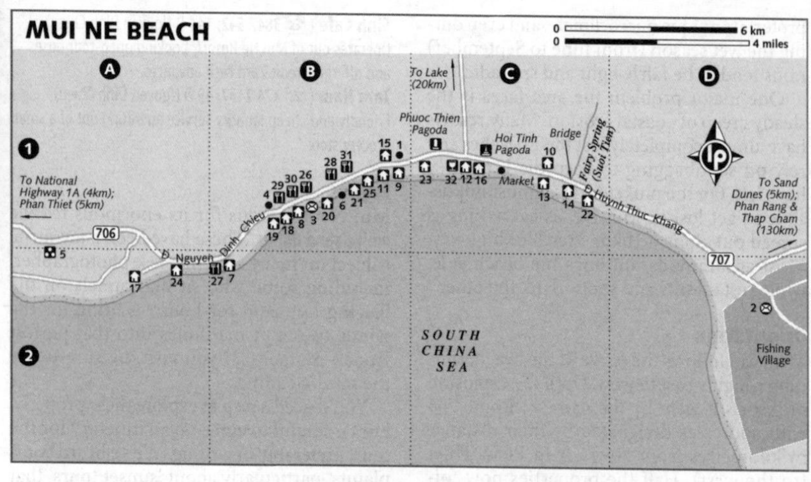

INFORMATION
Fami Tour Office....................1 B1
Main Post Office....................2 D2
Post Office Branch....................3 B1
Sinh Café....................(see 16)
Tam Nam....................4 B1

SIGHTS & ACTIVITIES
Airwaves....................(see 18)
Jibes....................(see 9)
Po Shanu Cham Towers....................5 A2
Windchimes....................6 B1

SLEEPING
Allez Boo Resort....................7 B2
Bamboo Resort....................(see 3)
Bien Dua Resort....................(see 32)
Bon Bien Resort....................(see 8)
Canary Beach Resort....................(see 22)
Cham Villas....................8 B1
Dynasty Beach Resort....................(see 16)
Full Moon Resort....................9 B1
Golden Sunlight Guesthouse....................10 C1
Hai Yen Guesthouse....................(see 32)
Hiep Hoa Resort....................11 B1
Hoang Kim Golden....................12 C1
Indochina Dreams....................(see 11)
Kim Ngan Guesthouse....................(see 23)
L'Anmien Resort....................(see 7)
Little Mui Ne Cottages....................13 C1
Lu Hoang Guesthouse....................(see 23)
Lucy Resort....................14 C1
Mellow....................15 B1
Mui Ne Resort....................16 C1
Paradise Huts....................(see 9)
Romana Resort....................17 A2
Sailing Club....................18 B1
Seahorse Resort....................19 B1
Sunsea Resort....................20 B1
Sunshine Beach....................(see 11)
Suoi Tien Mui Ne Resort....................21 B1
Terracotta Resort & Spa....................(see 18)
Thai Hoa Mui Ne Resort....................22 C1
Tien Dat Resort....................23 C1
Victoria Phan Thiet Beach Resort....................24 A2
Vietnam-Austria House....................(see 9)
Wind Champ Resort....................25 B1

EATING
Ganesh....................(see 26)
Good Morning Vietnam....................26 B1
Guava....................(see 30)
Hoa Vien Brauhaus....................27 B2
Hoang Vu....................28 B1
Hoang Vu....................(see 1)
Lam Tong....................(see 9)
Le Chasseur Blanc....................(see 31)
Luna d'Autunno....................29 B1
Peaceful Family Restaurant....................30 B1
Snow....................31 B1

DRINKING
Gecko....................(see 30)
Pogo....................32 C1
Wax....................(see 25)

Activities

Jibes (☎ 384 7405; www.windsurf-vietnam.com; 90 Đ Nguyen Dinh Chieu; 🕒 7.30am-6pm) is a surfer's heaven, offering lessons and renting state-of-the-art gear like windsurfers (one hour/half-day/full-day US$12/30/45), surfboards (one hour/half-day/full-day US$7.50/15/25), kitesurfers (one hour/half-day/full-day US$50/100/140) and kayaks (one hour/half-day/full-day US$5/13/25). Insurance is extra.

Airwaves (☎ 3847 440; www.airwaveskitesurfing.com; 24 Đ Nguyen Dinh Chieu), based at the Sailing Club (see p312), is another outfit offering kitesurfing, windsurfing and sailing lessons, plus equipment rentals.

Windchimes (☎ 0909-720 017; www.windsurfing-vietnam.com) is another reliable option, operating out of Saigon Mui Ne Resort at 56 Đ Nguyen Dinh Chieu.

Sleeping

Mui Ne is the escape of choice for expats working in HCMC and affluent Vietnamese seeking to escape the big-city smoke, meaning that the smarter accommodation is often full during weekends and holidays. This has encouraged a number of properties with mid-range standards to demand top-end prices and even genuine budget options are thin on the ground, but then unlike Nha Trang most places here come with a beachfront location.

However, the sheer volume of options on offer means that there is still value for money to be found at every budget, but this is definitely one of the few places on the coast where it is smart to book ahead.

BUDGET

Hai Yen Guesthouse (☎ 384 7243; www.muinebeach.net/haiyen; 132 Đ Nguyen Dinh Chieu; r US$10-20;) A little cracker, the friendly Hai Yen has cheap fan rooms and a good selection of chilled (air-con) rooms set behind a new swimming pool. There is beachfront access, plus a small restaurant.

our pick **Thai Hoa Mui Ne Resort** (☎ 384 7320; www.thaihoaresort.com; 56 Đ Huynh Thuc Khang; r US$10-25;) One of the last places on the Mui Ne strip, which also makes it one of the best value. Bungalows front onto a spacious garden ,and the more expensive ones are up close and personal with the beach. Fan rooms run to US$15, while air-con kicks in from US$20. Worth the journey.

Vietnam-Austria House (☎ 384 7047; ngothikimhong@hotmail.com; Km13.5; r US$10-20;) One of the old-school places in Mui Ne, this is good value but a little cramped – they have somehow squeezed a small pool into the complex. The cheap rooms have shared bathrooms, but US$15 earns some privacy for ablutions. The most expensive rooms are near the beachfront.

Bien Dua Resort (Coconut Beach; ☎ 384 7241; 136 Đ Nguyen Dinh Chieu; r US$10-20;) At this small French-run place, the bungalow-style rooms are great value and include some beachfront browsing. Cheaper rooms have fan; all rooms have hot water and TV.

Hoang Kim Golden (☎ 384 7689; www.hoangkim-golden.com; 140 Đ Nguyen Dinh Chieu; r US$10-45;) This old timer was undergoing major renovations during the time of our visit, meaning there aren't that many budget rooms left for the taking. All rooms are set in bungalows near the small swimming pool and beachfront. The cheap rooms are pretty bare with fan and attached bathroom.

Lu Hoang Guesthouse (☎ 350 0060; 106 Đ Nguyen Dinh Chieu; r US$15-20;) This upmarket villa looks like a swanky private house, but it offers good-value lodgings. The effusive owner has decorated the rooms with care and attention to detail, including superb bathrooms for this price range. No direct beach access is the only drawback.

Wind Champ Resort (☎ 384 7001; www.windchamp.com; 68 Đ Nguyen Dinh Chieu; r US$15-25;) This spacious backpacker resort is reminiscent of Ko Phan Ngan or the way things used to be in Mui Ne before land prices rocketed. Thatched bungalows are set amid coconut palms, and many face the beach. It's also a base for water activities and is just a crawl from the happening Wax bar (p314).

Hiep Hoa Resort (☎ 384 7262; hiephoatourism@yahoo.net; 80 Đ Nguyen Dinh Chieu; r US$20-25;) Barely scraping into the budget category, but it's cheap by Mui Ne standards, this intimate little resort has a lush garden and atmospheric rooms. Go on, be a devil, splash US$5 for the sea view.

More? Oh yes, there are many more:

Golden Sunlight Guesthouse (☎ 374 3124; hiephoatourism@yahoo.net; 19B Đ Nguyen Dinh Chieu; r US$10) Alright, so it's not on the beach and right at the end of town, but it's a friendly place with clean, airy rooms with fan and attached bathroom.

Mellow (☎ 374 3086; 117C Đ Nguyen Dinh Chieu; r US$10-25;) On the 'wrong' (nonbeach) side of town, no frills, but some thrills in the attached bar-restaurant. The cheaper rooms share bathrooms (with hot water) and toilets.

Kim Ngan Guesthouse (☎ 384 7046; kimnganvilla@yahoo.com; Km13; r US$15-25;) This family-run guesthouse is set in a modern villa by the beach. Rooms are basic, but include TV and hot water.

MIDRANGE

Indochina Dreams (☎ 384 7271; www.indochinadream.com; 74 Đ Nguyen Dinh Chieu; r US$30-35;) Small in size, big in character, this dreamy spot has just five bungalows decorated with terracotta tiles and bamboo furnishings. The popular bar-restaurant on the street side is a good place to while away an evening.

Lucy Resort (☎ 384 7801; www.lucyresort.net; Km18; r US$30-60;) This bungalow resort is clustered around a coconut grove and includes a figure-eight pool overlooking the beach. The US$30 fan rooms are a bit optimistic, but the deluxe bungalows by the beach have plenty of charm.

Canary Beach Resort (☎ 384 7258; www.canaryresort.com.vn; 60 Huynh Thuc Khang; r US$35-65;) The end of the road as far as accommodation in Mui Ne is concerned, this is reflected in the good-value rates. There are 70 rooms, all featuring a smart trim, but the different prices reflect size of the room and proximity to the beach. The free-form pool is impressive.

our pick **Full Moon Resort** (Trang Tron; ☎ 384 7008; www.windsurf-vietnam.com; 84 Đ Nguyen Dinh Chieu; r US$30-90;) The committed owners have consistently upgraded this place, one of the first resorts on the Mui Ne strip, to keep up with the competition. Beachfront bungalows are very atmospheric with wall hangings and jacuzzi-like bathtubs. Family rooms are available that include a sofa bed for the kiddies.

Tien Dat Resort (☎ 384 7989; www.tiendatresort.com; 94A Đ Nguyen Dinh Chieu; r US$37-70;) The 'Blue Waves' resort has 100 rooms and bungalows, making it a good option for a last-minute booking, especially as it is not averse to promotional rates. Check out the old motorbike collection in front of the hotel, a resting place for Jawas, MZs and ancient Mobylettes, plus a Russian Taz limousine.

Mui Ne Resort (☎ 384 7542; www.sinhcafevn.com; 144 Đ Nguyen Dinh Chieu; r 560,000-880,000d;) Under the stewardship of the Sinh Café, this is a smart midrange resort, more flashpacker than backpacker. The rooms are spotless and the staff friendly. There is a great pool surrounded by lush foliage, plus a beach strip. The restaurant is huge, to accommodate the open-bus tourists who swarm into the place several times a day on their compulsory pit stop.

Paradise Huts (☎ 384 7177; www.chezninavn.com; 86 Đ Nguyen Dinh Chieu; r US$40;) Also known as Chez Nina, in case you were wondering about the website, these pretty bungalows are housed in a leafy garden in the middle of Mui Ne. If the beautiful beach doesn't do it for you, check out the sumptuous Nina Spa at 165 Đ Nguyen Dinh Chieu, set in an old wooden house with a pool out front.

Dynasty Beach Resort (☎ 384 7816; www.dynastyresorts.com; 140A Đ Nguyen Dinh Chieu; r US$45-55;) Designed in the Hoi An retro style of a Vietnamese trading town, this resort has rooms that are good value thanks to their spacious and bright layout overlooking the beach. There is a large beachfront pool next to the beach.

Little Mui Ne Cottages (☎ 384 7550; www.littlemuine.com; 10B Huynh Thuc Khang; r incl breakfast US$60-160;) Set amid extensive gardens, this is quite an oasis that promotes its personal service. The cottages are generously spread out so it doesn't feel too crowded and the huge pool is big enough for laps. Other nice touches include internet access and use of bicycles. Not so nice are the tax and service charges on top.

Still can't decide? We know the feeling:

Suoi Tien Mui Ne Resort (☎ 384 7146; suoitienmuineresort@vnn.vn; 60 Đ Nguyen Dinh Chieu; r US$20-70;) This friendly, family-run place occupies a fine strip of sand and now has a little pool as well. Fan rooms are pricey, but the air-con rooms are reasonable.

Sunshine Beach Resort (☎ 384 7788; www.sunshine-beach.com; 82 Đ Nguyen Dinh Chieu; r US$26-43;) This likeable little resort offers great-value rooms with private terrace and there are no hidden extras for taxes or credit-card payments.

Sunsea Resort (☎ 384 7700; www.sunsearesort-muine.com; 50 Đ Nguyen Dinh Chieu; r US$50-70;) The beautiful bungalows here are like African-style *bandas*, set around a sculptured garden dotted with coconut palms. Inviting pool rounds things off.

Bon Bien Resort (☎ 374 1081; www.bonbienresort.com; 30 Đ Nguyen Dinh Chieu; r US$60-80;) Just about midrange by Mui Ne standards, this smart new resort is offering some enticing rates to fill the beds.

TOP END

Most of the places at the top end usually charge an extra 10% tax and 5% service.

Sailing Club (☎ 384 7440; www.sailingclubvietnam.com; 24 Đ Nguyen Dinh Chieu; r US$66, bungalows US$88-126;) At this sophisticated and stylish resort the sensibly priced rooms include designer furnishings, wood trim and private balconies. The two beachfront bungalows are a worthy indulgence. The beachside pool includes a great bar-restaurant overlooking the sea, which is open to all-comers for a meal or a drink.

Terracotta Resort & Spa (☎ 384 7610; www.terracottaresort.com; 28 Đ Nguyen Dinh Chieu; r US$85-230;) One of several new resorts to have opened its doors, this place has bungalows offering a high standard of comfort without sacrificing atmosphere. Choose from the pool or the manicured sand; there is a beach bar by night.

Seahorse Resort (☎ 384 7507; www.seahorseresortvn.com; Km11; r US$109-220;) An elegant escape, the bungalows here are set amid a coconut-tree-shaded garden that follows the contours of the land. Bungalows are grouped together in quads around a garden and include traditional Vietnamese art and furnishings, plus Balinese-style alfresco bathrooms. The Hippocampe Restaurant has a fine location overlooking the pool and beach.

Cham Villas (☎ 374 1234; www.chamvillas.com; 32 Đ Nguyen Dinh Chieu; r incl breakfast US$120-160;) The most boutique of many 'boutique' resorts in Mui Ne, there are just 16 stylish villas available here, so it does tend to fill up quickly. Verdant gardens surround the large pool and there is strip of private beach. Wi-fi included.

our pick **Victoria Phan Thiet Beach Resort** (☎ 381 3000; www.victoriahotels-asia.com; Km9; r US$180-680;) The original luxury resort in Mui Ne (yes, ignore the name, it's not really in Phan Thiet), the Victoria remains one of the best addresses in town. The gorgeous open-plan bungalows feature huge bathrooms with deep tubs and Balinese-style outdoor showers. There is a lengthy strip of beach and two pools. The kids club is handy for parents wanting a little break now and then, plus the restaurant has an impressive and eclectic menu.

And the roll-call goes on:

Bamboo Resort (☎ 384 7007; www.bamboovillageresortvn.com; 38 Đ Nguyen Dinh Chieu; r US$88-190;) This long-running resort has had a makeover, bringing it back into contention with the big boys. Bamboo decor predominates and facilities include two pools and a kiddies play area.

Romana Resort (☎ 374 1289; www.romanaresort.com.vn; Km8; r US$98-358;) Designed in Romanesque style with fountains and statues, this place isn't shy to offer promotions. Villas each include a private pool, starting from US$118 in low season.

Allez Boo Resort (☎ 374 1081; www.allezboo.com; 8 Đ Nguyen Dinh Chieu; r US$100-430;) It's hard to believe this place is related to the original backpacker bar of Pham Ngo Lao, as it is all about style: colonial-style decor in the rooms, very modern facilities, including a huge pool and jacuzzi, plus a lively bar.

L'Anmien Resort (☎ 374 1888; www.lanmienresort.com; 12A Đ Nguyen Dinh Chieu; r US$224-800;) Just about to open its doors as we were in town, this looks like it will be the most sophisticated place on the beach.

Plus, there are a couple of high-flying places further afield from Mui Ne:

Pandanus Resort (☎ 384 9849; www.pandanusresort.com; Ap Thien Ai; r US$119-229;) The curious name aside, this is a smart resort in a similar style to Furama near Danang. Discount packages available online. It is located just north of Mui Ne village near the red dunes.

Princess d'Annam (☎ 368 2222; www.princessannam.com; Ke Ga; r US$300-1200;) Claiming to be Vietnam's first all-villa resort, this is unashamed luxury, located on a private stretch of beach about 30km south of Mui Ne.

Eating

our pick **Lam Tong** (☎ 384 7598; 92 Đ Nguyen Dinh Chieu; dishes 25,000-75,000d; breakfast, lunch & dinner) It doesn't look like much, sandwiched in between the fancy-pants resorts of Mui Ne, but this family-run beachfront restaurant serves some of the best food in town. Fresh seafood is popular and affordable – the place is always busy with a mix of travellers and locals. There are also some tables right on the sand.

Peaceful Family Restaurant (Yen Gia Quan; ☎ 374 1019; 53 Đ Nguyen Dinh Chieu; dishes 30,000-70,000d; lunch & dinner) A long-running local restaurant, the family here serve up traditional Vietnamese cuisine under a breezy thatched roof. Prices have remained fairly stable here, while other places have been rounding them up, making it a good bet.

Hoang Vu (Double Wheels Restaurant; ☎ 384 7525; Km12.2 & 121 Đ Nguyen Dinh Chieu; dishes 40,000-90,000d; lunch & dinner) Like many successful businesses in Vietnam, this one has cloned itself into two restaurants. The menu is predominantly Asian, with Vietnamese, Chinese and Thai tastes on offer. The setting is very atmospheric and the service attentive.

our pick **Hoa Vien Brauhaus** (☎ 374 1383; www.hoavien.vn; 2A Đ Nguyen Dinh Chieu; mains 50,000-150,000d; lunch & dinner) Freshly brewed draft Pilsner Urquell is the big draw here, although it feels a bit different to be sipping it overlooking the South China Sea. The huge restaurant offers some Czech and international dishes, as well as a good selection of Vietnamese food and a dizzying array of live seafood (thankfully not served live, in most cases).

Snow (☎ 374 3123; 109 Đ Nguyen Dinh Chieu; mains 50,000-150,000d; lunch & dinner;) This is an ubertrendy place by Mui Ne standards, finished in minimalist white and popular with Russians who may be missing the snow of a cold winter. One of the only places offering sushi and sashimi, it also has international and Vietnamese offerings. Free pick-ups from your hotel.

Le Chasseur Blanc (☎ 374 1222; www.chasseurblanc.com; 97 Đ Nguyen Dinh Chieu; mains 80,000-200,000d; lunch & dinner;) Ostensibly the leading French restaurant in Mui Ne, but as well as serving succulent steaks and duck, it also offers some unexpected meats such as crocodile, kangaroo and ostrich. Artfully decorated, there is also free wi-fi for customers, plus a pool table.

Luna d'Autunno (☎ 384 7591; 51A Đ Nguyen Dinh Chieu; mains 80,000-200,000d; 🕑 lunch & dinner) A sophisticated Italian restaurant, Luna is well represented in the region from Hanoi to Phnom Penh. Prices are higher than most in Mui Ne, but the pizzas and pastas are authentic and the seafood specials have an Italian twist.

Other good eateries:

Ganesh (☎ 374 1330; 57 Đ Nguyen Dinh Chieu; mains 40,000-140,000d; 🕑 lunch & dinner) A stylish Indian-run restaurant offering authentic flavours from the homeland.

Guava (☎ 374 1330; 57 Đ Nguyen Dinh Chieu; mains 40,000-140,000d; 🕑 lunch & dinner) A southern relative of the trendy Nha Trang spot, Guava Mui Ne is more restaurant than bar, offering fresh seafood, fusion flavours and a generous cocktail menu.

Good Morning Vietnam (☎ 384 7585; www.goodmorningviet.com; Km11.8; mains 60,000-140,000d; 🕑 lunch & dinner) Part of the popular chain of Italian restaurants, this place pioneered the idea of offering free hotel pick-ups to bridge the distance of the strip.

Drinking

It wouldn't be a (wind/kite) surf spot without a legion of beachside bars, and Mui Ne can deliver.

Pogo (☎ 0909-479 346; 138 Đ Nguyen Dinh Chieu) A little way from the main action, it is worth hopping along to Pogo for the chilled atmosphere. The open-air bar features lively decoration, free pool, some sorted sounds and big beanbags for crashing on.

Wax (☎ 384 7001; Wind Champ Resort; 68 Đ Nguyen Dinh Chieu) Tucked away on the beachfront in Wind Champ Resort, this is one of the livelier bars in town and stays open later than most. Good tunes, a mammoth drink list and beachside flopping draw the crowds.

Gecko (☎ 3741 033; 51 Đ Nguyen Dinh Chieu) If you are looking for something a bit more sophisticated, this bar-restaurant has an impressive cocktail list. Or try an ice cream or smoothie by day and take advantage of the free wi-fi.

Jibes (☎ 3847 405; 90 Đ Nguyen Dinh Chieu) Unofficial HQ of the kitesurfing brigade, this beachside cafe-bar is a relaxing place for a drink, but it quietens down by night when the party crowd is elsewhere.

Getting There & Away

Mui Ne is no longer the dead-end town (literally, not metaphorically) it once was, as there are both north and south links to Hwy 1A. The newer northern link is a scenic stretch, passing deserted beaches and a beautiful lake ringed with water lilies, which allows the open-tour buses to pass through Mui Ne without backtracking, reducing journey times.

Open-tour buses are the most convenient option for Mui Ne, as most public buses serve Phan Thiet. Several companies have daily services to/from HCMC (US$6, four hours), Nha Trang (US$7, five hours) via Ca Na (US$4, 1½ hours), and Dalat (US$8, 5½ hours). A local bus makes trips between Phan Thiet bus station and Mui Ne, departing from the Coopmart, on the corner of Đ Nguyen Tat Thanh and Đ Tran Hung Dao, every 15 minutes. A *xe om* ride from Phan Thiet to Mui Ne will cost around 50,000d.

Getting Around

Mui Ne is so spread out that it's difficult to wander about on foot when it's so hot. There are plenty of *xe om* drivers to take you up and down the strip; no trip should cost more than 10,000d to 20,000d, depending on how far you want to go. For something more comfortable, **Mai Linh** (☎ 389 8989) operates meter taxis, although call ahead to book later in the evening or ask the restaurant or bar to assist.

Given that the area isn't highly populated and it's not on the main highway, this is not a bad place to hire a bicycle or motorbike through your hotel or one of the travel agencies. However, take care, as traffic is moving pretty fast and accidents involving tourists have been known to happen.

PHAN THIET

☎ 062 / pop 168,400

Before the discovery of Mui Ne, Phan Thiet was an emerging resort town in its own right, but it has been eclipsed by the new kid on the block. Phan Thiet is traditionally known for its *nuoc mam* (fish sauce), producing 16 to 17 million litres of the stinky stuff per annum. The population includes descendants of the Cham, who controlled this area until 1692. During the colonial period the Europeans lived in their own segregated ghetto stretching along the northern bank of the Phan Thiet River, while the Vietnamese, Cham, Southern Chinese, Malays and Indonesians lived along the southern bank.

The river flowing through the centre of town creates a small **fishing harbour**, which is always chock-a-block with boats, making for a photo opportunity. To get to Phan Thiet's **beachfront**, turn off Đ Tran Hung Dao (Hwy

1A) into Đ Nguyen Tat Thanh – the road opposite the **Victory Monument**, an arrow-shaped concrete tower with a cluster of victorious patriots around the base.

The main attraction of Phan Thiet is the **Ocean Dunes Golf Club** (☎ 382 3366; www.vietnamgolfresorts.com; 1 Đ Ton Duc Thang; per round from US$70), a top-notch 18-hole, par 72 course designed by Nick Faldo, near the beachfront at the Novotel. Very reasonably priced golf package tours are available if you book from HCMC – visit the website or contact the resort's HCMC **marketing office** (☎ 08-824 3460; New World Hotel, 76 Đ Le Lai).

Orientation & Information

Phan Thiet is built along both banks of the Phan Thiet River (also known as the Ca Ty and the Muong Man River). Hwy 1A becomes Đ Tran Hung Dao as it runs through town.

Binh Thuan Tourist (☎ 3816 821; www.binhthuantourist.com; 82 Đ Trung Trac; ⏲ 7-11am & 1.30-5pm Mon-Fri, 8-10.30am Sat & Sun) Tourist maps and information.

Sleeping & Eating

Unless you're here for the golf, you're much better off staying in nearby Mui Ne (see p308). Serious golfers might like to try **Novotel Ocean Dunes & Golf Resort** (☎ 3822 393; www.accorhotels-asia.com; 1 Đ Ton Duc Thang; r US$70-135; ❄ 💻 🏊), sitting pretty between the golf course and a private stretch of beach. The hotel's Seahorse Restaurant is the best restaurant in town, serving up local seafood (dishes US$5 to US$15). There is also a branch of Mogambo's (which is a popular spot in Saigon) in the clubhouse, overlooking the green. Discounted golf packages, including accommodation, are available from just US$110.

Getting There & Around

Phan Thiet bus station (Ben Xe Binh Thuan; ☎ 382 1361; Đ Tu Van Tu; ⏲ 5.30am-3.30pm) is on the northern outskirts of town. Phan Thiet is on Hwy 1A, 198km east of HCMC, 250km from Nha Trang and 247km from Dalat. The nearest train station to Phan Thiet is 12km west of town in dusty little Muong Man.

TA CU MOUNTAIN

The highlight here is the **white reclining Buddha** (Tuong Phat Nam). At 49m long, it's the largest in Vietnam. The pagoda was constructed in 1861, but the Buddha was only added in 1972. It has become an important pilgrimage centre for Buddhists, who stay overnight in the pagoda's dormitory. Foreigners can't do this without police permission, but there is a **guesthouse** (☎ 386 7484; r 200,000d; ❄) on the mountain.

The mountain is just off Hwy 1A, 28km south from Phan Thiet, from which the Buddha is a beautiful two-hour trek, or a two-minute cable-car ride (55,000d return) and a short, but steep, hike.

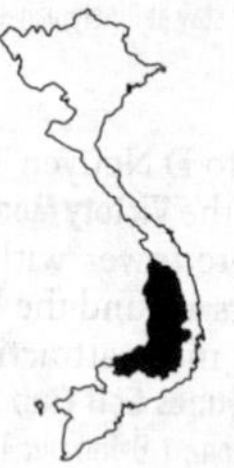

Central Highlands

The beauty of the central highlands is that there's plenty of space to disappear into. The undulating landscape that once sheltered VC soldiers down the Ho Chi Minh Trail now offers an intriguing refuge for travellers. There's a rugged charm to its villages and valleys, waterfalls and winding roads, and except at the former French hill station of Dalat, foreigners are still quite a rarity.

Most people come here to visit Montagnard (hill-tribe) villages; the further off the beaten track you travel, the more unspoiled an existence you'll find. Likewise the natural attractions in the vicinity are simple, rustic affairs. Most don't rate as must-sees, just pleasant pit stops if you're roving about on your own.

In 2001 and 2004 protests erupted in Buon Ma Thuot, Pleiku and other parts of the highlands, objecting to the government's resettlement and land policies and alleged discrimination against Montagnards. While things seem quiet now, international human-rights groups continue to report instances of ill-treatment of ethnic minorities. As for the natural landscape, it's beautiful but in some places marred – first by Agent Orange in the American War, then by slash-and-burn agriculture, now by expanding farms and dams.

Despite its fraught history, the central highlands are safe and easy to travel. Dalat is perfect for a weekend's respite from the heat, the rest of the highlands for a week-long immersion in a life far from the madding crowd.

HIGHLIGHTS

- Learn about the Montagnard way of life in the villages around **Kon Tum** (p339)
- Enjoy the fresh air and French flair of **Dalat** (opposite), Vietnam's mountain resort
- Hop on a motorbike and hit the twists and turns of the **Ho Chi Minh Trail** (p334)
- Challenge your heart rate with an adventure trip in the hills **around Dalat** (p320)
- Get foggy as you approach the thundering **Dray Sap and Dray Nur Falls** (p333)

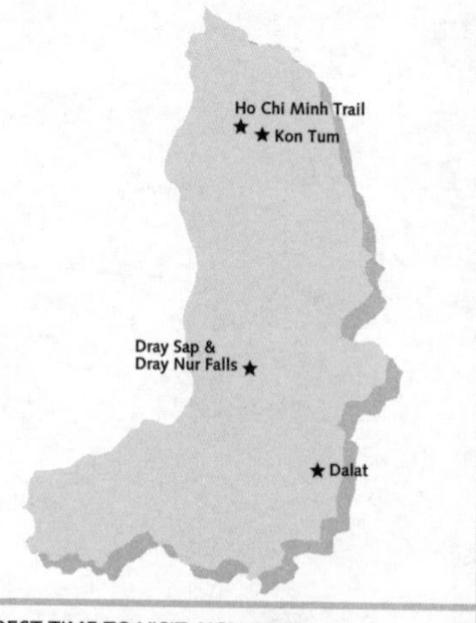

- ELEVATION: 200–2598M
- BEST TIME TO VISIT: NOV–MAR

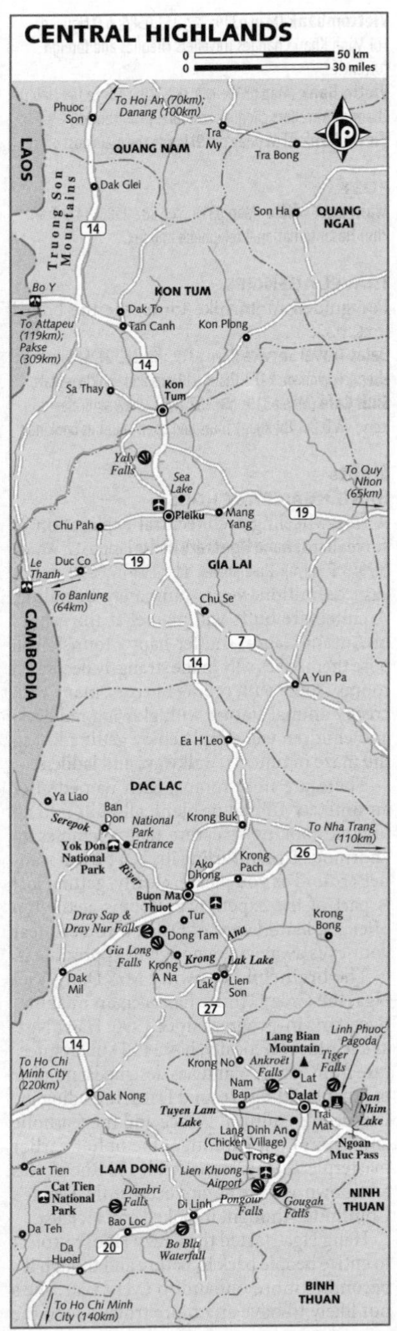

Getting There & Away

The region has airports at Dalat, Buon Ma Thuot and Pleiku; all have flights from HCMC, Hanoi and Danang. There are no trains servicing this region.

By road you can access Dalat via Hwy 20 from HCMC or Phan Rang. Hwy 14 is the main north–south route, passing through Buon Ma Thuot, Pleiku and Kon Tum. Pleiku is connected to the coast by Hwy 19, which hits Hwy 1A near Quy Nhon. Similarly, Buon Ma Thuot can be reached from Ninh Hoa, just north of Nha Trang, by Hwy 26. There are frequent buses on all these routes, but only Dalat is served by open-tour buses.

DALAT

☎ 063 / pop 189,523 / elev 1475m

You could call Dalat Bizarro Vietnam – it's spring-like cool instead of tropical hot, the town is dotted with elegant French-colonial villas instead of squat socialist architecture, and the farms around are thick with strawberries and flowers, not rice. As a highland resort it's been welcoming tourists for a century, and it has all the attractions – natural and tricked-out – to prove it.

The French came first, fleeing the heat of Saigon. They left behind not only their holiday homes but also the vibe of a European town and the local bohemian artists' predilection for swanning around in berets. The Vietnamese couldn't resist adding little touches to, shall we say, enhance Dalat's natural beauty. Whether it's the Eiffel Tower–shaped radio tower, the horse-drawn carriages or the zealously colourful heart-shaped cut-outs at the Valley of Love, this is a town that takes romance very seriously – yea, unto the full extent of kitsch.

But don't let the Disneyfied feel stop you from enjoying the very pretty scenery and utterly charming town. This used to be hunting territory too, described in the 1950s as 'abounding in deer, roe, peacocks, pheasants, wild boar, black bear, wild caws, panthers, tigers, gaurs and elephants'. Unfortunately hunters were so efficient that only taxidermied specimens remain, in the local museum.

Dalat is a big draw for domestic tourists – it's Le Petit Paris, the honeymoon capital and the City of Eternal Spring (daily temperatures hover between 15°C and 24°C) all rolled into one. They tend to come in summer, while the dry season (December to March) is the best time to visit. The wet season takes over for the rest of the year, but even then mornings normally remain dry, allowing time for sightseeing before the downpours begin.

History

Home to Montagnards for centuries, 'Da Lat' means 'river of the Lat tribe' in their language. The first European to 'discover' the area was Dr Alexandre Yersin in 1893 (see p293). The city was established in 1912 and quickly became fashionable with Europeans. At one point during the French-colonial period, some 20% of Dalat's population was foreign, as evidenced by the 2500-odd chateau-style villas scattered around the city.

During the American War, Dalat was spared by the tacit agreement of all parties concerned. Indeed, it seems that while South Vietnamese soldiers were being trained at the city's military academy and affluent officials of the Saigon regime were relaxing in their villas, VC cadres were doing the same thing not far away (also in villas). On 3 April 1975 Dalat fell to the North without a fight.

Orientation

Dalat's sights are well spread out. The terrain in and around the city is hilly, so walking or cycling can be demanding despite the cool temperatures.

The Central Market, set in a hollow, marks the middle of the town. Most of the midrange accommodation is clustered here, while budget places are to the north (along Đ Truong Cong Dinh and Đ Phan Dinh Phung) and northeast (along Đ Bui Thi Xuan). To the southeast the 'Eiffel Tower' of the main post office is a useful landmark.

Information

INTERNET ACCESS

Blue Net (Map p319; ☎ 091-881 5189; 26 Đ Nguyen Chi Thanh; per hr 6000d; ⏲ 7.30am-11pm)

Internet & Game Online (Map p319; 1C Đ Bui Thi Xuan; per hr 3000d)

MEDICAL SERVICES

Lam Dong General Hospital (Map p319; ☎ 382 1369; 4 Đ Pham Ngoc Thach)

MONEY

Banks with ATMs (Map p319) Agribank, Sacombank and Vietin Bank are clustered at Hoa Binh Sq (Khu Hoa Binh).

Vietcombank (Map p319; ☎ 351 0586; 6 Đ Nguyen Thi Minh Khai) Changes travellers cheques and foreign currencies.

Vietin Bank (Map p319; ☎ 382 2495; 1 Đ Le Dai Hanh) Changes travellers cheques and foreign currencies.

Vietin Bank ATM (Map p319) Inside the main post office.

POST

Main post office (Map p319; ☎ 382 2586; 14 Đ Tran Phu) Has international telephone and fax.

TRAVEL AGENCIES

For guided motorbike tours, see the boxed text, p325.

Dalat Travel Service (Map p319; ☎ 382 2125; dalattravelservice@vnn.vn; 7 Đ 3 Thang 2) Tours and vehicle rentals.

Sinh Cafe (Map p319; ☎ 382 2663; www.sinhcafevn.com; 4A Đ Bui Thi Xuan) Tours and open-tour bus bookings.

Sights

HANG NGA CRAZY HOUSE

A free-wheeling architectural exploration of surrealism, **Hang Nga Crazy House** (Map p319; ☎ 382 2070; 3 Đ Huynh Thuc Khang; admission 12,000d) defies easy definition, yet is ultimately beguiling. Architecture buffs will marvel at the echoes of Antoni Gaudi, shutter-happy tourists will pose themselves silly in the strangely decorated rooms (some with ceiling mirrors, many with creepy animal statues with glowing red eyes) and children will simply enjoy getting lost in the maze of tunnels, walkways and ladders.

There are nine rooms, each named after an unlikely animal or plant, all built into an organic-looking structure that resembles an enormous tree unfurling itself. You can wander around as you please; clearly, getting lost is part of the experience. Rooms at the top offer a splendid view of Dalat, if you can tear your eyes away long enough to appreciate it.

The brainchild of owner Mrs Dang Viet Nga, the Crazy House has been an imaginative work-in-progress since 1990. Hang Nga, as she's known locally, has a PhD in architecture from Moscow and has designed a number of other buildings around Dalat, including the Children's Cultural Palace and the Catholic church in Lien Khuong. One of her earlier masterpieces, the 'House with 100 Roofs', was torn down as a fire hazard because the People's Committee thought it looked antisocialist.

Hang Nga started the Crazy House project to entice people back to nature and though it's becoming more outlandish every year, she's not likely to have any more trouble with the

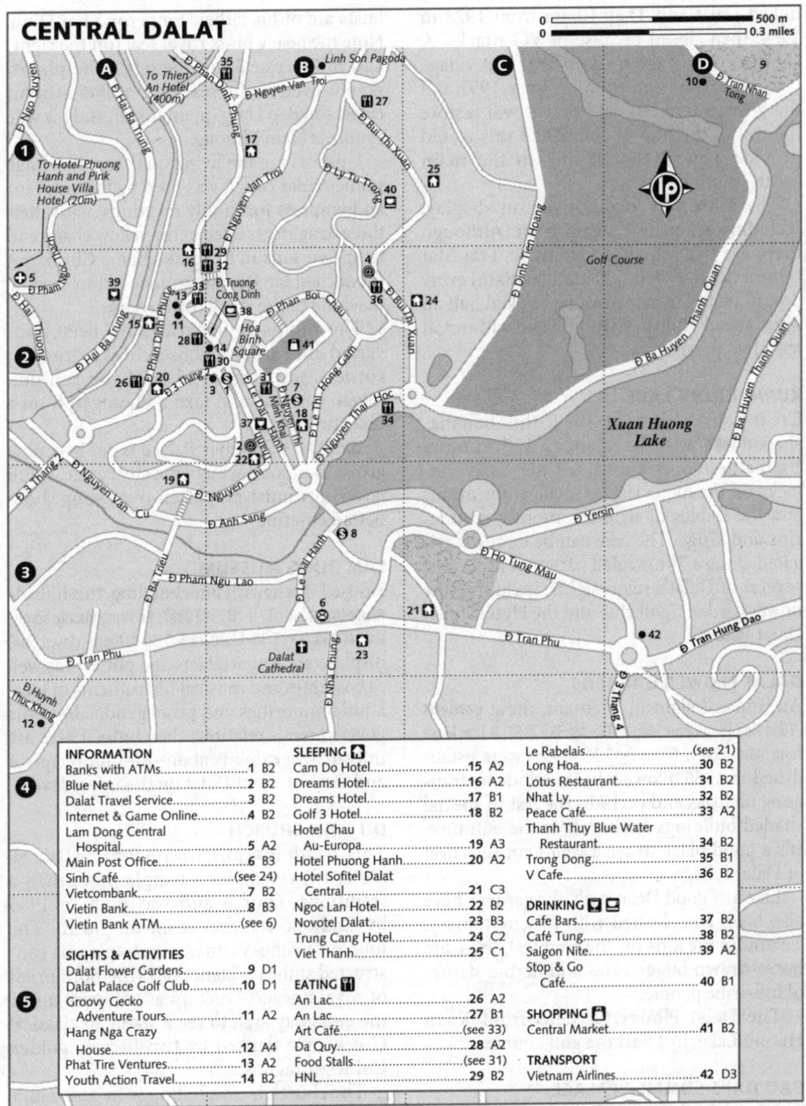

authorities. Her father, Truong Chinh, was Ho Chi Minh's successor, serving as Vietnam's second president from 1981 until his death in 1988. There's a display about him in one of the ground-floor spaces (part living room, part limestone cave).

If an hour or so spent in the embrace of this kitschy extravaganza isn't enough for you, you can opt to stay overnight (rooms US$35 to US$114) and see what waking up in Alice's Wonderland must feel like.

CRÉMAILLÈRE RAILWAY STATION

Dalat's pretty **train station** (Map p321; Ga Da Lat; ☎ 383 4409; 1 Đ Quang Trung; admission free; ⏰ 6.30am-5pm) is now largely decorative. The cog-railway linked Dalat and Thap Cham from 1928 to 1964, then closed because of VC attacks. A short section of the track to Trai Mat village (see p326) has been running since 1997 and the government has said that it will restore the rest of the line. If completed this would provide a great tourist link to the main north–south lines.

There are old locomotives on display, including a Japanese steam train. Although there are five scheduled trains to Trai Mat (return ticket 80,000d, 30 minutes, 8km) every day, in reality tickets must be booked half an hour ahead and they won't leave without at least two passengers.

XUAN HUONG LAKE

Created by a dam in 1919, this banana-shaped **lake** was named after a 17th-century Vietnamese poet known for her daring attacks on the hypocrisy of social conventions and the foibles of scholars, monks, mandarins and kings. The lake can be circumnavigated along a 7km sealed path that leads past several of Dalat's main sights, including the flower gardens, golf club and the Hotel Sofitel Dalat Palace.

DALAT FLOWER GARDENS

An unusual sight in Vietnam, these **gardens** (Vuon Hoa Thanh Pho; Map p319; ☎ 382 2151; Đ Tran Nhan Tong; admission 10,000d; 🕒 7.30am-4pm) were established in 1966. Flowers here include hydrangeas, fuchsias and orchids, the last in special shaded buildings to the left of the entrance. It's a good place to see a well-kept selection of Dalat foliage.

Like any good Dalat park, the gardens have also been embellished with kitschy topiary. To amuse the kids (or the couples), there are horse-drawn buggy rides and heroic statues of hill-tribe people.

The Dalat Flower Gardens front Xuan Huong Lake, just past the golf course.

BAO DAI'S SUMMER PALACE

This art deco–influenced **villa** (Dinh 3; Map p321; off Đ Trieu Viet Vuong; admission 8000d; 🕒 7-11am & 1.30-4pm) was constructed in 1933 and was one of three palaces Bao Dai kept in Dalat. The decor has not changed in decades and the place has the feel of an oversized, faded dollhouse.

In Bao Dai's office, the life-sized white bust above the bookcase is of the man himself (he died in 1997); the smaller gold and brown busts are of his father, Emperor Khai Dinh. Note the heavy brass royal seal (on the right) and military seal (on the left). The photographs over the fireplace are of Bao Dai, his eldest son Bao Long (in uniform), and his wife Empress Nam Phuong.

Upstairs are the living quarters. The huge semicircular couch was used by the emperor and empress for family meetings, with their three daughters seated in the yellow chairs and their two sons in the pink chairs. Check out the ancient tan Rouathermique infrared sauna machine in the small linen room.

The rooms at the rear have been converted into one of those cheesy dress-up corners, where from 15,000d you can don 'royal' costume and take a photograph on a fake throne.

Bao Dai's Summer Palace is set in a pine grove, 2km southwest of the city centre. Cloth coverings must be placed over your shoes before entering.

LAM DONG MUSEUM

Housed in a newish pink building, this hillside **museum** (Map p321; ☎ 382 0387; 4 Đ Hung Vuong; admission 4000d; 🕒 7.30-11.30am & 1.30-4.30pm, closed Sun) displays ancient artefacts and pottery, as well as costumes and musical instruments of local ethnic minorities and propaganda about the government's relations thereunto. There are informative exhibits about Alexandre Yersin and the history of Dalat on the upper level.

DU SINH CHURCH

This **church** (Map p321; Đ Huyen Tran Cong Chua; admission free) resembles a temple more than a traditional church and was built in 1955 by Catholic refugees from the north. The four-post, Sino-Vietnamese steeple was constructed at the insistence of a Hue-born priest of royal lineage. Look up as you pass under the entryway arch to see a statue in classical Greek style flanked by two fiercely golden Chinese dragons.

The church is on a hilltop with panoramic views in all directions. To get there, walk 500m southwest up the road from the former **Couvent des Oiseaux** (Đ Huyen Tran Cong Chua), now a teachers' training college.

Activities

ADVENTURE SPORTS

Dalat's cool climate and mountainous surrounds lend themselves to all kinds of outdoor

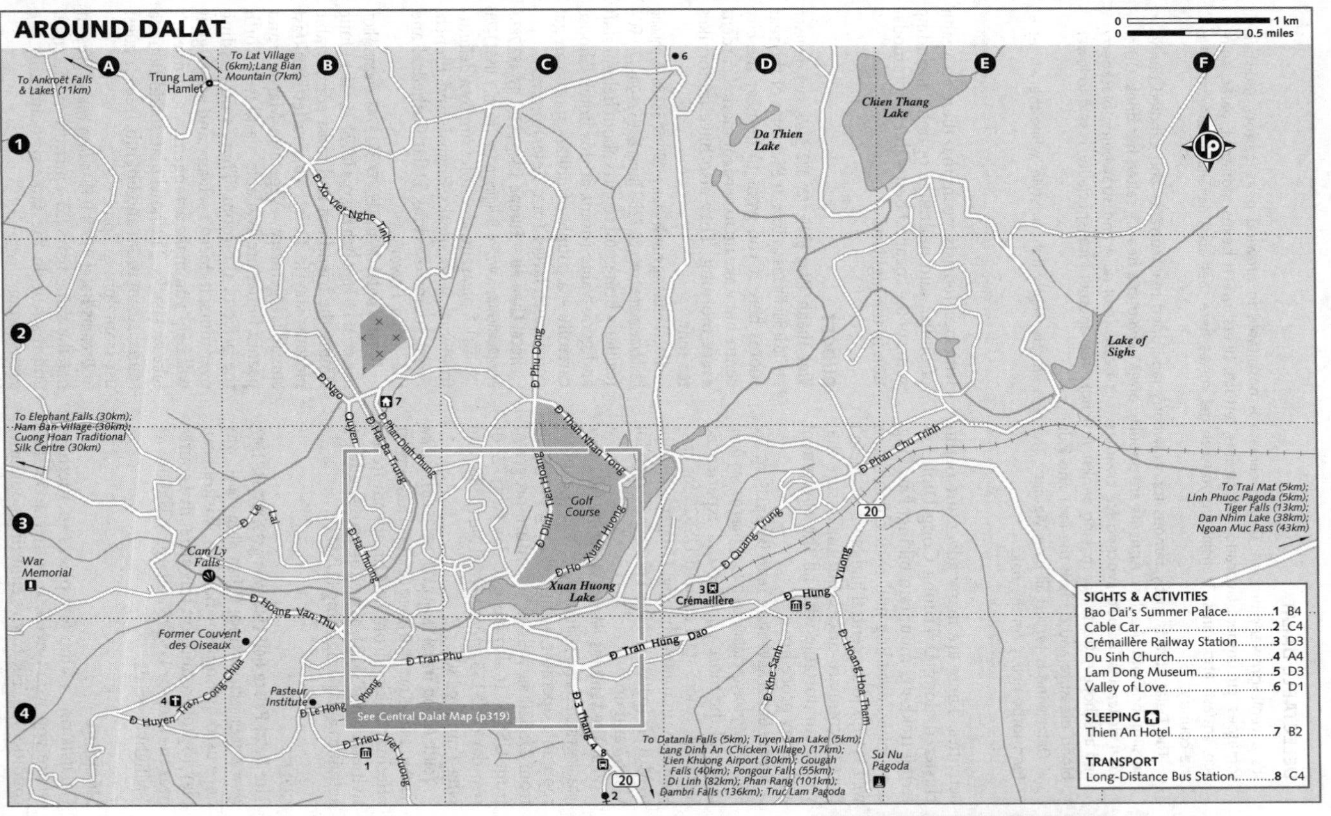
AROUND DALAT
0 1 km
0 0.5 miles
To Ankroët Falls & Lakes (11km)
Trung Lam Hamlet
To Lat Village (6km);Lang Bian Mountain (7km)
Da Thien Lake
Chien Thang Lake
Lake of Sighs
Đ Xo Viet Nghe Tinh
Đ Ngo Quyen
Đ Phan Dinh Phung
Đ Hai Ba Trung
Đ Phu Dong
Đ Than Nhan Tong
Đ Dinh Tien Hoang
Golf Course
Đ Ho Xuan Huong
Xuan Huong Lake
Đ Phan Chu Trinh
Đ Quang Trung
Crémaillère
Đ Hung Vuong
Đ Tran Hung Dao
Đ Tran Phu
Đ Khe Sanh
Đ Hoang Hoa Tham
Su Nu Pagoda
Đ 3 Thang 4
20
Đ Hai Thuong
Đ Le Lai
Cam Ly Falls
War Memorial
Đ Hoang Van Thu
Former Couvent des Oiseaux
Đ Huyen Tran Cong Chua
Pasteur Institute
Đ Le Hong Phong
Đ Trieu Viet Vuong
See Central Dalat Map (p319)
To Elephant Falls (30km); Nam Ban Village (30km); Cuong Hoan Traditional Silk Centre (30km)
To Trai Mat (5km); Linh Phuoc Pagoda (5km); Tiger Falls (13km); Dan Nhim Lake (38km); Ngoan Muc Pass (43km)
To Datanla Falls (5km); Tuyen Lam Lake (5km); Lang Dinh An (Chicken Village) (17km); Lien Khuong Airport (30km); Gougah Falls (40km); Pongour Falls (55km); Di Linh (82km); Phan Rang (101km); Dambri Falls (136km); Truc Lam Pagoda
SIGHTS & ACTIVITIES
Bao Dai's Summer Palace....1 B4
Cable Car....2 C4
Crémaillère Railway Station....3 D3
Du Sinh Church....4 A4
Lam Dong Museum....5 D3
Valley of Love....6 D1
SLEEPING
Thien An Hotel....7 B2
TRANSPORT
Long-Distance Bus Station....8 C4

DELECTABLE DALAT

It's a vegie-grower's heaven: Dalat's climate is hospitable to growing peas, carrots, radishes, tomatoes, cucumbers, avocados, capsicums, lettuce, beets, green beans, potatoes, garlic, spinach, squash and yams. Translation: you can get meals here that are unavailable elsewhere in the country.

The Dalat area is justly famous for strawberry jam, dried blackcurrants and candied plums, persimmons and peaches. Apricots are popular, often served in a heavily salted hot drink. Other local delicacies include avocado ice cream, sweet beans (*mut dao*) and strawberry, blackberry and artichoke extracts (for making drinks). Artichoke tea, another local speciality, is said to lower blood pressure and benefit the liver and kidneys.

Dalat wine is served all over Vietnam. The reds are pleasantly light in style, while the whites tend to be heavy on the oak.

activities. There are many adventure outfits clustered along Đ Truong Cong Dinh, offering trekking, mountain biking, kayaking, canyoning, abseiling and rock climbing, as well as trips to the central highlands. It doesn't hurt to compare prices, but make sure that you're comfortable with all the equipment and safety procedures.

Groovy Gecko Adventure Tours (Map p319; ☎ 383 6521; www.groovygeckotours.net; 65 Đ Truong Cong Dinh) is one of the more popular and experienced agencies. Prices start around US$25 for canyoning or mountain biking. Longer bike trips to Mui Ne (p308) or Nha Trang (p280) go for US$63 and up.

Phat Tire Ventures (Map p319; ☎ 382 9422; www.phattireventures.com; 73 Đ Truong Cong Dinh) is another reputable operator, with trekking programs from US$20 as well as adventure programs from US$30. It also has one-day (US$72) or two-day (US$155) rides to Mui Ne (p308) and Nha Trang (p280).

Youth Action Travel (Map p319; ☎ 351 0357; www.youthactiontravel.com; 45 Đ Truong Cong Dinh) has similar offerings (biking from US$20, adventure activities from US$28), as well as team-building activities and paragliding (US$80).

GOLF

The **Dalat Palace Golf Club** (Map p319; ☎ 382 1202; www.vietnamgolfresorts.com; Đ Tran Nhan Tong) was once used by Emperor Bao Dai. Visitors can play 18-hole rounds on this attractive course near the lake for US$95 and up. Ask about its Twilight Specials.

Sleeping

Dalat is one of the few places in Vietnam where you won't need to bother about air-conditioning. The town's enduring popularity with local tourists means that there's a wealth of budget and midrange options, including some of the cheapest best-value accommodation in the highlands.

BUDGET

Viet Thanh (Map p319; ☎ 382 3369; savy@hcm.vnn.vn; 16 Đ Bui Thi Xuan; r US$6-8) Pick one of the rear rooms here if you want to be near the city centre but wake up to verdant market gardens every morning. They also have motorbikes for rent.

Hotel Phuong Hanh (Map p319; ☎ 383 8839; phuonghanhhotel@gmail.com; 80-82 Đ 3 Thang 2; r US$8-20; 💻) We regularly hear good reports about helpful staff and good-value rooms at this hotel. Choose carefully – a couple of dollars more can get you a much larger (or quieter) room.

Hotel Chau Au – Europa (Map p319; ☎ 382 2870; europa@hcm.vnn.vn; 76 Đ Nguyen Chi Thanh; r US$11-20; ❄ 💻) A pleasant, airy hotel run by a delightful owner who speaks English and French. Front rooms overlook Dalat Cathedral and the 'Eiffel Tower'.

Dreams Hotel (Map p319; ☎ 383 3748; dreams@hcm.vnn.vn; 151 Đ Phan Dinh Phung; r US$20-25; 💻) Quite simply the friendliest and most comfortable place to stay in Dalat. The buffet breakfast spread is legendary – Vegemite, Marmite and peanut butter are available – and well worth the price of the room. There's no hassling over tours: it doesn't sell any and although it will help you make arrangements, it doesn't take kickbacks. The hotel's latest addition is a sauna, steam room and hot tub, free for guest use from 4pm to 7pm.

Dreams Hotel (164B Đ Phan Dinh Phung) Yes, it has the same name, it's just down the road, and it's run on the same principles by the same owner.

Thien An Hotel (Map p321; ☎ 352 0607; thienanhotel@vnn.vn; 272A Đ Phan Dinh Phung; r US$18-20; 💻) Continuing the winning family tradition, this hotel (run by the brother of the owner of Dreams) provides spacious rooms, glorious breakfasts and warm hospitality. It's a little further out for those who want to avoid the town's neon lights, and free bicycles are provided.

The quiet lane off Đ Hai Thuong opposite the Lam Dong General Hospital is home to a cluster of decent budget hotels. The only downside is that you have to walk up a steep hill to get home every night. Choices include:

Hotel Phuong Hanh (Map p319; ☎ 356 0528; 7/1 Đ Hai Thuong; r US$4-6; 💻) The predecessor to the hotel of the same name along Đ 3 Thang 2, this is in a well-maintained older building with lots of character.

Pink House Villa Hotel (Map p319; ☎ 381 5667; pink_063@yahoo.com; 7 Đ Hai Thuong; s/d US$7/10; 💻) With a large garden and high ceilings in every room, this hotel is quite the pleasant oasis.

MIDRANGE

Trung Cang Hotel (Map p319; ☎ 382 2663; www.sinhcafevn.com; 4A Đ Bui Thi Xuan; r US$20-30; 💻) There's still a newish feel to this smart Sinh Cafe operation, with good, clean rooms. A breakfast buffet is included in the price. Open-tour buses stop right outside.

Cam Do Hotel (Map p319; ☎ 382 2732; www.camdohotel.com.vn; 81 Đ Phan Dinh Phung; r US$30-45, ste US$60; 💻) A one-time backpackers' oasis, Cam Do has been completely transformed into a smart midrange hotel. Rooms are as you'd expect in this range, including complimentary in-room tea service.

Golf 3 Hotel (Map p319; ☎ 382 6042; golf3.dalat@vinagolf.vn; 4 Đ Nguyen Thi Minh Khai; r US$50-85, ste US$100-120; ❄ 💻) Smack in the centre of town, this hotel has extremely comfortable rooms with nice fittings (including safety boxes) and a pleasant ambience. Views from the rooftop cafe are stellar.

Novotel Dalat (Map p319; ☎ 382 5777; www.novotel.com; 7 Đ Tran Phu; s US$49-64, d US$55-70, ste US$79-85; ❄ 💻) In a respectfully refurbished 1932 building, the Novotel retains a wealth of old-world charm with its old-fashioned gated lift, splendid high ceilings and period light fittings. Rooms are a little small but have all the mod-cons.

TOP-END

Ngoc Lan Hotel (Map p319; ☎ 382 2136; www.ngoclanhotel.vn; 42 Đ Nguyen Chi Thanh; r US$85-125, ste US$145-385; ❄ 💻) This Dalat stalwart has been transformed into a spiffy new hotel with a boutique feel, all clean white with stylish purple accents. There's a dash of colonial character with the wooden floors and French windows; everything else is impeccably modern.

Hotel Sofitel Dalat Palace (Map p319; ☎ 382 5444; www.sofitel.com; 12 Đ Tran Phu; s US$236-296, d US$250-310, ste US$436-500; ❄ 💻) The *grande dame* of Dalat hotels (1922) has unimpeded views of Xuan Huong Lake. Inside, the niceties of French-colonial life have been splendidly preserved, from claw-foot tubs and working fireplaces to sumptuous chandeliers and paintings. Perfect for immersing yourself in a slice of transplanted European extravagance.

Eating

Dalat has an appealing selection of smart restaurants that make the most of the local produce (see opposite). For cheap eats in the day, head to the upper level of the **Central Market** (Cho Da Lat; Map p319). At night, **food stalls** (Đ Nguyen Thi Minh Khai) materialise out of nowhere on the wide steps at the street's market end.

VIETNAMESE

Art Cafe (Map p319; ☎ 351 0089; 70 Đ Truong Cong Dinh; dishes 20,000-70,000d; 🕒 lunch & dinner) Owned by an artist whose work adorns the walls, this elegant, bamboo-accented eatery has intimate tables and soothing soft lighting. Linger over a glass of wine to admire the artwork. The menu features Vietnamese dishes with a twist, including plenty of vegetarian options.

Trong Dong (Map p319; ☎ 382 1889; 220 Đ Phan Dinh Phung; mains 20,000-80,000d; 🕒 lunch & dinner) A friendly and unpretentious eatery, cleverly decorated with mirrors. Try the grilled shrimp paste on sugar cane or the sautéed rabbit.

Da Quy (Wild Sunflower; Map p319; ☎ 351 0883; 49 Đ Truong Cong Dinh; dishes 25,000-55,000d; 🕒 lunch & dinner) It has an upmarket ambience but low prices, and earns rave reviews from travellers of all tastebuds. Try the traditional claypot dishes, such as with fish or shrimp.

Long Hoa (Map p319; ☎ 382 2934; longhoarestaurant@yahoo.com.vn; 6 Đ 3 Thang 2; dishes 25,000-100,000d; 🕒 lunch & dinner) A cosy bistro-style place, run by a Francophile owner and dressed up with images of France. Westerners come here for the Vietnamese food Vietnamese come here to try the steaks. Top off your meal with a glass of Dalat wine or some home-made yoghurt.

HNL (Map p319; ☎ 383 5505; 94 Đ Phan Dinh Phung; dishes 25,000-120,000d; ⌚ lunch & dinner) Painted in kooky pastels and with a classic motorbike as its centrepiece, this cosy restaurant serves interesting Vietnamese dishes – along with pizza to keep the kids happy. If you're feeling all revved up after dinner, there's a karaoke lounge upstairs.

Lotus Restaurant (Map p319; ☎ 382 3457; 1A Đ Nguyen Thi Minh Khai; dishes 25,000-120,000d; ⌚ lunch & dinner) Right by Hoa Binh Square, this restaurant has rooftop terrace seating as well as an enclosed dining area with Chinese-influenced decor; the former is better for people-watching; the latter is a warmer option in winter. The food is excellent and service is prompt, though they don't speak much English.

Nhat Ly (Map p319; ☎ 382 1651; 88 Đ Phan Dinh Phung; dishes 30,000-120,000d; ⌚ lunch & dinner) A very local place that serves hearty meals, including a sumptuous hotpot that really hits the spot. There's also rabbit and frog on the menu.

VEGETARIAN

An Lac (Map p319; ☎ 382 2025; 71 Đ Phan Dinh Phung; meals 10,000d; ⌚ breakfast, lunch & dinner) There's an English menu here, and options range from noodle soups to rice and *banh bao* (steamed rice-flour dumplings stuffed with a savoury filling).

An Lac (Map p319; ☎ 383 3717; 26 Đ Bui Thi Xuan; meals 10,000d; ⌚ breakfast, lunch & dinner) Another one of the same name and incredibly popular with the locals.

INTERNATIONAL

V Cafe (Map p319; ☎ 352 0215; 1/1 Đ Bui Thi Xuan; dishes 25,000-79,000d; ⌚ lunch & dinner) A travellers' favourite, this cute bistro hung with Chinese lanterns serves a mix of Asian and Western mains. Service is very good and you can choose dessert from the small spread on the counter.

Thanh Thuy Blue Water Restaurant (Map p319; ☎ 353 1668; thanhthuy@cattuonggroup.vn; 2 Đ Nguyen Thai Hoc; dishes 30,000-105,000d; ⌚ breakfast, lunch & dinner) With an unbeatable location right on the lake, this restaurant serves a mixed-up menu of mostly Cantonese fare, with some Vietnamese and Western dishes as well (fancy some pizza with your dim sum?). The food is all right but the view and vibe are what people come for.

Le Rabelais (Map p319; ☎ 382 5444; 12 Đ Tran Phu; set lunch/dinner US$22/55, degustation menu US$65; ⌚ breakfast, lunch & dinner) For fine French dining, the signature restaurant at the Sofitel is the place to go. The impressive dining room oozes gentility at every turn. Leave the kids at home if they're under 12, and while away the night like the French might have, with a *digestif* and live piano music.

Drinking

While Dalat has a lively night market scene, its cafes and bars are a pretty tame lot. The best thing is to go where the locals go: to the lively strip of **cafe-bars** (Đ Le Dai Hanh). The music isn't great but it's perfect for people-watching while knocking back a few beers.

Saigon Nite (Map p319; ☎ 382 0007; 11A Đ Hai Ba Trung) Your classic dive – people come for the beer, pool and company, not for the decor. There's a friendly bartender and the place stays open till late.

Peace Cafe (Map p319; ☎ 382 2787; http://peacedalat.googlepages.com; 64 Đ Truong Cong Dinh) Attached to Peace Hotel, this noisy cafe is always packed, no doubt because the women who run it do their darnedest to round up every passing traveller. There's no hassle once you're seated and it's a good place to meet other backpackers (and in the day, Easy Riders too).

Stop & Go Cafe (Map p319; ☎ 382 8458; duyviet@hoadalat.net; 2A Đ Ly Tu Trong; ⌚ 7am-7pm) This little bohemian oasis is run by a beret-wearing poet in the front room of his house. He'll happily recite his poetry while serving you homemade cake or (if you're female) proffering a flower from his abundant garden.

Cafe Tung (Map p319; 6 Hoa Binh Sq) A famous hang-out for Saigonese intellectuals in the 1950s, Cafe Tung remains exactly as it was then, serving only tea, coffee, hot cocoa, lemon soda and orange soda to the sound of mellow French music.

Shopping

Dalat is a good place to pick up some of the food that the region is famous for (see p322). You could also pick up coffee if you're not passing Buon Ma Thuot (see p331). The shops in and around the Central Market (Map p319) are a good place to browse and bargain.

Getting There & Away

AIR

Vietnam Airlines (Map p319; ☎ 383 3499; 2 Đ Ho Tung Mau) has daily services to HCMC and Hanoi. Lien Khuong Airport is 30km south of the city.

EASY DOES IT

For many travellers, the highlight of their trip to the central highlands is an off-the-beaten-track motorcycle tour with an Easy Rider. Besides the romance of cruising down endless highways, the Easy Riders' stock-in-trade is good company and insider knowledge, providing a brief but intimate window into highland life.

The flip side to the popularity of the Easy Riders is that now everyone claims to be one. In central Dalat, you can't walk down the street without being invited (sometimes harassed) for a tour. Some Easy Riders have banded together to protect 'their' brand, donning blue jackets and charging membership fees. Similarly, in Danang (said by some to be where they started out before they gained guidebook-endorsed eminence) and Hoi An, the Easy Rider moniker applies to other packs of motorcycle guides, with jackets of different colours.

Whether you're speaking to a jacket-wearing chap or an indie-spirited upstart, it's prudent to find out just what they can show you that you can't see on your own. Easy Riders don't come cheap. The going rate now is US$20 or more. Extended trips starting at US$50 per day run across the central highlands, across the south, even all the way north to Hanoi. It's also good to gauge the rider's command of English; some travellers have complained that when they've hired Easy Riders in pairs, one does all the talking while the other barely speaks any English.

Not every jacketed Easy Rider is a good guide and many freelance riders are perfectly talented guides (perhaps because they don't have a 'brand' behind them). In the convoluted politics of the motorcycle-guide world, some freelancers now disdain the term Easy Rider and call themselves Free Riders or just plain motorcycle guides.

Before you commit to a long-haul trip, it's a good idea to test a rider out with a day trip: Is he a safe driver? Can you spend the next 48 hours or more with him? Are your bags safely strapped on the bike? Is the seat padded and the helmet comfortable (and clean)? Most riders can produce a logbook of glowing testimonials from past clients; also, check internet forums for recommendations.

BUS

Dalat's **long-distance bus station** (Map p321; Đ 3 Thang 4) is 1km south of Xuan Huong Lake, although many private services can make pick-ups and drop-offs at your hotel. Services are available to most of the country, including several to HCMC (110,000d, six to seven hours), Phan Rang (40,000d, 4½ hours), Nha Trang (88,000d, new road four hours, old road seven hours) and Buon Ma Thuot (65,000d, four hours).

Dalat is a major stop for open-tour buses. Sinh Cafe (see p318) has a daily bus to Mui Ne (120,000d, four hours) and Nha Trang (100,000d, five hours).

CAR & MOTORBIKE

From HCMC, taking the inland (Hwy 20) route to Dalat is faster than taking the coastal route (Hwy 1A). From Nha Trang, a new road shaves almost 70km off the old-road distance, and offers spectacular views to boot – a dream for motorbikers and cyclists. Besides wending across forested hills for much of the way, the road hits a height of 1700m at Hon Giao mountain, where it follows a breathtaking 33km pass.

The following are road distances from Dalat: Di Linh (82km), Nha Trang (140km), Phan Rang (108km), Phan Thiet (247km) and HCMC (308km). Hwy 27 runs along a scenic route to Buon Ma Thuot (200km); the road is scheduled to be improved in 2009.

Getting Around

TO/FROM THE AIRPORT

The Vietnam Airlines shuttle bus between Lien Khuong Airport and Dalat (35,000d, 30 minutes) is timed around flights, leaving from the door of the terminal and, in Dalat, from in front of 40 Đ Ho Tung Mau, two hours before each departure.

Private taxis can be hired to make the trip for around US$12, while a motorbike taxi should cost about US$10.

BICYCLE

Pedal power is a great way of seeing Dalat, but the hilly terrain and long distances between the sights make it hard work. Several hotels rent out bicycles and some provide them free to guests. It's also worth looking into cycling tours (see p320).

MOTORBIKE

Dalat is too hilly for *cyclos*, but a motorbike is a good way of getting around. For short trips around town (15,000d), *xe om* drivers can be flagged down around the Central Market area. Self-drive motorbikes are US$6 to US$8 per day.

TAXI & CAR

Taxis are easy to find; if you need to call for one, try **Mai Linh** (☎ 352 1111) or **Dalat Taxi** (☎ 355 6655). Daily car rentals (with a driver) cost around US$40; ask your hotel or try Dalat Travel Service (see p318).

AROUND DALAT

Valley of Love

When even the locals find the place tacky, you know it's reached new depths of kitschiness. This park surrounding a lake in a **valley** (Thung Lung Tinh Yeu, or Vallee d'Amour; Map p321; Đ Phu Dong Thien Vuong; adult/child 10,000/5000d; 🕑 7am-5pm) is attractive in its own right but burdened with the responsibilities of its name (given by Dalat University students in 1972). Romantically-themed props and statues (surprisingly, a couple are nude) are scattered across its landscaped gardens, and the lake can get woefully noisy with the splashing of paddle boats, canoes and motorboats.

Adding to the surreal atmosphere are the 'Dalat cowboys': Vietnamese guides dressed as American cowboys, in the most cliché-ridden sense of the word. They rent horses to tourists for a guided tour around the lake. You'll have to pay them if you take their picture.

The Valley of Love is 5km north of Xuan Huong Lake. It's a popular stop for tour buses.

Tuyen Lam Lake

Also known as Quang Trung Reservoir, this is an artificial **lake** (Ho Tuyen Lam; admission free) created by a dam in 1980. The hill to the right of the lake is crowned by **Truc Lam Pagoda** (admission free). Despite its popularity, the sprawling grounds and temple don't feel crowded, and the views of the lake are wonderful. If you'd like a little spiritual recharge, enquire about the sessions at the **meditation centre** (🕑 6am-5pm).

From the lake shore, the road over the dam to the right leads to a small recreation area with **boat rides** (200,000-300,000d). To the left, the road winds around the lake past fish and vegetable farms, ending at the tiny Fairy Rock Field Tourism Resort. It claims to be 'ecotourism' but there's a sad elephant tethered to a tree.

Hiking and canoeing are possible in the area; ask the adventure companies in Dalat (see p320).

Tuyen Lam Lake is about 7km outside Dalat. Take Hwy 20, turn right at the signpost 5km from town and continue for 2km. The fun way to get here is by **cable car**, though it's not for the faint-hearted. From the **Cable Car Station** (Cap Treo; Map p321; ☎ 383 7938; off Đ 3 Thang 4; adult one-way/return 40,000/60,000d, child one-way/return 20,000/30,000d; 🕑 7-11.30am & 1.30-5pm) in Dalat, it runs along a 2.3km wire over majestic pine forests to the hill where Truc Lam Pagoda stands.

Linh Phuoc Pagoda

This ornate **complex** (admission free) consists of the main temple and a new pagoda that was close to completion at the time of research. Both are heavily decorated in ceramic mosaics made from deliberately broken crockery. Remove your shoes before entering the main hall, which is dominated by a 5m-high Buddha.

The seven-storey **pagoda** houses an 8½-tonne bell that was used to ring in the millennium in 2000. It's now covered in Post-it notes – the faithful write down their wish, then strike the bell to send the wish to the Buddha's attention. For the best views, climb all the way to the top of the pagoda via the increasingly steep and narrow staircases.

Linh Phuoc Pagoda is in Trai Mat, 9km from Dalat. It can be reached by the train that runs from the Crémaillère Railway Station (see p319) or by *xe om*.

Lang Bian Mountain

Also called Lam Vien Mountain, this **mountain** (☎ 063-383 9088; admission 7000d) has five volcanic peaks ranging in altitude from 2100m to 2400m. Of the two highest peaks, the eastern one is known by the woman's name K'Lang while the western one bears a man's name, K'Biang. Only the upper reaches of the mountain remain forested, whereas just half a century ago the foothills had lush foliage that sheltered many wild animals. The hike up to the top's spectacular views takes three to four hours from the ticket booth.

Lang Bian Mountain is about 13km north of Dalat. Follow Đ Xo Viet Nghe Tinh until you reach Tung Lam Hamlet. Continue straight on (northwest) rather than to the left. On bicycle it takes about 45 minutes.

Minority Villages

There are two minority villages a short drive from Dalat, both unremarkable despite their popularity. If you're interested in hill-tribe life, you're better off heading to Buon Ma Thuot (see p328) or one of the other highland towns.

Less than 1km from the base of Lang Bian Mountain is **Lat Village** (pronounced 'lak'), a community of about 6000 people spread across nine hamlets. Only five of the hamlets are actually Lat; residents of the other four are members of the Chill, Ma and Koho tribes. It's a sleepy little place with a few handicraft shops. Sometimes it hosts wine-drinking sessions or gong performances for tour groups.

Lang Dinh An (Chicken Village) has the distinction of having a giant concrete chicken caught mid-strut in the village centre. The statue is part of a long-dysfunctional water system, and used to crow as water was pumped. It's home to about 600 people of the Koho people, now largely Vietnamised, and offering the same woven objects and 'cultural' activities as Lat Village. The village is on Hwy 20, 17km from Dalat.

Cuong Hoan Traditional Silk Centre

This is a small family-run **factory** (☎ 063-385 2338; Nam Ban) where you can inspect the entire process of silk production: the sorting of locally grown cocoons, boiling them and unravelling the thread, then dyeing the threads and weaving them into shimmering new fabric. You can even sample the cooked grub (they have a nutty flavour). There are some beautiful garments and lengths of cloth for sale.

The centre is in Nam Ban Village, 30km west of Dalat, near Elephant Falls (see right). Many Easy Riders stop here.

Waterfalls

There are a number of other waterfalls of varying interest value near Dalat. None are royally spectacular and quite a few have dwindled in size as more dams are built in the region.

The two most popular falls are Datanla Falls and Elephant Falls because they're convenient to Dalat. There are a number of other waterfalls in the area; they are more useful as waypoints if you're exploring the countryside on your own wheels.

DATANLA FALLS

This is the closest **waterfall** (admission 5000d) to Dalat, which dooms it to popularity even though the cascade is quite modest. Follow the paved path down to the falls. In 2007 a **bobsled ride** (adult one-way/return 25,000/35,000d, child under 1.2m one-way/return 10,000/15,000d) was added for those who'd rather steer themselves down a winding elevated track. Along with the loud music and weekend crowds, this once-peaceful spot has become quite a circus.

The waterfalls are about 7km south of Dalat. Take Hwy 20 and turn right about 200m past the turn-off to Tuyen Lam Lake. It's well signposted.

ELEPHANT FALLS

A popular stop on the Easy Rider trail, these imposing curved **falls** (admission free) are best seen from below. An uneven and sometimes hazardous path heads down to the base of the waterfall. It's also possible to inch behind the falls, but watch your footing very carefully (unless you have mountain goat–like agility) and expect to get wet.

Nearby, the **Linh An Pagoda** (2004) has been built to take advantage of the good feng shui of having water in front and a mountain behind. Inside, the three large Buddhas are flanked by two multi-armed Buddhas. More statues lurk in the garden out the back, including a particularly jolly giant – a Happy Buddha with neon halos and a room built into his ample belly.

The falls are situated near Nam Ban village, 30km west of Dalat. You can combine this with a visit to Cuong Hoan Traditional Silk Centre (left).

OTHER WATERFALLS

Tiger Falls (Thac Hang Cop; admission 6000d) is named after the local legend of a ferocious tiger living in a nearby cave. There are good hiking trails in the area; make arrangements in Dalat. The falls are about 14km east of Dalat. Follow Đ Hung Vuong to Trai Mat village and continue for another 3.5km from the local train station to a left-hand turn (signposted). From here it's another 3km along a very rough dirt road to the falls.

Ankroët Falls and Lakes (admission free) are 18km northwest of Dalat and were created as part of a hydroelectric project. The waterfall is about 15m high.

Gougah Falls (admission 5000d) is 36km from Dalat towards HCMC. It's only 500m from the highway so it's easy to get to.

Pongour Falls (admission 6000d) is the largest in the area when the dam above the river hasn't siphoned off all its water. If you don't feel like walking down to the falls, check out the view from the reconstructed royal pavilion. The original structure was built for Emperor Bao Dai's hunting expeditions. The falls are signposted on the right about 50km towards HCMC from Dalat and 6km off the highway.

DI LINH

elevation 1010m

The town of Di Linh (pronounced 'zee ling', also known as Djiring) is known for tea, which is grown on giant plantations founded by the French. Only a few decades ago the region was famous for its tiger hunting but as in Dalat, the wild animals are long gone. However the forests outside town are still good for bird-watching.

The 32m-high **Bo Bla Waterfall** (admission 5000d) is on the east side of Hwy 20, 16km southwest of Di Linh, near the village of Lien Dam. There's a steep 25-minute walk down to the base of the falls.

Di Linh is 226km northeast of HCMC and 82km southwest of Dalat on Hwy 20. It's a pleasant drive, passing tea and coffee plantations and houses with racks of silk worms.

BAO LOC

pop 141,528

The heartbeats of Bao Loc are tea, silk and the cultivation of mulberry leaves that make up the silkworms' diet. Roadside rest stops offer free samples of the local tea. There are also a few guesthouses here, making it a practical place to break the journey between HCMC (180km) and Dalat (118km); Easy Riders often stop here.

Nearby **Dambri Falls** (admission 10,000d) is one of the highest (90m), most magnificent and easily accessible waterfalls in Vietnam. For some incredible views, ride the **vertical cable car** (5000d) or trudge up the steep path to the top of the falls.

To reach Dambri Falls, turn off the main highway north of Bao Loc and follow the road for 18km through tea and mulberry plantations. The high peak to your right is May Bay Mountain.

NGOAN MUC PASS

elev 980m

Known to the French as Bellevue Pass, **Ngoan Muc Pass** is 43km from Dalat, 64km from Phan Rang, and 5km from Dan Nhim Lake (altitude 1042m). On a clear day you can see the ocean, 55km away. As the highway winds down the mountain it passes under two gargantuan water pipes that link the lake with the hydroelectric power station at the base of the pass.

South of the road (to the right as you face the ocean) you can see the steep tracks of the crémaillère (cog railway) linking Thap Cham with Dalat (p319). At the top of the pass there's a waterfall next to the highway, pine forests and the old Bellevue train station.

BUON MA THUOT

☎ 050 / pop 312,000 / elev 451m

A prospering modern town, Buon Ma Thuot (pronounced 'boon me tote'; also spelled as Ban Me Thuot) has outgrown its rustic origins – the Ede name translates as 'Thuot's father's village' – but alas, without acquiring any new charms. Inundated by traffic from three highways and powdered by orange-brown dust, its only saving grace is coffee. The region grows some of the best coffee in Vietnam, plenty of which is sold and drunk in town.

Most travellers stop in Buon Ma Thuot en route to the attractions around it: Yok Don National Park, a couple of striking waterfalls and heaps of minority villages. The province is home to 44 ethnic groups, including some who have migrated here from the north. Among indigenous Montagnards, the dominant groups are the Ede, Jarai, M'nong and Lao. However the government's policy of assimilation has been effective: nearly all of the Montagnards now speak Vietnamese fluently.

Before WWII, this was a centre for big-game hunting, attracting Emperor Bao Dai, but the animals have all but disappeared. Towards the end of the American War, Buon Ma Thuot was a strategic but poorly defended South Vietnamese base. It fell to the North in a one-day surprise attack in March 1975, pushing the South into a retreat from which it never recovered.

The rainy season around Buon Ma Thuot lasts from May to October, though downpours are usually short. Because of its lower elevation, Buon Ma Thuot is warmer and more humid than Dalat; it is also very windy.

Information

MEDICAL SERVICES

Dak Lak General Hospital (☎ 385 2665; 2 Đ Mai Hac De)

THE PEOPLE OF THE MOUNTAIN

The uneasy relationship in the central highlands between the Montagnards and the Vietnamese majority dates back centuries, when Vietnamese expansion pushed the tribes up into the mountains. While French-colonial rule recognised the Montagnards as a separate community, South Vietnam later attempted to assimilate them through such means as abolishing tribal schools and courts, prohibiting the construction of stilt houses and appropriating their land.

In response the Montagnards formed nationalist guerrilla movements, the best-known of which was the Front Unifié de Lutte des Races Opprimées (FULRO) or the United Front for the Struggle of the Oppressed Races. In the 1960s Montagnard tribes were courted by the US as allies against North Vietnam, and were trained by the CIA and US Special Forces.

They paid dearly for this after the war, when government policies brought more ethnic Vietnamese into the highlands, along with clampdowns on education in native languages and religious freedom (many Montagnards belong to unauthorised churches). Many Montagnards have been relocated to modern villages, partly to discourage slash-and-burn agriculture but this also speeds up assimilation.

In 2001 and 2004, Montagnard protests erupted, which the government quickly and some say violently suppressed. International human-rights groups point to more deaths than the government admits to, and thousands of Montagnards fled to Cambodia or the US afterwards. Ask the ethnic Vietnamese and many will probably repeat the state's line that the protests were the work of outsiders. Talk to any organisation that works with the Montagnards and you'll hear a different story: one of continuing government surveillance, harassment, religious persecution and abuse. Most of this is kept out of the public eye, but it's plain to see that Montagnard communities are still very much poor and marginalised on their own lands.

MONEY

Agribank (☎ 385 3930; 37 Đ Phan Boi Chau) Changes currency and travellers cheques.
BIDV ATM (6 Đ Le Duan)
Donga Bank (☎ 385 8654; 9 Đ Phan Chu Trinh) Makes foreign-currency exchanges and has an ATM.
Vietin Bank ATM (6 Đ Le Duan)

POST & INTERNET ACCESS

Main post office (☎ 385 2612; 1 Đ No Trang Long) Also has internet access.

TRAVEL AGENCIES

These agencies offer tours of the surrounding villages, waterfalls, Lak Lake and Yok Don National Park.

DakLak Tourist (☎ 385 8243; daklaktour@dng.vnn.vn; 51 Đ Ly Thuong Kiet) On the ground floor of Thanh Cong Hotel.
Damsan Tours (☎ 385 2505; damsantour@dng.vnn.vn; 212-214 Đ Nguyen Cong Tru) Attached to the Damsan Hotel.
Vietnam Highland Travel (☎ 385 5009; highlandco@dng.vnn.vn; 24 Đ Ly Thuong Kiet) With an office in Thanh Binh Hotel, this agency has experienced guides who specialise in homestays and trekking trips well off the beaten track.

TRAVEL PERMITS

Permits are required to visit minority villages in the area, except for Ako Dhong (see right) and Ban Don (see p332). Any of the local travel agencies can make the arrangements.

Sights

VICTORY MONUMENT

Smack in the centre of town, this **monument** commemorates the events of 10 March 1975 when VC and North Vietnamese troops liberated the city. It's one of the most interesting pieces of socialist realist sculpture, consisting of a column supporting a central group of figures holding a flag, with a modernist arch forming a rainbow over a concrete replica tank.

The frieze, starting from the right-hand side of the column, shows hill-tribe people with traditional gongs and a communal wine vessel. On the rear panel minority women are shown hugging a proud soldier, while on the left side there's a glimpse into a socialist future, peopled with happy nurses, farmers, industrial workers and children. It's a far cry from the reality of the situation, as many of the hill-tribe people fought with the Americans and suffered for it after the war (with continuing allegations of discrimination and mistreatment).

AKO DHONG VILLAGE

At the northern end of Buon Ma Thuot is this **Ede village**, a neat little community of

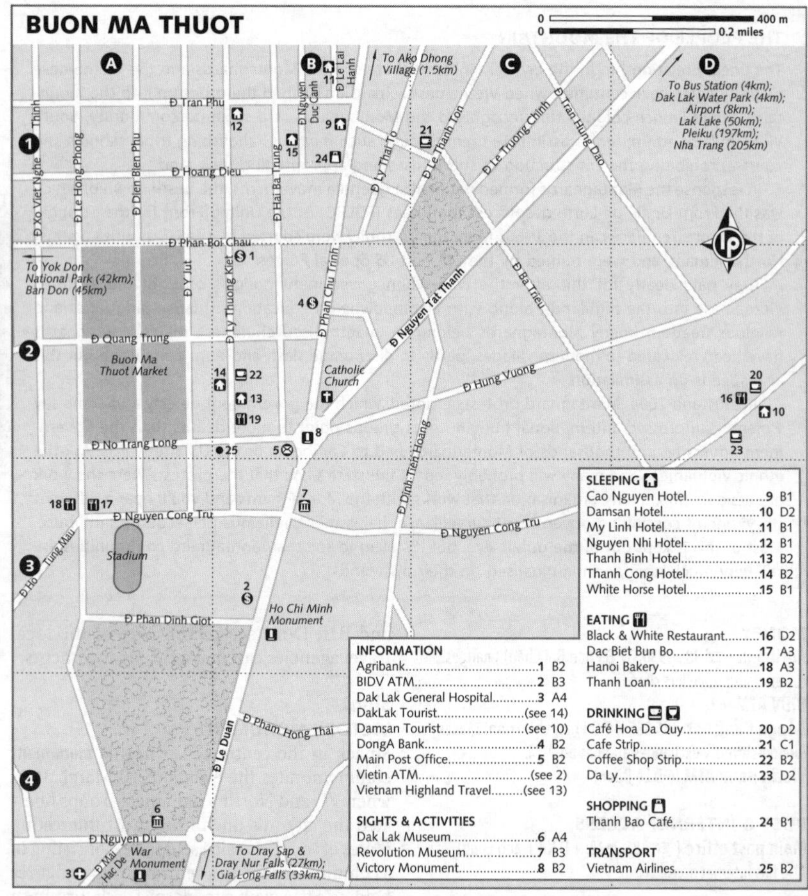

stilt-house suburbia. Strolling around the village makes for a pleasant break from the downtown din, and you may be able to find some locals at work weaving traditional fabrics.

The village is about 1.5km from the centre of town and makes an easy walk. Take Đ Phan Chu Trinh north and hang a left on Đ Tran Nhat Duat. The village is about 500m down the road, bordered to the east by Yang Sing Hotel and to the west by a cemetery.

DAK LAK MUSEUM

This musty, little-visited **museum** (☎ 385 0426; 4 Đ Nguyen Du; admission 10,000d; 🕒 7.30-11am & 2-5pm) has a small display of cultural artefacts and photographs about indigenous minority groups. The Ho Chi Minh quotation, posted boldly over a golden bust of him in the main hall, blithely declares that all ethnic minorities are 'the children of Vietnam' and 'blood brothers' to the Vietnamese.

The museum is housed in the Bao Dai Villa, a grand French-colonial building that was one of the emperor's many residences.

REVOLUTION MUSEUM

If you're lucky enough to find it open, this little **museum** (☎ 385 0426; 1 Đ Le Duan; admission 10,000d; 🕒 7.30-11am & 2-5pm Wed-Sun) focuses on the city's role during the American War.

DAK LAK WATER PARK

Strictly in the 'if you have time to kill' category, the waterslides at **Dak Lak Water Park** (☎ 395 0381;

Đ Nguyen Chi Thanh; admission adult/child 35,000/25,000d; 9am-6pm) are a passable diversion on a hot afternoon. It's about 4km from the centre of town, just before the bus station.

Sleeping

BUDGET

Thanh Binh Hotel (385 3812; 24 Đ Ly Thuong Kiet; r 150,000-180,000d;) Conveniently located in the middle of the guesthouse strip, this hotel has narrow, dark corridors that open up to large, comfortable rooms.

My Linh Hotel (381 5353; mylinhhotel@yahoo.com; 27-29 Đ Le Dai Hanh; r 150,000-400,000d;) Aspiring to boutique status, this mini-hotel has comfortable rooms and modern decor. The massive if worn top-floor suite sleeps 10 and is a bargain at 400,000d, but access is only through the 4th-floor massage-service level.

Nguyen Nhi Hotel (385 9868; 164 Đ Ly Thuong Kiet; r US$15;) A pleasant, welcoming mini-hotel, though no one in the family speaks English. Rooms are spacious and get lots of light.

Thanh Cong Hotel (385 8243; daklaktour@dng.vnn.vn; 51 Đ Ly Thuong Kiet; r US$15-28;) One of the nicer places along this stretch, this hotel has a wide range of good rooms, all with bathtubs.

MIDRANGE

White Horse Hotel (Khach San Bach Ma; 381 5656; whitehorsehotelvn@yahoo.com; 7-13 Đ Nguyen Duc Canh; r US$20-38, ste US$40-42;) Even the floors are polished to a gleam at this immaculate establishment. Rooms come with all the nice touches and the better ones have in-room computers.

Damsan Hotel (3851 234; www.damsanhotel.com.vn; 212-214 Đ Nguyen Cong Tru; r US$30-40;) For those who must have their swimming pool and tennis court, Damsan Hotel has these, a restaurant and nice rooms as well. Rooms at the back look over lush coffee plantations.

Cao Nguyen Hotel (385 5960; www.daklaktourist.com.vn; 65 Đ Phan Chu Trinh; r US$33-40;) This is the kind of hotel that advertises its massage and karaoke services in prominent neon lights. Still, the carpeted rooms look decent, if a little worn around the edges.

Eating

It's hard to scare up good grub in Buon Ma Thuot. Some hotels (Thanh Cong, White Horse, Damsan and Cao Nguyen) have restaurants but none are particularly outstanding.

Hanoi Bakery (385 3609; 123-125 Đ Le Hong Phong; pastries 5000d) Part bakery, part general store, this popular neighbourhood joint is known for its pastries and breads, as well as stocks of cheese and chocolate.

Thanh Loan (385 4960; 22 Đ Ly Thuong Kiet; meals 15,000d; lunch & dinner) There's only one thing on the menu: roll-your-own rice-paper rolls, with green vegies and herbs, fried pork, crunchy rice paper and raw garlic. Dunk the rolls in either a meaty broth or a mixture of fish sauce and chilli. It's a light meal, but full of fresh flavours.

Dac Biet Bun Bo (381 0135; 10 Đ Le Hong Phong; meals 15,000d; breakfast, lunch & dinner) Another one-dish wonder, this popular eatery serves hearty beef noodles in a spicy broth.

Black & White Restaurant (384 1245; 171 Đ Nguyen Cong Tru; dishes 30,000-180,000d; lunch & dinner) Across from Damsan Hotel, this stylish restaurant has an extensive menu of good Vietnamese fare. More adventurous diners might want to try the turtle, sparrow or pigeon dishes.

Drinking

You can't stop by the coffee capital of Vietnam without sampling some of the local brews. Try the streets around Đ Le Thanh Ton where there are dozens of **cafes** (Đ Le Thanh Ton) to explore. Some also serve alcohol.

Café Hoa Da Quy (385 1304; 173 Đ Nguyen Cong Tru) This stylish yet cosy three-storey bar-cafe is a popular night-time spot and good for watching what's going on at the Damsan Hotel. The rooftop seating is pleasant and cool.

Da Ly (381 2243; 188 Đ Nguyen Cong Tru) There are great views over a coffee plantation from the garden of this chic cafe.

Shopping

Stock up on coffee here – the price is lower and the quality higher than in HCMC or Hanoi. You can buy whole beans or ground coffee at around 60,000d per 500g; better varieties cost more. Good places to buy the brown gold include **Thanh Bao Café** (385 4164; 32 Hoang Dieu), as well as along the guest-house strip on Đ Ly Thuong Kiet.

Getting There & Around

AIR

There are daily **Vietnam Airlines** (395 4442; 17-19 Đ No Trang Long) flights from HCMC and Hanoi, and services four times a week from Danang. The airport is 8km east of town. A taxi should cost about 100,000d.

BUS

Buon Ma Thuot's **bus station** (71 Đ Nguyen Chi Thanh) is about 4km from the centre, with plenty of services to Dalat (65,000d, four hours) and Pleiku (70,000d, four hours).

CAR & MOTORBIKE

Hwy 26 links the coast with Buon Ma Thuot, intersecting Hwy 1A at Ninh Hoa (157km), 34km north of Nha Trang. The road is surfaced and in good condition, though fairly steep. Hwy 14 to Pleiku (199km) is excellent. Hwy 27 is a scenic sealed road connecting Buon Ma Thuot with Dalat (200km, via Lak Lake). Though full of twists and turns, it's mainly in good condition and was scheduled for expansion in 2009.

TAXI

Try the local operation: **Mai Linh** (☎ 381 9819).

AROUND BUON MA THUOT

☎ 050

Yok Don National Park

The largest of Vietnam's nature reserves, **Yok Don National Park** (Vuon Quoc Gia Yok Don; ☎ 378 3049; yokdonecotourism@vnn.vn) has been gradually expanded and today encompasses 112,102 hectares of mainly dry deciduous forest. The park runs all the way up to the border with Cambodia, with the beautiful Serepok River flowing through it.

Yok Don is home to 67 mammal species, 38 of which are listed as endangered in Indochina and 17 of those endangered worldwide. The park habitat accommodates elephant, tiger and leopard, as well as nearly 250 different species of bird – including a pair of critically endangered giant ibis (Thaumatibis gigantea). More common wildlife includes deer, muntjac, monkey, and snake. In recent years previously unknown animals like the Canisauvus, a species of wild dog, have been discovered.

Within the park's boundaries are four minority villages, predominantly M'nong but also with Ede and Lao people. Three villages are accessible while the fourth is deep inside the park. The M'nong are a matrilineal tribe known for their skills in capturing wild elephants.

The delicate balance between ecological conservation and the preservation of local cultures is a challenge, considering the poverty of the region's people and their traditional means of survival (eg hunting). However, the Vietnamese government is working with international agencies such as the UN Development Programme (UNDP) to manage this balance, aiming towards education and community participation in conservation practices.

To explore the national park, you'll have to either engage your own guide from Buon Ma Thuot (see p329) or pick one up at the park entrance. Guides (US$30 per day for up to three persons) are available to lead treks (additional US$15 for camping overnight and US$10 per meal); there's also a US$5 boat fee to cross the Serepok River. It's possible to arrange a night visit to see the park's nocturnal inhabitants (US$200 for up to six people).

Elephant rides and treks (see the boxed text, opposite) can also be arranged. A direct booking at the park costs US$20 per hour per elephant or US$100 to US$120 for a full-day trek.

SIGHTS & ACTIVITIES

Most of the tourist action centres on the village of **Ban Don** in Ea Sup district, 45km northwest of Buon Ma Thuot. The village is 5km beyond the turn-off into the national park and often gets overrun with busloads of visitors, particularly at the **Ban Don Tourist Centre** (☎ 378 3020; ttdl.buondon@gmail.com). Traditional activities such as gong performances and drinking wine from a communal jug (everybody drinks at the same time through very long straws) are held for the edification of foreigners. Near the Tourist Centre a 200m-long bamboo **suspension bridge** (10,000d) crosses the Serepok River – a pretty, shaded walk but there's nothing 'ethnic' about it.

There are the neglected ruins of a 13th-century Cham tower called **Yang Prong** 35km north of Ban Don at Ya Liao, near the Cambodian border. A permit and guide are necessary to visit this spot.

SLEEPING & EATING

At the park entrance, 5km southeast of Ban Don, **Yok Don Guesthouse** (☎ 378 3049; r US$15; ❄) has rooms with hot water. You can also overnight at one of three **forest stations** (US$5) located 7km, 17km and 25km into the park. These are simple huts used by park rangers.

In Ban Don, contact **Ban Don Tourist Centre** (☎ 378 3020; ttdl.buondon@gmail.com) about staying in minority **stilt houses** (per person US$5) or **bungalows** (US$12). The bungalows are either

AN ELEPHANT'S LIFE

Behind the apparently glorious status of the elephant in Vietnam is a tortured history spanning centuries. Prized by kings, these gentle and intelligent creatures were trapped around present-day Yok Don National Park by M'nong hunters. The animals were then tamed through savage beatings before being presented as royal gifts or put to work by the tribe.

And what work it was – elephants were (and still are) used as combination bulldozers, fork-lifts and semitrailers. Now they're more often seen in the lucrative tourist industry, lugging people through the forests or as part of minority festivals.

It's not necessarily a better life. Many elephants were trapped as babies so that they would be easier to train – neglecting the fact that they need their mother's milk up to the age of four in order to develop healthily. It's also easy to overestimate what adult elephants can tolerate. Elephant skin appears to be rough and impermeable, but it's as sensitive as human skin, vulnerable to sunburn, dirt and infections.

Another misconception is that elephants are strong, even indefatigable, but their spines were not designed to carry heavy burdens for extended periods of time. Above all, they need 250kg of food a day – an expensive undertaking, even for the most successful owner.

Before you decide on an elephant ride, take a closer look at the animal and its work environment:

- The elephant should have a shaded area to rest, with clean water and food. There should be enough slack in the chain so that it can move around. Given enough space, elephants don't defecate where they eat (who would want to?).
- The seat placed on the elephant should be made of light bamboo, not heavy wood, and there should be about seven layers of padding between the seat and the skin. There should be rubber hoses to line the binding ropes, or they will abrade the skin horribly.
- The elephant should work for only four or five hours a day, bearing up to only two adults at a time.
- The elephant caretaker should not have to use the bullhook or whip on the elephant with every command.

Though elephant trapping was banned In 1990, it was not strictly enforced. Vietnam's native elephant species has been listed as endangered since 1976 and it's estimated that only a few hundred elephants remain in the highlands. Without elephant sanctuaries or alternative employment, their fate seems grim: a lifetime of tourist rides, illicit employment in logging and construction, or, if the money runs out, abandonment or death.

Compiled with assistance from Jin Pyn Lee

beside the lake or out on nearby Aino Island, reached via a rickety series of bamboo suspension bridges. There is a restaurant in Ban Don, which sometimes hosts performances of gong music and dancing for a group tour.

GETTING THERE & AROUND

Local buses head from Buon Ma Thuot bus station to Yok Don National Park (20,000d, hourly, 40km). Motorbike taxis in Buon Ma Thuot can take you to the park for around US$8/12 one way/return.

Dray Sap & Dray Nur Falls

Located on the Krong Ana River, these stunning **waterfalls** (☎ 321 3194; admission 10,000d) offer good riverside trekking opportunities. From the car park, the first one is the 100m-wide **Dray Sap** ('smoky falls' in Ede). For a better view, head down the path beside the river to a suspension bridge that crosses the river.

Across the bridge, follow the path through cornfields for another 250m. It leads to another bridge overlooking the 30m-wide **Dray Nur** waterfall. At the end of this bridge is a dirt path that brings you closer to Dray Nur.

It's possible to hike from Dray Nur to the Gia Long Falls, but you'll need to engage a guide. The trail runs for about 4km and takes about 1½ hours.

To reach the falls, follow Đ Le Duan until it becomes Đ Nguyen Thi Dinh and eventually

THE HO CHI MINH TRAIL

This legendary route was not one but many paths that formed the major supply link for the North Vietnamese and VC during the American War. Supplies and troops leaving from the port of Vinh (see p198) headed inland along mountainous jungle paths, crossing in and out of Laos, and eventually arrived near Saigon. With all the secrecy, propaganda and confusion regarding the trail, it's hard to say how long it was in full; estimates range from over 5500km (said the US military) to more than 13,000km (boasted the North Vietnamese).

While elephants were initially used to cross the Truong Son Mountains into Laos, eventually it was sheer human power that shouldered supplies down the trail, sometimes supplemented by ponies, bicycles or trucks. Travelling from the 17th Parallel to the vicinity of Saigon took about six months in the mid-1960s; years later, with a more complex network of paths, the journey took only six weeks but it was still arduous going.

Each man started out with a 36kg pack of supplies as well as a few personal items (eg a tent, spare uniform and antisnake venom). What lay ahead was a rugged and mountainous course, plagued by flooding, disease and the constant threat of American bombing. At their peak, more than 500 American air strikes hit the trail everyday and more ordnance was dropped on it than was used in all the theatres of war in WWII.

Despite these shock-and-awe tactics and the elaborate electronic sensors along the McNamara Line, the trail was never blocked. Most of it has returned to the jungle, but you can still follow sections of the trail today. Note that this is usually the more developed trail from the early 1970s, as the older trail was over the border in Laos. The Ho Chi Minh Highway is the easiest way to get a fix, an incredible mountain road running along the spine of the country. Starting near Hanoi, it passes through some popular tourist destinations and former battlefields, including the Phong Nha Cave (p202), Khe Sanh (p212), Aluoi (p212), Kon Tum (p338) and Buon Ma Thuot (p328) on its way to Saigon. The most spectacular sections include the roller-coaster ride through the Phong Nha–Ke Bang National Park, where looming karsts are cloaked in jungle, and pretty karsts north of the Phong Nha Cave are punctuated with traditional villages.

Travel this route by car (or 4WD), motorbike or even bicycle if you are training for the King of the Mountains jersey; or arrange a tour through the Easy Riders (p325) in Dalat or one of the leading motorbike touring companies in Hanoi (p507). **Explore Indochina** (www.exploreindochina.com) specialise in trail tours.

Hwy 14 heading south. After 12km look left for the sign for the turn-off to the waterfalls. Drive for another 11km through a small industrial zone, then farmland, before you arrive at the entrance to the falls.

A longer but more picturesque route involves continuing on Đ Nguyen Thi Dinh until you're about 16km out of town and crossing the bridge there. Continue for another 5km and turn left about 500m past the markets. This road will bring you to the entrance in another 6km.

Gia Long Falls

Further down the road from Dray Sap and Dray Nur is this shorter **waterfall** (☎ 363 8456; admission 10,000d), named for the first emperor of the Nguyen dynasty. He wanted to have a bridge built across the river but it was never completed; remnants are still visible through the overgrowth. The falls' future is in doubt as the new Buon Kuop Dam has been built upstream and may eventually poach the water supply.

The Gia Long Falls are a further 7km along the road from Dray Sap and Dray Nur. It can be reached on foot from Dray Nur if you have a guide to lead you.

Lak Lake

The largest natural body of water in the central highlands, **Lak Lake** (Ho Lak) covers 700 hectares in the rainy season, shrinking in the dry season to 400 hectares surrounded by rice paddies. While there are pockets of tourist development, it's nowhere as orchestrated as what you'd get at Ban Don Village (see p332).

The scenery around the lake is a postcard portrait of rural life, which sufficiently impressed Emperor Bao Dai that he built yet another of his palaces overlooking the lake (see opposite). There are two minority villages around the lake that often receive visitors. On the south shores near the town of Lien Son lies **Jun village**, a fairly traditional M'nong settlement filled with rattan and wooden stilt houses. The villagers are surprisingly non-plussed about visitors, even though DakLak Tourist has a small set-up and runs elephant rides (US$30 per hour). The second village of **M'lieng** is on the southwestern shore and can be reached by elephant or boat; enquire at DakLak Tourist.

If you're interested in staying overnight, Mr Duc at **Cafe Duc Mai** (☎ 358 6280; 268 Đ Nguyen Tat Thanh) can organise a mattress in one of several traditional stilt longhouses (US$5), or the usual gong concerts, elephant rides, and kayaking or walking tours.

SLEEPING & EATING

Lak Resort (Du Lich Ho Lak; ☎ 358 6164; Lien Son; r US$10, bungalows US$30, shared longhouse US$5; 💻 🏊) Run by DakLak Tourist, this resort has a range of rooms – from nice new modern ones to backpacker-basic shared facilities – in a quiet lakeside location. There's also a pool and a restaurant (meals 80,000d). The resort is committed to employing at least 51% M'nong staff.

Bao Dai Villa (☎ 358 6164; Lien Son; r US$25-45) DakLak Tourist also owns the former emperor's palace on the hill above Lak Resort. There are six enormous rooms, dressed up with photographs of the emperor and empress; the view outside the window is much more appealing. More royal portraits adorn the restaurant (meals 80,000d).

GETTING THERE & AWAY

Lak Lake is located on the mountainous road between Dalat (154km southeast) and Buon Ma Thuot (50km north). It's regularly visited on the Easy Rider trail. A day trip on the back of a motorbike from Buon Ma Thuot should cost around 120,000d, including waiting time. All the tour agencies in Buon Ma Thuot offer tours (see p329).

Public buses to Lak Lake leave regularly from the Buon Ma Thuot bus station (16,000d).

PLEIKU

☎ 059 / pop 236,982 / elev 785m

The busy but ho-hum capital of Gia Lai province, Pleiku (or Playcu) is better known as a strategic American and South Vietnamese base during the American War than for any postwar accomplishments. It makes an adequate pit stop, but there's little to detain a traveller for more than a few hours. Torched by departing South Vietnamese soldiers in 1975, the city was rebuilt in the 1980s with help from the Soviet Union, which thoroughly explains its lack of appeal today.

In 2001 and 2004 Pleiku was the scene of Montagnard protests against the government (see the boxed text, p329); the latter promptly responded by prohibiting foreigners from visiting the area. While these rules have gradually been relaxed and the province is safe for travel, you'll need a permit to visit the minority villages around here. Venturing out without one is not recommended, unless you enjoy being questioned by the police.

In 1965 the VC shelled a US compound in Pleiku, and killed eight Americans. This attack was used as a justification by US President Lyndon Johnson to begin a relentless bombing campaign against North Vietnam and the rapid build-up of US troops, who, until then, were supposed to be in a noncombat role.

TO DIE JARAI

The Jarai minority of the Pleiku area honour their dead in graveyards set up like miniature villages. These graveyards are located to the west of the village, where the sun sets.

Each grave is marked with a shelter or bamboo stakes. Carved wooden figures are placed along the edge, often pictured in a squatting position with their hands over their faces in an expression of mourning. Placed on the grave is a jar that represents the deceased person, and objects that the deceased might need in the next world are buried with them.

For seven years after the death, relatives bring food to the grave and pass death anniversaries at the gravesite, mourning and celebrating the deceased by feasting and drinking rice wine. After the seventh year, the spirit is believed to have moved on from the village and the grave is abandoned.

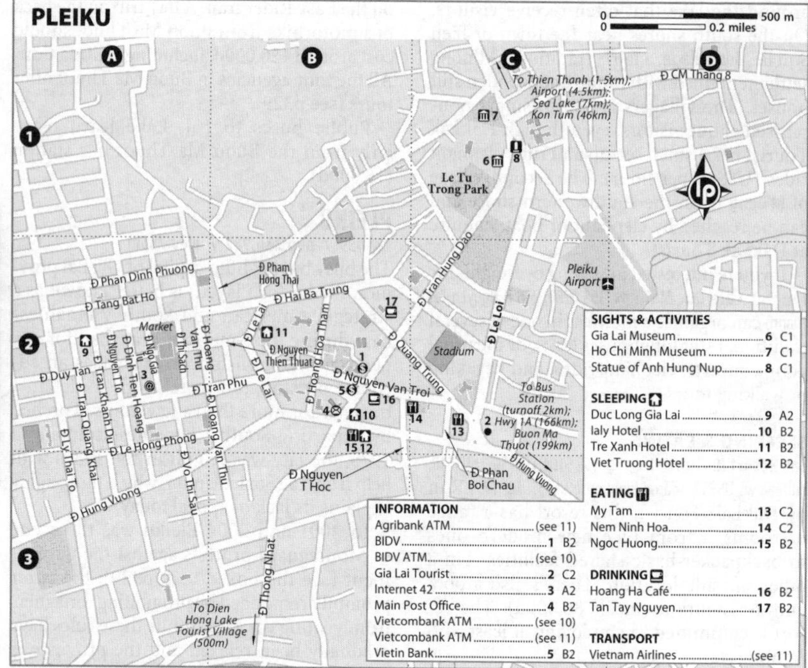

When US troops departed in 1973 the South Vietnamese kept Pleiku as their main combat base in the area. They fled the advancing VC in 1975, and the civilian population of Pleiku and nearby Kon Tum fled with them. The stampede to the coastline along the only road, Hwy 7, became known as the 'Convoy of Tears' as they were relentlessly attacked by North Vietnamese forces en route; it's estimated that only a quarter or a third of the 100,000 people survived.

Information

You need a permit and guide to visit villages in Gia Lai province. This puts off many travellers, who usually skip Pleiku and head north to Kon Tum. Gia Lai Tourist can arrange the permit and guide as part of one of its packages.

Agribank ATM (18 Đ Le Lai) In the Tre Xanh Hotel.
BIDV (☎ 389 7539; 1 Đ Nguyen Van Troi) Foreign-currency and travellers-cheque exchange, and credit-card advances.
BIDV ATM (89 Đ Hung Vuong) In the foyer of the Ialy Hotel.
Gia Lai Tourist (☎ 387 4571; www.gialaitourist.com; 215 Đ Hung Vuong) Has English- and French-speaking guides who lead a variety of tours, including trekking and programs catering for war veterans.
Internet 42 (42 Đ Dinh Tien Hoang; per hr 3000d)
Main post office (☎ 387 2123; 69 Đ Hung Vuong)
Vietcombank ATM (89 Đ Hung Vuong) In the foyer of the Ialy Hotel.
Vietcombank ATM (18 Đ Le Lai) In the Tre Xanh Hotel.
Vietin Bank (☎ 387 1216; 1 Đ Tran Hung Dao) Foreign-currency and travellers' cheque exchange, and credit-card advances.

Sights

MUSEUMS

Pleiku has two museums, neither of them remarkable and both often closed.

The **Ho Chi Minh Museum** (☎ 382 4276; 1 Phan Dinh Phuong; admission free; 8-11am & 1-4.30pm Mon-Fri) offers the usual paeans to Uncle Ho, with an emphasis on his affinity for hill-tribe people and their love for him. There are also displays about Bahnar hero Anh Hung Nup (1914–98), who led the hill tribes against the French and Americans. There's a **statue of Anh Hung Nup** (cnr Đ Le Loi & Đ Tran Hung Dao) nearby.

The **Gia Lai Museum** (☎ 382 4520; Đ Tran Hung Dao; admission 10,000d) is at a new location, with hill-tribe artefacts and photographs about Pleiku's role during the American War.

SEA LAKE

Bien Ho, or Sea Lake, is a deep mountain lake about 7km north of Pleiku. It is believed to have been formed from a prehistoric volcanic crater. Because it's the town's main water source, there's little development around the lake and it's possible to swim in the green water (though few do). The surrounding area is beautiful and can be viewed from a tiered terrace.

Sleeping

Viet Truong Hotel (☎ 382 4515; 84 Đ Hung Vuong; r 140,000d; ❄) The spiral staircase is a little dark, but this hotel has large rooms, basic bathrooms and a central location directly opposite the Ialy Hotel.

Dien Hong Lake Tourist Village (☎ 371 6450; Đ Ho Dien Hong; r US$15-20; ❄) For peace and quiet away from the city centre, opt for this neat row of bungalows on the shore of an artificial lake. Rooms are newish and come with all the mod-cons, and it's only 1km away from town.

Ialy Hotel (☎ 382 4843; ialyhotel@dng.vnn.vn; 89 Đ Hung Vuong; r 220,000-400,000d; ❄) An ageing hotel in the town centre, with passable rooms and city views. The price includes breakfast Vietnamese-style (noodles and tepid coffee).

Duc Long Gia Lai (☎ 387 6303; thienhc@diglgroup.com; 95-97 Đ Hai Ba Trung; r US$20; ❄ 💻) Not much English is spoken here, but that doesn't detract from the smart and spotless rooms that are the best value in town. The more expensive rooms have balconies and corner tubs.

Tre Xanh Hotel (Green Bamboo Hotel; ☎ 371 5787; 18 Đ Le Lai; r 280,000-380,000d; ❄ 💻) Next to the fancy plaza of the same name, this hotel has nice, carpeted rooms with all the usual comforts. Rooms at the front have good views of the highlands.

Eating & Drinking

Ngoc Huong (☎ 382 2796; 76 Đ Hung Vuong; dishes 15,000-70,000d; 🕒 lunch & dinner) An unpretentious restaurant with standard Vietnamese fare. There's no English menu, but the staff will let you walk into the kitchen and point at what you want.

Nem Ninh Hoa (80 Đ Nguyen Van Troi; meals 30,000d; 🕒 lunch & dinner) A casual eatery that serves freshly grilled pork for roll-your-own spring rolls.

My Tam (☎ 382 1293; 3 Đ Quang Trung; meals 30,000d; 🕒 lunch & dinner) A hole-in-the-wall joint where the house speciality is roasted chicken, crisped to perfection and served with rice cooked with tomato and garlic.

Thien Thanh (☎ 382 7011; 58 Đ Pham Van Dong; meals 100,000d; 🕒 lunch & dinner) If you'd like a little scenery along with your dinner, try this restaurant nestled in a valley. It overlooks pretty rice fields and specialises in goat or beef grilled in bamboo. An English menu is available.

Hoang Ha Cafe (☎ 382 4573; 26 Đ Nguyen Van Troi) A pair of solemn arowana fish greet you at the entrance to this three-storey cafe. The decor is as modern as it gets in Pleiku, and there's a good range of cocktails.

BORDER CROSSING: BO Y–PHOU KEAU

The Bo Y–Phou Keau border crossing lies 86km northeast of Kon Tum and 119km northwest of Attapeu (Laos). Although it opened to tourists in 2006, some locals will swear that it isn't. Lao and Vietnamese visas are not available at this border.

Coming from Vietnam, buses leave Pleiku at 8am daily for Attapeu (225,000d, eight hours, 250km), continuing to Pakse (280,000d, 12 hours, 440km). Kon Tum Tourist can arrange for you to join the bus when it passes through Kon Tum at 10am (to Attapeu 220,000d, six hours, 200km; to Pakse 320,000d, 10 hours, 420km). In the opposite direction, buses leave Attapeu (110,000 kip to Kon Tum) and Pakse (160,000 kip to Kon Tum) every day.

There are also buses from Quy Nhon twice a week, passing through Pleiku and Kon Tum en route to Attapeu and Pakse. The schedule fluctuates and it's best to inquire at the bus station for the latest details.

Crossing the border independently can be a challenge. On the Vietnam side, the nearest major town is Ngoc Hoi, which can be reached by bus (25,000d, 1½ hours, 60km) from Kon Tum. You'll have to catch a minibus or *xe om* from Ngoc Hoi to cover the 14km to the border. On the Laos side, things are even quieter and you'll be at the mercy of passing traffic to hitch a ride onwards.

Tan Tay Nguyen (☎ 387 4217; 24 Đ Quang Trung) With a thatched longhouse looking onto a garden bar, this is a comfortable place to while away the time over a drink.

Getting There & Around

The local office of **Vietnam Airlines** (☎ 382 4680; 18 Đ Le Lai) is located in Tre Xanh Hotel. It can book tickets on the daily flights to Hanoi, HCMC and Danang. The airport is about 5km from the town and accessible by taxi (50,000d) or *xe om*.

Pleiku's newish **bus station** (Ben Xe Duc Long Gia Lai; ☎ 382 9021; 45 Đ Ly Nam De) is located about 2.5km southeast of town. It's also one of the nicest looking and least harassing stations around. Regular buses head to Buon Ma Thuot (70,000d, four hours), Kon Tum (15,000d, one hour) and Quy Nhon (70,000d, four hours). It's also possible to catch buses to Cambodia (see the boxed text, p341) and Laos (see the boxed text, p337).

For a taxi call **Mai Linh** (☎ 371 7979).

Pleiku sits at the intersection of Hwys 14 and 19, linking it to Buon Ma Thuot (199km), Quy Nhon (186km) and Kon Tum (47km). From Pleiku it's 550km to HCMC and 424km to Nha Trang.

KON TUM

☎ 060 / pop 137,190 / elev 525m

If you like dusty little towns with not much going on, you'll love Kon Tum. It's less a destination in itself than a jumping-off point for visiting the region. Most foreigners who pass here are on their way to see Montagnard villages (there are 700 dotting the area), to pick up the Ho Chi Minh Trail (see the boxed text, p334) or to cross the border to Laos (see the boxed text, p337). Besides a couple of Bahnar villages on the edge of town, there's little in the way of conventional sightseeing spots – which for some travellers might be a reason to linger.

Kon Tum saw its share of combat during the American War. A major battle between the South and North Vietnamese took place in and around Kon Tum in the spring of 1972, when the area was devastated by hundreds of American B-52 raids. In March 1975 the South withdrew from the province after Buon Ma Thuot fell to the North and many civilians joined them in the 'Convoy of Tears'.

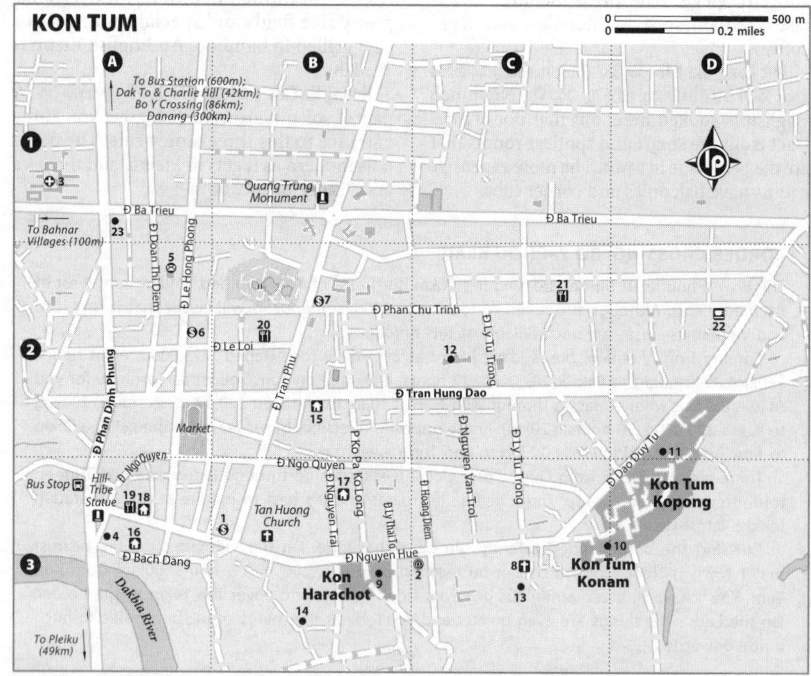

More recently, in the 2004 protests against government policies in the highlands, Montagnards in Kon Tum province clashed with police and soldiers. On the surface things have cooled off, but relations between Montagnards and the authorities remain fraught.

Information

BIDV (☎ 386 2340; 1 Đ Tran Phu; ⏰ closed Sat) Has an ATM, exchanges US dollars and gives cash advances on major credit cards.
BIDV ATM (205 Đ Le Hong Phong) In the post office.
Internet cafe (21 Đ Nguyen Hue)
Kon Tum General Hospital (☎ 386 2565; 224A Đ Ba Trieu)
Kon Tum Tourist (☎ 386 1626; ktourist@dng.vnn.vn; 2 Đ Phan Dinh Phung) Located in the Dakbla Hotel, this agency has English-speaking staff who can arrange tours and homestays to Bahnar and Jarai villages, and trekking or hunting trips. Ask for Mr Huynh, who's a font of information on the region.
Main post office (☎ 386 2361; 205 Đ Le Hong Phong)
Vietcombank (☎ 391 3519; 108D Đ Le Hong Phong)
Vietin Bank (☎ 391 0714; 92 Đ Tran Phu)

INFORMATION	
BIDV	**1** B3
BIDV ATM	(see 5)
Internet Café	**2** C3
Kon Tum General Hospital	**3** A1
Kon Tum Tourist	**4** A3
Main Post Office	**5** A2
Vietcombank	**6** A2
Vietin Bank	**7** B2
SIGHTS & ACTIVITIES	
Hill-Tribe Museum	(see 12)
Immaculate Conception Cathedral	**8** C3
Kon Harachot	**9** B3
Kon Tum Konam	**10** C3
Kon Tum Kopong	**11** D2
Seminary	**12** C2
Vinh Son 1 Orphanage	**13** C3
Vinh Son 2 Orphanage	**14** B3
SLEEPING	
Family Hotel	**15** B2
Indochine Hotel	**16** A3
Thinh Vuong Hotel	**17** B3
Viet Tram	**18** A3
EATING	
Dakbla's	**19** A3
Nghia II	**20** B2
Quan 58	**21** C2
DRINKING	
Eva Cafe	**22** D2
TRANSPORT	
Vietnam Airlines	**23** A1

Sights

MONTAGNARD VILLAGES

There are several clusters of Bahnar villages on the periphery of Kon Tum, where cows, pigs, chickens and children – sometimes as naked as the animals around them – ramble nonchalantly through the dirt lanes. These neighbourhoods look (and are) significantly poorer than the town itself. Village life centres on the traditional *rong* house (*nha rong*), a tall thatched-roof community house built on stilts. The stilts were originally for protection from elephants, tigers and other animals. *Rong* houses are usually locked, unless they're hosting community meetings, weddings, festivals or prayer sessions.

The three closest village clusters lie to the east, south and west of the town. The village cluster to the east is the original Kon Tum village that the modern town grew out of. It's made up of two villages: **Kon Tum Konam** (Lower Kon Tum) and **Kon Tum Kopong** (Upper Kon Tum), each with its own *rong* house. To the south of town is the village **Kon Harachot**, in the middle of which lies the Vinh Son 2 orphanage (see the boxed text, p340). The cluster to the west is near the hospital and comprises about five villages.

Generally the local people welcome tourists and it's fine to wander around the village. But ask permission before pointing a camera into people's faces or homes. Some of the older people might be conversant in French but not English. You also probably won't see people in traditional garb unless they're on their way to Mass in the Bahnar language, held on Sunday nights at the Immaculate Conception Cathedral.

If you can afford to spend several days here, Kon Tum Tourist (left) can arrange village homestays. Because the guides here are careful not to intrude too frequently on any one village, visitors are always welcomed and traditions remain intact. Day trips are also available from about US$25 for a guide and an additional US$2 to US$12 per person, depending on the places visited. Permits are no longer required, but be on the safe side by checking in with Kon Tum Tourist before you venture off on your own.

IMMACULATE CONCEPTION CATHEDRAL

This is a beautiful French wooden **cathedral** (Đ Nguyen Hue) with a dark front, sky-blue trim and wide terraces. Inside it's light, airy and elegant. The heart of the 160-year-old Kontum diocese, it serves primarily the ethnic minority community and the altar is bedecked in traditional woven fabrics.

SEMINARY & HILL-TRIBE MUSEUM

This lovely old Catholic **seminary** (Đ Tran Hung Dao; admission free; 8-11am & 2-4pm Mon-Sat) wouldn't look out of place in a provincial French village. Built in 1934, it has a chapel with beautiful wood carvings and a **'Traditional Room'** upstairs that functions as an unofficial museum of hill-tribe life and the Kon Tum diocese. You may have to ask one of the Seminary residents to unlock the museum for you.

Sleeping

Viet Tram (386 9269; 162 Đ Nguyen Hue; r US$10-15;) A simple family-run mini-hotel with clean rooms, though it's starting to look a little rundown. Room prices can be bargained down if you skip the air-conditioning.

Family Hotel (386 2448; phongminhkt@yahoo.com; 55 & 61 Đ Tran Hung Dao; r US$10-25;) This mini-hotel has a range of good rooms with nice bathrooms, perhaps a touch heavy on the pastel palette. The real kicker is the garden courtyard, set back from the main road, where breakfast is served in a pretty, peaceful setting.

Thinh Vuong Hotel (391 4729; 16B Đ Nguyen Trai; r 160,000-180,000d;) Tucked away on a quiet residential street, this is an airy, friendly mini-hotel with spacious rooms. The hotel doesn't serve breakfast but there are some *pho* shops around the corner.

Indochine Hotel (386 3334; www.kontumtourism.com; 30 Đ Bach Dang; r US$45-50, ste US$80;) Rooms are comfortable and most have lovely views of the highlands, but otherwise this place is not as swish as you might expect.

Eating & Drinking

Nghia II (72 Đ Le Loi; dishes 10,000d; lunch & dinner) A casual and cheap eatery serving good vegetarian fare.

Dakbla's (386 2584; 168 Đ Nguyen Hue; dishes 20,000-80,000d; lunch & dinner) One of Kon Tum's few bona fide restaurants, Dakbla's has a standard Vietnamese menu spiced up with meats like wild boar and frog. The decor provides

SUFFER THE LITTLE CHILDREN

A popular 'sightseeing' stop for tourists passing through Kon Tum are the Vinh Son 1 and 2 orphanages, run by the Sisters of the Miraculous Medal. Each orphanage is home to about 200 mostly Montagnard children. Not all are orphans – some have been placed here by families who are unable to support them.

Although both orphanages welcome visitors and foreign support, having large groups of tourists suddenly descend upon them can be disruptive to the children's lessons and other learning activities. Like children anywhere in the world, the kids are happy to be distracted, particularly by foreigners keen to fawn upon and cuddle them. They enjoy these feel-good moments, but you have to wonder about the emotional impact if this becomes their typical interaction with foreigners.

If you plan to visit, please avoid giving the children sweets or candy; their minders and dentists will thank you for it. Consider bringing some fruit or nutritious fresh food instead. Other possible gifts are clothing, toys and school supplies, though it's hard to precisely anticipate what's needed.

Monetary contributions are of course appreciated, but standards of transparency and accountability are not what Westerners are used to. Another way to contribute is through an intermediary, such as California-based **Friends of Vinh Son Montagnard Orphanage** (www.friendsofvso.org), Pennsylvania-based **Friends of Central Highlands, Vietnam** (www.fochvn.org) or American NGO **East Meets West Foundation** (www.eastmeetswest.org); the latter runs a dental program for the orphanages and other education projects in the highlands. There are many orphanages and projects in Kon Tum (and all over Vietnam) that need help – it doesn't hurt to spread the tourist largesse around.

Vinh Son 1 is just behind the Immaculate Conception Cathedral on Đ Nguyen Hue. Vinh Son 2 is in Kon Harachot, a small village at the southern edge of town; it's at the end of the second dirt track on the right after the small paddock.

BORDER CROSSING: LE THANH–O YADAW

Opened in December 2007, this is the newest border crossing in the area, 90km from Pleiku and 64km from Ban Lung, Cambodia. Visas are available on arrival in Cambodia, but not in Vietnam.

The road on the Cambodian side gets unfavourable reports, although it's supposed to improve soon. Bus schedules are prone to change, so check with the bus station or Gia Lai Tourist in Pleiku to get the latest information.

From Pleiku there is a local bus leaving several times a day for Moc Den (21,000d, two hours, 80km), where another bus (30,000d, 15km) heads to the border. After entering Cambodia at O Yadaw, you'll have to ask around for a taxi (US$50) or motorbike (US$15) to Banlung.

At the time of research, there was no bus service from Ban Lung to Pleiku. You'll have to get your own transport to the border, then wait for a bus heading to Moc Den or Duc Co (15,000d); from either town you can connect to Pleiku. There are *xe om* waiting on the Vietnamese side, who will avow that there are no bus services to Pleiku in order to drive a hard bargain.

the requisite local colour with tribal artefacts glowering down on diners.

Quan 58 (☎ 386 3814; 58 Đ Phan Chu Trinh; hotpot 70,000d; ⏲ lunch & dinner) All goat, all the time. This modest operation will serve you goat just about any way you might want to eat it: steamed (*de hap*), grilled (*de nuong*), sautéed (*de xao lan*), curried (*de cari*) and the ever-popular hotpot (*lau de*).

Eva Coffee (☎ 386 2944; evacoffee2002@yahoo.com; 1 Đ Phan Chu Trinh) A cosy neighbourhood cafe with plenty of quirk, from the treehouselike setting to the solemn tribal masks overhead. A nice place to unwind with a beer or coffee, as local couples have established.

Getting There & Around

The local **Vietnam Airlines** (☎ 386 2282; 129 Đ Ba Trieu; ⏲ closed Sun) office can handle air-travel bookings; the nearest airport is in Pleiku.

Kon Tum's **bus station** (Đ 279 Phan Dinh Phung) has plenty of services to Pleiku (15,000d, one hour) and Danang (130,000d, four hours). Buses to Pleiku also make pick-ups along Đ Phan Dinh Phung across the street from Dakbla Hotel. It's possible to head for the border with Laos from here (see the boxed text, p337).

From Kon Tum, Hwy 14 runs to Pleiku (49km south) and Danang (300km north).

Kon Tum is easy to traverse on foot, but *xe om* are in ready supply. It shouldn't cost more than 10,000d to get anywhere on the back of a bike. If you need a taxi, try **Mai Linh** (☎ 395 5555).

AROUND KON TUM

Dak To & Charlie Hill

The obscure **Dak To outpost**, 42km north of Kon Tum, was a major battlefield during the American War. In 1972 it was the scene of intense fighting and one of the last big battles before American troops pulled out.

Dak To has become popular with visiting groups of US veterans as well as a few VC veterans. There are two Russian tanks on display, an old airstrip and a war memorial; you probably won't find much of interest if you're not a war buff but you could seek out the well-tended *rong* house.

About 5km south of Dak To is **Charlie Hill**. The hill was a fortified South Vietnamese stronghold before the VC tried to overrun it. The South Vietnamese officer in charge, Colonel Ngoc Minh, decided that he would neither surrender nor retreat and the battle became a fierce fight to the death. Unusual for a guerrilla war, this was a prolonged battle. The VC laid siege for 1½ months before they managed to kill Colonel Minh and 150 South Vietnamese troops. Although largely forgotten in the West, the battle is well known even now in Vietnam, largely because the fight was commemorated by a popular song, *Nguoi O Lai Charlie* (The People Stayed in Charlie).

Charlie Hill is visible from the airstrip but off-limits to visitors. It was heavily mined during the war and may still be unsafe to climb.

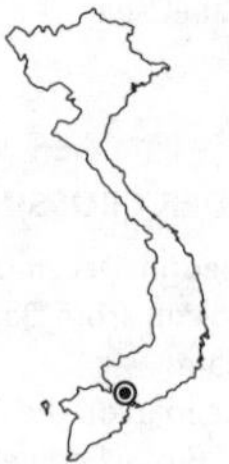

Ho Chi Minh City

Fasten your seatbelts as Ho Chi Minh City is a metropolis on the move – and we're not just talking about the motorbikes that throng the streets. Saigon, as it's known to all but city officials, is Vietnam at its most dizzying: a high-octane city of commerce and culture that has driven the whole country forward with its limitless energy. It is a living organism that breathes life and vitality into all who settle here, and visitors cannot help but be hauled along for the ride.

Saigon is a name so evocative that it conjures up a thousand jumbled images. Wander through timeless alleys to ancient pagodas or teeming markets, past ramshackle wooden shops selling silk, spices and baskets, before fast-forwarding into the future beneath sleek skyscrapers or at designer malls, gourmet restaurants and minimalist bars. The ghosts of the past live on in the churches, temples, former GI hotels and government buildings that one generation ago witnessed a city in turmoil, but the real beauty of Saigon's urban collage is that these two worlds blend so seamlessly into one.

Whether you want the finest hotels or the cheapest guesthouses, the classiest restaurants or the most humble street stalls, the designer boutiques or the scrum of the markets, Saigon has it all. The Saigon experience is about so many things – memorable conversations, tantalising tastes and moments of frustration – yet it will not evoke apathy. Stick around this conundrum of a city long enough and you may just unravel its mysteries.

HIGHLIGHTS

- Step back into the turbulent past at the **History Museum** (p355) and the **War Remnants Museum** (p354)
- Experience the Chinese pagodas of colourful **Cholon** (p359), before heading to the atmospheric **Giac Vien Pagoda** (p364)
- Discover the secrets of Vietnamese cuisine at one of the city's many gourmet restaurants, like **Huong Lai** (p374) or **Hoa Tuc** (p374)
- Hit the town for a big night out Saigon style by trawling leading bars such as hip **Vasco's** (p379), classy **Q Bar** (p379) or, for live music, **Acoustic Bar** (p379), before washing up in **Pham Ngu Lao** (p380)
- Unearth some trinkets or chow down on local delicacies in **Ben Thanh Market** (p384)

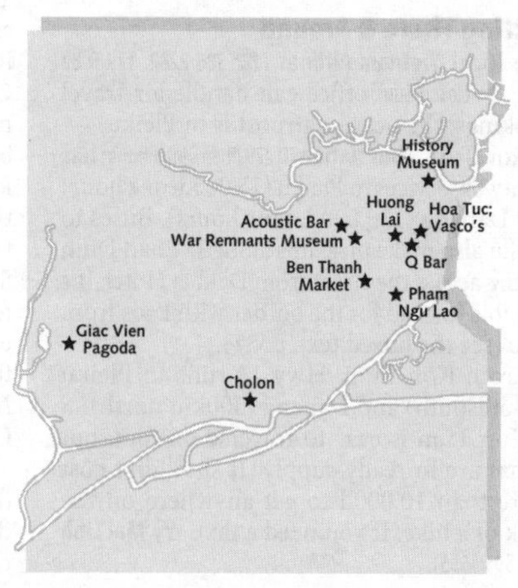

TELEPHONE CODE: 08	POPULATION: 7 MILLION+	BEST TIME TO VISIT: NOV–FEB

HISTORY

Saigon was originally part of the kingdom of Cambodia and, until the 17th century, was a small port town known as Prey Nokor. As more and more settlers moved south it was absorbed by Vietnam and became the base for the Nguyen Lords.

Saigon was captured by the French in 1859, and named the capital of Cochinchina a few years later. The city served as the capital of the Republic of Vietnam from 1956 until 1975, when it fell to advancing North Vietnamese forces and was renamed Ho Chi Minh City by the Hanoi government.

The official government census only counts those who have official residence permits, and, today, as many as one-third of the population could be living here illegally. Some of these illegal residents lived in the city before 1975, but their residence permits were transferred to rural re-education camps after reunification. Many have simply sneaked back into the city, although without a residence permit they cannot own property or a business.

Explosive growth is evident in a slew of satellite suburbs beyond the centre and a glut of high-rise buildings, joint-venture hotels and colourful shops downtown. Downsides include the sharp increase in traffic, pollution and other urban ills, but a more open-minded new generation may infuse HCMC's chaotic growth with a more globally conscious attitude.

ORIENTATION

In reality, HCMC is not so much a city as a small province stretching from the South China Sea almost to the Cambodian border. Rural regions make up about 90% of the land area of HCMC and hold around 25% of the municipality's population; the other 75% is crammed into the remaining 10% of land, which constitutes the urban centre.

HCMC is divided into 16 urban districts (*quan*, derived from the French *quartier*) and five rural districts *(huyen)*. It is city growing fast, with many new developments underway in up-and-coming residential areas such as An Phu in District 2, or Saigon South, also known as District 7.

The majority of places and sights described in this chapter are located in District 1, the district still officially known as Saigon (although many residents still refer to the whole city as Saigon just to confuse things), which includes the backpacker district of Pham Ngu Lao, and the more upmarket area of Dong Khoi, host to the city's best assortment of restaurants, bars and boutiques. The city's neoclassical and international-style buildings,

HO CHI MINH CITY IN...

One Day

Start your morning with a steaming bowl of *pho* (rice-noodle soup), the soup that built a nation, before strolling among the shops and galleries lining Đ Dong Khoi. Make your way to the **Museum of Ho Chi Minh City** (p355), then have lunch at nearby **Quan An Ngon** (p373), the place to sample a wide variety of Vietnamese delicacies. Continue your journey into the past at the **Reunification Palace** (p353) and the **War Remnants Museum** (p354). In the evening, catch the sunset and stunning views from the rooftop bar of the **Sheraton Saigon** (p372), followed by an elegant meal at **Huong Lai** (p374), a restaurant that helps disadvantaged children and former street kids. Have a nightcap at one of the many bars around the centre of town. Đ Dong Du, Đ Le Thanh Ton and Đ Pasteur are all good hunting grounds.

Two Days

Kick off the day at bustling **Ben Thanh Market** (p384), where you can grab a bite while loading up on knick-knacks, sweets and conical hats. Then take a taxi to **Cholon** (p359) for a visit to the historic pagodas of HCMC's Chinatown. Have lunch in a local diner, then pay a final pagoda visit to **Giac Lam** (p363), HCMC's oldest and arguably most impressive pagoda. As the afternoon wanes, treat yourself to a massage or spa treatment at **L'Apothiquaire** (p366), a welcome reward for tired limbs. Suitably reinvigorated, start the fun all over again with a decadent meal at one of the many superb international restaurants in the Dong Khoi area. End the night at one of HCMC's most happening night spots, such as **Acoustic Bar** (p379) or **Apocalypse Now** (p381).

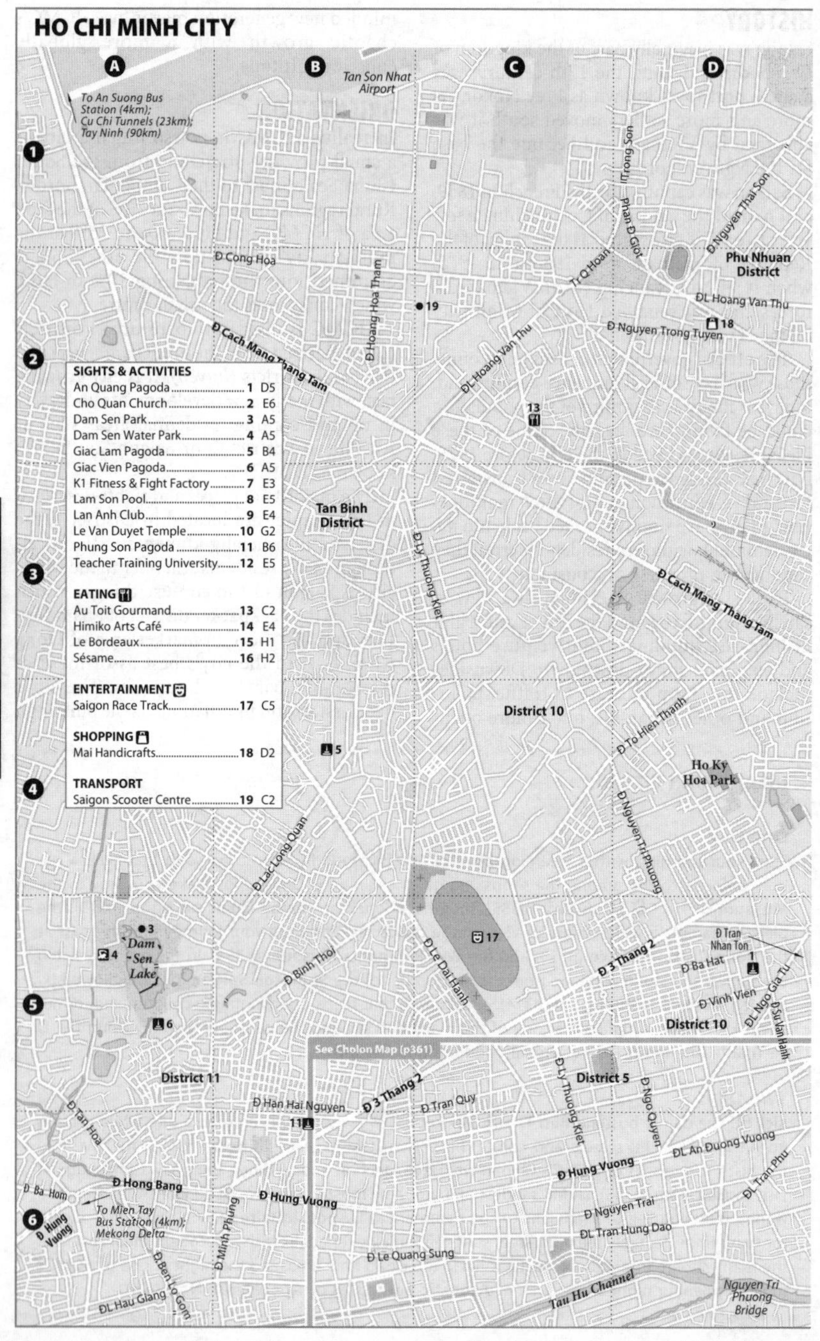
HO CHI MINH CITY
A
B
C
D
1
2
3
4
5
6
To An Suong Bus Station (4km); Cu Chi Tunnels (23km); Tay Ninh (90km)
Tan Son Nhat Airport
SIGHTS & ACTIVITIES
An Quang Pagoda 1 D5
Cho Quan Church 2 E6
Dam Sen Park 3 A5
Dam Sen Water Park 4 A5
Giac Lam Pagoda 5 B4
Giac Vien Pagoda 6 A5
K1 Fitness & Fight Factory 7 E3
Lam Son Pool 8 E5
Lan Anh Club 9 E4
Le Van Duyet Temple 10 G2
Phung Son Pagoda 11 B6
Teacher Training University 12 E5
EATING
Au Toit Gourmand 13 C2
Himiko Arts Café 14 E4
Le Bordeaux 15 H1
Sésame 16 H2
ENTERTAINMENT
Saigon Race Track 17 C5
SHOPPING
Mai Handicrafts 18 D2
TRANSPORT
Saigon Scooter Centre 19 C2
Đ Cong Hoa
Đ Hoang Hoa Tham
Đ Cach Mang Thang Tam
Tr Q Hoan
Phan Đ Giot
Đ Nguyen Thai Son
Phu Nhuan District
ĐL Hoang Van Thu
Đ Nguyen Trong Tuyen
Tan Binh District
Đ Ly Thuong Kiet
District 10
Đ To Hien Thanh
Ho Ky Hoa Park
Đ Nguyen Tri Phuong
Đ Lac Long Quan
Đ Le Dai Hanh
Đ Binh Thoi
Đ 3 Thang 2
Đ Tran Nhan Ton
Đ Ba Hat
Đ Vinh Vien
ĐL Ngo Gia Tu
Đ Su Van Hanh
Dam Sen Lake
District 11
See Cholon Map (p361)
Đ Han Hai Nguyen
Đ Tran Quy
District 5
Đ Ngo Quyen
ĐL An Đuong Vuong
Đ Tan Hoa
Đ Hong Bang
Đ Hung Vuong
ĐL Tran Phu
Đ Ba Hom
To Mien Tay Bus Station (4km); Mekong Delta
Đ Minh Phung
Đ Nguyen Trai
ĐL Tran Hung Dao
Đ Le Quang Sung
Đ Ben Lo Gom
ĐL Hau Giang
Tau Hu Channel
Nguyen Tri Phuong Bridge
HO CHI MINH CITY

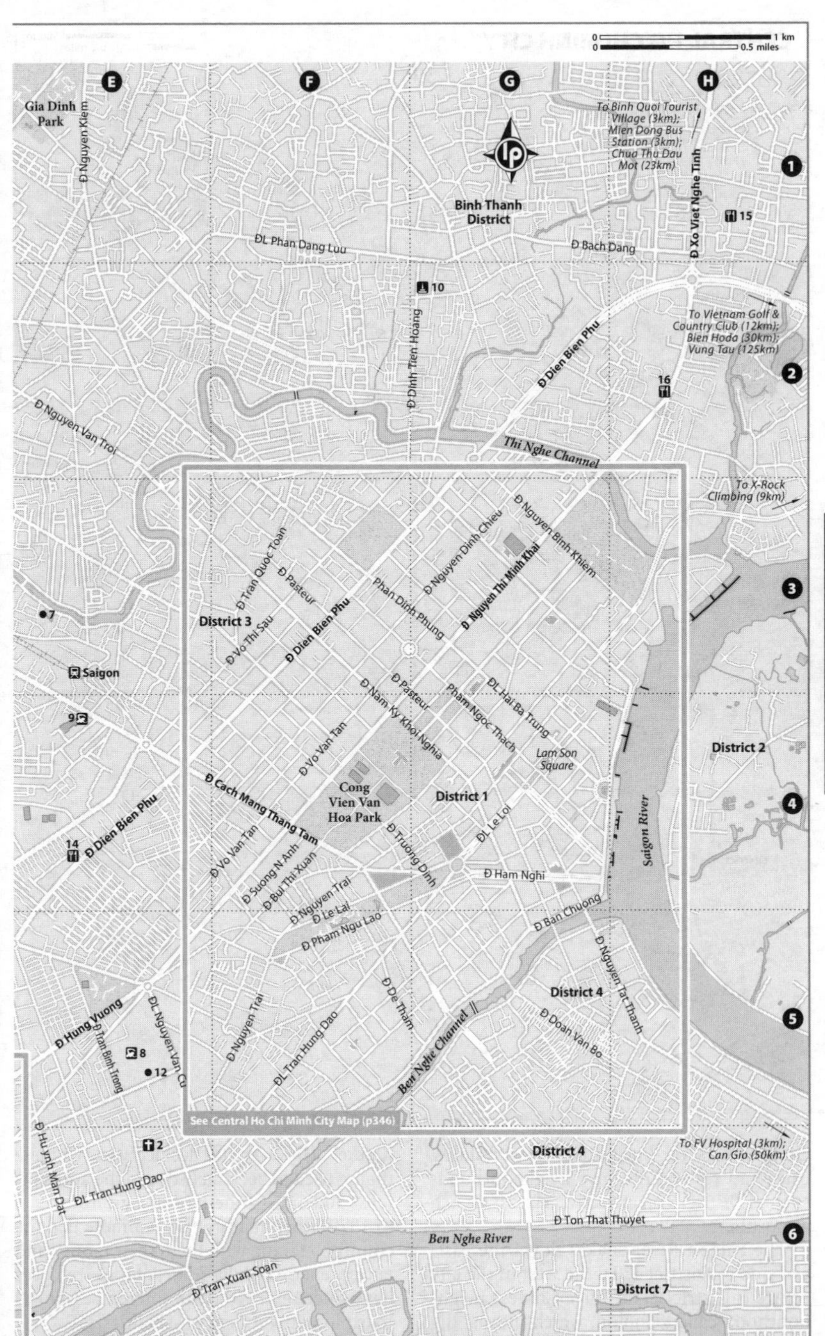

Gia Dinh Park
Đ Nguyen Kiem
To Binh Quoi Tourist Village (3km); Mien Dong Bus Station (3km); Chua Thu Dau Mot (23km)
Binh Thanh District
ĐL Phan Dang Luu
Đ Bach Dang
Đ Xo Viet Nghe Tinh
To Vietnam Golf & Country Club (12km); Bien Hoda (30km); Vung Tau (125km)
Đ Dinh Tien Hoang
Đ Dien Bien Phu
Đ Nguyen Van Troi
Thi Nghe Channel
To X-Rock Climbing (9km)
Đ Tran Quoc Toan
Đ Pasteur
Đ Nguyen Dinh Chieu
Đ Nguyen Binh Khiem
Đ Nguyen Thi Minh Khai
Phan Dinh Phung
District 3
Đ Vo Thi Sau
Đ Dien Bien Phu
Saigon
Đ Pasteur
Đ Nam Ky Khoi Nghia
Pham Ngoc Thach
ĐL Hai Ba Trung
Lam Son Square
District 2
Đ Vo Van Tan
Đ Cach Mang Thang Tam
Cong Vien Van Hoa Park
District 1
Saigon River
Đ Dien Bien Phu
ĐL Le Loi
Đ Truong Dinh
Đ Vo Van Tan
Đ Suong N Anh
Đ Bui Thi Xuan
Đ Ham Nghi
Đ Nguyen Trai
Đ Le Lai
Đ Pham Ngu Lao
Đ Ban Chuong
Đ Nguyen Tat Thanh
District 4
Đ De Tham
Đ Hung Vuong
Đ Tran Binh Trong
ĐL Nguyen Van Cu
Đ Nguyen Trai
ĐL Tran Hung Dao
Ben Nghe Channel
Đ Doan Van Bo
See Central Ho Chi Minh City Map (p346)
Đ Huynh Man Dat
To FV Hospital (3km); Can Gio (50km)
District 4
ĐL Tran Hung Dao
Đ Ton That Thuyet
Ben Nghe River
Đ Tran Xuan Soan
District 7

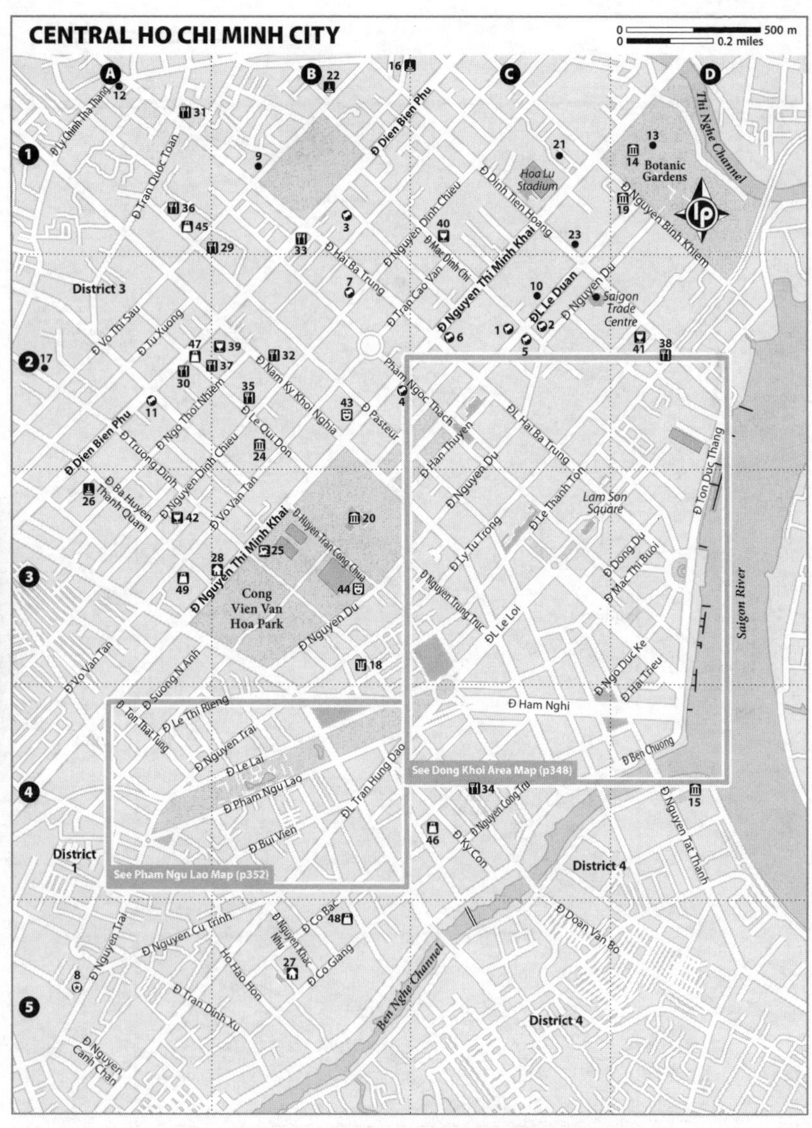

along with its tree-lined streets set with shops, cafes and restaurants, give neighbourhoods such as District 3 an attractive, almost French atmosphere.

The Saigon River snakes down the eastern side of District 1. To the west of the city centre is District 5, the huge Chinese neighbourhood called Cholon, which means 'Big Market'. However, it is decidedly less Chinese than it used to be, largely due to the anticapitalist and anti-Chinese campaign from 1978 to 1979, when many ethnic Chinese fled the country – taking with them their money and entrepreneurial skills. Many of these refugees have since returned (with foreign passports) to explore investment possibilities.

INFORMATION
American Consulate 1 C2
British Consulate 2 C2
British Council (see 2)
Cambodian Consulate 3 B1
Chinese Consulate 4 B2
Dutch Consulate 5 C2
French Consulate 6 C2
German Consulate 7 B2
Immigration Police Office 8 A5
Maple Dental Clinic 9 B1
Phuong Nam Bookshop 10 C2
Thai Consulate 11 A2

SIGHTS & ACTIVITIES
Binh Soup Shop 12 A1
Botanic Gardens 13 D1
History Museum 14 D1
Ho Chi Minh Museum 15 D4
Jade Emperor Pagoda 16 B1
L'Apothiquaire 17 A2
Mariamman Hindu Temple 18 B3
Military Museum 19 D1
Reunification Palace 20 B3
Saigon Yoga 21 C1
Temple of King Hung Vuong (see 14)
Tran Hung Dao Temple 22 B1
University of Social Sciences & Humanities 23 C1
War Remnants Museum 24 B2
Workers' Club 25 B3
Xa Loi Pagoda 26 A3

SLEEPING
Dan Le Hotel (see 27)
Guest House California (see 27)
Miss Loi's Guesthouse 27 B5
Ngoc Son (see 27)
Saigon Star Hotel 28 B3

EATING
Au Lac do Brasil 29 B1
Au Manoir de Khai 30 A2
Banh Xeo 46A 31 A1
Banh Xeo Muoi Xiem (see 32)
Beefsteak Nam Son 32 B2
La Camargue 33 B1
L'En Tete 34 C4
Ngoc Suong 35 B2
Pho Hoa 36 A1
Serenata 37 B2
Sushi Bar 38 D2
Vegetarian Food Stalls (see 26)

DRINKING
Acoustic Bar 39 B2
Hoa Vien 40 C1
Lush 41 D2
Yoko 42 A3

ENTERTAINMENT
Butterfly 43 B2
Conservatory of Music 44 B3
Golden Dragon Water Puppet Theatre (see 25)

SHOPPING
Cham Khanh 45 A1
Chle (see 35)
Dan Sinh Market 46 C4
Dolezza House 47 A2
Galerie Quynh 48 B5
Vinh Loi Gallery 49 A3

The 7km trip into town from the airport should cost around 80,000d to 100,000d in a metered taxi. There is also an airport bus (3000d) that drops you right in central HCMC (see p386). From the train station (Ga Sai Gon; p386), a *xe om* to Pham Ngu Lao costs about 25,000d; a taxi will be more like 50,000d. Saigon's intercity bus stations are a long way out, meaning almost airport-style fares to get into town; public buses from the bus stations also pass by the central Ben Thanh Market (3000d), but these usually stop running about 6pm. Open-tour buses will unload you directly into Pham Ngu Lao.

Note that addresses presented in this chapter as, for example, 197/15, mean that the building is down an alley starting at that number on the relevant street. So a hotel located at 197/15 D Pham Ngu Lao is not on Đ Pham Ngu Lao, but is located down a side alley starting at that point.

Maps

Accurate and up-to-date maps of HCMC are available at bookstores in Districts 1 and 3; a reliable, central source is Fahasa Bookshop (right).

INFORMATION

For up-to-date information on what's going on in town, check out **The Word HCMC** (www.wordhcmc.com) or **Asialife HCMC** (www.asialifehcmc.com), both quality listings magazines available around the city.

Bookshops

The best area to look for maps, books and stationery is along the north side of ĐL Le Loi, between the Rex Hotel and Đ Nam Ky Khoi Nghia, in the Dong Khoi area (Map p348). There are many small, privately run shops as well as large government-run ones.

On Đ De Tham, around Đ Pham Ngu Lao (Map p352), there is a handful of shops dealing in used paperbacks. Vendors on foot sell pirated paperbacks, but we know you wouldn't dream of buying a photocopied Lonely Planet.

Fahasa Bookshop (Map p348; ⏰ 8am-10pm) Đ Dong Khoi (☎ 3822 4670; 185 Đ Dong Khoi); ĐL Nguyen Hue (☎ 3822 5796; 40 ĐL Nguyen Hue) Government-run bookshop with dictionaries, maps and general books in English and French.

Phuong Nam Bookshop (Map p346; ☎ 3822 9650; 2A ĐL Le Duan; ⏰ 8am-9.30pm) Has imported books and magazines in English, French and Chinese.

Cultural Centres

British Council (Map p346; ☎ 3823 2862; www.britishcouncil.org/vietnam; 25 ĐL Le Duan) Next to British Consulate.

Institute of Cultural Exchange with France (Idecaf; Map p348; ☎ 3829 5451; 31 Đ Thai Van Lung) Plus Le Jardin (p375).

Emergency

Emergency (☎ 115)
Fire (☎ 114)
Information (☎ 1080)
Police (☎ 113)

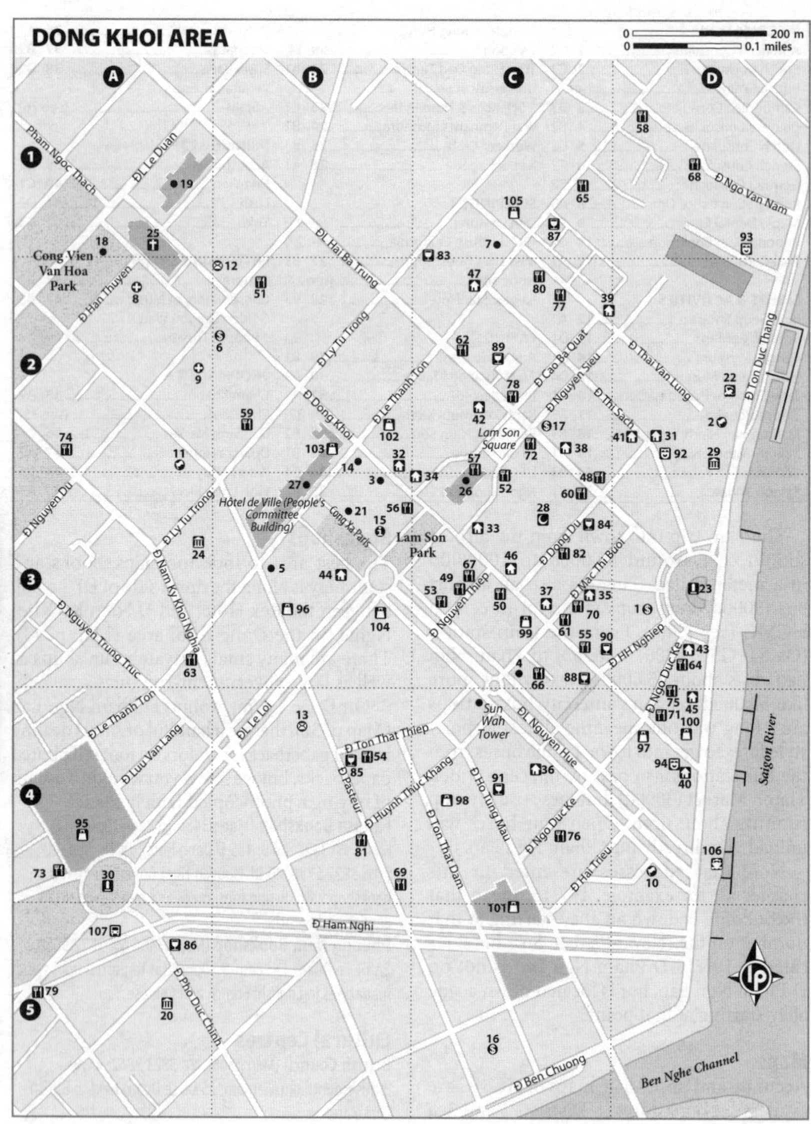

Internet Access

Internet access is widely available in HCMC. The largest concentration of internet cafes is in Đ Pham Ngu Lao (Map p352), with around 30 places along Đ Pham Ngu Lao, Đ De Tham and Đ Bui Vien. In the downtown area (Map p348), there are internet cafes along Đ Le Thanh Ton and Đ Dong Du.

However, most hotels and guesthouses now offer internet for guests, with a couple of terminals in the lobby or free wi-fi in the rooms. Five-star hotels charge a fortune for the privilege. There are also plenty of restaurants, bars and cafes offering free wi-fi for customers; add this to the growing number of hotels and it is not hard to get that online fix.

INFORMATION
ANZ Bank 1 D3
Asiana Travel Mate (see 15)
Australian Consulate 2 D2
Buffalo Tours (see 40)
Canadian Consulate (see 6)
DHL (see 12)
Exotissimo (see 48)
Fahasa Bookshop 4 C3
Fahasa Bookshop 3 B3
Federal Express 5 B3
HCMC Family Medical Practice (see 19)
HSBC 6 B2
Institute of Cultural Exchange with France 7 C1
International Medical Centre 8 A2
International SOS 9 A2
Japanese Consulate 10 D4
Lao Consulate 11 A2
Main Post Office 12 B2
New Zealand Consulate (see 6)
Post Office 13 B4
Saigon Tourist 14 B2
Tourist Information Center 15 B3
Vietcombank 17 C2
Vietcombank 16 C5

SIGHTS & ACTIVITIES
Aqua Day Spa (see 46)
Cong Vien Van Hoa 18 A1
Diamond Superbowl 19 A1
Fine Arts Museum 20 A5
Glow 21 B3
Legend Hotel 22 D2
Me Linh Square 23 D3
Museum of Ho Chi Minh City 24 A3
Notre Dame Cathedral 25 A1
Opera House 26 C3
People's Committee Building (Hôtel de Ville) 27 B3
Saigon Central Mosque 28 C3
Ton Duc Thang Museum 29 D2
Tran Nguyen Hai Statue 30 A4

SLEEPING
A & Em Hotel 31 D2
Asian Hotel 32 B2
Caravelle Hotel 33 C3
Continental Hotel 34 C3
Dong Do Hotel 35 C3
Duxton Hotel 36 C4
Huong Sen Hotel 37 C3
Indochine Hotel 38 C2
King Star Hotel 39 C2
Majestic Hotel 40 D4
Northern Hotel 41 D2
Park Hyatt Saigon 42 C2
Renaissance Riverside Hotel 43 D3
Rex Hotel 44 B3
Riverside Hotel 45 D4
Sheraton Saigon 46 C3
Spring Hotel 47 C2

EATING
3T Quan Nuong (see 54)
Annam Gourmet Shop 48 C3
Augustin 49 C3
Brodard Café 50 C3
Casbah 51 B2
Centro Caffe 52 C3
Ciao Café 53 C3
Fanny 54 B4
Gardenstadt 55 C3
Givral 56 B3
Gloria Jean's Coffee (see 50)
Highlands Coffee 57 C2
Hoa Tuc (see 89)
Hoi An 58 D1
Huong Lai 59 B2
Indian Canteen (see 28)
Java Coffee Bar 60 C3
Juice 61 C3
K Café 62 C2
La Fenetre de Soleil 63 A3
La Fourchette 64 D3
La Hostaria 65 C1
Lac Thai 66 C3
Le Jardin (see 7)
Lemon Grass 67 C3
Mandarine 68 D1
Mogambo 69 B4
Nam Kha 70 C3
On the 6 71 D4
Pacharan 72 C2
Pho 2000 73 A4
Quan An Ngon 74 A2
Restaurant 13 75 D4
Seoul House 76 C4
Skewers 77 C2
Tandoor 78 C2
Temple Club (see 54)
Tin Nghia 79 A5
Veggy's 80 C2
Warda (see 66)
X Café 81 B4
Xu (see 72)
Zan Z Bar 82 C3

DRINKING
Alibi (see 80)
Blue Gecko Bar 83 C1
Café Latin 84 C3
Cantina Central 85 B4
Kool Beer Store 86 A5
Q Bar (see 26)
Refinery (see 89)
Saigon Saigon Bar (see 33)
Samsara (see 50)
Sheridan's Irish House 87 C1
Underground 88 C3
Vasco's 89 C2
Velvet 90 C3
Vino (see 89)
Voodoo 91 C4

ENTERTAINMENT
Apocalypse Now 92 D2
Cage 93 D1
Diamond Plaza Cinema (see 19)
Maxim's Dinner Theatre 94 D4
Samsara (see 50)

SHOPPING
Ben Thanh Market 95 A4
Blue Space Gallery (see 20)
Chi Chi 96 B3
Diamond Plaza (see 19)
Dogma 97 D4
Huynh Thuc Khang Street Market 98 C4
Khai Silk 99 C3
Lacquer & Oil (see 20)
Nguyen Freres 100 D4
Old Market 101 C5
Parkson Plaza 102 B2
Song 103 B2
Tax Department Store 104 B3
Vietnam Quilts 105 C1

TRANSPORT
Bach Dang Jetty 106 D4
Ben Thanh Bus Station 107 A5
Boats for Hire (see 106)
Bonsai River Cruise (see 106)

Media

Hotels, bars and restaurants around HCMC carry free entertainment magazines, such as *The Word HCMC*, plus old-timers like *The Guide*, a weekly supplement published by the *Vietnam Economic Times* (VET).

There is also an eclectic selection of foreign newspapers and magazines for sale in recommended bookstores and smarter hotels. Street vendors wander the popular Dong Khoi and Pham Ngu Lao areas touting magazines, but check the cover date and bargain over price.

Medical Services

FV Hospital (Franco-Vietnamese Hospital; off Map pp344-5; ☎ 3411 3333; www.fvhospital.com; 6 Đ Nguyen Luong Bang, Tan Phu Ward, District 7; 24hr) French-, Vietnamese- and English-speaking physicians; superb care and equipment.

HCMC Family Medical Practice (Map p348; ☎ 24hr emergency 3822 7848; www.vietnammedicalpractice.com; Diamond Plaza, 34 ĐL Le Duan; 24hr) Well-run practice with branches in Hanoi and Danang.

International Medical Centre (Map p348; ☎ 3827 2366; ☎ 24hr emergency 3865 4025; fac@hcm.vnn.vn;

RENAMING THE PAST

One of the main battlegrounds for the hearts of Vietnamese during the last four decades has been the naming of Vietnam's provinces, districts, cities, towns, streets and institutions. Some places have borne three or more names since WWII and, often, more than one name is still used.

When French control of Vietnam ended in 1954, almost all French names were replaced in both the North and the South. Saigon's Rue Catinat, a familiar name to anyone who has read Graham Greene's *A Quiet American*, was renamed Đ Tu Do (Freedom). Since reunification it has been known as Đ Dong Khoi (Uprising). Later, in 1956, the US-backed government changed the names of some provinces and towns in the South in an effort to erase from popular memory the Viet Minh's anti-French exploits, which were often known by the places in which they occurred. The village-based southern communists, who by this time had gone underground, continued to use the old designations and boundaries in running their regional and local organisations. The peasants – now faced with two masters – quickly adapted to this situation, using one set of place names when talking to South Vietnamese officials and a different set of names when dealing with the communists.

After reunification, the first task of Saigon's provisional government was to rename the southern capital Ho Chi Minh City, a decision confirmed in Hanoi a year later. The new government began changing street names considered inappropriate, dropping English and French names in favour of Vietnamese ones. The only French names still in use are those of Albert Calmette (1893–1934), developer of a tuberculosis vaccine; Marie Curie (1867–1934), who won the Nobel Prize for her research into radioactivity; Louis Pasteur (1822–95), chemist and bacteriologist; and Alexandre Yersin (1863–1943), discoverer of the plague bacillus.

Despite the ongoing attempts at renaming, the most important streets are unlikely to change names. Some even object to officialdom's intrusion into the name game. Saigon, after all, is still the preferred name for the majority of southerners who live there.

1 Đ Han Thuyen; 24hr) A nonprofit organisation with English-speaking French doctors.

International SOS (Map p348; ☎ 3929 8424, 24hr emergency 3829 8520; www.internationalsos.com; 65 Đ Nguyen Du; 24hr) Has an international team of doctors who speak English, French, Japanese and Vietnamese.

Maple Dental Clinic (Map p346; ☎ 3820 1999; 72 Đ Vo Thi Sau; 8am-8pm Mon-Fri, 9am-5pm Sat) Dental care (including emergencies) from English-speaking dentists.

Money

There are several exchange counters in the arrivals hall at Tan Son Nhat Airport, just after clearing customs, and most offer the official rates. There are also ATMs available here.

Banks with 24-hour ATMs dispense dong only, to a maximum amount of 2,000,000d per day, with the exception of ANZ which will churn out 4,000,000d. Visa or MasterCard cash advances for larger amounts of dong, as well as US dollars, can be handled at bank counters during banking hours. All of these banks also exchange travellers cheques, charging less commission when exchanging for dong. Try the following:

ANZ Bank (Map p348; ☎ 3829 9319; 11 Me Linh Sq) Has a 24-hour ATM.

HSBC (Map p348; ☎ 3829 2288; 235 Đ Dong Khoi) Offers a secure 24-hour ATM.

Sacombank (Map p352; ☎ 3836 4231; www.sacombank.com; 211 Đ Nguyen Thai Hoc) Conveniently located in the backpacker zone, with 24-hour ATM.

Vietcombank (Map p348; closed Sun & last day of the month) Đ Ben Chuong (☎ 3829 7245; 29 Đ Ben Chuong); Lam Son Sq (19 Lam Son Sq); The eastern building of the Ben Chuong branch is for foreign exchange only, but is worth the visit just to see the stunningly ornate interior.

Post

HCMC's grandiose French-style **main post office** (Map p348; ☎ 3829 6555; 2 Cong Xa Paris; 7am-9.30pm) is right next to Notre Dame Cathedral. Built between 1886 and 1891, it is the largest post office in Vietnam and worth visiting just for its architecture.

Countless other post-office branches are scattered around town; see Map p348 and Map p361 for locations. Like the main post office, many of these also keep late hours.

The following private carriers operate near the main post office:

DHL (Map p348; ☎ 3823 1525; 2 Cong Xa Paris; 7.30am-5pm Mon-Fri)

Federal Express (Map p348; ☎ 3829 0995; www.fedex.com; 146 Đ Pasteur; 🕑 7am-8pm Mon-Fri, 7am-2pm Sat)

Telephone

International and domestic phone calls can be made from post offices and better hotels. Hotel prices for local calls vary, so be sure to ask the price beforehand.

International calls can also be made over the internet at most internet cafes; rates start at around 3000d per minute, though you can call for free (computer to computer) through Skype.

Tourist Information

Tourist Information Center (Map p348; ☎ 3822 6033; www.vietnamtourism.com; 4G Le Loi; 🕑 8am-8pm) This smart information centre distributes city maps and brochures and offers limited advice about goings-on in Saigon. Privately run, but reasonably helpful; there's also a tour operator and currency exchange here.

Travel Agencies

HCMC's official government-run travel agency is **Saigon Tourist** (Map p348; ☎ 3829 8914; www.saigontourist.net; 49 Đ Le Thanh Ton; 🕑 8-11.30am & 1-5.30pm). The agency owns, or is a joint-venture partner in, more than 70 hotels and numerous restaurants around town, plus a car-rental agency, golf clubs and assorted tourist traps.

There's a plethora of other travel agencies in town, virtually all of them joint ventures between government agencies and private companies. These places can provide cars, book air tickets and extend visas. Competition is keen and you can often undercut Saigon Tourist's tariffs by a reasonable margin if you shop around. Many agencies have multilingual guides.

Most tour guides and drivers are not paid that well, so if you're happy with their service, tipping is common. Many travellers on bus tours to Cu Chi or the Mekong Delta, for example, collect a kitty (say US$1 or US$2 per person) and give it to the guide and driver at the end of the trip.

We suggest visiting several tour operators to see what's being offered to suit your taste and budget. Plenty of cheap tours – of varying quality – are sold around Pham Ngu Lao. One worthwhile strategy is to grill other travellers who've just returned from a tour.

Another appealing option is to arrange a customised private tour with your own car, driver and guide. Travelling this way provides maximum flexibility, and split between a few people it can be surprisingly affordable.

For customised tours, **Sinhbalo Adventures** (Map p352; ☎ 3837 6766; www.sinhbalo.com; 283/20 Đ Pham Ngu Lao) is one of the best in Saigon. Sinhbalo specialises in cycling trips, but also arranges innovative special-interest journeys to the Mekong Delta, central highlands and further afield. We've been using and recommending the company for more than a decade now.

Hanoi-based **Handspan Adventure Travel** (Map p352; ☎ 3925 7605; www.handspan.com; 7th fl, Titan Bldg, 18A Đ Nam Quoc Cang) have a branch office in Ho Chi Minh City and are known for their quality tours.

Other recommended operators include:

BUDGET AGENCIES

Delta Adventure Tours (Map p352; ☎ 3920 2112; www.deltaadventuretours.com; 267 Đ De Tham)
Innoviet (Map p352; ☎ 3295 8840; www.innoviet.com; 158 Đ Bui Vien)
Kim Travel (Map p352; ☎ 3920 5552; www.kimtravel.com; 270 Đ De Tham)
Sinh Café (Map p352; ☎ 3836 7338; www.sinhcafevn.com; 246 Đ De Tham)

MIDRANGE & TOP-END AGENCIES

Asiana Travel Mate (Map p348; ☎ 3825 0615; www.asianatravelmate.com; 4G Đ Le Loi)
Buffalo Tours (Map p348; ☎ 3827 9170; www.buffalotours.com; Satra House, Ste 601, 58 Đ Dong Khoi)
Exotissimo (Map p348; ☎ 3827 2911; www.exotissimo.com; 20 Đ Hai Ba Trung)

DANGERS & ANNOYANCES

HCMC is the most theft-ridden city in Vietnam; don't become a statistic. See p482 for advice on how to avoid street crime. Be especially careful along the Saigon riverfront, where motorbike 'cowboys' operate and specialise in bag snatching.

Scams

One of the more common rip-offs in HCMC involves *cyclo* drivers demanding exorbitant sums at the end of a tour. Rather than hopping blithely into the seat when the driver smilingly says, 'price up to you', clearly negotiate a fair price up front (consider 100,000/200,000d for a half-day/full-day tour). If more than one person is travelling make sure you're negotiating the price for both and not a per-passenger fee. It sometimes pays to sketch out numbers and pictures with pen and paper so all parties

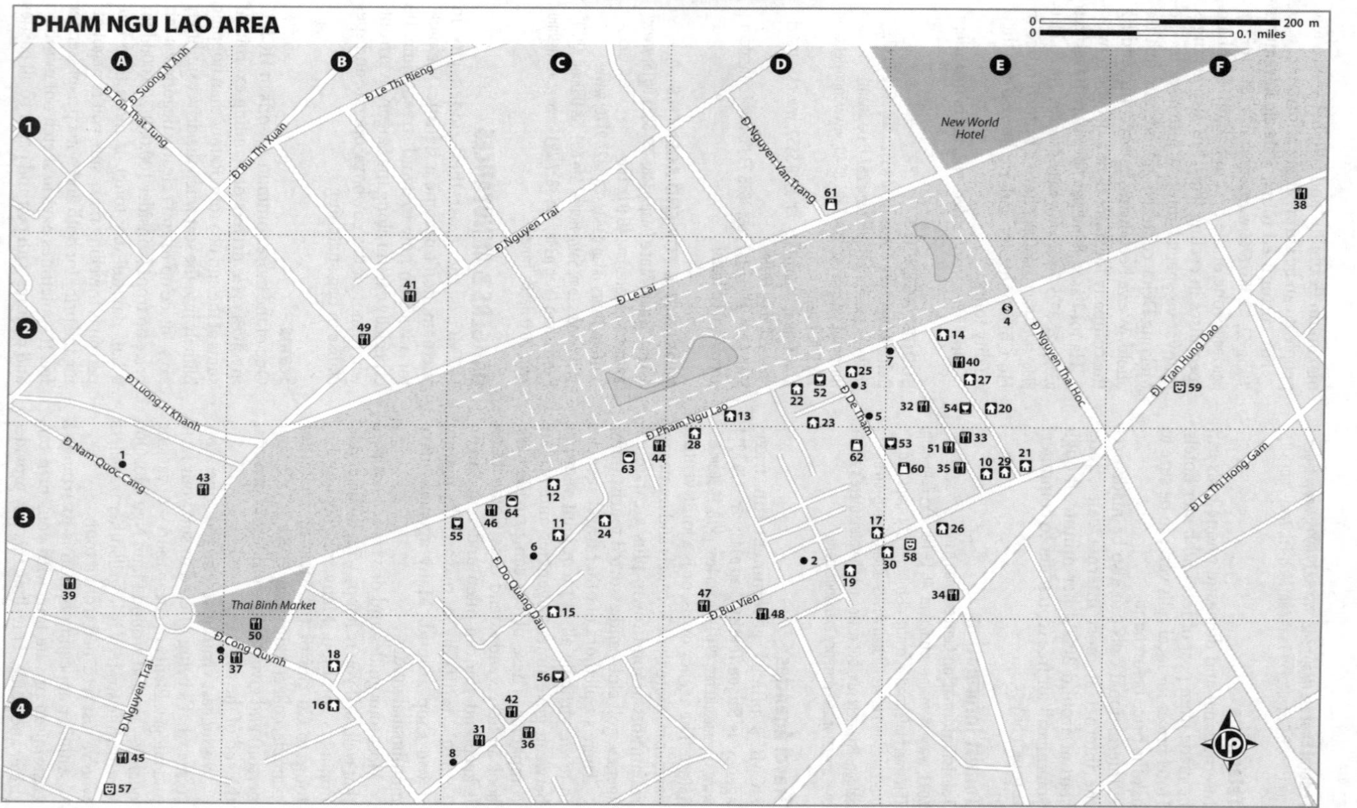
PHAM NGU LAO AREA
0 200 m
0 0.1 miles
A
B
C
D
E
F
1
2
3
4
New World Hotel
Thai Binh Market
Đ Suong N Anh
Đ Ton That Tung
Đ Bui Thi Xuan
Đ Le Thi Rieng
Đ Nguyen Trai
Đ Nguyen Van Trang
Đ Le Lai
Đ Nguyen Thai Hoc
ĐL Tran Hung Dao
Đ Le Thi Hong Gam
Đ Pham Ngu Lao
Đ De Tham
Đ Do Quang Dau
Đ Bui Vien
Đ Luong H Khanh
Đ Nam Quoc Cang
Đ Cong Quynh
Đ Nguyen Trai

INFORMATION
Delta Adventure Tours .... (see 52)
Handspan Adventure Travel 1 A3
Innoviet 2 D3
Kim Travel 3 D2
Sacombank 4 E2
Sinh Cafe 5 D2
Sinhbalo Adventures 6 C3

SIGHTS & ACTIVITIES
Bi Saigon 7 E2
Relax House 8 C4
Vietnamese Traditional Massage Institute 9 A4

SLEEPING
An An Hotel 10 E3
Bich Duyen Hotel 11 C3
Canadian Hotel 281 .... 12 C3
Elios Hotel 13 D2
Giant Dragon Hotel 14 E2
Ha Vy Hotel 15 C3
Hotel 127 .... 16 B4
Hotel 64 .... 17 D3
Hotel MC 184 .... 18 B4
Kim's 19 D3
Kim's Cafe .... (see 3)
Lac Vien Hotel 20 E2
Le Le Hotel .... (see 14)
Lien Ha Hotel 21 E3
Mai Phai Hotel 22 D2
Nga Hoang 23 D2
Ngoc Minh Guesthouse 24 C3
Orient Hotel 25 D2
Quyen Thanh Hotel 26 E3
Saigon Comfort Hotel 27 E2
Sao Nam Hotel .... (see 40)
Spring House Hotel 28 D3
Vuong Hoa Hotel 29 E3
Yellow House 30 E3

EATING
Akbar Ali 31 C4
Asian Kitchen 32 E2
Bobby Brewers .... (see 30)
Bread & Butter 33 E3
Café Zoom 34 E3
Chi's Café 35 E3
Co-op Mart .... (see 39)
Coriander 36 C4
Dinh Y 37 B4
Falafellim 38 F1
Hanoi Mart 39 A3
Hong Hoa Mini-Market .... (see 5)
Margherita 40 E2
Mon Hue 41 B2
Mumtaz 42 C4
Phap Hoa 43 A3
Pho 24 .... 44 C3
Pho Hung 45 A4
Pho Quynh 46 C3
Sozo 47 D3
Stella 48 D3
Tan Hai Van 49 B2
Thai Bin Market 50 B4
Zen 51 E3

DRINKING
Allez Boo Bar 52 D2
Eden 53 E3
Le Pub 54 E2
Long Phi 55 C3
Santa Café 56 C4

ENTERTAINMENT
Galaxy Cinema 57 A4
Go2 .... 58 E3
Gossip Club 59 F2

SHOPPING
Blue Dragon 60 E3
Gaya 61 D1
Sapa 62 D3

TRANSPORT
Saigon Railways Tourist Services 63 C3
Sapaco 64 C3
Vietnam Vespa Adventure .... (see 34)

agree. Unfortunately, 'misunderstandings' do happen; unless the *cyclo* driver has pedalled you to all the districts of HCMC, US$25 is not the going rate.

That said, don't just assume the driver is trying to cheat you. It's a tough living, especially as the city government is trying to phase out the *cyclos* entirely.

SIGHTS

Although HCMC lacks the obvious aesthetic virtues of its rival to the north, the city provides some fascinating sights for the wanderer, from little-visited pagodas hidden down quiet lanes, to museums, historic sites and teeming markets all set against the chaotic pastiche that is the urban scene. First-time visitors often focus exclusively on District 1, where many of the sights are found. Those with more than a day in the city can take in central HCMC, the pagodas in Cholon, and further afield, leaving enough time to explore the Saigon less visited.

Central Area

REUNIFICATION PALACE

Time has stood still here since 30 April 1975, a slightly scary thought. The striking modern architecture and the slightly eerie feeling you get as you walk through its deserted halls make **Reunification Palace** (Dinh Thong Nhat; Map p346; ☎ 3829 4117; 106 Đ Nguyen Du; admission 15,000d; 7.30-11am & 1-4pm) one of the most fascinating sights in HCMC. The building was once the symbol of the South Vietnamese government, which hundreds of thousands of Vietnamese and 58,183 Americans died trying to save.

The first communist tanks to arrive in Saigon rumbled towards this building on the morning of 30 April 1975, then known as Independence Palace or the Presidential Palace. After crashing through the wrought-iron gates – in a dramatic scene recorded by photojournalists and shown around the world – a soldier ran into the building and up the stairs to unfurl a VC flag from the 4th-floor balcony. In an ornate 2nd-floor reception chamber, General Minh, who had become head of the South Vietnamese state only 43 hours before, waited with his improvised cabinet. 'I have been waiting since early this morning to transfer power to you', Minh said to the VC officer who entered the room. 'There is no question of your transferring power', replied the officer. 'You cannot give up what you do not have.'

In 1868 a residence was built on this site for the French governor-general of Cochinchina and gradually it expanded to become Norodom Palace. When the French departed, the palace became home for South Vietnamese President Ngo Dinh Diem. So unpopular was Diem that his own air force bombed the palace in 1962 in an unsuccessful attempt to kill him. The president ordered a new residence to be built on the same site, this time with a sizeable bomb shelter in the basement. Work was completed in 1966, but Diem did not get to see his dream house as he was killed by his own troops in 1963. The new building was named Independence Palace and was home to South Vietnamese President Nguyen Van Thieu until his hasty departure in 1975.

Norodom Palace, designed by Paris-trained Vietnamese architect Ngo Viet Thu, is an outstanding example of 1960s architecture. It has an airy and open atmosphere and its spacious chambers are tastefully decorated with the finest modern Vietnamese art and crafts. In its grandeur, the building feels worthy of a head of state.

The ground-floor room with the boat-shaped table was often used for conferences. Upstairs in the **Presidential Receiving Room** (Phu Dau Rong, or Dragon's Head Room; the one with the red chairs in it), the South Vietnamese president received foreign delegations. He sat behind the desk, the chairs with dragons carved into the arms were used by his assistants, and the chair facing the desk was reserved for foreign ambassadors. The room with gold-coloured chairs and curtains was used by the vice president. You can sit in the former president's chair and have your photo taken.

In the back of the structure are the president's living quarters. Check out the model boats, horse tails and severed elephants' feet. The 3rd floor has a card-playing room with a bar and a movie-screening chamber. This floor also boasts a terrace with a heliport where a derelict helicopter still languishes. The 4th floor has a dance hall and casino.

Perhaps most interesting of all is the basement with its telecommunications centre, war room and network of tunnels, with the best map of Vietnam you'll ever see pasted on the wall.

Reunification Palace is not open to visitors when official receptions or meetings are taking place. English- and French-speaking guides are on duty during opening hours. There is a viewing room where you can watch a video about Vietnamese history in a variety of languages. The national anthem is played at the end of the tape and you are expected to stand up – it would be rude not to.

WAR REMNANTS MUSEUM

Once known as the Museum of Chinese and American War Crimes, the **War Remnants Museum** (Bao Tang Chung Tich Chien Tranh; Map p346; ☎ 3930 5587; 28 Đ Vo Van Tan; admission 15,000d; ⏰ 7.30am-noon & 1.30-5pm) is consistently the most popular museum in HCMC with Western tourists. Many of the atrocities documented here were well publicised in the West, but rarely do Westerners have the opportunity to hear the victims of US military action tell their own stories.

US armoured vehicles, artillery pieces, bombs and infantry weapons are on display outside. Many photographs illustrating US atrocities are from US sources, including photos of the infamous My Lai Massacre (p270). There is a model of the notorious tiger cages used by the South Vietnamese military to house Viet Cong (VC) prisoners on Con Son Island and a guillotine used by the French on Viet Minh 'troublemakers'. There are also pictures of deformed babies, their defects attributed to the USA's widespread use of chemical herbicides.

In a final gallery, there's a collection of posters and photographs showing support for the antiwar movement.

There are few museums in the world that drive home so well the point that war is horribly brutal and that many of its victims are civilians. Even those who supported the war would have a difficult time not being horrified by the photos of children affected by US bombing and napalming. You'll also have the rare chance to see some of the experimental weapons used in the war, which were at one time military secrets, such as the *fléchette*, an artillery shell filled with thousands of tiny darts. On the downside, it remains a very one-sided story and many of the labels are woefully propagandist.

The War Remnants Museum is in the former US Information Service building, at the intersection with Đ Le Quy Don. Explanations are in Vietnamese, English and Chinese. Though a bit incongruous with the museum's theme, **water-puppet theatre** is staged in a tent on the museum grounds (see p382).

Look out for the **Requiem Exhibition**, housed in a small compound near the entrance to the site. Compiled by legendary war photographer

Tim Page (p356), this striking collection of photos documents the work of photographers on both sides of the conflict and includes works by Larry Burrows and Robert Capa. Attempts are underway to reprint the collection and house it in a new gallery in the main hall.

MUSEUM OF HO CHI MINH CITY

Housed in a grand neoclassical structure built in 1886 and once known as Gia Long Palace (later, the Revolutionary Museum), the **Museum of Ho Chi Minh City** (Bao Tang Thanh Pho Ho Chi Minh; Map p348; ☎ 3829 9741; 65 Đ Ly Tu Trong; admission US$1; 🕑 8am-4pm) is a singularly beautiful and impressive building.

The museum displays artefacts from the various periods of the communist struggle for power in Vietnam. The photographs of anticolonial activists who were executed by the French appear out of place in the gilded, 19th-century ballrooms, but the contrast gives a sense of the immense power and pomposity of the colonial French. There are photos of Vietnamese peace demonstrators in Saigon demanding the departure of US troops, and a dramatic photo of Thich Quang Duc, the monk who made headlines worldwide in 1963 when he burned himself to death in protest against the policies of President Ngo Dinh Diem (see p229).

The information plaques are in Vietnamese only, but some of the exhibits include documents in French or English, and many others are self-explanatory if you know some basic Vietnamese history (if you don't, see the History chapter on p27). The exhibitions cover the various periods in the city's 300-year history.

Among the most interesting artefacts on display is a long, narrow rowing boat *(ghe)* with a false bottom in which arms were smuggled. Nearby is a small diorama of the Cu Chi Tunnels. The adjoining room has examples of infantry weapons used by the VC, and various South Vietnamese and US medals, hats and plaques. A map shows communist advances during the dramatic collapse of South Vietnam in early 1975. There are also photographs of the liberation of Saigon.

Deep beneath the building is a network of reinforced concrete bunkers and fortified corridors. The system, branches of which stretch all the way to Reunification Palace, included living areas, a kitchen and a large meeting hall. In 1963 President Diem and his brother hid here before fleeing to Cha Tam Church (p363). The network is not currently open to the public because most of the tunnels are flooded.

In the garden behind the museum is a Soviet tank, and a US Huey UH-1 helicopter and anti-aircraft gun. In the garden fronting Đ Nam Ky Khoi Nghia is more military hardware, including the American-built F-5E jet used by a renegade South Vietnamese pilot to bomb the Presidential Palace (now Reunification Palace) on 8 April 1975.

The museum is located a block east of Reunification Palace.

HISTORY MUSEUM

The stunning Sino French–style building that houses the **History Museum** (Bao Tang Lich Su; Map p346; ☎ 3829 8146; Đ Nguyen Binh Khiem; admission 15,000d; 🕑 8-11am & 1.30-4.30pm Tue-Sun) was built in 1929 by the Société des Études Indochinoises. It's worth a visit just to view the architecture.

The museum has an excellent collection of artefacts that illustrate the evolution of the cultures of Vietnam, from the Bronze Age Dong Son civilisation (which emerged in 2000 BC) and the Funan civilisation (1st to 6th centuries AD), to the Cham, Khmer and Vietnamese. There are many valuable relics taken from Cambodia's Angkor Wat.

At the back of the building on the 3rd floor is a **research library** (☎ 3829 0268; 🕑 Mon-Sat) with numerous books about Indochina from the French-colonial period.

Across from the entrance to the museum you'll see the elaborate **Temple of King Hung Vuong**. The Hung kings are said to have been the first rulers of the Vietnamese nation, having established their rule in the Red River region before it was invaded by the Chinese.

The museum is just inside the main gate to the city zoo and botanic gardens (p369), where the east end of ĐL Le Duan meets Đ Nguyen Binh Khiem.

MILITARY MUSEUM

Just a short distance from the history museum is a small **military museum** (Bao Tang Quan Doi; Map p346; ☎ 3822 9387; 2 ĐL Le Duan) devoted to Ho Chi Minh's campaign to liberate the south. Inside is of minor interest, but some US, Chinese and Soviet war material is on display outdoors, including a Cessna A-37 of the South Vietnamese Air Force and a

TIM PAGE

Tim Page experienced a very different Vietnam from the one visitors see today. It was 'Nam, the war was in full flow and he was a war photographer risking all on the frontline. He was the Hunter S Thompson of photojournalists, larger than life and not averse to getting into scrapes, several of which nearly cost him his life, including taking shrapnel in the brain in 1969.

We consider the Requiem Exhibition, on permanent show at the War Remnants Museum. 'I was gobsmacked to learn that Requiem is more visited than Reunification Palace', he laughs. 'We are in discussions to secure a new exhibition space in the main hall, as it's a real shame it is located in an old barracks', he laments. His plan is to house it in a gallerylike space and charge a small entrance fee to raise funds for the Indochina Media Memorial Foundation that trains a new generation of independent Vietnamese journalists.

He reflects nostalgically on the old days. 'Most of the big attractions in Saigon are linked to history, to events from the '60s and '70s, the stuff of folklore and legend', he states. 'Maybe it's time to turn this into an experience, like the blue plaques in London but for wartime Saigon, covering famous residents and famous events.' No doubt Tim Page himself would be worthy of a plaque or two. We talk about the ghosts of the past and his old haunts in Saigon. 'Café Brodard is always mentioned, but now it's a Gloria Jeans. That's insulting really', he says with a hint of mischief. With the Continental Shelf long gone and the Rex 'gone mad', Page finds his Saigon by sitting on a plastic stool on the side of the road, the street cafes little changed in four decades. 'Underground (p379) is a good meeting place these days', he offers, 'opposite the old Reuters office during the war. Downstairs was Minh the Tailor who invented the TV anchorman suit.'

We come back to Requiem and discuss the defining shots in the exhibition. 'Larry Burrows was an incredible photographer, his images are almost cinematic in their quality', he suggests. Burrows was killed in a helicopter crash in 1971 and several of his pictures are in the exhibition. 'Henri Huet's image that looks through the legs of US soldiers at the distressed Vietnamese beyond is very powerful', he adds, perhaps subconsciously recalling that Huet died in the same helicopter crash as Burrows.

The story of his old friend Sean Flynn resurfaces, the son of Errol Flynn, who disappeared in Cambodia in 1970, presumed kidnapped and killed by the Khmer Rouge. 'A lot of people are interested in the story, there are a lot of scripts floating around out there', he says, although the impression is that he doesn't approve of most of them. Perhaps for Page it is too personal as the search for Sean Flynn was his 'quest for the holy grail'. He might be too old to play himself in a Hollywood flick about 1970, but don't rule out a film about Tim Page in the next few years – he has lived more lives than most.

Tim Page is a renowned photojournalist and writer whose work has appeared in magazines, newspapers and exhibitions all over the world. He returned to Vietnam to put together the Requiem Photographic Exhibition at the War Remnants Museum, which chronicles the work of photojournalists on both sides of the conflict. Visit www.timpage.com.au for more on his work or pick up a copy of his books Page after Page, Derailed in Uncle Ho's Victory Garden *or* Nam.

US-built F-5E Tiger with the 20mm nose gun still loaded. The tank on display is one of the tanks that broke into the grounds of Reunification Palace on 30 April 1975.

FINE ARTS MUSEUM

A classic yellow-and-white building with a modest Chinese influence, the **Fine Arts Museum** (Bao Tang My Thuat; Map p348; ☎ 3829 4441; www.baotangmythuattphcm.vn; 97A Đ Pho Duc Chinh; admission 10,000d; 🕒 9am-4.30pm Tue-Sun), houses one of the more interesting collections in Vietnam, ranging from lacquer- and enamelware to contemporary oil paintings by Vietnamese and foreign artists. If that doesn't sound enticing, just come to see the huge hall with its beautifully tiled floors. The 1st floor includes a display of officially accepted contemporary art: most of it is just kitsch or desperate attempts to master abstract art, but occasionally something brilliant is displayed here. Much of the recent art is for sale and prices are reasonable.

The 2nd floor has older, politically correct art. Some of it is pretty crude: pictures of heroic figures waving red flags, children with rifles, a wounded soldier joining the Communist Party, innumerable tanks and weaponry, grotesquely presented Americans and God-like reverence for Ho Chi Minh. However, it's worth seeing if only because Vietnamese artists managed not to be as dull and conformist as their counterparts in Eastern Europe sometimes were. Once you've passed several paintings and sculptures of Uncle Ho, you will see that those artists who studied before 1975 managed to somehow transfer their own aesthetics onto the world of their prescribed subjects. Most impressive are some drawings of prison riots in 1973 and some remarkable abstract paintings.

The 3rd floor has a good collection of older art dating back to the 4th century, including Funan-era sculptures of Vishnu, the Buddha and other revered figures (carved in both wood and stone), which resemble styles of ancient Greece and Egypt. You will find here the best Cham pieces outside of Danang, and also interesting are the many pieces of Indianised art, such as stone elephant heads, which likely originate from Angkor in Cambodia.

HO CHI MINH MUSEUM

This **museum** (Khu Luu Niem Bac Ho; Map p346; ☎ 3840 0647; 1 Đ Nguyen Tat Thanh; admission 5000d; 🕐 7.30-11.30am & 1.30-5pm) is in the old customs house in District 4, just across Ben Nghe Channel from the quayside end of ĐL Ham Nghi. Nicknamed the 'Dragon House' (Nha Rong), it was built in 1863. The link between Ho Chi Minh and the museum building is tenuous: 21-year-old Ho, having signed on as a stoker and galley boy on a French freighter, left Vietnam from here in 1911 and thus began 30 years of exile in France, the Soviet Union, China and elsewhere.

The museum houses many of Ho's personal effects, including some of his clothing (he was a man of informal dress), sandals, his beloved US-made Zenith radio and other memorabilia. The explanatory signs in the museum are in Vietnamese, but if you know something about Uncle Ho (p35) you should be able to follow most of the photographs and exhibits.

TON DUC THANG MUSEUM

This small, seldom-visited **museum** (Bao Tang Ton Duc Thang; Map p348; ☎ 3829 7542; 5 Đ Ton Duc Thang; admission 5000d; 🕐 7.30-11.30am & 1.30-5pm Tue-Fri) is dedicated to Ton Duc Thang, Ho Chi Minh's successor as president of Vietnam, who was born in Long Xuyen, An Giang province, in 1888. He died in office in 1980. Photos and displays illustrate his role in the Vietnamese Revolution, including a couple of very lifelike exhibits that represent the time he spent imprisoned on Con Son Island (p409).

The museum is on the waterfront, half a block north of the **Tran Hung Dao statue**.

JADE EMPEROR PAGODA

Built in 1909 by the Cantonese (Quang Dong) Congregation, the **Jade Emperor Pagoda** (Phuoc Hai Tu or Chua Ngoc Hoang; Map p346; 73 Đ Mai Thi Luu) is a real gem among Chinese temples. It is one of the most spectacularly colourful pagodas in HCMC, filled with statues of phantasmal divinities and grotesque heroes. The pungent smoke of burning joss sticks fills the air, obscuring the exquisite woodcarvings decorated with gilded Chinese characters. The roof is covered with elaborate tile work, while the statues, which represent characters from both the Buddhist and Taoist traditions, are made of reinforced papier-mâché. The pagoda is dedicated to the Emperor of Jade, the supreme Taoist god.

Inside the main building are two especially fierce and menacing figures. On the right (as you face the altar) is a 4m-high statue of the general who defeated the Green Dragon (depicted underfoot). On the left is the general who defeated the White Tiger, which is also being stepped on.

The Taoist Jade Emperor (or King of Heaven, Ngoc Hoang), draped in luxurious robes, presides over the **main sanctuary**. He is flanked by his guardians, the Four Big Diamonds (Tu Dai Kim Cuong), so named because they are said to be as hard as diamonds.

Out the door on the left-hand side of the Jade Emperor's chamber is another room. The semi-enclosed area to the right (as you enter) is presided over by Thanh Hoang, the Chief of Hell; to the left is his red horse. Other figures here represent the gods who dispense punishments for evil acts and rewards for good deeds. The room also contains the famous **Hall of the Ten Hells** – carved wooden panels illustrating the varied torments awaiting evil people in each of the Ten Regions of Hell.

On the other side of the wall is a fascinating little room in which the **ceramic figures** of 12 women, overrun with children and wearing colourful clothes, sit in two rows of six. Each of the women exemplifies a human characteristic, either good or bad (as in the case of the woman drinking alcohol from a jug). Each figure represents one year in the 12-year Chinese calendar. Presiding over the room is Kim Hoa Thanh Mau, the Chief of All Women.

The Jade Emperor Pagoda is in a part of the city known as Da Kao (or Da Cao). To get here, head to 20 Đ Dien Bien Phu and walk half a block to the northwest.

XA LOI PAGODA

Famed as the repository of a sacred relic of the Buddha, **Xa Loi Pagoda** (Map p346; 89 Đ Ba Huyen Thanh Quan) was built in 1956. In August 1963 truckloads of armed men under the command of President Ngo Dinh Diem's brother, Ngo Dinh Nhu, attacked Xa Loi Pagoda, which had become a centre of opposition towards the Diem government. The pagoda was ransacked and 400 monks and nuns, including the country's 80-year-old Buddhist patriarch, were arrested. This raid and others elsewhere helped solidify opposition among Buddhists to the regime, a crucial factor in the US decision to support the coup against Diem. This pagoda was also the site of several self-immolations by monks protesting against the Diem regime and the American War.

Women enter the main hall of Xa Loi Pagoda by the staircase on the right as you come in the gate, and men use the stairs on the left. The walls of the sanctuary are adorned with paintings depicting the Buddha's life.

Xa Loi Pagoda is in District 3 near Đ Dien Bien Phu. A monk preaches every Sunday from 8am to 10am. On days of the full moon and new moon, special prayers are held from 7am to 9am and 7pm to 8pm.

TRAN HUNG DAO TEMPLE

This small **temple** (Map p346; 36 Đ Vo Thi Sau; 6-11am & 2-6pm Mon-Fri) is dedicated to Tran Hung Dao, a national hero who in 1287 vanquished Mongol emperor Kublai Khan's invasion force, said to have numbered 300,000 men. The temple is one block northeast of the telecommunication dishes that are between Đ Dien Bien Phu and Đ Vo Thi Sau.

NOTRE DAME CATHEDRAL

Built between 1877 and 1883, **Notre Dame Cathedral** (Map p348; Đ Han Thuyen) is set in the heart of HCMC's government quarter. The cathedral faces Đ Dong Khoi. It is neo-Romanesque with two 40m-high square towers tipped with iron spires, which dominate the square here. In front of the cathedral (in the centre of the square bounded by the main post office) is a statue of the Virgin Mary. If the front gates are locked, try the door on the side of the building that faces Reunification Palace.

Unusually, this cathedral has no stained-glass windows, which were damaged in fighting during WWII. A number of foreign travellers worship here and the priests are allowed to add a short sermon in French or English to their longer presentations in Vietnamese. The 9.30am Sunday Mass might be the best one for tourists to attend.

MARIAMMAN HINDU TEMPLE

This is the only **Hindu temple** (Chua Ba Mariamman; Map p346; 45 Đ Truong Dinh) still in use in HCMC and is a little piece of southern India in the centre of town. Though there are only a small number of Hindus in HCMC, this temple is also considered sacred by many ethnic Vietnamese and ethnic Chinese. Indeed, it is reputed to have miraculous powers. The temple was built at the end of the 19th century and dedicated to the Hindu goddess Mariamman.

The lion to the left of the entrance used to be carried around the city in a street procession every autumn. In the shrine in the middle of the temple is Mariamman, flanked by her guardians Maduraiveeran (to her left) and Pechiamman (to her right). In front of the Mariamman figure are two linga (stylised phalluses that represent the Hindu god Shiva). Favourite offerings placed nearby often include joss sticks, jasmine, lilies and gladioli. The wooden stairs on the left (as you enter the building) lead to the roof, where you'll find two colourful towers covered with innumerable figures of lions, goddesses and guardians.

After reunification, the government took over the temple and turned part of it into a factory for joss sticks. Another section was occupied by a company producing seafood for export, which was dried on the roof in the sun.

Mariamman Hindu Temple is only three blocks west of Ben Thanh Market. Remove your shoes before stepping onto the slightly raised platform.

SAIGON CENTRAL MOSQUE

Built by South Indian Muslims in 1935 on the site of an earlier mosque, the **Saigon Central Mosque** (Map p348; 66 Đ Dong Du) is an immaculately clean and well-kept island of calm in the middle of the bustling Dong Khoi area. In front of the sparkling white-and-blue structure, with its four nonfunctional minarets, is a pool for the ritual ablutions required by Islamic law before prayers. Take off your shoes before entering the sanctuary.

The simplicity of the mosque is in marked contrast to the exuberance of Chinese temple decoration, and the rows of figures facing elaborate ritual objects in Buddhist pagodas. Islamic law strictly forbids using human or animal figures for decoration.

There are not that many Indian Muslims remaining in HCMC, as most of the community fled in 1975. As a result, prayers – held five times a day – are sparsely attended, except on Friday, when several dozen worshippers are present.

There are 12 other mosques serving the 5000 or so Muslims in HCMC.

PEOPLE'S COMMITTEE BUILDING

HCMC's gingerbread **People's Committee Building** (Hôtel de Ville; Map p348), one of the city's most prominent landmarks, is the home of the Ho Chi Minh City People's Committee. Built between 1901 and 1908, the Hôtel de Ville is situated at the northwestern end of ĐL Nguyen Hue, facing the river. The former hotel is notable for its gardens, ornate facade and elegant interior lit with crystal chandeliers. It's one of the most photographed buildings in Vietnam. At night, the exterior is usually covered with thousands of geckos feasting on insects.

Unfortunately, you'll have to content yourself with admiring the exterior only. The building is not open to the public and requests by tourists to visit the interior are aggressively denied.

OPERA HOUSE

A grand colonial building with a sweeping staircase, the **Opera House** (Nha Hat Thanh Pho; Map p348; ☎ 3829 9976; Lam Son Sq), also known as the Municipal Theatre, is hard to miss at the intersection of Đ Dong Khoi and ĐL Le Loi. For information on performances held here, see p382.

CONG VIEN VAN HOA PARK

Next to the old Cercle Sportif, which was an elite sporting club during the French-colonial period, the bench-lined walks of **Cong Vien Van Hoa Park** (Map p348) are shaded with avenues of enormous tropical trees. There is also an exhibition of contemporary sculpture, which looks like it will become as permanent a fixture as the old trees.

In the morning, you can often see people here practising the art of *thai cuc quyen*, or slow-motion shadow boxing. Within the park is also a small-scale model of Nha Trang's most famous Cham towers.

This place still has an active **sports club** that is possible to visit. It has 11 tennis courts, a passable swimming pool and a clubhouse, all of which have a faded colonial feel about them. The tennis courts are available for hire at a reasonable fee and hourly tickets are on sale for use of the pool.

There are also Roman-style baths and a coffee shop overlooking the colonnaded pool. Other facilities include a gymnasium, table tennis, weights, wrestling mats and ballroom-dancing classes.

Cong Vien Van Hoa Park is adjacent to Reunification Palace. There are entrances across from 115 Đ Nguyen Du and on Đ Nguyen Thi Minh Khai.

BINH SOUP SHOP

It might seem strange to introduce a noodle-soup restaurant as a sight, but there is more to **Binh Soup Shop** (Map p346; ☎ 3848 3775; 7 Đ Ly Chinh Tha Thang, District 3; noodle soup 30,000d) than meets the eye. The Binh Soup Shop was the secret headquarters of the VC in Saigon. It was from here that the VC planned its attack on the US embassy and other places in Saigon during the Tet Offensive of 1968. One has to wonder how many US soldiers ate here, completely unaware that the staff were all VC infiltrators. By the way, the *pho* makes it a worthwhile stop for lunch or breakfast.

Cholon

A treasure trove of interesting Chinese-style temples awaits in Cholon (District 5) – it's well worth heading over to Chinatown for a half-day or more to explore. Aside from the temples and pagodas, you can sample some excellent Chinese and Vietnamese food or have a swim at one of the water parks, if you're all templed out.

While you're roaming, stroll over to the strip of **traditional herb shops** (Map p361; Đ Hai Thuong Lan Ong) between Đ Luong Nhu Hoc and Đ Trieu Quang Phuc for an olfactory experience you won't soon forget. The streets here are filled with amazing sights, sounds and rich herbal aromas.

QUAN AM PAGODA

One of Cholon's most active pagodas, **Quan Am Pagoda** (Map p361; 12 Đ Lao Tu) was founded by the Fujian Congregation in the early 19th century and displays obvious Chinese influences. It's named for the Goddess of Mercy, Quan The Am Bo Tat whose statue lies hidden behind a remarkably ornate exterior.

Fantastic ceramic scenes decorate the roof and depict figures from traditional Chinese plays and stories. The tableaux include ships, village houses and several ferocious dragons. Other unique features of this pagoda are the gold-and-lacquer panels of the entrance doors. Just inside, the walls of the porch are murals, in slight relief, of scenes of China from around the time of Quan Cong. There are elaborate woodcarvings above the porch.

In the courtyard behind the main sanctuary, in the pink-tiled altar, is a figure of A Pho, the Holy Mother Celestial Empress, while Quan The Am Bo Tat, dressed in white embroidered robes, stands nearby.

PHUOC AN HOI QUAN PAGODA

Built in 1902 by the Fujian Congregation, **Phuoc An Hoi Quan Pagoda** (Map p361; 184 Đ Hung Vuong) is one of the most beautifully ornamented pagodas in HCMC. Of special interest are the many small porcelain figures, the elaborate brass ritual objects and the fine woodcarvings on the altars, walls, columns and hanging lanterns. From the exterior, look out for the ceramic scenes, each containing innumerable small figurines, which decorate the roof.

To the left of the entrance is a life-size figure of the sacred horse of Quan Cong. Before leaving on a journey, people make offerings to the horse, then stroke its mane and ring the bell around its neck. Behind the main altar, with its stone and brass incense braziers, is Quan Cong, to whom the pagoda is dedicated.

TAM SON HOI QUAN PAGODA

The **Tam Son Hoi Quan Pagoda** (Chua Ba Chua; Map p361; 118 Đ Trieu Quang Phuc) was built by the Fujian Congregation in the 19th century, and retains much of its original rich ornamentation. The pagoda is dedicated to Me Sanh, the Goddess of Fertility and is particularly popular with local women who come here to pray for children.

Among the striking figures presented in this pagoda is the deified General Quan Cong with his long black beard. He's found to the right of the covered courtyard. Flanking him are two guardians, the Mandarin General Chau Xuong on the left and the Administrative Mandarin Quan Binh on the right. Next to Chau Xuong is Quan Cong's sacred red horse.

Across the courtyard from Quan Cong is a small room containing ossuary jars and memorials in which the dead are represented by their photographs. Next to this chamber is a small room containing the papier-mâché head of a dragon of the type used by the Fujian Congregation for dragon dancing.

Tam Son Hoi Quan Pagoda is located close to 370 ĐL Tran Hung Dao.

THIEN HAU PAGODA

Built by the Cantonese Congregation in the early 19th century, this large **pagoda** (Ba Mieu, Pho Mieu or Chua Ba; Map p361; 710 Đ Nguyen Trai) is dedicated to Thien Hau and always has a mix of worshippers and visitors, who mingle beneath the large coils of incense suspended overhead.

It is believed that Thien Hau (also known as Tuc Goi La Ba) can travel over the oceans on a mat and ride the clouds to wherever she pleases. Her mobility allows her to save people in trouble on the high seas. The Goddess is very popular in Hong Kong and Taiwan, which might explain why this pagoda is included on so many tour-group itineraries.

Though there are guardians to each side of the entrance, it is said that the real protectors of the pagoda are the two land turtles that live here. There are intricate ceramic friezes above the roof line of the interior courtyard. Near the huge braziers are two miniature wooden structures in which a small figure of Thien Hau is paraded around the nearby streets on the 23rd day of the third lunar month.

On the main dais are three figures of Thien Hau, one behind the other, all flanked by two servants or guardians. To the left of the dais is a bed for Thien Hau. To the right is

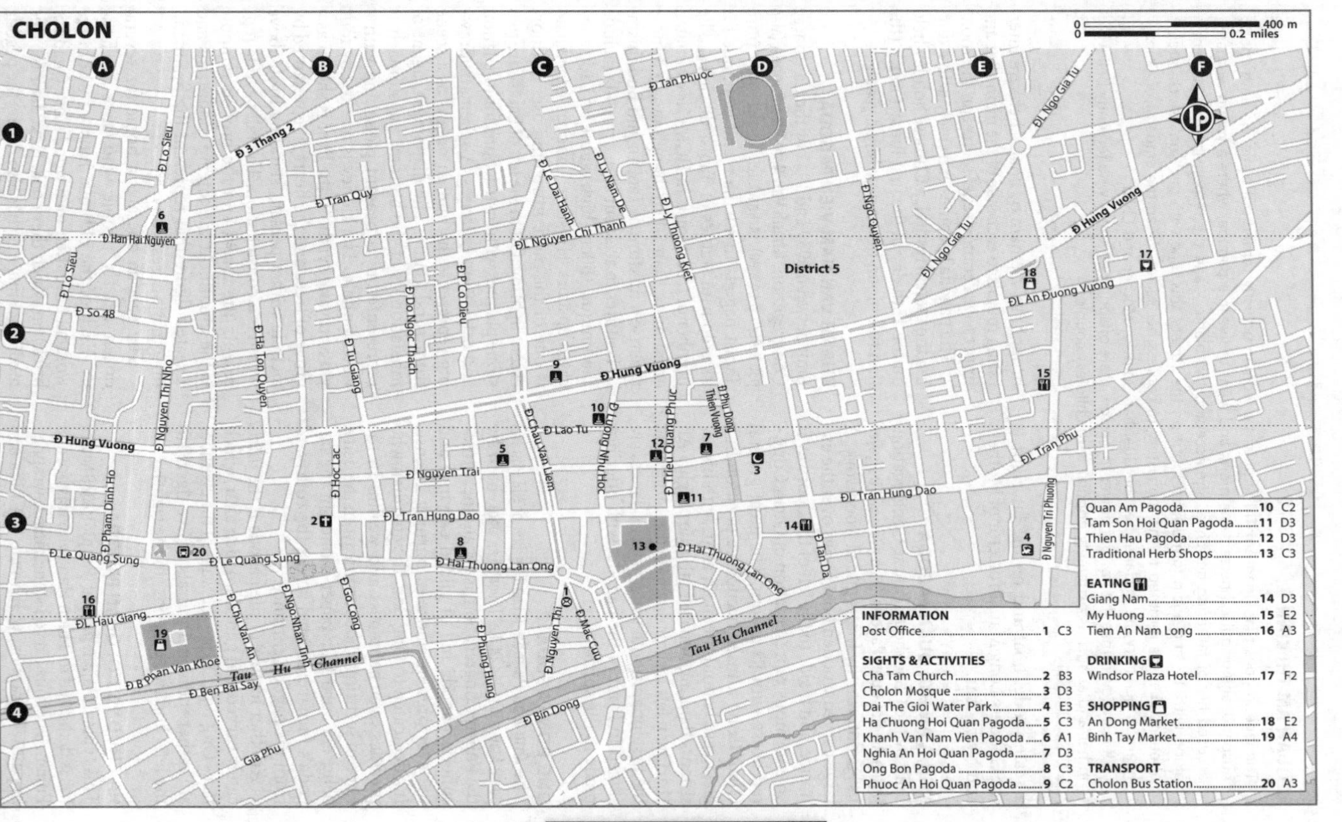
CHOLON
0 400 m
0 0.2 miles
District 5
Tau Hu Channel
Đ Hung Vuong
ĐL Ngo Gia Tu
ĐL An Duong Vuong
ĐL Tran Phu
Đ Nguyen Tri Phuong
Đ Ngo Quyen
ĐL Tran Hung Dao
Đ Tan Da
Đ Hai Thuong Lan Ong
Đ Phu Dong Thien Vuong
Đ Trieu Quang Phuc
Đ Ly Thuong Kiet
Đ Tan Phuoc
Đ Ly Nam De
Đ Le Dai Hanh
ĐL Nguyen Chi Thanh
Đ Luong Nhu Hoc
Đ Lao Tu
Đ Chau Van Liem
Đ Mac Cuu
Đ Nguyen Thi
Đ Phung Hung
Đ Bin Dong
Đ Nguyen Trai
Đ P Co Dieu
Đ Do Ngoc Thach
Đ Tran Quy
Đ Tu Giang
Đ Hoc Lac
Đ Go Cong
Đ Ngo Nhan Tinh
Đ 3 Thang 2
Đ Ha Ton Quyen
Đ Le Quang Sung
Đ Chu Van An
Đ Ben Bai Say
Gia Phu
Đ Lo Sieu
Đ Han Hai Nguyen
Đ Nguyen Thi Nho
Đ B Phan Van Khoe
Đ Pham Dinh Ho
ĐL Hau Giang
Đ So 48
INFORMATION
Post Office 1 C3
SIGHTS & ACTIVITIES
Cha Tam Church 2 B3
Cholon Mosque 3 D3
Dai The Gioi Water Park 4 E3
Ha Chuong Hoi Quan Pagoda 5 C3
Khanh Van Nam Vien Pagoda 6 A1
Nghia An Hoi Quan Pagoda 7 D3
Ong Bon Pagoda 8 C3
Phuoc An Hoi Quan Pagoda 9 C2
Quan Am Pagoda 10 C2
Tam Son Hoi Quan Pagoda 11 D3
Thien Hau Pagoda 12 D3
Traditional Herb Shops 13 C3
EATING
Giang Nam 14 D3
My Huong 15 E2
Tiem An Nam Long 16 A3
DRINKING
Windsor Plaza Hotel 17 F2
SHOPPING
An Dong Market 18 E2
Binh Tay Market 19 A4
TRANSPORT
Cholon Bus Station 20 A3

QUAN AM THI KINH

The legend goes that Quan Am Thi Kinh was a woman unjustly turned out of her home by her husband. She disguised herself as a monk and went to live in a pagoda, where a young woman accused her of fathering her child. She accepted the blame – and the responsibility that went along with it – and again found herself out on the streets, this time with her 'son'. Much later, about to die, she returned to the monastery to confess her secret. When the emperor of China heard of her story, he declared her the Guardian Spirit of Mother and Child.

It is believed that she has the power to bestow male offspring on those who fervently believe in her and as such is extremely popular with childless couples.

a scale-model boat and on the far right is the Goddess Long Mau, Protector of Mothers and Newborns.

NGHIA AN HOI QUAN PAGODA

Built by the Chaozhou Chinese Congregation, **Nghia An Hoi Quan Pagoda** (Map p361; 678 Đ Nguyen Trai) is noteworthy for its gilded woodwork. A large carved wooden boat hangs over the entrance, and inside to the left of the doorway is an enormous representation of Quan Cong's red horse with its groom. The great general Quan Cong himself occupies a position in a glass case behind the main altar, with his assistants flanking him on both sides. Nghia An Hoi Quan lets its hair down on the 14th day of the first lunar month when various dances are staged in front of the pagoda, with offerings made to the spirits.

ONG BON PAGODA

The **Ong Bon Pagoda** (Chua Ong Bon or Nhi Phu Hoi Quan; Map p361; 264 ĐL Hai Thuong Lan Ong), built by the Fujian Congregation, is yet another atmospheric pagoda full of gilded carvings and the ever-present smoke of burning incense. It's dedicated to Ong Bon, the guardian who presides over happiness and wealth. In the hope of securing good fortune from the deity, believers burn fake paper money in the pagoda's furnace, located across the courtyard from the pagoda entrance.

Another feature of the pagoda is the intricately carved and gilded wooden altar, which faces Ong Bon. Along the walls of the chamber are rather indistinct murals of five tigers (to the left) and two dragons (to the right).

HA CHUONG HOI QUAN PAGODA

This typical Fujian **pagoda** (Map p361; 802 Đ Nguyen Trai) is dedicated to Thien Hau, who was born in Fujian. The four carved stone pillars, wrapped in painted dragons, were made in China and brought to Vietnam by boat. There are interesting murals to each side of the main altar and impressive ceramic relief scenes on the roof.

The pagoda becomes extremely active during the **Lantern Festival**, a Chinese holiday held on the 15th day of the first lunar month (the first full moon of the new lunar year).

KHANH VAN NAM VIEN PAGODA

Built between 1939 and 1942 by the Cantonese Congregation, **Khanh Van Nam Vien Pagoda** (Map p361; 46/5 Đ Lo Sieu) is said to be the only pure Taoist pagoda in Vietnam and is unique for its colourful statues of Taoist disciples. The number of true Taoists in HCMC is estimated at no more than 5000, though most Chinese practise a mixture of Taoism and Buddhism.

Features to seek out at this pagoda include the unique 150cm-high statue of Laotse located upstairs. His surreal, mirror-edged halo is one of the more intriguing uses of fluorescent lighting. Off to the left of Laotse are two stone plaques with instructions for inhalation and exhalation exercises. A schematic drawing represents the human organs as a scene from rural China. The diaphragm, agent of inhalation, is at the bottom; the stomach is represented by a peasant ploughing with a water buffalo. The kidney is marked by four yin and yang symbols, the liver is shown as a grove of trees and the heart is represented by a circle with a peasant standing in it, above which is a constellation. The tall pagoda represents the throat and the broken rainbow is the mouth. At the top are mountains and a seated figure that represent the brain and imagination, respectively.

The pagoda operates a home for several dozen elderly people who have no family. Each of the old folk, most of whom are women, have their own wood stove (made of brick) on which they cook. Next door is a free medical clinic, which is also run by the pagoda and offers Chinese herbal medicines and acupuncture treatments to the community. If you would like to support this venture you can leave a donation with the monks.

Prayers are held daily from 8am to 9am. In order to reach the pagoda, turn off Đ Nguyen Thi Nho, which runs perpendicular to Đ Hung Vuong (between Nos 269B and 271B).

CHA TAM CHURCH

Cha Tam Church, with its facade of white and lime-green trim, was built around the turn of the 19th century. It has a sleepy, tropical feel to it, a far cry from its role during one of Saigon's more harrowing epochs.

President Ngo Dinh Diem and his brother Ngo Dinh Nhu took refuge in **Cha Tam Church** (Map p361; 25 Đ Hoc Lac) on 2 November 1963, after fleeing the Presidential Palace during a coup attempt. When their efforts to contact loyal military officers (of whom there was almost none) failed, Diem and Nhu agreed to surrender unconditionally and they revealed where they were hiding.

The coup leaders sent an M-113 armoured personnel carrier to the church and the two were taken into custody. However, before the vehicle reached central Saigon the soldiers had killed Diem and Nhu by shooting them at point-blank range and then repeatedly stabbing their bodies.

When news of the deaths was broadcast on radio, Saigon exploded with rejoicing. Portraits of the two were torn up and political prisoners, many of whom had been tortured, were set free. The city's nightclubs, which had closed because of the Ngos' conservative Catholic beliefs, were reopened. Three weeks later the US president, John F Kennedy, was assassinated. As his administration had supported the coup against Diem, some conspiracy theorists speculated that Diem's family orchestrated Kennedy's death in retaliation.

The statue in the tower is of François Xavier Tam Assou (1855–1934), a Chinese-born vicar apostolic (delegate of the pope) of Saigon. Today, the church has a very active congregation of 3000 ethnic Vietnamese and 2000 ethnic Chinese. Masses are held daily.

Cha Tam Church is at the western end of ĐL Tran Hung Dao.

CHOLON MOSQUE

The clean lines and lack of ornamentation of the **Cholon Mosque** (Map p361; 641 Đ Nguyen Trai) contrast starkly with nearby Chinese and Vietnamese Buddhist pagodas. In the courtyard is a pool for ritual ablutions. Note the tiled niche in the wall (*mihrab*) indicating the direction of prayer, which is towards Mecca. The mosque was built by Tamil Muslims in 1935, but since 1975 it has served the Malaysian and Indonesian Muslim communities.

Greater HCMC

Although Cholon has a high density of pagodas, there are several particularly striking ones further out.

GIAC LAM PAGODA

Believed to be the oldest pagoda in greater HCMC, **Giac Lam Pagoda** (Map pp344-5; 118 Đ Lac Long Quan) dates from 1744. It's a fantastically atmospheric place full of gilded statues, colourful wall panels (depicting among other things the path to enlightenment as well as the tortures awaiting those condemned to hell) with one of the country's most impressive stupas (32m tall). For the sick and elderly, the pagoda is a minor pilgrimage sight, as it contains a bronze bell that, when rung, is believed to answer the prayers posted by petitioners. Home to several monks, the Buddhist pagoda also incorporates aspects of Taoism and Confucianism. It is well worth the trip out here from the centre and is one of the city's cultural relics.

The pagoda is set in a peaceful, gardenlike setting with the **tombs** of venerated monks to the right of the two-tiered pagoda gate. The looming Bodhi located in the front garden was the gift of a monk from Sri Lanka in 1953. Next to the tree is a gleaming white statue of Quan The Am Bo Tat standing on a lotus blossom, a symbol of purity.

Inside the reception area of the **main building** is the 18-armed Chuan De, another form of the Goddess of Mercy. Carved hardwood columns bear gilded Vietnamese inscriptions, with the portraits of great monks from previous generations (and dragons hidden in clouds) looking down on the proceedings.

The main **sanctuary** lies in the next room, filled with countless gilded figures. On the dais in the centre of the back row sits A Di Da, the Buddha of the Past (Amitabha), easily spotted by his colourful halo. The fat laughing fellow, seated with five children climbing all over him, is Ameda, the Buddha of enlightenment, compassion and wisdom. On the altars along the side walls of the sanctuary are various Bodhisattvas and two 10-panelled drawings: the first depicts the Judges of the 10 Regions of Hell and the various gruesome treatments meted out to the unworthy. Next to it are 10 more panels showing scenes from Thich Ca Buddha's life from birth to enlightenment.

The red-and-gold Christmas tree–shaped object is a wooden altar bearing 49 lamps and 49 miniature Bodhisattva statues. People pray for sick relatives or ask for happiness by contributing kerosene for use in the lamps. Petitioners' names and those of ill family members are written on slips of paper, which are attached to the branches of the 'tree'.

The frame of the large bronze bell in the corner resembles a bulletin board because petitioners have attached to it lists of names: those of people seeking happiness and those of the sick and the dead, placed there by relatives. It is believed that when the bell is rung, the sound will resonate to the heavens, carrying with it the attached supplications.

Prayers here consist of chanting to the accompaniment of drums, bells and gongs, and they follow a traditional rite which is seldom performed these days. Prayers are held daily from 4am to 5am, 11am to noon, 4pm to 5pm and 7pm to 9pm.

Giac Lam Pagoda is about 3km from Cholon in the Tan Binh district, and is best reached by taxi or *xe om*.

GIAC VIEN PAGODA

Architecturally similar to Giac Lam, this striking **pagoda** (Map pp344-5; Đ Lac Long Quan; 7-11.30am & 1.30-7pm) also shares its atmosphere of scholarly serenity, although Giac Vien is less visited and in a more rural setting near Dam Sen Lake in District 11. The pagoda was founded by Hai Tinh Giac Vien in the late 1700s. It is said that Emperor Gia Long, who died in 1819, used to worship at Giac Vien. The pagoda remains a marvellously preserved artefact from the past, boasting some 100 lavish carvings of various divinities.

Hidden behind a warren of winding streets, the pagoda, like Giac Lam, has several impressive **tombs** on the right leading up to the pagoda itself. Funeral tablets line the first chamber, while the second chamber is dominated by a statue of Hai Tinh Giac Vien holding a horse-tail switch. Nearby portraits depict his disciples and successors. Opposite Hai Tinh Giac Vien is a representation of the 18-armed Chuan De, who is flanked by two guardians.

The main **sanctuary** is on the other side of the wall behind the Hai Tinh Giac Vien statue. The dais is set behind a fantastic brass incense basin with fierce dragon heads emerging from each side. On the altar to the left of the dais is Dai The Chi Bo Tat; on the altar to the right is Quan The Am Bo Tat. The Guardian of the Pagoda is against the wall opposite the dais. Nearby is a 'Christmas tree' similar to the one in Giac Lam Pagoda. Lining the side walls are the Judges of the 10 Regions of Hell (holding scrolls) and 18 Bodhisattvas.

Prayers are held daily from 4am to 5am, 8am to 10am, 2pm to 3pm, 4pm to 5pm and 7pm to 9pm.

PHUNG SON PAGODA

This **pagoda** (Phung Son Tu or Chua Go; Map pp344-5; 1408 ĐL 3/2) is extremely rich in statuary made of bronze, wood, ceramic and beaten copper. It's peopled with a mix of gilded and beautifully carved statues (some painted). This Vietnamese Buddhist pagoda was built between 1802 and 1820 on the site of structures from the Funan period, dating back at least to the early centuries of Christianity. Other foundations of Funanese buildings have also been discovered here.

Once upon a time, it was decided that Phung Son Pagoda should be moved to a different site. The pagoda's ritual objects – bells, drums, statues – were loaded onto the back of a white elephant, but the elephant slipped because of the great weight and all the precious objects fell into a nearby pond. This event was interpreted as an omen that the pagoda should remain at its original location. All the articles were retrieved except for the bell, which locals say was heard ringing, until about a century ago, whenever there was a full or new moon.

The main dais, with its many levels, is dominated by an enormous gilded A Di Da Buddha seated under a canopy flanked by long mobiles resembling human forms without heads. To the left of the main dais is an altar with a statue of Bodhidharma, who brought Buddhism from India to China. The statue, which is made of Chinese ceramic, has a face with Indian features.

Phung Son Pagoda is in District 11. Prayers are held three times a day, from 4am to 5am, 4pm to 5pm and 6pm to 7pm. The main entrances are locked most of the time, but the side entrance (to the left as you approach the building) is open during prayer times.

LE VAN DUYET TEMPLE

Dedicated to Marshal Le Van Duyet (1763–1831), this **temple** (Map pp344-5; Đ Dinh Tien Hoang) is also his burial place, alongside his wife. The marshal was a South Vietnamese general and viceroy who helped put down the Tay Son Rebellion (p31) and reunify Vietnam. When the Nguyen dynasty came to power in 1802, he was elevated by Emperor Gia Long to the rank of marshal. Le Van Duyet fell out of favour with Gia Long's successor, Minh Mang, who tried him posthumously and desecrated his grave. Emperor Thieu Tri, who succeeded Minh Mang, restored the tomb, thus fulfilling a prophecy of its destruction and restoration. Le Van Duyet was considered a national hero in the South before 1975, but is disliked by the communists because of his involvement in the expansion of French influence.

Among the items on display are a portrait of Le Van Duyet, some of his personal effects (including European-style crystal goblets) and other antiques. There are two wonderful life-size horse statues on either side of the entrance to the third and last chamber, which is kept locked.

During celebrations of Tet and on the 30th day of the seventh lunar month (the anniversary of Le Van Duyet's death), the tomb is thronged with pilgrims. Vietnamese used to come here to take oaths of good faith if they could not afford the services of a court of justice.

There are tropical fish on sale for visitors. The caged birds that are for sale are bought by pilgrims and freed to earn merit. The birds are often recaptured (and liberated again).

The temple is reached by heading north from the city centre on Đ Dinh Tien Hoang, all the way to ĐL Phan Dang Luu; it's easy to spot from the southeast corner.

AN QUANG PAGODA

This **pagoda** (Map pp344-5; Đ Su Van Hanh) gained some notoriety during the American War as the home of Thich Tri Quang, a powerful monk who led protests against the South Vietnamese government in 1963 and 1966. When the war ended he was held under house arrest and later placed in solitary confinement for 16 months until his eventual release.

An Quang Pagoda is on Đ Su Van Hanh, near the intersection with Đ Ba Hat, in District 10.

CHO QUAN CHURCH

Built by the French about 100 years ago, **Cho Quan Church** (Map pp344-5; 133 Đ Tran Binh Trong; 4-7am & 3-6pm Mon-Sat, 4-9am & 1.30-6pm Sun) is one of the largest churches in HCMC. Jesus on the altar has a neon halo, though the best reason to come here is for the view from the belfry (a steep climb). The church is between ĐL Tran Hung Dao and Đ Nguyen Trai. Sunday masses are held at 5am, 6.30am, 8.30am, 4.30pm and 6pm.

ACTIVITIES

Bowling

Diamond Superbowl (Map p348; ☎ 3825 7778; Diamond Plaza, 34 ĐL Le Duan; 10am-1am) This is a 32-lane bowling alley right in the centre of town. It's very popular with locals thanks to fluorescent bowling balls and state-of-the-art scoring. Attached is a large amusement centre with billiards, a video-game arcade and shops.

Climbing

X-Rock Climbing (☎ 2210 9192; www.xrockclimbing.com; 503A ĐL Nguyen Duy Trinh, D2) Saigon's leading climbing wall, so get in some practice for Cat Ba or Halong Bay by scaling the 26m wall here. Prices start from around US$10 per person. Grab a taxi to navigate here.

Gyms & Pools

Even if you don't make it to one of Saigon's water parks (p369) or to Cong Vien Van Hoa Park (p359), some of HCMC's finer hotels have gyms with attractive swimming pools attached. You needn't stay there to swim, but you'll have to pay an admission fee of US$10 to US$25 per day. Hotels that offer access to their pools include the **Legend** (Map p348; ☎ 3823 3333; 2A Đ Ton Duc Thang, District 1), Park Hyatt Saigon (p372), Majestic Hotel (p372), Renaissance Riverside Hotel (p372) and Rex Hotel (p372).

There are a number of less-expensive public pools and these pools charge by the hour, which works out to be pretty cheap, if you're staying only a short time.

Lam Son Pool (Map pp344-5; ☎ 3835 8028; 342 Đ Tran Binh Trong, District 5; admission per hr 8000d, after 5pm 10,000d; 8am-8pm) Offers an Olympic-sized pool.

Lan Anh Club (Map pp344-5; ☎ 3862 7144; 291 Cach Mang Thang Tam, District 10; admission gym/pool 50,000d/30,000d; ⏰ pool 6am-9pm) Good gym here.

Workers' Club (Map p346; ☎ 3930 1819; 55B Đ Nguyen Thi Minh Khai, District 3; admission per hr 10,000d)

Golf

Vietnam Golf and Country Club (Cau Lac Bo Golf Quoc Te Viet Nam; off Map pp344-5; ☎ 280 0101; www.vietnamgolfcc.com; Long Thanh My Village, District 9; driving range per 50 balls US$2.50, full round weekday/weekend US$90/120) Situated about 15km east of central HCMC, and the first in Vietnam to provide night golfing under floodlights. As well as 36-holes of golf, other facilities include tennis courts and a swimming pool.

If you're serious about golf, one of Vietnam's best courses is located at the Novotel in Phan Thiet (p315). There is another in Dalat (p322). Visit www.vietnamgolfresorts.com for more information on the courses and reasonably priced golf package tours.

Massages & Spas

HCMC offers some truly fantastic hideaways for pampering, the perfect antidote to a frenetic day spent dodging motorbikes. While many midrange and upmarket hotels offer massage services, some are more legitimate than others. Check out www.spasvietnam.com for extensive reviews of places and online bookings.

Vietnamese Traditional Massage Institute (Map p352; ☎ 3839 6697; 185 Đ Cong Quynh; per hr 40,000-50,000d, sauna 30,000d; ⏰ 9am-9pm) Sure, it's not the classiest act in town, but it does offer inexpensive, no-nonsense massages performed by well-trained blind masseurs from the Ho Chi Minh City Association for the Blind.

Relax House (Map p352; ☎ 3404 2284; 242 Đ Bui Vien; ⏰ 10am-11pm) A small place for those on a small budget, it offers pedicures, manicures and foot massages.

L'Apothiquaire (Map p346; ☎ 3932 5181; www.lapothiquaire.com; 64A Đ Truong Dinh; per hr hot stone US$45; ⏰ 9am-9pm; 🏊) Long considered the city's most elegant spa, this award-winning place is housed in a pretty, white mansion tucked down a quiet alley, with numerous services available. Guests enjoy body wraps, massages, facials, foot treatments and herbal baths, and L'Apothiquaire makes its own line of lotions and cosmetics. Members (or those on a package) have free use of the pool and sauna.

Glow (Map p348; ☎ 3823 8368; www.glowsaigon.com; 106 Đ Nguyen Hue, Eden Mall, per hr massage US$28; ⏰ 10am-8pm) Trendy spa in the heart of downtown, set in a mall that used to be an old French cinema. It's almost like a little boutique hotel, and offers an array of aromatherapy facial treatments, body treatments and therapeutic massage.

Aqua Day Spa (Map p348; ☎ 3827 2828; www.aquadayspasaigon.com; Sheraton Saigon, 88 Đ Dong Khoi; ⏰ 10am-11pm) One of HCMC's fanciest hotel spas, this beautiful space offers a range of treatments, including warm-stone massage, herbal scrubs, foot pampering and back massages.

Yoga & Martial Arts

There are several places in town to take yoga classes, including the calming L'Apothiquaire (left). If you're interested in martial arts, the best place to see (or try) *thai cuc quyen* is at Cong Vien Van Hoa Park (p359).

Saigon Yoga (Map p346; ☎ 3910 5181; www.saigonyoga.com; 10F Đ Nguyen Thi Minh Khai; per class/month US$14/115; ⏰ 8am-7pm) A small studio (tucked down a narrow alley) offering Vikram, Ashtanga, Vinyasa and power yoga, as well as pilates classes taught by US and Singaporean instructors. Short-term visitors can take advantage of seven days of unlimited yoga for US$25.

K1 Fitness & Fight Factory (Map pp344-5; ☎ 091-833 7111; www.teamminetti.com; 346 Đ Ben Van Dong; per class US$40; ⏰ 9am-6pm Mon-Fri) A fight club, and the place to improve your technique. The full-contact kickboxing dojo is run by Frenchman David 'Serial Striker' Minetti.

WALKING TOUR

Although HCMC is a sprawling metropolis – and growing by the day – there is still some rewarding exploring to be had on foot. This walking tour covers the city centre, District 1 (officially known as 'Saigon'), and can be done in one, stimulus-filled day.

Begin your excursion bright and early on **Đ Pham Ngu Lao (1)**, a teeming area of colourful shops and backpacker cafes. Skip the greasy eggs and bacon and instead grab a bowl of steaming *pho* at the excellent **Pho Quynh** (**2**; p374). Or wander a few blocks to **Pho 2000** (**3; p374**), which serves tasty noodles to locals, foreigners and former US president Bill Clinton.

Cross the road and enter the vast indoor **Ben Thanh Market** (**4**; p384), which is at its bus-

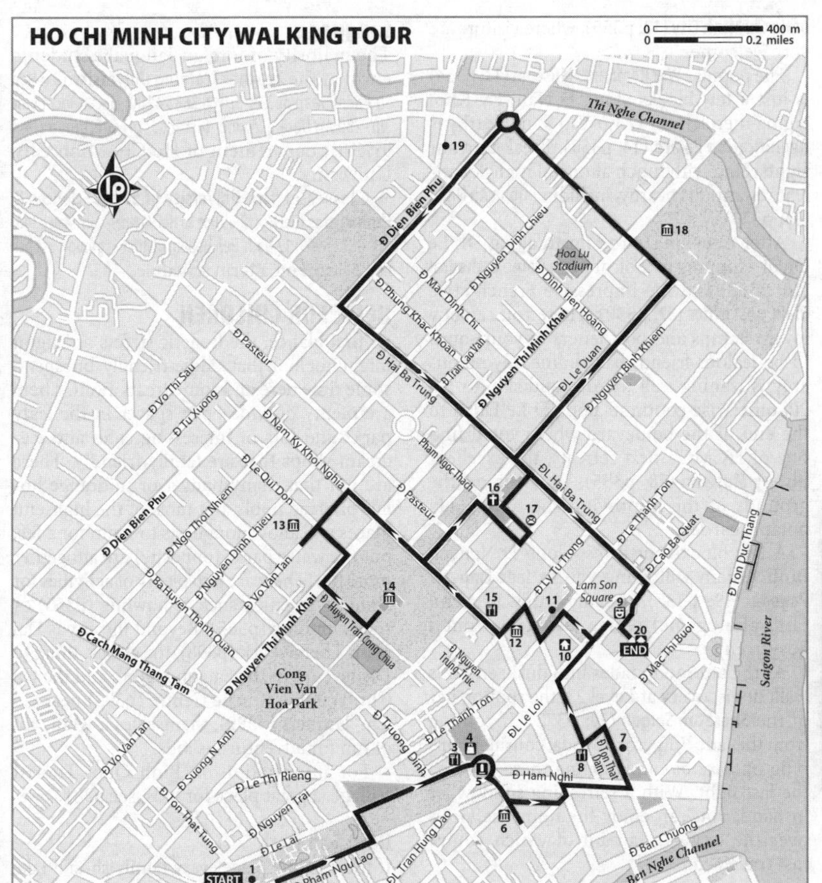

WALK FACTS

Start Pham Ngu Lao
End Sheraton Saigon
Distance 5km
Duration approximately 6 hours

tling best in the morning. After exploring the market, cross the massive roundabout (very carefully!), where you'll see a statue of **Tran Nguyen Hai (5)** on horseback. One short block south, on Đ Pho Duc Chinh, is the quaint **Fine Arts Museum** (**6**; p356), where you can tour some exhibits, and peek in some excellent galleries behind the museum. Zigzag east to ĐL Ham Nghi and turn north again on Đ Ton That Dam to stroll through the colourful outdoor **street market (7)**. Swing left and cool off at the **X Café** (**8**; p378), which serves some great ice cream in an inviting classical villa. Continue north to ĐL Le Loi, Saigon's commercial heart, which leads towards the grand and thoughtfully restored **Opera House** (**9**; p359).

One short block before the theatre, turn left at the **Rex Hotel** (**10**; p372) and head up ĐL Nguyen Hue. Just ahead, at the northern end of the boulevard, is the stately colonial-era People's Committee Building, also known as the **Hôtel de Ville** (**11**; p359). Admire it from the outside as requests to visit the interior are denied. However, a one-block walk south on Đ Le Thanh Ton will bring you to the **Museum**

of Ho Chi Minh City (**12**; p355), where visitors are very welcome.

The popular **War Remnants Museum** (**13**; p354) is just a few blocks along Đ Nam Ky Khoi Nghia then left on Đ Vo Van Tan. Nearby is **Reunification Palace** (**14**; p353). Break up your sightseeing with lunch at one of many excellent restaurants nearby, including **Quan An Ngon** (**15**; p373).

After refuelling, stroll north along ĐL Le Duan, stopping to look at **Notre Dame Cathedral** (**16**; p358) and the impressive French-style **main post office** (**17**; p350). There you can buy lovely stamps and post letters to your soon-to-be-jealous friends back home. If your energy is waning, call it a day and skip to No 20, otherwise continue along Đ Le Duan to the end of the boulevard where you'll find one of HCMC's best retreats, the excellent **History Museum** (**18**; p355), which is on the grounds of the improving zoo and shady botanic gardens.

A few blocks northwest along Đ Nguyen Binh Khiem will bring you to **Jade Emperor Pagoda** (**19**; p357), a remarkably peaceful (and photogenic) refuge just steps from a busy avenue.

As the afternoon fades into dusk, end this walk of discovery at Level 23, the rooftop bar of the **Sheraton Saigon** (**20**; p372). If coming from the Jade Emperor Pagoda, consider hopping on a *xe om* and zipping there to catch the last light. With a refreshing sundowner in hand, you can enjoy the immense views over the city – a fair bit of which you've just traversed.

COURSES

Cooking

Many of the major hotels offer cooking classes, although usually at rates to match the tariffs. For something a little different, try one of the following:

Vietnam Cookery Centre (☎ 3512 7246; www.vietnamcookery.com; M1 Cu Xa Tan Tang, Ward 25, Binh Thanh District; per person US$39) offers a half-day initiation course for lunch or dinner involving five dishes and a souvenir handbook to remember the tricks of the trade. Lunch classes from 9.30am, dinner classes from 3.30pm. See the website for full details of the address and how to get here.

Bi Saigon (Map p352; ☎ 3836 0678; www.bisaigon.com; 185/26 Đ Pham Ngu Lao, District 1; per person per dish US$20) organises private cooking classes on request.

Language

The majority of foreign-language students enrol at the **Teacher Training University** (Dai Hoc Su Pham; Map pp344-5; ☎ 3835 5100; ciecer@hcm.vnn.vn; 280 An Duong Vuong, District 5; private/group class US$6/4), a department of Ho Chi Minh City University.

Classes at the **University of Social Sciences & Humanities** (Dai Hoc Khoa Hoc Xa Hoi Va Nhan Van; Map p346; ☎ 3822 5009; 12 Dinh Tien Hoang, District 1; group class per hr US$4) run on a term schedule.

HCMC FOR CHILDREN

At first glance, the frenetic streets of Saigon might not look that kiddie-friendly, but spend some time here and some treats await. There are plenty of wide-open spaces in the leafy parks and lots of interesting cafes and ice-cream shops that are family friendly. There are not that many budget or midrange hotels offering pools, but most of the high-end places will allow nonguests to swim for a fee, but the water parks (opposite) are altogether more fun. There are also plenty of activities for children to enjoy such as bowling (p365) or rock climbing (p365). Beyond the city is Dai Nam Theme Park (p398), the closest thing to Disneyland in the Saigon region, and the Cu Chu Wildlife Rescue Centre (p393) near Cu Chi Tunnels (p390), themselves a whole lot of fun for adventurous kids.

For information on Binh Quoi Tourist Village, a great place for kids, see p381.

Dam Sen Park

If there is one place every family should take kids in this city, then **Dam Sen Park** (Map pp344-5; ☎ 858 7826; 3 Đ Hoa Binh; www.damsenpark.com.vn; adult/child 25,000/15,000d; 🕑 7am-9pm) is it. It includes a wide variety of amusements, such as paddle-boat rides around a lake lined with dragons. There are rides that include a monorail snaking through the park – a good way to get your bearings – plus a roller coaster, Ferris wheel and bumper cars. There are also plenty of parks and theme areas, such as orchid gardens, an aviary and a dinosaur park. On weekends the bandstand sees a range of shows, which feature singing and dancing warriors, rabbits and hip-hop stars all under the age of 12. Fishing is allowed in the lakes. There's also a water park (opposite) on the grounds. Dam Sen Park is located in District 11, northwest of Cholon. Entry includes the grounds and some of the attractions, but not the rides.

Water Parks

Outside the city centre, a couple of water parks offer cool relief from the heat. Anyone with kids and a half-day to spare will quickly come to appreciate these wet playgrounds on a sweltering day. To duck the crowds, avoid going on weekends and public holidays.

Dam Sen Water Park (Map pp344-5; ☎ 3858 8418; www.damsenwaterpark.com.vn; 3 Đ Hoa Binh; admission 35,000-75,000d; ⏰ 9am-6pm) has water slides, rivers with rapids (or slow currents) and rope swings for flips (or belly flops).

Dai The Gioi Water Park (Map p361; ☎ 3853 7867; 600 Đ Ham Tu, District 5; admission 30,000-60,000d; ⏰ 8am-9pm Mon-Fri, 10am-9pm Sat & Sun) is a good spot if you happen to be in Cholon, with a large pool and slides.

Botanic Gardens

One of the first projects undertaken by the French after they established Cochinchina as a colony was to found these lush **gardens** (Thao Cam Vien; Map p346; ☎ 3829 3901; 2 Đ Nguyen Binh Khiem; adult/child 10,000/5000d; ⏰ 7am-10pm). Though once one of the finest such gardens in Asia, they're now more a pleasant place for a stroll under giant tropical trees. The emphasis is on the fun fair, with kids' rides, a fun house, miniature train, house of mirrors and more.

There is also a zoo here, which, while hardly up there with Singapore Zoo, is much better than it once was and might divert the children. However, plans are under way for an all new Saigon Safari Park in Cu Chi District and all the animals from here will be relocated if and when it eventually opens.

Standing just inside the main gate (Đ Nguyen Binh Khiem on the eastern end of ĐL Le Duan) you'll be flanked by two striking architectural gems, the impressive Temple of King Hung Vuong and the History Museum (p355).

TOURS

There are surprisingly few day tours of HCMC itself available, although most local travel agents can work something out for a fee. Hiring a *cyclo* for a half-day or full day of sightseeing is an interesting option, but be sure to agree on the price before setting out (most drivers charge around US$1 per hour).

There are heaps of organised tours to the outlying areas such as the Cu Chi Tunnels (p390), Tay Ninh (p393)and the Mekong Delta (p413). Some tours are day trips and other are overnighters. The best-value tours are available from cafes and agencies in the Pham Ngu Lao area (see p351).

FESTIVALS & EVENTS

Tet (First day of first lunar month) The whole city parties and then empties out for family breaks. Đ Nguyen Hue is closed off for a huge flower exhibition and everyone exchanges lucky money.

Saigon Cyclo Race (mid-March) Professional and amateur *cyclo* drivers find out who's fastest; money raised is donated to local charities.

Festival at Lang Ong (Thirtieth day of seventh lunar month) People pray for happiness and the health of the country at the Ong Bon Temple (p362) in HCMC's Binh Thanh district; plays and musical performances are staged.

SLEEPING

District 1 is the undisputed lodging capital of HCMC, though the decision whether to go east (upmarket) or west (cheaper) depends on what you're after. Budget travellers often head straight to the Pham Ngu Lao area (Map p352), where cheap-ish hotels and budget cafes line the streets. Those seeking fancy-pants places head to the Dong Khoi area (Map p348), home to the city's best hotels, restaurants and bars.

Hotel rates have risen dramatically in the past couple of years, pretty much doubling across the board. This means HCMC is no longer the bargain it once was, but with the global economic crisis beginning to have an impact, this trend may slowly reverse.

Budget

Most budget travellers head to Pham Ngu Lao, as it is an easy place to hunt for a hotel or guesthouse on foot. Lugging your bags around makes you a prime target for touts, so consider dropping your gear at one of the travellers cafes and exploring from there. Most won't mind keeping an eye on your luggage and they'll be happy to tell you about their tour programs. If you book ahead, most hotels will fetch you at the airport for between US$5 and US$10.

PHAM NGU LAO

Three streets – Đ Pham Ngu Lao, Đ De Tham and Đ Bui Vien – along with a warren of intersecting alleys form the heart of this backpacker ghetto, with more than 100 places to stay. Among the options are countless family-run guesthouses (US$10 to US$20), newer, spiffier hotels (US$25 to US$50), and even the odd dorm. We have highlighted some of the better places here, but there are dozens more comfortable options and new places opening all the time.

Yellow House (Map p352; ☎ 3836 8830; yellowhousehotel@yahoo.com; 31 Đ Bui Vien; dm/s/d US$7/13/17;) One of the few hotels to offer dorm beds, they might not be as cheap as they were, but this is the new Saigon. Yellow House has two dormitories (a mixed seven-bed and a three-bed for men or women – whoever arrives first) as well as private rooms, but these are similar to what is on offer elsewhere. Breakfast included.

Kim's (Map p352; ☎ 3836 8584; 91 Đ Bui Vien; r US$10-15;) This small hotel is not part of the Mekong empire that is Kim Café, but an independent family-run pad with good-value rooms. Their rates have remained mercifully low in these inflationary times.

Ha Vy Hotel (Map p352; ☎ 3836 9123; 16-18 Đ Do Quang Dau; r US$12-17;) Located at the western end of the district, the Ha Vy is a reliable bet thanks to well-kept rooms with a choice of air-con or fan.

Mai Phai Hotel (Map p352; ☎ 3836 5868; maiphaihotel@saigonnet.vn; 209 Đ Pham Ngu Lao; r US$14-30;) One place we have stayed in a few times over the years, as the service is friendly and rooms are well furnished. Bonus features include a lift and free wi-fi.

our pick **Madame Cuc's** (madamcuc@hcm.vnn.vn; r US$15-25;) Hotel 127 (Map p352; ☎ 836 8761; 127 Đ Cong Quynh); Hotel 64 (Map p352; ☎ 836 5073; 64 Đ Bui Vien); Hotel 184 (Map p352; ☎ 836 1679; 184 Đ Cong Quynh) A three-in-one recommendation here; this trio of places is run by the welcoming Madame Cuc. All the hotels offer clean and spacious rooms with friendly service. There's free tea, coffee and fruit all day; breakfast and a simple dinner are included in the room rates.

Sao Nam Hotel (Map p352; ☎ 3920 6472; haohiep@yahoo.com; 175/5 Đ Pham Ngu Lao; r US$16-25;) Tucked away in a quiet alley, the 'Southern Star' has 22 rooms that feature sparkling new tiles and bathrooms, plus TV and fridge. Free internet for guests.

Quyen Thanh Hotel (Map p352; ☎ 3836 8570; thanhdahotel@vnn.vn; 212 Đ De Tham; r US$17-20;) One of the original places in this part of town, the place is decked in balconies with plants, and sits on one of liveliest corners in town, though perhaps not ideal for light sleepers. There is a busy souvenir shop on the ground floor.

Le Le Hotel (Map p352; ☎ 3836 8787; 171 Đ Pham Ngu Lao; r US$17-28;) Located at the central end of Pham Ngu Lao, this is a smart mini-hotel with wooden furnishings. Credit cards accepted.

Orient Hotel (Map p352; ☎ 3920 3993; www.orienthotel.vn; 274 Đ De Tham; r US$17-40;) One of the biggest hotels on De Tham with a whacking 70 rooms, this is teetering towards midrange. Smart rooms, breakfast included, free internet and a lift.

Oh yes, there are more:

Vuong Hoa (Map p352; ☎ 3836 9491; 36 Đ Bui Vien; dm US$3;) Probably the cheapest beds in town. The dorms here feature six beds per room – very simple, very cheap. Downstairs is an internet cafe.

Nga Hoang (Map p352; ☎ 3920 3356; www.yellowhousevn.com; 269/19 Đ Pham Ngu Lao; r US$8-20;) Another of the Yellow House family, this is a friendly place and rates include breakfast.

Bich Duyen Hotel (Map p352; ☎ 3837 4588; bichduyenhotel@yahoo.com; 283/4 Đ Pham Ngu Lao; r US$18-27;) Very friendly place on a popular alley off Pham Ngu Lao, with free internet for guests.

CO GIANG AREA

For a quieter alternative to Pham Ngu Lao, about 10 minutes' walk south, is a string of good guesthouses in the quiet alley connecting Đ Co Giang and Đ Co Bac (Map p346). To reach the guesthouses, walk southwest on Đ Co Bac and turn left after you pass the *nuoc mam* (fish sauce) shops.

Dan Le Hotel (Map p346; ☎ 3836 9651; 171/10 Đ Co Bac; s/d US$11/16;) A smart new minihotel in the midst of these alleys, the Dan Le is cracking value. All rooms include a tidy trim, but it is worth being a VIP for the night for more space. There's also a little roof terrace up top.

our pick **Miss Loi's Guesthouse** (Map p346; ☎ 3837 9589; missloi@hcm.fpt.vn; 178/20 Đ Co Giang; r US$12-25;) The original Co Giang guesthouse. We first crashed here back in 1995 and the homely atmosphere prevails today, although the rooms have definitely been upgraded. Miss Loi is an attentive host with helpful staff and the rates include a light breakfast.

The budget beat goes on:

Ngoc Son (Map p346; ☎ 3836 4717; ngocsonguesthouse@yahoo.com; 178/32 Đ Co Giang; r US$10-15;) Small guesthouse with good value rooms. Motorbikes for hire.

Guest House California (Map p346; ☎ 3837 8885; guesthousecalifornia-saigon@yahoo.com; 171A Đ Co Bac; r US$15-28;) 'Such a lovely place…' or so the Eagles might have said. Intimate, friendly and clean.

Midrange

Although Pham Ngu Lao has traditionally been seen as better value, there are some pretty good deals in the Dong Khoi area, but it is best to book ahead in this desirable part of town.

PHAM NGU LAO

Giant Dragon Hotel (Map p352; ☎ 3836 1935; gd-hotel@hcm.vnn.vn; 173 Đ Pham Ngu Lao; r US$20-30;) Looming large over the nearby bar and restaurant strip, rooms here are good value for money given the extras like bathtubs and hairdryers that mini-hotels just don't have. The US$30 rooms are more like suites, with sofas and city views. Breakfast included.

Lien Ha Hotel (Map p352; ☎ 3837 5582; lienhahotel@yahoo.com; 28/2 Đ Bui Vien; r US$21-42;) Having been merged with the old Ki Hotel, this large place offers 53 rooms with creative decorations in bamboo and paper. Extras include bathrobes, free internet (wired or wireless) and a rooftop pool, one of few in this area.

Spring House Hotel (Map p352; ☎ 3837 8312; www.springhotelvietnam.com; 221 Đ Pham Ngu Lao; r US$22-40;) Furnished in bamboo and rattan, this is a cosy hotel in the middle of the PNL strip. Rooms come in many shapes in sizes, but include the same fundamentals. Friendly spot.

Canadian Hotel 281 (Map p352; ☎ 3837 8666; www.canadianhotel281.multiply.com; 281 Đ Pham Ngu Lao; r US$22-40;) There are only 10 rooms in this cool, crisp (Canadian?) hotel, all with inviting linen and internet connection. Room 201 is a worthy investment.

Lac Vien Hotel (Map p352; ☎ 3920 4899; www.lacvienhotel.com; 28/12 Đ Bui Vien; r US$32-55;) One of the smarter set on Bui Vien, the Lac Vien is popular with well-heeled travellers thanks to the sharp rooms that feature tasteful furnishings, flat-screen TVs and modern bathrooms. Wi-fi included.

Elios Hotel (Map p352; ☎ 3838 5584; www.elioshotel.vn; 233 Đ Pham Ngu Lao; r US$58-100;) This swish new hotel is proof of the continued gentrification of the Pham Ngu Lao area. The rooms are stylish, with silks, a safe and flat-screen TV. Breakfast is included at the rooftop Blue Sky Restaurant, with huge views over Saigon.

More good places:

Ngoc Minh Guesthouse (Map p352; ☎ 3837 6407; www.ngocminh-hotel.com; 283/11 Đ Pham Ngu Lao; r US$20-40;) Bright and friendly guesthouse with rooftop terrace and 24-hour internet access.

Saigon Comfort Hotel (Map p352; ☎ 3837 6516; www.saigoncomfort.com; 175/21 Đ Pham Ngu Lao; r US$30-45;) Smart place with friendly staff, amenities include safety deposit box and free wi-fi.

An An Hotel (Map p352; ☎ 3837 8087; www.anan.vn; 40 Đ Bui Vien; r US$36-45;) Smart, skinny place with businesslike rooms including safety deposit boxes and internet access.

DONG KHOI AREA

If you want to base yourself in the city centre, you'll find a good number of well-appointed hotels along Đ Dong Khoi or near the Saigon River.

our pick **Indochine Hotel** (Map p348; ☎ 3822 0082; www.indochinehotel.com; 40-42 ĐL Hai Ba Trung; r US$30-50, ste US$65;) Location, location, location, you know the old adage. For this price, this place really has it nailed. Formerly the uninspiring Fimex Hotel, it has been given a full facelift and offers smart, creatively decorated rooms in the heart of town.

Spring Hotel (Map p348; ☎ 3829 7362; springhotel@hcm.vnn.vn; 44-46 Đ Le Thanh Ton; s/d incl breakfast from US$36/45;) This is a welcoming hotel just a block away from a whole string of restaurants and bars on the popular Le Thanh Ton strip. The rooms aren't as big as some but make up for it with artful decoration.

King Star Hotel (Map p348; ☎ 3822 6424; kingstarhotelsaigon@yahoo.com.vn; 8A ĐL Thai Van Lung; r US$40-80;) Completely refurbished in 2008, this hotel is now verging on the 'boutique-business' look. The decoration is very contemporary and cool, with all rooms featuring flat-screen TVs and snazzy showers.

Riverside Hotel (Map p348; ☎ 3822 4038; www.riversidehotelsg.com; 18 Đ Ton Duc Thang; s/d from US$59/69;) Blink and you'll miss this place with the Renaissance hotel (p372) looming overhead, but this Riverside delivers excellent value for money for the prime location. The decor is kind of '90s, but surely that will soon be in fashion again?

Northern Hotel (Map p348; ☎ 3825 1751; www.northernhotel.com.vn; 11A Đ Thi Sach; r US$69-129;) Brand new in late 2008, the rooms here are some of the smartest in town for this kind of money. The bathrooms are a cut above average, plus there's a rooftop bar and gym.

Other contenders:

A & Em Hotel (Map p348; ☎ 3824 1695; www.a-emhotels.com; 4A Đ Thi Sach; r US$28-64;) Close to Apocalypse Now (p381) for night owls, this is part of a new chain whose branches are springing up all over town. Affordable style.

Dong Do Hotel (Map p348; ☎ 3827 3637; www.dongdohotel.com; 35 Đ Mac Thi Buoi; r US$30-60;) Central but still quiet, the rooms here feature some ornate woodwork. Suites are huge with corner baths; standard rooms are small.

Huong Sen Hotel (Map p348; ☎ 3829 1415; www.huongsenhotel.com.vn; 66-70 Đ Dong Khoi; s/d from US$58/69;) Long-running government place with great location. Popular with tour groups, so book ahead.

Asian Hotel (Map p348; ☎ 3829 6979; asianhotel@hcm.fpt.vn; 150 Đ Dong Khoi; s/d incl breakfast from US$60/70;) A very central contemporary hotel with three-star standard rooms. Opt for deluxe or suite if you want a view.

DISTRICT 3

Saigon Star Hotel (Map p346; ☎ 930 6290; www.saigonstarhotel.com.vn; 204 Đ Nguyen Thi Minh Khai; r US$50-60;) Although it is slightly showing its age – reflected in the rates – this warrants a mention for families as it has a good location opposite Cong Vien Van Hoa Park. Its rooftop restaurant has fine views of Reunification Palace.

HO CHI MINH CITY

Top End

Most of HCMC's top-notch hotels are concentrated in District 1 and most of these are in the Dong Khoi area. Rates went through the roof during 2007, but may be scaled back. Some won't even publish rates, just offering 'rate of the day'. Most charge an extra 10% tax and 5% service; some don't include breakfast. Check the small print.

Continental Hotel (Map p348; ☎ 3829 9252; www.continentalvietnam.com; 132-134 Đ Dong Khoi; r US$129;) A classic Saigon landmark, the Continental provided the backdrop for much of the action in Graham Greene's novel *The Quiet American*. Originally dating from the turn of the 19th century, the last major renovation unfortunately removed some of the famous features such as the 'Continental shelf' balcony cafe so loved by war correspondents. Rooms are roomy indeed and include wood-panelled ceilings.

Rex Hotel (Map p348; ☎ 3829 2185; www.rexhotelvietnam.com; 141 ĐL Nguyen Hue; r from US$135;) The Rex has recently had an overhaul, propelling it into the five-star bracket, although this may be in part down to generosity towards the government owners Saigon Tourist. Built in 1950, it was once the haunt of US army officers. Rooms are now looking much better than they were, and amenities include a pool and popular rooftop bar.

Caravelle Hotel (Map p348; ☎ 3823 4999; www.caravellehotel.com; 19 Lam Son Sq; r from US$188;) One of the first luxury hotels to re-open its doors in postwar Saigon, the Caravelle still sets a high standard. Rooms are fully decked out and spread over 16 floors. The rooftop Saigon Saigon Bar (p379) is a spectacular place to have a cocktail in the early evening.

our pick Majestic Hotel (Map p348; ☎ 3829 5517; www.majesticsaigon.com.vn; 1 Đ Dong Khoi; r from US$219;) With a pedigree dating back to 1925, this is a venerable place with smart colonial-themed rooms. Dollar for dollar it may not have the best rooms in town, but the 'olde-worlde' atmosphere makes it a romantic option. Take a dip in the courtyard pool on a hot afternoon or take a cocktail on the rooftop bar on a breezy evening. Breakfast and fruit basket included.

Park Hyatt Saigon (Map p348; ☎ 3824 1234; saigon.park.hyatt.com; 2 Lam Son Sq; d from US$260;) Setting the standard as the smartest hotel in Saigon, the Park Hyatt has a prime location opposite the Opera House. The neoclassical structure is as easy on the eye as the lavishly appointed rooms. There's an inviting pool, the acclaimed Xuan Spa, and a highly regarded (yet affordable) Italian restaurant, Opera.

Among many more, these are standouts:

Duxton Hotel (Map p348; ☎ 3822 2999; www.duxton.com.au; 63 Đ Nguyen Hue; r from US$115;) Good value at this end of the range, this smart business hotel is well located for exploring on foot.

Renaissance Riverside Hotel (Map p348; ☎ 3822 0033; reservations@renaissance-saigon.com; 8-15 Đ Ton Duc Thang; d from US$160;) A towering riverside skyscraper with smart rooms and slick service. The cinematic river views are worth the extra dollars.

Sheraton Saigon (Map p348; ☎ 3827 2828; www.sheraton.com/saigon; 88 Đ Dong Khoi; r from US$200;) The Sheraton lives up to expectations with luxurious rooms, an excellent spa, an elegant pool and rooftop bar with 360-degree views.

EATING

Hanoi may have more lakes and colonial charm, but HCMC is the culinary heavyweight of Vietnam. Restaurants here range from dirt-cheap sidewalk stalls to atmospheric villas, each adding a unique twist to traditional Vietnamese flavours. As well as delicious regional fare, Saigon offers a welcoming dose of world cui-

DISH BY DISH: SAIGON'S GREATEST HITS

Trawling through Saigon's food-filled streets for a culinary catch is one of the great pleasures of the Vietnam experience, but with such an array of temptations – and never enough time – the hardest part of an epicurean exploration is knowing where to begin. The following (highly subjective) list includes some of our favourite Vietnamese and foreign bites and where to find them.

For more on great eating in HCMC, visit www.noodlepie.com, an excellent foodie insider's guide to Saigon written by a *bun cha* (rice vermicelli with roasted pork and vegetables)–loving expat. Also check out gastronomyblog.com, an insight on Saigon and Vietnamese cuisine from the resident 'gastronomer'.

- Best *pho* (rice-noodle soup) – **Pho 24** (p374)
- Best *banh xeo* (prawn and pork-filled pancake) – **Banh Xeo 46A** (below)
- Best *bo tung xeo* (grilled beef) – **3T Quan Nuong** (p374)
- Best vegetarian – **Zen** (p377)
- Best fresh seafood – **Ngoc Suong** (p374)
- Best dining for a cause – **Huong Lai** (p374)
- Best street food – the 50-odd stalls of **Ben Thanh Market** (p384)
- Best Indian – **Mumtaz** (p375)
- Best French – **Le Toit Gourmand** (p376)
- Best ice cream – **X Cafe** (p378)
- Best setting for *ca phe sua da* (iced milk coffee) – **Serenata** (p377)

sine, with Indian, Japanese, Thai, French, Italian and East–West fusions well represented.

Good foodie neighbourhoods include the Dong Khoi area, with a concentration of top-quality restaurants, as well as nearby District 3. Pham Ngu Lao's eateries, attempting to satisfy every possible culinary whim, are generally less impressive but good value. Chinese fare rules Cholon, although restaurants here can seem sparser than pagodas on a casual stroll through the area. There are also a few escapes further afield for those willing to undertake the adventure.

English menus are common in most restaurants these days.

Vietnamese

Banh Xeo 46A (Map p346; ☎ 3824 1110; 46A Đ Dinh Cong Trang; mains 20,000-40,000d) Locals will always hit the restaurants that specialise in a single dish and this renowned spot has some of the best *banh xeo* in town. These Vietnamese rice-flour crêpes stuffed with bean sprouts, prawns and pork (vegetarian versions available) are the stuff of legend.

our pick **Quan An Ngon** (Map p348; ☎ 3825 7179; 138 Đ Nam Ky Khoi Nghia; mains 20,000-90,000d; ⏲ lunch & dinner) Always heaving with locals and foreigners alike, this is one of the most popular places in town for the taste of street food in stylish surroundings. Set in a leafy garden ringed by food stalls, each cook serves up a specialised traditional dish, ensuring an authentic taste. Follow your nose and browse the stalls.

Restaurant 13 (Map p348; ☎ 3823 9314; 15 Đ Ngo Duc Ke; mains 30,000-90,000d; ⏲ lunch & dinner) Popular with a generation of adventure-tour leaders, this is one of a handful of numbered eateries in this area that do tasty, no-nonsense Vietnamese favourites.

Mon Hue (Map p352; ☎ 6240 5323; 98 Đ Nguyen Trai; mains 30,000-60,000d; ⏲ lunch & dinner) Hue's cuisine is justly famous beyond the borders of old Annam (the former Chinese name for Vietnam) and was once the preserve of emperors. Mon Hue is an up-and-coming chain of restaurants that offers a good introduction to the cuisine for those who don't make it to the old capital. Open late.

Beefsteak Nam Son (Map p346; 188 Đ Nam Ky Khoi Nghia; mains 30,000-60,000d; ⏲ lunch & dinner) If you are craving a steak and can't afford the fancier places, this is a real bargain. Local steaks, Australian imports and even some cholesterol-friendly ostrich on the menu.

Other good Vietnamese places:

Ban Xeo Muoi Xiem (Map p346; ☎ 3829 6415; 190 D Nam Ky Khoi Nghia; mains 25,000-50,000d; ⏲ lunch &

dinner) Emerging *ban xeo* chain, which does more than 35 varieties, including vegetarian options like mushroom.

PHO SHOPS

Noodle soup is available all day long at street stalls everywhere. A large bowl of delicious beef noodle soup usually costs between 20,000d and 25,000d. Just look for the signs that say '*pho*'.

Pho Quynh (Map p352; 323 Đ Pham Ngu Lao; pho from 25,000d) Occupying a bustling corner on Pham Ngu Lao, this place always seems to be packed with diners and most of them are Vietnamese, which is a good sign. Specialises in *pho bo kho*, a stewlike broth which is delicious.

Pho 24 (Map p352; ☎ 3821 8122; 271 Đ Pham Ngu Lao; mains from 30,000d) It may be the leading noodle-soup chain in the country, but this is no McPho. Choose your cuts of meat and enjoy a steaming bowl accompanied by a veritable jungle of herbs. Plenty of other locations around the city.

Also recommended:

Pho Hoa (Map p346; ☎ 829 7943; 260C Đ Pasteur; *pho* 25,000d) Long-running, highly regarded *pho* shop in District 3.

Pho 2000 (Map p348; ☎ 3822 2788; 1-3 Đ Phan Chu Trinh; pho 30,000d; 🕒 6am-2am) Near Ben Thanh Market, Pho 2000 is where former US president Bill Clinton stopped by for a bowl.

Pho Hung (Map p352; ☎ 3838 5089; 241 Đ Nguyen Trai; pho 30,000d; 🕒 6am-3am) Popular *pho* place, near backpackersville, which is open into the early hours.

FOOD STALLS

Markets always have a side selection of food items, often on the ground floor. Clusters of food stalls can be found in Thai Binh (Map p352), Ben Thanh (p384) and An Dong markets (Map p385).

Sandwiches with a French look and a very Vietnamese taste are sold by street vendors. Fresh baguettes are stuffed with something resembling pâté (don't ask) and cucumbers seasoned with soy sauce. A sandwich costs between 10,000d and 20,000d, depending on the fillings.

Gourmet Vietnamese

Despite the price surge of recent years, the top Vietnamese restaurants are still pretty good value compared with expensive Western capitals. It is still possible to eat very well for around US$15 to US$20, although forget that if you are quaffing the vino. It is advisable to book ahead at all the following places.

our pick **Huong Lai** (Map p348; ☎ 3822 6814; 38 Đ Ly Tu Trong; mains 40,000-120,000d; 🕒 lunch & dinner) Set in the airy loft of an old French-era shophouse, this is dining with a difference. All staff here are from disadvantaged families or are former street children and receive on-the-job training, education and a place to stay. Many have gone on to secure jobs at top hotels and restaurants. A must for beautifully presented traditional Vietnamese food.

Ngoc Suong (Map p346; ☎ 3930 0071; 172H Đ Nguyen Dinh Chieu, District 3; mains 50,000-500,000d; 🕒 lunch & dinner) Ask a sample of well-to-do Saigonese where to go for seafood and the chances are they will recommend Ngoc Suong. So successful has it been that there are now three buildings clustered around the junction of Nguyen Dinh Chieu and Le Quy Don.

Mandarine (Map p348; ☎ 3822 9783; 11A Đ Ngo Van Nam; mains 60,000-250,000d; 🕒 lunch & dinner) Offering a tempting array of dishes from all regions of the country, and traditional music performances that have a calming effect, even with a crowd. The menu includes mouth-watering Hanoi-style *cha ca* (filleted fish slices grilled over charcoal).

Temple Club (Map p348; ☎ 3829 9244; 29 Đ Ton That Thiep; mains 70,000-200,000d; 🕒 lunch & dinner) This classy establishment is housed on the 2nd floor of a stunning colonial-era villa and has been decked out in spiritual motifs. The menu includes delightful dishes such as fish with tamarind or shrimp in coconut milk. The spirited cocktails are a good way to prepare for the experience.

3T Quan Nuong (Map p348; ☎ 3821 1631; 29 Đ Ton That Thiep; mains 70,000-120,000d; 🕒 lunch & dinner) The address look familiar? That is because this breezy barbecue restaurant is set on the rooftop above Temple Club (above). Choose from a range of meat, fish, seafood and vegies and fire it up right there on the table.

Hoa Tuc (Map p348; ☎ 3825 1676; 74/7 ĐL Hai Ba Trung; mains 80,000-240,000d; 🕒 lunch & dinner) A newcomer on the fine Vietnamese dining scene, it is a good place for social butterflies with Vasco's, the Refinery and Vino (see p378) all in the same courtyard.

Xu (Map p348; ☎ 824 8469; 1st fl, 75 Đ Hai Ba Trung; mains 90,000-270,000; 🕒 11.30am-midnight) This super stylish restaurant-lounge serves up a menu of Vietnamese-inspired fusion dishes. The name means coin and it is expensive, but well worth the flutter. Top service, a classy wine list and the happening lounge-bar round things off nicely.

our pick **Sésame** (Map pp344-5; ☎ 3899 3378; triangle ghvn@hcmc.netnam.vn; 153 Đ Xo Viet Nghe Tinh, Binh Thanh district; set meals 100,000-180,000d; 11.30am-2pm Tue-Fri, 7-10pm Fri & Sat) A hospitality training school for disadvantaged children, Sésame was originally set up by the French NGO Triangle Génération Humanitaire. The menu is Franco-Vietnamese, prepared with fresh local ingredients, and dishes are beautifully presented. It is worth the trek out here to experience the attentive service.

Nam Kha (Map p348; ☎ 828 8309; 46 Đ Dong Khoi; mains around 200,000d; lunch & dinner) This is one of Saigon's best-known designer restaurants, quite literally, as it is run by the Khai Silk group. The setting is striking with a reflective pool set amid Romanesque pillars. The menu is all about aromatic Vietnamese flavours.

More gastronomic delights await:

Lemon Grass (Map p348; ☎ 3822 0496; 4 Đ Nguyen Thiep; mains 50,000-100,000d; lunch & dinner) Long-running place over three floors. It can be a bit touristy but many locals still rate the place. Reservations essential.

Hoi An (Map p348; ☎ 823 7694; 11 Đ Le Thanh Ton; mains 70,000-220,000d; lunch & dinner) Under the same ownership as Mandarine, this graceful Chinese-style place has an antique motif and cuisine from central Vietnam.

Other Asian

Asian Kitchen (Map p352; ☎ 3836 7397; 185/22 Đ Pham Ngu Lao; mains 15,000-60,000d) A reliable Pham Ngu Lao cheapie, the menu here includes some Chinese, Indian and Japanese, plus vegetarian options. There is a handful tables outside. Free wi-fi.

My Huong (Map p361; ☎ 3856 3586; 131 Đ Nguyen Tri Phuong; mains 20,000-60,000d; lunch & dinner) When in Chinatown, do as the Chinese do and head to this popular restaurant with all sorts of tasty dishes, including an impressive noodle soup with duck.

Tiem An Nam Long (Map p361; ☎ 3969 4659; 47 Đ Pham Dinh Ho; mains 30,000-50,000d; lunch & dinner) Another Cholon special, this is near Binh Tay Market and has earned a loyal following thanks to its tasty wok-fried dishes. Has an English menu.

Coriander (Map p352; ☎ 3837 1311; 185 Đ Bui Vien; mains 35,000-70,000d; lunch & dinner) It is one of the smaller Thai restaurants in the city, but it punches above its weight with authentic Siamese delights. The green curry is zesty indeed.

our pick **Mumtaz** (Map p352; ☎ 3837 1767; 226 Đ Bui Vien; mains 65,000d; lunch & dinner) It may be a relative newcomer to the city, but everyone is raving about the quality of the curries. Try the succulent fish tikka dishes or a classic like chicken *chettinaad*.

Tandoor (Map p348; ☎ 3930 4839; 74/6 Đ Hai Ba Trung; mains around 70,000d; lunch & dinner) Recently relocated to a prime spot opposite the Park Hyatt, this long-running Indian restaurant serves a good range of North Indian favourites and offers affordable set meals.

Lac Thai (Map p348; ☎ 3823 7506; 71/2 Đ Mac Thi Buoi; meals 100,000d; lunch & dinner) This slither of an alley is earning a name for itself for some good restaurants and this is the Thai contribution, set in a colonial-era house with an unexpected rooftop for romantics.

K Café (Map p348; ☎ 3824 5355; 2 Đ Hai Ba Trung; meals US$5-20; lunch & dinner) Right in the thick of the action, this Japanese restaurant is always brimming with customers. Salmon-skin rolls and fresh sashimi make for a decadent dinner.

Other options:

Giang Nam (Map p361; cnr Đ Tan Hang & Đ Tan Da; mains 25,000d; lunch) The place for noodle soup if you are hankering for some broth in Cholon. There's no menu, just the dish, or two, of the day.

Indian Canteen (Map p348; ☎ 3823 2159; 66 Đ Dong Du; dishes 25,000-50,000d) Cult curries behind the Saigon Central mosque. Meals include iced tea and bananas.

Tan Hai Van (Map p352; ☎ 3925 0824; 162 Đ Nguyen Trai; mains 25,000-75,000d; 24hr) The Chinese place to come if you have an attack of the midnight munchies; it never closes.

Akbar Ali (Map p352; ☎ 3836 4205; 240 Đ Bui Vien; mains around 60,000d; lunch & dinner) Near Mumtaz, this small Indian place is popular with Indian expats, which is always a reliable sign. Friendly service.

Seoul House (Map p348; ☎ 3829 4297; 37 Đ Ngo Duc Ke; mains 50,000-200,000d; lunch & dinner) Follow the (Korean) crowd to this long-running restaurant.

Sushi Bar (Map p346; ☎ 823 8042; 2 Đ Le Thanh Ton; sushi from 50,000d; lunch & dinner) Set on a frenzied intersection; enjoy the show over delicious Japanese bites. Delivery available until 10pm.

French

Unsurprising given its heritage, HCMC has a fine selection of French restaurants, from the casual bistro to haute cuisine.

Le Jardin (Map p348; ☎ 3825 8465; 31 Đ Thai Van Lung; mains from 65,000d; lunch & dinner Mon-Sat) This

CITY ESCAPES

An Phu or District 2 is a very popular quarter with resident expats in Saigon and there are plenty of new places opening up to cater for this affluent crowd. It might feel a bit cliquey if you don't get invited by someone you know, but good places by the river include:

The Deck (☎ 3744 6632; www.thedecksaigon.com; 33 D Nguyen U Di) Stylish riverside place looking more than a touch like FCC Angkor in Siem Reap. Restaurant with fusion flavours and international plates.

River Café (☎ 3744 4111; Riverside Apts, 53 Vo Truong Toan) Another popular riverside place, that is expat-tastic on a Sunday when they have a brunch buffet and live jazz.

place is consistently popular with French expats seeking an escape from the busier boulevards. It has a wholesome bistro-style menu with a shaded terrace cafe in the outdoor garden.

L'En Tete (Map p346; ☎ 3821 4049; 139 Đ Nguyen Thai Binh; mains from 130,000d; 5pm-midnight) Somewhat hidden away from the District 1 action, this 1st-floor restaurant has dishes like sole fillet with tangerine sauce. Live piano or jazz most nights.

La Camargue (Map p346; ☎ 3520 4888; 191 Đ Hai Ba Trung; mains from 180,000d; lunch & dinner) Long one of the grand dames of French dining in Saigon, this place has relocated to a lovely new location with an open plan 1st-floor terrace. The menu includes such home-style cooking as rabbit saddle.

Le Toit Gourmand (Map pp344-5; ☎ 09-0822 5884; 31/4 Đ Hoang Viet, Ward 4 Tan Binh; set meals from US$35; lunch & dinner) This is currently the gastronomic retreat in Saigon, like being invited to the private home of a leading chef. The set menus offer tastings like tuna cerviche, langoustine ravioli or foie gras spring rolls. Divine cheeses and desserts to finish. Mmmm.

Come on, it was French Indochine after all:

Augustin (Map p348; ☎ 3829 2941; 10 Đ Nguyen Thiep; mains from 100,000d; lunch & dinner Mon-Sat) Well-established French bistro-restaurant that remains popular with those in the know.

La Fourchette (Map p348; ☎ 3829 8143; 9 Đ Ngo Duc Ke; mains from US$8; lunch & dinner) Much loved little French restaurant in a central location. The menu includes tender meats.

Le Bordeaux (Map pp344-5; ☎ 3899 9831; 7-8 Đ D2, Binh Than district; mains 150,000-400,000d; lunch & dinner) One of the city's best French restaurants serves delicate scallops, succulent sea bass and other delights.

Au Manoir de Khai (Map p346; ☎ 3930 3394; 251 Đ Dien Bien Phu; mains from US$15; lunch & dinner) It is a touch pretentious, but there is no doubting the pedigree of this five-star place set in a lovely 'manor'.

International Cuisine

Stella (Map p352; ☎ 3836 9220; 119 Đ Bui Vien; mains 35,000-125,000d; lunch & dinner) A class apart from some of the budget places here, this predominantly Italian place has lasagne, gnocchi and pizzas. The coffee is also in the major league.

Pacharan (Map p348; ☎ 3825 6824; 97 Đ Hai Ba Trung; tapas 40,000-150,000d; lunch & dinner) Spread over three floors in one of the most desirable locations in town, Pacharan bites include succulent chorizo, marinated anchovies and chillied *gambas*, plus some more substantial mains like an authentic paella for two. The rooftop terrace is a great place to sample some Spanish wine.

Warda (Map p348; ☎ 3824 1374; 71/7 Đ Mac Thi Buoi; 50,000-235,000d; 11am-midnight) Suitably located in a medinalike alley off Mac Thi Buoi, this is a chic place with sensuous flavours from Morocco to Persia. Lamb and prune tagine, sizzling kebabs, it's all here, including the inevitable shishas for an after-dinner puff.

On the 6 (Map p348; ☎ 3823 8866; 6 Đ Dong Khoi; light bites US$3-17; lunch & dinner) Set in a spacious property on Dong Khoi, this is the place to try tapas teasers from famous chef Didier Corlou. The bites are delicious and affordable. Upstairs in the restaurant, they are very (think elite Paris) expensive.

Skewers (Map p348; ☎ 3829 2216; 8A/1/D2 Đ Thai Van Lung; mains US$5-18; lunch & dinner) The Mediterranean menu here takes in all stops from the Maghreb to Marseilles, with the accent on … skewers. It's an atmospheric place with an open-plan kitchen, and usually draws a crowd.

La Hostaria (Map p348; ☎ 3823 1080; 17B Đ Le Thanh Ton; pizzas 110,000-180,000d; lunch & dinner) A homely trattoria-style place, this is a nice place to immerse yourself in Italian cuisine. The risottos include salmon and caviar, plus fish specials such as scallop and artichoke skewers. Delivery available.

Zan Z Bar (Map p348; ☎ 3822 7375; 41 Đ Dong Du; meals US$6-22; ⏲ 10.30am-midnight) An ultrahip diner on Dong Du, this place has quickly generated a buzz thanks to its Pacific-Rim fusion cuisine. Try chilli crab noodles or the excellent pita pizzas. Definitely one of the 'in' places.

Cepage (Map p348; ☎ 3823 8733; Lancaster Bldg, 22 Đ Le Thanh Ton; mains 150,000-350,000d; ⏲ lunch & dinner) An impressive addition to the international dining scene, Cepage is a trendy wine bar with a lounge downstairs and a serious foodie place upstairs. Try the 'black box' – a mystery three-course set lunch for 130,000d.

Au Lac do Brasil (Map p346; ☎ 3820 7157; 238 Đ Pasteur; set dinner 390,000d; ⏲ lunch & dinner) For a taste (and then some) of Brazil, head to Au Lac. Decked out with Carnaval-themed paintings, this *churrascaria* (barbecue restaurant) serves all-you-can-eat steak (and 11 other cuts of meat), just like back in Rio. Plus a new à la carte menu.

And some more:

Falafellim (Map p352; ☎ 3915 1733; 97 Đ Pham Ngu Lao; falafels around 40,000d; ⏲ 10am-10pm) Friends of the falafel should make their way here, a hole-in-the-wall fast food–style place with bargain bites.

Mogambo (Map p348; ☎ 3825 1311; 50 Đ Pasteur; mains 50,000-100,000d; ⏲ lunch & dinner) Some residents swear this place has the best burgers in town. A good menu of Tex-Mex and Americana.

Gartenstadt (Map p348; ☎ 3822 3623; 34 Đ Dong Khoi; set lunch 99,000d; ⏲ 10.30am-midnight) A long-running German place with good-value set lunches and home-made sausages.

Backpacker Cafes

Western backpackers tend to easily outnumber the Vietnamese on Đ Pham Ngu Lao and Đ De Tham, which is the axis of HCMC's budget-eatery haven.

Café Zoom (Map p352; 169A Đ De Tham; mains 30,000-70,000d; ⏲ breakfast, lunch & dinner) Paying homage to the classic Vespa, this buzzing place has a great location for watching the world go by. The menu includes great burgers with original toppings, plus a mix of Italian and Vietnamese favourites.

Chi's Cafe (Map p352; ☎ 3920 4874; 40/27 Đ Pham Ngu Lao; mains 30,000-70,000d; ⏲ breakfast, lunch & dinner) Close by is Chi's, one of the better budget cafes in the area with big breakfasts, Western favourites and some local dishes.

Bread & Butter (Map p352; ☎ 3836 8452; 40/24 Đ Pham Ngu Lao; mains 40,000-70,000d) Tiny place on hotel alley that is popular with resident English teachers. The pub food includes staples like fish and chips, pies and burgers.

Among many more, standouts these are:

Kim Cafe (Map p352; ☎ 836 8122; 268 Đ De Tham; mains 20,000-50,000d; ⏲ breakfast, lunch & dinner) One of the original cafes here. The prices are still extremely reasonable and the food reliable.

Margherita (Map p352; ☎ 3837 0760; 175/1 Đ Pham Ngu Lao; mains 20,000-80,000d) Another golden oldie, this place turns out Vietnamese, Italian and Mexican food at a steal.

Vegetarian

The largest concentration of vegetarian restaurants is around the Pham Ngu Lao area. On the first and 15th days of the lunar month, food stalls around the city, especially in the markets, serve vegetarian versions of meaty Vietnamese dishes. While these stalls are quick to serve, they're usually swamped on these special days. Be patient, as it's worth the wait.

Dinh Y (Map p352; ☎ 3836 7715; 171B Đ Cong Quynh; mains from 15,000d) Run by a friendly Cao Dai family, this is in a very 'local' part of Pham Ngu Lao near Thai Binh Market. The food is delicious and cheap, plus there's an English menu.

Zen (Map p352; ☎ 3837 3713; 185/30 Đ Pham Ngu Lao; mains 20,000-45,000d) It has been in various locations down the years, but the food at this place is consistently good and cheap. From braised mushrooms in claypot to fried tofu with chilli and lemongrass, the menu is packed with goodness.

More vegie action:

Tin Nghia (Map p348; ☎ 3821 2538; 9 ĐL Tran Hung Dao; mains from 15,000d; ⏲ 7am-8.30pm) Opposite Ben Thanh Market, the setting is simple, but the Buddhist owners turn out some traditional treats.

Phap Hoa (Map p352; 9 Đ Nguyen Trai; mains from 20,000d) Another vegetarian place, this one near Thai Binh Market. It's always heaving at lunchtime.

Cafes, Bakeries & Ice Cream

All the following places offer free wi-fi these days.

Serenata (Map p346; ☎ 3930 7436; 6D Đ Ngo Thoi Thien; ⏲ 7.30am-10pm Mon-Sat) Down the same lively alley as the happening Acoustic Bar (p379), this grand house is the perfect setting for a coffee. The garden is scattered with tables around a pond-filled courtyard, making it a romantic retreat. It also features occasional live music.

Sozo (Map p352; ☎ 09-8972 2468; 176 Đ Bui …30am-10pm Mon-Sat) A classy little cafe in th… …get end of town, the attractions here include cultured coffee, doughy cinnamon rolls, home-made cookies and other sweet treats. Best of all, the cafe trains and employs poor, disadvantaged Vietnamese. Use the free wi-fi to spread the word.

Bobby Brewers (Map p352; ☎ 3610 2220; 45 Đ Bui Vien) This is a contemporary cafe set over three floors, and the range of coffees here is professional. There are also juices, sandwiches, pastas and salads, plus movies upstairs.

Fanny (Map p348; ☎ 3821 1633; 29-31 Đ Ton That Thiep) Set in the lavish French villa that houses Temple Club (p374), Fanny creates excellent Franco-Vietnamese ice cream in a healthy range of tropical-fruit flavours, including durian and lychee.

Centro Caffe (Map p348; ☎ 3827 5946; 11-13 Lam Son Sq) Just about as central as it gets, this place has original Italian coffee in every shape and size. There is also a menu of Italian food.

Gloria Jean's Coffee (Map p348; ☎ 3822 3966; 131 Đ Dong Khoi) While it is kind of strange to recommend an Australian coffee chain to Vietnam first-timers, this is the historic Brodard Café, immortalised by Graham Greene in *The Quiet American*.

Java Coffee Bar (Map p348; ☎ 3823 0187; 38-42 Đ Dong Du; 🕓 7.30am-midnight) This stylish corner cafe has hard-hitting espressos and silken smoothies, not forgetting some of the comfiest lounge chairs around.

Himiko Arts Café (Map pp344-5; www.himikokoro.com; 324B Đ Dien Bien Phu; 🕓 10am-11pm) Run by a Vietnamese artist who trained in Japan, this place occasionally falls foul of the artistically staid authorities. A coffee shop and gallery combined, these are unusual surroundings for a drink.

X Café (Map p348; ☎ 3914 2142; 53 Đ Pasteur) Set in a lovely old colonial-era villa, downstairs is cool and minimalist, and upstairs has sofas and balconies with regular films. X also marks the spot for one of the strongest Long Island Iced Teas in town, served in a disturbingly tall glass.

Cafe culture is big in Saigon:

Casbah (Map p348; ☎ 090 555 9468; 57 Đ Nguyen Du) Hidden away down an alley near the main post office, this is an attractive setting for a coffee or a cocktail.

Ciao Café (Map p348; ☎ 3823 1130; 74 Đ Nguyen Hue; 🕓 7.30am-10pm) This is a grand place to sip coffee and while away some time while admiring the wooden interior and tiled floors.

Givral (Map p348; ☎ 3829 2747; 169 Đ Dong Khoi) A landmark place that has fine views towards the Opera House and the busy junction.

Highlands Coffee (Map p348; Lam Son Sq) Part of a successful nationwide chain, this garden branch sits behind the Opera House.

Juice (Map p348; ☎ 3829 6900; 49 Đ Mac Thi Buoi) Tardis-like, this small shopfront is set over four floors with fresh juices and smoothies plus healthy snacks.

La Fenetre de Soleil (Map p348; ☎ 3822 5209; 135 Đ Le Thanh Ton) Housed on the 2nd floor of an old French house, this bohemian hideaway includes a four-poster bed. Juices, shakes, coffees and ice cream.

Self-Catering

The city's markets and street stalls are a great place to assemble a fresh meal. If you don't feel like going anywhere, **Chez Guido** (☎ 3898 3747; www.chezguido.com; mains 30,000-150,000d; 🕓 9am-11pm) is the *tour de force* of take outs. The menu offers a mind-boggling cornucopia of international cuisine but specialises in Italian food. Download a menu online.

Two big supermarkets near Pham Ngu Lao are **Hanoi Mart** and **Co-op Mart** (Map p352; Đ Cong Quynh), just down the street from each other.

Other places to try:

Annam Gourmet Shop (Map p348; 16 Đ Hai Ba Trung; 🕓 9am-8pm) A small but high-class shop stocking imported cheeses, wines, chocolates and all the other delicacies you won't find elsewhere.

Hong Hoa Mini-Market (Map p352; Hong Hoa Hotel, 185/28 Đ Pham Ngu Lao; 🕓 9am-8pm) Small but packed with toiletries, alcohol and Western junk food, such as chocolate bars.

Veggy's (Map p348; 15 Đ Thai Van Lung; 🕓 9am-8pm) Carries a quality selection of imported foods, wine and sauces, as well as fresh produce and frozen meats.

DRINKING

Wartime Saigon was known for its riotous nightlife. Liberation in 1975 put a real dampener on the fun and games, but the pubs and clubs are well and truly back in business. However, periodic 'crack-down, clean-up' campaigns – allegedly to control drugs, prostitution and excessive noise – continue to keep the city's nightlife on the early side for a city of this size.

Pubs & Bars

Happening HCMC is concentrated around the Dong Khoi area, with everything from dive pubs to designer bars. However, places in this area often close around 1am, as they are under the watchful gaze of the local authorities. Pham Ngu Lao rumbles on into the wee hours.

DONG KHOI AREA & CENTRAL HCMC

One area that is particularly easy to browse is the courtyard off 74 Hai Ba Trung, where there are several lively spots, including the newly located **Vasco's** (Map p348; ☎ 3824 2888; 74/7D ĐL Hai Ba Trung). Long one of the hippest places in town, the recipe remains the same with great drinks, pool tables and bar food, plus DJs and events.

Almost next door are a couple more lively places: **Vino** (Map p348; ☎ 3299 1315; 74/17 ĐL Hai Ba Trung) is the inviting shop window for a leading wine importer so always has a great selection of tipples, while **The Refinery** (Map p348; ☎ 3823 0509; 74/7C ĐL Hai Ba Trung) is more of a bistro-bar with good cocktails and appetising snacks.

Underground (Map p348; ☎ 3829 9079; 69 Đ Dong Khoi; 🕑 10am-midnight) Going Underground? Expats commute here after work, drawn to the familiar tube sign that lights the way to the perennial draft-beer happy hour and top bar food.

Sheridan's Irish House (Map p348; ☎ 3823 0793; 17/13 Đ Le Thanh Ton; 🕑 11am-late) This is a pretty authentic Irish pub for anyone yearning for the Emerald Isle. It recently doubled in size, but remains cozy and serves a dangerous selection of Irish whiskies plus good pub grub.

Voodoo (Map p348; ☎ 3915 2836; 92 Đ Ho Tung Mau) Surely a candidate for the longest bar in town, this friendly spot in the centre of town serves some regional beers like Huda and generous measures. Has classic indie anthems on the MP3, plus a couple of dart boards.

Lush (Map p346; ☎ 09-1863 0742; 2 Đ Ly Tu Trong) The decor is very manga here, with cool graphics plastering the walls. This place draws a mixed crowd that lounges around the central bar to people watch. Features heavy beats, regular DJs and some pool tables hidden out the back.

Alibi (Map p348; ☎ 3822 3240; 11 Đ Thai Van Lung) A happening lounge-bar with Latin grooves, Alibi (ala-bee for French speakers) is reasonably priced for the style factor. Regular late-night events, plus a French bistro menu.

our pick **Acoustic Bar** (Map p346 ☎ 3930 2239; 6E1 Đ Ngo Thoi Nhiem) The leading live-music venue in town, Acoustic pays homage to Jimi Hendrix, John Lennon and other rock 'n' roll legends. Vietnam's leading musicians flock here for cameo cover versions and, judging by the numbers that turn up nightly, the crowd just can't get enough.

Yoko (Map p346; ☎ 3933 0577; 22A Đ Nguyen Thi Dieu) Another place to appreciate some live music, the blend here could be anything from indie rock to country and western, and kicks off around 9pm nightly. Small stage, comfy chairs and revolving art-works keep it cool.

Q Bar (Map p348; ☎ 3823 3479; 7 Lam Son Sq) The mother of all trendy nightspots in HCMC, Q Bar seems to have been around almost as long as the Opera House. An enduring and endearing spot, it pulls the beautiful people thanks to hip music and sophisticated decor. It's on the side of the Municipal Theatre, across from the Caravelle Hotel.

Bars, bars and more bars:

Blue Gecko Bar (Map p348; ☎ 3824 3483; 31 Đ Ly Tu Trong) Popular Aussie bar with seriously cold beer, regular music, pool tables and plenty of screens for sport.

DRINKS WITH A VIEW

See the city in style from a rooftop bar, while sipping a frozen margarita. It's well worth the extra dong to enjoy the frenetic pace of life on the streets from a lofty vantage point. Among our favourite spots at sunset:

Caravelle Hotel (p372; 🕑 11am-late) One of the first high-rise bars to open, Saigon Saigon has great views and some alfresco tables. No more happy hour, but live music.

Majestic Hotel (p372; 🕑 4pm-midnight) This is a great spot for a sundowner, as the top-floor Bellevue Bar has a panoramic view of the river and a certain colonial-era cachet.

Rex Hotel (p372; 🕑 4-11pm) The Rex wins the kitsch award, with its plaster animals, empty birdcages and various other tat, but the view over Le Loi is superb.

Sheraton Saigon (p372; 🕑 4pm-midnight) The highest of the downtown bars, this is a great place to see the sheer size of HCMC. Last stop 23rd floor, with live music and food.

Windsor Plaza Hotel (Map p361; ☎ 3833 6688; 18 Đ An Duong Vuong, District 5; 🕑 5-11pm) For a reverse angle, try the 24th floor of this Cholon hotel, where the 360-degree views put the downtown in perspective.

MOTORBIKE MADNESS

Home to a passionate, if practical motorbike culture, HCMC has some energising vantage points from which to watch the endless procession of passing two-wheelers. The Dong Khoi area is a particularly fine place to be on weekend and holiday nights, when the streets fill with cruisers of all ages and styles. Everyone's dressed to impress, with two, three or four packed to a bike, and you can almost taste the electricity in the air (or are those fumes?) as the young and restless check each other out through the handlebars of their matching Honda Futures. The mass of slow-rolling humanity is so thick on Đ Dong Khoi that crossing the street is like moving (cautiously, mind you; see p506 for tips!) through a swarm of honeybees. Despite the apparent chaos of 10 or more lanes of traffic hurtling toward each other at each intersection, most of the time the swarms part and the motorbikes glide smoothly around each other like a choreographed pageant.

Even if you don't want to join the parade, you can still bag some great seats to the nightly streetside spectacle. Here are some of our favourite places in town to catch the action (which is far better than TV – and most organised sporting events for that matter).

- **Highlands Coffee** (Map p348) Without a doubt, one of the most buzzing motorbike vantage points in the country.
- **Traffic circle** (Map p346; cnr Pham Ngoc Thach & Tran Cao Van) This huge landmark roundabout is ringed with cafes and restaurants, and there's never a dull moment on the road.
- **Cyclo Bar** On the ground floor of the Majestic Hotel (Map p348), Cyclo Bar is one of the fancier places to keep the motor running.
- **Café Zoom** (Map p352) Dedicated to the original HCMC motorbike, the Vespa, this friendly cafe has top views of a city in motion.
- **Pho 2000** (Map p348) Pho fit for a president with big views to Ben Thanh Market and the Le Loi junction.

Café Latin (Map p348; ☎ 3822 6363; 19 Đ Dong Du) Strange name for a sports bar, but it works thanks to a central location, some big, big screens and a loyal following.

Cantina Central (Map p348; ☎ 3914 4697; 51 Đ Ton That Thiep) Primarily a Mexican restaurant, but this also means they stir up the best frozen margaritas in town.

Hoa Vien (Map p346; ☎ 3829 0585; 28 Đ Mac Dinh Chi) An unexpected find in the backstreets of HCMC, this Czech restaurant brews up fresh pilsner daily.

Kool Beer Store (Map p348; 177 Đ Ham Nghi) Beers come in every shape and size here, not to mention shade. A veritable beer emporium.

Velvet (Map p348; ☎ 3823 3978; 26 Đ HH Nghiep) This glam lounge-bar remains popular with Vietnamese movers and shakers thanks to DJs and promotions.

PHAM NGU LAO

When it comes to nightlife, the Pham Ngu Lao area has several buzzing spots, in addition to the traveller cafes that often draw a lingering crowd.

Le Pub (Map p352; ☎ 3837 7679; www.lepub.org; 175/22 Đ Pham Ngu Lao) The name sums it up perfectly, British pub meets French cafe-bar, and the result is popular with expats and travellers alike. An extensive beer list, nightly promotions, cocktail jugs and pub grub draw them in.

Allez Boo Bar (Map p352; ☎ 3837 2505; 187 Đ Pham Ngu Lao) Long the leading backpacker drinking den in this area, it has relocated across the road and gone ever-so-slightly more upmarket, but not much. A merry-go-round of punters and late-night action upstairs ensures its popularity.

Eden (Map p352; ☎ 3836 8154; 185/22 Đ De Tham) A popular bar-restaurant with red lanterns over the bar (no, not those sort of red lights), the friendly staff are dressed in traditional *ao dai*. Late drinks, plus a huge food menu.

Other bars here:

Long Phi (Map p352; 325 Đ Pham Ngu Lao) One of the PNL originals, this French-run bar stays open late and sometimes hosts live bands.

Santa Café (Map p352; cnr Đ Bui Vien & Đ Do Quang Dau) Tiny little bar-restaurant on a lively corner. There is cheap beer and a predominantly Italian menu.

ENTERTAINMENT

Pick up *The Word HCMC*, *Asialife HCMC* or *The Guide* to find out what's on during your stay in Saigon. Monthly listings include art shows, live music and theatre performances happening around town. You can also stop by the Opera House (p359) to see what's on, as it often stages worthwhile plays, and musical and dance performances.

Binh Quoi Tourist Village (off Map pp344-5; ☎ 3899 1831, dinner cruise bookings 829 8914; www.binhquoiresort.com.vn; 1147 Đ Xo Viet Nghe Tinh, Binh Thanh district; boat rides 25,000-75,000d, dinner adult/child 140,000/80,000d; 11am-2pm & 5-8pm Sun & holidays, buffet dinner 5-8pm Sat) This 'village' is actually a full-on resort run by Saigon Tourist, with boat rides, water-puppet shows, tennis courts and amusements for the kids. The weekend buffet dinner, with a dazzling variety of traditional Vietnamese regional specialities, is served along a canal lit with floating lanterns and accompanied by live traditional music. Call ahead for the latest schedule of performances.

If you don't mind getting carted around on a tour package, the dinner cruises can be fun and are followed by a traditional music or water-puppet performance at the village. The park also puts in a plug for Vietnam's ethnic minorities by staging their traditional weddings accompanied by folk music.

Binh Quoi Tourist Village is 8km north of central HCMC. You can get here by taxi (around 80,000d).

Bonsai River Cruise (Map p348; ☎ 3910 5095; www.bonsaicruise.com.vn) Set onboard a wooden dragon boat, the Bonsai offers a range of river cruises with lunch, dinner or a sundowner. They even offer a floating cooking course for something different. Dinner shows include live music, which makes a real night of it.

Maxim's Dinner Theatre (Map p348; ☎ 829 6676; 15 Đ Dong Khoi; 11am-11pm) Something of a Saigon legend, located next to the Majestic Hotel, this supper club is better recommended for its music performances than for the food. The menu offers Vietnamese, Chinese and Western dishes, including the adventurous sea slug. The live music includes everything from Vietnamese folk music to slow smoochy tunes. Reservations are recommended.

Cinemas

There are plenty of international-standard cinemas *(rap)* in the city centre, several of which show English-language blockbusters.

Popular cinemas:

Diamond Plaza Cinema (Map p348; ☎ 3825 7751; Diamond Plaza, 34 Đ Le Duan) Three screens with films in original language plus Vietnamese subtitles.

Galaxy Cinema (Map p352; ☎ 3920 6688; 230 Đ Nguyen Trai) One of the best in town, near Pham Ngu Lao.

Institute of Cultural Exchange with France (Idecaf) (Map p348; ☎ 3829 5451; 31 Đ Thai Van Lung) Screens French-language films.

Nightclubs

Most of the following dance clubs don't really warm up until after 10pm; ask around popular bars about the latest greatest places.

Apocalypse Now (Map p348; ☎ 3824 1463; 2C Đ Thi Sach) Others have come and gone, but 'Apo' has been around since the early days and remains one of the must-see clubs. A sprawling place with a big dance floor and an outdoor courtyard for cooling off, it's quite a circus, with travellers, expats, Vietnamese movers and shakers, plus the odd hooker (some odder than others). The music is thumping and it's apocalyptically rowdy.

Cage (Map p348; 3A Đ Ton Duc Thang) Arguably the most international of clubs in town right now, Cage is set in an old warehouse near the Saigon Legend Hotel. Its sleek decor and guest DJs make this a good place for a big night out.

GAY & LESBIAN HO CHI MINH CITY

Though there are few openly gay venues in town, HCMC's popular bars and clubs are generally gay-friendly. Most of the bars in the Pham Ngu Lao area can be considered gay-friendly in the sense that the crowd is mostly international travellers. In the Dong Khoi area, Lush (p379) attracts a good, mixed crowd with heavy beats, but it doesn't have a dance floor. Apocalypse Now (above) attracts a small gay contingent among an otherwise straight crowd, with loud anthems and a spacious dance floor. **Samsara** (Map p348; ☎ 3862 2630; 2nd fl, 131 Đ Dong Khoi), above the Brodard Café (now Gloria Jean's) is a mainly gay affair, with waiters in shirtless vests, good DJs and an action-packed dance floor. Friday and Saturday nights are the times to go.

A word of warning regarding masseurs: masseurs travel on bicycle through the streets of Pham Ngu Lao area, rattling a small bell to announce their services. They often offer cheap massages along with other services, but some of them try to extort money afterwards. As things can sometimes get nasty, it's best to avoid them altogether.

Go2 (Map p352; ☎ 3836 9575; 187 Đ De Tham) For all-night action, go to this little club located above a street-level bar. It attracts a fun crowd of drunks and dancers thanks to the party atmosphere. Upstairs is a rooftop bar to cool off or retreat from the smoke.

Rave on:

Butterfly (Map p346; 96 Đ Nguyen Thi Minh Khai) Lively local nightclub on the junction with Pasteur that is packed by the midnight hour.

Gossip Club (Map p352; ☎ 3824 2602; 79 Đ Tran Hung Dao) Housed in the Dai Nam Hotel, this long-running club heats up at the weekend, when expats and locals come out to play.

Theatre

Conservatory of Music (Nhac Vien Thanh Pho Ho Chi Minh; Map p346; ☎ 3824 3774; 112 Đ Nguyen Du; performances 7.30pm Mon-Fri Mar-May & Oct-Dec) Performances of both traditional Vietnamese and Western classical music are held at the conservatory, near Reunification Palace.

The city's Opera House (p359) is also known as the Municipal Theatre (but Opera House is so much more romantic). There are weekly programs, such as Eastern European-style gymnastics, classical music or traditional Vietnamese theatre. Performances typically begin at 8pm.

Saigon Race Track

Saigon Race Track (Cau Lac Bo The Thao Phu To; Map pp344-5; ☎ 3855 1205; 2 Đ Le Dai Hanh, District 11; admission 10,000d; noon-4pm Sat & Sun) When South Vietnam was liberated in 1975, one of the Hanoi government's policies was to ban debauched, capitalistic pastimes such as gambling. Horse-racing tracks – mostly found in the Saigon area – were shut down. However, the government's need for hard cash caused a rethink and the track re-opened in 1989.

Like the state lottery, the track has proven extremely lucrative. But grumbling about where the money is going has been coupled with widespread allegations about the drugging of horses. The minimum legal age for jockeys is 14 years; many look like they're pushing 10.

The overwhelming majority of gamblers are Vietnamese, as this is one of the few legal forms of gambling. There is no rule prohibiting foreigners from joining in the fun of risking their dong. The minimum legal bet is 10,000d and, for the high rollers hoping to become a dong billionaire, the sky's the limit. Form guides are available for 3000d for those who are serious about their bets.

It is all slightly surreal and can add another angle to the Saigon experience. A taxi from downtown will cost about 70,000d.

Water Puppets

Although it originates in the north, the art has migrated to HCMC in the last decade – in part because of its popularity with tourists. The main venue to see this art form is the **Golden Dragon Water Puppet Theatre** (Map p346; ☎ 3930 2196; www.goldendragonwaterpuppet.com; 55B Nguyen Thi Minh Khai; entry 50,000d). Shows start at 6.30pm and 8pm and last about 50 minutes.

It is also possible to see the puppets, rather incongruously, at the War Remnants Museum (p354; admission 30,000d) and at the History Museum (p355; admission 30,000d). Schedules vary, but shows tend to start when a group of five or more customers has assembled. Expect a 20-minute show, performed by skilled and imaginative puppeteers.

SHOPPING

HCMC's teeming streets are like the Elysian Fields for intrepid shopping souls. While there's much junk being peddled to the tourist masses, there are also plenty of great discoveries just waiting to be unearthed. The hunting grounds include sprawling markets, antique stores, silk and fabric boutiques and speciality stores selling ceramics, ethnic fabrics, lacquered bamboo and custom-made clothing. And although the art scene is better up north, HCMC has a growing number of galleries selling everything from lavish oil paintings to photographs and vintage propaganda posters.

There are also the quirkier gems like miniature *cyclos*, and helicopters made from beer and soda cans – one place to browse for these is at the War Remnants Museum (p354) gift shop.

The best place to begin any shopping journey is the gallery- and boutique-lined Đ Dong Khoi and the streets that intersect with it. This is also the place to look for high-quality handicrafts. Better deals can be found in Pham Ngu Lao, although the selection is less extensive. If you're pressed for time, several shopping centres are reliable one-stop destinations, including the sleek, high-end **Diamond Plaza** (Map p348; 34 Đ Le Duan); the popular **Parkson Plaza** (Map p348; 41-45 Đ Le Thanh Ton) with clothing and cosmetics; and the inspiringly named (and cheaper) **Tax Department Store** (Map p348; cnr Đ Nguyen Hue & Đ Le Loi).

One thing worth remembering for those coming on a shorter break is that Vietnam manufactures a lot of rucksacks, suitcases and other expensive forms of luggage, all of which are available in Saigon very cheaply. There are shops all over District 1 stocking Lowe Alpine, North Face, Samsonite and more, mostly original and way cheaper than back home. So don't worry about too much shopping, just buy another bag.

Arts & Handicrafts

Blue Dragon (Map p352; 222 Đ De Tham) Popular souvenir store in Pham Ngu Lao, which stocks objets d'art made from recycled motorbike parts, among other things.

Dogma (Map p348; ☎ 3822 7318; 29A Dong Khoi; 9am-10pm) This little store stocks reproduction propaganda posters and has emblazoned them on coffee mugs, coasters and T-shirts. Several branches around the city.

Mai Handicrafts (Map pp344-5; ☎ 3844 0988; maivn@hcm.vnn.vn; 298 Đ Nguyen Trong Tuyen, Tan Binh district) Fair-trade shop dealing in ceramics, ethnic fabrics and other gift items which, in turn, support disadvantaged families and street children.

Nguyen Freres (Map p348; 2 Đ Dong Khoi) Stocks a lovely assortment of antique furnishings and textiles, pillowcases, silks, pottery and lamps.

Vietnam Quilts (Map p348; ☎ 3825 1441; www.vietnam-quilts.org; 26/1 Đ Le Thanh Ton) Hidden away down an alley opposite Sheridan's, this is the place to buy handmade quilts, sewn by the rural poor, in support of a sustainable income.

Clothing

Saigon is fast emerging as a stylish stop in Southeast Asia. There are plenty of places where you can shop for chic apparel or opt for a custom-made *ao dai*, the couture symbol of Vietnam. This quite flattering outfit of silk tunic and trousers is tailored at shops in and around Ben Thanh Market and around the Rex and Continental Hotels. There are also male *ao dai* available, which are a looser fit and come with a silk-covered head wrap to match.

Cham Khanh (Map p346; ☎ 3820 6861; 256 Đ Pasteur, District 3) This is one of several *ao dai* shops on this stretch of Đ Pasteur. It sells particularly colourful pieces and is a reliable place for getting an *ao dai* made.

The Dong Khoi neighbourhood is awash with tempting shops selling contemporary clothing. Some will also custom-tailor clothing and shoes, and turnaround usually takes a few days. A survey of the neighbourhood around Đ Pasteur and Đ Le Thanh Ton yields at least two dozen boutiques; Đ Dong Khoi and Đ Ngo Duc Ke or Đ Dong Du reveal yet more.

Souvenir T-shirts are prevalent in town, with bargain deals available from vendors along ĐL Le Loi in the city centre, or Đ De Tham in the Pham Ngu Lao area. Prices start at US$2 for a printed T-shirt and US$5 for an embroidered one.

Original clothing stores:

Chi Chi (Map p348; ☎ 3824 7812; 138 Đ Pasteur) Designer shop with classy fabrics and fine designs; custom-tailoring offered here.

Chle (Map p346; ☎ 3912 0162; 138 Đ Nguyen Dinh Chieu) Another designer silk store specialising in clothing for women, plus a range of homewares and accessories.

Dolezza House (Map p346; ☎ 3821 7724; 26A Đ Le Quy Don) Fun and funky fashion for women here, plus some accessories, and there's a little cafe to mull over the best buys.

Gaya (Map p352; ☎ 3925 1495; 1 Đ Nguyen Van Trang) Designer lifestyle shop and gallery that includes Romyda Keth's collection, a leading Cambodian-French designer from this region.

Khai Silk (Map p348; ☎ 3829 1146; 107 Đ Dong Khoi) This is one of many branches in HCMC of this nationwide silk empire. Expensive but high quality.

CARVED SEALS

One item found in every self-respecting bureaucrat's desk is a carved seal. Indeed, no functioning administrator, communist or otherwise, can exist without the official stamps and seals that are the raison d'être for legions of clerks. This need is well-catered for by the shops strung out along the street just north of the New World Hotel (opposite side of ĐL Ham Nghi and just west of Ben Thanh Market). In Cholon you can find shops making these seals along Đ Hai Thuong Lan Ong.

Most Vietnamese also own carved seals bearing their name (an old tradition borrowed from China). You can have one made, too, but ask a local to help translate your name into Vietnamese. You might want to get your seal carved in Cholon using Chinese characters; these are certainly more artistic (though less practical) than the romanised script used by the Vietnamese today.

THIS COFFEE TASTES LIKE...

Vietnamese coffee is some of the most popular around and is exported all over the world. It is also a pretty good buy for lovers of the bean. The best grades are from Buon Ma Thuot and the beans are roasted in butter. Lovers of weasels and strange things should get their hands on *ca phe chon* ('weasel coffee', No 8 of the signature Trung Nguyen brand). These coffee beans are fed to weasels first, then harvested from their droppings before being sold to you. Brew and enjoy.

Some of the city's major markets are a good place to browse, although Ben Thanh Market (Map right), is more expensive than most.

Sapa (Map p352; ☎ 3836 5163; 223 Đ De Tham) Small store incorporating ethnic fabrics and designs with modern styling; also sells gifts and jewellery.

Song (Map p348; ☎ 3824 6986; 76D Đ Le Thanh Ton) A central boutique that specialises in sophisticated linens and cottons for men and women.

Galleries

HCMC is brimming with art galleries. Good places to browse are the handful of galleries around the Fine Arts Museum (p356) and along Đ Dong Khoi. You'll find excellent top-quality works at the following places: **Blue Space Gallery** (Map p348; ☎ 3821 3695; 1A Đ Le Thi Hong Gam; 9am-6pm), **Lacquer & Oil** (Map p348; ☎ 3821 2320; 97A Đ Pho Duc Chinh; 9am-5.30pm) and **Vinh Loi Gallery** (Map p346; ☎ 930 5006; www.galerievinhloi.com; 41 Đ Ba Huyen Thanh Quan, District 3; 9am-6pm). Any of these places will ship worldwide. For low-quality reproductions of famous paintings, visit the painting shops along Đ Bui Vien (Map p352) in Pham Ngu Lao.

Galerie Quynh (Map p346; ☎ 3836 8019; www.galeriequynh.com; 65 Đ De Tham) Don't turn around thinking you have missed this place, as it is located in a very backstreet part of town. This is one of the best-known galleries in the city – probably *the* place for Vietnamese contemporary art.

Markets

There are markets all over HCMC and all of them are interesting places to see local life unfold. Markets are also a good place to pick up conical hats and *ao dai* if you bargain with confidence.

BEN THANH MARKET

The most central of all markets is **Ben Thanh Market** (Cho Ben Thanh; Map p348; cnr ĐL Le Loi, ĐL Ham Nghi, ĐL Tran Hung Dao & Đ Le Lai). The market and surrounding streets make up one of the city's liveliest areas. Everything that's commonly eaten, worn or used by the Saigonese is available here: vegetables, meats, spices, sweets, tobacco, clothing, hardware and so forth. There's also a healthy selection of souvenir items. However, you will need to bargain efficiently here, as prices are usually higher than elsewhere.

Known to the French as Les Halles Centrales, it was built in 1914 from reinforced concrete; the central cupola is 28m in diameter. The main entrance, with its belfry and clock, has become a symbol of HCMC. Opposite the belfry, in the centre of the traffic roundabout, is an equestrian **statue** of Tran Nguyen Hai, the first person in Vietnam to use carrier pigeons. At the base of it, on a pillar, is a small white bust of Quach Thi Trang, a Buddhist woman who was killed during antigovernment protests in 1963.

HUYNH THUC KHANG STREET MARKET

This **street market** (Map p348; Đ Huynh Thuc Khang & Đ Ton That Dam) in the Dong Khoi area sells almost everything. The area was known as the 'electronics black market' until early 1989, when it was legalised.

There are still electronic goods of all sorts – from mosquito zappers to DVD players – but the market has expanded enormously to include just about everything to satisfy your material needs.

OLD MARKET

Despite the name, the **Old Market** (Map p348; Đ Ham Nghi) is not the place to find antiques, although it is quite old. This is the place to buy imported food, wine, shaving cream, shampoo and so on. However, if its Vietnamese name, Cho Cu, is written or pronounced without the correct tones it means 'penis'; your *cyclo* driver will no doubt be much amused if you ask for this. Perhaps directions are a better bet – the Old Market can be found on the north side of Đ Ham Nghi between Đ Ton That Dam and Đ Ho Tung Mau.

DAN SINH MARKET

Also known as the War Surplus Market, **Dan Sinh Market** (Map p346; 104 Đ Yersin) is the place to shop for authentic combat boots or rusty (perhaps less authentic) dog tags. It's also the best market for electronics and other types of imported industrial machinery.

Dan Sinh is next to Phung Son Tu Pagoda. The front part is filled with stalls selling automobiles and motorbikes, but directly behind the pagoda building you can find reproductions of what is touted as second-hand military gear.

Stall after stall sells everything from handy gas masks and field stretchers to rain gear and mosquito nets. You can also find canteens, duffel bags, ponchos and boots. Anyone planning on spending time in a combat zone should consider picking up a second-hand flak jacket, as prices are reasonable.

BINH TAY MARKET

Cholon's main market is **Binh Tay Market** (Map p361; ĐL Hau Giang), a Chinese-style architectural masterpiece with a great clock tower in the centre. Much of the business here is wholesale. This is very popular with tour-group itineraries, so a lot of foreigners pass through here.

AN DONG MARKET

Cholon's other indoor market, **An Dong** (Map p361; ĐL An Duong Vuong), is very close to the intersection of ĐL Tran Phu and ĐL An Duong Vuong. This market is four storeys high and is crammed with shops. The 1st floor carries nothing but clothing, including imported designer jeans, the latest pumps from Paris and *ao dai*. The basement is a gourmet's delight of small restaurants – a perfect place to lunch on the cheap.

GETTING THERE & AWAY

Air

Tan Son Nhat Airport was one of the three busiest in the world in the late 1960s. Even today, the runways are still lined with lichen-covered, mortar-proof aircraft-retaining walls, hangars and other military structures.

The majority of domestic flights in the country are operated by Vietnam Airlines. Newer budget airline Jetstar Pacific is providing some much needed competition on several routes, while Vasco flies between HCMC and the Con Dao Islands. For more details on international air travel see p493.

Boat

Hydrofoils (adult/child 160,000/80,000d, 1¼ hours) depart for Vung Tau (p399) almost hourly from Bach Dang jetty (Map p348) on Đ Ton Duc Thang. For more information contact **Greenlines** (☎ 3821 5609) or **Petro Express** (☎ 3821 0650), which are both located at the jetty. In Vung Tau you will board the hydrofoil at Cau Da pier, opposite the Hai Au Hotel.

Bus

Intercity buses depart from and arrive at a variety of bus stations around HCMC and are well served by local bus services from Ben Thanh Market. HCMC is one place where the open-tour buses really come into their own, as they depart and arrive in the very convenient Pham Ngu Lao area. This saves an extra local bus journey or taxi fare. Most of the open-tour companies sell tickets to Mui Ne (around US$5), Nha Trang (around US$9) and Dalat (around US$8), plus there are night buses to Nha Trang (around US$12). **Phuong Trang** (Puta Travel; ☎ 3837 9879; www.putatravel.com.vn) is a major new player serving the above routes plus Can Tho (80,000d) in the Mekong Delta.

Mien Tay bus station (Ben Xe Mien Tay; off Map pp344-5; ☎ 3825 5955) serves all areas south of HCMC, which basically means the Mekong Delta. This huge station is about 10km west of HCMC in An Lac, a part of Binh Chanh district (Huyen Binh Chanh). Buses and minibuses from Mien Tay serve most towns in the Mekong Delta, using air-conditioned express buses and premium minibuses. For a smattering of prices, see the relevant destination in the Mekong Delta chapter.

Buses to locations north of HCMC leave from the immensely huge and busy **Mien Dong bus station** (Ben Xe Mien Dong; off Map pp344-5; ☎ 3829 4056), in Binh Thanh district, about 5km from central HCMC on Hwy 13 (Quoc Lo 13; the continuation of Đ Xo Viet Nghe Tinh). The station is just under 2km north of the intersection of Đ Xo Viet Nghe Tinh and Đ Dien Bien Phu. Note that express buses depart from the east side, and local buses connect with the west side of the complex.

Buses to Tay Ninh, Cu Chi and points northwest of HCMC depart from the newer **An Suong bus station** (Ben Xe An Suong; off Map pp344-5), in District 12, way to the west of the centre. To get here, head all the way out on Đ Cach Mang Thang Tam and Đ Truong Chinh. The station is close to the flyover for Quoc Lo 1 (Hwy 1). Note that it's not really worth using local buses to visit Tay Ninh and Cu Chi, as many of the smaller tunnel sites are off the main highways, making it a nightmare to navigate.

INTERNATIONAL BUS

There are also international bus services connecting HCMC and Phnom Penh, Cambodia. There are plenty of companies running this route these days, most with departures from the Pham Ngu Lao area, including **Sapaco** (Map p352; ☎ 3920 3623; 309 Pham Ngu Lao), which has eight services a day in either direction between 6.30am and 2pm, costing US$12. These buses are now all direct, so there is no longer the need to change vehicle at the border.

Car & Motorbike

Inquire at almost any tourist cafe, travel agent or hotel to arrange car rental. Just remember that your rental will include a driver, as it's illegal for foreigners to drive in Vietnam without a Vietnamese license. The agencies in the Pham Ngu Lao area generally offer the lowest prices. Also check with the travel agencies listed earlier in this chapter (p351), or check out newcomer **Budget Car Rental** (☎ 3930 1118; www.budget.com.vn) which offers new cars with English-speaking drivers at reasonable rates.

Motorbikes are available in the Pham Ngu Lao area for around US$10 per day if you will be taking the bike out of town, although this is one city where it helps to have experience. Check the quality of the helmet provided as it may be worth investing in a better one for a long trip.

Train

Trains from **Saigon train station** (Ga Sai Gon; Map pp344-5; ☎ 3823 0105; 1 Đ Nguyen Thong, District 3; ticket office 🕑 7.15-11am & 1-3pm) serve coastal cities to the north of HCMC.

Purchase tickets from **Saigon Railways Tourist Services** (Map p352; ☎ 3836 7640; fax 3837 5224; 275C Đ Pham Ngu Lao; 🕑 7.30-11.30am & 1-4.30pm) to avoid any commission, or from most travel agents for a small fee. For details on fares, see the relevant destination in the other chapters of this book.

For details on the Reunification Express service see p508.

GETTING AROUND

To/From the Airport

Tan Son Nhat Airport is 7km northwest of central HCMC. Metered taxis are the easiest option between the airport and the city centre, and cost around 80,000d to 100,000d. You'll be enthusiastically greeted by taxi drivers after you exit the terminal; most are OK, but make sure that the driver agrees to use the meter and it is switched on *after* you get in the car. **Sasco Taxi** (☎ 3844 6448), just past the baggage carousels, has a counter where you can prepay (100,000d) for a taxi.

Be aware that taxi drivers will probably recommend a 'good and cheap' hotel, and deliver you to a hotel for a commission; if you haven't planned where you're going, this is not a bad system per se. Problems may arise, however, when you ask a taxi driver to take you to a place that doesn't pay commission. The driver may tell you the hotel is closed, burned down, is dirty and dangerous, or anything to steer you somewhere else.

To get to the airport from town you can call a taxi (see p388). Some cafes in the Pham Ngu Lao area do runs to the airport – these places even have sign-up sheets where you can book share-taxis for US$3 per person.

Most economical is the air-conditioned airport bus 152 (3000d), going to and from the airport. Buses leave the airport approximately every 15 minutes and make regular stops along Đ De Tham (Pham Ngu Lao area) and international hotels along Đ Dong Khoi, such as the Caravelle and the Majestic. Buses are labelled in English, but you might also look for the words 'Xe Buyt San Bay'. This service only operates between 6am and 7pm.

Consider a motorbike taxi a last resort, as the traffic is even more manic if you are trying to balance baggage. Drivers can't access the airport, so you will need to walk outside and negotiate: 50,000d to the city centre is the going rate.

Bicycle

For pedal power devotees, a bicycle can be a great, if slow, way to get around the city. Bikes can be rented from a number of places, including hotels, cafes and travel agencies.

Bicycle parking lots are usually just roped-off sections of pavement. For about 2000d you can safely leave your bicycle, bearing mind that theft is a big problem. Your bicycle will have a number written on the seat in chalk or stapled to the handlebars and you'll be given a reclaim chit. Don't lose it. If you come back and your bicycle is gone, the parking lot is supposedly required to replace it.

Boat

It's easy to hire a motorised 5m-long boat to tour the Saigon River. There's always someone hanging around the Bach Dang jetty area looking to charter a boat. Ask them to bring it to you, rather than you going to the boat.

The price should be around US$8 per hour for a small boat or US$15 to US$30 for a larger, faster craft. Since you hire boats by the hour, some will go slowly because they know the meter is running. You might want to set a time limit at the start. Interesting destinations for short trips include Cholon (along Ben Nghe Channel) and the botanical gardens (along Thi Nghe Channel). Note that both channels are fascinating, but filthy and a little whiffy, as raw sewage is discharged into the water. Tourists regard the channels as an attraction, but the government considers them an eyesore and has attempted to move residents out. The channels will eventually be filled in and the water diverted into underground sewerage pipes. Of course, although cruising the Saigon River can be interesting, it pales in comparison with the splendour of the canals in the Mekong Delta.

Ferries across the Saigon River leave from the Bach Dang jetty dock at the foot of Đ Ham Nghi and run every half-hour or so between 4.30am and 10.30pm.

Bus

Traditionally, few tourists have made use of the city buses, but this may start to change as they are cheap and plentiful, serving some important destinations around town. They are also safer than *cyclos* and *xe oms*.

There are now more than 130 local bus routes around the city and beyond. There is a useful and free *Ho Chi Minh Bus Route Diagram* (map to you and me) available at the Ben Thanh bus station (Map p348).

Some useful numbers from Ben Thanh include the 152 to Tan Son Nhat Airport, 149 to Saigon train station, 1 to Binh Tay Market in Cholon, 102 to Mien Tay bus station and 26 to Mien Dong bus station. All buses have air-con and uniformed drivers, and the average ticket price is just 3000d. Buy your ticket on board from the attendant.

Car & Motorbike

Travel agencies, hotels and cafes are all in the car-rental business. Most vehicles are relatively recent Japanese- or Korean-made machines – everything from saloons to minibuses. Not long ago, classic American cars (complete with tail-fins and impressive chrome fenders) were popular as 'wedding taxis', but these have all been hoovered up by collectors and are rarely seen.

If you're brave you can rent a motorbike and really earn your 'I Survived Saigon' T-shirt. Many say this is the fastest and easiest way to get around the city – or to the hospital, if you don't know what you're doing. Even if you're an experienced biker, make sure you've spent some time observing traffic patterns before venturing forth.

Motorbike rentals are ubiquitous in places where tourists tend to congregate – the Pham Ngu Lao area is as good as any. Ask at the cafes. A 100cc motorbike can be rented for US$7 to US$10 per day, including some sort of helmet, and your passport may be kept as collateral. Before renting one make sure it's in good working order.

Saigon Scooter Centre (Map pp344-5; ☎ 848 7816; www.saigonscootercentre.com; 25/7 Đ Cuu Long, Tan Binh district; ⏰ 10am-5pm Mon-Sat) is a reliable source for restored classic Vespa and Lambretta scooters, which are also rented out by the day. Daily rates start from US$10 and discounts are offered for long-term rentals. For an extra fee it is possible to arrange a one-way service, with a pick-up of the bikes anywhere in Vietnam.

On a similar theme, **Vietnam Vespa Adventure** (Map p352; ☎ 09-0365 2068; www.vietnamvespaadventure.com), which operates out of Café Zoom (p377) offers guided tours around southern Vietnam, including a loop up the back road from Vung Tau to Mui Ne and some beautiful trails through the mountains near Dalat.

Cyclo

No longer the icon that it once was, the *cyclo* still makes its appearance along certain streets, particularly along Đ Pham Ngu Lao and around Đ Dong Khoi. Although some Vietnamese still enjoy them, use has declined significantly in the day of the motorbike and taxi, and tourists are largely the beneficiaries of this poorly paid trade. In HCMC, a few of the older riders are former South Vietnamese army soldiers and quite a few know at least basic English, while others are quite fluent. Some drivers have stories of war, 're-education', persecution and poverty to tell (and will often gladly regale you with tales over a bowl of *pho* or a beer at the end of the day).

In an effort to control HCMC's traffic problems, there are dozens of streets on which *cyclos* are prohibited. As a result, your driver must often take a circuitous route to avoid these trouble spots (and possible fines levied by the police) and may not be able to drop you at the exact address. Try to have some sympathy as it is not the driver's fault.

Short hops around the city centre will cost around 10,000d to 20,000d; District 1 to central Cholon costs about 30,000d. Overcharging tourists is the norm, so negotiate a price beforehand and have the exact change ready. You can rent a *cyclo* for around 30,000d per hour, a fine idea if you will be doing a lot of touring; most *cyclo* drivers around the Pham Ngu Lao area can produce a sample tour program.

You should enjoy *cyclos* while you can, as the municipal government plans to phase them out, and it won't be too long before the cyclo disappears entirely from the city's streets.

Motorbike Taxi

Far more prevalent and much faster than the *cyclo* taxis is the *xe om* (sometimes called a *Honda om*), or motorbike taxi. *Xe om* drivers usually hang out on their parked bikes on street corners, looking for passengers, and will usually wave you down first. When looking for one, it's highly unlikely that you'll have to walk more than 10 steps before being offered a ride. The accepted rate is 10,000d to 20,000d for short rides (Pham Ngu Lao to Dong Khoi area for instance) or you can charter one for around US$2 per hour or US$10 per day.

Taxi

Metered taxis cruise the streets, but it is worth calling ahead if you are off the beaten path. Lots of companies in HCMC offer metered taxis and charge almost exactly the same rates. The flagfall is around 12,000d to 15,000d for the first kilometre. Most rides in the city centre cost just a couple of bucks. Note that cranky meters are much less common here than in Hanoi.

The following contact details are for HCMC's main taxi companies.

Ben Thanh Taxi (☎ 3842 2422)
Future Taxi (☎ 3818 1818)
Mai Linh Taxi (☎ 3822 6666)
Saigon Taxi (☎ 3823 2323)
Vina Taxi (☎ 3811 1111)
Vinasun Taxi (☎ 3827 7178)

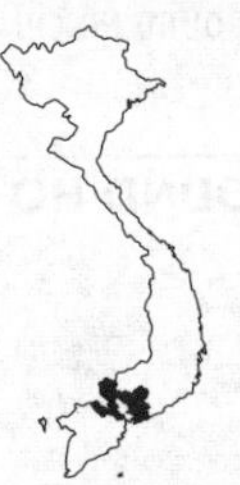

Around Ho Chi Minh City

As Ho Chi Minh City (HCMC) continues its insatiable expansion in every direction, swallowing up rural communities and country backwaters, finding a respite from urban life has become quite a challenge. Thankfully, there are still some rewarding escapes, such as wild forests, inviting beaches and fascinating historical and cultural sights, just a short journey from town.

One of the region's big hitters is Cat Tien National Park, a Unesco-rated biosphere boasting a startling variety of flora and fauna. Visitors can go bird-watching, explore hiking trails, overnight in a crocodile swamp and (optimistically) spot signs of Vietnam's rarest wildlife. The Con Dao Islands offer a similarly pristine environment, albeit of a tropical-island variety. A former prison colony under the French and US regimes, Con Dao today boasts largely undiscovered beaches, empty coastal roads and a healthy ecosystem complete with coral reefs and colonies of green sea turtles, one of Vietnam's best places to see them in the wild.

Other fine beaches stretch east of the bustling beach town of Vung Tau. Although lacking the popularity of Mui Ne and Nha Trang further up the coast, there are some idyllic hideaways here for those seeking a quiet beach holiday far from the madding crowd.

More popular than HCMC's nearby beaches and forests, however, is the underground maze of the Cu Chi tunnels, where VC guerrillas once lived, fought and, in many cases, died. Nearby, the fairy-tale Cao Dai Temple is a surreal backdrop to learning about Vietnam's unique syncretic religion. Both these destinations are extremely popular day excursions from HCMC.

HIGHLIGHTS

- Comb the beautiful beaches, snorkel coral reefs or motorbike the empty coastal roads on the **Con Dao Islands** (p407)
- Hike, bike or track down shy wildlife in the lush forests of **Cat Tien National Park** (p406).
- Make a road trip up the coast to explore the endless sands of **Long Hai** (p403) and **Ho Coc** (p405)
- Experience the surreal, subterranean life of the Viet Cong in the claustrophobic **Cu Chi Tunnels** (p390).
- Attend a religious service at Tay Ninh's cotton candy **Cao Dai Great Temple** (p395)

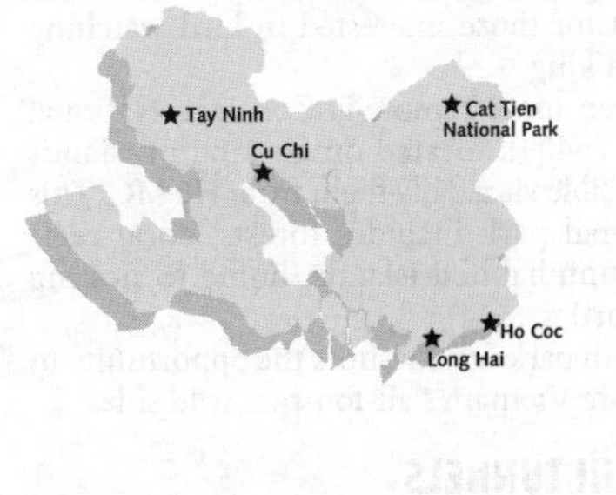

- ELEVATION: 30M
- BEST TIME TO VISIT: DEC–MAR

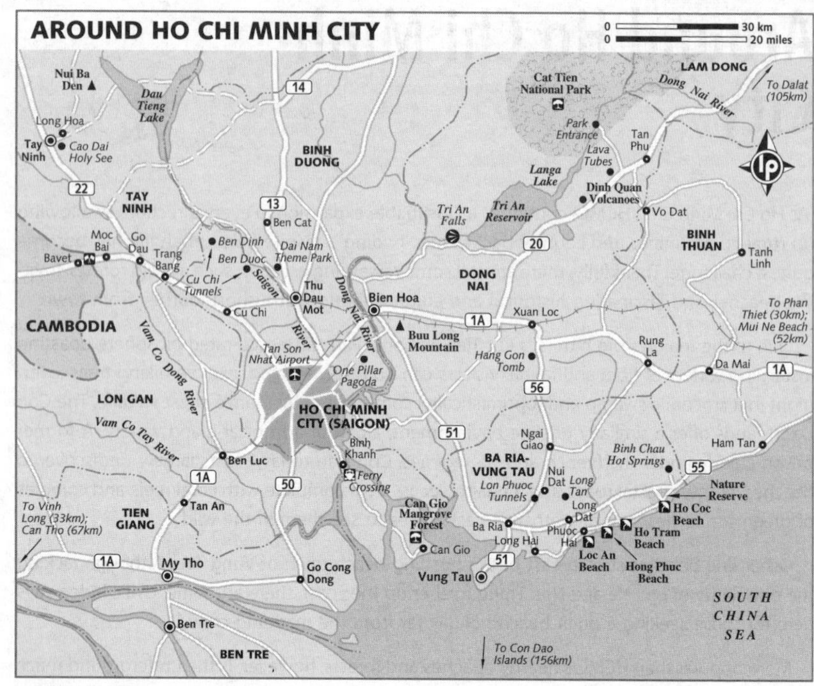

National Parks

Two notable national parks are found in this southern slice of Vietnam. Cat Tien National Park (p406), a few hours from HCMC, makes a delightful detour between HCMC and Dalat for those interested in bird-watching and hiking.

Even more remote is Con Dao National Park (p409), located on a string of islands accessible via a daily flight from HCMC. This national park includes forests, coral reefs and uninhabited islands, home to nesting sea turtles.

Both parks give visitors the opportunity to explore Vietnam's all-too-rare wild side.

CU CHI TUNNELS

If the tenacious spirit of the Vietnamese can be symbolised by a place, then few candidates make a stronger case than the **tunnels of Cu Chi** (☎ 3794 8823; www.cuchitunnel.org.vn). Cu Chi is a district of greater HCMC and has a population of about 200,000 (it had about 80,000 residents during the American War). At first glance there is little evidence here to indicate the intense fighting, bombing and destruction that occurred in Cu Chi during the war. To see what went on, you have to dig deeper – underground.

The tunnel network of Cu Chi became legendary during the 1960s for its role in facilitating Viet Cong (VC) control of a large rural area only 30km to 40km from HCMC. At its height the tunnel system stretched from the South Vietnamese capital to the Cambodian border; in the district of Cu Chi alone there were more than 250km of tunnels. The network, parts of which were several storeys deep, included innumerable trapdoors, constructed living areas, storage facilities, weapons factories, field hospitals, command centres and kitchens.

The tunnels facilitated communication and coordination between the VC-controlled enclaves, isolated from each other by South Vietnamese and American land and air operations. They also allowed the VC to mount surprise attacks wherever the tunnels went – even within the perimeters of the US military base at Dong Du – and to disappear suddenly into hidden trapdoors without a trace. After ground operations against the tunnels claimed large numbers of US casualties and proved ineffective, the Americans resorted to massive firepower, eventually turning Cu Chi's 420 sq km into what the authors of *The Tunnels of Cu Chi* (Tom Mangold and John Penycate) have called 'the most bombed, shelled, gassed, defoliated and generally devastated area in the history of warfare'.

Cu Chi has become a place of pilgrimage for Vietnamese school children and communist-party cadres. Two sections from this remarkable tunnel network (which are enlarged and upgraded versions of the real thing) are open to the public. One is near the village of Ben Dinh and the other is 15km beyond at Ben Duoc. Most tourists visiting the tunnels end up at Ben Dinh, the favourite of bus tours; those seeking more of a surreal, funhouse atmosphere could head to Ben Duoc.

History

The tunnels of Cu Chi were built over a period of 25 years that began sometime in the late 1940s. They were the improvised response of a poorly equipped peasant army to its enemy's high-tech ordnance, helicopters, artillery, bombers and chemical weapons.

The Viet Minh built the first dugouts and tunnels in the hard, red earth of Cu Chi (ideal for their construction) during the war against the French. The excavations were used mostly for communication between villages and to evade French army sweeps of the area.

When the VC's National Liberation Front (NLF) insurgency began in earnest around 1960, the old Viet Minh tunnels were repaired and new extensions were excavated. Within a few years the tunnel system assumed enormous strategic importance, and most of Cu Chi district and the nearby area came under VC control. In addition Cu Chi was used as a base for infiltrating intelligence agents and sabotage teams into Saigon. The stunning attacks in the South Vietnamese capital during the 1968 Tet Offensive were planned and launched from Cu Chi.

In early 1963 the Diem government implemented the Strategic Hamlets Program, under which fortified encampments, surrounded by many rows of sharp bamboo spikes, were built to house people who had been 'relocated' from communist-controlled areas. The first strategic hamlet was in Ben Cat district, next to Cu Chi. However, the VC were able to tunnel into the hamlets and control them from within, so that by the end of 1963 the first showpiece hamlet had been overrun.

The series of setbacks and defeats suffered by the South Vietnamese forces in the Cu Chi area rendered a complete VC victory by the end of 1965 a distinct possibility. In the early months of that year, the guerrillas boldly held a victory parade in the middle of Cu Chi town. VC strength in and around Cu Chi was one of the reasons the Johnson administration decided to involve US troops in the war.

To deal with the threat posed by VC control of an area so near the South Vietnamese capital, one of the USA's first actions was to establish a large base camp in Cu Chi district. Unknowingly, they built it right on top of an existing tunnel network. It took months for the 25th Division to figure out why they kept getting shot at in their tents at night.

The US and Australian troops tried a variety of methods to 'pacify' the area around Cu Chi, which came to be known as the Iron Triangle. They launched large-scale ground operations involving tens of thousands of troops but failed to locate the tunnels. To deny the VC cover and supplies, rice paddies were defoliated, huge swathes of jungle bulldozed, and villages evacuated and razed. The Americans also sprayed chemical defoliants on the area aerially and a few months later ignited the tinder-dry vegetation with gasoline and napalm. But the intense heat interacted with the wet tropical air in such a way as to create cloudbursts that extinguished the fires. The VC remained safe in their tunnels.

BORDER CROSSING: MOC BAI–BAVET

This busy border crossing is the fastest way to get between HCMC and Phnom Penh, crossing via Moc Bai–Bavet. Numerous traveller cafes in the Pham Ngu Lao area (p351) sell bus tickets between the capitals for around US$12, with most buses departing between about 6am and 2pm. Allow about six hours for the trip, including time spent on border formalities. Cambodian visas (US$20) are issued at the border, although you'll need a passport-sized photo. Moc Bai has become a major duty-free shopping zone for the Vietnamese, with a handful of hypermarkets. Across the border, Bavet is a mini Macau complete with half-a-dozen or more casinos.

Unable to win this battle with chemicals, the US army began sending men down into the tunnels. These 'tunnel rats', who were often involved in underground fire fights, sustained appallingly high casualty rates.

When the Americans began using German shepherd dogs, trained to use their keen sense of smell to locate trapdoors and guerrillas, the VC began washing with American soap, which gave off a scent the canines identified as friendly. Captured US uniforms were put out to confuse the dogs further. Most importantly, the dogs were not able to spot booby traps. So many dogs were killed or maimed that their horrified handlers then refused to send them into the tunnels.

The USA declared Cu Chi a free-strike zone: little authorisation was needed to shoot at anything in the area, random artillery was fired into the area at night, and pilots were told to drop unused bombs and napalm there before returning to base. But the VC stayed put. Finally, in the late 1960s, American B-52s carpet-bombed the whole area, destroying most of the tunnels along with everything else around. The gesture was almost symbolic by then because the USA was already on its way out of the war. The tunnels had served their purpose.

The VC guerrillas serving in the tunnels lived in extremely difficult conditions and suffered serious casualties. Only about 6000 of the 16,000 cadres who fought in the tunnels survived the war. Thousands of civilians in the area were killed. Their tenacity was extraordinary considering the bombings, the claustrophobia of living underground for weeks or months at a time and the deaths of countless friends and comrades. Some wry southerners privately ask why they bothered, as looking at Vietnam today, they argue capitalism has triumphed in the end.

The villages of Cu Chi have since been presented with numerous honorific awards, decorations and citations by the government, and many have been declared 'heroic villages'. Since 1975 new hamlets have been established and the population of the area has more than doubled; however, chemical defoliants remain in the soil and water, and crop yields are still poor.

The Tunnels of Cu Chi, by Tom Mangold and John Penycate, is a powerful book documenting the story of the tunnels and the people involved on both sides.

Sights

THE TUNNELS

Over the years the VC developed simple but effective techniques to make their tunnels difficult to detect or disable. Wooden trapdoors were camouflaged with earth and branches; some were booby-trapped. Hidden underwater entrances from rivers were constructed. To cook they used 'Dien Bien Phu kitchens', which exhausted the smoke through vents many metres away from the cooking site. Trapdoors were installed throughout the network to prevent tear gas, smoke or water from moving from one part of the system to another. Some sections were even equipped with electric lighting.

Ben Dinh

The most visited of the tunnel sites, this small, renovated section of the **tunnel system** (admission 65,000d) is near the village of Ben Dinh, about 50km from HCMC. In one of the classrooms at the visitors centre, a large map shows the extent of the network; the area shown is in the northwestern corner of greater HCMC. The tunnels are marked in red, VC bases in light grey and the river in light blue (the Saigon River is at the top). Fortified villages held by South Vietnamese and US forces are marked in grey, while blue dots represent the American and South Vietnamese military posts that were supposed to ensure the security of nearby villages. The dark blue area in the centre is the base of the US 25th Infantry Division. Most prearranged tours do not take you to this former base, but it is not off limits and you can arrange a visit if you have your own guide and driver.

To the right of the large map are two cross-section diagrams of the tunnels. The bottom diagram is a reproduction of one used by General William Westmoreland, the commander of US forces in Vietnam (1964–68). The Americans seemed to have had their intelligence information right, although the tunnels did not pass under rivers, nor did the guerrillas wear headgear underground.

The section of the tunnel system presently open to visitors is a few hundred metres south of the visitors centre. It snakes up and down through various chambers along its 50m length. The tunnels are about 1.2m high and 80cm across, and are unlit. Some travellers find them too claustrophobic for comfort. A knocked-out M-41 tank and a bomb crater are near the exit, which is in a reforested eucalyptus grove.

Be warned that this site tends to get crowded, and you can feel like you're on a tourist conveyor belt most days.

Ben Duoc

Many Vietnamese and the odd foreign visitor make it to the **Ben Duoc tunnels** (admission 65,000d). The tunnels here have been enlarged to accommodate tourists and feature a number of sights within the underground chambers themselves. The emphasis here is more on the fun fair rather than the history of the tunnels. Hence visitors can don guerrilla costumes and gear before scraping through the tunnels in order to feel like a 'real' VC soldier. Inside are bunkers, a hospital and a command centre that played a role in the 1968 Tet Offensive, and the set pieces include tables, chairs, beds, lights, and dummies outfitted in guerrilla gear (aside from your fellow tourists, that is). Although it's amusing, it's not exactly the way the real tunnels once looked – which were cramped and largely barren, more like those found at Ben Dinh.

Perhaps more moving than the underground chambers is the small **Ben Duoc temple** built in 1993 in memory of the Vietnamese killed at Cu Chi. It's flanked by a nine-storey tower with a flower garden in front.

CU CHI WAR HISTORY MUSEUM

The small **Cu Chi War History Museum** (Nha Truyen Thong Huyen Cu Chi; admission US$1) is not actually at the tunnel sites but just off the main highway in the central area of the town of Cu Chi. Almost all of the explanations are in Vietnamese. There are a few gruesome photos showing civilians who were severely wounded or killed following American bombing raids, and a list of VC guerrillas killed in the Cu Chi area. Overall, it's rather disappointing and doesn't warrant a visit. Most travellers find HCMC's War Remnants Museum (p354) far more edifying.

Tours

An organised tour is the easiest way to visit the Cu Chi tunnels and these are very good value. Most of the cafes in the Pham Ngu Lao area in HCMC run half-day trips to the tunnels for US$6 or combined full-day tours to the Cu Chi tunnels and Cao Dai Great Temple (p395) for around US$8. For something a little different, try the half-day boating trip (US$12) to the tunnels organised by Delta Adventure Tours (p351).

Getting There & Around

Cu Chi district covers a large area, parts of which are as close as 30km to central HCMC. The Cu Chi War History Museum is closest to the city, while the Ben Dinh and Ben Duoc tunnels are about 50km and 65km, respectively, from central HCMC. It is very difficult to visit by public transport, as it involves several changes of bus. Tay Ninh buses pass though Cu Chi, but getting from the town of Cu Chi to the tunnels by public transport is tough.

Hiring a taxi in HCMC and driving out to Cu Chi is not all that expensive, especially if the cost is shared by several people. The easiest way to do this is to stop by one of the budget travel cafes in Pham Ngu Lao (p351) and arrange a car, or flag a taxi who will agree to charge for driving time only. See p388 for details on local taxi companies.

A visit to the Cu Chi tunnel complex can easily be combined with a stop at the headquarters of the Cao Dai sect in Tay Ninh. A taxi for an all-day excursion to both should cost about US$50 or so.

Cu Chi Wildlife Rescue Centre

Just a few kilometres down the road from the tunnels of Ben Dinh, this **rescue centre** (www.wildlifeatrisk.org; admission free) is a welcome addition to the sites around Cu Chi. It's a small centre dedicated to the protection of wildlife that has been confiscated from owners or illegal traders. Animals here include Asiatic black bear, otter, gibbon and even a leopard. The centre is expanding its enclosures to create more comfortable habitats and there is an informative display on the rather depressing state of wildlife in Vietnam, including the 'room of death' featuring a host of traps and baits. Donations welcome or purchase some of the merchandise on sale. It's tough to navigate these back roads on your own, so talk to a travel agent about incorporating it into a Cu Chi Tunnels trip.

TAY NINH

☎066 / pop 42,000

Tay Ninh town, the capital of Tay Ninh province, serves as the headquarters of one of Vietnam's most intriguing indigenous religions, Cao Daism. The Cao Dai Great Temple

NGUYEN CHUONG

Nguyen Chuong works in the frontline of defence against the illegal trade in wildlife in Vietnam, a trade that is booming thanks to domestic consumption and increasing demand from neighbouring giants like China. So what drew him into this line of work? 'I love the animals of Vietnam, so I wanted to try and help protect them', he tells me. 'It is a great opportunity as we run the only wildlife rescue centre in southern Vietnam.' So it is rewarding work? 'Yes, definitely, as I see these animals in terrible conditions in markets and can bring them into a secure and safe environment at our centre. I feel like I am directly contributing to the conservation of wildlife in my country', he says emphatically.

We move on to the more depressing aspects of the job. 'I see so many animals in our markets being mistreated and we only have limited space for more wildlife at our rescue centre', he laments, 'therefore we have to focus on endangered species which are most at risk. But I hate to see any animals mistreated'.

We discuss the future of wildlife in Vietnam. 'The abuse of wildlife and the illegal trade in Vietnam is such a big issue that it won't change for some time', he says resignedly. 'The Vietnamese have used wildlife for thousands of years for thousands of different reasons. The big problem now is that the wildlife has a commercial value both at home and abroad.' But is there room for optimism? 'With so many people joining the fight against this cruelty, I think it is possible to provide a safe environment for our animals, but we will need more space to house and rehabilitate them', he says with a grin.

He believes there are several important approaches in the battle against traffickers and poachers. 'First we need to educate everyone in Vietnam about the effects we are having on our animal population and this is really the key', he states. 'Also, we could strengthen the law to punish the perpetrators in this trade, plus provide more space to look after these animals once they are rescued.'

On a more light-hearted note, I ask him about troublesome wildlife. 'Even the easiest animals can be hard to work with, as they are from the wild', he points out. 'Cobras and other venomous snakes are hard to handle and quite dangerous, but they are a protected species and we need to save them.'

And what can visitors do to help in the protection of Vietnam's wildlife? 'Try to avoid any products which involve wildlife, like snake wine', he offers. 'Think about the places you choose to eat and try to avoid places with wildlife on the menu, as otherwise you are indirectly supporting the wildlife trade.'

Nguyen Chuong works as the manager of Kiem Lam Cu Chi (Cu Chi Animal Rescue) and is responsible for saving trafficked or mistreated animals and bringing them to the Cu Chi Wildlife Rescue Centre, run in cooperation with international NGO, Wildlife at Risk (www.wildlifeatrisk.org).

at the sect's Holy See is one of the most striking structures in all of Asia. Built between 1933 and 1955, the temple is a rococo extravaganza combining the conflicting architectural idiosyncrasies of a French church, a Chinese pagoda, Hong Kong's Tiger Balm Gardens and Madame Tussaud's Wax Museum.

Tay Ninh province, northwest of HCMC, is bordered by Cambodia on three sides. The area's dominant geographic feature is Nui Ba Den (Black Lady Mountain), which towers above the surrounding plains. Tay Ninh province's eastern border is formed by the Saigon River. The Vam Co River flows from Cambodia through the western part of the province.

Because of the once-vaunted political and military power of the Cao Dai, this region was the scene of prolonged and heavy fighting during the Franco-Viet Minh War. Tay Ninh province served as a major terminus of the Ho Chi Minh Trail during the American War, and in 1969 the Viet Cong captured Tay Ninh town and held it for several days.

During the period of conflict between Cambodia and Vietnam in the late 1970s, the Khmer Rouge launched a number of cross-border raids into Tay Ninh province and committed atrocities against civilians. Several cemeteries around Tay Ninh are stark reminders of these events.

Information

Tay Ninh Tourist (☎ 382 2376; tanitour@hcm.vnn.vn; 210B Đ 30/4) is located in the Hoa Binh Hotel (p396). Tay Ninh's **post office** (Đ 30/4) is down the street, but it does not offer internet services.

Sights

CAO DAI HOLY SEE

Home to the **Cao Dai Great Temple** (Thanh That Cao Dai), the Cao Dai Holy See, founded in 1926, is 4km east of Tay Ninh, in the village of Long Hoa. As well as the Great Temple, the complex houses administrative offices, residences for officials and adepts, and a hospital of traditional Vietnamese herbal medicine, which attracts people from all over the south for its treatments. After reunification the government 'borrowed' parts of the complex for its own use (and perhaps to keep an eye on the sect).

Prayers are conducted four times daily in the Great Temple (suspended during Tet). It's worth visiting during prayer sessions – the one at noon is most popular with tour groups from HCMC – but don't disturb the worshippers. Only a few hundred priests participate in weekday prayers, but during festivals several thousand priests, dressed in special white garments, may attend.

The Cao Dai clergy has no objection to photographing temple objects, but do not photograph people without their permission, which is seldom granted. However, it is possible to photograph the prayer sessions from the upstairs balcony, an apparent concession to the troops of tourists who come here every day.

It's important that guests wear modest and respectful attire inside the temple, which means no shorts or sleeveless T-shirts, although sandals are OK as footwear must be removed before entering.

Set above the front portico of the Great Temple is the **divine eye**. Americans often comment that it looks as if it were copied from the back of a US$1 bill. Lay women enter the Great Temple through a door at the base of the tower on the left. Once inside they walk around the outside of the colonnaded hall in a clockwise direction. Men enter on the right and walk around the hall in an anticlockwise direction. Hats must be removed upon entering the building. The area in the centre of the sanctuary is reserved for Cao Dai priests.

A **mural** in the front entry hall depicts the three signatories of the 'Third Alliance Between God and Man': the Chinese statesman and revolutionary leader Dr Sun Yat-sen (1866–1925) holds an ink stone; while the Vietnamese poet Nguyen Binh Khiem (1492–1587) and French poet and author Victor Hugo (1802–85) write 'God and Humanity' and 'Love and Justice' in Chinese and French (Nguyen Binh Khiem writes with a brush; Victor Hugo uses a quill pen). Nearby signs in English, French and German each give a slightly different version of the fundamentals of Cao Daism.

The Great Temple is built over nine levels, representing the nine steps to heaven, with each level marked by a pair of columns. At the far end of the sanctuary, eight plaster columns entwined with multicoloured dragons support a dome representing the heavens. Under the dome is a giant star-speckled blue globe with the 'divine eye' on it.

The largest of the seven chairs in front of the globe is reserved for the Cao Dai pope, a position that has remained vacant since 1933. The next three chairs are for the three men responsible for the religion's law books. The remaining chairs are for the leaders of the three branches of Cao Daism, represented by the colours yellow, blue and red.

On both sides of the area between the columns are two pulpits similar in design to the *minbar* in mosques. During festivals the pulpits are used by officials to address the assembled worshippers. The upstairs balconies are used if the crowd overflows.

Up near the altar are barely discernible portraits of six figures important to Cao Daism: Sakyamuni (Siddhartha Gautama, the founder of Buddhism), Ly Thai Bach (Li Taibai, a fairy from Chinese mythology), Khuong Tu Nha (Jiang Taigong, a Chinese saint), Laozi (the founder of Taoism), Quan Cong (Guangong, Chinese God of War) and Quan Am (Guanyin, the Goddess of Mercy).

LONG HOA MARKET

Several kilometres south of the Cao Dai Holy See complex is **Long Hoa Market** (🕑 5am-6pm). This large market sells meat, food staples, clothing and pretty much everything else you would expect to find in a rural marketplace. Before reunification the Cao Dai sect had the right to collect taxes from the merchants here.

CAO DAISM

A fascinating fusion of East and West, Cao Daism *(Dai Dao Tam Ky Pho Do)* is a syncretic religion born in 20th-century Vietnam that contains elements of Buddhism, Confucianism, Taoism, native Vietnamese spiritualism, Christianity and Islam – as well as a dash of secular enlightenment thrown in for good measure. The term Cao Dai (meaning high tower or palace) is a euphemism for God. There are an estimated two to three million followers of Cao Daism worldwide.

History

Cao Daism was founded by the mystic Ngo Minh Chieu (also known as Ngo Van Chieu; born 1878), a civil servant who once served as district chief of Phu Quoc Island. He was widely read in Eastern and Western religious works and became active in seances. In 1919 he began receiving revelations in which the tenets of Cao Dai were set forth.

Cao Daism was officially founded as a religion in 1926, and over the next few decades attracted thousands of followers, with the Cao Dai running Tay Ninh province as an almost independent feudal state. By 1956 the Cao Dai were a serious political force with a 25,000-strong army. Having refused to support the VC during the American War, the sect feared the worst after reunification. And for good reason: all Cao Dai lands were confiscated by the new communist government and four members of the sect were executed in 1979. Only in 1985, when the Cao Dai had been thoroughly pacified, were the Holy See and some 400 temples returned to their control.

Philosophy

Much of Cao Dai doctrine is drawn from Mahayana Buddhism, mixed with Taoist and Confucian elements (Vietnam's 'Triple Religion'). Cao Dai ethics are based on the Buddhist ideal of 'the good person' but incorporate traditional Vietnamese beliefs as well.

The ultimate goal of the Cao Dai disciple is to escape the cycle of reincarnation. This can only be achieved by refraining from killing, lying, luxurious living, sensuality and stealing.

The main tenets of Cao Daism are the existence of the soul, the use of mediums to communicate with the spiritual world and belief in one god – although it also incorporates the duality of the Chinese yin and yang. In addition to seances, Cao Dai practices include priestly celibacy, vegetarianism and meditative self-cultivation.

According to Cao Daism, history is divided into three major periods of divine revelation. During the first period God's truth was revealed to humanity through Laotse (Laozi) and figures associated with Buddhism, Confucianism and Taoism. The human agents of revelation during the second period were Buddha (Sakyamuni), Mohammed, Confucius, Jesus and Moses. The third and final revelation is the product of the 'Third Alliance Between God and Man', which is where seances play a part. Disciples believe that Cao Daism avoids the failures of the first two periods because spirits of the dead guide the living. Among the contacted spirits who lived as Westerners are Joan of Arc, William Shakespeare, Vladimir Ilyich Lenin and Victor Hugo, who was posthumously named the chief spirit of foreign missionary works owing to his frequent appearance.

All Cao Dai temples observe four daily ceremonies, held at 6am, noon, 6pm and midnight. These rituals, during which dignitaries wear ceremonial dress, include offerings of incense, tea, alcohol, fruit and flowers. All Cao Dai altars have the 'divine eye' above them, which became the religion's official symbol after Ngo Minh Chieu saw it in a vision.

If all this sounds like just what you've been waiting for, you can always join up. Read more on the official Cao Dai site: www.caodai.org.

Sleeping & Eating

There is no real reason to stay here as Ho Chi Minh City is within commuting distance. But there are some options if you're running late:

Anh Dao Hotel (☎ 382 7306; 146 Đ 30/4; r 150,000-200,000d) Located 500m west of Hoa Binh Hotel. Breakfast included.

Hoa Binh Hotel (☎ 382 1315; 210 Đ 30 Thang 4; r 220,000-350,000d;) Five kilometres from the Cao Dai Great Temple, this is a classic Soviet-era concrete slab; rates include breakfast.

Both hotels have in-house restaurants, but there's better Vietnamese food right next door to the Hoa Binh Hotel at **Thanh Thuy** (☎ 382 7606; Đ 30 Thang 40; mains 35,000-70,000d). The menu has no prices, but the cost is reasonable and portions generous.

Getting There & Away

Tay Ninh is on Hwy 22 (Quoc Lo 22), 96km from HCMC. The road passes through **Trang Bang**, the place where the famous photograph of a severely burnt young girl, Kim Phuc, screaming and running, was taken by a journalist during a US napalm attack. Read more about her story in *The Girl in the Picture* (1999) by Denise Chong. There are several Cao Dai temples along Hwy 22, including one (which was under construction in 1975) that was heavily damaged by the VC.

There are buses from HCMC to Tay Ninh that leave from the An Suong bus station (Ben Xe An Suong) in Tan Binh district, but these do not pass via the Cu Chi Tunnels.

As there's no public transport to Cu Chi from Tay Ninh, hire a motorbike in Tay Ninh. Look for *xe om* drivers in front of the hotels. It will probably cost about US$6 for a return trip. It's easier to join a tour from HCMC in this case.

An easy way to get to Tay Ninh is by chartered taxi on a day trip that includes Cu Chi. An all-day return trip from HCMC to both should cost around US$50.

NUI BA DEN

☎ 066

Fifteen kilometres northeast of Tay Ninh, **Nui Ba Den** (Black Lady Mountain; adult/child 10,000/5000d) rises 850m above the rice paddies, corn, cassava (manioc) and rubber plantations of the surrounding countryside. Over the centuries Nui Ba Den has served as a shrine for various peoples of the area, including the Khmer, Chams, Vietnamese and Chinese, and there are several interesting **cave temples** here. The summits of Nui Ba Den are much cooler than the rest of Tay Ninh province, most of which is only a few dozen metres above sea level.

Nui Ba Den was used as a staging area by both the Viet Minh and the VC, and was the scene of fierce fighting during the French and American Wars. At one time there was a US Army firebase and relay station at the summit, which was later, ironically, defoliated and heavily bombed by US aircraft.

The name Black Lady Mountain is derived from the legend of Huong, a young woman who married her true love despite the advances of a wealthy Mandarin. While her husband was away doing military service, she would visit a magical statue of Buddha at the mountain's summit. One day Huong was attacked by kidnappers but, preferring death to dishonour, she threw herself off a cliff. She then reappeared in the visions of a monk who lived on the mountain, and he told her story.

The hike from the base of the mountain to the main temple complex and back takes about 1½ hours. Although steep in parts, it's not a difficult walk – plenty of older pilgrims in sandals make the journey to worship at the temple. Around the temple complex are a few stands selling snacks and drinks.

If you need more exercise, a walk to the summit and back takes about six hours. The fastest, easiest way is via the **chair lift** (one way/return adult 30,000/50,000d, child 15,000/25,000d) that shuttles the pilgrims up and down the hill. For a more exhilarating descent, try the 'slideway', a sort of winding track that drops 1700m around the mountain and is the closest thing to the luge in Vietnam.

At the base of the mountain there are lakes and manicured gardens and (as with many such sacred sites in Asia) a mix of religious and tacky amusement park–style attractions: paddle boats for hire and a choo-choo train to save the weary a bit of walking.

Very few foreign tourists visit the mountain, but it's a popular place for Vietnamese people. Because of the crowds, visiting on Sunday or during a holiday or festival is a bad idea.

Nui Ba Den appears prominently in a recent memoir published by a former American soldier, *Black Virgin Mountain: A Return to Vietnam* by Larry Heinemann.

Sleeping & Eating

Not really a place to overnight if you can help it. However, there are old A-frame bungalows and camping at **Nha Nghi Thuy Dong** (☎ 362 4204; bungalows 150,000d, A-frame platform tents 80,000d). Bungalows are situated about 500m inside the main entrance gate, on the side of the lake. Each bungalow has a basic squat toilet, and shared showers. Tent accommodations have shared toilets and cold showers. Monks at the nearby Trung Pagoda can prepare you traditional vegetarian meals with a day's advance notice. The food is free, but a contribution is advisable.

Thuy Dong Restaurant (mains 30,000-60,000d) is attached to the bungalow complex and has breezy views of the lake. There are also a few nearby food stalls and kiosks selling cold drinks and souvenirs.

Getting There & Away

There is limited public transport to Nui Ba Den. If you're not travelling with your own wheels, the easiest way to reach the site is to take a *xe om* from Tay Ninh for around 60,000d return.

ONE PILLAR PAGODA

☎ 08

Modelled on Hanoi's One Pillar Pagoda, this structure is similar but not identical. The One Pillar Pagoda of Thu Duc, Hanoi's original pagoda was built in the 11th century, destroyed by the French in 1954 and rebuilt by the Vietnamese; HCMC's version was constructed in 1958. Officially known as **Nam Thien Nhat Tru** (Chua Mot Cot Thu Duc; ☎ 3896 0780; 1/91 Đ Nguyen Du), most people call it the One Pillar Pagoda of Thu Duc.

When Vietnam was partitioned in 1954, Buddhist monks and Catholic priests wisely fled south to avoid persecution and continued to practise their religion. One monk from Hanoi who travelled south in 1954 was Thich Tri Dung. After his arrival in Saigon, Thich petitioned the South Vietnamese government for permission to construct a replica of Hanoi's famous One Pillar Pagoda. However, President Ngo Dinh Diem was a Catholic with little tolerance for Buddhist clergy and denied permission. Nevertheless, Thich and his supporters raised the funds and built the pagoda in defiance of the president's orders.

At one point the Diem government ordered the monks to tear down the temple, but they refused even though they were threatened with imprisonment for not complying. Faced with significant opposition, the government's dispute with the monks reached a standoff. However, the president's attempts to harass and intimidate the monks in a country that was 90% Buddhist did not go down well and ultimately contributed to Diem's assassination by his own troops in 1963.

The pagoda is in Thu Duc district, 15km northeast of central HCMC. Traveller cafes and travel agencies in HCMC (p351) should be able to put together a customised tour to the pagoda or to arrange a car and driver for you.

DAI NAM THEME PARK

There have been many attempts at theme parks in Vietnam, but few have come close to the real deal. However, this has all just changed with the arrival of **Dai Nam Theme Park** (Lac Canh Dai Nam Van Hien; ☎ 0650 351 2660; www.laccanhdainamvanhien.vn; 🕑 9am-5pm, weekends & holidays to 9pm; adult/child 150,000/75,000d, zoo 20,000d), located about 30km from HCMC on Hwy 13. The roller-coaster is serious stuff with corkscrews and loops, plus there is a sky dive and a log flume. There are plenty of rides for smaller kiddies and a safari park–style zoo with white tigers, white rhinos and other big animals. Plans are afoot to open a huge water park here during 2009. Local bus 18 runs from Ben Thanh to Dai Nam daily.

CAN GIO

☎ 08

Notable for its extensive mangrove forest, which some say acts as nature's check on the growing pollution of the city, Can Gio is a low palm-fringed island some 25km southeast of HCMC. The island, which is at the intersection between the Saigon River and the sea, was created by silt washing downstream. It is hard-packed mud rather than sandy beach, so attracts only a few international visitors and the area remains relatively undeveloped.

The principal attraction here is **Can Gio mangrove forest** (Lam Vien Can Gio; ☎ 3874 3069; admission 15,000d). Formed by sediment deposits from the Dong Nai and Long Tau Rivers, this forest contains a high degree of biodiversity with more than 200 species of fauna and 50 species of flora. However, as with many 'ecotourism' activities in Vietnam, **Saigon Tourist** (www.cangioresort.com.vn) has got in on the act and turned the experience into a bit of an event. Kayaking in the mangroves is a great concept, but the animal circus just doesn't do it for us.

Minor attractions here include the **Can Gio Museum**, which has displays on the wildlife of the forest, along with exhibits relating to local war history, as the nearby **Rung Sac base** was used by guerrillas during the war and has been recreated for visitors. The island is also home to the **Can Gio Forest Park**, a monkey sanctuary that houses at least a hundred simians, but take care: like monkeys everywhere, the line between cheeky and dangerous is very fine. One area of the mangrove forest is famous for its salt production, **Van Sat**, where there is a saltwater pool to bathe in rather like the Dead Sea, plus a display of saltwater crocodiles, although luckily not in the same location. Also of interest is **Dam Doi** or Bat Swamp, an area where fruit bats nest.

Though much smaller than the Cao Dai Great Temple at Tay Ninh, Can Gio boasts a **Cao Dai temple** of its own. It's near the large **market**, which is made very conspicuous by some rather powerful odours. Seafood and salt are the local specialities. The vegetables, rice and fruit are all imported by boat from around HCMC.

Adjacent to the local shrimp hatchery is a **vast cemetery** and **war memorial** (Nghia Trang Liet Si Rung Sac), 2km from Can Gio Market. Like all such sites in Vietnam, the praise for bravery and patriotism goes entirely to the winning side and there is nothing said about the losers. Indeed, all of the former war cemeteries containing remains of South Vietnamese soldiers were bulldozed after liberation – a fact that still causes much bitterness.

The southern side of the island faces the sea, creating a **beachfront** nearly 10km long. Unfortunately a good deal of it is inaccessible because it's been fenced off by shrimp farmers and clam diggers. Nevertheless, there is a point about 4km west of the market where a dirt road leads off the main highway to HCMC, heading towards the beach. At the beach there are a handful of stalls selling food and drinks. The hills of the Vung Tau Peninsula are clearly visible on a clear day.

Getting There & Away

Can Gio is about 60km southeast of central HCMC, and the fastest way to make the journey is by car or motorbike (about two hours).

There's a ferry crossing (motorbike/car 2000/10,000d) 15km from HCMC at Binh Khanh (Cat Lai), a former US naval base. The road is paved all the way from HCMC to Can Gio. Once you get past the ferry, there is little traffic and the sides of the road are lined with mangrove forests. The motorbike ride is a day out in itself, making two wheels a good option for experienced riders. Upon arrival at the Dan Xay Bridge, switch to a boat (around 150,000d) to explore the various sights around the mangroves.

BUU LONG MOUNTAIN

Given the number of tourist pamphlets that tell you that **Buu Long Mountain** (admission 10,000d) is the 'Halong Bay of the south', you'd be forgiven for thinking that it must be an incredible place. In truth Buu Long Mountain is more like a small hill and definitely no Halong Bay, but it's a peaceful place to escape the crowds of HCMC.

The summit is 60m (mountain, they're having a laugh!) above the car park, and there are several walking trails. The top of the mountain is marked by the **Buu Phong Pagoda**, originally dating from the 17th century, from where you can look over **Long An** (Dragon Lake). There is some pretty countryside scenery, a bit of bird-watching and sweeping views of the rural farms along the Dong Nai River.

There are cold drinks and noodles at a few refreshment shops, but we recommend trying out the food at the small **vegetarian restaurant** (meals 20,000-40,000d; breakfast & lunch) at the top of the mountain.

Buu Long Mountain is 32km from central HCMC near Bien Hoa and is best reached by car or motorbike.

TRI AN FALLS

An 8m-high and 30m-wide cascade on the Song Be (Be River), the Tri An Falls are at their most spectacular in late autumn, when the river's flow is at its greatest. Tri An Falls are in Dong Nai province, 36km from Bien Hoa and 68km northeast of HCMC (via Thu Dau Mot).

Further upstream is **Tri An Reservoir** (Ho Tri An), a large artificial lake fed from the forest highlands around Dalat and created by the Tri An Dam. Completed in the early 1980s with Soviet assistance, the dam and its adjoining hydroelectric station supplies the bulk of HCMC's electric power.

VUNG TAU

064 / pop 195,400

A popular escape from the city for expats and locals alike, Vung Tau has long been overlooked by travellers as they rush up the coast to Mui Ne or Nha Trang. Perhaps not for much longer thanks to the beautiful new coastal road connecting Vung Tau to Phan Thiet and Mui Ne via some idyllic and empty beaches. Vung Tau rocks at weekends when HCMC exiles descend in numbers, but it is blissfully quiet during the week. Vung Tau's beaches have been a favourite of the Saigonese since French colonists first began coming here around 1890. It's changed a bit since then and is now big and brash, with a somewhat seedy underbelly, as the infamous case of UK glam rocker Gary Glitter highlighted during 2005–06.

Known under the French as Cap St Jacques, Vung Tau is on a peninsula jutting into the South China Sea, about 128km southeast of HCMC. The beaches here aren't Vietnam's best, but Vung Tau is a convenient beach fix from HCMC via the memorable hydrofoil ride. Oil is big business here, so the horizon is regularly dotted with oil tankers, and the industry has attracted a surprisingly large population of Russians to the city, who also make up a significant percentage of the tourists.

Orientation

Vung Tau's peninsula is punctuated by Small Mountain (Nui Nho) to the south and Big Mountain (Nui Lon) in the north. Popular Back Beach (Bai Sau) stretches for kilometres, with a wide, sandy beach and a long strip of guesthouses and hotels. There are new beach developments beyond here, including Chi Linh and Dong Hai beaches. You'll find the downtown action at Front Beach (Bai Truoc), which has been redeveloped into a series of attractive parks with marble pavements (expensive sidewalk!), but there's not much in the way of sand. If you're looking for a quiet, but pebbly beach, head for tranquil Mulberry Beach (Bai Dau), up the northwest coast.

Information

The official website for Vung Tau is at www.baobariavungtau.com and although you might be put off by the 'Agent of Communist Party of Ba Ria Vung Tau province' there are some quite useful links. Or try www.vungtauinfo.com.

International SOS (☎ 385 8776; 1 Đ Le Ngoc Han; 24hr) International standards, international prices.

Internet Cafe (4A Đ Ba Cu) Reliable connection in town centre.

Le Loi Hospital (☎ 383 2667; 22 Đ Le Loi) Main hospital.

Main post office (8 Đ Hoang Dieu) Located at the ground level of the Petrovietnam Towers building.

OSC Vietnam Travel (☎ 385 2008; www.oscvietnamtravel.com.vn; 9 Đ Le Loi) Vung Tau's leading travel agency sells a decent city map (20,000d) and offers a host of unique trips, including an old -battlefield tour.

Vietcombank (☎ 385 2024; 27-29 Đ Tran Hung Dao) Exchanges cash, travellers cheques and offers credit-card advances. It also has an ATM at the Rex Hotel.

Sights & Activities

Welcome to Rio di Vietnam, where a **giant Jesus** (admission free, parking 2000d; 7.30-11.30am & 1.30-5pm) stands atop Small Mountain with arms outstretched to embrace the South China Sea. The Vietnamese claim this is the highest Jesus statue in the world at 32m, a good 6m taller than His illustrious Brazilian cousin. It is possible to ascend to the arms for a panoramic view of Vung Tau. At His foot is a sad collection of monkeys and snakes in cramped cages, plus a couple of major field guns.

A kilometre or so northwest, the 1910 **lighthouse** (admission 2000d; 7am-5pm) boasts a spectacular 360-degree view of Vung Tau. From Cau Da Pier on Đ Ha Long, take a sharp right on the alley north of the Hai Au Hotel, then roll on up the hill.

The **White Villa** (Bach Dinh or Villa Blanche; Đ Tran Phu; admission 20,000d) was the weekend retreat of French governor Paul Doumer (later French President) and is a gorgeous, grand colonial-era residence that smacks of boutique hotel for the future. It is possible to wander the extensive gardens and spot art-nouveau features on the ageing exterior. Inside is some Ming pottery retrieved from shipwrecks off the coast. The villa sits about 30m above the road, up a winding lane.

Pagodas dot the length of Đ Ha Long, but pretty **Hon Ba pagoda** sits offshore on an islet – *the* place to be if low tide coincides with sunrise.

THE LONG TAN MEMORIAL CROSS

Nearly 60,000 Australian soldiers were involved in the American War throughout the 1960s and 1970s. The Long Tan Memorial Cross commemorates a particularly fierce battle that took place on 18 August 1966 between Australian troops and Viet Cong fighters. Originally erected by Australian survivors of the battle, the current cross is a replica installed by the Vietnamese in 2002. It is located about 18km from Ba Ria town or 55km from Vung Tau, near the town of Nui Dat. It is no longer necessary to arrange a permit to visit and can be combined with the seldom visited Lon Phuoc tunnels, an underground network similar to that at Cu Chi. Hook up with a *xe om* driver or contact OSC Travel (left).

Along Front Beach, heading towards Mulberry Beach, there are cafe-bars on the hillside facing the ocean. On weekends you'll hear local amateurs belting out the ballads *du jour,* backed by live bands. It's like karaoke, only…good.

If you have had enough of the salty sea, there are a couple of swimming pools: **Seagull & Dolphin** (Đ Thuy Ban, Back Beach). The pools are almost opposite the Imperial Plaza and both charge 50,000d for the day. **Vung Tau Beach Club** (www.vungtausurf.com; 8 Đ Thuy Ban), in the same area, offers kite surfing and surfing classes.

Oh, one more thing: where in Vietnam do you think you'll see greyhound racing? **Lam Son Stadium** (☎ 380 7309; 15 Đ Le Loi; admission 20,000d; 🕒 7-10.30pm Sat) is the place.

Sleeping

During weekends and holidays, Vung Tau's hundred or so hotels can get heavily booked, so it is sensible to book ahead.

BACK BEACH

There's a string of older midrange hotels on the western side of Small Mountain if you can't find a room on Back Beach.

Song Bien (☎ 352 3311; 131A Đ Thuy Van; d 150,000-300,000d; ❄) This is one of a cluster of places in this area. The prices here are reasonable and there is a touch (but only a touch, mind you) more decorative flair than in some of the neighbours' places.

Vungtau Intourco Resort (☎ 385 3481; www.intourcoresort.com; 1A Đ Thuy Van; r from 680,000d, bungalows from 960,000d; ❄) One of the only places located on the beach in this strip, this resort has pretty gardens and a free-form pool. Rooms are sophisticated enough and the bungalows would be a good investment for families.

Sammy Hotel (☎ 385 4755; www.sammyhotelvt.com; 157 Đ Thuy Van; r US$50-69; ❄ 💻) One of the smartest hotels this side of Small Mountain, Sammy has slick modern rooms with all the trimmings. There's no pool but it is possible to use one of the pools in the oceanfront park.

FRONT BEACH

Rex Hotel (☎ 385 2135; rex.osc@hcm.vnn.vn; 1 Đ Le Quy Don; s/d from US$32/36; ❄ 💻 🏊) A long-running hotel facing the seafront, this hotel is very good value thanks to the spacious and smart (if slightly dated) rooms and a good range of amenities including a pool and tennis courts.

Lan Rung Resort & Spa (☎ 352 6010; lanrungresort@vnn.vn; 3-6 Đ Ha Long; r US$55-100; ❄ 💻 🏊) One of the newest and smartest hotels in town, the Lan Rung is also one of the few places with a beachside setting, albeit a rocky one. The rooms are pristine and include heavy wooden furniture, plus all the usual extras. The pool is set overlooking the sea, plus there are seafood and Italian restaurants.

Grand Hotel (☎ 385 6888; www.grand.oscvn.com; 2 Đ Nguyen Du; r from US$60; ❄ 💻 🏊) It is indeed one of the grandest in town, offering smart rooms with safety deposit box and bathrobes. The pool is particularly nice, shaded by a huge banyan tree.

MULBERRY BEACH

My Tho Guesthouse (☎ 355 1722; 45 Đ Tran Phu; r 150,000-200,000d; ❄) This place is very rough and ready, but has a good location right on the water's edge. Probably only worth it if you can score a seafront room.

Binh An Village (☎ 351 0016; www.binhanvillage.com; 1 Đ Tran Phu; r & ste US$85-250; ❄ 💻 🏊) *The* desirable address in Vung Tau, the oasis that is Binh An Village feels like it has been transported straight from Bali. The bungalows are beautifully decorated with Asian antiques and set amid serene oceanfront scenery. There are two swimming pools, one ocean-fed and one freshwater, both near the sea's edge. There's also a good open-air restaurant here, with live jazz most weekend nights and à la carte cuisine.

Eating & Drinking

The road along Back Beach, Đ Thuy Van, is crammed with *com pho* shops and seafood restaurants. The nightlife is low key compared with HCMC or Nha Trang, although the oil industry ensures there is a working-girl edge to the nightlife.

FRONT BEACH

Viet An (☎ 385 3735; 1 Đ Hoang Dieu; mains 30,000-100,000d) This shady garden restaurant is located on a peaceful side street and offers an enticing combination of Vietnamese fish and seafood or 100% halal Indian food.

Ali Baba (☎ 351 0685; 7 Đ Nguyen Trai; mains around 60,000d) A popular Indian restaurant in the middle of town. We suggest the Tandoori kebab platter or one of the excellent seafood curries. This place also offers a delivery service.

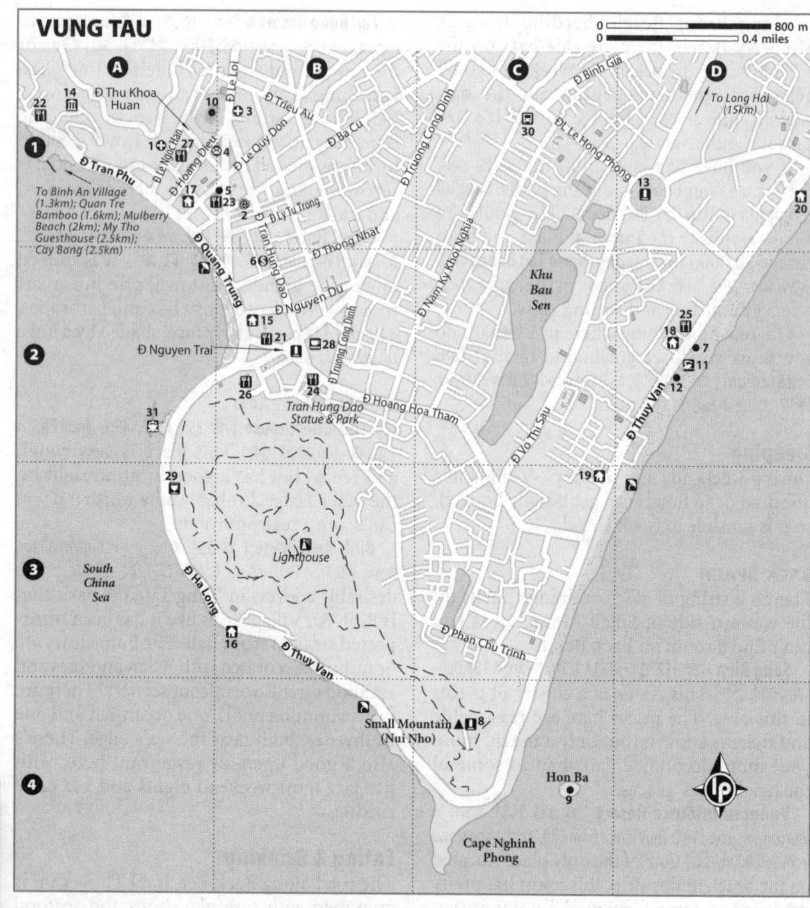

Good Morning Vietnam (☎ 385 6959; 6 Đ Hoang Hoa Tham; www.goodmorningviet.com; meals 60,000-160,000d; 🕐 breakfast, lunch & dinner) Another outpost of this coastal chain, this is the place for authentic Italian in Vung Tau. Pizzas from 70,000d.

Black Cat (☎ 361 2652; 10 Đ Tran Phu; meals 50,000-150,000d) The Black Cat team are famous for their bespoke burgers and this place doesn't disappoint. Located in the same spot as the Irish-themed Duck Bar.

Plein Sud (☎ 351 1570; 152A Đ Ha Long; mains 50,000-150,000d) One of the most atmospheric restaurants in town has a Mediterranean feel with an alfresco terrace, plus pool table, internet and bar. The menu includes an ever-changing series of specials, including fresh fish and seafood, plus wood-fired pizza and tapas.

More to consider:

Blue Note Cafe (☎ 532 247; 6 Đ Tran Hung Dao) One of the coolest cafes in this cafe neighbourhood; there is a shady terrace and free wi-fi.

Essentials (☎ 351 1294; 6 Đ Le Quy Don; 🕐 7.30am-9pm) Little shop selling international treats like cereal, cheese and chocolate.

Red Parrot (☎ 351 2563; 6 Đ Le Quy Don) This bar has a pool table, cold beers and cheap bar snacks.

Tommy's Bar (☎ 385 3554; 94 Đ Ha Long) Long-running expat bar with cold beers and an Aussie crowd.

BACK BEACH

Imperial Plaza (☎ 352 6688; 159 Đ Thuy Van) This shiny new shopping centre is not only a good respite from the heat on a blazing day, but it offers a healthy array of dining options. Downstairs is

INFORMATION		
International SOS	1	A1
Internet Café	2	B1
Le Loi Hospital	3	B1
Main Post Office	4	A1
OSC Vietnam Travel	5	B1
Vietcombank	6	B2
SIGHTS & ACTIVITIES		
Dolphin Pool	7	D2
Giant Jesus	8	C4
Hon Ba Pagoda	9	C4
Lam Son Stadium	10	A1
Oceanfront Park	11	D2
Seagull Pool	(see 7)	
Vung Tau Beach Club	12	D2
War Monument	13	D1
White Villa	14	A1
SLEEPING		
Grand Hotel	15	B2
Lan Rung Resort & Spa	16	B3
Rex Hotel	17	A1
Sammy Hotel	18	D2
Song Bien	19	C3
Vungtau Interco Resort	20	D1
EATING		
Ali Baba	21	B2
Black Cat	22	A1
Essentials	23	A1
Good Morning Vietnam	24	B2
Imperial Plaza	25	D2
Plein Sud	26	B2
Viet An	27	A1
DRINKING		
Blue Note Café	28	B2
Red Parrot	(see 23)	
Tommy's Bar	29	A3
TRANSPORT		
Bus Station	30	C1
Cau Da Pier	31	A2

a branch of the popular Highlands Coffee, with great frappes and shakes. Upstairs, the food court is perfect for those experiencing indecisiveness, with a Pho 24 outlet, a pizza joint, a juice stall and New Zealand ice cream. Easy.

MULBERRY BEACH

Mulberry Beach's main road has several good seafood places overlooking the water.

Cay Bang (☎ 383 8522; 69 Đ Tran Phu; mains 30,000-200,000d; 🕑 11am-10pm) With a great location on the water, this is one of the most popular seafood restaurants in town and draws a huge crowd at the weekend for the shellfish.

Quan Tre Bamboo (☎ 383 6157; 7 Đ Tran Phu; mains 40,000-180,000d; 🕑 lunch & dinner) Another tip-top seafood place that does the full monty like lobster or king crab. Good views of the Mary and Baby Jesus statue from the upstairs terrace.

Getting There & Away

From Mien Dong bus station in HCMC, air-con minibuses (from 40,000d, two hours, 128km) leave for Vung Tau throughout the day until around 4.30pm. From Vung Tau's **bus station** (192A Đ Nam Ky Khoi Nghia) to Mulberry Beach or Back Beach, a *xe om* will cost around 20,000d.

It's much more enjoyable to catch a hydrofoil if you have the extra dollars. **Greenlines** HCMC (☎ 08-3821 5609); Vung Tau (☎ 351 0720) and **Petro Express hydrofoil** HCMC (☎ 08-3821 0650); Vung Tau (☎ 351 5151) both run regular services to HCMC (adult/child 160,000/80,000d, 75 minutes). There are regular services throughout the day and additional boats at weekends, when it pays to book ahead. In Vung Tau the boat leaves from Cau Da pier, opposite the Hai Au Hotel.

Getting Around

Vung Tau is easily traversed on two wheels. Guesthouses can arrange bicycle hire (per day US$2); motorbikes cost US$7 to US$10 per day. Or just make eye contact with that *cyclo* or *xe om* driver on the corner.

LONG HAI

☎ 064

If Vung Tau is all a bit bling for you, then consider an escape to Long Hai, a less-commercialised seaside retreat within a couple of hours' drive of HCMC. The fishing village of Long Hai, now only 15km northeast of Vung Tau thanks to a new bridge, has a pretty white-sand beach and the area benefits from a microclimate that brings less rain than other parts of the south. This is why Bao Dai, the last emperor of Vietnam, built a holiday residence here (now the Anoasis Beach Resort).

Long Hai is a peaceful place to visit during the week, but it loses its local character on the weekends when Vietnamese tourists (and the occasional busload of Chinese visitors) pack the sands. While there are a couple of low-key resorts in the Long Hai vicinity, Western travellers have yet to arrive in numbers, so if you're looking for a lively spot with dining and nightlife action, Mui Ne (p308) is the better choice.

Sights & Activities

The western end of Long Hai's beach is where fishing boats moor and is not so clean. However, the eastern end is pretty, with white

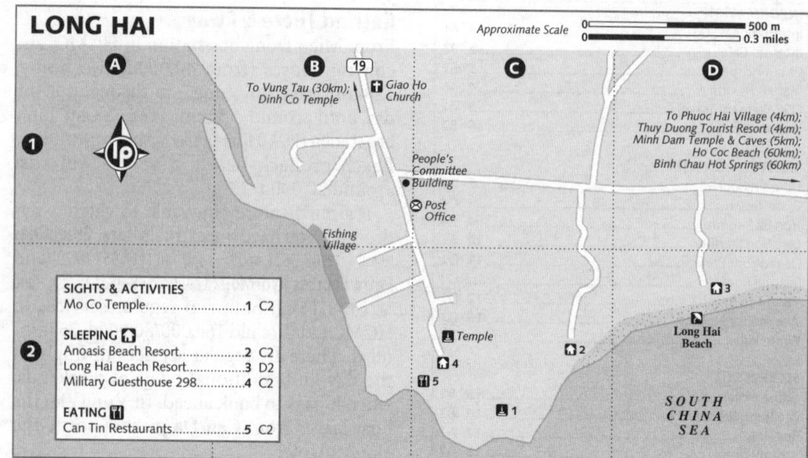

sand and swaying palms. For an even prettier beach, keep heading east.

After the Tet holiday, Long Hai hosts an annual major **fishermen's pilgrimage festival**, where hundreds of boats come from afar to worship at **Mo Co Temple**.

Apart from the beaches, there are several sites in the area well worth exploring. At Minh Dam, 5km from Long Hai, there are **caves** with historical connections to the Franco–Viet Minh and American Wars. Although the caves are little more than spaces between the boulders covering the cliff-face, VC soldiers bunked here off and on between 1948 and 1975; you can still see bullet holes in the rocks from the skirmishes that took place. Steps hewn into the rock-face lead up to the caves, with spectacular views over the coastal plains at the top.

Nearby there is a **mountain-top temple** with more great panoramic views of the coastline.

If you are heading to/from Hwy 1A or Mui Ne, north of Long Hai, a less-travelled route is along coastal Rte 55.

Sleeping

Military Guesthouse 298 (Doan an Dieu Duong 298; ☎ 386 8316; Rte 19; r 180,000-250,000d; ❄) Where Rte 19 runs out of road, this spacious complex is run by the navy, helping to explain the prime beachfront location. Some buildings were being upgraded at the time of writing, so prices may rise. Cheaper rooms are fan only.

Thuy Duong Tourist Resort (☎ 388 6215; www.thuyduongresort.com.vn; r US$42-160; ❄ 💻 🏊) This huge place sprawls across the coastal road and is located about 4km south of Long Hai. Rooms here come in every shape and size, including suites and villas. The beach here is particularly beautiful, with large boulders for kids to clamber around. Day entry is 40,000d.

Long Hai Beach Resort (☎ 366 1355; www.longhaibeachresort.com; Provincial Rd 44; r US$140-340; ❄ 💻 🏊) A newer resort about 500m east of Anoasis, the recipe is perhaps borrowed from its neighbour, although the end result is not quite as charming. Some bungalows front the beach and facilities include a tennis court, pool and gym.

Anoasis Beach Resort (☎ 386 8227; www.anoasisresort.com.vn; Provincial Rd 44; bungalows incl breakfast US$153-325; ❄ 💻 🏊) Emperor Bao Dai's former residence is one of the most charming beachside retreats on the south coast, the bungalows and cottages set in immaculate gardens fronting the beautiful private beach. Diversions include cycling, fishing, tennis and, of course, massage. Weekday rates are slightly lower than the weekend rates listed above.

Eating

There's a rustic cluster of thatch-roof beachside restaurants called **Can Tin 1**, **2**, **3** and **4** (mains around 30,000-90,000d; 🕐 7am-7pm) near Military Guesthouse 298. These serve reliable Vietnamese cuisine, including fresh seafood dishes. Dine, relax in a deckchair and then take a dip.

Getting There & Away

Long Hai is 124km from HCMC and takes about two hours to reach by car. The 15km road between Vung Tau and Long Hai will cost about 50,000d by *xe om* or about 180,000d by meter taxi one way.

LOC AN BEACH

☎ 064

A beautiful road winds along the coast from Long Hai to Binh Chau, crossing through the town of Phuoc Hai before passing by a dune-covered beach and the small **Loc An Resort** (☎ 388 6377; www.locanresort.com; d 240,000-500,000d;). Situated on a lagoon about 50m from the palm-shaded beach, this welcoming guesthouse offers clean, comfortable rooms. Boats shuttle guests to the beach and back for free. The restaurant (mains 40,000d to 80,000d) has a terrace and serves decent seafood, plus there's a pool table.

HO TRAM BEACH

☎ 064

Another 5km east of Loc An, there's a lovely stretch of sand that's blissfully undeveloped, for the time being. The big draw in this area is the **Ho Tram Beach Resort & Spa** (☎ 378 1525; www.hotramresort.com; bungalow incl breakfast US$110-220;), a beautifully landscaped complex dotted with attractive bungalows. Now under the management of Life Resorts, each has high ceilings and unique furnishings and layouts. There's also a spa, a beach bar and an open-sided restaurant (mains 100,000d to 200,000d) that's open to nonguests and is worth the experience if you're passing through the area.

Nearby is a huge construction called the Ho Tram Strip, which will see a new Sanctuary Resort and a 'strip' of shops and restaurants. Change is coming.

HO COC BEACH

☎ 064

The coastal road just keeps on snaking its way northeast and about 12km or so from Ho Tram you'll arrive at the remote and beautiful Ho Coc Beach. Golden sands, rolling dunes and clear waters, along with the lack of development, make it a real draw – particularly on weekdays, when you'll have the beach largely to yourself. As elsewhere along the coast, weekends bring crowds of Vietnamese tourists.

The area around the beach is part of an 11,000-hectare rainforest that was designated a nature reserve in 1975. Most of the larger wildlife was exterminated or else relocated for safety reasons (most of the elephants were sent to Thailand), but plenty of birds and monkeys can be spotted in the forest. Guides for the walking trails can be hired for about 80,000d a day. Inquire at Huong Phong Ho Coc (below).

Sleeping & Eating

There are only a few accommodation choices right at the beach, all of which have decent adjoining restaurants that serve great seafood options.

Huong Phong Ho Coc (☎ 387 8145; www.huongphong.com, in Vietnamese; bungalows 180,000-350,000d;) A rustic resort with a prime location near the beach, this place could be a wonderful retreat with a little imagination and investment. The cottages are pretty basic, but include TV, fridge and (cold water) bathroom. The 350,000d buys you air-con.

Hotel Ven Ven (☎ 379 1121; www.kimsabai.com; r 300,000-500,000d;) Although it lacks the beachside location of its rivals, this is a pretty place to stay with lush gardens. The rooms are smart and include quads (rooms not bikes) for 500,000d, plus some more expensive bungalows.

Saigon-Ho Coc (☎ 387 8175; bungalows US$100-134;) This place is also known as Prosperity House, and you'll be needing some prosperity to stay here after the comprehensive upgrade in 2008! It offers stylish bungalows, but tax and service is extra. Weekday discounts are available.

Getting There & Away

There's little public transport out here, but some of the budget cafes in HCMC offer overnight trips to Ho Coc. **Saigon Tourist** (☎ 08-3829 8914; www.saigontourist.net; 49 Đ Le Thanh Ton, HCMC) puts together trips to Ho Coc that include a visit to Binh Chau Hot Springs Resort (p406). This also makes for a great day trip on a motorbike from Vung Tau. The new road is in decent shape, and it's a particularly magical ride past sand dunes with lovely ocean views on certain stretches of the road between Ho Tram and Ho Coc. It is possible to continue all the way to Phan Thiet and Mui Ne, with the option of a circuit up through Dalat and back to Saigon.

BINH CHAU HOT SPRINGS

☎ 064

About 150km from HCMC, and 60km northeast of Long Hai, is **Binh Chau Hot Springs** (Suoi Khoang Nong Binh Chau; admission 25,000d) and the **Binh Chau Hot Springs Resort** (☎ 387 1131; www.saigonbinhchauecoresort.com; r incl breakfast US$34-100, bungalow US$100-267).

Chief among the attractions on this 35-hectare site is an outdoor hot-spring-fed swimming pool (admission 40,000d), although visitors wanting the full experience might opt for a soak in a mudbath (130,000d). The pool temperature is around 37°C, and the minerals in the water are said to be beneficial to bones, muscles and skin, and are able to improve blood circulation and mental disorders. There's also a spa, with massages available. On-site are a golf practice range, tennis court, restaurant and playground.

The rooms at the resort are airy and clean, with trim furnishings, but the cheaper options are on the small side. Bungalows provide roomier quarters for families. Rates include free entry, plus fancier rooms include bonuses like a free mud bath or free eggs. Whoopee!

Until about just over a decade ago there was wildlife in the area, including tigers and elephants, but it seems humans have nearly won the area over. In 1994 six elephants were captured near the springs, but after a few months of keeping them as pets their captors turned them over to the zoo in HCMC. Nowadays the only wildlife you are likely to spot are ceramic lions, cheetahs and panthers, which decorate the marshes around the springs.

The hottest spring reaches 82°C, which is hot enough to boil an egg in 10 to 15 minutes. Vietnamese visitors boil eggs in the bamboo baskets set aside for this purpose. There are a couple of giant chicken statues decorating the springs where you too can boil up a snack for yourself, with raw eggs on sale. Kitsch indeed.

Getting There & Away

The resort is in a compound 6km north of the village of Binh Chau. The road connecting Rte 55 to Binh Chau is a smooth ride, thanks to funds donated by the Australian government in the 1990s.

Good highway or not, there's no public transport, so arrange a motorbike or car; if you choose the latter, try to find some travellers to share the expense.

CAT TIEN NATIONAL PARK

☎ 061 / elev 700m

One of the outstanding natural treasures of the region, the 72,000-hectare **Cat Tien National Park** (☎ 366 9228; www.namcattien.net; adult/child 50,000/20,000d; 7am-10pm) comprises an amazingly biodiverse region of lowland tropical rain forest. The hiking, mountain biking and bird-watching are the best in Southern Vietnam. Always call ahead for reservations as the park can accommodate only a limited number of visitors. However, a word of caution, visitors rarely see any of the larger mammals resident in the park, so don't come expecting to encounter rhinos and tigers.

In the 2nd century AD, the Cat Tien area was a religious centre of the Funan empire, and ancient Oc-Eo cultural relics have been discovered in the park. Cat Tien was hit hard by defoliants during the American War, but the large old-growth trees survived and the smaller plants have recovered. Just as importantly, the wildlife has made a comeback and in 2001 Unesco added Cat Tien National Park to its list of biosphere reserves. Since then, infrastructure has improved markedly with decent overnight options. It's worth spending at least two full days here, if possible.

Fauna in the park includes 326 bird species, 100 types of mammal, 79 types of reptile, 41 amphibian species, plus an incredible array of insects, including 400 or so species of butterfly. Many of these creatures are listed as rare and endangered, including the Javan rhinoceros. Considered one of the rarest mammals in the world, this unusual rhino exists only in the Cat Loc area of Cat Tien (although there are believed to be only five to seven remaining in the park) and on the island of Java, in Indonesia. Leopards are also believed to roam here. Rare birds in the park include the orange-necked partridge, green peafowl and Siamese fireback. There is also a healthy population of monkeys. Leeches are a less desirable member of the local fauna so come prepared, especially during the wet season.

Elephants are present in the park, but their presence has caused some controversy. In the early 1990s a herd of 10 hungry elephants fell into a bomb crater, created during the American War, just outside of Cat Tien. Local villagers took pity on the elephants and dug out a ramp to rescue them. Tragically, since then a number of villagers have been killed by rampaging elephants. Theoretically, the problem could have been 'solved' by shooting the elephants, but the Vietnamese government wasn't willing to risk the wrath of international environmental groups. However, none of these organisations has come up with the funds for relocating the elephants, some of which were finally removed to zoos. In the longer term such conflicts are likely to be repeated because of the increasing competition between Vietnam's wildlife and its growing population for the same living space.

Cat Tien also boasts a wide range of evergreen, semideciduous and bamboo forests; some 1800 species of plants thrive in the park.

Cat Tien National Park can be explored on foot, by mountain bike, by 4WD and also by boat along the Dong Nai River. There are many well-established hiking trails in the park, though the catch is you'll need to hire a **guide** (per half-/full day 100,000/200,000d), as well as transportation to and from the start of the trail (4WDs can also be rented for 160,000d per hour).

Highly recommended is an overnight visit to the **Crocodile Swamp** (Bau Sau), which is a 9km drive from the park headquarters and you have to trek the last 4km to the swamp; the walk takes about three hours return. It may be possible for smaller groups (four or less) to spend the night at the ranger's post here. It's a good place to view the wildlife that comes to drink in the swamp. Another evening activity is the **night safari** (200,000d) that the park offers. Wherever you decide to go, be sure to book a guide in advance and take plenty of insect repellent.

A new addition to the park is the **Dao Tien Endangered Primate Centre**, located on an island in the Dong Nai River near the park entrance. It is still in its infancy, but in time will no doubt welcome visitors like the famous centre in Cuc Phuong National Park (p196).

The park lies 150km northeast of HCMC and 40km south of Buon Ma Thuot and straddles the border of three provinces – Lam Dong, Dong Nai and Binh Phuoc.

Sleeping & Eating

Accommodation comes in the form of wooden huts or more comfortable concrete **bungalows** (☎/fax 366 9228; hut US$20, bungalow US$25-30; [icon] [icon]) near the park headquarters. The facilities are in reasonable condition for the price, but don't expect too many frills. There is a pool and a tennis court here. It is possible to pitch a tent at the park's campsite (30,000d), but you'll need your own gear. Two basic bungalows are also under construction at Bau Sau, which will be available for US$15 per night.

There are several small restaurants near the park entrance, including a simple thatch-roof canteen (mains 25,000d to 50,000d), which opens from 7am to 10pm, and a full-on restaurant (mains 30,000d to 70,000d) serving heartier fare just down the path. This place is open from 7am to 8pm.

Getting There & Away

Whichever way you come, you'll be dropped off at the park office, 100m before the ferry across the Dong Nai River to park headquarters. Buy your entrance ticket from the park office, which includes the price of the ferry crossing.

The most common approach to the park is from Hwy 20, which connects HCMC with Dalat. To reach the park, follow the narrow 24km road, which branches west from Hwy 20 at Tan Phu, 125km north of HCMC and 175km south of Dalat. The road to the park is signposted at the junction, and with your own wheels getting there shouldn't be a hassle.

By bus, take any Dalat-bound service (40,000d or so, four hours) and ask the driver to let you off at Vuon Quoc Gia Cat Tien. From this junction, you can hire a motorbike (they're always around) to take you the remaining 25km to the park (around 60,000d).

Another approach to Cat Tien National Park is to take a boat across Langa Lake and then go by foot from there. **Dalat Holidays/Phat Tire Ventures** (☎ 063-382 9422; www.phattireventures.com) is a reputable eco-tour operator in Dalat and is a good place to inquire about this.

Although many travel agencies from HCMC operate tours to the park, we've received mixed reviews about the budget agencies. For a reputable customised birding, bike or hiking tour, contact Sinhbalo Adventures (p351).

CON DAO ISLANDS

☎ 064 / pop 1650

Isolated from the mainland, the Con Dao Islands are one of the star attractions in Vietnam. Long the Alcatraz of Indochina, and the preserve of political prisoners and undesirables, this place is now turning heads thanks to its striking natural beauty. Con Son, the largest of this chain of 15 islands and islets, is ringed with lovely beaches, coral reefs and scenic bays, and remains partially covered in thick forests. In addition to hiking, diving and exploring empty coastal roads and deserted beaches, there are some excellent wildlife-watching opportunities.

Con Son Island (with a total land area of 20 sq km) is also known by its Europeanised Malay name, Iles Poulo Condore (Pulau Kundur), which means 'Island of the Squashes'. Although it seems something of an island paradise, Con Son was once hell on earth for the thousands of prisoners who languished in confinement during the French- and American-backed regimes.

Roughly 80% of the land area in the island chain is part of Con Dao National Park, which protects Vietnam's most important **sea turtle nesting grounds**. For the last decade the World Wildlife Foundation (WWF) has been working with local park rangers on a long-term monitoring program. During nesting season (May to September) the park sets up ranger stations to rescue threatened nests and move them to the safe haven of hatcheries.

Other interesting sea life around Con Dao includes the **dugong**, a rare and seldom-seen marine mammal in the same family as the manatee. Dugongs live as far north as Japan, and as far south as the subtropical coasts of Australia. Their numbers have been on a steady decline, and increasingly efforts are being made to protect these gentle creatures. Major threats include coastal road development, which causes the destruction of shallow-water beds of seagrass, the dugongs' staple diet.

Con Dao is one of those rare places in Vietnam where there are virtually no structures over two storeys, and where the traveller's experience is almost hassle-free. So far, it's not even necessary to bargain at the local market. Owing to the relatively high cost and the inaccessibility of the islands, mass tourism has thankfully been kept at bay.

Even today, most visitors to Con Son are package-tour groups of former VC soldiers who were imprisoned on the island. The Vietnamese government generously subsidises these jaunts as a show of gratitude for their sacrifice. Foreign tourists are still few and far between, though their numbers are on the rise.

The driest time to visit Con Dao is from November to February, although the seas are

NATIONAL HIGHWAY 20: ROADSIDE ATTRACTIONS

Langa Lake

The HCMC–Dalat road (Hwy 20) spans this reservoir, which is crossed by a bridge. Lots of floating houses, where families harvest the fish underneath, can be seen here. It's a very scenic spot for photography, and most tourist vehicles on the HCMC–Dalat road make a short pit stop here.

Volcanic Craters

Near Dinh Quan on Hwy 20 there are three volcanoes, now extinct, but nonetheless very impressive. The craters date from the late Jurassic period, about 150 million years ago. You'll have to do a little walking to see the craters. One is on the left-hand side of the road, about 2km south of Dinh Quan, and another on the right-hand side about 8km beyond Dinh Quan, towards Dalat.

Underground Lava Tubes

A bit beyond the volcanic craters, towards Dalat, are underground lava tubes. These rare caves were formed as the surface lava cooled and solidified, while the hotter underground lava continued to flow, leaving a hollow space. Lava tubes differ sharply in appearance from limestone caves (the latter are formed by underground springs). While limestone caves have abundant stalactites and stalagmites, the walls of lava caves are smooth.

The easiest way to find the lava tubes is to first find the teak forest on Hwy 20 between the Km120 and Km124 markers. The children who live around the forest can point you to the entrance of the lava tubes. However, you are strongly advised *not* to go into the tubes by yourself. It's best to have a guide and, furthermore, inform someone responsible where you are going. You definitely need to take a torch (flashlight).

calmest from March to July. The rainy season lasts from June to September, but there are also northeast and southwest monsoons from September to November that can bring heavy winds. In November 1997 typhoon Linda unleashed her fury here: 300 fishing boats were lost, reefs were wiped out and the forests flattened. September and October are the hottest months, though even then the cool island breezes make Con Dao relatively comfortable when compared with HCMC or Vung Tau.

Change has been almost glacial compared with the mainland resorts of Nha Trang and Mui Ne, but things are starting to move. The arrival of the super-luxurious Six Senses residences is a sign of the times, although as the name suggests, they are for purchase, and not a resort. Watch this space.

History

Occupied at various times by the Khmer, Malays and Vietnamese, Con Son Island also served as an early base for European commercial ventures in the region. The first recorded European arrival was a ship of Portuguese mariners in 1560. The British East India Company maintained a fortified trading post here from 1702 to 1705 – an experiment that ended when the English on the island were massacred in a revolt by the Makassar soldiers they had recruited on the Indonesian island of Sulawesi.

Con Son Island has a strong political and cultural history, and an all-star line-up of Vietnamese revolutionary heroes (many streets are named after them) were incarcerated here. Under the French, Con Son was used as a major prison for opponents of French colonialism, earning a reputation for the routine mistreatment and torture of prisoners. In 1954 the island was taken over by the South Vietnamese government, which continued to utilise its remoteness to hold opponents of the government (including students) in horrendous conditions. During the American War the South Vietnamese were joined here by US forces.

Information

The **national park headquarters** (☎ 383 0150; vqgcdao@hcm.vnn.vn; 29 Đ Vo Thi Sau; 🕙 7-11.30am & 1.30-5pm Mon-Fri, 7.30-11am & 2-4.30pm Sat) is a good place to get information. Since the military controls access to parts of the national park, stop here first to have staff brief you on possible island excursions and hikes; this office also distributes a useful free handout on hikes around the island. Some hiking trails have interpretive signage in English and Vietnamese. The headquarters also has an exhibition hall with displays on the diversity of local forest and marine life, threats to the local environment, and local conservation activities.

> **PENNILESS IN PARADISE**
>
> Before flying out to the Con Dao Islands be sure to get ample funds as there are no banks or ATMs.

Several internet cafes are found in town, including one attached to the **post office** (cnr Đ Tran Phu & Nguyen Thi Minh Khai; 🕙 8am-8pm).

Sights & Activities

CON DAO NATIONAL PARK

From March to November it's possible to do a beautiful and leisurely two-hour **trek** starting from near the airport runway, but you'll definitely need a local guide to do this (about US$7 for the outing). The walk leads through thick forest and mangroves, and past a hilltop stream to **Bamboo Lagoon** (Dam Tre). This spot is stunning and there's good snorkelling in the bay. You might even consider arranging for a boat to come and pick you up.

A hike that you can do yourself is a 1km walk (about 25 minutes each way) through rainforest to **Ong Dung Bay**. The trail begins a few kilometres north of town. On the road to the trailhead, you'll also pass the ruins of the Ma Thien Lanh Bridge, which was built by prisoners under the French occupation. The bay itself has only a rocky beach, although there is an interesting display of coral 300m off shore.

Rainbow Divers (www.divevietnam.com) were based on the island, but the authorities are being very cautious when it comes to sites, so they have suspended operations for now. Check their website for updates. There are some excellent dives among the coral reefs around the islands. During the dry season (November to May) visibility is good and dives are less likely to be cancelled.

CON SON ISLAND

Con Son town is a sleepy seafront settlement that would make a perfect location for a

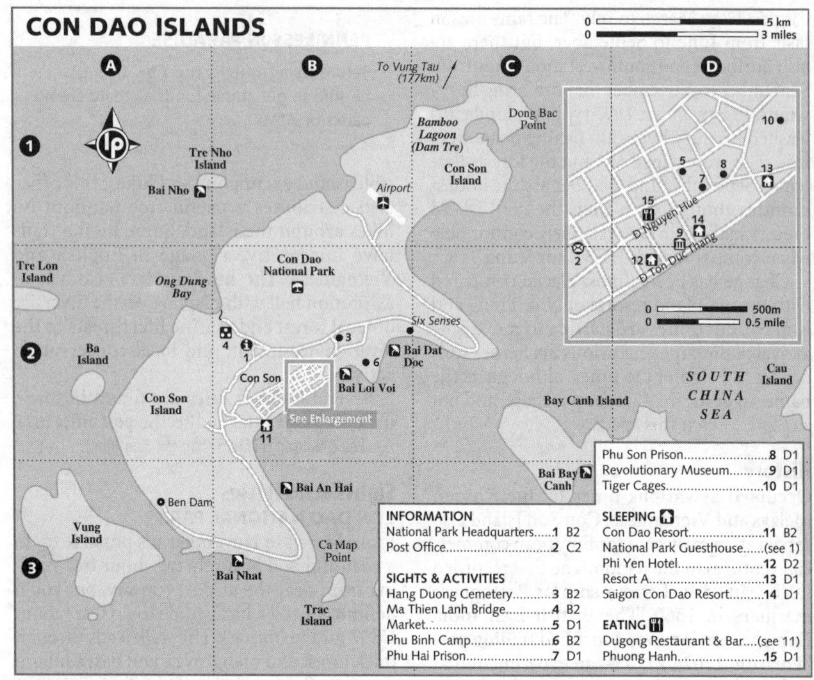

period film. All three of the town's hotels are on Đ Ton Duc Thang, along a strip of forlorn single-storey French villas (most are abandoned and in disrepair, but nonetheless photogenic). Nearby is the local **market**, which is busiest between 7am and 8am.

The main sights on Con Son Island are a museum, several prisons and a cemetery. If you visit the museum first you can buy a ticket for 35,000d that will get you a guided tour of the museum and prisons – very good value.

The **Revolutionary Museum** (7-11am & 1.30-5pm Mon-Sat) is next to Saigon Con Dao Hotel and has exhibits on Vietnamese resistance to the French, communist opposition to the Republic of Vietnam, and the treatment of political prisoners (including some gruesome photos of torture). There is also a mock-up of the islands and some curiously embalmed animals – including a monkey smoking a pipe.

Phu Hai Prison, a short walk from the museum, is the largest of the 11 prisons on the island. Built in 1862, the prison houses several enormous detention buildings, one with about 100 shackled and emaciated mannequins that are all too lifelike. Equally eerie are the empty solitary cells with ankle shackles (the decree on the walls in Vietnamese means 'no killing fleas' – prisoners were not allowed to dirty the walls). Nearby is the equally disturbing **Phu Son Prison.**

The notorious **Tiger Cages** were built by the French in the 1940s. From 1957 to 1961 nearly 2000 political prisoners were confined in these tiny cells. Here there are 120 chambers with ceiling bars, where guards could watch down on the prisoners like tigers in a zoo, and another 60 solariums with no roof at all.

Over the course of four decades of war, some 20,000 people were killed on Con Son and 1994 of their graves can be seen at **Hang Duong Cemetery**. Sadly, only 700 of these graves bear the name of the victims. Vietnam's most famous heroine, Vo Thi Sau (1933–52), was the first woman executed by a firing squad on Con Son, on 23 January 1952. Today's pilgrims come to burn incense at her tomb, and make offerings of mirrors and combs, symbolic because she died so young. In the distance behind the cemetery you'll see a huge **monument** symbolising three giant sticks of incense.

Phu Binh Camp is also part of the main tour, though it's outside of town. Built in 1971 by the Americans, this one has 384 chambers and was known as Camp 7 until 1973, when it closed following evidence of torture. After the Paris Agreements in 1973, the name was changed to Phu Binh Camp.

CON SON BEACHES & OTHER ISLANDS

On Con Son there are several good beaches worth seeking out. Inquire at the hotels about snorkelling-gear rental for about 60,000d per day. **Bai Dat Doc** is a beautiful beach with a long stretch of sand, although part of this has now been cornered by the new Six Senses residences. Keep an eye out for dugongs frolicking in the water.

Bai Nhat is small and very nice, though it's exposed only during low tide. **Bai An Hai** looks appealing, but there are a good number of fishing boats moored nearby, and a few too many sandflies. **Bai Loi Voi** is another option, but there can be a fair bit of rubbish and lots of sea shells.

The best beaches of all are on the smaller islands, such as the beautiful white-sand beach on **Tre Lon**. Perhaps the best all-round island to visit is **Bay Canh**, which has lovely beaches, old-growth forest, mangroves, coral reefs (good snorkelling at low tide) and sea turtles (seasonal). There is a fantastic two-hour walk to a functioning French-era **lighthouse**.

Sleeping & Eating

Three of Con Son's hotels are on the main road facing the bay in town.

Phi Yen Hotel (☎ 383 0168; 34 Đ Ton Duc Thang; s/d 180,000/240,000d;) This is pretty basic compared with the atmospheric resorts dotted about the island, but is cheap enough if you are looking to save some cash. Still, you're in the wrong part of Vietnam to be doing that. Air-con, hot water and some sea views.

Resort A (☎ 383 0111; www.atcvietnam.com; 8 Đ Ton Duc Thang; bungalow from US$30, villa US$60-90;) 'A' offers rooms in old converted villas dating back to the French-colonial era, although luckily they have been upgraded since. Some include period wooden furniture. There are also two spacious thatch-roof stilt houses relocated here from Hoa Binh, all set in lovely gardens. Resort A offers good deals via its website, includes seafood meals, some booze and transport. Plus free wi-fi that works.

Saigon Con Dao Resort (☎ 383 0155; www.saigoncondao.com; 18 Đ Ton Duc Thang; s US$35-65, d US$42-72;) Another property playing the colonial card, this place is set in a cluster of old French buildings about 400m south of Resort A, and offers smart but not particularly stylish rooms, some with ocean views. Most visitors end up here on package tours booked through the Saigon Tourist office (p351) in HCMC.

Con Dao Resort (☎ 383 0939; www.condaoresort.com.vn; 8 Đ Nguyen Duc Thuan; r US$45-80, ste US$120;) The smartest place on Con Dao,

THE RETURN OF THE GREEN SEA TURTLE

Two decades ago the fate of the Green Sea Turtle *(Chelonia mydas)* in Con Dao was in jeopardy. They were prized for their meat, and their shells had value as souvenirs. To make matters worse, the turtles' numbers were decimated by destructive fishing practices. And yet, today, following a decade of local and foreign initiatives, the turtle has made a remarkable comeback. One of Vietnam's most important sea-turtle nesting sites lies scattered around the shores of the Con Dao archipelago. The World Wildlife Foundation (WWF) has given substantial help, as have other international organisations, by setting up conservation stations on the islands of Bay Canh, Tre Lon, Tai and Cau. According to WWF, since 1995 more than 300,000 hatchlings have been released into the sea. In 2006, 85% of sea-turtle eggs hatched successfully – the highest percentage in Vietnam. Later that year WWF also launched a satellite tracking program (the first of its kind in Vietnam) to give conservation workers a better understanding of migration patterns, as well as key habitats used by the turtles for feeding and mating. Though the population is on the rise, many turtles still die after nesting, often by getting ensnared in fishing nets.

Visitors wishing to see the turtles in their natural habitat can arrange a trip to Bay Canh Island and spend the night at the conversation site. (Turtles only lay their eggs at night, each one producing three to 10 nests with an average of 70 eggs.) The best time to see them is during the nesting season, which is from May to September. For information on trips, inquire at Con Dao National Park headquarters (p409). Tours prices vary from US$50 to US$100.

this resort has its own stretch of private beach, as well as an inviting swimming pool. It lies about 600m south of town and offers smart and stylish rooms with beach or mountain views. It is also home to the Dugong Restaurant and Bar, the best diner in town with mains from 50,000d to 120,000d.

All the other hotels also have restaurants, but if you want to mix it with the locals, try **Phuong Hanh** (☎ 383 0180; 38C Đ Nguyen Hue; mains 30,000-80,000d), a welcoming restaurant in the centre of town.

Plus a real cheapie:

National Park Guesthouse (☎ 383 0150; vqgcdao@hcm.vnn.vn; 29 Đ Vo Thi Sau; r 180,000d) Run by the national park department, this place has basic rooms, some with views towards the nearby peaks. However, we have heard reports of things disappearing here, so take care with valuables. It's 2km north of town.

Getting There & Around

AIR

With its upgraded airport, there are now daily flights between Con Son Island and Ho Chi Minh City (US$54 one way), operated by Vasco (Vietnam Air Services Company). The tiny airport is about 15km from the town centre. All of the hotels on the island provide free transport both to and from the airport. Although it's advisable to book your hotel in advance, you can often show up and grab a seat on one of the hotel shuttle vans that meet the planes.

BOAT

If you want to explore the islands by boat, hire one from the national park office. A 12-person boat costs around 1,500,000d per day.

MOTORBIKE & BICYCLE

Some of the main sites on Con Son, such as the Revolution Museum and Phu Hai Prison, are within walking distance of town, but to get further afield a motorbike is ideal. All of the hotels rent motorbikes for about US$7 to US$10 per day (bicycles cost around US$2 per day). There are good coastal cycling routes, such as from town to Bai Nhat and onto the tiny settlement of Ben Dam, some gentle ups and downs and, thankfully, little motorised traffic.

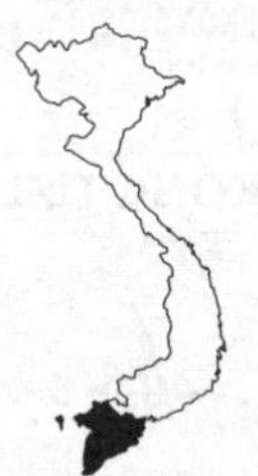

Mekong Delta

The 'rice bowl' of Vietnam, the Mekong Delta is an idyllic landscape carpeted in a dizzying variety of greens. It is a water world where boats, houses and even markets float upon the endless rivers, canals and streams that flow through like life-giving arteries. Battling with nature and the seasons, the people produce one of the most bountiful rice harvests on earth.

The delta, which alone yields enough rice to feed Vietnam with a healthy surplus, was formed by sediment deposited by the Mekong. The process continues today, with silt deposits extending the shoreline by as much as 80m per year, although the effects of climate change could see this growth reverse dramatically in coming decades. The river is so large that it has two daily tides. Lush with rice paddies, the delta plain also nourishes the cultivation of sugar cane, fruit and coconut. Although the area is primarily rural, it is one of the most densely populated regions in Vietnam and nearly every hectare is intensively farmed.

The uniquely southern charm with its welcoming introduction to life along the river is the real draw, and visitors can explore quaint riverside towns, sample fruits traded in the colourful floating markets or dine on home-cooked delicacies before overnighting as a homestay guest or on a traditional boat. There are also bird sanctuaries, rustic beach getaways like Hon Chong and impressive Khmer pagodas in the regions around Soc Trang and Tra Vinh.

Those seeking a tropical hideaway will find it on Phu Quoc, an island dotted with pretty beaches, freshwater springs and empty dirt roads, ideal for motorbike adventures. Good diving and powdery white-sand beaches have earned it the status of 'the next big thing', with a mix of cheap bungalows and five-star resorts lining the uncrowded coastline.

HIGHLIGHTS

- Experience life up close and personal at one of the many **homestays** (p425) around Vinh Long
- Meander along the canals between **My Tho** (p415) and **Ben Tre** (p420) then step ashore a lush river island to feast on fresh fish
- Seek out striking Khmer pagodas and learn about the Mekong's first inhabitants in **Tra Vinh** (p426)
- Explore floating fish farms and Cham villages around the traditional town of **Chau Doc** (p449)
- Leave your worries behind on the blissful beaches of idyllic **Phu Quoc Island** (p464)

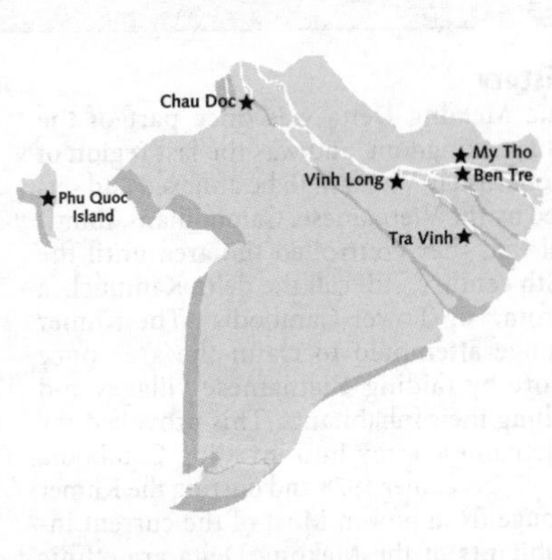

- ELEVATION: 0–3M
- BEST TIME TO VISIT: NOV–MAR

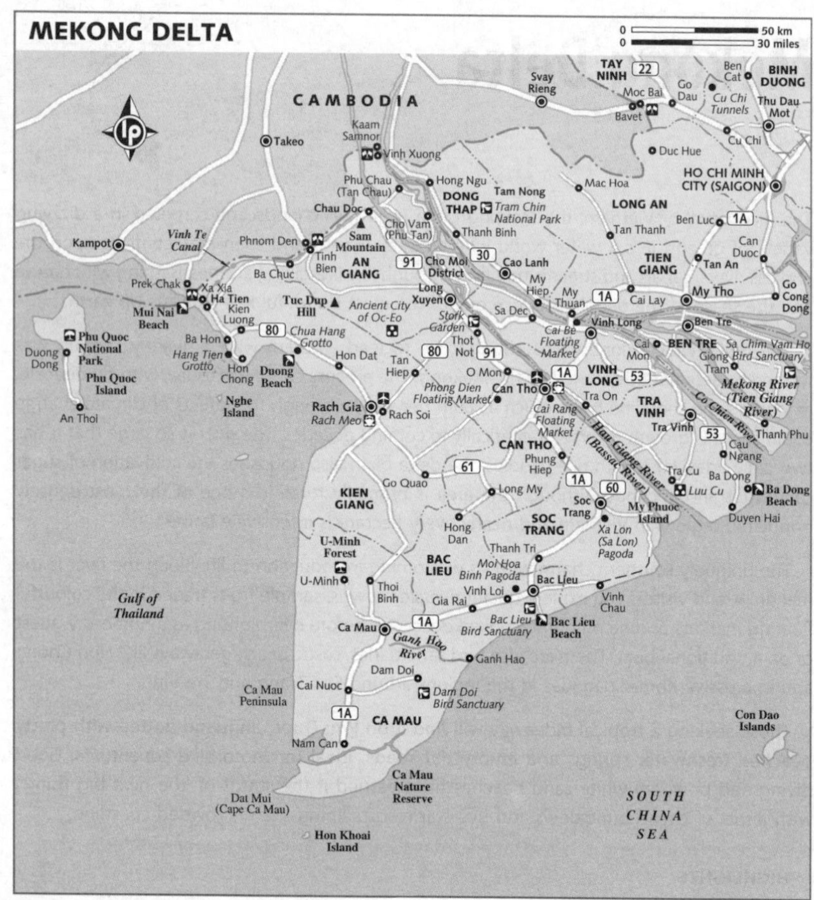

History

The Mekong Delta was once part of the Khmer kingdom, and was the last region of modern-day Vietnam to be annexed and settled by the Vietnamese. Cambodians, mindful that they controlled the area until the 18th century, still call the delta Kampuchea Krom, or 'Lower Cambodia'. The Khmer Rouge attempted to claim the area once more by raiding Vietnamese villages and killing their inhabitants. This provoked the Vietnamese army into invading Cambodia on 25 December 1978 and ousting the Khmer Rouge from power. Most of the current inhabitants of the Mekong Delta are ethnic Vietnamese, but there are also significant populations of ethnic Chinese and Khmer, as well as a few Chams. For more information on the story of the Khmer people and their place in the Mekong Delta region, see p431.

When the government introduced collective farming to the delta in 1975, production fell significantly and there were food shortages in Saigon, although farmers in the delta easily grew enough to feed themselves. The Saigonese would head down to the delta to buy sacks of black-market rice, but to prevent 'profiteering' the police set up checkpoints and confiscated rice from anyone carrying more than 10kg. All this ended in 1986 and farmers in this region have since propelled Vietnam to become one of the world's largest rice exporters.

WARNING: BIRD FLU ALERTS

Although bird flu comes and goes as a media story in the West, there are persistent if small outbreaks in Vietnam. While these rarely affect the average tourist, they often lead to the temporary closure of bird sanctuaries in the region to avoid the risk of avian-human contact. To avoid disappointment, call ahead if planning a long trip to a specific bird sanctuary.

Getting There & Around

Most travellers head to the Mekong Delta on an organised tour – a cheap and easy way to get a taste of the delta. Those travelling on their own will have greater access to areas off the beaten track, with many little-visited places to discover.

There are excellent bus connections throughout the delta, as there are so many major population centres. As well as public buses, private operator **Mai Linh** (☎ 08-3929 2929) connects most major towns with Ho Chi Minh City (HCMC).

Travel by express minibus is cheap, efficient and comfortable (though sometimes crowded). The ultimate way to see the delta, however, is by private car, bicycle or rented motorbike. Two-wheeling around the delta is good fun, especially getting lost among the maze of country roads.

With the opening of several border crossings between Vietnam and Cambodia, including the river border at Vinh Xuong (near Chau Doc) and the land border at Xa Xia (near Ha Tien), many travellers are choosing these delta routes ahead of the original land crossing at Moc Bai. Cambodian visas are available on arrival at all border crossings.

Wherever you travel in the delta, be prepared for ferry crossings. Fruit, soft drinks and sticky rice-based snacks are sold in the ferry waiting areas.

TOURS

Numerous travel agents in HCMC offer inexpensive tours. See p351 for a list of recommended companies. The cheapest tours are sold around the Pham Ngu Lao area. Shop around before you book, and remember that you usually get what you pay for. This is not to say pricey tours are necessarily better, but sometimes 'rock-bottom' means all you will get is a brief glance at the region from a packed bus full of other tourists. The cost largely depends on how far from HCMC the tour goes. The standard of accommodation, transport, food and the size of the group will be other determining factors.

MY THO

☎ 073 / pop 180,000

Gateway to the Mekong Delta, for some whirlwind visitors on a day trip to the delta region, this is the Mekong Delta. The slow-paced, at least compared with HCMC, capital of Tien Giang province, My Tho is an important market town, but for the famous floating markets, it is necessary to continue on to Can Tho (p434). The riverfront makes for a pleasant stroll and the town is easily explored on foot.

My Tho was founded in the 1680s by Chinese refugees fleeing Taiwan for political reasons. The Chinese population is small these days, the people having been driven out in the late 1970s when their property was seized by the government. The economy is based on tourism, fishing and the cultivation of rice, coconuts, bananas, mangoes, longans and citrus fruit.

Orientation

Sprawling along the bank of the northernmost branch of the Mekong River, My Tho is laid out in a regular grid pattern.

The bus station is 3km west of town. Coming from the bus station, you enter My Tho on Đ Ap Bac, which turns into Đ Nguyen Trai (oriented west–east).

Parallel to the Mekong River is Đ 30 Thang 4 (also written as Đ 30/4), named for Saigon Liberation Day.

Information

The official tourism authority for Tien Giang province, **Tien Giang Tourist** (Cong Ty Du Lich Tien Giang; ☎ 387 3184; www.tiengiangtourist.com; 8 Đ 30 Thang 4; 🕑 7am-5pm) has an impressive new home on the riverfront, but service is a bit sleepy for individual travellers. You're better off enquiring at the tourism desks found at hotels. **Mekong Tour** (☎ 387 4324; congdoantourist@hcm.vnn.vn; 61 Đ 30 Thang 4), attached to the Trade Union Hotel, offers a range of excursions including bicycle tours (with an overnight homestay) and boat tours to the floating markets. Most trips are priced at group rates (boat/bicycle excursion per

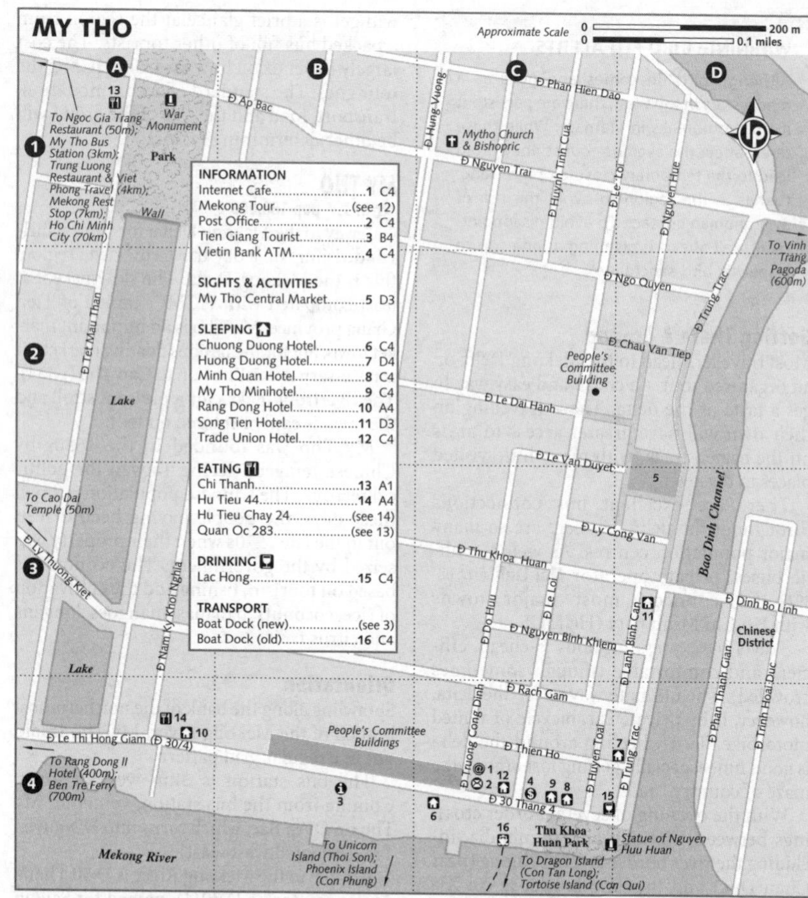

person US$7/12), so you'll have to negotiate if you're on your own.

There's a **Vietin Bank ATM** (cnr Đ 30 Thang 4 & Đ Le Loi) near the Trade Union Hotel. The **post office** (59 Đ 30 Thang 4) has an internet cafe next door.

Sights

CAO DAI TEMPLE

If you missed the one in Tay Ninh (p395), My Tho has its own colourful but smaller **Cao Dai Temple** (Đ Ly Thuong Kiet) that's worth a look. It's west of the town centre between Đ Dong Da and Đ Tran Hung Dao.

MY THO CENTRAL MARKET

This **market** (Đ Trung Trac & Đ Nguyen Hue) is in an area of town that is closed to traffic. The streets are filled with stalls selling everything from fresh food and bulk tobacco to boat propellers. In an attempt to clear these streets, the local government has built a three-storey concrete monstrosity on the riverside, intending to relocate vendors inside. With the high rent and taxes, however, most sellers prefer to take their chances on the street.

VINH TRANG PAGODA

The monks at **Vinh Trang Pagoda** (60A Đ Nguyen Trung Truc; admission free; 9-11.30am & 1.30-5pm), a beautiful and well-maintained sanctuary, provide a home for orphans, disabled and other needy children. Donations are always welcome.

The pagoda is about 1km from the city centre. To get here, take the bridge east across the river on Đ Nguyen Trai and after 400m turn left. The entrance to the sanctuary is about 200m from the turn-off, on the right-hand side of the building as you approach it from the ornate gate.

Tours

Boat trips are the highlight of a visit to My Tho. The small wooden vessels can navigate the mighty Mekong (barely), but the target for most trips is cruising past pleasant rural villages through the maze of small canals. Depending on what you book, destinations usually include a coconut-candy workshop, a honey-bee farm (try the banana wine) and an orchid garden.

The My Tho People's Committee has a near-monopoly on boat travel, charging around US$25 for a two- to three-hour tour. Private touts operate customised tours cheaper than the 'official' rates (per hour around 75,000d), however they are illegal and there's a small chance the boatman may be fined by the river cops. The best place to look for these freelancers is along the riverfront, but they'll find you first.

Sleeping

Trade Union Hotel (Khach San Cong Doan; ☎ 387 4324; congdoantourist@hcm.vnn.vn; 61 Đ 30 Thang 4; r 100,000-220,000d; ❄) This old and rambling place is

THE RIVER OF NINE DRAGONS

The Mekong River is one of the world's great rivers and its delta is one of the world's largest. The Mekong originates high in the Tibetan plateau, flowing 4500km through China, between Myanmar (Burma) and Laos, through Laos, along the Laos–Thailand border, and through Cambodia and Vietnam on its way to the South China Sea. At Phnom Penh (Cambodia), the Mekong River splits into two main branches: the Hau Giang (Lower River, also called the Bassac River), which flows via Chau Doc, Long Xuyen and Can Tho to the sea; and the Tien Giang (Upper River), which splits into several branches at Vinh Long and empties into the sea at five points. The numerous branches of the river explain the Vietnamese name for the Mekong: Song Cuu Long (River of Nine Dragons).

The Mekong's flow begins to rise around the end of May and reaches its highest point in September; it ranges from 1900 to 38,000 cubic metres per second depending on the season. A tributary of the river that empties into the Mekong at Phnom Penh drains Cambodia's Tonle Sap Lake. When the Mekong is at flood stage, this tributary reverses its direction and flows into the Tonle Sap, acting as one of the world's largest natural flood barriers. Unfortunately, deforestation in Cambodia is disturbing this delicate balancing act, resulting in more flooding in Vietnam's portion of the Mekong River basin.

In recent years seasonal flooding has claimed the lives of hundreds and forced tens of thousands of residents to evacuate from their homes. In some areas inhabitants are not able to return to their homes until the waters fully recede several months later. Floods cause millions of dollars worth of damage and have a catastrophic effect on regional rice and coffee crops.

Living on a flood plain presents some technical challenges. Lacking any high ground to escape flooding, many delta residents build their houses on bamboo stilts to avoid the rising waters. Many roads are submerged or turn to muck during floods; all-weather roads have to be built on raised embankments, but this is expensive. The traditional solution has been to build canals and travel by boat. There are thousands of canals in the Mekong Delta – keeping them properly dredged and navigable is a constant but essential chore.

A further challenge is keeping the canals clean. The normal practice of dumping all garbage and sewage directly into the waterways behind the houses that line them is taking its toll. Many of the more populated areas in the Mekong Delta are showing signs of unpleasant waste build-up. The World Wildlife Foundation (WWF) is one organisation that's working with local and provincial governments to improve conservation techniques and sponsoring environmental education and awareness programs.

Life in the waters of the Mekong includes copious catfish, one of the rarest being the giant Mekong catfish, the largest freshwater fish in the world, which can reach 3m in length. Further north in Cambodia and Laos, the freshwater Irrawaddy dolphin is still present in small pockets. As well as bountiful fish, there are also many varieties of water snakes, turtles and aquatic insects. To learn more, visit **WWF Greater Mekong Programme** (www.worldwildlife.org).

good value if you aren't bothered by the creakiness of the rooms. Triples from 120,000d and quads for 220,000d can't be bad. More-expensive rooms include hot water; all have TV and fridge.

Rang Dong Hotel (☎ 387 4400; 25 Đ 30 Thang 4; r 130,000-150,000d; ❄) Still popular with budget travellers, this family-run place has good-value rooms, including 3rd-floor offerings that face a terrace with river views.

Rang Dong II Hotel (☎ 397 0085; Đ Le Thi Hong Giam; r US$16-22; ❄ 💻) This newer hotel offers a smarter touch than its namesake (above), but is not so central.

Song Tien Hotel (☎ 387 2009; 101 Đ Trung Trac; r 160,000-260,000d; ❄) At this reliable midrange option, the rooms include satellite TV, a minibar and hot water. The 'suites' have fancier furniture. There is also a lift and reasonably legit massage.

Chuong Duong Hotel (☎ 387 0875; www.chuongduonghotel.com; 10 Đ 30 Thang 4; r 350,000-500,000d; ❄) The daddy of all hotels in My Tho, it has a superb riverside location and all rooms overlook the Mekong. Spot the early-morning swimmers doing their exercise in the river or join them if you feel brave. Rooms come with all the obvious amenities. The restaurant here is worth a visit for its range of dishes, plus there is a lively coffee shop.

Other offerings:

Huong Duong Hotel (☎ 387 2011; 33 Đ Trung Trac; r 100,000-200,000d; ❄) Just about overlooking the river, this budget hotel has good-value rooms and a rooftop cafe.

Minh Quan Hotel (☎ 397 9979; 69 Đ 30 Thang 4; r 300,000-650,000d; ❄ 💻) Judged on rooms alone, this is the smartest place in town, with inviting decor and free wi-fi. But the rooftop coffee shop bangs out loud tunes until 11pm or so.

My Tho Minihotel (☎ 387 2543; 67 Đ 30 Thang 4; r 130,000-200,000d; ❄) The cheap riverside rooms run from singles to quads but none have hot water.

Otherwise, overnight in the rarely visited hotel on Phoenix Island (opposite) or opt for a homestay around Ben Tre or Vinh Long (p425).

Eating & Drinking

My Tho is known for a special vermicelli soup, *hu tieu my tho,* which is richly garnished with fresh and dried seafood, pork, chicken and fresh herbs. It is served either with broth or dry and can also be made vegetarian.

Although *hu tieu* can be found at almost any eatery in town, there's a handful of specialty restaurants. Carnivores should try **Hu Tieu 44** (44 Đ Nam Ky Khoi Nghia; soups 15,000d), while vegetarians can indulge at **Hu Tieu Chay 24** (24 Đ Nam Ky Khoi Nghia; soups 10,000d).

Quan Oc 283 (☎ 397 0372; 283 Đ Tet Mau Than; mains 10,000-100,000d; 🕑 lunch & dinner) This is the place to come for a bargain seafood barbecue. Point at the platters out the front, piled high with clams, scallops, mussels and snails, or venture behind to the tanks of live fish, crab and shrimp. Busting with locals and lots of beer.

Mekong Rest Stop (☎ 385 8676; www.mekongreststop.com.vn; Hwy 60; mains 30,000-120,000d) About 8km west of town, this complex includes a thatched-roof restaurant and some of the best bathrooms this side of HCMC. While it serves a good assortment of fresh seafood and traditional dishes amid the lush gardens, it does get overrun with tour groups passing through the delta.

Lac Hong (☎ 397 6459; 3 Đ Trung Trac; drinks 5000-25,000d) Set in a gorgeous old colonial-era trading house on the riverfront, this place has real style and wouldn't be out of place in downtown HCMC. Downstairs are lounge chairs and free wi-fi, upstairs breezes and river views. Live music on Thursdays.

Other worthy contenders:

Chi Thanh (☎ 387 3756; 279 Đ Tet Mau Than; mains 15,000-80,000d) This small restaurant does a steady trade in tasty Chinese and Vietnamese fare, with a menu in English.

Ngoc Gia Trang (☎ 387 2742; 196 Đ Ap Bac; mains 25,000-70,000d; 🕑 lunch & dinner) This friendly spot sits among greenery on the road into My Tho from HCMC. The large menu is well translated in English and French.

Trung Luong (☎ 385 5441; Hwy 60; meals 25,000-95,000d; 🕑 lunch & dinner) The original Mekong rest stop, this place has an extensive garden. Bag a table by the river and try the elephant ear fish.

Getting There & Around

BOAT

My Tho's car ferry (per person/motorbike 1000/5000d) to Ben Tre province is due to be replaced by the new bridge during 2009, which will greatly reduce travel time between the two towns. It currently leaves from Ben Pha Rach Mieu station about 1km west of My Tho city centre.

Tourist boats to explore the delta have traditionally left from the dock opposite the Trade Union Hotel. However, when the new construction is complete at the Tien Giang Tourist complex, there will be fancy new

RICE PRODUCTION

The ancient Indian word for rice, *dhanya* ('sustainer of the human race'), is apt when describing the importance of this 'white gold' to the Vietnamese.

A Vietnamese fable tells of a time when rice did not need to be harvested. Instead, it would be summoned through prayer and arrive in each home from the heavens in the form of a large ball. One day a man ordered his wife to sweep the floor in preparation for the coming of the rice, but she was still sweeping when the huge ball arrived and struck it by accident, causing it to shatter into many pieces. Since then, the Vietnamese have had to toil to produce rice by hand.

While some remote parts of Vietnam today are similar to how they would have been centuries ago – women in *non bai tho* (conical hats) irrigating fields by hand, farmers stooping to plant the flooded paddies and water buffalo ploughing seedbeds with harrows – things are steadily becoming more mechanised as Vietnam ramps up its production.

Rice is the single most important crop in Vietnam and involves up to 50% of the working population. While always playing an important role in the Vietnamese economy, its production intensified considerably as a result of economic reforms, known as *doi moi* ('renovation'), in 1986. The reforms helped transform Vietnam from a rice importer to exporter in 1989. Today rice is a substantial part of the country's earnings and the country is the second largest exporter after Thailand. In 2007 Vietnam produced 36 million tonnes of rice, exporting 4.3 million tonnes, and earning around US$1.4 billion.

The importance of rice in the diet of the Vietnamese is evident in the many rice dishes available, including *banh xeo* (rice omelette), *chao* (rice porridge) and extremely potent *ruou gao* (rice wine), to name a few. Vietnam's ubiquitous *com pho* (rice-noodle soup) restaurants serve white rice *(com)* with a variety of cooked meat and vegetables, as well as *pho*.

Rice plants take three to six months to grow, depending on the type and environment. In Vietnam the three major cropping seasons are winter-spring, summer-autumn and the wet season. When ready to harvest, the plants are thigh-high and in about 30cm of water. The grains grow in drooping fronds and are cut by hand, then transported by wheelbarrows to thrshing machines that separate the husk from the plant. Other machines are used to 'dehusk' the rice (for brown rice) or 'polish' it (for white rice). At this stage, brown carpets of rice spread along roads to dry before milling are a familiar sight.

In 2006, Vietnam, along with Thailand, announced a ban on growing genetically engineered varieties of rice, citing health concerns. The announcement came in the wake of scandals caused by the US and China contaminating the global rice supply with unapproved and illegal genetically engineered rice varieties.

wharfs for arrivals and departures, probably another attempt to corner the market for boat tours.

BUS

My Tho is served by buses leaving HCMC from the Cholon and Mien Tay bus stations (p385). Buses from Cholon have the added advantage of dropping passengers right in My Tho, as opposed to the bus station outside of town. The trip takes 1½ hours.

The **My Tho bus station** (Ben Xe Khach Tien Giang; 4am-5pm) is several kilometres west of town. To get there from the city centre, take Đ Ap Bac westward and continue on to Hwy 1A (Quoc Lo 1).

Buses to HCMC (24,000d, two hours) leave when full from the early morning until about 5pm. There are also daily bus services to most points in the Mekong Delta, including Can Tho (40,000d, four hours).

CAR & MOTORBIKE

The drive from HCMC to My Tho along Hwy 1A, by car or motorbike, takes around two hours. Road distances from My Tho are 16km to Ben Tre, 66km to Vinh Long, 70km to HCMC and 104km to Can Tho.

AROUND MY THO

Phoenix Island

Until his imprisonment by the communists for his antigovernment activities and the consequent dispersion of his flock, the Coconut Monk (Ong Dao Dua; p420) led a small community on Phoenix Island (Con

THE COCONUT MONK

The Coconut Monk was so named because he once ate only coconuts for three years; others claim he only drank coconut juice and ate fresh young corn. Whatever the story, he was born Nguyen Thanh Nam in 1909, in what is now Ben Tre province. He studied chemistry and physics in France at Lyon, Caen and Rouen from 1928 until 1935, when he returned to Vietnam, got married and had a daughter.

In 1945 the Coconut Monk left his family in order to pursue a monastic life. For three years he sat on a stone slab under a flagpole and meditated day and night. He was repeatedly imprisoned by successive South Vietnamese governments, which were infuriated by his philosophy of achieving reunification through peaceful means. He died in 1990.

Plaques on the 3.5m-high porcelain jar (created in 1972) on Phoenix Island (Con Phung) tell all about the Coconut Monk. He founded a religion, Tinh Do Cu Si, which was a mixture of Buddhism and Christianity. Representations of Jesus and the Buddha appeared together, as did the Virgin Mary and eminent Buddhist women, together with the cross and Buddhist symbols. Today only the symbols remain, as the Tinh Do Cu Si community has dissolved from the island.

Phung), a few kilometres from My Tho. In its heyday the island was dominated by a somewhat trippy open-air **sanctuary** (admission 5000d; 8-11.30am & 1.30-6pm). The dragon-emblazoned columns and the quirky tower, with its huge metal globe, must have once been brightly painted, but these days the whole place has become faded, rickety and silent. Nevertheless, it is seriously kitsch, with a model of the Apollo rocket set among the Buddhist statues. With some imagination you can almost picture how it all must have appeared as the Coconut Monk presided over his congregation, flanked by enormous elephant tusks and seated on a richly ornamented throne. Private boat operators can include the island as part of an organised tour.

If you really wish to be at one with the island, it is possible to spend the night at the simple **Con Phung Hotel** (075 382 2198; r 100,000-200,000d;). The VIP quarters have river views, but all rooms include TV, fridge and hot water. The restaurant serves a range of delta-flavour dishes (mains 50,000d to 120,000d).

Dragon Island

Famed for its well-known **longan orchards**, Dragon Island (Con Tan Long) makes for a pleasant stop and stroll. The lush, palm-fringed shores of the island are lined with wooden fishing boats, and some of the residents of the island are shipwrights. There are some small restaurants and cafes on the island, which is just a five-minute boat trip from My Tho.

Other Islands

Two other islands in the vicinity, **Tortoise Island** (Con Qui) and **Unicorn Island** (Thoi Son) are popular stops for the coconut candy and banana wine workshops. On Tortoise Island is an excellent restaurant, the **Du Lich Xanh Con Qui** (361 0988; set menu 70,000-100,000d; lunch). It's a peaceful thatched-roof setting, surrounded by water hyacinths. Although you can visit these islands as part of a package tour from HCMC, you'll have much more freedom if you hire a boat yourself in My Tho. Budget around US$12 to US$16 for a three- or four-hour cruise, making stops along the way.

BEN TRE

075 / pop 120,000

As tourism took off in the Mekong Delta, the picturesque little province of Ben Tre was always one ferry beyond the tourist traffic of My Tho and consequently has developed at a more languid pace. That could be all set to change with the new bridge about to open, finally plugging Ben Tre into the big time. The town's sleepy waterfront, lined with ageing villas, makes for a pleasant stroll, and there's some good exploring to be had in the rustic settlement across the bridge to the south of the centre. This is also a good place to arrange boat trips (see p423) in the area, particularly for those wanting to escape the tour buses.

Ben Tre is particularly famous for its *keo dua* (coconut candy). Many local women work in small factories making these sweets, spending their days boiling cauldrons of sticky coconut mixture, before rolling it out and cutting sections off into squares, and finally wrapping them into paper for sale.

Information

Ben Tre Tourist Office (☎ 382 9618; ttdhdulichbt@hcm.vnn.vn; cnr Đ Hai Ba Trung & Đ Dong Khoi; 7-11am & 1-5pm) rents out bikes, boats, canoes. It also arranges various Mekong excursions.

Ben Tre has a number of **internet cafes** (per hr 4000d), plus you'll find internet access at the **main post office** (3/1 Đ Dong Khoi).

You can stock up on cash at **Vietinbank** (☎ 382 2507; 42 Đ Nguyen Dinh Chieu; Mon-Fri), which is open on weekdays only.

Sights

In the centre of Ben Tre is the **Vien Minh Pagoda** (Đ Nguyen Trai), which is also the head office of the Buddhist Association of Ben Tre province. An interesting feature of pagoda is a large white statue of Quan The Am Bo Tat (Goddess of Mercy), set in the front courtyard. The Chinese calligraphy that adorns the pagoda was written by an old monk.

The **Ben Tre Museum** (Bao Tang Ben Tre; Đ Hung Vuong; 8am-11am & 1-5pm) is set in an ageing but atmospheric old yellow villa. It has the usual assortment of rusty weapons and American War paraphernalia, along with rousing images of Ho Chi Minh.

LE VAN SINH

Everyone who travels through Vietnam knows the Sinh Café, pioneer of the Open Tour bus ticket (see p503). A lesser-known fact is that Le Van Sinh (just Sinh to friends) was the brains behind this empire, establishing it back in the early 1990s, together with a string of backpacker crashpads in Pham Ngu Lao.

Sinh's family was from the Cai Be area of the Mekong Delta and he has been drawn back to his roots time and time again. Growing up in Saigon, he spent family holidays back in the delta, learning about the slower paced life in rural areas. In the late 1980s, Sinh was working as an engineer, but life was about to take a dramatic change in course. Working first as a hotel receptionist, then a tour guide, he founded Sinh Café in 1992. This was where he met some of the early Lonely Planet authors in Vietnam such as Robert Storey and Mason Florence and helped them forge new trails into emerging areas at a time when travel in Vietnam was still tough.

One of his real passions is cycling: 'Cycling always brings me back to the time of "subsidised by the government" when everyone used to use bikes to get around,' laughs Sinh. That was the old image of Vietnam, the ubiquitous bicycle, but today times are changing. 'The highways are becoming too crowded with traffic, polluted and a little bit dangerous, so bicycles are the best way to enjoy the scenery and get off the beaten track,' he continues.

Family connections aside, why the Mekong Delta? 'Cycling in the far north or even the central highlands requires some experience and endurance, but for the pancake flat Mekong, everyone can manage a few days exploring on two wheels,' enthuses Sinh. 'It doesn't matter whether a serious cyclist or a city slicker, there are so many routes in the Mekong to enjoy and explore.'

Sinh knows more routes than most and his preferred trails are through the lesser-known areas of the Mekong Delta. 'My favourite backroads include the small trail under the shade of coconut palms that runs from Ben Tre through Mo Cay and the pretty town of Tra Vinh to Can Tho,' says Sinh. 'Most tourists only experience Hwy 1A on the way to Can Tho, but this is another world.' He also rates the loop from Chau Doc via Sam Mountain and Ba Chuc back to the popular border town.

But Sinh's love affair with the delta region goes beyond two wheels. 'The waters travel thousands of kilometres to meet the sea,' he continues. 'I have always been interested in waterways, as it is such a great way to relax in a hammock, cruising along the river. The system of canals and floating markets here is incredible and so different that all tourists should see it.'

And the next big thing in the Mekong Delta, from someone who has pioneered many a route before? 'That has to be the villages around Ben Tre,' states Sinh, 'as the new bridge link to My Tho will make this whole area so much more accessible.'

Le Van Sinh is the owner of Sinhbalo Adventures (www.sinhbalo.com), specialising in Mekong Delta tours. He has travelled almost every road in the country on two wheels, assisting a generation of Lonely Planet authors in discovering new routes and attractions.

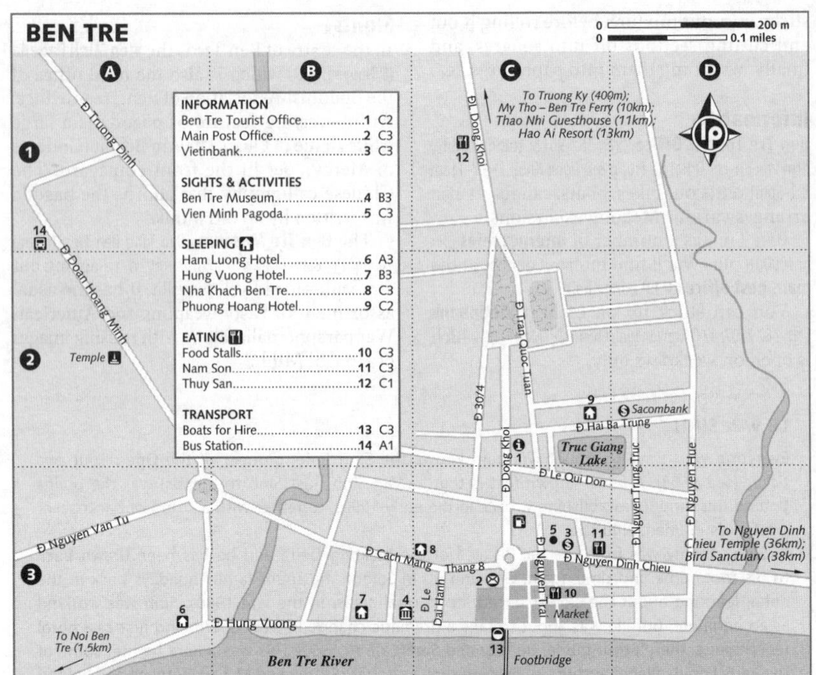

Sleeping

Phuong Hoang Hotel (☎ 382 1385; 28 Đ Hai Ba Trung; r 50,000-180,000d; ❄) Overlooking the small lake in town, this place is slightly old and decrepit, but then there is nowhere else in town offering a room for just US$3 with fan. You pays your money, you makes your choice.

Nha Khach Ben Tre (☎ 382 2339; 5 Đ Cach Mang Thang 8; r 130,000-360,000d; ❄) Coming to you courtesy of the Communist Party, this is one of the best-value places in town. Rooms are slightly stark and dated, but include extras like TV, fridge and hot water. There is a breezy cafe downstairs, but it can attract a karaoke crowd when party members are in-house.

Hung Vuong Hotel (☎ 382 2408; 166 Đ Hung Vuong; r 240,000-560,000d; ❄ 💻) The best all-rounder in Ben Tre, it has an attractive riverfront location with cheaper rooms in the old wing and some smarter, newer rooms. Tiled floors, polished wood furnishings and modern bathrooms make for a good deal. The in-house restaurant is very reasonably priced and overlooks the riverfront.

Ham Luong Hotel (☎ 356 0560; www.hamluongtourist.com.vn; 200 Đ Nguyen Van Tu; r 350,000-1,200,000d; ❄ 💻 🏊) A gleaming new hotel on the riverfront (the entrance is on Đ Hung Vuong), the Ham Luong is clearly betting on the bridge to bring it success. The modern rooms are nicely furnished and there's even a swimming pool, unheard of in little old Ben Tre.

For something a little different, head out of town to the rustic if slightly dated **Thao Nhi Guesthouse** (☎ 386 0009; thaonhitours@yahoo.com; Hamlet 1, Tan Thach village; r 100,000-250,000d; ❄), a more traditional place set amid abundant greenery, about 11km north of town. Hearty meals include excellent elephant ear fish, and there's free bike rental. As it's difficult to find, hire a *xe om* to take you there.

Eating

Nam Son (☎ 382 2873; 40 Đ Phan Ngoc Tong; mains 20,000-60,000d; 🕑 lunch & dinner) Centrally located, this place draws a lively local crowd thanks to its popular grilled chicken, best washed down with lashings of draught beer.

Thuy San (☎ 383 3777; 210B ĐL Dong Khoi; mains 30,000-90,000d) One of the more sophisticated restaurants in town; the kitchen turns out traditional Vietnamese served amid faux greenery.

Noi Ben Tre (☎ 382 2492; Đ Hung Vuong; mains 30,000-150,000d; ⌚ lunch & dinner) A multistorey barge moored in the river, this place doesn't cruise, but it does draw a healthy breeze by night. The menu is extensive and includes everything you can imagine and some things you can't.

Hao Ai (☎ 361 0785; Hamlet 2, Tan Thach village; set lunches 70,000-100,000d; ⌚ lunch) Set in lush landscaped gardens, this attractive island restaurant does a roaring trade with tour groups exploring the delta by boat. There are enough pavilions for independent travellers to hide away and generous set menus are available for two or more. Get here by hiring a private boat from Ben Tre or My Tho.

For ultracheap eats, head to the market, which has plenty of **food stalls** (plates around 10,000d).

Getting There & Away

The My Tho–Ben Tre ferry (motorbike/person 5000/1000d, 15 minutes one way) has long been the only option between the two towns, but the new bridge will open in 2009, cutting down the journey time and putting Ben Tre on the tourist map.

Public buses stop at the **bus station** (Đ Doan Hoang Minh) west of the town centre. Private minibuses also make the Ben Tre–HCMC run daily (2½ to three hours, eight daily), including Mai Linh (p415), which charges 39,000d.

Getting Around

Slow boats can be rented at the public pier near the market. Here you can figure on about 60,000d to 80,000d per hour, with a minimum of two hours cruising the local canals. Check with the boat drivers who hang around near the end of the footbridge.

AROUND BEN TRE

Bird Sanctuary

The locals make a real flap about the storks that nest at **San Chim Vam Ho Bird Sanctuary** (☎ 385 8669; admission 10,000d; ⌚ 7-11am & 1-7pm), as a stork sitting on the back of a water buffalo is the quintessential image of the Mekong waterways. The sanctuary is 38km east of Ben Tre town. Ben Tre Tourist (p421) has speedboats that can make the round trip in about two hours, or slow boats that take about five hours. Compare the going rates at Ben Tre Tourist with what freelance boat operators charge.

To get there overland, follow Đ Nguyen Dinh Chieu east out of town for 20km to Giong Tram. Turn left onto the windy, rural dirt road leading to Trai Tu K-20 (Prison K-20); you'll reach the prison after 11km (and may see hundreds of prisoners out tilling the fields), then turn right and drive the final 7km to Vam Ho.

VINH LONG

☎ 070 / pop 130,000

It may not be the largest town in the Mekong, but as a major transit hub it can be noisy and chaotic nonetheless. Escape the mayhem on the riverfront, where there are plenty of cafes and restaurants. Despite a lack of in-town attractions, Vinh Long is the gateway to island life and some worthwhile sites, including Cai Be floating market, abundant orchards and atmospheric homestays, which can be a highlight of a Mekong journey. Vinh Long is the capital of Vinh Long province and situated about midway between My Tho and Can Tho.

Information

Cuu Long Tourist (☎ 382 3616; www.cuulongtourist.net; 1 Đ 1 Thang 5; ⌚ 7am-5pm) One of the more switched-on state-run tour outfits in the region, it can arrange local homestays (see p425).

Main post office (Đ Hoang Thai Hieu) Plus internet access.

Vietinbank (☎ 382 3109; 143 Đ Le Thai To) Exchanges cash and travellers cheques.

Sights

MEKONG RIVER ISLANDS

What makes a trip to Vinh Long worthwhile is not the town but the beautiful islands dotting the river. The islands are dedicated to agriculture, especially the growing of tropical fruits which are shipped to markets in HCMC.

To visit the islands you can charter a boat through Cuu Long Tourist for around US$10 per person or pay substantially less for a private operator (from US$5 per hour).

You can also take the public ferry (3000d) to one of the islands and then walk around on your own; however, this isn't as interesting as a boat tour, since you won't cruise the narrow canals.

Some of the more popular islands to visit include **Binh Hoa Phuoc** and **An Binh Island**, but there are many others. This low-lying region is as much water as land and houses are generally built on stilts.

CAI BE FLOATING MARKET

This bustling **river market** (⌚ 5am-5pm) is worth including on a boat tour from Vinh Long, but it is best to arrive early in the morning.

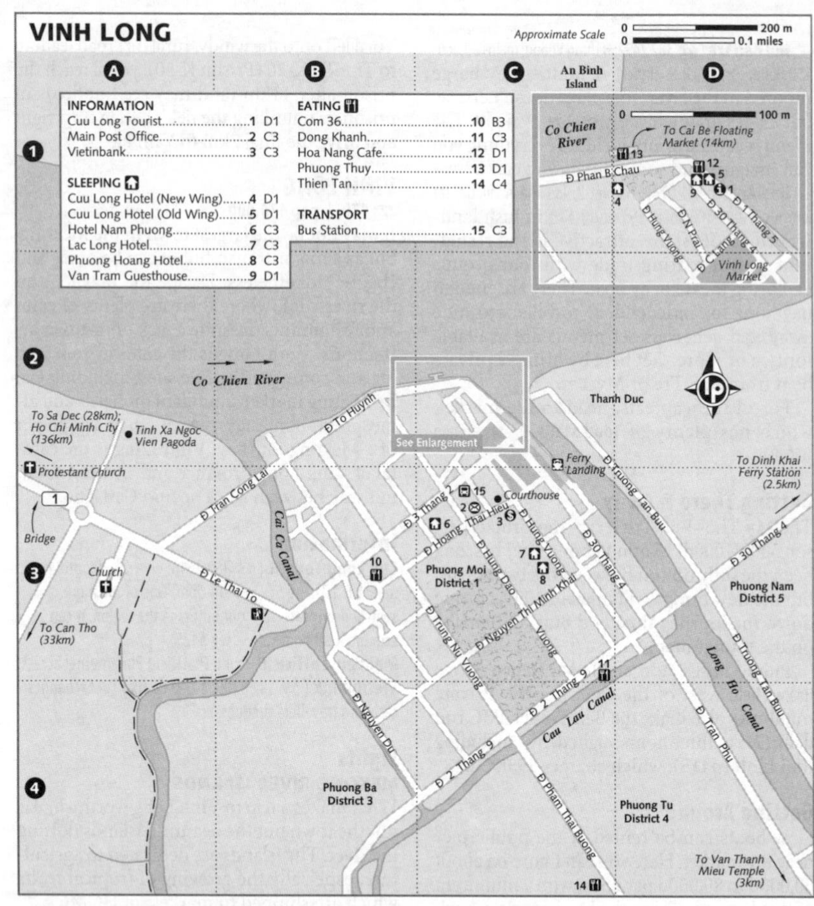

Wholesalers on big boats moor here, each specialising in just a few types of fruit or vegetable. Customers cruise the market in smaller boats and can easily find what they're looking for, as larger boats hang samples of their goods from tall wooden poles.

One interesting thing you won't see at other floating markets is the huge Catholic cathedral on the riverside – a popular and memorable backdrop for photographs.

It takes about an hour to reach the market from Vinh Long, but most people make detours on the way there or back to see the canals or visit orchards. For those travelling on an organised tour of the delta, it is customary to board a boat here, explore the islands and moor in Vinh Long before continuing to Can Tho.

VAN THANH MIEU TEMPLE

One surprise in Vinh Long is the large and beautiful **Van Thanh Mieu Temple** (Phan Thanh Gian Temple; Đ Tran Phu) by the river. It's unusual as far as Vietnamese temples go, as it's a Confucian temple, which is rare in southern Vietnam. The front hall honours local hero Phan Thanh Gian, who led an uprising against the French colonists in 1930. When it became obvious that his revolt was doomed, Phan killed himself rather than be captured by the colonial army.

The rear hall, built in 1866, has a portrait of Confucius above the altar. The building was designed in the Confucian style and looks like it was lifted straight out of China.

Van Thanh Mieu Temple is 3km southeast of town. Don't confuse it with the much smaller **Quoc Cong Pagoda** (Đ Tran Phu), which you'll pass along the way.

Tours

Cuu Long Tourist offers a variety of boat tours ranging from three to five hours in length, as well as overnight excursions, although you can also arrange these with local operators. Destinations include small canals, fruit orchards, brick kilns, a conical palm hat workshop and the Cai Be floating market (p423). Plan on about US$30 (per small group) for a day-long boat trip, slightly less with independent guides.

Sleeping

See the boxed text 'Homestays in the Delta, below, for homestay options beyond the town. Cuu Long Tourist can help arrange bookings and transport to these charming but rustic spots.

Lac Long Hotel (☎ 383 6846; 2H Đ Hung Vuong; r 100,000-250,000d;) Set in a street with a string of good-value guesthouses, the Lac Long offers free wi-fi for guests, an unexpected bonus. Rooms are clean and include TV, fridge and hot-water showers. Air-con kicks in from 150,000d.

Phuong Hoang Hotel (☎ 382 2156; 2R Đ Hung Vuong; r 130,000-250,000d;) Almost next door to the Lac Long, the Phuong Hoang offers no-nonsense value with spacious rooms (albeit with small bathrooms), plus TV and hot water.

Van Tram Guesthouse (☎ 382 3820; 4 Đ 1 Thang 5; r US$10-16;) A small place with just five rooms, the real adventure here is the location near the riverfront and lively market. Small size means bigger rooms which come with hot water showers and a balcony to watch the action below.

Hotel Nam Phuong (☎ 382 2226; khachsannamphuongvl@yahoo.com; 11 Đ Le Loi; r US$14-24;) This smart new hotel stands out above the competition thanks to eight storeys. The rooms are well finished and some include bathtubs. Just US$18 buys a triple and US$20 a quad.

Cuu Long Hotel (☎ 382 3656; www.cuulongtourist.net; 1 Đ 1 Thang 5; r old wing 100,000-220,000d, new wing 360,000-600,000d;) This government-run hotel is spread across two wings which couldn't be more different in character. The decaying old wing has a great location on the riverside, but is in sorry shape. The newer wing is a smart if characterless hotel that is the choice of abode for most midrange tour groups.

HOMESTAYS IN THE DELTA

One of the highlights of any Vietnam trip is experiencing a homestay with one of the friendly Mekong families. Here, you get a taste of local customs by sharing a home-cooked meal and possibly a few glasses of rice wine before retiring to your bed near the river. Although many tourists book through group tours in HCMC, there's no reason you can't do it yourself. The following options all charge around US$15 per night, which includes a night's sleep, dinner and breakfast the next morning. Note that most hosts are unlikely to speak much English, but welcome foreign guests just the same. Most of the places listed below are perched on the banks of a river or canal. Vinh Long is probably the best centre in which to arrange a homestay.

Mai Quoc Nam (☎ 070 385 9912; Phuan 1 hamlet, Binh Hoa Phuoc village, Long Ho District) A short hop by boat from Vinh Long, Mai Quoc Nam has a modern concrete building in front, but attractive wooden bungalows hidden away in a garden setting at the back. The owners can help arrange boat trips around the canals.

Sau Giao (☎ 070 385 9019; Binh Thuan 2 hamlet, Hoa Ninh village, Long Ho District) With the passing away of Mr Sau Giao, the traditional wooden house with a pretty bonsai garden is only serving lunch (set meals 70,000d to 100,000d) However, his daughter has kept the homestay tradition alive in a nearby property. Bicycle hire is also available.

Song Tien (☎ 070 385 8487; An Thanh hamlet, An Binh village, Long Ho District) Across the Co Chien River from Vinh Long, this friendly place offers beds in small bungalows with stop and drop toilets. The landscaping here is particularly lush with citrus trees and the owners are known to bust out the mandolin from time to time for a bit of traditional singing for their guests.

Tam Ho (☎ 070 385 9859; info@caygiong.com; Binh Thuan 1 hamlet, Hoa Ninh village, Long Ho district) About 1.5km from Vinh Long, Tam Ho is a working orchard run by a friendly, welcoming family. One of the hosts bears a striking resemblance to Ho Chi Minh. Private rooms are available but the canal can be noisy, day and night.

Eating & Drinking

Com 36 (☎ 383 6290; 36 Đ Hoang Thai Hieu; mains 15,000-35,000d; ⌚ lunch & dinner) This is the real Vietnamese deal, with bare-bones furnishing, no decor and no English menu, but the authentic food is displayed behind a glass counter so just point and eat.

Dong Khanh (☎ 382 2357; 49 Đ 2 Thang 9; mains 30,000-70,000d; ⌚ lunch & dinner) For a varied menu, try the popular Dong Khanh, where dishes include squid with mushrooms and a filling fish hotpot. The tablecloths add a touch of class, as does the English-language menu.

Thien Tan (☎ 382 4001; 56/1 Đ Pham Thai Buong; mains 30,000-80,000d; ⌚ lunch & dinner) Missing the Sunday barbie (BBQ, not blonde doll) back home? This place has delicious barbecued dishes, as well as *ca loc nuong tre* (fish cooked in bamboo) and *ga nuong dat set* (chicken cooked in clay).

Hoa Nang Cafe (Đ 1 Thang 5; drinks 5,000-20,000d) Perched on the riverbank, this is a good place to enjoy an iced coffee or scented tea in the morning or quaff your first beer upon returning from the Mekong excursion without fear of falling off the sampan when it wobbles.

Other options:

Vinh Long Market (Đ 3 Thang 2) A good spot for delicious local fruit and a range of inexpensive street snacks.

Phuong Thuy (Đ Phan B Chau; mains 30,000-100,000d; ⌚ lunch & dinner) Great location on the riverside, but it can fill up with tour groups, detracting from the atmosphere.

Getting There & Away

BOAT

Cargo boats sometimes take passengers from Vinh Long all the way to Chau Doc (near the Cambodian border); enquire locally, near the ferry landing, if this sounds like an adventure.

BUS

Frequent buses go between Vinh Long and HCMC (from 38,000d, three hours; by minibus 63,000d). They leave HCMC from Cholon and Mien Tay bus stations (p385). You can also get to Vinh Long from Can Tho (25,000d), My Tho, Tra Vinh and other points on the Mekong Delta. Vinh Long's **bus station** (Đ 3 Thang 2) is conveniently located in the middle of town.

CAR & MOTORBIKE

Vinh Long is just off Hwy 1A, 33km from Can Tho, 66km from My Tho and 136km from HCMC.

TRA VINH

☎ 074 / pop 96,000

The boulevards of Tra Vinh are still lined with shady trees, one of the prettiest towns in the Mekong Delta, harking back to an earlier era. Boasting more than 140 Khmer temples scattered about the province, Tra Vinh is a quiet place for exploring the Mekong's little-touted Cambodian connection. The town itself sees little tourist traffic, owing to its somewhat isolated location on a peninsula. Getting here by public transport is a straight up and back trip, because no big car ferries cross the rivers here, but cyclists and motorbikers can take some nice backroads connecting to Ben Tre.

About 300,000 ethnic Khmer live in Tra Vinh province. At first glance they might seem to be an invisible minority since they all speak fluent Vietnamese and there's nothing outwardly distinguishing about their clothing or lifestyle. However, digging a little deeper quickly reveals that Khmer culture is alive and well in this part of Vietnam. Many of its numerous pagodas have schools to teach the Khmer language and many Tra Vinh locals can read and write Khmer at least as well as Vietnamese. For more information, see the boxed text on p431.

Vietnam's Khmer minority are almost all followers of Theravada Buddhism. If you've visited monasteries in Cambodia, you may have observed that Khmer monks are not involved in growing food and rely on donations from the local community. Here in Tra Vinh, Vietnamese guides will proudly point out the monks' rice harvest as one of the accomplishments of liberation. To the Vietnamese government, nonworking monks were seen as parasites. The Khmers don't necessarily see it the same way and continue to donate funds to the monasteries surreptitiously.

Between the ages of 15 and 20, most boys set aside a few months to live as monks (they decide themselves on the length of service). Khmer monks are allowed to eat meat, but they cannot kill animals.

There is also a small but active Chinese community in Tra Vinh, one of the few such communities that remain in the Mekong Delta region.

Information

Tra Vinh Tourist (☎ 385 8556; tvtourist@yahoo.com; 64 Đ Le Loi; ⌚ 7.30-11am & 1.30-5pm) is probably the friendliest outfit in the Mekong. The staff can

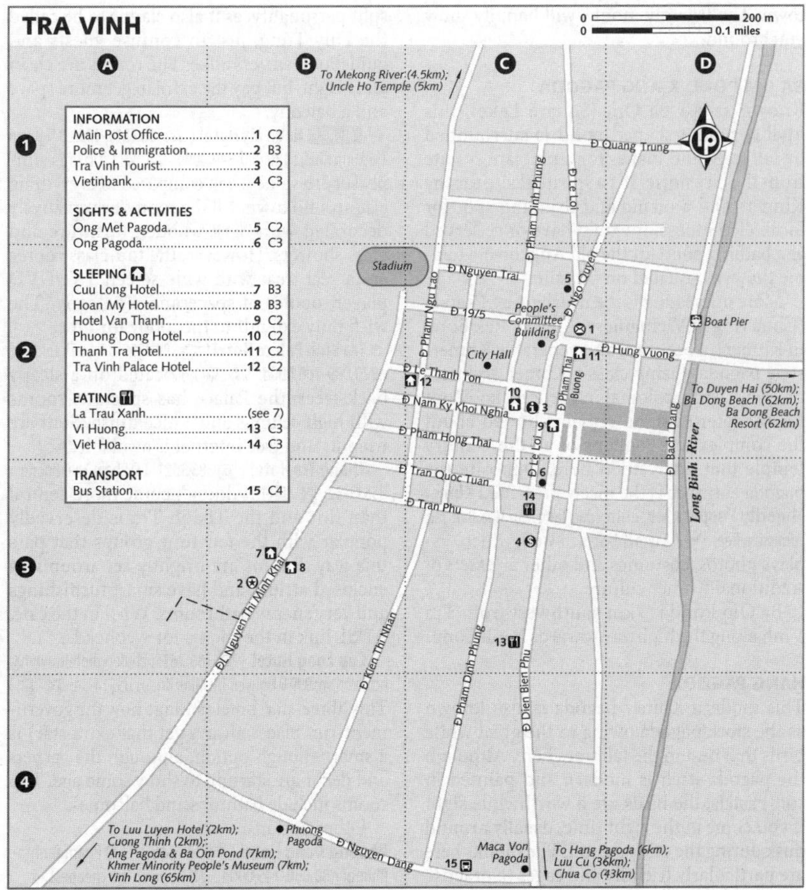

provide regional travel info and book various trips to sites around the province, though the boat trips are the most interesting. A Tra Vinh tourist map includes the town and province, and is available here.

The **main post office** (Đ Hung Vuong) has an attached internet cafe. **Vietinbank** (☎ 386 3827; 15A Đ Dien Bien Phu) exchanges foreign currencies and handles cash advances. There's also an ATM at Cuu Long Hotel.

Sights

ONG PAGODA

The very ornate, brightly painted **Ong Pagoda** (Chua Ong & Chua Tau; cnr Đ Pham Thai Buong & Đ Tran Quoc Tuan) is a fully fledged Chinese pagoda and a very active place of worship. The red-faced god on the altar is deified general Quan Cong. He is believed to offer protection against war and is based on a historical figure, a soldier of the 3rd century. You can read more about him in the Chinese classic *The Romance of the Three Kingdoms.*

The Ong Pagoda was founded in 1556 by the Fujian Chinese Congregation, but has been rebuilt a number of times. Recent visitors from Taiwan and Hong Kong have contributed money for the pagoda's restoration, which explains why it is in such fine shape.

ONG MET PAGODA

The chief reason for visiting the large Khmer **Ong Met Pagoda** (Chua Ong Met; Đ Ngo Quyen) is its accessibility, as it's right in the centre of town. The friendly monks will happily show you around.

BA OM POND & ANG PAGODA

Known as Ao Ba Om (Square Lake), this idyllic, square-shaped pond is surrounded by tall trees and makes for a pleasant respite from the city noise. It's a spiritual site for the Khmers and a picnic and drinking spot for local Vietnamese. It would have once served as a bathing pond for the old Angkor-era temple that was situated on this site.

More interesting is the nearby Ang Pagoda (Chua Ang in Vietnamese; Angkor Rek Borei in Khmer), a beautiful and venerable Khmer-style pagoda, fusing classic Khmer architecture with some colonial influences. Look out for the laterite stone remains dotted about the complex, the remains of a 10th century temple that once stood here. Opposite the pagoda entrance is the nicely presented **Khmer Minority People's Museum** (Bao Tang Van Hoa Dan Tac; admission free; 7-11am & 1-5pm Fri-Wed), which displays photos, costumes and other artefacts of traditional Khmer culture.

Ba Om Pond is 7km southwest from Tra Vinh along the highway towards Vinh Long.

HANG PAGODA

This modern Khmer pagoda is also known as the stork pagoda owing to the great white birds that nest in the tall trees here. Although the pagoda itself is modern and painted in soft pastels, the birds are a worthwhile sight if you come at the right time, usually around dusk during the rainy season. The monks here are particularly friendly and eager to practise their English skills. Chua Hang is located 6km south of town on Đ Dien Bien Phu.

UNCLE HO TEMPLE

The highly unusual (particularly in these southern parts) **Uncle Ho Temple** (Den Tho Bac; 7-11am & 1-5pm) is dedicated, of course, to the late president Ho Chi Minh, and contains a shrine to Ho as well as a small museum displaying photos of his life. The temple was built in 1971, while the war was still in progress, and there's a downed US aircraft on the grounds. The Uncle Ho Temple is at Long Duc commune, 5km north of Tra Vinh town.

Sleeping

Hotel Van Thanh (385 8567; 151 Đ Le Loi; r 180,000-220,000d) This place seems to suffer from a split personality, as it also claims to be called the Duy Tung, just to confuse guests and guidebook writers alike. The rooms are clean and bright, but pay the extra to get more space and a balcony.

our pick **Hoan My Hotel** (386 2211; 105A Đ Nguyen Thi Minh Khai; r 180,000-340,000d) This is simply superb value when compared to everything else around town. All the rooms are creatively decorated with dark wooden furniture and glass showers. However, the top-class rooms are a real treat with wide-screen TV, DVD player, oodles of space and a balcony. The wi-fi only extends to the lobby for now.

Tra Vinh Palace Hotel (386 4999; 3 Đ Le Thanh Ton; r 220,000-300,000d) Located on a sleepy backstreet, the Palace has spacious rooms with high ceilings and a nice finish. Staff are friendly and free internet is available.

Thanh Tra Hotel (385 3621; 1 Đ Pham Thai Buong; r US$12-32) It doesn't come more central than this and the Thanh Tra is deservedly popular with the few tour groups that pass this way. Rooms are brightly set around an enclosed atrium and have smart furnishings and very snazzy bathrooms. Wi-fi in the cafe, ADSL link in the rooms for webheads.

Cuu Long Hotel (386 2615; cuulonghoteltravinh@hcm.vnn.vn; 999 Đ Nguyen Thi Minh Khai; r US$14-34) This 'three-star' hotel (strange how the government-run places always get that extra star) is a smart enough option, although the carpets and decor are starting to show some age. Top rooms include bathtubs and balconies.

Other options:

Phuong Dong Hotel (386 5486; 1A Đ Pham Dinh Phung; r 80,000-145,000d) One of the cheapest places in town, it's pretty basic and not exactly spotless, but then rooms start at just five bucks.

Luu Luyen Hotel (384 2306; 16 Đ Nguyen Thi Minh Khai; r 180,000-450,000d) A little out of the way on the road to Vinh Long; the rooms are smart and stylish, plus there is a good restaurant next door.

Eating

Vi Huong (386 4045; 37A Đ Dien Bien Phu; mains 10,000-30,000d) A cheap and cheerful local hole-in-wall, the Vi Huong sticks with wholesome traditional dishes like sour soup, fish in clay pot and pork with rice.

Cuong Thinh (384 8428; 18A Đ Nguyen Thi Minh Khai; mains 20,000-120,000d) A huge open plan restaurant, Cuong Thinh is popular for its traditional mains and palm-lined ambience. It's 2km south of town on the road to Vinh Long.

La Trau Xanh (☎ 386 2615; 999 Đ Nguyen Thi Minh Khai; mains 20,000-150,000d) Hiding behind the facade of the Cuu Long Hotel, this restaurant has a pleasant setting under a huge thatched roof. This is as international as it gets in Tra Vinh and tempting dishes include steamed sea-bass and shrimp in coconut sauce.

Viet Hoa (☎ 386 3046; 80 Đ Tran Phu; mains 30,000d) One of the most popular restaurants in town, this is run by a Chinese family who stuck around. Greatest hits include a famous fish kebab and some bubbling hotpots.

Getting There & Away

Tra Vinh is 65km from Vinh Long and 205km from HCMC. Buses to HCMC depart regularly (60,000d, 4½ hours) from Tra Vinh's intercity bus station on Đ Nguyen Dang, on the south side of town. **Mai Linh** (☎ 386 8686) charges 85,000d for the privilege of riding in its minibus.

AROUND TRA VINH

Chua Co

A Khmer monastery, Chua Co is interesting because the grounds form a bird sanctuary. Several types of stork and ibis arrive here in large numbers before sunset to spend the night. There are many nests here, so take care not to disturb the birds when visiting.

Chua Co is 43km from Tra Vinh. Travel 36km to Tra Cu then follow the sandy road for 7km to the monastery.

Luu Cu

Some **ancient ruins** are found at Luu Cu, south of Tra Vinh near the shores of the Hau Giang River. The ruins include brick foundations similar to those found at pre-Angkorian Chenla temples in Cambodia. There have been a series of archaeological digs here and the site is now protected. It's 10km from the town of Tra Cu (36km from Tra Vinh).

Ba Dong Beach

This yellow-sand beach is quite a looker compared with other 'beaches' in the Mekong Delta, but the real attraction at Ba Dong Beach is the peace and quiet, as it sees very few visitors during the week. Weekends can get packed with regional visitors. The big event here – well worth attending if you happen to be in the area – is the **Khmer Ok Om Bok Festival**, featuring colourful boat races. It's held on a weekend in late October or November – ask for details at Tra Vinh Tourist (p426).

Tra Vinh Tourist operates the only accommodation on the beach. **Ba Dong Beach Resort** (☎ 373 9559; badongresort@hcm.vnn.vn; d/bungalow 150,000/200,000d; ❄) offers tidy little bungalows (and simpler rooms) with ocean views and hot-water bathrooms. Rates include breakfast, and there's a seafood restaurant attached.

To get here from Tra Vinh, head 50km along the paved road to Duyen Hai and follow the bumpy dirt road for 12km until you reach the beach. About five buses a day make the trip from Tra Vinh to Duyen Hai (18,000d), from where you can hire a *xe om* (about 30,000d) to take you to the beach.

SA DEC

☎ 067 / pop 108,000

The sleepy former capital of Dong Thap province, Sa Dec is a peaceful town of tree-lined streets and fading colonial villas, with orchards and flower markets ringing the town. It has a minor claim to fame as the setting for *The Lover*, a film by Jean-Jacques Annaud based on the novel by Marguerite Duras. One of the classic French villas used in the film is now a guesthouse and can be seen across the river from the market area.

Groups doing a whirlwind tour of the Mekong Delta often make a lunch stop here and drop in on the nurseries.

Information

The **post office** (cnr Đ Hung Vuong & Quoc Lo 80) also has a handy internet cafe next door. There's a **Vietcombank ATM** (251A Đ Nguyen Sinh Sac) at the Bong Hong Hotel.

Sights

HUONG TU PAGODA

Of classic Chinese design is the Huong Tu Pagoda (Chua Co Huong Tu), where a bright white statue of Quan The Am Bo Tat standing on a pedestal adorns the grounds. Don't confuse this place with the adjacent **Buu Quang Pagoda** (Đ Hung Vuong), which is somewhat less glamorous.

NURSERIES

The **nurseries** (vuon hoa; 🕑 8-11am & 1-5pm) operate year-round, though they are practically stripped bare of their flowers just before Tet. Note that domestic tourists from HCMC arrive in droves on Sundays and the nurseries

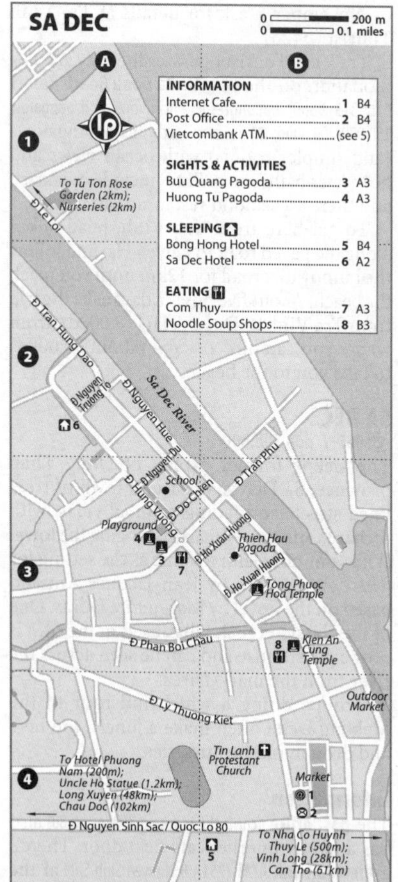

are a major sightseeing attraction around the Tet festival holiday.

There are many small operators here, each with a different speciality. The most famous garden is called the **Tu Ton Rose Garden** (Vuon Hong Tu Ton; 8-11am & 1-5pm), which has over 500 different kinds of rose in 50 different shades and colours.

Sleeping & Eating

Not many foreigners overnight in Sa Dec, but there are some hotels if you get stuck.

Hotel Phuong Nam (386 7867; hotelphuongnam@yahoo.com; 384A Đ Nguyen Sinh Sac; r 80,000-200,000d;) Rooms here are well tended and include wooden floors. Wi-fi is a real surprise in this neck of the woods.

Sa Dec Hotel (386 1430; 108/5A Đ Hung Vuong; r with fan/air-con from US$9/16;) The government-owned pad in town, this place is right at the end of Hung Vuong. Rooms are spacious and some include bathtub and balcony, but they do feel a bit mothballed. Breakfast is included.

Bong Hong Hotel (386 8288; 251A Đ Nguyen Sinh Sac; r US$10-22, ste US$32;) The smartest pad in town, the upper rooms are the most appealing and include balconies. Breakfast is included, and there are tennis courts next door and a good thatched-roof restaurant at the back.

Nha Co Huynh Thuy Le (091-396 7586; thanhctydl@yahoo.com.vn; r US$15;) This wonderfully atmospheric house on the riverfront was once the residence for the family of novelist Marguerite Duras, and Sa Dec the inspiration for her semi-autobiographical work *The Lover*. The house is a Sino-French design, the interior Chinese woodwork and shrine is incredible, and the rooms are charming if basic. Shared bathrooms are located at the back of the property.

Com Thuy (386 1644; 439 Đ Hung Vuong; mains 15,000-30,000d) One of the few restaurants around town; the food is good, but the bizarre expressions on the fish in the big tank are even more of a diversion.

Further south on Đ Hung Vuong are a few good **noodle-soup shops** (soups around 10,000d).

Getting There & Away

Sa Dec is midway between Vinh Long and Long Xuyen and accessible by bus, minibus and car. Some travel companies offer overnight boat trips from Sa Dec to Chau Doc as part of a tour: try Kim Travel (p351) in HCMC.

CAO LANH

067 / pop 150,000

A new town carved from the jungles and swamps of the Mekong Delta region, Cao Lanh is big for business, but it doesn't draw a lot of tourists. Its main appeal is as a base to explore bird sanctuaries and Rung Tram (Tram Forest), both major attractions reachable by boat.

Information

Dong Thap Tourist (385 5637; dothatour@hcm.vnn.vn; 2 Đ Doc Binh Kieu) is a friendly, helpful outfit that can arrange boat and other tours of the surrounding area. A boat-station **branch office** (382 1054) handles boat tours from a landing in My Hiep village.

THE STORY OF KAMPUCHEA KROM

Visitors to some Mekong provinces may be surprised to find Khmer towns whose inhabitants speak a different language, follow a different brand of Buddhism and have a vastly different history and culture to their Vietnamese neighbours. Though the Khmer are a minority in the Mekong, they were the first inhabitants here, with an ancestry dating back more than 2000 years.

Kampuchea Krom (meaning 'Lower Cambodia') is the unofficial Khmer name for the Mekong Delta region, whose indigenous inhabitants are the Khmer Krom, an ethnic minority living in southern Vietnam. The Khmer Krom trace their origins back to the 1st century AD, to the founding of Funan, a maritime empire that stretched from the Malay peninsula to the Mekong. Archaeologists believe Funan was a sophisticated society that built canals, traded in precious metals and had a high level of political organisation as well as agricultural know-how. Following the Funan came the Chenla empire (630–802 AD), and then the Khmer empire, the mightiest in Southeast Asia, which saw the creation of Angkor Wat among other great achievements. By the 17th century, however, the empire was in ruins, under pressure from the expansionist Thais and Vietnamese. This was a time of rising power for the Vietnamese empire which began expanding south, conquering first the Cham empire before setting their sights on Khmer lands in the Mekong Delta.

According to some historians, there were around 40,000 Khmer families living around Prey Nokor when the Vietnamese arrived in the 1600s, following the granting of settlement rights by King Chey Chettha in 1623. Prey Nokor was an important port for the Cambodian kingdom and was renamed Saigon in 1698. Waves of Vietnamese settlers populated the city as other colonists continued south. Prior to their arrival there were 700 Khmer temples scattered around south Vietnam. Over the next century the Khmer Krom fought and won some minor victories in the region, expelling the intruders, only to lose their gains in new rounds of attacks.

When the French subjugated Indochina in the 19th century, the hope of an independent Kampuchea Krom would be forever destroyed. Although the ethnic Khmer were a majority in southern Vietnam at that time, the French didn't incorporate the colony with Cambodia but made it a separate protectorate called Cochinchina. On 4 June 1949, the French formally annexed Kampuchea Krom, a day of sorrow for many Cambodians, although the writing had been on the wall centuries earlier as the area was colonised.

Since independence in 1954, the Vietnamese government has adopted a policy of integration and forced assimilation (the Khmer Krom must take Vietnamese family names and the Vietnamese language among other things). According to the Khmer Kampuchea-Krom Federation (KKF), many atrocities have been committed against the minority in the last four decades, and the Khmer Krom continue to suffer persecution. They report difficult access to Vietnamese health services, religious discrimination (Khmer Krom are Theravada Buddhists, unlike Vietnam's Mahayana Buddhists) and also racial discrimination. Several monks have been defrocked for nonviolent protest in recent years and the Cambodian government has even assisted in deporting some agitators according to Human Rights Watch.

The Khmer are the poorest segment of the population. Even their numbers remain a contentious topic. Vietnam reports one million Khmer Krom, who are called 'Nguoi Viet Goc mien' (Vietnamese of Khmer origin) by Vietnamese officials, while KKF claims there are seven million Khmer living in southern Vietnam. For more information about the ongoing struggles of the Khmer Krom, visit www.khmerkrom.org.

Internet access is available at the **post office** (85 Đ Nguyen Hue). Exchange cash at the **Vietinbank** (☎ 382 2030; Đ Nguyen Hue).

Sights

DONG THAP MUSEUM

The impressive looking **Dong Thap Museum** (Đ Pham Huu Lau; admission free; 7-11.30am & 1.30-5pm) is among the best museums in the Mekong. The 1st floor displays an anthropological history of Dong Thap province, with exhibits of tools, sculpture, models of traditional houses and a few stuffed animals. The 2nd floor is devoted to war history and, of course, to Ho Chi Minh. All interpretive signs are in Vietnamese.

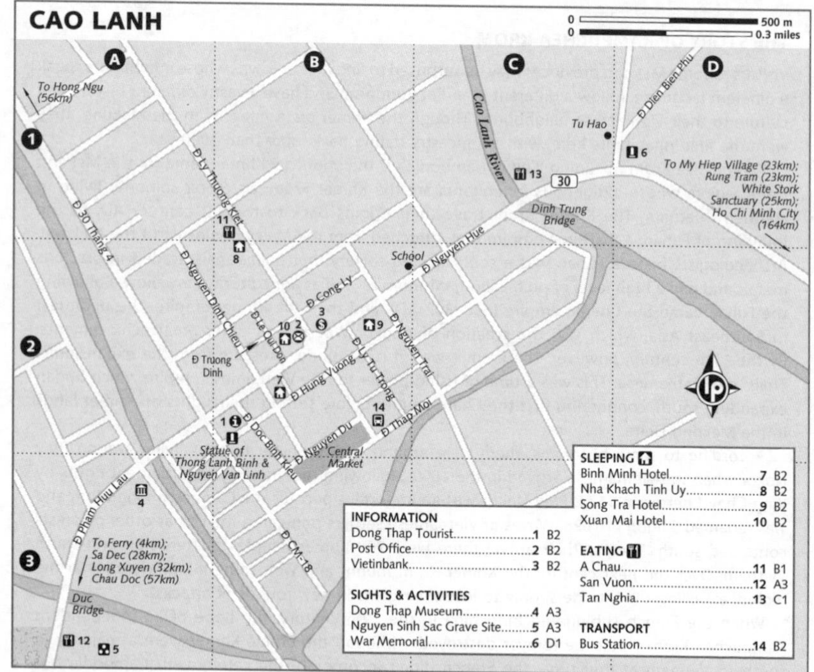

WAR MEMORIAL

Situated on the eastern edge of town off Hwy 30, the War Memorial (Dai Liet Si) is Cao Lanh's most prominent landmark. This socialist-style sculpture features a clamshell-shaped building with a large Vietnamese star alongside a hammer and sickle; concrete statues of victorious peasants and soldiers front the building. The surrounding grounds are decked out with the graves of over 3000 VC who died while fighting in the American War.

NGUYEN SINH SAC GRAVE SITE

Another significant tomb in Cao Lanh is that of Nguyen Sinh Sac (1862–1929). Nguyen's main contribution to Vietnamese history was being Ho Chi Minh's father. His tomb (Lang Cu Nguyen Sinh Sac) occupies 1 hectare about 1km southwest of Cao Lanh.

Although various plaques (in Vietnamese) and tourist pamphlets extol Nguyen Sinh Sac as a great revolutionary, there is little evidence confirming that he was involved in the anticolonial struggle against the French, but his son more than made up for it.

Sleeping

Binh Minh Hotel (☎ 385 3423; 157 Đ Hung Vuong; r 80,000-150,000d;) The rooms are pretty simple here, but the friendly, English-speaking schoolteacher makes it a worthwhile place to stay. Bathrooms are cold water only and there are no real frills on display.

Xuan Mai Hotel (☎ 385 2852; 33 Đ Le Qui Don; r 150,000-180,000d;) Still the best value in town, this mini-hotel has neat and tidy rooms, all finished with bathtubs and hot water. It is located just behind the post office and rates include breakfast.

Nha Khach Tinh Uy (☎ 387 2669; 48 Đ Ly Thuong Kiet; r 240,000-360,000d;) Another Communist Party special; the boys in red are obviously doing alright as their hotels are quite smart these days. This place has large airy rooms with polished floors. Suites, while pricey, are enormous and large enough to accommodate a family or politburo chief.

Song Tra Hotel (☎ 385 2624; 178 Đ Nguyen Hue; r US$22-43;) It is a bit of a Soviet-style edifice from the exterior, but the rooms are in pretty good shape. All include big windows, satellite TV, a minibar and hot water. There is also a lift.

Eating

Cao Lanh is famous for *chuot dong* (rice-field rats) so it's as good a place as any to sample the local delicacy.

A Chau (☎ 385 2202; 42 Đ Ly Thuong Kiet; mains 15,000-60,000d) Head here for the tasty *banh xeo* (fried pancakes), a house speciality that you roll up and dip in fish sauce. The *lau de* (goat hotpot) is also a winner.

San Vuon (☎ 387 1988; 57 Đ Pham Huu Lau; mains 35,000-85,000d) This place is a peaceful retreat from the downtown bustle and is set amid extensive gardens. The sizeable menu includes the usual panoply of dishes such as frog and rat or the more conventional grilled beef or chicken.

Tan Nghia (☎ 387 1989; 331 Đ Le Duan; mains 40,000-100,000d) Arguably the most sophisticated restaurant in town, this place has a likeable setting next to the river. The menu includes a good range of meats and seafood and it pulls a regular crowd.

Getting There & Around

There are regular buses to both My Tho (27,000d, 2½ hours) and Vinh Long (20,000d, 1½ hours). The road between Cao Lanh and Long Xuyen is beautiful but has few buses.

The sights around Cao Lanh are best visited by river. Although you could possibly arrange something privately with boat owners, you'll probably find it easier – though slightly more expensive – to deal with Dong Thap Tourist (p430). Plan on spending US$25 to US$30 for a half-day boat tour.

AROUND CAO LANH

White Stork Sanctuary

To the northeast of Cao Lanh is a bird sanctuary (Vuon Co Thap Muoi) for white storks. The sanctuary only covers 2 hectares, but the birds seem mostly undisturbed by the nearby farmers. The storks are accustomed to people and are fairly easy to spot, as they feed in the mangrove and bamboo forests. They live in pairs and don't migrate with the seasons, so you can see them at any time of year.

There are no roads as such to the bird sanctuary, so getting there requires a trip by boat. Dong Thap Tourist (p430) can arrange speedboats (US$30 per hour, one hour) or slow boats (US$5 per person up to 20 people, three hours). In the dry season, you have to plan your boat trip according to the two daily tides – at low tide the canals can become impassable.

Many travellers include a trip to White Stork Sanctuary with a visit to Rung Tram (see below).

Rung Tram

Southeast of Cao Lanh and accessible by boat tour is the 52-hectare **Rung Tram** (Xeo Quyt Forest; admission 8000d; 🕒 7am-5pm) near My Hiep village. The area is one vast swamp with a beautiful thick canopy of tall trees and vines. It's one of the last natural forests left in the Mekong Delta and by now probably would have been turned into a rice paddy were it not for its historical significance. During the American War the VC had a base here called Xeo Quyt, where top-brass VC lived in underground bunkers. But don't mistake this for another Cu Chi Tunnels – it's very different.

Only about 10 VC were here at any given time. They were all generals who directed the war from here, just 2km from a US military base. The Americans never realised that the VC generals were living right under their noses. Naturally, they were suspicious about that patch of forest and periodically dropped some bombs on it to reassure themselves, but the VC remained safe in their underground bunkers.

During the rainy season a 20-minute boat tour (8000d) by canoe takes you past old bunkers and former minefields along narrow canals filled with ever-present dragonflies and water hyacinths. During the dry season you can explore this area on foot.

Access to Rung Tram is most popular by boat and many visitors combine a visit with a trip to White Stork Sanctuary. You can also try hiring a speedboat from Cao Lanh to Rung Tram, which takes around 30 minutes (depending on the tides). It is also possible to reach the forest by road if you are travelling by car or motorbike. From My Hiep, you can also hire a slow boat (US$20, seating up to 10 persons) that takes around 40 minutes to make the 2km journey to Rung Tram.

Tram Chim National Park

Due north of Cao Lanh in Tam Nong district (Dong Thap province) is **Tram Chim National Park** (Tram Chim Tam Nong; entry free), which is notable for its **eastern sarus cranes** *(Grus antigone sharpii)*. More than 220 species of bird have been identified within the reserve, but ornithologists will be most interested in the rare red-headed cranes, which grow to an impressive 1.5m high. Seeing these birds, however, requires a considerable commitment (time, effort and money), so it's really for bird enthusiasts only.

The birds nest here from about December to May; from June to November they migrate to northwest Cambodia, so schedule your visit to coordinate with the birds' travel itinerary if you want to see them. The birds are early risers, though you might get a glimpse when they return home in the evening. During the day, the birds are engaged in the important business of eating.

Tam Nong is a sleepy town 45km from Cao Lanh. The one-way drive takes about one hour by car; it's also possible to get there by boat. Speedboats or slow boats can be arranged from Dong Thap Tourist (p430). From the guesthouse in Tam Nong it takes another hour by small boat (around 500,000d) to reach the area where the cranes live and another hour to return. Add to this whatever time you spend (perhaps an hour) staring at your feathered friends through binoculars (bring your own), and then the requisite one to four hours to return to Cao Lanh, depending on your mode of transport.

The state-run **guesthouse** (r US$10-18) in Tam Nong is just before the bridge heading into town, and doubles as the national park headquarters, but has pretty basic rooms. Tam Nong shuts down early so if you want to eat dinner here, make arrangements before 5pm.

CAN THO

☎ **071 / pop 330,000**

The epicentre of the Mekong Delta, Can Tho is the largest city in the region and feels like a veritable metropolis after a few days exploring the backwaters. As the political, economic, cultural and transportation centre of the Mekong Delta, it's a buzzing town with a lively waterfront and an appealing blend of narrow backstreets and wide boulevards that make for some rewarding exploration. It is also the perfect base for nearby floating markets, the major draw for tourists who come here to boat along the many canals and rivers leading out of town.

Information

MEDICAL SERVICES

Hospital (Khoa Khan Benh; ☎ 382 0071; 4 Đ Chau Van Liem)

MONEY

Golf Hotel Can Tho (2 Đ Hai Ba Trung) Has an ATM.

Vietcombank (☎ 382 0445; 7 ĐL Hoa Binh) Has foreign-currency exchange and a 24-hour ATM.

Vietinbank (9 Đ Phan Dinh Phung) Credit-card cash advances can be arranged here.

POST

Main post office (2 ĐL Hoa Binh) Postal services and internet access.

TOURIST INFORMATION

Can Tho Tourist (☎ 382 1852; www.canthotourist.com.vn; 20 Đ Hai Ba Trung; 7am-5pm & 6-8pm) Staff at this provincial tourism authority are very helpful and speak both English and French. Decent city maps are available here, as well as general information on attractions in the area. There is also a booking desk for **Vietnam Airlines** (☎ 382 4088)

Sights & Activities

CAN THO MUSEUM

The enormous, well-presented **Can Tho Museum** (☎ 381 3890; 1 ĐL Hoa Binh; admission free; 8-11am & 2-5pm Tue-Thu, 8-11am & 6.30-9pm Sat, Sun & holidays) has exhibits of the history of Can Tho resistance during foreign rule as well as displays on the culture and history of the province. There's a life-size pagoda and ample English signage.

MUNIRANGSYARAM PAGODA

The ornamentation of **pagoda** (36 ĐL Hoa Binh) is typical of Khmer Theravada Buddhist pagodas: it doesn't have any of the multiple Bodhisattvas and Taoist spirits common in Vietnamese Mahayana pagodas. In the upstairs sanctuary a 1.5m-high representation of Siddhartha Gautama, the historical Buddha, sits serenely under a Bodhi Tree.

Built in 1946, the Munirangsyaram Pagoda serves the Khmer community of Can Tho, which numbers about 2000.

ONG TEMPLE

In a fantastic location facing the Can Tho River, Chua Ong (Ong Temple) is set inside the **Guangzhou Assembly Hall** (Đ Hai Ba Trung) and is one of the most interesting religious sites in town. It was originally built in the late 19th century to worship Kuang Kung, a deity symbolising loyalty, justice, reason, intelligence, honour and courage, among other merits. It is designed to symbolise the Chinese character for nation, with rows of enclosed sections laid out symmetrically. Approaching the

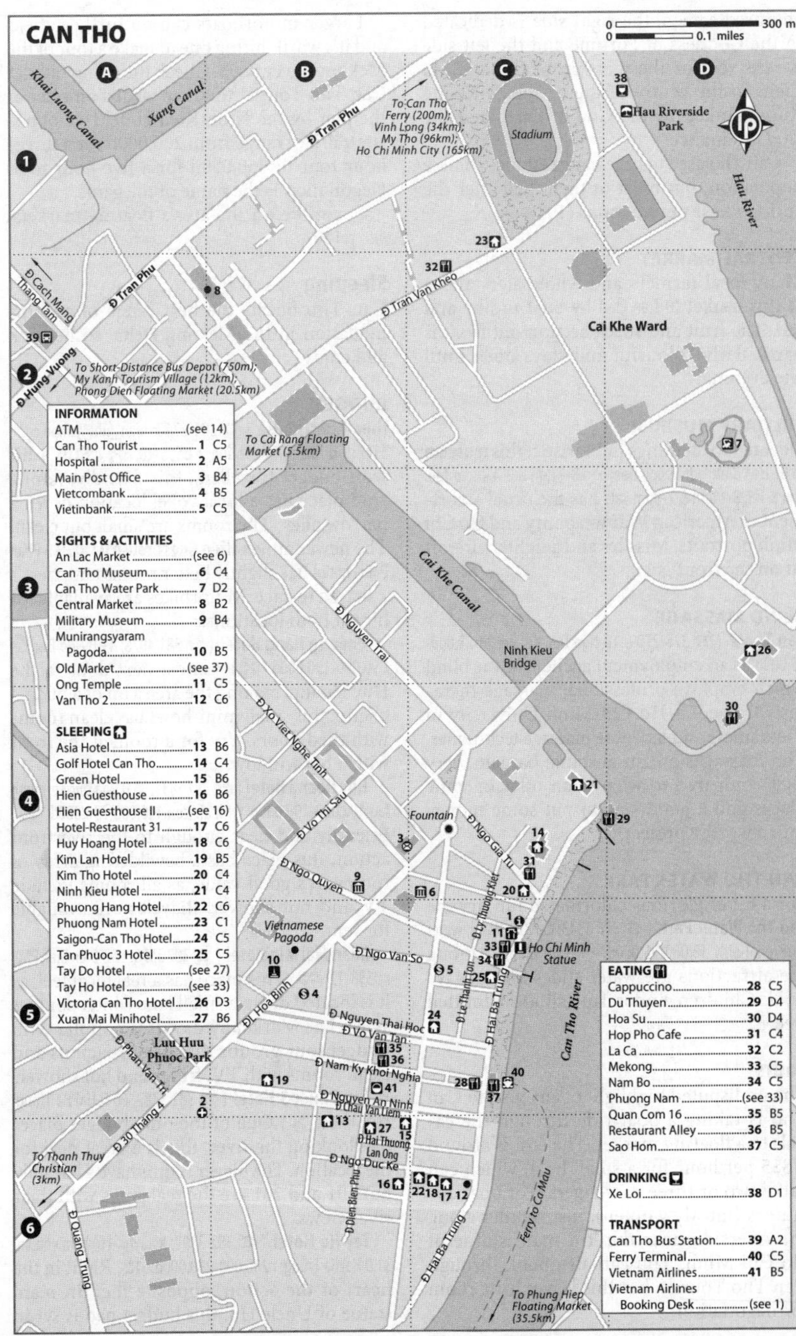
CAN THO
0 300 m
0 0.1 miles
Khai Luong Canal
Xang Canal
Đ Tran Phu
To Can Tho Ferry (200m); Vinh Long (34km); My Tho (96km); Ho Chi Minh City (165km)
Stadium
Hau Riverside Park
Hau River
Đ Cach Mang Thang Tam
Đ Tran Van Kheo
Cai Khe Ward
Đ Hung Vuong
To Short-Distance Bus Depot (750m); My Kanh Tourism Village (12km); Phong Dien Floating Market (20.5km)
To Cai Rang Floating Market (5.5km)
Cai Khe Canal
Đ Nguyen Trai
Ninh Kieu Bridge
Đ Xo Viet Nghe Tinh
Đ Vo Thi Sau
Fountain
Đ Ngo Gia Tu
Đ Ngo Quyen
Đ Ly Thuong Kiet
Vietnamese Pagoda
Đ Ngo Van So
Ho Chi Minh Statue
Đ Le Thanh Ton
Đ Hai Ba Trung
Can Tho River
ĐL Hoa Binh
Đ Nguyen Thai Hoc
Đ Vo Van Tan
Luu Huu Phuoc Park
Đ Phan Van Tri
Đ Nam Ky Khoi Nghia
Đ Nguyen An Ninh
Đ Chau Van Liem
Đ 30 Thang 4
Đ Hai Thuong Lan Ong
Đ Ngo Duc Ke
To Thanh Thuy Christian (3km)
Đ Dien Bien Phu
Ferry to Ca Mau
Đ Quang Trung
To Phung Hiep Floating Market (35.5km)

INFORMATION
ATM (see 14)
Can Tho Tourist 1 C5
Hospital 2 A5
Main Post Office 3 B4
Vietcombank 4 B5
Vietinbank 5 C5

SIGHTS & ACTIVITIES
An Lac Market (see 6)
Can Tho Museum 6 C4
Can Tho Water Park 7 D2
Central Market 8 B2
Military Museum 9 B4
Munirangsyaram Pagoda 10 B5
Old Market (see 37)
Ong Temple 11 C5
Van Tho 2 12 C6

SLEEPING
Asia Hotel 13 B6
Golf Hotel Can Tho 14 C4
Green Hotel 15 B6
Hien Guesthouse 16 B6
Hien Guesthouse II (see 16)
Hotel-Restaurant 31 17 C6
Huy Hoang Hotel 18 C6
Kim Lan Hotel 19 B5
Kim Tho Hotel 20 C4
Ninh Kieu Hotel 21 C4
Phuong Hang Hotel 22 C6
Phuong Nam Hotel 23 C1
Saigon-Can Tho Hotel 24 C5
Tan Phuoc 3 Hotel 25 C5
Tay Do Hotel (see 27)
Tay Ho Hotel (see 33)
Victoria Can Tho Hotel 26 D3
Xuan Mai Minihotel 27 B6

EATING
Cappuccino 28 C5
Du Thuyen 29 D4
Hoa Su 30 D4
Hop Pho Cafe 31 C4
La Ca 32 C2
Mekong 33 C5
Nam Bo 34 C5
Phuong Nam (see 33)
Quan Com 16 35 B5
Restaurant Alley 36 B5
Sao Hom 37 C5

DRINKING
Xe Loi 38 D1

TRANSPORT
Can Tho Bus Station 39 A2
Ferry Terminal 40 C5
Vietnam Airlines 41 B5
Vietnam Airlines Booking Desk (see 1)

engraved screen, the right side is dedicated to the Goddess of Fortune and the left side is reserved for the worship of General Ma Tien. In the centre of the temple is Kuang Kung flanked by the God of Earth and the God of Finance.

Can Tho used to have a large ethnic-Chinese population, but most of them fled after the anti-Chinese persecutions (1978–79).

CENTRAL MARKET

Many local farmers and wholesalers arrive at this **market** (Đ Tran Phu) by boat to buy and sell. The fruit and snack section out front is particularly colourful and stays open until late evening.

MILITARY MUSEUM

Devoted to all things militaristic, this **museum** (6 ĐL Hoa Binh; admission free; 8-11am & 2-4.30pm Tue, Thu & Fri, 8-11am & 7-9pm Sat) has the usual assortment of American War weaponry and Ho Chi Minh portraits. Missiles and a fighter aircraft sit on the front lawn.

BLIND MASSAGE

Van Tho 2 (☎ 375 2709; 1B Ngo Duc Ke; per hr 25,000-45,000d) is an employment agency for the blind which employs professional massage therapists trained at Ho Chi Minh University in Vietnamese and Japanese massage techniques. The massages are an absolute bargain, very legit compared to what is on offer in some places and a good way to put some money into a worthy project.

CAN THO WATER PARK

For a bit of glorious chlorinated fun, try the **Can Tho Water Park** (☎ 376 3343; Cai Khe Ward; water park/pool only 40,000/25,000d; 9am-6pm). Among the attractions are water slides and a wave pool. Children under 1m tall are admitted free.

Tours

The undisputed highlight of any visit to Can Tho is taking a boat ride through the canals to a floating market. The cost is around US$5 per hour for a small boat, which can carry two or three passengers. For boat operators (mostly women), just wander along the riverside near the 'tin man' statue of Ho Chi Minh. You can also book through Can Tho Tourist, but this leaves little room for negotiation.

Larger motorboats can go further afield and it's worth hiring one to make a tour of the Mekong River itself. Check the going rates at Can Tho Tourist then see what's on offer at the pier by the Ninh Kieu Hotel (see opposite). Prices range from 200,000d for a three-hour tour to 350,000d for a five-hour tour. Negotiation is the name of the game.

For more on the area's floating markets, see p440.

Sleeping

Can Tho boasts the best range of accommodation in the Mekong Delta, so lie back and enjoy.

BUDGET

Hien Guesthouse (☎ 381 2718; hien_gh@yahoo.com; 118/10 Đ Phan Dinh Phung; r US$5-10;) Still a hit with budget travellers, this friendly, family-run place has a local yokel location down a narrow alley. The rooms are small but clean. The newer annex **Hien Guesthouse II** (106/3 Đ Phan Dinh Phung) has slightly better rooms and there's a shared terrace. Motorbikes are available for hire at both locations.

Phuong Hang Hotel (☎ 381 4978; 41 Đ Ngo Duc Ke; r 90,000-130,000d;) Almost next door to the Huy Hoang, making the area a bit of a budget ghetto, this small mini-hotel has clean rooms with tiled floors. Try for a room at the front with a big window.

Huy Hoang Hotel (☎ 382 5833; 35 Đ Ngo Duc Ke; r with fan 100,000-190,000d, with air-con 140,000-230,000d;) Friendly and near enough to the riverfront action, this place has a bewildering array of rooms. It's good value, as all rooms include TV and hot shower. Bicycles are available for rent.

Xuan Mai Minihotel (☎ 382 3578; 17 Đ Dien Bien Phu; r US$8-12;) This place has a real local feel, as it is located down a small lane which doubles as An Lac Market by day. It is popular with budget tour groups thanks to spacious and clean rooms with TV, fridge and hot shower.

Tan Phuoc 3 Hotel (☎ 381 3782; 60 Đ Hai Ba Trung; r US$10-14;) One of the only budget places overlooking the river, this is a great deal for the location. The bigger rooms have a bathtub, but 101 and 201 are the real gems with their river views.

Tay Ho Hotel (☎ 382 3392; kstayho-ct@hcm.vnn.vn; 31 Đ Hai Ba Trung; r 200,000-280,000d;) Right in the heart of the action, opposite the 'tin man' statue of Uncle Ho, this budget pad is set in

A NIGHT UPON THE MEKONG

As well as homestays, guesthouses, hotels and resorts, it is also now possible to spend the night onboard a boat on the Mekong River. This is a good way to explore more of the waterways that make up this incredible region and helps bring you closer to life on the river. Five of the more interesting options include the following:

Bassac (☎ 0710-382 9540; www.transmekong.com) Offers a range of three beautiful wooden boats for small groups. The standard itinerary is an overnight between Cai Be and Can Tho, but custom routes are possible.

Delta Adventure Tours (☎ 08-3920 2112; www.deltaadventuretours.com) This budget travel agency operates a comfortable overnight boat between Sa Dec and Chau Doc, offered as part of their HCMC to Chau Doc or Phnom Penh trips.

Exotissimo Sampans (☎ 08-3827 2911; www.exotissimo.com) The ultimate in Mekong exclusivity, tour operator Exo offers these romantic sampans for couples to explore the delta at their own pace. Expensive, but very memorable.

Le Cochinchine (☎ 08-3993 4552; www.lecochinchine.com) Luxurious converted rice barge that is akin to a floating hotel. The main route is My Tho to Can Tho via Cai Be and Vinh Long.

Mekong Eyes (☎ 0710-246 0786; www.mekongeyes.com) A stunningly converted traditional rice barge, the name plays on the ever-present eyes painted on every boat in the delta. This stylish boat travels between Can Tho and Cai Be, but is also available for charter.

As well as these options, there are also a couple of boats plying the waters between HCMC and Phnom Penh or Siem Reap, including **Pandaw Cruises** (www.pandaw.com) and the **Tuom Teav** (www.cfmekong.com).

one of the few surviving colonial-era buildings on the riverfront. Unsurprisingly this means high ceilings, but a real bonus is the shuttered doors opening onto riverfront balconies for the rooms at the front. The owner is quite a character.

Or consider the following:

Green Hotel (☎ 381 0777; 31 Đ Chau Van Liem; r 180,000-280,000d; ❄ 🖳) Newish place with sharp rooms and free wi-fi for laptop-toting road warriors.

Hotel-Restaurant 31 (☎ 382 5287; 31 Đ Ngo Duc Ke; r US$6-15; ❄) There's a certain convenience to staying in a restaurant for the idle of nature. Fan rooms are tiny but the big air-con rooms are fine. Cheap meals from 15,000d to 40,000d.

Phuong Nam Hotel (☎ 376 3959; 118/9/39 Đ Tran Van Kheo; r US$13-22; ❄) Smart, not-so-mini hotel (seven-storeys), with big bathrooms and wi-fi. Away from the centre but good value.

MIDRANGE

Kim Lan Hotel (☎ 381 7049; www.kimlanhotel.com; 138A Đ Nguyen An Ninh; r US$25-28; ❄ 🖳) Just another skinny mini-hotel from the outside, there is more to this model than meets the eye. The chic rooms include contemporary furnishings in bamboo and wood, plus art works on the wall. Solar-powered water (thumbs up) and free wi-fi complete the picture.

Tay Do Hotel (☎ 382 7009; www.taydohotel.vnn.vn; 61 Đ Chau Van Liem; r US$25-35; ❄ 🖳) So three stars is pushing it a bit, but this is a smart hotel with a full range of amenities. All rooms include satellite TV and most have bathtubs and balconies. Breakfast is included.

Ninh Kieu Hotel (☎ 382 1171; 2 Đ Hai Ba Trung; r old wing US$30-35, new wing US$45-80; ❄) It may belong to the army but this hotel is a world away from boot camp. It has an enviable location on the riverfront and occupies several buildings, but the new wing is considerably smarter than the dated old wing.

Saigon-Can Tho Hotel (☎ 382 5831; www.saigoncantho.com; 55 Đ Phan Dinh Phung; s US$38-50, d US$49-62; ❄ 🖳) This hotel has a good range of rooms, and prices have remained static for a while now, making it good value. Deluxe rooms are like suites and come with flat-screen TVs and fruit basket. All rooms have safety deposit boxes and guests enjoy free internet access, including wi-fi.

our pick **Kim Tho Hotel** (☎ 322 2288; www.kimtho.com; 1A Đ Ngo Gia Tu; r US$40-120; ❄ 🖳) A smart new hotel, verging on the boutique, it sets a new standard for midrange properties in town. The rooms are stylish throughout and include designer bathrooms. The US$50 river-view rooms are a great deal. There is also a rooftop coffee bar.

Being Can Tho, there are more options:

Asia Hotel (☎ 381 2800; asiahotel@hcm.vnn.vn; 91 Đ Chau Van Liem; r US$25-34;) A long-running midrange place; the deluxe rooms have large balconies. Rates include breakfast.

My Khanh Tourism Village (☎ 384 6260; www.mykhanh.com; 335 Đ Lo Vong Cung, Phong Dien District; r US$25-40;) Located 12km southwest of Can Tho, this small, lushly landscaped complex has concrete bungalows with attractive furnishings.

TOP END

Golf Hotel Can Tho (☎ 381 2210; www.golfhotel.vnn.vn; 2 Đ Hai Ba Trung; r US$80-300;) This huge hotel overshadows everything else on the riverfront. The rooms are smart enough, with some great views from the upper floors, but you may find better value in some of the newer midrange places. Hotel facilities include a health club and a beauty salon; breakfast included.

Victoria Can Tho Hotel (☎ 381 0111; Cai Khe Ward; www.victoriahotels-asia.com; r US$128-282;) This hotel defines style and sophistication in the Mekong Delta. Designed with a French colonial look, the rooms are set around an inviting pool that looks out over the river. Rooms are delightful and facilities include an excellent restaurant, an open bar and a new riverside spa. There are plenty of activities on offer, including cycling tours and cooking classes. The hotel operates the Lady Hau, a converted rice barge, for breakfast or dinner cruises.

Eating

Can Tho has the best range of restaurants in the Mekong Delta. Browse the riverfront for a choice of cafes and restaurants or venture into town in search of specialities such as fish, frog and turtle.

Restaurant Alley (Đ Nam Ky Khoi Nghia; mains 15,000-40,000d) If you fancy skipping the main tourist scene on the riverfront, then try this small alley between Đ Dien Bien Phu and Đ Phan Dinh Phung where there are about a dozen local restaurants scattered on both sides of the street. Barbecued meats, seafood hotpots and simple vegetables, it's all here.

Quan Com 16 (☎ 382 7326; 45 Đ Vo Van Tan; mains 15,000-45,000d) This long-running place is a bit of a Can Tho institution with locals. It has relocated down the road, but thankfully the recipe remains the same: piles of freshly cooked fish, meat and vegetable dishes and fast service.

Mekong (☎ 382 1646; 38 Đ Hai Ba Trung; mains 20,000-60,000d; 8am-2pm & 4-10pm) Right opposite the 'tin man' statue, this has long been a travellers' favourite thanks to a good blend of local and international food at very reasonable prices. It's the closest thing to a riverfront bar by night with a few tables spilling onto the street.

Hop Pho Cafe (☎ 381 5208; 6 Đ Ngo Gia Tu; mains 20,000-75,000d) For discount designer dining, look no further than this stylish cafe-restaurant. Choose from indoor or outdoor, upstairs or downstairs – this place is huge, as is the drinks list. Standard Vietnamese fare at fair prices, affordable drinks and free wi-fi. Note that food service stops around 9pm.

Phuong Nam (☎ 381 2077; 48 Đ Hai Ba Trung; mains 25,000-65,000d) Next door to the Mekong, this place offers a similar ambience, but has the slight advantage of an upstairs terrace for people-watching.

Cappuccino (☎ 346 1981; Đ Hai Ba Trung; mains 30,000-75,000d; lunch & dinner) This Italian restaurant may not look that stylish but looks can be deceiving, as the menu features some delicious dishes at absurdly affordable prices. Pastas, risottos, pizzas, plus US$4 mains such as veal escalope with mushroom sauce. Oh and did we mention the Mexican and Vietnamese food, plus the tempting tiramisu?

Nam Bo (☎ 382 3908; 50 Đ Hai Ba Trung; mains 30,000-90,000d; lunch & dinner) When it comes to setting, this restaurant has it, housed in an elegantly restored shophouse overlooking the river. The menu offers well-presented Vietnamese dishes as well as some affordable international offerings or you can just sit on the terrace and enjoy a glass of wine.

Thanh Thuy Christian (☎ 384 0207; 149 Đ 30 Thang 4; mains 40,000-70,000d; 8am-11pm) This goat-meat specialty restaurant serves traditional curried goat or if you're feeling a bit lively, try the goat-scrotum hotpot. The restaurant is a few kilometres out of town. Look for the sign on your left, just beyond the junction with Đ Tran Hoang Na.

our pick **Sao Hom** (☎ 381 5616; 50 Đ Hai Ba Trung; mains 40,000-80,000d; 8am-midnight) Set in the (now upmarket) former market, Sao Hom has an atmospheric riverside setting. The menu includes Vietnamese, international and some fusion dishes, including crispy spring rolls for a change and some tandoori dishes. It is very popular at lunch and remains one of Can Tho's most alluring spots.

THE FRUITS OF VIETNAM

One of the great rewards of travelling through the Mekong is sampling the extraordinary array of fruits available at markets, orchards and street stalls all over the region. Fruits worth sampling include the following:

buoi (pomelo) – this gargantuan grapefruit has thick skin and sweeter, less acidic fruit than ordinary grapefruit
chom chom (rambutan) – a tiny fiery-red fruit with hairy skin and tender sweet white flesh; most prevalent during the rainy season (May to October)
du du (papaya) – Vietnam boasts 45 species of papaya; it's great in juices or raw when ripe (orange to red flesh), and used in tangy salads when green
dua (pineapple) – another common Mekong fruit, some aren't so sweet; locals sometimes doctor them up with salt and chilli powder
khe (starfruit) – a five-pointed, shiny skinned fruit that is intensely juicy
mang cau (custard apple) – inside this fruit's bumpy green skin lie black pips surrounded by white flesh, which does indeed taste very much like custard
mang cut (mangosteen) – a violet, tennis-ball-sized fruit; break it open to reveal delectable white flesh inside
mit (jackfruit) – giant and blimp-shaped, this fruit contains chewy yellow segments; it's loaded with vitamins
nhan (longan) – this tiny fruit has light-brown skin, a translucent juicy white pulp and is used for many purposes in the Mekong (it's even dried and used for kindling)
oi (guava) – with green, edible skin and pink flesh, the guava is loaded with vitamins and is great raw or in juice
sau rieng (durian) – this huge spiky fruit has a memorable odour and its creamy rich interior has a taste somewhat resembling custard; you'll either love it or hate it
thanh long (dragon fruit) – unusual in appearance, dragon fruit is a large red fruit with spiky fronds tipped with green. It has a mild, crisp flesh with numerous edible seeds
trai vai (lychee) – very common, this small, round red spiky fruit has a white fleshy inside, which is particularly sweet
xoai (mango) – mangoes come in several varieties; the sweetest are large round ones with bright yellow skin. The best mango season is April and May when the heat ripens them to perfection
vu sua (star apple) – a round, smooth fruit that produces a sweet, milky juice (its name means 'milk from the breast')

Or try one of the following:

La Ca (☎ 376 2793; 118/15A Đ Tran Van Kheo; mains 20,000-200,000d; ⏲ 8am-10pm) This stylish barbecue restaurant is fun, unless you happen to be a suckling pig, the house speciality. Staff are on rollerskates to speed up service.

Hoa Su (☎ 382 0717; Cai Khe Ward; mains 40,000-85,000d) Located near the Victoria Hotel, this restaurant is very popular with well-to-do locals on an evening out.

Du Thuyen (☎ 381 0841; Đ Hai Ba Trung; mains 40,000-120,000d) A floating restaurant set over three floors, it's all aboard from 8pm.

Drinking

Xe Loi (☎ 346 0362; Hau Riverside Park; ⏲ 5pm-late) Or Cyclo Club to you and me, this is the most happening nightspot in Can Tho. The huge gardens include plenty of tables and even a fake beach on the riverside. Inside the sort of Wild West-ish saloon is a full-on nightclub with DJs and regular live music. Free entry unless there is an event, but drinks are pricey.

Getting There & Away

AIR

There is now a functioning airport in Can Tho, although the only connections are to Hanoi (1,536,000d) with **Vietnam Airlines** (☎ 384 4320; 64 Đ Nguyen An Ninh), so most tourists will continue to arrive by road or boat.

BUS

There are buses leaving HCMC from Mien Tay bus station (from 60,000d, five hours). Express minibuses save almost an hour, but cost about 80,000d. There are also services to Soc Trang (25,000d, one hour), My Tho (40,000d, three hours), Long Xuyen (30,000d, 1½ hours) and Chau Doc (50,000d, three hours).

Can Tho's **main bus station** (cnr Đ Nguyen Trai & Đ Tran Phu) is about a kilometre north of town. The short-haul bus depot, 300m south of the corner of Đ 30 Thang 4 and Đ Mau Than, is good for getting to Soc Trang and the Phung Hiep floating market.

BOAT

There are several boat services to other cities in the Mekong Delta, including hydrofoils to Ca Mau (100,000d, three to four hours), passing through Phung Hiep.

CAR & MOTORBIKE

Whether you travel by car or motorbike, the ride from HCMC to Can Tho along Hwy 1A takes about four hours. There is one ferry crossing at Binh Minh (in Can Tho). The Can Tho ferry runs from 4am through to 2am. There is a new bridge under construction which will speed things up, but it has been severely delayed (2010–11) after a tragic collapse in 2007.

To get from ĐL Hoa Binh in Can Tho to the ferry crossing, go along Đ Nguyen Trai to the main bus station and turn right onto Đ Tran Phu.

Getting Around

These makeshift vehicles are unique to the Mekong Delta and the main form of transport around Can Tho. A *xe loi* is essentially a two-wheeled wagon attached to the rear of a motorbike, creating what resembles a motorised *cyclo*, but with four wheels touching the ground rather than two. Fares around town should be about 10,000d per person (they can carry two, or sometimes more).

AROUND CAN THO

Arguably the biggest drawcard of the delta is its colourful **floating markets**, which are on the banks of wide stretches of river. Most market folk set out early to avoid the daytime heat, so try to visit between 6am and 8am and beat the tourist tide. The real tides, however, are also a factor as bigger boats must often wait until the water is high enough for them to navigate.

Some of the smaller, rural floating markets are disappearing, largely because of improved roads and access to private and public transport. Many of the larger markets near urban areas, however, are still going strong.

Rural areas of Can Tho province, renowned for their durian, mangosteen and orange orchards, can easily be reached from Can Tho by boat or bicycle.

Cai Rang Floating Market

Just 6km from Can Tho in the direction of Soc Trang is Cai Rang, the biggest floating market in the Mekong Delta. There is a bridge here that serves as a great vantage point for photography. The market is best before 9am, although some vendors hang out until noon. It is quite an experience to see this in full swing, but it is well worth getting up extra early to beat the tour group crowds or you may end up seeing almost as many foreigners as market traders.

Cai Rang can be seen from the road, but getting here is far more interesting by boat. From the market area in Can Tho it takes about an hour by river, or you can drive to the Cau Dau Sau boat landing (by the Dau Sau Bridge), from where it takes only about 10 minutes to reach the market.

Phong Dien Floating Market

Perhaps the best floating market in the Mekong Delta, Phong Dien has fewer motorised craft and more stand-up rowing boats. It's less crowded than Cai Rang and there are far fewer tourists. The market is at its bustling best between 6am and 8am. It is 20km southwest of Can Tho and most get here by road.

It is theoretically possible to do a whirlwind boat trip here, visiting the small canals on the way and finishing back at the Cai Rang floating market. This journey should take approximately five hours return from Can Tho.

Stork Garden

On the road between Can Tho and Long Xuyen, **Vuon Co** (admission 2000d; 5am-6pm) is a 1.3-hectare stork sanctuary. It is a popular stop for group tours coming to view the thousands of resident storks, but is often closed due to a bird flu risk. There is a tall wooden viewing platform to see the storks chattering away in their nests; the best times of day are around dawn and dusk.

Vuon Co is in the Thot Not district, about 15km southeast of Long Xuyen. Look for a sign in the hamlet of Thoi An saying 'Ap Von Hoa'. Coming from Can Tho the sign is on the west side of the road, immediately after a small bridge. It is a couple of kilometres off the main highway – reachable on foot within 30 minutes, or hire a motorbike taxi for about 15,000d.

SOC TRANG

☎ 079 / pop 115,000

Soc Trang isn't the most charming of Mekong towns, but it is an important centre for the

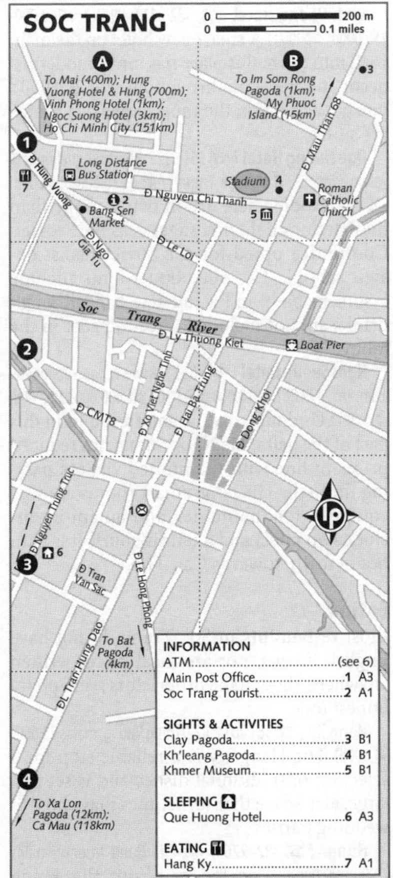

Khmer people who make up 28% of the province's population. It's a useful base for exploring some impressive Khmer temples in the area, although you can probably pass on these if Cambodia is on your radar. There is a colourful annual festival (usually in November) and, if you're in the vicinity at the right time, it's worth checking this out.

Information

Soc Trang Tourist (☎ 382 1498; www.soctrangtourism.com; 131 Đ Nguyen Chi Thanh; 🕑 8-11am & 1.30-5pm) is next door to the Phong Lan 2 Hotel, but little English is spoken.

ATMs are available at the Que Huong Hotel. The **main post office** (☎ 382 0051) is at 1 ĐL Tran Hung Dao.

Sights

KH'LEANG PAGODA

Except for the rather garish paint job, this **pagoda** (Chua Kh'leang; Đ Nguyen Chi Thanh) could have been transported straight from Cambodia. Originally built from bamboo in 1533, it had a complete rebuild in 1905 (this time using concrete). There are seven religious festivals held here every year, drawing people from outlying areas of the province.

Several monks reside in the pagoda, which also serves as a base for over 150 novices who come from around the Mekong Delta to study at Soc Trang's College of Buddhist Education across the street. The monks are friendly and happy to show you around the pagoda and discuss Buddhism.

KHMER MUSEUM

This **museum** (Bao Tang Tinh Soc Trang; ☎ 382 2983; 23 Đ Nguyen Chi Thanh; admission free; 🕑 7.30-11am & 1.30-4.30pm Mon-Fri) is dedicated to the history and culture of Vietnam's Khmer minority. It doubles as a sort of cultural centre, and traditional dance and music shows are periodically staged here for larger groups.

The Khmer Museum is opposite Kh'leang Pagoda and often appears closed; you may have to rouse someone to let you in.

CLAY PAGODA

Buu Son Tu (Precious Mountain Temple) was founded over 200 years ago by a Chinese family named Ngo. Today the temple is better known as **Chua Dat Set** (163 Đ Mau Than 68), or Clay Pagoda.

Unassuming from the outside, this pagoda is highly unusual in that nearly everything inside is made entirely of clay. These objects were hand-sculpted by the monk Ngo Kim Tong. From the age of 20 until his death at 62, this ingenious artisan dedicated his life to decorating the pagoda. He made the hundreds of statues and sculptures that adorn the interior today.

Entering the pagoda, visitors are greeted by one of Ngo's greatest creations – a six-tusked clay elephant, which is said to have appeared in a dream of Buddha's mother. Behind this is the central altar, which was fashioned from more than five tonnes of clay. In the altar are a thousand Buddhas seated on lotus petals. Other highlights include a 13-storey Chinese-style tower over 4m tall. The tower features 208 cubby holes, each with a mini-Buddha figure inside, and is decorated with 156 dragons.

The pagoda also features two giant candles (200kg and 2.6m tall) that burn in honour of the great artist.

Though some of the decor borders on kitsch, the pagoda is an active place of worship, and totally different from the Khmer and Vietnamese pagodas elsewhere in Soc Trang. The resident monk, Ngo Kim Giang, is the younger brother of the artist and a delightful man to chat with about the pagoda. He speaks excellent French although very little English.

The Clay Pagoda is within walking distance of the town centre. Needless to say, the clay objects in the pagoda are fragile so explore with care. Donations are welcome.

IM SOM RONG PAGODA

This large, beautiful Khmer pagoda was built in 1961 and is notable for its well-kept gardens. A plaque on the grounds honours the man who donated the funds to build the pagoda. There are many monks in residence here, most of whom are very friendly.

Im Som Rong Pagoda is over 1km east of Soc Trang on the road to My Phuoc Island. When you reach the main gate it is a 300m walk futher along a dirt track to the pagoda itself.

Festivals & Events

OC BOM BOC FESTIVAL

Once a year, the Khmer community turns out for the Oc Bom Boc Festival (known as Bon Om Touk or the Water Festival in Cambodia), with longboat races on the Soc Trang River. This event attracts visitors from all over Vietnam and even Cambodia. First prize is more than US$1000, so it's not difficult to see why competition is so fierce.

The races are held according to the lunar calendar on the 15th day of the 10th moon, which roughly means November. The races start at noon, but things get jumping in Soc Trang the evening before. Hotel space is at a premium during the festival.

Sleeping

Hung Vuong Hotel (☎ 362 4666; 6/24 Đ Hung Vuong; r 120,000-200,000d; ❄) Tucked away down a side road off the main drag into town, this new mini-hotel is great value, with nice linen on the beds and sparkling floors.

Vinh Phong Hotel (☎ 362 6111; 89 QL1; r 160,000-250,000d; ❄ 💻) A smart new hotel on the main road into town, this place has funky modernist decor and free wi-fi throughout. For 200,000d you get a bathtub; the most expensive rooms are suites.

Que Huong Hotel (☎ 361 6122; khachsanquehuong@yahoo.com; 128 Đ Nguyen Trung Truc; r 220,000-550,000d; ❄ 💻) Rooms here are in better shape than the exterior might first suggest, as the People's Committee opted for the Soviet-realist design school. The 400,000d rooms include a sunken bath and a full-size bar, although drinks are not included. Free internet in the lobby.

Ngoc Suong Hotel (☎ 361 3108; www.ngocsuonghotel.com; Km 2127 QL1; r 220,000-350,000d, ste 400,000-800,000d; ❄ 🏊) Undoubtedly the smartest digs in this part of the delta, the Ngoc Suong has reduced prices in line with the limited visitors passing through. The large smart rooms are well equipped for the money and amenities include two pools and a tennis court. It is 3km out of town, towards Can Tho.

Eating

Most restaurants in Soc Trang do not have English menus, nor are meal prices written anywhere, though the proprietors seem pretty honest folk.

Hang Ky (☎ 361 2034; 67 Đ Hung Vuong; mains 20,000-80,000d) The Hang Ky is a reliable stop for a selection of traditional dishes and is set in a large, airy space that sometimes plays host to wedding parties.

Hung (☎ 382 2268; 6/24 Đ Hung Vuong; mains 20,000-90,000d) Located opposite the Hung Vuong Hotel, this is one of the best restaurants in town. Hung is a huge eating space with delicious grilled meat and fish and is perpetually busy.

Mai (☎ 361 5511; 85A Đ Hung Vuong; mains 20,000-150,000d; 🕑 lunch & dinner) Spread over two floors, this local diner is always packed thanks to its cheap draught beer and extensive collection of live seafood.

Getting There & Away

Long-distance buses stop at the station on Đ Nguyen Chi Thanh, just down the street from Soc Trang Tourist. Buses run between Soc Trang and most Mekong cities, including Can Tho (from 25,000d) and Ca Mau (from 50,000d). Regular vans travel to HCMC (95,000d, around six hours).

AROUND SOC TRANG

Bat Pagoda

This is one of the Mekong Delta's most unusual sights and has become a favourite stop-off for both foreign and domestic tourists. Sadly a fire ripped through the compound in 2007 and it has yet to be restored.

The Bat Pagoda (Chua Doi) is a large monastery compound. Upon entering through an archway, you'll almost immediately hear the screeching of the large colony of resident fruit bats. There are literally hundreds of these creatures hanging from the fruit trees, although colony numbers are thought to have been halved by the fire. The largest bats weigh about 1kg and have a wingspan of about 1.5m.

Fruit bats are not toilet trained, so watch out when standing under a tree, or bring an umbrella. In the evening the bats spread their wings and fly out to invade orchards all over the Mekong Delta, much to the consternation of farmers, who are known to trap the bats and eat them. Inside the monastery the creatures are protected and the bats seem to know this and stick around.

The best times for visiting are early morning and at least an hour before sunset, when the bats are most active. Around dusk hundreds of bats swoop out of the trees to go foraging.

The monks are very friendly and don't ask for money, although it doesn't hurt to leave a donation. The pagoda is decorated with gilt Buddhas and murals paid for by overseas Vietnamese contributors. In one room there's a life-size statue of the monk who was the former head of the complex. There's also a beautifully painted Khmer longboat here of the type used at the Oc Bom Boc Festival.

The Bat Pagoda is about 4km west of Soc Trang. You can catch a motorbike taxi or easily walk here in under an hour. About 3km out of town towards the pagoda the road splits into two – take the right fork and continue for 1km.

Xa Lon (Sa Lon) Pagoda

This magnificent, classic Khmer pagoda was originally built in wood more than 200 years ago. In 1923 it was completely rebuilt, but proved to be too small. From 1969 to 1985, the present-day large pagoda was slowly built as funds trickled in from donations. The ceramic tiles on the exterior of the pagoda are particularly stunning.

As at other pagodas, the monks lead an austere life. They eat breakfast at 6am and seek alms until 11am, when they hold a one-hour worship. They eat again just before noon and study in the afternoon – they do not eat dinner.

At present around 25 monks reside here. The pagoda also operates a school for the study of Buddhism and Sanskrit.

The temple is 12km from Soc Trang, towards Ca Mau, on Hwy 1A.

BAC LIEU

☎ 0781 / pop 136,000

Few people stop in Bac Lieu, but birders may find themselves passing through en route to the excellent bird sanctuary near town. Of the 800,000 people living in the surrounding province, about 8% are of Chinese or Cambodian origin.

The town has a few elegant but forlorn French colonial buildings, like the impressive **Fop House** (now used as a community sports centre), but little else.

Farming is a difficult occupation in this region because of saltwater intrusion, and the province is better known for its healthy longan orchards. In addition to this, the enterprising locals eke out a living from fishing, oyster collection and shrimp farming, as well as salt production, obtained by evaporating saltwater ponds that form immense salt flats.

Information

The helpful **Bac Lieu tourist office** (☎ 382 4272; 2 Đ Hoang Van Thu; 7-11am & 1-5pm) is next to the Bac Lieu Hotel. Some English is spoken and basic town maps are available, as is information about trips to the bird sanctuary (p444).

The **post office** (☎ 382 4242; 20 Đ Tran Phu) is off the main roundabout. **Sacombank** (☎ 393 2200; B2 Đ Tran Phu), which can exchange currency, is on the same street.

Sleeping & Eating

In addition to those listed here, there are numerous inexpensive guesthouses (rooms cost around US$10) that dot the road into town from Soc Trang.

Hoang Cung Hotel (☎ 382 3362; 1B/5 Đ Tran Phu; r 160,000-250,000d;) The best-value place in town, this hotel offers clean and comfortable rooms, the best with balconies overlooking a large palm at the back. It's about 1km from the roundabout in the direction of Soc Trang (across from the Khmer pagoda gate).

Cong Tu Hotel (☎ 395 3304; 13 Đ Dien Bien Phu; r 300,000-500,000d; ❄) This is a rare old colonial gem that is decidedly showing its age but carries the decay off with a certain charm. The smarter rooms have a balcony and high ceilings but the carpet tells you how long it was since the last renovation. The restaurant (mains 30,000d to 80,000d) here is one of the better spots in town.

Bac Lieu 2 (☎ 382 4951; 89/3 Đ Tran Phu Lo 1; mains 20,000-70,000d) Located on the road to Soc Trang, this long-running local favourite offers a good range of Vietnamese classics in clean surroundings. It's about 700m north of the roundabout towards Soc Trang.

Getting There & Around

The bus station is on the main road into town, 1km west of the centre. From here you can catch regular buses to Ho Chi Minh City (105,000d), Ca Mau (30,000d) and Soc Trang (25,000d).

For trips to outlying areas (including the bird sanctuary), you can arrange a taxi through the Bac Lieu tourist office or by calling ☎ 392 2922.

AROUND BAC LIEU

Bac Lieu Bird Sanctuary

One of more interesting sights in this sleepy corner of the Mekong Delta, **Bac Lieu Bird Sanctuary** (Vuon Chim Bac Lieu; ☎ 383 5991; admission 15,000d; 🕑 7.30am-5pm) is notable for its 50-odd species of bird, including a large population of graceful white herons. It is surprisingly popular with Vietnamese tourists, but foreign visitors are rare, probably because Bac Lieu is so out of the way.

Whether or not you see any birds depends on what time of year you visit. Bird populations are at their peak in the rainy season – approximately May to October. The birds hang around to nest until about January, then fly off in search of greener pastures. There are basically no birds here from February until the rainy season begins again.

The drive is only 5km but the road is in poor shape. The rest of the trek is through dense (and often muddy) jungle. Bring plenty of repellent, good shoes, water and binoculars.

Pay the admission fee when you reach the entrance of the bird sanctuary. You can (and should) hire a guide here, as you may get lost without one. The guides aren't supposed to receive money, so tip them discreetly; most guides do not speak English. Transport and guides can also be arranged at the Bac Lieu tourist office (see p443), but hiring a guide there will cost considerably more.

Moi Hoa Binh Pagoda

This Khmer pagoda (Chua Moi Hoa Binh or Se Rey Vongsa) is 13km south of Bac Lieu along Hwy 1A. The pagoda is uniquely designed and chances are good that the monastery's enormous tower will catch your eye even if you're not looking for it. As pagodas in Vietnam go, it's relatively new, having first been built in 1952. The tower was added in 1990 and is used to store the bones of the deceased. There is a large and impressive meeting hall in front of the tower.

Most Khmer people in the area head for monastery schools in Soc Trang in order to receive a Khmer education. Apart from the small contingent of student monks, very few students study at the Moi Hoa Binh Pagoda.

CA MAU

☎ 0780 / pop 176,000

Built on the swampy shores of the Ganh Hao River, Ca Mau is the capital and largest city in Ca Mau province. It occupies the southern tip of the Mekong Delta, a remote and inhospitable area that wasn't cultivated until the late 17th century. The province of Ca Mau was devastated by Typhoon Linda in 1997.

Owing to the boggy terrain, this area has the lowest population density in southern Vietnam. Ca Mau lies in the middle of Vietnam's largest swamp and is known for its voracious mosquitoes.

Ca Mau has developed rapidly in recent years, but the actual town itself is rather dull. The main attractions here are the nearby swamps and forests, which can be easily explored by boat. Bird-watchers and aspiring botanists get excited about stork-sighting opportunities and swamp ecology. Speak to Ca Mau Tourist before undertaking trips to these outlying attractions.

Information

Interesting boat trips – two days and two nights to Nam Can, Dat Mui (Cape Ca Mau), the Da Bac Islands and the U-Minh

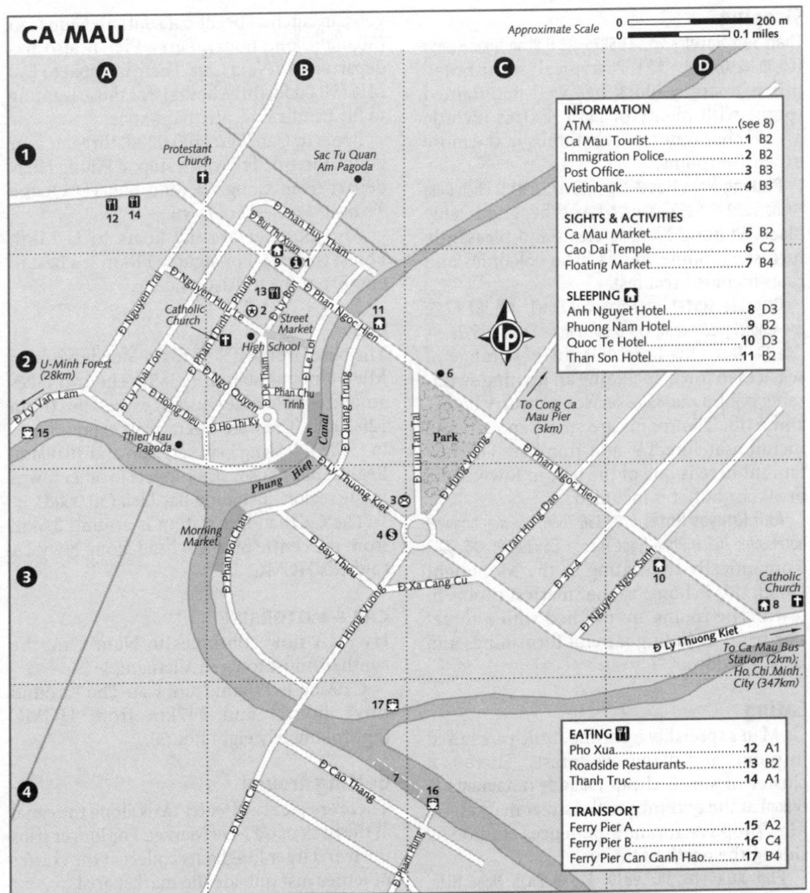

Forest – can be organised at **Ca Mau Tourist** (Cong Ty Du Lich Minh Hai; ☎ 383 1238; 3-5 Đ Ly Bon; 8-11am & 1-5pm). Other services available here include foreign-currency exchange, car and boat rentals, and visa extensions.

Near the post office, **Vietinbank** (☎ 383 8677; 94 Đ Ly Thuong Kiet) offers foreign-currency exchange and cash advances. There's an ATM located inside the Anh Nguyet Hotel.

In an emergency, seek medical help at **Ca Mau Hospital** (Benh Vien Ca Mau; ☎ 383 1015; Đ Ly Thuong Kiet). Better still, head to HCMC.

Sights

CA MAU MARKET

This is a wholesale **market** (6am-6pm) and not really a place for people to shop. The animal life on display – such as fish and turtles – is cleaned, packed into crates, frozen and sent to HCMC by truck. It's an interesting place to wander around – it certainly bears little resemblance to the supermarkets at home. However, animal rights advocates will not be pleased.

There's also a **floating market** (6am–mid-afternoon) here.

CAO DAI TEMPLE

Though not as large as the one in Tay Ninh (p393), this **Cao Dai Temple** (Đ Phan Ngoc Hien) is still a very impressive place and it's staffed by friendly monks. The temple was built in 1966 and to this day still seems to be fairly active.

Sleeping

Than Son Hotel (☎ 381 5825; 23 Đ Phan Ngoc Hien; r 100,000-250,000d; ❄) A typical mini-hotel, this five-storey block has well-maintained rooms with plenty of light. Extras include TV and hot water, plus bathtubs in the more expensive rooms.

Phuong Nam Hotel (☎ 383 1752; 91 Đ Phan Dinh Phung; r 250,000-350,000d; ❄) Another good-value place, Phuong Nam is clean and pleasantly furnished. Some rooms have balconies and rates include breakfast.

Quoc Te Hotel (International Hotel; ☎ 382 6745; www.hotelquocte.com; 179 Đ Phan Ngoc Hien; r US$22-60; ❄ 💻) This hotel has the best range of services in town, including an inviting swimming pool, a massage service for weary bodies and a lift. The rooms are smart enough and include satellite TV and minibar. The restaurant here is one of the best in town and a breakfast buffet is included.

Anh Nguyet Hotel (☎ 356 7666; www.anhnguyethotel.com; 207 Đ Phan Ngoc Hien; r US$29-59; ❄ 💻) Romantically translating as the Moonlight Hotel, this is home to the smartest rooms in town. The rooms are finished with a three-star trim, including tasteful furnishings and large windows.

Eating

Ca Mau's speciality is shrimp, which are raised in ponds and mangrove forests. There is a cluster of small, cheap **roadside restaurants** (Đ Ly Bon) at the entrance to the street market. Ca Mau's top restaurant experiences are side by side in the north of town:

Pho Xua (☎ 382 9830; 126 Đ Phan Ngoc Hien; mains 30,000-80,000d) The menu here is heavy on shrimp, seafood and fish dishes. It's quite a stylish place for Ca Mau, set amid landscaped gardens.

Thanh Truc (☎ 382 0021; 126 Đ Phan Ngoc Hien; mains 30,000-80,000d) Right next door to the Pho Xua, this is the place to sample a bubbling hotpot or the popular grilled meat dishes.

Getting There & Away

BOAT

Ca Mau has several piers with boat services around the region. Three to four hydrofoils a day travel between Ca Mau and Rach Gia (the boat docks in Rach Meo, about 2km from Rach Gia). This departs from Ferry Pier Can Ganh Hao daily between 7.30am and 1pm (100,000d, three hours). This pier is also where you can catch a speedboat south to Nam Can (50,000d, one hour). Ferry Pier B also has departures to Nam Can. There is a boat to Dai Mui (90,000d, three hours), for those wanting to hit Land's End, Vietnam-style.

Boats to Can Tho (100,000d, three to four hours, three daily), with a stop in Phung Hiep, depart from Cong Ca Mau pier (Đ Quang Trung), 3km east of town.

Also popular are the boats to U-Minh Forest (below). For a guided tour, it's best to enquire at the tourist office.

BUS

The buses from HCMC to Ca Mau leave from Mien Tay bus station (p385). The trip takes around eight to nine hours by express bus (from 120,000d). There are several daily express buses to HCMC leaving between 5am and 10.30am. Regular daily buses also connect to other towns in the region, including Bac Lieu (30,000d).

The Ca Mau bus station is around 2.5km from the centre of town; head along Hwy 1A towards HCMC.

CAR & MOTORBIKE

Hwy 1A now continues to Nam Can, the southernmost town in Vietnam.

Ca Mau is 178km from Can Tho (around three hours) and 347km from HCMC (approximately eight hours).

Getting Around

There are plenty of water taxis along the canal at the back of Ca Mau Market. For longer trips upriver, larger longboats collect at the cluster of jetties just outside the market area.

AROUND CA MAU

U-Minh Forest

The town of Ca Mau borders the U-Minh Forest, a huge mangrove forest covering 1000 sq km of Ca Mau and Kien Giang provinces. Local people use certain species of mangrove as a source of timber, charcoal, thatch and tannin. When the mangroves flower, bees feed on the blossoms, providing both honey and wax. The area is an important habitat for waterfowl.

The U-Minh Forest, which is the largest mangrove forest in the world beyond the Amazon basin, was a favourite hideout for the VC during the American War. US patrol boats were frequently ambushed here and the VC regularly planted mines in the canals. The Americans responded with chemical defoliation, which made their enemy more visible while doing enormous damage to the forests. Replanting efforts at first failed because the soil was so toxic, but gradually the heavy rainfall has washed the dioxin out to sea and the forest is returning. Many eucalyptus trees have also been planted here because they have proved to be relatively resistant to dioxin.

Unfortunately the mangrove forests are being further damaged by clearing for shrimp-farming ponds, charcoal production and woodchipping. The government has tried to limit these activities, but the conflict between nature and humans continues. The conflict will probably get worse before it gets better, because Vietnam's population is still growing rapidly.

The area is known for its birdlife, but these creatures have also taken a beating. Nevertheless, twitchers will enjoy a boat trip around Ca Mau, although the flocks of birds aren't nearly as ubiquitous as the swarms of mosquitoes.

Ca Mau Tourist (p444) offers all-day tours of the forest by boat. Once you have established a price (US$140 but seemingly negotiable) with these guys, you can also talk to the locals down at Ferry Pier A to see if there are better deals.

Dam Doi Bird Sanctuary

About 45km southeast of Ca Mau lies **Dam Doi Bird Sanctuary** (admission 15,000d; ⌚ dawn-dusk). Storks are the largest and most easily spotted birds here, making their nests in the tall trees. Remember that birds will be birds – they don't like humans to get too close and they leave their nests early in the morning in search of food.

Ca Mau Tourist offers a full-day tour by boat to the sanctuary for US$120 (one to 10 people).

NAM CAN

☎ 0780

Except for a minuscule fishing hamlet (Tran De) and an offshore island (Hon Khoai), Nam Can stakes its claim as the southernmost town in Vietnam. Few tourists come to this isolated community, which survives mainly from the shrimp industry.

At the southern tip of the delta is the **Ca Mau Nature Reserve**, sometimes referred to as Ngoc Hien Bird Sanctuary. It's one of the least developed and most protected parts of the Mekong Delta region. Shrimp farming is prohibited here. Access is by boat.

If you're looking to visit another remote spot, you can hire a boat to take you to Dat Mui (Cape Ca Mau), the southwestern tip of Vietnam. Motorbikes can whisk you from Dat Mui to the stone marking Vietnam's southern tip, about 2km beyond. However, few people find this worthwhile.

Getting There & Away

Hwy 1A links Nam Can with Ca Mau, but the speedboat (50,000d, one hour) is the most popular form of transport. There are also speedboats on to Dat Mui (55,000d, 1½ hours).

LONG XUYEN

☎ 076 / pop 240,000

In this relatively affluent town that doubles as the capital of An Giang province, industries include agriculture, fish processing and cashew nuts. Aside from a few sites, a lively market, and perhaps a short trip along the river, there's little to detain travellers here.

Long Xuyen was once a stronghold of the Hoa Hao sect. Founded in 1939, the sect emphasises simplicity in worship and does not believe in temples or intermediaries between humans and the Supreme Being. Until 1956 the Hoa Hao had an army and constituted a major military force in this region.

The town's other claim to fame is being the birthplace of Vietnam's second president, Ton Duc Thang. There is a museum in town dedicated to Bac Ton (Uncle Ton) as well as a large statue bearing his likeness.

Information

An Giang Tourist (☎ 384 1036; www.angiangtourimex.com.vn; Dong Xuyen Hotel; ⌚ 7-11am & 1-5pm) is located inside the Dong Xuyen Hotel. Some English is spoken and they should be able to put you in touch with a guide to Oc-Eo (p449).

Vietcombank (☎ 384 1075; 1 Đ Hung Vuong; ⌚ Mon-Fri) offers cash advances on credit cards and also exchanges travellers cheques. The **Vietinbank** (☎ 384 1704; 20-22 Đ Ngo Gia Tu), near the post office, offers internet access next door.

Sights

LONG XUYEN CATHOLIC CHURCH

One of the largest churches in the Mekong Delta, **Long Xuyen Catholic Church** (Đ Tran Hung Dao; ⌚ 7.30am-5.30pm) is an impressive modern structure that boasts a 50m-high bell tower. It was constructed between 1966 and 1973 and can seat 1000 worshippers.

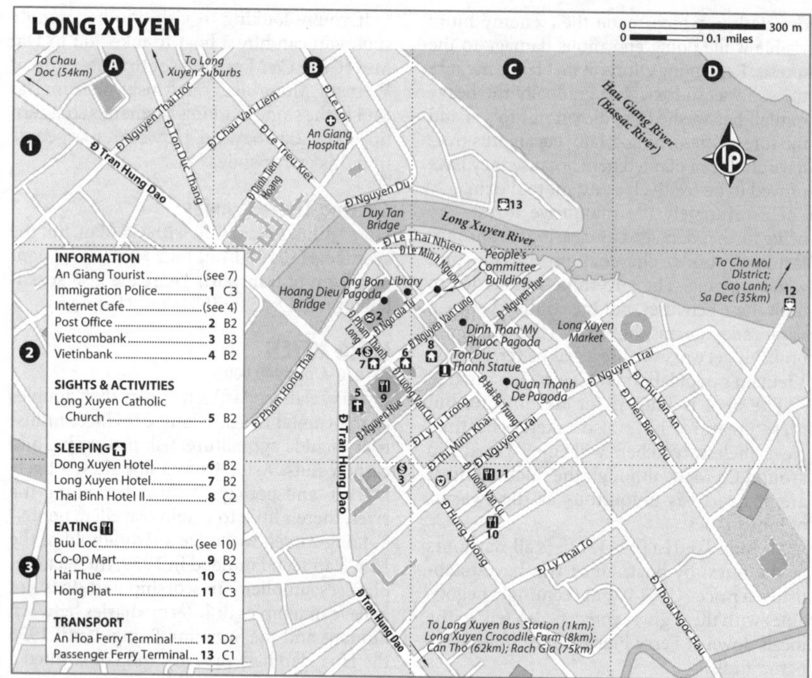

CHO MOI DISTRICT

Across the river from Long Xuyen, Cho Moi district is known for its rich groves of fruit such as bananas, durians, guava, jackfruit, longans, mangoes, mangosteens and plums.

Cho Moi district can be reached by boat from the ferry terminal.

LONG XUYEN CROCODILE FARM

For a close-up view of the reptile that once ruled the Mekong, this **farm** (☎ 383 1298; longxuyencrocodilefarm@yahoo.com; 44/1A Đ Tran Hung Dao; admission 5000d; 7am-6pm) is home to thousands of crocodiles ranging in size from 10cm to 4m. The meat and skin of these animals is largely exported, though some Vietnamese drop in to buy fresh or frozen crocodile meat (50,000d to 150,000d per kilogram). The farm lies 8km south of town on the road to Can Tho.

Sleeping & Eating

Thai Binh Hotel II (☎ 384 7078; 4 Đ Nguyen Hue A; r 80,000-250,000d;) The cheapest digs in town, but you'll be planning the great escape if you choose the small cheapies here. The air-con rooms are a better deal and include a balcony.

Long Xuyen Hotel (☎ 384 1927; longxuyenhotel@hcm.vnn.vn; 19 Đ Nguyen Van Cung; r 230,000-350,000d;) One of the state-owned specials in town, this place could probably do with an overhaul, but prices remain reasonable in the meantime. Rooms include satellite TV, hot water and shared balconies, plus there is a Vietcombank ATM.

Dong Xuyen Hotel (☎ 394 2260; dongxuyenag@hcm.vnn.vn; Đ 9A Luong Van Cu; r 350,000-670,000d, ste 700,000d;) Opposite the Long Xuyen Hotel, this is the smartest place in town. The rooms are nicely furnished in wood and include the usual suspects like a minibar. The staff are friendly and helpful and speak good English.

Hong Phat (☎ 384 2359; 242/4 Đ Luong Van Cu; mains 25,000-70,000d) This restaurant features air-conditioning, a bonus on a hot day. English menus, grilled meats, plenty of seafood and friendly staff make it a reliable choice.

Self caterers planning a longer boat trip might try the giant **Co-Op Mart** (Đ Luong Van Cu) or there are a couple more dining options on the Luong Van Cu restaurant drag:

Hai Thue (☎ 384 5573; 245/3 Đ Luong Van Cu; mains 15,000-40,000d) A good stop for cheap but authentic Vietnamese food.

Buu Loc (☎ 384 4401; 246/3 Đ Luong Van Cu; mains 20,000-40,000d) Another popular local place for filling meals, but no English menu.

Getting There & Away

BOAT

To get to the Long Xuyen ferry dock from Đ Pham Hong Thai, you'll need to cross Duy Tan Bridge and turn right. Passenger ferries leave from here to Sa Dec and other delta destinations.

From the An Hoa ferry terminal you can also catch boats to Cao Lanh and Sa Dec.

BUS

The buses heading from HCMC to Long Xuyen leave from the Mien Tay bus station (p385; from 85,000d).

Long Xuyen bus station (Ben Xe Long Xuyen; ☎ 385 2125; opposite 96/3B Đ Tran Hung Dao) is at the southern end of town. Buses from Long Xuyen to Can Tho, Chau Doc and Rach Gia leave from here.

Long Xuyen is 62km from Can Tho, 126km from My Tho and 189km from HCMC.

AROUND LONG XUYEN

Ancient City of Oc-Eo

It's hard to believe, but many centuries ago, Oc-Eo was the Saigon of its day, both the port and commercial centre for this part of the Mekong Delta. During the 1st to 6th centuries AD, when southern Vietnam and southern Cambodia were under the rule of the Indian-influenced Cambodian kingdom of Funan, Oc-Eo was a major trading city. Much of what is known about the Funan empire, which reached its height during the 5th century AD, comes from contemporary Chinese sources and the excavations at Oc-Eo and Angkor Borei in neighbouring Cambodia. The excavations have uncovered evidence of contact between Oc-Eo and what is now Thailand, Malaysia and Indonesia, as well as Persia and the Roman Empire.

An elaborate system of canals around Oc-Eo was once used for both irrigation and transportation, prompting Chinese travellers of the time to write about 'sailing across Funan' on their way to the Malay peninsula. Most of the buildings of Oc-Eo were built on piles and pieces of these structures indicate the high degree of refinement achieved by Funanese civilisation. Artefacts found at Oc-Eo are on display in HCMC at the History Museum (p355) and Fine Arts Museum (p356), and in Hanoi at the History Museum (p97).

Though there is in fact very little to see here today, the remains of Oc-Eo are not far from Long Xuyen. Enquire at An Giang Tourist (p447) for guides and travel information. Oc-Eo is most accessible during the dry season. Special permission may be required to visit if there are archaeological digs taking place.

CHAU DOC

☎ 076 / pop 102,000

Draped along the banks of the Hau Giang River (Bassac River), Chau Doc sees plenty of travellers passing through on the river route between Cambodia and Vietnam (p455). It is a likeable little town with significant Chinese, Cham and Khmer communities. Its cultural diversity – apparent in the mosques, temples, churches and nearby pilgrimage sites – makes it a fascinating place to explore even if you aren't continuing to Cambodia. Taking a boat trip to the Cham communities across the river is another highlight, while the bustling market and peaceful waterfront provide fine backdrops to a few days of relaxing before heading out.

Information

There's **internet** (🕑 7am-9pm) in the courtyard of Chau Doc's main **post office** (☎ 386 9200; 2 Đ Le Loi). Foreign currency can be exchanged at **Vietinbank** (☎ 386 6497; 68-70 Đ Nguyen Huu Canh).

Local travel agencies where you can buy boat transport to Phnom Penh and book half- and full-day boat trips on the Mekong include **Mekong Tours** (☎ 386 8222; www.mekongvietnam.com; 14 Đ Nguyen Huu Canh) and **Delta Adventure** (☎ 356 3810; www.deltaadventuretours.com; 53 Đ Le Loi), part of the Kim Travel empire.

Sights

CHAU PHU TEMPLE

In 1926 this **temple** (Dinh Than Chau Phu; cnr Đ Nguyen Van Thoai & Đ Gia Long) was built to worship the Nguyen dynasty official Thoai Ngoc Hau, who is buried at Sam Mountain (p453). The structure is decorated with both Vietnamese and Chinese motifs. Inside are funeral tablets bearing the names of the deceased and some biographical information about them.

MOSQUES

Domed and arched **Chau Giang Mosque**, in the hamlet of Chau Giang, serves the local Cham

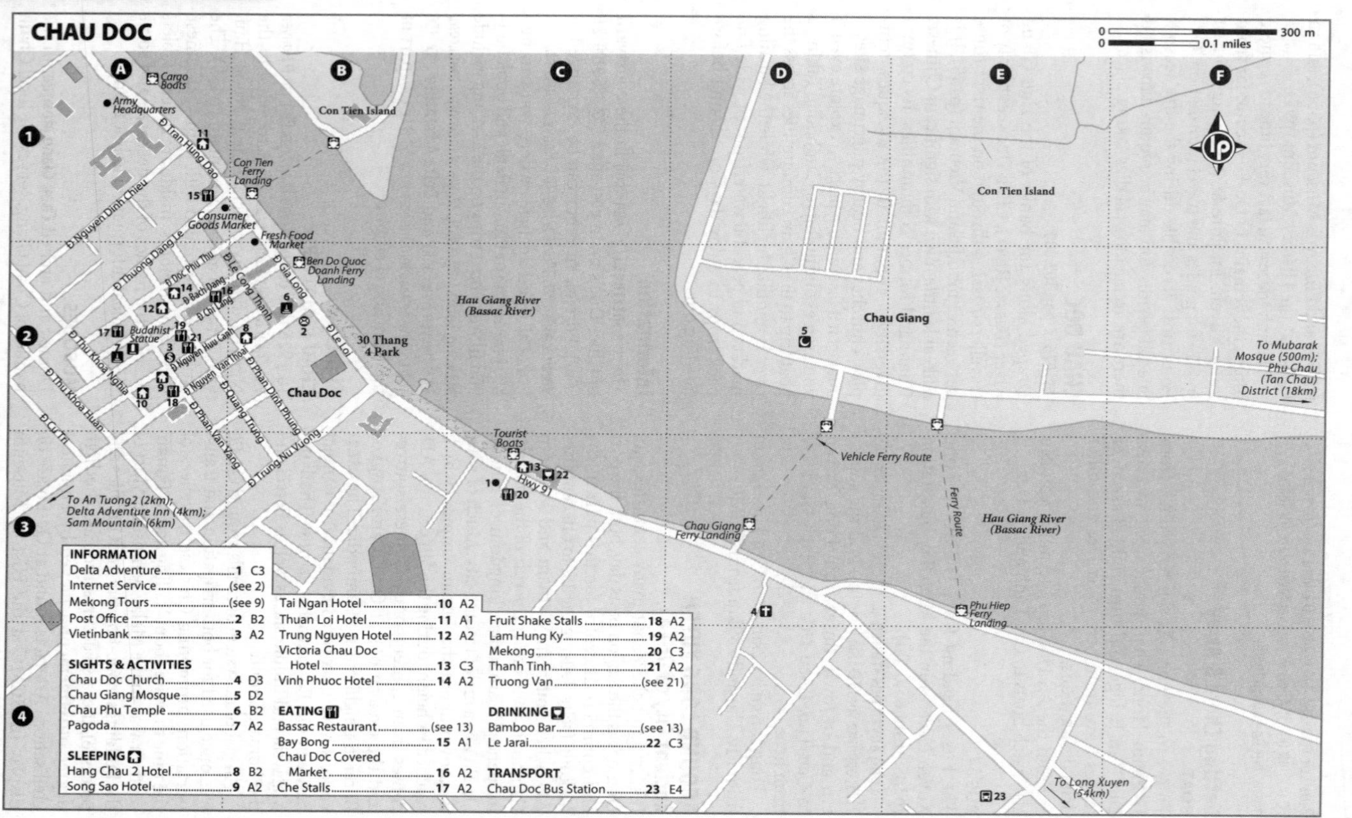
CHAU DOC
0 300 m
0 0.1 miles
A
B
C
D
E
F
1
2
3
4
Cargo Boats
Army Headquarters
Con Tien Island
Đ Tran Hung Dao
Con Tien Ferry Landing
Consumer Goods Market
Fresh Food Market
Ben Do Quoc Doanh Ferry Landing
Đ Nguyen Dinh Chieu
Đ Thuong Dang Le
Đ Doc Phu Thu
Đ Bach Dang
Đ Chi Lang
Đ Le Cong Thanh
Đ Gia Long
Đ Le Loi
Buddhist Statue
Đ Thu Khoa Nghia
Đ Nguyen Huu Canh
Đ Nguyen Van Thoai
Đ Phan Dinh Phung
Đ Quang Trung
Đ Phan Van Vang
Đ Trung Nu Vuong
Đ Thu Khoa Huan
Đ Cu Tri
30 Thang 4 Park
Chau Doc
Hau Giang River (Bassac River)
To An Tuong2 (2km); Delta Adventure Inn (4km); Sam Mountain (6km)
Tourist Boats
Hwy 91
Chau Giang
Chau Giang Ferry Landing
Vehicle Ferry Route
Ferry Route
Phu Hiep Ferry Landing
Hau Giang River (Bassac River)
To Mubarak Mosque (500m); Phu Chau (Tan Chau) District (18km)
To Long Xuyen (54km)
INFORMATION
Delta Adventure 1 C3
Internet Service (see 2)
Mekong Tours (see 9)
Post Office 2 B2
Vietinbank 3 A2
SIGHTS & ACTIVITIES
Chau Doc Church 4 D3
Chau Giang Mosque 5 D2
Chau Phu Temple 6 B2
Pagoda 7 A2
SLEEPING
Hang Chau 2 Hotel 8 B2
Song Sao Hotel 9 A2
Tai Ngan Hotel 10 A2
Thuan Loi Hotel 11 A1
Trung Nguyen Hotel 12 A2
Victoria Chau Doc Hotel 13 C3
Vinh Phuoc Hotel 14 A2
EATING
Bassac Restaurant (see 13)
Bay Bong 15 A1
Chau Doc Covered Market 16 A2
Che Stalls 17 A2
Fruit Shake Stalls 18 A2
Lam Hung Ky 19 A2
Mekong 20 C3
Thanh Tinh 21 A2
Truong Van (see 21)
DRINKING
Bamboo Bar (see 13)
Le Jarai 22 C3
TRANSPORT
Chau Doc Bus Station 23 E4

Muslims. To get there, take the car ferry from Chau Giang ferry landing in Chau Doc across the Hau Giang River. From the ferry landing, walk inland from the river for 30m, turn left and walk 50m.

The **Mubarak Mosque** (Thanh Duong Hoi Giao), where children study the Quran in Arabic script, is also on the river bank opposite Chau Doc. Visitors are permitted, but you should avoid entering during the calls to prayer (five times daily) unless you are a Muslim.

There are other small mosques in the Chau Doc area. They are accessible by boat but you'll need a local guide to find them all.

FLOATING HOUSES

These houses, whose floats consist of empty metal drums, are both a place to live and a livelihood for their residents. Under each house, fish are raised in suspended metal nets: the fish flourish in their natural river habitat; the family can feed them whatever scraps are handy; and catching the fish requires less exertion than fishing. You can find these houses floating around Chau Doc and get a close-up by hiring a boat (but please be respectful of their privacy). To learn more about the workings of these fish cages, see p452.

Sleeping

As well as these places in Chau Doc, there are a couple more accommodation options out near Sam Mountain for those who want to get away from it all. Most hotels here charge in US dollars, probably thanks to the overland connection with Cambodia.

Vinh Phuoc Hotel (☎ 386 6242; 12 Đ Quang Trung; r US$6-20; ❄ 💻) Popular budget hotel that has friendly staff with a good knowledge of the delta region. Rooms range from cheapies with fan to smarter air-con options with hot water. The restaurant (mains 25,000d to 60,000d) is good value and there are usually some beer drinkers lurking around.

Thuan Loi Hotel (☎ 386 6134; hotelthuanloi@hcm.vnn.vn; 18 Đ Tran Hung Dao; r US$7-10; ❄) This is the only cheap hotel with a riverside location and it uses it to its best advantage with a floating restaurant set under a thatched roof. The rooms are not so atmospheric but are good value. Fan rooms are cold water only, so it's worth investing in a bigger air-con room.

Song Sao Hotel (☎ 356 1777; songsaohotel@yahoo.com; 12-13 Đ Nguyen Huu Canh; r US$11-15; ❄) This central hotel overlooks the local pagoda and is popular with midrange tour groups passing through town. The rooms have wood furnishings, but some are better than others and include balconies, so shop around.

our pick **Trung Nguyen Hotel** (☎ 386 6158; trunghotel@yahoo.com; 86 Đ Bach Dang; r US$12-17; ❄ 💻) Following a facelift, this is definitely the best of the budget places, with a trim and panache that is decidedly more midrange. Rooms feature a bit more decorative verve than the competition and added benefits include free wi-fi or internet, plus breakfast. We like it.

Victoria Chau Doc Hotel (☎ 386 5010; www.victoriahotels-asia.com; 32 Đ Le Loi; r US$155-240, online rates from US$115; ❄ 💻 🏊) Seriously stylish for Chau Doc, the Victoria is built in classic colonial style. With a striking location on the riverfront, the grand rooms here have timber floors, inviting bathtubs and classy drapes. The swimming pool overlooks the busy riverfront action and there is a small spa upstairs.

Some cheapies dotted around town include the following:

Hang Chau 2 Hotel (☎ 386 8891; hangchau2agg@hcm.vnn.vn; 10 Đ Nguyen Van Thoai; r US$10-12; ❄) A friendly mini-hotel with spacious rooms and little touches like balconies or leather armchairs.

Tai Ngan Hotel (☎ 386 6435; tainganfood@yahoo.com; 11 Đ Nguyen Huu Canh; r US$10-12; ❄) A reliable place with some spacious rooms with a balcony overlooking the plaza.

Eating

RESTAURANTS

Mekong (☎ 386 7381; 41 Đ Le Loi; mains 30,000-80,000d; 🕐 lunch & dinner) Located directly opposite the Victoria Chau Doc Hotel, this restaurant has a large covered section or an outdoor area in front of the gracefully decaying old villa. A good spot for Vietnamese greatest hits at affordable prices.

Lam Hung Ky (☎ 386 6745; 71 Đ Chi Lang; mains 30,000-60,000d) There's a strip of Chinese restaurants on Chi Lang, including the busy Lam Hung Ky, complete with the usual strung-up ducks and chickens. It serves good food, despite the menu offering misleadingly unappetising items like 'instant boiled assorted meats'.

Bay Bong (☎ 386 7271; 22 Đ Thuong Dang Le; mains 35,000-75,000d; 🕐 lunch & dinner) It doesn't look like much, but the food is really something. According to Mekong explorer Le Van Sinh (p421), it's the best in the delta, specialising

FISH FARMING & BIOFUEL

Fish farming constitutes around 20% of Vietnam's total seafood output and is widely practised in An Giang province, in the region near the Cambodian border. The highest concentration of 'floating houses' with fish cages can be observed on the banks of the Hau Giang River (Bassac River) in Chau Doc, near its confluence with the mighty Mekong.

The fish farmed here are two members of the Asian catfish family, basa (*Pangasius bocourti*) and tra (*P hypophthalmus*). It is interesting to note that even with two tides a day here, there is no salt water in the river. Around 18,000 tonnes of fish are exported annually, primarily to European and American markets (as well as Australia and Japan), in the form of frozen white fish fillets.

The two-step production cycle starts with capturing fish eggs from the wild, usually sourced in the Tonle Sap Lake in Cambodia, followed by raising the fish to a marketable size – usually about 1kg. Fish are fed on a kind of dough made by the farmers from cereal, vegetables and fish scraps. The largest cage measures 2000 cubic metres and can produce up to 400 tonnes of raw fish in each 10-month production cycle.

One of the more interesting developments affecting fish farming was announced in 2006, when Saigon Petrol and An Giang Fisheries Import-Export Company (Agifish) agreed to set up a joint venture to produce biofuel from the fat of the tra and basa catfish. Some 400,000 tonnes of the two fish are consumed annually in the Mekong River provinces, and if some of its by-products could be utilised the effects would be groundbreaking. One kilogram of fish fat can yield 1L of bio-diesel fuel, according to specialists, meaning some 60,000 tonnes of bio-diesel fuel could be made yearly if all the tra and basa fat could be utilised from the processing plants in the region. Agifish claims that the biofuel will be more efficient than diesel, is nontoxic and will generate far fewer fumes. Agifish believes this business will eventually be a boon to the local economy, to local fish farmers who will earn more money, and even to the environment. Those who've gotten a whiff of *nuoc mam* (fish sauce) and thought, 'you can power a dump truck on this stuff' aren't far off the mark.

in hotpots and soups, as well as fresh fish dishes. Try the *ca kho to* (stewed fish in a clay pot) or *canh chua* (sweet-and-sour soup).

Bassac Restaurant (☎ 386 5010; 32 Đ Le Loi; mains US$6-18) The most sophisticated dining experience in Chau Doc is to be found here at the Victoria Chau Doc Hotel. The menu includes some delightfully presented Vietnamese food, as well as a wonderful selection of international dishes to make the mouth water. Desserts are devilish or there is more simple fare at the Bamboo Bar.

Other options:

Thanh Tinh (☎ 386 5064; 13 Đ Quang Trung; mains 15,000-30,000d) This place translates as 'to calm the body down' and it will do just that for vegetarians looking for a reliable menu.

Truong Van (☎ 386 6567; 15 Đ Quang Trung; mains 20,000-40,000d) Nothing fancy here, just good Vietnamese food at decent prices.

QUICK EATS

To sample the best *sinh to* (fruit shakes) in town, look out for the stalls on the corner of Đ Phan Van Vang and Đ Nguyen Van Thoai.

At night, you can also try a variety of cool dessert *che* (dessert soups) at *che* stalls on Đ Bach Dang, next to the pagoda. There are also lots of other inexpensive stalls with large whiteboard menus displaying their wares.

The **Chau Doc Covered Market** (Đ Bach Dang) has delicious Vietnamese food (plates 7000d to 15,000d).

Drinking & Entertainment

It may be best to leave the disco clothes in the bag, as Chau Doc is a pretty sleepy place.

Le Jarai (32 Đ Le Loi; ⏰ 4-11pm most nights) Moored on the river behind the Victoria Hotel, this boat makes a pleasant setting for a cocktail if it is not chugging up the river. Or try the lobby bar in the hotel, which has a colonial ambience and a pool table.

An Tuong 2 (admission from 20,000d; ⏰ 8pm-midnight, Thu-Sun) This is the local disco in town, or rather more accurately 2km from town on the road to Sam Mountain. It is usually the preserve of local boys and some working girls unless there is a big event kicking off.

Getting There & Away

BOAT

No-frills cargo boats run twice weekly between Chau Doc and Ha Tien via the Vinh Te Canal (negotiable from 150,000d to 200,000d, eight to 12 hours), which straddles the Cambodian border; it's an interesting 95km trip. Departures are at 5am from a tiny pier (near 60 Đ Trung Hung Dao). There are plans for a fast boat service during the lifetime of this book. For information on travelling into Cambodia see p455 or p456.

Delta Adventure (p449) offers a couple of boat options out of Chau Doc, including a day cruise to Sa Dec or a two-day cruise to HCMC via Vinh Long and a night in a homestay.

BUS

The buses from HCMC to Chau Doc leave from the Mien Tay bus station (p385). The Mai Linh express bus can make the run in six hours and costs around 110,000d. To Can Tho is just 50,000d by express bus.

The Chau Doc bus station (Ben Xe Chau Doc) is east of town towards Long Xuyen. Buses from Chau Doc leave here for Long Xuyen, Can Tho, Rach Gia and Ha Tien.

CAR & MOTORBIKE

By road, Chau Doc is approximately 117km from Can Tho, 181km from My Tho and 245km from HCMC.

The Chau Doc–Ha Tien road is 100km in length and is slowly improving. As you approach Ha Tien, the land turns into a mangrove forest that is infertile and almost uninhabited. The drive takes about three hours, and it's possible to visit Ba Chuc and Tuc Dup en route. If you don't plan to drive yourself, *xe om* drivers typically charge about US$15 to US$20 for this route or arrange a car through travel agencies or hotels in town.

Getting Around

Xe loi can be hired around town for around 10,000d. Motorbikes are available for rent through most guesthouses and cost US$10/5 for a full/half day.

Boats to Chau Giang district (across the Hau Giang River) leave from two docks: vehicle ferries depart from Chau Giang ferry landing (Ben Pha Chau Giang), opposite 419 Đ Le Loi; smaller, more frequent boats leave from Phu Hiep ferry landing (Ben Pha FB Phu Hiep), a little further southeast.

Vehicle ferries to Con Tien Island depart from the Con Tien ferry landing (Ben Pha Con Tien) at the river end of Đ Thuong Dang Le; you can catch boats to Chau Giang and Phu Chau (Tan Chau) from the Ben Do Quoc Doanh ferry landing on Đ Gia Long, opposite the post office.

Private boats (50,000d for a couple of hours), which are rowed standing up, can be hired from either of these spots, and are highly recommended for seeing the floating houses and visiting nearby Cham minority villages and mosques. Motorboats (100,000d per hour) can be hired in the same area.

AROUND CHAU DOC

Phu Chau (Tan Chau) District

Traditional silk making has made Phu Chau (Tan Chau) district famous throughout southern Vietnam. The **market** in Phu Chau has a selection of competitively priced Thai and Cambodian goods.

To get to Phu Chau district from Chau Doc, take a boat across the Hau Giang River from the Phu Hiep ferry landing, then catch a ride on the back of a *xe om* (about 40,000d) for the 18km trip to Phu Chau district.

Sam Mountain

This is a holy mountain for Vietnamese, offering striking views over the surrounding countryside. There are dozens of pagodas and temples, many of them set in caves, around Sam Mountain (Nui Sam), which is about 6km southwest of Chau Doc via Đ Nguyen Van Thoai. The Chinese influence is evident and Sam Mountain is also a favourite spot for ethnic Chinese.

Climbing the peak is a highlight of a visit to Sam Mountain. The views from the top are excellent (weather permitting) and you can gaze over Cambodia. There's a military outpost on the summit, a legacy of the days when the Khmer Rouge made cross-border raids and massacred Vietnamese civilians.

Walking down is easier than walking up, so if you want to cheat, have a motorbike take you to the summit. The road to the top is a pretty ride on the east side of the mountain. Veer left at the base of the mountain and turn right after about 1km where the road begins its climb.

You can walk down along a peaceful, traffic-free trail on the north side, which will bring you to the main temple area. The summit road

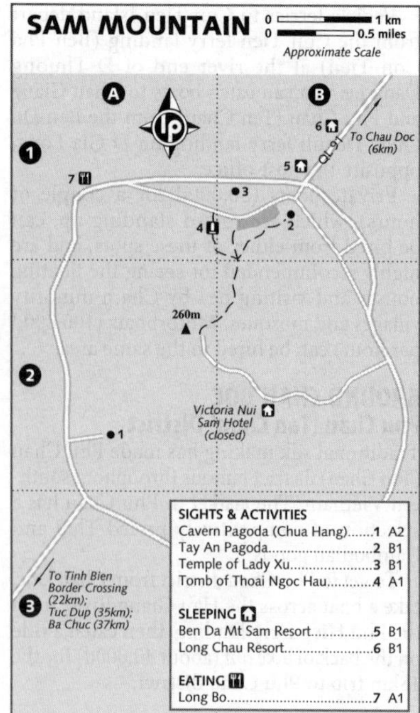

has been decorated with amusement-park ceramic dinosaurs and the like. But there are also some small shrines and pavilions, which add a bit of charm and also remind you that this is indeed Vietnam and not Disneyland.

Tay An Pagoda

This pagoda (Chua Tay An) is renowned for the fine carving of its hundreds of religious figures, most of which are made of wood. Aspects of the building's architecture reflect Hindu and Islamic influences. The first chief monk of Tay An Pagoda (founded in 1847) came from Giac Lam Pagoda in Saigon. Tay An was last rebuilt in 1958.

The main gate is of traditional Vietnamese design. Above the roof are figures of lions and two dragons fighting for possession of pearls, chrysanthemums, apricot trees and lotus blossoms. Nearby is a statue of Quan Am Thi Kinh, the Guardian Spirit of Mother and Child.

In front of the pagoda are statues of a black elephant with two tusks and a white elephant with six tusks. Around the pagoda are monks' tombs. Inside are Buddha statues adorned with psychedelic disco lights.

TEMPLE OF LADY XU

Founded in the 1820s, the Temple of Lady Xu (Mieu Ba Chua Xu) faces Sam Mountain, not far from Tay An Pagoda. The first building here was made of bamboo and leaves; the last reconstruction took place in 1972.

According to legend, the statue of Lady Xu used to stand at the summit of Sam Mountain. In the early 19th century Siamese troops invaded the area and, impressed with the statue, decided to take it back to Thailand. But as they carried the statue down the hill, it became heavier and heavier, and they were forced to abandon it by the side of the path.

One day some villagers who were cutting wood came upon the statue and decided to bring it back to their village in order to build a temple for it; but it weighed too much for them to budge. Suddenly, there appeared a girl who, possessed by a spirit, declared herself to be Lady Xu. She announced to them that 40 virgins were to be brought and that they would be able to transport the statue down the mountainside. The 40 virgins were then summoned and carried the statue down the slope, but when they reached the plain, it became too heavy and they had to set it down. The people concluded that the site where the virgins halted had been selected by Lady Xu for the temple construction and it's here that the Temple of Lady Xu stands to this day.

Offerings of roast whole pigs are frequently made here, providing an interesting photo opportunity. The temple's most important festival is held from the 23rd to the 26th day of the fourth lunar month, usually late May or early June. During this time, pilgrims flock here, sleeping on mats in the large rooms of the two-storey resthouse next to the temple.

Tomb of Thoai Ngoc Hau

A high-ranking official, Thoai Ngoc Hau (1761–1829) served the Nguyen Lords and, later, the Nguyen dynasty. In early 1829, Thoai Ngoc Hau ordered that a tomb be constructed for himself at the foot of Sam Mountain. The site he chose is not far from Tay An Pagoda.

The steps are made of red 'beehive' stone *(da ong)* brought from the southeastern part of Vietnam. In the middle of the platform is the tomb of Thoai Ngoc Hau and those of his wives, Chau Thi Te and Truong Thi Miet. Nearby are several dozen other tombs where his officials are buried.

BORDER CROSSING: VINH XUONG–KAAM SAMNOR

One of the most enjoyable ways of entering Cambodia is via this crossing located just northwest of Chau Doc along the Mekong River. If coming from Cambodia, get a visa; if you're leaving Vietnam, Cambodian visas are available at the crossing, but minor overcharging is common.

Several companies in Chau Doc sell boat tickets taking you from Chau Doc to Phnom Penh via the Vinh Xuong border. **Hang Chau** (Chau Doc ☎ 076-356 2771; Phnom Penh ☎ 012-883 542) departs Chau Doc at 8.30am and Phnom Penh at noon and costs US$24. It also offers a slower service which involves changing boat at the border and a local bus ride into Phnom Penh costing US$16.

The more upmarket **Blue Cruiser** (www.bluecruiser.com; HCMC ☎ 08-3294 5766; Phnom Penh ☎ 023 990 441) pulls out at 8.30am and 1.30pm, costing US$35. It takes about four hours, including the border check. More expensive again is the **Victoria Hotels express boat** (www.victoriahotels-asia.com) which runs from the Victoria Chau Doc Hotel to Phnom Penh. At US$80 per person, it tends to be exclusive to Victoria Hotel guests.

Some adventurous travellers like to plot their own course. Catch a minibus from Chau Doc to the border at Vinh Xuong (US$1, one hour). The border posts here are some way apart so hire a *xe om* (US$1) to carry you from building to building to deal with the lengthy bureaucracy. There are separate offices for immigration and customs on both sides of the border, so it can end up taking as much as an hour. Luggage has to be x-rayed on the Vietnamese side of the border. Once officially in Cambodia at Kaam Samnor, arrange a speedboat to Neak Luong (US$4 per person, US$25 for the boat, one hour). Once in Neak Luong, change to a local bus (5000r, regular departures) to Phnom Penh, which will terminate at the Central Market.

Cavern Pagoda

The Cavern Pagoda (Chua Hang, also known as Phuoc Dien Tu) is halfway up the western side of Sam Mountain. The lower part of the pagoda includes monks' quarters and two hexagonal tombs in which the founder of the pagoda, a female tailor named Le Thi Tho, and a former head monk, Thich Hue Thien, are buried.

The upper section has two parts: the main sanctuary, in which there are statues of A Di Da (the Buddha of the Past) and Thich Ca Buddha (Sakyamuni, the Historical Buddha); and the cavern. At the back of the cave behind the sanctuary building is a shrine dedicated to Quan The Am Bo Tat.

According to legend, Le Thi Tho came from Tay An Pagoda to this site half a century ago to lead a quiet, meditative life. When she arrived, she found two enormous snakes, one white and the other dark green. Le Thi Tho soon converted the snakes, which thereafter led pious lives. Upon her death, the snakes disappeared.

SLEEPING & EATING

There is now quite a bustling community at the base of Sam Mountain, with several hotels and resorts lining the street.

Long Chau Resort (☎ 076-386 1249; www.vamcotravel.com; QL 91; r 160,000-320,000d; ❄) Once known as the Delta Adventure Inn, this pretty compound of bungalows sits amid the rice paddies about 4km outside Chau Doc on the way to Sam Mountain. There are great views to the holy mountain and the rooms are good value with smart air-con options starting at just 200,000d. There is also an attractive restaurant set in the centre of a lily pond.

Ben Da Mt Sam Resort (☎ 076-386 1745; bendanuisam@hcm.vnn.vn; QL 91; r 265,000-390,000d; ❄) The rooms at this immense government hotel are smart enough and some overlook the extensive gardens. As well as satellite TV and minibar, breakfast is included.

Long Bo (☎ 076-386 1479; Khom Vinh Tay1; mains 40,000-90,000d) This is a bit of a legend among Chau Doc locals, a grilled meat restaurant offering such delights as *bo lui xa* (beef wrapped around lemongrass). Cook it yourself on the hot coals brought to your table. It's 1km west of the Temple of Lady Xu.

GETTING THERE & AWAY

Most people get here by rented motorbike or on the back of *xe om* (about 30,000d one-way). However, there are also local buses heading this way from Chau Doc, costing just 5000d, a real money saver.

BA CHUC

Ba Chuc or the Bone Pagoda stands as a grisly reminder of the horrors perpetrated by the

Khmer Rouge. Between 1975 and 1978 Khmer Rouge soldiers regularly crossed the border into Vietnam and slaughtered innocent civilians. Over the border, things were even worse, where nearly two million Cambodians were killed during the period of Pol Pot's Democratic Kampuchea regime.

Between 12 April and 30 April 1978, the Khmer Rouge killed 3157 people at Ba Chuc. Only two people are known to have survived. Many of the victims were tortured to death. The Vietnamese government might have had other motives for invading Cambodia at the end of 1978, but certainly outrage at the Ba Chuc massacre was a major justification.

Two other notable pagodas at Ba Chuc are Chua Tam Buu and Chua Phi Lai. The Bone Pagoda has a common tomb housing the skulls and bones of more than 1100 victims. This resembles Cambodia's Choeung Ek killing fields, where thousands of skulls of Khmer Rouge victims are on display. Near the skull collection is a temple that displays graphic and gruesome photos taken shortly after the massacre. The display is both fascinating and horrifying and you will need a strong stomach.

Ba Chuc is located close to the Cambodian border; to reach it, follow the road that runs along the canal from Chau Doc to Ha Tien. Turn off this main road onto Hwy 3T and follow it for 4km. A round-trip by *xe om* will cost about US$6.

TUC DUP HILL

elev 216m

Because of its network of connecting caves, Tuc Dup Hill served as a strategic base of operations during the American War. *Tuc dup* is Khmer for 'water runs at night' and it is also known locally as 'Two Million Dollar Hill', in reference to the amount of money the Americans sank into securing it. Tuc Dup is 35km from Chau Doc and 64km from Long Xuyen.

This is a place of historical interest but there isn't much to see. It might be worth the trip if you're visiting Ba Chuc.

HA TIEN

☎ 077 / pop 93,000

Ha Tien may be part of the Mekong Delta, but lying on the Gulf of Thailand it feels a world away from the ricefields and rivers that typify the region. There are dramatic limestone formations peppering the area, which are home to a network of caves, some of which have been turned into temples. Plantations of pepper trees cling to the hillsides. On a clear day, Phu Quoc Island is easily visible to the west. The town itself has a sleepy charm, with crumbling colonial villas and a colourful riverside market. Visitor numbers have recently soared thanks to the opening of the nearby border with Cambodia at Xa Xia–Prek Chak and the new fast boat service to Phu Quoc. Oh yes, Ha Tien is on the map. And the map is getting bigger thanks to major expansion plans that will see the city spread southwest along the coast.

Ha Tien was a province of Cambodia until 1708. In the face of attacks by the Thai, the Khmer-appointed governor, a Chinese immigrant named Mac Cuu, turned to the Vietnamese for protection and assistance. Mac Cuu thereafter governed this area as a fiefdom under the protection of the Nguyen Lords. He was succeeded as ruler by his son, Mac Thien Tu. During the 18th century the area was invaded and pillaged several times by the Thai. Rach Gia and the southern tip of the Mekong Delta came under direct Nguyen rule in 1798.

During the Khmer Rouge regime, Cambodian forces repeatedly attacked Vietnamese territory and massacred thousands of civilians here. The entire populations of Ha Tien and nearby villages (in fact, tens of thousands of people) fled their homes. Also during this period, areas north of Ha Tien along the Cambodian border were sown with

BORDER CROSSING: TINH BIEN–PHNOM DEN

This little-used border crossing is less convenient for Phnom Penh–bound travellers, but may be of interest for those who savour the challenge of obscure border crossings. The border is in a remote area with little in the way of transport and has been rather eclipsed by the newer crossing of Xa Xia near Ha Tien, which offers a more convenient link between Phu Quoc Island and the colonial era towns of Kep and Kampot in Cambodia.

Arrange a *xe om* from Chau Doc (about 60,000d) to the border and then a share taxi (US$3 per seat, US$20 charter) on to Ta Keo from Phnom Den.

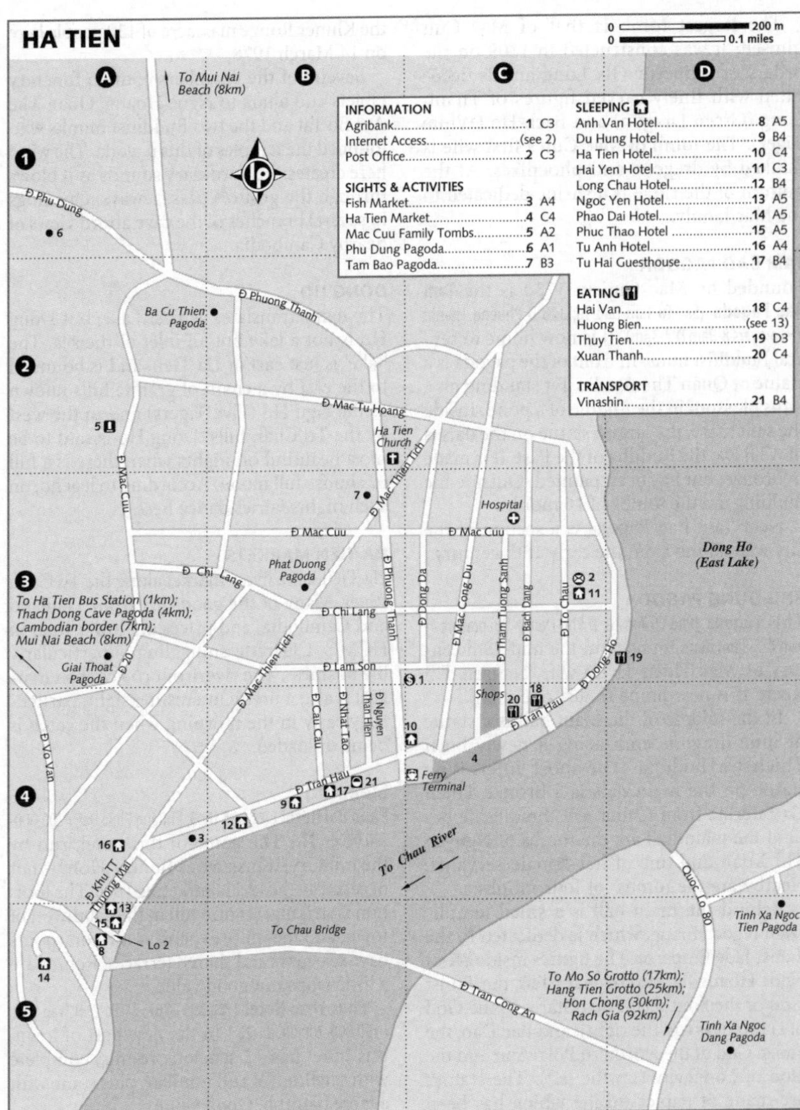

mines and booby traps, some of which have yet to be cleared.

Information

The **post office** (☎ 385 2190; 3 Đ To Chau; 🕑 7am-10pm) also offers internet access. **Agribank** (☎ 385 2055; 37 Đ Lam Son) is one block from the waterfront and has an ATM.

Sights

MAC CUU FAMILY TOMBS

Not far from town are the **Mac Cuu Family Tombs** (Lang Mac Cuu; Đ Mac Cuu), known locally as Nui Lang, the Hill of the Tombs. Several dozen relatives of Mac Cuu are buried here in traditional Chinese tombs decorated with figures of dragons, phoenixes, lions and guardians.

The largest tomb is that of Mac Cuu himself; it was constructed in 1809 on the orders of Emperor Gia Long and is decorated with finely carved figures of Thanh Long (Green Dragon) and Bach Ho (White Tiger). The tomb of Mac Cuu's first wife is flanked by dragons and phoenixes. At the bottom of the ridge is a shrine dedicated to the Mac family.

TAM BAO PAGODA

Founded by Mac Cuu in 1730 is the **Tam Bao Pagoda** (Sac Tu Tam Bao Tu; 328 Đ Phuong Thanh; prayers 8-9am & 2-3pm). It is now home to several Buddhist nuns. In front of the pagoda is a statue of Quan The Am Bo Tat standing on a lotus blossom in the middle of a pond. Inside the sanctuary, the largest statue on the dais is of A Di Da, the Buddha of the Past. It is made of bronze, but has been painted. Outside the building are the tombs of 16 monks.

Near Tam Bao Pagoda is a section of the city wall dating from the early 18th century.

PHU DUNG PAGODA

This **pagoda** (Phu Cu Am Tu; Đ Phu Dung; prayers 4-5am & 7-8pm) was founded in the mid-18th century by Mac Thien Tich's wife, Nguyen Thi Xuan. It is now home to just one monk.

In the middle of the main hall is a statue of nine dragons embracing a newly born Thich Ca Buddha. The most interesting statue on the main dais is a bronze Thich Ca Buddha from China. On the hillside behind the main hall are the tombs of Nguyen Thi Xuan and one of her female servants. Nearby are the tombs of four monks.

Behind the main hall is a small temple, Dien Ngoc Hoang, which is dedicated to the Taoist Jade Emperor. The figures inside are of Ngoc Hoang flanked by Nam Tao, the Taoist God of the Southern Polar Star and the God of Happiness (on the right); and Bac Dao, the Taoist God of the Northern Polar Star and the God of Longevity (on the left). The statues are made of papier-mâché which has been moulded over bamboo frames.

To get to the Phu Dung Pagoda, turn off Đ Phuong Thanh at No 374.

THACH DONG CAVE PAGODA

Also known as Chua Thanh Van, this is a subterranean Buddhist temple 4km from town. To the left of the entrance is the Stele of Hatred (Bia Cam Thu), which commemorates the Khmer Rouge massacre of 130 people here on 14 March 1978.

Several of the chambers contain funerary tablets and altars to Ngoc Hoang, Quan The Am Bo Tat and the two Buddhist monks who founded the temples of this pagoda. The wind here creates extraordinary sounds as it blows through the grotto's passageways. Openings in several branches of the cave afford views of nearby Cambodia.

DONG HO

The name translates as East Lake, but Dong Ho is not a lake but an inlet of the sea. The 'lake' is just east of Ha Tien, and is bounded to the east by a chain of granite hills known as the Ngu Ho (Five Tigers) and to the west by the To Chan hills. Dong Ho is said to be most beautiful on nights when there is a full or almost-full moon. According to legend, on such nights fairies dance here.

HA TIEN MARKETS

Ha Tien has a lively market along the To Chau River. Many of the goods are from Thailand and Cambodia, and prices are lower than in HCMC. Cigarette smuggling is particularly big business. The riverfront *cho ca* (fish market) is also a pretty interesting sight, particularly early in the morning when the catch is being unloaded.

Sleeping

Phao Dai Hotel (385 1849; Phuong Phao Dai; r 100,000-200,000d;) The name of this hotel, run by the military, translates as Bunker Hotel – not necessarily the ideal marketing ruse. The location is striking, set on a hill in the southwest of town, and the more expensive air-con rooms have sea views and shared terraces. Rooms are a little worn but good value.

Phuc Thao Hotel (395 0767; 31 Lo 2, Đ Tran Hau; r 150,000-200,000d;) In the new part of town, this hotel has 33 spacious rooms, complete with satellite TV and minibar, plus some with a large bathtub. Good value.

Tu Anh Hotel (385 2622; 170 Đ Mac Thien Tich; r 150,000-250,000d;) This smart mini-hotel is a good deal, offering a window and air-con in every room. The well-tended rooms include a TV and fridge, plus hot water, and the service is friendly.

Hai Yen Hotel (385 1580; 15 Đ To Chau; r 150,000-350,000d;) Next to the post office, this is one of the old timers by Ha Tien standards. A huge place, it has expanded into two connected wings; rooms are well finished in wood and pricier options have a bath and river view.

Anh Van Hotel (☎ 395 9222; www.anhvanhotel.com; Lo 2, Đ Tran Hau; r 150,000-400,000d; ❄ 💻) Set in the new part of town near the bridge, this hotel is one of the best all-rounders in town. Cheaper rooms lack a window, but are brimming with amenities. The 320,000d rooms are worth the investment, with smart bathrooms and river views.

Du Hung Hotel (☎ 395 1555; duhunghotel@yahoo.com.vn; 17A Đ Tran Hau; r 170,000-250,000d; ❄) Right in the middle of the main drag, this is a great little hotel with good-value rooms. Opt for one of the corner rooms with expansive views of the river and coast. Wood furnishings, hot showers and a lift.

Long Chau Hotel (☎ 395 2740; hotellongchau@yahoo.com; 36 Lo 7; r 200,000-250,000d; ❄ 💻) OK, so it looked like it was in the middle of a building site when we visited, but once the riverfront park is finished, this place will have a prime location. Currently it has the best furnishings in town and the more expensive rooms include a riverfront balcony and bathtub. Very promising.

Ha Tien Hotel (☎ 395 2093; 36 Đ Tran Hau; r 300,000-700,000d; ❄ 💻) Just about holding on to the crown of Ha Tien's best hotel, but by no means the best value, this place has smart rooms. Out the front is an open-air restaurant where the included breakfast is taken, but it strangely doesn't serve meals to nonguests.

And the list goes on:

Tu Hai Guesthouse (☎ 385 2549; Đ Tran Hau; r 100,000; ❄) A cheap guesthouse on the main street. Rooms are basic but good value, with air-con and hot water.

Ngoc Yen Hotel (☎ 395 2953; 12 Đ Khu Trung Tam Thuong Mai; r 150,000-250,000d; ❄) Smart mini-hotel in the newer part of town with generously proportioned rooms.

Eating & Drinking

Ha Tien's speciality is an unusual variety of coconut that can only be found in Cambodia and this part of Vietnam. These coconuts contain no milk, but the delicate flesh is delicious. Restaurants all around the Ha Tien area serve the coconut flesh in a glass with ice and sugar.

Xuan Thanh (☎ 385 2197; 20 Đ Tran Hau; mains 20,000-60,000d; 🕑 lunch & dinner) You know you have hit the coast when shrimp is the cheapest dish on the menu. This local eatery has an English menu boasting a range of seafood and grills, plus cheap breakfasts.

Huong Bien (☎ 385 2072; Đ Khu Trung Tam Thuong Mai; mains 20,000-60,000d) This old favourite has recently relocated to the new part of town near the bridge. The menu remains blissfully simple with fewer than 20 dishes, but it draws a local crowd.

Other places in town:

Hai Van (☎ 385 0344; 4 Đ Tran Hau; mains 25,000-75,000d) This riverfront restaurant is popular for weddings and serves good Vietnamese, Chinese and Western meals.

Thuy Tien (☎ 385 1828; Đ Dong Ho) Overlooking Dong Ho, this is a nice spot for an iced coffee or sundowner beer.

Getting There & Away

BOAT

Passenger ferries dock at the ferry terminal, which is opposite the Ha Tien Hotel. There is a new fast boat service from Ha Tien to Phu Quoc Island (190,000d one-way, 1½ hours), which is operated by **Vinashin** (Ha Tien ☎ 395 9060; 11 Đ Tran Hau; Phu Quoc ☎ 077-399 6456). Services should be daily by the time you read this. It departs Ha Tien at 8am and returns from Phu Quoc at 2pm. There is also a slower old boat costing 120,000d, but it doesn't look like it's built for the high seas. Note that the water can get pretty choppy if there are high winds.

BUS

Buses from HCMC to Ha Tien leave three times daily from the Mien Tay bus station (p385); the trip (from 96,000d) takes nearly 10 hours. Faster express services are operated by Mai Linh costing 132,000d.

Ha Tien bus station (Ben Xe Ha Tien) is on the main road to Mui Nai Beach and the Cambodian border, about 1km from the centre. Buses leave from here to Chau Doc (from 35,000d) and Rach Gia (30,000d by public bus, 45,000d with Mai Linh), among other destinations.

CAR & MOTORBIKE

Ha Tien is 92km from Rach Gia, 95km from Chau Doc, 206km from Can Tho and 338km from HCMC.

AROUND HA TIEN

There are many islands off the coast between Rach Gia and the Cambodian border. Some locals make a living gathering swiftlet nests (the most important ingredient of that famous

Chinese delicacy, bird's-nest soup), on the islands' rocky cliffs.

Beaches

The beaches in this part of Vietnam face the Gulf of Thailand. The water is incredibly warm and calm here, like a placid lake. The beaches are OK for bathing and diving but hopeless for surfing.

Mui Nai (Stag's Head Peninsula) is 8km west of Ha Tien; it supposedly resembles the head of a stag with its mouth pointing upward. On top is a lighthouse and there are sand beaches on both sides of the peninsula. Mui Nai is accessible by road from both Ha Tien and Thach Dong Cave Pagoda (admission person/car 2000/10,000d).

There are dozens of simple restaurants overlooking the beach, and several budget guesthouses in the area, including **Kim Ngan** (☎ 077-395 1661; r 180,000-250,000d; ❄), with rooms clustered in bungalows around a garden, all just a stroll to the beach.

There's no public transport to the beach. A *xe om* here should set you back around 30,000d.

Other beaches include **No Beach** (Bai No), which does have a beach lined with coconut palms despite the name, and shady **Bang Beach** (Bai Bang). Both are several kilometres west of Ha Tien and can be reached from the road to Mui Nai Beach.

Hang Tien Grotto

About 25km towards Rach Gia from Ha Tien, Hang Tien Grotto served as a hideout for Nguyen Anh (later Emperor Gia Long) in 1784, when he was being pursued by the Tay Son Rebels. His fighters found zinc coins buried here, a discovery that gave the cave its name, Coin Grotto. Hang Tien Grotto is accessible by boat from the ferry terminal in Ha Tien. The trip takes about an hour.

Hon Giang Island

About 15km from Ha Tien and accessible by small boat, Hon Giang Island has a lovely, secluded beach.

HON CHONG

☎ 077

Home to the nicest stretch of beach on the Mekong Delta mainland, this small and secluded beach resort is undeveloped by Vietnamese standards. In fact development seems to have gone into reverse, with an air of abandonment, as the beachfront action moves to the nearby island of Phu Quoc. If you want some peace and calm, this might be a good place to lie low, as it sees few foreign travellers. The attractions here are Chua Hang Grotto, Duong Beach and Nghe Island. While they are a far cry from the stunning 3000-plus islands and grottoes of Halong Bay, the stone formations here are indeed photogenic.

Hon Chong lies along both sides of the road from Ba Hon, curving along the coast. Hotels and resorts dot the road, which terminates at Chua Hang Grotto.

Chua Hang Grotto

Chua Hang Grotto is entered through a Buddhist temple set against the base of a hill. The temple is called **Hai Son Tu** (Sea Mountain Temple). Visitors light incense and offer prayers here before entering the grotto itself, whose entrance is located behind the altar. Inside is a statue of Quan The Am Bo Tat.

Duong Beach

Running north from Chua Hang Grotto, this beach (Bai Duong) is named for its long -needled *duong* (pine trees). During weekends or holidays, the southern area can get busy with Vietnamese tourists – and their beloved karaoke – but otherwise the 3km stretch of coast is quite tranquil.

Although this is easily the prettiest beach in the Mekong Delta, don't expect any white sand. The waters around the delta contain heavy concentrations of silt, so the beach sand tends to be hard while in the water it's muddy, which can be off-putting. Still, the water is reasonably clear here and the beach is known for its spectacular sunsets.

From the busy southern end of the beach (near Chua Hang Grotto) you can see remnants of **Father and Son Isle** (Hon Phu Tu) several hundred metres offshore; it was said to be shaped like a father embracing his son, but the father was washed away in 2006. Boats can be hired at the shore to row out for a closer look.

Nghe Island

This is the most beautiful island in the area and is a favourite pilgrimage spot for Buddhists. The island contains a **cave temple** (Chua Hang) next to a large statue of Quan The Am Bo Tat, which faces the sea. The area where you'll find the cave temple and statue is called Doc Lau Chuong.

Finding a boat to the island is not too difficult, though it is much cheaper if you round up a group. Enquire at the Hon Trem Resort (right). You can also rent a speedboat for the day for 1,500,000d from the Tan Phat restaurant (right). The boat seats up to 20, and the captain can take you on a tour of four islands in the area. Tourists are not permitted to stay on the island.

Sleeping

The hotels are completely booked when Buddhists arrive to worship 15 days before and one month after Tet. Another worship deluge occurs in March and April. The following hotels are listed in order as you approach them on the main (and only) road into town.

Green Hill Guesthouse (☎ 385 4369; 905 Hon Chong; d US$17-25; ❄) Set in an imposing villa on a hilltop over Duong Beach, this is a friendly, family-run place with a range of spacious rooms. The communal balcony on the 2nd floor is a breezy place, while the room of choice is on the top floor if available.

An Hai Son Resort (☎ 375 9226; anhaison@hcm.vnn.vn; Bai Gieng Hamlet; r 240,000-340,000d; ❄ 💻) The best-value lodgings in Hon Chong, this resort has an extensive garden with rooms dotted throughout the bungalows and villas. The cheaper rooms are actually better thanks to stylish furnishings and, conversely, more space. The more expensive quads are too cramped with all the beds. There's a tennis court and massage services, plus breakfast is included.

My Lan Hotel (☎ 375 9044; mylanhotel@vnn.vn; r 160,000-250,000d; ❄) Sometimes spelt Milan, it lacks the style of its namesake, but the rooms are good value. Some are so white as to be on the clinical side, while others are roomy with bright windows.

Diem My Hotel (☎ 375 9216; 1022 Hamlet 3; r 70,000-160,000d; ❄) The 'pink place', this is the cheapest pad in town. It seems to have been designed back-to-front with air-con rooms at the back and cheaper fan rooms at the front with sea views.

Binh An Hotel (☎ 385 4332; 1030 Hamlet 3; r 180,000-240,000d; ❄) This old trade-union-run hotel has spacious rooms set amid extensive gardens. The old fan rooms are making way for an upgraded new wing during 2009. There's also a beachfront restaurant.

Hon Trem Resort (☎ 385 4331; ctycpdulichkg@vnn.vn; r/bungalow US$36/48; ❄ 💻) The smartest place in town by some stretch, the Hon Trem is draped over a hillock towards the end of the main strip. The hexagonal bungalows are attractively set overlooking the sea and include a large bed with light linen and generous baths. They even feature safes for valuables. The gardens are well kept and there is a reputable restaurant overlooking the beach. Breakfast included.

Eating

Aside from special orders prepared at your hotel, there are **thatched-roof restaurants** (mains 20,000-70,000d) along the beach and **food stalls** (mains around 20,000d) near the entrance of Chua Hang Grotto. For just a few dollars, you can point to one of the live chickens, which will be summarily executed and barbecued for you.

Hong Ngoc (coconuts around 5000d) Just near the entrance gate to the Chua Hang Grotto, this is a good place to sample delicious Ha Tien coconuts.

Tan Phat (☎ 375 9943; Hamlet 3; mains 30,000-60,000d; ❄) Located a kilometre or so before Duong Beach, this seafood restaurant looks like a tumbledown shack from the outside, but it has pavilions over the water with good views of the local fishing fleet.

Getting There & Away

Hon Chong is 32km from Ha Tien towards Rach Gia. The access road branches off the Rach Gia–Ha Tien highway at the small town of Ba Hon. Buses can drop you off at Ba Hon, from where you can hire a motorbike to continue the journey on to Hon Chong (around 50,000d).

There's also a direct bus service from Rach Gia to Hon Chong (30,000d, 2½ hours, three daily). It departs from the **Ben Xe Ha Tien bus station** (Đ 30 Thang 4) in Rach Gia and in Hon Chong from outside the Huong Bien Guesthouse.

Greenlines (☎ in HCMC 08-3914 7806; www.greenlines.com.vn) operates a boat service from Hon Chong to Phu Quoc Island (160,000d, one hour), but the schedule is very erratic. When running, boats leave Hon Chong at 10am and 2pm, or Phu Quoc at 8.30am and 12.30pm.

RACH GIA

☎ 077 / pop 180,000

Rach Gia is something of a southern boom town, flush with funds from the thriving port on the Gulf of Thailand, but also benefiting from a serious injection of Viet Kieu money, as former boat people ride the wave of development. The population includes significant numbers of both ethnic Chinese and ethnic Khmers. Most travellers give the busy centre short shrift, heading straight to the port for boats to Phu Quoc Island. Those who linger can explore the lively waterfront and bustling backstreets, where there are some inexpensive seafood restaurants.

With its easy access to the sea and the proximity of Cambodia and Thailand, fishing, agriculture and smuggling are profitable trades in this province. The area was once famous for supplying the large feathers used to make ceremonial fans for the Imperial Court.

Like Ha Tien, there are big plans for the expansion of Rach Gia. New suburbs have been carved out along the coastline to the south of the centre and this looks to be where much of the action will shift in years to come, with new hotels and malls under construction.

Information

Benh Vien Hospital (☎ 394 9494; 80 Đ Nguyen Trung Truc) One of the better medical facilities in the Mekong Delta; privately operated.

Kien Giang Tourist (Du Lich Lu Hanh Kien Giang; ☎ 386 2081; ctycpdulichkg@vnn.vn; 5 Đ Le Loi; 🕑 7am-5pm). Provincial tourism authority.

Main post office (☎ 387 3008; 2 Đ Mau Than) Centrally located near the river and has the usual attached internet services.

Vietcombank (☎ 386 3178; 2 Đ Mac Cuu) Offers a 24-hour ATM.

Sights

RACH GIA MUSEUM

The **Rach Gia Museum** (☎ 386 3727; 21 Đ Nguyen Van Troi; admission free; 🕑 7-11am Mon-Fri plus 1-5pm Mon-Wed) is housed in a gem of a colonial-era building, but was once again under wraps for a renovation when we visited. The collection includes some Oc-Eo artefacts and pottery.

NGUYEN TRUNG TRUC TEMPLE

This **temple** (18 Đ Nguyen Cong Tru) is dedicated to Nguyen Trung Truc, a leader of the resistance campaign of the 1860s against the newly arrived French. Among other exploits, he led the raid that resulted in the burning of the French warship *Esperance*. Despite repeated attempts to capture him, Nguyen Trung Truc continued to fight until 1868, when the French took his mother and a number of civilians hostage and threatened to kill them if he did not surrender. Nguyen Trung Truc turned himself in and was executed by the French in the marketplace of Rach Gia on 27 October 1868.

The first temple structure was a simple building with a thatched roof; over the years it has been enlarged and rebuilt several times. In the centre of the main hall is a portrait of Nguyen Trung Truc on an altar.

PHAT LON PAGODA

This large Cambodian Theravada Buddhist pagoda, whose name means Big Buddha, was founded about two centuries ago. Though all of the three dozen monks who live here are ethnic Khmers, ethnic Vietnamese also frequent the pagoda.

Inside the sanctuary *(vihara)*, figures of the Thich Ca Buddha wear pointed hats. Around the exterior of the main hall are eight small altars. The two towers near the main entrance are used to cremate the bodies of deceased monks. Near the pagoda are the tombs of about two dozen monks. Prayers are held here daily from 4am to 6am and 5pm to 7pm.

TAM BAO PAGODA

This **pagoda** (🕑 prayers 4.30-5.30am & 5.30-6.30pm), which dates from the early 19th century, is near the corner of Đ Thich Thien An and Đ Ngo Quyen. Rebuilt in 1913, the garden contains numerous trees sculpted as dragons, deer and other animals.

CAO DAI TEMPLE

This small **Cao Dai Temple** (189 Đ Nguyen Trung Truc) was constructed in 1969 and is worth a peek if you missed the Great Temple in Tay Ninh.

Sleeping

There are clusters of hotels near the bus station on Đ Le Thanh Ton and near the boat pier on Đ Tu Do, both good hunting grounds.

Hoang Cung Hotel (☎ 387 2655; 26 Đ Le Thanh Ton; r 100,000-250,000d) A good deal, thanks to its spacious rooms; there's cheap fan rooms and a range of air-con deals that include a sort of suite with armchairs, bathtub and bas-relief on the wall.

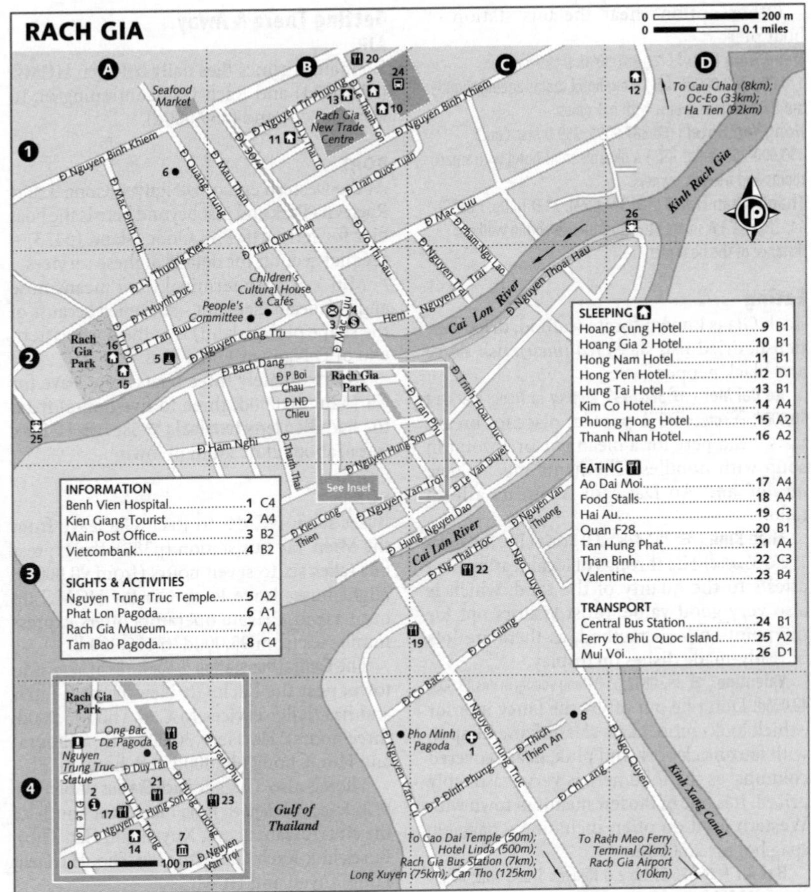

Hung Tai Hotel (☎ 387 7508; 30/4 Đ Le Than Thon; r 100,000-250,000d; ❄) This friendly hotel has a good spread of rooms, all including satellite TV and fridge, but not necessarily hot water. Not so sure about the erotic pictures in the shower.

Phuong Hong Hotel (☎ 386 6138; 5 Đ Tu Do; r 120,000-200,000d; ❄ 💻) A friendly little spot that is conveniently close to the boat pier; the staff speak pretty good English here. Rooms are small but clean and some include hot water and air-con.

Hotel Linda (☎ 391 8818; Lo 1 Đ 3/2; r 160,000-400,000d; ❄ 💻) One of the first hotels to open its doors in the new seafront suburb of town, it has some of the smartest rooms in Rach Gia. The priciest rooms are corner suites with two balconies and a massage bath, but the decoration is tasteful throughout. The cheapest rooms are a tight squeeze.

Kim Co Hotel (☎ 387 9610; 141 Đ Nguyen Hung Son; r 200,000-250,000d; ❄ 💻) The most centrally located of the hotels, the Kim Co is a masterclass in pastel shades. The rooms are in very good shape, some including decadent bathtubs, making it tempting value. Free wi-fi available.

Hoang Gia 2 Hotel (☎ 392 0980; www.hoanggiahotels.com.vn; 31 Đ Le Than Thon; r 200,000-400,000d; ❄ 💻) A cut above the competition near the bus station, this hotel features inviting beds with soft sheets and is rounded off with tasteful furnishings and bathtubs. Free wi-fi for guests.

Other options near the bus station or boat pier:

Hong Nam Hotel (☎ 387 3090; Đ Ly Thai To; r 120,000-300,000d; ❄) A big hotel that is ageing slightly but has spacious rooms with balconies.

Hong Yen Hotel (☎ 387 9095; 259 Đ Mac Cuu; r 150,000-250,000d; ❄) A likeable mini-hotel with smart rooms and friendly owners.

Thanh Nhan Hotel (☎ 394 6694; 21 Đ Tu Do; r US$9-14; ❄ 💻) A smart little guesthouse within walking distance of the boat pier.

Eating

Rach Gia is known for its seafood, dried cuttlefish, dried fish slices *(ca thieu)*, fish sauce and black pepper.

Ao Dai Moi (☎ 386 6295; 26 Đ Ly Tu Trong; breakfast 10,000d; 🕑 breakfast) A popular place for breakfasts, head here for a mean *pho* or a won ton soup with noodles. The name means 'new *ao dai*' and Ao Dai Moi is run by a local tailor.

Than Binh (☎ 387 4780; 2 Đ Nguyen Thai Hoc; mains 15,000-35,000d) The throngs of locals eating here attests to the quality of the food, which is also very good value. Most visitors opt for the point-and-eat method, as there are lots of ready-made dishes on display.

Valentine (☎ 392 0852; 35 Đ Hung Vuong; mains 15,000-40,000d) Don't be put off by the fancy interior ,which looks more like a classic karaoke spot, with faux brickwork and pink, heart-covered columns, as the food here is very reasonably priced. It is one of the few menus in town with Western food on offer, including a passable spag bol for 25,000d.

Hai Au (☎ 386 3740; 2 Đ Nguyen Trung Truc; mains 20,000-200,000d) An expensive restaurant by local standards, it is worth the investment for the great location on the side of the Cai Lon River. Choose from an air-con interior or the livelier terrace. Seafood is popular, including crayfish and crab. Free wi-fi on tap.

Cheap, tasty Vietnamese food is sold from **food stalls** (Đ Hung Vuong) between Đ Bach Dang and Đ Le Hong Phong.

Other reliable places:

Tan Hung Phat (☎ 386 7599; 118 Đ Nguyen Hung Son; mains 20,000-50,000d) This small restaurant has a big selection of fish and seafood dishes.

Quan F28 (☎ 386 7334; 28 Đ Le Than Thon; mains 20,000-80,000d; 🕑 lunch & dinner) Convenient for the bus station hotels, this is lively by night and does inexpensive molluscs – shrimp, snails, blood cockles and the like.

Getting There & Away

AIR

Vietnam Airlines flies daily between HCMC (536,000d) and Rach Gia, continuing on to Phu Quoc Island (459,000d).

BOAT

At the western end of Đ Nguyen Cong Tru is Rach Gia Park and just beyond here is the boat pier for ferries to Phu Quoc Island (p473) – see that section for details of these services.

Mui Voi ferry terminal (*mui* means nose and *voi* means elephant – so named because of the shape of the island) is at the northeastern end of Đ Nguyen Thoai Hau.

Approximately three boats daily leave for Ca Mau (10,000d, three to five hours) from the **Rach Meo ferry terminal** (☎ 381 1306; 747 Đ Ngo Quyen), about 2km south of town.

BUS

Buses from HCMC to Rach Gia leave from the Mien Tay bus station (p385); the express bus takes six to seven hours (from 90,000d). Night buses leave Rach Gia for HCMC up until 11pm. Private operators offers express minibuses from 95,000d to 110,000d.

The **Central bus station** (Đ Nguyen Binh Khiem) is in town, near the Rach Gia New Trade Center, and has daily services to Can Tho (45,000d, three hours), Ha Tien (30,000d, three hours) and Hon Chong (30,000d, two hours).

There's also a bigger **Rach Gia bus station** (Ben Xe Rach Soi; 78 Đ Nguyen Trung Truc), 7km south of the city (towards Long Xuyen and Can Tho). Buses link Rach Gia with Can Tho, Ha Tien, Long Xuyen and HCMC.

CAR & MOTORBIKE

Rach Gia is 92km from Ha Tien, 125km from Can Tho and 248km from HCMC.

PHU QUOC ISLAND

☎ 077 / pop 85,000

Phu Quoc is everything a tropical island is supposed to be. It is fringed with exquisite white-sand beaches lined with swaying palms and gently lapping turquoise waters. Onshore are pretty fishing villages and, further inland, dense tropical jungle as an exotic backdrop. Opt for adventures by diving the reefs, sea kayaking in the bays or exploring the backroads on a motorbike, or live the life of a lotus eater by lounging on the beach, indulging in a massage and dining on fresh seafood. Tourism is set to take off in Phu Quoc, with the Vietnamese touting it as the next Phuket. For now, Phu Quoc remains blissfully undeveloped beyond Long Beach and there is a great choice of accommodation from family bungalows to five-star resorts. If mass tourism isn't your thing, then Phuk-et, pack your bags today before the world discovers this divine destination.

The tear-shaped island lies in the Gulf of Thailand, 45km west of Ha Tien and 15km south of the coast of Cambodia. At 48km long (with an area of 1320 sq km), Phu Quoc is Vietnam's largest island and its most politically contentious: Phu Quoc is claimed by Cambodia who call it Koh Tral and this explains why the Vietnamese have built a substantial military base covering much of the northern end of the island. It was only granted to Vietnam by the French in 1949, as part of the formal annexation of the Mekong Delta.

Phu Quoc Island served as a base for the French missionary Pigneau de Behaine during the 1760s and 1780s. Prince Nguyen Anh, who later became Emperor Gia Long, was sheltered here by Behaine when he was being hunted by the Tay Son Rebels.

Phu Quoc is not really part of the Mekong Delta and doesn't share the delta's extraordinary ability to produce rice. The most valuable crop is black pepper, but the islanders here have traditionally earned their living from the sea. Phu Quoc is also famous in Vietnam for its production of high-quality fish sauce *(nuoc mam)*.

The island has some unusual hunting dogs, which have ridgebacks, curly tails and blue tongues and are said to be able to pick up their masters' scent from over 1km away (the *nuoc mam* their masters eat certainly helps). Unfortunately, the dogs have decimated much of the island's wildlife.

Despite the impending development (of a new international airport, a golf course and a casino), much of this island is still protected since becoming a national park in 2001. **Phu Quoc National Park** covers close to 70% of the island, an area of 31,422 hectares.

Phu Quoc's rainy season is from July to November. The peak season for tourism is midwinter, when the sky is blue and the sea is calm, but it can get pretty damn hot around April and May.

Orientation

The island's chief fishing port is **Duong Dong**, on the central west coast, also home to the small airport. To the south of here is **Long Beach**, the most developed area of the island, where most of the hotels and resorts are located. There are several small lanes heading from the main Đ Tran Hung Dao drag down to Long Beach and some of these shelter some of the nicest places to stay and eat, feeling more like the island getaway one would imagine.

The town itself is not that exciting, though the markets are mildly interesting, including the excellent night market with its delicious food stalls. The old bridge in town is a good vantage point to photograph the island's fishing fleet crammed into the narrow channel.

The main shipping port is **An Thoi** at the southern tip of Phu Quoc Island, but the town has fallen off the map as far as most travellers are concerned, as boats now dock at **Bai Vong** on the east of the island. However, it is still the embarkation point for day trips to the An Thoi Islands (p468).

Information

The **post office** (Map p469; Đ 30 Thang 4) is in downtown Duong Dong.

Several hotels and resorts now provide free internet to their guests, either the wired or wireless variety. **Buddy Ice Cream** (☎ 399 4181; 26 Đ Nguyen Trai) offers free internet to customers and has a couple of computers, plus free wi-fi.

There are plenty of ATMs located in resorts on Long Beach.

Sights & Activities

BEACHES

Long Beach

Long Beach (Bai Truong; Map p466) is indeed a long, spectacular stretch of sand from Duong Dong southward along the west coast, almost to An Thoi port. The southern end of the beach is known as Tau Ru Bay (Khoe Tau Ru). The water is crystal clear and the beach is lined with coconut palms, but for now development has all been concentrated in the northern section near Duong Dong.

Long Beach is easily accessible on foot (just walk south from Duong Dong's Cau Castle), but a motorbike or bicycle is necessary to reach some of the remote stretches towards the southern end of the island. The beach around the family-run guesthouse area is a particularly popular spot. There are a few bamboo huts where you can buy drinks, but bring water if planning a long hike along this beach.

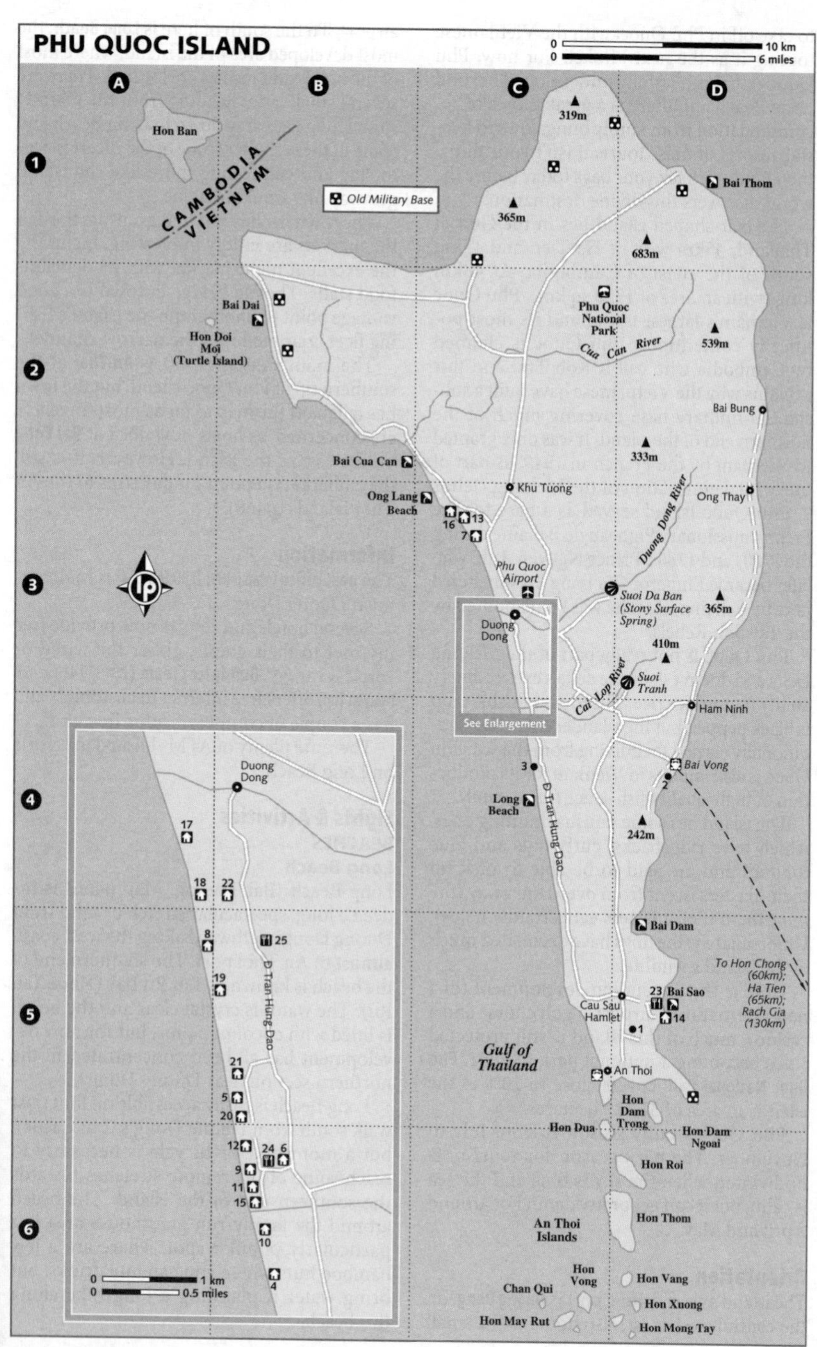
PHU QUOC ISLAND
0 10 km
0 6 miles
Hon Ban
CAMBODIA
VIETNAM
Old Military Base
319m
365m
683m
Bai Thom
Phu Quoc National Park
Cua Can River
539m
Bai Dai
Hon Doi Moi (Turtle Island)
Bai Bung
333m
Bai Cua Can
Khu Tuong
Ong Thay
Duong Dong River
Ong Lang Beach
16
13
7
Phu Quoc Airport
Suoi Da Ban (Stony Surface Spring)
365m
Duong Dong
410m
Suoi Tranh
Cai Lop River
Ham Ninh
See Enlargement
3
Bai Vong
2
Long Beach
D Tran Hung Dao
242m
Bai Dam
To Hon Chong (60km); Ha Tien (65km); Rach Gia (130km)
23
Bai Sao
14
Cau Sau Hamlet
1
Gulf of Thailand
An Thoi
Hon Dam Trong
Hon Dua
Hon Dam Ngoai
Hon Roi
Hon Thom
An Thoi Islands
Hon Vong
Hon Vang
Chan Qui
Hon Xnong
Hon May Rut
Hon Mong Tay
Duong Dong
17
18
22
8
25
19
D Tran Hung Dao
21
5
20
12
24
6
9
11
15
10
4
0 1 km
0 0.5 miles

INFORMATION	
ATM	(see 17)
Vietnam Airlines Office	(see 17)
SIGHTS & ACTIVITIES	
Coconut Tree Prison	1 D5
Mui Duong Watersports	2 D4
Phu Quoc Pearl Farm	3 C4
Searama	(see 9)
SLEEPING	
Beach Club	4 B6
Bo Resort	(see 16)
Cassia Cottage	5 B5
Charm	6 B6
Chen La Resort	7 C3
Duong Dong Resort	(see 22)
Gecko Jacks	(see 14)
Kim Hoa Resort	8 A5
La Veranda	9 B6
Lam Ha Eco Resort	10 B6
Lien Hiep Thanh Hotel	11 B6
Luna Resort	(see 8)
Mai House	12 B6
Mango Bay	13 C3
My Lan	14 D5
Nhat Lan	15 B6
Phu Quoc Resort Thang Loi	16 C3
Saigon-Phu Quoc Resort	17 A4
Sasco Blue Lagoon Resort	18 A4
Sea Star Resort	19 B5
Thai Tan Tien Guesthouse	(see 10)
Thanh Hai	(see 24)
Thanh Kieu Beach Bungalows	20 B5
Tropicana Resort	21 B5
Voi Vang Hotel	22 B4
EATING	
Ai Xiem	23 D5
Charm	(see 6)
Gop Gio	(see 8)
Le Bistrot	24 B6
My Lan	(see 14)
Pepper Tree	(see 9)
Pepper's Pizza & Grill	25 B5
Restaurant Carole	(see 8)
DRINKING	
Luna Resort Bar	(see 8)
Eden	(see 9)
Rainbow Bar	(see 20)

Bai Cua Can & Bai Ong Lan

The most accessible of the northern beaches, Bai Cua Can (Map p466) is about 11km from Duong Dong. It remains mercifully quiet during the week, but can get busy at weekends. Just south of here is Bai Ong Lan (Map p466), with a series of sandy bays sheltered by rocky headlands. There are several midrange resorts in this area which are popular with those wanting to get away from it all.

Bai Dai & Bai Thom

These are both remote beaches in the north. Bai Dai (Map p466) is in the far northwest and Bai Thom (Map p466) is on the northeastern coast. The newer road to Bai Dai cuts down on motorbike time and red dust in your face. It is very rare for either beach to be crowded for the time being. The road from Bai Dai to Bai Thom via Ganh Dau is very beautiful, passing through dense forest with tantalising glimpses of the coast below.

With the military finally loosening their grip on beaches around the island, both these stretches of sand are accessible any time.

Bai Sao & Bai Dam

Two beautiful white-sand beaches along the southeastern part of the island are Bai Sao (Map p466) and Bai Dam (Map p466), situated just a few kilometres from An Thoi. There are a couple of beachfront restaurants at Bai Sao. North of here is Bai Vong (Map p466) where the fast boats from the mainland dock, home to the Mui Duong Watersports, which offers jetskiing, waterskiing and other aquatic fun.

Just south of these beaches is undeveloped Bai Khem (Map p466), one of the most beautiful beaches on the island but one of the few remaining areas that is under military control and closed to the public.

NATIONAL PARK

Phu Quoc's poor soil and lack of surface water have disappointed farmers for generations, although their grief has been the island's environmental salvation. About 90% of the island is forested and the trees now enjoy official protection. Indeed, this is the last large stand of forest in the south.

The forest is most dense in the northern half of the island. The area is a forest reserve (Khu Rung Nguyen Sinh). You'll need a motorbike or mountain bike to get through the reserve. There are a few primitive dirt roads, but no real hiking trails.

SUOI DA BAN

Compared with the waterlogged Mekong Delta, Phu Quoc has very little surface moisture, but there are several springs originating in the hills. The most accessible of these is **Suoi Da Ban** (Stony Surface Spring; Map p466; admission 1000d, motorbike 1000d). It's a white-water creek tumbling across some attractive large granite boulders. There are deep pools and it's nice enough for a dip. Bring plenty of mosquito repellent.

Another pretty waterfall is **Suoi Tranh** (admission 1000d, motorbike 1000d), which is reachable by a 10-minute walk through the forest from the ticket counter.

AN THOI ISLANDS

Just off the southern tip of Phu Quoc are the tiny An Thoi Islands (Quan Dao An Thoi; Map p466). These 15 islands and islets can be visited by chartered boat, and it's a fine area for sightseeing, fishing, swimming and snorkelling. Hon Thom (Pineapple Island) is about 3km in length and is the largest island in the group. Other islands here include Hon Dua (Coconut Island), Hon Roi (Lamp Island), Hon Vang (Echo Island), Hon May Rut (Cold Cloud Island), the Hon Dams (Shadow Islands), Chan Qui (Yellow Tortoise) and Hon Mong Tay (Short Gun Island). As yet, there is no real development on the islands, but expect some movement in the next few years.

Most boats depart from An Thoi on Phu Quoc, but you can make arrangements through hotels and resorts on Long Beach. You can also inquire at the dive operators (see below), as they have boats heading down there regularly for diving. Boat trips are seasonal and generally do not run during the rainy season.

DIVING & SNORKELLING

Although Nha Trang is arguably the best all-round dive destination in Vietnam, there is also plenty of underwater action around Phu Quoc, However, the diving season is only during the dry months from November to May. Two fun dives cost from US$60 to US$80 depending on the location. Snorkelling trips are US$20.

Reputable **Rainbow Divers** (Map p469; ☎ 0913-400 964; www.divevietnam.com; Đ Tran Hung Dao; ⏰ 9am-6pm) was the first to set up shop on the island and offers a wide range of diving and snorkelling trips. As well as their walk-in office, they are well represented at resorts on Long Beach.

There are several other dive operators on the island:

Coco Dive Center (Map p469; ☎ 398 2100; www.cocodivecenter.com; 58 Đ Tran Hung Dao) Long running operator with its HQ in Nha Trang.

Searama (Map p466; ☎ 399 4577; searama@hotmail.fr; 91 Đ Tran Hung Dao) Newer outfit catering to the French market and others.

Vietnam Explorer (Map p469; ☎ 384 6372; www.divingvietnam.com; 36 Đ Tran Hung Dao) Well-known outfit which also operates out of Nha Trang

X Dive (Map p469; ☎ 399 4877; x-dive@hotmail.com; 12 Đ Tran Hung Dao) Newcomer offering similar kind of trips.

KAYAKING

There are several places to rent kayaks along Bai Sao beach, and its protected, fairly calm waters make for a smooth ride. In addition to locals who hire out boats, you can ask at restaurants along the beach: **My Lan** (Map p466; ☎ 399 0779) and **Ai Xiem** (Map p466; ☎ 399 0510). The going rate is about 60,000d per hour.

PHU QUOC PEARL FARM

On an isolated stretch of Long Beach, **Phu Quoc Pearls** (Map p466; ☎ 398 0585; www.treasuresfromthedeep.com; ⏰ 8am-5pm) is a requisite stop if you're in the market for pearls. A small shop sells pearl necklaces and earrings, and wall panels describe (in English) how the oysters yield their bounty. There's a small cafe on site. Avid pearl hunters can find cheaper wares at kiosks in the village of Ham Ninh, but at least you have a guarantee of authenticity here.

COCONUT TREE PRISON

Being a relatively remote and forested island (and an economically marginal area of Vietnam), Phu Quoc was useful to the French colonial administration as a remote prison. The Americans took over where the French left off and housed about 40,000 VC prisoners here.

The island's main penal colony was known as the **Coconut Tree Prison** (Nha Lao Cay Dua; Map p466) and is near An Thoi town. Though it's considered an historic site, plans to open a museum here have stalled. It's still used as a prison, so not surprisingly, few visitors come to check it out.

CAU CASTLE (DINH CAU)

According to the tourist brochures, Duong Dong's main attraction is **Cau Castle** (Dinh Cau; Map p469; Đ Bach Dang; admission free). In fact, it's less of a castle, more of a combination temple and lighthouse. It was built in 1937 to honour Thien Hau (Goddess of the Sea), who provides protection for sailors and fishermen. The 'castle' is worth a quick look and gives you a good view of the harbour entrance. Around sunset, locals stroll along the promenade leading from the castle to Đ Tran Hung Dao.

FISH SAUCE FACTORY

OK, so it's not your average sightseeing attraction, but more than a few have enjoyed a visit to the **distillery** (Map p469; admission free; ⏰ 8-11am & 1-5pm) of Nuoc Mam Hung Thanh, the

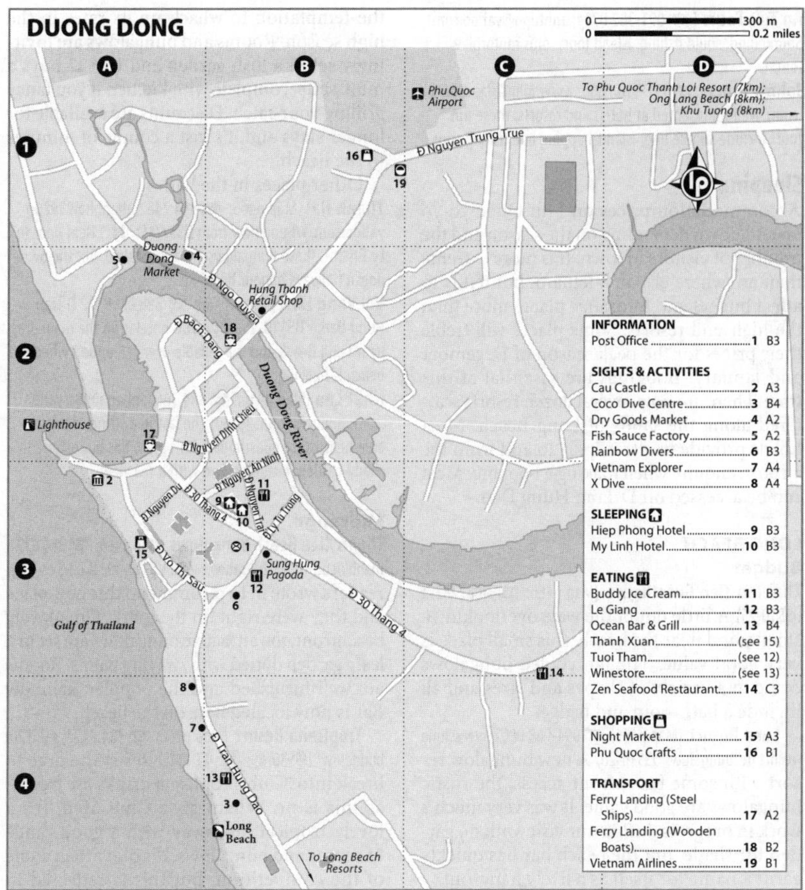

largest of Phu Quoc's fish-sauce makers. At first glance, the giant wooden vats may make you think you've arrived for a wine tasting, but one sniff of the festering *nuoc mam* essence brings you right back to reality. It's actually not so bad after a few minutes.

Most of the sauce produced is exported to the mainland for domestic consumption, though an impressive amount finds its way abroad to kitchens in Japan, North America and Europe.

The factory is a short walk from the **markets** in Duong Dong. There is no admission charge to visit, although you'd be best off taking a guide along unless you speak Vietnamese. Keep in mind that although *nuoc mam* makes a wonderful gift for your distant relatives, you may not be able to take it out of the country. Vietnam Airlines, among other carriers, has banned it from its planes.

Tours

Your best bet for booking tours is through your hotel or resort, as there's no government-run tourist office in Duong Dong. Most travellers get around the island by rental motorbike. There are a handful of English-speaking motorbike guides on the island.

For organised snorkelling tours, consider contacting the recommended dive companies (opposite). There are some other specialised companies offering boat excursions and fishing trips. Try the following:

An Tu's Tours (☎ 091-382 0714; anhtupq@yahoo.com) Snorkelling, squid fishing, island tours, plus motorbike rental.

John's Tours (☎ 091-910 7086; www.johnsislandtours.com) Well represented at hotels and resorts, these fun tours include snorkelling, island-hopping and fishing trips.

Sleeping

Accommodation prices on Phu Quoc yo-yo up and down depending on the season and the number of visitors in town. It is more extreme than anywhere else in Vietnam, but tends to affect budget and midrange places more than the high-end resorts. Some places will treble their prices for the peak season of December and January. Bookings are essential at this time. There are now several dozen resorts scattered along the sands of Long Beach. Most hotels provide free transport to and from the airport; enquire when making a booking. Most can be accessed off Đ Tran Hung Dao.

LONG BEACH

Budget

Thai Tan Tien Guesthouse (Map p466; ☎ 384 7782; r US$10-25) A little out of the way, overlooking a small pond near the beach, this small place is very good value. The fan-cooled bungalows come in a variety of shapes and sizes and all include a bathroom and fridge.

Luna Resort (Map p466; ☎ 094-968 0801; www.luna-resort.de; bungalows US$10-20) A new bungalow resort with some beachfront access; the rustic bungalows are good value. It was very much a work in progress during our visit, with no garden for shade, but the beach bar has quickly earnt a name for itself as a lively hang-out.

Lien Hiep Thanh Hotel (Map p466; ☎ 384 7583; r US$10-50; ❄) Also known somewhat more easily as the Family Hotel, this pretty complex includes 21 bungalows and rooms. Beachfront rooms include air-con and hot water, but prices rocket in high season. There's a small restaurant on the beach.

Beach Club (Map p466 ☎ 398 0998; www.beachclubvietnam.com; r US$15-28) This chilled retreat, run by an English-Vietnamese couple, is a great place to escape the bustle of the main drag. The bungalows are very spacious if simple. The owner is a great source of local info if he's around, plus there is a breezy beachside restaurant for stunning sunsets.

our pick **Lam Ha Eco Resort** (Map p466; ☎ 384 7369; r/bungalow US$17/22; ❄) Consistently one of the best-value places on Phu Quoc, it even resists the temptation to whack up its rates in the high season. Rooms and bungalows are invitingly set in a lush garden and US$22 buys a mini-suite, complete with kitchen if you fancy grilling your catch. Discounts are available for longer stays and it's just a couple of minutes to the beach.

Other places in the hat:

Thanh Hai (Map p466; ☎ 384 7482; thanhhai99926@yahoo.com; r/bungalow from US$7/15; ❄) Next door to Le Bistrot, these bungalows are a great deal, but the owner doesn't always honour bookings.

Voi Vang Hotel (Map p466; ☎ 398 0899; 72 Đ Tran Hung Dao; r US$10-25; ❄) This hotel is on the main drag near Long Beach and is a reliable overspill option when the beach is heaving.

Nhat Lan (Map p466; ☎ 384 7663; nhatlan98@yahoo.com; bungalow US$15-40) The last in a string of affordable beachfront guesthouses, this place has bungalows in a shady garden, including two with a sea view.

Midrange

Thanh Kieu Beach Bungalows (Map p466; ☎ 384 8394; thanhkieucocobeach@yahoo.com; r US$20-40; 💻) Several readers wrote in to recommend this new place and they were right on the mark. On a lovely beachfront, the attractive bungalows are set in a leafy garden dotted with swaying palms. Rooms are well furnished and the popular Rainbow Bar is now located here on the beach.

Tropicana Resort (Map p466; ☎ 384 7127; r US$20, bungalows US$30-65; ❄ 💻 🏊) Resist the urge to break into 'Club Tropicana drinks are free…' as this is no Wham-style Club Med. It's a lovely tropical hideaway with a good range of rooms and bungalows. It's older than some of the competition, but this is reflected in lowered rates. There is a swimming pool, decent restaurant and pristine sand. Staff speak English and French.

our pick **Sea Star Resort** (Map p466; ☎ 398 2161; www.seastarresort.com; r US$30, bungalow US$35-55; ❄) A fun and friendly place to stay. The management have a quirky sense of humour but definitely know how to look after their guests. The extensive compound includes 37 rooms and bungalows, many fronting on to a manicured stretch of sand with sea-view balconies. Prices drop by about 20% in the low season, making it our deal of the day.

Charm (Map p466; ☎ 329 1296; www.phuquoccharm.com; r US$45-65; ❄ 💻) There is a certain wholesome charm to this self-proclaimed place. While the rooms are not quite as atmospheric as the traditional garden restaurant, they are extremely smart for this kind of money. The decor is very tasteful and comes with all the trimmings, which makes up for the short walk (five minutes) to the beach.

Mai House (Map p466; ☎ 384 7003; maihouseresort@yahoo.com; r US$55-75; 🖳) This small resort is designed with personal space in mind, which means they have carefully chosen not to cram as many bungalows as possible into the available space. The design and detail are very attractive, although there is no air-con for those who like to (quite literally) chill.

There are also some major resorts that cater to Vietnamese tourists, and these are good value if not brimming with character:

Duong Dong Resort (Map p466; ☎ 398 3111; www.duongdongresorts.com; r US$24-29, bungalow US$49; ❄ 🖳 🏊) This place doesn't look that glamorous, but it's good value and fronts the beach.

Kim Hoa Resort (Map p466; ☎ 384 8969; www.kimhoaresort.com; r US$25-35, bungalow US$30-55; ❄ 🖳 🏊) Almost next door to the Duong Dong, this is a major hotel-resort which includes a number of solid beachfront bungalows and a swimming pool.

Top End

Cassia Cottage (Map p466; ☎ 384 8395; www.cassiacottage.com; r US$98-109; ❄ 🖳 🏊) A new boutique-style resort on Long Beach. The rooms here include handsome furnishings and are set amid a flourishing garden. Some include a pool view or sea view, plus there is a pretty garden restaurant with beachside tables.

our pick **La Veranda** (Map p466; ☎ 398 2988; www.laverandaresort.com; r from US$150; ❄ 🖳 🏊) Still the most stylish place to stay on Phu Quoc, La Veranda is designed in colonial style and is small enough to remain intimate, with just 44 rooms. There is a pool with a kiddies' area, a stylish spa and all rooms feature large beds and designer bathrooms. The beach is very pretty and the excellent Pepper Tree Restaurant offers the finest dining in town.

There are a couple more big resorts on the main drag:

Saigon-Phu Quoc Resort (Map p466; ☎ 384 6510; www.vietnamphuquoc.com; 1 Đ Tran Hung Dao; r US$108-190; ❄ 🖳 🏊) This smart resort features rooms in villas or smart bungalows, most with views over the beach. Check the website for seasonal deals.

Sasco Blue Lagoon Resort (Map p466; ☎ 399 4499; www.sasco-bluelagoon-resort.com; r US$140-280; ❄ 🖳 🏊) Next door to the Saigon-Phu Quoc, this is one of the biggest resorts on the island with bungalows, a huge pool and a long beachfront.

ONG LANG BEACH

Although it is rockier and less beautiful than Long Beach, Ong Lang Beach, 7km north of Duong Dong near the hamlet of Ong Lang, is unquestionably less crowded. Definitely book ahead if planning to stay around here.

Phu Quoc Resort Thang Loi (Map p466; ☎ 398 5002; www.phu-quoc.de; bungalows US$15-33) Set on an isolated hillock overlooking Ong Lang, this resort is a real retreat with bungalows set under the shade of cashew nut, palm and mango trees. The staff are friendly and helpful and the restaurant offers good food at fair prices. Email ahead for reservations.

Mango Bay (Map p466; ☎ 090-338 2207; www.mangobayphuquoc.com; bungalows US$60-210) Set around a small cove near Ong Lang, this ecofriendly resort uses solar panels and organic and recycled building materials. The bungalows all include a private terrace and they have larger family rooms. All in all it's a romantic getaway for those who want some privacy.

And there are a couple more exclusive hideaways:

Bo Resort (Map p466; ☎ 0913-640 520; www.boresort.com; bungalows US$48-84; 🖳) Set on a jungle-clad hill overlooking Ong Lang, this French-run resort offers intimacy and seclusion, plus good food.

Chen La Resort (Map p466; ☎ 399 5895; www.chenla-resort.com; bungalows US$120-240; ❄ 🖳 🏊) Newly opened in November 2008, this is a striking new addition to the accommodation offerings on Phu Quoc.

BAI SAO

My Lan (Map p466; ☎ 399 0779; bungalows US$15-20) For the time being, this is one of the only places to stay on this lovely beach. My Lan has charming if rustic bungalows with wood floors, thatch roof and cold-water showers. There is an excellent restaurant here offering fresh seafood on the beach.

Gecko Jacks (Map p466; ☎ 399 9800; www.geckojacks.com) This is a new resort under development, but currently only the bar and restaurant are up and running. Visit the website to follow the progress, as it looks promising.

DUONG DONG

Most travellers prefer to stay at the beach, but downtown Duong Dong has some guesthouses if the beach is bursting at the seams.

Hiep Phong Hotel (Map p469; ☎ 384 6057; tangk_xuan@yahoo.com; 17 Đ Nguyen Trai; r 150,000-250,000d; ❄ 🖳) A very friendly, family-run hotel in the middle of town. The rooms include air-con, satellite TV, fridge and hot water, something you won't find on the beach at this price. Free internet and wi-fi.

My Linh Hotel (Map p469; ☎ 384 8674; 9 Đ Nguyen Trai; r US$10-25; ❄) Just a few doors down from Hiep Phong, this mini-hotel offers a similar sort of deal with solid wooden beds and some balconies. Plus English-speaking staff.

Eating

Many of the recommended resorts have excellent restaurants, often with a beachside location or a sunset view. Guests staying at more remote resorts such as those at Ong Lang Beach tend to eat in, as it is a long way into town.

Some of the standout places include **Charm** (mains 30,000-120,000d), which has a beautiful setting in a traditional Vietnamese style compound that feels more Hoi An than Phu Quoc, and the **Pepper Tree** (mains US$6-20) at La Veranda Resort, which offers some divine French cuisine, as well as elegant Vietnamese dishes.

For something a bit more local, try the restaurants in the fishing village of Ham Ninh. There are several along the pier (end of the road), including **Kim Cuong I** (Map p466; ☎ 384 9978; Ham Ninh; mains 30,000-80,000d).

LONG BEACH & DUONG DONG

The **night market** (Đ Vo Thi Sau) is one of the most atmospheric (and affordable) places to dine in Duong Dong. There are a dozen or more stalls serving a delicious range of Vietnamese seafood, grills and vegetarian options. Look for a local crowd, as they are a discerning bunch or try the excellent **Thanh Xuan** (Map p469; Đ Vo Thi Sau; 🕑 dinner), which offers freshly barbecued fish and seafood.

Buddy Ice Cream (Map p469; ☎ 399 4181; 26 Đ Nguyen Trai; dishes 20,000-140,000d) This ice-cream shop and information centre is a good stop for budget travellers looking for free internet or impartial advice. The New Zealand ice cream is great, plus there are pizzas, sausages and more.

Restaurant Carole (Map p466; ☎ 384 8884; 88 Đ Tran Hung Dao; mains 25,000-160,000d) This place is French in accent, but the menu includes a whole lot of fresh Vietnamese seafood, such as the signature shrimps in cognac or pastis. The prices are very reasonable for international dining.

our pick **Le Bistrot** (Map p466; ☎ 398 2200; 118/2 Đ Tran Hung Dao; meals 28,000-120,000d; 🕑 7am-late) Tucked away an the atmospheric lane, this French garden restaurant offers French home cooking at a distinctly Vietnamese price, making it a great place. The menu includes some Italian and Vietnamese dishes, plus French cheeses and profiteroles. It stays open late as a lively bar with pool table.

Gop Gio (Map p466; ☎ 384 7057; 78 Đ Tran Hung Dao; mains 30,000-70,000d) This long-running Vietnamese restaurant has a leafy terrace and is popular for its fresh seafood, with dishes such as shrimp with mango or steamed grouper with ginger.

Ocean Bar & Grill (Map p469; ☎ 399 4268; 60 Đ Tran Hung Dao; mains 40,000-100,000d; 🕑 lunch & dinner) This is a tiny little tapas bar-grill located on the main road into town. The bites are light, so mix and match, but know well that the wine selection is the best in town thanks to the attached winestore.

Pepper's Pizza & Grill (Map p466; ☎ 384 8773; 89 Đ Tran Hung Dao; mains 40,000-150,000d; 🕑 lunch & dinner) Almost opposite Carole, Pepper's is home to the best pizzas on the island, according to long-term residents. Other items include steaks, ribs and the like.

Zen Seafood Restaurant (Map p469; ☎ 399 4555; Đ 30 Thang 4; mains 40,000-150,000d 🕑 lunch & dinner) The sculpted garden here is indeed quite Zen, with fountains, streams and pools. Popular with Vietnamese high-rollers looking for seafood or suckling pig.

There are a couple of reliable local restaurants side by side on the road into town:

Tuoi Tham (Map p469; ☎ 384 6368; Đ Tran Hung Dao; mains 20,000-50,000d) Another popular local place with good food and a welcoming atmosphere.

Le Giang (Map p469; ☎ 384 6444; 289 Đ Tran Hung Dao; mains 20,000-60,000d) A wide range of Vietnamese favourites here, plus an upstairs terrace to catch a breeze.

BAI SAO

To get to these places, follow the paved road a few kilometres north of An Thoi and look for the 'My Lan' sign on the right, which leads down a dirt track to the beach.

Ai Xiem (Map p466; ☎ 399 0510; Bai Sao; mains 40,000-100,000d; 🕑 lunch & dinner) Gorgeously located on the inviting white sands of Bai Sao beach, this place has succulent barbecued seafood and great fish in clay pot meals. Tables are on the sands, a few metres from lapping waves.

My Lan (Map p466; ☎ 399 0779; Bai Sao; mains 40,000-120,000d; 🕑 lunch & dinner) About 400m south of Ai Xiem, My Lan offers similarly good seafood and the same beachside allure.

Drinking

There aren't a whole lot of bars on Phu Quoc Island, as a lot of folk tend to stick around their resorts by night. However, there are a few beachfront places that are worth the walk.

Run by the same crew who made the once-upon-a-lifetime-ago Nha Trang institution a legendary good time, the friendly Rainbow Bar (Map p466) is located right on the beach by the Thanh Kieu Resort. Similarly lively is the Luna Resort bar (Map p466) with a central location on the sand.

Eden (Map p466; ☎ 399 4208) Next door to La Veranda, this is an outpost of the popular Pham Ngu Lao bar-restaurant (p380). It has a fine location with tables on the sand and a covered interior with pool tables and internet access.

Shopping

Phu Quoc doesn't really afford the shopping opportunities of somewhere like Hoi An just yet, but the **night market** (Cho Den Dinh Cau; Đ Vo Thi Sau) has some interesting stalls.

Phu Quoc Crafts (Map p469; ☎ 399 5606; www.phuquoccrafts.com; 109 Đ Nguyen Trung Truc) Located right opposite the airport, this cafe-gallery has a nice range of locally made handicrafts, such as candles, bags and cutlery. The cafe is a good place to wait for a flight, with tasty shakes and light meals.

Getting There & Away

With the opening of the Vietnam–Cambodia border at Xa Xia–Prek Chak, it is becoming very popular to visit Phu Quoc as part of a loop through the Mekong Delta and the south coast of Cambodia. This is now very easy thanks to a new fast boat connecting Phu Quoc and Ha Tien, plus there are fast boats and daily flights connecting Rach Gia and Phu Quoc. There are persistent rumours of a fast boat service to Sihanoukville or Kep in Cambodia, both closer than the Vietnamese mainland, so keep your ear to the ground.

AIR

There are six flights per day between HCMC and Phu Quoc Island, all operated by **Vietnam Airlines** (☎ 398 2320; 122 Đ Nguyen Trung Truc). However, demand can still be pretty high in peak season so book ahead.

A popular round trip between HCMC and Phu Quoc is to travel overland through the Mekong Delta, take a ferry to the island from Rach Gia or Ha Tien and, tanned and rested, take the short one-hour flight back to HCMC (820,000d).

BOAT

There are now fast boats connecting both Ha Tien and Hon Chong to Phu Quoc Island, both considerably shorter crossings than from Rach Gia. For details of these new services, see the Ha Tien (p459) and Hon Chong (p461) entries in this chapter.

Numerous companies operate speedy hydrofoils between Rach Gia and Phu Quoc. Various boats leave in both directions daily between 7am and 8.30am, and again between 12.30pm and 1.30pm. Ticket prices for the 2½-hour journey are 250,000d for adults, 170,000d for children. Tickets must be purchased in advance, although you can usually find a seat by booking as little as 30 minutes ahead.

Hydrofoil companies include **Super Dong** (☎ Rach Gia 077-387 8475, Phu Quoc 077-398 0111), **Duong Dong Express** (☎ Rach Gia 077-387 9765, Phu Quoc 077-399 0747) and **Hai Au** (☎ Rach Gia 077-387 9455, Phu Quoc 077 -399 0555). All have offices by the dock in Rach Gia and in Duong Dong. Most travel agents can book your passage for the same fare.

All passenger ferries departing and arriving at Phu Quoc now use the dock at Bai Vong on the eastern side of the island.

Getting Around

TO/FROM THE AIRPORT

Phu Quoc's airport is pretty much in central Duong Dong. The motorbike drivers at the airport will charge you about US$1 to US$2 to most places on Long Beach, but are notorious for trying to cart people off to where they can collect a commission. If you know where you want to go, tell them you've already got a reservation.

BICYCLE

If you can ride a bicycle in the tropical heat over these dusty, bumpy roads, all power to you. Bicycle rentals are available through most hotels from US$2 per day.

BUS

There is a skeletal bus service between An Thoi and Duong Dong. Buses run perhaps once every hour or two. A bus (20,000d) waits for the ferry at Bai Vong to take passengers to Duong Dong. Several hotels operate shuttles or will offer free transfers for guests.

BORDER CROSSING: XA XIA–PREK CHAK

The recently opened Xa Xia–Prek Chak crossing has been long anticipated, connecting Ha Tien with Kep and Kampot on Cambodia's south coast. This makes it possible to link the beautiful island of Phu Quoc with the Cambodian coast. There are currently no cross-border bus services here, but it is simple enough with a combination of local transport. Take a *xe om* (motorbike taxi) from Ha Tien to the border (US$2) and then arrange a *xe om* on to Kompong Trach (US$3), Kep (US$6) or Kampot (US$9). It is also possible to charter a taxi from the border to Kampot (US$40), Kep (US$30) or Kompong Trach (US$20).

MOTORBIKE

You won't have to look for the motorbike taxis – they'll find you. Some polite bargaining may be necessary. For short runs within the town, 10,000d should be sufficient. Otherwise, figure on around 30,000d for about 5km. From Duong Dong to Bai Vong will cost you about 50,000d or so.

Motorbikes can be hired from most hotels and bungalows for around US$7 (semi-automatic) to US$10 (automatic) per day. The cheaper bikes tend to be pretty old and in poor condition, so inspect them thoroughly before setting out. Most places prefer not to rent out overnight, so make sure you are clear on the arrangements before taking the bike.

TAXI

There are several metered taxi companies operating on the island. **Mai Linh** (☎ 397 9797) is reliable and drivers always use the meter. It costs about 150,000d from Duong Dong to the dock at Bai Vong.

Directory

CONTENTS

ACCOMMODATION

Vietnam offers beds for every budget – from bargain basements to sky-high super-hotels – and we cover them all. Beyond the main cities, many hotels in Vietnam quote prices in a mix of Vietnamese dong and US dollars. The lower dong price is usually reserved for locals, while foreigners pay the higher dollar price. Prices are quoted in dong or dollars throughout this book based on the preferred currency of the particular property.

When it comes to budget, we are talking about guesthouses or hotels where the majority of rooms cost less than US$20. These are usually family-run guesthouses, mini-hotels or, usually the least-appealing option, state-run guesthouses stuck in the '70s. Budget rooms generally come well equipped for the money, so don't be surprised to find air-con, hot water and a TV for 10 bucks.

Moving on to midrange, we are referring to rooms in the US$20 to US$75 range, which buys some pretty tasty extras in Vietnam. At the lower end of this bracket, many of the hotels are similar to budget hotels but with bigger rooms or balconies. Flash a bit more cash and three-star touches are available, such as access to a swimming pool, and a hairdryer hidden away somewhere.

At the top end are a host of international-standard hotels and resorts that charge from US$75 a room to US$750 a suite. Some of these are fairly faceless business hotels, while others ooze opulence or resonate with history. There are some good deals when compared with the Hong Kongs and Singapores of this world, so if you fancy indulging yourself, Vietnam is a good place to do it. Most hotels at the top end levy a tax of 10% and a service charge of 5%, displayed as ++ ('plus plus') on the bill.

Be aware that some budget and midrange hotels also apply the 10% tax. Check carefully before taking the room to avoid any annoying shocks on departure.

Accommodation options are limited in off-the-beaten-track destinations in the far north and the central highlands. Usually there will just be a few guesthouses and basic hotels. However, in major towns and along the coastal strip, there is now an excellent range of accommodation, including some of the world's biggest names, such as Sofitel and Six Senses.

BOOK ACCOMMODATION ONLINE

For more accommodation reviews and recommendations by Lonely Planet authors, check out the online booking service at www.lonelyplanet.com. You'll find the true, insider lowdown on the best places to stay. Reviews are thorough and independent. Best of all, you can book online.

PRACTICALITIES

- **Electricity** The usual voltage is 220V, 50 cycles, but sometimes you encounter 110V, also at 50 cycles, just to confuse things. Electrical sockets are usually two-pin.
- **Laundry** Most guesthouses and hotels have cheap laundry services, but check there is a dryer if the weather is bad. There are also dry-cleaning outlets in every town.
- **Newspapers & Magazines** *Vietnam News* and the *Saigon Times* are propagandist English-language dailies. Popular listings mags include the *Guide*, which covers the whole country, plus *AsiaLife* and *The Word* in Ho Chi Minh City.
- **Radio & TV** *Voice of Vietnam* hogs the airwaves all day and is pumped through loudspeakers in many rural towns. There are several TV channels and a steady diet of satellite stuff.
- **Weights & Measures** The Vietnamese use the metric system for everything except precious metals and gems, where they follow the Chinese system.

Peak tourist demand for hotel rooms comes at Christmas and New Year, when prices may rise by as much as 25%. There is also a surge in many cities during Tet, when half of Vietnam is on the move. Try to make a reservation at these times so as not to get caught out. During quiet periods it is often possible to negotiate a discount, either by email in advance or over the counter on arrival, as there is a surplus of hotel beds in many destinations.

Passports are almost always requested on arrival at a hotel. It is not absolutely essential to hand over your actual passport, but at the very least you need to hand over a photocopy of the passport details, visa and departure card.

Accommodation prices listed in this book are high-season prices for rooms with attached bathroom, unless stated otherwise. An icon is included if air-con is available; otherwise, assume that a fan will be provided.

Camping

Perhaps because so many Vietnamese spent much of the war years living in tents, as either soldiers or refugees, camping is not yet the popular pastime it is in the West.

Some innovative private travel agencies in Ho Chi Minh City (HCMC) and Hanoi offer organised camping trips to national parks, plus camping out in beauty spots such as Halong Bay (p139). See Travel Agencies in Hanoi (p87) and HCMC (p351).

Guesthouses & Hotels

Many of the large hotels *(khach san)* and guesthouses *(nha khach* or *nha nghi)* are government owned or joint ventures. There has also been a mushrooming of mini-hotels – small, smart private hotels that represent good value for money. The international hotel chains are now well represented in Hanoi and HCMC.

There is considerable confusion over the terms 'singles', 'doubles', 'double occupancy' and 'twins', so let's set the record straight here. A single contains one bed, even if two people sleep in it. If there are two beds in the room, that is a twin, even if only one person occupies it. If two people stay in the same room, that is double occupancy. In some hotels 'doubles' means twin beds, while in others it means double occupancy.

While many of the newer hotels have lifts, older hotels often don't and the cheapest rooms are at the end of several flights of stairs. It's a win-win-win situation: cheaper rooms, a bit of exercise and better views! Bear in mind that power outages are possible in

HOTELS FROM HELL

It is hardly unique to the country, but there are quite a lot of hotel scams in Vietnam. They are mostly, but not exclusively, happening in Hanoi, although keep the radar up in most of the major cities. Copycat hotels, dodgy taxi drivers, persistent touts – all this is possible and more. Overcharging is a concern, as is constant harassment to book a tour. However, most guesthouse and hotel operators are decent folk and honest in their dealings with tourists. Don't let the minority ruin your Vietnam experience. For more on horror hotels in Hanoi, see p104.

some towns and this can mean 10 flights of stairs just to get to your room in a tall, skinny HCMC-style skyscraper.

Many hotels post a small sign warning guests not to leave cameras, passports and other valuables in the room. Most places have a safety deposit system of some kind, but if leaving cash (not recommended) or travellers cheques, be sure to seal the loot in an envelope and have it counter-signed by staff. However, many readers have been stung when leaving cash at cheaper hotels, so proceed with caution.

Homestays

Homestays are a popular option in parts of Vietnam, but some local governments are more flexible than others about the concept. Homestays were pioneered in the Mekong Delta (p425), where it has long been possible to stay with local families. At the opposite end of the map, there are also homestays on the island of Cat Ba (p150).

Many people like to stay with ethnic minority families in the far north of Vietnam. Mai Chau (p168) was the first place to offer the chance to stay with the hospitable White Thai families. Sapa (p176) is the number-one destination to meet the hill tribes in Vietnam and it is possible to undertake two- or three-day treks with an overnight stay in a H'mong or Dzao village. If you are serious about homestays throughout the north, consider contacting one of the travel agencies (p87) or motorbike touring companies (p507) that can help organise things. Vietnam is not the sort of country where you can just drop in and hope things work out, as there are strict rules about registering foreigners who stay overnight with a Vietnamese family.

Resorts

Resorts have really taken off in the last few years, particularly along the beautiful coastline. Top beach spots such as China Beach, Nha Trang and Mui Ne all have a range of sumptuous places for a spot of pampering. Wild and isolated strips of tropical coastline in between are slowly being snapped up and ultra-exclusive resorts are under development. Up-and-coming destinations such as Phu Quoc Island are fast catching up with the mainland. Beach resorts in Vietnam are pretty good value compared with other parts of the world, so if you have the money to spend, it is worth the experience staying in a top-end resort.

There are a number of eco-resorts in the mountains of the north and the far-flung corners of Bai Tu Long Bay, a trend that looks set to continue. There are also plans afoot to develop some eco-resorts in national parks, such as Cat Tien and Con Dao. However, 'eco-resort' remains a much used and abused term in this region, so take a good look at the website of the property before making a booking.

ACTIVITIES

If you are looking for action, Vietnam can increasingly deliver. Biking and hiking are taking off up and down the country, while offshore there is kayaking and surfing above the water and diving and snorkelling beneath. If it all sounds like too much hard work, rent a motorbike and let the engine take the strain.

Cycling

For distances near and far, cycling is an excellent way to experience Vietnam. A bicycle can be rented in most tourist centres from just US$2 a day.

The flatlands of the Mekong Delta region are an ideal place for a long-distance ride through the back roads. The entire coastal route along Hwy 1 is an alluring achievement, but the insane traffic makes it tough going and dangerous. A better option is the newer inland route, Hwy 14, also known as the Ho Chi Minh Highway (not to be confused with the original wartime trail), which offers stunning scenery and little traffic.

North of the old Demilitarised Zone (DMZ), cycling is a bad idea in the winter months, particularly if heading from the south to the north, thanks to the massive monsoon winds which blow from the north. There are some incredible, and incredibly challenging, rides through the Tonkinese Alps (Hoang Lien Mountains) of the north, but the opportunity to get up close and personal with the minority peoples of the region makes it more than worth the while.

For some laughs, as well as the lowdown on cycling in Vietnam, visit the website www.mrpumpy.net.

Diving & Snorkelling

The most popular scuba-diving area in Vietnam is around Nha Trang (p295).

There are several reputable dive operators here, whose equipment and training is up to international standards. Phu Quoc Island (p468) is another popular spot.

It is also possible to hire snorkelling gear and scuba equipment at several beach resorts along the coast, including Cua Dai Beach (p260), Ca Na (p307) and China Beach (p243).

The Con Dao Islands (p407) have the potential to be the next big thing in underwater exploration in Vietnam and dive operators are sniffing around.

Golf

Mark Twain once said that playing golf was 'a waste of a good walk' and apparently Ho Chi Minh agreed with him. Times have changed and government officials can often be seen fraternising on the fairways.

All over East Asia playing golf wins considerable points in the 'face game', even if you never hit a ball. For maximum snob value you need to join a country club, and in Vietnam memberships start at around US$10,000. Most golf clubs will allow you to pay a guest fee.

The best golf courses in Vietnam are located in Dalat (p317) and Phan Thiet (p314), but there are also plenty of courses in and around Hanoi and HCMC.

For information about golf package deals visit www.vietnamgolfresorts.com.

Kayaking

Kayaking has taken off around Halong Bay in the past few years, following in the footsteps of Krabi in Thailand. Several companies offer kayaking itineraries around the majestic limestone pinnacles, including overnights on islands in the bay. Even the standard Halong Bay tours now include the option of kayaking through the karsts for those who want the experience without the effort. Leading beach destinations also offer sea kayaks for rent, only without the dramatic scenery.

Motorbiking

Motorbiking through Vietnam's 'deep north' is unforgettable. For those seeking true adventure there is no better way to go. If you are not confident riding a motorbike, it's comparatively cheap to hire someone to drive it for you. Also highly recommended are 4WD trips in the north, though the mobility of two wheels is unrivalled. Motorbikes can traverse trails that even the hardiest 4WD cannot follow. Just remember to watch the road when the scenery is sublime.

Another up-and-coming route is to follow the Ho Chi Minh Highway (p334), which runs the spine of the country from north to south.

Rock Climbing

It is still early days, but with the sheer range of limestone karsts found up and down the country, it is only a matter of time before the word gets out. For now, Halong Bay (p139) and Cat Ba Island (p148) are emerging as the premier spots, but in time Ninh Binh (p192) and Phong Nha (p202) could offer some competition.

Surfing, Kitesurfing & Windsurfing

Surfing and windsurfing have only recently arrived on the scene, but these are quickly catching on in popularity. The best place to practise these pursuits is at Mui Ne Beach (p308), but experienced surfers should head for China Beach in Danang (p235). Kitesurfing has really taken off and is now one of Mui Ne's biggest draws for thrillseekers.

Trekking

Vietnam offers excellent trekking opportunities, notably in its growing array of national parks and nature reserves. There are ample opportunities to hike to minority villages in the northwest, northeast and central highlands regions. Anything is possible, from half-day hikes to an assault on Fansipan, Vietnam's highest mountain. The best bases from which to arrange treks are Sapa (p176), Bac Ha (p186) and Cat Ba (p148), all in northern Vietnam; Bach Ma National Park (p232) in central Vietnam; and Cat Tien (p406) and Yok Don (p332) National Parks in the south. Tour operators in Hanoi and HCMC offer a variety of programs featuring hiking and trekking, but it may be better to wait until you arrive in a trekking hub such as Sapa or Dalat before planning an itinerary, as this allows more flexibility than signing up for an all-inclusive tour. Rangers at the leading parks can also help in crafting some experiences if you turn up in a national park with no clear plans.

Bear in mind that it may be necessary to arrange special permits, especially if you plan to spend the night in remote mountain villages where there are no hotels.

BUSINESS HOURS

Vietnamese people rise early and consider sleeping in to be a sure indication of illness. Offices, museums and many shops open between 7am and 8am and close between 5pm and 6pm. Post offices keep longer hours and are generally open from 6.30am to 9pm. Banks are generally open from 8am to 11.30am and 1pm to 4pm during the week and 8am to 11.30am on Saturday.

Most government offices are open on Saturday until noon but are closed on Sunday. Most museums are closed on Monday while temples and pagodas are usually open every day from around 5am to 9pm.

Many of the small, privately owned shops, restaurants and street stalls stay open seven days a week, often until late at night.

Lunch is taken very seriously and virtually everything shuts down between noon and 1.30pm. Government workers tend to take longer breaks, so figure on getting nothing done between 11.30am and 2pm.

In this book, opening hours are only included when they differ from these standard hours.

CHILDREN

Children get to have a good time in Vietnam, mainly because of the overwhelming amount of attention they attract and the fact that almost everybody wants to play with them. However, this attention can sometimes be overwhelming, particularly for blond-haired, blue-eyed babes. Cheek pinching, or worse still (if rare), groin grabbing for boys, are distinct possibilities, so keep them close. For the full picture on surviving and thriving on the road, check out Lonely Planet's *Travel with Children*, which has a rundown on health precautions for kids and advice on travel during pregnancy.

Practicalities

When it comes to feeding and caring for babies, almost anything and everything is available in the major cities of Vietnam, but supplies dry up quickly in the countryside. Cot beds are available in international-standard midrange and top-end hotels, but not elsewhere. There are no safety seats in rented cars or taxis, but some Western restaurants can usually find a highchair when it comes to eating.

Breastfeeding in public is quite common in Vietnam, so there is no need to worry about crossing a cultural boundary. But there are few facilities for changing babies other than the usual bathrooms. You'll need to pack a baby bag everywhere you go. For kiddies who are too young to handle chopsticks, most restaurants also have cutlery.

The main worry throughout Vietnam is keeping an eye on what strange things infants are putting in their mouths. Their natural curiosity can be a lot more costly in a country where dysentery, typhoid and hepatitis are commonplace. Keeping their hydration levels up and insisting they use sunscreen, despite their protests, is also important.

However, on the upside, there are some great things to put in kids' mouths in the right circumstances. The range of fruit in Vietnam is staggering and includes the weird and wonderful dragon fruit, as well as delectable mangoes. Most major destinations now have a good combination of delicious local food to experiment with, as well as comfort food from home when you need something familiar.

Sights & Activities

There is plenty to do in big cities to keep kids interested, though in most smaller towns and rural areas boredom may set in from time to time. The zoos, parks and some of the best ice-cream shops in the region are usually winners. Children visiting the south should not miss HCMC's water parks (p369), while Hanoi's must is a water-puppet performance (p115).

Nature lovers with children can hike in one of Vietnam's expansive national parks or nature reserves. Cuc Phuong National Park (p196) is home to the excellent Endangered Primate Rescue Centre, where endangered species of monkeys are protected and bred. This is a great place to see gibbons gallivanting about their safe houses and to learn about the plight of our furry friends.

With such a long coast, there are some great beaches for young children to enjoy, but pay close attention to any playtime in the sea, as there are some big riptides at many of the most popular beaches. Some popular beaches have warning flags and lifeguards, but at quieter beaches, parents should test the current first. Parents with younger children may prefer to opt for a resort with a pool or head to somewhere such as Phu Quoc Island (p464), which is more sheltered than the mainland. Halong Bay (p139) is a must, as sleeping on the boat is an adventure for many children, plus they get to explore caves and islands that look like they come out of a fairy tale.

CLIMATE CHARTS

The climate of Vietnam varies considerably from region to region. Although the entire country lies in the tropics and subtropics, local conditions vary from frosty winters in the far northern hills to year-round, subequatorial warmth in the Mekong Delta.

For more climate information, take a look at When to Go (p17).

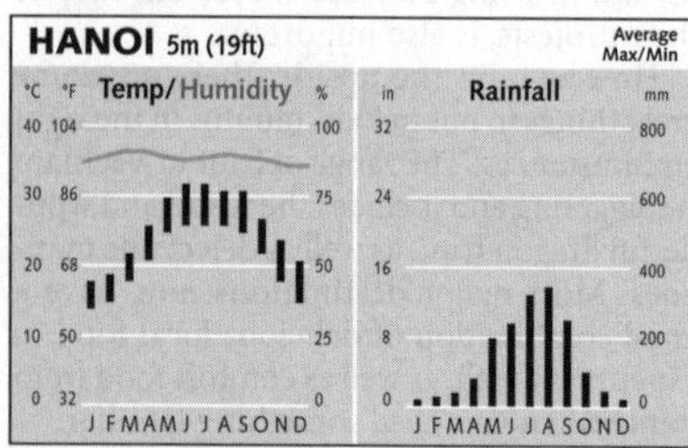

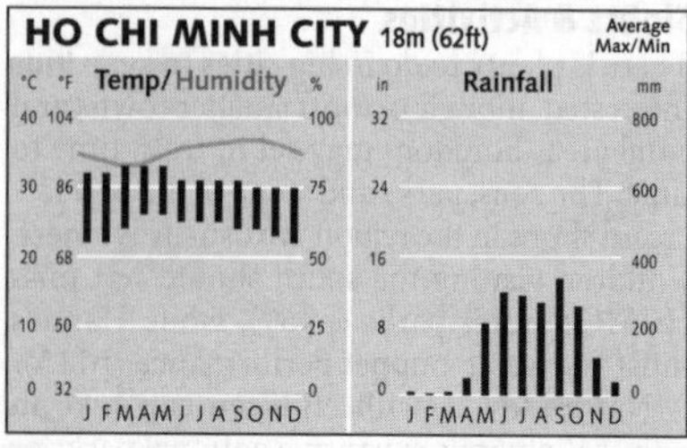

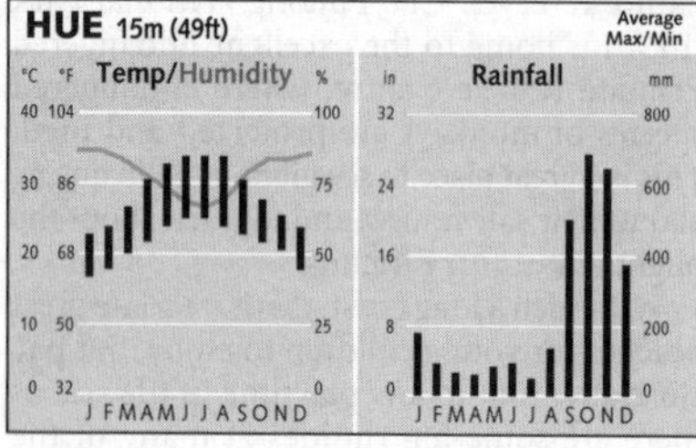

COURSES

Cooking

For the full story on cooking courses, check out the Food & Drink chapter (p70).

Language

There are Vietnamese-language courses offered in HCMC, Hanoi and elsewhere. To qualify for student-visa status you need to enrol at a bona fide university, as opposed to a private language centre or with a tutor. Lessons usually last for two hours per day, and cost from US$5 (university) to US$15 (private) per hour.

It is important to decide whether to study Vietnamese in Hanoi or HCMC, as the northern and southern dialects are quite different. Many have been dismayed to discover that if they studied in one city they could not communicate clearly in the other. For more details, see under Language Courses in Hanoi (p103) and Ho Chi Minh City (p368).

CUSTOMS

Enter Vietnam by air and the whole procedure only takes a few minutes. When entering overland, expect to attract a bit more interest, particularly at remote borders.

Duty-free allowances are the standard 200 cigarettes and a bottle of booze variety. Visitors can bring unlimited foreign currency into Vietnam, but large sums (US$7000 and greater) must be declared upon arrival.

DANGERS & ANNOYANCES

Beggar Fatigue

Just as you're about to dig into the scrumptious Vietnamese meal you've ordered, you feel a tug on your shirt sleeve. This latest 'annoyance' is a bony, eight-year-old boy holding his three-year-old sister in his arms. The little girl has a distended stomach and her hungry eyes are fixed on your full plate.

This is the face of poverty. How do you deal with these situations? If you're like most of us, then not very well. Taking the matter into your own hands by giving out money or gifts to

> **GOVERNMENT TRAVEL ADVICE**
>
> The following government websites offer travel advisories and information on current hot spots:
>
> **Australian Department of Foreign Affairs** (☎ 1300 139 281; www.smarttraveller.gov.au)
>
> **British Foreign Office** (☎ 0845-850-2829; www.fco.gov.uk/countryadvice)
>
> **Canadian Department of Foreign Affairs** (☎ 800-267 6788; www.dfait-maeci.gc.ca)
>
> **US State Department** (☎ 888-407 4747; http://travel.state.gov)

people on the streets can cause more damage than good. The more people are given handouts, the more reliant and attracted to life on the streets they become. When money is tight, people recognise that life on the streets is no longer so fruitful. This will hopefully discourage parents and 'pimps' forcing children and beggars onto the streets.

One way to contribute and help improve the situation is to invest just a few hours to find out about local organisations that work with disadvantaged people; these groups are far more likely to make sure contributions are used in the most effective way possible to help those who need it.

However, if you want to do something on the spot, at least avoid giving money or anything that can be sold. The elderly and the young are easily controlled and are ideal begging tools. If you are going to give something directly to a beggar, it's better to give food than money; take them to a market or stall and buy them a nutritious meal or some fruit to be sure they are the only beneficiaries.

Noise

Remember Spinal Tap? The soundtrack of Vietnam is permanently cranked up to 11. Not just any noise, but a whole lot of noises that just never seem to stop. At night there is most often a competing cacophony from motorbikes, discos, cafes, karaoke clubs and restaurants; if your hotel is near any or all of these, it may be difficult to sleep.

Fortunately most noise subsides around 10pm or 11pm, as few places stay open much later than that. Unfortunately, however, Vietnamese are up and about from around 5am onwards. This not only means that traffic noise starts early, but you may be woken up by the crackle of loudspeakers as the Voice of Vietnam cranks into life at 5am in small towns and villages. It's worth trying to get a room at the back of a hotel.

One last thing…don't forget the earplugs!

Prostitution

Karaoke clubs and massage parlours are ubiquitous throughout Vietnam. Sometimes this may mean an 'orchestra without instruments', or a healthy massage to ease a stiff body. However, more often than not, both of these terms are euphemisms for some sort of prostitution. There may be some singing or a bit of shoulder tweaking going on, but ultimately it is just a polite introduction to something naughtier. Legitimate karaoke and legitimate massage do exist in the bigger cities, but as a general rule of thumb, if the place looks small and sleazy, it most probably is.

> **PLANET OF THE FAKES**
>
> You'll probably notice a lot of cut-price Lonely Planet *Vietnam* titles available as you travel around the country. Don't be deceived. These are pirate copies, churned out on local photocopiers. Sometimes the copies are very good, sometimes awful. The only certain way to tell is price. If it's cheap, it's a copy. Look at the print in this copy…if it is faded and the photos are washed out, then this book will self-destruct in five seconds.

Scams

Con artists and thieves are always seeking new tricks to separate naive tourists from their money and are becoming more savvy in their ways. We can't warn you about every trick you might encounter, so maintain a healthy scepticism and be prepared to argue when unnecessary demands are made for your money.

Beware of a motorbike-rental scam that some travellers have encountered in HCMC. Rent a motorbike and the owner supplies an excellent lock, insisting you use it. What he doesn't tell you is that he has another key and that somebody will follow you and 'steal' the bike at the first opportunity. You then have to pay for a new bike, as per the signed contract.

More common is when your motorbike won't start after you parked it in a 'safe' area with a guard. But yes, the guard knows somebody who can repair your bike. The mechanic shows up and quickly reinstalls the parts they removed earlier and the bike works again. That will be US$10, please.

Beware of massage boys who, after a price has been agreed upon, try to extort money from you afterwards by threatening to set the police on you (these threats are generally empty ones).

The most common scam most visitors encounter is the oldest in the book. The hotel of choice is 'closed' or 'full', but the helpful taxi driver will take you somewhere else. This has been perfected in Hanoi, where there are often several hotels with the same name in the same area. Book by telephone or email in advance and stop the scammers in their tracks.

Despite an array of scams, however, it is important to keep in mind the Vietnamese are not always out to get you. One concerning trend we're noticing in Vietnam, relative to neighbouring countries such as Cambodia and Laos, is a general lack of trust in the locals on the part of foreigners. Try to differentiate between who is good and bad and do not close yourself off to every person you encounter.

Sea Creatures

If you plan to spend your time swimming, snorkelling and scuba diving, familiarise yourself with the various hazards. The list of dangerous creatures that are found in seas off Vietnam is extensive and includes sharks, jellyfish, stonefish, scorpion fish, sea snakes and stingrays. However, there is little cause for alarm as most of these creatures avoid humans, or humans avoid them, so the number of people injured or killed is very small.

Jellyfish tend to travel in groups, so as long as you look before you leap into the sea, avoiding them should not be too hard. Stonefish, scorpion fish and stingrays tend to hang out in shallow water along the ocean floor and can be very difficult to see. One way to protect against these nasties is to wear plastic shoes in the sea.

Theft

The Vietnamese are convinced that their cities are full of criminals. Street crime is commonplace in HCMC and Nha Trang, and on the rise in Hanoi, so it doesn't hurt to keep the antennae up wherever you are.

HCMC is the place to really keep your wits about you. Don't have anything dangling from your body that you are not ready to part with, including bags and jewellery, which might tempt a robber. Keep an eye out for the Saigon cowboys – drive-by thieves on motorbikes – they specialise in snatching handbags and cameras from tourists on foot and taking *cyclos* (pedicabs) in the city.

Pickpocketing, which often involves kids, women with babies and newspaper vendors, is also a serious problem, especially in the tourist areas of HCMC. Many of the street kids, adorable as they may be, are very skilled at liberating people from their wallets.

Avoid putting things down while you're eating, or at least take the precaution of fastening these items to your seat with a strap or chain. Remember, any luggage that you leave unattended for even a moment may grow legs and vanish.

There are also 'taxi girls' (sometimes transvestites) who approach Western men, give them a big hug, often more, and ask if they'd like 'a good time'. Then they suddenly change their mind and depart, along with a mobile phone and wallet.

We have also had reports of people being drugged and robbed on long-distance buses. It usually starts with a friendly passenger offering a free Coke, which turns out to be a chloralhydrate cocktail. You wake up hours later to find your valuables and new-found 'friend' gone.

Despite all this, don't be overly paranoid. Although crime certainly exists and you need to be aware of it, theft in Vietnam does not seem to be any worse than what you'd expect anywhere else. Don't assume that everyone's a thief – most Vietnamese are honest.

Undetonated Explosives

For more than three decades four armies expended untold energy and resources mining, booby-trapping, rocketing, strafing, mortaring and bombarding wide areas of Vietnam. When the fighting stopped most of this ordnance remained exactly where it had landed or been laid; American estimates at the end of the war placed the quantity of unexploded ordnance (UXO) at 150,000 tonnes.

Since 1975 more than 40,000 Vietnamese have been maimed or killed by this leftover ordnance. While cities, cultivated areas and well-travelled rural roads and paths are safe for travel, straying from these areas could land you in the middle of danger.

Never touch any rockets, artillery shells, mortars, mines or other relics of war you may come across. Such objects can remain lethal for decades. And don't climb inside bomb craters – you never know what undetonated explosive device is at the bottom.

You can learn more about the issue of landmines from the Nobel Peace Prize–winning **International Campaign to Ban Landmines** (ICBL; www.icbl.org), or visit the **Halo Trust** (www.halotrust.org) or **Mines Advisory Group** (MAG; www.maginternational.org) websites, both British organisations specialising in clearing landmines and UXO around the world. Cluster munitions were recently outlawed in a treaty signed by more than 100 countries, the usual suspects declining to sign: visit www.stopclustermunitions.org.

DISCOUNT CARDS

Senior Cards

There are no 'senior citizen' discounts for pensioners, as all foreigners who can afford to fly to Vietnam are considered affluent enough to pay in full.

Student & Youth Cards

Ditto for student cards. Carry one if you are travelling through the region, but it will gather dust in your wallet while you are in Vietnam.

EMBASSIES & CONSULATES

With the exception of those for Cambodia, China and Laos, Hanoi's embassies and HCMC's consulates do very little visa business for non-Vietnamese.

It's important to realise what your country's embassy can and can't do to help if you get into trouble. Generally speaking, it won't be much help if the trouble you're in is remotely your own fault. Remember that you are bound by the laws of the country you are in. Your embassy won't be sympathetic if you end up in jail after committing a crime, even if such actions are legal in your own country.

In genuine emergencies you might get some assistance, but only if other channels have been exhausted. If you have all your money and documents stolen, you might get some assistance with getting a new passport, but a loan for onward travel is out of the question.

The following are some of the embassies and consulates found in Vietnam.

Australia (www.ausinvn.com) Hanoi (Map pp84-5; ☎ 3831 7755; 8 Đ Dao Tan, Ba Dinh District); HCMC (Map p348; ☎ 3829 6035; 5th fl, 5B Đ Ton Duc Thang)
Cambodia Hanoi (Map pp88-9; ☎ 3942 4788; 71A P Tran Hung Dao); HCMC (Map p346; ☎ 3829 2751; 41 Đ Phung Khac Khoan)
Canada (www.dfait-maeci.gc.ca/vietnam) Hanoi (Map pp88-9; ☎ 3734 5000; 31 Đ Hung Vuong); HCMC (Map p348; ☎ 3854 5025; 10th fl, 235 Đ Dong Khoi)
China Hanoi (Map pp88-9; ☎ 8845 3736; 46 P Hoang Dieu); HCMC (Map p346; ☎ 3829 2457; 39 Đ Nguyen Thi Minh Khai)
France Hanoi (Map pp88-9; ☎ 3943 7719; P Tran Hung Dao); HCMC (Map p346; ☎ 3829 7231; 27 Đ Nguyen Thi Minh Khai)
Germany Hanoi (Map pp88-9; ☎ 3845 3836; 29 Đ Tran Phu); HCMC (Map p346; ☎ 3829 1967; 126 Đ Nguyen Dinh Chieu)
Japan Hanoi (Map pp84-5; ☎ 3846 3000; 27 Pho Lieu Giai, Ba Dinh District); HCMC (Map p348; ☎ 3822 5341; 13-17 ĐL Nguyen Hue)
Laos Danang (Map p236; 16 Đ Tran Qui Cap); Hanoi (Map pp88-9; ☎ 3942 4576; 22 P Tran Binh Trong); HCMC (Map p348; ☎ 3829 7667; 93 Đ Pasteur)
Netherlands HCMC (Map p346; ☎ 3823 5932; 29 ĐL Le Duan)
New Zealand Hanoi (Map p92; ☎ 3824 1481; nzembhan@fpt.vn; Level 5, 63 P Ly Thai To); HCMC (Map p348; ☎ 3822 6907; 41 Đ Nguyen Thi Minh Khai)
Philippines Hanoi (Map pp88-9; ☎ 3943 7948; 27B P Tran Hung Dao)
Singapore Hanoi (Map pp88-9; ☎ 3823 3965; 41-43 Đ Tran Phu)
Sweden Hanoi (Map pp84-5; ☎ 3726 0400; 2 Đ Nui Truc)
Thailand Hanoi (Map pp88-9; ☎ 3823 5092; 63-65 P Hoang Dieu); HCMC (Map p346; ☎ 3932 7637; 77 Đ Tran Quoc Thao)
UK (www.uk-vietnam.org) Hanoi (Map p92; ☎ 3936 0500; Central Bldg, 31 Pho Hai Ba Trung); HCMC (Map p346; ☎ 3829 8433; 25 ĐL Le Duan)
USA (http://usembassy.state.gov/vietnam) Hanoi (Map pp84-5; ☎ 3772 1500; 7 P Lang Ha, Ba Dinh District); HCMC (Map p346; ☎ 3822 9433; 4 ĐL Le Duan)

FESTIVALS & EVENTS

Major religious festivals in Vietnam have lunar dates; check against any Vietnamese calendar for the Gregorian dates. If you know when Tet kicks off, simply count from there.

Special prayers are held at Vietnamese and Chinese pagodas when the moon is full or a thin sliver. Many Buddhists eat only vegetarian food on these days, which, according to the Chinese lunar calendar, fall on the 14th and 15th days of the month and from the last day of the month to the first day of the next month.

Tet (Tet Nguyen Dan) The Big One! The Vietnamese Lunar New Year is Christmas, New Year and birthdays all rolled into one. Lasting from the first to seventh days of the first moon, the Tet Festival falls in late January or early February. See p54 for more on Tet. Travel is difficult at this time, as transport is booked up and many businesses closed.
Holiday of the Dead (Thanh Minh) It's time to honour the ancestors with a visit to graves of deceased relatives. Fifth day of the third moon.
Buddha's Birth, Enlightenment and Death A big celebration at Buddhist temples and pagodas with lively processions. Eighth day of the fourth moon.
Summer Solstice Day (Tiet Doan Ngo) Keep the epidemics at bay with offerings to the spirits, ghosts and the God of Death. Fifth day of the fifth moon.

Wandering Souls Day (Trung Nguyen) Second in the pecking order to Tet; offerings are made for the wandering souls of the forgotten dead. Fifteenth day of the seventh moon.
Mid-Autumn Festival (Trung Thu) A fine time for foodies with moon cakes of sticky rice filled with lotus seeds, watermelon seeds, peanuts, the yolks of duck eggs, raisins and other treats. Fifteenth day of the eighth moon.
Confucius' Birthday Happy birthday to China's leading philosophical export. Twenty-eighth day of the ninth moon.
Christmas Day (Giang Sinh) Needs no introduction; this is not a national holiday, but is celebrated throughout Vietnam, particularly by the sizeable Catholic population.

FOOD

Vietnamese cuisine has become a favourite throughout the Western world and a journey through Vietnam is a gastronomic treat. For the full story on Vietnamese cuisine, see p61.

GAY & LESBIAN TRAVELLERS

Vietnam is a relatively hassle-free place for homosexuals. There are no official laws on same-sex relationships in Vietnam, nor much in the way of individual harassment.

That said, the government is notorious for clamping down on gay venues, and places that are covered in the mass media are 'coincidentally' closed down days later. Most gay venues keep a fairly low profile. There are, however, healthy gay scenes in Hanoi and HCMC, evidenced by unabashed cruising around certain lakes in Hanoi (p115) and the thriving cafe scene in HCMC (p381).

Homosexuality is still far from accepted in the wider community, though the lack of any laws keeps things fairly safe. Major headlines were made in 1997 with Vietnam's first gay marriage, and again in 1998 at the country's first lesbian wedding, in the Mekong Delta. However, displaying peculiar double standards, two weeks later government officials broke up the marriage of the women and the couple signed an agreement promising not to live together again.

With the vast number of same-sex travel partners – gay or otherwise – checking into hotels throughout Vietnam, there is little scrutiny over how travelling foreigners are related. However, it would be prudent not to flaunt your sexuality. As with heterosexual couples, passionate public displays of affection are considered a basic no-no.

Utopia (www.utopia-asia.com) features gay travel information and contacts, including detailed sections on the legality of homosexuality in Vietnam and some local gay terminology.

HOLIDAYS

Politics affects everything, including public holidays. After a 15-year lapse, religious holidays were re-established in 1990. The following are public holidays in Vietnam:
New Year's Day (Tet Duong Lich) 1 January
Anniversary of the Founding of the Vietnamese Communist Party (Thanh Lap Dang CSVN) 3 February – the date the party was founded in 1930.
Liberation Day (Saigon Giai Phong) 30 April – the date on which Saigon's surrender is commemorated nationwide as Liberation Day.
International Workers' Day (Quoc Te Lao Dong) 1 May
Ho Chi Minh's Birthday (Sinh Nhat Bac Ho) 19 May
Buddha's Birthday (Phat Dan) Eighth day of the fourth moon (usually June).
National Day (Quoc Khanh) 2 September – commemorates the Declaration of Independence by Ho Chi Minh in 1945.

INSURANCE

Insurance is a *must* for Vietnam, as the cost of major medical treatment is prohibitive. Although you may have medical insurance in your own country, it is probably not valid while you are in Vietnam. A travel insurance policy to cover theft, loss and medical problems is the best bet.

There is a wide variety of policies available, so check the small print. Some insurance policies specifically exclude such 'dangerous activities' as riding motorbikes, diving and even trekking. Check that the policy covers an emergency evacuation in the event of serious injury.

INTERNET ACCESS

The internet is widely available throughout towns and cities in Vietnam. There is everything from trendy cybercafes to computer terminals in the lobbies of hotels and guesthouses, plus public internet access in many Vietnamese post offices. Many of the budget and midrange hotels in major cities offer free internet in the lobby. Midrange and some top-end places offer free access in the room for those travelling with a laptop.

The cost of internet access generally ranges from 3000d to 10,000d per hour, depending on where you are and what the competition is like. Printing usually costs around 1000d per page and scanning about 2000d a page.

Wi-fi access is spreading fast. Hanoi, HCMC and other big towns have plenty of cafes and bars offering free access. However, be careful when signing up to unsecure networks in busy places, as you don't know who is viewing your computer. Many of the leading hotels also offer wi-fi, but in keeping with the five-star tradition, it is not a free service.

Remember that the power-supply voltage will vary from that at home. The best investment is a universal AC adapter, which will enable you to plug it in anywhere without frying the innards of your equipment. For more information on travelling with a portable computer, see www.teleadapt.com.

LAUNDRY

It is easy to get your laundry done at guesthouses and cheaper hotels for just a few US dollars. There have, however, been a number of reports of gross overcharging at certain hotels, so make sure you check the price beforehand.

Budget hotels do not have clothes dryers, as they rely on the sunshine – so allow at least a day and a half for washing and drying, especially during the wet season. You can also elect to wash your own clothes as washing powder is cheap and readily available.

LEGAL MATTERS

Civil Law

On paper it looks good, but in practice the rule of law in Vietnam is a fickle beast. Local officials interpret the law any way it suits them, often against the wishes of Hanoi. There is no independent judiciary. Not surprisingly, most legal disputes are settled out of court.

Drugs

The drug trade has made a comeback in Vietnam with plentiful supplies making it overland along the porous Lao border. The country has a very serious problem with heroin these days and the authorities are clamping down hard. Life sentences or the death penalty are liberally handed out.

Marijuana and, in the northwest, opium are readily available, but giving in to this temptation is a risk. There are many plain-clothes police in Vietnam and, if you're arrested, the result might be a large fine and/or a long prison term.

Police

Vietnamese police are the best that money can buy. Police corruption is an everyday reality and has been acknowledged in official newspapers. If something does go wrong, or if something is stolen, the police can't do much more than prepare an insurance report for a negotiable fee.

Hanoi has warned all provincial governments that any police caught shaking down foreign tourists will be fired and arrested. The crackdown has dented the enthusiasm of the police to confront foreigners directly with demands for bribes, but it still happens in more out-of-the-way places.

MAPS

Most bookshops in Vietnam stock a good range of maps. A must for its detailed road maps of every province is the *Viet Nam Administrative Atlas,* published by Ban Do. It is perfect for cyclists or motorbikers looking for roads less travelled and costs less than US$10 in hardback.

Ban Do also publishes reasonable tourist maps of HCMC, Hanoi, Danang, Hue and a few other cities. Unfortunately, maps of smaller towns are practically nonexistent. Most of the listings mags produced in Vietnam have city maps of Hanoi and HCMC, and there are some good hand-drawn 3D maps of Hanoi, Hue and Sapa available from Covit, a local publisher.

Vietnamese street names are preceded with the words Pho, Duong and Dai Lo – on the maps and in the text in this book, they appear respectively as P, Đ and ĐL.

MONEY

The first currency of Vietnam is the dong, which is abbreviated to 'd'. Banknotes come in denominations of 500d, 1000d, 2000d, 5000d, 10,000d, 20,000d, 50,000d, 100,000d, 200,000d and 500,000d. Now that Ho Chi Minh has been canonised (against his wishes), his picture is on *every* banknote. Coins are also in circulation, although they are more common in the cities, and include 500d, 1000d and 5000d. The second currency is the US dollar and that needs no introduction.

The dong has experienced its ups and downs. The late 1990s Asian economic crisis, which wreaked severe havoc on the regional currencies, caused the dong to lose about 15% of its US-dollar value. Since then the dong has stabilised at around 16,000d to 17,000d to the US dollar.

Where prices on the ground are quoted in dong, we quote them in this book in dong. Likewise, when prices are quoted in dollars, we follow suit. While this may seem inconsistent, this is the way it's done in Vietnam and the sooner you get used to thinking comparatively in dong and dollars, the easier your travels will be.

For a smattering of exchange rates at the time of going to print, see the inside front cover of this book.

ATMs

It used to be just a couple of foreign banks in Hanoi and HCMC that offered ATMs, but Vietnamese banks have now got into this game in a big way. Vietcombank has the best network in the country, including most of the major tourist destinations and all the big cities. Agribank, Vietin Bank and Sacombank are also well represented. Every branch stocks a useful leaflet with a list of their nationwide ATMs. Withdrawals are issued in dong, and there is a single withdrawal limit of 2,000,000d (about US$125). However, you can do multiple withdrawals until you hit your own account limit. ANZ offers 4,000,000d withdrawals per transaction. Most banks charge 20,000d per transaction. Cash advances for larger amounts of dong, as well as US dollars, can be arranged over the counter during office hours.

Bargaining

Some bargaining is essential in most tourist transactions. Remember that in Asia 'saving face' is important, so bargaining should be good-natured. Smile and don't get angry or argue. In some cases you will be able to get a 50% discount or more, at other times this may only be 10%. And once the money is accepted, the deal is done. Don't waste time getting stressed if you find out someone else got it for less; it is about paying the price that is right for you, not always the local price.

Black Market

The black market operates quite openly. Private individuals and some shops and restaurants will exchange US dollars for dong and vice versa. While the practice is technically illegal, law enforcement is virtually nonexistent. Ironically, black market exchange rates are usually *worse* than the official exchange rates, so the only advantage is the convenience of changing money when and where you like.

If people approach you on the street with offers to change money at rates better than the official one, you can rest assured that you are being set up for a rip-off. Fake notes or too few notes, they will get you somehow. Remember, if an offer seems too good to be true, that's because it probably is.

Cash

Most major currencies can be exchanged at leading banks in Vietnam, but away from the tourist centres the US-dollar remains king. Vietcombank is the most organised of the local banks for changing cash and can deal with euros, pounds and pretty much anything else you are packing. The US dollar exchange rate worsens the further you get from the tourist trail, so stock up on dong if you are heading into remote areas. In small towns it can be difficult to get change for the larger notes, so keep a stack of smaller bills handy. Changing US$100 will make you an instant millionaire.

It's a good idea to check that any big dollar bills you take do not have any small tears or look too tatty, as no-one will accept them in Vietnam.

You cannot legally take dong out of Vietnam but you can reconvert reasonable amounts of it into US dollars on departure.

Most land border crossings now have some sort of official currency exchange, offering the best rates available in these remote parts of the country.

Credit Cards

Visa, MasterCard and JCB cards are now widely accepted in all major cities and many tourist centres. However, a 3% commission charge on every transaction is pretty common; check first, as some charge higher commissions than others. Some merchants also accept Amex, but the surcharge is typically 4%. Better hotels and restaurants do not usually slap on an additional charge.

If you wish to obtain a cash advance from Visa, MasterCard and JCB, this is possible at Vietcombank branches in most cities, as well as at some foreign banks in HCMC and Hanoi. Banks generally charge a 3% commission for this service. This is handy if you want to take out large sums, as the ATMs have low daily limits.

Tipping

Tipping is not expected in Vietnam, but it is enormously appreciated. For a person who earns US$100 per month, a US$1 tip is significant. Upmarket hotels and some restaurants may levy a 5% service charge, but this may not make it to the staff. If you stay a couple of days in the same hotel, try and remember to tip the staff who clean your room.

You should also consider tipping drivers and guides – after all, the time they spend on the road with you means time away from home and family. Typically, travellers on minibus tours will pool together to collect a communal tip to be split between the guide and driver.

It is considered proper to make a small donation at the end of a visit to a pagoda, especially if a monk has shown you around; most pagodas have contribution boxes for this purpose.

Travellers Cheques

It is wise not to rely entirely on travellers cheques by keeping a reasonable stash of US dollars to hand. Travellers cheques can only be exchanged at authorised foreign-exchange banks, but these aren't found throughout Vietnam.

If you only have travellers cheques, stock up on US dollars at a bank, which will usually charge anywhere from 0.5% to 2% commission to change them into cash. Vietcombank charges no commission for exchanging Amex travellers cheques; a reasonable 0.5% for other types.

If your travellers cheques are in currencies other than US dollars, they may be useless beyond the major cities. Hefty commissions are the norm if they can be exchanged at all.

PHOTOGRAPHY

Memory cards are pretty cheap in Vietnam, which is fortunate given the visual feast awaiting even the amateur photographer. Most internet cafes can also burn photos on to a CD or DVD to free up storage space. It's worthwhile bringing the attachment for viewing your files on the big screen, as many hotels come equipped with televisions.

Colour print film is widely available and prices are pretty reasonable at about US$2.50 for a roll of 36 print film. Slide film can be bought in Hanoi and HCMC, but don't count on it elsewhere. Supplies of black-and-white film are rapidly disappearing, so bring your own.

Photo-processing shops are located all over Vietnam and developing costs are about US$4 per roll depending on the print size selected. The quality is generally very good. Processing slide film is best saved for somewhere else. Printing digital shots is fairly cheap and works out at between 1000d and 2000d a photo.

Cameras are reasonably priced in Vietnam but the selection is limited. All other camera supplies are readily available in major towns, but soon dry up in remote areas.

The Vietnamese police usually don't care what you photograph, but on occasion they get pernickety. Obviously, don't photograph sensitive sites such as airports and border checkpoints. Don't even think of trying to get a snapshot of Ho Chi Minh in his glass sarcophagus!

Photographing anyone, particularly hill-tribe people, demands patience and the utmost respect for local customs. Photograph with discretion and manners. It's always polite to ask first and if the person says no, don't take the photo. If you promise to send a copy of the photo, make sure you do. For plenty of tips on better travel photography, pick up a copy of Lonely Planet's *Travel Photography.*

POST

Every city, town, village and rural subdistrict in Vietnam has some sort of post office *(buu dien)*. Post offices all over the country keep long hours, from about 6.30am to 9pm including weekends and public holidays (even Tet).

Vietnam has a quite reliable post service these days. Gone are the days of your stamps being steamed off and your postcards being delivered to the rubbish bin. International postal rates are similar to those in European countries. Postcards cost from 7000d to 10,000d depending on the destination.

Items mailed from anywhere other than large towns and cities might take a month to arrive at their international destination. Airmail service from HCMC and Hanoi takes approximately five to 10 days to get to most Western countries. Express-mail service (EMS), available in the larger cities, is twice as fast as regular airmail and everything is registered.

Private couriers such as FedEx, DHL and UPS are reliable for transporting small parcels or documents.

Poste restante works well in post offices in Hanoi and HCMC. Foreigners must pay a small service charge for each letter received through the poste restante. Receiving even a small package from abroad can cause a headache and large ones will produce a migraine. If the parcel contains books, documents, CDs, DVDs or dangerous goods it's possible that a lengthy inspection will be required, which could take weeks.

SHOPPING

Vietnam has some fantastic shopping opportunities so it is well worth setting aside half a day or more to properly peruse what's on offer. Hot spots include Hanoi, Hoi An and HCMC, each of which has a tempting selection of everything from avant-garde art to sumptuous silk suits. Some of the best buys on the block include gorgeous glazed pottery, classic lanterns, 'almost' antiques, embroidered tablecloths, fine furnishings, and lavish silk and linen creations in designer boutiques.

Art & Antiques

There are several good shops where you can hunt for art and antiques, but Vietnam has strict regulations on the export of real antiques, so be sure the items are allowed out of the country. Most reputable shops can provide the necessary paperwork.

Both traditional and modern paintings are popular items. Cheaper mass-produced stuff is touted in souvenir shops and by street vendors. More sophisticated works are displayed in art galleries, with paintings from US$50 to US$500, but some of the hottest Vietnamese artists now fetch up to 10 times that. It's important to know that there are forgeries around – just because you spot a painting by a 'famous Vietnamese artist' does not mean that it's an original. If you are planning on a serious investment, then it is best to deal with a reputable gallery.

A Vietnamese speciality is the 'instant antique', such as a teapot or ceramic dinner plate, with a price tag of around US$2. Of course, it's OK to buy fake antiques as long as you aren't paying genuine prices.

Clothing

Forget the rubber sandals and pith helmets, Vietnam is emerging as a regional design centre and there are some extravagant creations in the boutiques of Hanoi and HCMC. Beautiful silk dresses cost a fraction of what they would at home, and men can get in on the action with some flamboyant shirts or sharp suits.

Ao dai (*ow*-zai in the north, *ow*-yai in the south) is the national dress for Vietnamese women and is a popular item to take home. Ready-made *ao dai* cost from US$15 to US$30, but custom-made numbers can cost a lot more and may be necessary due to size differences. There are *ao dai* tailors nationwide, but those in the tourist centres are more familiar with foreigners.

These days more and more hill-tribe gear is finding its way to shops in Hanoi and HCMC. It is brightly patterned stuff, but you may need to set the dyes yourself (try soaking the clothes in some salty water overnight) so those colours don't bleed all over the rest of your clothes. Alternatively, put it in a plastic bag and wait until you get home.

Women all over the country wear conical hats to keep the sun off their faces, though they also function as umbrellas in the rain. The best-quality conical hats are produced in the Hue area.

T-shirts are ever popular items with travellers. A printed shirt starts from 20,000d while an embroidered design will cost about 50,000d.

Handicrafts

Hot items on the tourist market include lacquerware, boxes and wooden screens with mother-of-pearl inlay, ceramics, colourful embroidery, silk greeting cards, wood-block prints, oil paintings, watercolours, blinds made of hanging bamboo beads, reed mats, carpets, jewellery and leatherwork.

War Souvenirs

In places frequented by tourists, it's easy to buy what looks like equipment left over from the American War. However, almost all of these items are reproductions and your chances of finding anything original are slim.

The fake Zippo lighters engraved with platoon philosophy are still one of the hottest-selling items. You can pay extra to get one that's been beaten up to look like a war relic, or just buy a brand-new shiny one for less.

TELEPHONE & FAX

For the all-important numbers like emergency services and the international access code, check out the Quick Reference section on the inside cover of this book.

Every city has a **general information service** (☎ 1080) that provides everything from phone numbers and train and air timetables to exchange rates and the latest football scores. It even provides marriage counselling or bedtime lullabies for your child – no kidding! You can usually be connected to an operator who speaks English or French.

Fax

Most post offices and hotels offer fax services. Hotels charge considerably more than the post office.

International Calls

Charges for international calls from Vietnam have dropped significantly in the past few years. With the introduction of Voice Over Internet Protocol (VOIP), international phone calls to most countries cost a flat rate of just US$0.50 per minute. The service is easy to use from any phone in the country; just dial ☎ 17100, the country code and the number.

International and domestic long-distance calls can be made at hotels, but it's expensive at the smarter places. However, many of the cheaper hotels and guesthouses now operate VOIP services that are very cheap. Another option is to make these calls from post offices, which have handy displays telling you the cost of the call.

Using services such as Skype can save considerable money or you can hook up with a fellow Skype user for free. Most internet cafes also provide webcams, so you can see family and friends while catching up on the gossip.

Reverse charges or collect calls are possible to most, but not all, Western countries including Australia, Canada, France, Japan, New Zealand, the UK and the USA.

Local Calls

Phone numbers in Hanoi, HCMC and Haiphong have eight digits. Elsewhere around the country phone numbers have seven digits. Telephone area codes are assigned according to the province.

Local calls can usually be made from any hotel or restaurant phone and are often free. Confirm this with the hotel so you don't receive any unpleasant surprises when you check out. Domestic long-distance calls are reasonably priced and cheaper if you dial direct. Save up to 20% by calling between 10pm and 5am.

Mobile (Cellular) Phones

Vietnam is putting a lot of money into its cellular network. Vietnam uses GSM 900/1800, which is compatible with most of Asia, Europe and Australia but not with North America.

If your phone has roaming, it is easy enough, although reasonably expensive, to make calls in Vietnam. Another option is to buy a SIM card with a local number to use in Vietnam.

There are at least half a dozen mobile phone companies battling it out in the local market with gimmicks galore to attract new customers. All these companies have offices and branches nationwide.

TIME

Vietnam is seven hours ahead of Greenwich Mean Time/Universal Time Coordinated (GMT/UTC). Because of its proximity to the equator, Vietnam does not have daylight-saving or summer time. When it's noon in Vietnam it is 9pm the previous day in Vancouver, midnight in New York, 5am in London and 3pm in Sydney.

TOILETS

The issue of toilets and what to do with used toilet paper causes some confusion. In general, if there's a wastepaper basket next to the toilet, that is where the toilet paper goes, as many sewage systems cannot handle toilet paper.

Toilet paper is seldom provided in the toilets at bus and train stations or in other public buildings. You'd be wise to keep a stash of your own with you at all times while on the move.

Another thing to be mentally prepared for is squat toilets. For the uninitiated, a squat toilet has no seat for you to sit on while reading this guidebook; it's a hole in the floor. The only way to flush it is to fill the conveniently placed bucket with water and pour it into the hole. Most hotels will have Western-style loos, but squats are the norm in older hotels and public places.

The scarcity of public toilets is more of a problem for women than for men. Vietnamese men often urinate in public. Women might find roadside toilet stops easier if wearing a sarong.

TOURIST INFORMATION

Tourist offices in Vietnam have a different philosophy from the majority of tourist offices worldwide. These government-owned enterprises are really travel agencies whose primary interests are booking tours and turning a profit. Don't come here hoping for freebies.

Vietnam Tourism and Saigon Tourist are old examples of this genre, but nowadays every province has at least one such organisation. Travel cafes, budget agencies and your fellow travellers are a much better source of information than any of the so-called 'tourist offices'.

There are now privately operated, though fairly helpful, tourist offices in Hanoi and Ho Chi Minh City.

TRAVELLERS WITH DISABILITIES

Vietnam is not the easiest of places for travellers with disabilities, despite the fact that many Vietnamese are disabled as a result of war injuries. Tactical problems include the chaotic traffic, a lack of pedestrian footpaths, a lack of lifts in smaller hotels and the ubiquitous squat toilets.

That said, with some careful planning it is possible to have a relatively stress-free trip to Vietnam. Find a reliable company to make the travel arrangements and don't be afraid to double-check things with hotels and restaurants yourself. In the major cities many hotels have lifts and disabled access is improving. Bus and train travel is not really geared for disabled travellers, but rent a private vehicle with a driver and almost anywhere becomes instantly accessible. As long as you are not too proud about how you get in and out of a boat or up some stairs, anything is possible, as the Vietnamese are always willing to help.

You might try contacting the following organisations:

Accessible Journeys (☎ 610-521 0339; www.disabilitytravel.com)
Mobility International USA (☎ 54-1343 1284; www.miusa.org)
Royal Association for Disability and Rehabilitation (Radar; ☎ 020-7250 3222; www.radar.org.uk)
Society for Accessible Travel & Hospitality (SATH; ☎ 212-447 7284; www.sath.org)

Lonely Planet's **Thorn Tree** (www.lonelyplanet.com) is a good place to seek the advice of other travellers.

VISAS

Tourist visas allow visitors to enter and exit Vietnam at Hanoi, HCMC and Danang airports or at any of its plentiful land borders, shared with Cambodia, China and Laos.

Tourist visas are valid for a single 30-day stay. The government often talks about issuing visas on arrival to certain favoured nationalities, but as yet this sensible scheme has failed to materialise beyond the immediate Asean neighbours. Arranging the paperwork for a Vietnamese visa has become fairly straightforward, but it remains expensive and unnecessarily time-consuming. Processing a tourist-visa application typically takes four or five working days in countries in the West.

It is possible to arrange a visa on arrival through a Vietnamese travel agent. They will need passport details in advance and will send a confirmation for the visa to be issued at your airport of arrival.

In Asia the best place to pick up a Vietnamese visa is Cambodia, where it costs around US$30 and can be arranged the same day. Bangkok is also a popular place as many agents offer cheap packages with an air ticket and visa thrown in.

If you plan to spend more than a month in Vietnam, or if you plan to exit Vietnam and enter again from Cambodia or Laos, arrange a three-month multiple-entry visa. These cost around US$95 in Cambodia, but are not available from all Vietnamese embassies.

In our experience personal appearance influences the reception you receive from airport immigration – if you wear shorts or scruffy clothing, or look dirty or unshaven, you can expect problems. Try your best to look 'respectable'.

Business Visas

Business visas are usually valid for three or six months, and allow multiple entries and the right to work. Getting a business visa has now become cheap and easy, although prices are about double those of a tourist visa. It is generally easier to apply for a business visa once in Vietnam, after having arrived on a tourist visa. Or pick one up in Cambodia.

Re-Entry Visas

It's possible to enter Cambodia or Laos from Vietnam and then re-enter without having to apply for another visa. However, you must apply for a re-entry visa *before* you leave Vietnam. If you do not have a re-entry visa, you will have to go through the whole visa process again.

Re-entry visas are easiest to arrange in Hanoi or HCMC, but you will almost certainly have to ask a travel agent to do the paperwork for you. Travel agents charge about US$25 for this service and can complete the procedure in a day or two.

Student Visas

A student visa is usually arranged after your arrival. It's acceptable to enter Vietnam on a tourist visa, enrol in a Vietnamese language course and then apply at the immigration police for a change in status. In reality, the easiest way to do it is to contact a travel company and have them help you make the application.

Visa Extensions

If you've got the dollars, they've got the rubber stamp. Tourist-visa extensions officially cost as little as US$10, but it is easier to pay more and sort this out through a travel agency. Getting the stamp yourself can be a bureaucratic nightmare. The procedure takes two or three days and you can only extend one time for 30 days.

In theory you should be able to extend your visa in any provincial capital. In practice it goes smoothest in major cities, such as HCMC, Hanoi, Danang and Hue, which cater to regular visitors.

VOLUNTEERING

There are fewer opportunities for volunteering than one might imagine in a country such as Vietnam. This is partly due to the sheer number of professional development workers based here, and the fact that development is a pretty lucrative industry these days.

For information on volunteer work opportunities, chase up the full list of nongovernment organisations (NGOs) at the **NGO Resource Centre** (☎ 04-3832 8570; www.ngocentre.org.vn; Hotel La Thanh, 218 Pho Doi Can, Hanoi), which keeps a database of all of the NGOs assisting Vietnam. Check out the website of Service Civil International for some specific options in Vietnam, including the SOS Village in Viet Tri, north of Hanoi, and the **Friendship Village** (www.vietnamfriendship.org), established by veterans from both sides to help victims of Agent Orange.

Or try contacting the following organisations if you want to help in some way:

15 May School (www.15mayschool.org) A school in HCMC for disadvantaged children, which provides free education and vocational training.

Street Voices (www.streetvoices.com.au) Donate your skills, time or money to help give street children career opportunities. Street Voices' primary project is KOTO Restaurant (p109); check its website to see what you can do to help in Vietnam or Australia.

The other avenue is professional volunteering through an organisation back home that offers one- or two-year placements in Vietnam. One of the largest is **Voluntary Service Overseas** (VSO; www.vso.org.uk) in the UK, but other countries have their own organisations, including **Australian Volunteers International** (AVI; www.australianvolunteers.com) and **Volunteer Service Abroad** (VSA; www.vsa.org.nz). The UN also operates its own volunteer program; details are available at www.unv.org. Other general volunteer sites with links all over the place include www.worldvolunteerweb.com, www.volunteerabroad.com and www.idea list.org.

WOMEN TRAVELLERS

Like Thailand and other predominantly Buddhist countries, Vietnam is relatively free of serious hassles for Western women. But it is a different story for some Asian women, particularly those who are young. It's not uncommon for an Asian woman accompanied by a Western male to be stereotyped as a Vietnamese prostitute. The fact that the couple could be married, or friends, doesn't seem to occur to everyone, or that the woman may not be Vietnamese at all. Asian women travelling in Vietnam with a Western male companion have occasionally been on the receiving end of verbal abuse.

However, there's no need to be overly paranoid. Things have improved as more Vietnamese people are exposed to foreign visitors.

Sanitary napkins are available in larger cities, though tampons are harder to find.

WORK

As Vietnam has taken its place on the global stage, all sorts of work opportunities for Westerners have opened up. Generally speaking, the best-paid Westerners living in Vietnam are those working for international organisations or foreign companies, but many of these jobs are secured before arrival in the country.

Foreigners who look like Rambo have occasionally been approached by Vietnamese talent scouts wanting to recruit them to work as extras in war movies, but for most travellers the main work opportunities are teaching a foreign language.

English is by far the most popular foreign language with Vietnamese students, but some students also want to learn French. There is also a limited demand for teachers of Japanese, German, Spanish and Korean.

Government-run universities in Vietnam hire some foreign teachers. Pay is generally around US$5 to US$10 per hour, but benefits such as free housing and unlimited visa renewals are usually thrown in.

There is also a budding free market in private language centres and home tutoring; this is where most newly arrived foreigners seek work. Pay in the private sector is slightly better, at about US$8 to US$15 per hour, but these private schools won't offer the same extras as a government-run school. Private tutoring usually pays even better, at around US$10 to US$25 per hour.

Finding teaching jobs is quite easy in places such as HCMC and Hanoi, and is sometimes possible in towns that have universities. Pay in the smaller towns tends to be lower and work opportunities fewer.

Looking for employment is a matter of asking around – jobs are rarely advertised. The longer you stay, the easier it is to find work – travellers hoping to land a quick job and depart two months later will be disappointed. Check out the website www.livinginvietnam.com for job opportunities.

Transport

CONTENTS

GETTING THERE & AWAY

ENTERING VIETNAM

It's possible to enter Vietnam by train, plane, automobile and other forms of transport. Air is popular for those holidaying in Vietnam, while bus is the most common means of transport for those travelling extensively throughout the region. The train ride from Kunming in China's Yunnan province to Hanoi is spectacular, but the train is currently suspended on the Chinese side, necessitating a train–bus combination. Entering from Cambodia, the boat ride down the Mekong River from Phnom Penh to Chau Doc is also memorable.

Formalities at Vietnam's international airports are generally smoother than at land borders, as the volume of traffic is greater. That said, crossing overland from Cambodia and China is now relatively stress-free. Crossing the border between Vietnam and Laos remains somewhat trying.

Passport

There are no 'suspect' stamps that will prevent foreigners from visiting Vietnam, but some Vietnamese who live overseas may be given a harder time by immigration and customs than non-Vietnamese visitors. Arranging a visa remains essential before arrival in Vietnam, but these can be obtained from embassies worldwide or through Vietnamese travel agents in advance (see p506). Most ASEAN visitors no longer need a visa to visit, but contrary to persistent rumours, all other nationalities need a visa for the time being.

AIR

Airports & Airlines

There are three international airports in Vietnam. **Tan Son Nhat airport** (SGN; ☎ 08-3845 6654) serves Ho Chi Minh City (HCMC) and is Vietnam's busiest international air hub. Hanoi's **Noi Bai airport** (HAN; ☎ 04-3827 1513) is the destination of choice for those concentrating on northern Vietnam, while a handful of international flights also serve **Danang airport** (DAD; ☎ 051-1383 0339), a useful gateway to the charms of central Vietnam. There are also plans to upgrade Nha Trang (Cam Ranh) and Phu Quoc airports to international gateways.

Vietnam Airlines (www.vietnamairlines.com.vn) Hanoi (☎ 04-3832 0320); HCMC (☎ 08-3832 0320) is the state-owned flag carrier, and the majority of flights into and out of Vietnam are joint operations between Vietnam Airlines and foreign operators.

Vietnam Airlines has a modern fleet of Airbuses and Boeings and the level of service on its international flights is starting to catch up with its larger rivals. However, on the domestic front, cancellations and late flights are still possible.

Many international flights leaving Hanoi connect through HCMC, but it's a

> **THINGS CHANGE...**
>
> The information in this chapter is particularly vulnerable to change. Check directly with the airline or a travel agent to make sure you understand how a fare (and ticket you may buy) works and be aware of the security requirements for international travel. Shop carefully. The details given in this chapter should be regarded as pointers and are not a substitute for your own careful, up-to-date research.

CLIMATE CHANGE & TRAVEL

Climate change is a serious threat to the ecosystems that humans rely upon, and air travel is the fastest-growing contributor to the problem. Lonely Planet regards travel, overall, as a global benefit, but believes we all have a responsibility to limit our personal impact on global warming.

Flying & Climate Change

Pretty much every form of motor travel generates CO_2 (the main cause of human-induced climate change) but planes are far and away the worst offenders, not just because of the sheer distances they allow us to travel, but because they release greenhouse gases high into the atmosphere. The statistics are frightening: two people taking a return flight between Europe and the US will contribute as much to climate change as an average household's gas and electricity consumption over a whole year.

Carbon Offset Schemes

Climatecare.org and other websites use 'carbon calculators' that allow jetsetters to offset the greenhouse gases they are responsible for with contributions to energy-saving projects and other climate-friendly initiatives in the developing world – including projects in India, Honduras, Kazakhstan and Uganda.

Lonely Planet, together with Rough Guides and other concerned partners in the travel industry, supports the carbon offset scheme run by climatecare.org. Lonely Planet offsets all of its staff and author travel.

For more information check out our website: lonelyplanet.com.

headache. Passengers have to claim their bags and check in again before boarding the international flight.

AIRLINES FLYING TO & FROM VIETNAM

All phone numbers are in Hanoi (area code 04) unless otherwise stated.

Aeroflot (airline code SU; ☎ 3771 8742; www.aeroflot.com)
Air Asia (airline code AK; ☎ 3928 8282; www.airasia.com)
Air France (airline code AF; ☎ 3825 3484; www.airfrance.fr)
Asiana Airlines (airline code OZ; ☎ 3831 5141; www.us.flyasiana.com)
Cathay Pacific (airline code CX; ☎ 3826 7298; www.cathaypacific.com)
China Airlines (airline code CI; ☎ 3824 2688; www.china-airlines.com)
China Eastern Airlines (airline code MU; ☎ 3883 4618; www.flychinaeastern.com)
China Southern Airlines (airline code CZ; ☎ 3771 6611; www.cs-air.com)
Eva Air (airline code BR; ☎ 3936 1500; www.evaair.com)
Japan Airlines (airline code JL; ☎ 3826 6693; www.jal.co.jp)
Jetstar Pacific (airline code 3K; www.jetstar.com/vn)
Korean Air (airline code KE; ☎ in HCMC 08-3824 2878; www.koreanair.com)
Lao Airlines (airline code QV; ☎ 3822 9951; www.laoairlines.com)
Lufthansa (airline code LH; ☎ in HCMC 08-3829 8529; www.lufthansa.com)
Malaysia Airlines (airline code MY; ☎ 3826 8820; www.malaysiaairlines.com)
Philippine Airlines (airline code PR; ☎ in HCMC 08-3822 2241; www.philippineair.com)
Qantas (airline code QF; ☎ 3933 3025; www.qantas.com.au)
Shanghai Airlines (airline code FM; ☎ in HCMC 3930 8888; www.shanghai-air.com)
Singapore Airlines (airline code SQ; ☎ 3826 8888; www.singaporeair.com)
Thai Airways (airline code TG; ☎ 3826 6893; www.thaiair.com)
Tiger Airways (airline code TR; ☎ 3824 5868; www.tigerairways.com)
United Airlines (airline code UA; ☎ in HCMC 08-3823 1833; www.unitedairlines.com)

Tickets

Shop around and it is possible to find a good deal to Vietnam. If there are no obvious bargains to Hanoi or HCMC, then consider buying a discounted ticket to Bangkok or Hong Kong and picking up a flight or travelling overland on to Vietnam.

It's hard to get reservations for flights to/from Vietnam during holidays, especially Tet, which falls between late January and mid-February. If you will be in Vietnam during Tet, make reservations well in advance or you may find yourself marooned in a regional airport along the way. The chaos begins a week before Tet and can last for about two weeks after it.

Be aware that Vietnam is not the only country to celebrate the Lunar New Year, as it falls at the same time as Chinese New Year. Many people hit the road at this time, resulting in overbooked airlines, trains and hotels all over Asia.

Asia

Although many Asian countries now offer competitive deals, Bangkok, Singapore and Hong Kong are still the best places to shop around for discount tickets.

CAMBODIA

Vietnam Airlines currently has a monopoly on the Phnom Penh to HCMC route, with several flights a day. There are no direct flights from Phnom Penh to Hanoi, only via HCMC or Vientiane. Vietnam Airlines also offers numerous services daily between Siem Reap and HCMC and a couple of more expensive flights direct to Hanoi. Jetstar Pacific plans to launch services to both Phnom Penh and Siem Reap from HCMC.

CHINA

Vietnam Airlines now offers links from Hanoi to several major cities in China, including Beijing, Guangzhou, Kunming and Shanghai. These routes are shared with Air China, China Southern Airlines, China Eastern Airlines and Shanghai Airlines, respectively. The only direct flights between HCMC and mainland China are to Beijing and Guangzhou.

HONG KONG

Vietnam Airlines and Cathay Pacific jointly operate daily services between Hong Kong and both Hanoi and HCMC. The open-jaw option is a popular deal, allowing you to fly into one and out of the other.

JAPAN

ANA, Japan Airlines and Vietnam Airlines connect Hanoi and HCMC with Osaka and Tokyo. There are also less frequent services to Nagoya and Sapporo.

LAOS

Both Lao Airlines and Vietnam Airlines operate daily flights between Vientiane and Hanoi or HCMC (usually via Phnom Penh). There are also regular flights between Luang Prabang and Hanoi every week.

MALAYSIA

Malaysia Airlines and Vietnam Airlines have daily connections between Kuala Lumpur and both Hanoi and HCMC, but Air Asia is gaining favour thanks to discounted fares.

SINGAPORE

Singapore Airlines and Vietnam Airlines have daily flights from Singapore to both Hanoi and HCMC. Jetstar and Tiger Airways are cheaper budget carriers and e-tickets can be booked via their websites.

SOUTH KOREA

Asiana Airlines, Korean Air and Vietnam Airlines all fly the Seoul–HCMC route, so there's at least one flight offered per day. There are also several direct Seoul–Hanoi flights per week, plus services to Busan.

TAIWAN

Airlines connecting Hanoi and HCMC with Taipei or Kaohsiung include China Airlines, Eva Air and Vietnam Airlines.

THAILAND

Bangkok has traditionally been the most popular gateway to Vietnam. Air France, Thai Airways and Vietnam Airlines offer daily connections from Bangkok to Hanoi and HCMC. Air Asia is a cheaper option to both Hanoi and HCMC.

One popular choice is an open-jaw ticket that involves a flight to either HCMC or Hanoi, an overland journey to the other city, and a flight back to Bangkok.

Australia

Fares between Australia and Asia are relatively expensive considering the distances involved. Most of the cheaper flights between Australia and Vietnam involve stopovers at Kuala

> **DEPARTURE TAX**
>
> There is an international departure tax of US$14 from the main airports at Hanoi, HCMC and Danang. However this is now included in the ticket price so there is no need to pay in cash at the airport.

Lumpur, Bangkok or Singapore, but Qantas and Vietnam Airlines have services linking Brisbane, Melbourne, Perth and Sydney with either Hanoi or HCMC.

The following are good places to pick up tickets in Australia:

Flight Centre (☎ 133 133; www.flightcentre.com.au)
STA Travel (☎ 1300 733 035; www.statravel.com.au)

Canada

Discount tickets from Canada tend to cost a bit more than those sold in the USA. For the lowdown on cheap fares, contact **Travel Cuts** (☎ 800-667 2887; www.travelcuts.com), which has offices across the country.

Continental Europe

Although London is the discount-travel capital of Europe, major airlines and big travel agents usually have offers from all the major cities on the continent.

Recommended agents with branches across France:

Nouvelles Frontières (☎ 08 25 00 07 47; www.nouvelles-frontieres.fr)
Voyageurs du Monde (☎ 01 40 15 11 15; www.vdm.com)

Reliable agencies in Germany:

Just Travel (☎ 089-747 33 30; www.justtravel.de)
STA Travel (☎ 0180-545 64 22; www.statravel.de)

From other countries in Europe, try the following agencies in Italy, Netherlands and Spain.

Airfair (☎ 0206-20 51 21; www.airfair.nl; Netherlands)
Barcelo Viajes (☎ 902 11 62 26; www.barceloviajes.com; Spain)
CTS Viaggi (☎ 064 62 04 31; www.cts.it; Italy)
NBBS Reizen (☎ 0206-20 50 71; www.nbbs.nl; Netherlands)

New Zealand

The best way to get from New Zealand to Vietnam is to use one of the leading Asian carriers like Malaysian, Singapore or Thai. Good agencies to start shopping around for tickets:

Flight Centre (☎ 0800 243 544; www.flightcentre.co.nz)
STA Travel (☎ 0508 782 872; www.statravel.co.nz)

UK & Ireland

From London there are some great fares to Asia, although prices to Vietnam are not as cheap as to Bangkok or Hong Kong. There are oodles of agencies in the UK. Some of the best bets:

Flightbookers (☎ 087-0010 7000; www.ebookers.com)
North South Travel (☎ 012-4560 8291; www.northsouthtravel.co.uk) North South Travel donates part of its profit to projects in the developing world.
STA Travel (☎ 087-0160 0599; www.statravel.co.uk)
Trailfinders (☎ 084-5050 5891; www.trailfinders.co.uk)

USA

Discount travel agents in the USA are known as consolidators. San Francisco is the ticket-consolidator capital of America, although some good deals can be found in Los Angeles, New York and other big cities.

Useful online options in the USA:

- www.cheaptickets.com
- www.lowestfare.com
- www.sta.com
- www.travelocity.com

LAND

Vietnam shares land borders with Cambodia, China and Laos and there are plenty of border crossings open to foreigners with each neighbour: a big improvement on a decade ago. The downside is that it is still not possible to get a Vietnamese visa on arrival at any of these borders. See opposite for a snapshot view of things; the Vietnamese border name appears first.

Border Crossings

It is essential to have a Vietnamese visa before rocking up to the border, as they are not issued at land crossings. There are currently 17 or so international land borders: seven shared with Cambodia, seven with Laos and three with China. More may open during the lifetime of this book, so ask around in Hanoi or HCMC for the latest information. Border opening hours may vary slightly, but standard times when foreigners are allowed to cross are usually 7am to 5pm daily.

There are now legal money-changing facilities on the Vietnamese side of these border crossings, which can deal with US dollars and some other key currencies, including Chinese renminbi, Lao kip and Cambodian riel. Avoid black marketeers, as they have a well-deserved reputation for short-changing and outright theft.

Travellers at the border crossings are occasionally asked for an 'immigration fee' of some kind, although this is less common than

BORDER CROSSINGS

Country	Border Crossing	Connecting	Visa on Arrival
Cambodia	Moc Bai–Bavet	HCMC–Phnom Penh	Cambodia (Y)/Vietnam (N)
	Vinh Xuong–Kaam Samnor	Chau Doc–Phnom Penh	Cambodia (Y)/Vietnam (N)
	Xa Xia–Prek Chak	Ha Tien–Kep	Cambodia (Y)/Vietnam (N)
	Tinh Bien–Phnom Den	Chau Doc–Takeo	Cambodia (Y)/Vietnam (N)
	Le Tanh–O Yadaw	Pleiku–Ban Lung	Cambodia (Y)/Vietnam (N)
	Xa Mat–Trapaeng Thlong	Tay Ninh–Kompong Cham	Cambodia (Y)/Vietnam (N)
	Loc Ninh–Trapaeng Sre	Loc Ninh–Snuol	Cambodia (Y)/Vietnam (N)
China	Youyi Guan–Huu Nghi Quan (Friendship Gate)	Hanoi–Nanning	China (N)/Vietnam (N)
	Lao Cai–Hekou	Hanoi–Kunming	China (N)/Vietnam (N)
	Mong Cai–Dongxing	Mong Cai–Dongxing	China (N)/Vietnam (N)
Laos	Lao Bao–Dansavanh	Dong Ha–Savannakhet	Laos (Y)/Vietnam (N)
	Bo Y–Phou Keua	Pleiku–Attapeu	Laos (N)/Vietnam (N)
	Cha Lo–Na Phao	Dong Hoi–Tha Kaek	Laos (N)/Vietnam (N)
	Nam Can–Nong Haet	Vinh–Phonsavan	Laos (Y)/Vietnam (N)
	Cau Treo–Nam Phao	Vinh–Tha Kaek	Laos (Y)/Vietnam (N)
	Nam Xoi–Na Meo	Thanh Hoa–Xam Nua	Laos (N)/Vietnam (N)
	Tay Trang–Sop Hun	Dien Bien Phu–Muang Khua	Laos (Y)/Vietnam (N)

it used to be. We crossed at several remote border posts when researching this book, and were only asked for a 'health certificate' fee (US$1) at the Xa Xia border near Ha Tien.

CAMBODIA

Cambodia and Vietnam share a long frontier with a glut of border crossings. Cambodian visas are now available at all crossings. The Moc Bai–Bavet border (p391) is the traditional favourite for a cheap and quick way between HCMC and Phnom Penh. For those willing to take their time, it is much nicer to meander through the Mekong Delta and travel by river between Chau Doc and Phnom Penh. The new crossing at Xa Xia–Prek Chak is a great way to link the Cambodian coast with the Mekong Delta or Phu Quoc Island, while the Le Thanh–O Yadaw crossing (p341) looks set to be a popular way to link the central highlands of Vietnam with Cambodia's remote northeast. One-month Cambodian visas are issued on arrival at all Cambodian border crossings for US$20, but overcharging is common at all borders except Bavet.

Moc Bai–Bavet

The most popular border crossing between Cambodia and Vietnam is Moc Bai (p391), which connects Vietnam's Tay Ninh province with Cambodia's Svay Rieng province. There are plenty of daily direct services between Phnom Penh and HCMC (via Moc Bai), departing between 6am and midday, taking about six hours and costing an average of US$12. If you're travelling during a major Cambodian holiday, this route can take as long as 12 hours due to the Neak Luong ferry crossing.

Vinh Xuong–Kaam Samnor

A more leisurely alternative to the Moc Bai crossing is the Vinh Xuong–Kaam Samnor border (p455) near Chau Doc. This offers the advantage of a leisurely look at the Mekong Delta without the hassle of backtracking to HCMC. There are slow boats or smart speedboats plying this route, plus it is possible to plot your own course with a combination of boat and bus.

There are several companies that offer luxury boat cruises between HCMC and Phnom Penh or Siem Reap via this border: the international player **Pandaw Cruises** (www.pandaw.com) and Cambodian company **Toum Teav Cruises** (www.cfmekong.com). Pandaw is an expensive option favoured by high-end tour companies, while Toum Teav is smaller and is well regarded for the personal service and excellent food.

Other Crossings

While it's open season when it comes to border crossings between Vietnam and Cambodia, many are a little out of the way for the average traveller. There are also rumours that a ferry

TRANSPORT

CHINA GUIDEBOOKS CONFISCATED

Travellers entering China by road or rail from Vietnam report that Lonely Planet *China* guidebooks have been confiscated by border officials. The guidebook's maps show Taiwan as a separate country, and this is a sensitive issue. If you are carrying a copy of Lonely Planet's *China* guide, consider putting a cover on the book to make it less recognisable and, just to be safe, copy down any crucial details you might need while in China.

may soon link Sihanoukville and/or Kep with Vietnam's Phu Quoc Island.

The newly opened Xa Xia–Prek Chak crossing has been long anticipated, connecting the Mekong Delta town of Ha Tien with Kep and Kampot. This also offers the prospect of linking the Cambodian coast with Phu Quoc Island, as there are new fast-boat services from Ha Tien. As this is a fairly new crossing there is still little in the way of regular transport, but expect bus services to start at some stage. For now, it is possible to take a *xe om* from Kompong Trach (US$4), Kep (US$6) or Kampot (US$9) to the border, cross into Vietnam and take another *xe om* to Ha Tien (US$2 to US$3). It is also possible to charter a taxi or minibus from the border to Kampot (US$40), Kep (US$30) and Kompong Trach (US$20), although this is generally easier in the other direction.

The Tinh Bien–Phnom Den (p456) crossing has been open for some time now, but is rarely used as most travellers prefer the Mekong crossing at Kaam Samnor or the new Prek Chak crossing to the south. A *xe om* can be arranged in Chau Doc (about US$5) or Ha Tien (about US$10), or private vehicles for around US$25 and US$50, respectively. On the Cambodian side, Phnom Den lies about 60km southeast of Takeo town and a seat in a share taxi will cost about US$2.50.

There is another new border crossing in Vietnam's central highlands at Le Tanh–O'Yadaw (p341), offering connections between Pleiku and Banlung in Ratanakiri province. Roads on the Vietnamese side are in good shape and NH19 in Cambodia is being overhauled, bringing the journey time down to just six hours. There are no direct bus services, but the combination of buses and motorbikes or share taxis is reasonably painless.

There are a cluster of border crossings in the southwest of Vietnam that connect with obscure towns in Cambodia and are not really on the radar. The Xa Mat–Trapaeng Phlong and Loc Ninh–Trapaeng Sre crossings are both off NH7 in Cambodia and the Xa Mat crossing could be useful for those planning to visit the Cao Dai temple (p395) when travelling to or from HCMC.

CHINA

There are currently three border checkpoints where foreigners are permitted to cross between Vietnam and China: Huu Nghi Quan (the Friendship Pass), Lao Cai and Mong Cai. It is necessary to arrange a Chinese visa in advance (US$30 for three months, add US$30 for same-day service) through the embassy in Hanoi (p483). The embassy's visa section is open between 8.30am and 11am.

Set your watch when you cross the border as the time in China is one hour ahead. Cross-border trade rumbles on all night, but foreigners can only cross during standard hours.

Youyi Guan–Huu Nghi Quan (Friendship Gate)

The busiest border crossing (p158) between Vietnam and China is located at the Vietnamese town of Dong Dang, 164km northeast of Hanoi. It connects Hanoi with Nanning and is on the overland route to Yuanshou and Hong Kong. Dong Dang is an obscure town, about 18km north of bustling Lang Son.

There is a twice-weekly international train between Beijing and Hanoi, departing on Tuesdays and Fridays at 6.30pm, which stops at Huu Nghi Quan (Friendship Pass). You can board or get off at numerous stations in China. The entire Hanoi–Beijing run is about 2951km and takes approximately 48 hours, including a three-hour delay at the border checkpoint. In the other direction, it leaves Beijing at 4.16pm on Thursdays and Sundays.

Train tickets to China are more expensive in Hanoi, so some travellers prefer to buy a ticket to Dong Dang, cross the border and then buy another ticket on the Chinese side. While this plan involves a motorbike to the border and a bus or taxi on to Pingxiang, it helps avoid the three-hour delay while the international train is given the once over at the border checkpoint, plus avoids having to cross the border in the middle of the night.

Lao Cai–Hekou

There's a 762km railway linking Hanoi with Kunming in China's Yunnan province, but the Chinese side has been out of action for a while. The border town on the Vietnamese side of this border crossing (p184) is Lao Cai, 294km from Hanoi. On the Chinese side, the border town is Hekou, 468km south of Kunming.

It is possible to take the train as far as Lao Cai on the Vietnamese side, transfer to the border by *xe om* or taxi, cross into Hekou and arrange a bus to Kunming. There are several train services a day from Hanoi to Lao Cai, so it's easy to combine a stop at Sapa (p176) by bus before returning to Lao Cai when crossing this way.

Mong Cai–Dongxing

Vietnam's third (but seldom-used) border crossing (p155) with China can be found at Mong Cai in the northeast of the country, opposite the Chinese city of Dongxing. It might be useful for anyone planning to travel between Halong Bay and Hainan Island, but otherwise it is well out of the way.

LAOS

There are seven (and counting) overland crossings between Vietnam and Laos. Thirty-day Lao visas are now available at the busier borders, but currently not at Nam Xoi, Na Phao and the Phou Keua border. We have received scores of letters complaining about immigration and local-transport hassles on the Vietnamese side of these borders; in fact, these border crossings are probably second only to Hanoi hotel scams in the volume of email they generate. Lies about journey times are common: yes, it really does take almost 24 hours to get from Hanoi to Vientiane and not 12. Worse are the devious drivers who stop the bus in the middle of nowhere and renegotiate the price. Transport links on both sides of the border can be very hit and miss, so don't use the more remote borders unless you have plenty of time, and patience, to spare.

Lao Bao–Dansavanh

Known as Lao Bao–Dansavanh (p216), this is the most popular border crossing between Laos and Vietnam and is usually the most hassle-free. The border town of Lao Bao is on Hwy 9, 80km west of Dong Ha. Just across the border is the southern Lao province of Savannakhet, and the first town you come to is Sepon. There is an international service from Hue to Savannakhet (US$20, nine hours, departing at 6am every second day) that passes through Dong Ha (US$12, 7½ hours, around 8am). Coming in the other direction there are daily buses from Savannakhet at 10pm.

Cau Treo–Nam Phao

Vietnam's Hwy 8 hits Laos at the Keo Nua Pass (734m), known as Cau Treo (p202) in Vietnamese, and Kaew Neua in Lao.

The nearest Vietnamese city of any importance is Vinh, 96km east of the border. On the Lao side it's about 200km from the border to Tha Khaek via Lak Sao. Most people use this border when travelling on the direct buses between Hanoi and Vientiane, but this is no picnic. In fact it's a set menu from hell. The journey takes about 24 hours and the buses get progressively more dangerous and overcrowded. The bus hardly stops for bathrooms or meals, but stops randomly when the driver fancies a sleep. Invariably the bus arrives at the border at an ungodly hour. Almost everyone ends up wishing they had flown. If you are a sucker for punishment, travel agents and guesthouses in Hanoi and Vientiane can help set you up, literally, for somewhere in the region of US$25 or so. A more sane option might be to do it in stages, stopping in Vinh and Tha Khaek along the way.

Other Crossings

The Nam Can–Nong Haet border (p201) links Vinh with Phonsavan and the Plain of Jars. There are regular(ish) buses connecting these two towns.

There is a border at Cha Lo–Na Phao (p205) that links Dong Hoi and Tha Khaek, but very few travellers have used it until now. Two buses connect these cities each week.

Arguably the most remote of remote borders is at Na Meo–Nam Xoi (p199) which connects Thanh Hoa, 153km south of Hanoi, with the town of Xam Nua and the famous Pathet Lao caves of Vieng Xai. This involves several changes of transport and a lot of overcharging. Check out the box details if you dare.

The remote crossing at Bo Y–Phou Keau (p337) links Kon Tum and Quy Nhon with Attapeu and Pakse. It involves a roller-coaster ride on the Lao side of the border. Transport is still not all that regular, but several Vietnamese-run buses link Attapeu and Pleiku (US$10, 12 hours). There are also local minivans (80,000k) departing between 7am and 10am to/from Ngoc Hoi, on the Ho Chi Minh Highway about 14km east of Bo Y. Finally, there are direct buses from Quy Nhon to Pakse, but Lao visas are not available at this border.

The latest border to open is Tay Trang–Sop Hun (p174) which connects Dien Bien Phu with Muang Khua on the Lao side. There are currently four buses a week in either direction, taking seven hours or more. Attempting it in shorter hops is very tough due to a lack of local transport.

Bus

It is possible to cross into Vietnam by bus from Cambodia or Laos. The most popular way to or from Cambodia are the international buses via the Moc Bai–Bavet border crossing. When it comes to Laos, many travellers take the nightmare bus between Vientiane and Hanoi via the Cau Treo crossing, or the easier route from Savannakhet in southern Laos to Hue in central Vietnam via the Lao Bao border crossing.

Car & Motorbike

It is theoretically possible to travel in and out of Vietnam by car or motorbike, but only through borders shared with Cambodia and Laos. However, in reality the bureaucracy makes this a real headache. It is generally easy enough to take a Vietnamese motorbike into Cambodia or Laos, but very difficult in the other direction. It is currently not possible to take any sort of vehicle into China from Vietnam.

Drivers of cars and riders of motorbikes will need the vehicle's registration papers, liability insurance and an International Driving Permit, in addition to a domestic licence. Most important is a *carnet de passage en douane*, which is effectively a passport for the vehicle and acts as a temporary waiver of import duty.

Train

Several international trains link China and Vietnam. The most scenic stretch of railway is between Hanoi and Kunming via Lao Cai, but at the time of research trains were not operating on the Chinese side. The mammoth journey from Hanoi to Beijing via Lang Son is also a possibility. There are no railway lines linking Vietnam with Cambodia or Laos.

RIVER

There is a river border crossing between Cambodia and Vietnam on the banks of the Mekong. Regular fast boats ply the route between Phnom Penh in Cambodia and Chau Doc in Vietnam via the Vinh Xuong–Kaam Samnor border. There are also several luxury river boats with cabins running all the way to the temples of Angkor at Siem Reap in Cambodia.

TOURS

Package tours to Vietnam are offered by travel agencies worldwide. Nearly all these tours follow one of a dozen or so set itineraries. Tours come in every shape and size from budget trips to ultimate indulgences, and those booked outside Vietnam are not bad value when you tally everything up (flights, hotels, transport). Then again, it's a cheap country for travelling.

It's easy enough to fly into Vietnam and make the travel arrangements with a tour company upon arrival (see p506). The main saving through booking before arrival is time, and if time is more precious than money, a pre-booked package tour is probably right for you. There are also plenty of good Vietnam-based operators who can plan your visit in advance. Some of the best are listed below.

Almost any good travel agency can book you on a standard mad-dash minibus tour around Vietnam. More noteworthy are the adventure tours arranged for people with a particular passion. These include speciality tours for cyclists, trekkers, war veterans, culture vultures and gourmet travellers.

For a rewarding trip to Vietnam, you might like to try contacting the following tour providers:

AUSTRALIA

Adventure World (☎ 02-8913 0755; www.adventureworld.com.au) Adventure tours to Vietnam, as well as Cambodia and Laos.

Griswalds Vietnamese Vacations (☎ 02-9564 5040; www.vietnamvacations.com.au) Popular Australian company offering affordable adventures.

Intrepid Travel (☎ 1300 360 667; www.intrepidtravel.com) Small-group tours for all budgets with an environmental, social and cultural edge.

Peregrine (☎ 02-9290 2770; www.peregrine.net.au) Small-group and tailor-made tours supporting responsible tourism.

Wide Eyed Tours (☎ 02-9290 2770; www.wideeyedtours.com) Set up by former Intrepid tour leaders, this company offers tours all over Vietnam and has an office in the Old Quarter of Hanoi.

FRANCE

Compagnie des Indes & Orients (☎ 01 53 63 33 40; www.compagniesdumonde.com) Offers organised tours that cover every corner of Vietnam.

Intermedes (☎ 01 45 61 90 90; www.intermedes.com) Offers specialised private tours.

La Route des Indes (☎ 01 42 60 60 90; www.larotedesindes.com) High-end tours with an academic edge.

NEW ZEALAND

Adventure World (☎ 09-524 5118; www.adventureworld.co.nz) A wide range of adventure tours covering the country.

Pacific Cycle Tours (☎ 03-972 9913; www.bike-nz.com) Mountain bike tours through Vietnam, plus hiking trips to off-the-beaten-path destinations.

UK

Audley Travel (☎ 016-0423 4855; www.audleytravel.com) Popular tailor-made specialist covering all of Vietnam.

Cox & Kings (☎ 020-7873 5000; www.coxandkings.co.uk) Well-established high-end company, strong on cultural tours.

Explore (☎ 012-5276 0100; www.exploreworldwide.com) Small-group adventure holidays, with lots of Vietnam itineraries.

Hands Up Holidays (☎ 077-6501 3631; www.handsupholidays.com) A new company bringing guests close to the people of Vietnam through its responsible holidays with a spot of volunteering.

Symbiosis (☎ 020-7924 5906; www.symbiosis-travel.com) Small bespoke travel company with an emphasis on cycling and diving.

Wild Frontiers (☎ 020-7376 3968; www.wildfrontiers.co.uk) Adventure specialist with themed tours like Apocalypse Now.

USA

Asia Transpacific Journeys (☎ 800-642 2742; www.asiatranspacific.com) Group tours and tailor-made trips across the Asia-Pacific region.

Distant Horizons (☎ 800-333 1240; www.distant-horizons.com) Educational tours for discerning travellers.

Geographic Expeditions (☎ 800-777 8183; www.geoex.com) Well-established high-end adventure -travel company.

Global Adrenaline (☎ 800-825 1680; www.globaladrenaline.com) Luxury adventures for the experienced traveller.

Tour Operators in Vietnam

Buffalo Tours (☎ 04-3828 0702; www.buffalotours.com; 11 Pho Hang Muoi, Hanoi) Popular travel company run by a former Intrepid guide.

Destination Asia (☎ 08-3844 8071; www.destination-asia.com; 143 Đ Nguyen Van Troi, Phu Nhuan district, HCMC) High-end travel company for the discerning visitor.

Exotissimo (☎ 04-3828 2150; www.exotissimo.com; 26 Tran Nhat Duat, Hanoi) Leading regional player with a good range of tours, including cycling and trekking.

Sinhbalo Adventures (☎ 08-8337 6766; www.sinhbalo.com; 283/20 Đ Pham Ngu Lao, District 1, HCMC) The leading cycling specialist with tours to the Mekong Delta and the northern mountains.

Sisters Tours (☎ 04-3562 2733; www.sisterstoursvietnam.com; 37 Đ Thai Thinh, Hanoi) Locally owned high-end company working with the US market.

GETTING AROUND

AIR

Airlines in Vietnam

Vietnam Airlines (www.vietnamairlines.com.vn) is the leading local carrier, although budget carrier **Jetstar Pacific Airlines** (www.jetstar.com/vn/en/index.html) is growing fast thanks to its affordable fares.

Most travel agents do not charge any more than when you book directly with the airline, as they receive a commission. Note that you will need a passport in order to make a booking on all domestic flights.

Vietnam Airlines has come a long way and many (but still not all) branch offices accept credit cards for the purposes of ticket purchases. The airline has retired its ancient Soviet-built fleet and purchased new Western-made aircraft.

BICYCLE

A great way to get around Vietnam's towns and cities is to do as the locals do and ride a bicycle. During rush hours, urban thoroughfares approach gridlock, as rushing streams of cyclists force their way through intersections

FARE'S FAIR?

This is the million dong question. Am I being quoted the right fare, or are they completely ripping me off? Well there is no easy answer, but here are some guidelines to help you navigate the maze.

Airfares are fixed, although web fares differ depending on when you book and what dates you want to travel. Rail fares are also fixed, although naturally there are different prices for different classes. Bus fares are a bit more complicated. If you buy the ticket from the point of departure (ie the bus station), then the price is fixed and very reasonable. However, should you board the bus along the way, then there is a chance the driver or conductor will overcharge. This gets more prevalent in more remote areas, where prices may be four or five times what the locals pay. Most boat fares for ferries or hydrofoils are fixed, but not for small local boats in places like the Mekong Delta.

When it comes to local transport, local bus prices are fixed and displayed by the door. Taxis are mostly metered and very cheap, but some taxis have dodgy meters that run fast. *Xe om* and *cyclo* fares are most definitely not fixed and you need to bargain. Prices throughout this book are indicative and the actual price of a local ride depends on the wiliness of the driver and your negotiating skills.

without the benefit of traffic lights. In the countryside, Westerners on bicycles are often greeted enthusiastically by locals who don't see that many foreigners pedalling around.

Long-distance cycling is popular in Vietnam. Much of the country is flat or only moderately hilly, and the major roads are in good shape. Safety, however, is a considerable concern. Bicycles can be transported around the country on the top of buses or in train baggage compartments. Lonely Planet's *Cycling Vietnam, Laos & Cambodia* gives the lowdown on cycling through Vietnam.

Decent bikes can be bought at a few speciality shops in Hanoi and HCMC, but it's better to bring your own if you plan on cycling over long distances. Mountain bikes are preferable, as large potholes or unsealed roads are rough on the rims, but a touring bike is fine for coastal routes or the Mekong Delta. Basic cycling safety equipment and authentic spare parts are also in short supply, so bring all this from home. A bell or horn is mandatory – the louder the better.

Hotels and some travel agencies rent bicycles for about US$2 to US$5 per day and it is a great way to explore some of the smaller cities like Hue or Nha Trang. There are innumerable bicycle-repair stands along the side of the roads in every city and town in Vietnam.

Groups of foreign cyclists touring Vietnam are a common sight these days, and there are several tour companies that specialise in bicycle trips.

BOAT

Vietnam has an enormous number of rivers that are at least partly navigable, but the most important by far is the Mekong River and its tributaries. Scenic day trips by boat are possible on rivers in Hoi An, Danang, Hue, Tam Coc and even HCMC, but only in the Mekong Delta are boats used as a practical means of transport.

Boat trips are also possible on the sea. Cruising the islands of Halong Bay is a must for all visitors to northern Vietnam. In the south, a trip to the islands off the coast of Nha Trang is popular.

In some parts of Vietnam, particularly the Mekong Delta, there are frequent ferry crossings. Don't stand between parked vehicles on the ferry as they can roll and you could wind up as the meat in the sandwich.

BUS

Vietnam has an extensive network of dirt-cheap buses that reach the far-flung corners of the country. Until recently, few foreign travellers used them because of safety concerns and overcharging, but the situation has improved dramatically with modern buses and fixed-price ticket offices at most bus stations.

Bus fleets are being upgraded as fast as the roads, so the old French, American and Russian buses from the '50s, '60s and '70s are becoming increasingly rare. On most popular routes, modern Korean buses are the flavour of the day. Most of these offer air-con and comfortable seats, but on the flipside most of them are equipped with TVs and dreaded karaoke machines. You can ignore the crazy kung fu videos by closing your eyes, but you'd need to be deaf to sleep through the karaoke sessions – ear plugs are recommended.

Figuring out the bus system is not always that simple. Many cities have several bus stations, and responsibilities are divided according to the location of the destination (whether it is north or south of the city) and the type of service being offered (local or long distance, express or nonexpress).

Short-distance buses, mostly minibuses, depart when full (ie jam-packed with people and luggage). They often operate throughout the day, but don't count on many leaving after about 4pm. However, there are also now private companies offering smart minibuses with pre-allocated seats on short and medium-distance routes, such as **Mai Linh Express** (www.mailinh.vn). Nonexpress buses and minibuses drop off and pick up as many passengers as possible along the route, so try to avoid these. The frequent stops make for a slow journey.

Express buses make a beeline from place to place. This is the deluxe class and you can usually be certain of there being enough space to sit comfortably.

It is also perfectly feasible to kick in with some fellow travellers and charter your own minibus. Many drivers refuse to drive after dark because the unlit highways are teeming with bicycles and pedestrians who seem oblivious to the traffic. However, if you like living dangerously, there are now plenty of overnight sleeper buses with reclining seats.

Be aware that luggage is easily pilfered at toilet stops unless someone is looking after it. No matter how honest your fellow passengers might seem, never accept drinks from them, as there is a chance you may be drugged and robbed.

When arriving by bus, it is generally better to try and arrange a metered taxi on to your hotel or guesthouse of choice, as *xe oms* and *cyclos* tend to demand ridiculous prices.

Reservations & Costs

Reservations aren't required for most of the frequent, popular services between towns and cities, but it doesn't hurt to purchase the ticket the day before if you're set on a specific departure time. Most major bus stations now have ticket offices with official prices clearly displayed. Always buy a ticket from the office, as bus drivers are notorious for overcharging. Small private minibuses fill up fast, as they are faster and more comfortable, so book these tickets ahead also.

Costs are negligible, though on rural runs foreigners are typically charged anywhere from twice to 10 times the going rate. If you have to battle it out with the bus driver, it is helpful to determine the cost of the ticket for locals before starting negotiations. As a benchmark, a typical 100km ride is between US$2 and US$3.

Open Tours

In backpacker haunts throughout Vietnam, you'll see lots of signs advertising 'Open Tour', 'Open Date Ticket' or 'Open Ticket'. These are bus services catering mostly to foreign budget travellers, but increasing numbers of Vietnamese are using the services due to convenient central departure points. The air-con buses run between HCMC and Hanoi and passengers can hop on and hop off the bus at any major city along the route.

Prices are still very reasonable by international standards. A through ticket from Ho Chi Minh City to Hanoi costs around US$40, depending on the exact route. Sample prices include the following:

Route	Price (US$)
Ho Chi Minh City–Dalat	6
Ho Chi Minh City–Mui Ne	6
Ho Chi Minh City–Nha Trang	9
Nha Trang–Hoi An	12
Hoi An–Hue	6
Hue–Hanoi	14

The downside to the open tour concept is that operators depend on kickbacks from a very elaborate and well-established network of sister hotels and restaurants along the way, making the whole experience feel like being part of the herd. On the plus side, the buses depart from central places, such as the Pham Ngu Lao area in HCMC, avoiding an extra journey to the bus station.

Buying shorter point-to-point tickets on the open-tour buses costs a bit more but you achieve more flexibility, including the chance to take a train, rent a motorbike or simply change plans.

Nevertheless, cheap open-tour tickets are a temptation and many people go for them. A couple of shorter routes to try are HCMC–Dalat and HCMC–Mui Ne Beach, two places that are not serviced by train.

If you are set on open-tour tickets, look for them at budget cafes in HCMC and Hanoi. From the original Sinh Café (see p351 for details of the HCMC branch) concept a decade ago, there are now lots of companies in on this game. Buses vary in size and standard, so a good rule of thumb is to turn up and check out the bus before committing to a company. Sinh Café, if you manage to hook up with the original and not an imitation, still has a good reputation.

CAR & MOTORBIKE

Having your own set of wheels gives you maximum flexibility to visit remote regions and stop when and where you please. Car hire usually includes a driver. Motorbike hire is good value and this can be self-drive or with a driver.

Driving Licence

In order to drive a car in Vietnam, you need a Vietnamese licence and an International Driving Permit, usually issued by your automobile association back home. This effectively means it is easy enough for expatriates to arrange, but pretty complicated for visitors. When it comes to renting motorbikes, it's a case of no licence required.

Fuel & Spare Parts

By international standards, fuel is pretty cheap in Vietnam. Fuel is readily available throughout the country, but prices rise in rural areas. Even the most isolated communities usually have someone selling petrol out of Fanta or Johnnie Walker bottles. Some sellers mix this fuel with kerosene to make a quick profit – use it sparingly, in emergencies only.

When it comes to spare parts, Vietnam is awash with Japanese motorbikes, so it is easy to get parts for Hondas, Yamahas or Suzukis, but finding a part for a Ducati is another matter. Likewise for cars, spares for Japanese cars are easy to come by, as are spares for international brands manufactured in Vietnam like Ford and Mercedes. But if you are driving something obscure, whether with two wheels or four, bring substantial spares.

Hire

The major considerations are safety, the mechanical condition of the vehicle, the reliability of the rental agency, and your budget.

CAR & MINIBUS

Self-drive rental cars have yet to make their debut in Vietnam, which is a blessing in disguise given traffic conditions, but cars with drivers are popular and plentiful. Renting a vehicle with a driver and guide is a realistic option even for budget travellers, providing there are enough people to share the cost.

Hanoi and HCMC have an especially wide selection of travel agencies that rent vehicles. For sightseeing trips around HCMC or Hanoi, a car with driver can also be rented by the day. It costs about US$30 to US$60 per day, depending on the car.

Renting a minibus (van) is good value for larger groups, as they hold between eight and 15 passengers. They are also a smart option for small groups planning to travel long distances at night, as everyone can stretch out.

For the rough roads of northwestern Vietnam, the vehicle of choice is a 4WD. Without one, the muddy mountain roads can be treacherous. In Vietnam, 4WDs come in different flavours – the cheapest are Russian made, although these are increasingly rare, while more cushy Korean and Japanese vehicles with air-con are about twice the price. Expect to pay about US$80 to US$100 a day for a decent 4WD in the far north of Vietnam.

MOTORBIKE

Motorbikes can be rented from cafes, hotels, motorbike shops and travel agencies. If you don't fancy the challenge, there are plenty of local drivers willing to act as a chauffeur and guide for around US$6 to US$10 per day.

Renting a 100cc moped runs from US$5 to US$10 per day, usually with unlimited mileage. To tackle the mountains of the north, it is best to get a slightly more powerful bike such as a Honda Bonus or Minsk. For the ultimate experience in mountains of the north, consider joining a motorbike tour to discover the secret backroads; see p507 for more on motorbike touring companies.

Most places will ask to keep your passport until you return the bike. Try and sign some sort of agreement clearly stating what you are renting, how much it costs, the extent of compensation and so on. To learn more about potential scams, see p481.

Insurance

If you are travelling in a tourist vehicle with a driver, then it is almost guaranteed to be insured. When it comes to motorbikes, many rental bikes are not insured and you will have to sign a contract agreeing to a valuation for the bike if it is stolen. Make sure you have a strong lock and always leave it in guarded parking where available.

Do not even consider renting a motorbike if you are daft enough to be travelling in Vietnam without insurance. The cost of treating serious injuries can be bankrupting for budget travellers.

Road Conditions & Hazards

Road safety is definitely not one of Vietnam's strong points. The intercity road network of two-lane highways is becoming more and more dangerous. High-speed, head-on collisions between buses, trucks and other smaller vehicles (such as motorbikes and bicycles) have become a sickeningly familiar sight on the major highways. Vietnam does not have an efficient emergency-rescue system, so if something happens on the road, it could be some time before help arrives and a long way to even the most basic of medical facilities. Locals might help in extreme circumstances, but in most cases it will be up to you or your guide to get you to the hospital or clinic.

In general, the major highways are hard surfaced and reasonably well maintained, but seasonal flooding can be a problem. A big typhoon can create potholes the size of bomb craters. In some remote areas, roads are not surfaced and transform themselves into a sea of mud when the weather turns bad – such roads are best tackled with a 4WD vehicle or motorbike. Mountain roads are particularly dangerous: landslides, falling rocks and runaway vehicles can add an unwelcome edge to your journey. The occasional roadside shrine often indicates where a bus has plunged into the abyss.

For motorbikers, serious sunburn is a major risk and well worth preventing. The cooling breeze prevents you from realising how badly you are burning until it's too late. Cover up exposed skin and use a strong sunscreen. Bikers also must consider the opposite problem – occasional heavy rains. A rainsuit or poncho is essential, especially during the monsoon season.

Road Rules

Basically, there aren't many; arguably any. Size matters and the biggest vehicle wins by default. Be particularly careful about children on the road. It's common to find kids playing hopscotch in the middle of a major highway. Livestock on the road is also a menace; hit a cow on a motorbike and you'll both be hamburger.

Although the police frequently stop drivers and fine them for all sorts of real and imagined offences, speeding is the flavour of the month. New speed limits are surprisingly slow, probably a way to ensure more revenue from fines. In cities, there is a rule that you cannot turn right on a red light. It's easy to run afoul of this law in Vietnam and the police will fine you for this offence.

Honking at all pedestrians and bicycles (to warn them of your approach) is not road rage, but considered an essential element of safe driving – larger trucks and buses might as well have a dynamo-driven horn. There is no national seatbelt law and the locals often laugh at foreigners who insist on using seatbelts.

Legally a motorbike can carry only two people, but we've seen up to six on one vehicle…plus luggage! This law is enforced in major cities, but ignored in rural areas.

> **HELMET LAW**
>
> It is now compulsory to wear a helmet when riding a motorbike in Vietnam, even when travelling as a passenger. Consider investing in a decent imported helmet if you are planning extensive rides on busy highways or winding mountain roads, as the local eggshells don't offer much protection. Better-quality helmets, such as the imported 'Index' models, are available in major cities from US$20 to US$30.

HITCHING

Hitching is never entirely safe in any country in the world, and we don't recommend it. Travellers who decide to hitch should understand that they are taking a potentially serious risk. People who do choose to hitch will be safer if they travel in pairs and let someone know where they are planning to go.

LOCAL TRANSPORT

Bus

The bus systems in Hanoi and HCMC have improved immeasurably in the past few years. Get your hands on a bus map and it is now possible to navigate the suburbs cheaply and efficiently. Some of the most popular sights in Hanoi and HCMC are accessible by public transport, making for a cheap visit. There are also local bus networks in most major towns and cities, although it's hard to use them without some local language skills. Many travellers prefer other fast and economical options, such as meter taxis and motorbike taxis.

Cyclo

The *cyclo* (*xich*-lo), from the French *cyclo-pousse,* offers cheap and environmentally friendly transportation around Vietnam's main cities.

Groups of *cyclo* drivers always hang out near major hotels and markets, and many speak at least broken English. To make sure the driver understands where you want to go, it's useful to bring a city map. Bargaining is imperative. Settle on a fare before going anywhere or you're likely to get stiffed.

As a basic rule, short rides around town should cost about 10,000d. For a longer ride or a night ride, expect to pay double that or more. It pays to have the exact change when taking a *cyclo,* as drivers may claim they don't have change. *Cyclos* are cheaper by time rather than distance. A typical price is about US$2 per hour.

There have been many stories of travellers being mugged by their *cyclo* drivers in HCMC so, as a general rule of thumb, it's safe to hire *cyclos* only during the day. When leaving a bar late at night, take a meter taxi.

Taxi

Western-style taxis with meters, found in most major cities, are very, very cheap by international standards and a safe way to travel around at night. Average tariffs are about 10,000d to 15,000d per kilometre. However, there are many dodgy taxis roaming the streets of Hanoi and HCMC and the meters are clocked to run at two or three times the normal pace. Only travel with reputable or recommended companies. See the Getting Around sections in relevant cities for listings.

Xe Om

The *xe om* (*zay*-ohm) is a motorbike that carries one passenger, like a two-wheeled taxi. *Xe* means motorbike, and *om* means hug (or hold), so you get the picture. Getting around by *xe om* is easy, as long as you don't have a lot of luggage.

Fares are comparable with those for a *cyclo,* but negotiate the price beforehand. There are plenty of *xe om* drivers hanging around street corners, markets, hotels and bus stations. They will find you before you find them…

TOURS

We are drowning in letters complaining about the quality of bottom-end budget tours being peddled in HCMC and Hanoi. Some are better than others, but remember the old adage that 'you get what you pay for'. Tour-operator gimmicks like 'one free beer' or '10 minutes of internet' are not a promising sign.

Renting a car with a driver and guide gives you the chance to design a tailor-made itinerary for you and your companions. Seeing the country this way is almost like independent travel, except that it's more comfortable, less time-consuming and allows for stops anywhere, or everywhere, along the way.

The cost varies considerably. At the high end are tours booked through government travel agencies and upmarket tour companies, while budget and midrange companies can usually arrange something just as enjoyable at a cheaper price.

The price typically includes accommodation, a guide, a driver and a car. The cost of the car depends largely on the type of vehicle.

HOW TO CROSS THE STREET AND LIVE TO TELL THE TALE

If you don't want to wind up like a bug on a windshield, pay close attention to a few pedestrian survival rules when crossing the street, especially on the streets of motorbike-crazed HCMC and Hanoi. Foreigners frequently make the mistake of thinking that the best way to cross a busy street in Vietnam is to run quickly across it. This does not always work in practice, and could get you creamed. Most Vietnamese cross the street slowly – very slowly – giving the motorbike drivers sufficient time to judge their position so they can pass on either side. They won't stop or even slow down, but they will try to avoid hitting you. Just don't make any sudden moves. Good luck!

Once you've settled on an itinerary, get a copy from the travel agency. If you find that your guide is making it up as they go along, ignoring the agreed itinerary, that piece of paper is your most effective leverage.

A good guide can be your translator and travelling companion, and can usually save you as much money along the way as they cost you. A bad guide can ruin your trip. If possible, you should meet your guide before starting out – make sure that this is someone you can travel with.

If you choose to travel with a freelance guide, you are usually responsible for their travel expenses, but if you pay for a package through a company, any expenses for the guide and driver should be included.

For trips in and around big cities like HCMC and Hanoi, you'll often find women working as guides. However, it seems relatively few women are employed as guides on long-distance trips.

For a list of recommended tour companies in Vietnam, see p500. For recommended budget and midrange operators running tours throughout Vietnam, check the listings under the major town or city in the relevant area.

Motorbike Tours

Specialised motorbike tours through Vietnam are growing in popularity. It is a great way to get off the trail and explore the mountainous regions of the north and centre of the country – two-wheels can reach the parts that four-wheels sometimes can't, by traversing small trails and traffic-free back roads. A little experience helps, but many of leading companies also offer tuition for first-timers. Mounting a Minsk to take on the peaks of the north is one of Vietnam's defining moments and should not be missed.

Foreign guides charge considerably more than local Vietnamese guides. Based on a group of four people, you can expect to pay around US$100 per person per day for an all-inclusive tour that provides motorbike rental, petrol, guide, food and accommodation. Some of the best companies running trips in the north include the following:

Explore Indochina (☎ 09-1352 4658; www.exploreindochina.com) Run by back-road explorer Digby and Minsk master mechanic Cuong, these guys have biked all over the country and can take you to the parts others cannot reach. They even helped Jeremy Clarkson and co on their recent ride for BBC *Top Gear*. Minsks and 650cc Urals available. Prices from US$150 per day.

Free Wheelin' Tours (☎ 04-3747 0545; www.freewheelin-tours.com) Run by Fredo (Binh in Vietnamese), who speaks French, English and Vietnamese, this company has its own homestays in the northeast, plus 4WD trips. Prices start from US$100 per day for a group of four.

Offroad Vietnam (☎ 04-3904 5049; www.offroadvietnam.com) This is a Vietnamese-run company, and these guys generate really good feedback from their guests. Honda bikes from 125cc to 250cc. Tours from US$100 per day.

Voyage Vietnam (☎ 04-3926 2373; www.voyagevietnam.net) Another locally run outfit, this company is quickly earning itself a good reputation. Hondas, Yahamas and Minsks. Prices start from around US$100 per day.

For more on the Easy Riders operating out of Dalat, see p325. There are a host of other motorbike and bicycle day trips covered under individual towns throughout this book.

TRAIN

The 2600km Vietnamese railway system, operated by **Vietnam Railways** (Duong Sat Viet Nam; ☎ 04-3747 0308; www.vr.com.vn), runs along the coast between HCMC and Hanoi, and also links the capital with Hai Phong and northern towns. While sometimes even slower than buses, trains offer a more relaxing way to get around and more room than the jam-packed buses. The trains are also considered safer than the country's kamikaze bus fleet.

Vietnam's railway authority has been rapidly upgrading trains and facilities – with air-con sleeping berths and dining cars available now on express trains – and lowering the price for foreigners. Foreigners and Vietnamese are now charged the same price, a big change from a few years ago when foreigners were charged 400% more.

The train journey between Hanoi and HCMC takes from 30 to 41 hours, depending on the train. The slowest express train on this route takes 41 hours. There are also local trains that only cover short routes, but these can crawl along at 15km/h, as there is only one track with many passing points and local trains have the lowest priority. Vietnam is planning a massive overhaul of its rail network in the next decade, including the introduction of high-speed trains in partnership with Japan.

Petty crime is a problem on Vietnamese trains. While there doesn't seem to be organised pack-napping gangs, such as those in India, thieves have become proficient at grabbing packs through the windows as trains pull out of stations. Always keep your bag nearby and lock or tie it to something, especially at night.

Another hazard is children throwing rocks at the train. Passengers have been severely injured this way and many conductors insist that you keep down the metal window shield. Unfortunately, however, these shields also obstruct the view.

Bicycles and motorbikes must travel in the freight car. Just make sure that the train you are on has a freight car (most have) or your bike will arrive later than you do.

Eating is easy, as there are vendors at every station who board the train and practically stuff food, drinks and cigarettes into your pockets. The food supplied by the railway company, included in the ticket price on some long journeys, isn't Michelin-starred, but it fills the void. It's a good idea to stock up on your favourite munchies before taking a long trip.

Odd-numbered trains travel south and even-numbered ones travel north. The fastest train service is provided by the Reunification Express (see the boxed text below), which runs between HCMC and Hanoi, making only a few short stops en route. If you want to stop at some obscure point between the major towns, use one of the slower local trains or catch a bus.

Aside from the main HCMC–Hanoi run, three rail-spur lines link Hanoi with the other parts of northern Vietnam. One runs east to the port city of Hai Phong. A second heads northeast to Lang Son, crosses the border and continues to Nanning, China. A third goes northwest to Lao Cai and on to Kunming, China.

Several Reunification Express trains depart from Hanoi and HCMC every day. The train schedules change frequently. The timetables for all trains are posted on the Vietnam Railway website and at major stations. Another excellent resource is the **Man in Seat Sixty-One** (www.seat61.com), the top international train website. Most travel agents and some hotels keep a copy of the latest schedule on hand. In HCMC call or visit the **Saigon Railways Tourist Service** (☎ 08-3836 7640; 275C Đ Pham Ngu Lao, District 1) in the Pham Ngu Lao area.

It's important to realise that the train schedule is 'bare-bones' during the Tet festival. The Reunification Express is suspended for nine days, beginning four days before Tet and continuing for four days afterwards.

THE REUNIFICATION EXPRESS

Construction of the 1726km-long Hanoi–Saigon railway, the Transindochinois, began in 1899 and was completed in 1936. In the late 1930s the trip from Hanoi to Saigon took 40 hours and 20 minutes at an average speed of 43km/h. During WWII the Japanese made extensive use of the rail system, resulting in Viet Minh sabotage on the ground and US bombing from the air. After WWII, efforts were made to repair the Transindochinois, major parts of which were either damaged or had become overgrown.

During the Franco-Viet Minh War, the Viet Minh engaged in sabotage against the rail system. At night the Viet Minh made off with rails to create a 300km network of tracks (between Ninh Hoa and Danang) in an area wholly under their control – the French quickly responded with their own sabotage.

In the late 1950s the South, with US funding, reconstructed the track between Saigon and Hue, a distance of 1041km. But between 1961 and 1964 alone, 795 Viet Cong attacks were launched on the rail system, forcing the abandonment of large sections of track (including the Dalat spur).

By 1960 the North had repaired 1000km of track, mostly between Hanoi and China. During the US air war against the North, the northern rail network was repeatedly bombed. Even now clusters of bomb craters can be seen around virtually every rail bridge and train station in the north.

After reunification the government immediately set about re-establishing the Hanoi–Ho Chi Minh City rail link as a symbol of Vietnamese unity. By the time the Reunification Express trains were inaugurated on 31 December 1976, 1334 bridges, 27 tunnels, 158 stations and 1370 shunts (switches) had been repaired.

Today the Reunification Express chugs along slightly faster than the trains did in the 1930s, at an average speed of 50km/h.

REUNIFICATION EXPRESS FARES FROM HANOI

Station	Soft seat air-con	Top hard air-con (6 berth)	Bottom soft air-con (4 berth)
Vinh	140,000d	163,000d	208,000d
Dong Hoi	243,000d	282,000d	360,000d
Hue	320,000d	405,000d	518,000d
Danang	368,000d	448,000d	574,000d
Nha Trang	635,000d	810,000d	1,037,000d
HCMC	758,000d	878,000d	1,125,000d

Classes

There are four main classes of train travel in Vietnam: hard seat, soft seat, hard sleeper and soft sleeper. These are also split into air-con and non air-con options. Presently, air-con is only available on the faster express trains. Hard-seat class is usually packed, and is tolerable for day travel, but it is not much fun for overnight journeys. Soft-seat carriages have vinyl-covered seats rather than the uncomfortable hard benches, while express trains have been upgraded in recent years across both classes.

A hard sleeper has three tiers of beds (six beds per compartment). Because of limited head room and the climb, the upper berth is cheapest, followed by the middle berth and finally the lower berth. There is sometimes no door to separate the compartment from the corridor. Soft sleeper has two tiers (four beds per compartment) and all bunks are priced the same. These compartments all have a door. Fastidious travellers will probably want to bring a sleep sheet, sleeping bag and/or pillow case with them, although 'clean' linen is provided. Trains classified as SE are the smartest and fastest, while those referred to as TN are slower and older – very '90s.

There are also quite a lot of private operators offering carriages on popular routes these days. This was pioneered by Victoria Hotels to offer guests at their Sapa property a luxurious way to travel between Lao Cai and Hanoi, but lots of companies now offer private carriages on this run. There is also a luxury service running between Nha Trang and HCMC.

Costs

Ticket prices vary depending on the train, and the fastest trains are naturally the most expensive. See above for some sample fares from Hanoi to stations south. For all the details on trains from Hanoi to Haiphong see p138; Hanoi to Lao Cai see p184; and Hanoi to Lang Son see p158.

Reservations

The supply of train seats is frequently insufficient to meet demand. Reservations for all trips should be made at least one day in advance. For sleeping berths, it is wise to book several days before the date of departure. You'll need to bring your passport when buying train tickets.

Many travel agencies, hotels and cafes sell train tickets for a small commission, and this can save considerable time and trouble. It's a good idea to make reservations for onward travel as soon as you arrive in a city.

Health

CONTENTS

Health issues and the quality of medical facilities vary enormously depending on where and how you travel in Vietnam. Many of the major cities are now very well developed, although travel to rural areas can expose you to a variety of health risks and inadequate medical care.

Travellers tend to worry about contracting infectious diseases when in the tropics, but infections are a rare cause of serious illness or death in travellers. Pre-existing medical conditions such as heart disease, and accidental injury (especially traffic accidents), account for most life-threatening problems.

A bout of sickness, however, is a relatively common thing. Fortunately most common illnesses can either be prevented with some common-sense behaviour or be treated easily with a well-stocked traveller's medical kit.

HEALTH ADVISORIES

It's usually a good idea to consult your government's travel-health website before departure, if one is available:

Australia (www.dfat.gov.au/travel)
Canada (www.travelhealth.gc.ca)
New Zealand (www.mfat.govt.nz/travel)
UK (www.dh.gov.uk/Policyandguidance/Healthadvicefortravellers/fs/en)
US (www.cdc.gov/travel)

The following advice is a general guide only and does not replace the advice of a doctor trained in tropical medicine.

BEFORE YOU GO

Pack any medications in their original, clearly labelled, containers. A signed and dated letter from your doctor describing your medical conditions and medications, including generic names, is also a good idea. If carrying syringes or needles, be sure to have a physician's letter documenting their medical necessity. If you have a heart condition, bring a copy of your ECG taken just prior to travelling.

If you happen to take any regular medication bring double your needs in case of loss or theft. In Vietnam you can buy many medications over the counter without a doctor's prescription, but it can be difficult to find some of the newer drugs, particularly the latest antidepressant drugs or blood-pressure medications.

INSURANCE

Even if you are fit and healthy, don't travel without health insurance – accidents do happen. Declare any existing medical conditions – the insurance company *will* check if the problem is pre-existing and will not cover a traveller if it is undeclared. Some adventure activities such as rock climbing require extra coverage. If your health insurance doesn't cover you for medical expenses abroad, consider getting extra insurance – check our website (www.lonelyplanet.com) for more information. If you're uninsured, emergency evacuation is expensive; bills of US$100,000 are not unknown. Find out in advance if the insurance plan will make payments directly to providers or if they reimburse you later for overseas health expenditures. Note that doctors often expect payment in cash in Vietnam.

Some prefer a policy that pays doctors or hospitals directly rather than having to pay on the spot and claim later. If claiming later, keep all the relevant documentation. Some policies ask you to call a centre in your home country where an immediate assessment of your problem is made.

RECOMMENDED VACCINATIONS

The only vaccine required by international regulations is yellow fever. Proof of vaccination will only be required if you have visited a country in the yellow-fever zone within the six days prior to entering Vietnam. If travelling to Vietnam from Africa or South America you should check to see if you require proof of vaccination.

Specialised travel-medicine clinics are your best source of information; they stock all available vaccines and will be able to give specific recommendations for you and your trip. The doctors will take into account factors such as past vaccination history, the length of your trip, activities you may be undertaking, and underlying medical conditions such as pregnancy.

Most vaccines don't produce immunity until at least two weeks after they're given, so visit a doctor four to eight weeks before

REQUIRED & RECOMMENDED VACCINATIONS

The World Health Organization (WHO) recommends the following vaccinations for travellers to Southeast Asia:

- Adult diphtheria and tetanus – single booster recommended if you've had none in the previous 10 years. Side effects include a sore arm and fever.
- Hepatitis A – provides almost 100% protection for up to a year; a booster after 12 months provides at least another 20 years' protection. Mild side effects such as headache and a sore arm occur for between 5% and 10% of people.
- Hepatitis B – now considered routine for most travellers. Given as three shots over six months. A rapid schedule is also available, as is a combined vaccination with Hepatitis A. Side effects are mild and uncommon, usually a headache and sore arm. Lifetime protection occurs in 95% of people.
- Measles, mumps and rubella – two doses of MMR are required unless you have had the diseases. Occasionally a rash and flulike illness can develop a week after receiving the vaccine. Many young adults require a booster.
- Polio – in 2002, no countries in Southeast Asia reported a single case of polio. Only one booster is required as an adult for lifetime protection. Inactivated polio vaccine is safe during pregnancy.
- Typhoid – recommended unless your trip is less than a week and only to developed cities. The vaccine offers around 70% protection, lasts for two or three years and comes as a single shot. Tablets are also available; however, the injection is usually recommended as it has fewer side effects. Sore arm and fever may occur.
- Varicella – if you haven't had chickenpox, discuss this vaccination with your doctor.

Long-term Travellers

These vaccinations are recommended for people travelling for more than one month, or those at special risk:

- Japanese B Encephalitis – three injections in all. A booster is recommended after two years. A sore arm and headache are the most common side effects reported. Rarely, an allergic reaction comprising hives and swelling can occur up to 10 days after any of the three doses.
- Meningitis – single injection. There are two types of vaccination: the quadrivalent vaccine gives two to three years' protection; meningitis group C vaccine gives around 10 years' protection. Recommended for long-term travellers aged under 25.
- Rabies – three injections in all. A booster after one year will provide 10 years of protection. Side effects are rare – occasionally a headache and sore arm.
- Tuberculosis – adult long-term travellers are usually recommended to have a TB skin test before and after travel, rather than the vaccination. Note: one vaccine is given in a lifetime.

departure. Ask the doctor for an International Certificate of Vaccination (otherwise known as the yellow booklet), which will list all the vaccinations administered.

For information on current immunisation recommendations for Vietnam, contact the international team of doctors at the **Family Medical Practice** (www.doctorkot.com) in Hanoi (p86) and Ho Chi Minh City (HCMC; p349). They can provide the latest information on vaccinations, malaria and dengue-fever status, and offer general medical advice regarding Vietnam.

See the boxed text, p511, for possible vaccinations you may require.

MEDICAL CHECKLIST

Recommended items for a personal medical kit:

- antibacterial cream, eg Muciprocin
- antibiotics for skin infections, eg Amoxicillin/Clavulanate or Cephalexin
- antibiotics for diarrhoea, eg Norfloxacin or Ciprofloxacin; Azithromycin for bacterial diarrhoea; and Tinidazole for giardiasis or amoebic dysentery
- antifungal cream, eg Clotrimazole
- antihistamines for allergies, eg Cetrizine for daytime and Promethazine for night
- anti-inflammatories, eg Ibuprofen
- antinausea medication, eg Prochlorperazine
- antiseptic for cuts and scrapes, eg Betadine
- antispasmodic for stomach cramps, eg Buscopa
- contraceptives
- decongestant for colds and flus, eg Pseudoephedrine
- DEET-based insect repellent
- diarrhoea 'stopper', eg Loperamide
- first-aid items such as scissors, plasters (Band Aids), bandages, gauze, thermometer (electronic, not mercury), sterile needles and syringes, safety pins and tweezers
- indigestion medication, eg Quick Eze or Mylanta
- iodine tablets (unless you are pregnant or have a thyroid problem) to purify water
- laxatives, eg Coloxyl
- migraine medication (your personal brand), if a migraine sufferer
- oral-rehydration solution for diarrhoea, eg Gastrolyte
- paracetamol for pain
- permethrin (to impregnate clothing and mosquito nets) for repelling insects
- steroid cream for allergic/itchy rashes, eg 1% to 2% hydrocortisone
- sunscreen and hat
- throat lozenges
- thrush (vaginal yeast infection) treatment, eg Clotrimazole pessaries or Diflucan tablet
- urine alkalisation agent, eg Ural, if you're prone to urinary tract infections.

INTERNET RESOURCES

There is a wealth of travel-health advice on the internet. For further information, our **website** (www.lonelyplanet.com) is a good place to start. The **World Health Organization** (WHO; www.who.int/ith/) publishes a superb book called *International Travel & Health,* which is revised annually and is available free online. Another website of general interest is **MD Travel Health** (www.mdtravelhealth.com), which provides complete travel-health recommendations for every country and is updated daily. The **Centers for Disease Control and Prevention** (CDC; www.cdc.gov) website also has good general information.

FURTHER READING

Lonely Planet's *Healthy Travel – Asia & India* is a handy pocket-sized book that is packed with useful information including pre-trip planning, emergency first aid, immunisation and disease information and what to do if you get sick on the road.

Other good recommended references include *Traveller's Health* by Dr Richard Dawood as well as *Travelling Well* by Dr Deborah Mills – check out the website (www.travellingwell.com.au).

IN TRANSIT

DEEP VEIN THROMBOSIS (DVT)

Deep vein thrombosis (DVT) occurs when blood clots form in the legs during plane flights, chiefly because of prolonged immobility. The longer the flight, the greater the risk. Though most blood clots are reabsorbed uneventfully, some may break off and travel through the blood vessels to the lungs, where they may cause life-threatening complications.

The chief symptom of DVT is swelling or pain of the foot, ankle or calf, usually on just one side. When a blood clot travels to the lungs, it may cause chest pain and difficulty in breathing. Travellers with any of these symptoms should immediately seek medical attention.

To prevent the development of DVT on long flights you should walk about the cabin, stretch your legs and contract the leg muscles while sitting, drink plenty of fluids, and avoid alcohol. Also, try to avoid tobacco before and after flights.

JET LAG & MOTION SICKNESS

Jet lag is common when crossing more than five time zones; it results in insomnia, fatigue, malaise or nausea. To avoid jet lag try drinking plenty of fluids (nonalcoholic) and eating light meals. Upon arrival, seek exposure to natural sunlight and readjust your schedule (for meals, sleep etc) as soon as possible.

Antihistamines such as dimenhydrinate (Dramamine) and meclizine (Antivert, Bonine) are usually the first choice for treating motion sickness. Their main side effect is drowsiness. A herbal alternative is ginger, which works like a charm for some people.

IN VIETNAM

AVAILABILITY OF HEALTH CARE

The significant improvement in Vietnam's economy has brought with it some major advances in public health, but rural areas can still pose a problem when it comes to finding good health care. Foreigners with hard cash will receive the best treatment available, but even big bucks cannot buy blood tests or X-rays when the local clinic doesn't even have the most basic supplies. If you become seriously ill in rural Vietnam, get to HCMC or Hanoi as quickly as you can. If you need any type of surgery or other extensive treatment, don't hesitate to fly to Bangkok, Hong Kong or another renowned medical centre as soon as possible.

Government hospitals in Vietnam are overcrowded and basic. In order to treat foreigners, a facility needs to obtain a special license and so far only a few have been provided. The private clinics in Hanoi and HCMC should be your first port of call. They are familiar with the local resources and can organise evacuations if necessary. The contact details of the best medical facilities in Vietnam are listed in the Hanoi (p86) and HCMC (p349) chapters. These are the only cities where you are likely to find health facilities that come close to meeting the standard of developed countries.

Self-treatment may be appropriate if your problem is minor (eg travellers' diarrhoea), you are carrying the appropriate medication and you cannot attend a recommended clinic. If you think you may have a serious disease, especially malaria, do not waste time – travel to the nearest quality facility to receive attention. It is always better to be assessed by a doctor than to rely on self-treatment.

Buying medication over the counter is not recommended, as fake medications and poorly stored or out-of-date drugs are common. Check the expiry dates on all medicines. If you need special medication then take it with you.

INFECTIOUS DISEASES

Dengue

This mosquito-borne disease is becoming increasingly problematic throughout Southeast Asia, especially in the cities. As there is no vaccine available it can only be prevented by avoiding mosquito bites. The mosquito that carries dengue bites day and night, so use insect-avoidance measures at all times. Symptoms include high fever, severe headache and body ache (dengue was once known as 'breakbone fever'). Some people develop a rash and experience diarrhoea. There is no specific treatment, just rest and paracetamol – do not take aspirin as it increases the likelihood of haemorrhaging. See a doctor to be diagnosed and monitored.

Filariasis

This is a mosquito-borne disease that is very common in the local population, yet very rare in travellers. Mosquito-avoidance measures are the best way to prevent this disease.

Hepatitis A

A problem throughout the region, this food- and water-borne virus infects the liver, causing jaundice (yellow skin and eyes), nausea and lethargy. There is no specific treatment for hepatitis A, you just need to allow time for the liver to heal. All travellers to Vietnam should be vaccinated against hepatitis A.

Hepatitis B

The only sexually transmitted disease that can be prevented by vaccination, hepatitis

B is spread by body fluids, including sexual contact. In some parts of Southeast Asia up to 20% of the population are carriers of hepatitis B, and usually are unaware of this. The long-term consequences can include liver cancer and cirrhosis.

Hepatitis E

Hepatitis E is transmitted through contaminated food and water and has similar symptoms to hepatitis A, but is far less common. It is a severe problem in pregnant women and can result in the death of both mother and baby. There is currently no vaccine, and prevention is by following safe eating and drinking guidelines.

HIV

The official figures on the number of people with HIV/AIDS in Vietnam are vague, but are on the rise. Health-education messages relating to HIV/AIDS are visible all over the countryside, but the official line is that infection is largely limited to sex workers and drug users. Condoms are widely available throughout Vietnam.

Influenza

Present year-round in the tropics, influenza (flu) symptoms include high fever, muscle aches, runny nose, cough and sore throat. It can be very severe in people over the age of 65 or in those with underlying medical conditions such as heart disease or diabetes; vaccination is recommended for these individuals. There is no specific treatment, just rest and paracetamol.

Japanese B Encephalitis

While a rare disease in travellers, at least 50,000 locals are infected with Japanese B Encephalitis each year in Southeast Asia. This viral disease is transmitted by mosquitoes. Most cases occur in rural areas, and vaccination is recommended for travellers spending more than one month outside of cities. There is no treatment, and a third of infected people will die while another third will suffer permanent brain damage.

Malaria

For such a serious and potentially deadly disease, there is an enormous amount of misinformation concerning malaria. You must get expert advice as to whether your trip actually puts you at risk. Many parts of Vietnam, particularly city and resort areas, have minimal to no risk of malaria, and the risk of side effects from the tablets may outweigh the risk of getting the disease. For most rural areas, however, the risk of contracting the disease far outweighs the risk of any tablet side effects. Travellers to isolated areas in high-risk regions such as Ca Mau (p444) and Bac Lieu (p443) provinces, and the rural south, may like to carry a treatment dose of medication for use if symptoms occur. Remember that malaria can be fatal. Before you travel, seek medical advice on the right medication and dosage for you.

Malaria is caused by a parasite transmitted by the bite of an infected mosquito. The most important symptom of malaria is fever, but general symptoms such as headache, diarrhoea, cough or chills may also occur. Diagnosis can only be made by taking a blood sample.

Two strategies should be combined to prevent malaria – mosquito avoidance, and antimalarial medications. Most people who catch malaria are taking inadequate or no antimalarial medication.

Travellers are advised to prevent mosquito bites by taking these steps:

- Choose accommodation with screens and fans (if not air-conditioned).
- Impregnate clothing with permethrin in high-risk areas.
- Sleep under a mosquito net impregnated with permethrin.
- Spray your room with insect repellent before going out for your evening meal.
- Use a DEET-containing insect repellent on exposed skin. Wash this off at night, as long as you are sleeping under a mosquito net. Natural repellents such as citronella can be effective, but must be applied more frequently than products containing DEET.
- Use mosquito coils.
- Wear long sleeves and trousers in light colours.

MALARIA MEDICATION

There are various medications available. The effectiveness of the Chloroquine and Paludrine combination is now limited in Vietnam. Common side effects include nausea (40% of people) and mouth ulcers. It is generally not recommended.

Lariam (Mefloquine) has received a lot of bad press, some of it justified, some not. This weekly tablet suits many people. Serious side effects are rare but include depression, anxiety, psychosis and seizures. Anyone with a history of depression, anxiety, other psychological disorders or epilepsy should not take Lariam. It is considered safe in the second and third trimesters of pregnancy. It is around 90% effective in Vietnam. Tablets must be taken for about four weeks after leaving the risk area.

Doxycycline, taken as a daily tablet, is a broad-spectrum antibiotic that has the added benefit of helping to prevent a variety of tropical diseases, including leptospirosis, tick-borne disease, typhus and melioidosis. The potential side effects include photosensitivity (a tendency to sunburn), thrush in women, indigestion, heartburn, nausea and interference with the contraceptive pill. More serious side effects include ulceration of the oesophagus – you can help prevent this by taking your tablet with a meal and a large glass of water, and never lying down within half an hour of taking it. It must be taken for four weeks after leaving the risk area.

Malarone is a new drug combining Atovaquone and Proguanil. Side effects are uncommon and mild, most commonly nausea and headaches. It is the best tablet for scuba divers and for those on short trips to high-risk areas. It must be taken for one week after leaving the risk area.

Derivatives of Artesunate are not suitable as a preventive medication, but they are useful treatments under medical supervision.

A final option is to take no preventive medication but to have a supply of emergency medication should you develop the symptoms of malaria. This is less than ideal, and you'll need to get to a good medical facility within 24 hours of developing a fever. If you choose this option the most effective and safest treatment is Malarone (four tablets once daily for three days). Other options include Mefloquine and quinine but the side effects of these drugs at treatment doses make them less desirable. Fansidar is no longer recommended.

Measles

Measles remains a problem in some parts of Vietnam. This highly contagious bacterial infection is spread via coughing and sneezing. Many people born before 1966 are immune as they had the disease in childhood. Measles starts with a high fever and rash and can be complicated by pneumonia and brain disease. There is no specific treatment.

Rabies

This uniformly fatal disease is spread by the bite or lick of an infected animal – most commonly a dog or monkey. Seek medical advice immediately after any animal bite and commence postexposure treatment. Having a pretravel vaccination means the postbite treatment is greatly simplified. If an animal bites you, gently wash the wound with soap and water, and apply an iodine-based antiseptic. If you are not vaccinated you will need to receive rabies immunoglobulin as soon as possible.

Schistosomiasis

Schistosomiasis (also called bilharzia) is a tiny parasite that enters your skin after you've been swimming in contaminated water – travellers usually only get a light infection and hence have no symptoms. If you are concerned, you can be tested three months after exposure. On rare occasions, travellers may develop 'Katayama fever'; this occurs some weeks after exposure, as the parasite passes through the lungs and causes an allergic reaction. Symptoms are coughing and fever. Schistosomiasis is easily treated with medications.

STDs

Sexually transmitted diseases include herpes, warts, syphilis, gonorrhoea and chlamydia. People carrying these diseases often have no signs of infection. Condoms will help prevent gonorrhoea and chlamydia but not warts or herpes. If after a sexual encounter you develop any rash, lumps, discharge or pain when passing urine seek immediate medical attention. If you have been sexually active during your travels, have an STD check on your return home.

While abstinence from sexual contact is the only 100% effective prevention, using condoms is also effective. Condoms are widely available throughout Vietnam; when purchasing, ensure the package hasn't been stored in the sun as the rubber could have deteriorated.

Tuberculosis

Tuberculosis (TB) is rare in short-term travellers. Medical and aid workers, and long-term travellers who have significant contact with the local population, should take precautions, however. Vaccination is usually only given to children under the age of five, but adults at risk are recommended to have pre- and post-travel TB testing. The main symptoms are fever, cough, weight loss, night sweats and tiredness.

Typhoid

This serious bacterial infection is spread via food and water. It gives a high, slowly progressive fever and headache, and may be accompanied by a dry cough and stomach pain. It is diagnosed by blood tests and treated with antibiotics. Vaccination is recommended for all travellers spending more than a week in Vietnam, or travelling outside of the major cities. Be aware that vaccination is not 100% effective so you must still be careful with what you eat and drink.

Typhus

Murine typhus is spread by the bite of a flea whereas scrub typhus is spread via a mite. These diseases are rare in travellers. Symptoms include fever, muscle pains and a rash. You can avoid these diseases by following general insect-avoidance measures. Doxycycline will also help prevent them.

TRAVELLERS' DIARRHOEA

Travellers' diarrhoea is by far the most common problem affecting travellers – between 30% and 50% of people will suffer from it within two weeks of starting their trip. In over 80% of cases, travellers' diarrhoea is caused by a bacteria (there are numerous potential culprits), and therefore responds promptly to treatment with antibiotics. Treatment with antibiotics will depend on your situation – how sick you are, how quickly you need to get better, where you are and so on.

Travellers' diarrhoea is defined as the passage of more than three watery bowel-actions within 24 hours, plus at least one other symptom such as fever, cramps, nausea, vomiting or feeling generally unwell.

Treatment consists of staying hydrated. Rehydration solutions like Gastrolyte are the best for this. Antibiotics such as Norfloxacin, Ciprofloxacin or Azithromycin will kill the bacteria quickly.

Loperamide is just a 'stopper' and doesn't get to the cause of the problem. It is helpful if you have to go on a long bus ride, but don't take Loperamide if you have a fever, or blood in your stools. Seek medical attention quickly if you do not respond to an appropriate antibiotic.

Amoebic Dysentery

Amoebic dysentery is very rare in travellers but is often misdiagnosed by poor-quality labs in Southeast Asia. Symptoms are similar to bacterial diarrhoea (eg fever, bloody diarrhoea and generally feeling unwell). You should always seek reliable medical care if you have blood in your diarrhoea. Treatment involves two drugs: Tinidazole or Metroniadzole to kill the parasite in your gut and then a second drug to kill the cysts. If left untreated complications such as liver or gut abscesses can occur.

Giardiasis

Giardia lamblia is a parasite that is relatively common in travellers. Symptoms include nausea, bloating, excess gas, fatigue and intermittent diarrhoea. 'Eggy' burps are often attributed solely to giardiasis, but work in Nepal has shown that they are not specific to this infection. The parasite will eventually go away if left untreated but this can take months. The treatment of choice is Tinidazole, with Metronidazole being a second-line option.

ENVIRONMENTAL HAZARDS

Air Pollution

Air pollution, particularly vehicle pollution, is an increasing problem in most of Vietnam's major cities. If you have severe respiratory problems speak with your doctor before travelling to any heavily polluted urban centres.

This pollution also causes minor respiratory problems such as sinusitis, dry throat and irritated eyes. If troubled by the pollution leave the city for a few days and get some fresh air.

Food

Eating in restaurants is the biggest risk factor for contracting travellers' diarrhoea. Ways to avoid it include eating only freshly cooked food, and avoiding shellfish and food that has been sitting around in buffets. Peel all fruit, cook vegetables, and soak salads in iodine water for at least 20 minutes. Eat in busy restaurants with a high turnover of customers.

SCORCHED OEUF POLICY

There have been periodic outbreaks of avian influenza, or bird flu, in Vietnam in the past few years. Dozens of people have died and the threat of human-to-human transmission remains real. Now the HN-51 strain has gone global, Vietnam is no longer in the spotlight. However, when outbreaks occur, eggs and poultry are usually banished from the menu in many hotels and restaurants. Even where eggs are available, we recommend a scorched oeuf policy. Ensure they are well cooked in whatever shape or form they come. No runny omelettes, no sunny-side up. Don't take risks or you might end up with egg on your face.

Heat

Many parts of Vietnam are hot and humid throughout the year. For most people it takes at least two weeks to adapt to the hot climate. Swelling of the feet and ankles is common, as are muscle cramps caused by excessive sweating. Prevent these by avoiding dehydration and excessive activity in the heat. Take it easy when you first arrive. Don't eat salt tablets (they aggravate the gut) but do drink rehydration solution and eat salty food. Treat cramps by stopping activity, resting, rehydrating with double-strength rehydration solution and gently stretching.

Dehydration is the main contributor to heat exhaustion. Symptoms include feeling weak, headache, irritability, nausea or vomiting, sweaty skin, a fast, weak pulse and a normal or slightly elevated body temperature. Treatment involves getting out of the heat and/or sun, fanning the victim and applying cool wet cloths to the skin, laying the victim flat with their legs raised and rehydrating with water containing a quarter of a teaspoon of salt per litre. Recovery is usually rapid, though it is common to feel weak for some days afterwards.

Heatstroke is a serious medical emergency. Symptoms come on suddenly and include weakness, nausea, a hot dry body with a body temperature of over 41°C, dizziness, confusion, loss of coordination, seizures and eventually collapse and loss of consciousness. Seek medical help and commence cooling by getting the person out of the heat, removing their clothes, fanning them and applying cool wet cloths or ice to their body, especially to the groin and armpits.

Prickly heat is a common skin rash in the tropics, caused by sweat being trapped under the skin. The result is an itchy rash of tiny lumps. Treat by moving out of the heat and into an air-conditioned area for a few hours and by having cool showers. Creams and ointments clog the skin so they should be avoided. Locally bought prickly-heat powder can be helpful.

Tropical fatigue is common in long-term expats based in the tropics. It's rarely due to disease and is caused by the climate, inadequate mental rest, excessive alcohol intake and the demands of daily work in a different culture.

Insect Bites & Stings

Bedbugs don't carry disease but their bites are very itchy. They live in the cracks of furniture and walls and then migrate to the bed at night to feed on you. You can treat the itch with an antihistamine. You can try to prevent or minimise bites by using your own sheet-sleeping bag cover. Lice inhabit various parts of your body but most commonly your head and pubic area. Transmission is via close contact with an infected person, although body lice can come from contaminated bedclothes. They can be difficult to treat and you may need numerous applications of an antilice shampoo such as permethrin, or in the case of body lice, with medicated creams or ointments. Pubic lice are usually contracted from sexual contact.

Ticks are contracted during walks in rural areas. They are commonly found behind the ears, on the belly and in armpits. If you have had a tick bite and experience symptoms such as a rash (at the site of the bite or elsewhere), fever or muscle aches you should see a doctor. Doxycycline prevents tick-borne diseases.

Leeches are found in humid forest areas. They do not transmit any disease but their bites are often intensely itchy for weeks afterwards and can easily become infected. Apply an iodine-based antiseptic to any leech bite to help prevent infection.

Bee and wasp stings mainly cause problems for people who are allergic to them. Anyone with a serious bee or wasp allergy should carry an injection of adrenalin (eg an Epipen) for emergency treatment. For others pain is the

DRINKING WATER

The number-one rule is *be careful of the water*. Ice can be particularly risky; if you don't know for certain that the water is safe, assume the worst. However, a lot of the ice in Vietnam comes from factories introduced by the French, so it is as safe as the bottled water. Following these rules will help you avoid water-borne diseases:

- Never drink tap water.
- Bottled water is generally safe – check the seal is intact at purchase.
- Boiling water is the most efficient method of purifying it.
- The best chemical purifier is iodine. It should not be used by pregnant women or people who suffer from thyroid problems.
- Water filters should filter out viruses. Ensure your filter has a chemical barrier such as iodine. and a small pore size, ie less than four microns.

main problem – apply ice to the sting and take painkillers.

Jellyfish

Most jellyfish in Vietnamese waters are not dangerous, just irritating. First aid for jellyfish stings involves pouring vinegar onto the affected area to neutralise the poison. Do not rub sand or water onto the stings. Take painkillers, and seek medical advice of you feel ill in any way after being stung. Take local advice if there are dangerous jellyfish around and keep out of the water.

Parasites

Numerous parasites are common in local populations in Vietnam, however most of these are rare in travellers. The two rules to follow if you wish to avoid parasitic infections are to wear shoes and to avoid eating raw food, especially fish, pork and vegetables. A number of parasites are transmitted via the skin by walking barefoot including strongyloides, hookworm and cutaneous larva migrans.

Skin Problems

Fungal rashes are common in humid climates. There are two common fungal rashes that affect travellers. The first occurs in moist areas that get less air such as the groin, armpits and between the toes. It starts as a red patch that slowly spreads and is usually itchy. Treatment involves keeping the skin dry, avoiding chafing and using an antifungal cream such as Clotrimazole or Lamisil. *Tinea versicolor* is also common – this fungus causes small, light-coloured patches, most commonly on the back, chest and shoulders. Consult a doctor.

Cuts and scratches become easily infected in humid climates. Take meticulous care of any cuts and scratches to prevent complications such as abscesses. Immediately wash all wounds in clean water and apply antiseptic. If you develop signs of infection (increasing pain and redness) see a doctor. Divers and surfers should be particularly careful with coral cuts as they become easily infected.

Snakes

Vietnam is home to many species of both poisonous and harmless snakes. Assume all snakes are poisonous and never try to catch one. Always wear boots and long pants if walking in an area that may have snakes. First aid in the event of a snake-bite involves pressure immobilisation via an elastic bandage firmly wrapped around the affected limb, starting at the bite site and working up towards the chest. The bandage should not be so tight that the circulation is cut off, and the fingers or toes should be kept free so the circulation can be checked. Immobilise the limb with a splint and carry the victim to medical attention. Do not use tourniquets or try to suck the venom out. Antivenom is available only in major cities.

Sunburn

Even on a cloudy day sunburn can occur rapidly. Always use a strong sunscreen (at least factor 30), making sure to reapply after a swim, and always wear a wide-brimmed hat and sunglasses outdoors. Avoid lying in the sun during the hottest part of the day (from 10am to 2pm). If you become sunburnt, stay out of the sun until you have recovered, apply cool compresses and take painkillers for the discomfort. One percent hydrocortisone cream applied twice daily is also helpful.

WOMEN'S HEALTH

Pregnant women should receive specialised advice before travelling. The ideal time to travel is in the second trimester (between 16 and 28 weeks), during which the risk of pregnancy-related problems is at its lowest and pregnant women generally feel at their best. During the first trimester there is a risk of miscarriage and in the third trimester complications such as premature labour and high blood pressure are possible. It's wise to travel with a companion.

Always carry a list of quality medical facilities available at your destination and ensure you continue your standard antenatal care at these facilities. Avoid rural travel in areas with poor transportation and medical facilities. Most of all, ensure travel insurance covers all pregnancy-related possibilities, including premature labour.

Malaria is a high-risk disease in pregnancy. WHO recommends that pregnant women do *not* travel to areas that have Chloroquine-resistant malaria. None of the more effective antimalarial drugs are completely safe in pregnancy.

Travellers' diarrhoea can quickly lead to dehydration and result in inadequate blood flow to the placenta. Many of the drugs used to treat various diarrhoea bugs are not recommended in pregnancy. Azithromycin is considered safe.

In the urban areas of Vietnam, supplies of sanitary products are readily available. Birth control options may be limited so bring adequate supplies of contraception. Heat, humidity and antibiotics can all contribute to thrush. Treatment is with antifungal creams and pessaries such as Clotrimazole. A practical alternative is a single tablet of Fluconazole (Diflucan). Urinary tract infections can be precipitated by dehydration or long bus journeys without toilet stops; bring suitable antibiotics.

TRADITIONAL MEDICINE

A number of traditional medical treatments are practised in Vietnam. Herbal medicine, much of it imported from China, is widely available and sometimes very effective. As with Western medicine, self-diagnosis is not advisable – see a doctor. Traditional Chinese doctors are found wherever a large Chinese community exists, including HCMC, Hanoi and Hoi An.

If you visit traditional Chinese doctors, you might be surprised by what they discover about your body. For example, the doctor will almost certainly take your pulse and then may perhaps tell you that you have a 'slippery' or 'thready' pulse. They have identified more than 30 different kinds of pulse. A pulse could be empty, prison, leisurely, bowstring, irregular or even regularly irregular. The doctor may then examine your tongue to see if it is slippery, dry, pale, greasy, has a thick coating or possibly no coating at all. The doctor, having discovered your ailment, such as wet heat, as evidenced by a slippery pulse and a red greasy tongue, will prescribe the proper herbs for your condition.

Once you have a diagnosis you may be treated by moxibustion, a traditional treatment whereby various types of herbs, rolled into what looks like a ball of fluffy cotton, are held near the skin and ignited. A slight variation of this method is to place the herb on a slice of ginger and then ignite it. The idea is to apply the maximum amount of heat possible without burning the patient. This heat treatment is supposed to be very good for diseases such as arthritis.

It is common to see Vietnamese people with long bands of red welts on their necks, foreheads and backs. Don't worry, this is not some kind of hideous skin disease, but rather a treatment known as *cao gio*, literally 'scrape wind'. In traditional Vietnamese folk medicine, many illnesses are attributed to 'poisonous wind', which can be released by applying eucalyptus oil or tiger balm and scraping the skin with a spoon or coin, thus raising the welts. The results aren't pretty, but the locals say this treatment is good for the common cold, fatigue, headaches and other ailments. Whether the cure hurts less than the disease is something one can only judge from experience.

Another technique to battle bad breezes is called *giac hoi*. This one employs suction cups, typically made of bamboo or glass, which are placed on the patient's skin. A burning piece of alcohol-soaked cotton is briefly put inside the cup to drive out the air before it is applied. As the cup cools, a partial vacuum is produced, leaving a nasty-looking but harmless red circular mark on the skin, which goes away in a few days. Looks pretty weird on the forehead though!

There is some solid evidence attesting to the efficacy of acupuncture. Some major surgical operations have been performed using acupuncture as the only anaesthetic (this works best on the head). In this case, a small electric current (from batteries) is passed through the needles.

If done properly the practice doesn't hurt. Knowing where to insert the needle is crucial. Acupuncturists have identified more than 2000 insertion points, but only about 150 are commonly used. The exact mechanism by which acupuncture works is not fully understood. Practitioners talk of energy channels or meridians that connect the needle insertion point to the particular organ, gland or joint being treated. The acupuncture point is sometimes quite far from the area of the body being treated.

Nonsterile acupuncture needles pose a genuine health risk in this era of AIDS. You would be wise to purchase your own acupuncture needles if you plan on having this treatment in Vietnam.

Language

CONTENTS

LANGUAGES IN VIETNAM

Vietnamese is the official language of Vietnam, and it is spoken throughout the country. There are dialectical differences between the north, central and southern regions. There are also dozens of different languages spoken by the various ethnic minorities, particularly in the central highlands and in the far north of the country. Khmer, the Cambodian language, is spoken in parts of the Mekong Delta, and Lao and various Chinese dialects are evident in areas bordering Laos and China.

The Vietnamese people's knowledge of foreign languages reflects their country's relationship with foreign powers – cordial or otherwise – in recent history.

Much of Vietnam's elder generation still speak French, while many middle-aged Vietnamese speak Russian and other Eastern European languages – many of these people spent time in countries like Russia, Bulgaria and the former East Germany during the Cold War (at least until it thawed in the late 1980s). Today, however, Vietnam's youth has fully embraced the English language. A fair number of young people also study Japanese, French and other Western European languages.

The most widely spoken foreign languages in Vietnam are Chinese (Cantonese and Mandarin), English and French, more or less in that order. People in their 50s and older (who grew up during the colonial period) are much more likely to understand some French than southerners of the successive generation, for whom English was indispensable for professional and commercial contacts with the Americans. Some southern Vietnamese men – former combat interpreters – speak a quaint form of English peppered with all sorts of charming southern-American expressions such as 'y'all come back' and 'it ain't worth didley squat', pronounced with a perceptible drawl. Apparently, they worked with Americans from the deep south, carefully studied their pronunciation and diligently learned every nuance.

Many of the Vietnamese who can speak English – especially former South Vietnamese soldiers and officials – learned it while working with the Americans during the war. After reunification, almost all of them spent periods of time ranging from a few months to 15 years in 're-education camps'. Many of these former South Vietnamese soldiers and officials will be delighted to renew contact with Americans, with whose compatriots they spent so much time, often in very difficult circumstances, more than half a lifetime ago.

These days almost everyone has a desire to learn English. If you're looking to make contacts with English students, the best place is at the basic food stalls in university areas.

Spoken Chinese (both Cantonese and Mandarin) is making a definite comeback after years of being supressed. The large number of free-spending tourists and investors from Taiwan and Hong Kong provide the chief motivation for studying Chinese. In addition, cross-border trade with mainland China has been increasing rapidly and those who are able to speak Chinese are well positioned to profit from it.

After reunification, the teaching of Russian was stressed all over the country. With the collapse of the USSR in 1991, all interest in studying Russian ground to a screeching halt. Most Vietnamese who bothered to learn the language have either forgotten it or are in the process of forgetting it.

VIETNAMESE

The Vietnamese language *(Kinh)* is a fusion of Mon-Khmer, Tai and Chinese elements. Vietnamese derived a significant percentage of its basic words from the nontonal Mon-Khmer languages. From the Tai languages came certain grammatical elements and tonality. Chinese gave Vietnamese most of its literary, technical and governmental vocabulary, as well as its traditional writing system.

The following list of words and phrases will help get you started. If you'd like a more comprehensive guide to the language, pick up a copy of Lonely Planet's pocket-sized *Vietnamese Phrasebook*.

The variation in vocabulary between the Vietnamese of the north and that of the south is indicated in this chapter by (N) and (S) respectively.

WRITTEN VIETNAMESE

For centuries, the Vietnamese language was written in standard Chinese characters *(chữ nho)*. Around the 13th century, the Vietnamese devised their own writing system called *chữ nôm* (or just *nôm*), which was created by combining two Chinese words or by using single Chinese characters for their phonetic value. Both writing systems were in use until the 20th century – official business and scholarship was conducted in *chữ nho*, while *chữ nôm* was used for popular literature. The Latin-based *quốc ngữ* script, widely used since WWI, was developed in the 17th century by Alexandre de Rhodes (see the boxed text, right). *Quốc ngữ* served to undermine the position of Mandarin officials, whose power was based on traditional scholarship in *chữ nho* and *chữ nôm*, scripts that were largely inaccessible to the masses.

The Vietnamese treat every syllable as an independent word, so 'Saigon' is spelt 'Sai Gon' and 'Vietnam' is written as 'Viet Nam'. Foreigners aren't too comfortable with this system – we prefer to read 'London' rather than 'Lon Don'. This leads to the notion that Vietnamese is a 'monosyllabic language', where every syllable represents an independent word. This idea appears to hark back to the Chinese writing system, where every syllable is represented by an independent character and each character is treated as a meaningful word in its own right. In reality, Vietnamese appears to be polysyllabic, like English. However, writing systems do influence people's perceptions of their own language, so the Vietnamese themselves will insist that their language is monosyllabic – it's a debate probably not worth pursuing.

ALEXANDRE DE RHODES

One of the most illustrious of the early missionaries was the brilliant French Jesuit scholar Alexandre de Rhodes (1591–1660). De Rhodes first preached in Vietnamese only six months after arriving in the country in 1627, and he is most recognised for his work in devising *quốc ngữ*, the Latin-based phonetic alphabet in which Vietnamese is written to this day. By replacing Chinese characters with *quốc ngữ*, de Rhodes facilitated the propagation of the gospel to a wide audience.

Over the course of his long career, de Rhodes travelled back and forth between Hanoi, Macau, Rome and Paris, seeking support and funding for his missionary activities and battling both Portuguese colonial opposition and the intractable Vatican bureaucracy. In 1645 he was sentenced to death for illegally entering Vietnam to proselytise, but was expelled instead; two of the priests with him were beheaded.

For his contributions, de Rhodes gained the highest respect from the Vietnamese (in the south, anyway), who called him *cha caả* (father). A memorial statue of de Rhodes stands in central Saigon.

Most of the names of the letters of the *quốc ngữ* alphabet are pronounced like the letters of the French alphabet. Dictionaries are alphabetised as in English except that each vowel/tone combination is treated as a different letter.

Most of the consonants of the Romanised Vietnamese alphabet are pronounced more or less as they are in English with a few exceptions. Vietnamese doesn't use the English letters 'f', 'j', 'w' and 'z'.

To help you make sense of what is (for most non-Vietnamese) a very tricky writing system, the words and phrases in this language guide include pronunciations that use a written form more familiar to English speakers. The same symbols as *quốc ngữ* are used for marking the tones.

For example, Vietnamese **d** and **gi-** are represented with 'z', **đ** with 'd', **ph-** with 'f', **x** with 's', **-ng** with 'm', **-nh** with 'ny' etc.

SYMBOL & PRONUNCIATION

c, k	**ğ**	an unaspirated 'k'
đ	**đ**	(with crossbar) as in 'do'
d	**z/y**	(without crossbar) as the 'z' in 'zoo' (N); as the 'y' in 'yes' (S)
gi-	**z/y**	as a 'z' (N); as a 'y' (S)
kh-	**ch**	as the 'ch' in German *buch*
ng-	**ng**	as the '-nga-' sound in 'long ago'
nh-	**ny**	as the 'ny' in 'canyon'
ph-	**f**	as in 'farm'
r	**z/r**	as 'z' (N); as 'r' (S)
s	**s/sh**	as 's' (N); as 'sh' (S)
tr-	**ch/tr**	as 'ch' (N); as 'tr' (S)
th-	**t**	a strongly aspirated 't'
x	**s**	like an 's'
-ch	**k**	like a 'k'
-ng	**ng**	as the 'ng' in 'long' but with the lips closed; sounds like English 'm'
-nh	**ng**	as in 'singing'

TONES

For Westerners, the hardest part of studying Vietnamese is learning to differentiate between the tones. There are six tones in spoken Vietnamese. Thus, every syllable in Vietnamese can be pronounced six different ways. For example, depending on the tones, the word *ma* can be read to mean 'phantom', 'but', 'mother', 'rice seedling', 'tomb' or 'horse'.

The six tones of spoken Vietnamese are represented by five diacritical marks in the written language (the first tone is left unmarked). These should not be confused with the four other diacritical marks that are used to indicate special consonants and vowels.

The following examples show the six different tone representations:

ma (ghost): middle of the vocal range
mà (which): begins low and falls lower
mả (tomb): begins low, dips and then rises to higher pitch
mã (horse): begins high, dips slightly, then rises sharply
mạ (rice seedling): begins low, falls to a lower level, then stops
má (mother): begins high and rises sharply

A visual representation looks something like this:

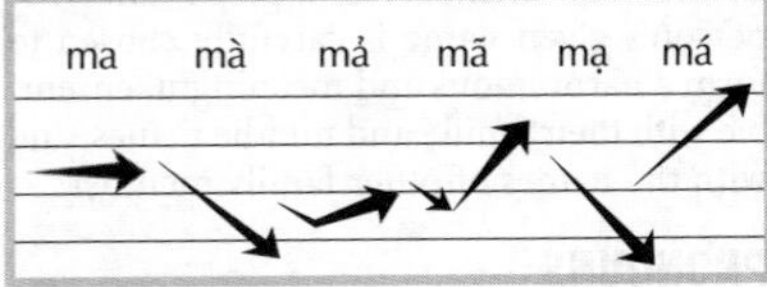

GRAMMAR

Vietnamese grammar is fairly straightforward, with a wide variety of possible sentence structures. Nouns have no masculine, feminine or plural forms, and verbs have only one form regardless of gender, person or tense. Instead, tool words and classifiers are used to show a word's relationship to its neighbours. For example, in the expression *con mèo (của) tôi* (my cat), *con* is the classifier, *mèo* is the noun, *của* means 'of/belong to' (and can be omitted), and *tôi* is the personal pronoun 'I'.

PROPER NAMES

Most Vietnamese names consist of a family name, a middle name and a given name, in that order. Thus, if Henry David Thoreau had been Vietnamese, he would have been named Thoreau David Henry and would have been addressed as Mr Henry – people are called by their given name, but to do this without using the title Mr, Mrs or Miss is considered as expressing either great intimacy, or arrogance of the sort a superior would use with his or her inferior.

In Vietnamese, Mr is *Ông* if the man is of your grandparents' generation, *Bác* if he is of your parents' age, *Chú* if he is younger than your parents and *Anh* if he is in his teens or early 20s. Mrs is *Bà* if the woman is of your grandparents' age and *Bác* if she is of your parents' generation or younger. Miss is *Chị* or *Em* unless the woman is very young, in which case *Cô* might be more appropriate. Other titles of respect are *Thầy* (Buddhist monk or male teacher), *Bà* (Buddhist nun), *Cha* (Catholic priest) and *Cô* (Catholic nun).

There are 300 or so family names in use in Vietnam, the most common of which is Nguyen (which is pronounced something like 'nwee-en'). About half of all Vietnamese have the surname Nguyen! When women marry, they usually (but not always) take their husband's family name. The middle name may be purely ornamental, may indicate the sex of its bearer or may be used by all the male members of a given family. A person's given name is carefully chosen to form a harmonious and meaningful ensemble with their family and middle names, and with the names of other family members.

PRONOUNS

I
tôi — doy

you
ông — awm (to an older man)
bà — baà (to an older woman)
anh — aang (to a man your own age)
cô — ğaw (to a woman your own age)

he
anh ấy — ang áy

she
cô ấy — ğó áy

we
chúng tôi — júm doy

they
họ — họ

ACCOMMODATION

Where is there a (cheap) ...?
đâu có ... (rẻ tiền)? — đoh ğó ... (zả đee·ùhn)

camping ground
nơi cắm trại — ner·ee ğúhm chại

hotel
khách sạn — kaák saạn

guesthouse
nhà khách — nyaà kaák

What is the address?
Địa chỉ là gì?
đee·ụh cheẻ laà zeè

Could you write the address down, please?
Bạn có thể viết giùm địa chỉ được không?
baạn ğó tẻ vee·úht zòom đee·ụh jeẻ đuhr·ẹrk kawm

I need to leave at ... o'clock (tomorrow morning).
Tôi phải đi lúc ... giờ (sáng mai).
doy faỉ đee lúp ... zèr (saáng mai)

How much does a room cost?
Giá một phòng là bao nhiêu?
zaá mạwt fòm laà bow nyee·oo

I'd like (a) ...
Tôi muốn ... — doy moo·úhn ...

bed
cái giường — ğaí zuhr·èrng

single room
phòng đơn — fòm dern

double-bed
giường đôi — zuhr·èrng đoy

room
phòng — fòm

room with two beds
phòng gồm hai giường ngủ — fòm gàwm hai zuhr·èrng ngoỏ

room with a bathroom
phòng có phòng tắm — fòm ğó fòm dúhm

to share a dorm
ở chung phòng nội trú — ẻr jum fòm nọy choó

air-conditioning
máy lạnh — máy laạng

bathroom
phòng tắm — fòm dúhm

blanket
mền — mèn

fan
quạt máy — gwaạt máy

hot water
nước nóng — nuhr·érk nóm

laundry
giặt ủi — zụht oỏ·ee

mosquito net
màng — maàng

reception
tiếp tân — dee·úhp duhn

room
phòng — fòm

room key
chìa khóa phòng — chee·aà kwaá fòm

1st-class room
phòng loại 1 — fòm lwaị mạwt

2nd-class room
phòng loại 2 — fòm lwaị hai

MAKING A RESERVATION
(for written and phone inquiries)

To ...	
Đến ...	đén ...
From ...	
Từ ...	dùhr ...
Date	
ngày tháng	ngày taáng
I'd like to book ...	
Làm ơn cho tôi đặt trước một ...	laàm ern jo doy đụht truhr·érk mạwt ...
in the name of ...	
tên là ...	den laà ...
from ... (date)	
Từ ...	dùhr ...
until ...	
Đến ...	đén ...
credit card	
thẻ tín dụng	tả dín zoọm
number	
số	sáw
expiry date	
hết hàng	hét haàng

sheet
ra trãi giường zaa chaĩ zuhr·èrng
toilet
nhà vệ sinh nyaà vẹ sing
toilet paper
giấy vệ sinh záy vẹ sing
towel
khăn tắm kúhn dúhm

How much is it ...?
Giá bao nhiêu ...? zaá bow nyee·oo ...
per night
một đêm mạwt đem
per person
một người mạwt nguhr·eè

May I see it?
Tôi có thể xem phòng được không?
doy ğó tẻ sam fòm đuhr·ẹrk kawm
Where is the bathroom?
Phòng tắm ở đâu?
fòm dúhm ẻr đoh
Where is the toilet?
Nhà vệ sinh ở đâu?
nyaà vẹ sing ẻr đoh
I'm leaving today.
Hôm nay tôi rời đay.
hawm nay doy zer·eè đay
We're leaving tomorrow.
Ngày mai chúng tôi rời đay.
ngày mai júm doy zer·eè đay

CONVERSATION & ESSENTIALS

Hello.
Xin chào. sin jòw
Goodbye.
Tạm biệt. daạm bee·ụht
Yes.
Vâng. (N)/*Dạ.* (S) vuhng/yạ
No.
Không. kawm
Please.
Làm ơn. laàm ern
Thank you (very much).
Cảm ơn (rất nhiều). ğaảm ern (zúht nyee·oò)
You're welcome.
Không có chi. kawm ğó jee
Excuse me. (often used before questions)
Xin lỗi. sin lõy
Sorry.
Xin lỗi. sin lõy
How are you?
Có khỏe không? ğáw kwả kawm
Fine, thank you. And you?
Khỏe, cám ơn. kwả ğaảm ern
Còn bạn thì sao? kwả ğòn baạn teè sow
Good night.
Chúc ngủ ngon. júp ngoỏ ngon
What's your name?
Tên là gì? den laà zeè
My name is ...
Tên tôi là ... den doy laà ...
Where are you from?
Bạn từ đâu đến? baạn dùhr đoh đén
I'm from ...
Tôi đến từ ... doy đén tùhr ...
I like ...
Tôi thích ... doy tík ...
I don't like ...
Tôi không thích ... doy kawm tík ...
I want ...
Tôi muốn ... doy moo·úhn ...
I don't want ...
Tôi không muốn ... doy kawm moo·úhn ...

DIRECTIONS

Where is ...?
ở đâu ...? ẻr đoh ...
Go straight ahead.
Thẳng tới trước. tủhng der·eé chuhr·érk
Turn left.
Sang trái. saang chaí
Turn right.
Sang phải. saang fai

SIGNS

Lối Vào	Entrance
Lối Ra	Exit
Hướng Dẫn	Information
Mở	Open
Đóng	Closed
Cấm	Prohibited
Cảnh Sát/Công An	Police
Nhà Vệ Sinh	Toilets/WC
Đàn Ông	Men
Phụ Nữ	Women

at the corner
ở góc đường ẻr góp đuhr·èrng
at the traffic lights
tại đèn giao thông dại đèn zow tawm
behind
đằng sau đùhng sow
in front of
đằng trước đùng chuhr·érk
far
xa saa
near (to)
gần gùhn
opposite
đối diện đóy zee·ụhn
north
bắc búhk
south
nam naam
east
đông đawm
west
tây day

beach
bãi biển baĩ beẻ·uhn
boulevard
đại lộ đại lạw
bridge
cầu ğóh
island
đảo đỏw
main square
quảng trường chính gwaảng chuhr·èrng jíng
market
chợ trường jẹr chuhr·èrng
mountain
núi noo·eé
quay
bến tàu bén dòh
river
sông sawm
sea
biển beẻ·uhn
square (in a city)
công viên ğawm vee·uhn
street
phố/đường (N/S) fáw/đuhr·èrng
temple
chùa joo·ùh

HEALTH

I'm sick.
Tôi bị đau.
doy beẹ đoh
It hurts here.
Chỗ bị đau ở đây.
jãw beẹ đoh ẻr đay
Please take me to the hospital.
Làm ơn đưa tôi bệnh viện.
laàm ern đuhr·uh doy bẹn vee·ụhn

dentist
nha sĩ nyaa seẽ
doctor
bác sĩ baák seẽ
pharmacy
nhà thuốc tây nyaà too·úhk day

I'm ...
Tôi bị ... doy beẹ ...
asthmatic
suyễn sweẽ·uhn
diabetic
bệnh đái đường bẹn đái đuhr·èrng
epileptic
động kinh đạwm ğing

I'm allergic to ...
Tôi bị dị ứng với ... doy beẹ zeẹ úhrng ver·eé ...
antibiotics
thuốc kháng sinh too·úhk kaáng sing
aspirin
thuốc giảm đau too·úhk zaảm đoh
penicillin
thuốc pênicilin too·úhk pe·nee·see·lin
bees
con ong ğon om
peanuts
đậu phọng đọh fọm

backache
đau lưng đoh luhrng
diarrhoea
tiêu chảy dee·oo jảy
dizziness
chóng mặt jóm mụht

LANGUAGE

EMERGENCIES

Help!
Cứu tôi! ğuhr·oó doy
There's been an accident!
Có tai nạn! ğó dai naạn
I'm lost.
Tôi bị lạc đường. doi beẹ laạk đuhr·èrng
Leave me alone!
Thôi! toy
Thief!
Ăn cắp! uhn ğúhp
Pickpocket!
Móc túi! móp doo·eé
Please call ...
Làm ơn gọi ... laàm ern gọy ...
an ambulance
xe cứu thương sa ğúuhr·oó tuhr·erng
a doctor
bác sĩ baák seẽ
the police
công an ğawm aan

fever
bệnh sốt bẹn sáwt
headache
nhức đầu nyúhrk đoh
malaria
sốt rét sáwt zét
nausea
buồn nôn boo·ùhn nawn
stomach ache
đau bụng đoh bụm
toothache
nhức răng nyúhrk zuhng
vomiting
ói óy
antiseptic
thuốc khử trùng too·úhk kủhr chùm
condoms
bao dương vật bow zuhr·erng vụht
contraceptive
cách ngừa thai ğaák nguhr·ùh tai
insect repellent
thuốc chống muỗi too·úhk jáwm moõ·ee
medicine
y thuốc ee too·úhk
mosquito coils
hương đốt chống muỗi (N) huhr·erng đért jáwm moõ·ee
nhang chống muỗi (S) nyaang jáwm moõ·ee
sanitary pads
băng vệ sinh buhng vẹ sing
sunblock cream
kem chống nắng ğam jáwm núhng
tampons
ống băng vệ sinh áwm buhng vẹ sing

LANGUAGE DIFFICULTIES

Do you speak English?
Bạn có nói được tiếng Anh không?
baạn ğó nóy đuhr·ẹrk díng aang kawm
Does anyone here speak English?
Có ai biết nói tiếng Anh không?
ğó ai bee·úht nóy díng aang kawm
What does that mean?
Nghĩa là gì?
ngee·ũh laà zeè
I (don't) understand.
Tôi (không) hiểu.
doy (kawm) heẻ·oo
Could you write it down, please?
Xin viết ra giùm tôi.
sin vee·úht zaa zùm doy
Can you show me (on the map)?
Xin chỉ giùm (trên bản dồ này).
sin jeẻ zùm (chen baản dàw này)

NUMBERS

1	*một*	mạwt
2	*hai*	hai
3	*ba*	baa
4	*bốn*	báwn
5	*năm*	nuhm
6	*sáu*	sóh
7	*bảy*	bảy
8	*tám*	dúhm
9	*chín*	jín
10	*mười*	muhr·eè
11	*mười một*	muhr·eè mọt
19	*mười chín*	muhr·eè jín
20	*hai mươi*	hai muhr·ee
21	*hai mươi mốt*	hai muhr·ee máwt
22	*hai mươi hai*	hai muhr·ee hai
30	*ba mươi*	ba muhr·ee
90	*chín mươi*	jín muhr·ee
100	*một trăm*	mạwt chuhm
200	*hai trăm*	hai chuhm
900	*chín trăm*	jín chuhm
1000	*một nghìn* (N)	mạwt ngyìn
	một ngàn (S)	mọt ngaàn
10,000	*mười nghìn* (N)	muhr·eè ngyìn
	mười ngàn (S)	muhr·eè ngaàn
1,000,000	*một triệu*	mạwt chee·oọ
2,000,000	*hai triệu*	hai chee·oọ
first	*thứ nhất*	túhr nyúht
second	*thứ hai*	túhr hai

PAPERWORK

name	*tên*	den
nationality	*quốc gia*	gwáwk zaa
address	*địa chỉ*	đee·ụh jeẻ
date/place of birth	*ngày/nơi sinh*	ngày/ner·ee sing
sex/gender	*giới tính*	zer·eé díng
passport (number)	*(số) hộ chiếu*	(sáw) hạw jee·oó
visa	*thị thực*	teẹ tụhrk

QUESTION WORDS

Who?	*Ái?*	aí
What?	*Cái gì?*	ğaí zeè
What is it?	*Cái này là cái gì?*	ğaí này laà ğaí zeè
When?	*Khi nào?*	kee nòw
Where?	*Ở đâu?*	ẻr đoh
Which?	*Cái nào?*	ğaí nòw
Why?	*Tại sao?*	tại sow
How?	*Làm sao?*	laàm sow

SHOPPING & SERVICES

I'd like to buy ...
Tôi muốn mua ...
doy moo·úhn moo·uh ...

How much is this?
Cái này giá bao nhiêu?
ğaí này zaá bow nyee·oo

I want to pay in dong.
Tôi muốn trả bằng tiền Việt Nam.
doy moo·úhn chả bùhng đee·ùhn vee·ụht naam

I don't like it.
Tôi không thích nó.
doy kawm tík nó

May I look at it?
Tôi có thể xem được không?
doy ğó tẻ sam đuhr·ẹrk kawm

I'm just looking.
Tôi chỉ ngắm xem.
doy jeẻ ngúhm sam

It's cheap.
Cái này rẻ.
ğaí này zả

It's too expensive.
Cái này quá mắc.
ğaí này gwaá múhk

I'll take it.
Tôi lấy cái này.
doy láy ğaí này

Do you accept ...?
Bạn có nhận ... không?
bạn kó nyụhn ... kawm

credit cards	*thẻ tín dụng*	tả dín zụm
travellers cheques	*xét du lịch*	sát zoo lịk

more	*nhiều hơn*	nyee·oò hern
less	*ít hơn*	ít hern
smaller	*nhỏ hơn*	nyỏ hern
bigger	*lớn hơn*	lérn hern

I'm looking for ...
Tôi tìm ...
doy dìm ...

a bank	*ngân hàng*	nguhn haàng
the church	*nhà thờ*	nyaà tèr
the city centre	*trung tâm thành phố*	chum duhm taàng fáw
the ... embassy	*sự quan ...*	sụr gwaan ...
the hospital	*nhà thương*	nyaà tuhr·erng
my hotel	*khách sạn của tôi*	kaák saạn ğoỏ·uh doy
the market	*chợ*	jẹr
the museum	*viện bảo tàng*	vee·ụhn bỏw daàng
the police	*cảnh sát*	ğaảng saát
the post office	*bưu điện*	buhr·oo đee·ụhn
a public phone	*phòng điện thoại*	fòm đee·ụhn twaị
a restaurant	*nhà hàng*	nyaà haàng
a public toilet	*phòng vệ sinh*	fòm vẹ sing
tourist office	*văn phòng hướng dẫn du lịch*	vuhn fòm huhr·érng zũhn zoo lịk

TIME & DATES

What time is it?
Mấy giờ rồi? máy zèr zòy
It's (eight) o'clock.
Bây giờ là (tám) giờ. bay zèr laà (dúhm) zèr
When?
Khi nào? kee nòw
now
bây giờ bay zèr
in the morning
sáng saáng
in the afternoon
chiều jee·oò
in the evening
tối dóy
today
hôm nay hawm nay
tomorrow
ngày mai ngày mai

Monday	*thứ hai*	túhr hai
Tuesday	*thứ ba*	túhr baa
Wednesday	*thứ tư*	túhr duhr
Thursday	*thứ năm*	túhr nuhm
Friday	*thứ sáu*	túhr sóh
Saturday	*thứ bảy*	túhr bảy
Sunday	*chủ nhật*	jỏo nhụht

January	*tháng giêng*	taáng zee·uhng
February	*tháng hai*	taáng hai
March	*tháng ba*	taáng baa
April	*tháng tư*	taáng tuhr
May	*tháng năm*	taáng nuhm
June	*tháng sáu*	taáng sóh
July	*tháng bảy*	taáng bảy
August	*tháng tám*	taáng dúhm
September	*tháng chín*	taáng jín
October	*tháng mười*	taáng muhr·eè
November	*tháng mười một*	taáng muhr·eè mạwt
December	*tháng mười hai*	taáng muhr·eè hai

TRANSPORT

Public Transport

What time does the (first)... leave/arrive?
Chuyến ... (sớm nhất) chạy lúc mấy giờ?
jwee·úhn ... (sérm nyúht) jạy lúp máy zèr
boat
tàu/thuyền dòw/twee·ùhn
bus
xe buýt sa beét
plane
máy bay máy bay
train
xe lửa sa lủhr·uh

I'd like a ... ticket.
Tôi muốn vé ...
doy moo·úhn vá ...
one way
đi một chiều đee mạt jee·oò
return
khứ hồi kúhr haw·eè
1st class
hạng nhất haạng nyúht
2nd class
hạng nhì haạng nyeè

I want to go to ...
Tôi muốn đi ...
doy moo·úhn đee ...
How long does the trip take?
Chuyến đi sẽ mất bao lâu?
jwee·úhn đee sã múht bow loh
What time does it arrive?
Mấy giờ đến?
máy zèr đén
The train has been cancelled.
Chuyến xe lửa bị hủy bỏ.
jwee·úhn sa lủhr·uh beẹ hweẻ bỏ
How long will it be delayed?
Nó sẽ bị đình hoãn bao lâu?
nó sã beẹ đìng hwaãn bow loh

the first
đầu tiên đòw dee·uhn
the last
cuối cùng ğoo·eé ğùm
bus station
bến xe bén sa
ticket office
phòng bán vé fòm baán vá
timetable
thời biểu ter·eè beẻ·oo
sleeping berth
giường ngủ zùhr·erng ngoỏ
railway station
ga xe lửa gaa sa lủhr·uh

Private Transport

I'd like to hire a ...
Tôi muốn thuê ...(N) doy moo·úhn twe ...
Tôi muốn mướn ...(S) doy moo·úhn muhr·érn ...
car
xe hơi sa her·ee
motorbike
xe moto sa mo·to
bicycle
xe đạp sa đạp
cyclo (pedicab)
xe xích lô sa sík law

LANGUAGE

Is this the road to ...?
Con đường nầy có dẫn đến ...?
ğon đuhr·èrng này ğó zũhn đén ...
How many kilometres to ...?
... cách đây bao nhiêu ki-lô-mét?
... ğaák đay bow nyee·oo kee·law·mét
Where's a service station?
Trạm xăng ở đâu?
chaạm suhng ẻr doh
Please fill it up.
Làm ơn đổ đầy bình.
laàm ern đỏ đày bìng
I'd like ... litres.
Tôi muốn ... lít.
doy moo·úhn ... léet

diesel
dầu diesel zòh dee·sel
leaded petrol
dầu xăng có chì zòh suhng ğó jeè
unleaded petrol
dầu xăng zòh suhng
highway
xa lộ saa lạw
map
bản đồ baản đàw

(How long) Can I park here?
Chúng tôi có thể đậu xe được (bao lâu)?
júm doy ğó tẻ dọh sa đuhr·ẹrk (bow loh)
I need a mechanic.
Chúng tôi cần thợ sửa xe.
júm doy ğùhn tẹr súhr·uh sa
The car/motorbike has broken down (at ...)
Xe bị hư (tại ...).
sa beẹ huhr (daị ...)
The car/motorbike won't start.
(Xe hơi/Xe moto) không đề được.
(sa her·ee/sa mo·to) kawm đè đuhr·ẹrk
I have a flat tyre.
Bánh xe tôi bị xì.
baáng sa doy beẹ seè
I've run out of petrol.
Tôi bị hết dầu/xăng.
doy beẹ hét zòh/suhng

TRAVEL WITH CHILDREN

Is there a/an ...?
Ở đây có ...? ẻr đay ğó ...
I need a/an ...
Tôi cần ... doy ğùhn ...
baby change room
phòng thay quần áo cho em bé fòm tay gwùhn ów jo am bá
car baby seat
ghế ngồi trong xe cho em bé gé ngòy chom sa jo am bá
child-minding service
dịch vụ giữ trẻ em zịk voọ zũhr chả am
children's menu
thực đơn cho trẻ em tụhrk đern jo chả am
disposable nappies/diapers
tã lót daã lót
(English-speaking) babysitter
người giữ trẻ em (nói tiếng Anh) nguhr·eè zũhr chả am (nóy díng aang)
highchair
ghế cao cho em bé gé kow jo am bá
potty
bô cho trẻ em bo jo chả am
stroller
xe đẩy cho em bé sa đay jo am bá

Do you mind if I breastfeed here?
Xin lỗi tôi có thể cho con tôi bú ở đây không?
sin lõy doy ğó tẻ jo ğon doy bóo ẻr đay kawm
Are children allowed?
Trẻ em có được phép vào không?
chả am ğó đuhr·ẹrk fáp vòw kawm

HILL-TRIBE LANGUAGES

The task of neatly classifying the different hill tribes of Vietnam is not an easy one. Ethnologists typically classify the Montagnards by linguistic distinction and commonly refer to three main groups (which further splinter into vast and quite complex subgroupings). The Austro-Asian family includes the Viet-Muong, Mon-Khmer, Tay-Tai and Meo-Dzao language groups; the Austronesian family includes Malayo-Polynesian languages; and the Sino-Tibetan family encompasses the Chinese and Tibeto-Burmese language groups. In addition, within a single spoken language there are often myriad dialectical variations.

The following words and phrases should prove useful if you are visiting members of the larger Vietnamese hill tribes. If you're planning on spending a considerable amount of time within Vietnam's hill-tribe areas, consider taking Lonely Planet's *Hill Tribes Phrasebook* with you. For more information on hill tribes and the areas they inhabit, see p285.

TAY

Also known as the Ngan, Pa Di, Phen, Thu Lao and Tho, the Tay belong to the Tay-Thai language group.

Hello.	*Pá prama.*
Goodbye.	*Pá paynó.*
Yes.	*Mi.*
No.	*Boomi.*
Thank you.	*Đay fon.*
What's your name?	*Ten múng le xăng ma?*
Where are you from?	*Mu'ng du' te là ma?*
How much is this?	*Ău ni ki lai tiên?*

H'MONG

The H'mong are also known as Meo, Mieu, Mong Do (White H'mong), Mong Du (Black H'mong), Mong Lenh (Flower H'mong), Mong Si (Red H'mong). They belong to the H'mong-Dzao language group, but their spoken language resembles Mandarin Chinese.

Hello.	*Ti nấu/Caó cu.*
Goodbye.	*Caó mun'g chè.*
Yes.	*Có mua.*
No.	*Chúi muá.*
Thank you.	*Ô chờ.*
What's your name?	*Caó be hua chan'g?*
Where are you from?	*Caó nhao từ tuả?*
How much is this?	*Pố chố chá?*

DZAO

Also known as Coc Mun, Coc Ngang, Dai Ban, Diu Mien, Dong, Kim Mien, lan Ten, Lu Gang, Tieu Ban, Trai and Xa, this tribe belongs to the Mong Dzao language group.

Hello/Goodbye.	*Puang tọi.*
Yes.	*Mái.*
No.	*Mái mái.*
Thank you.	*Tỡ dun.*
What's your name?	*Mang nhi búa chiên nay?*
Where are you from?	*May hải đo?*
How much is this?	*Pchiả nhăng?*

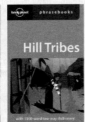

Glossary

For food and drink terms, see Eat Your Words on p70. For information on the Vietnamese language and pronunciation, see the Language chapter (p521).

A Di Da – Buddha of the Past
Agent Orange – toxic, carcinogenic chemical herbicide used extensively during the American War
am duong – Vietnamese equivalent of Yin and Yang
Amerasians – children borne of unions between Asian women and US servicemen during the American War
American War – Vietnamese name for what is also known as the Vietnam War
Annam – old Chinese name for Vietnam, meaning 'Pacified South'
ao dai – Vietnamese national dress worn by women
apsaras – heavenly maidens
ARVN – Army of the Republic of Vietnam (former South Vietnamese army)

ba mu – midwife. There are 12 'midwives', each of whom teaches newborns a different skill necessary for the first year of life: smiling, sucking, lying on their stomachs, and so forth.
Ba Tay – a term used to refer to Western women, meaning 'Mrs Westerner'
ban – mountainous village
bang – congregation (in the Chinese community)
bar om – literally 'holding' bars associated with the sex industry. Also known as 'karaoke om'.
bonze – Vietnamese Buddhist monk
buu dien – post office

cai luong – Vietnamese modern theatre
Cao Daism – indigenous Vietnamese religion
Cham – ethnic minority descended from the people of Champa
cham cui – acupuncture
Champa – Hindu kingdom dating from the late 2nd century AD
Charlie – nickname for the Viet Cong, used by US soldiers
chua – pagoda
chu nho – standard Chinese characters (script)
Cochinchina – the southern part of Vietnam during the French-colonial era
com pho – rice and rice-noodle soup
crémaillère – cog railway
cyclo – pedicab or bicycle rickshaw

Dai The Chi Bo Tat – an assistant of *A Di Da*
dan bau – single-stringed zither that generates an astounding magnitude of tones
dan tranh – 16-stringed zither
den – temple
Di Lac Buddha – Buddha of the Future
dikpalaka – gods of the directions of the compass
dinh – communal meeting hall
DMZ – Demilitarised Zone, a strip of land that once separated North and South Vietnam
doi moi – economic restructuring or reform, which commenced in Vietnam in 1986
dong – natural caves. Also Vietnamese currency.
do son – drums
DRV – Democratic Republic of Vietnam (the old North Vietnam)

ecocide – term used to describe the devastating effects of the herbicides sprayed over Vietnam during the American War

fléchette – experimental US weapon. An artillery shell containing thousands of darts.
Funan – see *Oc-Eo*

garuda – half human-half bird
gom – ceramics

hai dang – lighthouse
hat boi – classical theatre in the south
hat cheo – Vietnamese popular theatre
hat tuong – classical theatre in the north
ho ca – aquarium
Ho Chi Minh Trail – route used by the North Vietnamese Army and Viet Cong to move supplies to the South
Hoa – ethnic Chinese, one of the largest single minority groups in Vietnam
hoi quan – Chinese congregational assembly halls
Honda Dream – classic model of Honda motor-scooter seen throughout Vietnam
huong – perfume
huyen – rural district

Indochina – Vietnam, Cambodia and Laos. The name derives from Indian and Chinese influences.

kala-makara – sea-monster god
kalan – a religious sanctuary
khach san – hotel
Khmer – ethnic Cambodians

Khong Tu – Confucius
kich noi – spoken drama
Kinh – Vietnamese language
Kuomintang – Chinese Nationalist Party, also known as KMT. The KMT controlled China between 1925 and 1949 until defeated by the communists.

li xi – lucky money distributed during the Vietnamese Lunar New Year
liberation – 1975 takeover of the South by the North. Most foreigners call this 'reunification'.
Lien Xo – literally, Soviet Union. Used to call attention to a foreigner
linga – stylised phallus which represents the Hindu god Shiva

MAAG – Military Assistance Advisory Group, set up to instruct troops receiving US weapons on how to use them
mai son – lacquer
manushi-buddha – Buddha who appeared in human form
moi – derogatory word meaning 'savages', mostly used by ethnic Vietnamese to describe hill-tribe people
Montagnards – term meaning highlanders or mountain people, used to refer to the ethnic minorities who inhabit remote areas of Vietnam
muong – large village unit made up of *quel* (small stilt-houses)

naga – Sanskrit term for a mythical serpent being with divine powers; often depicted forming a kind of shelter over the Buddha
nam phai – for men
napalm – jellied petrol (gasoline) dropped and lit from aircraft; used by US forces with devastating repercussions during the American War
nha hang – restaurant
nha khach – hotel or guesthouse
nha nghi – guesthouse
nha rong – large stilt house, used by hill tribes as a kind of community centre
nha tro – dormitory
NLF – National Liberation Front, the official name for the VC
nom – Vietnamese script, used between the 10th and early 20th centuries
nu phai – for women
nui – mountain
nuoc mam – fish sauce, added to almost every main dish in Vietnam
NVA – North Vietnamese Army

Oc-Eo – Indianised Khmer kingdom (also called Funan) in southern Vietnam between the 1st and 6th centuries
Ong Bon – Guardian Spirit of Happiness and Virtue
Ong Tay – a term used to refer to Western men, meaning 'Mr Westerner'
Orderly Departure Program (ODP) – carried out under the auspices of the UN High Commissioner for Refugees (UNHCR), and designed to allow orderly resettlement of Vietnamese political refugees
OSS – US Office of Strategic Services. The predecessor of the CIA.

pagoda – traditionally an eight-sided Buddhist tower, but in Vietnam the word is commonly used to denote a temple
phong thuy – literally, 'wind and water'. Used to describe geomancy. Also known by its Chinese name, feng shui.
PRG – Provisional Revolutionary Government, the temporary Communist government set up by the VC in the South. It existed from 1969 to 1976.

quan – urban district
Quan Cong – Chinese God of War
Quan The Am Bo Tat – Goddess of Mercy
quoc am – modern Vietnamese literature
quoc ngu – Latin-based phonetic alphabet in which Vietnamese is written

rap – cinema
Revolutionary Youth League – first Marxist group in Vietnam and predecessor of the Communist Party
roi can – conventional puppetry
roi nuoc – water puppetry
ruou (pronounced xeo) – rice wine
RVN – Republic of Vietnam (the old South Vietnam)

salangane – swiftlet
sao – wooden flute
sao la – antelopelike creature
shakti – feminine manifestation of Shiva
song – river
SRV – Socialist Republic of Vietnam (Vietnam's official name)
Strategic Hamlets Program – program (by South Vietnam and the USA) of forcibly moving peasants into fortified villages to deny the VC bases of support
sung – fig tree
Tam Giao – literally, 'triple religion'. Confucianism, Taoism and Buddhism fused over time with popular Chinese beliefs and ancient Vietnamese animism.
Tao – the Way. The essence of which all things are made.
Tet – Vietnamese Lunar New Year
thai cuc quyen – Vietnamese for t'ai chi
Thich Ca Buddha – the historical Buddha Sakyamuni, whose real name was Siddhartha Gautama

Thien Hau Thanh Mau – Goddess of the Sea and Protector of Fishermen and Sailors
thong nhat – reunification. Also a common term for the Reunification Express train.
thuoc bac – Chinese medicine
toc hanh – express bus
Tonkin – the northern part of Vietnam during the French-colonial era. Also the name of a body of water in the north (Tonkin Gulf)
truyen khau – traditional oral literature

UNHCR – UN High Commissioner for Refugees

VC – Viet Cong or Vietnamese Communists
Viet Kieu – overseas Vietnamese
Viet Minh – League for the Independence of Vietnam, a nationalistic movement that fought the Japanese and French but later became communist-dominated
VNQDD – Viet Nam Quoc Dan Dang. Largely middle-class nationalist party.

xang – petrol
xe Honda loi – wagon pulled by a motorbike
xe lam – tiny three-wheeled trucks used for short-haul passenger and freight transport
xe loi – wagon pulled by a motorbike in the Mekong Delta region
xe om – motorbike taxi, also called *Honda om*
xich lo – *cyclo*, from the French *cyclo-pousse*

The Authors

NICK RAY

Coordinating Author, South-Central Coast, Ho Chi Minh City, Around Ho Chi Minh City, Mekong Delta

A Londoner of sorts, Nick comes from Watford, the sort of town that makes you want to travel. He has been visiting Vietnam for about 15 years, first as a traveller and later as a tour leader for adventure-travel companies. Living in nearby Phnom Penh, Vietnam is his backyard of sorts and he has co-authored *Cycling Vietnam, Laos & Cambodia*, as well as the *Cambodia* book, for Lonely Planet. Nick has been to almost every province from Ha Giang in the north to Ca Mau in the south. He stayed south for this edition of the book and was glad to finally make it to the beautiful islands of Phu Quoc and Con Dao.

YU-MEI BALASINGAMCHOW

North-Central Vietnam, Central Vietnam, Central Highlands

Yu-Mei first visited Vietnam in 2002, when she went kayaking in Halong Bay in the middle of winter and was almost cast out to sea by the currents. Subsequent (less harrowing) visits to the country have revolved around getting her fill of street food and *ca phe sua da*, and being mistaken as Vietnamese. She lives in Singapore and, in between other writing on travel, history, culture and the arts, has co-authored a popular history of Singapore. This is her first guidebook for Lonely Planet.

IAIN STEWART

Hanoi, Northeast Vietnam, Northwest Vietnam

Iain Stewart first visited Vietnam in 1991 when he was part of the first wave of travellers to explore the country after the American War. At that time all foreigners were called *Ling Xo* (Soviets) by the locals, who only had contact with nationalities from the communist bloc. Times have changed but Vietnam remains as fascinating as ever. Iain's been a travel writer since 1997, writing guidebooks for several publishers and covering terrain as diverse as Ibiza and Indonesia, but this was his first gig in Vietnam. For this guide Iain rode a motorbike around the northwest, climbed karst cliffs in Cat Ba and even survived Vietnam's toughest challenge – crossing the street in Hanoi.

LONELY PLANET AUTHORS

Why is our travel information the best in the world? It's simple: our authors are passionate, dedicated travellers. They don't take freebies in exchange for positive coverage so you can be sure the advice you're given is impartial. They travel widely to all the popular spots, and off the beaten track. They don't research using just the internet or phone. They discover new places not included in any other guidebook. They personally visit thousands of hotels, restaurants, palaces, trails, galleries, temples and more. They speak with dozens of locals every day to make sure you get the kind of insider knowledge only a local could tell you. They take pride in getting all the details right, and in telling it how it is. Think you can do it? Find out how at **lonelyplanet.com**.

CONTRIBUTING AUTHORS

Dr Trish Batchelor wrote the Health chapter (p510). Trish is a general practitioner and travel-medicine specialist who works at the CIWEC Clinic in Kathmandu, Nepal, as well as being a medical advisor to the Travel Doctor New Zealand clinics.

Robyn Eckhardt wrote the Food & Drink chapter (p61), and the foodie itinerary on p130. Kuala Lumpur–based Robyn has been living and eating in Asia for 14 years. She's food editor for *Time Out Kuala Lumpur*, and also writes for *Wall Street Journal Asia* and *Travel + Leisure*. Having once called Saigon home, she returns often for fixes of *banh mi* and *bun*.

David Lukas wrote the Environment chapter (p74). David is a naturalist who lives on the edge of Yosemite National Park, but he developed a strong love for Southeast Asia on a year-long rainforest ecology study in Borneo. He has contributed environment and wildlife chapters to nearly 30 Lonely Planet guides including *Vietnam, Cambodia, Laos & the Greater Mekong; Thailand's Islands & Beaches; Thailand; Bangkok;* and *Borneo*.

Behind the Scenes

THIS BOOK

This is the 10th edition of *Vietnam*. Nick Ray was the coordinating author and he was skilfully assisted by Iain Stewart and Yu-Mei Balasingamchow. They worked with the text from *Vietnam* 9 which was written by Nick Ray, Peter Dragicevich and Regis St Louis. *Vietnam* 8 was prepared by Nick Ray and Wendy Yanagihara. *Vietnam* 7 was researched by Mason Florence and Virginia Jealous. The Food & Drink chapter for this edition was written by Robyn Eckhardt and David Lukas wrote the Environment chapter. This guidebook was commissioned in Lonely Planet's Melbourne office, and produced by the following:

Commissioning Editor Tashi Wheeler
Coordinating Editor Katie O'Connell
Coordinating Cartographer Jacqueline Nguyen
Coordinating Layout Designer Carlos Solarte
Managing Editor Lauren Hunt
Managing Cartographers David Connolly, Hunor Csutoros
Managing Layout Designer Laura Jane
Assisting Editors Jocelyn Harewood, Charlotte Harrison, Helen Koehne, Gabrielle Stefanos
Assisting Cartographers Ildiko Bogdanovits, Diana Duggan, David Kemp
Assisting Layout Designer Cara Smith
Cover Designer Rebecca Dandens
Language Content Coordinators Quentin Frayne & Branislava Vladisavljevic
Project Manager Chris Love

Thanks to Lucy Birchley, Sally Darmody, Eoin Dunlevy, Chris Girdler, Nicole Hansen, Indra Kilfoyle, Yvonne Kirk, John Mazzocchi, Lauren Meiklejohn

THANKS

NICK RAY

As always, so many people have been instrumental in helping to put this book together. First thanks to my wonderful wife Kulikar Sotho who has joined me on many a trip to Vietnam. Travel has been considerably enlivened by our two children, Julian and Belle, although they only get to do the gentle bits for now. Thanks to Mum and Dad for their constant support and encouragement, which carried me to faraway lands from a young age.

Many people in Vietnam were very helpful along the way. In no particular order, many thanks to Linh, Vinh, Truong, Digby, Cuong, Diep, Marcus, Nghi, Rowan, Nicola, Seb, Matt, Brigdhe, Lan, Long, Matt, Dan, Andreas and many more. Additional thanks to Pete Murray for introductions in Saigon and Nick Ross from *The Word HCMC* for pointers.

THE LONELY PLANET STORY

Fresh from an epic journey across Europe, Asia and Australia in 1972, Tony and Maureen Wheeler sat at their kitchen table stapling together notes. The first Lonely Planet guidebook, *Across Asia on the Cheap*, was born.

Travellers snapped up the guides. Inspired by their success, the Wheelers began publishing books to Southeast Asia, India and beyond. Demand was prodigious, and the Wheelers expanded the business rapidly to keep up. Over the years, Lonely Planet extended its coverage to every country and into the virtual world via lonelyplanet.com and the Thorn Tree message board.

As Lonely Planet became a globally loved brand, Tony and Maureen received several offers for the company. But it wasn't until 2007 that they found a partner whom they trusted to remain true to the company's principles of travelling widely, treading lightly and giving sustainably. In October of that year, BBC Worldwide acquired a 75% share in the company, pledging to uphold Lonely Planet's commitment to independent travel, trustworthy advice and editorial independence.

Today, Lonely Planet has offices in Melbourne, London and Oakland, with over 500 staff members and 300 authors. Tony and Maureen are still actively involved with Lonely Planet. They're travelling more often than ever, and they're devoting their spare time to charitable projects. And the company is still driven by the philosophy of *Across Asia on the Cheap*: 'All you've got to do is decide to go and the hardest part is over. So go!'

A big thanks also to Le Van Sinh for all the effort he put into early editions of this book and once again helping out with information and tips along the way. Thanks to my co-authors Iain and Yu-Mei for all their work in other parts of Vietnam. And a big thanks to the in-house team at Lonely Planet who carry this from conception to reality. Finally, thanks to all the readers who have written in; you're all part of the big picture.

IAIN STEWART

Many thanks to all my family, especially darling Fiona, for putting up with me decamping on yet another extended tropical, exotic jaunt. In Vietnam I couldn't have managed without the help, support and friendship of Chien and Ocean Tours, and my pals Thanh, Hien and 'Harry Potter' who came along for the long ride around the northeast. A special mention to the Cat Ba crew – Erik, Slo 'in seach of the one' Carrington and Vinh – beautiful Lan Ha Bay has a chance of staying that way with you guys around. Thanks as well to An Wu and Offroad Vietnam for on-the-road support and convincing me that I had to cover the northwest on a motorbike. I was also greatly assisted by local experts Tommy and Chai (great hike!) in Sapa, and Mr Nghe in Bac Ha. Finally a big shout to Matt Law for all his Hanoi input and also to Brice, Jimmy Pham and the Hwy 4 crew.

YU-MEI BALASINGAMCHOW

Thanks to all the lovely people who shared their advice, tips and tricks along the way, especially Wong Waisan, Erica Denison, Toby Huynh, Tan Soon Meng, Dinh Minh Khue, Thuong Trinh, Duong Thu Truyen, Lan Anh, Nguyen Luong Thien, Quy Nguyen, Dawn Phillips, Ann Knight, Patrick Ryan, Sam Miller, Nick Keegan, Francis Fee, Thanh Ha, Tran Xuan Duc, Tran Tien Nam, Duong Huynh Yang, Jin Pyn Lee, Deanna Ng and Chia Yan Wei. Thanks also to family and friends at home, especially Mom and Dad, Yu-Hui and Suzie for minding the cats (and much else), Joyce, Shereen, Wan, Darren, Mel, Chee Foong, Jude and Sarah.

OUR READERS

Many thanks to the travellers who used the last edition and wrote to us with helpful hints, useful advice and interesting anecdotes:

A Maria Abrecht, Gary Adams, Jose Manuel Aguilar, Stefano Albisini, Carlo Alcos, Yvonne Alcos, Christopher Alexander, Ines Alvarez, Joe Alvaro, Thea Andersson, Minni Anko, Suzan Arets, Jeff Arnold, Benjamin August, Craig Austin **B** John Bailey, Rohan Barker, Cecil & Colette Barnard, Alison Barnfather, Annie Barry, Constanze Barten, Geoff Bartlett, Julianne Becker, Philip Bell, David Berg, Kathy Best, Kevin Beswick, Burjis Bhathena, Matthew Bigham, Ron Black, Rachel Blackamore, Bettina Blass, Ignacio Blat Andres, Kathryn Blatch, Suzanne Blogg, Chelsea Boehr, Michaela Bonfert, Ole Botnen Eide, Douglas Boulton, Robert Bouwhuis, Elin Brask, Kathleen Breslin, Fred Broussard, Thomas Buechler, Simon Burdon, Collin Burger, Helen Burke, Francis Burt, Stephen Byrne **C** Frederike Campman, Marc Chahin, Rachael Chan Chan, Yoke Cheng Cheam, Mei Ling Chong, Jeff Chorney, Katerina Chrissochou, Andre Christ, Steve Church, Jane Church, James Clark, Candice Coady, Richard Coe, Ken Coleman, Ann Collaery, Martyn Collins, Nicolas Combremont, Lucy Conn, Annerly Cooper, Kristy Coulter, Brian Coxon, Murray Crosswell, Alice Crowley, Robert Crowley, Kim Cruickshank, Martin Cumming, Aidan Cunniffe, Sophie Curtis **D** Tu Kien Dang, Lynley Davidson, Jill De Leijer, Wim De Paepe, David De Rango, Igor De Ruitz, Manuel De Tommasi, Wilma & Michel De Winter, Cathy Degaytan, Mark Degaytan, Mathijs & Jessie Den, James Denyer, Robert Derash, Andreas Dernbach, Mark Deumer, Ego Yao Di Ozlu, Pieter Dierckx, Anja Dijkema, Jeff Diverres, Mark Doggett, Kareen Du Mont D'Athelia, Chelsea Duke, Doug Durst, Christian Dutilh **E** Rachel Ellison, Moritz Eppenstein, Ville Etelapaa **F** Bill Fabi, Libby Fainsilber, Simon Faithfull, Delia Farlam, Trudi Faulkner, Brian Federnassum, Michael Finn, Christian Fischer, Mhairi Fleming, Dave Flooks, Kerry Kennedy Flynn, Brendan Foley, Sean Fox, Paolo Franchetto, Lucas Franchi, Neil Franklin, Megan Fraser, Liz Frazer, Justin Frydman **G** Charlotte Gareis, Richard Gauthier, Michelle Gee, Philip Geenen, Jane Gentle, Trevor Giblin, Marlies Giesbers, Dawn Gill,

SEND US YOUR FEEDBACK

We love to hear from travellers – your comments keep us on our toes and help make our books better. Our well-travelled team reads every word on what you loved or loathed about this book. Although we cannot reply individually to postal submissions, we always guarantee that your feedback goes straight to the appropriate authors, in time for the next edition. Each person who sends us information is thanked in the next edition – and the most useful submissions are rewarded with a free book.

To send us your updates – and find out about Lonely Planet events, newsletters and travel news – visit our award-winning website: **lonelyplanet.com/contact**.

Note: we may edit, reproduce and incorporate your comments in Lonely Planet products such as guidebooks, websites and digital products, so let us know if you don't want your comments reproduced or your name acknowledged. For a copy of our privacy policy visit lonelyplanet.com/privacy.

Ashley Goldstraw, Eric Gothberg, Richard Gough, Jessica Green, Robin Greif, Stuart Greif, Peter Gremse, Wendy Gregory-Walker, Elisabeth Grill, Colin Grinnell, Annette Grobly, Julie Grogan, Alain Grootaers, Helmut Grossmann, Michael Gulvin, Melanie Gunn, Anett Gyuricza **H** Anja Hadamek, Tina Haley, Elinor Hallström, Mijnke Hamel, Susan Hanley, Patrick Hanlon, Peter Hansen, Emma Hardwick, Toby Harris, Vebjørn Haugerud, Simone Hauser, Lorna Hayley, John Hayward, Brett Hearn, Shannon Heit, Samira Helaoui, Halo Hero, William Herron, Peter Hibbard, Christopher Hill, Iris Hinterberger, Lewis Hitchcock, Kelly Hobbs, Nadine Hoffmann, Brian Holgate, Matt Holmes, Thomas Honey, Erik Hoogcarspel, Esmaralde Hoorweg, Tobias Hörnfeldt Röhr, Sheena Horning, Esther Horrevorts, Berta Hortiguela, Scott Howell, Trevor Howett, Bob Huff, Jakobien Huisman, Rhett Hutchence **I** Megan Ireland, Jo-Anne Irving, Miwa Ishigami, Marie Iskenius **J** K Jackson, Philip Jackson, Jan Jacobs, Fabrice Jannot, Celine Jansen, Stan Jansky, Fiona Jenkins, Sharon Johnson, Celia Jones, Christopher Jones **K** Maria Katonak, Alan Kennedy, Julia Kenny, Elizabeth Keymer, Ralf Keysselitz, Dave Kho, Alex Kiefer, Tu Kien, Margot Kilgour, Randy King, Gareth Kinsella, Edwin Knox, Xieheng Kong, Kon Konovalov, Chris Kopec, Jan Kronhede-Jensen, Astrid Kueffer, Claudia Kuenstler, Lal Kuruppu **L** Lotte Lacet, Linda Lansfield, Nicole Lavergne, Collin Lawrence, Zach Lawryk, Hy Khuong Le, Kim Anh Le, Daniel Le, Jason Leichter, Dave Lemke, Ken Leybourne, Sue Liao, Susan Lieu, Patricia Liscio, Giorgia Liviero, Paul Longworth, Kerry Lyall, Jane Lynch **M** Claudia Maettig, John Maginness, Laurent Maillefer, Joe Manning, Paul Mark, Rebecca Marland, Jeff Marshall, Jonathan Matchett, Alison Matthews, Juergen Maussner, Christoph-Erik Mayer, Nicholas Mayne, Jo McArthur, Rowan McClean, Chris McDonald, Mick McGrath, Keith McKay, Mary McKay, Grant McMillan, Sally Meadows, Ronald Meyerq, Jeremy Milk, Kate Mills, Richard Mills, Severine Minot, Jess Miranda, Annett Mohnert, Funky Monkey, Bruce Moon, Lauren Moore, Ashley Morden, Ignacio Morejon, Marvin Moreno, Simon Morley, Monica Müllhaupt, Ian Munro, Tom Munro, Jani Mustonen **N** Landon Nabb, Laura Najjar, Barbara Nardelli, Zarni Ne Win, Rosemary Neuman, Jonathan Newton, Cuong Nguyen, Quynh Nguyen Nhu, Jan Tijs Nijssen, Beth Noble, Judith Norell, Joachim Norum, Dan Noviskey, Sebastiaan Numan **O** Rebecca Occhiuto, Ryan O'Keven, Adriana Okuma, Marinus Onder De Linden, Dustin Ooley, Bosse Orrhult **P** Jan Panman, Sonia Paradis, Pedro Pastrano, Claudia Patschka, Brooke Pearson, Matt Pepe, Laure Perrier, Ros Perry, Jay Phang, Sarah Pickering, Caprioli Piercarlo, Katerina Pintova, Matt Pirie, David Pizer, Francis Pope, Steve Pope-Carter, Rom Port, Russell Porteus, John Price, Hans-Christian Pulver **Q** Stans Quik **R** David Ragg, Linda Rawles, Francis Reardon, Pat Reid, Hoi Lun Reumann, Caroline & Julia Rhodes, Donna Ridge, Steve Rieger, Gemma Riley, Doyle Roberts, Jonny Robinson, Phil Robinson, Roberto Roman, Nick Ross, Jeremie Ross-Latour, Valerie Ross-Wilson, Cerise Roth-Vinson, Lodovico Ruggeri, Joe Rush **S** Linda Sabatini, Michelle Sabatini, Sharon Saunders, Emer Savage, Paolo Scampini, Annett Schlenker, Anne Schneider, Carolyn Schuch, Peter Schuetterle, David Schulman, Ralph Schwer, Bryan Scott, Pamela Sekhon, Crepaldi Sergio, Markus Sesser, Alex Sharp, Charlotte Shaw, Clive Shepherd, Luna Shepherd, Dmitry Shinkarenko, Brian Shook, Susan Si, Gemma Slate, Paul Slemmons, Mike Slone, Peter Smiar, Jack Smith, Matt Smith, Shelley Smith, Jessi Snow, Melissa Sommerville, Enrico Soresini, Pamela Southern, Kerry Stephens, Peter Stewart, Joseph Stimpfl, Ann Stoughton, Bill Stoughton, Tamara Stowe, Maria Svensson, Arjan Syrier, Istvan Szucs, Monika Szyszlowska **T** Raymond Ta, Ye Chiong Tan, Chee-Hian Tan, Rourou Tan, Jack Tattis, JR Tattis, Dan Taylor, Julia Teng, Marlies Terpstra, Luu Thai, Susan Thai, Richard Thompson, Bill Thornton, Sue Thornton, Christian Thorsen, Mark Tiernan, John Tierney, Jacek Tombinski, Kristin Tømmervaag, Karin Tordy, John Tran, Thi Mai Tram Tran, Katherine Trelstad, Pip Tschudin **V** Tan V, Cor Valk, Nicole van de Waterbeemd, Marc van der Heijde, Arjan van der Horst, Nanda van der Horst, Gerben van driel, Martin van Iersel, Hoang van Truong, Jaap van Weeghel, Caris Vanghetti, Jussi Varjunen, Martha Vasquez, Elliot Vermes, Gill Vine, Benedicte Viola **W** Rupert Walker, Jennie Walsh, Jerry Ward, Kaye Warner, Grant Watson, Reynold Weidenaar, Louise Welcome, Sanny Wensveen, Ulf Wessendorf, Jochem Westeneng, Alan White, Jodie Wilkinson, Vicki Willcock, John Williams, Anthony Wilson, Taj Wilson, Cornelia Wintergerst, Johann Wojta, Ben Wood, David Wood, Kevin Wortz, Sylvia Wuensche **Z** Nina Zaech, Ombretta Zanetti

ACKNOWLEDGMENTS

Many thanks to the following for the use of their content:

Globe on title page ©Mountain High Maps 1993 Digital Wisdom, Inc.

Internal photographs p126 (#6) Siegfried Grassegger/imagebroker/Alamy; p128 (#3) Nicholas Pitt/Digital Vision/Alamy. All other photographs by Lonely Planet Images, or as credited, and by Grant Dixon p127 (#1); Greg Elms p129 (#1), p130 (#5); Mason Florence p131 (#2); David Greedy p125; Rachel Lewis p126 (#1); Stu Smucker p132.

Index

000 Map pages
000 Photograph pages

000 Map pages
000 Photograph pages

INDEX

INDEX

000 Map pages
000 Photograph pages

INDEX

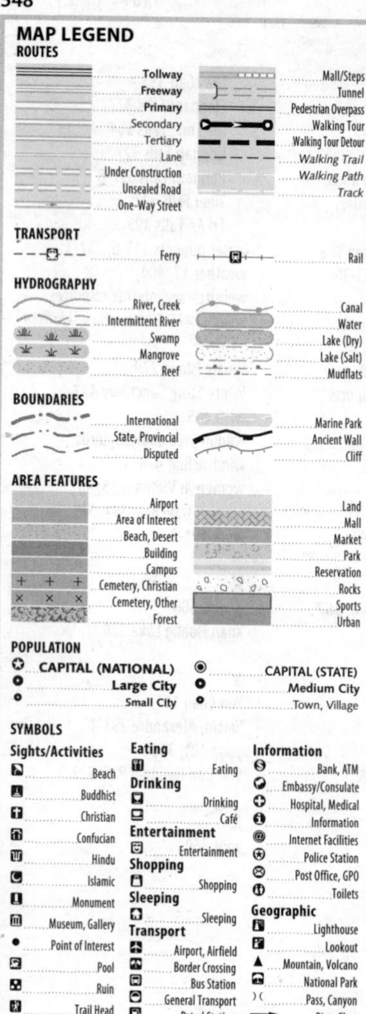

LONELY PLANET OFFICES

Australia

Head Office
Locked Bag 1, Footscray, Victoria 3011
☎ 03 8379 8000, fax 03 8379 8111
talk2us@lonelyplanet.com.au

USA

150 Linden St, Oakland, CA 94607
☎ 510 250 6400, toll free 800 275 8555
fax 510 893 8572
info@lonelyplanet.com

UK

2nd fl, 186 City Rd,
London EC1V 2NT
☎ 020 7106 2100, fax 020 7106 2101
go@lonelyplanet.co.uk

Published by Lonely Planet Publications Pty Ltd
ABN 36 005 607 983

Cover photograph: People watching the fishing boats on the water at Mui Ne; Micah Wright/Lonely Planet Images. Many of the images in this guide are available for licensing from Lonely Planet Images: www.lonelyplanetimages.com.

Printed by SNP Security Printing Pte Ltd, Singapore.